Tom Veitch

D0783533

FOURTH EDITION

SENSATION

AND

PERCEPTION

FOURTH EDITION

SENSATION

AND

PERCEPTION

STANLEY COREN
University of British Columbia

LAWRENCE M. WARD
University of British Columbia

JAMES T. ENNS
University of British Columbia

Harcourt Brace College Publishers

Fort Worth   Philadelphia   San Diego   New York   Orlando   Austin   San Antonio
Toronto   Montreal   London   Sydney   Tokyo

Publisher	Ted Buchholz
Acquisitions Editor	Tina Oldham
Senior Project Editor	Kay Kaylor
Production Manager	Erin Gregg
Book Designer	Burl Sloan
Cover Illustration	© 1993 Dennis Farris

Requests for permission to make copies of any part of the work should be mailed to: Permissions Department, Harcourt Brace & Company, 8th Floor, Orlando, Florida 32887

Address for Editorial Correspondence: Harcourt Brace College Publishers, 301 Commerce Street, Suite 3700, Fort Worth, TX 76102

Address for Orders: Harcourt Brace & Company, 6277 Sea Harbor Drive, Orlando, FL 32887; 1-800-782-4479 or 1-800-433-0001 (in Florida)

ISBN: 0-15-500103-5

Library of Congress Catalog Card Number: 92-75501

Printed in the United States of America

3 4 5 6 7 8 9 0 1 2   0 3 9   9 8 7 6 5 4 3 2 1

For permission to use copyrighted material, the publisher is grateful to the following: *Chapter 1 opener:* Reginald Neal (1909–1992), *Square of Three—Yellow and Black (1964).* Acrylic and lithograph on canvas, 32 5/8" x 32 5/8", New Jersey State Museum Collection. Circle F Purchase Award; Kramer, Hirsch and Carchidi Foundation Purchase Award; Tec-Torch Company, Inc. Purchase Award; "Art from New Jersey Three," FA 1968.73; *Chapter 2:* © George Hall/Woodfin Camp & Assoc.; *Color Insert:* © 1993 Mary Ann Fittipaldi; *Chapter 3:* Courtesy of Deric Bownds and Stanley Carlson, University of Wisconsin; *Chapter 4:* Christian Delbert Photography/The Picture Cube; *Chapter 6:* © Henry Groskinsky; *Figure 6-1:* Courtesy of J.O. Pickles. From *An Introduction to the Physiology of Hearing,* 2nd Edition, by James O. Pickles, copyright 1988 Academic Press; *Figure 6-2:* Courtesy of J.O. Pickles. From *An Introduction to the Physiology of Hearing,* 2nd Edition, by James O. Pickles, copyright 1988 Academic Press; *Chapter 8:* Stock Yard; *Chapter 9:* Jeffry Myers/Stock, Boston; *Chapter 10:* Martin Rogers/Stock, Boston; *Chapter 12:* © Peter L. Chapman; *Chapter 13:* Ed Carlin/The Picture Cube; *Chapter 14:* William Johnson/Stock, Boston; *Chapter 15:* David Aronson/Stock, Boston; *Chapter 16:* Harcourt Brace Photo/Richard Watherwax; *Chapter 18:* A.T. Willett/The Image Bank; *Appendix:* © 1988 Bruce Iverson, BSc.

Preface. . .

Take away the sensations of softness, moisture, redness, tartness, and you take away the cherry. Since it is not a being distinct from these sensations; a cherry, I say, is nothing but a congeries of sensible impressions or ideas perceived by various senses; which ideas are united into one thing. . . ."

George Berkeley, 1713

Virtually everything we know about our world has entered our minds through our senses. We all realize that without even some of our senses, our experiences would be incredibly limited. Consider the impossible problem of explaining the difference between the color blue and the color green to a person who has been blind since birth. Or how would you explain to a person who has no taste buds how the tastes of chocolate and vanilla differ from each other? Such aspects of the world will never exist for these individuals. For the blind person, salt and pepper differ only in taste. For the person with no ability to taste, salt and pepper differ only in color. For those of us who have senses of sight, hearing, taste, touch, and smell, our world is a continuous flow of changing percepts. Each new sensation carries with it information about our world.

This book provides an introduction to the study of sensation and perception. It has been revised substantially since the third edition, and has been updated with several hundred new references. These changes reflect many of the recent findings that have emerged, or coalesced into meaningful patterns, since the completion of the third edition. We have rewritten all of the chapters, with some sections revised "from the ground up." We have tried to retain the general structure and organization of the third edition so that the book will still feel familiar to our previous users. We have also retained all those features that instructors felt made the previous editions such useful teaching tools. For instance, concrete examples are used throughout the text in order to make the subject matter "come alive" for students. Whenever possible, common or natural instances of perceptual phenomena are described during the discussion of the concepts underlying them. Each chapter is preceded by an outline that serves as a preview to its contents. These outlines also provide a structure to guide students as they review the chapters.

Although terms are defined when they are introduced in the text, a glossary is provided at the end of each chapter as well. Any item printed in **boldface** in the text is also listed in the chapter glossary. Students will find that these glossaries serve as a succinct review and chapter summary. They can also be used for self-testing and study purposes.

One special feature of our textbook is the inclusion of more than 100 *Demonstration Boxes.* Each box describes a simple demonstration designed to allow students actually to experience many of the perceptual phenomena described in the text. Most require only the stimuli in the box itself, or commonplace items that can be found in most homes or dormitory rooms. The majority of these demonstrations require only a few moments of preparation, and we feel that this is time well spent in improving understanding of the concepts under discussion and in maintaining student interest. Some instructors have reported that having students perform the demonstrations in class has been very useful. In such cases the demonstrations may also serve as the focal point for a lecture or for classroom discussion.

For a bit of amusement, this edition also includes a cartoon at the end of each chapter. The humorous aspect of each cartoon depends upon knowledge of a particular term, concept, or principle described in the chapter, so "getting the joke" requires that the student has read the material.

This textbook is designed to survey the broad range of topics generally included under the heading of *sensation and perception*. The reader will notice that no single theory of perception is championed. In general, we have attempted to be as eclectic as possible, describing the various viewpoints in areas of controversy and attempting to present a balanced overview so that instructors of different opinions might be comfortable using the book.

The topics in this book were selected on the basis of our experience in teaching our own courses; therefore, much of the material has already been class tested. We have included three chapters—*Attention, Speech and Music,* and *Individual Differences*—that are not always seen in sensation and perception textbooks. These areas have attracted a good deal of experimental work in recent years, and they are sufficiently relevant to many issues in perception that we felt students should be aware of their existence.

In order to keep the book to a manageable size, we have occasionally been selective in our coverage. It was our first priority to cover the central concepts of each topic in enough detail to make the material clear and coherent. To have included all the topics ever classified as part of the field of sensation and perception, we would have had to present a "grocery list" of concepts and terms, each treated superficially. Such an alternative was unacceptable to us.

Each of the chapters has been written so that it is relatively self-contained and independent of the other chapters. When this is not completely possible, such as when material from other chapters is used in a discussion, the location of that information is always cited. This has been done to provide instructors with maximum flexibility in the sequence of chapter presentation. By altering the sequence in which chapters are presented, an instructor can impress his or her orientation upon the material. A brief appendix on some basic aspects of neurophysiology has also been provided, and may be used where needed.

We have organized the book by sensory systems, with the first half of the book covering the basic physiology and sensory responses and the second half covering those topics involving more complex and cognitive interactions. Chapters 1 and 2 provide an introduction to the problems of sensation and perception along with methodological and theoretical aspects of psychophysical measurement. Chapters 3, 4, and 5 cover the physiology and basic sensory qualities of vision; Chapters 6 and 7 do the same for audition; and Chapters 8 and 9 cover the chemical and mechanical senses. These first nine chapters thus cover the major topics usually grouped together under the heading of *sensation*. Chapters 10 through 15 cover the perception of space, form, speech and music, time and motion, perceptual constancies, and the perceptual aspects of attention. Chapters 16, 17, and 18 look at how individual factors such as age, experience, learning, gender, culture, drugs, and personality variables may affect the perceptual response. Thus the last nine chapters cover the topics most frequently grouped together as *perception*.

Those of you who have encountered earlier versions of this book will notice that we have added a new author (James T. Enns). His insights have helped us to expand and update our coverage of the field, and he adds a bit of a new "flavor" to the writing. In our attempts to collect and interpret the information for this textbook, we have been assisted at various stages by a number of people. Specifically, we would like to thank the personnel of the University of British Columbia's *Human Neuropsychology and Perception Laboratory, Psychophysics Laboratory,* and *Attention Laboratory,* with special thanks to David Wong and Juliet Armstrong, for assisting with library work and all of the small but necessary chores that eat up innumerable hours of a textbook writer's time.

In addition, we would like to thank Barry S. Anton, University of Puget Sound; Ira H. Bernstein, University of Texas, Arlington; Janet D. Larson, John Carroll University; Robert M. Levy, Indiana State University; Susan Petry, Adelphi University; Charles E. Sternhein, University of Maryland, College Park; and Benjamin Wallace, Cleveland State University, for their helpful comments and suggestions after reviewing this edition.

Finally, the reader might notice that there is no dedication page. This is not to say that we do not wish to dedicate the book to anyone. It reflects the fact that too many people have been important in our personal and professional lives to list on any single page (no matter how small the print). Perhaps it is best simply to dedicate this book to all of those researchers who have provided the knowledge that we have attempted to organize and review between these covers, and to all of those researchers who will provide further insights into sensation and perception for future authors to collate, review, digest, wonder at, and learn from.

S.C.
L.M.W.
J.T.E.

Contents

PREFACE / V

CHAPTER 1
SENSATION AND PERCEPTION / 3
Aspects of the Perceptual Process / 12
Theories of Perception / 13
The Plan of the Book / 15

CHAPTER 2
PSYCHOPHYSICS / 19
Detection / 21
Identification / 33
Discrimination / 39
Scaling / 46

CHAPTER 3
THE VISUAL SYSTEM / 65
Light / 66
The Structure of the Eye / 66
Neural Responses to Light / 79
The Visual Pathways / 84
The Visual Cortex / 90

CHAPTER 4
BRIGHTNESS AND SPATIAL
FREQUENCY / 103
Photometric Units / 104
Factors in Brightness Perception / 107
Visual Acuity / 114
Spatial Frequency Analysis / 118

Spatial Context Effects / 129
Temporal Context Effects / 136
Darkness Perception / 139

CHAPTER 5
COLOR / 145
Color Stimulus / 146
The Physiology of Color Vision / 156
Color Perception / 169

CHAPTER 6
THE AUDITORY SYSTEM / 181
Sound / 182
The Structure of the Ear / 187
Electrical Activity of the Auditory Nerve /
201
The Auditory Pathways / 204
The Auditory Cortex / 207

CHAPTER 7
HEARING / 213
Detection of Sounds / 214
Subjective Dimensions of Sounds / 231
Auditory Scene Analysis / 245

CHAPTER 8
TASTE AND SMELL / 253
The Gustatory (Taste) Sense / 254
The Olfactory (Smell) Sense / 267

CHAPTER 9
TOUCH AND PAIN / 285

The Skin Senses / 286
Touch / 293
Kinesthesis / 301
Warmth and Cold / 307
Pain / 313

CHAPTER 10
SPACE / 327

Types of Depth Perception / 328
Pictorial Depth Cues / 329
Physiological Cues for Depth / 338
Motion and Motion Parallax / 339
Binocular Depth Perception / 341
Interaction of Depth Cues / 351
Perception of Direction / 354
Development of Space Perception / 357

CHAPTER 11
FORM / 365

The Problem of Visual Form Perception / 366
Contour Detection and Feature Extraction / 368
Perceptual Organization / 375
Object Recognition and Identification / 390
Theories of Object Identification / 398

CHAPTER 12
SPEECH AND MUSIC / 407

Music / 408
Speech / 417

CHAPTER 13
TIME AND MOTION / 443

Time / 444
Motion / 453

CHAPTER 14
THE CONSTANCIES / 483

The Task of Perception / 484
Perceptual Constancies / 486
Size Constancy / 487
Shape Constancy / 497
Lightness or Whiteness Constancy / 501
Color or Hue Constancy / 504
Other Constancies / 506

CHAPTER 15
ATTENTION / 511

Varieties of Attention / 512
Orienting / 512
Filtering / 521
Searching / 528
Expecting / 539
Theories of Attention / 542

CHAPTER 16
DEVELOPMENT / 549

Perception in Infants / 550
Perceptual Change through Childhood / 565
Perceptual Change in Adults / 571

CHAPTER 17
LEARNING AND EXPERIENCE / 579

Experience and Development / 580
Sensory-Motor Learning / 588

Context and Meaning / 595

Environmental and Life History Differences / 601

CHAPTER 18
INDIVIDUAL DIFFERENCES / 617

Physiological Differences / 618

Gender Differences / 627

Personality and Cognitive Style Differences / 632

APPENDIX
PRIMER OF NEUROPHYSIOLOGY / 639

Neurons and the Nervous System / 640

The Nature of Neural Activity / 641

Techniques to Measure Neural Function / 643

REFERENCES / 649

AUTHOR INDEX / 717

SUBJECT INDEX / 735

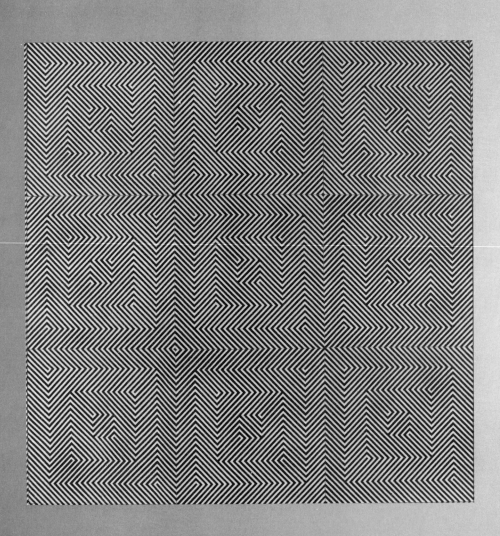

Chapter ... 1

SENSATION AND PERCEPTION

Aspects of the Perceptual Process

Theories of Perception

The Plan of the Book

*C*an you answer the following questions? What color is the sky? Which is warmer—fire or ice? Which tastes sweeter—sugar or vinegar? Which has a stronger smell—burning wood or burning rubber? Which sounds louder—a chirping bird or the crack of a rifle? Such questions probably seem quite trivial, and the answers obvious. Well, perhaps we should phrase the questions differently. How do you know what color the sky is? How do you know how hot fire is relative to ice? How do you know that sugar is sweet? Again, you might feel that the answers are obvious. You see the color of the sky, you feel the temperatures of a flame and an ice cube, and you taste the sweetness of sugar—in other words, the answers come through your senses.

Let us push our questioning one step further. How do you know anything about your world? You might say that you learn from books, television, radio, films, lectures, or the actual exploration of places. And how do you obtain the information from these sources? Again, the answer is through your senses. In fact, without your senses of vision, hearing, touch, taste, and smell, your brain, the organ that is responsible for your conscious experience, would be an eternal prisoner in the solitary confinement of your skull. You would live in total silence and darkness. All would be a tasteless, colorless, feelingless, floating void. Without your senses, the world would simply not exist for you. The philosopher Thomas Hobbes recognized this fact in 1651 when he wrote, "There is no conception in man's mind which hath not at first, totally or by parts, been begotten upon the organs of sense." The Greek philosopher Protagoras stated the same position around 450 B.C. when he said, "Man is nothing but a bundle of sensations."

You may protest that this is a rather extreme viewpoint. Certainly, much of what we know about the world does not arrive through our eyes, ears, nose, and other sense organs.

We have complex scientific instruments, such as telescopes, that tell us about the size and shape of the universe by analyzing images too faint for the human eye to see. We have sonar to trace out the shape of the sea bottom, which may be hidden from our eyes by a hundred feet of water. We have spectrographs to tell us about the exact chemical composition of many substances, as compared to the crude chemical sensitivity of our noses and tongues.

Although such pieces of apparatus exist to measure phenomena not directly available to our senses, this does not alter the fact that it is the *perception of the scientist* that constitutes the subject matter of every science. The eye of the scientist presses against the telescope or examines the photograph of the distant star. The ear of the scientist listens to the sound of sonar tracing out the size and distance of objects, or the scientist's eyes read the sonograph. Although the tongue of the scientist does not taste the chemical composition of some unknown substance, the eye, aided by the spectrograph, provides the data for analysis. Really, the only data that reach the mind of the scientist come not from instruments but from the scientist's senses. The instrument he or she is looking at can be perfectly accurate, yet if the scientist misreads a digital readout, or does not notice a critical shift in the operation of a measurement device, the obtained information is wrong and the resulting picture of the world is in error. The minds of the scientist, the nonscientist, our pet dog sniffing about the world, or a fish swimming about in a bowl—in fact, the minds of all living, thinking organisms—are prisoners that must rely on information smuggled in to them by the senses. Your world is what your senses tell you. The limitations of your senses set the boundaries of your conscious existence.

Because our knowledge of the world is dependent on our senses, it is important to know how our senses function. It is also important to know how well the world that is created by our senses corresponds to external reality (that is, the reality measured by scientific instruments). At this point, you may be smiling to yourself and thinking, "Here comes another academic discourse that will attempt to make something that is quite obvious appear to be complex." You might be saying to yourself, "I see my desk in front of me because it is there. I feel my chair pressing against my back because it is there. I hear my phone ringing because it contains a bell that makes sounds. What could be more obvious?" Such faith in your senses is a vital part of existence. It causes you to jump out of the way of an apparently oncoming car, thus preserving your life. It provides the basic data that cause you to step back from a deep hole, thus avoiding a fall and serious bodily harm.

Such faith in our senses is built into the very fabric of our lives. As the old saying goes, "Seeing is believing." Long before the birth of Christ, Lucretius stated this article of faith when he asked, "What can give us surer knowledge than our senses? With what else can we distinguish the true form from the false?" Perhaps the most striking example of this faith is found in our courts of law, where people's lives and fortunes rest solely on testimony via the eyes and ears of witnesses. A lawyer might argue that a witness is corrupt or lying, or even that his memory has failed, but no lawyer would have the audacity to suggest that her client should be set free because the only evidence available was what the witnesses saw or heard. Certainly no sane person would charge the eye or ear with perjury!

The philosophical position that perception is an immediate, almost godlike knowledge of external reality has been championed not only by popular sentiment, but also by philosophers of the stature of Immanuel Kant (1724–1804). Unfortunately, it is wrong. Look at the drawings shown in Figure 1-1. Clearly, they are all composed of outlined forms on various backgrounds. Despite what your senses tell you, A, B, and C are all perfect squares. Despite the evidence of your senses, D is a perfect circle, the vertical lines in E are both straight, and the lines marked X and Y in F are both the same length.

The ease with which we use our senses— seeing, apparently through the simple act of opening our eyes, or touching, apparently by merely pressing our skin against an object— masks the fact that perception is an extremely sophisticated activity of the brain. Perception calls on stores of memory data. It requires subtle classifications, comparisons, and myriad decisions before any of the data in our senses become our conscious awareness of what is "out there." Contrary to what you may think, the eyes do not see. Many individuals have perfectly functioning eyes yet have no sensory impressions. They cannot perceive because they have injuries in those parts of the brain that receive and interpret messages from the eyes. Epicharmus knew this in 450 B.C. when he said, "The mind sees and the mind hears. The rest is blind and deaf."

"So what?" you mutter to yourself. "So sometimes we make errors in our perceptions. The real point is that the senses simply carry a picture of the outside world to the brain. The picture in the brain represents our percept. Of course if we mess up the brain we will distort or destroy perception." Again, this answer is too simple. If we look outside and see a car, are we to believe that a picture of a car is present somewhere in our brain? If we notice that a traffic light is green, are we to believe that some part of the brain has turned green? And suppose such images were present in the brain, carried without distortion from the senses— would this help us to see? Certainly, images in the brain would only be of value if some other eyes in the head would look at these pictures and interpret them. If this were the case, we

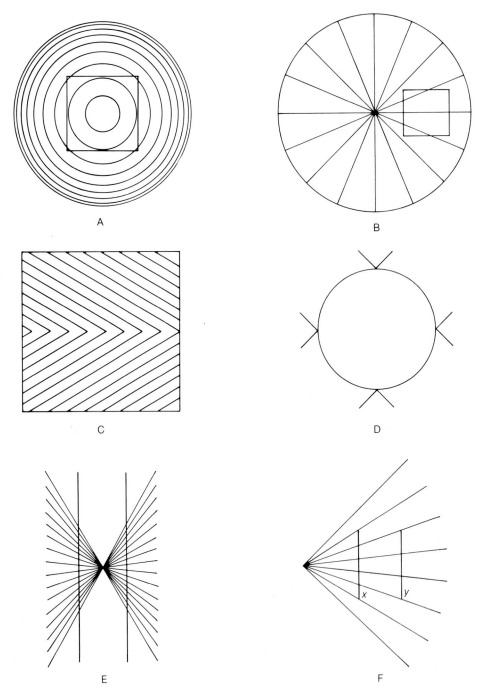

Figure 1-1   *Some instances where the senses tell lies.*

would be left with the question of how these internal eyes see. Thus, we would eventually be forced to set up an endless chain of pictures and eyes and pictures and eyes, because the question of who is perceiving the percept, and how, still remains.

If we are to understand perception we must consider it in its natural context. Sensation and perception are some of the many complex processes that occur in the continuing flow of individual behavior. No clear line exists between perception and many other behavioral activities. No perception gives direct knowledge of the outside world; rather such knowledge is the end product of many processes. The wet-looking black spot on the edge of a desk could be the place where ink was spilled. Of course, this percept could be wrong. The ink may be dry, or the spot might not be there at all. The desk that is seen and touched might not really exist. We might be dreaming, drugged, or hallucinating. Too extreme, you say? Consider the following example that actually happened to one of the authors of this textbook. One night he walked across the floor of his darkened home. In the dim gloominess of the night, he saw his dog resting on the floor, clearly asleep. When he bent to touch the dog, he found that it was a footstool. He stepped back, somewhat startled at his stupidity, only to bump against the cold corner of a marble-topped coffee table. When he reached back to steady himself, he found that the corner of the table was, in fact, his dog's cold nose. Each of these perceptions—dog, stool, table, and dog again—seemed, when first received in consciousness, to be accurate representations of reality. Yet, sensory data are not always reliable. Sometimes they can be degraded or not completely available. No sudden break seems to occur between perceiving or sensing an object and guessing the identity of an object. In some respects, we can say that all perception of objects requires some guessing. Sensory stimu-

lation provides the data for our hypotheses about the nature of the external world, and it is these hypotheses that form our perceptions of the world. The importance of what we have been discussing is that no matter how convincing a percept may be, it still may be wrong, as is shown in Demonstration Box 1-1.

Many human behaviors have been affected by the fallible and often erroneous nature of our percepts. For example, the most elegant of the classic Greek buildings, the Parthenon, is bent. The straight, clean lines, which bring a sense of simple elegant grandeur, are actually an illusion. If we schematically represent the east wall of the building as it appears, it is square (as shown in Figure 1-2A). Actually, the Parthenon was built in a distorted fashion in order to offset a series of optical illusions. As a result of a common visual distortion, we find that placing angles above a line (much as the roof is placed over the architrave) causes the line to appear slightly bowed. One form of this illusion is shown as Figure 1-2B, where the ends of the horizontal line appear slightly higher than the center. If the Parthenon were built physically square, it would appear to sag as a result of this visual distortion. This is shown in an exaggerated manner in Figure 1-2C. The sagging does not appear, because the building has been altered to compensate for the distortion. Figure 1-2D illustrates what an undistorted view of the Parthenon would look like. The upward curvature is more than 6 cm on the east and west walls and almost 11 cm on the longer north and south sides.

The vertical features of the Parthenon (such as the columns) were inclined inward in order to correct for a second optical illusion in which the features of rising objects appear to fall outward at the top. Thus, if we projected all of the columns of the Parthenon upward, they would meet at a point somewhat less than 2 km above the building. Furthermore, the corner columns were made thicker because when

DEMONSTRATION BOX 1-1   The Fraser Spiral

Look at the figure here. It clearly looks like a spiral, converging toward the center. How much would you be willing to bet that it is a spiral? On the basis of your perception alone, would you ever believe that it is actually a set of concentric circles? It actually *is* a set of circles, and you can verify this for yourself. Place one finger on any line making up the "spiral". Place a finger from the other hand beside it, and carefully trace the line around with this finger while not moving the first finger. Eventually the moving finger will come back to the stationary one, since the lines that appear spiral are all part of a set of concentric circles (see Fraser, 1908; Stuart & Day, 1988; Taylor & Woodhouse, 1980, for variations of this illusion). This shows that no matter how convincing a perception might be, since it is based on an *interpretation* of the stimuli reaching us, our conscious experience may be wrong.

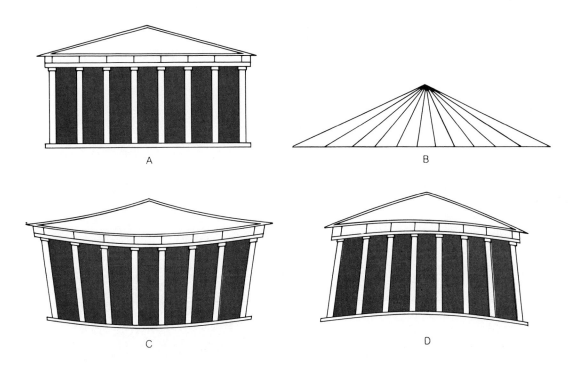

Figure 1-2   *(A) The Parthenon as it appears; (B) an illusion that should cause the Parthenon to appear as (C); (D) the way the Parthenon is built to offset the illusion.*

equally thick columns were seen against the sky, they appeared to be thinner than those seen against the darker background formed by the interior wall.

These were conscious corrections made by the Greek architects. To quote one of them, Vitruvius, writing around 30 B.C., "For the sight follows gracious contours, and unless we flatter its pleasure by proportionate alterations of these parts (so that by adjustment we offset the amount to which it suffers illusions) an uncouth and ungracious aspect will be presented to the spectators." In other words, the Parthenon appears to be square, with elegant straight lines, because it has been consciously distorted to offset perceptual distortions. If it were geometrically square, it would not be perceptually square.

It is amazing to discover the degree to which our conscious experience of the world can differ from the physical (scientific) reality. Although some perceptual distortions are only slight deviations from physical reality, some can be quite complex and surprising, such as that shown in Demonstration Box 1-2.

Such distortions, in the form of disagreements between percept and reality, are quite common. We call them **illusions,** and they occur in predictable circumstances for normal observers. The term illusion is drawn from the Latin root *illudere,* meaning "to mock," and in a sense they do mock us for our unthinking reliance on the validity of our sensory impressions. Every sensory modality is subject to distortions, illusions, and systematic errors that misrepresent the outside environment to our

DEMONSTRATION BOX 1-2   Gears and Circles

The pattern shown in this box should be viewed in motion. Move the book around so the motion resembles that which you would make if you were swirling coffee around in a cup without using a spoon. Notice that the six sets of concentric circles seem to show radial regions of light and dark that appear to move in the direction you are swirling the book. They look as though they were covered by a liquid surface tending to swirl with the stimulus movement.

A second effect has to do with the center circle that seems to have gearlike teeth. As you swirl the array, the center gear seems to rotate, but in a direction *opposite* to that of the movement of the outer circles. Some observers see it moving in a jerky, steplike manner from one rotary position to another and other observers see a smooth rotation. Of course, there is no *physical* movement within the circles, and the geared center circle is also unchanging, despite your conscious impression to the contrary.

DEMONSTRATION BOX 1-3   A Subjective Color Grid

The figure in this box consists of a series of thinly spaced diagonal black lines alternating with white spaces. Study this figure for a couple of seconds, and you will begin to see faint, almost pastel streaks of orange-red and other streaks of blue-green. For many observers, these streaks tend to run vertically up and down the figure crossing both white and black lines; for others, they seem to form a random, almost fishnetlike pattern over the grid. These colors are not present in the stimulus; hence they are *subjective*, or *illusory*, colors.

consciousness. We experience illusions of touch, taste, and hearing, as well as vision. Virtually any aspect of perception you might think of can be subject to these kinds of errors. For instance, such basic and apparently simple qualities as the brightness of an object or its color may be perceptually misrepresented, as shown in Demonstration Box 1-3.

Many perceptual errors are merely amusing, such as those in Demonstration Boxes 1-1 and 1-2, whereas others may be thought-provoking as in Demonstration Box 1-3. Still others may lead to some embarrassment or annoyance, such as might have been felt by the artisan who created the picture frame shown in Figure 1-3A. Although his workmanship is faultless, he has been undone because the grain of the wood is too prominent. Despite the fact that the picture is perfectly rectangular, it appears to be distorted. Unfortunately, some perceptual errors or illusions are quite serious. Figure 1-3B shows a surgeon probing for a bullet. She is using a fluoroscope, which presents the outline of the patient's ribs, and her probe is positioned so it is exactly on line with the bullet lodged below the rib. As you can see, it appears that she will miss and her probe will pass above the bullet despite the fact that the probe is angled perfectly. Figure 1-3C shows an even more disastrous occurrence of an illusion. It represents a radar screen with various flight regions marked across its face. The two oblique streaks represent jet aircraft approaching the control region, both flying at about 950 kph. The information displayed is similar to data that an air traffic controller might use. From it he might conclude that if these two aircraft continue in the same direction, they will pass each other with a safe distance between them. At the moment represented here, however, these aircraft are traveling toward each other on the same line. If they are flying at the same altitude, it is very likely that they will collide.

These examples illustrate how important discrepancies between perception and reality

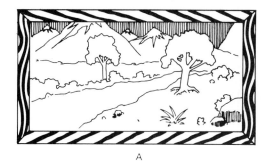

A

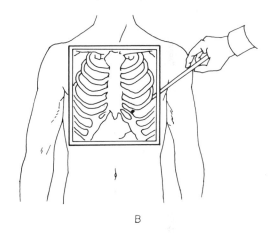

B

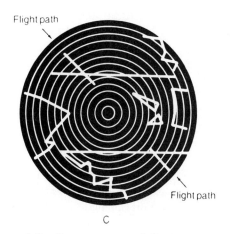

C

Figure 1-3 *Some perceptual distortions in common situations.*

can be. Therefore it becomes important for us to know how our perceptions arise, how much we can rely on them, under what circumstances they are most fallible, and under what conditions our perceptions most accurately present a picture of the world. An exploration of these questions is the purpose of this book.

ASPECTS OF THE PERCEPTUAL PROCESS

The study of perception is diverse. Partly this is the result of the length of time that perceptual problems have been studied. The Greek philosophers, the pre-Renaissance thinkers, the Arabic scholars, the Latin scholastics, the early British empiricists, the German physicists, and the German physicians who founded both physiology and psychology considered issues in sensation and perception to be basic. When Alexander Bain wrote the first English textbook on psychology in 1855, it was entitled *The Senses and the Intellect*, with the most extensive coverage reserved for sensory and perceptual functions. The major portion of both theorizing and empirical work produced by Wilhelm Wundt, who is generally credited with founding experimental psychology, was oriented toward sensation and perception. In addition to the diversity caused by a long and varied history, perception theory has been affected by many "schools" of thought. Each has its own theoretical viewpoint and its own set of methodological techniques. Thus we encounter psychophysicists, gestaltists, functionalists, analytic introspectionists, transactionalists, sensory physiologists, sensory-tonic theorists, "new look" psychologists, efferent theorists, artificial intelligence experts, and computational psychologists, to name but a few. Some theorists (such as certain behaviorists) deny the existence of, or at least deny our ability to study, the conscious event we call perception. Despite

this chorus of diverse voices and viewpoints, a consensus seems to have formed about the important aspects of perceptual study.

Before we look at the major areas of emphasis in the study of perceptual processes, let us first offer a disclaimer. We realize that it is difficult, perhaps impossible, and most certainly unwise to attempt to draw sharp lines separating one field of inquiry from another. However, certain problem areas or orientations characterize certain groups of investigators, and these seem to be definable. The study of **sensation,** or sensory processes, is concerned with the first contact between the organism and the environment. Thus, someone studying sensation might look at the way in which electromagnetic radiation (light) is registered by the eye. This investigator would look at the physical structure of the sense organ and would attempt to establish how sensory experiences are related to physical stimulation and physiological functioning. These types of studies tend to focus on less complex (although not less complicated) aspects of our conscious experience. For instance, these investigators might study how we perceive brightness, loudness, or color; however, the nature of the object having a given brightness, sound, or color would not make much difference to them.

Someone who is interested in the study of **perception** is interested in our conscious experience of objects and object relationships. For instance, the sensory question might be, "How bright does the target appear to be?", while the perceptual questions would be, "Can you identify that object?", "Where is it?", "How far away is it?", and "How large is it?" In a more global sense, those who study perception are interested in how we form a conscious representation of the outside environment, and in the accuracy of that representation. However, those of you who have difficulty in drawing a hard and fast line between the concepts of perception and sensation can rest easy. Since

Thomas Reid introduced the distinction in 1785, some investigators have urged its use and others have totally ignored it, choosing to treat sensation and perception as a unitary problem.

Cognition is a term used to define a very active field of inquiry in contemporary psychology. The word itself is quite old, probably first introduced by St. Thomas Aquinas (1225–1274). He divided the study of behavior into two broad divisions: *cognition*, meaning how we know the world, and *affect*, which was meant to encompass feelings and emotions. Today's definition of cognition is as broad as that of Aquinas. Although many investigators use the term to refer to memory, association, concept formation, language, and problem solving (all of which simply take the act of perception for granted), other investigators include the processes of attention and the conscious representation and interpretation of stimuli as part of the cognitive process. In other words, cognition tends to be somewhere between the areas that were traditionally called *perception* and *learning*, and it incorporates elements of both. The similarity between many of the problems studied by cognitive psychologists and those studied by perceptual psychologists is best evidenced by the fact that both often publish in the same journals and on similar topics.

Information processing is a relatively general term used to emphasize all the processes that finally lead to identification and interpretation of stimuli. This approach focuses on how information about the external world is operated on (processed) to produce our conscious percepts and guide our actions. Information processing is typically assumed to include a *registration* or sensory phase, an *interpretation* or perceptual phase, and a *memoric* or cognitive phase. Thus, instead of being a separate subdiscipline, the information processing approach attempts to integrate sensation, perception, and cognition within a common framework. It relies upon a **levels-of-processing** analysis in which each stage of sensory processing, from the first registration of the stimulus on the receptor to the final conscious representation entered into memory, is systematically analyzed.

None of these labels should be taken as representing inflexible, or completely separate, areas of study. At a recent professional meeting one well-known psychologist lamented, "When I first started doing research, people said I studied perception. After a while, they said I studied cognition. Now they say that I am studying human information processing. I don't know what is going on—I've been studying the same set of problems for the last 10 years!"

THEORIES OF PERCEPTION

In the same way that there are many aspects of perception, there are also many theoretical approaches to perceptual problems. One important approach may be called **biological reductionism.** It is based on the presumption that for any given aspect of the observer's sensation, a corresponding physiological event occurs. According to this approach, the main goal of the perception researcher is to isolate these underlying physiological mechanisms. The search for specific neural units, pathways, or processes that correspond to specific sensory experiences is common to such theories. One recent example is the work of Margaret Livingstone and David Hubel (1988), who view the visual system as a set of channels, each containing specific neural units that process or extract specific information from incoming data.

Other theoretical approaches are often less bound to a specific class of mechanism. For example, **direct perception** involves a set of theories that begins with the premise that all the information needed to form the conscious percept is available in the stimuli that reach our receptors. Certain aspects of the stimulation produced by any particular object or environmental situation are *invariant* predictors of certain properties, such as the actual size, shape, or distance of the object being viewed. These **invariants** are fixed properties of the stimulus even though the observer may be moving or changing viewpoints, causing continuous changes in the optical image that reaches the eye. This stimulus information is automatically extracted by the perceptual system because it is relevant to survival. Invariants provide information about **affordances,** which are simply action possibilities available to the observer, such as picking an object up or going around it. The label *direct perception* was given to such theories by J. J. Gibson (for example, 1979), who argued that this information is directly available to the perceiver and is not based on any higher-level cognitive processing or computation.

A number of perceptual theorists, whose thinking has been influenced by developments in the branch of computer science called artificial intelligence, have adopted an alternative approach. Their theories are usually presented in the form of computer programs or computational systems that might allow machines directly to interpret sensory information in the same manner that a human observer might. Typical of such theorists is David Marr (1982), who began with the general presumption made in direct perception that all of the information needed is in the stimulus inputs. It differs from direct perception theory in that it involves the piecing together of information based on some simple dimensions in the stimulus, such as boundaries and edges, line endings, or particular patterns where stimuli meet. This process of interpretation or synthesis is believed to require a number of computations and several stages of analysis that often can be specified as mathematical equations or steps in a computer program. This added requirement of calcu-

lating features of objects or aspects of the environment from aspects of the stimuli reaching the observer has resulted in the label **computational theories** for this approach. At the highest levels, certain aspects of specific computational theories often require fairly high-powered mathematics, including non-Euclidean geometry, Lie algebras, Fourier analysis, and so forth.

A much older (but still active) theoretical approach begins with the recognition that our perceptual representation of the world is much richer and more accurate than might be expected on the basis of the information contained in the stimuli available at any one moment in time. Theories to explain this fact often begin with the suggestion that perception is much like reasoning. In addition to the information available to our sense organs at the moment, we can also use information based on our previous experience, our expectations, and so forth. This means, for example, that a visual percept may depend on other sources of information, some nonvisual in nature, some arising from our past history and cognitive processing strategies. The similarity of some of these mechanisms to reasoning leads us to refer to this type of theory as **intelligent perception.** This approach, which probably originated with Helmholtz in 1867, survives today in the work of researchers such as Irvin Rock (1983) who have a more cognitive orientation. These theories are also called **constructive theories** of per-ception, since our final conscious impression may involve combining a number of different factors to "construct" the final percept.

It is quite likely that each of these approaches is useful in describing some aspects of the perceptual process (see Coren & Girgus, 1978; Uttal, 1981). However, different orientations tend to lead researchers in different directions, searching for different types of mechanism. Each approach is likely to be valid for some parts of the problem and irrelevant to others. This is a common occurrence in many areas of endeavour. For instance, a metallurgist might look at a bridge and consider its material components, whereas a civil engineer might look at the load-bearing capacity of the entire structure, and a city planner might look at the same bridge in terms of traffic flow. At first glance the various views may seem to have little overlap, since the city planner does not care about the specific shape of the bridge structure, and the engineer only cares about the structural aspects of the beams, not their specific alloy constituents. Yet each level of analysis is valid for some specific set of questions. This book addresses the problem of how people build a conscious representation of their environment through the use of information reaching their senses. We follow the lead of many contemporary theorists and try to use data from all levels of the perceptual process, and we include discussions in terms of several different theoretical positions, in order to give an integrated view of the process of perception. After all, the label we apply to our approach is of considerably less importance than the understanding we attain.

THE PLAN OF THE BOOK

The orientation of this book is implicit rather than explicit. Although theories are introduced and discussed in the various chapters, no all-encompassing theoretical orientation has been adopted. We have chosen to be "militantly eclectic" in our orientation. Thus, this text is mostly concerned with perceptual and sensory *processes*. In general, the presentation of the material follows a levels-of-processing approach, in that the first half of the book is concerned with the more basic sensory processes and is organized around specific sensory systems, such as vision or audition, and the second half of the book is concerned with the more clearly perceptual processes that have strong cognitive influences and are often not bound to any single sensory modality.

We have tried to make the individual chapters relatively self-contained. We begin by explaining how sensations and perceptions are measured (Chapter 2). We then proceed with the physiological structures and the basic sensory capacities associated with vision (Chapters 3 through 5), hearing (Chapters 6 and 7), and the chemical and mechanical senses (Chapters 8 and 9). For those who feel a bit "rusty" about some of the very basic physiological facts, we have also included a "Primer of Neurophysiology" as an appendix. Chapters 10 through 15 deal with problems that have traditionally been treated as part of classical perception—our perceptual representation of space, time, motion, form, and size. The more cognitive aspects of perception are also introduced in this section, in those chapters that deal with the issues of music, speech perception, and attention. The last three chapters (16 through 18) deal with perceptual diversity, including many of the factors that make the perceptual experience of one individual different from that of another, such as the normal aging process, life history, experience, learning, and personality factors.

You will notice that each chapter includes several Demonstration Boxes. These are experimental demonstrations that you can perform for yourself using stimuli provided in the book or materials that are easily found around a house or living quarters. They illustrate many aspects of perceptual processes. Quite often they demonstrate concepts that are difficult to put into words, but that, when experienced, are immediately understandable. These demonstrations are an integral part of the book, and you are encouraged to try them. In the same way that perception involves interaction with the world, these demonstrations allow you to interact with your senses in a controlled manner and to gain insight into yourself.

We hope this book will provide you with some understanding of the limits and the abilities of your senses. This knowledge should expand your comprehension of many behavioral phenomena that depend on perception as a first step. Perception seems to be the final judge of the truth or the falsity of everything we encounter as part of our human experience. How often have you heard the phrase, "Seeing is believing" or "I didn't believe it until I saw it with my own two eyes"? Yet you have already seen in this chapter that such faith in the truthfulness of our conscious percepts is often misplaced. In 500 B.C., Parmenides considered how perception can deceive us, summarizing his feelings in these words: "The eyes and ears are bad witnesses when they are at the service of minds that do not understand their language." In this book we will try to teach you their language.

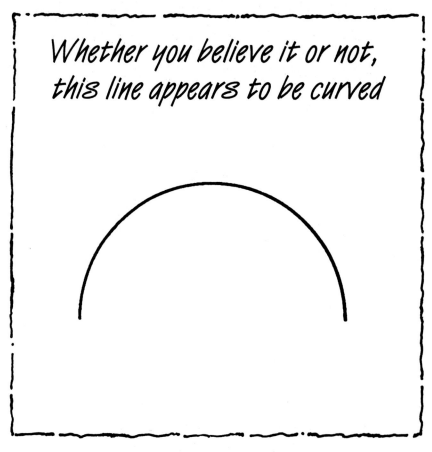

Some illusions are more illusory than others!

GLOSSARY

The following definitions are specific to their use in this book.

Affordances   A set of actions that a specific object or environmental situation *affords* or makes available to the perceiver.

Biological reductionism   The theoretical premise that each sensory experience is associated with particular physiological events.

Cognition   The process of knowing, incorporating both perception and learning.

Computational theories   Theories that involve the presumption that certain perceived qualities require computation and that these computations can be precisely described mathematically.

Constructive theories   Theories that maintain that perception may involve the integration of several sources of information, and may be affected by cognitive factors and experience.

Direct perception   The theoretical position that all of the information needed for the final conscious percept is in the stimulus array and that no computations or inferences are required to extract its meaning.

Illusions   Distortions or incongruencies between percept and reality.

Information processing   The process by which stimuli are registered in the receptors, identified, and stored in memory.

Intelligent perception   The theoretical presumption that cognitive processes and experience can affect perception.

Invariants   Aspects of the stimulus situation that are always present in the stimulus and are good predictors of object properties such as size, shape, or distance.

Levels-of-processing analysis   Analysis of the contribution of each stage of processing to the final percept, beginning with the receptor and continuing through cognitive mechanisms.

Perception   The conscious experience of objects and object relationships.

Sensation   Simple conscious experience associated with a stimulus.

Chapter ...

PSYCHOPHYSICS

Detection

  Method of Constant Stimuli

  Method of Limits

  Adaptive Testing

  Signal Detection Theory

Identification

  Information Theory

    • Channel Capacity

Discrimination

  Weber's Law

  Signal Detection Theory in Discrimination

  Reaction Time

Scaling

  Indirect Scaling: Fechner's Law

  Direct Scaling

    • Catagory Judgment

    • Magnitude Estimation: Stevens' Law

    • Cross-Modality Matching

  Multidimensional Psychological Scaling

  Context and Bias

*T*he ocean liner glides slowly though the thick, stormy night. Somewhere in the murk is the entrance to New York Harbor. The ship is in a heavily traveled trade route, and the crew must continually be alert for possible collisions with other ships. With the visibility near zero, the captain is forced to rely solely on the ship's radar for information about where those ships might be. The radar operator is watching her screen intently, searching for an "echo" caused by the presence of another ship nearby. She is also wrestling with a fundamental psychophysical problem, that of **detection.** She is trying to answer the question, "Is there anything there?"

She is sure she sees an echo. Now the question becomes "What is it"? Is it an echo from another ship or just a "ghost," a false echo often encountered in stormy weather? The radar operator is facing a second basic problem: **identification.** We normally solve the detection and identification problems quickly and automatically, since we generally encounter stimuli that are strong and clear. The complex nature of the processes involved in detection and identification usually becomes apparent only when conditions make stimuli weak and unclear, such as in a thick fog.

The echo turns out to be a "ghost," and the order is given to the helmsman to maintain the current heading (compass direction). The helmsman now becomes concerned with whether the compass needle is centered on the desired heading. At this moment, he is asking himself, "Has the needle drifted slightly toward the north?" If so, he must compensate by turning the wheel so that the needle moves back to the desired compass point. His task evokes the fundamental psychophysical process of **discrimination.** "Is this stimulus different from that one?" is the general discrimination question.

Finally, through the clearing weather, the entrance to New York Harbor appears. The ship is taken in tow by a tugboat and maneuvered toward its berth at the dock. The captain of the tugboat peers from his bridge, carefully judging the distance between the ship and the concrete wall of the pier. He must repeatedly ask himself, "How far does the ship appear to be from the pier?" Questions such as "How much of X is there?" are part of another fundamental psychophysical problem, called **scaling.**

These four problems, *detection, identification, discrimination,* and *scaling,* are fundamental concerns of the area of perceptual psychology called *psychophysics.* Psychophysics owes its name and origin to Gustav Theodor Fechner (1801–1887), a physicist and philosopher who set out to determine the relationship between the magnitude of a sensation experienced in the mind and the magnitude of the physical stimulus that gave rise to it. Hence the name psychophysics (from the Greek roots *psyche,* or "mind," and *physike,* which refers to naturally occurring phenomena). Fechner not only established the philosophical rationale for studying the relations between sensations and physical stimuli but also developed many of the experimental methods still in use today. These ways of collecting and analyzing data are employed in every aspect of the study of sensation and perception (see, for example, Laming, 1986) and in many other areas of psychology, including social, personality, environmental, developmental, and clinical psychology (Baird & Noma, 1978; Grossberg & Grant, 1978; Wegener, 1982).

Many perceptual and cognitive psychologists continue to work on Fechner's original problems. They have been called *fundamental psychophysicists* because they study the fundamental psychophysical concepts themselves (such as detection or discrimination) rather than use psychophysical methods to study a sensory system such as vision or audition (Ward, 1991). Because of the current revolution in the cognitive sciences, along with the cumulative progress of more than 130 years of psychophysics itself, fundamental psychophysics is beginning to emerge as a discipline in its own right. It has many theoretical concepts, empirical studies, and methods to contribute to psychology. As you read this chapter, keep in mind that although psychophysics emphasizes methods, the concepts it introduces are so fundamental to the rest of perceptual psychology that they are usually taken for granted.

DETECTION

The basic task for any sensory system is to detect the presence of energy changes in the environment. These changes may take the form of electromagnetic (light), mechanical (sound, touch, movement, muscle tension), chemical (taste, smell), or thermal (heat, cold) stimulation. The problem of detection is centered around the problem of how much of a stimulus is necessary for an individual to be consciously aware of its presence (that is, to see, hear, or otherwise sense it). Classically, this minimal amount of energy has been called the **absolute threshold.** In 1860 Fechner defined a *threshold stimulus* as one that "lifted the sensation or sensory difference over the threshold of consciousness." Below some critical intensity of the stimulus, a person would not be able to detect it. As soon as this threshold intensity is exceeded, however, we would expect the observer always to detect its presence.

We can represent this hypothetical relation using a graph called a **psychometric function.** Along the *ordinate* (or vertical axis) of the graph, we plot the proportion of stimulus presentations for which an observer is expected to say "yes" to the question, "Did you see (or hear, feel, etc.) the stimulus?" Along the *abscissa* (or horizontal axis) of the graph are plotted the values of the stimulus magnitude.

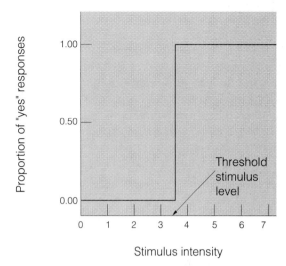

Figure 2-1   *Absolute threshold.*

These data have been plotted in Figure 2-1 using arbitrary units for stimulus intensity. Notice that the proportion of presentations on which the stimulus is detected takes a sudden step up from 0 to 1.00 when the stimulus reaches a value of 3.50. The absolute threshold indicated by this ideal psychometric function is thus 3.50.

Method of Constant Stimuli

How do we measure absolute thresholds? Let us conduct a relatively simple but typical experiment to measure the absolute threshold of hearing. In this experiment an observer sits in a soundproof room wearing headphones. The experimenter selects a set of tones that all have the same frequency but vary in intensity around the probable threshold intensity. These tones are presented, one at a time, to the observer. Each stimulus is presented many times in a prearranged, irregular order. The observer is simply required to respond "yes" when the stimulus is detected and "no" when it is not.

This procedure is called the **method of constant stimuli,** a name derived from the fact that a fixed or constant set of stimuli is chosen beforehand. Some typical data obtained with this method are presented graphically in Figure 2-2, where we plot the proportion of "yes" responses (simply the number of "yes" responses divided by the number of stimulus presentations for each stimulus intensity).

We see in Figure 2-2 that as the stimulus energy increases, the relative number of times the observer says "yes" (meaning the stimulus was perceived) gradually increases. These S-shaped curves, called *ogives*, are obtained commonly with the method of constant stimuli in all sensory systems. Notice that our psychophysical experiment did not find the sharp transition from "not sensing" to "sensing" that we expected from Figure 2-1. Instead we find that the likelihood that a person will report the stimulus increases gradually as the stimulus intensity increases. So where is the absolute threshold?

With no dramatic transition point to define the absolute threshold, we must make a somewhat arbitrary decision. If the stimulus is def-

initely above threshold the observer should detect it every time. If it is definitely below the threshold the observer should never detect it. It seems sensible to say that some place in between these extremes we cross the threshold. Thus the threshold stimulus is defined as that intensity where the probability of saying "yes" is the same as the probability of saying "no" (each equals 0.50). This corresponds to the stimulus intensity that the subject would detect 50% of the time.

Notice that we use the term *probability* in this context. Proportions (as in Figure 2-2) represent actual data, whereas probabilities are predicted (or theoretical) proportions. In Figure 2-2 we show graphically how the threshold can be determined. Simply run a horizontal line from the 0.50 value on the ordinate until it intersects the data curve. A line dropped vertically from this point now marks the absolute threshold (which is about 3.50 energy units for this observer). Although this halfway point on the psychometric function (a probability detection of 0.50) is the generally agreed upon value for the threshold, it is an arbitrary value. For certain specific purposes other researchers have used different threshold values (for example, 0.60 or 0.75).

Although the method of constant stimuli can give good estimates of absolute threshold, it has the drawback of being quite time-consuming. Pretesting is often needed to find the general location of the threshold, and then a large number of trials are presented at each intensity level. Sometimes fewer trials may be used, but this method is not time-efficient, and many trials are "wasted" because they yield information about stimuli that are far from the threshold (Simpson, 1988; Watson & Fitzhugh, 1990). The amount of time spent in determining a sensory threshold is especially important in a clinical setting, such as testing a patient's eyesight for a prescription for glasses. Doctors and patients prefer to avoid methods involving hours of testing.

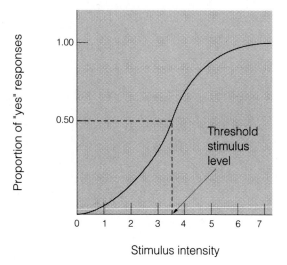

Figure 2-2   *Typical data from method of constant stimuli in detection.*

The time-consuming nature of the method of constant stimuli leads to another problem. The method is not very useful for measuring how thresholds change over a brief time period, since it depends on the threshold remaining constant until enough trials are completed. If the threshold changes during the administration of the necessary trials, the method will give an average value that represents neither the original nor the final threshold.

Method of Limits

One way to avoid some of the problems of the method of constant stimuli is to estimate the threshold point directly rather than trace out the entire psychometric function. One of the oldest of such methods is called the **method of limits.** Emil Kraepelin created that name in 1891, because a stimulus series always ends when the observer reaches a limit or a point of change in judgment. In this technique, the experimenter begins by presenting an observer with a stimulus (say, a pure tone) at an intensity high enough to be easily heard and then decreases its intensity in small steps until the observer reports, "I no longer hear it." This is

called a *descending series*. On alternate trials the experimenter starts with a tone that cannot be heard and increases the intensity until the observer reports "I hear it." This is termed an *ascending series*. Such a method gives a fairly quick measurement of the threshold.

When thresholds are measured with the method of limits, the "absolute threshold" for hearing is not a fixed value as we first proposed. For instance, we might find that in one descending series the observer could no longer detect the stimulus when presented with a tone intensity of 50, but in the next descending series a stimulus intensity of only 43 was still detected. It seems that the threshold varies from measurement to measurement, or from moment to moment. Demonstration Box 2-1 shows how you personally can experience this threshold variability.

Why does the threshold seem to vary from moment to moment? As early as 1888, Joseph Jastrow speculated on the reason for the variability of the threshold over time. He theorized that lapses of attention, slight fatigue, and other psychological changes could cause fluctuation of the threshold. In addition, there are more fundamental reasons to expect the threshold to fluctuate.

DEMONSTRATION BOX 2-1   The Variability of the Threshold

For this demonstration you will need a wristwatch (or a clock) that ticks. Place the watch on a table and move across the room so that you can no longer hear the ticking. If the tick is faint, you may accomplish this merely by moving your head away some distance. Now gradually move toward the watch. Note that you are actually performing a method of limits experiment, since the sound level steadily increases as you approach the watch. At some distance from

the watch you will begin to hear the source of the sound. This is your momentary threshold. Now hold this position for a few moments and you will notice that occasionally the sound will fade and you may have to step forward to reach threshold, whereas at other times it may be noticeably louder and you may be able to step back and still hear it. These changes are a result of your changing threshold sensitivity.

We tend to assume that in a threshold measurement experiment the only stimulus present is the stimulus we are asking our observer to detect. This is not the case. A constantly present and ever-changing background of sensation exists no matter what stimulus we present to the observer. If you place both of your hands over your ears to block out the room noises, you will hear a sound one observer poetically called "the sound of waves from a distant sea," and another, somewhat less poetically, "the faint hissing of radio static." Similarly, if you sit in a completely light-proof room in absolute darkness, you do not see complete blackness. Your visual field appears to be filled with a grayish mist (which has been termed "cortical gray"), and occasionally you can even see momentary bright pinpoint flashes here and there. Any stimulus we ask an observer to detect must compete with this spontaneously generated fluctuating background. It is as though every stimulus to be detected is superimposed on a background of noise generated within the observer. By *noise* we mean any background sensation other than the one to be detected, which means that we can have visual as well as auditory noise. As this *endogenous*, or internal, noise level changes, so does our measured threshold, in the same way that a person standing in the midst of a crowd finds she can not hear the person she is conversing with when the crowd gets particularly noisy.

Some experimenters have resorted to the introduction of experimentally controlled background noise caused by external stimuli other than the one to be detected (*exogenous* noise) in order to achieve more constant conditions. Under these conditions they have a more accurate idea of the noise level with which the stimulus is competing, since the imposed noise is much more intense and "swamps" the endogenous noise. Many of the experiments we will discuss have employed such a controlled background noise level.

Adaptive Testing

The method of limits is still somewhat inefficient, because only the stimuli near the threshold (at the end of the testing series) give any information. All of the very intense (or very weak) stimuli at the beginning of a test series are thus wasted. **Adaptive testing** procedures are used to keep the test stimuli "hovering around" the threshold by *adapting* the sequence of stimulus presentations to the observer's responses. Consider, for example, one such technique called the **staircase method.** In one application of this procedure we might start with a descending set of stimuli. Each time the observer says, "Yes, I hear it" we *decrease* the stimulus intensity by one step. At some point the stimulus will become too weak to be heard and the observer will say, "No, I don't hear it." At this point we do not end the series, as we did in the method of limits, but rather reverse its direction. Thus we now *increase* the stimulus intensity by one step. We continue with this pattern, decreasing the stimulus when the observer says "yes" and increasing it when the observer says "no." In this way the value of the test stimulus flips back and forth around the threshold value as shown in Figure 2-3. The advantage of this procedure is that it allows the experimenter to "track" the threshold over time, even if sensitivity is continually changing, such as after administration of a drug or after adaptation to different background stimuli (Bekesy, 1949; Jesteadt, 1980).

The staircase method is the simplest example of the use of adaptive testing to find thresholds. Using the observer's previous responses as a basis for choosing the next stimulus to be presented allows the experimenter to zero in on the threshold quickly and efficiently, with few wasted trials, and with a high degree of reliability (Kaernbach, 1991). In our example we used the rule, "Increase intensity by one step if the response to the previous stimulus was 'no' and decrease intensity by one step if the previ-

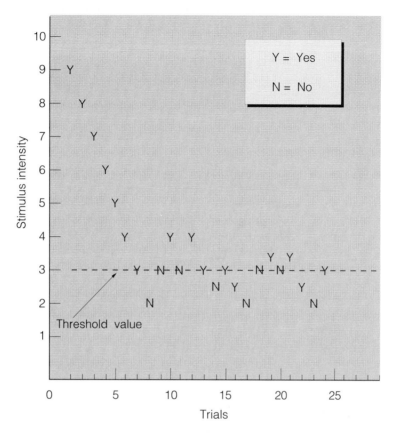

Figure 2-3   *A portion of a trial-by-trial record (called a track) from a run of an adaptive testing technique using a descending staircase procedure where the intensity is decreased on detection ("yes") and increased when not detected ("no").*

ous response was 'yes.'" This is called a *1 up–1 down* rule. Other rules can be used, however, to increase the precision of the method, to avoid judgment biases, or to achieve certain statistical properties in the data. Other adaptive testing rules that have been suggested are 1 up–2 down and 1 up–3 down, in which a sequence of two or three "yes" responses at each stimulus level is required before the stimulus intensity is reduced by one step. Also, the intensity step in adaptive testing is usually a constant, preselected increase or decrease in intensity. However, in some methods the step size is changed adaptively as well (for example, Kaernback, 1991).

Let us consider some examples of approximate absolute threshold values as measured by these methods. The human visual system is so sensitive that a candle flame can be seen from a distance of more than 48 kilometers (30 miles) on a dark, clear night. The auditory system can detect the ticking of a wristwatch in a quiet room at a distance of 6 meters (20 feet)— sensitivity beyond this point would allow us to hear the sound of air molecules colliding. As for our other senses, we can taste one teaspoon of sugar dissolved in 7 1/2 liters (2 gallons) of water, and smell one drop of perfume diffused through the volume of an average three-room apartment (Galanter, 1962).

Signal Detection Theory

Some of you may have been bothered by one aspect of the psychophysical measurement techniques we have discussed. Although we are studying an observer's sensory capacities, we have not talked about the probability that an observer *detects* a stimulus. Rather, we have only looked at the probability that the observer says, "Yes, I hear it (or see it)." We can imagine that if an observer feels that this is a "test" of some sort, and wants to appear to be quite sensitive, the person might say "yes" on almost every trial. What is to prevent this from happening? Although we might argue that people are basically honest, and would not lie about whether or not they heard or saw a stimulus, this is not the sort of guarantee upon which scientists would like to rest their conclusions. We are not criticizing the reliability of observers in psychophysical experiments; most are quite sincere and honest. Rather, we are pointing out that with the very low stimulus energies used in most detection experiments, observers may be unsure as to whether a stimulus was present or not, and may adopt some "strategy" for responding. For example, an observer may decide not to let too many trials go by with only "no" responses, so as not to appear to be "hard of hearing."

In an attempt to establish some control over subjects' guessing patterns, experimenters began to insert **catch trials,** on which no stimulus was presented. Experimenters reasoned that if observers were honest in their reports, they would respond "no" on these catch trials. If the "yes" response came too frequently on catch trials, the observer was cautioned against guessing. Alternatively, researchers attempted to adjust the calculated threshold to account for the guesses, or simply discarded the data. Over many experiments, however, it became clear that the observers were not trying to fool anyone. Somehow their behavior was reasonable, even though it was not clear what they were doing. One possible reason for these honest "mistakes" seems to be that the observers' decision-making behavior interacts with their sensory processes to give rise to "biased" estimates of thresholds. This explanation led to the development of a set of techniques that were designed to measure observers' response "bias" directly and to provide a bias-free estimate of sensory sensitivity (which is what classical threshold measurements were supposed to do).

The new procedures form a system called **signal detection theory** (see Egan, 1975; Gescheider, 1985; Green & Swets, 1966). This mathematically based theory assumes that the observer is not a passive receiver of stimuli, but rather an active decision-maker who makes difficult perceptual judgments under conditions of uncertainty. The procedures used in signal detection experiments also involve catch trials where no signal is present, but the data from these trials are treated in a systematic way.

The basic experimental setup for signal detection studies is shown in Table 2-1. The experiments use two types of "stimulus" presentations (shown at the left of the table). A *signal absent* presentation is like a classical catch trial on which no stimulus is presented and observers see or hear only the noise generated by their sensory system. *Signal present* is a trial on which the experimenter actually presents the target stimulus (which is, of course, superimposed on the endogenous noise in the sensory system). Two responses are possible in the experiment (shown at the top of the table).

Table 2-1 Outcomes of a Signal Detection Experiment

	RESPONSE	
Signal	*Yes*	*No*
Present	Hit	Miss
Absent	False alarm	Correct negative

Yes indicates that the observer thinks a stimulus was presented on a particular trial (that is, signal present), and *No* indicates that the observer thinks the signal was absent. The combination of two possible stimulus presentations and two possible responses leads to four possible outcomes on a given trial (indicated by the four cells of the table). When the signal is present and the response is "yes," the observer has made a **hit.** But if the observer responded "yes" when the signal was absent, then a **false alarm** has been made. The other cells are called **misses** and **correct negatives** for obvious reasons.

Consider a typical signal detection experiment designed to measure an observer's ability to detect a tone. The tone for a given experiment will be constant in intensity. After a ready signal, the observer is required to respond by pushing one button to indicate, "Yes, the signal tone was present" and a different button to signify, "No, it was not." Table 2-2 shows a typical response pattern when the signal was presented on 50% of the trials, and no signal was presented for the remaining 50%. This **outcome matrix** shows the proportion of trials on which the four possible results occurred.

Notice that on 25% of the trials, when the signal was absent the observer responded, "Yes, the signal was present." Why would the observer report that a signal was present when it was not? First, clearly the observer is not always sure that what was heard was actually the signal. Thus, many nonsensory aspects of the situation might influence the response pattern.

Consider the effect of the observer's expectations. An observer who knows that the signal is given on almost every trial might respond "yes" to even the faintest or most ambiguous of sensations (perhaps even generated by endogenous noise from the nervous system). This is sensible behavior if the stimulus occurs most of the time, because on these "doubtful" trials the observer will quite often be correct. However, if the signal rarely occurs, the observer would be less tempted by ambiguous, faint sensations, and might wait to experience a stronger sensation before saying "yes."

If our description of what the observer is doing is correct, then we should be able to change the response pattern by changing the expectations, even though the person's sensitivity would remain the same. Typical results from the same observer in Table 2-2 are presented in Table 2-3. In one case the signal was present on 90% of the trials, and in the other on only 10% of the trials. Notice that when the signal is occurring frequently the observer says "yes" often. This results in a high proportion of hits, but also a high proportion of false alarms. The observer says "no" more often when expecting the signal only occasionally, thus reducing the proportion of false alarms, but also

Table 2-2   Outcome Matrix (Proportions) When Stimulus Is Present 50% of the Time

	RESPONSE	
Signal	*Yes*	*No*
Present	0.75	0.25
Absent	0.25	0.75

Table 2-3   Outcome Matrices (Proportions) for Two Different Conditions

STIMULUS PRESENT 90% OF THE TIME		
	Response	
Signal	Yes	No
Present	0.95	0.05
Absent	0.63	0.37

STIMULUS PRESENT 10% OF THE TIME		
	Response	
Signal	Yes	No
Present	0.35	0.65
Absent	0.04	0.96

reducing the proportion of hits. How, then, do we measure the observer's sensitivity? Using our previous definition of an absolute threshold as the stimulus intensity at which the probability of detecting a signal is 0.50, the tone is clearly above threshold in the case where the stimulus was presented 90% of the time, but below threshold when the stimulus was only presented 10% of the time. This does not make sense, since neither the tone's intensity nor the observer's sensitivity has changed. Obviously, we need some way of separating the observer's sensitivity from the observer's decision strategy.

Let us begin such an analysis by exploring how the observer's responses change for a particular signal strength as we vary expectations by varying the relative frequency with which the signal occurs. We will obtain proportions of hits and false alarms separately for each different signal probability, as we just discussed. If these proportions of hits and false alarms are plotted against each other as in Figure 2-4, we

obtain a **receiver operating characteristic curve** (abbreviated **ROC curve**), which displays the relation between proportions of hits and false alarms as the decision conditions change. This terminology was inherited from the communications engineers who first developed a form of signal detection theory. A more descriptive term is *isosensitivity curve* (where the root *iso* means "same"), indicating that the curve represents the range of possible outcome matrices for one, unchanging, level of sensitivity. As in the previous example, Figure 2-4 shows that when the signal is rare, the observer says "no" on a large proportion of trials even when the signal was presented. At the high end of the curve, where the signal occurs frequently, the observer says "yes" on a large proportion of the trials even when the signal did not occur.

An ROC curve reflects an observer's response pattern for one signal strength. If we increase the strength of the signal we find that the curve has a more pronounced bow, as shown by the curved black line in Figure 2-4. If we decrease the signal strength, the curve becomes flatter and approaches the 45-degree line, which represents chance responding. Thus, the location and shape of the ROC curve varies with signal strength. An alternative way to interpret an ROC curve is in terms of differences in the sensitivity of different observers to a signal of a particular strength. Thus, the two curves in Figure 2-4 could be interpreted as reflecting the sensitivity of a single observer to stimuli of different strength (greater sensitivity shown by more bow and distance from the diagonal), or they could be curves of two different observers with different sensitivities to the same signal strength.

We may also vary the observer's response pattern, while holding the signal intensity constant, by varying the perceived importance of a given response. For instance, if we pay 10 cents for every hit and nothing for correct rejections, misses, or false alarms, the optimal strategy is

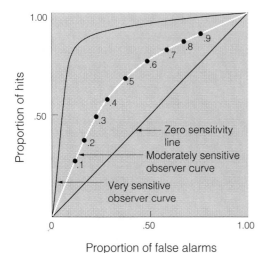

Figure 2-4 *ROC curves. Notice how the shape of the curve changes for a given signal strength and different levels of sensitivity. The black dots on the white curve represent results with indicated probability of signal presentation.*

to guess "yes" on every trial, since there are no penalties for a wrong "yes," and no rewards or penalties at all for "no" responses. This strategy would maximize the amount of money that can be earned in the test situation. Contrast this to a situation where we deduct 10 cents for each false alarm and pay nothing for hits, correct rejections, or misses. Here, a reasonable observer would minimize the losses by saying "no" on every trial. Actually most situations fall somewhere between these two extremes. For instance, we might pay our observer 10 cents for every correct response (hit or correct rejection) and deduct 5 cents for every wrong response (false alarm or miss). This situation, in which "yes" and "no" responses have equal value, is depicted in the matrix of numbers shown in Table 2-4. Such a set of rewards and penalties is called a **payoff matrix.** Changing the payoff matrix changes an observer's response pattern in much the same way as varying an observer's expectations concerning stimulus frequency. By systematically varying the payoff matrix of an experiment, we can vary an observer's numbers of hits and false alarms and produce an ROC curve similar to that generated by varying the relative frequency of signals. Thus an observer's *motives* as well as *expectations* affect responses during the detection experiment. Note that it is the observer's *response pattern* (for example, the overall number of "yes" responses) that varies as the ROC curve is produced, *not the sensitivity to the stimulus.* Because the motivation in this case is manipulated by varying the payoff

matrix, and thus the amount of money paid to an observer, this type of experiment has been given the snide name "sweatshop psychophysics."

Perhaps the theoretical and methodological bases for signal detection will become clearer if we look at the detection problem from a different angle. We have said that even when no stimulus is present an observer's sensory systems are still active, generating sensory noise. The amount of noise varies from moment to moment. This fluctuation in noise level is probably caused by the operation of physiological, attentional, and other variables on the sensory and perceptual systems of the observer. Signal detection theorists represent these fluctuations in the form of a **probability distribution,** which is a theoretical summary of many trials in an experiment. This distribution is graphed in Figure 2-5 as the *signal absent curve.* The abscissa represents the amount of sensory activity (or sensation level), and the ordinate can be thought of as the relative likelihood of occurrence of any particular sensation level over the whole set of trials. This means that even in the absence of any external signal, the observer experiences some level of sensation that is represented by a particular location along the abscissa. The relative frequency of each level experienced is represented by the height of the curve at that point.

When a signal is actually presented, it occurs against this background of sensory noise. Of course, the signal produces some sensory response of its own, which then adds to whatever amount is already present. The net effect is the creation of a new distribution of sensory activity, the *signal present curve,* which is a theoretical summary of many signal trials. The average level of activity elicited by the signal added to the sensory noise is more intense than that of the noise alone. This is shown by the fact that the mean of the signal present curve is shifted toward higher values of the sensory activity axis in Figure 2-5. When the signal

Table 2-4 A Typical Payoff Matrix for a Psychophysical Experiment

	RESPONSE	
Signal	*Yes*	*No*
Present	10¢	−5¢
Absent	−5¢	10¢

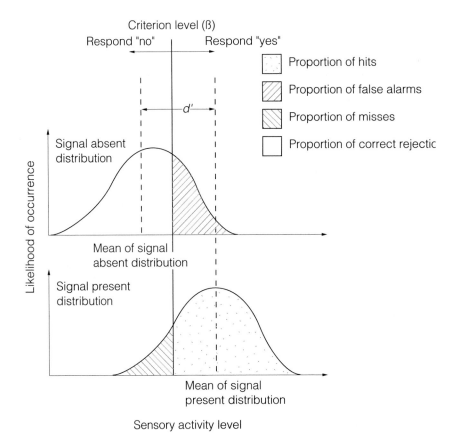

Figure 2-5   *Illustration of how signal absent and signal present distributions result in hits, misses, false alarms, and correct negatives for a particular criterion setting. Notice that the two curves are actually plotted on the same axes—they are separated for clarity. The curves would overlap if plotted together.*

is weak, however, it will not add enough sensory activity to make the two distributions (signal absent versus signal present) completely distinct. The two distributions in Figure 2-5 would overlap if drawn on the same set of axes. You can see from Figure 2-5 that some levels of sensation could result either from presentations of the signal or from noise alone.

Imagine you are an observer trying to decide whether a signal has just been presented. The only information you have is the intensity of your experienced sensation. Remember, however, that sometimes the noise produces a sensation that is just as intense as that pro-

duced by the signal, as shown in Figure 2-5. As a rational being, you would probably solve this problem by setting a **criterion** or cutoff point for sensation level. This is the value you are willing to accept as indicating that a signal was most likely present. If you experience a sensation level below the criterion level (to the left of the vertical solid line in Figure 2-5), you respond "no"; if it is above (to the right of) the criterion level, you respond "yes." This simplifies the problem greatly, since you must only decide, based on your motives and expectations, where to put the criterion. From that point on, the level of sensation you experience more or less automatically determines your response. The criterion level is usually symbolized with the Greek letter ß **(BETA).**

If this is what the observer is doing, then we can specify the expected proportions of hits and false alarms depending on where the observer places the criterion. According to signal detection theory, the proportions of the various outcomes observed in an experiment (see Table 2-1) may be represented as the proportion of the *area* under the appropriate probability distribution curve to the right or left of the criterion location. Thus, if Figure 2-5 represents an actual situation in which the observer says "yes" whenever the experienced sensation level is above (to the right of) the criterion level, the proportion of signal present trials on which a "yes" response would be given (the proportion of hits) is represented by the area under the signal present curve to the right of the criterion. Similarly, the proportion of false alarms is represented by the area under the signal absent curve to the right of the criterion, since that is the proportion of trials on which the sensation level generated by the sensory system in the absence of a signal would be expected to exceed the criterion level set for the "yes" response. The other two possible outcomes are also represented in Figure 2-5.

The motivation and expectation effects on an observer's decision behavior in a detection experiment are now interpretable. Essentially, these variables affect the placement of the criterion and, hence, the proportion of hits and false alarms. For instance, suppose the observer is a radiologist looking for a light spot as evidence of cancer in a set of chest x-rays (see, for example, Swensson, 1980). If the radiologist thinks she has found such a spot, she calls the patient back for additional tests. The penalty for a false alarm (additional tests when no cancer is present) only involves some added time and money on the part of the patient, whereas the penalty for a miss (not catching an instance of real cancer) might be the patient's death. Thus, the radiologist may set a criterion value

that is quite low (lax), not wanting to miss any danger signals. This means she will have many hits and few misses, but also quite a few false alarms, a situation shown in Figure 2-6A. Conversely, if the observer is a radar operator looking for blips on a screen signifying enemy

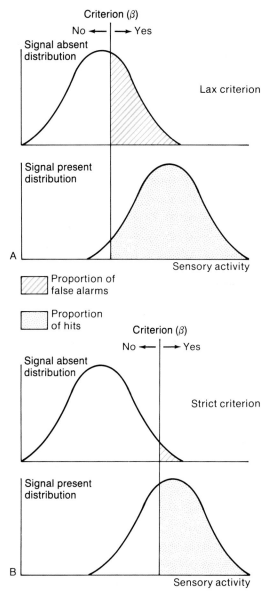

Figure 2-6 *The effect of motives or expectations on criterion placement and proportion of hits and false alarms.*

missiles, he might be much more conservative. Here the penalty for a false alarm could be war, while the penalty for a miss might be only a few seconds lost in sounding the alarm. He would set a high (strict) criterion in order to avoid false alarms, but at the penalty of reducing the number of hits. This would be equivalent to the situation shown in Figure 2-6B. Each point on any given ROC curve (such as Figure 2-4) actually represents a different criterion setting.

Although we indicated that the location of the criterion alters the pattern of responses, we did not mention the effect of criterion location on the sensitivity of the observer. This is because no such effect exists. In signal detection theory, sensitivity refers to the average amount of sensory activity generated by a given signal as compared with the average amount of noise-generated activity. This is similar to the everyday use of the word *sensitivity*. Thus, a radio receiver that produces a large electrical response, allowing a weak signal to be heard above the background static, is more sensitive than one that produces only a small electrical response to that signal, which may then be obscured by static and noise.

Within our present framework, the perceptual analog of sensitivity is the distance between the centers (means) of the signal absent and the signal present distributions. This represents the difference in average sensation levels as a function of the presence or absence of a signal. We call this distance measure of sensitivity d', which is pronounced "d prime" (see Figure 2-5). When the distributions are far apart, and overlap very little, as in Figure 2-7B, d' is large and the ROC curve is far from the diagonal and sharply curved. When the distributions are close together, and overlap to a great extent, d' is relatively small, as in Figure 2-7A. The corresponding ROC curve is close to the diagonal, which you may remember represents zero sensitivity. Signal detection theory attempts to measure an observer's sensitivity to a signal independently of the decision strategy, although it acknowledges that both factors can

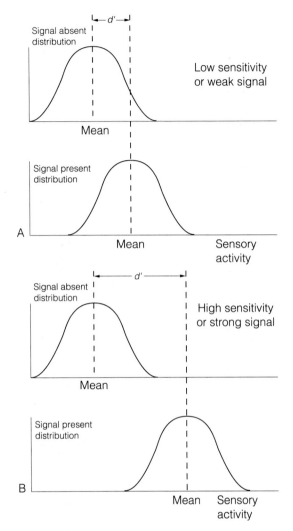

Figure 2-7 *The effect of sensitivity and signal strength on* d'.

affect the actual responses made in the experimental setting. This theory has become an indispensable part of modern psychophysics, even appearing in some adaptive measurement techniques for thresholds (for example, Kaernbach, 1990). Instructions for calculating d' and ß using proportions of hits and false alarms obtained from any typical signal detection experiment (for example, Tables 2-2 and 2-3) can be found in Computation Box 2-1.

IDENTIFICATION

The doctor listened very carefully, paused for a moment to adjust the stethoscope to a more comfortable position, and listened again to the sounds emanating from the patient's chest. The sounds were quite clear and distinct. The problem was to decide whether they indicated a normal or a pathological heartbeat. This doctor is facing a problem that does not involve stimulus detection, for the sounds are clearly above the detection threshold. However, it does involve the identification of the occurrence of one of a number of possible alternative stimuli. To identify a stimulus is one of the major tasks that the perceptual system is asked to perform.

The difficulty of any identification task depends, in part, on the number of possible stimulus alternatives among which an observer is asked to distinguish. Consider an observer who claims she can identify her favorite brand of cola. Suppose we gave her two unmarked glasses of cola and asked her to sample them and try to select her own favorite brand. If she did select the correct brand we would not be very surprised, since she would be expected to select her own brand 50% of the time by chance alone, even if her taste buds were nonfunctional. If our "expert" selected her own brand out of 25 brands presented to her, we would be much more likely to take her claim seriously, since the probability that she would by chance alone find her brand out of 25 alternatives is only 1/25. Measures of the difficulty of the recognition task must therefore take into account the number of stimulus alternatives.

Information Theory

To solve the problem of specifying the difficulty of an identification task, psychologists in the early 1950s turned to ideas developed by engineers to assess the performance of radio and telephone communications systems. Books by Shannon and Weaver (1949) and by Wiener

(1961) made it clear that the problems faced by the psychophysicist and by the communications engineer were quite similar. The engineer deals with a message that is transmitted through a communication channel and decoded by someone or something at the receiver end. The degree to which the final decoded message reflects the original message depends on the ability of the system to transmit information without distortion (this is what is meant by the *fidelity* of a system), and on the complexity of the input. The psychophysicist has an analogous problem. Stimulus information is transmitted to an observer through a sensory system, and it is then decoded in the central nervous system. The degree to which the observer's identification of the stimulus corresponds to the actual stimulus input will be affected both by the ability of the sensory system to handle the stimulus input without distortion and by the complexity of the input.

The quantitative system for specifying the characteristics of the input message is known as **information theory.** What we will present here as information theory is actually a system of measurement. The amount of information in a given stimulus display is defined so that the nature of the object being measured is irrelevant. What, then, do we mean by *information*? We mean what the everyday use of the word implies. If you tell us that this week will contain a Sunday morning, you have conveyed very little information, since we know that every week contains a Sunday morning. If you tell us that this Sunday morning a parade will be held in honor of Jiffy the Kangaroo, you have conveyed a great deal of information because you have specified which one out of a large number of possible alternative events will occur.

One way to quantify information is to define it in terms of the questions a person must ask to discover which member of a stimulus set has occurred. Suppose there were only two possible alternatives, A or B, and you wanted to determine which of them was the target. You

COMPUTATION BOX 2-1   Calculation of Signal Detection Measures d' and β

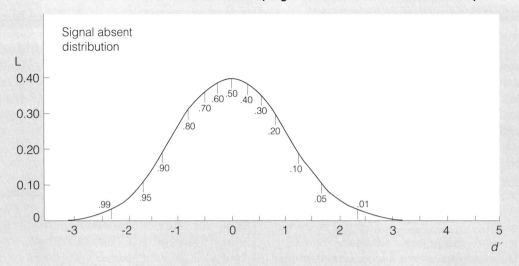

To calculate *d'* and ß using a simple graphic procedure, you will need the sheet of transparent overlay (found inside the front cover) and the diagram of the signal absent distribution above. First, tear the overlay along the perforated line to separate the *criterion* and *signal present distribution* portions as indicated.

Next, from the outcome of a signal detection experiment, you will need the proportions of *hits* and *false alarms*. As an example, we will use the data from Table 2-2.

TO CALCULATE *d'*

1. Put the sheet containing the criterion on top of the diagram of the signal absent distribution. Make sure that the horizontal line of the criterion sheet is superimposed on the horizontal axis of the distribution.

2. Slide the criterion sheet across the sheet below until the criterion (vertical line) is positioned so that it cuts the signal absent distribution curve at the point that represents the proportion of false alarms. From Table 2-2 this

is 0.25, so you must estimate the placement between the marked numbers.

3. Holding the criterion sheet stationary, add the *signal present distribution* sheet to the stack, positioning it so that the horizontal axis is aligned with the other horizontal axes. Adjust it so the criterion meets the signal present distribution curve at the point representing the proportion of *hits* (in this example it is 0.75).

4. The final stack of 2 overlay sheets on top of the signal absent distribution should look something like the figure on page 35. Notice you can see through the overlay sheets to the *d'* scale printed on the signal absent distribution diagram. The *d'* value can then be read off that scale as the point where the vertical line (which is marked "Read *d'* " and represents the mean of the signal present distribution) intersects the *d'* scale (about 1.35 in the figure on page 35—interpolate carefully).

Now try calculating the values of *d'* for the two sets of data in Table 2-3. You should find that *d'* is about 1.35, the same as for the data

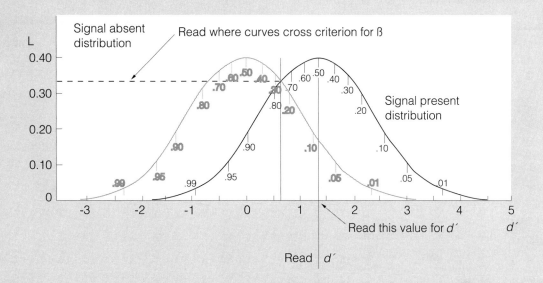

Signal absent distribution

Read where curves cross criterion for ß

Signal present distribution

Read this value for d´

Read | d´

of Table 2-2, in spite of the vast differences in hit and false alarm rates (compare with Figure 2-6).

TO CALCULATE ß

To measure the criterion, calculating ß requires one small computational step in additon to looking at the graphs.

1. Align a straight-edge (ruler or piece of paper) parallel to the superimposed horizontal axes of your pile (without sliding the sheets around) and position it vertically so that you are measuring the height of the curve where the criterion and the *signal present curve* meet. Read off the value corresponding to the height from the vertical axis (labeled "L" for "Likelihood") where the straight-edge crosses it (around 0.34).

2. Next read the height of the curve where the criterion crosses the *signal absent curve*. (In this example this is the same, with a height of 0.34).

3. To calculate ß, divide the height (the L axis value) for the *signal present distribution* by the height for the *signal absent distribution*. In the figure below, this is 0.34/0.34 = 1.00, or ß = 1.00.

Try calculating ß for the two sets of data in Table 2-3. You should find that, because of the very different hit and false alarm rates in the two data sets, the ß values are also very different. The top data set shows a lax criterion with ß less than 1.00 (here around 0.30), while the lower data set demonstrates a conservative criterion with ß greater than 1.00 (here a bit more than 4.00).

You should save your sheets of transparent overlay with the book so you can use them for other d' and ß calculations. Also note that, although this graphical method is accurate enough for quick estimates of d' and ß, psychophysicists use precise numerical tables or complex equations to arrive at these measures with the accuracy needed for research.

need only ask, "Is it *A*?" to determine unambiguously which alternative had been designated as the target. If you received an answer of "No" you would know immediately that the target was *B*. If you had to determine which of four stimuli, *A*, *B*, *C*, or *D*, had been chosen as the target, you could determine it with two questions. The answer to the question, "Is it *A* or *B*?" reduces your number of possible alternatives to two, since a "No" answer reveals that it is either *C* or *D*, while a "Yes" indicates that it is *A* or *B*. We already know that only one more question is necessary in order to identify the correct item. Each necessary question, structured to eliminate exactly *half* of the alternatives, defines a **bit** (from *bi*nary dig*it*) of information.

The number of bits of information needed to determine exactly one stimulus alternative is the logarithm to the base 2 of the total number of equally likely stimulus alternatives. The logarithm of a number *n* to the base 2, which is written $\log_2 n$, is the power to which the number 2 must be raised to equal *n*. Thus, if we have four alternatives we must raise 2 to the second power (that is, $2^2 = 2 \times 2 = 4$) and $\log_2 4 = 2$. Similarly, Table 2-5 gives the corresponding number of bits for *n* alternatives (a more detailed table can be found in Garner, 1962). Each time the number of stimulus alternatives is doubled, the amount of information rises by one bit. Of course, for intermediate values the number of bits will not be a whole number (for example, seven alternatives gives 2.81 bits).

Channel Capacity

It is important at this point to define the concept of **information transmission.** Let us consider an observer as a sort of communication channel. Our observer may be represented as in Figure 2-8. A stimulus is presented to the observer, who is asked to try to identify it. By identification we mean giving a response that is the correct, agreed-on label for the particular stimulus presented. We can say that information is transmitted by the observer to the extent the responses match the labels of the stimuli presented. That is, if the observer is presented with a stimulus, and gives the correct label as a response, information (the correct label) has been transmitted through the channel (the observer). If the response matches the stimulus perfectly for all stimuli, then the observer is a perfect information transmitter.

Consider an example in which we randomly call out letters from a set containing 8 items: *A B C D F G H X*. If the observer correctly identifies (response) the letter that we have called out (stimulus), then he has transmitted 3 bits of information ($\log_2 8$). Suppose identification is not perfect; that is, only some of the information is being transmitted. For instance, if the observer hears a faint "eee" sound, with the first part of the letter cut off, he does not know exactly which letter was called out. However, he can eliminate *A*, *F*, *H*, and *X*,

Table 2-5 Log$_2$n for Selected Numbers

NUMBER OF STIMULUS ALTERNATIVES (*n*)	NUMBER OF BITS ($\log_2 n$)
2	1
4	2
8	3
16	4
32	5
64	6
128	7
256	8

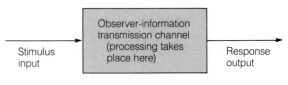

Figure 2-8   *A human information channel.*

which have no "eee" sound; hence, he has reduced the number of stimulus alternatives by half, and we would say that 1 bit of information has been transmitted. In general, the greater the probability that the observer will identify the stimulus—that is, the more he "picks up" from the presentations—the more information he is capable of transmitting.

Consider a hypothetical experiment in which each of 4 stimuli are presented 12 times and observers are asked to identify which stimulus was presented. The data from such an experiment can be presented in a **confusion matrix,** as is shown in Table 2-6 for three observers.

Observer A shows perfect information transmission because every time stimulus 1 is presented it is correctly identified; every time 2 is presented it is named correctly; and so forth. There are never any errors, or *confusions*. Observer B shows poorer information transmission. Note that when stimulus 2 is presented, it is called stimulus 2 most of the time, but sometimes it is called stimulus 1 and sometimes stimulus 3. When the response is "2," however, there is a fair likelihood that it is stimulus 2. Observer B is better than observer C, who seems to be responding without reference to the stimulus presented. Observer C is transmitting none of the available stimulus information. Formulas for computing the amount of information transmitted in such a confusion matrix may be found in Garner and Hake (1951).

How many bits of stimulus information can an observer transmit perfectly? Let us first look at a group of stimuli selected from a one-dimensional physical continuum, such as sound or light intensity. The number of stimuli from one continuum that an observer can identify perfectly has been found to be surprisingly small. For the identification of tones varying only in frequency, Pollack (1952) found it to be about 5 different tones, which is equivalent to about 2.3 bits of stimulus information. Garner (1953) found much the same result for sound intensity, around 2.1 bits. Eriksen and Hake (1955) measured several visual continua and found information transmission to be limited to 2.34 bits for light intensity, 2.84 bits for size, and 3.08 bits for wavelength. Overall, the number of stimuli that may be perfectly identified on any single continuum turns out to be approximately 7 plus or minus 2 (7 ± 2), depending on the particular stimulus continuum being tested (Miller, 1956).

This limit is called the observer's **channel capacity.** A typical measurement of channel capacity is shown in Figure 2-9. Notice that even though we increase the amount of information

Table 2-6 Stimulus-Response Matrices for Three Observers

OBSERVER A:
PERFECT INFORMATION TRANSMISSION

Stimulus	Response			
	1	2	3	4
1	12			
2		12		
3			12	
4				12

OBSERVER B:
SOME INFORMATION TRANSMISSION

Stimulus	Response			
	1	2	3	4
1	8	4		
2	2	8	2	
3		2	8	2
4			4	8

OBSERVER C:
NO INFORMATION TRANSMISSION

Stimulus	Response			
	1	2	3	4
1	3	3	3	3
2	3	3	3	3
3	3	3	3	3
4	3	3	3	3

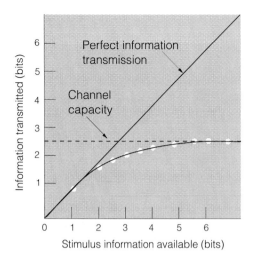

Figure 2-9 *Channel capacity. The straight diagonal represents perfect information transmission. The curve represents typical performance. The dotted horizontal line is channel capacity.*

available in the display, our observer has reached the limit of identification (about 2.5 bits) and can transmit no more information.

Several theories have been proposed to explain this general finding. In the most popular of these views, the limit reflects cognitive or response processes (for example, Braida & Durlach, 1988; Gravetter & Lockhead, 1973; Luce, Green, & Weber, 1976; Marley & Cook, 1984). A less popular theory is that the limit is set by the response characteristics of sensory neurons, and is thus an absolute limit for a single sensory continuum (Norwich, 1981).

Seven seems to be a very small number of stimuli to be able to identify. Each of us knows that musicians, for example, seem able to identify (indeed sing) hundreds of different songs. Every one of us can certainly identify dozens of faces and thousands of words. How can this be, in light of our inability to transmit more than about 3 bits of information per stimulus dimension?

One consideration might be that stimuli in the everyday world are more widely spaced

than typical laboratory stimuli and are therefore more discriminable. However, there is no such simple relationship between discriminability and identification performance (Braida & Durlach, 1988; Norwich, 1981; Pollack, 1952). Another possible explanation is that our everyday performance is improved because of practice or repetition. Except in extreme cases, however, where a person might have years of intensive training on a single dimension, the practice effect is also not large enough to explain our everyday performance. For instance, you may hear a new word today and later identify that word with ease, even though you have only encountered it once. You can also distinguish this word from every other word in your vocabulary. We are not at all surprised at such a performance, yet this type of identification may involve the transmission of some 16 bits of information (or more, depending on the total number of words in your vocabulary). Given that our channel capacity is so limited for any single stimulus dimension, how can this occur? The answer involves the *number of dimensions* along which the stimulus varies.

For example, Pollack (1953) found that if he varied only sound frequency, information transmission averaged about 1.80 bits, whereas if he varied only intensity information transmission was about 1.70 bits. When both dimensions were varied simultaneously, however, information transmission was 3.10 bits. This is more than was obtained for either dimension separately, although lower than the 3.50 bits expected if the information transmissions on the separate dimensions were simply summed. Nonetheless, the more dimensions along which the stimulus varies, the better the identification performance. Certain ways of combining dimensions seem to produce better performance by making stimuli "stand out" more clearly, or by capitalizing on the small gains obtainable from familiarity (Lockhead, 1970; Monahan & Lockhead, 1977). Thus, by proper selection of stimulus dimensions, Anderson and Fitts (1958) were able to obtain information transmission levels of 17 bits on a single flashed stimulus. This means that their observers could perfectly identify 1 stimulus out of more than 131,000 alternative stimuli.

The importance of stimulus dimensions and how they are combined has led modern investigators to place less emphasis on the *quantity* of information available and more emphasis on the *quality*, or kind, of information and the characteristics of the information processor (see Cutting, 1987; Garner, 1974; Neisser, 1967). The basic ideas of information theory, especially those associated with the number of stimulus alternatives, have been important in calling attention to critical issues in identification. Although other methods, based on signal detection methods, are sometimes used to measure identification (for example, Snodgrass & Corwin, 1988), information theory has taken its place as a foundation concept, and modern researchers use its methods and assumptions in many different situations.

DISCRIMINATION

The artist glances at the model's hair and then back down at the paint on the palette. He mutters to himself, "Still not the same." He daubs a bit more black, mixes the color thoroughly, and glances up again. "That is a perfect match," he grunts. This artist is engaging in an act of discrimination. He is determining whether two colors are the same or different. He does not care what the color actually is—it can be cocoa, burnt sienna, or just plain brown—he cares only whether or not the paint matches his model's hair color. Discrimination problems ask the question, "Is this stimulus different from that one?"

The study of discrimination has focused on the question, "By how much must two stimuli differ in order to be discriminated as not the same?" Suppose we are comparing a computer and a typewriter. Are they the same or different? The answer depends on what aspects are being compared. Both have keyboards and can print words, so they are the same in that way. But computers can compute and typewriters cannot, so they are different too. To avoid such confusions, the standard discrimination experiment involves variation of stimuli along only one dimension. Thus, in a study of the discrimination of weights we might hold the size and shape of our stimuli constant and vary only the weight.

In a typical study, observers are presented with pairs of stimuli and asked to make the response "heavier" or "lighter" or some similar set of judgments appropriate to the stimulus dimension being judged. Observers are not permitted to say "same," since it has been shown that even when they feel they are just guessing, observers are more often correct than incorrect. Therefore, not allowing "same" judgments yields a more accurate estimate of discrimination performance (Brown, 1910). One stimulus intensity, called the **standard,** is the stimulus that the others are judged against. The standard appears on every trial and is compared to a graded set of similar stimuli differing only along the dimension being studied. These graded stimuli make up the set of **comparison stimuli.** This is a variant of the method of constant stimuli (which, you may remember, is used to determine the absolute threshold) in which the standard is added. We are also measuring a threshold here, but this is a threshold for the perception of a difference between the standard and other stimuli. It is called a **difference threshold.**

Typical results from an experiment in discrimination of lifted weights are displayed in Figure 2-10. In this experiment, the standard (a 100-g weight) was presented with each comparison stimulus (82 to 118 g in 1-g steps) over 700 times. We need only plot the proportion of the presentations on which each comparison

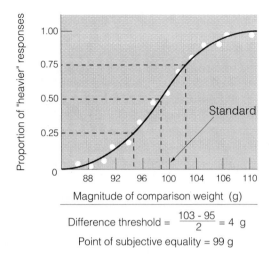

Difference threshold = $\dfrac{103 - 95}{2}$ = 4 g

Point of subjective equality = 99 g

Figure 2-10   *Typical data from the method of constant stimuli in discrimination with calculations of difference threshold and point of subjective equality.*

stimulus was judged "heavier" than the standard, since the proportion of "lighter" judgments can be obtained by subtraction. Notice that the shift in the probability of "heavier" judgments is not very abrupt, as it would be if the threshold were always a single, unique value (see Figure 2-1). Rather we find a gradual change in the probability of a "heavier" response as the comparison stimulus changes from much lighter than the standard to much heavier. Again, this S-shaped psychometric function can be fitted with a smooth curve. We have done this (by eye) to the data in Figure 2-10. Since the curve changes gradually, we again must decide how we will define the threshold for a stimulus to be called "different" (either lighter or heavier) than the standard. Clearly the point on the curve where the comparison stimulus was called "lighter" half of the time and "heavier" half of the time (a proportion of 0.50) is not appropriate. This point, usually called the **point of subjective equality,** probably represents the stimulus that appeared most like the standard, since the choices are evenly divided on either side of it. The stimulus

for which the proportion of heavier judgments is equal to 1.00 represents perfect discrimination (because here a physically heavier stimulus is judged heavier 100% of the time). The stimulus for which the proportion of heavier judgments is equal to 0.50 represents perception of no difference. Therefore, the point where the proportion of heavier judgments is equal to 0.75 (halfway between 0.50 and 1.00) represents a value where the *difference* is noted 50% of the time. Following similar reasoning, the stimulus for which the proportion of heavier judgments is equal to 0.25 is the point at which a stimulus difference in the lighter direction is noted 50% of the time. By convention, we take the interval from the 0.25 point to the 0.75 point, called the **interval of uncertainty,** and divide it by 2 to obtain the difference threshold. The difference threshold for the data in Figure 2-10 is about 4 g. This means that when standard and comparison stimuli are separated by 4 g, the subject will be able to detect the difference between them about half the time. The difference threshold is the average of the threshold for "greater than" and the threshold for "less than." It represents the threshold for "different" averaged across the direction of the differences.

If discrimination is good, very small differences between stimuli will be noticed. This corresponds to a small difference threshold. In Figure 2-11 the black line shows a good discriminator with a difference threshold of 0.50 units, whereas the white line shows a poor discriminator with a difference threshold of 2.00 units. As the difference threshold increases in size and discrimination ability decreases, the curve begins to flatten. The extreme of no discrimination at all would be represented by a horizontal line parallel to the abscissa at a proportion of heavier judgments equal to 0.50.

You may have noticed an interesting aspect of the data pictured in Figure 2-10: the point of subjective equality is not equal to the standard. The stimulus that *appears* to be equal to the standard of 100 g is actually 1 g lighter. This is

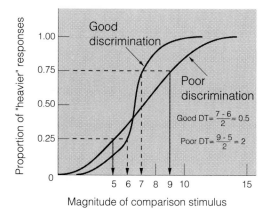

Figure 2-11 *Difference thresholds (DTs) for observers of different sensitivity.*

a typical result in many psychophysical experiments involving the presentation of stimuli that are separated in time. The stimulus presented first (generally the standard) is judged to be less intense than the later stimulus. This effect has been named the **negative time error** (because the standard is judged as less intense than it should be). Fechner (l860/1966) and Wolfgang Kohler (1923) thought this error was caused by the fading of the image or the memory trace of the sensation of the standard with the passage of time. However, work done with auditory stimuli has shown that with proper selection of a time interval, the error can be positive rather than negative (Kohler, 1923). Such errors are probably the result of particular cognitive or judgmental factors involved in judging stimuli in the context of others. Such comparison processes, as we shall see later, influence even the most apparently simple perceptual tasks (Hellstrom, 1979, 1985).

Weber's Law

Is the difference threshold a fixed value for any given sense modality? Does it vary as a function of the nature of the stimulus input or the state of the observer? Following the lead of Ernst Heinrich Weber (1834), Fechner (1860/1966) conducted an experiment in which he measured the difference thresholds for lifted weights using standard weights of different magnitudes. In Figure 2-12 we have plotted for some illustrative data the size of the difference threshold against the magnitude of the standard. First, notice that the difference threshold is not constant. It is larger for larger standards. In fact the difference threshold increases roughly linearly with the magnitude of the standard. The intuitive force of this relation is well illustrated in an example proposed by Galanter (1962): "If in a room with ten candles you had to add one more in order to detect an increase in illumination, then if the room contained one hundred it would be necessary to add ten candles in order to detect the same apparent increase in illumination ... " (p.133). This relation between the size of the difference threshold and the magnitude of the standard is called **Weber's law.**

Weber's law is written as

$$\Delta I = kI$$

where ΔI (delta I) is the size of the difference threshold, I is the intensity (magnitude) of the standard stimulus, and k is a constant. The constant k, called the **Weber fraction** is equal to $\Delta I/I$ (divide both sides of the equation by I

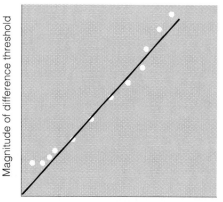

Figure 2-12 *Effect of intensity of standard on difference threshold.*

DEMONSTRATION BOX 2-2   Weber's Law

It is easy to demonstrate Weber's law for the perception of heaviness. You will need three quarters, two envelopes, and your shoes. Take one quarter and put it in one envelope and put the remaining two quarters in the other. If you now lift each envelope gently and put it down (use the same hand), it is quite easy to distinguish the heavier envelope. Now insert one envelope into one of your shoes and the other envelope into your second shoe, and lift them one at a time. The weight difference should be almost imperceptible. In the first instance the targets differed by the weight of the quarter and the difference was discriminated easily. In the second instance, although the weight differential was the same (one quarter), the overall stimulus intensity was greater because shoes weigh much more than the envelopes and the quarters alone.

and simplify). This constant, which is usually less than 1, indicates the proportion by which a standard stimulus must be changed so the change can be detected 50% of the time. Weber's law asserts that the Weber fraction is the same for any intensity of standard stimulus. For example, in a weight judgment experiment with a Weber fraction of 0.02, to discriminate a comparison stimulus as heavier than a 2-g standard the comparison weight must be 0.04 g (2 x 0.02 = 0.04) heavier than the standard. To discriminate a comparison stimulus as heavier than a 200-g standard, it must be 4 g heavier (200 x 0.02 = 4). A simple demonstration of Weber's law is given in Demonstration Box 2-2.

The Weber fraction can be interpreted as a measure of the overall sensitivity of a sensory system to differences along a stimulus continuum. The larger the Weber fraction for a stimulus dimension, the larger the relative stimulus difference needed for discrimination. Note that k has no specific units (such as grams) and so does not depend on the physical scale used to measure I and ΔI. Thus, we can compare Weber fractions across different stimulus dimensions without having to worry about how the stimulus values were measured. The Weber fraction represents the average ratio of difference

threshold size to the size of the standard level at which the difference threshold was measured, over an entire range of standard values. Table 2-7 presents typical Weber fractions for a variety of continua. As you can see, some of the ks are relatively large (for example, those for brightness and loudness), and some are quite small (for example, electric shock).

How well does Weber's law fit the data? For many years there was considerable argument about this issue. Measurements were taken in many sense modalities to check the relation. The clearest picture of the results is given by

Table 2-7 Typical Weber Fractions ($\Delta I/I$) (Based on Teghtsoonian, 1971)

CONTINUUM	WEBER FRACTION
Brightness	0.079
Loudness	0.048
Finger span	0.022
Heaviness	0.020
Line length	0.029
Taste (salt)	0.083
Electric shock	0.013
Vibration (fingertip)	
60 Hz	0.036
125 Hz	0.046
250 Hz	0.046

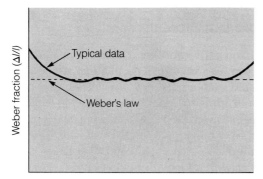

Figure 2-13 Typical data for test of Weber's law. The dotted line is predicted by Weber's law: $\Delta I/I = k$.

plotting the value of the Weber fraction, $\Delta I/I$, against the standard stimulus intensity. If the Weber fraction is constant, we should see a horizontal line, parallel to the horizontal axis. Figure 2-13 shows a composite of data from many sound intensity discrimination experiments. Deviation from the expected constancy can be seen at both extremes. Although these deviations look large, this is only because we have plotted the stimuli in logarithmic units. The flat part of the curve actually covers most of the total range of intensities used. Thus, Weber's law is a useful summary in spite of the deviation of the data from a perfect fit. Moreover, even the deviations are beginning to be understood (see Green 1976; Norwich, 1987).

Signal Detection Theory in Discrimination

Although signal detection theory was presented (and first developed) in the context of the detection problem, it can be extended to the discrimination situation. To use the signal detection procedure to assess discrimination, we must redesign the method of constant stimuli experiment so the observer is asked to say which of two very similar stimuli was actually presented on a given trial. This is like an identification experiment with only two stimuli.

The signal detection theory analysis of this experiment is quite similar to that used for the detection situation. Instead of trying to ascertain whether the sensation experienced on a given trial came from the signal present or the signal absent distribution, the observer must decide whether it is from the Signal 1 or Signal 2 distribution. If the stimuli were very similar the sensory response curves would overlap when plotted on the same set of axes, and an observer would be faced with a situation very much like that faced by the observer in the absolute detection situation. Look back at Figure 2-5 and mentally relabel the two distributions "Signal 1" and "Signal 2." Two stimuli can give rise to a variety of different sensation levels, with different probabilities. Since the curves cover the same general area of the sensation axis, there is no way to be certain which stimulus elicited a given sensation level on any one trial. The best the observer can do is to place a criterion somewhere on the sensation axis, and simply determine whether the sensation level experienced is above or below that criterion. If above, the appropriate response would be that the presented stimulus was a 2; if below, a 1. Just as in the absolute detection situation, where the observer places the criterion will greatly affect the proportions of different responses. In turn, criterion placement will be affected by the observer's expectations as to the relative frequency of presentation of the two stimuli, and by the observer's motivational biases.

As in the detection experiment, different criterion placements will define an isosensitivity curve when we plot the proportion of hits against the proportion of false alarms. The measure of sensitivity to the difference between the two stimuli is still called d' and is still unaffected by changes in the criterion. Actually, d' is determined by the physical difference between the two stimuli and the sensitivity of the observer's sensory system; both are factors that determine the difference between the average levels of sensation evoked by the stimuli. Thus, d' represents a measure of just how discriminable two very similar stimuli are. As such, it is closely related to the difference threshold and to the Weber fraction (Treisman, 1976).

Reaction Time

We have been looking at stimuli that are difficult to discriminate correctly. Even when we are working with stimuli well above the difference threshold, we may feel that some discriminations are easier to make than others. For example, most people feel that red is more easily differentiated from green than from orange. However, methods that depend on observers making errors cannot be used to measure interstimulus differences in detectability or discriminability in situations where there are no errors, as when all stimuli or differences are well above threshold. To measure such differences, we must use one of the oldest techniques in sensory psychology: we must measure **reaction time.** Reaction time is defined as the time between the onset of a stimulus and the beginning of an overt response. The concept was first introduced in 1850 by one of the early giants in perception and physiology, Hermann von Helmholtz, who used it as a basis for a crude measure of the speed of neural conduction in a limb.

There are two varieties of reaction time. **Simple reaction time** involves pressing or releasing a telegraph key (or making some other simple, stereotyped response) immediately on detecting a stimulus. **Choice reaction time** involves making one of several responses depending on the stimulus presented (for example, press the right-hand key for a red stimulus and the left-hand key for green).

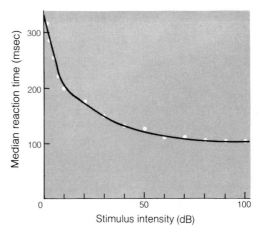

Figure 2-14 *Effect of stimulus intensity on simple reaction time (based on Chocolle, 1940).*

Simple reaction times are generally used in detection paradigms. We have known for a long time that the less intense a stimulus, the slower the reaction time. Figure 2-14 shows typical median reaction times to the onset of a tone plotted against the stimulus intensity (Chocolle, 1940). When the stimulus intensity is low and near the detection threshold (although it is still quite detectable), the reaction times are longer. Similar results have been obtained for visual stimuli (Cattell, 1886; Grice, Nullmeyer, & Schnizlein, 1979). Simple reaction time can also be used to measure discrimination. When observers must react as soon as they detect a change in stimulus intensity, we find that the smaller the change (either an increase or a decrease), the longer the reaction time (Welford, 1980).

Choice reaction time has been used in studies of discrimination and identification. These reaction times tend to be somewhat longer than simple reaction times (Posner, 1978). The classic discrimination experiment using reaction time was done by Henmon (1906). In this experiment the observer had two response keys—one for each hand. In one instance, the observer was presented with pairs of lines differing only in length and was told to depress the key corresponding to the side on which the line was longer. Henmon found that the smaller the difference between the line lengths, the longer the reaction time. He reported similar results for colors and tones.

A striking example of the relation between choice reaction time and the discriminability of stimuli used a slightly different technique. Shallice and Vickers (1964) required observers to sort decks of cards into piles according to which of two lines on the cards appeared longer. The total time it took to sort the cards was the measure of discriminability. This measure is, of course, the sum of a number of reaction times, where we consider the sorting of each card as a single response. The standard stimulus in this experiment was a 4.5-cm line. In the data shown in Table 2-8, we see that the smaller the difference between the two lines on the cards, the longer the sorting time. You can experience a similar effect by trying Demonstration Box 2-3.

Crossman (1953) argued that such reaction time differences are related both to the discriminability of the stimuli and to the amount of information they contain. We are referring to information in the technical sense

Table 2-8 Differences in Reaction Time as a Function of Differences in Line Lengths Measured via Card Sorts (Based on Shallice & Vickers, 1964)

DIFFERENCE IN LENGTH (cm)	SORTING TIME (sec)
1.1	39.4
0.9	40.0
0.7	40.1
0.5	41.0
0.4	42.0
0.3	42.9
0.2	46.5
0.1	52.4

discussed in the section on identification. If this is the case, then we would expect choice reaction times to increase as we increase the number of response alternatives, and indeed, this result has been known for many years. Merkel (1885) showed with number stimuli that choice reaction time increased as the number of response alternatives increased (see Table 2-9).

Hick (1952) attempted to explain these results by postulating that the observer extracts information from the stimulus display at a constant rate (compare Norwich, 1981), so the

---

DEMONSTRATION BOX 2-3   Reaction Time and Stimulus Discriminability

Take a deck of common playing cards and select out of it 10 of the picture cards (Kings, Queens, and Jacks) and 10 numbered cards from the red suits (hearts and diamonds) to make a new deck of 20 cards. Compose another deck of 20 by using the numbered cards (include the Aces) of the black suits (clubs and spades). Shuffle each deck separately and place it in front of you, face down. Next you need a clock or a watch with a sweep second hand. Wait until the second hand reaches the 12, pick up one of the decks and begin to sort it into two piles. The first deck gets sorted into number and picture cards; the second gets sorted into spades and clubs. Note the time it takes to sort each deck. You may want to repeat the task a couple of times so that you are sorting smoothly. Notice that the sorting time for the spades and clubs (a more difficult task since it involves making small form discrimination on similarly colored cards) is longer than the easier discrimination task of sorting picture and number cards.

Table 2-9 Reaction Time As a Function of Number of Stimulus Alternatives (Based on Merkel, 1885)

NUMBER OF ALTERNATIVES	REACTION TIME (msec)
1	187
2	316
3	364
4	434
5	487
6	534
7	570
8	603
9	619
10	632

more information that must be obtained from the display, the longer the reaction time. In an experimental situation where a display of lights served as stimuli and finger pressings of telegraph keys served as responses, he found a linear function relating reaction time and the logarithm of the number of equally likely stimulus alternatives. This relation, called **Hick's law,** states that choice reaction time is a linear function of the amount of information in the stimulus (at least up to 3 bits—see Longstreth, 1987). This means, for example, that we can only directly compare choice reaction times between conditions in which the number of response alternatives is the same. You may demonstrate effects of the number of stimulus

alternatives on reaction time by trying Demonstration Box 2-4.

SCALING

The dog trainer glanced at her new St. Bernard pupil and estimated his shoulder height to be 75 cm and his weight to be 80 kg. In so doing she was estimating scale values of her pupil's height and weight. Scaling attempts to answer the question, "How much of X is there?" X can be a physical (stimulus) magnitude, a sensation magnitude, or the magnitude of such other complex psychological variables as similarity or even pleasantness.

A **scale** is a rule by which we assign numbers to objects or events. The scale attempts to represent numerically some property of those objects or events (see Mitchell, 1986). A variety of different types of representations may be established, and each has its own characteristics (see Luce & Narens, 1987; Narens & Luce, 1986; Stevens, 1946). The most primitive and unrestricted type of scale is a **nominal scale.** Its etymology specifies its nature, since *nomin* is derived from the Latin word for "name." When numbers are assigned in a nominal scale, they serve only as identity codes or surrogate names. The numbers imply nothing more

---

DEMONSTRATION BOX 2-4   Number of Stimulus Alternatives and Reaction Time

Take a deck of playing cards and separate 16 cards using only the low numbers Ace, 2, 3, and 4. Next, make up another deck of 16 cards using 2 each of the 5, 6, 7, 8, 9, 10, Jack, and Queen. Now shuffle each deck. Measure the time it takes to sort each deck into piles by number (4 piles for the first and 8 for the second deck) using a watch or clock with a sweep second hand as you did in Demonstration Box 2-3. Notice that the reaction time becomes longer (measured by sorting time) as the number of alternative stimuli that must be recognized and responded to becomes greater. Thus, sorting the 4-stimuli deck is more rapid than sorting the 8-stimuli deck.

about the quantity of some property than does the number on a baseball uniform.

Whenever it is possible to say that one object or event contains more or less of the property than some other object or event, we can create an **ordinal scale** of that property. An ordinal scale ranks items on the basis of some quantity. An example might be the "Best Seller" or "Top Fifty" lists that order books or records on the basis of how many have been sold. Although this scale is more useful for measurement than a nominal scale, we are still restricted in our use of the numbers on an ordinal scale since all that is represented is *order* or ranking, not actual quantities.

A third type of scale is the **interval scale.** It not only answers the questions implied by the labels "more" or "less" but also tells "by how much." It employs not only the sequential properties of numbers but also their spacing, or the *intervals* between them. A good example of an interval scale is the scale of temperature represented by the common household thermometer. Here the size of the difference between 10 deg and 20 deg C (50 deg and 68 deg F) is exactly the same as between 40 deg and 50 deg C (104 deg and 122 deg F). Such scales are very useful, since most statistical techniques can be meaningfully applied to interval scale values. Interval scales suffer from one major drawback, however. They do not have a *true* zero point; rather, convenience or convention usually dictates where the zero will be. Thus, in the centigrade scale of temperature, the zero point is the triple point of pure water (the temperature at which water exists simultaneously as vapor, liquid, and ice).

The most numerically powerful scale is the **ratio scale.** Creation of this type of scale is possible only when equality, rank order, equality of intervals and of ratios, and a true zero point can be experimentally determined. Unfortunately, ratio scales are more often found in the physical than in the behavioral sciences.

Such things as mass, density, and length can be measured on ratio scales since the zero points are not arbitrary. For example, 0 g represents the complete absence of mass, and we can meaningfully say that 10 g is twice as massive as 5 g. Negative values of mass exist only in the fantasies of dieters.

All sensory qualities cannot be scaled in the same way. Some perceptual experiences have an underlying aspect of intensity (for instance, brightness), whereas others do not (such as color). When we are dealing with a stimulus or experience for which it makes sense to ask "How much?" or "How intense?" we have a **prothetic continuum** (Stevens & Galanter, 1957). With prothetic continua, changes from one level of sensation to another come about by adding or subtracting from what is present. Thus, when we increase the weight of a stimulus, the corresponding sensation of "heaviness" increases. Prothetic continua can be meaningfully measured on scales of any of the types we have discussed (although some restrictions may be imposed—see Bolanowski & Geschieder, 1991). In nonprothetic continua, changes in the physical stimulus result in a change in the apparent *quality* rather than the apparent *quantity* of a stimulus. When we have a stimulus or experience for which the only question it makes sense to ask is "What kind?" we are dealing with a **metathetic continuum.** Thus, a change in the wavelength of a light may cause its appearance to change from red to green. Psychologically, there is no quantitative difference between these two hues; they just appear to be different. It makes no sense to ask if red is "more" or "less" than green. Occasionally both types of continua will be present in the same sense impressions. For instance, in touch, the amount of pressure applied is a prothetic continuum, but the location of the touch is a metathetic continuum. Metathetic continua must be measured with nominal scales (compare Schneider & Bissett, 1981).

Indirect Scaling: Fechner's Law

When the perceptual investigator attempts to establish a sensory scale for which numbers will be assigned to the intensity of sensations, two alternative approaches are available. The first is a **direct scaling** procedure in which individuals are asked simply to assign a value to the magnitude of the sensation. Many early psychologists distrusted the accuracy of such direct reports. For this reason **indirect scaling** methods, based upon discrimination ability, formed the basis for the first psychological scales. We should note that using an indirect procedure is not necessarily bad. After all, we measure temperature indirectly, using the height of a column of mercury as our indicator. In fact, some have argued that the best way to measure psychological magnitude would be very similar to how temperature is measured (for example, Ward, 1991).

The first person to attempt to describe the relation between stimulus intensity and sensation intensity was Gustav Theodor Fechner. To do this, he had to invent a way to measure the magnitudes of sensations. As his starting point, he assumed that since the minimal difference in stimulus intensity that can be sensed is the difference threshold, our subjective impression of the size of the difference between any two stimuli separated by the amount of one difference threshold (the **just noticeable difference** or **jnd**) must always be the same regardless of the physical magnitude of the two stimuli. Thus, if we take two dim lights that are separated by one difference threshold, and we take two lights that are much more intense, but again separated from each other by one difference threshold, we should perceive the two pairs of stimuli as differing by equal sensory steps (equal *jnds*). This assumption allowed Fechner to create a scale of sensation magnitude by simply counting *jnds*. A stimulus at absolute threshold intensity was assumed to generate 0 units of sensation magnitude; a stimulus intensity 1 difference threshold above absolute threshold was assumed to generate 1 unit of sensation magnitude (1 *jnd*); a stimulus intensity 2 difference thresholds above absolute threshold was assumed to generate 2 units of sensation magnitude (2 *jnds*); and so forth. Thus the number of *jnds* "measured" the sensation intensity. The *jnd* was the "unit" of a sensation scale (since all were assumed to represent equal increments of sensation) just as the centimeter (or inch) is the unit of a length scale (since all represent equal increments of length).

Next, Fechner assumed that Weber's law (the difference threshold increases as a fixed proportion of the stimulus magnitude) was correct. As we have seen, it does hold over a wide range of stimuli. The combination of this assumption with that of the equality of all *jnds* led Fechner to conclude that when we are judging the apparent intensity of stimuli, a small physical change in a weak stimulus will produce the same change in the perceived intensity of a stimulus as a large physical change in a strong stimulus. This means that sensation intensity grows rapidly with changes in stimulus intensity for weak physical stimuli and more slowly as the physical stimulus is made more intense.

The relation between the sensation intensity and the intensity of the physical stimulus implied by Fechner's assumptions (and a few other technical ones) is shown graphically in Figure 2-15. This curve is described by the equation

$$S = (1/k) \log_e (I/I_0)$$

where S is the magnitude of sensation a stimulus elicits (number of *jnds* above 0 at absolute threshold), I/I_0 is the physical magnitude of the stimulus [intensity (I) relative to the absolute threshold stimulus magnitude (I_0)], $1/k$ is the inverse of the Weber fraction ($k = \Delta I/I$) and $\log_e$ is the natural logarithm (logarithm to the base e). This equation is called Fechner's law (Baird

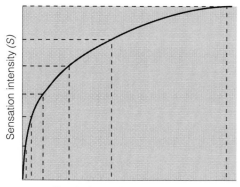

Figure 2-15 *Fechner's law. It takes larger and larger differences between stimuli (Is) as stimulus intensity increases to give rise to the same size differences between sensations (Ss).*

& Noma, 1978, and Falmagne, 1985, show how this equation is derived). Notice that $1/k$ will be different for different sensory and psychological continua, since it is the inverse of the Weber fraction for the continuum scaled. For many years Fechner's law was used in practical applications, such as building concert halls, to predict how people would respond to stimuli of various intensities. In addition it was thought to be consistent with physiological data, such as the approximately logarithmic increase in firing rate in sensory neurons with increases in stimulus intensity. Most recently, psychophysicists often have found that scales of sensation intensity based on discrimination measures, such as d', are logarithmically related to stimulus intensity.

Direct Scaling

Since Fechner's time, many psychophysicists have insisted that indirect scaling is neither necessary nor preferable. Because we are interested in the *apparent* intensity of a stimulus to an observer, why not simply require judgments based on how intense a stimulus *seems* to be?

The observer's responses could then be used directly to establish a scale of measurement.

This method was first attempted in 1872 by one of Fechner's contemporaries, a Belgian investigator named Plateau. To test Fechner's law he had eight artists mix a gray that was halfway between a particular black and white. Notice that this requires direct relative judgments of three stimuli: black, white, and gray. Fechner's law predicts that this psychological midpoint should correspond to the average of the logarithm of the physical intensity of the black stimulus and that of the white stimulus. Unfortunately the results, although somewhat similar to the prediction, did not fully support Fechner's law. Rather, the grays mixed by Plateau's artists seemed to fall halfway between the cube roots (1/3 power) of the intensities of the black and the white stimuli. This numerical discrepancy suggests that Fechner's law may only be an approximation to the relation between physical and sensory intensity, which could be better described by a power function such as $S = I^{1/3}$. Such mathematical deviations are important, because a major purpose of scaling is to make possible *precise* descriptions of relations between physical and perceptual quantities, such as the intensities of physical stimuli and those of the sensations they give rise to.

Category Judgment

An investigator named Sanford was among those who first attempted to measure sensation directly. As early as 1898, he had developed a technique that involved having observers judge a number of envelopes, each of which contained different weights. The subjects were instructed to sort the weights into 5 categories. Category 1 was to be used for the lightest weights, and category 5 for the heaviest, with the remaining weights distributed in the other categories in such a way that the intervals between the category boundaries would be subjectively equal. Thus, the difference in sensation between the upper and the lower boundaries of category 1 should be the same as that for category 2. In other words, all categories should be the same size. This method has been called **category scaling** or **equal interval scaling.** This process is similar to an identification task, except that category scaling usually involves fewer categories than stimuli. Also, it is assumed that no correct or incorrect answer exists in category scaling, since the very nature of the experiment seems to imply that we cannot know in advance what a correct category assignment might be. Happily, sensation scales produced from category judgments have been found to be relatively stable over several different manipulations, including the labels applied to the categories (numbers versus words) and the number of categories used (Stevens & Galanter, 1957).

If the observer has spaced the category boundaries equally in terms of the magnitudes of the sensory differences between them, we can, without making any other assumptions, mark off equal category intervals (to represent the midpoints of the categories) along the ordinate of a graph and label them with the numbers the categories represent. On this graph we can plot the average category label assigned to each stimulus intensity over several trials. The curve obtained for typical data (Figure 2-16) is concave downward and approximates the curve predicted by Fechner's law (Figure 2-15). The fact that we can predict the shape of the category scale from simple discrimination data is quite an impressive feat. To Sanford this seemed to support the contention that a logarithmic relation exists between physical stimulus intensity and perceived magnitude.

Magnitude Estimation: Stevens's Law

Although in category judgments observers are responding directly to variations in stimulus

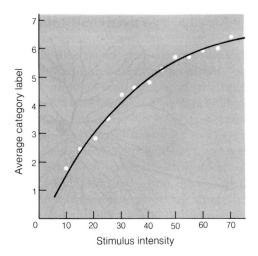

Figure 2-16   *Some typical data from a category judgment experiment. The dots represent average category judgments of the various stimulus intensities.*

magnitude, some "indirectness" is still involved. Stimuli that are similar but that give rise to discriminably different sensations may be grouped into the same category. Also, responses are limited to a few category labels. S. S. Stevens popularized a procedure called **magnitude estimation** that avoids these problems. The method is so simple and direct that one wonders why it had to be "invented" at all. In this procedure, observers are simply asked to assign numbers to stimuli on the basis of how intense they appear to be. Stimuli are usually judged one at a time and the sole restriction on responses is that only numbers larger than zero can be used.

Consider a typical modern magnitude estimation experiment (for example, Zwislocki & Goodman, 1980), in which we wish to scale the loudnesses of a set of pure tones. We would ask observers to assign a number to the sensation (loudness) elicited by each tone so that their impression of the magnitude of the number matched the loudness of the tone. We would tell the observers that they could use any positive number, including decimals or fractions. We would also tell them not to pay attention to any stimuli presented earlier or the responses they might have given to these stimuli, but to concentrate on matching a number to the loudness of the current stimulus.

As you can see, this is a very direct way to attempt to measure sensation. As you might also guess, the numbers chosen may vary widely from observer to observer or even from stimulus to stimulus. Thus, this method often requires either an average over many observers or an average over many trials per observer to achieve stable results. Although many researchers prefer magnitude estimation because they believe that the resulting scale has ratio scale properties, lively debate still centers on this issue (Bolanowski & Gescheider, 1991; Stevens, 1975).

Stevens originally expected the results of his experiments to confirm Fechner's law. However, when he plotted the data from an experiment on the magnitude estimation of loudness (Stevens, 1956), he found that the graph differed from what Fechner's law had led him to expect. The equation he found that best described the relation of the median magnitude estimates to the stimulus intensities was $L = aI^{0.6}$ where L is the subjective loudness obtained through the observer's magnitude estimates, a is a constant, I is the physical intensity of the sound, and 0.6 is a power to which I is raised. In succeeding years, Stevens and a host of others produced magnitude estimation scales for a multitude of sensory continua. All of these scales seemed to be related to the physical stimulus intensities by the general relation

$$S = aI^m$$

where S is the measure of the sensation intensity and m is a characteristic exponent (power) that differs for different sensory continua.

Since this relation states that the magnitude of the sensation is proportional to the intensity of the physical stimulus raised to some power (m), this relation is often called the **power law** or, after its popularizer, **Stevens's law.**

In the power law the magnitude of the sensation difference, given a difference in stimulus intensity, depends on the size of the exponent. In general, the exponent for any one continuum is quite stable. As long as the experimental situation is kept reasonably standard, and the same measures of physical stimulus intensity are used (Myers, 1982), the average exponents produced by different groups of observers for the same continuum are quite similar. Some of them are small fractions (0.30 for brightness); some are close to 1 (for line length); and others are substantially greater than 1 (3.50 for electric shock). Some typical exponents for several continua are given in Table 2-10.

If we plot some of the relations between judged sensory intensity and physical stimulus intensity, we find that the curves for power functions with different exponents (m) have dramatically different shapes. This can be seen in Figure 2-17. With exponents of less than 1 (for example, brightness), the curves are concave downward, meaning that as the stimulus becomes more intense, greater differences in stimulus intensity are needed to produce the same degree of difference in sensation intensity. When exponents are greater than 1 (for example, electric shock), the curves are concave upward, meaning that as stimuli become more intense, the same physical stimulus difference produces an even larger perceptual difference than at lower stimulus intensities. Since each sensory continuum might give a different curve describing the relation between sensory and physical intensity, it is fortunate that a simple procedure exists that allows us to estimate the power function from any set of data. If we plot the logarithms of the magnitude

Table 2-10 Representative Exponents of the Power Functions Relating Sensation Magnitude to Stimulus Magnitude (Based on Stevens, 1961)

CONTINUUM	EXPONENT	STIMULUS CONDITIONS
Loudness	0.6	Both ears
Brightness	0.33	5° target—dark
Brightness	0.5	Point source—dark
Lightness	1.2	Gray Papers
Smell	0.55	Coffee odor
Taste	0.8	Saccharine
Taste	1.3	Sucrose
Taste	1.3	Salt
Temperature	1.0	Cold—on arm
Temperature	1.6	Warmth—on arm
Vibration	0.95	60 Hz—on finger
Duration	1.1	White noise stimulus
Finger span	1.3	Thickness of wood blocks
Pressure on palm	1.1	Static force on skin
Heaviness	1.45	Lifted weights
Force of handgrip	1.7	Precision hand dynamometer
Electric shock	3.5	60 Hz—through fingers

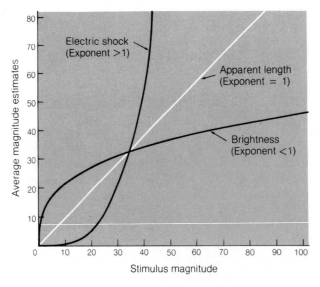

Figure 2-17   *Power functions for brightness, length, and electric shock. Notice how the shape of the curve changes as the exponent changes.*

estimates (the numbers observers assign to their sensations) against the logarithms of the stimulus intensities, any curve of the general form $S = aI^m$ will appear as a straight line. In Figure 2-18 the curves in Figure 2-17 have been replotted in this way. We can now estimate m from the curve by measuring with a ruler the distances marked Δy and Δx in Figure 2-18 and computing $m = \Delta y/\Delta x$. The constant a is the antilogarithm of the point at which the line crosses the ordinate. More sophisticated methods of estimating the parameters in Stevens's law and those in Fechner's law are described by Thomas (1983). Demonstration Box 2-5 allows you to perform a magnitude estimation experiment for yourself.

You might wonder why category judgments seem to give a logarithmic relation that supports Fechner's law, whereas magnitude estimates are related to stimulus magnitude by a power law. Actually, Stevens and Galanter (1957) found that category judgments only approximately fit a logarithmic relation. Since then several investigators (Marks, 1968, 1974; Gibson & Tomko, 1972; Ward, 1971, 1972, 1974) have shown that category judgments also fit the power law, but with exponents (m) that are about half the size of those produced by magnitude estimation.

Marks (1974) and Torgerson (1961) have suggested that these different results reflect different but equally valid ways of judging the same sensory experience. For example, if my 10-kg dog and my 100-kg brother both gain 1 kg in weight, we may ask, "Which one gained more?" If we make an equal interval judgment (analogous to that required for category scaling), the answer is neither, since both have increased by 1 kg. If we make an equal ratio judgment (magnitude estimate), my dog has increased his body weight by 10% and my brother by only 1%. Thus, my dog registered a much greater proportional gain. Both judgments require estimates of the magnitude of a single event, and both are useful, but the scales (and resultant stimulus-sensation curves) are different (see also Marks, 1979; Popper, Parker, & Galanter, 1986).

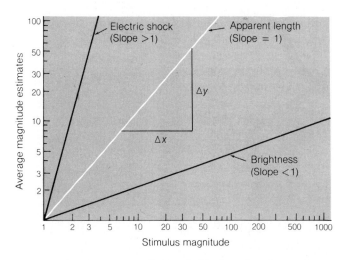

Figure 2-18 *The same power functions as in Figure 2-17 plotted on logarithmic axes. In such "log-log" plots, all power functions become straight lines, with the slope of the straight line determined by the exponent (m) of the power function.*

DEMONSTRATION BOX 2-5　Magnitude Estimation of Loudness

To produce a graded set of sound intensities for this demonstration you will need a long ruler, a coin (we have designed the demonstration for a quarter), an empty tin can or water glass, a soft towel, and a friend. Place the can on the folded towel and have your friend drop the coin from the designated height so that the coin hits the can on its edge only once and then falls onto the towel (silently, we hope). You should sit with your back to the apparatus.

Ask your friend to drop coins onto the can from heights of 1, 10, 70, 100, and 200 cm in some mixed order. For each sound so produced, call out a number whose magnitude you feel matches the loudness of the sound. You may use any numbers you think appropriate as long as they are greater than 0, including decimals and fractions. Your friend should record the height from which the coin was dropped and the number you gave in each instance. Do this for two or three runs through the stimuli (in different

irregular orders) and then average the numbers you called out for each height.

To determine if these judgments follow a power law, plot them on the log-log coordinates provided on the accompanying graph. The vertical axis represents the average magnitude estimates spaced logarithmically and the horizontal axis represents the sound intensities spaced logarithmically (based on the height of the coin drop). Draw the straight line that best fits (by eye) the data points. Usually the data points fall close to such a line, and any deviations around it are usually fairly random. You can compute the exponent directly (m in the power law $S = aIm$) by computing the slope of the straight line on the graph. To do this, pick two points on the line and measure Δx and Δy with a ruler as done in Figure 2-18. Now divide Δy by Δx and you should get a value somewhere around 0.30. This is half of the 0.60 value for loudness in Table 2-10 because we have measured sound intensity differently here.

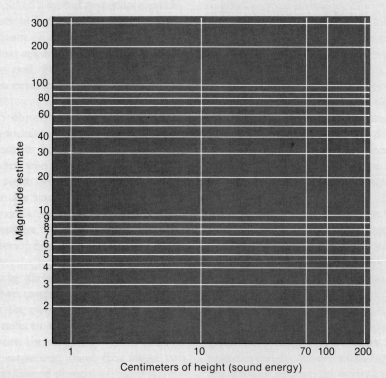

Other investigators disagree that the category and magnitude scales are equally valid. Some (for example, Krueger, 1989) favor category scales (and resulting exponents), whereas others favor magnitude estimation scales (for example, Stevens, 1975; Zwislocki & Goodman, 1980). Still others suggest combinations of the two (such as Borg, 1982) or refinements of one or the other (such as Berglund, 1991; Guirao, 1991). Since both methods and their variants do give reliable results, which one to use is still a matter of taste. However, care must be taken when the results are interpreted.

Cross-Modality Matching

If the size of the exponent varies with the nature of the response, you might wonder whether these scales tell us more about how humans use numbers than they do about how sensation varies with stimulus intensity (see Baird, 1975; Baird, Lewis, & Romer, 1970). To counter such criticism, Stevens invented a scaling procedure that does not use numbers at all. In this technique, an observer adjusts the intensity of a stimulus until it appears to be as intense as another stimulus from a different sensory continuum. Thus, an observer might be asked to squeeze a handgrip until the pressure felt was as strong as a particular light was bright. This procedure is called **cross-modality matching,** since the observer is asked to match sensation magnitudes across sensory modalities. Actually, the version of magnitude estimation described earlier is also a form of cross-modality matching in which the number continuum is matched to a stimulus continuum (compare Oyama, 1968; Stevens, 1975).

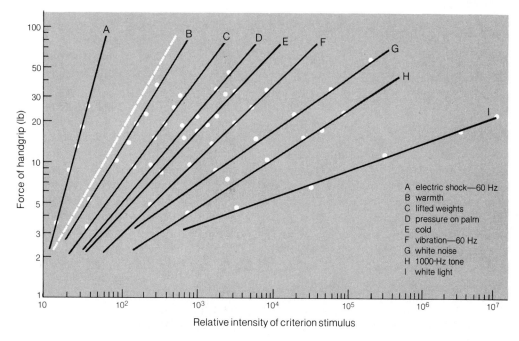

Figure 2-19 *Cross-modality matching data for nine different psychological stimulus continua with force of handgrip as the response continuum. Because the values on both axes are logarithmically spaced, all of the straight lines indicate power function relations between stimulus and response magnitude. The dashed white line has an exponent of 1.0. (From S. S. Stevens, in W. A. Rosenblith (Ed.),* Sensory Communication. *New York: Wiley, 1961. Copyright 1961 by the MIT Press.)*

When we plot the data from cross-modality matching experiments on log-log axes (as we did for magnitude estimation experiments), we find that the average matches fall onto a straight line. Despite the fact that the observers no longer make numerical estimates, the data still obey the power law for sensation intensities. Figure 2-19 shows this for a number of modalities matched against handgrip pressure.

Cross-modality matching is often more difficult to use than direct magnitude estimation because the subject must adjust one of the sensory continua to give a response, rather than simply reporting a number or category label. Nonetheless, because of its conceptual simplicity and its relation to the foundations of measurement theory (Luce, 1990; Ward, 1991; Zwislocki, 1991), most modern psychophysicists agree that it is probably the best basis for the measurement of psychological magnitude (Gescheider & Bolanowski, 1991).

Because psychophysicists want to obtain as accurate an estimate of the exponent as possible in order to describe the relation between the physical stimulus and its perceived magnitude with maximum precision, new refinements of the classical scaling procedures are always being introduced. For instance, a recent modification of the cross-modality matching technique makes the task somewhat easier for the observer, and seems to give somewhat more reliable results. In this procedure, called **mixed-modality scaling** (Ward 1982a), observers don't actually match sensation magnitudes. Instead, they judge two different sets of sensory stimuli (for instance, lights and sounds), both of which are intermixed in the same experiment. Observers try to use the same scale as the stimuli alternate between the modalities. The experimenter later uses sophisticated mathematical techniques to determine the relation between the two sets of judgments and also to estimate the exponents of the power functions for the two sensory modalities (Stevens & Marks, 1980).

The theoretical importance of techniques such as cross-modality matching or mixed-modality scaling rests in the exponents derived from them for the power law. Remarkably, the exponents usually agree regardless of the technique used to estimate them (for example, Ward, 1986). In addition, they generally agree with the values obtained from traditional magnitude estimation techniques (Teghtsoonian, 1975). Given all the evidence, the power law still seems to be a reasonable first approximation to the description of how sensory intensity is related to stimulus intensity.

Multidimensional Psychological Scaling

Sometimes researchers have difficulty demonstrating the exact relationship between variations in stimuli and our sensory impressions. This is a particular problem for metathetic continua where, as we noted earlier, the changes in the physical stimulus result in a change in the quality, rather than the intensity, of the sensation. It is also a problem in situations where the relevant physical dimensions are complex, are unknown, or do not seem to correspond directly to any psychological dimension. For example, Ekman (1954) asked how our impression of color (hue) varies as we vary the wavelength of light. He obtained observers' ratings of how similar the colors were for various pairs of stimuli ranging in wavelength from 434 nm to 674 nm. As we explain in Chapter 5, hue varies with wavelength qualitatively rather than quantitatively. Ekman (1954) presented his data in the form of a **similarity matrix** in which pairs of stimuli that were seen to be more similar received higher similarity ratings. In the example shown in Table 2-11, each entry represents the similarity rating (on a 1–10 scale) for the pair of stimuli with the wavelengths in the corresponding row and column. Notice that low wavelength stimuli, which ap-

Table 2-11 A Similarity Matrix for the Observers in
Ekman's (1954) Color Perception Experiment

WAVELENGTHS	445	465	504	537	584	600	651	674
445	—	9	7	6	2	2	7	8
465		—	8	7	2	2	6	7
504			—	9	6	5	2	2
537				—	7	6	3	2
584					—	8	4	3
600						—	5	4
651							—	9
674								—

pear blue, have higher similarity ratings with the high wavelength stimuli, which appear red, than with the medium wavelength stimuli, which appear yellow. Table 2-11 contains many numbers, and it is not easy to discern a simple relationship from data presented in this way.

An elegant procedure for uncovering the psychological structure implicit in such data matrices was developed by Torgerson (1958) and Shepard (1962, 1974, 1980), and elaborated and extended by several others (for example, Carroll & Chang, 1970; Kruskal, 1964). The central idea behind this procedure, known as **multidimensional scaling,** is that data representing psychological similarity can be represented as physical distance in a spatial map. The more similar two psychological entities are, the closer together they are placed in the map; the more dissimilar they are, the further apart. Although these ideas are quite simple and intuitive, it requires a computer program to discover the map implied by the data (see Shiffman, Reynolds, & Young, 1981).

An illustration of a spatial map that represents the data collected by Ekman (1954) is shown in Figure 2-20. The computer program provided the positioning of the points representing the various wavelength stimuli. The lines and labels that have been drawn on the map are there simply to help you "see" the structure uncovered by the program. The

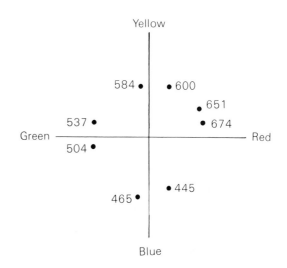

Figure 2-20 A multidimensional scaling map based on the color similarity data in Table 2-11 (based on Shepard, 1962).

structure illustrated in Figure 2-20 is the color circle that has been found to be so useful in predicting color mixtures (see Figure 5-8). The axes required to represent this color circle can be interpreted to represent two *dimensions,* one representing opponent variations from red–green and the other from blue–yellow. As Chapter 5 explains, these dimensions can now be shown to result from characteristic response patterns of neurons in the higher brain centers of the visual system. Finally, the coordinates of the points representing the stimuli can be interpreted as interval scales of the psychological or physiological dimensions revealed by the map. Thus, multidimensional scaling provides a way both to represent the structure of complex data matrices and to obtain meaningful scales of psychological attributes that do not correspond in any simple way to physical dimensions.

Some psychological entities are best thought of in terms of common and distinctive features, rather than in terms of continuous spatial dimensions (Tversky, 1977). For example, the letters of the alphabet have been characterized in terms of distinctive features such as lines of different orientation and curvature (see Chapter 11). **Hierarchical clustering,** a procedure related to multidimensional scaling but differing in terms of the final representation, is sometimes helpful in describing perceived relationships among such sets of stimuli (Johnson, 1967). This procedure also relies heavily on the use of computer programs, but instead of representing stimuli as points on a map, stimuli are represented as the "leaves" on a "tree," or as "clusters" of stimuli of different degrees of similarity. Together, hierarchical clustering analysis and multidimensional scaling provide a set of powerful psychophysical scaling methods when stimuli vary in ways that cannot be described as simple variations in intensity along a single physical continuum.

Context and Bias

Part of the circus strongman's job was to carry various members of the animal cast onto the circus train. One visitor watched in amazement as one after another he lifted the dancing ponies and placed them in their railroad car. "Aren't they heavy?" asked the visitor. "Not if you've just carried three elephants," came the reply.

The essence of this apocryphal tale is that no stimulus can be appreciated in isolation. Stimuli are always seen in the context of the stimuli that precede and surround them. Thus, sportscasters of average height look like midgets when interviewing professional basketball players but like giants when interviewing professional jockeys. They have not, of course, changed size, but their apparent size has changed as a result of the frame of reference provided by the heights of those around them. Contextual effects have long been known to influence judgments of sensory magnitude in many psychophysical tasks, even when the context is in another modality than the one being judged. You can experience this kind of context effect by using Demonstration Box 2-6.

Helson (1964) attempted to explain how context can affect our judgments of sensation magnitudes. In Helson's theory, the organism is

---

DEMONSTRATION BOX 2-6   The Effect of Visual Context on Judged Weight

You will need two envelopes for this demonstration. One should be rather small (about 7 by 13 cm or so) and one should be large (approximately 20 by 28 cm). Put 15 nickels in each envelope. With the same hand, lift the large envelope and next lift the small. Which appears to be heavier? You will probably feel that the small envelope was considerably heavier although the weights were physically equal. This is an example of how a visual context (the envelope size) can alter our perception of heaviness. The same weight in the context of a smaller container seems heavier than when judged in the context of a larger container.

thought to accommodate itself to the changing environment around it. This accommodation involves establishing an internal *reference level* against which all other stimuli are judged. Stimuli below this reference, or **adaptation level,** are judged to be weak and stimuli above it to be intense. Stimuli at or near the adaptation level are judged to be medium or neutral. It is significantly more difficult to discriminate stimuli that are both on the same side of the adaptation level than to discriminate stimuli, equally close together, that appear on different sides of the adaptation level (Streitfeld & Wilson, 1986). This implies that all judgments are relative. A stimulus is not simply weak or intense; it is weak or intense compared to the subjective adaptation level.

For Helson, adaptation levels are established by pooling the effects of three classes of stimuli. The first class is called **focal stimuli.** These stimuli are the center of an observer's attention and are usually the ones being judged. Clearly the magnitude of these stimuli will in some way determine the observer's judgments, which is the basic assumption of all scaling procedures. The second class of stimuli is called **background stimuli.** These stimuli occur closely in space and/or time to the focal stimulus, providing the immediate background against which a focal stimulus is judged. The final set of stimuli is called **residual stimuli.** These stimuli are not current for the observer, but are the residue of stimuli the observer has experienced in the past. To be more concrete, consider the sportscasters surrounded by basketball players or jockeys. The physical height of the sportscaster is the focal stimulus. The background stimuli are the heights of the surrounding athletes. The residual stimuli are the heights of all persons previously encountered, including athletes. The adaptation level is formed from a weighted combination (like an average) of all of these stimuli.

Adaptation level theory can explain many perceptual context effects such as certain vi-

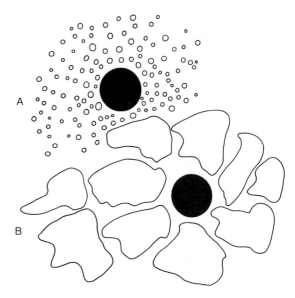

Figure 2-21 *The circle surrounded by smaller elements appears larger than the circle surrounded by larger elements, although both are the same size (based on Coren & Girgus, 1978).*

sual illusions (Coren & Girgus, 1978). For instance, consider Figure 2-21. The two black circles are physically the same size, although they appear to be different. It is easy to understand this illusory effect if you recognize that when you are looking at circle A, the adaptation level is shifted toward the smaller size of the surrounding elements, whereas when you are looking at circle B, the adaptation level is shifted toward the larger size of the elements in that region. Because of this, circle A is above the adaptation level established for its immediate vicinity, and hence appears larger, and circle B is below the adaptation level in its region, and hence appears smaller.

Context can have major effects on judgments of perceptual quantities, such as sensation magnitude. Different researchers disagree about the specifics of how stimuli interact, which stimuli are involved, and the specific way in which comparisons with a context occur, although all accept the fact that context does affect perception (Anderson, 1975; Di-Carlo & Cross, 1990; Marks, Szczesiul, & Ohlott, 1986). Context effects have been shown to affect all aspects of psychological scaling, including category judgments (Parducci, 1965; Ward, 1972), and magnitude estimations and cross-modality matches (Marks, 1988; Poulton, 1985; Ward, 1973, 1979, 1987). Furthermore, when we ask whether the effects are only upon the response assigned to the sensations (for example, ß in signal detection) or upon what is actually perceived, recent evidence seems to indicate that both the actual sensory experience of a stimulus and the responses used to describe it are affected by context (Algom & Marks, 1990; Schneider & Parker, 1990).

Context effects suggest that no simple relation may exist between stimulus magnitude and sensory magnitude. What we perceive is not simply a photographic reproduction of the stimuli in the environment, but is affected by the myriad forces that impinge upon us now and have impinged upon us in the past, since these forces provide the context for the perceptual situation in which we presently find ourselves. Perception is an active process, and processes within the observer are sometimes more important in determining the sensory experience than are factors in the external environment.

The psychophysical measurement techniques introduced in this chapter appear in many disguises throughout the rest of the book. We usually do not stop to identify specific techniques or the rationale for using them. The methods by which perceptual data are collected are important, however, because the measurement technique will frequently interact with the phenomena to be measured. We find, for example, that when we look at raw

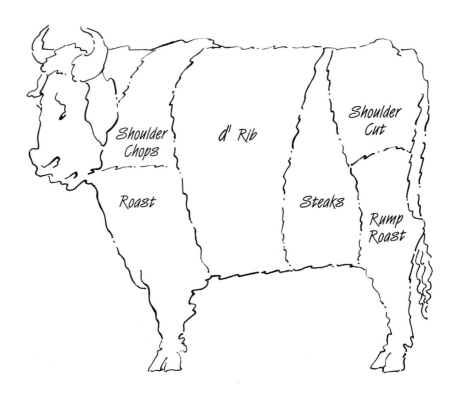

identification scores in one experiment, red and green are equally discriminable from orange because the individual hues are correctly recognized 100% of the time. In contrast, when we measure reaction times, it takes longer to discriminate red from orange than green from orange, indicating a difference in discriminability. Is this a contradiction of fact? Not necessarily. Each method of measurement is tuned to a different task, and often each measures a different psychological function. In everyday language you could say that the answer you get depends on the question you ask.

GLOSSARY

The following definitions are specific to their use in this book.

Absolute threshold The minimal amount of energy required to detect a stimulus; defined as the 50th percentile of a psychometric function from a method of constant stimuli experiment.

Adaptation level A subjective reference point against which stimuli are both quantitatively and qualitatively judged.

Adaptive testing A method for measuring threshold in which the sequence of stimuli presented to an observer is adapted to the observer's responses to previous stimuli.

Background stimuli An adaptation level theory term for stimuli that form a context for a focal stimulus but are not judged by an observer.

Beta (ß) In signal detection theory, the criterion sensation level that separates a "yes" response from a "no" response.

Bit The amount of information in a stimulus measured by the logarithm to the base 2 of the number of stimulus alternatives.

Category scaling A psychophysical scaling method in which stimuli are grouped in a predetermined number of categories on the basis of their perceived intensity. Also called equal-interval scaling.

Catch trials Trials where no stimulus is presented. Used in threshold measuring experiments.

Channel capacity The limit to the number of bits of information an observer can transmit on a single stimulus dimension.

Choice reaction time Reaction time to make different responses to different stimuli.

Comparison stimuli A graded set of stimuli differing along a specific dimension that are to be judged relative to a standard stimulus.

Confusion matrix Matrix (table) in which the entries are the number of occasions on which a given response (column labels) was made to a given stimulus (row labels) in an absolute identification experiment.

Correct negative A signal detection theory term for a signal absent trial on which the observer's response is "no."

Criterion In signal detection theory, a sensation level that differentiates "yes" from "no" responses (*see* Beta).

Cross-modality matching A scaling procedure in which the observer adjusts the intensity of a stimulus until it appears to be as intense as another stimulus from a different sensory continuum.

d′ In signal detection theory, the distance between the means of the signal absent and the signal present distributions; a measure of sensory sensitivity.

Detection A psychophysical problem involving being aware that a stimulus is present.

Difference threshold The minimum amount of stimulus change needed for two stimuli to be perceived as different; defined as the interval of uncertainty divided by 2 in a method of constant stimuli experiment.

Direct scaling A procedure in which individuals are asked to assess directly the intensity of a sensation.

Discrimination A psychophysical problem involving noticing a difference between stimuli.

Equal interval scaling *See* Category scaling.

False alarm A signal detection theory term for a signal absent trial to which the observer's response is "yes."

Fechner's law The logarithmic relation, proposed by Fechner, between the intensity of sensation and the intensity of physical stimulus, $S = (1/k) \log_e (I/I_0)$.

Focal stimuli An adaptation level theory term for

stimuli at the center of an observer's attention, usually those being judged.

Forced choice   A paradigm in which several observation intervals are presented to an observer who must make a choice as to which interval contained the stimulus with a specified property (e.g., the more intense stimulus).

Hierarchical clustering   A psychological scaling procedure that represents the relations among stimuli as "leaves" on a "tree."

Hick's law   A law stating that choice reaction time is a linear function of the amount of information in the stimuli to be differentiated.

Hit   A signal detection theory term for a signal present trial on which the response is "yes."

Identification   A psychophysical problem involving naming stimuli.

Indirect scaling   Any method, often based on discrimination ability, by which sensation intensity is measured indirectly.

Information theory   A quantitative system for measuring the difficulty of an identification task in terms of the logarithm to the base 2 of the number of stimulus alternatives that must be distinguished.

Information transmission   The degree to which the output of an information channel (for example, an observer in an identification experiment) reflects the information input to it.

Interval of uncertainty   In a discrimination experiment, the difference between the stimulus intensity judged greater than the standard 25% of the time and that judged greater 75% of the time.

Interval scale   A scale in which differences between adjacent values are meaningful, but in which no absolute zero point exists.

Just noticeable difference (jnd)   The subjective experience of the difference threshold; the sensation difference between two stimuli separated by one difference threshold.

Magnitude estimation   A psychophysical scaling procedure requiring the observer to assign numbers to stimuli on the basis of the intensity of the sensations they arouse.

Metathetic continuum   A stimulus continuum for which quantitative stimulus changes cause qualitative sensation changes, such as wavelength of light and hue.

Method of constant stimuli   A method for determining thresholds in which each of a number of stimuli above and below the proposed threshold are presented and judged repeatedly.

Method of limits   A method for determining thresholds in which stimulus intensity is systematically increased or decreased until a change in response occurs.

Miss   A signal detection theory term for a signal present trial on which the observer's response is "No."

Mixed-modality scaling   A psychophysical scaling procedure in which observers make judgments (including magnitude estimations, category judgments, or cross-modality matches) of stimuli from two different sensory continua on the same scale.

Multidimensional scaling   A psychological scaling procedure in which the perceived similarities between stimuli are represented as physical distances in a spatial map.

Negative time error   In discrimination experiments, when the point of subjective equality is less than the value of the standard stimulus.

Nominal scale   A scale in which scale values can only be used as names of objects or events, thus reflecting only identity.

Ordinal scale   A scale involving the ranking of items on the basis of more or less of some quantity.

Outcome matrix   In signal detection theory, a matrix containing the proportions of trials on which the four possible outcomes occurred.

Payoff matrix   In signal detection theory, a set of rewards and penalties given an observer based on performance in a psychophysical experiment.

Point of subjective equality   The comparison stimulus intensity that appears most like the standard in a discrimination experiment.

Power law   The relation that the magnitude of sensation varies as the intensity of the physical stimulus raised to some power. Also known as Stevens's Law, $S = aI^m$.

Probability distribution   A graphic representation of the likelihood that a given event will occur.

Prothetic continuum   A stimulus continuum for which quantitative stimulus changes cause quantitative sensation changes, such as intensity of sound and loudness.

Psychometric function   The relation between the proportion of responses of a particular type (for example, "heavier") and the intensity of the stimulus.

Ratio scale   A measurement scale in which the rank order, spacing, and ratios of the numbers assigned to events have meaning; it also has an absolute zero point.

Reaction time   The interval between the onset of a stimulus and the beginning of an overt response.

Receiver operating characteristic (ROC) curve   In signal detection theory the graph of probabilities of hits (ordinate) versus false alarms (abscissa) generated by criterion changes.

Residual stimuli   In adaptation level theory, stimuli that are no longer present but affect the current adaptation level.

ROC curve   *See* Receiver operating characteristic curve.

Scale   A rule by which numbers are assigned to objects or events.

Scaling   A psychophysical problem involving the measurement of how much of something is present.

Signal detection theory   A mathematical, theoretical system that formally deals with both decisional and sensory components in detection and discrimination tasks.

Similarity matrix   A matrix whose entries are the perceived similarities between pairs of stimuli; *see* multidimensional scaling.

Simple reaction time   Reaction time for simply detecting the onset of a stimulus.

Staircase method   A method for measuring absolute thresholds in which the experimenter alters the direction of changes in stimulus intensity each time the observer changes his or her response.

Standard   A stimulus against which the comparison stimuli are judged in a discrimination experiment.

Stevens's law   *See* Power law.

Weber fraction   The proportion by which the standard stimulus must be increased in order to detect change, $k = \Delta I / I$.

Weber's law   The relation that the size of the difference threshold increases linearly with the size of the standard, $\Delta I = kI$.

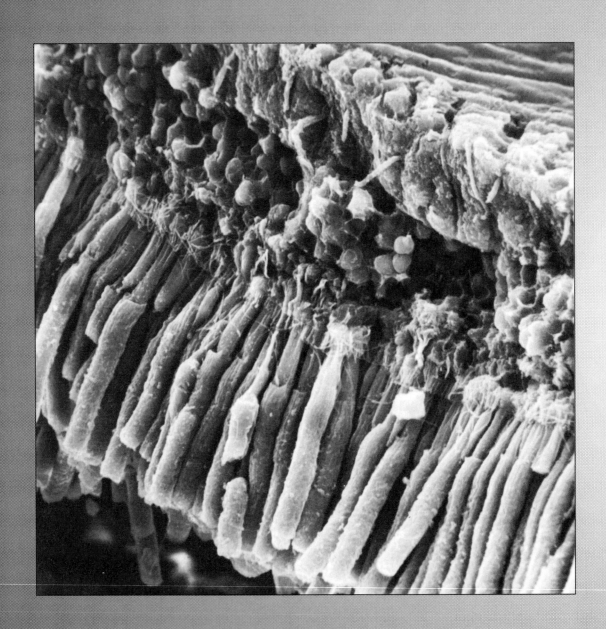

Chapter ... 3

THE VISUAL SYSTEM

Light

The Structure of the Eye

The Crystalline Lens

The Retina

The Fovea

Rods and Cones

Neural Responses to Light

Retinal Responses and Receptive Fields

Parvo and Magno Ganglion Cells

The Visual Pathways

The Geniculostriate System

The Tectopulvinar System

The Visual Cortex

Receptive Fields in the Visual Cortex

Organization of the Primary Visual Cortex

The Temporal Lobes: A System for Knowing "What?"

The Parietal Lobes: A System for Knowing "Where?"

Additional Visual Maps

Although perception occurs within the brain, your only real contact with the external environment is through your sense organs. Recalling the old saying, "The eyes are the windows to the world," it is clear that the physical properties of this "window" will affect the nature of your perception in the same manner that the physical properties of a glass window will affect your view. If the window is colored, your perception of the world will be tinted. If the window is dark, or dirty, your ability to discern objects will be reduced. If the window is curved so as to magnify the images, your perception of the size of objects viewed through the glass may also be distorted. Thus, it is important for you to know the nature of the "window" through which you look at the world, or, more simply, to understand the physiological makeup of the eye.

LIGHT

Each of the sensory systems is maximally responsive to a different form of physical stimulation. Taste and smell respond to chemical stimuli, touch to mechanical pressure, and hearing to the vibration of air molecules. The physical stimulus for sight is electromagnetic radiation. We call the particular form of electromagnetic radiation that produces a visual response *light.*

In 1704, Sir Isaac Newton advanced the theory that light, or for that matter any form of electromagnetic radiation, acts as if it were a stream of particles traveling in a straight line. Nowadays each particle is called a **quantum,** and a quantum of light is called a **photon.** The intensity of light is then given by the number of photons. Although this conception of light is extremely useful in physics, it is only important to the understanding of vision when we deal with stimuli that are relatively dim. At low levels of light, intensities are often described as the number of photons reaching the visual receptors. The smallest amount of light possible is a single photon.

Light often acts as if it were a stream of particles, but at other times it acts as if it were made up of waves. James Clerk Maxwell (1873) showed that light not only travels in a straight line but also as an oscillating wave. He suggested that if we consider the change in the electromagnetic field surrounding the train of photons, we can treat light as purely a wave phenomenon, with the wavelength defined as the physical distance between the peaks of the photon waves.

Electromagnetic energy can have wavelengths over a broad range, varying from trillionths of a centimeter to many kilometers. Very short wavelengths are not visible, nor are very long wavelengths. As can be seen in Figure 3-1, very short wavelengths include gamma rays, x-rays, and ultraviolet rays. Longer wavelengths range from those we call electricity to the broadcasting wavelengths associated with television and radio (which may be more than 100 m in length). The section of the electromagnetic spectrum we see as visible light is really quite small, extending from 380 to about 760 nanometers. A **nanometer** is a billionth of a meter and is usually abbreviated *nm.* Perceptually, variations in wavelengths correspond roughly to the hue or color of light. In normal eyes, wavelengths of about 400 nm are seen as violet, 500 nm as blue-green, 600 nm as yellow-orange, and 700 nm as red. However, the perception of color depends on more than wavelength, as you will learn in Chapter 5.

THE STRUCTURE OF THE EYE

Most vertebrate eyes, from those of fish to those of mammals, have a similar basic structure (Berman, 1991). A schematic diagram of

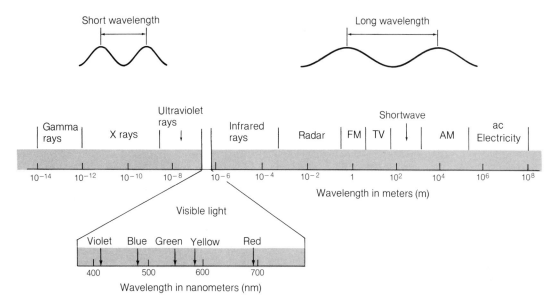

Short wavelength   Long wavelength

Visible light

Violet   Blue   Green   Yellow   Red

400   500   600   700

Wavelength in nanometers (nm)

Figure 3-1 *Electromagnetic radiation spectrum, with the region containing visible light enlarged.*

the human eye is shown in Figure 3-2. The eyes lie in protective bony sockets within the skull and are spherical structures about 20–25 mm in diameter. The outer covering, which is seen as the "white" of the eye, is a strong elastic membrane called the **sclera.** Because the eye is not made of rigid materials, it maintains its shape by means of fluid pressure from within.

The front of the eye contains a region where the sclera resembles a clear, domelike window, about 13 mm in diameter, called the **cornea** (Martin & Holden, 1982). The cornea is the first optically active element in the eye. It serves as a simple fixed lens that begins to gather light and to concentrate it. Because the cornea bulges forward, it allows reception of light from a region slightly behind the observer as shown in Demonstration Box 3-1 (p. 69).

Behind the cornea is a small chamber filled with a watery fluid called **aqueous humor.** This fluid is similar in nature to the cerebral spinal fluid that bathes the inner cavities of the brain. This is not surprising, since embryological evidence has shown that the neural components of the eye develop from the same structures that eventually form the brain.

When you look at a human eye, your attention is usually captured by a ring of color. This colored membrane, surrounding a central hole, is called the **iris.** When you say that a person has brown eyes, you really are saying that the person has brown irises. The color of the iris, which may vary from blue through black, is genetically determined in the same way as is skin color. The function of the iris seems to be to control the amount of light entering the eye. It may be of some interest to note that although blue eyes seem to have been viewed as more appealing by some Western poets, dark irises, such as brown or black, more effectively shield the eye from light. The light enters through the hole in the iris, which is called the **pupil.** The size of the pupil is controlled by a reflex. When the light is bright the pupil may contract to as little as 2 mm in diameter, whereas in dim light

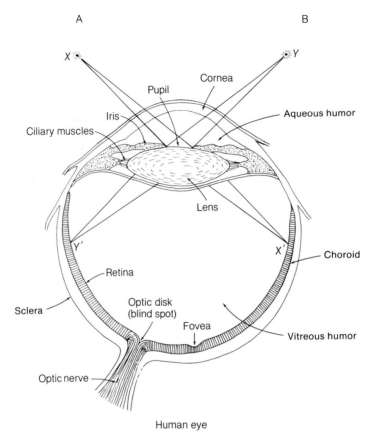

A   B

X

Y

Cornea

Pupil

Iris

Aqueous humor

Ciliary muscles

Lens

Y'

X'

Choroid

Retina

Sclera

Optic disk
(blind spot)

Fovea

Vitreous humor

Optic nerve

Human eye

Figure 3-2 *Structure of the human eye, with a demonstration of the image formation of two targets (X and Y).*

it may dilate to more than 8 mm. This is about a sixteenfold change in the area of the aperture. Demonstration Box 3-2 shows how you may observe the effect of light on pupil size.

The constriction of the pupil serves an important function. Despite the fact that the eye needs light to function, there are some advantages to viewing the world with a small pupil. Although the amount of light entering the eye is reduced, imperfections in the lens produce fewer distortions with a small pupil, and the depth of focus (which is the range of distances over which objects are simultaneously in focus) is vastly increased. We might say that the eye takes advantage of better light by im-

proving its optical response. In dim light, the ability of the eye to resolve or discriminate details (called **acuity**) is less important than the increased sensitivity obtained by increasing the amount of light entering the eye; thus the pupil increases in size to let in more light. The pupil size also changes as a function of emotional and attentional variables. Under conditions of high interest the eye tries to gather more light and the pupil tends to be large, a cue often used by smart traders as an index of a customer's interest in an item. Clever customers often negate the usefulness of this cue in bargaining situations by wearing dark glasses. Similarly, the dimness of candlelight

DEMONSTRATION BOX 3-1   Vision "behind" the Eye

It is easy to demonstrate that the visual field actually extends to a region somewhat behind the eye. In order to do this, simply choose a point that is some distance in front of your head and stare at it. Now raise your hand to the side of your head as shown in the figure, with your index finger extended upward. Your hand should be out of view when you stare at the distant point. Now, wiggle your finger slightly, and bring your hand slowly forward until the wiggling finger is just barely visible in your peripheral vision. At this point stop and, with your head as still as possible, move your finger directly in toward your head. You will notice that your hand will touch a point on your temple somewhat behind the location of the eye, indicating that you were actually seeing somewhat, "behind yourself."

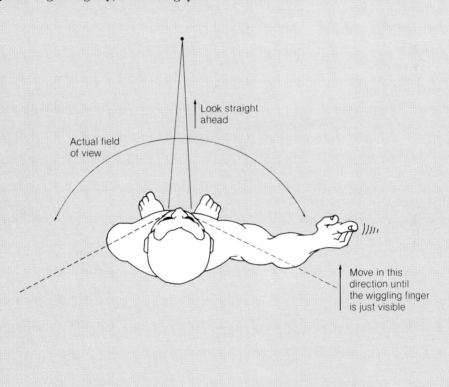

Look straight ahead

Actual field of view

Move in this direction until the wiggling finger is just visible

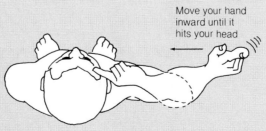

Move your hand inward until it hits your head

DEMONSTRATION BOX 3-2   The Pupillary Light Reflex

For this demonstration you need a friend. Dim the light in the room, but leave enough light so that you can still see the size of the pupil. Notice how large your friend's pupil appears to be under these conditions. Now turn on an overhead light or shine the beam of a flashlight into your friend's eye and note how the pupil constricts. Removal of the light will cause the pupil to dilate again. The light reflex of the pupil was the first reflex ever studied by Whytt (1751), who is credited with the discovery of reflex action. It is still sometimes called *Whytt's reflex.*

---

dilates the pupils and makes lovers appear to be more attentive and interested.

The Crystalline Lens

Most vertebrate eyes contain a **lens,** located directly behind the pupillary aperture. Since the curvature of the lens determines the amount by which the light is bent, its shape is critical in bringing an image into focus at the rear of the eye. The process by which the lens varies its focus is called **accommodation.** The lens changes focus by changing its shape (Dalziel & Egan, 1982). The natural shape of the human lens tends to be spherical, but when the ciliary muscles that control it relax, the pressure of the fluid in the eyeball and the tension of the zonal fibers connecting the lens to the inside wall of the eye cause it to flatten. Under these conditions, distant objects should be in focus. Contraction of the ciliary muscles, from which the lens is suspended, takes some of the tension from the lens and it regresses to a more spherical shape. When the lens is rounder, near objects are in focus. The effect of lens shape on point of focus is shown in Figure 3-3.

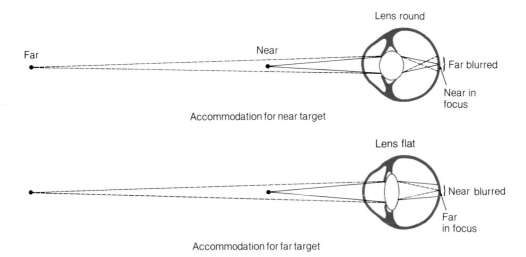

Figure 3-3   Accommodation (focusing) of an image by changing the shape of the crystalline lens of the eye.

An individual's age is important in determining the focusing ability of the lens. The ability to accommodate is not present at birth. For a newborn infant, until about the age of 1 month, only images of objects that are approximately 19 cm away are in focus (Dobson & Teller, 1978; Teller & Movshon, 1986). Images of targets closer or farther away than 19 cm are proportionally blurred. However, during the second month of infancy, the accommodative system begins to respond more adaptively (see Chapter 16).

The ability of the lens to change focus decreases with age after about age 16. This is because the inner layers of the lens die and lose some of their elasticity (Weale, 1986), and it thus becomes more difficult for the ciliary muscles to change the lens's curvature to accommodate to a near object. This results in a form of **refractive error** (light bending or focusing error) called **presbyopia,** which simply translates to "old sighted." Functionally, this condition increases the **near point** distance. The near point refers to how close an object may be brought to the eye before it can no longer be held in focus and becomes blurry. Thus, older persons without corrective lenses often may be seen holding reading material abnormally far from their face in order to focus it adequately.

Another interesting feature of the lens is the fact that it is not perfectly transparent. The lens is tinted somewhat yellow, and the density of this yellow tint increases with age (Coren, 1987; Coren & Girgus, 1972a). The yellow pigment screens out some of the ultraviolet light entering the eye. Animals with clear lenses (such as many birds and insects) can see ultraviolet light, as can people who have had their lenses surgically removed (for example, Emmerton, 1983; Hardie & Kirschfeld, 1983). The yellow pigment in the lens also screens out some of the blue light, and thus somewhat alters color perception. For example, you may have heard individuals arguing whether a particular color was blue or green. If they are different ages, the source of the argument may lie in the fact that, because the lens yellows with age, each is viewing the world through a different yellow filter.

As we noted earlier, the major purpose of the lens is to focus the image in the eye. An eye having normal accommodative (focusing) ability is called **emmetropic.** Sometimes the cornea has too much or too little curvature, or alternatively, the shape of the eye is too short or too long, so that the accommodative capacity of the lens is not sufficient to bring targets into focus. If the eye is too short, or if the light rays are not bent sharply enough by the cornea, distant objects are seen quite clearly, but it is difficult to bring near objects into focus. The common term for this is *farsightedness,* and the technical term is **hypermetropia.** If the eye is too long, or if the light rays are bent too sharply by the cornea, near objects are sharply in focus, but distant objects are blurry. This condition is called *nearsightedness* or **myopia.** The optical situations that result from these difficulties are shown in Figure 3-4.

The Retina

The large chamber of the eye is filled with a jellylike substance called **vitreous humor.** This substance is generally clear, although shreds of debris can often be seen floating in it. Try steadily viewing a clear blue sky and note the shadows that move across it as your eyes scan back and forth; these shadows are from floating debris in the vitreous humour.

The image formed by the optical system of the eye is focused on a screen of neural elements at the back of the eye called the **retina.** The term *retina* derives from the Latin word meaning *"net,"* because when an eye is opened up surgically (or its interior viewed with an optical device such as an ophthalmoscope), the most salient feature is the netlike system of

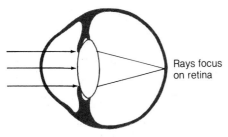

Emmetropic eye (normal)

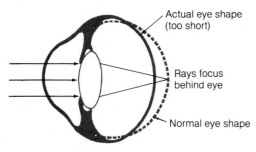

Hypermetropic eye (farsighted)

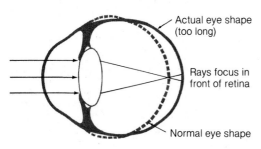

Myopic eye (nearsighted)

Figure 3-4 *Three common refractive conditions of the eye.*

blood vessels lining the inner cavity of the eye. Demonstration Box 3-3 shows how you can observe these blood vessels in your own eyes.

The sheet of neural elements that makes up the retina extends over most of the interior of the eye. In diurnal or daylight-active animals, the retina is backed by a light-absorbing dark layer called the **pigment epithelium** or **choroid coat.** This dark pigment layer serves the same purpose as the black inner coating in a photographic camera, reducing the amount of reflected and scattered light that could blur or fog the image. In nocturnal or night-active animals, where the detection of light is more important than image clarity, the light that penetrates the retina is reflected back through the retina by a shiny surface known as the **reflecting tapetum.** This permits the light to pass through the retina twice (once as it enters and once as it is reflected out), effectively doubling its intensity. Although this results in a sizable increase in sensitivity, it also results in a noticeably blurred image. This is especially true at higher illumination levels. The existence of this reflecting surface explains why a cat's eyes seem to glow in the dark when a flashlight is pointed toward them.

The retina consists of three major layers of neural tissue and is about the thickness of a sheet of paper (see Figure 3-5). It is here that the light is changed or *transduced* into a neural response. The outermost layer of the retina, closest to the scleral wall, contains the **photoreceptors.** Two types of photoreceptors are distinguishable on the basis of their shapes: long, thin, cylindrical cells, called **rods,** and shorter, thicker, somewhat more tapered cells, called **cones.** The outer segments of these cells contain pigments that absorb the light and start the visual process. The next level of the retina consists of **bipolar cells,** which are neurons with two long extended processes. One end makes synapses with the photoreceptor; the other end makes synapses with the large retinal **ganglion cells** in the third layer of the retina.

In addition to photoreceptors, bipolars, and ganglion cells, the retina also contains two types of cells that have lateral connections. Closest to the receptor layer are the **horizontal cells.** These cells typically have short dendrites and a long horizontal process that extends some distance across the retina. The second set of lateral interconnecters are called **amacrine cells.** These large cells, which are

DEMONSTRATION BOX 3-3 Mapping the Retinal Blood Vessels

For this demonstration you will need a pocket penlight and a white paper or light-colored wall. Hold the penlight near the outside canthus (corner) of your eye. Now, shaking the bulb up and down you will see a netlike pattern on the light surface. This pattern is generated by the movements of the shadows of your retinal blood vessels across your retina. By steadily shaking the bulb with one hand and tracing the shadows with the other, you can produce a map of your own retinal blood vessels.

found between the ganglion and bipolar cells, seem to interact with spatially adjacent units. Actually, more than 30 types of amacrine cells, differing in size and chemical properties, have been isolated (Masland, 1986). Both the horizontal and amacrine cells modify the visual signal and allow adjacent cells in the retina to communicate and interact with one another (Kolb, Nelson, & Mariani, 1981; Naka, 1982; Tomita, 1986).

Light reception occurs within the rod and cone cells. Contrary to what we might expect, the orientation of rods and cones is inverted, with the pigment-bearing end pointing toward the rear of the eye rather than toward the lens. Thus, the retina may be viewed as if it were a transparent carpet lying upside down on the floor of a room, with the pile of the carpet corresponding to the rods and cones. The incoming light must therefore pass through the carpet (the retina) before reaching the photoreceptors. Although this arrangement might appear to be somewhat counterproductive, it actually makes good sense. The photoreceptors

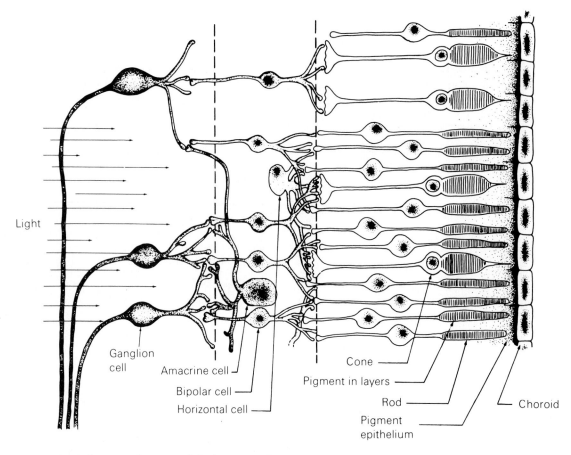

Light

Ganglion
cell

Amacrine cell

Bipolar cell

Horizontal cell

Cone

Pigment in layers

Rod

Pigment
epithelium

Choroid

Figure 3-5   *Schematic diagram of the human retina.*

need a rich oxygen supply, and to meet this
need there are many blood vessels in the ep-
ithelial layer at the rear of the eye. If the retina
were "right-side up," these blood vessels would
partially block light input to the photoreceptors. Therefore, the "upside-down" organization is more functional.

The Fovea

Not all parts of the retina are of equal importance in the perceptual process. The most important section of the human retina is located
in the region around the **optic axis,** an imagi-

nary line from the center of the fovea that
passes through the center of the pupil (see Figure 3-2). If we view a human retina through an
ophthalmoscope we note a yellow patch of pigment located in the region of the origin of the
optic axis. This area is called the **macula lutea**
(or just *macula*), which translates to "yellow
spot." Demonstration Box 3-4 describes a procedure in which you can see your own macula.

In the center of the macula is a small depression that looks much like the imprint of a
pinpoint about 1/3 mm in diameter. This
small circular depression is called the **fovea
centralis,** or translated, the "central pit." The
fovea is critical in visual perception. Whenever

DEMONSTRATION BOX 3-4   The Macular Spot

Under appropriate conditions it is possible to see the macular spot in your own eye. In order to do this you will need a dark blue or purple piece of cellophane. Brightly illuminate a piece of white paper with a desk lamp. Now, while looking at the paper with one eye, quickly bring the piece of cellophane between your eye and the paper. Now as you look at the paper you see what appears to be a faint circular shadow in the center of it. The sight of the shadow may only last for a couple of seconds. Sometimes its visibility can be improved by moving the cellophane in front of and away from your eye, so that you have a flickering colored field. Some individuals can see the spot when staring at a uniform blue field, such as a clear summer sky. This percept is caused by the fact that the yellow pigment in the macula absorbs the blue light and does not let it pass. This causes a circular shadow, which can be briefly seen. It is often called *Maxwell's spot,* after James Clerk Maxwell, who noticed its presence during some color-matching experiments.

you "look" directly at a target, it means that the eyes are rotated so that the image of the target falls on the foveal region.

The fovea, which is schematically depicted in Figure 3-6, is quite unique in its structure. In the center of the foveal depression, the upper layers of cells are apparently pushed away so that the light passes through a much thinner cellular layer before reaching the photoreceptors. The photoreceptors themselves are densely packed in this region. The central part of the fovea contains only cones; no rods are present at all. Foveal cones have a different shape than the more peripheral cones depicted in Figure 3-5. They are much longer and thinner (often only 0.001 mm in diameter), so that they somewhat resemble rods.

In a laborious study, Osterberg (1935) examined the retina of a human eye that had been removed as the result of an accident. By

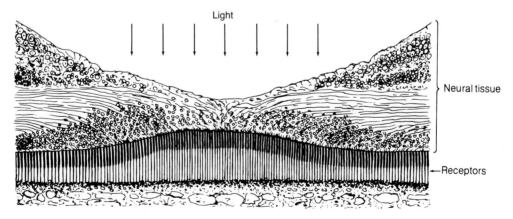

Figure 3-6   *Sketch of a cross section through the fovea. Light comes from the direction of the top of the page.*

fixing the fresh retina in a suitable fluid, it is possible to preserve it indefinitely. He counted the number of rods and cones in this human retina, demonstrating that no rods are present in the center of the fovea. The number of cones rapidly decreases with increasing distance from the fovea. The number of rods, on the other hand, rapidly increases with increasing distance from the foveal region, reaching a peak at about 20 degrees of visual angle from the fovea and then decreasing again. This general distribution (shown in Figure 3-7) has been verified in recent computer mappings of the retina (Curciao, Sloan, Packer, Hendrickson, & Kalina, 1987).

Rods and Cones

The presence of two types of retinal photoreceptors suggests the existence of two types of visual functions. In the early 1860s the retinal anatomist Max Schultze found that nocturnal animals, such as owls, have retinas that contain only rods. Animals that are diurnal, or only active during the day, such as the chip-

munk or pigeon, have retinas that are all cones. Animals that are active in the twilight, or during both day and night, such as rats, monkeys, and humans, have retinas composed of both rods and cones. On the basis of these observations, Schultze offered what has been called the **duplex retina theory** of vision. He maintained that there are two separate visual systems. One is for vision under dim light conditions and is dependent on the rods; the other is for vision under daylight or bright conditions and is dependent on the cones. Vision under bright light is called **photopic** (which translates to "light vision"), while vision under dim light is called **scotopic** ("dark vision").

Some early clinical observations (von Kries, 1895) support the idea that the eye contains two different visual systems. For instance, individuals whose retinas contain no rods, or only nonfunctioning rods, seem to have normal vision under daylight conditions. However, as soon as the light dims beyond a certain point (into what might be called a twilight level of intensity), they lose all sense of sight and become functionally blind. These individuals suffer from **night blindness.** The implication is that in the absence of rods, scotopic vision is ab-

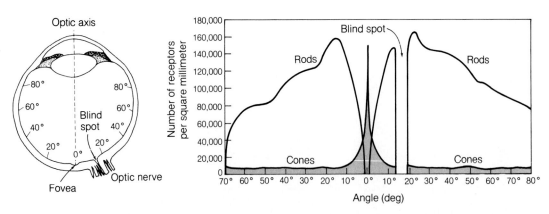

Figure 3-7   *The distribution of rods and cones in the human retina. The left figure gives the locations on the retina of the "angle" relative to the optic axis on the right figure (modified from Lindsay & Norman, 1977).*

sent. A quite different pattern is found for individuals who lack functioning cones. These people find normal levels of daylight quite painful, totally lack color vision, and have very poor visual acuity. Under dim levels of illumination, however, they function normally. Such individuals, who suffer from **day blindness,** provide evidence that a functioning cone system is necessary for normal photopic vision and for the perception of color. The specifics of the perception of brightness and color are discussed in Chapters 4 and 5.

Before a rod or a cone can signal the presence of light, it must first interact with the light in some way. Chemically, such interaction involves absorbing, or capturing, one or more photons. Any substance that absorbs light is called a *pigment*. A substance that absorbs a lot of light would appear to be darkly pigmented, since most of the photons hitting it would be absorbed and very few would be reflected to the eye of the viewer. As we noted earlier, the outer segments of both the rods and the cones contain visual pigments. If you turn back to Figure 3-5, you will see the pigments arranged in layers in the outer segments of the photo receptors. For rods, the photosensitive pigment is arranged in a stack of around 2000 tiny disks, like coins inside a tube; for cones, the pigment is part of a single large, elaborately folded membrane that forms the layers of photosensitive material.

Rods and cones do not contain the same pigment. The first successful isolation of the pigment in rods occurred in 1876 when Franz Boll isolated a brilliant red pigment from the frog retina (which contains predominantly rods). He noted that this pigment bleached, or lost its apparent coloration, when exposed to light. This reaction indicated that the substance was photosensitive. He further noted that the pigment regenerated itself in the dark. Thus, it fulfilled the elementary requirements of the visual pigment in that it responded by changing chemically in the presence of light,

yet it remained capable of resynthesizing itself. Kuhne took up the study of this pigment in 1877 and, in one extraordinary year, laid the groundwork for our understanding of its action. This pigment has been named **rhodopsin** (which means "visual red" rather than "visual purple" as it is sometimes called). In the century since the work by Boll and Kuhne, we have been able to work out much of the photochemical reaction in rhodopsin.

Basically, rhodopsin is a compound made up of two parts: **retinal,** a complex organic molecule derived from vitamin A, and **opsin,** a protein that has the capacity to act as an enzyme. As is the case for many organic compounds, the retinal component can exist in several different shapes called *isomers*. When a molecule of rhodopsin absorbs a photon of light it isomerizes, or changes shape, and then splits into its two component parts. A complex sequence of events, outlined in Figure 3-8, then begins. This involves the activation of several enzymes, resulting in the breakdown of the molecule that normally keeps the cell membrane open to allow the flow of sodium ions (Schoenlein, Peteanu, Mathies, & Shank, 1991; Stryer, 1987). (In order to understand what happens next, you should know a little about how information is transmitted to and by neurons and receptors. If you are a bit unsure in this area, you should stop and read the "Primer of Neurophysiology" included as an Appendix at the back of the book.) Once the flow of sodium ions into the rod stops, the rod cell **hyperpolarizes,** that is, the normally negative charge of −40 millivolts (mv) across the cell membrane becomes even more negative, perhaps −70 to −80 mv. This hyperpolarization indicates that the rod has been stimulated by light (Hubbell & Bownds, 1979; Schnapf & Baylor, 1987).

To be ready for another response this process must be reversed. The rhodopsin regenerates in the dark from the retinal and opsin with the help of vitamin A and a set of enzymes. Some evidence has been found

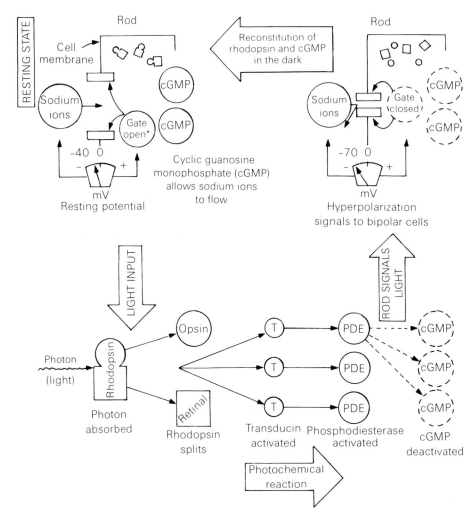

Figure 3-8 *The rod response cycle that transforms the capture of a photon to hyperpolarization, which signals that light has been received.*

indicating that light actually provides the energy to resynthesize rhodopsin, although this process is somewhat too complex to discuss here (Blazysnski & Ostroy, 1981; Rodieck, 1973). Notice that vitamin A is vital to the resynthesis, and in the absence of vitamin A, rhodopsin cannot be formed. In isolated communities where fish products or appropriate vegetables are not available, the absence of vitamin A in the diet results in "epidemics" of night blind-

ness, as people's rods become nonfunctional (Wald, 1968).

The identification and analysis of cone pigments has proved to be more difficult and elusive than that of rhodopsin. However, we have learned that a purple-colored pigment called **iodopsin** ("visual purple") is present in the cone cells of some birds. On exposure to light, iodopsin breaks down into retinal and another form of opsin. The opsin found in cones is often called **photopsin** to distinguish it from that in rods, which is called **scotopsin.** Photopsin is a slightly different protein from the opsin found in rods. The retinal, however, appears to be the same in rods and cones. Research indicates that all photopigments, regardless of the animal species studied, are composed of the same retinal and a specific protein or opsin that is characteristic of each pigment (Dartnall, 1967; Metzler & Harris, 1978). The biochemical events that lead to hyperpolarization in the presence of light, as we have outlined, are believed to be similar for both rods and cones (Bridges, 1986; Schnapf & Baylor, 1987). In their resting states, these receptors release a steady flow of neurotransmitters. Hyperpolarization of these cells causes this flow to stop, thereby stimulating the bipolar cells. The bipolar cells in turn stimulate the ganglion cells. At the same time, complex interactions occur between neighboring bipolar and ganglion cells via the horizontal and amacrine cells that connect to them. The axons of the ganglion cells then carry the resulting neural signals out of the eye toward the brain.

NEURAL RESPONSES TO LIGHT

The axons of the retinal ganglion cells extend in a transverse fashion across the retina and gather together to exit the eye by means of a hole through the retina and the scleral wall. The resulting bundle of axons forms the **optic nerve.** Through the center of the optic nerve come the blood vessels that sustain the metabolic needs of the eye. Since the optic nerve must penetrate the retina, this region contains no photoreceptors. Thus, no visual response occurs to light striking this portion of the retina, and it is appropriately called the **blind spot.** The neural axons that form the optic nerve have a distinctive circular pattern as they exit the eye, and this has led anatomists to refer to this as the **optic disk.** You may easily demonstrate the absence of vision in this region of the retina by referring to Demonstration Box 3-5.

The output of the retina is transmitted to the brain via the optic nerve. The nerve impulses transmitted via the ganglion cell axons

---

DEMONSTRATION BOX 3-5   The Blind Spot

The region of the retina where the optic nerve leaves the eye contains no photoreceptors and thus is blind. You may demonstrate this for yourself by using the figure here. Close your left eye and with your right eye look at the X in the figure. Keeping your eye on the X, move the page toward you. At some point the little open square will seem to disappear. At this point its image is falling on your blind spot. Notice that when you have the page at the correct distance, not only does the square seem to disappear, but also the line appears to run continuously through the area where the square should be. This indicates that we automatically "fill in" missing information. We fill it in with material that is similar to nearby visible material. This accounts for why you are not normally aware of the blind spot. You are simply supplying the missing information to fill in this "hole" in the visual field.

that make up the optic nerve are not "raw" sense data but are the result of a large amount of neural processing that has already taken place in the retina itself. In order to understand how much processing has occurred, you might consider that each human eye contains some 120 million rods and another 5 million cones. Each optic nerve contains only about 1 million axons. Clearly, then, each receptor cell does not have its own private pipeline to the brain, but rather the responses of a large number of photoreceptors may be represented in one optic nerve fiber. This occurs when the combined activity of the 125 million rods and cones, plus the output of several million more intervening bipolar, horizontal, and amacrine cells, converge upon the much smaller number of ganglion cells. We will soon see how the information is modified as it is collected.

Since the information carried to the brain by a single ganglion cell can represent the combined activity of a large number of rods and cones, a single ganglion cell may respond to light from a sizable region of the retina. Such a region of the retina, in which light alters the firing rate of a cell, is called that cell's **receptive field.** Thus, a single ganglion cell receives information coming from a substantial zone of receptor cells in the retina. In order to understand how visual information is processed, we must know how specific ganglion cells respond to various forms of light stimuli. Before attempting to comprehend this, however, it is important for you to understand the nature of neural responses in general, and how they are measured experimentally. If you have not already done so, you might want to read the "Primer of Neurophysiology" in the Appendix.

Retinal Responses and Receptive Fields

Most contemporary studies of the response of retinal ganglion cells to light have followed the lead of Hartline (1940) and Kuffler (1953), who inserted an electrode through the eye of an anesthetized cat and recorded from single ganglion cells in the retina. Generally one finds that when a single small spot of light is displayed on the screen, thereby stimulating the retina of the animal observing it, three different types of cell responses may be elicited, depending on the location of the spot in the field. The type of response that is most typically expected when a neuron is excited involves a burst of neural impulses immediately following the onset of the stimulus. This response has been dubbed an **on response.** Alternatively, the cell can give a burst of impulses coincident with the termination of a stimulus. Such a response is termed an **off response.** Some responses are hybrids because both presentation and removal of the stimulus causes a burst of neural impulses. These are designated **on-off responses.** Typical examples of these responses are shown in Figure 3-9.

When investigators use very small stimulus lights (about 0.20 mm in diameter), the nature of the retinal ganglion cell response tends to vary from on, through on-off, to off, depending

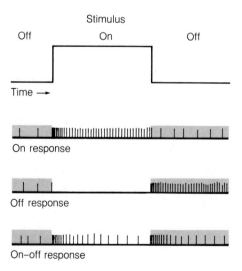

Figure 3-9   *On, off, and on-off neural responses in the retinal ganglion cells.*

on the location of the stimulus. A map of the shape of the overall receptive field of the retinal ganglion cell (the region of retinal stimulation to which the cell responds) shows that the responses are distributed circularly with two distinct zones within each receptive field. One receptive field has a relatively circular center that gives on responses when stimulated. That is, the ganglion cell responds with an on response to the onset of a light stimulus. The outer portion of the receptive field gives the opposite result. That is, the onset of a light in that region inhibits the response of the cell, but the termination of the light coincides with a burst of activity. Between these two regions, roughly at the boundary between the on and off regions, is a narrow region where on-off responses occur. Typical receptive fields are shown in Figure 3-10, where on response regions are marked by "+" and off by "−" (remember, on-off responses occur at the border between these regions).

As Figure 3-10 indicates, some receptive fields have the opposite organization, with the central region giving off responses and the surrounding region showing on responses. The retina contains approximately equal numbers of off-center and on-center cells. The ganglion cells that show the on- and off-center responses are visibly different. Apparently, the off-center cells make contact with their respective bipolar and amacrine cells at a more peripheral level in the retina (closer to the photoreceptors) than do the on-center cells (Kaneko, Nishimura, Tachibana, & Shamai, 1981; Nelson, Kolb, Robinson, & Mariani, 1981). Furthermore, evidence suggests that specific amacrine cells, with different neurotransmitters, may shape particular receptive field properties in ganglion cells (Dacey, 1988; Masland, 1986).

Parvo and Magno Ganglion Cells

It has long been known that ganglion cells come in a wide range of shapes and sizes (Cajal, 1893). However, only quite recently have researchers come to general agreement

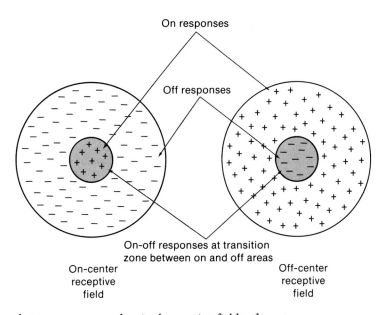

Figure 3-10   *Circular center-surround retinal receptive fields of two types.*

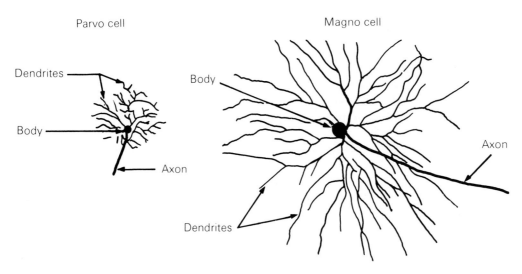

Parvo cell

Magno cell

Figure 3-11   *Examples of parvo and magno cells, taken from a cat retina and laid flat for illustration purposes (from Boycott & Waessle, 1974).*

on a classification system (Rodieck & Brening, 1983). As shown in Figure 3-11, the most obvious dimension along which ganglion cells vary is that of size. Cells with smaller bodies have come to be known as **parvo cells,** and those with larger bodies are called **magno cells** (*parvo* and *magno* are Latin terms for "small" and "large"). These names actually refer to the layers of the lateral geniculate nucleus to which these cells send information, as we will see shortly. You should also be aware that a number of other labeling schemes exist for the distinction between large and small ganglion cells, including **X** and **Y cells,** and *beta* and *alpha cells,* respectively. These terms are not exactly equivalent, and may include other important definitional characteristics as well as the size of the cell body. We now know that a wide range of anatomical and physiological characteristics is associated with these obvious differences in size (for example, Bishop, 1984; Shapley, 1990; Shiller, 1986).

Figure 3-11 shows that parvo ganglion cells have branches that extend over a much smaller area than the branches of magno ganglion cells. This means that magno cells have a much broader range when it comes to communicating with neighboring cells. Proportionally, there are many more parvo cells than magno cells, and they differ in terms of their distribution across the retina. Virtually no magno cells have been found in the foveal region, and the number of magno cells increases as we move outward into the peripheral retina.

Also associated with these differences in anatomy are a number of important functional characteristics. These have been summarized in Table 3-1. For instance, magno cells send neural impulses along their axons at speeds of about 40 m per second. This is very fast when compared with the parvo cells, which have conduction speeds of only 20 m per second. Although both parvo and magno cells have receptive fields with the center-surround, on-off arrangement we have described, the physically smaller parvo cells also have smaller center-surround receptive fields.

The characteristic neural response patterns of parvo and magno cells also differ. When parvo cells are stimulated they respond in a rather sustained manner, continuing their neural activity as long as the stimulus remains.

Table 3-1   Selected Anatomical and Physiological Differences between Parvo and Magno Ganglion Cells, along with Some Possible Consequences for Behavior

	PARVO GANGLION CELLS	MAGNO GANGLION CELLS
Anatomical Differences	small cell body dense branching short branching majority of cells	large cell body sparse branching long branches minority of cells
Physiological Differences	slow conduction rate sustained response small receptive field low-contrast sensitivity color-sensitive	rapid conduction rate transient response large receptive field high-contrast sensitivity color-blind
Possible Behavioral Consequences	detailed form analysis spatial analysis color vision	motion detection temporal analysis depth perception

Magno cells, on the other hand, have a much more transient response. They tend to give only a brief burst of activity when the stimulus comes on, or when it goes off, and they tend to return to their baseline rate quickly thereafter.

Another parvo–magno difference is illustrated in Figure 3-12. Part A shows a schematic drawing of the receptive field of a retinal ganglion cell, in which half of the field is evenly illuminated with light and the other half is dark. Suppose we now switched the illumination to the pattern shown as B or C. If we were stimulating a parvo cell it would continue to respond exactly as it had been responding. In other words, as long as the same amount of illumination is present in the center and surround, the parvo cell does not distinguish between the different locations of illumination. However, any switch in the pattern of illumination will provoke a vigorous response in a magno cell. Since changes in the distribution of illumination across a region of the field are usually caused by movement of an object, the usual interpretation is that magno cells may be specialized for movement detection, whereas parvo cells are specialized for the analysis of stationary patterns (Kruger, 1981). However, several other lines of data suggest that the attributes to which each type of cell responds may be more complex (for example, Shapley, 1990; Sherman, 1985).

The analysis of ganglion cells in some species, such as cats, has made it necessary to add a third class of ganglion cell to the existing parvo-magno distinction. These have been called **W cells** by some (Stone & Hoffman, 1972) and *gamma ganglion cells* by others (Boycott & Waessle, 1974). These tiny cells conduct impulses very slowly (10 m per second) and can have complex receptive field properties (Bishop, 1984; Schiller, 1986). The sluggish manner in which these cells respond in cats, along with

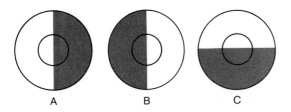

Figure 3–12   *If the illumination pattern on a center-surround receptive field was half light and half dark as shown in A, and then was shifted to a new orientation (either B or C), a parvo ganglion cell would not respond to a change, whereas a magno ganglion cell would respond*

their absence in the retinas of monkeys and humans, has led most researchers to assume that the basic analysis of the visual scene is done by the parvo and magno ganglion cells (for example, Sherman, 1985).

THE VISUAL PATHWAYS

As we noted earlier, the axons of the retinal ganglion cells gather together and exit from the eye at the blind spot. This bundle of axons, which forms the optic nerve, is the beginning of the pipeline of information that eventually ends in the brain. However, two distinct anatomical routes lead to the common end point, and each carries somewhat different information.

The primary visual pathway is the **geniculostriate system;** the secondary pathway is the **tectopulvinar system.** Both begin in the same fashion, with the information traveling out of the eyes along the optic nerves. As can be seen in Figure 3-13, the two optic nerves come together at a point that looks like an *X*. This point is called the **optic chiasm** (from the Greek letter *X*, or *chi*). In lower animals, the optic nerve from the right eye crosses completely to the left side of the head and vice versa. In many mammalian species, particularly those who use combined input from the two eyes to obtain better depth perception, some of the fibers do not cross (this will be discussed more fully in Chapter 10). In primates, such as humans, approximately one-half of the optic nerve fibers cross to the opposite side of the head. These are the fibers that represent the two inside or *nasal* (near the nose) retinas. Those from the outside or *temporal* (near the temples) halves of each retina do not cross but continue on the same side. Such an arrangement implies that the two halves of the visual field project to opposite sides of the brain. To keep the situation straight, you should also remember what is happening optically. Since the

crystalline lens in the eye reverses the image up-down and right-left, this means that the right visual field is projected onto the nasal half of the retina of the right eye and the temporal half of the retina of the left eye. The axons from the left half of each retina (or left *hemiretinas*) terminate in the left side of the brain. Thus, information from the right side of your field of view is represented upside down in the left side of your "brain," and vice versa, as shown in Figure 3-13.

As we begin to trace the visual pathways, we will need a few maps to help us. A general map is given in Figure 3-14. We will provide you with a few additional ones as we progress.

The Geniculostriate System

Beyond the optic chiasm, the pathway is no longer called the optic nerve but rather the **optic tract.** The most important relay center for most of the sensory information reaching the brain is a large body in the midbrain known as the **thalamus.** For most primates the major termination for the optic tract is reached after the fibers pass around the hypothalamus and synapse in the **lateral geniculate nucleus** of the thalamus. The cells in the lateral geniculate are arranged in six layers, each of which contains a **topographic map** of the visual field. A *topographic map* has points that correspond to spatially related points in the visual field, or on the retina. Later we will find that the brain contains many other such maps of the visual field (Orban, 1984).

As in the case with the retinal ganglion cells, lateral geniculate cells do not respond to visual stimuli unless the stimulation occurs within their receptive fields. Thus, a particular lateral geniculate neuron provides information about the location of an object in space, because it responds only to those objects projected onto the patch of retinal receptors that define its receptive field. These receptors, in

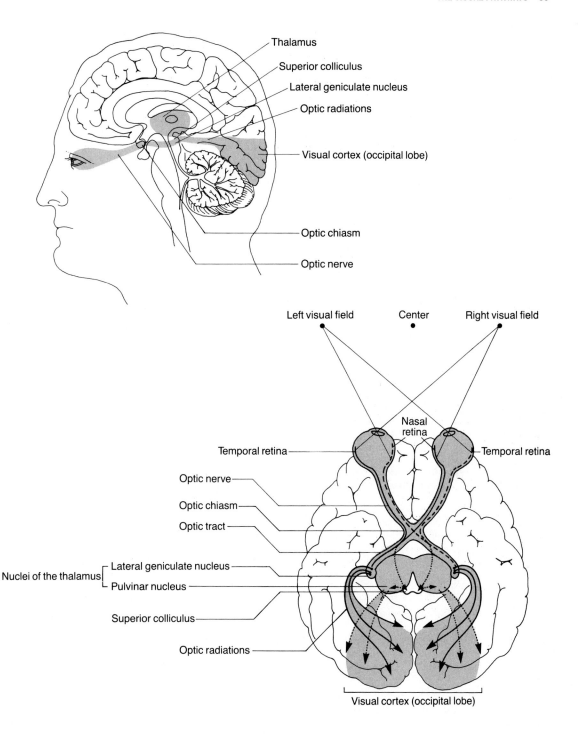

Figure 3-13 *The visual pathways from the eye to the visual cortex.*

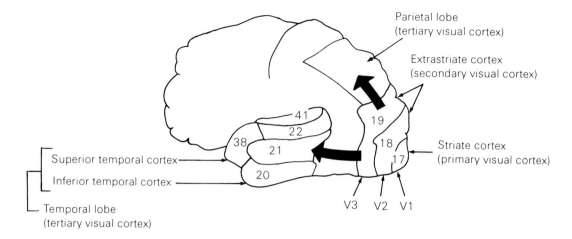

Figure 3-14   *The principal visually responsive regions of the cortex, and associated regions, with Brodmann's numbering of the areas (see p. 88), and several alternate labeling systems.*

turn, respond only to objects in a particular region of the visual field. Generally, the receptive fields of the lateral geniculate cells are similar to those of the retinal ganglion cells. If we map the receptive field of a lateral geniculate cell by projecting points of light onto a screen in the visual field in front of an animal, we find that the cell response appears similar to that of a retinal ganglion cell. For instance, most such cells have an *on* center and an *off* surround, or the reverse.

Figure 3-15 illustrates the layering of cells in the lateral geniculate nucleus. Note first that the layers alternate between those receiving input from the left eye and those receiving signals from the right eye. Another salient division among the six layers is that between the small (parvo) cells and large (magno) cells (Lennie, Trevarthen, Van Essen, & Waessle, 1990; Livingstone & Hubel, 1988; Shapley, 1990).

Parvo cells in the upper four layers of the lateral geniculate nucleus receive their input primarily from the parvo ganglion cells in the retina; magno cells in the lower two layers receive signals from the magno ganglion cells. It should not be surprising, then, that these two cell types in the lateral geniculate have parvo-

like and magno-like responses to stimuli, similar to those we outlined in Table 3-1. For instance, the lateral geniculate cells that receive inputs from the parvo cells have a center-surround organization like those shown in Figure 3-10, in which the positive or negative responses depend on the specific wavelengths of light (which we see as colors). On the other hand, most magno cells respond similarly to all wavelengths of light. Magno cells are also more sensitive than parvo cells to the magnitude of the change in luminance at an edge (Lehmkuhle, Kratz, Mangel, & Sherman, 1981; Shapley, 1990). This has been interpreted to mean that there is a division into two parallel streams of visual information processing. Specifically, a slow-acting channel handles form and color vision, and a faster-acting one handles movement perception. This separation into different channels begins in the retina, continues into the lateral geniculate nucleus, and, as we shall see later, is maintained by many other areas of the brain that process visual information (Bishop, 1984; Schiller, 1986).

Electrophysiological studies of the lateral geniculate have shown that its neurons are spontaneously active, meaning that these cells are always producing neural impulses, even if

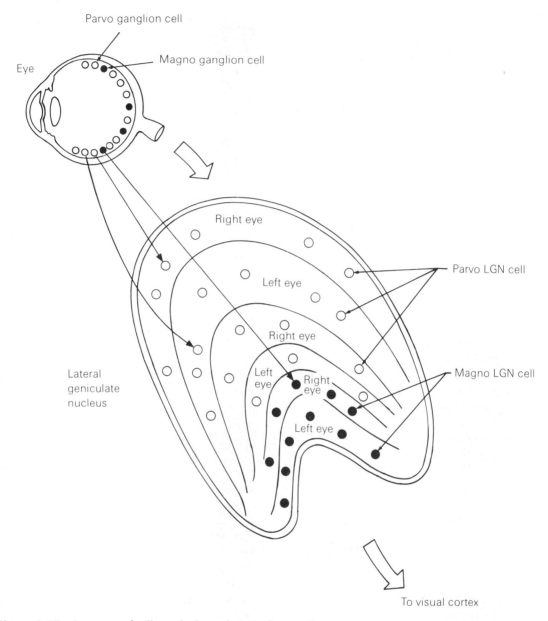

Parvo ganglion cell

Magno ganglion cell

Eye

Right eye

Parvo LGN cell

Left eye

Right eye

Left eye

Right eye

Magno LGN cell

Left eye

Lateral geniculate nucleus

To visual cortex

Figure 3-15 *Layering of cells in the lateral geniculate nucleus.*

the retina is in the dark. Although this may seem a bit surprising, spontaneous activity is a characteristic of most brain cells. We do not fully understand why this occurs. However, this continuing train of neural impulses does augment the information coding capacity of the cells, since signals from one neuron to another

may either be *excitatory* (causing an increase in the firing rate over the resting, or baseline, activity level) or *inhibitory* (causing a decrease in activity relative to the baseline).

As we mentioned earlier, some cells in the lateral geniculate respond differentially not only to the location of a light, but also to its color (DeValois & Jacobs, 1984; Hurvich, 1981). For instance, DeValois and DeValois (1975) reported that one type of cell in the lateral geniculate of monkeys responded with an increase in firing rate when the center of the receptive field was stimulated by a red spot of light, whereas it showed an *off* response (a decrease in activity relative to the spontaneous firing rate) when the center was stimulated by a green light. Such color-responsive cells are, of course, most likely to be from the parvocelluar system. One conclusion from the existence of cells organized in this way is that both color and location information may be encoded in the same cells. We will encounter this concept again in Chapter 5.

Another important feature of cells in the lateral geniculate nucleus is that they receive neural signals not only from the retina, but also from higher visual centers in the cortex. These returning signals, called **back projections,** represent a form of feedback based on previous information that has already been sent to the brain. Some estimates of the percentage of lateral geniculate inputs that are back projections are as high as 80% (Shiller, 1986). This is the first instance we have encountered along the visual pathway where the processing of information is being influenced both in a *bottom-up* fashion, through input from the retina, and in a *top-down* fashion, through back projections from the cortex. Such complex interactions are quite common in the processing of visual information.

The axons of the lateral geniculate neurons exit in the form of a large fan of fibers called **optic radiations,** as shown in Figure 3-13. These fibers eventually synapse with cells in the cortex in the rear (or posterior) portion of the brain. This area is known as the **occipital lobe.** Several alternate labels have been used to refer to this region of the brain. The traditional system for locating parts of the cortex is the numbering system devised by Brodmann (1914), based on the appearance of cells. In Brodmann's system this primary area of visual function, that is, the place where the fibers from the lateral geniculate terminate, is designated **Area 17.** A modern labeling scheme that is growing in popularity refers to this same area as the **primary visual cortex,** or simply **V1.**

Yet another popular term for this region is the **striate** ("striped") **cortex,** since when it is sliced vertically following chemical staining it has a distinct banded appearance. Some of the geniculate fibers also project to an area adjacent to Area 17, which Brodmann called **Area 18.** Also known as **V2** (short for **secondary visual cortex**), it is one of the many regions now known generally as the **extrastriate cortex** (the term *extra* here has the meaning of "beyond"). Areas 17, 18, and 19 each contain a separate topographic map in which each point of the visual field is represented by a separate region in the cortex. More than 20 such maps have already been identified in the primate cortex (for example, De Yoe & Van Essen, 1988; Van Essen, 1985), and this number seems to grow each year. This proliferation of knowledge about the brain has forced researchers to begin naming these maps separately. Some of these areas are named in Figure 3-14, and will be discussed shortly.

The Tectopulvinar System

A second pathway to the visual cortex is also indicated in Figure 3-13. This pathway begins when a number of fibers from the optic tract branch off to go toward the brain stem. Most pictures of the brain do not show the brain stem or midbrain structures because they are hidden by the cortex. In Figure 3-16 we have shown schematically where these structures are located, and we have marked off some of the areas of concern to us.

The visual center in the brain stem is, in an evolutionary sense, much older and more primitive than those of the cortex. In animals it

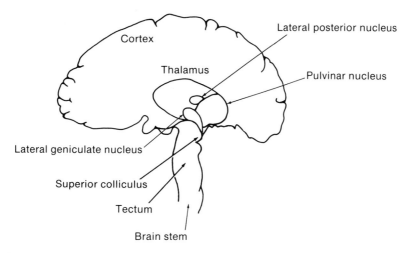

Figure 3-16 *The visually responsive areas of the thalamus and optic tectum.*

is known as the **tectum,** and for some animals, such as birds, almost all visual processing occurs here. The part of the tectum that receives most of the incoming fibers is the upper pair of what appear to be four bumps on the back (or dorsal) surface of the brain stem; these are known as the **superior colliculi.** Not all of the retinal ganglion cell types project to the superior colliculi, however. The vast majority of cells whose axons make up this pathway appear to be of the magno type in primates and of the magno and W type (or gamma type) in other animals, such as cats. Parvo inputs are found only in the geniculostriate system, while magno cells are found in both major pathways (Orban, 1984). Actually, there is some dispute as to whether the cells in the tectopulvinar system are really magno cells, or only cells that have similar functional characteristics to magno cells. For convenience, we will use the label "magno" to refer to cells that operate like magno cells as well as to cells that are indisputably magnocellular.

Cells in the upper layers of the superior colliculi have receptive fields that are arranged in an orderly topographic manner—the front (or anterior) portion represents the central visual field, and the back (posterior) region represents the visual periphery. As one might expect, given the magnocellular input from the retina, these receptive fields are not very sensitive to details of shape (such as orientation) or to color, but they are quite sensitive to motion and location. In deeper layers the cells begin to exhibit an interesting property—in addition to being activated by visual stimuli, they can also be driven by auditory and tactile stimuli. This suggests that the superior colliculi are a site for at least some forms of integration between sensory modalities.

As with other visual centers in the brain, we must keep in mind that the inputs to the superior colliculi are not only from the retina. This area also receives inputs in the form of back projections from the primary visual area of the cortex (V1) as well as from an extra striate area thought to be a center for visual motion processing (the *medial temporal* region, which overlaps area 22 in Figure 3-14, p. 86). Both of these back projections are primarily of the magnocellular type, thus contributing to the view that the superior colliculi are important in the analysis of movement and location. (We will return to this topic in Chapter 15.)

From the superior colliculi the pathway continues to the thalamus. However, rather than projecting to the lateral geniculate nucleus, the pathways go to the **pulvinar** and the **lateral posterior nuclei,** which are located nearby (see Figure 3-16). From here, the fibers project to the cortex. None are destined for the primary visual cortex (Area V1), but rather they connect to cells in the secondary visual areas (Area V2 and beyond).

Do the two different pathways to the visual cortex serve different perceptual functions? In simple terms, it seems that the geniculostriate system is involved in the fine-grained perception of patterns and colors, whereas the tectopulvinar system seems to coordinate the localization of objects in space, the guidance of eye movements, and gross pattern perception (Van Essen, 1985; Ungerleider & Mishkin, 1982). The most dramatic demonstrations of these separate functions come from studies of lower vertebrates. In one study, Schneider (1969) showed that removal of the lateral geniculate of the golden hamster left the animal with an inability to recognize patterns, whereas removal of the superior colliculi left it with the ability to recognize patterns but with an inability to localize them well enough to approach them. Deficits in spatial localization and depth perception have also been shown for cats when the tectopulvinar system is blocked (Ogasawara, McHaftie, & Stein, 1984). This result is consistent with the idea that the two anatomical visual pathways serve the different functions of localization and recognition, although some overlap in function seems likely.

THE VISUAL CORTEX

The visual cortex contains more than 100 million neurons. Only a small fraction of these have been thoroughly studied in attempts to discover their response characteristics. What we do know is based largely on research in which electrical impulses are recorded (using microelectrodes) from single cells, employing techniques similar to those used in the mapping of the receptive fields for the retinal ganglion and lateral geniculate cells. Much of the pioneering work was done by David Hubel and Torstein Wiesel, who received the Nobel prize in 1981.

We have already mentioned that several places in the cortex contain a rather direct topographic map of the external visual world, with specific points in the environment corresponding to specific regions in the cortex. This mapping was established first for Area V1 solely on the basis of clinical data from cases of accident or war injury, where penetrating missile wounds had injured specific parts of the cortex. When a piece of the occipital cortex is so damaged, the patient is blind in part of the visual field. Such a damaged area is technically called a *lesion,* and the blind patch in the visual field is called a **scotoma** (meaning "dark spot"). Through the measurement of such lesions, the correspondence between sections of cortex and parts of the visual field can be mapped, although the cortical map does not correspond exactly with the external scene in all of its dimensions. For instance, the fovea is represented by an inordinately large quantity of cortex relative to its actual size on the retina. This is in accord with its disproportionate importance relative to other retinal regions. When we say that points on the cortex correspond to points in the visual field, we do not mean to imply that if you are looking at a house there is a house-shaped pattern of electrical excitation in the cortex. Rather, this indicates only that the analysis of features nearby in the visual field occurs within cortical neurons in adjacent patches of cortex.

Receptive Fields in the Visual Cortex

Following the methodological procedures of Hubel and Wiesel (1962, 1979), many investigators have mapped receptive fields of cortical cells in animals. Usually, recording electrodes have been placed (or implanted) in cortical cells in V1. Next, the electrical responses of this cortical cell are measured as stimuli are projected on a screen in front of the animal. We illustrate this procedure in Figure A-5 in the Appendix (DeValois, Yund, & Hepler, 1982; Heggelund, 1981a, 1981b). When cortical cells are mapped in this way, the familiar circular on and off regions found for ganglion and lateral geniculate cells are still present. However, the majority of the measured receptive fields have elongated central regions, which make them most responsive to lines and edges. This type of cell, which Hubel and Wiesel labeled a **simple cell,** never seems to respond to diffuse illumination covering the whole screen. Sometimes such cells respond, although grudgingly, to small spots of light. However, because of the elongation of the central region of the receptive field, the best stimulus for such a cell is a dark or light bar or line flashed in the appropriate location in the receptive field.

Figure 3-17 shows the receptive fields that might be mapped from several simple cells. Beneath each of them you will see the stimulus that produces the maximal response for each of these receptive fields. Notice that in every case the edge between the light and the dark must be at a particular orientation in a particular location. If the edge of the line is flashed on the receptive field at a different angle, a greatly reduced response, or perhaps no response at all, may be obtained. For this reason such cortical cells are said to have **orientation specificity,** which is something cells with circular center-surround receptive fields do not have.

Other kinds of neurons in the visual cortex seem to be tuned to even more complicated pattern properties of the stimulus. These more elaborate feature-analyzing neurons have been labeled **complex cells.** They have larger receptive fields than those of simple cells, although

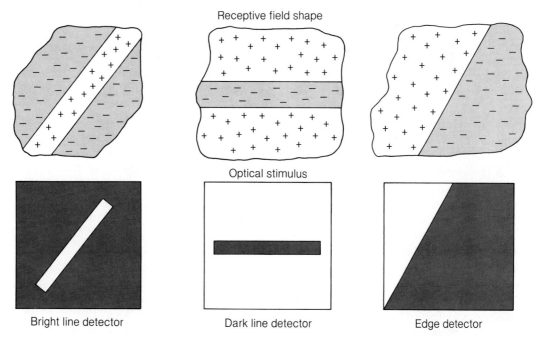

Figure 3-17 *Receptive fields of "simple" cortical cells: "+" indicates a region in the receptive field that gives an on response, and "−" indicates an off response.*

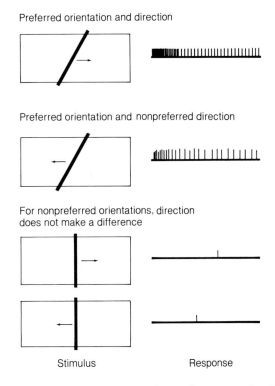

Preferred orientation and direction

Preferred orientation and nonpreferred direction

For nonpreferred orientations, direction does not make a difference

Stimulus   Response

Figure 3-18   *Some typical complex cortical cell responses.*

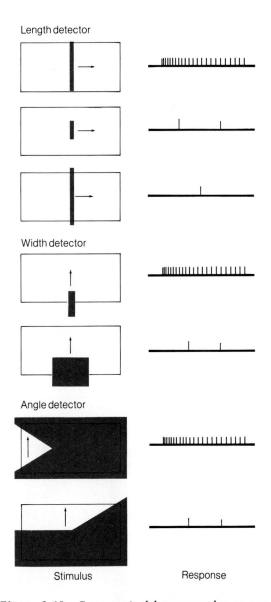

Length detector

Width detector

Angle detector

Stimulus   Response

Figure 3-19   *Some typical hypercomplex or special complex cortical cell responses.*

their size may vary tremendously. Like simple cells, complex cells respond maximally to stimuli of a particular orientation. However, they rarely respond to any flashing patterns. They prefer a bar or edge moving somewhere within the receptive field, and its location does not appear to be particularly important. In other words, complex cells seem to generalize their response over a wider area of the visual field. Figure 3-18 shows the response of a complex cell to two different moving light slits, one in the preferred and the other in a nonpreferred orientation. Notice that both direction of movement and orientation of the line are important factors in determining the response.

Complex and simple cells do not exhaust the types of cells recorded in the cortex. At a slightly more sophisticated level are certain **special complex cells,** often called **hypercom-** **plex cells.** These respond not only to the orientation and to the direction of movement of the stimulus, but also to the length, width, or other features of shapes, such as the presence of corners. Figure 3-19 shows an example of some hypercomplex cell responses.

Organization of the Primary Visual Cortex

Simple, complex, and hypercomplex cells are not randomly intermixed in the visual cortex. Instead, particular cell types are organized spatially into an incredibly detailed structure. The cortex in V1 is arranged in six layers, numbered 1 to 6, beginning with the outermost (surface) layer. These layers are depicted in Figure 3-20. Several additional sublayers have also been identified, as can be seen, for example, in Layer 4. To assist your understanding of these layers, you should be aware of a general organizing principle of the visual cortex—cells in the middle layers tend to receive input directly from the lateral geniculate nucleus; cells in the outer layers send signals to extrastriate regions; and cells in the innermost layers receive back projections from extrastriate visual centers and provide more immediate feedback to cells in the outer layers.

The cell layer in V1 receiving inputs directly from the lateral geniculate body is Layer 4C. A majority of the cells here have the simple circular center-surround receptive field found at lower levels of the visual system. The cell classification system we saw in the retina and in the lateral geniculate nucleus is also preserved in Layer 4C—magno cells are found in the top half (labeled Layer 4C α and in Figure 3-20), and parvo cells are found in the lower half (labeled Layer 4C β).

Above this level, in Layers 2, 3, and 4B, we find cells that connect with extrastriate regions of the cortex. They too appear to preserve the parvo-magno distinction, although in a somewhat different form. A cell-staining technique

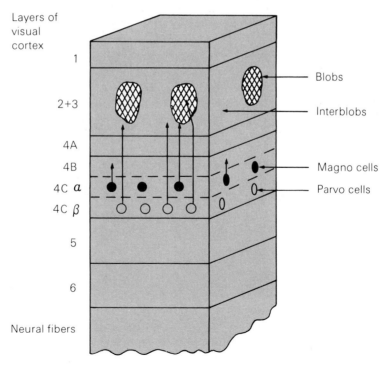

Figure 3-20 *Location of various visually responsive cells in the layers of the striate cortex (also known as Area 17 or primary visual cortex).*

has shown a fine pattern of groups of darkly stained cells in Layers 2 and 3, each about 0.20 mm in diameter, which can be seen against a background of lighter cells (Wong-Riley, 1979). These dark regions have been called **blobs,** and the light regions **interblobs.** Examination of the connections between these cells and cells in Layer 4C shows that blob cells receive input from both parvo and magno cells, whereas, interblob cells receive input only from the parvo cells. The thin Sublayer 4B, which lies just above layer 4C α, receives only magno cell input (Livingston & Hubel, 1984; Shapley, 1990).

When tested for functional selectivity, blob cells are highly sensitive to color and to contrast, but not to orientation or movement. Interblob cells respond selectively to the orientation of an edge, but do not differentiate between edges of different colors. Cells in Sublayer 4B are also not sensitive to color, but they are selective for both orientation and movement. A typical cell in Sublayer 4B will respond to an edge moving only in a particular direction.

Layers 5 and 6 also contain specialized cells that remind us of the parvo-magno distinction. Receptive fields of cells in Layer 5 are quite large and sensitive to the direction of stimulus movement, whereas those of cells in Layer 6 are rather long, narrow, and directionally sensitive. Although cells in these deep layers are not as well understood as those in the outer layers, this arrangement does suggest that the specialization of function in parallel pathways is present throughout the brain.

Cells sensitive to various orientations are not randomly distributed either. Instead, cells with a particular orientation sensitivity tend to be aligned in a column, as shown in Figure 3-21. As we move across the top of the cortex, the orientation specificity shifts by about 10 deg per column. Moving in the other direction, we encounter columns of cells that have the same orientational sensitivity. However, each column now receives inputs from a slightly differ-

ent section of the visual field, thus forming a sort of "slab" of cells with a specific orientational tuning.

One final aspect of the organization of the cortex must be mentioned. Each cortical cell tends to be more responsive to one particular eye than to the other, hence showing a relative **eye dominance.** These inputs are also spatially separated, with a slab of cells responding to one eye located next to one driven by the other eye. These are systematically arranged in alternating stripes across the cortex. A region of cortex containing all 360 deg of orientational specificity, and including a region responsive to both the left and the right eye, forms a larger unit that is sometimes called a **hypercolumn,** (see Figure 3-21). Such a piece of cortex might be between 0.50 and 1.00 mm square, and 2.00 mm deep.

This catalog of cell types and arrangements does not exhaust all of the forms of special receptive field properties that may be perceptually important. We shall mention others when we talk about brightness, spatial frequencies, color, and depth perception in later chapters. For the moment, however, these give us a general idea of the types of visual analysis that may be monitored at the single-cell level in the primary and secondary visual cortex.

Such a detailed architecture, spatial arrangement, and specificity at the cellular level is bound to elicit theoretical speculation. For example, the existence of orientation-specific or feature-specific cells in the cortex suggests that pattern perception may take place by decomposing visual stimuli into component features or contours. These would then be resynthesized later according to some plan or template (Frisby, 1980). Many pattern recognition machines have been built using this principle. For instance, the machine that reads the numbers on your bank check is tuned to respond to certain highly stylized, numerical stimuli by matching the patterns on paper to internally represented codes. Unfortunately, in mammalian species the significance of such

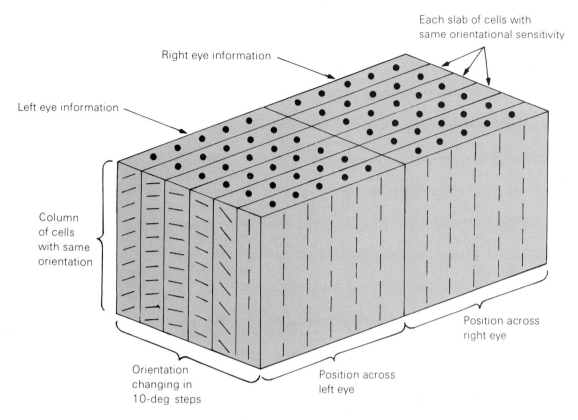

Figure 3-21 *Diagram of a hypercolumn, which is a small region of visual cortex containing inputs from both eyes, and all visual orientations, separated spatially, as shown.*

feature extraction cells for the perceptual process has not yet been determined. Evidence has also shown that removal of large areas of the primary visual cortex (and hence most of these orientation-specific cells), although greatly reducing visual acuity, does not have the massively disruptive effects one might expect if higher-level perception were directly dependent on extraction of simple features by these cells (for example, Lehmkule, Kratz, & Sherman, 1982). Furthermore, we now know that if we alter an animal's visual experience from birth, we can alter the distribution of orientations and features to which cortical cells are responsive. The significance of such changes will be discussed in Chapter 17 when we deal with the effects of experience. As Barlow

(1985) has pointed out, it is very difficult to go directly from single-cell responses to higher-level perceptual phenomena. It is often more useful to go the other way, from the perceptual phenomena to the search for a physiological unit that might support it.

The Temporal Lobes: A System for Knowing "What?"

Both the geniculostriate and tectopulvinar systems have inputs to the secondary visual areas, V2 and V3. From here the information seems to travel in one of two distinctly different pathways (Mishkin, Ungerleider, & Macko, 1983). One of these pathways is to the temporal lobes of the brain, which roughly correspond to the region directly behind the temples of your skull (Rockland & Pandya, 1981). Additional maps of the visual field are present here, and some very complex processing of visual stimuli takes place. In order to localize these *tertiary* or "third-order" visual areas, review Figure 3-14.

The first part of this region to be studied was the lower portion, called the **inferotemporal cortex.** The visual significance of this section of cortex was accidentally discovered by Kluver and Bucy in 1937 while observing monkeys who had undergone surgery that removed most of both temporal lobes. They called the syndrome **psychic blindness.** The animals could reach for, and accurately pick up, small objects; hence, they were clearly not blind. However, they appeared to have lost the ability to identify objects by sight. An example of this is shown in what was named the **concentration test.** Here, a piece of food or a metal object is presented to the monkey approximately every 30 seconds. A normal monkey will eat the food and discard the nail or steel nut after examination by mouth. Within a few trials, a normal monkey will let the metal objects pass by and select only the food. For animals with inferotemporal lobe loss, however, both the food and the inedible object were picked up virtually every trial. The animal seemed to show no evidence of learning to discriminate visually between the targets. Wilson (1957) found that such monkeys could discriminate between an inverted and an upright "L" by touch, yet with inferotemporal lesions they could not make the same discrimination visually.

This syndrome is similar to a human defect called **visual agnosia** (Kolb & Whishaw, 1980), which recently received popular attention in the book *The Man Who Mistook His Wife for a Hat* (Sacks, 1987). Patients with visual agnosia can see all parts of the visual field, but the objects they see mean nothing to them. Patients with lesions of the right temporal lobe also show deficits on a variety of visual tests. For instance, they have difficulty placing pictures in a sequence that relates a meaningful story or pattern. They also have difficulty learning to recognize new faces. Furthermore, such patients make poor visual estimates of the number of dots in an array, have difficulty recognizing overlapping figures, have poor memory for nonsense forms, and generally have poor picture memory. We will say more about such agnosias when we consider some clinical conditions in Chapter 18.

Some investigators have begun to map single neurons in the inferotemporal cortex. Microelectrode recordings from the monkey brain have produced startling results, suggesting that neurons found in this part of the brain have amazing response specificities. Although this research area is quite new, neurons sensitive to size, shape, color, orientation, and direction of movement have already been discovered in this region of the brain (Desimone, Albright, Gross, & Bruce, 1980; Desimone, Schein, Moran, & Ungerleider, 1985). One study reported that one neuron produced its best response when the stimulus was the outline of a monkey's paw. Gross, Rocha-Miranda, and Bender (1972) reported that one day they discovered a cell that seemed unresponsive to any light stimulus. When they waved a hand in front of the stimulus screen, however, they elicited a very vigorous response from the previously unresponsive neuron. They then spent the next 12 hours testing various paper cutouts in an attempt to find out what feature triggered this specific unit. When the entire set of stimuli were ranked according to the strength of the response they produced, they could not find any simple physical dimension that correlated with this rank order. However, the rank order of stimuli, in terms of their ability to drive the cell, did correlate with their apparent similarity (at least for the experimenters) to the shadow of a monkey's hand. The relative adequacy of a few of these stimuli in producing a neural response is shown in Figure 3-22. Inter-

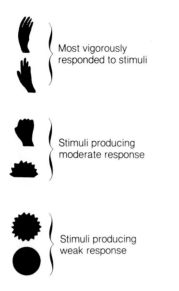

Most vigorously
responded to stimuli

Stimuli producing
moderate response

Stimuli producing
weak response

Figure 3-22 *The stimuli in the figure were used to excite a neuron in the inferotemporal cortex of a monkey. Notice that the more handlike a stimulus is, the more vigorous the response.*

estingly enough, fingers pointing downward elicited very little response when compared to fingers pointing upward or to the side. An animal looking at his own hand would most likely see a hand with fingers pointing upward. Such complex response specificity has been observed a number of times in this region of the cortex (Desimone & Gross, 1979).

Even more startling degrees of stimulus analysis seem to be emerging from a region of the temporal lobe called the **superior temporal cortex.** Here cells have been found in monkeys that responded selectively to faces (Bruce, Desimone, & Gross, 1981) and even to particular movements of faces, such as back-and-forth or rotation (Perrett & Mistlin, 1987). The more realistic and monkeylike the face, the stronger the response. Distorting the stimulus by removing the eyes, scrambling the features, or presenting a cartoon caricature resulted in a weaker response. Kendrick and Baldwin (1987)

have found similar cells in sheep that respond preferentially to sheep faces and, interestingly, to human faces as well. Thus, it seems possible that your temporal cortex might contain a template for the perception of your grandmother, your car, or many other familiar stimulus shapes.

The Parietal Lobes: A System for Knowing "Where?"

The second distinctive visual pathway that continues from areas V2 and V3 goes to the **parietal lobe** of the cortex. You may want to refer back to Figure 3-14 to locate this tertiary visual region. Monkeys with lesions in the parietal cortex have no difficulty learning to identify objects by sight alone; however, they have a great deal of difficulty learning to respond correctly on the basis of relative spatial location (Mishkin, Lewis, & Ungerleider, 1982; Pohl, 1973). For instance, monkeys trained to respond to the food source that is "closer to the landmark object" are unable to perform this task following parietal lesions, although similar lesions in the temporal cortex leave performance on this task at a high level. Humans with brain damage to the parietal cortex also appear to be impaired on tasks that require relative location judgments, but not on tasks that require object identification (for example, Posner, 1988). We will discuss this topic in greater detail in Chapter 15.

Additional Visual Maps

We mentioned earlier that many alternate maps of the visual field are present in the cortex. More than 20 have been described for primates, with more than a dozen of these in the temporal cortex, at least 3 in the occipital region, several in the parietal cortex, and others

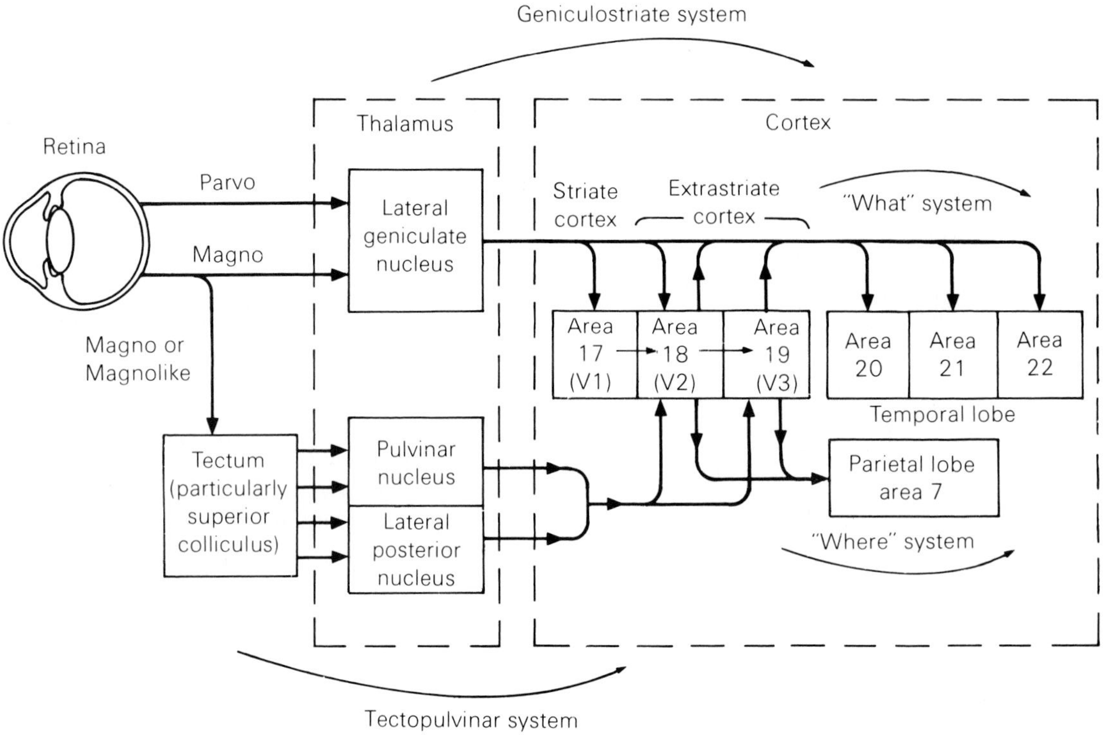

Figure 3-23   *A highly schematic overview of the visual system, indicating the two visual pathways to the cortex and their connections with the major subcortical and cortical centers. The two pathways from secondary cortex to tertiary cortical areas are also shown.*

scattered around the brain (DeYoe & Van Essen, 1988; Maunsell & Newsome, 1987; Van Essen, 1984). The pattern of innervations, beginning with the parvo and magno ganglion cells of the retina, can become quite complex (see Figure 3-23).

Why do so many different maps of the visual field exist? To begin with, you must remember that the function of the visual system is not to re-create an image of the outside world in the brain, since nobody is in there to look at such an image. The function of the visual system is to recognize objects, locate them in space, and eventually assist the organism to act appropriately. A number of investigators have suggested that each map of the visual field is set up to extract some subset of properties

from the visual image (for example, Cowey, 1981; Desimone et al., 1985; Livingstone & Hubel, 1988; Phillips, Zeki, & Barlow, 1984). Thus, one map might be relatively specialized for color, another for orientation or movement, yet another for distance or texture, and so forth. By performing these analyses of different visual attributes in parallel, rather than in series, much more processing can be accomplished in a short period of time (Ballard, Hinton, & Sejnowski, 1983). The reason for the topographic mapping may be to isolate "an object" with "a property" with "a specific location in space" (Treisman, 1986). We will encounter these concepts again when we talk about object and form perception in Chapter 11. For now, one important consequence of the *parallel mapping* of visual brain function is that the destruction of any one of these cortical maps may produce only subtle disruptions of visual processing, rather than massive and global deficits, such as a total loss of the ability to read type on paper.

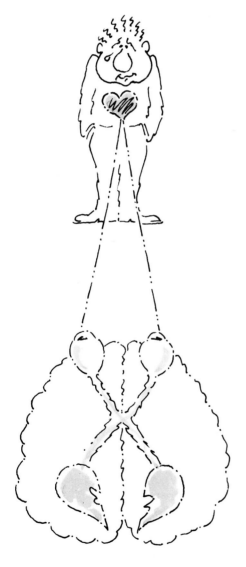

Poor Fred's heart is broken at Cathy's optic chiasm

GLOSSARY

The following definitions are specific to their use in this book.

Accommodation The process by which the lens of the eye varies its focus.

Acuity The ability of the eye to resolve or discriminate details.

Amacrine cells Large, laterally interconnecting neurons found in the retina near the ganglion cell layer.

Aqueous humor The fluid occupying the small chamber between the cornea and the lens of the eye.

Area 17 According to Brodmann's numbering system, another name for the primary visual cortex, which is one part of the occipital lobe of the brain receiving inputs from the geniculostriate system. Also known as V1, primary visual cortex, and striate cortex.

Area 18 and Area 19 Secondary visual cortex receiving inputs from both the geniculostriate and tectopulvinar systems. Also known as V2 and V3, respectively.

Back projections Inputs coming to a particular region of the brain from another region that is farther along the visual stream. These inputs may provide feedback based on previous information that has already been processed by the brain.

Bipolar cells Neural cell in the retina between the photoreceptor and ganglion cells.

Blind spot Portion of retina through which optic nerve passes and therefore an area without photoreceptors. This region shows no response to light.

Blobs Regions of cells in Layers 2 and 3 of the primary visual cortex that become dark in response to chemical staining. These cells receive signals from both the parvo cells and the magno cells of Layer 4C and are highly sensitive to color and to contrast.

Choroid coat *See* Pigment epithelium.

Complex cells Cells in the visual cortex that respond to feature such as line orientation and direction of movement.

Concentration test Method for determining the ability to discriminate objects following inferotemporal lobe loss.

Cones Short, thick, tapering cells in the photoreceptive layer of the retina, responsible for bright-light and color vision.

Cornea The transparent, domelike part of the sclera of the eye.

Day blindness   Visual difficulty under bright-light conditions, caused by the absence or nonfunctioing of cones.

Duplex retina theory   The concept of two separate visual systems, rod-dependent for dim-light vision, and cone-dependent for bright-light vision.

Emmetropic   Refers to an eye with normal accommodative ability.

Extrastriate cortex   V2 and beyond in the cortex; also the secondary and tertiary visual cortex areas.

Eye dominance   Refers to the fact that most cortical receptive cells can be driven better by one eye than the other.

Fovea centralis   A small depression in the retina that contains mostly cones and in which acuity is best.

Ganglion cells   Third layer of the retina through which neural signals travel, after the photoreceptor and bipolar cells.

Geniculostriate system   The primary visual pathway passing through the lateral geniculate nucleus to the striate cortex.

Horizontal cells   Retinal cells with short dendrites and a long axonal process that extends horizontally.

Hypercolumn   A small piece of visual cortex, sensitive to input from both eyes and to a full range of orientational specificity.

Hypercomplex cells   Cortical cells that respond to complex stimulus features regardless of where they occur in the receptive field.

Hypermetropia   Farsightedness.

Hyperpolarization   The change of the electrical potential of a cell toward increasing negativity.

Inferotemporal cortex   A cortical region located in the temporal lobes of the brain, which may be associated with recognition abilities and, pathologically, with visual agnosia.

Interblobs   The area between the blobs of Layers 2 and 3 of the primary visual cortex. These cells receive signals from the parvo cells of Layer 4C and are sensitive to the orientation of a visual edge, but not to the color of the edge.

Iodopsin   The cone pigment present in some birds.

Iris   The opaque, colored membrane controlling the amount of light entering the eye by changing the size of the pupil.

Lateral geniculate nucleus   The first major relay center in the geniculostriate system for optic nerve fibers leaving the retina. It is in the thalmus in primates.

Lateral posterior nucleus   A visual center in the thalamus, part of the tectopulvinar system.

Lens   A transparent body in the eye. It can change shape, thus altering the focus of the retinal image.

Macula lutea   A yellow pigmented area centered over the fovea.

Magno cells   Large, fast-conducting retinal ganglion cells that are important for motion perception. Also known as Y cells and alpha cells.

Myopia   Nearsightedness.

Nanometer (nm)   A billionth of a meter (a millionth of a millimeter).

Near point   The nearest point to which an object may be brought to an eye and still remain in focus on the retina.

Night blindness   The inability to see under low-light (twilight) conditions, caused by an absence of functioning rods.

Occipital lobe   The rear portion of the brain, which serves as the primary visual processing center.

Off response   A neural response commencing with the termination of a stimulus.

On response   A neural response commencing with the onset of a stimulus.

On-off response   A burst of neural responses given at both the onset and the termination of a stimulus.

Opsin   Protein part of the rhodopsin pigment.

Optic axis   Hypothetical line from the center of the pupil to the fovea, used as a reference point for distances across the eye.

Optic chiasm   The point at which the two optic nerves meet and the nasal fibers cross to the contralateral side.

Optic disk   The region of the retina where the optic nerve leaves the eye. *See* Blind spot.

Optic nerve   The collection of axons from retinal ganglion cells as they exit the eye.

Optic radiations   The large fans of neural fibers spreading out from the lateral geniculate nucleus to the occipital cortex.

Optic tract   The path of the optic nerve once it is past the optic chiasm.

Orientation specificity   A property whereby cortical cells respond selectively to visually presented lines or edges of a particular orientation.

Parietal lobe   A portion of the cortex above the occipital lobe; one of the tertiary visual centers involved in the processing of information about object location.

Parvo cells Small, slow-conducting ganglion cells that are important for detailed pattern and color vision. Also known as X cells and beta cells.

Photon A quantum of light energy.

Photopic Refers to vision under bright-light conditions.

Photopsin The protein segment of the photochemical in cones.

Photoreceptors Photosensitive cells in the retina (rods and cones).

Pigment epithelium The light-absorbing dark layer at the back of the retina in diurnal animals. Also called choroid coat.

Presbyopia Farsightedness found in older individuals.

Primary visual cortex Primary area of visual function in the occipital lobe. Also known as Area 17, V1, and striate cortex.

Psychic blindness The condition in which animals are able to locate objects yet are unable to identify them.

Pulvinar nucleus A visual center in the thalamus.

Pupil The opening in the iris of the eye through which light enters.

Quantum The smallest amount possible of any form of electromagnetic radiation. *See* Photon.

Receptive fields For any particular cell, the region of the visual field in which a stimulus can produce a response.

Reflecting tapetum The shiny surface backing the retina in some nocturnal animals.

Refractive error Light-bending or focusing error.

Retina The rear portion of the eye containing photoreceptors and several types of sensory neurons.

Retinal Part of the rhodopsin pigment, similar to vitamin A.

Rhodopsin The photopigment found in rods.

Rod Long, thin, cylindrical photoreceptors in the retina, responsible for low-light vision.

Sclera Strong, elastic outer covering, seen as the "white" of the eye.

Scotopic Refers to vision under low-light conditions.

Scotoma A localized blind spot.

Scotopsin The protein portion of rhodopsin in rods.

Secondary visual cortex Brodmann's Areas 18 and 19 in the occipital lobe. Also known as V2 and V3.

Simple cell A cortical cell that responds to lines or edges of a particular orientation and location.

Special complex cells *See* Hypercomplex cells.

Striate cortex Area 17 in the occipital lobe. Also known as V1 and primary visual cortex.

Superior colliculi The termination point of the optic fibers on the brain stem.

Superior temporal cortex An area of the temporal lobe whose cells show a high degree of response specificity to visual stimuli.

Tectopulvinar system A secondary pathway to the visual cortex that includes nuclei in the brain stem and thalamus.

Tectum A primitive visual center in the brain stem.

Topographic map An area of the brain in which points in visual space are represented in the neural tissue in a spatially related manner.

Thalamus A large mass of neural tissue located at the base of the cerebrum, which serves as a major "switching center" for sensory information.

V1 Area 17 in primates. Also known as primary visual cortex and striate cortex.

V2 and V3 Areas 18 and 19 in primates. Also known as secondary visual cortex.

Visual agnosia A syndrome in which all parts of the visual field are seen, but the objects seen are without meaning.

Vitreous humor The jellylike substance filling the large chamber of the eye.

W cells Slow-conducting visual cells in cats whose function is not yet fully established. Also called gamma cells.

X cells Parvo ganglion cells in cats. Also beta cells.

Y cells Magno ganglion cells in cats. Also alpha cells.

Chapter ...

4

BRIGHTNESS AND SPATIAL FREQUENCY

Photometric Units

Factors in Brightness Perception

  Adaptation

  Retinal Locus

  Wavelength

  Time and Area

  Maximum Sensitivity

Visual Acuity

Spatial Frequency Analysis

  Spatial Fourier Analysis

  Modulation Transfer Function

  Neural Spatial Frequency Channels

    • Neurons as Spatial Filters

Spatial Context Effects

  Brightness Contrast

  Brightness Assimilation

Temporal Context Effects

Darkness Perception

*T*he following scene must have played countless times on cinema screens in Grade-B horror movies:

It is night, and in the darkness two old ragged beachcombers can barely be seen moving along the water's edge. Suddenly, one stops.

"Hey, Charlie, I think there's something out there."

"W-What is it?"

"I can't make it out. It's some sort of glow. It's too dim to make out what it is."

This scene illustrates the most basic property of vision, namely, that it depends on the presence of light. The most primitive visual percepts are simply reactions to the intensity of the incoming energy. These responses are represented in consciousness as a brightness or glow. We often sense the presence of light before sufficient energy exists for us to apprehend shape or form. Thus, the next line in the above scenario usually goes, "It's getting brighter," and then as the energy becomes sufficient to apprehend the object itself, "Oh my God! It's some sort of creature!" As we shall see, the perception of brightness is much more complex and surprising than the script of this particular film.

Photometric Units

Electromagnetic energy, or light, can vary along three dimensions: intensity, wavelength, and duration (see Chapter 3). All dimensions are important in the perception of brightness, although brightness varies most directly with intensity. Of course, to make sense of the perceptual effects, we must first be able to specify the physical intensity of the stimulus. This is not as simple as it seems.

Light measurement, or **photometry,** is based on the visual effects produced by visible radiation. Photometric units are used to describe the stimulus, and these units are, by convention, expressed in terms of energy. Unfortunately, over the years a confusing array of

photometric units was developed, most of them designed for some specific purpose by some technical or academic subdiscipline. The result was chaos. Even among the most scholarly scientists, few can tell you how many *nits* there are in an *apostilb* or a *blondel,* or how any of these units are related to a *candle* or a *lambert.* In 1960, an International Conference on Weights and Measures established a uniform system of measurement called the *System International d'Unites* (known commonly as the **SI System**). Throughout this book we use the **standard units** established by this system. Should your reading bring you into contact with some of the older forms of photometric measurement, we suggest you look at a more advanced text such as Wyszecki and Stiles (1967) to make sense of the quantities involved.

Basically, light can reach the eye in two ways: (1) directly from a radiating source such as a light bulb, a fluorescent tube, a firefly, or the sun, or (2) indirectly by reflection from surfaces that have radiant energy falling upon them, such as walls and paper. Different types of measures are used for these different types of light input. All photometric units, however, are ultimately based on the amount of light emitted from a single candle. The nature of this *standard candle*, its photic energy, and the specific measures derived from it have been fixed (albeit somewhat arbitrarily) by an international body called the *Commission Internationale de l'Eclairage*, or **CIE.**

Each different aspect of light is designated by its own name and requires a different measurement unit. These are summarized in Figure 4-1 for a situation in which a projector is shining light on a screen. Let us begin with the light measures that can be taken with a photometer (a physical light measuring device). The amount of energy coming from a light source (for example, the projector bulb) is called its **radiance.** The unit of radiance is the standard candle, which produces an energy of slightly more than 0.001 watt at a wavelength

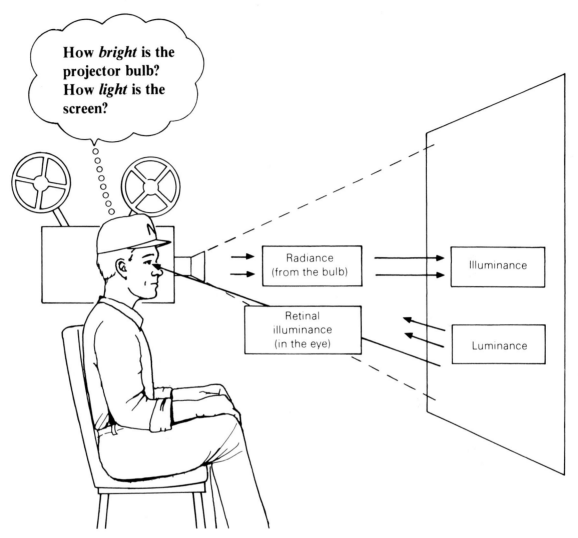

Figure 4-1 *The relationship between various physical measures of light and psychological judgments of brightness and lightness.*

of 555 nm. This quantity of luminous energy is called a **lumen.** The amount of light falling on a surface (such as the screen) is another photometric quantity called **illuminance.** The amount of light reflected from a surface is called its **luminance,** and the *percentage* of light falling on a surface that is reflected is called its **reflectance**. Reflectance is thus simply the percentage of luminance compared to illuminance. The amount of light reaching the

retina is called the **retinal illuminance.** Table 4-1 summarizes these photometric quantities and explains how they are measured, the units used, and some of their specific properties.

Vision researchers are interested in two important subjective measures of light intensity. These measures are not of physical quantities but refer to our perceptual responses to light. The first of these is **brightness,** or the phenomenal impression of the amount of light

Table 4-1   Photometric Units

PHOTOMETRIC TERM	WHAT IS MEASURED	UNIT	HOW MEASURED	COMMENTS
Radiance or luminous flux	Radiant energy from a light source	Lumen	A candela is the light of a 1-lumen source at a distance of 1 m shone on a square meter	Defined in terms of a standard candle (candela)
Illuminance	Light falling on a surface	Lux	1 lumen/m^2	As the source moves farther away illuminance decreases
Luminance	Light reflected from a surface	Candelas per square meter	Luminance = $\dfrac{\text{Illuminance} \times \text{Reflectance}}{100}$	Independent of distance of eye from surface
Reflectance (albedo)	Proportion of light reflected from surface	Percentage reflectance	Reflectance = $\dfrac{\text{Luminance}}{\text{Illuminance}} \times 100$	Really ratio of reflected to incident light
Retinal illuminance	Amount of light incident on the retina	Trolands	1 candela/m^2 seen through pupil of 1 mm^2 area	Roughly 0.0036 lumens/m^2 through a 1-mm^2 pupil

that is being emitted from a source or reflected from a surface. *Brightness* is therefore the psychological attribute corresponding to the physical measures of *illuminance* (if the light source is being viewed) and *luminance* (if a reflecting surface is being viewed). The second subjective measure of light intensity is **lightness,** or the phenomenal impression of the percentage of reflected light relative to the total light falling on a surface. *Lightness* (sometimes referred to as *whiteness*) is therefore the psychological correlate to the physical measure of *reflectance*. It refers to the observer's impression of whether the pigment of a reflecting surface is white, gray, or black (Fiorentini, Baumgartner, Magnussen, Shiller, & Thomas, 1990; Walraven, Enroth-Cugell, Hood, McLeod, & Schnapf, 1990). In this chapter we will focus on *brightness* perception, returning to the discussion of *lightness* perception in Chapter 14.

Why is it necessary to distinguish between the various physical measurements we can make and the psychological judgment of brightness? Because the perception of brightness cannot be explained simply by the amount of light reaching the eye. As we noted in Chapter 2, when we plot the sensation of light intensity against the physical stimulus intensity, we get a nonlinear relationship. The apparent brightness measured by a direct scaling technique (such as magnitude estimation) grows approximately as the cube root of the physical intensity (to be precise, the phenomenal sensation is proportional to the light intensity raised to the 0.33 power). This means that if you had a theater stage illuminated by 8 lights, and you wished to increase the perceived brightness of the area, doubling the number of lights to 16 would not double the perceived brightness but would only increase it

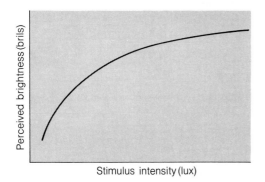

Figure 4-2 The nonlinear relationship between stimulus intensity and brightness.

by one-third. If you wanted to double the phenomenal brightness, you would have to increase the number of lights to 64.

Figure 4-2 shows the general shape of this relationship graphically. Notice that the curve in Figure 4-2 greatly resembles the logarithmic curve of Fechner's law (remember Chapter 2, and particularly Figure 2-15). For this reason, various photometric values, such as the brightness scales used in television studios, are frequently presented in logarithmic units, especially when designed for visual purposes. This roughly equalizes the sizes of the sensory changes as a function of changes in physical intensity. The unit of brightness in the graph in Figure 4-2 is the **bril**, which was suggested by S. S. Stevens. Each bril represents about one-tenth of a log unit above threshold, in much the same way that a decibel (see Chapter 6) represents one-tenth of a log unit above threshold in audition.

FACTORS IN BRIGHTNESS PERCEPTION

Adaptation

The perception of brightness depends on the current state of sensitivity of your eye in much

the same way that the brightness of a photographic image depends on the sensitivity of the film. An amount of light that may produce a faint image on insensitive film may produce an overly bright image on very sensitive film. You are probably aware of the effects of your eyes' changing sensitivity when you walk from a darkened room into the bright sunlight, only to find that everything appears to be so bright and "washed out" that a few moments must pass before objects are clearly visible. The opposite occurs when you walk from a bright outside into a darkened movie theater. Now everything appears to be very dark, and objects are difficult to resolve in the gloom. After a while you can discern objects, although the accommodation to the darkness takes somewhat longer than the adaptation to the brighter environment. We call the process of adaptation to a darker environment **dark adaptation** and that to a brighter environment **light adaptation.** Although we cannot slip off our daylight retina and put on the twilight one in the way that we change film in a camera to accommodate changes in lighting conditions, the sensitivity of our eyes changes through these two adaptation processes.

We can monitor directly the changes in sensitivity associated with dark adaptation. First, we adapt an observer to bright light by putting the individual in a brightly lit room for a few minutes; then we turn off the lights. Now we test to find the observer's *absolute threshold* for the detection of a light shone onto a fairly large region of the retina. This is done at fixed time intervals after the onset of darkness, using one of the standard psychophysical methods outlined in Chapter 2. Such an experiment usually reveals that the observer at first needs relatively strong stimuli to reach threshold; however, the eye rapidly becomes more sensitive over the first or second minute, at which point sensitivity begins to stabilize at a level about 100 times more (2 log units) than when we initially turned off the lights. After

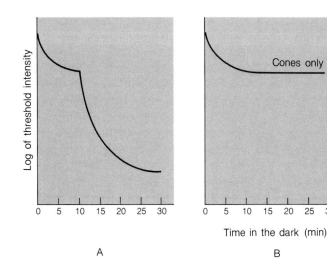
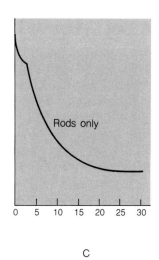

Figure 4-3   (A) *The normal time course of dark adaptation,* (B) *dark adaptation in the cones (or central fovea), and* (C) *dark adaptation in the rods (or periphery).*

about 10 minutes of darkness, the sensitivity begins to increase rapidly again. During this second period, the threshold drops quickly for 5 or 10 minutes, then again stabilizes, reaching a relatively constant level after about one-half hour. When we graph the change in threshold for a typical observer, as we have done in Figure 4-3A, we can see a break, or *kink*, in the sensitivity curve. The kink indicates a change in the rate of dark adaptation.

When a sudden transition or break is found in a curve, it often suggests that a second mechanism or process has come into operation. This is confirmed in the present case by the fact that a marked change in conscious perception occurs near this sharp break in the curve. For instance, if we used a greenish light (or nearly any color, for that matter) to measure the threshold, the observer would be able to identify the color throughout the first 10 minutes or so of the test session. At about the point at which the threshold suddenly begins to drop again, the test stimulus would seem to lose its color and become grayish. An old proverb is based on this loss of color vision

under dim levels of illumination: "At night, all cats are gray."

In Chapter 3 we talked about the differences between rods and cones. At that time, we reviewed evidence indicating that rods were found predominantly in animals active during the twilight hours (or in conditions of dim illumination), whereas cones are found predominantly in the retinas of animals that are active during daylight. It was suggested that cones provide **photopic** or daylight vision (including the perception of color), and rods provide **scotopic** or twilight vision. Humans have rods *and* cones; hence, the two segments of the dark adaptation curve represent separate rod and cone contributions. The cones seem rapidly to reach their level of maximal sensitivity. The rods take longer to adapt. When they do, the threshold begins to drop, but at the expense of a loss in color vision. The point at which the adaptation of the rods catches up to that of the cones is the break in the dark adaptation curve shown in Figure 4-3A.

We can verify this explanation of the kink in the dark adaptation curve experimentally.

Suppose we return to the experimental situation we used to track the course of dark adaptation. Now we change the stimulus so that we focus a tiny pencil of light only on the central fovea when we take threshold measurements. Since the central fovea contains only cones (Chapter 3), this method will allow us to track dark adaptation in cones. Such an experiment gives us the data shown in Figure 4-3B. Notice that this looks just like the first segment of the curve in Figure 4-3A. No second increase in sensitivity occurs, no matter how long we continue in darkness. To demonstrate the lower or rod portion of the curve we repeat the experiment, but now we focus our pencil of light about 20 deg from the center of the fovea, where the retina contains predominantly rods. When we do this, we get the curve shown in Figure 4-3C, in which the first rapid change (attributable to cone action) is almost completely absent.

An even more spectacular way to show the separate rod and cone origin for the two portions of the dark adaptation curve was provided by Hecht and Mandelbaum (1938). They placed a normal observer on a diet deficient in vitamin A for 57 days. Because this vitamin is critical for the synthesis of rhodopsin, the pigment in rods, the diet effectively eliminated the action of these receptors. After 57 days, the observer had a dark adaptation curve similar to that in Figure 4-3B. Not only was the rod portion of the curve almost totally absent, but the individual was almost completely "night-blind"

and unable to see dimly illuminated targets. The observer completely recovered when he went back to his normal diet. Perhaps similar naturally occurring instances have given carrots (a vegetable high in vitamin A) their reputation for being "good for the eyes." This experiment tells us that the advantage found in carrots is specific to scotopic, or "night" vision.

Overall, these experiments indicate that two separate physiological mechanisms are involved in the perception of brightness: the cone system for brighter illumination and the rod system for dimmer illumination. Some evidence suggests that when bright light is present, and the cones are active, they actually inhibit or "turn off" the action of the rods (Drum, 1981).

Much remains to be learned about the nature of the adaptation process. Clearly, any incoming light will bleach the available photopigments in the rods and cones, and time will be needed for them to regenerate. As more pigment becomes available, the sensitivity of the eye should increase. Although such a process does seem to play a role (MacLeod, 1978), dark adaptation also involves changes in the sensitivity and responsiveness of neural processes (Green & Powers, 1982; Shapley & Enroth-Cugell, 1984). Later in this chapter we shall see that even higher level cognitive processes may influence our perception of brightness. Demonstration Box 4-1 allows you to see the effects of dark adaptation for yourself.

DEMONSTRATION BOX 4-1   Dark Adaptation

To show the dramatic increase in sensitivity associated with dark adaptation you should first carefully blindfold one eye. Use a couple of cotton balls and some tape to do this. After about 30 minutes darken the room, or step into a reasonably dark closet. Remove the blindfold and compare the sensitivity of your two eyes by alternately opening one eye at a time. The dark-adapted eye should see quite well in the dim illumination, but the other eye will be virtually blind.

Retinal Locus

As we saw in Figure 3-7, rods and cones are unevenly distributed across the retina. The central fovea contains only cones, which are less sensitive to weak stimuli, whereas the more sensitive rods are more plentiful in the periphery. Suppose the apparent brightness of a light depended directly on the sensitivity of the stimulated receptors, as well as on the intensity of the light. If that were the case, then moving a constant light stimulus across the dark-adapted retina, stimulating less sensitive cones near the fovea and more sensitive rods in the periphery, should change the apparent brightness of the light. This has been verified experimentally (Drum, 1980; Osaka, 1981). Peripheral targets appear brighter. This finding is also embodied in a bit of folk wisdom. At some time in antiquity people noted that looking directly at a dim object, such as a star, could cause it to disappear from view. For this reason, early astronomers would often look at a point off to the side of a star in order to let its image fall upon the more sensitive peripheral retina (containing mostly rods). This technique allows such a dim target to be perceived more clearly. If you try this yourself, look at a point about 20 deg from the star you wish to see. This would allow the star's image to fall on the part of the retina where the density of rods is greatest and would give you maximum sensitivity.

Wavelength

The wavelength of the light stimulating the eye will also affect our perception of brightness. For instance, yellow light (medium wavelengths) almost always appears to be brighter than blue light (short wavelengths). The usual procedure for assessing the relative brightness of lights of different colors is to use a *bipartite target*—a circular target that has been divided

in half. One half contains the *standard color* that is to be matched in brightness, and the other half is the *comparison color* that is adjustable. Systematically pairing various colors and then matching their apparent brightness provides a set of measures of the relative amounts of energy needed to produce equal sensations of brightness for various wavelengths of light. For convenience, the wavelength requiring the least energy to equal the brightness of the standard is set at a value of 1.00. All other wavelengths, being less effective in producing the brightness sensation, are assigned values less than 1, depending on their relative brightnesses.

Once this conversion has been made, a **luminosity curve** can be plotted as in Figure 4-4. Notice that we actually have two curves in this figure. The first, labeled *photopic*, represents the results from the matching experiment if the standard is at daylight levels of light intensity. It has a peak sensitivity for wavelengths around 555 nm, and the apparent brightness falls off rapidly for shorter (toward the blue) or longer (toward the red) wavelengths. If we repeat this matching experiment under conditions where the standard is quite dim, so only rod vision is operating, the observer will not be aware of the color of the stimuli, and both halves of the field will appear gray regardless of their wavelength. Nonetheless, some wavelengths will still look brighter than others. Thus, we can map out the luminosity curve marked *scotopic* in Figure 4-4. Under these conditions the curve is somewhat different, with a peak around 505 nm. This curve is shifted toward the short wavelengths, suggesting that we are more sensitive to blue light under dim viewing conditions.

The change in the apparent brightness of light of different wavelengths as the intensity is changed was first described by the Czechoslovak phenomenologist Johannes E. Purkinje, and in his honor this phenomenon is referred to as the **Purkinje shift.** He first noted the change while looking at his garden as twilight

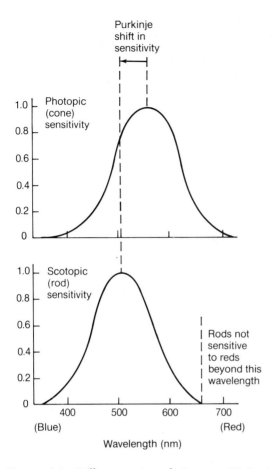

Figure 4-4 *Differences in relative sensitivity to various wavelengths under photopic and scotopic illumination conditions.*

was falling. As the light dimmed, the apparent brightnesses of the various colors began to change. Reds that had been bright relative to blues and greens began to look darker, while the bluer tones appeared relatively brighter. Because scotopic vision lacks the sensation of color, daylight greens or blues change to moonlight grays, while daylight reds change to moonlight blacks. Demonstration Box 4-2 allows you to experience this shift in sensitivity for yourself.

There is an interesting application of the Purkinje shift. You may remember from watch-

ing war movies that the briefing rooms next to air strips or the control rooms of ships and submarines are often depicted as illuminated by red light. This red is not used solely for dramatic effect in the film, but is actually used in such settings. Rods are relatively insensitive to the red end of the spectrum; hence red light is virtually equivalent to no light at all for the rods. However, the cones still function at these longer wavelengths when stimulus intensity is sufficient, so the cones may be used while the rods are beginning to dark adapt. The dashed line in the bottom part of Figure 4-4 shows a wavelength beyond which the rods no longer function while the cones still do. Thus, pilots about to fly night missions, or sailors about to stand the night watch, can be briefed or can check their instruments under red illumination, and then go directly into the dark without waiting the many minutes necessary to completely dark adapt.

Time and Area

In addition to the intensity, wavelength, and retinal location of the stimulus, our ability to detect a spot of light depends on other stimulus properties. For instance, a photographer taking a picture under dim illumination may have to lengthen the exposure time to collect enough light to adequately register the image on the film. In bright sunlight a short exposure will usually do. Actually the same amount of physical energy is necessary to expose the film properly in each case; it just takes longer to collect the requisite amount under dim illumination. In physics this relationship is known as the **Bunsen-Roscoe law.** This law describes the photochemical reaction of any light-sensitive substance, whether film or visual pigment. We find a similar trade-off between stimulus duration and stimulus intensity in the absolute threshold for vision. We can express this relationship using simple algebra. If we define C as

---

DEMONSTRATION BOX 4-2   The Purkinje Shift

For this demonstration you will need a dark room and some way of providing a light whose intensity you can vary without altering its color. A good method is to use a television set as a light source. This may be done by tuning the set to an unused channel and turning the contrast control to a minimum. This reduces the visibility of the random dots that normally appear on the screen. Now, if you darken the room so that the television is the only source of illumination, the brightness control on the set will be a means of controlling the room light. An alternate procedure in the absence of a television is to turn on a light in a room and enter a closet, shutting the door after you. The amount of light entering the closet can be controlled by opening the door by differing amounts. Turning your back to the door allows for a diffusion of the light to any target that you wish to be illuminated. Unfortunately, if the outside room is well lit, opening the door by a few centimeters will provide a good deal of light: hence, control of illumina-tion may be improved by dimming the light in the outside room.

Now, look at Color Plate 1. Here we have two colored spots, one blue and one red. When viewed in moderate or bright light (the brightness control on the television is set to high, or the closet door is more widely ajar), the blue and the red spot appear to be approximately equal in brightness. Now, make the light very dim (close the door almost completely, or turn down the brightness control on the television). In the bright light, you were viewing the spots with cone vision. Now, if you dim the lights sufficiently, only rod vision will be activated. After 5–10 minutes, as your eye dark adapts, the blue spot will appear to be significantly brighter than the red spot. In fact, the red spot may actually disappear. The effect may be accentuated by staring at the white spot. This shifts the images away from the fovea to an area of the retina containing a greater number of rods.

---

the critical amount of light energy necessary to reach threshold, I as the stimulus intensity, and T as the stimulus duration, the relation-ship is $T \times I = C$. When applied to vision, this is known as **Bloch's law.**

This means that for a weak stimulus we must increase the length of time it is presented in order for it to be detected, whereas a more intense stimulus can be presented for a shorter duration and still be detected. This time-versus-intensity trade-off only works over stimulus durations less than about one-tenth of second. This limiting value may vary a bit, being somewhat longer for the completely dark-adapted eye and somewhat shorter for the very light-adapted eye (Montellese, Sharpe, & Brown, 1979). If the duration is greater than about one-tenth of a second, the probability that a stimulus will be detected is no longer affected by stimulus duration, but depends only on stimulus intensity. Like many other things in vision, Bloch's law only holds under certain circumstances. For instance, it holds better in the periphery (where many rods are present) than in the fovea (Gottlieb, Kietzman, & Berhaus, 1985), and it may also depend on the wavelength of the stimuli used (Schwartz & Loop, 1984).

The size of a stimulus is also important in determining its detectability. In chapter 3, we noted that a good deal of convergence occurs in the visual system, meaning that a number of rods or cones may synapse with the same bipolar cell, and several bipolar cells may converge upon the same retinal ganglion cell. Consider a hypothetical example. Suppose four units of neurotransmitter per second are sufficient to activate a bipolar cell, and that bipolar cell has four receptors making synapses with it. If we provide a tiny spot of light, which is only strong enough to elicit one unit of neurotransmitter per second from the retinal receptor, and the light is only wide enough to stimulate two receptors, clearly the bipolar cell will not respond. If we double the size of the stimulus so all four receptors are illuminated, however, the bipolar cell will receive a total of four units of neurotransmitter per second and will become activated. Thus, as the area of a stimulus increases (even though its intensity does not change), the likelihood increases that we will recruit enough photoreceptors to begin a chain of neural activity that will allow us to detect it.

An alternative way of conceptualizing this is in terms of retinal receptive fields, such as those illustrated in Figure 3-10. Increasing the stimulus size might be thought of as "filling in" the center of the receptive field with light, thus adding more on responses to the overall activity.

For relatively small areas, covering visual angles of 10 minutes (10') of arc or less (about 1 mm viewed at arm's length), a trade-off relationship exists between area and intensity. If A signifies the area stimulated, and I and C are again stimulus intensity and critical amount of light energy, respectively, we can describe the relationship as $A \times I = C$. This is known as **Ricco's law.** Thus, if we increase the intensity of a stimulus we can decrease its size and still be able to detect it, and vice versa for a decrease in stimulus intensity.

For stimulus sizes greater than 10' in visual angle, increasing the area has a reduced effect. The effect of area on detection for larger stimuli is described by $\sqrt{A} \times I = C$. In other words, for larger stimuli a greater increase in area is needed to achieve the same compensation for a decrease in stimulus intensity. This second area-intensity relationship is known as **Piper's law.** Beyond 24 deg of visual angle, no further benefit is gained by increasing the size of the stimulus, and the likelihood of detection depends solely on light intensity. The change in the summation function seems to be due to changes in the nature or degree of neural convergence in the periphery (Lie, 1980; Randsom-Hogg & Spillmann, 1980).

The brightness effects caused by summation of neural responses converging on a single retinal ganglion cell can be used as a tool to study the organization of neurons in the retina. For instance, the circular receptive field of a ganglion cell, with an on-center and an off-surround (see Chapter 3), affects brightness sensitivity (Spillman, Randsom-Hogg, & Oehler, 1987; Teller, 1980; Westheimer, 1965; 1967). The experimental procedure is in most ways like any other test of visual sensitivity—an *absolute threshold* is measured for a small spot of light at a specific location in the visual field. This procedure differs in that the threshold is measured when the test spot, instead of being presented in total darkness, is superimposed on top of a disk of light that is above threshold, and the subject has to detect the slightly brighter small spot. Figure 4-5 shows the results of an experiment where a small spot (2' in diameter) is used as the test stimulus and is shown on disks of varying diameter. For small background disks, as the size of the background disk increases, the intensity of the test spot must be increased to maintain threshold detection. This is because the background disk is exciting more of the same central (on-responding) region of the receptive field that

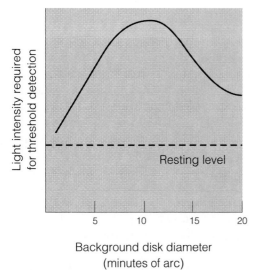

Figure 4-5 *The intensity required for threshold detection of a spot of light that is 2 minutes of arc in diameter, plotted as a function of the diameter of a background disk of light that is above threshold (based on Westheimer, 1967).*

the test spot is exciting. In other words, the test spot is competing with the background disk and making less and less of a contribution to the overall apparent brightness. However, for disk sizes of 10' of arc and greater, the relation is reversed. Further increases in the size of the background disk actually make the test spot easier to detect. This suggests that the inhibitory (off-responding) surround of the receptive field has been stimulated by the background disk, thereby allowing the test spot once again to make a larger relative contribution to the excitation of the on-center region. Researchers often use the peak in the threshold function in Figure 4-5 as a measure of the diameter of the on-center of a receptive field, and the point where the curve levels off again as a measure of the size of the off or inhibitory region (Spillman, Randsom-Hogg, & Oehler, 1987). Some researchers refer to this curve as the **Westheimer function**, after the researcher who first reported it (Westheimer, 1965, 1967).

Maximum Sensitivity

After this discussion, you may be wondering just what the ultimate limit of sensitivity might be if the stimulus was adjusted to the optimal wavelength, size, duration, and retinal position, and the observer was fully dark-adapted. The classic experiment to answer this question was conducted by Hecht, Schlaer, and Pirenne (1942), who found that the lowest absolute threshold for vision is only 6 quanta of light (photons). Further computations showed that detection occurred if each of 6 photons stimulated a different rod. Theoretically, we cannot get any more sensitive than this. Even at higher levels of illumination, however, it is possible to show that fluctuations of only a few photons may affect our perception of brightness, thus showing the exquisite sensitivity of the eye as a light detector (Krauskopf & Reeves, 1980; Zuidema, Gresnight, Bouman, & Koenderink, 1978).

VISUAL ACUITY

Visual acuity refers to the ability of the visual system to resolve details. There are different types of visual acuity, each dependent on the specific task or specific detail to be resolved. The type of visual acuity most commonly measured is **recognition acuity**, which was introduced by Herman Snellen (1862). He created the familiar *eye chart* found in most ophthalmologists' or optometrists' offices, consisting of rows of letters of progressively smaller size. The observer is asked to identify the letters on the chart, and the size of the smallest letters correctly identified determines acuity. Acuity is usually measured relative to the performance of a normal observer. Thus, an acuity of 6/6 indicates that an observer is able to identify letters at a distance of 6 m that a normal observer can also read at that distance (you may be more familiar with the designation 20/20;

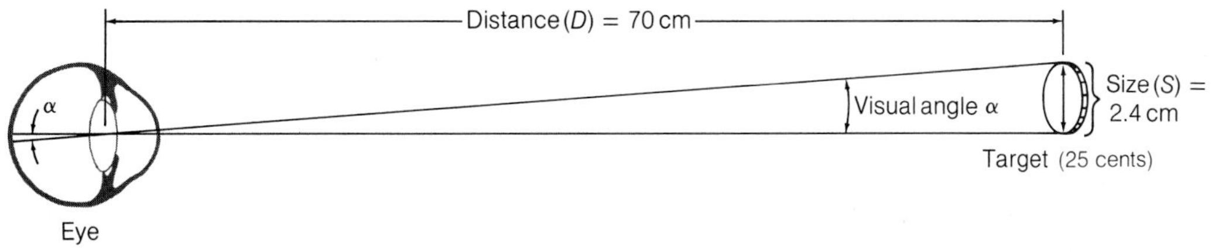

Distance $(D) = 70\,\text{cm}$

Visual angle α

Size $(S) = 2.4\,\text{cm}$

Target (25 cents)

Eye

Figure 4-6 *Computation of the size of the visual angle of the image of a quarter viewed a distance of 70 cm (approximately arm's length), where the observer's line of sight is perpendicular to the lower edge of the coin. Tangent of visual angle = size/distance; therefore $\tan \alpha = S/D = 2.4/70 = 0.034$. Thus, α is approximately 2 deg.*

6 m is equivalent to 20 ft). In other words, the measured acuity is normal. An acuity of 6/9 (or 20/30) means that an observer is able to read letters at 6 m that are large enough for a normal observer to read at a distance of 9 m. Here, the visual acuity is less than normal.

A more general means of specifying the limits of acuity is to use the minimum **visual angle** of a detail that can be resolved. The visual angle is a measure of the size of the retinal image. Figure 4-6 shows what is meant by visual angle and demonstrates a simple computation based on the size and the distance of the object. A normal observer can reliably resolve details of 1' of arc (about the size of a quarter seen at a distance of 81 m, which is nearly the length of a football field), although different tasks often produce different limits of acuity (Beck & Schwartz, 1979).

The identification of letters on a Snellen chart is not the best way to measure acuity, because letters differ in their degree of identifiability. For instance, O and Q, or P and F, are easily confused, whereas L and W, or O and I, are quite easy to discriminate. Because these differences might affect acuity measurements, Hans Landolt (1889) introduced a different task that used circles with a gap in them as targets (see Figure 4-7). The gap can be oriented up, down, to the right, or to the left, and the observer's task is to indicate the position of the gap. The circles differ in size and the smallest detectable gap is the measure of acuity.

A variety of other tasks is used to measure visual acuity. The most primitive measure of acuity is the specification of the smallest target of any type that can be detected. The relationship between brightness perception and the

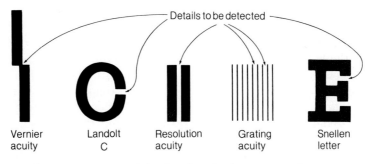

Details to be detected

| Vernier acuity | Landolt C | Resolution acuity | Grating acuity | Snellen letter |

Figure 4-7 *Some typical acuity targets and the details to be discriminated.*

acuity task is most apparent for this task, where the target is a light line or spot against a dark background, or a dark line or spot against a light background. **Vernier** or **directional acuity** requires an observer to distinguish a broken line from an unbroken line. **Resolution** or **grating acuity** is measured by an observer's ability to detect a gap between two bars, or the orientation of a grid of lines. This particular form of acuity task has certain theoretical implications, which we will discuss in the next section. Figure 4-7 shows examples of the above-mentioned acuity targets with arrows pointing to the crucial detail. Notice that each detail is merely a region of the field where the luminance changes.

It is reasonable to expect that the minimum resolvable detail size would be determined by the size of the retinal receptors or the size of retinal receptive fields. Thus, in order to determine that two spots of light are present, it would seem to be necessary to have at least one unstimulated retinal receptor (or receptive field) between two light-stimulated retinal receptors (or receptive fields). Surprisingly, for tasks such as vernier acuity, people can resolve much finer details than might be expected on the basis of these considerations. Under optimal conditions, acuities of 5 seconds (a second of arc is 1/3600 of a degree) or less are possible, despite the fact that the smallest receptive fields are around 25 times larger than this (Klein & Levi, 1985; Westheimer, 1979). In fact, this is about one-sixth the diameter of the smallest retinal cones. Resolution of details less than about 10 seconds is often referred to as **hyperacuity,** since visual performance seems to have gone beyond the limit of resolution imposed by the physical size of the receptors. Some theorists explain this paradox by proposing models of complex neural circuitry and statistical pooling of neural responses (Carlson, 1983; Wilson, 1986). Others believe that the responses of single cells can account for hyperacuity, but that these cells are higher up in the

chain of processing than ganglion cells. For instance, electrophysiological evidence exists that a vernier stimulus (such as the broken line in Figure 4-9) excites a different orientation-tuned simple cell in the primary visual cortex (see Chapter 3) than a line without the break (Swindale & Cynader, 1986). If so, this would suggest that hyperacuity might exist because higher-level cells are specifically tuned to particular "acuity details," such as gaps, breaks, or offsets.

Because acuity tasks are closely related to brightness discrimination, it is not surprising to find that acuity varies as a function of the many factors shown to be important in the perception of brightness. For instance, the adaptive state of the eye determines the minimum details that can be discriminated under particular viewing conditions (Lie, 1980). Thus, if you step out of the bright sunlight into a dim room, you may find it impossible to read even the large type of the headlines of a newspaper for a few moments. As your eyes adapt to the dim surroundings, however, you can soon easily read even fine print. Even a brief flash of light, bright enough to alter an observer's state of adaptation, markedly reduces an observer's ability to detect and recognize acuity targets (Miller, 1965).

The detection of details in acuity targets also shows an interaction between time and stimulus intensity, very much like that described by Bloch's law for brightness detection. This means that we can increase the likelihood that a detail will be detected either by increasing the difference between the intensity of the target and that of its background, or by increasing the amount of time the observer views the stimulus. Although Bloch's law only holds for times less than 100 msec for brightness detection, the trade-off between time and intensity holds for up to 300 msec in acuity tasks in which observers are trying to detect pattern details (Kahneman, 1966; Kahneman, Norman, & Kubovy, 1967).

DEMONSTRATION BOX 4-3   Visual Acuity as a Function of Retinal Location

Visual acuity is best in the fovea. The range of clear vision extends less than 10 deg away from the foveal center. Lay this book flat on the table and view the accompanying diagram from a distance of approximately 12 cm. Cover your left eye with your left hand and look directly at the point marked $0°$.

Without moving your right eye, you will note that the letter over the $0°$ mark is relatively clear, and that the letter at $5°$ is also legible. However, the letters at $10°$ and beyond begin to appear fuzzy, and the letters at $40°$ and $50°$ are virtually unreadable.

K	B	X	M	P	A	S
+	+	+	+	+	+	+
$50°$	$40°$	$30°$	$20°$	$10°$	$5°$	$0°$

Retinal position is also as important for acuity as it is for brightness perception (Jennings & Chapman, 1981). The figure in Demonstration Box 4-3 allows you to experience the drastic reductions in visual acuity for targets that are imaged some distance from the fovea. When we measure relative acuity for various locations on the retina, we find that it varies, as shown in Figure 4-8. Notice that acuity is best in the central fovea and drops off rapidly as we

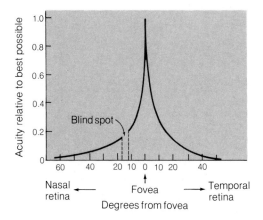

Figure 4-8 The distribution of visual acuity across the retina.

move into the periphery. This curve looks remarkably like the distribution of cones across the retina diagramed in Figure 3-7. It also looks much like the distribution of parvo ganglion cells in the retina (Peichl & Wassle, 1979). Direct physiological measurements of the responsiveness of parvo and magno cells show that parvo cells have smaller receptive fields and sustain their responses to stationary stimuli. This has led a number of researchers to suggest that the limits of visual acuity are set by the prevalence of parvo cells, or cells with characteristics similar to parvo cells, which are best designed for detection and analysis of small details in stationary visual arrays (Andrews & Pollen, 1979; Robson, 1980).

The part of the retina that is highest in visual acuity contains mostly cones, which send their signals to parvo ganglion cells. Since cones operate only at higher levels of illumination, we could predict that acuity would be better at higher illumination levels. When we measure the relationship between acuity and illumination directly, we obtain the curve shown in Figure 4-9. Notice that when the illumination is low, in the scotopic (rod) range, acuity is poor, and it improves only slightly as

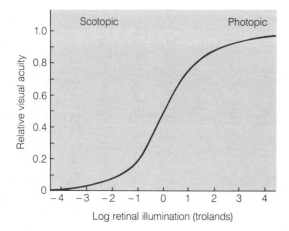

Figure 4-9 *The effect of illumination on visual acuity.*

the light intensity is increased. However, as we begin to shift into the photopic (cone) range, acuity improves rapidly. Of course, at too a high a light level, the acuity is reduced again because of the effects of glare (not shown). Demonstration Box 4-4 provides a stimulus figure and instructions for demonstrating the relationship between acuity, contrast, and illumination.

One aspect of the relationship between acuity and illumination has important implications for some common situations. In 1789 Lord Maskelyne, director of the Royal Greenwich Observatory, noticed that he became noticeably nearsighted at night. This was because he had a tendency to accommodate his eye for an inappropriately near distance, even when the object of interest was far away, a condition called *night myopia* (Leibowitz, Post, Brandt, & Dichgans, 1982). The resulting reduction of acuity degrades the sharpness of the retinal image, interfering with one's ability to see details under twilight and nighttime observation conditions. This may be an important component in nighttime driving accidents (Leibowitz & Owens, 1977).

DEMONSTRATION BOX 4-4   Acuity, Contrast, and Illumination

You will need your variable intensity light source again for this demonstration (either television or closet). First read the text in this box under very bright illumination. Make a note of the line on which you begin to be unable to read all the words. This is the limit of your contrast acuity under these conditions. Now dim the light source and read the text again, noting the line on which the words begin to become unreadable. This shows the extent to which your visual acuity is dependent on the apparent contrast of the forms you are seeing. Apparent contrast increases along with the illumination level, serving both to make the text seem darker and to make the background page seem lighter. If you are still able to read this line under the bright illumination condition, then begin this demonstration again with a dimmer initial source of light. If you are still able to read this line, make the light source even dimmer.

SPATIAL FREQUENCY ANALYSIS

Spatial Fourier Analysis

A complete description of the relationship between brightness perception and acuity must take into account a great deal of information. Imagine any test pattern of light. Next realize that when this pattern stimulates the eye, there are 125 million or more retinal receptors per eye, each receiving an amount of light ranging from zero up to many millions of units. Pity the poor perceptual researcher who must now find a method of describing all of this activity (not to mention the poor brain that must interpret it). If we had to catalog every point of light and its intensity before we could understand the major phenomena associated with brightness and acuity, our information about these topics would be limited indeed. Many researchers realized this and began to look for some reasonably small set of relationships among the variables that affect brightness perception that could be used to describe visual arrays, hoping that such a simplified description might yield deeper insight into these phenomena.

In some ways, the most successful attempt to summarize brightness and acuity data to date has involved the use of a mathematical technique based upon **Fourier's theorem.** This theorem states that it is possible to analyze any

pattern of stimuli into a series of sine waves. In Chapter 6 we apply this theorem to complex sound waves, in which sound pressure level varies over time in an irregular but repeated pattern. For our current problem we are concerned with how light intensity varies across space, namely across the retinal image. According to Fourier's theorem we can analyze *any* such complex pattern of light intensity across space into a series of simpler sine wave patterns, each of which would be seen as a regularly varying pattern of light and dark, if seen alone.

You might recall from your study of trigonometry that a sine wave is a regular, smooth, periodically repeating function that can be precisely specified mathematically. Figure 4-10A shows a graph of a sine wave, and beside it a distribution of light that varies in the

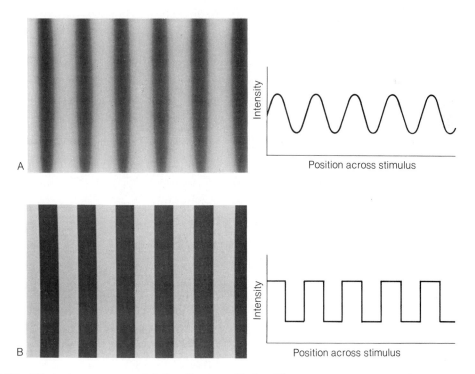

Figure 4-10 (A) *A sine wave spatial distribution of light,* (B) *a square wave spatial distribution of light (based on Cornsweet, 1970).*

same way, growing more intense where the function rises and less intense where it fails. Such a pattern is called a **sine wave grating,** because the intensity of reflected light from the page varies sinusoidally as we move horizontally across the figure, and the whole pattern forms a sort of blurry grating or grid. When applied to light distributions, Fourier's theorem states that by adding together (or *synthesizing*) a number of such gratings, we can produce *any* specified light distribution. Moreover, although individual sine wave patterns have only gradual changes in intensity, by adding many of them together we can even produce light distributions that contain sharp corners, such as the one shown in Figure 4-10B. Figure 4-10B is called a **square wave grating** because the light changes are sharp and give a boxlike intensity pattern. Successive addition of the appropriate frequencies of sine waves (or more accurately, the sine wave variations in light intensity that they represent) gradually gives a better and better approximation of the sharp corners of

the square wave grating as can be seen in Figure 4-11.

You might think that adding sine waves can only give you repeating patterns or gratings such as those in Figure 4-10. This is not true. According to the rules of Fourier synthesis, *any* pattern, whether repeating or not, can be created from combination of appropriate sine waves. Thus Figure 4-12 shows a single bright bar on a dark background. Below it are the first few sine wave variations in intensity that would be added to produce the bar. Notice that after only the fourth wave pattern has been added, we have already started to create single bright feature. Addition of other sine waves will ultimately make the bar sharper.

If we take this approach to describing the patterns of light that act as stimuli to our visual systems, we no longer have to catalog the intensity of every point in the pattern. Now we can describe a light pattern precisely with a relatively compact mathematical expression indicating the particular set of sine wave gratings to

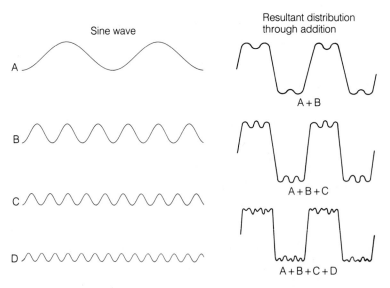

Figure 4-11 *Gradually adding higher frequency sine waves of lower amplitude to the distribution leads to better approximations of a square wave through the process of Fourier synthesis.*

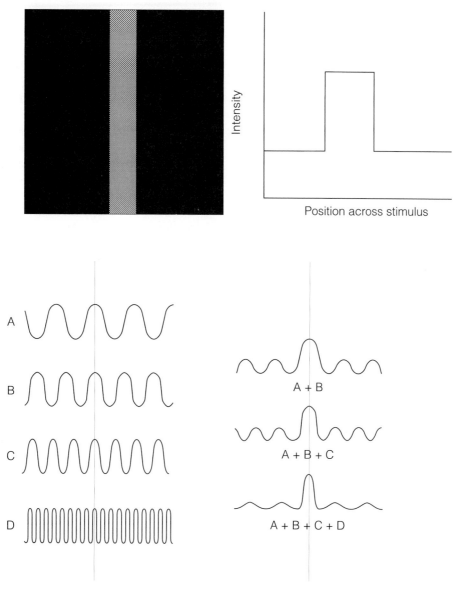

Figure 4-12 *Gradually adding higher frequency sine waves of the same amplitude to the distribution leads to an approximation of a single bright bar of light (based on Weisstein, 1980).*

be added together to reproduce it. Even if the mathematics sometimes become complex, the resulting description is still far simpler than a catalog of the light hitting 125 million or more individual retinal receptors. (See Levine & Shefner, 1981; Weisstein, 1980; or Graham, 1989, for a more complete introduction to Fourier analysis of visual patterns.)

Modulation Transfer Function

Fourier analysis (breaking up a pattern into its component sine waves) and *Fourier synthesis* (adding together a set of sine wave variations to create a more complex pattern) provide more than a simple shorthand for the description of light patterns. They serve as powerful tools that may be used to analyze how the visual system responds to stimuli. Consider for a moment how we might test the fidelity of a photographic system (that is, how well the final photo reproduces the actual light variations in the real world). The simplest way of doing this is to use a series of gratings, such as those shown in Figure 4-13. Some of the gratings will have very broad bars and spaces. In such gratings the light intensity rises and falls slowly across the spatial extent of a surface; hence they are said to have *low spatial frequencies* (the frequency of changes in light intensity across each unit of space is low). Other gratings will have narrow bars and spaces. In these gratings the light intensity changes frequently across the same extent of space; hence they are said to have *high spatial frequencies.* Now we will photograph each grating to see how well it is reproduced. At some point, when the bars and spaces become quite narrow, the system will reach its limit. The photographic lens will no longer be able to resolve the individual bars, and all of the bars and spaces will merge into a gray blur. This is the same type of task we would use to measure the *resolution acuity* or *grating acuity* of human observers, except that here we are looking at the resolution acuity of an optical system.

When photographic engineers do this type of analysis for an optical system, they measure its resolution in terms of the maximum number of lines per inch that can be resolved. Since very finely packed arrays of lines, corresponding to high spatial frequencies, cannot be resolved and are simply blurred, we say that optical systems *attenuate* the high-frequency components of the pattern. A graphic or mathematical description of the way in which certain spatial frequencies are accurately reproduced but others are lost because the system cannot resolve them is called the **spatial modulation transfer function.** A *modulation* is just a change, so spatial modulation refers to light-intensity changes over some spatial distance. Thus the spatial modulation transfer function measures a system's ability to "transfer" accurately the original spatial modulation from the target stimulus through the system to final decoding.

Spatial modulation can be described using physical measurements of light on both the

A   B   C

Figure 4-13   The effect of spatial frequency on the apparent brightness and contrast of pattern. Notice that the higher frequency pattern (C) *has less apparent contrast than the lower frequency pattern* (B).

light and dark regions of an image. From these measurements, vision scientists construct a measure called a **contrast ratio.** Various specific forms of this ratio exist, but the most commonly used ones compare the *difference* between the most and least intense illuminations and divide through by some average or pooled estimate of the overall amount of light. One example of this, called the Michaelson contrast ratio, takes the following form:

Contrast ratio = $(L_{max} - L_{min}) / (L_{max} + L_{min})$

where L_{max} refers to the maximum luminance value in the image and L_{min} refers to the minimum luminance value. The *contrast ratio* is very useful as a summary of spatial changes in an image because it is not affected by overall changes in illumination, but only by the magnitude of the differences between the most and least intense stimuli. Thus uniformly increasing the total amount of light falling on an image or grating will have the same effect as multiplying each L term in the equation by a constant value that will leave the computed contrast ratio unchanged (see Walraven et al., 1990, for a more complete discussion of contrast ratios).

To assess the visual system's limitations in resolving changes in light intensity over space, a procedure called **contrast matching** is used to measure the modulation transfer function in humans. Consider gratings A and B in Figure 4-13. Although both are square wave gratings, they differ in terms of their physical *contrast ratio*—grating A has a smaller contrast ratio than B since the maximum difference in A is between black and mid-gray, while in B it is between the same black and a brighter, white region. Now consider the difference between gratings B and C. Both are square wave gratings, but B has a lower spatial frequency (wider bars) than C. Despite the fact that the physical contrast is the same (both are the same black ink with the same white interspaces), the perceived contrast (the apparent difference between light and dark regions) is much less for

the higher frequency, with the black looking a bit lighter and the white a bit darker in C than in B. You can increase this difference by propping the book up and stepping back a foot or two. In a contrast matching task, observers would be asked to match the apparent contrast of such targets (or more usually sine wave gratings) by adjusting the intensities of the light and the dark regions until the apparent contrast of the two patterns matched. In this way, we could map the differences in visibility of various spatial frequencies. The reduced contrast in C suggests that the visual system is not doing as good a job in transferring that pattern from the real world to your consciousness.

An alternative method of measuring sensitivity to various spatial frequencies involves measuring the *contrast threshold*—the amount of contrast needed for you to detect that a grating is present, rather than a uniform gray. Either of these techniques will give us a representation of how sensitivity changes as we change the spatial frequency of the stimuli. In these ways we can map out the modulation transfer function where the stimulus modulations (or intensity changes in the environment) are being transferred to (detected in) in the observer's conscious experience of the pattern.

When we measure a typical modulation transfer function for a human observer, it looks like the solid line shown in Figure 4-14. Notice that the contrast threshold ratio is plotted backwards (for example, with higher contrast thresholds lower on the vertical axis). This is done so that when we view the figure, the height of the curve will represent the observer's sensitivity. Clearly, the curve is highest at around 6 cycles per degree (6 cycles of the sine wave over each degree of visual angle). This shows that human observers are most sensitive in this region, meaning that they can see stimuli with this spatial frequency even if the contrast ratio is quite low. Sensitivity decreases rapidly for the higher spatial frequencies, meaning that observers need more contrast to see these

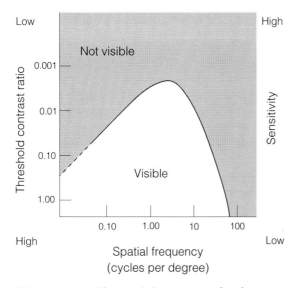

Figure 4-14 *The modulation transfer function, which shows the relative visibility of targets of various spatial frequencies.*

stimuli. This loss at higher frequencies is probably a result of the fact that the eye is an optical system, containing a lens, and any such system has a high-frequency cutoff. Notice also that some resolution is lost in the lower spatial frequencies (less than 6 cycles per degree). This loss results from the fact that as the bars and spaces become wider, the neural sharpening processes (lateral inhibition, which we will discuss later) become less effective. Apparently intensity changes are most effective in producing the phenomenal impression of brightness differences when these changes occur at intermediate spatial frequencies (as determined by the Fourier analysis). When intensity changes occur too frequently within the visual image they are difficult to resolve. Similarly, when the physical changes are too infrequent, there is no perception of brightness differences.

The modulation transfer function provides a convenient basis for predicting the apparent brightness of many types of stimulus configurations. Furthermore, as a summary of the spatial

frequencies we can detect at any given contrast level, it serves as a measure of our visual acuity. For instance, if you draw a horizontal line across Figure 4-14, at any contrast level, only the frequencies for which the transfer function curve is above the line will be visible.

Since the modulation transfer function serves as a kind of summary of our visual acuity and responsiveness to light, we can use it to compare the visual resolution ability of various groups of individuals. For instance, we know changes occur in the modulation transfer function as we grow older, with a general reduction in sensitivity to higher spatial frequencies. These changes accurately predict not only reductions in visual acuity with age, but also changes in certain aspects of our depth perception *(stereopsis)* measured by other techniques (Greene & Madden, 1987). Figure 4-15 shows the modulation transfer functions from groups of 20-, 50-, and 80-year-olds (Owsley,

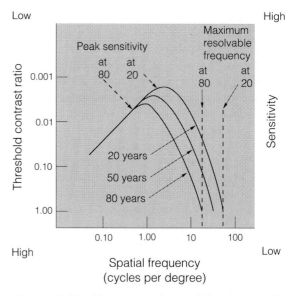

Figure 4-15 *Changes in the modulation transfer function with age, showing the loss of sensitivity for high spatial frequencies and a general reduction in sensitivity (based on data from Owsley, Sekuler, & Siemensen, 1983).*

Sekuler, & Siemensen, 1983). Notice that the highest frequency visible steadily drops with age (meaning that smaller details or narrower stripes cannot be seen). This might be expected if the optical quality or focusing ability of the lens was diminishing (see Chapter 16). Notice also that the peak sensitivity (the highest point on the curve) is lower for older individuals, indicating that visual responsiveness is lower (more contrast is needed to reach threshold). Finally, the peak sensitivity, representing the spatial frequency that would appear to be brightest, is also shifting toward lower frequencies, suggesting that wider stripes or gratings are more effective stimuli for older observers. All of this acuity and brightness response information, and more, can be derived from comparing modulation transfer functions, which explains the popularity of this method of data presentation.

Neural Spatial Frequency Channels

Imagine an extremely self-assured scientist sitting at a home computer, complete with all of the programs necessary to do Fourier analyses of any light patterns that might happen to be of importance or interest, thinking, "If I find Fourier analysis so useful in analyzing patterns of light, maybe the visual system does too. Perhaps the visual system is set up to conduct some sort of spatial frequency analysis for any given pattern of light. Certainly, if it did, it would benefit from the same sort of concise description of the incoming light pattern that I obtain, and could thus also avoid the separate analysis of millions of responses of millions of individual photoreceptors."

Actually, this suggestion is not as strange as it might seem. At a general level, the first stage of spatial frequency analysis can be accomplished by mechanisms that we know exist and have already discussed. These mechanisms are the circularly organized retinal receptive fields described in Chapter 3. Recall that each of these has an excitatory (or *on*) region that, when stimulated by light, gives an increase in neural response rate, and an inhibitory (or *off*) region that gives a decrease in the neural response rate when stimulated by light (and a burst of responses upon the light's termination). Before we discuss how such a system can conduct a spatial frequency analysis, we must first introduce a bit of terminology. Every cycle of a sine wave grating has both a dark and a light phase, as we saw in Figure 4-10. This means that the dark stripe (or the light stripe) would be one-half of the sine wave cycle. Now we can tell you that every circular receptive field is "tuned" to a sine wave frequency whose *half cycle* is equal to the size of its central excitatory or inhibitory region. To visualize this type of structure, consider Figure 4-16.

Suppose we have an on-center receptive field of the size illustrated in the figure. If the spatial frequency is too low, (that is, the stripes are too wide), the fields of illumination will fall on both the center and the surround. Even though the central *on* region of the field is stimulated, an equal degree of stimulation of the inhibitory surrounding *off* regions occurs. Because of lateral inhibitory interactions, the two types of responses tend to cancel each other out. Thus, the total response of the ganglion cell with this receptive field is low. Now consider the other extreme, where the spatial frequency is very high, and many stripes fall across the field. The *on* and *off* regions of the field would each be stimulated by about equal proportions of light and dark, again producing little or no net response. Finally, consider a spatial frequency in which the half-cycle width is approximately the same as the central region of the receptive field. If the bright stripe now covers the central region of the *on* center cell, a vigorous *on* response will occur. There will be little inhibition from the surrounding *off* region, which lies mostly in darkness from the dark half of the cycle. Thus, the net response to this grating would be relatively stronger than to

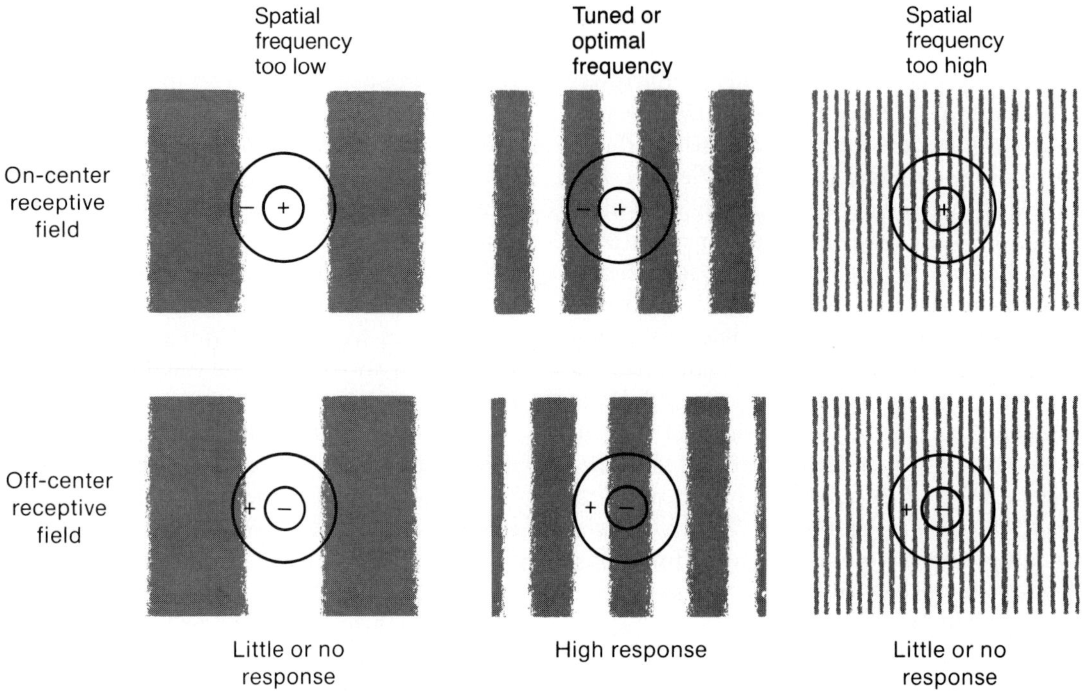

Figure 4-16 *A demonstration of how a circular receptive field organization of a particular size can perform a crude spatial frequency analysis.*

any other size grating. Notice that the same sort of analysis of spatial frequency can occur in the off-center cell, but here the optimal response is obtained when the dark half of the cycle is over the central region of the receptive field. Each receptive field is maximally responsive to a specific spatial frequency of light intensity changes.

This crude analysis of spatial frequencies could serve as the first step of a Fourier decomposition of the incoming stimulus pattern if a few additional requirements were met. First, there must be a broad range of receptive field sizes so that "tuning" would be fine enough to approximate sufficiently many of the spatial frequencies that make up the pattern. This requirement seems to be easily fulfilled since, as we noted in Chapter 3, parvo and magno cells differ in their ranges of receptive field size,

with parvo cells tuned for higher spatial frequencies than magno cells. Thus, the visual system may contain a number of different channels, each tuned to a different range of spatial frequencies. There is some evidence that the magnolike lower spatial frequency channels interact with and can inhibit the parvolike higher spatial frequency channels (Hughes, 1986; Olzak, 1986). Moreover, a model assuming as few as six such channels (or receptive field sizes) can explain some of the remarkable feats of acuity people are capable of, namely the hyperacuity that we discussed earlier where resolution ability is better than would be predicted on the basis of the physical size of the retinal receptors (Bradley & Skottun, 1987; Wilson, 1986).

Of course, for such Fourier analysis to be of value perceptually, higher-level cells must be present, perhaps in the visual cortex, that preserve the spatial frequency information extracted by the tuned receptive fields of the retinal ganglion cells. There is evidence that such cells exist in the cortex. These cells have not only preferred edge orientations to which they respond maximally, but also preferred ranges of spatial frequency (Derrington & Fuchs, 1981; DeValois, Albrecht, & Thorell, 1982; DeValois & DeValois, 1987). Although the existence of such cells does not prove that Fourier analysis occurs in the visual system, it at least suggests that the equipment to perform such an analysis does exist.

Neurons As Spatial Filters

Visually sensitive cells in the brain that work together to perform a crude Fourier analysis of the visual image are often referred to as **neural filters.** The term *filter* is used here because these cells are thought to respond by firing most rapidly when a specific visual pattern excites them and firing much less rapidly to any other patterns. In effect they are filtering out all but a select set of stimuli and passing on information about only those they are "tuned" for, much like a radio tuner passes on to the amplifier only information carried on a specific radio frequency. The cells we are considering respond by firing more or less, depending on the extent to which the spatial frequencies in the image match the filter characteristics.

It has been suggested that the center-surround cells we described in Figure 4-15 are themselves the results of the actions of neural filters occurring more peripherally in the visual system, some of which are still hypothetical and have not yet been physically isolated. The more peripheral filters probably are formed from networks of connections between neurons in the retina. These filters are really quite simple. If we look at their response pattern over a single slice of space we find that most of them increase their responsiveness toward

the center of the field and then tail off again, giving us a familiar bell-shaped distribution as shown in the leftmost part of Figure 4-17A. These distributions, which were mathematically described by Carl Fredrich Gauss, are called *Gaussian distributions*. Filters with distributions of response can have either wide or narrow spreads, and low or high peaks (compare the leftmost distributions in 4-17A and B).

Another important feature is that these filters can either be excitatory (meaning that neural responses increase the likelihood that other nearby neurons will react) or inhibitory (neural responses decrease the likelihood that other nearby neurons will react). Combining an excitatory and an inhibitory distribution has the same arithmetic effect as subtracting the actual numbers representing the inhibitory distribution of responses from those representing the excitatory distribution. Hence the spatial filter that results from the combination of these is referred to as the **difference of Gaussian filters,** or more affectionately, **DOG filters,** (Marr, 1982).

Note that the net effect of combining two bell-shaped spatial filters, where the wider one is effectively subtracted from the narrower, is to create a filter with all the essential characteristics of an on-center receptive field as seen in *A*. An off-center receptive field can be modeled by simply subtracting the narrower of the two bell-shaped curves from the wider one, as shown in *B*. Both of these arrangements are plausible for ganglion cells, since these cells have inputs from other cells with receptive fields in a variety of sizes. This has led many computational vision scientists to build models of the retina with DOG filters (Fiorentini, Baumgartner, Magnussen, Shiller, & Thomas, 1990; Marr, 1982; Rodieck, 1965; Wilson & Bergen, 1979; Wilson & Gelb, 1984).

Simple cortical cells have also been modeled as filters represented by other mathematical equations. One of the more popular models involves a combination of a bell-shaped curve

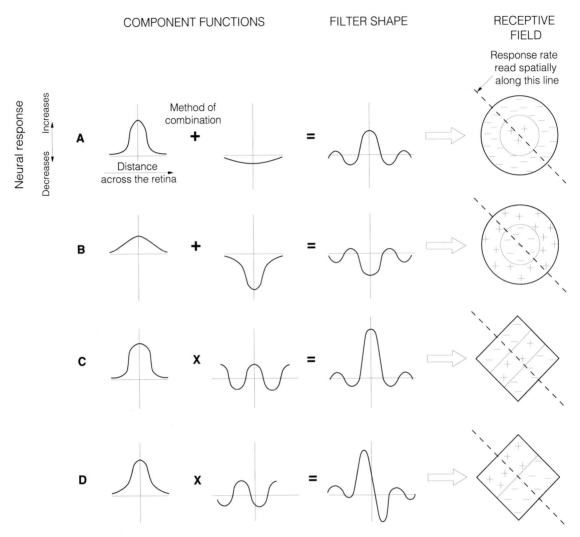

COMPONENT FUNCTIONS   FILTER SHAPE   RECEPTIVE FIELD

Figure 4-17 Subtracting one bell-shaped curve from another of a different width yields a difference of Gaussian function, which performs spatial filtering like a center-surround ganglion cell (as in A *and* B). *Multiplying a bell-shaped curve with a sine function produces a Gabor function, which performs like an orientation specific line detection* (C) *or edge detection* (D) *cell in the visual cortex.*

with another well-known and mathematically describable distribution of responses, namely the sine function. This filter is referred to as a **Gabor filter,** after Dennis Gabor, the Nobel-Prize-winning physicist who analyzed such filters and used them to develop the theory upon which holography is based. The main charac-

teristic that distinguishes the Gabor from the DOG filter is that when a sine wave filter is multiplied with a Gaussian filter, it results in a new filter that has orientation in two dimensions. This allows the filter to detect bars of a specific tilt in the image or edges, depending on how the sine wave peaks are aligned with the peak of the bell-shaped filter (see Figures 4-17C and D). As with the DOG filter, Gabor filters are used by many computational vision scientists because they are thought to be plausible models of the way in which the primary visual cortex processes a visual image (Daugman, 1980; Watson, 1983; Webster & DeValois, 1985; Wilson, Levi, Maffei, Rovamo, & DeValois, 1990). Notice that DOG filters give us center-surround receptive fields, while Gabor filters give orientation-specific line and edge detectors, such as those described in Chapter 3. Some visual physiologists are beginning to regard the processing of information in the visual system as the application of a complex series of filters to the incoming information (for example, Van Essen, Anderson, & Felleman, 1992). Others argue that even if we cannot find specific physiological mechanisms that correspond to Gaussian and sine wave filters, the use of these mathematical concepts to describe differences among various visual feature detectors may help to simplify our understanding of them. At the very least, these concepts allow computational vision scientists to represent feature-specific cells in mathematical terms for later use and manipulation in their theories.

Although spatial frequency analysis and visual filtering seem to provide useful or promising approaches to the problems of brightness and acuity, they do not give us the complete answer. Our final perception of a particular brightness, size, or detail resolution involves the operation of all levels of the perceptual system. In later chapters we shall see how spatial frequency analysis is useful in understanding some aspects of form perception (Chapter 11), and also how cognitive and other higher-level factors interact with the basic sensory mechanisms we have discussed so far to determine our perception of complex stimuli in our environment (Chapters 14 and 15).

SPATIAL CONTEXT EFFECTS

Brightness Contrast

Strange as it may seem, our perception of the brightness of objects often depends more on the luminance of adjacent objects than on the luminance of the object itself. Figure 4-18 demonstrates this phenomenon. Here we have four small squares, each of which is surrounded by a larger square. The central squares are all printed in the same gray; thus, the amount of light that reaches your eye from each is the same. Notice, however, that the apparent brightnesses of these small squares are not equal. Their brightnesses depend on their backgrounds, with the grays printed on dark backgrounds appearing lighter than the grays printed on light backgrounds. This effect is called **simultaneous brightness contrast.**

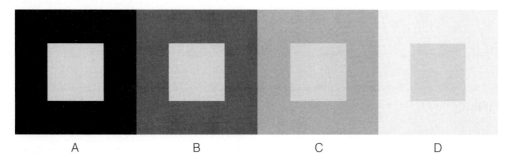

A   B   C   D

Figure 4-18 *Simultaneous brightness contrast, showing how the background can alter the perception of the central gray regions.*

DEMONSTRATION BOX 4-5   The Interaction of Luminance and Background

For this experiment you will need your variable light source again (either the closet or the television). Hold up Figure 4-18 and look at the central squares, with your light source providing a low (but not dim) level of illumination. As you increase the level of illumination from its lowest value, the center target in Square 1 should grow brighter. Now repeat the procedure while looking at the center target in Square 4. Notice that as the luminance level increases, this target square actually gets darker. Since all the center squares are identical in reflectance, the dif-

ferences in their apparent brightness depend solely on their backgrounds. This may seem strange because we tend to associate black with the absence of light. Since you are already in a room or a place that potentially can be darkened, turn off all the light sources and close your eyes (to eliminate any stray illumination). Notice that what you are seeing is not black, but rather a misty gray (often called *cortical gray*). Thus, the absence of light is gray, not black. Only in fields that contain some areas of bright illumination can real black be seen.

Everyday experience tells us that our conscious experience of brightness will increase as the amount of light reaching the eye increases. Unfortunately, our perceptual experiences sometimes defy such "common sense." Despite increases in the amount of light reaching the eye, the apparent brightness of a surface may actually *decrease* depending on the brightness of the background on which it rests. This surprising brightness paradox can be witnessed by following the instructions in Demonstration Box 4-5.

The fact that the central squares in Figure 4-18 vary in brightness as a function of the intensity of their background suggests that some form of spatial interaction is present, perhaps between adjacent retinal regions that are illuminated by the light reflected from the surfaces. Note again that surfaces on a light background, such as Square D in Figure 4-18, appear darker. The brightness response from the part of the retina exposed to Square D has been reduced. This suggests some sort of inhibition of the brightness response as a function of activity in surrounding retinal areas. Remember that in the previous section, during our discussion of spatial filters, we also en-

countered the idea of inhibition. There we saw that the responses of some spatial filters were thought to subtract from the responses going on in others.

Physiological evidence indicates that such inhibitory spatial interaction does take place in the eye. Most of this evidence has been collected from *Limulus* (the horseshoe crab), an animal commonly found on the eastern shores of the United States. *Limulus* has several sets of eyes, but the ones that are most important for research purposes are the lateral eyes, which are faceted (as in the eye of a fly). In such a *compound eye,* a separate optical system exists for each facet, and each has its own primitive retina. Since each eyelet has its own optic nerve, this arrangement spreads out the neural fibers in a way that makes research on separate fibers easier than in other animals.

With a dissecting microscope it is possible to separate out a single nerve fiber, drape it over an electrode, and record its electrical activity. Much of the work on the visual system of *Limulus* has been carried out in the laboratories of Nobel-prize-winner H. K. Hartline and his frequent collaborator Floyd Ratliff. They were able to demonstrate the inhibitory neural interactions between nearby receptors using a very simple, but elegant, experiment (Hartline & Ratliff, 1957).

Hartline and Ratliff first monitored the responses from the *eccentric cell,* which in *Limulus* is functionally equivalent to a ganglion cell, while the receptor attached to the cell was stimulated. The fact that the onset of the light increased the activity of the cell, of course, indicated that its activity was controlled by stimulation of the particular receptor they had illuminated. Let us call this ganglion-like cell and its receptor A. Next the researchers illuminated a receptor located a short distance away (call this one B). No increase occurred in the activity of A, indicating an absence of excitatory connections between A and B. Now the researchers again stimulated A and, while light remained on at A, turned on the light at B. Now they observed that the stimulation of B actually *decreased* the response of cell A. This experiment, which is shown diagrammatically in Figure 4-19, demonstrates that visual cells may be inhibited by the activity of adjacent visual

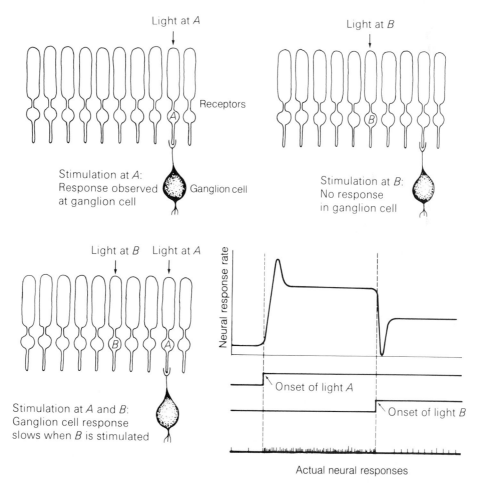

Figure 4-19 *Lateral inhibition: Stimulation at* A *produces a response in the ganglion cell, whereas stimulation at* B *does not. Stimulating* B *while* A *is active depresses* A's *response due to lateral inhibition (from Lindsay & Norman, 1977).*

units. This process is called **lateral inhibition** because the inhibition acts laterally (sideways) on adjacent cells. The amount of inhibition any given cell applies to its neighbors depends on how strongly it is responding, and on how close the cells are to each other. The more a cell is stimulated, and the closer it is to another cell, the more intensely it will inhibit the other.

It is now easier to understand why the central surface in Square A is seen to be brighter than the central surface in Square D in Figure 4-18. In the part of the retina exposed to the bright surround (Square D), many cells are active and, as a consequence of this activity, are actively inhibiting their neighbors. This inhibition from the bright surround should reduce the neural response rate in the central square, making it appear dimmer. The central square on the dark background does not receive as much inhibition from its less strongly stimulated neighbors. Since the amount of stimulation from the central squares is the same, but the cells exposed to central Square A are undergoing a lesser amount of inhibition, central Square A appears to be brighter. Thus, lateral inhibition provides a basis for explaining brightness contrast effects.

Lateral inhibition can also explain more complex effects observed in other stimulus configurations. Ever since the 1860s, when physicist and natural philosopher Ernst Mach studied patterns with an intensity distribution like that shown in Figure 4-20B, investigators have been intrigued by a brightness phenomenon that such a distribution generates (Weale, 1979). In this figure, we have a uniform dark and a uniform light area, with an intermediate zone that gradually changes from dark to light. However, when we look at the stimulus depicted in Figure 4-20A, we do not see a gradual change in brightness flanked by two uniform areas. Instead two bands or blurry lines are visible at the points marked by the arrows in the figure. One is darker than any other part of the figure, and the other is brighter. They are

called **Mach bands,** in honor of their discoverer Ernst Mach. Their presence can be explained by lateral inhibition.

We have indicated the location of some retinal cells illuminated by the Mach-band-producing pattern in Figure 4-20C. Cell *b* is stimulated by bright incoming light, but it is also strongly inhibited by the activity of the adjacent cells *a* and *c*. Cell *d* is stimulated to the

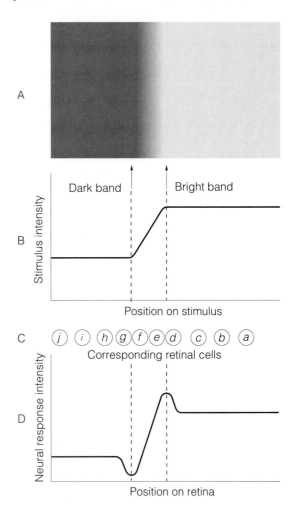

Figure 4-20 (A) *a Mach band pattern,* (B) *the actual distribution of stimulus intensity,* (C) *corresponding retinal cells (see the text), and* (D) *neural response intensity distribution* (A *and* B *based on Cornsweet, 1970).*

same extent as cell *b*. But on one side it is strongly inhibited by *c* and on the other side it is somewhat more weakly inhibited by *e*, which is not receiving as much light. The important thing to derive from this discussion is the fact that cells *b* and *d* have the same degree of stimulation, but *d* is less strongly inhibited. Thus, we might expect that its corresponding response would be more vigorous than that in cell *b*. This should cause the region around *d* to appear relatively brighter.

Next consider cell *i*. It is not stimulated very much, but neither are the nearby cells *h* and *j*. This means that *i* is not being strongly inhibited by surrounding units. Cell *g* is receiving the same small amount of stimulation as *i*. However, whereas *g* is weakly inhibited on one side by *h*, it is more strongly inhibited on the other side by *f*, which is responding more vigorously because of the higher intensity of light falling upon it. Thus, although *g* and *i* receive the same amount of stimulation, *g* is more strongly inhibited than *i*. This means that *g*'s response will be weaker, causing an apparently darker region to appear there.

The relationship between the input and the neural (and perceptual) response is diagramed in Figure 4-20D. It is quite easy to produce a Mach band pattern, as shown in Demonstration Box 4-6. It seems likely that a very wide array of brightness perception phenomena can be explained by theories that assume particular patterns of inhibitory and excitatory interactions between sensory neurons (see, for example, Cornsweet, 1985; Grossberg, 1987).

Brightness Assimilation

Even though brightness effects such as simultaneous brightness contrast and Mach bands can be explained by neural models based on mutual excitation and inhibition (for example, Arend & Goldstein, 1987; Ratliff, 1965), this does not

mean that higher-level cognitive processing plays no role. Unfortunately, brightness perception is quite complex, and in many instances predictions made from only lateral inhibitory or excitatory considerations can be wrong. One example can be seen in Figure 4-21. The two rings shown in this figure are composed of the same color of gray and lie atop the same sharp background edge of black and white. The only difference between the two rings is that thin black lines have been drawn through the ring in Figure 4-21B to connect the background edge from top to bottom. Despite the fact that lateral inhibition would lead you to expect that the half of the ring on the white background will be seen as darker than the half on the black background, the gray ring in *A* appears to be uniform in brightness. Compare this with the ring in *B*, which does show the expected simultaneous brightness contrast. It appears that the thin lines are enough to bias the interpretation of the display so it is seen as two half rings of different brightness laid side by side. The absence of the lines in *A* biases the perception of the ring toward a single-colored object, so no contrast effects are seen and both sides of the ring appear to be an "average" gray (Koffka, 1935).

Another example where cognitive effects may alter or override the effects of lateral inhibition on brightness is seen in Figure 4-22. The gray under the white stripes is identical to that under the black stripes. Notice, however, that the gray under the white stripes appears to be lighter than the gray under the black stripes. This is the opposite of the prediction we would make based on the action of lateral inhibition. The white stripes should *darken* the gray rather than *lighten* it. This phenomenal impression, which is the reverse of brightness contrast, is called **brightness assimilation** (Shapley & Reid, 1985).

Physiological contributions to brightness assimilation are suggested by the fact that it seems to occur only when the test stripes of

DEMONSTRATION BOX 4-6   Mach Band Patterns

Mach band patterns do not reproduce well in print. This is probably because the range of luminances possible from ink on paper is not very large. It is actually quite easy to produce your own Mach band pattern using a distribution of light. All you need is a card or a book that is opaque and has a straight edge, and a large light source. If you are in a room that has fluorescent or large frosted light fixtures in the ceiling, these produce a fine uniform source of illumination.

When you hold the card near a surface, you cast a shadow. As shown in the accompanying diagram, a full shadow appears under the surface and full light on the other side. In between is a graded shadow, the *penumbra*, which gradually moves from light to dark. Hold the card still and look at the brightness pattern—you will easily see the dark and light Mach bands. You may increase the visibility of the bands by moving the card closer to the surface. This reduces the size of the penumbra and makes the area of gradual change in intensity steeper, as shown in the diagram. Since this puts the bright and dim areas nearer one another, it enhances the effect of the inhibitory process.

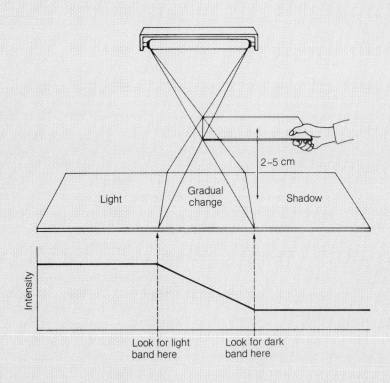

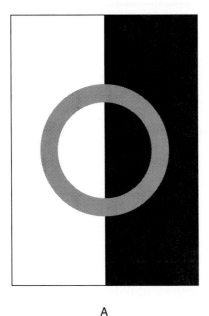

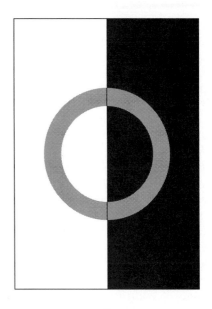

A   B

Figure 4-21 *Brightness contrast is influenced by the cognitive interpretation given to a form. The gray rings in A and B are identical, except for the thin black lines in B.*

white or black fall within the spatial summation zones of ganglion receptive fields as estimated by the Westheimer function we discussed earlier in this chapter (Westheimer, 1967). If the stimuli are increased in size to the point where the gray and white (or black) stripes taken together fall into the *off* or in-

hibitory region of the receptive field, then *brightness contrast* is once again observed (Anstis, 1975). However, cognitive factors such as *attention* may also play a role in this effect.

How you distribute your attention over a figure influences whether brightness contrast or brightness assimilation occurs. In general,

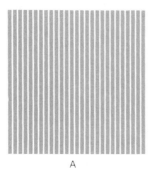

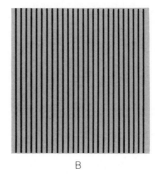

A   B

Figure 4-22 *Brightness assimilation, where the gray under the white stripes appears lighter than the gray under the black.*

the part of the visual field to which you are attending shows greater brightness contrast (Brussell & Festinger, 1973; Coren, 1969), whereas regions to which you are not attending show brightness assimilation (Festinger, Coren, & Rivers, 1970). Observers usually describe the pattern shown in Figure 4-22A as a *gray field with white lines on it* and Figure 4-22B as a *set of black lines on a gray background.* Festinger, Coren, and Rivers reasoned that the lines have a "figurelike" quality that captures the attention of observers. Since the gray is then a nonfigural background to which we pay little attention, it shows assimilation. If this is the case, then voluntary shifts in attention that focus concentration on the gray regions should alter the brightness effect from one of assimilation to one of contrast. The gray under the white stripes should now appear to be the darker member of the pair. This is exactly what happens (Festinger, et al., 1970). You can demonstrate this for yourself by focusing your concentration on the gray in Figure 4-22 for a few moments. Soon the grays will appear to differ in a contrast direction, rather than showing brightness assimilation.

Some brightness effects depend on other cognitive factors, such as the assumptions the observer makes about the nature of the world, or even the way in which regions of the visual field *appear* to be arranged, as well as on simple lateral inhibitory interactions (Flock & Nusinowitz, 1984; Gilchrist, Delman, & Jacobsen, 1983). We will have more to say about this in Chapter 14 when we discuss the issue of *lightness constancy.*

TEMPORAL CONTEXT EFFECTS

Brightness perception is affected not only by stimuli that lie adjacent to the test stimulus in space, but also is greatly affected by events that occur immediately prior in time. The temporal equivalent of simultaneous brightness contrast is called **successive brightness contrast.** It is most frequently studied by a procedure referred to as **selective adaptation.** The use of the word *adaptation* here involves the concept of **neural satiation,** or fatigue, which makes it quite different from the dark or light adaptation discussed earlier in the chapter. In this procedure, an observer is exposed to a stimulus with a specific attribute (for example, spatial frequency of 6 cycles per degree) for a moderately short time (from 20 seconds to several minutes). If a specific group of neurons is tuned to that particular frequency, they will, of course, immediately start responding when their optimal stimulus appears. If the stimulus remains in view for a long period of time, these neurons will continue to respond, until they are eventually too fatigued to respond vigorously any longer. Since this fatigue might last for a minute or two after exposure to the *adapting stimulus*, we have then effectively eliminated, or temporarily disabled, a particular group of spatial frequency channels, and this should be detectable perceptually.

Many of the findings supporting the idea of spatial frequency channels in the visual system arise from selective adaptation studies. For example, suppose we measure the modulation transfer function of an observer, which would produce the solid line in Figure 4-23. Now we have the observer stare for a while at a grating of about 6 cycles per degree (the adapting stimulus) to fatigue the spatial frequency channels associated with this middle range of frequencies. When we next measure the observer's transfer function, we get the results shown as the dotted line in Figure 4-23. Notice the depression in sensitivity around the adapted spatial frequency. This means it is now harder to detect gratings in this range of spatial frequencies, and larger values of physical contrast are

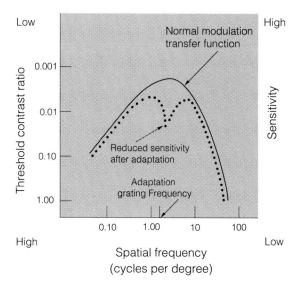

Figure 4-23 *Selective adaptation of a particular spatial frequency grating reduces the contrast sensitivity for a range of spatial frequencies similar to the adapting frequency.*

needed to produce the same perceptual effects. This is exactly what we would expect if the channels tuned to the adapting stimulus frequency have been fatigued, and hence no longer respond as effectively. Of course, if we used a different adapting stimulus, the region of reduced sensitivity would be different, depending on its spatial frequency (Graham, 1980; Harris, 1980).

A particularly interesting perceptual effect can be produced using this technique. Remember that spatial frequency roughly corresponds to the size of elements in a pattern. Thus, low spatial frequencies correspond to large elements, or in gratings to wide stripes, whereas high frequencies correspond to smaller elements. Suppose we somehow disabled all of our low spatial-frequency channels. With only the high-frequency channels operating, they would

be the major determinant of our responses to any stimuli, since the other channels are responding more weakly because of fatigue. Since the action of these higher-frequency channels usually signals the presence of higher spatial frequencies, we might expect that the pattern would appear to be dominated by high-frequency (smaller) elements compared with a situation where all channels were operating normally. Demonstration Box 4-7 allows you to demonstrate this effect for yourself.

One of the most important findings to emerge from selective adaptation studies of spatial frequency is that the adaptation, or neural satiation, is highly specific to a number of other features in addition to spatial frequency itself. For instance, adaptation to a particular spatial frequency is seen most strongly when the adapting and test gratings are equal in orientation, contrast, and wavelength (Anstis, 1975; Blakemore & Nachmias, 1971; Lovegrove & Over, 1973). You can observe this for yourself by trying out Part 2 in Demonstration Box 4-7. The original adaptation you experienced for vertical gratings should not transfer to horizontal gratings. This means that selective adaptation often involves several attributes, including not only spatial frequency, but orientation, color, and other factors.

While these interdependencies among adapted stimulus dimensions might at first appear to make the study of vision very difficult, researchers have also learned how to use them to learn more about the structure of the visual system. For instance, some have estimated how finely tuned orientation channels are by studying the extent to which spatial frequency adaptation generalizes to gratings that differ systematically in orientation from the adapting stimulus (Wilson, Levi, Maffei, Rovamo, & DeValois, 1990). In Chapter 5, we will see how the dependency between orientation and color response has also been studied using this technique.

DEMONSTRATION BOX 4-7   Selective Adaptation of Spatial Frequency Channels

PART 1

If you look at the figure, you will see that one of the squares on the left has broad bars (low spatial frequency) and the other has narrow bars (high spatial frequency). The pattern in *B* contains two gratings, both of which have the same spatial frequencies, but they are neither as high nor as low as the ones on the left. Hold the illustration about 80 cm away from you. Now look at the horizontal bar between the upper and lower patterns on the left for about 20 to 30 seconds. Move your gaze from one portion of the bar to another, but keep your eyes on the bar. As you look steadily at the bar, the channels tuned to low spatial frequencies from the upper part of your visual field and those tuned to the high spatial frequencies from the lower part of your visual field are fatiguing, or adapting. Now if you transfer your gaze quickly to the dot between the identical gratings in *B*, you will notice that they no longer seem to be the same. The top part of the grating now appears to be spaced more finely, with thinner stripes than those on the bottom. The low frequency channels have been disabled in the upper region of the visual field. With more high spatial frequency channels active, the percent is shifted toward higher frequencies; hence, the stripes are seen as smaller and more dense. The opposite effect is occurring in the lower region of the field.

PART 2

Now adapt yourself once again to the pair of gratings in *A* for 20 to 30 seconds. Then transfer your gaze to the pair of gratings in *C*. These horizontal gratings should not be influenced by the adaptation to *A* because spatial frequency adaptation is sensitive to orientation.

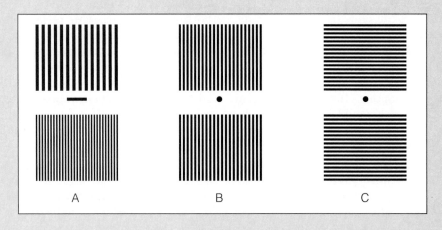

A   B   C

DARKNESS PERCEPTION

Although it might seem reasonable to assume that the perception of brightness and darkness are two ends of a single continuum, emerging evidence has shown that brightness and darkness perception are qualitatively different phenomena. This hypothesis was developed more than 30 years ago, based on an observation we have already mentioned, that increasing the illumination in a display does not cause all objects to appear brighter. Indeed, the brighter objects in the display become even brighter, but the objects that appeared to be dark originally become even darker—not brighter as we might expect (Jameson & Hurvich, 1964; Jung, 1961).

A physiological basis for a separate brightness and darkness system is already apparent at the retina. We saw in Chapter 3 that ganglion cells can be divided into two classes based on their receptive field organization. On-center, off-surround cells can be thought of as relative brightness detectors, whereas off-center, on-surround cells could serve as relative darkness detectors. Several facts add weight to this idea: (1) these two classes of receptive fields can be seen in both parvo and magno cells, (2) they are regularly distributed throughout the retina, and (3) their connections with higher visual centers are independent of one another (Perry & Silveira, 1988; Wassle, Peichl, & Boycott, 1983). It is therefore tantalizing to speculate that there are two systems of ganglion cells, one for the perception of brightness and one for the perception of darkness. The existence of two systems would certainly increase the ability of the visual system to respond to a much wider range of luminance levels (Fiorentini et al., 1990).

An important discovery by Slaughter and Miller (1981) makes it possible to test directly for the independence of the brightness and darkness systems in the retina. They applied a neurotransmitter called 2-amino-4-phosphonobutyrate, or **APB** to the retina of the mud puppy (an aquatic salamander). This caused all the on-center ganglion cells to become unresponsive to light; however, the off-center cells maintained their normal responses. Since then others have shown that APB blocks the responses of on-center ganglion cells and lateral geniculate nucleus cells in the cat and the monkey (Horton & Sherk, 1984; Sherk & Horton, 1984; Shiller, 1984; Shiller, Sandell, & Maunsell, 1986). Animals treated with APB show normal responses to *decreases* in light but are almost completely unable to detect light *increases*. However, they still show a normal response to oriented edges and to the motion of an edge in a particular direction, provided that the edge is defined by a decrease in light relative to the background.

Several researchers have demonstrated the independence of bright and dark systems in humans using selective adaptation. When observers were adapted to black gratings of a particular width (Burton, Nagshineh, & Ruddock, 1977) or to a black bar moving at a certain velocity (DeValois, 1977), they showed temporary fatigue in their ability to detect *black* gratings and black moving bars of similar size. However, they showed no evidence of fatigue to *white* gratings or white moving bars of the same size. Demonstration Box 4-8 allows you to observe the independence of the brightness and darkness perception systems.

DEMONSTRATION BOX 4-8   Independence of Brightness and Darkness Perception

For this demonstration you should first cover up the pair of gratings in *B* and then look at the gratings in *A* for about 30–60 seconds. Do this by moving your eyes back and forth along the dash between the two gratings, so each grating falls on a region of your retina that is equally far from the fovea. Now look at the pair of gratings in *B*. The black lines in the upper grating appear to be finer than those in the lower grating, even though they are physically identical to one another. The interpretation of this illusion is based on separate systems for brightness and dark-ness perception. The black bars in the upper grating in *A*, which are wider and hence more dominant, fatigue the *darkness* system more, whereas the wider white bars in the lower figure fatigue the *lightness* system more. When presented with equal white and dark stimuli in *B*, the dark response is weaker in the upper pattern, so dark appears less visible (finer bars), whereas the light response is weaker in the lower part of the visual field, making the white bars appear finer (based on Burton, Nagshineh, & Ruddock, 1977).

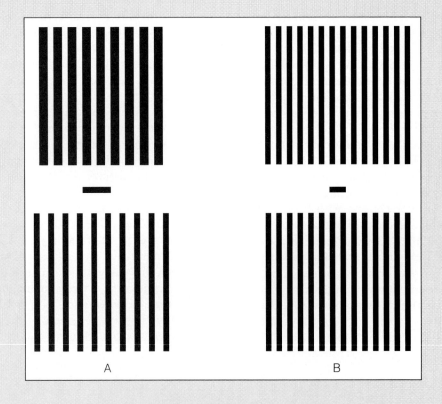

A   B

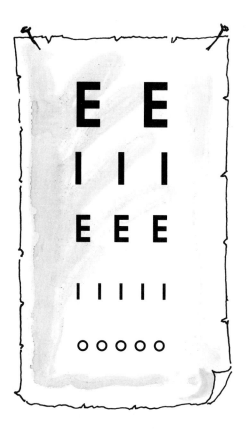

Old MacDonald had an eye chart

GLOSSARY

The following definitions are specific to their use in this book.

APB   A neurotransmitter that, when applied to the retina, causes all the on-center ganglion cells to become unresponsive to light but leaves the off-center cells functional.

Bloch's law   The trade-off relationship between stimulus duration and stimulus intensity in their effect on absolute threshold; $T \times I = C$.

Brightness   The phenomenal impression of the intensity of a light stimulus.

Brightness assimilation   The reverse of brightness contrast. Here, added light elements lighten a stimulus and added dark elements darken it.

Bril   A unit for measuring the apparent brightness of stimuli.

Bunsen-Roscoe law   The physical law defining the photochemical reaction of any light-sensitive substance as a function of the intensity and duration of light exposure.

CIE   The Commission Internationale de l'Eclairage; an international organization responsible for light measurement.

Contrast matching   A psychophysical procedure in which observers are asked to match two targets (often sine wave gratings) by adjusting the intensities of the light and the dark regions until the corresponding regions in the two patterns are apparently equal in brightness.

Contrast ratio   A physical measure of the difference between the light and dark regions in an image that is unaffected by overall changes in illumination. One common form of the ratio is $(L_{max} - L_{min}) / (L_{max} + L_{min})$, where L_{max} refers to the maximum luminance and L_{min} refers to the minimum luminance in the image.

Dark adaptation   The increase in visual sensitivity after a change from a higher to a lower level of illumination.

Difference of Gaussian filter   A mathematical description of a spatial filter based on the difference between two bell-shaped curves of different widths. Performs the function of a center-surround ganglion cell. Also called a DOG filter.

Directional acuity   *See* Vernier acuity.

DOG filter   *See* Difference of Gaussian filter.

Fourier's theorem   States that any periodic wave can be mathematically analyzed into a series of simple sine or cosine waves.

Gabor filter   A mathematical description of a spatial filter based on multiplying a bell-shaped curve with a sine wave. Performs the function of an oriented simple cortical cell.

Grating acuity   *See* Resolution acuity.

Hyperacuity   Resolution of details that are smaller than the diameter of one retinal receptor; usually, any acuity less than 10 seconds of visual angle.

Illuminance   The amount of light falling on a surface.

Lateral inhibition   The process of adjacent visual units inhibiting one another.

Light adaptation   The decrease in visual sensitivity after a change from a lower to a higher level of illumination.

Lightness   The phenomenal impression of the "grayness" of a surface. This judgment is related to the percentage of light that is reflected from a surface.

Lumen   The unit of radiance equal to the light emanating from a standard candle, which is slightly more than 0.001 watt at a wavelength of 555 nm.

Luminance   The amount of light reflected from a surface.

Luminosity curve   A plot of the relative brightness of different wavelengths.

Mach bands   The perception of dark and light lines at regions near abrupt changes in an intensity gradient.

Neural filter   Cells in the brain that are able to perform a crude Fourier analysis of the visual image by behaving like feature detectors for particular spatial frequencies.

Neural satiation   A process in which specific groups of neurons fatigue in response to optimal and continuous stimulation. This is the presumed cause of selective adaptation.

Photometry   The measurement of light.

Photopic   A term for high light (daylight) visibility conditions and vision under these conditions.

Piper's law   The trade-off relationship between area and intensity in the detection of stimuli between 10 and 24 deg of visual angle in size: $\sqrt{A} \times I = C$.

Purkinje shift   The change in the apparent brightness of different wavelengths as one goes from a light- to a dark-adapted state.

Radiance   The amount of energy emitted by a light source.

Recognition acuity   A type of visual acuity commonly measured by means of letter identification and scaled relative to a norm of identification at 6 m distance from the observer (6/6).

Reflectance   The proportion of incident light that a surface reflects.

Resolution acuity   The observer's ability to detect a gap between two lines, or the orientation of a grid of lines.

Retinal illuminance   The amount of light reaching the retina.

Ricco's law   The trade-off relationship between area and intensity in the detection of stimuli smaller than 10 minutes of visual angle in size; $A \times I = C$.

Scotopic   A term for low light (night) visibility conditions and vision under these conditions.

Selective adaptation   *See* Neural satiation.

Simultaneous brightness contrast   An effect through which a target area of a given luminance appears brighter when surrounded by a darker background than when surrounded by a lighter background.

Sine wave grating   A pattern of light intensity that varies from light to dark following sinusoidal gradations.

SI System   The System International d'Unites; a uniform system of measurement.

Spatial modulation transfer function   A graphical description of the way an optical system's ability to resolve spatial modulations (light intensity changes across space) varies with spatial frequency.

Square wave grating A pattern of light intensity with sharply alternating light and dark stripes.

Standard units Internationally agreed-on measures of photic energy.

Successive brightness contrast Brightness perception that is influenced by events occurring immediately prior to the test stimulus. It is the temporal analog of simultaneous brightness contrast.

Vernier acuity The measure of an individual's ability to distinguish a broken line from an unbroken line.

Visual acuity The ability of the eye to resolve details.

Visual angle A measure of the size of the retinal image.

Westheimer function A curve indicating that the ability to detect a small spot of light first declines and then improves as the diameter of a background disk is increased. This psychophysical procedure demonstrates the operations of center-surround ganglion cells.

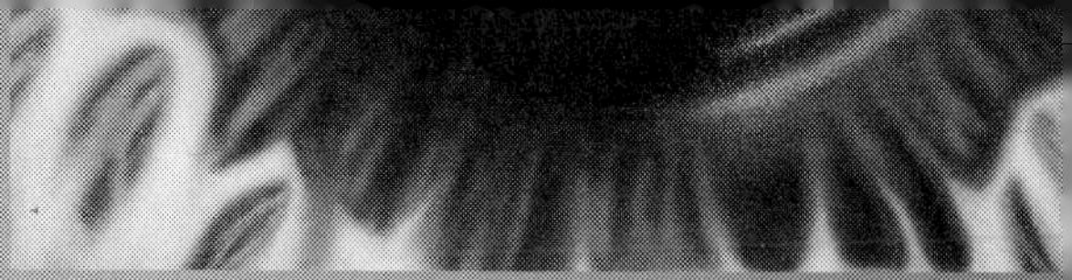

Chapter ...

5

COLOR

Color Stimulus

Color Appearance Systems

Color Mixture

CIE Color Space

The Physiology of Color Vision

Trichromatic Color Theory

- Color Vision Defects
- Physiological Basis of Trichromatic Theory

Opponent-Process Theory

- Physiological Basis of Opponent Process Theory

Color Channels and Cortical Coding

Color Perception

Intensity and Duration

Spatial Interactions

Age and Physical Condition

Cognitive Factors in Color Perception

- Memory for Color
- Culture and Color
- Color Impressions

OPPOSITE PAGE:
The Allegory of Painting BY JAN VERMEER.
OIL ON CANVAS, 47¼ X 39⅜.
KUNSTHISTORISCHES MUSEUM, VIENNA.

"My dad was color-blind, but didn't find out until he was nearly fifty. He was always doing strange things. He couldn't be trusted to pick tomatoes from the garden because he was always mixing up the ripe and the green ones. We finally suspected that something was wrong when he commented that he really admired cherry pickers for their ability to recognize shapes. 'After all,' he said, 'the only thing that tells 'em it's a cherry is the fact that it's round and the leaves aren't. I just don't see how they find 'em in those trees!'"

Like the student who told this tale, you may be surprised to learn how important color is in determining your ability to acquire information about the world. For instance, consider Figure 5-1. Although the figure appears to be a random collection of gray shapes, a word is hidden in it. Each letter is spelled out by a series of similar shapes. If you study the figure for a moment, you will begin to see how difficult it is to pick out the word (if you can do it at all), despite the fact that the shape and brightness information are there. In this task you are much like the color-blind person trying to pick out cherries among the leaves, by shape alone. Now flip to Color Plate 2, where we have added the dimension of color to the figure. Notice that in this color plate the word "leaps out." Thus, color provides an important stimulus dimension that aids in the localization and identification of targets. This explains why some occupations, such as air traffic control, require normal color vision (Kuyk, Veres, Lahey, & Clark, 1986). For some species, color vision is a matter of life and death. For instance, if honey bees lacked color vision, locating nectar-bearing flowers hidden among shrubs, grasses, or leaves would be almost impossible. The survival of this species may well depend on the ability to spot a glint of color that indicates the presence of blossoms.

COLOR STIMULUS

The human eye registers wavelengths between 360 and 760 nanometers (nm) as light. Sir Isaac Newton showed that stimuli of different wavelengths within this range produce different color sensations. Newton's experiment was quite simple. He took a glass prism and allowed sunlight to pass through it from a slit in a window shade. When he held a sheet of white paper on the other side of the prism, the light no longer appeared to be white; rather, it took

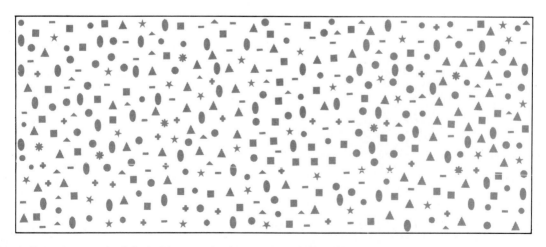

Figure 5-1 Can you find the hidden word? If not, turn to Color Plate 2.

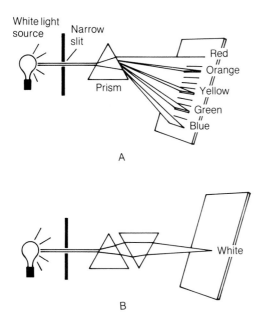

Figure 5-2 Newton's experiments: (A) *separation of white light into its various wavelengths gives the color spectrum*; (B) *recombination of spectral lights gives white light.*

the form of a colored spectrum, looking much like the arrangement of lights in a rainbow (see Figure 5-2A). Newton knew that light bends when passing through a prism, and that the amount of bending (technically called *refraction*) depends on wavelength. Longer wavelengths (600–700 nm) show less refraction, and and shorter wavelengths (400–500 nm) show more. Thus a prism takes various wavelengths of light, which make up sunlight, and separates them according to wavelength. The fact we see this spread of light as varying in hue shows that color perception depends on the wavelength of the light. Table 5-1 shows some typical color names associated with selected wavelengths of light.

Newton also inserted another prism (in the opposite orientation) so the light was refracted in the direction opposite to the effect of the original prism. This, of course, recombined all of these wavelengths into a single beam. When

he placed a piece of paper into this beam it again appeared to be white, with no hint of the original colors that went into the combination. This indicates that the sensation of white results from a mixture of many different wavelengths (see Figure 5-2B).

An important technical distinction should be made here. Figure 5-2 does not describe how white light is broken up into "colored light." Colored light does not exist; rather, what does exist is visible radiation of different wavelengths. If there were no observer there would be no color. Newton pointed this out when he said, "For the rays, to speak properly, are not coloured. In them is nothing else than a certain *Power* and *Disposition* to stir up a sensation of this or that Colour." When we talk about the color stimulus, we should actually speak of radiation of different wavelengths, since the sensations of red, green, blue, or any other color reside in the observer. Having made this technical distinction, we must admit that it is convenient to talk about red light or green light, and for the sake of brevity we will not hesitate to do so in some of our later descriptions. Remember, however, that when we refer to a "blue light," we are referring to those wavelengths of light that elicit the sensation of blue, namely, the shorter wavelengths in the visible spectrum.

Table 5-1 Wavelengths of Light and Associated Color Sensations

COLOR NAME	*WAVELENGTH (nm)*
Violet	450
Blue	470
Cyan	495
Green	510
Yellow-Green	560
Yellow	575
Orange	600
Red	660
Purple	Not a spectral color but a mixture of "red" and "blue"

Objects appear to be colored because they reflect to our eyes only selected wavelengths of light. Consider a common object, such as an apple with white light falling on it. It appears to be red. We have already seen that white light, such as sunlight, is a combination of all wavelengths. Since the light stimulus that reaches your eyes produces the sensation of red, all of the wavelengths except the longer (red-appearing) ones must have been absorbed by the surface of the apple. Colored objects or surfaces contain pigments that selectively absorb some wavelengths of light, while the rest are reflected and thus reach your eye. It is this selective "subtraction" of some wavelengths from the incoming light that gives an object its color. If a surface does not absorb any of the wavelengths reaching it but reflects them all uniformly, it appears white, rather than colored. Color filters work in much the same way, that is, by absorbing some wavelengths of light. For instance, if a white light is projected through a green filter, the resulting beam is green. This means that the filter has absorbed most of the long and short wavelengths, allowing only the medium range, or green-appearing, wavelengths to reach the eye.

Note that simply specifying the wavelength, or wavelengths, in a stimulus does not fully describe the way the color appears to an observer. For instance, a stimulus with a dominant wavelength of 570 nm may appear yellow, whereas another with the same wavelength composition might appear brown. For this reason, additional factors other than wavelength are used to classify colors.

Color Appearance Systems

Suppose you were marooned on a desert island that had a beach covered with colored pebbles. Lacking anything else to do, you set about the task of classifying the pebbles by color in some meaningful way. The first classification scheme that might come to mind would involve grouping them together on the basis of their hues. Thus, you would end up with a pile of red pebbles and another of green pebbles, and so forth. Once you have your piles of pebbles, you would next look for some meaningful arrangement for the piles. For instance, you might notice that orange seems to fall, in terms of appearance, somewhere between red and yellow. The yellow-greens, of course, seem to fall between yellow and green. Once you reach the blue end of your line of stones, however, you might find yourself running into a bit of a problem. The purple pebbles seem to fall somewhere between the blues and the reds. This means that a straight line arrangement is not adequate. Instead, you might arrange the pebbles as shown in Figure 5-3.

This crude color arrangement scheme is circular in form. You have probably seen it before in books on art, decorating, or design, where it is usually called the **color circle** or **color wheel.** In this arrangement, you have separated the colors according to hue, which is the psychological attribute that most clearly corresponds to variations in wavelength. Very often when we use the word *color*, in everyday

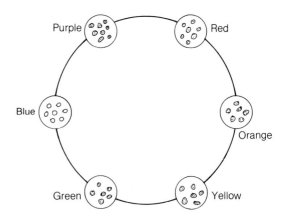

Figure 5-3 *A primitive color circle for encoding the colors of pebbles.*

life and in this chapter, we are actually referring to *hue.* Let us consider the effect of wavelength on sensation by looking at the effects
produced by pure, or **monochromatic,** stimuli.
A monochromatic stimulus contains only one
wavelength (from the Greek *mono* meaning
"one" and *chroma* meaning "color"). These
stimuli are similar to those found in the spectrum generated by Newton's prismatic separation of light and therefore are often called
spectral colors. Such monochromatic stimuli
do not produce all the hues found in the color
wheel. For instance, we find that no single
wavelength produces the sensation of purple.
This sensation requires a mixture of blue and
red wavelengths. Similarly, at no place in the
spectrum can we find a red that doesn't appear
to have a tinge of yellow. To achieve what appears to be true red, we must add a bit of blue
(short wavelength) light.

Meanwhile, back on the beach, our color-
wheel classification scheme based only on the
psychological attribute of hue seems incomplete. A close look at the piles of pebbles reveals marked color differences. For instance,
among the red pebbles you might find that
some are a deep red color whereas others are
pink; another group may be almost pure white
with only a hint of red. This observation corresponds to the physical dimension of **purity.**
Clearly the purest color would correspond to a
monochromatic or spectral hue, and as other
wavelengths or white light are added, the color
would become "washed out." This psychological attribute of color appearance is called **saturation.** It is quite easy to integrate saturation
into the color circle by simply placing white in
the center. Now imagine that the various degrees of saturation correspond to positions
along the spokes or radii emanating from the
center of the wheel. The center represents
white (or gray), and the perimeter represents
the purest or most saturated color possible.
Figure 5-4 shows the color wheel modified to
include saturation. Notice that the point corre-

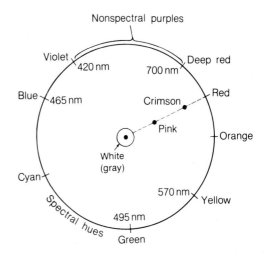

Figure 5-4 *The color circle modified to allow the
encoding of both hue and saturation. Spectral colors are on the outer rim; white is in the center.*

sponding to pink (a moderately desaturated
red) is plotted near the center along the line
connecting red and white, whereas crimson is
plotted farther from the center along the
same line.

To the average observer, hue and saturation do not completely describe all the visible
nuances of color. Two colors may match in
both of these attributes but still appear to be
different. For instance, a spot of blue light projected onto a screen would not appear to be the
same as another spot identical in all regards except that it has been dimmed by putting a light-
reducing filter in front of it. Thus, the sensory
attribute of **brightness** (which we discussed in
Chapter 4) must be worked into our system of
describing colors. Since we have already used
the two dimensions capable of being reproduced on a flat piece of paper, the addition of a
third color attribute (brightness) forces us to
use a solid instead of a flat representation.

The shape of the three-dimensional color
"space" can be derived from common observation if we recognize that at high brightness levels colors appear to be "washed out," whereas
at low brightness levels colors seem "weak" or

"muddy," meaning that they are of low saturation. Thus, the hue circle must shrink at these extremes, since saturation seems to vary over a confined range, and very high degrees of saturation are never observed at very high or very low levels of brightness.

If we combine the three psychological attributes of hue, saturation, and brightness, we get something that looks like Figure 5-5. It appears to be a pair of cones placed base to base. This is usually called the **color spindle** or **color solid.** The central core as we move up or down represents brightness and is composed of all the grays running from white (at the top) to black (at the bottom). We can imagine that at each brightness level, if we sliced through the color solid in the direction shown in the diagram, we would get a color circle in which the hue would be represented along the perimeter. Totally desaturated colors (the grays) are at the central core, as we have already noted; hence, saturation is represented by moving from the

center outward. This is the basic representation used in many color appearance systems. Probably the most popular in use among psychologists is the one developed by Munsell (1915) and modified by Newhall, Nickerson, and Judd (1943) to agree with the way typical observers arrange color stimuli. To actually classify colors you can use a **color atlas,** in which each page represents a horizontal or vertical slice through the color solid. Such atlases provide color samples that illustrate colors found in varying locations in the color solid, allowing the observer to identify and label any given test color.

Color Mixture

Pure colors of a single wavelength usually are produced under precise laboratory conditions. Most of the light reaching your eye is composed of a mixture of many different wavelengths. Generally, the **dominant wavelength** will determine what hue you see, although this is not always the case. When we combine two or more wavelengths of light, a new color, with a different psychological hue and saturation, is seen. Once the colors are mixed, the visual system can no longer determine the individual wavelengths that make up the mixture. Thus, you can have a pure yellow made up of only 570-nm light and another that matches it, composed of a mixture of a 500-nm green and a 650-nm red. You will not be able to distinguish between these hues, nor will you be able to isolate the red and the green that went into the mixture. Colors that appear to be the same but are made up of different wavelengths of light are called **metameric colors.**

Color mixtures fall into two types. The simplest to describe, called **additive color mixture,** occurs when we mix light. For instance, if we project a red circle on a screen, the light reaching the eye from the projected circle is red. If we project a blue circle on the screen so it par-

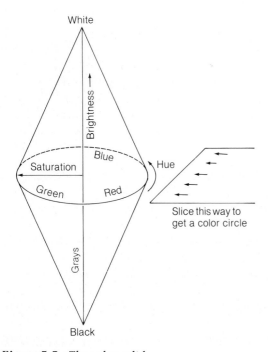

Figure 5-5   *The color solid.*

tially overlaps with the red circle, the light reaching the eye from the region where the circles overlap contains both blue and red. Thus, each new wavelength projected onto the screen *adds* to the mixture of wavelengths reaching the eye. Figure 5-6A shows what might occur if we use three projectors with the first projecting a red beam, the second a green beam, and the third a deep blue (almost violet) beam. If the circles of light are arranged so they partially overlap with one another, we get a series of additive mixtures. Where the red and the deep blue overlap, we get a reddish-purple generally called *magenta*. Where the deep blue and the green overlap, we get a lighter hue which is greenish-blue, usually called *cyan*. Something that some people find quite surprising happens where the red and green overlap—we get the sensation of yellow. Where all three beams overlap, we get the sensation of white. Demonstration Box 5-1 shows another way to get additive color mixtures.

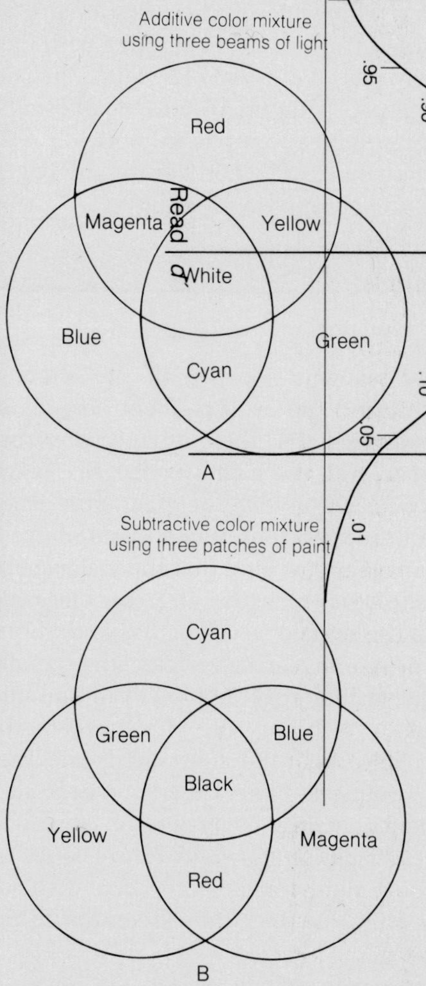

These results cannot be duplicated using paints. If you tried mixing all your paints together to get white, you would get a shade of gray or black instead. This is because pigments do not work in the same way as lights. Something that appears red, such as a tomato, will have a surface pigment that absorbs most of the short and medium wavelengths, reflecting to your eyes only the long (red) wavelengths. A pigment that gives you a color similar to grass green absorbs most of the long wavelengths and the short wavelengths, reflecting to your eyes, mainly middle wavelengths. Thus, when you mix the red and the green paints together, you have a mixture in which only the middle wavelengths are reflected by the green, yet these are absorbed by the red pigment. Hence you are essentially subtracting all of the wavelengths, leaving only a muddy gray.

Since pigments work by subtracting or absorbing wavelengths of light, a mixture of pigments is called a **subtractive color mixture.** Such mixtures produce colors that are considerably less predictable than mixtures of lights, because the wavelength-absorbing property of pigments is complex. For example, Figure 5-7 shows the wavelengths reflected by some typical pigments. When you see how irregularly they reflect the light, you can imagine the problems in predicting what the resultant mixes might reflect and absorb.

Suppose, however, that we are dealing with relatively simple pigments, where the yellow

Figure 5-6 *Color-mixture systems:* (A) *additive,* (B) *subtractive.*

DEMONSTRATION BOX 5-1   Color Mixture

There is a simple way to obtain additive color mixtures without using projected beams of light. Consider Color Plate 4A, in which you see a checkerboard of tiny red and green squares. In Color Plate 4B you see a yellow disk. Prop up the book so that you can see the color plates when you move across the room. Now, standing at a distance, look back at the figures. What formerly appeared to be red and green now appears to be yellow and should match the yellow disk. At a distance, the optics of the eye can no longer resolve the individual squares. The light from each of them smears, or blurs, across the retina giving rise to the color mixture effect.

This technique is similar to the technique used in your color television set. If you take a magnifying glass and hold it up to the screen, you will see that each region is made up of a series of tiny dots. When you sit at normal viewing distance, you can no longer resolve the individual dots. They have combined within the eye to give you an additive color mixture. A similar technique was used by the French painter Georges Seurat, who replaced the traditional irregular brush stroke used in painting with meticulously placed dots of color. Thus, instead of mixing paints on his palette, he allowed the mixture to be accomplished optically within the eye of the onlooker viewing the painting from an appropriate distance.

---

reflects only middle and long wavelengths, the cyan only short and middle wavelengths, and the magenta only the long and short wavelengths. If we now paint circles of these pigments so that they overlap, we get a crude representation of what would generally be expected in subtractive color mixtures. Since the

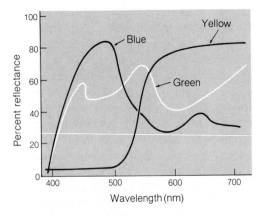

Figure 5-7 *The relative wavelength composition of a blue, a yellow, and a green pigment.*

yellow pigment absorbs all the short wavelengths, and the cyan pigment absorbs all the long wavelengths, their mixture absorbs both the short and the long wavelengths, leaving us only with the middle or green-appearing portion of the spectrum. When we combine yellow with magenta, we find that the yellow subtracts the short wavelengths and the magenta subtracts the middle wavelengths, so that only the long or red-appearing wavelengths remain. In a similar fashion, overlapping cyan and magenta leaves us with only the blue wavelengths, because all others are subtracted, and the mixture produces blue. Clearly, when all three pigments overlap everything is absorbed and we get black, as shown in Figure 5-6B. In general, it is more convenient to deal with additive color mixtures since they are easier to conceptualize.

The color circle, which we have already discussed, provides a convenient means of predicting the appearance of additive color mixtures. For example, suppose we mix a spectral red (about 650 nm) with a spectral yellow (about 570 nm). We can depict this as in Figure 5-8, where the resultant mixture is represented by the line connecting these two colors. If we combine the yellow and the red in equal proportions, we will get a color that corresponds to the dot in the center of the line. We can determine what this color will look like by simply drawing a line from the center of the color circle through the dot to the perimeter. When this is done, we find that we get an orange corresponding to about a 600-nm spectral stimulus. Increasing the amount of yellow shifts the point along the line in the direction closer to the yellow hue. Adding more red shifts the point along the line in the other direction.

You will notice that we started out with two spectral, or pure, hues (marked on the perimeter); however, the resultant mixed color is no longer on the perimeter but is closer to the center of the color circle. The purest colors possible (the spectral colors) are placed on the perimeter of the color circle; more desaturated colors are found closer to the center of the circle (nearer white or gray). From this we can conclude that any color mixture is less saturated than either of the two component colors

that went into it. No mixture of colors can ever be quite as saturated as a monochromatic or spectral color.

Mixing more than two hues (or hues containing more than a single wavelength) is a little more complex. If we mix three colors, the resultant color sensation would be given by the center of a triangle produced by connecting the three colors. If the amount of each hue differs, the center point of the triangle shifts toward the dominant hue.

CIE Color Space

An interesting effect occurs when we mix two colors that are exactly opposite to each other on the color circle. For instance, mixing a violet with a yellow along the lines shown in Figure 5-8 results in a colorless gray. This is because, when the proportions are correct, this mixture lies in the center of the circle. Colors whose mixture produces such an achromatic gray are known as **complementary colors.**

One of the most important facts about color mixtures emerged in the 1850s, when German physicist and physiologist Hermann von Helmholtz (1821–1894) and Scottish physicist James Clerk Maxwell (1831–1879) carried out a set of color matching experiments. They reported that by combining an appropriate set of three monochromatic light sources in appropriate amounts, they could match any other hue. These three wavelengths were to be known as **primaries.** Actually the choice of primaries is rather arbitrary. Primary colors need only be reasonably far apart, with the requirement that the mixture of any two of them alone will not match the third one.

Wright (1929) made a set of measurements in which observers matched the hue of the various spectral sensations. He selected as his primary colors a red of 650 nm, a green of 530 nm, and a blue of 460 nm. The observers matched the color of two patches of light,

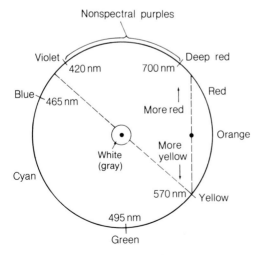

Figure 5-8 *Using the color circle to predict color mixtures.*

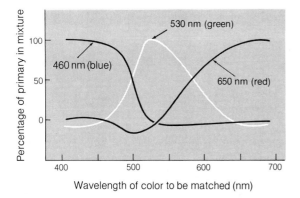

Figure 5-9 *The proportion of each primary (a 460-nm blue, a 530-nm green, and a 650-nm red) needed to match any spectral color.*

where the first was the test color and the second could contain any combination of the three primaries. Wright's results are shown in Figure 5-9, which indicates the relative amount of each of the three primaries needed to match any given wavelength. You might notice that

some of the values are negative. This indicates that some of the particular primary had to be added to the test sample in order to reduce its saturation to the point where it could be matched by a mixture of the two remaining primaries. In other words, some matches could be made only if one of the three primaries was not included in the mixture but was added to the test sample.

The fact that any given color can be matched by a mixture of three appropriately selected primary colors suggests an alternate way of specifying the hue of a stimulus, namely, in terms of the proportion (sometimes "negative") of the three primaries needed to reach this match. Geometrically this suggests a triangular space with a primary color at each corner. Color mixtures may then be represented in the same way as on the color circle. Thus yellow, which is a mixture of red and green, is represented by a point on the line between red and green. If we add more red the point moves toward the red primary, and if we

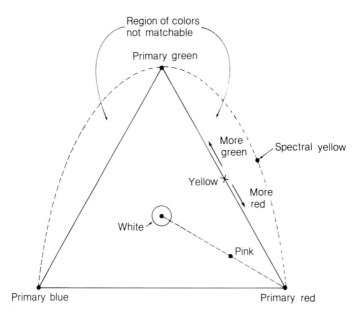

Figure 5-10 *Specifying colors using a color triangle.*

add more green it moves toward the green. As in the color circle, white is represented by a point in the middle, and is composed of an equal proportion of the three primaries. Also, as in the color circle, a red of lower saturation (the whitish-red or pink) would be represented by a point moved inward toward the center. Such a diagram is shown in Figure 5-10.

In 1931, a special body of the Commission Internationale de l'Eclairage (CIE) standardized the procedure for specifying the color of a stimulus. The group decided to use a color space created by the mixing of three primaries as described above. Unfortunately, if we select any three actual *spectral* primary colors, a number of perceptual and mathematical problems result. The major perceptual problem is that other spectral colors cannot be represented within the triangle. For instance, a pure spectral yellow cannot be represented (unless it is one of the primaries, which creates other problems), since any color mixture can never be as saturated as the pure spectral color itself. To solve this perceptual problem, the CIE selected three *imaginary* primary colors. They arranged the primaries at the corners of the triangle shown in Figure 5-11. These imaginary primary colors are more saturated than any

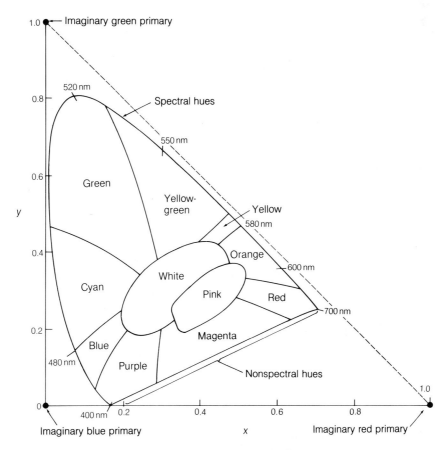

Figure 5-11 *The CIE chromaticity space, which is a variant of the color triangle system using three imaginary "super" primaries.*

real colors can be. (Remember, this is done so that all perceptually visible colors can be represented *within* the space.) Notice that we have labeled the horizontal and vertical axes of the triangle as x and y.

We can now represent *any* color as a point in the color space. We are able to plot a mixture of three colors by using a point that has only two spatial coordinates because the **CIE chromaticity space** has been arranged so that y represents the proportion of green in the mixture, and x represents the proportion of red. Clearly the proportions of red, green, and blue in any mixture must sum to a proportion of 1.00 (you can think of these as representing percentages where all the items must sum to 100% of the light). If we know the proportions of green and red in the mixture, we need only subtract these from 1.00 to find the proportion of blue. The actual colors that can be perceived do not fill the full triangle (remember the primaries we are using are imaginary "super-saturated" colors). Instead, they fill a horseshoe-shaped area with the spectral colors forming the outside boundary. We have labeled this area on the figure to show the regions filled by various colors. Thus, if we had a color $0.20x$ and $0.60y$, we would know that it is composed of 20% red, 60% green, and (subtracting from a total of 100%) 20% blue. Looking at the figure, you can find the point described by these x and y coordinates and see that this color would look green.

Notice that brightness is not represented anywhere on this diagram. As in the color space discussed earlier, brightness requires a third dimension. The color space in the figure can be pictured as a single slice through a three-dimensional color space, just as we demonstrated in Figure 5-5. This third dimension would be called z. Using the CIE color system we can specify and color stimulus by its **tristimulus values,** which are simply the x and y coordinates for the hue of the stimulus and a z coordinate for the brightness of the stimulus.

THE PHYSIOLOGY OF COLOR VISION

Thus far, we have dealt with the physical stimulus, some methods of specifying the appearance of a color, and some aspects of combining various wavelengths of light. None of these descriptions has specified how a particular color sensation arises. In order to understand this, we must deal with both physiological and psychological factors. Let us consider these factors in light of the two major theoretical positions that have emerged during the last 150 years.

Trichromatic Color Theory

Much research has focused on the physiological basis of color vision. One of the earliest findings was discussed in Chapter 4, where we reported that under scotopic levels of illumination, when only the rods are active, no color vision is found. On the basis of these observations, we concluded that cones are the retinal receptors that provide the first stage of the color response. Therefore, the first question becomes how the cones provide information about the wavelength of the incoming light.

Most people can discriminate among thousands of colors under a myriad of conditions. If brightness and saturation are held constant, the average human observer can discriminate at least 200 different hues. Suppose we wished to create an artificial eye with this same ability. The simplest procedure might seem to require a separate cone that responds to each of the discriminable hues. Unfortunately, such a scheme is not practical. For any given colored stimulus, we would have only 1/200 of the cones active, which means that our visual acuity would be much poorer than research has shown it to be. In addition, such a system would mean that our acuity measured under white illumination would be many times better than our acuity measured under monochromatic stimulation. Although visual acuity is lessened slightly when only color differences and no brightness differences are present in a pattern of stimuli, the acuity reduction is not very large (Mullen, 1990).

An alternate scheme would be to have only one type of retinal cone with 200 different code signals by which it could indicate the discriminable hues. This could be done via a sort of neural Morse code. Although such a code may play a part in some aspects of color vision (see the section on "Color Channels and Cortical Coding"), the evidence is still controversial. Research evidence suggests that each cone contains only one pigment. If so, how would the cone itself "recognize" the wavelength of the light? The only thing the cone "knows" is the amount of pigment that has been bleached. Although different wavelengths of light may bleach more or less pigment, simply increasing or decreasing the intensity of the stimulus could also cause the same variations in degree of bleaching. It thus seems unlikely a single cone would be able to discriminate 200 hues.

An answer was suggested almost 200 years ago by Thomas Young (1773–1829). Young proposed that only a few retinal receptor types, operating with different wavelength sensitivities, would be necessary to allow humans to perceive the number of colors they do. He further suggested that perhaps as few as three receptor types would suffice. His theoretical notion was revived in the 1850s, as we have already noted, when Helmholtz and Maxwell showed that normal observers need only three primaries to match any color stimulus. These data were taken as evidence for the presence of three different receptor types in the retina. Since the usual color-matching primaries consisted of a red, a green, and a blue, it was presumed that one receptor type was responsive

to long wavelengths, one to medium wavelengths, and one to short wavelengths of light. Since these receptors are cones, and cones operate by the bleaching of pigment, three hypothetical cone pigments were hypothesized. The first was called **erythrolabe** (from the Greek, meaning "red-catching"), another **chlorolabe** (meaning "green-catching"), and the third **cyanolabe** (meaning "blue-catching"). This **trichromatic theory** (from the Greek *tri* meaning "three" and *chroma* meaning "color") finds some very convincing support in the study of defective color vision.

Color Vision Defects

Virtually all individuals vary from what is usually called "normal" or "average" color vision in some way or another (Neitz & Jacobs, 1990). However, some people show drastic deficiencies in their ability to discriminate colored stimuli and, in popular speech, are said to suffer from **color blindness.** This term is much too strong, since only a very small percentage of individuals are totally incapable of discriminating colors. According to a trichromatic theory of color vision, we can predict five different varieties of color vision abnormality. The first, and most drastic, would be found in those who have no functioning cones. Since their sight would involve only the rod system, they would be expected to have no color discrimination ability. In addition, they should have relatively poor visual acuity (20/200 or less) and find photopic, or daylight, levels of illumination to be quite uncomfortable. It is estimated that only 1 in 300,000 individuals has no functioning cones at all (Sharpe & Nordby, 1989).

A slightly less drastic malady is one in which only one variety of cone is functioning in addition to the rods. With this problem, vision should be possible under both photopic and scotopic conditions, but the person would still lack any color discrimination ability. Any wavelength of light hitting one of the functioning rods (or the single-cone system) would produce some bleaching of the pigment. Even though different wavelengths might bleach different amounts, this would not allow color discrimination, since the response produced by any one wavelength of light can be matched by merely adjusting the intensity of any other. In other words, the individual with no functioning cones, or the one with only one functioning cone type, responds to light in much the way that a sheet of black-and-white film does. All colors are recorded simply as gradations in intensity of the response. Such individuals are called **monochromats** (from Greek *mono* meaning "one" and *chroma* meaning "color").

One might also suppose that some individuals, instead of lacking two or three sets of cones as does the monochromat, might only have one malfunctioning cone system. Given two functioning cone systems, these people should have some color perception, though it would differ from that of a normal observer. In effect, they should be able to match all other colors with a mixture of only two primaries. Such individuals are usually called **dichromats** (the Greek *di* means "two"). The existence of such individuals has been known since the 1700s. The English chemist John Dalton (1766–1844) was a dichromat, a fact he learned rather late in his life. Supposedly, it first came to his attention when he wore a scarlet robe to receive his PhD degree. Since he was a Quaker, and this sect shuns bright colors, his attire caused quite a stir until it became clear that woolen yarn dyed crimson or yarn dyed gray or dark blue-green appeared to be the same to him.

There are three predictable forms of dichromacy, depending on whether the red-, green-, or blue-responding cones are inoperative. The specific confusions are predictable from the color-matching curves of normal observers shown in Figure 5-9. Dalton's type of color defect is usually referred to as **protanopia** (the Greek prefix *proto* means "first," and red light is generally designated as the first primary). A protanope would be insensitive to long wavelengths normally perceived as red light. If a red light was made very much brighter than a green light, a protanope could easily confuse them, whereas a color-normal observer would perceive both that the red light was brighter than the green and that they differed in hue. When most individuals view a spectrum such as that produced by Newton's prism, they perceive six different colors, blending one into another. Dalton reported, "To me it is quite otherwise. I see only two, or at most three distinctions. These I should call yellow and blue, or yellow, blue, and purple. My yellow comprehends the red, orange, yellow, and green of others and my blue and purple coincide with theirs."

The most common form of dichromacy, involving a malfunction in the green cone system, is called **deuteranopia** (the Greek prefix *deuteros* means "second," and green light is by convention the second primary). Individuals with deuteranopia are able to respond to green light, but they cannot distinguish green from certain combinations of red and blue.

Trichromatic theory also predicts a third form of dichromacy caused by the absence or malfunction of the blue cone system. Although a name existed for this phenomenon, *tritanopia* (from the Greek *tritan*, for the "third" primary), no report of this difficulty was confirmed until about 1950, when a magazine article containing a color-vision test plate appeared as part of an intensive search througout England. This search resulted in the discovery of 17 tritanopes (Wright 1952). These individuals, instead of seeing the spectrum as composed of blue and yellow as do other dichromats, see the longer wavelengths as red and the shorter ones as bluish-green. The discovery of this last class of individuals provides strong support for a trichromatic theory of color vision.

Color vision defects are a fairly common problem. Some instances are relatively mild and result in what is called **anomalous trichromatism.** Color matches of individuals with this problem require more red **(protoanomaly)** or more green **(deuteranomaly)** than do those of normal observers. If we count all individuals with any form of color deficiency, we find that just over 8% of all males show color weaknesses, whereas slightly less than 0.05% of all females show similar deficits. Color defects are genetically transmitted, and recent studies have conclusively mapped the pattern of this transmission (Botstein, 1986; Nathans, 1987; Nathans, Piantanida, Eddy, Shows, & Hogness, 1986). The relevant genes are located on the X chromosome, of which females have two and males only one. If the single X chromosome of a male contains a deficient color vision gene, the male will have a color vision deficiency, whereas a deficient gene in one X chromosome of a female can be compensated for by a normal gene

in the other one. This explains why more males than females have color vision deficiencies.

What colors does a dichromat actually see? It is really not possible to know how the perceived colors of a dichromat compare with those seen by a color-normal observer. However, a glimpse into the visual world of the color defective has been provided by a rare person who was deuteranope in her left eye, but color-normal in her right eye. Graham and Hsia (1958) had this observer adjust the color seen by her normal eye so that it appeared to be the same hue as the color seen by her defective eye. The results of her matches are shown in Figure 5-12. As can be seen from this figure, the colors over the entire range of red to green (from about 700 to 502 nm) all appeared to have the same yellow hue (about 570 nm), and all of the colors from green to violet appeared to be blue (matching a 470-nm stimulus). The region that appears to be blue-green to the normal observer (around 502 nm) was perceived as a neutral gray in the defective eye. Knowledge of the nature of the color confusions among dichromats allowed Coren and Hakstian

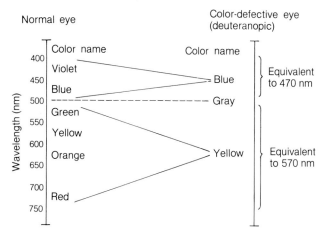

Figure 5-12 *Color matches of a normal eye to a "color-blind" (deuteranopic) eye in the same observer (based upon Graham & Hsia, 1958).*

DEMONSTRATION BOX 5-2   Color Vision Screening Inventory

To see if you may have a color-vision deficit simply take this test, which is the *Color Vision Screening Inventory** developed by Coren and Hakstian (1987, 1988). For each question you should select the response that best describes you and your behaviors. You can select from among the following response alternatives: *Never* (or almost never), *Seldom, Occasionally, Frequently, Always* (or almost always). Simply circle the letter corresponding to the first letter of your choice.

1. Do you have difficulty discriminating between yellow and orange?   N S O F A

2. Do you have difficulty discriminating between yellow and green?   N S O F A

3. Do you have difficulty discriminating between gray and blue-green?   N S O F A

4. Do you have difficulty discriminating between red and brown?   N S O F A

5. Do you have difficulty discriminating between green and brown?   N S O F A

6. Do you have difficulty discriminating between pale green and pale red?   N S O F A

7. Do you have difficulty discriminating between blue and purple?   N S O F A

8. Do the color names that you use disagree with those that other people use? N S O F A

9. Are the colors of traffic lights difficult to distinguish?   N S O F A

10. Do you tend to confuse colors?   N S O F A

Scoring instructions: Responses are scored 1 for *Never*, 2 for *Seldom*, 3 for *Occasionally*, 4 for *Frequently*, and 5 for *Always*. *Simply add together your scores for the 10 questions. If your score is 17 or higher, you have an 81% likelihood of failing a standard screening test for color vision. If your score is in this range you might want to get your color vision tested by your doctor or in a perception laboratory.*

*The *Color Vision Screening Inventory* is copyrighted by SC Psychological Enterprises Ltd., and is reprinted here with permission.

(1987, 1988) to develop a simple questionnaire that assesses whether individuals are likely to be color blind. You can test yourself with this questionnaire using Demonstration Box 5-2.

Physiological Basis of Trichromatic Theory

Although the data from color mixing and color defects seem to support a trichromatic theory of color vision, direct physiological evidence for the three cone pigments did not appear until the 1960s. The measurement procedure involved is conceptually simple but technically quite difficult (Brown & Wald, 1964; Marks, Dobelle & MacNichol, 1964; Bowmaker & Dartnell, 1980). It involves a device called a **microspectrophotometer.** With this device a narrow beam of monochromatic light is focused on the pigment-bearing outer segment of a cone. As tiny amounts of light of various wavelengths are passed through the cone, the amount of light absorbed at each wavelength is measured. The more light of a given wavelength that is absorbed by the cone pigment, the more sensitive the cone is to light of that particular wavelength. Such measurements were taken using cones from the retina of goldfish, monkeys, and finally from humans.

Although researchers are still refining the detailed description of the cone pigments (for example, MacNichol, 1986), the general pattern of the results is clear. There are three major groups of cones. A typical set of measurements, taken from a human eye that had to be surgically removed (Bowmaker & Dartnall, 1980), shows maximum absorptions in the ranges of 420, 534, and 564 nm, respectively. Figure 5-13 shows the relative absorption of these three pigments (where 1.00 is the maximum amount absorbed by the pigment). Clearly, on the basis of sensitivity peaks, we should call the short-wavelength-absorbing pigment "violet," the middle "yellow-green," and the long

"orange" if we wish to be more precise than using the traditional blue, green, and red labels. Also shown in Figure 5-13 is the relative sensitivity function for the rods in this same eye. These receptors have a maximum absorption of 498 nm when measured with the same technique.

Rushton (1962, 1965) introduced a similar technique measuring the photopigments in living human observers without a microspectrophotometer. First he sent a beam of light into the eye and took measurements on the amount of light reflected back out of the eye. By taking the difference between the amount of light sent and the amount reflected, he obtained an estimate of the amount of light at each wavelength absorbed by the photopigments in the intact human eye. Next he flooded the eye with light of a particular distribution. Thus, red light might be expected to activate the long-wavelength-catching pigment most strongly; hence it would, with continued exposure, be "bleached out." When he remeasured the amount of light absorbed at each wavelength, the difference between light reflected

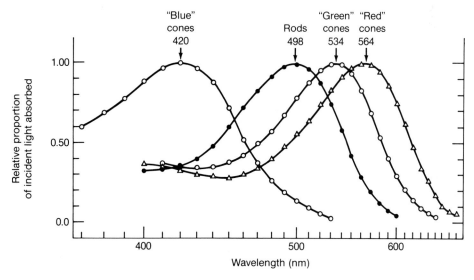

Figure 5-13 *The relative absorption of various wavelengths of light by the three different cone types and the rods of a human (based on Bowmaker & Dartnall, 1980).*

back by the "bleached" and "unbleached" retinas gave absorption curves similar to those shown in Figure 5-13 for pigments marked "red" and "green" in the fovea.

Rushton reasoned further that protanopes and deuteranopes, according to trichromatic theory, should be missing one or the other of the two longer wavelength pigments. When he used his procedure with color-defective observers, he found that they were missing the appropriate pigments. The receptors were physically there, since the density of cones is the same for normal and color defective individuals (Cicerone & Nerger, 1989), but the pigments seemed to be absent.

Rushton could not find evidence for cones containing blue-matching pigment in the fovea, which suggests that all observers are dichromats, specifically tritanopes, for small targets seen in central vision. This conclusion has been verified using psychophysical techniques as well (Bornstein & Monroe, 1978; Tuck & Long, 1990; Williams, MacLeod, & Hayhoe, 1981). Recent evidence based on destruction of blue cones in the monkey retina by prolonged exposure to short wavelength light has confirmed that no blue cones are present in a circular region 25 minutes of arc in diameter in the central fovea (for example, Sperling, 1986).

The relative rarity of blue cones probably also explains why blue contributes less than red or green to many aspects of the visual process (for example, Kaiser & Boynton, 1985).

Because the cones are differentially distributed across the retina (for example, Sperling, 1986), color response is different over different portions of the eye. The central foveal region is relatively blue-blind, and the ability to discriminate blue light first increases and then decreases with increasing distance from the fovea. The ability to see green diminishes with increasing distance from the fovea and disappears at about 40 degrees from the fovea. A similar pattern holds for the ability to discern red and yellow light, with color perception disappearing in the order green, red, yellow, and blue as distance from the fovea increases. In the far periphery of the retina, we are totally color-blind. The exact distance, however, depends on the size of the stimulus—we can discriminate the colors of larger stimuli farther out on the peripheral retina (Johnson, 1986). To see how your own color discrimination varies across the retina, try Demonstration Box 5-3.

We have already mentioned that color responses may differ among normal observers. Some of these differences are large enough to

---

DEMONSTRATION BOX 5-3   Color-Sensitive Zones on the Retina

Color perception is best in the central region of the retina (excluding the small central region of the fovea, which is blue-blind). You can observe the changes in color discrimination for different parts of the retina by taking a small orange piece of paper and placing it on a gray surface. Keeping your head fixed, look off to the side of the orange target. If you keep moving your eyes outward (away from the target), you stimulate more peripheral parts of the retina. Eventually you will reach a point where the orange will look yellowish, meaning that you have now imaged it beyond the red-sensitive zone. If you continue moving your eyes outward you may even hit a point where the orange no longer looks colored at all, but merely appears gray. Your eye will have to move farther to get these changes in color appearance if the orange patch is larger (see Johnson, 1986).

suggest that systematic differences may exist in cone photopigments between individuals (Alpern, 1979). One study involving 200 observers discovered that color-normal males are separated into two different types, based on color-matching tests involving red light (Neitz & Jacobs, 1986). Color-normal females were all similar in their color-matching behavior, but different from either of the two male types. The genetic basis for this variation is now understood. Using the techniques of molecular genetics, Nathans and his colleagues (Nathans, 1987; Nathans, Piantanida, Eddy, Shows, & Hogness, 1986) have identified the location and molecular structure of at least three genes on the X chromosome that determine the photopigments of the red-light cones. The distinctive genes responsible for the different photopigments are *autosomal recessive*, meaning that they are not usually expressed in females (females have two X chromosomes, so a gene that might cause a distinctive variation of the photopigment on one chromosome is usually blocked by the corresponding, more typical, gene on the other). However, the pattern is quite different for males. Since males have only one X chromosome, if that X chromosome carries a gene for the distinctive red photopigment, it will usually be created. This is similar to the explanation for why more males than females have color vision deficiencies.

Opponent-Process Theory

The German physiologist Ewald Hering (1878–1964) was not completely satisfied with a trichromatic theory of color vision. It seemed to him that human observers acted as if there were four, rather than three, primary colors. For instance, when observers are presented with a large number of color samples, and are asked to pick out those that appear to be *pure* (defined as not showing any trace of being a mixture of colors), they tend to pick out four

colors. These unique colors almost always include a red, a green, and a blue, as trichromatic theory predicts (Fuld, Wooten, & Whalen, 1981); however, they also include a yellow (Bornstein, 1973).

Boynton & Gordon (1965) showed that with the color names red, yellow, green, and blue, English-speaking observers can categorize the entire range of visible hues (some stimuli seem to require a combination term containing two primaries, such as yellow-green). The way adult observers distribute their hue names is shown in Figure 5-14, which indicates four overlapping hue-name categories corresponding to red, yellow, green, and blue. These results cannot be attributed simply to learning or language use. For example, Bornstein, Kessen, and Weiskopf (1976) showed that 4-month-old infants tend to see the spectrum as if it were divided into four hue categories. The investigators discovered this fact by repeatedly presenting a given wavelength of a light until the infants became visually bored and stopped looking at the light (a process called **habituation**). They next monitored how much time an infant spent looking at a second wavelength of light. They found that when the second wavelength was selected from another hue-name category (based on the adult data), the infants spent more time looking at it than they did at a wavelength selected from the

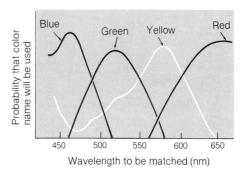

Figure 5-14   The relationship between color names and wavelengths.

same hue-name category. The infants acted as if stimuli in the same hue category were more similar than those from different categories; hence it seems they were categorizing hues into the same four groups that adults do.

Hering looked at another aspect of the subjective experience of hue. He noted that certain color combinations are never reported by observers, for instance, a yellowish-blue or a greenish-red. This led Hering to suggest hypothetical neural processes in which the four primaries were arranged in opposing pairs. One **opponent process,** would signal the presence of red or green, and a separate pair would signal blue or yellow. An example of such a process would be a neuron whose activity rate increased with the presence of one color (red) and decreased in the presence of its opponent color (green). Since the cell's activity cannot increase and decrease simultaneously, one could never have a reddish-green. A different "*opponent-process*" cell might respond similarly to blue and yellow. A third unit was suggested to account for brightness perception. This was called a *black-white opponent-process,* after the fact that black and white are treated psychologically as if they were "pure colors" (see Quinn, Wooten, & Ludman, 1985). But we need not limit the discussion to speculation based on color appearances alone since physiological evidence exists that bears directly on the issue of opponent-process coding of color information.

Physiological Basis of Opponent-Process Theory

When Hering first suggested an opponent-process mechanism for the neural encoding of hue information, no physiological evidence existed to support such a speculation. Perhaps the single most important finding of 20th-century sensory physiology was that neural responses are subject to both excitatory and in-hibitory influences caused by interaction between neighboring units. We introduced several such systems in Chapters 3 and 4. In fact, in Chapter 4 you saw that many brightness phenomena can be explained by the presence of a *spatially* opponent mechanism on the retina, where excitation in one region might cause inhibition in another. If we could also find *spectrally* opponent organization, where stimulation by one wavelength of light causes excitation in a cell, and stimulation by a wavelength in another region of the spectrum causes inhibition of that cell's neural response, then we would have a physiological unit that corresponds to the mechanism postulated by Hering.

The first evidence that different wavelengths of light could cause opponent effects in neural response was offered by Svaetichin (1956), who inserted an electrode into the cell layers of the retina of the goldfish. When he recorded the responses to light transmitted by the horizontal cells (units at the first cellular layer beyond the cones, as noted in Chapter 3), he found that responses varied depending on the wavelength of the light reaching the cones. These neural responses were not in the form of the typical action potential found in most neurons, but rather were graded shifts in the electrical polarization of the cells. Svaetichin found not only that the strength of response varied as the wavelength changed, but also, more importantly, that the electrical sign of the response was different for long and short wavelengths.

Figure 5-15 shows the pattern of responses recorded by Svaetichin & MacNicol (1958). Notice that the spectral sensitivities of the first two units are exactly what we would need for a blue-yellow cell and a red-green cell. For instance, the cell marked *red-green* would respond with a large positive signal if the unit is stimulated with a long-wavelength light (around 675 nm). This positive response could signal red. If the unit is stimulated with a greenish hue (around 500 nm), it would give its

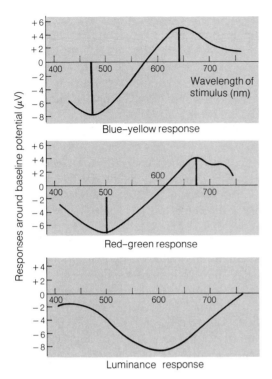

Figure 5-15 *Graded response of retinal cells to various wavelengths of light (based on Svaetichin & MacNicol, 1958).*

peak negative response, thus signaling the presence of green. If we simultaneously stimulated this unit with both a red and a green stimulus, the positive and negative responses would cancel each other and no signal would result. Thus, red and green oppose each other, and the same unit can never simultaneously signal both red and green. Such graded potentials are usually called **S potentials** after their discoverer, Svaetichin. The cells that give these responses are called *C-type* horizontal cells (where the *C* stands for *color*). Also notice that another form of cellular response is shown in the figure; it is marked *luminance*. This type of cell responds to the intensity of the light regardless of the wavelength. These *L-type* horizontal cells could be the basis of the black-white response hypothesized by Hering.

When we reach the level of the retinal ganglion cells, there is clearly an opponent-process coding; however, there is also a spatial distribution to these responses (Boynton, 1979; De Monasterio, 1978). The general form of this encoding involves the center-surround organization of receptive fields we discussed in Chapter 3. Suppose we shine a tiny red spot on the eye while recording from a retinal ganglion cell. In some cases, as the size of the spot increases, the vigorousness of the neural response increases up to some point. After that, further increases in the size of the red spot have no further influence on the cell's response. Notice that this is very different from the type of response seen when white light is used (as in Chapters 3 and 4), where increasing the size of the spot starts to produce a reduction of response rate as it begins to enter the inhibitory region of the receptive field. If we repeat the experiment with a green spot, we find that the cell appears unresponsive when the green spot is in the center of the receptive field; however, as the spot becomes larger, or is moved into the surround field, the resting level of activity is reduced. Thus, we have a cell that has the property of being excited by red and inhibited by green, if the stimulus is the appropriate size and in the appropriate location on the retina. Of course, an equal number of cells with the opposite organization (green excitatory center, red inhibitory surround), as well as cells in which the centers are inhibitory and the surrounds are excitatory, are also found. The visual system, having come upon a particular organizational scheme, seems to like to exhaust all combinations (see Gouras & Zrenner, 1981; Jacobs, 1986).

Further along in the visual system at the lateral geniculate nucleus, this particular arrangement can easily produce cells that generate a spectrally opponent signal with appropriate stimulus arrangements. DeValois and his co-workers (DeValois & DeValois, 1980) found that cells in the lateral geniculate of monkeys were also color-coded, similar to the color-coded retinal ganglion cells. These units showed a resting level of activity (in terms of neural responses per unit time) even in the absence of any light stimulation. When the eye was stimulated by large spots of light, the response pattern changed. Some cells responded more vigorously when the eye was stimulated with short wavelengths of light and decreased their response rate below their spontaneous (dark) activity level for long wavelengths of light. Other cells acted in an opposite manner. As with the S potentials, two different classes of cells were reported. Each had different patterns of response as a function of wavelength, similar to what is needed for a red-green and a blue-yellow cell. Since the lateral geniculate receives its input directly from the retinal ganglion cells, this is exactly the pattern of results

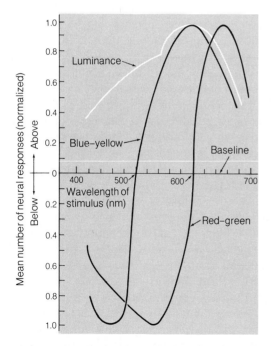

Figure 5-16 *The neural response rate for cells in the lateral geniculate relative to their resting response rate, for stimulation by lights of different wavelengths (based on DeValois & DeValois, 1975).*

that we would expect. Thus, returning to our example, if we have a red excitatory center in a receptive field, we should get increased response for a large-area red light, whereas the green inhibitory surround would completely ignore its presence. Conversely, a large green spot would cause an inhibitory response and be ignored by the red excitatory center, and so forth.

Typical responses from lateral geniculate cells can be seen in Figure 5-16. There are three cell types. One responds differentially to short and moderately long wavelengths (blue-yellow), one responds differentially to moderately short and long wavelengths (red-green), and one does not show different opponent processing, but rather responds simply to the amount of luminance reaching the eye. The spectrally tuned cells code both chromatic and spatial information in the responses. This means that whether a given wavelength will produce an increase or a decrease in neural response may also vary as the spatial position of the stimulus spot is varied within the receptive field of the cell.

How can a four-primary, opponent-process (or "push-pull") system exist when we already have provided physiological and psychophysical evidence indicating that the retina operates with a three-color pigment system? Hurvich and Jameson (1974) suggested a *neural wiring diagram* that indicates the way in which cones, each containing only one of three pigments, could produce opponent responses at the postretinal level. An example of such a diagram is shown in Figure 5-17. It requires only that certain cones excite cells further along in the system, and that other cones inhibit the response rates of those cells. Engineers hit on a similar system when they designed color television transmission. The color in the original scene is first analyzed into its red, green, and blue components by the camera, and then transformed into two color-difference (or opponent-process) signals (plus an intensity

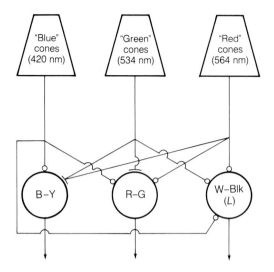

Figure 5-17 *Schematic diagram indicating how a three-pigment system might be connected to produce opponent-process neural responses. The lines represent the connections. The round and the flat connections differ in that one is excitatory and the other is inhibitory (which is arbitrary). Numbers indicate the wavelength of maximum sensitivity.*

signal). After reception, the signals are reconverted into red, green, and blue signals by the television set. This technique was selected because it required considerably less information to be transmitted through each channel, thus providing good fidelity and increased economy. Perhaps similar considerations of economy and fidelity underlie the organization of our visual systems.

Color Channels and Cortical Coding

A recent explosion of knowledge has occurred about how color information is encoded in the nervous system. Let us begin with the lateral geniculate, where the opponent-process color cells are found. As we indicated in Chapter 3, the lateral geniculate is composed of six well-defined layers (three receiving input from each eye). These layers can be subdivided on the

basis of the size of the cells in each. The upper four tiers are small cells and hence are called the *parvocellular* layers (from the Latin stem *parv*, meaning "small"), as opposed to the bottom two tiers, which are called the *magnocellular* layers (from the Latin *magno*, meaning "large").

The opponent color cells, which actually make up about 90% of the cells in the geniculostriate system, seem to be concentrated in the four parvocellular layers (Schiller & Logothetis, 1990). This has led to the speculation that we are dealing with two separate channels of visual information processing: the **parvocellular channel,** which carries color information, and the **magnocellular channel,** which carries brightness information (Livingstone & Hubel, 1988; Shapley, 1990). This is a bit of an oversimplification, since these two visual systems also differ in the way they contribute to the perception of form, motion, and depth (Lennie, Trevarthen, Waessle, & Van Essen, 1990). In addition, the magnocellular system, which is most concerned with brightness, is not completely insensitive to all aspects of color (Lennie et al., 1990; Shapley & Kaplan, 1989).

The separation of the color and brightness channels continues through the cortex. New physiological techniques have allowed us to study the organization of color processing in the brain. One technique involves a special stain or dye that reveals the presence of an enzyme (cytochrome oxidase) involved in the metabolic activity of a neural cell (Wong-Riley, 1979). Use of this stain has shown that activity in the primary visual cortex (V1, or area 17) is not uniform, but rather there are patches of activity, which show up as dark, slightly irregular oval regions, each about 0.20 mm in diameter. These regions (which bear the unsophisticated name of **blobs**) are arranged in a somewhat regular mosaic-like pattern as shown in Figure 5-18. Many investigators believe that the majority of the color-coded cells from the parvocellular channel end up in the blobs (Zrenner

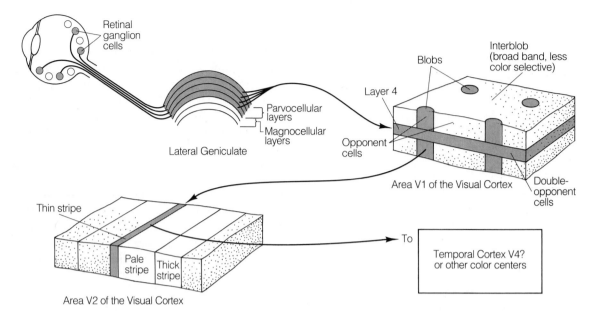

Figure 5-18 *The major color channel in the visual system is part of the parvocellular system, and is shown here, beginning with the eye, passing through the lateral geniculate, and then up through cortical regions V1 and V2.*

et al., 1990) while the regions between the blobs (called **interblob** regions, of course) receive only those parvocellular inputs that are more concerned with brightness; form; motion; and other, less color-coded information (Tootell, Silverman, Hamilton, DeValois, & Switkes, 1988).

If we use an electrode to record from the cells in a cortical blob, we find the usual opponent process that involves an increase in response when the eye is stimulated with some colors and a decrease in response when stimulated with others. Once again, a spatial factor is involved in this response. For example, stimulating the center of the cell's receptive field with red light would cause the cell to increase its activity, whereas stimulating the flanks with green light would cause the cell to decrease its activity. Layer 4 of the cortex contains cells that have a *double* opponent process. This does not mean that such cells are necessarily the result of a combination of two opponent-process

cells, but rather that they act as if two oppositely organized opponent-process cells were occupying the same area. Such a cell might increase its activity when the center of its receptive field is stimulated with red light, but actually decrease its firing when the surround is stimulated with red light. The opposite organization is seen for responses to green light in the same cell, with a green spot on the center of the receptive field producing a decrease in response and a green spot on the surround producing an increase in firing (Michael, 1985). The difference between opponent and double-opponent process cells can be seen in Figure 5-19. The color-only blob regions have mostly circular receptive fields and do not seem to have much orientation specificity. They are not very sensitive to motion processing and have lower visual acuity (compare Shapley, 1990).

The separation of color processing from other processing channels in the visual cortex continues through higher levels, with the color-

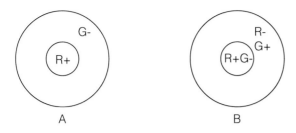

Figure 5-19 *Receptive fields of typical color-opponent* (A) *and double-opponent* (B) *cells, recorded in the cortex.*

weak magnocellular channel ending up in a different place than the less specifically color-coded parvocellular channel. In the secondary visual cortex (V2, or area 18), the organization shifts to "stripes" (this term is again based on the way in which regions accept various stains). The color-only areas concentrate into dark, *thin stripes;* the color-weak magnocellular inputs go into dark, *thick stripes;* and mixed inputs form wide, *pale stripes* (see Figure 5-18).

A number of researchers are investigating how color is processed beyond region V2. One suggestion is that the brain has a specific "color center," specialized for the processing of wavelength differences. Some studies have suggested that such an area exists for the macaque monkey in the temporal lobe of the cortex (known as the fourth cortical visual area, or V4) (Hubel & Livingstone, 1987). Recent studies in humans have used *positron emission tomography* (PET) scans, which measure blood flow in the cerebral cortex (Lueck et al., 1989). These studies suggest that a color processing center is located in the lower hind portion of the occipital cortex (around the lingual gyrus).

Although the evidence for a separate color center remains unconfirmed, the fact that hue and brightness information are processed in separate channels and places in the brain seems quite clear (Shapley, 1990; Zrenner et al., 1990). One striking example of this comes from a case history presented by Heywood, Wilson, and Cowey (1987). They described a traffic accident victim who was injured in the right temporal region of the brain (around where V4 would be in the monkey). After the injury he lost virtually all of his ability to discriminate hues; however, his ability to discriminate on the basis of brightness was left virtually unaffected.

Although our knowledge about the neural coding of colors is increasing some obvious puzzles are still left to be solved. One deals with the appearance of **subjective colors.** These are perceived colors in the absence of the appropriate wavelengths of light, which can be made to appear in certain flickering black-and-white displays (Festinger, Allyn, & White, 1971; Jarvis, 1977; Piggins, Kingham, & Holmes, 1972). The appearance of these colors is, at least on the surface, more consistent with some sort of neural Morse code carrying color information, rather than the spatial opponent-process system that contemporary physiological data seem to support (Young, 1977). Because of this inconsistency, subjective colors remain a puzzle. A procedure for creating subjective colors for yourself is shown in Demonstration Box 5-4. It is interesting to note that people who show color defects for real colors also show the same color defects for subjective colors (White, Lockhead, & Evans, 1977).

COLOR PERCEPTION

Although subjective colors baffle us at the moment, they do demonstrate that the wavelengths of light that are present are not the only factors that determine our perception of hue. A number of factors, such as stimulus intensity and duration, as well as the characteristics of surrounding stimuli, can also alter the perceived color.

DEMONSTRATION BOX 5-4   Subjective Colors

You have already encountered subjective colors in Demonstration Box 1-2, where colors appeared in a stationary stimulus. A more powerful set of subjective colors, produced by flickering black-and-white patterns, began as a toy invented by C. E. Benham in 1894. It was painted on a top and meant to be spun; hence the pattern is often referred to as **Benham's top.** The pattern is shown in the figure. Cut out this pattern (or carefully reproduce it), and mount it on a piece of thin cardboard. Punch a hole in the marked center region and insert a nail or a round pencil. Now spin the pattern as shown. Colors should appear when the pattern is spun at a moderate speed. If you are spinning it clockwise, the inner bands should be slightly red, the next yellow, then green, and the last blue or violet. The order of the colors should reverse if you spin the pattern counterclockwise. The color effects arise because of the specific patterns of flickering white and black set up by each band. These patterns mimic the flashing on-and-off light patterns used to study subjective colors in a laboratory setting.

If you alter the adaptive state of your eye by staring at a white surface for a minute, you will notice that the perceived colors on each line will be different (Karvellas, Pokorny, Smith & Tanczos, 1979).

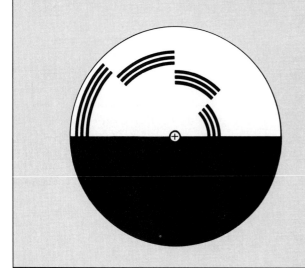

Intensity and Duration

Both physiological and psychophysical evidence now suggest that color and brightness information are carried by different visual channels (Bowen, 1981; Boynton, 1988; Faverau & Cavanagh, 1981). However, it is also clear that the perception of hue may interact with the intensity of the stimulus (for example, Emmerson & Ross, 1986). If intensity levels are low, only rods will be active and no color will be seen. But even beyond the cone threshold, the perceived hue of a stimulus will change depending on the stimulus intensity. Specifically, if we increase the intensity of red or yellow-green stimuli, they not only appear brighter but begin to take on a more yellow hue. Similarly, blue-greens and violets begin to appear bluer when the intensity is increased. This phenomenon is called the **Bezold-Brucke effect,** in honor of its two discoverers. It is quite easy to demonstrate, as is shown in Demonstration Box 5-5. Although the basis of the Bezold-Brucke effect is not yet fully understood, it is clearly neural in origin (Coren & Keith, 1970; Nagy, 1980). This effect may come about because the red-green opponent-process cells are slightly more sensitive than the blue-yellow cells. Thus, we can discriminate between red and green at lower intensity levels. Because the blue-yellow units become more active at higher intensity levels, hues tend to be dominated by these colors when stimuli are bright (Hurvich, 1981).

Prolonged exposure to colored stimuli also produces a shift in the perception of hue. For instance, if you viewed the world through a deep red filter for a sufficient period of time, you would find that when the filter was removed the world would take on a blue-green tint. This fatiguing of a specific color response is called **chromatic adaptation.** Scientists believe that these adaptation effects are due either to selective bleaching of one particular photopigment or to fatigue of one aspect of the neural response of an opponent-process system (for example, Vimal, Pokorny, & Smith, 1987). Suppose you look through a red filter for a long period of time. The red-catching pigment becomes bleached, or the red response in the red-green opponent-process cells become fatigued. Now, when you view a white surface, the absence of red pigment (or the weakness of the red response) causes the blue and green systems to account for a greater proportion of the total activity. This gives the white a cyan (blue-green) tint.

When such fatigue effects due to prolonged stimulation are localized (that is, confined to

---

DEMONSTRATION BOX 5-5   The Bezold-Brucke Effect

For this demonstration you will need three pieces of colored cellophane, glass, or celluloid to serve as color filters. One should be red, the other green, and the last yellow. Take a white sheet of paper that is brightly illuminated with room lighting, and cast a shadow over one-half of the paper. Looking through the red filter, you will notice that the hue of the red seen on the bright half of the paper is noticeably yellower than the hue seen on the shadowed portion. When you peer through the green filter, you should experience the same effect. However, looking through a yellow filter should not cause an apparent change in hue. Thus, the brighter you make a red or a green, the more yellow it will appear. This is a demonstration of the hue shift, associated with increasing stimulus intensity, called the Bezold-Brucke effect.

Another way to see this effect is simply to look at an incandescent light bulb (60–100 W) through the red or green filter. You will notice that the light bulb appears to be yellow, despite the presence of the filter. Since the red filter only allows the long (red) wavelengths of light to pass, and the green only allows the middle (green) wavelengths through, no yellow is reaching your eye. The yellow appearance of the bulb is caused by the Bezold-Brucke hue shift that occurs when the intensity of the stimulus is high.

DEMONSTRATION BOX 5-6   Color Afterimages

You can easily demonstrate negative or complementary color afterimages using Color Plate 6. Here you see four square patches of color: red, green, blue, and yellow. Notice the black *x* in the middle of this pattern. Stare at the black *x* for about 2 minutes while keeping the plate under reasonably bright illumination. At the end of this period, transfer your gaze to the black *x* to the right of the figure. You should see a pattern of colored squares that is the exact complement of the pattern originally viewed. Where the red patch was, you will see green; where the green patch was, you will see red; where the blue patch was, you will see yellow; and where the yellow patch was, you will see blue. These are the complementary color afterimages caused by the fatiguing of the various color responses during the time you were staring at the color patches.

---

one region of the retina), they are called **afterimages.** Demonstration Box 5-6 provides a stimulus for the production of color afterimages. You will notice when performing this demonstration that the hue of the afterimage tends to be a complementary hue of the stimulus producing the afterimage.

Spatial Interactions

In Chapter 4 you learned that the brightness of a stimulus could be affected by the intensity of adjacent stimuli. The general nature of the interaction was inhibitory, so that a bright surround made a central area appear dim. Inhibitory interactions between adjacent color systems can also occur, and these result in hue shifts. This phenomenon is called **simultaneous color contrast.** Consider Color Plate 3. Notice that this figure has four brightly colored patches, each of which surrounds a small central square. The square on the red patch appears to be slightly green, and that on the green appears to be slightly red. The square on the blue patch appears to be slightly yellow, and

that on the yellow patch appears to be slightly blue. However, each square is exactly the same gray. You might be able to increase the strength of this effect by viewing Color Plate 3 through a sheet of tracing paper or thin tissue.

Jameson and Hurvich (1964) suggested that color contrast arises from mechanisms similar to those that cause brightness contrast, namely, an active retinal neuron tends to inhibit the responding of adjacent neurons. In the case of the gray square on the red background, for example, we have a situation where the red response systems exposed to the surround are highly activated. In turn these active neurons will inhibit the red response in the neurons exposed to the central gray patch. Since the red and green responses are usually in balance, inhibition of the red response results in the emergence of the complementary, or opponent, green response in this region. A tinge of green hue is then seen in the gray. As one might expect, if this is truly an inhibitory interaction such as we observed in brightness effects, it should be possible to produce colored Mach bands in stimuli that, instead of varying in brightness as in Figure 4-20, vary in color (for example, from red to green). Ware and Cowan (1987) have demonstrated that such bands take on the colors predicted by simultaneous color contrast.

Contrast-induced colors act very much like real colors in their ability to produce other perceptual effects. For instance, Anstis, Rogers, and Henry (1978) induced very strong contrast colors on surrounded gray patches (as in Color Plate 3) and found that observers developed negative after-images to the contrast colors, just as though they had been viewing real colors.

Age and Physical Condition

An individual may have normal color vision when tested at one stage in the life span, but may show color discrimination defects when tested at a later stage. Although color vision can be reliably measured in 2-month-old infants (Mercer, Courage, & Adams, 1991), the aging process does seem to alter color vision. Perhaps this is because the crystalline lens of the eye grows more yellow as an individual ages; hence we look through a gradually darkening yellow filter (Coren, 1987; Coren & Girgus, 1972a). Other effects, such as the loss of cone pigment with age (Kilbride, Hutman, Fishman, & Read, 1986), may also account for changes in color vision. Generally speaking, aging seems to bring about a faster deterioration of blue vision (Schefrin & Werner, 1990; Verriest, 1974). Most individuals are unaware of such changes because the onset is quite slow; however, the effect gradually accumulates. Since the perception of hue is subjective, you seldom have opportunities to assess whether your hue perception agrees with that of others. Does your red appear to be the same as that of your friends? Clearly, this is an unanswerable question.

Physical conditions can also result in losses in the ability to discriminate colors. Such acquired color vision losses, called **dyschromatopsias,** can be caused by one of several diseases or physical conditions. One typical cause for loss of color vision is exposure to certain solvents and neurotoxins (Braun & Daigneault, 1989; Mergler, Bowler, & Cone, 1990). As in the case of aging, the most commonly observed losses are for sensitivity to blue (see Pokorny & Smith, 1986). Blue losses are observed also in diabetics (Lakowski, Aspinall, & Kinnear, 1972), individuals with glaucoma (Lakowski & Drance, 1979), and alcoholics (Reynolds, 1979). These color losses can be aggravated by a number of factors. For instance, diabetic women who take oral contraceptives show significantly greater discrimination losses in the blue range (Lakowski & Morton, 1977). Acquired problems with the red-green system are rarer and usually are associated with cone degeneration or optic nerve diseases (Pinkers & Marre, 1983).

Cognitive Factors in Color Perception

Although color is a basic sensory experience, certain nonsensory factors also affect the perceived color of an object. In addition, color may interact with other nonperceptual behaviors.

Memory for Color

The remembered color of a familiar object often differs from the object's actual color. When observers are shown color samples and later are asked to match them from an array of colored chips, systematic errors are made. Observers tend to pick chips of greater brightness when asked to remember bright colors and

DEMONSTRATION BOX 5-7   The McCollough Effect

The idea behind this demonstration is that, through repeated exposure to colored lines of a particular orientation, we develop a color aftereffect that is different for lines of different orientation. Some investigators feel that this process comes about because, with continued inspection, the cortical cells that are tuned to a particular combination of stimuli become fatigued. Thus, when we subsequently inspect a set of noncolored stimuli at the same orientation, these cells respond more weakly, which gives us color aftereffects (for example, Houck & Hoffman, 1986). The particular color seen is usually the complement to the fatigued color. Thus, for instance, if you fatigue the green response, normally white light will appear tinged with red; fatigue of the blue response will produce a yellow aftereffect; and so forth.

Several alternate explanations of the McCollough effect have been offered (for example, Day & Webster, 1989; Dodwell & Humphrey, 1990). One interesting possibility is based on learning effects similar to Pavlov's classical conditioning (Allan & Siegel, 1986; Skowbo, 1984; Sloane, Ost, Etheredge, & Henderlite, 1989). In this process the grid of lines serves as the conditioned stimulus (CS) and the color as the unconditioned stimulus (UCS) that produces the unconditioned response (UR—which might be seeing red bars). The pairing over time produces a conditioned color response (CR) that is the opposite of the UR (in this case, seeing green bars) that is evoked when the lined grid is presented by itself. Such a learning mechanism could explain why, under appropriate conditions, the color aftereffect may last for hours, days, or even weeks (Wolfe & O'Connell, 1986)

To see the effect for yourself, first notice that the figure in this box is completely achromatic. Now turn to Color Plate 5 and note the two colored grids, one containing vertical green lines and the other horizontal red lines. To selectively condition your visual system, simply look at the green grid for about 5 seconds, then shift your gaze to the

greater darkness when asked to remember dark colors (Bartleson, 1960; Newhall, Burnham, & Clark, 1957). When asked to remember and match colors of familiar objects with characteristic hues, we remember apples or tomatoes as being more red than the actual objects, bananas as being yellow, and grass as more green. Because of this memory effect, many film manufacturers have chosen to modify the spectral reproduction ability of colored film so the reproduced colors are richer than they are in nature. Since television engineers have not made a similar correction, color memory distortions may account for part of our feeling that the picture on a color television set is an unfaithful reproduction of real color.

Memory color effects tend to creep into certain other matching tasks. For instance, if you are asked to match the color of a Valentine's Day heart or an apple, both of which have been cut out of orange paper, you will match them with a redder hue than you would use to match an oval or a triangle cut out of the same material. A banana-shaped figure, or one labeled *lemon*, is matched with a yellower hue. It seems as if the remembered color blends with

red grid for another 5 seconds. Continue this alternation for about 2 or 3 minutes. Then look back at the figure in this box and you will find that it appears to be colored: The vertical white bars appear reddish and the horizontal bars appear greenish. Notice also that turning the book sideways, or tilting your head so the orientation of the lines changes on your retina, will change the colors of the lines.

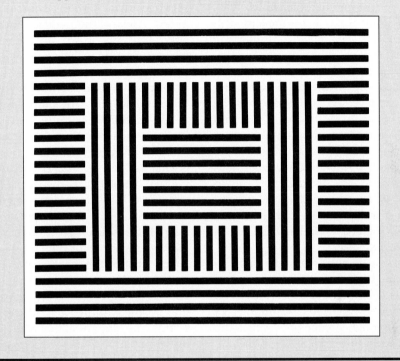

the observed stimulus, altering the percept toward the ideal, or prototypical, color of an object (Bruner, Postman, & Rodrigues, 1951; Delk & Fillenbaum, 1965; Harper, 1953; White & Montgomery, 1976). The color you remember is probably "better" than the color that is present; however, the color you see now may be tinged by hue supplied by your memory.

An interesting color phenomenon that some investigators believe is also caused by a learning or memory type of process, called the *McCollough effect,* is shown in Demonstration Box 5-7.

Culture and Color

As we noted earlier, an English speaker is content to describe hue differences using four basic categories: red, yellow, green, and blue. This is not the case for many other languages, some of which have no separate names for green and blue, or red and yellow. Some languages only distinguish red as a separate color and have no names for the other hues. It is often argued that language and perception interact, and that when separate names for separate sensory experiences exist, these labels make discriminations easier. In other words, the Lakuti tribe, who only have a single term for blue and green, may see the two colors as being more similar to each other than English speakers, who have separate words for these stimuli (Whorf, 1956). The suggestion that different language terms for colors indicate different perceptual abilities has been presented in many different forms. For instance, Robertson (1967) suggested that an evolutionary development has occurred both in the color-perceiving ability of humans and in the color terms encoded in the language. He suggested that the first discriminations were between red and green, and then the discrimination ability for yellow evolved, and finally that for blue. He analyzed a number of ancient languages and found such evolutionary trends. One could conclude from such evidence that the ancient Greeks were relatively weak in their ability to perceive colors because their language had a small set of color names.

Actually, when the ability of individuals to match, discriminate, or reproduce colors (rather than just to name colors) is measured directly, the picture changes. The number of color names in a language does *not* affect the ability to make such discriminations (Berlin & Kay, 1969; Bornstein, 1973; Bornstein, 1975). These findings indicate the danger, in the absence of perceptual measurements, of assuming that language usage directly reflects perceptual abilities.

Color Impressions

Color does more than provide us with additional information about stimuli; it also has emotional consequences (Hamid & Newport, 1989). It delights and depresses. It makes us feel warm or cold, tense or relaxed. For in-

stance, a manufacturer of detergent found that the color of the detergent box made a difference in how the user evaluated the strength of the detergent (Kupchella, 1976). Other data suggest that the color of pills or drug capsules may affect whether patients will take prescribed medications (Coffield & Buckalew, 1988). Apparently medications that are black, gray, tan, or brown are rejected, whereas, blues, reds, and yellows are readily accepted.

Color can even produce sensory impressions characteristic of other senses. It is almost universal to call the short-wavelength (blue) colors "cool," whereas the longer wavelengths (yellow) tend to be called "warm." Perhaps these labels arise because the cool of the night is first broken by the red of the dawn, with midday characterized by the yellow of sunlight and warmth. As the yellow begins to disappear and the blue of twilight begins to predominate, temperatures again grow cool. Many years and many generations of such an association might stamp this warm–cool relationship into our languages. In an era when the conservation of energy is important, it is interesting to note that people will turn a heat control to a higher setting in a blue room than they will in a yellow room. It is as if they are trying to compensate thermally for the coolness that has been visually induced (Boynton, 1971). Similarly, Alexander and Shansky (1976) showed that dark saturated colors are perceived as being associated with a greater sensation of "weight" or "heaviness." There is even some suggestion that the color of a substance can affect how it appears to smell to us (Zellner & Kautz, 1990). All these findings emphasize that color is a psychological achievement, not simply a direct effect of the physical variation of wavelengths of light. If you still doubt this statement, try turning back to Demonstration Box 1-3 (p. 10) or 5-4 to see colors develop in your mind where no physical variations in wavelength exist.

Isaac Newton and his assistant discover saturated colors

GLOSSARY

The following definitions are specific to their use in this book.

Additive color mixture A color mixture resulting from the addition of light of one wavelength to light of another, for example, projection of a blue light on top of a red light on a screen to produce magenta.

Afterimage A visual sensation that appears after an intense or prolonged exposure to a stimulus.

Anomalous trichromatism A defect in color vision in which color matches made by an individual are systematically different from normal, although the three primary color systems are still functioning.

Benham's top A black-and-white pattern that when rotated produces subjective colors.

Bezold-Brucke effect The shift in the apparent hue of a color as the intensity is changed.

Blobs   Dark, regularly spaced oval patches in the primary visual cortex (V1) that are identified by metabolic-sensitive dyes. Cells in *blob* regions are believed to process only color information from the parvocellular channel.

Brightness   The psychological impression of light intensity.

Chlorolabe   Green-sensitive cone pigment.

Chromatic adaptation   A weakened response to a color stimulus due to previous exposure to other chromatic stimuli.

CIE chromaticity space   A variant of the color triangle system, using three imaginary "super" primary colors.

Color atlas   A book in which each page represents a horizontal or a vertical slice through the color space.

Color blindness   A condition in which individuals lack the ability to make discriminations on the basis of wavelength of light.

Color circle   *See* Color wheel.

Color solid   *See* Color spindle.

Color spindle   A three-dimensional model in which the relationship between hue, brightness, and saturation are depicted.

Color wheel   A circular scheme in which colors are separated according to hue, with complementary colors placed directly across from each other.

Complementary colors   Colors whose mixture produces an achromatic gray or white.

Cyanolabe   Blue-sensitive cone pigment.

Deuteranomaly   A condition in which an individual's color matches require more green than those of a color-normal individual.

Deuteranopia   A form of color blindness associated with the confusion of reds and greens because of insensitivity in the green system.

Dichromats   Individuals whose color vision is defective, allowing all hues to be matched with two rather than three primaries.

Dominant wavelength   The wavelength of a monochromatic stimulus that best approximates the hue of a color mixture.

Dyschromatopsias   Acquired color vision losses.

Erythrolabe   Red-sensitive cone pigment.

Habituation   The process by which an observer ceases to respond, or reduces the magnitude of a response, to a repeated stimulus.

Hue   The term denoting the psychological attribute most clearly corresponding to wavelength of light and most often termed *color* in common language.

Interblob regions   Areas between the blobs in the primary visual cortex (V1), which process information that is less specifically color-coded than information in the blobs, for example, brightness, form, and motion.

Magnocellular channel   Refers to the information carried from the large cell layers of the lateral geniculate, which is mostly concerned with brightness, motion, form, and depth.

Metameric colors   Colors that appear to be the same but are composed of different wavelengths.

Microspectrophotometer   A device for measuring the amount of each wavelength of light emanating from microscopic target areas.

Monochromatic stimuli   Stimuli that contain only one wavelength of light.

Monochromats   Individuals who see color as simply gradations of intensity, because of the absence of any functioning cones.

Opponent process   A neural process that signals the presence of one color by increasing its activity and of an opposing color by decreasing its activity.

Parvocellular channel   Refers to the information carried to the cortex from the small cell layers of the lateral geniculate. When sent to the blobs in primary visual cortex (V1), this is mostly color information.

Primaries   Three monochromatic light sources that when combined in appropriate amounts can match any other hue.

Protoanomaly   A condition in which an individual's color matches require more red than those of a color-normal individual.

Protanopia   A form of color blindness resulting in the confusion of reds and greens because of insensitivity in the red system.

Purity   A spectrally pure stimulus is composed of only one wavelength, the more wavelengths in a light, the less pure it is.

S potentials   Graded electrical retinal-cell responses that vary in direction and strength depending on the wavelength of the stimulus.

Saturation   The psychological attribute of a color associated with "how much" of a hue is present.

Simultaneous color contrast   A process in which inhibitory interactions between adjacent color systems cause hue shifts.

Spectral colors   Pure monochromatic stimuli, such as those in a prismatic spectrum.

Subjective colors   Colors that are consciously experienced, but not associated with any wavelength change in the physical stimulus.

Subtractive color mixture   A color mixture resulting from the subtraction or absorption of light of various wavelengths, for example, the mixture of yellow and blue pigments to produce green.

Trichromatic theory   The theory that color vision is based on three primary responses.

Tristimulus values   The combination of the stimulus hue (x and y values) and brightness (z value) used in the CIE color system for determining any color stimulus.

Tritanopia   A color defect in which yellows and blues are confused because of reduced blue sensitivity.

Chapter ...

6

THE AUDITORY SYSTEM

Sound

A Simple Sound Wave

The Structure of the Ear

Evolution and Anatomy of the Ear

Physiology of the Human Ear

Mechanical Tuning on the Basilar Membrane

Mechanism of Transduction

Electrical Activity of the Auditory Nerve

The Auditory Pathways

Electrical Activity of the Lower Auditory Centers

The Auditory Cortex

*I*t is one of those strange historical occurrences that, while studying the physiology of the ear in order to help the deaf learn to deal with a world of sound, Alexander Graham Bell developed the telephone. Perhaps the conceptual leap was not all that large, for if the eye is our window to the world, then the ear must be our microphone. Modern scientists are still studying the physiology of the ear, and for some of them the goal is similar: an implanted prosthesis that can make the deaf hear again. In this chapter we will join these researchers in exploring the fascinating journey of sound waves down the ear canal in creating the conscious experience we call sound. In the process we will learn about a receptive device that fills a space of only 2 centimeters, but has more than 1 million moving parts (Hudspeth, 1985).

SOUND

Sound is a form of mechanical pressure. If you have ever attended a rock concert, you probably have felt the mechanical pulsations, especially those from the bass instruments, that cause the floor, the seat, or the air about you to vibrate. You are feeling the results of the movements of air molecules being pushed forward in waves by the cones of the speakers. Think about what happens when the lead guitarist plucks a guitar string, causing a sound. If you were up close you could see the string vibrate, moving rapidly back and forth in space. This movement causes the strand of steel to collide with the air molecules around it. These molecules in turn collide with others, causing air compression as the string moves forward and rarefaction as it moves back. The result is a **wave** of mechanical energy, as shown in Figure 6-1.

Sound waves are alternations of rarefaction and compression of an elastic medium (such as water, air, or walls) in which they travel and are created by rapid movements of a source in me-

chanical contact with this medium. The medium acquires some of the movement energy of the source and transfers it to other locations by means of collisions between the molecules of the medium. Sound waves can be transmitted for great distances, although the individual air molecules simply move back and forth over very small distances. The collisions of molecules, of course, are not perfectly efficient in transferring the original collision energy, so the wave tends to become less intense as it moves farther away from the original source. Consequently, its ability to move or vibrate other objects decreases. Since sound involves the vibration of parts of the medium through which it travels, it cannot pass through a vacuum. The necessity of a medium for the existence of sound waves was demonstrated by Robert Boyle in 1660, when he pumped the air out of a jar and then failed to hear the sounds made by a watch suspended by a thread in the jar.

The speed of sound varies according to the medium in which it travels. The elasticity and density of the medium are important, with sound traveling faster in a denser or more elastic substance where molecules are closer or more strongly connected to each other. Thus the speed of sound is faster in water (about 1360 m/sec) than in air (approximately 340 m/sec). Even at its fastest, the speed of sound is slow compared to that of electromagnetic waves such as light.

A Simple Sound Wave

The simplest sound wave is called *sinusoidal* because the trigonometric sine function describes it mathematically. When we plot the air pressure as it varies over time, we get the wave shown in the lower part of Figure 6-1. The **wavelength** (represented by the Greek letter λ, or *lambda*) is the distance from one peak of the wave to the next, representing a single

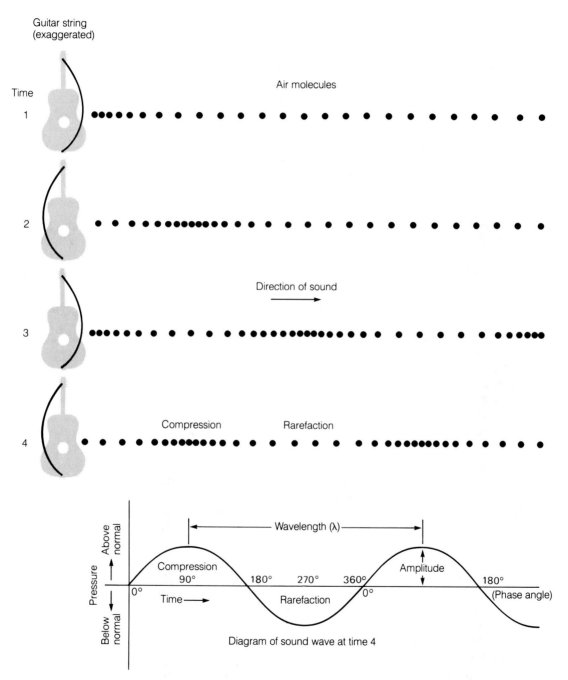

Figure 6–1 *The nature and description of a simple sound wave in air.*

cycle. The **frequency** (f) of the wave, by convention, is the number of cycles the wave is able to complete in one second. The unit used to measure frequency is the **hertz (Hz),** named after the German physicist Heinrich R. Hertz. One hertz is equivalent to one **cycle per second.** The frequency of a simple sound wave is the most important (but not the only) determinant of its pitch. The range of frequencies that seem to have pitch for most people is from about 20 to 20,000 Hz. Sounds below 20 Hz are sensed as vibration, whereas sounds above 20,000 Hz are not heard at all except by young children. Other animals, such as bats or dolphins, can hear frequencies several times as high as the upper limit for humans.

The intensity of a sound wave can be expressed in term of its **pressure amplitude.** This is a measure of compression or rarefaction in the air or other medium at the peaks or valleys of the sound wave. For a sine wave in air, the pressure amplitude is the maximum amount by which the wave causes the pressure (force per unit area expressed as dynes/cm^2) to differ from the normal atmospheric pressure (which is about 1 million dynes/cm^2). The maximum *pressure variation* the ear can tolerate is about 280 dynes/cm^2 above or below atmospheric pressure, whereas the minimum pressure variation detectable by average young adults is about 0.0002 dynes/cm^2. For these threshold-level sound waves, the air molecules are displaced (on average) about 0.0000000001 cm, which is about one-tenth the diameter of an average air molecule. Obviously the ear is an extremely sensitive organ with a broad response range.

In order to express conveniently this wide range of sound sensitivity, we use some special measures. When dealing with sound in terms of energy units, we can speak of the difference between two levels by asking how many powers of 10 (the logarithm) one energy level exceeds another. If one energy level is 1 million times greater than another (10^6 times greater), we

say that it is 6 **bels** greater (a measurement unit named after Alexander Graham Bell). It is more convenient, however, to speak in terms of **sound pressure level (SPL),** which represents the actual force against the ear, than in terms of sound energy. Because of the nature of the mathematical relationship between energy and pressure amplitude, the number of bels is doubled when we speak of ratios of sound pressure levels. Since a bel is a rather large unit relative to normal hearing levels, the unit most commonly used is the **decibel** (dB), which is one-tenth of a bel. The formula for decibels (dB) is

$$\text{Number of dB} = 20 \log (P/P_0)$$

where P is the sound pressure level we wish to express in decibels and P_0 is the standard reference level. The standard reference level is psychologically meaningful since it is near the average value of the threshold for sound (0.0002 dynes/cm^2) measured in young adults at 1000 Hz. Decibels are particularly suited to express the relationships between sound pressure levels, since they compress the large range of possible pressures into more manageable units. Table 6-1 gives typical values of sound pressure levels expressed in decibels for some representative sounds. The table shows that as the measured intensity of a sound increases,

Table 6-1   Sound Pressure Levels (Intensity Levels) of Various Sound Sources

SOURCE	SOUND LEVEL (dB)
Manned spacecraft launch (from 45 m)	180
Loudest rock band on record	160
Pain threshold (approximate)	140
Large jet motor (at 22 m)	120
Loudest human shout on record	111
Heavy auto traffic	100
Conversation (at about 1 m)	60
Quiet office	40
Soft whisper	20
Threshold of hearing	0

subjective loudness also increases. Intensity is the most important (but not the only) determinant of a sound's loudness.

A final important parameter of sound waves is **phase,** which is used in comparing two or more simple waves. *Phase* refers to the particular part of the compression-rarefaction cycle a wave has reached at a particular instant of time. If two waves are at exactly the same place in their respective cycles (so their peaks and valleys coincide), they are said to be **in phase.** If their peaks and valleys do not coincide, the two waves are **out of phase.** How much they are out of phase is expressed in terms of **phase angle.** A single cycle is assigned 360 deg (as in circular motion), usually beginning with 0 deg at a point of no compression or rarefaction, with the first peak pressure being 90 deg (see Figure 6-1). This means that any portion of a cycle can be specified by number of degrees from 0 to 360. If one wave is at its 90-deg point (its peak) when another wave is at its 180-deg point (crossing the zero pressure-difference line), then the two waves are 90 deg out of phase.

Since these waves consist of increases and decreases in mechanical pressure at various moments in time, different sound waves (patterns of pressure) that occur at the same time can interact with each other. If two same-frequency waves are perfectly in phase (0 deg out of phase), their peak and minimum pressures coincide; hence, they add strongly to each other's intensities.When two waves of the same frequency are 180 deg out of phase, one reaches its minimum when the other reaches its maximum and they cancel each other's effects; therefore, we would not be able to hear the interacting sound waves. This principle is used in what is called *active noise suppression* to cancel out unwanted noises. In a typical system a computer analyzes inputs from a microphone and then generates through a speaker sounds that are 180 deg out of phase with the unwanted sounds. They cancel the noise and it

is not heard. Your car may someday have such a noise-suppression system.

Everyday sounds are more complex than the simple sine waves we have been discussing. Only a few sound sources, such as tuning forks or electronic instruments, produce "pure" sine wave sounds. Sounds produced by musical instruments, the human voice, automobiles, waterfalls, and so on, have enormously complex cycles of compression and rarefaction. These complexities result from the interaction of many different waves of different frequencies and phases. Such complex wave forms produce the **timbre** of sounds (see Chapter 7 for a discussion of how this occurs). We can differentiate among the sounds of a trumpet, a clarinet, a piano, and a violin quite easily, because the waveforms they produce, even when they are playing the same musical "note," are quite different (see Figure 6-2). Demonstration Box 6-1 shows you how to experience our extraordinary ability to recognize complex sounds through their timbre.

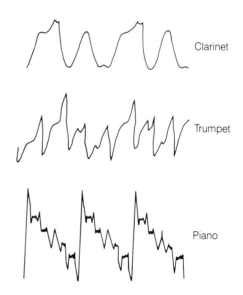

Figure 6–2 Complex sound waves produced by three musical instruments.

DEMONSTRATION BOX 6-1   Perception of Timbre

Perhaps the most primitive musical instrument is the human hand, used (usually in pairs) to clap rhythms. As in any musical instrument, the shape and orientation of the surrounding parts will alter the complex components of the resultant sound, hence the *timbre* that we hear. There seem to be only a few basic ways of clapping, and people have the remarkable ability to distinguish which is occurring from the sound alone (Repp, 1987). Try holding your hands in the configuration shown in part *A* of the figure so that your hands are aligned and flat. Clap a few times, listening closely to the sound. Now hold your hands in configuration *B*, with your hands oblique and slightly cupped. Clap a few times, again listening

closely to the sound. Position *B* generates more low frequency sounds in the mixture than position *A*. You should be able to distinguish the different claps quite clearly. You can also hear differences if the palms are crossed while clapping, or if you clap with your fingers around your palm, and so forth. It might be fun to have someone else now clap while you are not looking, and see if you can approximate what their hand positions are. If you can, you are responding to the timbre of the sounds, and performing some form of analysis of the complex sounds actually present into their constituent components, which then allows you to recognize their source.

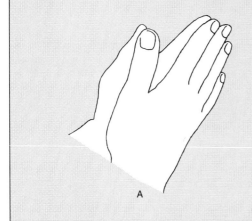

A

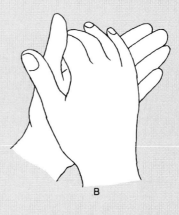

B

Complex sounds, such as those depicted in Figure 6-2, can be described most usefully by analyzing them into sets of simpler sine waves, which when added together would produce the more complicated waveforms. This method was invented by French scientist Jean B. J. Fourier in the course of his studies of heat conduction. Fourier proved a mathematical theorem that states, in essence, that *any* waveform that is continuous and periodic can be represented as the sum of a set of simple sine waves with appropriate wavelengths, phases, and amplitudes. Figure 6-3 shows an example of the decomposition of a complex wave form into such a set of sine waves, called **fourier components.** Speech sounds may also be analyzed

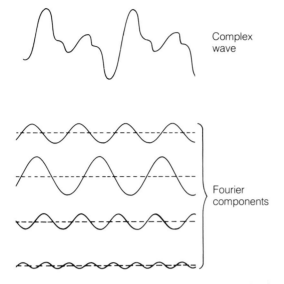

Figure 6–3 *Fourier components (sine waves) of a complex sound wave.*

into Fourier components, with results that are very useful for the understanding of speech perception (see Chapter 12). The ear itself acts as a sound analyzer, decomposing complex sounds into their individual components. This fact is known as **Ohm's acoustical law** after physicist George Ohm. You may demonstrate this effect for yourself using Demonstration Box 6-2.

THE STRUCTURE OF THE EAR

Evolution and Anatomy of the Ear

The human ear is a complex piece of biological engineering, yet biologists have traced its origins to simple organs in quite primitive animals (Stebbins, 1980; Bergeijk, 1967). All vertebrate ears seem to have evolved from the sense of touch. Whether primitive or advanced, they seem to be specializations of groups of cells with protruding hairs, much like those found on the skin of your arm. In fact, we can use the skin to demonstrate several phenomena associated with human hearing (Bekesy, 1960).

One of the first steps in the evolution of the modern mammalian ear was the *lateral line.* The lateral line is a horizontal linear array of nerve endings in the skin of fish and some amphibians from which protrude jellylike masses in which sensory hairs are embedded. As the water moves or vibrates because of sounds made by prey, predators, or other stimuli,

---

DEMONSTRATION BOX 6-2 Ohm's Acoustical Law

This demonstration is done with a piano or a guitar, but if neither is available use three glasses filled with water to different heights so that they produce a fairly high note, a middle note, and a low note when tapped with a butter knife. Now have some friends strike the high, middle, and low notes simultaneously a few times. Without telling you, have them drop out one note, sounding only two a few times, then put it back in. Notice that it is quite easy to determine which of the three notes was added or subtracted, despite the fact that the chord formed by these notes is quite a complex sound pattern. The individual sounds do not lose their identities, and can be discriminated from the others in the complex sound. With enough practice a person can learn to separate as many as six or seven different components of a complex chord or "clang." The separation of sound components by the auditory system is known as *Ohm's acoustical law.*

these sensory hairs bend, signaling the vibration to the animal's brain. For example, the lateral line system in one Antarctic fish is tuned very precisely to the vibrations made by the plankton it feeds on (Montgomery & MacDonald, 1987).

In addition to the lateral line system, some types of fish have primitive internal ears that work on much the same principles as do human ears. It is believed that these internal ears evolved from a specialized, deeply sunken part of the lateral line system. This part of the lateral line evolved into a primitive **labyrinth,** whose looping passages are filled with fluid. Into the fluid protrude hairs that bend when fluid movements are caused by sounds in the water outside. These hairs send the auditory information to the fish's brain by way of sensory nerves. In many of its elements, this system is quite similar to that found in humans, including the composition of the fluid in the labyrinth.

Mammals, birds, and the crocodilian reptiles have a more complex labyrinth that contains a **cochlea.** The cochlea is a specialized extension of the labyrinth that contains a long membrane covered with sensory cells from which, of course, hairs protrude. Its name (which means "shell") is derived from its coiled snail-shell appearance in mammals.

All mammalian ears have the same basic parts, although they differ somewhat in proportions (with the elephant of course having one of the largest). There are also differences in sensitivity. Bats, dolphins, and dogs have extraordinarily keen hearing over a very wide range of frequencies. The ears of mammals differ from those of birds, reptiles, and fish in that mammalian ears typically have three small bones to transmit vibrations to the labyrinth, rather than the single bone found in these other species. Bekesy (1960), in a series of detailed studies, established that all of these various types of ears function in a similar manner. He was able to link many of the performance differences with those in the physical properties of the ears (such as in the length of the cochlea). Thus, the human ear, with which we will be concerned in the remainder of this chapter, is part of a large family of roughly equivalent organs. This fact makes it possible to extend the results of studies of other mammalian ears to the human auditory system.

Physiology of the Human Ear

We shall now follow a sound wave through the structure of the human ear, and trace the neural pathways to the brain. The ear can be divided into three major parts; the **outer, middle,** and **inner ear.** Figure 6-4 is a schematic representation of the human ear. The most visible part of the outer ear is the **pinna,** which is the fleshy part visible from the outside. Only mammals have pinnae, and they function to channel the sound waves into the **external auditory meatus,** or *ear canal,* and to aid in the localization of sound (see Chapter 7). Some mammals, such as bats and dogs, have highly mobile pinnae that allow them partially to select the direction from which sounds are received.

The sound waves that enter the ear canal are channelled along it until they encounter the **eardrum** (or **tympanum**). The sound pressure at the eardrum is somewhat greater than that in the outside air for frequencies between 2000 and 7000 Hz and between 15,000 and 20,000 Hz because of resonances in the pinna and the ear canal that amplify these frequencies. The eardrum vibrates in resonance with the incoming sound waves, moving back and forth at a high rate for high-frequency sounds and more slowly for low-frequency sounds. As we mentioned when discussing sound, these vibratory movements are quite small. The detailed structure of the ear canal, the eardrum, and the air chambers of the middle ear all

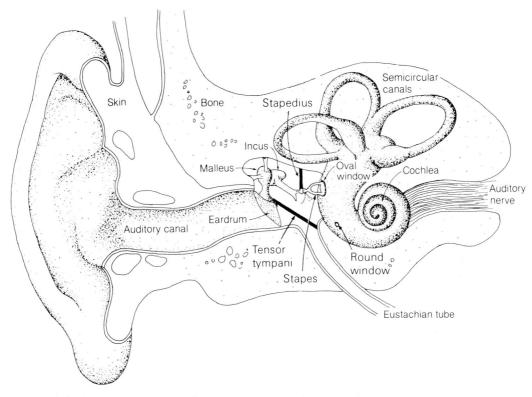

Figure 6–4 *The human ear (based on Lindsay & Norman, 1977).*

play a part in achieving the remarkable performance of the ear in responding efficiently to sounds (Rabbitt, 1990; Stinson & Khanna, 1989).

Beyond the eardrum is the middle ear, where we find a set of three tiny bones (ossicles): The **malleus** ("hammer"), the **incus** ("anvil"), and the **stapes** ("stirrup"). These bones transmit the vibrations of the eardrum to the transducer mechanism located in the inner ear via a small membranous opening called the **oval window.** When these bones fail to conduct sound vibrations for some reason, *conduction deafness* results. This condition can sometimes be relieved by surgery.

When functioning normally, the middle ear acts as an *impedance transformer*, a device that amplifies (or diminishes) the amount of pressure at a surface relative to the pressure applied to the transformer. This is necessary because the eardrum, to which the malleus is attached, is a large, easy-to-move flap of skin (low impedance), whereas the part of the inner ear that must be moved by the stapes, the oval window, is small and difficult to move (high impedance) because it is at the bottom of a long tube filled with fluid. To accomplish the impedance transformation, the middle ear increases the pressure applied to the oval window in three ways (Pickles, 1988). First, and most importantly, the area of the oval window is only about 1/15 that of the vibrating area of the eardrum. Elementary physics tells us that, when the same force is applied to two surfaces of different areas, the result is a greater force per unit area on the smaller surface. Hence this reduction in vibrating area increases the final pressure. The other two impedance-matching mechanisms are more subtle. They depend on the facts that the incus has a smaller lever arm than the malleus and that the eardrum buckles as it moves. These two processes increase the force applied by the stapes to the oval window and decrease the velocity of the oval window's movement relative to that of the eardrum. In total, the pressure at the stapes is increased by a factor of about 30 over that at the eardrum through these properties of the middle ear. The increase in the final pressure serves as a sort of mechanical amplifier and allows us to hear much fainter sounds than would be possible without it.

Another important aspect of the operation of the middle ear is exactly the opposite of amplification. For protective purposes, the arrangement of the middle ear can *decrease* the final pressure at the oval window in order to prevent damage to the ear caused by intense sounds. Sounds from low to moderate intensity cause the stapes to push directly on the fluid in the cochlea. For very intense sounds, however, the angle at which the stapes moves changes, and the force applied by the stapes to the cochlear fluid is greatly reduced. In addition, muscles attached to the malleus (*tensor tympani*) and to the stapes (*stapedius*) contract via neuromuscular reflexes when intense low-frequency sounds strike the ear, stiffening the ossicular chain and again decreasing the force applied at the oval window (see Figure 6-4). These mechanisms help to protect the ear from damage from long-lasting excessive stimulation by loud sounds.

The bones of the middle ear are surrounded by air. The air pressure is kept approximately equal to that of the surrounding atmosphere by means of the **eustachian tube,** which opens into the back of the throat. The equalization of pressure on either side of the eardrum is important, since a pressure differential would cause the membrane to bulge and

stiffen, resulting in less responsiveness of the eardrum to the sound striking it (Rabbitt, 1990). If the eustachian tube were not present, the pressure on the inner side would gradually drop because of absorption of the air by the surrounding tissue. However, the eustachian tubes (one for each ear) open briefly every time we swallow, allowing air to flow into the middle ear cavity from the mouth and lungs. This equalizes the air pressure on both sides of the eardrum. Sometimes, such as when we have a head cold, the eustachian tubes become blocked, and the pressure in the middle ear cannot be equalized to that of the outside air. Also, when we climb to cruising altitude in a commercial jetliner, the cabin pressure may become considerably lower than the pressure within our middle ear at the time of takeoff. Such inequalities in internal versus external air pressure can cause temporary hearing loss and even pain. The eustachian tubes can also be a route by which bacteria can travel to the middle ear and cause infections. This problem, called *otitis media,* often happens when infants or young children get colds, since their eustachian tubes are so short. In otitis media, fluid builds up in the middle ear, causing the eardrum to bulge painfully and sometimes to burst. Timely treatment by antibiotics usually relieves this condition before the symptoms become severe.

We have already noted that the footplate of the stapes rests on the oval window, which serves as the boundary between the middle and inner ear. This is the only place where the inner ear can directly receive sound vibrations. The oval window is at one end of one of the three canals that run the length of the cochlea, as can be seen from Figure 6-5. Two of these, the **vestibular** and the **tympanic canals,** are connected at the apex of the cochlea by an opening called the **helicotrema.** They are filled with a fluid resembling saltwater called *perilymph.* Since this fluid is relatively noncompressible, a point is needed where the pressure

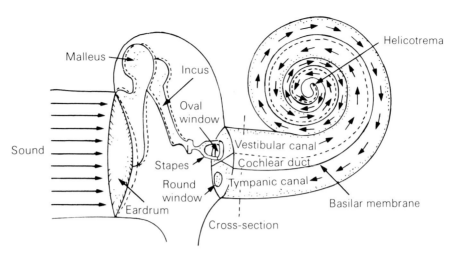

Figure 6–5 Movements of the eardrum in response to sound are transmitted by the ossicles to the fluid in the canals of the coiled cochlea.

from the vibration of the stapes at the oval window can be released. This release point is provided by the **round window,** a membrane at the base of the tympanic canal that opens onto the middle ear. When a movement of the stapes causes the fluid to move away from the oval window, the round window bulges. This indicates that some fluid has been displaced, causing corresponding displacements of the cochlear membranes.

The third canal of the cochlea, the **cochlear duct** or *scala media*), is relatively self-contained. It neither opens to the middle ear nor joins the vestibular or tympanic canals. It is formed by two membranes that run the length of the cochlea: **Reissner's membrane** and the **basilar membrane.** Together they form a rough triangle with the wall of the cochlea (Figure 6-6). The cochlear duct is filled with a different kind of fluid, called *endolymph,* which is more viscous than perilymph and contains many potassium ions. Reissner's membrane is very thin (only two cells thick) and has no function other than to form one wall of the cochlear duct. The basilar membrane is the functionally important one. In humans it is

about 3 cm long, is narrow (0.08 mm) near the base and wider (0.50 mm) at the apex, and is about 100 times stiffer at the base than at the apex. This tapering of the basilar membrane, which is in the opposite direction from that of the cochlea as a whole, is necessary to maintain the efficiency of transfer of energy between the middle and inner ears at low frequencies (Shera & Zweig, 1991). A third membrane within the cochlear duct is also important. The **tectorial membrane** extends into the cochlear duct from Reissner's membrane, and some of the hairs of the **organ of Corti** are embedded in it (Figure 6-7). The organ of Corti is the part of the cochlear duct that accomplishes the final transduction of the mechanical energy of a sound wave into electrochemical energy interpretable by the nervous system.

The organ of Corti rests on the basilar membrane along its entire length. It is composed of about 15,000 cells, which resemble the cells of the skin in that hairs protrude from them. The **tunnel of Corti** separates two sets of hair cells. A single row of about 3000 **inner hair cells** is found on the inner side (the left side in Figure 6-7), and three to five rows of

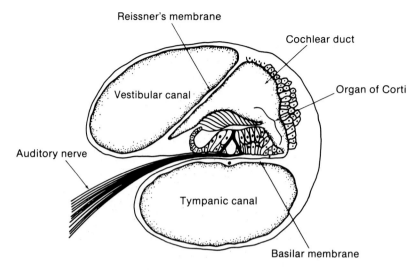

Figure 6–6 *Cross-section of the cochlea, revealing its three canals and the organ of Corti, the auditory receptor.*

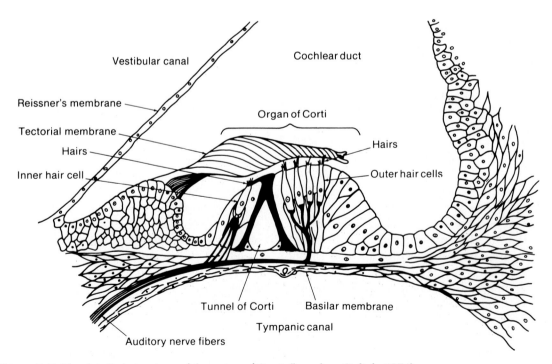

Figure 6–7 *The detailed structure of the organ of Corti (based on Gulick, 1971).*

outer hair cells are located on the outer side. Inner hair cells have about 40–60 hairs each, which extend into the endolymph that fills the cochlear duct, but which apparently do not touch the tectorial membrane (Lim, 1980). Each outer hair cell may have as many as 100–120 hairs protruding from it. The tallest of these hairs are firmly embedded in the tectorial membrane; the shorter hairs apparently do not touch the membrane. The hairs on outer hair cells are arranged in V or W-shaped rows, while those on the inner hair cells form straight rows (Photo 6-1).

In both kinds of hair cells, the graded set of hairs forms a **hair bundle.** Each hair bundle contains hairs that are connected to all of the surrounding hairs by thin filaments of a protein called *actin*. In addition, each shorter hair is connected at its tip to the side of its taller neighbor by another thin actin filament (Photo 6-2; Osborne, Comis, & Pickles, 1988; Pickles,

1988). Thus, all of the hairs in a hair bundle tend to move, or bend, as a unit, and if they bend in the direction toward the longer hairs, the actin filaments at the tips of the shorter hairs will pull on the cell membrane there.

About 30,000 nerve fibers, whose cell bodies are located in the **spiral ganglion,** form connections with the bases of the hair cells of each cochlea. About 95% of them, called **type I fibers,** make single connections with the *inner* hair cells at the same place where the fibers enter the cochlea. There are about 15 fibers per inner hair cell in the middle of the cochlea and about 3 to 4 per inner hair cell at the base and apex (Spoendlin & Schrott, 1989). The remaining 5% of the fibers from the spiral ganglion, called **type II fibers,** each make synaptic contact with about 10 *outer* hair cells located closer to the base than the fibers' point of entry into the cochlea. No individual outer hair cell receives more than about four such contacts

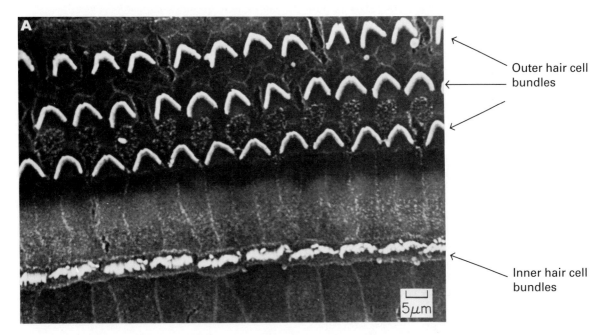

Outer hair cell bundles

Inner hair cell bundles

5μm

Photo 6–1 *Scanning electron micrograph of the organ of Corti from the top with the tectorial membrane removed to expose the hair bundles of the outer and inner hair cells (from Pickles, 1988).*

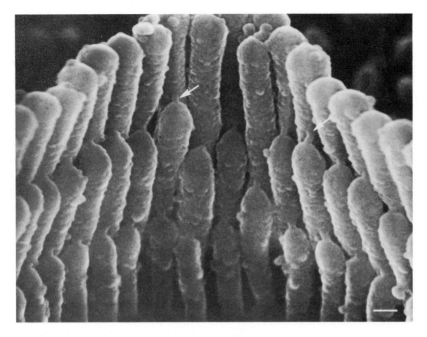

Photo 6–2 *Scanning electron micrograph of an outer hair cell hair bundle, showing the graded sizes of the hairs and the tip links connecting the tips of the shorter hairs to the sides of the taller ones.*

(Spoendlin, 1978). Figure 6-8 shows a general picture of how the fibers of the spiral ganglion cells innervate the cochlea. The type I fibers have a large diameter and are myelinated, whereas the type II fibers are smaller in diameter and are unmyelinated, and hence have slower neural conduction speeds. In addition, the two types of fibers come from ganglion cells that have a noticeably different shape (Kiang, Rho, Northrop, Liberman, & Ryugo, 1982). Given so many structural differences, it is likely these two sets of fibers carry different types of auditory information. One possibility is that information about sounds is carried by the fibers that innervate the inner hair cells, whereas the fibers that innervate the outer hair cells participate in a feedback loop that controls their mechanical properties and thereby modifies the responsiveness of the inner hair cells to sound (see section on "The Auditory Pathways," and Kim, 1985). The axons of these

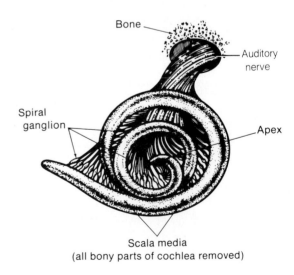

Bone

Auditory nerve

Spiral ganglion

Apex

Scala media
(all bony parts of cochlea removed)

Figure 6–8 *A view of the cochlea with the bone and other covering removed leaving only the soft membrane and neural tissue.*

spiral ganglion cells make up the auditory nerve, which is the neural pathway to the higher auditory centers in the brain.

Actually, the hair cells not only send information to the central nervous system, but they also receive outflow or *efferent innervation* from about 1800 neurons in the superior olive. The outer hair cells receive most of their efferent input from cells in the **superior olive** on the opposite or *contralateral* side of the head, through what is called the **crossed olivo-cochlear bundle.** The inner hair cells receive most of their efferent input from cells in a different part of the superior olive on the same or *ipsilateral* side of the head as the hair cell. These efferent inputs, especially those to the outer hair cells, may be involved in protecting the ear from damage by intense sounds (Puel, Bobbin, & Fallon, 1988), in sharpening the mechanical tuning curves of the basilar membrane (see "The Auditory Pathways"), and in attentional focusing (Pickles, 1988, and Chapter 15).

Mechanical Tuning on the Basilar Membrane

Sound waves cause the bones of the middle ear to vibrate, and the vibration of the last of these bones (the stapes) causes the oval window, and thus the cochlear fluid, to move back and forth at the same frequency. This movement causes pressure differences across the cochlear duct and movements in the basilar membrane, stimulating the sensory cells of the organ of Corti. Two important aspects of the transduction of mechanical energy into electrochemical energy are accomplished here. The first is the movements of the basilar membrane that result in the stimulation of the sensory cells, and the second is the actual transduction mechanism itself. We will discuss each of these in turn.

The movements of the cochlear fluid cause mechanical waves to travel down the basilar membrane from the base (near the oval window) to the apex. Such a wave is really a traveling bend or kink that moves down the length of the membrane, much like the motion when you crack a whip. Figure 6-9 is a schematic drawing of such a wave. The existence of these traveling waves was demonstrated by Georg von Bekesy (for example, 1960), who received the Nobel Prize for his work on the mechanics of the ear. The waves themselves travel very quickly, going from the base to the apex in about 3 msec (Kitzes, Gibson, Rose, & Hind, 1978). Each wave begins in the stiffer, narrower part of the basilar membrane, and travels toward the looser, broader part.

The variations in elasticity and width of the basilar membrane are responsible for the

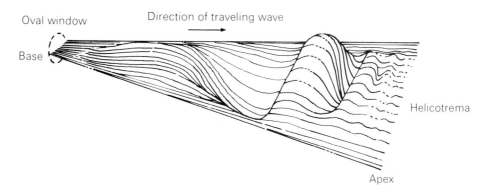

Figure 6–9 A traveling wave on the basilar membrane.

direction and the speed of the traveling wave. They are also mostly responsible for differences in the size or amplitude of the wave. Bekesy demonstrated that the basilar membrane reacts differently to sound stimuli of different frequencies. Although the entire membrane vibrates for any given stimulus, the traveling wave reaches a maximum at a different place along the basilar membrane for each different sound frequency. Traveling waves caused by low-frequency sounds grow steadily in size as they travel toward the apex of the membrane, and they do not reach a maximum until they arrive at a place near the apex. High-frequency sounds, however, cause traveling waves that reach their maximum near the base of the basilar membrane and then quickly dissipate, causing little deformation of the membrane near the apex. This is shown in Figure 6-10, which displays the amplitude of the traveling wave at different places along the basilar membrane for pure tones of three different frequencies (see also Greenwood, 1990). This characteristic action of the basilar membrane in response to sound allows us to discriminate among tones of different frequencies and also provides a basis for the isolation of particular frequency components in more complex sounds. Demonstration Box 6-3 shows a way to demonstrate the differences in the ability of sounds of low and high frequencies to travel down a membrane.

Modern measurements of the response of the basilar membrane have demonstrated that it is very sharply tuned to the frequency of the stimulating sound (Sellick, Patuzzi, & Johnstone, 1982), as indicated by the sharply peaked curves shown in Figure 6-10. It has been argued that variations in the stiffness and thickness of the basilar membrane along its length are not sufficient to explain these very sharp mechanical tuning curves (see Pickles, 1988). One alternative possibility is that an **active process** sharpens the mechanical tuning of the basilar membrane. Figure 6-11 illustrates how this process might work by adding energy to the wave just before it peaks, thereby raising the peak and making the drop off after the peak even sharper. Most models of this process involve the outer hair cells actively pushing against the tectorial membrane (for example, Geisler, 1991; Kim, 1985; Reuter & Zenner, 1990) or in other ways altering the response of the basilar membrane to the pressure waves in the cochlear canals (Zwicker, 1986). It is also possible that the stiffness of the outer

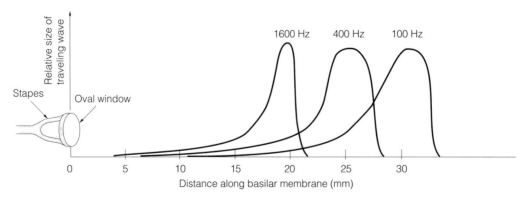

Figure 6–10 A graph of the relative sizes of traveling waves along the basilar membrane for three different frequencies of tone. Notice that as the frequency increases, the waves reach their maxima nearer the oval window and stapes (base).

DEMONSTRATION BOX 6-3   The Skin As a Model for the Basilar Membrane

The basilar membrane is set into vibration by incoming sound stimuli. How the membrane vibrates, however, depends on the frequency of the sound input. Low frequencies tend to cause vibrations of significant magnitude along the entire length of the membrane; high frequencies cause vibrations that are significant only near the base. You can easily demonstrate the frequency-specific nature of the vibration by using your finger as a model of the basilar membrane, since skin has about the same resiliency and elasticity. Place your finger in your mouth, resting your finger tip firmly against the front of your teeth. Now make a loud low sound (try to imitate the low sound of a foghorn), and notice that your entire finger seems to vibrate, perhaps all the way down to the knuckle at its base. Next make a high-pitched sound (try to imitate the whistling of a teakettle or the test tone on a TV station that has ended the day's broadcasting). Notice that the feeling of vibration covers only a tiny region, perhaps your fingertip, or down to the first joint. In a similar fashion, lower sound frequencies induce waves that extend over the length of the basilar membrane, whereas higher frequency waves are restricted spatially in their effects.

---

hair cells allows them to suppress the motion of the basilar membrane on the basal side of the peak, which could produce a similar effect on the sharpness of the tuning (Kolston, 1988). Both of these models depend on some form of efferent innervation of the outer hair cells that induces a modification of their mechanical action on the basilar membrane (Kim, 1985; Pickles, 1988).

One of the most startling manifestations of mechanical activity in the cochlea is the finding that sounds are actually *emitted* by the ear, and that these can be picked up by sensitive microphones inserted into the auditory canal (Kemp, 1978). Some of these **otoacoustic emissions** occur spontaneously, whereas others occur after sound input. One type is called *distortion product emissions*. These are thought to be the result of the inability of the basilar membrane to respond perfectly to two sounds at once. The frequency of the emitted sound can be predicted directly from the sounds presented to the ear. For two stimulus tones at different frequencies, the frequency of the distortion tone is always equal to twice the frequency of the lower tone (in Hz) minus the higher frequency. For example, for two simultaneous tones of 1000 and 1200 Hz, a distortion product at 800 Hz ($2 \times 1000 - 1200 = 800$) would be emitted. Otoacoustic emissions can be fairly intense (over 20 dB), and they differ depending on the average frequency of the two tones (Lonsbury-Martin, Harris, Stagner, Hawkins, & Martin, 1990). Figure 6-12 shows an example of an *audiogram* of the distortion product emissions recorded from a human ear. The variations in the intensity of these emissions with the average frequency of the input tones probably reflect the details of the mechanics of the basilar membrane and perhaps even how well parts of the cochlea are functioning.

Spontaneous otoacoustic emissions (which do not result from the input of tones) are probably indications of the active process that amplifies the traveling waves. An interesting

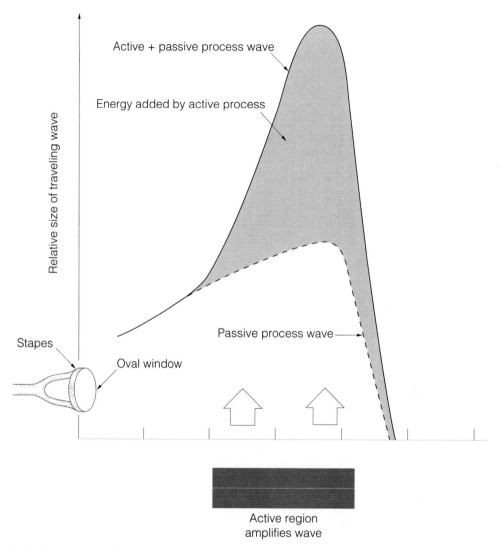

Figure 6–11 *Illustration of how the active process in the organ of Corti might sharpen mechanical tuning curves by amplifying traveling waves just before their peaks (based on Pickles, 1988).*

demonstration of this comes from the fact that the common drug aspirin is known to affect outer hair cell activity. Also, aspirin eliminates spontaneous emissions but not distortion product emissions in monkeys (Martin, Lonsbury-Martin, Probst, & Coats, 1988) and humans (Wier, Pasanen, & McFadden, 1988). This is probably because aspirin decreases the activity of the outer hair cells that cause spontaneous emissions. Such activity is closely related to the mechanisms proposed for the active process that is supposed to sharpen the traveling wave peaks (compare Talmadge, Tubis, Wit, & Long, 1991; van Dijk & Wit, 1990).

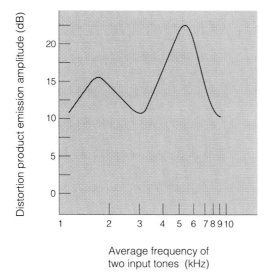

Figure 6–12 An acoustic emission audiogram showing the intensity of the sound emitted from the ear in response to stimulation by pure tone pairs of various average frequencies (based on Lonsbury-Martin, Harris, Stagner, Hawkins, & Martin, 1990).

Mechanism of Transduction

We have been discussing the ear as if it were a purely mechanical device. The organ of Corti, which rests on the basilar membrane, is the site of the transduction of sound energy from its mechanical form to the electrochemical energy needed for communication within the nervous system (see Appendix). The movements of the basilar membrane described earlier cause the basilar membrane and the tectorial membrane to move sideways with respect to one another. Since the outer hair cells are attached at their base to structures connected to the basilar membrane, and the longest of their hairs are embedded in the tectorial membrane, this results in a shearing force that causes these hairs to bend. The inner hair cell hairs are probably bent in a different way, most likely by the flow of the viscous fluid (en-

dolymph) in the cochlear duct caused by the movements of the basilar membrane (Dallos, 1978; Freeman & Weiss, 1990; Raftenberg, 1990). Although this seems to be a less efficient way of producing bending, there appear to be no differences in the absolute sensitivities of the inner and outer hair cells (Dallos, Santos-Sacchi, & Flock, 1982).

The mechanism by which the bending of hairs is transduced into electrical changes in the hair cells is thought to involve the *actin fibers* that link the tips of shorter hairs to their longer neighbors (Hudspeth, 1985; Pickles, Comis, & Osborne, 1984). Figure 6-13 illustrates what probably occurs. As shown in the figure, the tip of each shorter hair seems to have a pore that functions like a little "trap door" (Hudspeth, 1985). When the hair is standing straight, the trap door "rattles around" but is open only 20% of the time (shown closed in Figure 6-13A). Potassium ions, which have a positive charge, flow into the hair whenever these pores are open. The inward flow of positive charge is balanced by the outward flow of positive charge caused by other "pumps" elsewhere in the cell, maintaining the cell's resting membrane potential at about -60 millivolts (see Appendix). When the hair is bent in the direction of the tallest hairs, however, the filament attached to the trap door pulls on it and keeps it open more of the time, allowing more positive charge (potassium ions) to flow into the cell (Figure 6-13B). This causes a depolarization (making the inside of the cell more positive relative to the outside) of up to 20 millivolts (mV), which in turn releases neurotransmitter substances from the bottom of the hair cell. The release of these neurotransmitters results in stimulation of the dendrites of the spiral ganglion cells, which then generate the neural action potentials that communicate the presence of sound through the auditory nerve.

This model accounts for many properties of the auditory system. For example, because

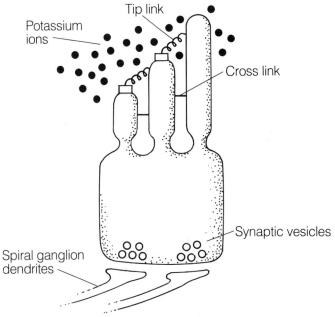

A. Hairs not bent—trap doors closed

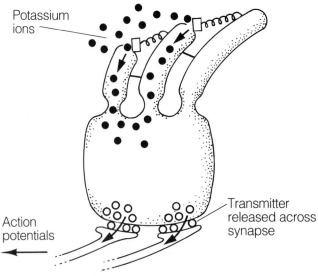

B. Hairs bent—trap doors open

Figure 6–13 *Model of transduction in hair cells.* A) No sound, hairs not bent, trapdoor closed, potassium ions excluded, no transmitter released, no action potentials; *(B)* Sound, hairs bent, trapdoor open, potassium ions enter, transmitter released, action potentials in auditory nerve.

the trap doors are constantly opening and closing, response to a sound can be very rapid, as data indicate it is (less than 1 msec). Moreover, because the process is probabilistic (hair-bending simply increases the probability that the door will be open at a given instant), it is capable of responding to very low levels of sound if averaged over a sufficiently long time. All in all, this seems a very good candidate for the correct model of transduction.

ELECTRICAL ACTIVITY OF THE AUDITORY NERVE

We have followed sound energy to the point where it is converted into patterns of electrical activity in the auditory nerve. These signals are now *spike potentials*; hence, in studying the neural processing of auditory information, we can use the same techniques of electrophysiological recording that we used to investigate the visual system. If you are unfamiliar with these procedures, now would be a good time to glance back at the Appendix. Basically, the technique involves inserting electrodes into cells in the auditory pathways and recording the electrical activity of individual neurons in response to a variety of sounds.

Although neurons possessing many different types of response characteristics are present in the auditory nerve, one type of neuron is extremely common. Such a neuron is often called a **tuned neuron** (tuned in the same sense that we "tune" a radio to receive accurately one particular station's broadcast frequency). Figure 6-14 shows the minimum intensity of sound of various frequencies that is needed to stimulate some typical tuned auditory neurons to respond above their resting rate. These are the neural equivalent of absolute thresholds (see Chapter 2). The curve in Figure 6-14 is called a **threshold response curve.** As can be seen from the figure, each neuron has a best, or characteristic, frequency

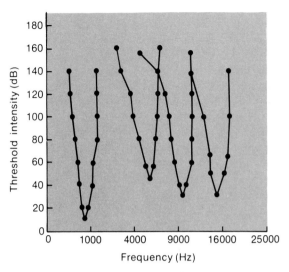

Figure 6–14 Threshold response curves for auditory nerve fibers in the cat (based on Whitfield, 1968).

for which its absolute threshold is lowest. The sensitivity of tuned neurons decreases (the threshold is higher) as we move away from the best frequency in either direction. Another way of looking at the tuning of such auditory neurons is to present a tone, varying in frequency, but fixed in intensity. A graph of the response rate of a tuned neuron treated in this way is often called a **tuning curve,** one example of which is shown in Figure 6-15. The auditory nerve contains neurons tuned to various frequencies spanning the entire range of hearing.

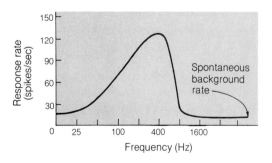

Figure 6–15 Tuning curve of a typical auditory nerve fiber (based on Lindsay & Norman, 1977).

The tuned nature of these cells probably comes about because of the mechanical properties of the basilar membrane (Khanna & Leonard, 1982; Pickles, 1988). Most of the tuned auditory nerve fibers that have been studied are connected to inner hair cells (Kiang et al., 1982; Liberman, 1982). Remember that different parts of the basilar membrane vibrate maximally to different frequencies of sound (see Figure 6-10), and this vibration causes the hair cells to bend and in turn to initiate the neural response. A hair cell will respond most strongly when a tone of a certain frequency creates a traveling wave on the basilar membrane that has its maximum amplitude at the location of that hair cell. The frequency of this tone will be the frequency to which the neuron that synapses with that hair cell is "tuned." Other frequencies of sound of the same intensity will cause less vigorous movement of the basilar membrane at that location, which in turn results in less vigorous bending of the hair of the hair cell, and consequently less vigorous responding of the neuron. Although the outer hair cells also show frequency tuning, their responses probably feed back on themselves through the crossed olivocochlear bundle, affecting their mechanical properties and thereby indirectly the responses of the inner hair cells (Kim, 1985; Pickles, 1988).

Further evidence for the interaction between inner and outer hair cells comes from a phenomenon called **two-tone suppression** (Rose, Galambos, & Hughs, 1959; Sachs & Kiang, 1968). This is seen when recording from an auditory fiber that is responding vigorously to a tone at its characteristic frequency. If a second tone of a different frequency that is moderately close to the tuned frequency is now briefly presented, the response rate in the tuned neuron drops. This effect may result from the mechanical action of outer hair cells stimulated by the second tone lessening the response of the basilar membrane, and thus of the inner hair cells, to the first tone. This is

supported by the fact that two-tone suppression disappears when outer hair cells have been selectively damaged by a drug (Schmiedt, Zwislocki, & Hamernik, 1980), and by the fact that it can be caused directly by stimulation of the outer hair cells (Geisler, Yates, Patuzzi, & Johnstone, 1990).

What is the nature of the information about intensity and frequency carried from the ear to the brain? One suggestion is that low frequencies may be encoded directly in the number of spike potentials in the neural response (Johnson, 1980; Rose, Brugge, Anderson, & Hind, 1967). Thus, if the frequency of the stimulus is 100 Hz, and if neurons fire at every pressure peak in the sound wave, the firing in the auditory nerve will tend to be approximately 100 Hz. This does not mean that any given individual neuron fires at this frequency. Rather, individual neurons seem to fire at fixed rates associated with the cycle of the sound wave. For example, one neuron may fire at every second peak of the wave (and thus at 50 Hz), whereas another may fire at every fifth peak (and thus at 20 Hz). This is called **phase-locking.** For a great many neurons firing out of phase with one another, one or more spikes will tend to occur at every peak of the wave, and thus a composite response rate of 100 Hz could be achieved. This ability of the auditory nerve to follow the frequency of the stimulating sound wave (up to about 4000 Hz) has been a central component of several theories of pitch perception (for example, Wever, 1979) that will be discussed in Chapter 7. What is important here is that the pattern of response of the whole auditory nerve rather than the responses of individual neurons may be significant in conveying information to the brain.

Although many cells in the auditory nerve may be tuned to the same characteristic frequency, their threshold intensities may vary over a range of about 20 dB (Evans, 1975). Once the intensity of a sound has exceeded a cell's threshold, further increases in intensity up to a level 30–50 dB above the threshold value will increase its rate of response. Further intensity increases beyond 30–50 dB above threshold will not cause the neuron to increase its rate of response, since the neuron is firing as fast as it can. Such a neuron is said to be **saturated.** On the other hand, as the intensity of the stimulus increases, other neurons, tuned to nearby frequencies (hence with a higher threshold for this particular sound input), may also be recruited, resulting in an increase in the number of neurons responding. This situation, where for any given sound input there is a population of neurons, all firing at different response rates, is represented for two levels of intensity in Figure 6-16A. Stimuli of different frequencies tend to cause different populations of neurons to fire above their background rates, as is shown in Figure 6-16B. Thus, the entire pattern of auditory activity changes with changes in the stimulus. Frequency seems to be indicated by *which* neurons are firing, whereas intensity seems to be roughly indicated by *how many* are firing (Whitfield, 1978), although the graded response rate of unsaturated fibers may still contribute to our experience of sound intensity (Viemeister, 1988).

Our increasing understanding of how the auditory nerve encodes frequency and intensity has allowed some people with hearing disabilities to recover some auditory ability. If the hair cells do not function normally, either because they were damaged or congenitally malformed, a person has a *sensorineural* hearing loss. This results in raised thresholds, distorted tuning curves, and sometimes in ringing in the ears (*tinnitus*) caused by hair cell or neural activity in the absence of sound.

Although it is difficult to do anything about too much neural activity, other than to mask it, people who have too little neural response to sounds can be helped. Recently, otologists have been able to implant in the ear devices (known as **cochlear implants**) that stimulate the auditory nerve electrically in response to external sounds (see Schindler & Merzenich, 1985). Modern cochlear implants first analyze the frequency composition of the sound into ranges of stimulus frequencies. The analysis and stimulating device is connected to a series of

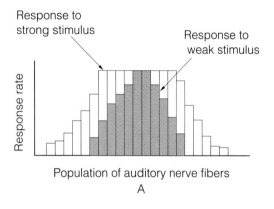

A

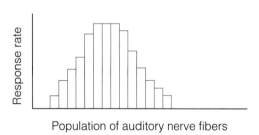

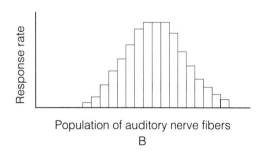

B

Figure 6–16 Hypothetical distributions of response rates for the population of auditory nerve fibers firing in response to (A) weak versus strong stimuli of the same frequency and (B) stimuli of the same strength but of different frequencies.

electrodes that have been implanted in the region of the hair cells at different points along the basilar membrane. Different regions along the membrane are then stimulated, based on the initial analysis of the frequencies, in an attempt to mimic the way traveling waves on the basilar membrane stimulates the hair cells. Deaf patients with such devices can discriminate the frequencies of different sounds (Townshend, Cotter, Van Compernolle, & White, 1987) and can even recognize speech sounds quite well, especially when a speech preprocessor is attached to the cochlear implant to isolate certain speech-relevant frequency changes (Blamey, Dowell, Brown, Clark, & Seligmen, 1987).

In the future, such devices may allow nearly a full range of hearing experience for people with this form of deafness (Miller & Spelman, 1990). For people who lack a viable auditory nerve, such as after some operations for cancer, there is hope that more central implants, such as in the cochlear nucleus, can provide useful hearing (Shannon & Otto, 1990).

THE AUDITORY PATHWAYS

Figure 6-17 diagrams the principle pathways taken by auditory information in the brain. These pathways are somewhat more complex

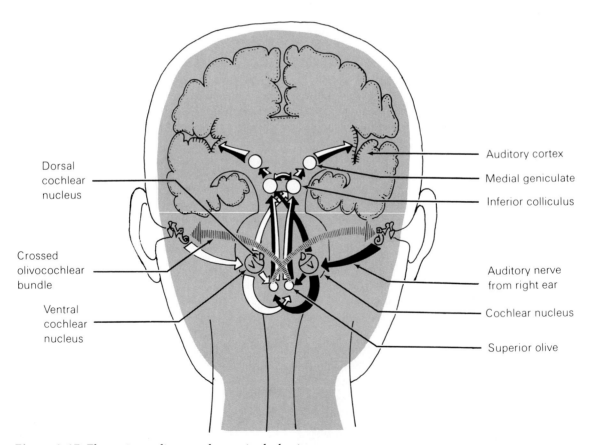

Figure 6–17 *The major auditory pathways in the brain.*

than the visual pathways. The axons of the spiral ganglion cells make up the auditory nerve, which projects to the **cochlear nucleus,** located in the lower back part of the brain. As shown in the figure, the auditory nerve fibers enter the **ventral** (front) **cochlear nucleus,** where each divides into at least two branches. One branch synapses with cells in the ventral cochlear nucleus, and the other proceeds to the **dorsal** (back) **cochlear nucleus.** The cells of the ventral cochlear nucleus send about half of their axons to the **superior olive** on the opposite side of the brain and half to that on the same side. The cells of the dorsal cochlear nucleus send all their axons to the opposite side of the brain, eventually to terminate in the **inferior colliculus.** Thus, most of the information from the right ear is sent to the left side of the brain, and vice versa. The two superior olives send most of their *afferent* (sensory input) fibers to the inferior colliculi (which are located just below the superior colliculi, discussed in Chapter 3). As mentioned earlier, special cells in the superior olives also send *efferent* fibers to synapse with the hair cells in the cochlea. One group of cells sends fibers to the inner hair cells, mostly on the same side of the brain (not shown in Figure 6-17). Another group sends efferent fibers

to synapse with the outer hair cells, mostly on the other side of the brain, via the crossed olivocochlear bundle. At the level of the inferior colliculus, considerable fiber-crossing takes place from one side of the brain to the other, so that each inferior colliculus has full information about what is occurring in the other.

Most cells in the inferior colliculi send axons to the **medial geniculate,** although a few axons go to the superior colliculus as well. Since the superior collicular pathway has been implicated in visual localization, perhaps the auditory fibers that go there also carry information about location. This sound localization information could then be related to visual data to yield a more complete "picture" of space (see Chapter 7).

From the medial geniculate, fibers project to a part of the temporal cortex often called the **primary auditory projection area,** or *A1* (or Brodmann's area 41). An adjacent area, called *A2* (Brodmann's area 42), also receives axons directly from the medial geniculate, although fewer of them. The surface aspects of these regions of the brain are pictured in Figure 6-18. Unfortunately, as can be seen from Figure 6-17, the vast majority of the auditory cortex is not on the surface, but is tucked into a fissure and

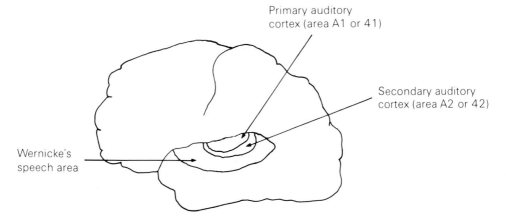

Figure 6–18 The principal auditorially responsive regions of the cortex (most not visible because they go into the fissures), with Brodmann's numbering of the areas and alternate labeling systems.

not visible in a standard side view of the brain. Several other areas process auditory stimuli, including areas adjacent to A1 and A2; some of the somatosensory cortex; and Wernicke's area (Brodmann's area 22), which processes speech stimuli. Like the primary visual cortex (V1), the primary auditory cortex is arranged in layers (six of them).

Electrical Activity of the Lower Auditory Centers

Many of the response patterns found in the fibers of the auditory nerve suggest that some form of auditory feature analysis is involved there. Although some of these neurons respond only to clicks or other stimuli that are not pure tones, the majority of the fibers are axons from tuned neurons. Recall that tuned neurons respond to a range of frequencies of pure-tone sounds, but each has a "preferred" band of frequencies to which it is most sensitive and to which it produces its maximum response. Similar "tuned" neurons are found in the cochlear nucleus, superior olive, inferior colliculus, and medial geniculate. Also, as described earlier for the auditory nerve, there is a region of nearby frequencies that produces an inhibition of response (as in two-tone suppression) in these same cells.

In addition to the frequency tuning of cells in the more central nuclei of the auditory pathway, a number of more complex neural response patterns appear. When Pfeiffer (1966) recorded from single neurons in the cochlear nucleus of adult cats, he found a variety of different types of neural responses to a simple tone. **On neurons** gave a burst of responses immediately after the onset of the tone bursts and then ceased responding, no matter how long the tone persisted. **Pauser neurons** exhibited a similar burst of firing at the onset of a tone, but this was followed by a pause and then a weaker, sustained response until the tone was turned off. **Choppers** gave repeated bursts of firing followed by short pauses, with the vigor of successive bursts decreasing. **Primarylike neurons** gave an initial vigorous burst of firing when the tone was turned on, and then the firing rate decayed to a lower level that was sustained for the duration of the tone. These primarylike neurons have been shown to be capable of encoding some critical aspects of speech sounds (Palmer, Winter, & Darwin, 1986).

In addition to these response patterns, a response analogous to the off responses observed in the visual system seems to exist for some neurons. These **off neurons** actually reduce their response rate below their spontaneous activity level at the onset of the tone and then give a burst of activity at its offset. An interesting variation of this is the presence of tuned cells that *reduce* their activity level when a stimulus different from the "best" one is present. One set of cells is reminiscent of the on-center/off-surround cells observed in the visual system (Chapter 3). Rather than have a receptive field that consists of a region in space, these cells have a receptive field consisting of a band of frequencies. For instance, the medial geniculate contains cells with "W-shaped" receptive field patterns. These neurons respond above their background rate of firing to a particular best frequency, and below the background rate for frequencies close to that frequency on either side. The firing rate gradually returns to background level for frequencies progressively more removed from the best frequency and its surrounding "worst" frequencies (Webster & Atkin, 1975).

Because different points along the basilar membrane vibrate most strongly for various different frequencies of sounds, we refer to the response of the basilar membrane as **tonotopic** (from the Greek *tono* for "tone" and *topus* for "place"). This means that sound frequencies are represented with a spatial code. This spatial encoding of frequency is preserved in the auditory nerve, because of the orderly way it innervates the cochlea, and throughout all of the auditory pathways (Martin, Webster, &

Service, 1988; Pickles, 1988; Rose, Galambos, & Hughes, 1960; Rouiller et al., 1989). The tonotopic organization of the basilar membrane is preserved even up to the primary auditory cortex. For example, in the A1 area of the cat brain, the preferred tuning of strips of cells goes from high to low frequencies in an orderly progression from the front to the back of the cortex (Harrison, Nagasawa, Smith, Stanton, & Mount, 1991; Merzenich, Knight, & Roth, 1975).

The finding that frequencies are spatially mapped into regions of the cortex has been confirmed in humans. One technique uses some ingenious measurements of the magnetic field created in the brain by its electrical response to sounds (Romani, Williamson, & Kaufman, 1982). For humans, the maximum brain activity observed in the auditory centers varies in depth (rather than from front to back as in the cat) as the frequency varies. Responses to high frequencies are deep, whereas those to low frequencies lie near the surface of the brain. A similar result has been obtained using *positron emission tomography*, which allows researchers to visualize areas of the brain that are most active during various activities, such as listening to sounds of different frequencies (Lauter, Herscovitch, Formby & Raichle, 1985; see Appendix). These results are consistent with the idea that the frequency of sound waves is coded mainly by place both on the basilar membrane and in the central auditory system.

THE AUDITORY CORTEX

Studies of nonhuman animals have provided us with most of the information we now possess about the physiology of sensory systems. For the lower levels of analysis, we can be fairly confident in generalizing the concepts to humans. When we begin to discuss the cortex, however, we are on shakier ground. The human cortex is more complex than that of most of the common experimental animals (such as the cat, the preferred subject of such studies), so generalization of findings to humans is more tenuous. Nonetheless, animal studies have yielded a significant amount of useful information on the activity of the auditory cortex.

Cells in the auditory cortex exhibit a variety of complex responses to sound stimuli. In the approximately 60% of the cells that respond to pure tones, there occur on responses, off responses, on-off responses, and more general excitatory and inhibitory responses (see Figure 6-19). These responses, of course, resemble the response patterns of cells in the visual system. The other 40% of the cells seem to respond selectively to more complex sounds, including noise bursts, clangs, or clicks.

An interesting type of neuron found in the auditory cortex of the cat is the **frequency sweep detector** (Whitfield & Evans, 1965). These cells respond only to sounds that change frequency in a specific direction and range. Some cells respond to increases but not to decreases in frequency in the same range. Others respond to decreases in frequency but not to increases. A third type responds only to increases in frequency for low-frequency tones. Since these types of stimuli are often encountered in speech and music, such detectors, if present in humans, could have an important role in speech and music perception. Certainly they have obvious utility for the cat, whose "war cries" and "love calls" consist of just these types of sounds. These cortical neurons respond to sound patterns in much the same way visual cortical neurons respond selectively to light patterns, For instance, cells in the cat auditory cortex respond with a unique pattern of activity to recordings of cat vocalizations (Watanabe & Katsuki, 1974). Interestingly, these cortical cells do not respond with the same pattern of activity to any of the individual components of the cat vocalization. This indicates that the cells are integrating the outputs of cells from lower levels of the auditory pathway that do respond to simpler components of the

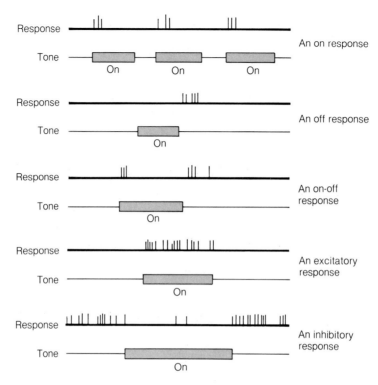

Figure 6–19 *Different types of response to pure tones recorded from neurons in the auditory cortex of the cat (based on Whitfield, 1967).*

sound pattern. We could say that the lower-level cells are detecting the various features of the vocalization and that the cortical cell is responding only to the combination of all the features (Whitfield, 1980).

There are even auditory analogues to the highly specific visual cells (face and paw detectors) observed in the temporal cortex (see Chapter 3). Cells are present in the auditory cortex of the squirrel monkey that are sensitive to the vocalizations of other squirrel monkeys (Swarbrick & Whitfield, 1972). Some of these cells are unresponsive to the presentation of simple tones, although they respond vigorously to the presentation of extremely complex vocalizations (Funkenstein, Nelson, Winter, Wolberg, & Newman, 1971). In macaque monkeys, destruction of areas A1 and A2 on the left side

of the brain abolishes their ability to discriminate such complex vocalizations (Heffner & Heffner, 1984). This implies that the monkey brain may contain a primitive analog to Wernicke's area (which is specialized for speech perception). On the other hand, some aspects of music perception seem to be predominantly handled by the auditory cortex on the right side of human brains (Coren, 1992; Zatorre, 1985).

Although these physiological findings are quite intriguing and suggestive, the ultimate test of any hypotheses about the significance of neural encoding or analysis of auditory patterns rests on data about an individual's actual auditory perceptions. In Chapter 7 we will consider *what* is heard and try to integrate it with what we have learned about *how* it is heard.

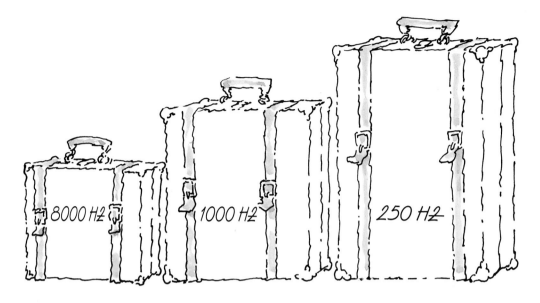

Recommended luggage for traveling waves

GLOSSARY

The following definitions are specific to their use in this book.

Active process A process by which energy is added to the traveling wave on the basilar membrane just before it peaks, possibly by means of outer hair cell motions.

Basilar membrane The membrane within the cochlea on which the organ of Corti lies.

Bel The basic unit used to measure the relative intensity of a sound wave.

Chopper A neuron that gives repeated bursts of impulses followed by short pauses, with the vigor of successive bursts decreasing, in response to presentation of a pure tone.

Cochlea A snail-shaped part of the labyrinth of the ear that contains the auditory receptors.

Cochlear duct One of the three canals in the cochlea. Also called the *scala media*.

Cochlear implant A device implanted in the cochlea that electrically stimulates the auditory nerve in a manner similar to the way it is stimulated by hair cell activity.

Cochlear nucleus A structure in the lower back part of the brain that receives input from the auditory nerve.

Crossed olivocochlear bundle Bundle of "efferent" nerve fibers extending from cells in the superior olive to the outer hair cells in the contralateral cochlea.

Cycle In sound, the completion of a full sequence of air rarefaction and compression.

Cycles per second The unit used to measure frequency of sound waves, usually referred to as *hertz*.

Decibel (dB) The unit used to measure sound intensity; one-tenth of a bel.

Dorsal cochlear nucleus The back half of the nucleus in the lower back part of the brain where the auditory nerve fibers end.

Eardrum The membrane at the end of the ear canal that vibrates in resonance with incoming sound waves.

Eustachian tubes A channel from the back of the throat to the middle ear; when we swallow it opens and allows the air pressure in the middle ear to equalize with the outside.

External auditory meatus The canal conducting sound waves to the eardrum. Also called the *ear canal*.

Fourier components Simple sine waves that add together to form a complex waveform.

Frequency   The number of cycles a sound wave completes in one second.

Frequency sweep detector   A neuron that responds only to sounds that change frequency in a specific direction and range.

Hair bundle   A graded set of hairs protruding from a hair cell in the cochlea and tending to move, or bend, as a unit.

Helicotrema   An opening, between the vestibular and tympanic canals, at the apex of the cochlea.

Hertz (Hz)   The unit (cycles per second) used to measure frequency of sound waves.

In phase   When two sound waves are at exactly the same place in their cycles at the same moment they are in phase.

Incus   One of the three middle-ear bones involved in sound condition to the cochlea. Also known as the *anvil*.

Inferior colliculi   Auditory processing centers in the midbrain that are the termini for cells of the superior olives.

Inner ear   The part of the ear containing the cochlea.

Inner hair cells   Cells found on the inner side of the tunnel of Corti.

Labyrinth   A structure of fluid-filled canals and chambers in the head that contains organs of hearing and the vestibular senses.

Malleus   The inner ear bone that is attached to the eardrum. Also called the *hammer*.

Medial geniculate   The brain structure that receives inputs from the inferior colliculus and sends axons to the auditory cortex.

Middle ear   The part of the ear consisting of the ossicles (malleus, incus, and stapes) that transmit the eardrum vibrations to the inner ear.

Off neurons   Neurons that reduce their firing rate below background at the onset of a tone and then give a burst of firing at its termination.

Ohm's acoustical law   The statement that the auditory system separates complex sounds into simple (Fourier) components.

On neurons   Neurons that fire immediately and exclusively after the onset of a tone.

Organ of Corti   The part of the cochlear duct that transduces mechanical sound wave energy into electrochemical energy interpretable by the nervous system.

Otoacoustic emissions   Emissions of sound by the ear, either spontaneously or in response to stimula-tion; spontaneous emissions may be related to the active process.

Out of phase   When the peaks and valleys of sound waves do not coincide over time.

Outer ear   The pinna, the auditory canal, and the eardrum.

Outer hair cells   Cells found on the outer side of the tunnel of Corti.

Oval window   A membrane in the cochlea that receives sound vibrations from the stapes.

Pauser neurons   Neurons, similar to on-response neurons, that exhibit an initial response to stimuli, followed by a pause, and then a weaker, sustained response until the stimulus stops.

Phase   The particular point in the compression-rarefaction cycle of a sound wave at one instant of time.

Phase angle   The degree to which one sound wave is out of phase with another, considering a complete cycle as 360 degrees.

Phase-locking   The tendency of individual neurons to fire at fixed points in the cycle of a sound wave.

Pinna   The fleshy visible part of the outer ear.

Pressure amplitude   A measure of the degree of compression or rarefaction at the peaks or valleys of a sound wave.

Primary auditory projection area   The area of the temporal cortex that receives most of the fibers from the medial geniculate. Also known as *A1*.

Primarylike neuron   A neuron that gives an initial burst of firing in response to a stimulus, and then continues firing at a lower level until the stimulus stops.

Reissner's membrane   One of two membranes making up the cochlear duct.

Round window   The membrane at the base of the cochlea facing the middle ear.

Saturated   The state in which a neuron cannot fire any faster, even if stimulus intensity is increased.

Sound pressure level (SPL)   The amount by which the pressure extended by a sound wave differs from atmospheric pressure, measured in decibels.

Spiral ganglion   The cells whose axons form the auditory nerve.

Stapes   The bone in the chain of middle ear ossicles that makes contact with the oval window; also called the *stirrup*.

Superior olives   The brain termini for axons leading from the ventral cochlear nuclei.

Tectorial membrane Within the cochlear duct, the membrane, extending from Reissner's membrane, in which some of the hairs of the organ of Corti are embedded.

Threshold response curve A graph of neural absolute threshold as a function of sound frequency.

Timbre A sound attribute associated with the components of a complex sound wave.

Tonotopic Characteristic of the place of response to a sound depending on the frequency of the sound.

Tuned neuron A neuron that responds optimally to tones of a particular frequency.

Tuning curve A graph showing the rate of firing of an auditory neuron for different tone frequencies; it usually has a single peak.

Tunnel of Corti A structure in the cochlea.

Two-tone suppression Inhibition of neural response to a characteristic frequency of sound that occurs when a second tone of a different frequency is presented; suppression occurs during and briefly after the presentation of the second tone.

Tympanic canal One of three canals running through the cochlea.

Tympanum *See* Eardrum.

Type I fibers Fibers extending from the spiral ganglion to the inner hair cells.

Type II fibers Fibers extending from the spiral ganglion to the outer hair cells.

Ventral cochlear nucleus The front half of the nucleus in the lower back part of the brain where the auditory nerve fibers end.

Vestibular canal One of three canals running though the cochlea.

Wave The pattern of air molecule motion that characterizes sound.

Wavelength The distance from one peak to the next of a sound wave.

Chapter ...

HEARING

Detection of Sounds

Temporal, Frequency, and Binaural Interactions

Auditory Masking

Sound Discrimination

Sound Localization

• Direction Cues: Simple Tones

• Direction and Distance Cues: Complex Sounds

• Physiological Mechanisms

Subjective Dimensions of Sounds

Loudness

Pitch

Theories of Pitch Perception

Auditory Scene Analysis

*T*ry a simple experiment. Scrape your fingernails or a piece of metal across the chalkboard in your classroom (before the professor arrives) and watch your classmates cringe. (Then apologize!) No one knows why this sound is so aversive to so many people. It isn't the high frequencies present because removing them makes little difference (Halpern, Blake, & Hillenbrand, 1986). Perhaps it is an ancient memory of the screams of predators or fellow primates in distress. Whatever the reason, the phenomenon demonstrates the powerful effects sound can have on behavior and the richness of the psychological experience of sound. In this chapter we shall investigate some of this richness, concentrating on the more basic sensations associated with our perception of sound. (Chapter 12 will deal with the more complex phenomena of speech and music perception).

DETECTION OF SOUNDS

The most elementary auditory experience is the detection of a sound. What is the minimum sound intensity we can hear? To determine an observer's absolute threshold for sound presented through earphones, we measure the threshold sound pressure level (see Chapters 2 and 6) using a microphone placed very close to the eardrum. This value is called the **minimum audible pressure.** This is a rather artificial situation, since the sound wave at the eardrum has already been somewhat amplified and distorted during its travels through the ear canal. Another, perhaps more natural, procedure would be to determine the absolute auditory threshold for an observer sitting in an open space that is free of echoes and other distortions. In this situation, sounds are presented by a speaker and the intensity of the threshold stimulus is measured at the location of the observer's head. This measurement of threshold is called the **minimum audible field** (indicating that

the intensity of the threshold stimulus was measured in a free field, rather than directly at the eardrum).

In a classic study at Bell Telephone Laboratories, Sivian and White (1933) systematically varied the frequency of a pure-tone stimulus as they took a series of threshold measurements under carefully controlled conditions. Their results are summarized in Figure 7-1. The absolute threshold varies for different frequencies of sound. The ear is most sensitive to sounds with frequencies between 1000 and 5000 Hz, being about 100 times less sensitive to a sound at 100 Hz than to a sound at 3000 Hz. Notice that the minimum audible field measurements are considerably lower than the minimum audible pressures. The most recent measurements give even lower minimum audible fields for frequencies higher than 250 Hz, especially in the region 2000 to 4000 Hz, where they are about 5 dB lower than the standard established by the International Standards Organization, which closely resembles Figure 7-1 (Betke, 1991).

Probably the most important reason for the lower thresholds in a free field is that the free-field situation allows resonances and amplifications from the shape of the pinna (the outer cup of the ear) and the ear canal to come into

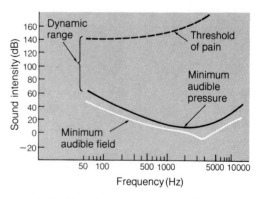

Figure 7-1 *The dynamic range of hearing from minimum audible intensities to the threshold of pain (based on Sivian & White, 1933).*

play. This is supported by the fact that we are most sensitive to sounds of 3000–4000 Hz in free-field presentation, which is also in the range of the natural resonance frequency of the external ear canal. Interestingly, screams of agony or terror, especially those of females, sometimes have peaks in the 3000 Hz range (Milne & Milne, 1967), and many speech sounds have important components in this range (see Chapter 12). You can demonstrate the effect of frequency on your ability to detect sounds using Demonstration Box 7-1.

The lower limit of sensitivity for the ear seems to be determined by the sound of blood rushing through the tiny vessels in the middle and inner ear, or perhaps by the random noise generated by motion of the air molecules (see Hudspeth, 1985), whereas the upper limit is determined by the stimulus intensity that produces pain. The difference between the absolute threshold and the pain threshold for a particular frequency of sound waves defines the **dynamic range** of the ear for that frequency (see Figure 7-1). For stimuli with frequencies between about 1000 and 5000 Hz the ear has a dynamic range of up to 150 dB, which is equivalent to a 7.5-millionfold increase in sound pressure from the weakest sound detectable to the most intense sound tolerable. Few stereo systems can approach the dynamic range with which you were born.

The dynamic range of the ear is distinct from the frequency range over which our ears respond to sound. Young adults can hear

---

DEMONSTRATION BOX 7-1   Sound Frequency and Threshold

Many people are aware of the problems associated with replaying recorded music so that it sounds as it did when it was recorded. Recording techniques reproduce the frequencies produced by musical instruments, but the replay is often at a lower intensity. Most of the sounds of musical instruments lie in frequency ranges where the absolute threshold is most affected by changes in frequency. Thus, unless you listen to recordings of an orchestra at reasonable intensity levels, you will not hear many of the frequencies produced by the instruments. Many high-quality audio amplifiers have been modified to include circuits that compensate for such psychological mechanisms. These circuits are set to emphasize very low and very high frequency sounds.

For this demonstration you will need a radio or another sound source that produces orchestral music. A cheaper unit, such as a portable radio or your car radio, both of which lack loudness compensation circuits, would be perfect. Find a station (or a record) where a full orchestra is playing. Turn down the sound and listen to the instruments you can hear. Now, gradually turn up the sound. As you do this, you will find that you become more aware of the bass violin and cello; the larger brass pieces, such as the tuba; and some of the lower notes of the harp or bassoon; as well as some of the higher tones from the violins, flutes, and piccolos. When the volume has been considerably increased so that you can hear the entire orchestra and many of the pieces (placing your ear close to the speaker helps), gradually turn down the volume again. Now many of the lower- and higher-frequency instruments seem to disappear as certain frequencies they produce drop below threshold. The middle frequencies of the orchestra, however, are still quite audible.

DEMONSTRATION BOX 7-2   High-Frequency Hearing Limits

You can make a simple test of your own high-frequency hearing using your television set. Turn it on and then lower the sound completely. Now lean over the back of your set and listen for a soft, high-pitched whine. If you can hear it, this means that you can detect frequencies on the order of 16,000 Hz. Now, try this test on someone who is considerably older than you are and then with someone who is much younger. You should find that the older individual cannot hear this sound, whereas the younger one can. You might also try moving away from the set (if possible) until you can just hear the sound. This is your *threshold distance*. Now have your other observers do the same and determine their threshold distances. The greater your threshold distance, the more sensitive your ear is to these high-frequency sounds.

---

sounds between about 20 and 20,000 Hz, and some young children can hear sounds with frequencies up to 27,000 Hz. Unfortunately, with age a progressive loss in sensitivity occurs, particularly for higher frequencies, so that this range gradually decreases as we grow older (see Chapter 16). Demonstration Box 7-2 provides a simple test for the upper range of your own hearing.

Temporal, Frequency, and Binaural Interactions

Several factors other than frequency and intensity determine our ability to detect sounds. One is the duration of the sound. The auditory system acts as if a fixed amount of sound energy is necessary to stimulate the ear sufficiently so that we hear a sound. It does not matter if this energy comes at a higher intensity over a shorter time interval or at a lower intensity over a longer time interval. In a sense, the auditory system adds together all of the sound energy received during a given time period, a phenomenon called **temporal summation.**

We can describe this relationship algebraically as $T = I \times D$, where I is the intensity of

the sound, D is its duration, and T is a constant threshold amount of energy. This simple formula says that any combination of intensity and duration that produces the same value (T) will be heard with the same likelihood. Thus, longer sounds can be less intense and still be heard with the same likelihood. For example, if a 50-msec sound at 10 dB is at threshold, then a 100-msec sound at 5 dB also would be at threshold. This relationship is a good approximation for sounds up to a duration of about 200 msec. Beyond 200 msec, increasing the stimulus duration has no effect on threshold intensity. This time–intensity trade-off is closely related to Bloch's law in the visual system, which we discussed in Chapter 4.

We also may increase the likelihood that a sound will be heard by increasing the number of different tones, or frequencies, that are presented together. Suppose we present an observer with two tones, neither of which would reach threshold by itself. Even if each tone is only about half the intensity needed for threshold, a sound will still often be heard. It seems that the nervous system adds the neural responses to the different tones, producing a composite response based on the sum of the intensities of the various single stimuli. The tones should not differ in frequency by too much, however, or their energies will not sum, and the threshold intensities will be the same as if we presented each tone alone.

Just as there was a critical duration beyond which temporal summation did not occur, there is a critical band of frequencies beyond which adding tones does not facilitate detection (Scharf, 1975). This critical band is not the same width for all frequencies, being much narrower for low frequencies than for high frequencies. Thus, if we start with a 400-Hz tone, adding a tone between 350 and 450 Hz will improve our ability to detect the sound, but adding a tone beyond these limits will not. If we started with a 5000-Hz tone, however, any added tone between about 4500 and 5500 Hz would improve our ability to detect the sound. The bandwidth is 100 Hz at the lower frequency but 1000 Hz at the higher. Figure 7-2 demonstrates how the critical bandwidth varies with frequency.

Another way to obtain a lower absolute threshold for sound is to present sounds to both ears, as opposed to only one. Presentations to one ear are called **monaural** (from the roots *mon* for "one" and *aural* for "ear"); presentations to two ears are called **binaural** (from the root *bi* for "two"). At first it was believed

that lower thresholds were obtained with binaural presentation because one of the ears was more sensitive than the other, and the most sensitive ear determined the absolute threshold (Sivian & White, 1933). However, later work demonstrated that the threshold for two-ear stimulation is about one-half of that for one-ear stimulation (Chocolle, 1962). An interesting aspect of the interaction between the ears is that the two stimuli do not have to occur simultaneously in the two ears. If the tones are presented to the ears one at a time, and the total stimulus duration of the combined input is less than 200 msec, the pair of tones will be detected even if each individual tone is only about one-half of the intensity needed to reach threshold when presented monaurally (Schenkel, 1967).

Auditory Masking

We have all been in a noisy meeting, convention, or theater and have found that we could not hear or understand a speaker well. When the crowd quiets down, however, we find that the speaker's voice is audible immediately. Whether a particular sound can be heard or not depends not only on its own intensity but also on the presence of other sounds in the environment. We just discussed how sounds can interact to facilitate detection; here the effects are reversed. We present an observer with a sound, which is audible by itself, and then add another sound only to find that the target sound can no longer be heard. We usually say that the second sound (the **masker**) is **masking** the first (the **target**). When target and masker are presented at the same time, we have **simultaneous masking.**

A masking sound does not simply make all other sounds more difficult to hear. Masking sounds act rather selectively. An elegant experiment demonstrating this was done by Zwicker (1958). He measured the threshold intensities

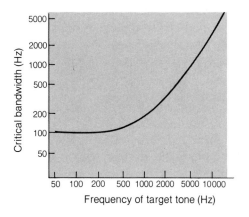

Figure 7-2 *The relation between critical bandwidth, within which added tones will facilitate detection, and frequency of target tone.*

for target tones of various frequencies presented both alone and together with a narrow band of noise with a middle frequency of 1200 Hz. He obtained the results shown in Figure 7-3. As you can see from the figure, the more intense the masking stimulus was, the more intense the target tone had to be for it to be audible. The most striking aspect of these data, however, is the asymmetry of the masking effect. Of course, the greatest masking is found for tones that have frequencies similar to the masker itself (the thresholds are highest for tones of frequencies around 1200 Hz). However, there is still a great deal of masking of tones higher in frequency than the masking sound (the threshold curves fall relatively slowly to the unmasked threshold curve on the right side of Figure 7-3), whereas tones of a lower frequency are relatively unaffected (the threshold curves fall quickly to the unmasked curve on the left of Figure 7-3). For people with sensorineural hearing loss (caused by damage to hair cells or auditory nerve cells), this "upward spread of masking" effect is even more pronounced (see, for example, Gagne, 1988).

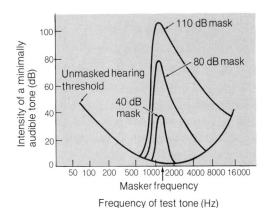

Figure 7-3 *Thresholds for a pure-tone target in the presence of a narrow band of masking noise centered at 1200 Hz. The higher the curve, the higher the threshold, hence the more effective the masking (based on Zwicker, 1958).*

You can experience some aspects of the frequency-specific effect of a masker by using Demonstration Box 7-3.

Why does added noise most effectively mask tones higher in frequency than itself? The answer may lie in the physiology of the ear. Turn back to Figure 6-12, which shows how the vibration pattern of the basilar membrane varies with the frequency of a pure tone. Notice that tones of low frequencies produce a very broad vibration pattern, extending over much of the membrane, whereas tones of higher frequencies produce vibration patterns nearer to the oval window and not extending as far along the membrane. Now look at Figure 7-4. Notice that when we have a weak test tone, and the masking noise is of a higher frequency than the target, the pattern of vibrations set up in the basilar membrane by the masking noise only extends part way up the membrane. Because the lower-frequency target tone vibrates more of the membrane, the target's pattern extends beyond the flank of the vibration pattern produced by the masker. Thus, the target is detectable. However, the vibration pattern produced by the target tone when the noise is of a lower frequency than the target is completely covered by the masker's vibration pattern, and it is thus not detectable as a separate tone. The intensity of the higher frequency test tone in the presence of low-frequency noise must be increased (to the "intense" level in Figure 7-4) before its own vibration pattern at last extends beyond that of the masker and the target can be detected as a separate tone.

We have just discussed how the upward spread of masking could be caused by the interaction of the patterns of excitation produced on the basilar membrane by the target and masking sounds. Of course, these vibration patterns would have their effects through stimulation of the hair cells at the appropriate places on the basilar membrane. However, another mechanism could be contributing to the mask-

DEMONSTRATION BOX 7-3   Auditory Masking

To experience several different masking phenomena you need two major sources of sound, one for a masking sound, and one for the target sound that will be masked. Good sources are the noise of a car engine for a masking sound and the car radio for a source of target sounds. If you have a car with a radio, get into it and turn on the radio without starting the engine. Find some music with a good range of frequencies. Classical music is best, but any music will do. Modern music with a lot of steel guitar (country) or electrically amplified guitar (rock) is also good. Take particular note of the high and the low frequencies. Turn the volume knob on the radio to an intensity where you can just barely hear these frequencies. Now start the car motor. Press on the accelerator (with the car out of gear!) to make the engine turn over at high revolutions per minute. This creates a source of intense broad-band masking noise. Now listen for the high and the low frequencies that were clearly audible in the music before you started the car engine. Turn up the volume until the high and low frequencies (which should now be masked) are just barely audible again and take notice of the difference between the volume settings before and after the noise was introduced. You could map out a masking curve for particular frequencies in a piece of music by varying the revolutions per minute of the motor to vary the intensity of the noise and by varying the frequency of the sounds whose audibility you are using as a criterion for radio volume adjustment. Note that even with intense masking noise, you can still hear the middle frequencies, where most of the singing is, while the higher and lower frequencies are masked. This is a reflection of the superior sensitivity of the ear to these frequencies. You also experience *speech masking* in your car. When the masking noise is of sufficient intensity (be careful not to damage your engine), even the middle frequencies (where most speech sounds occur) are masked, and you cannot understand the singer or the radio announcer.

ing pattern observed. In a manner similar to two-tone inhibition (see Chapter 6), neurons responding to the masker could be suppressing the actual activity of neurons responding to the target tone. There is some evidence from studies of auditory nerve fibers in cats that this mechanism is important for target frequencies well above the masker frequency (Delgutte, 1990).

Masking effects are not limited to situations in which target and masking sounds are presented simultaneously. If a masker is presented first, followed after some **interstimulus interval** by a brief target, any increase in the absolute threshold for the target is called **forward masking.** Many studies (see Zwislocki, 1978) have found, as you might expect, that forward masking increases as the intensity of the masking sound increases, and decreases as the interstimulus interval increases. For interstimulus intervals longer than 300 msec, no measurable forward masking occurs. Longer duration masking sounds produce more forward masking than do shorter duration ones, especially for interstimulus intervals shorter than 40 msec (Carlyon, 1988). In general, the

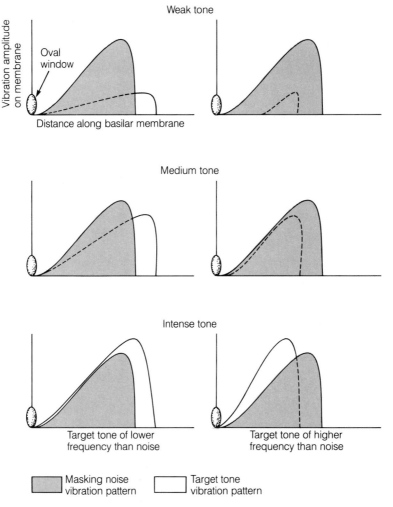

Figure 7-4 *The interactions of patterns of vibration of the basilar membrane resulting from a target and a noise stimulus (based on Scharf, 1964).*

lower the frequencies of *both* the target and mask pair, the more masking takes place (Jesteadt, Bacon, & Lehman, 1982). In addition, the same asymmetry we discussed for simultaneous masking shows up in forward masking: Little masking of target tones occurs with frequencies lower than the masker, but a great deal occurs for target tones of frequencies higher than the masker. It is unlikely, however, that we can explain all of these effects by inter-action of excitation patterns on the basilar membrane or by suppression of the neural response to the target by that to the masker, since the masker is no longer present when the target is presented at a later time. Some sort of interaction of more central neural processes must be involved. For the situation just discussed, it is likely that the masker is lowering the sensitivity of the hair cells, or their synapses with auditory nerve fibers, to stimulation by the target tone, thus raising the threshold for the target. It is also possible that more intense maskers cause the basilar membrane to "ring," or continue to vibrate, for up to 10 msec after it is turned off (Carlyon, 1988).

What happens when the target tone precedes the masker? Nothing, you might think; how could a sound that *follows* another affect our perception of the first sound, which has already been processed? Yet **backward masking** does occur, although somewhat differently from forward masking. For instance, your ability to hear a click may be reduced if another click follows it by as long as 25 msec (for loud masking clicks). Backward masking is more difficult to measure for tones than for clicks, because tones must extend longer in time, but it does occur. When a tone is masked with noise, the masker may have some effect on the threshold of a tone that is turned on up to 40 msec before the masker is turned on (Wright, 1964). The explanation of these backward masking effects is still not clear. One possibility is that inhibition caused by the masker could build up faster than excitation caused by the target tone, thus overlapping with it in time and canceling it to some extent, even when the target occurs appreciably earlier than the masker.

In addition to separating target and masker in time, we can separate them by presenting a target sound to one ear and a masking sound to the other. This is called **central masking,** since again there can be no interaction of the sounds on the basilar membrane and the masking is therefore assumed to take place in more central brain areas. When masker and target are presented to different ears, the masker must be about 50 dB more intense than when they are both presented to the same ear. Under these conditions the effect of the mask is usually much more symmetrical and does not spread so widely as we vary the frequency of the test tone (Zwislocki, Damianopoulos, Buining, & Glantz, 1967). Only when the frequency of the

masking sound is quite low (less than 200 Hz) is there appreciable asymmetry of masking (Billings & Stokinger, 1977).

Central interactions become very important when we consider the processing of more complex and meaningful sounds, such as speech (see Chapter 12). Interestingly, it is sometimes impossible to ignore components of complex sounds that are far from the target in frequency, resulting in what is called **informational masking** (Pollack, 1975; Watson, Kelly, & Wroten, 1976). This form of masking occurs when a masking sound is made up of several different frequencies chosen at random from trial to trial. When the mask is presented simultaneously with a target, the target is more difficult to detect *even if none of the frequencies is particularly close to the target frequency* (Neff & Green, 1987). However, no informational masking occurs when the masking sound ends before the target tone begins (Neff, 1991). It has been estimated that about 20% of the simultaneous masking of tones by noise is caused by informational masking (Lufti, 1990). Although the frequencies making up the masker do not have to be very near the frequency of the target tone, the farther away they are from the target tone's frequency, the less informational masking occurs (Leek, Brown, & Dorman, 1991). This indicates that informational masking might be caused by the inability to focus attention on the frequency of the target in the presence of other sounds with frequencies in the same range.

Sound Discrimination

In some respects the problem of masking is really a discrimination problem, of much the same sort as that discussed in Chapter 2. Basically, the observer's task is to *discriminate the target sound from the masking sound.* We may simplify this problem somewhat by asking the basic discrimination question for the perception of sound: "How different must two sounds be for the difference to be detected reliably?" To answer this question precisely, we must separate two of the physical dimensions along which a sound stimulus may differ: intensity and frequency.

Let us begin by considering our sensitivity to intensity differences. Riesz (1928), working at the Bell Telephone Laboratories, attempted to determine the limits of intensity discrimination. He used the Weber fraction (the proportion by which two stimuli must differ in order for the difference to be detected—see Chapter 2) as a measure of our ability to discriminate various sounds. Figure 7-5 shows Riesz's (1928) results for how the Weber fraction varies as the intensity of the standard (I) stimulus is varied. Notice that we have plotted four different curves for four different frequencies. As you can see, the size of the Weber fraction for intensity differences is smallest (discrimination is best) for stimuli in the middle range of frequencies (1000 and 4000 Hz). Increasing or decreasing the frequency decreases our ability to discriminate intensity differences, although such variations in discrimination with changes in frequency are not always found to be as large as those shown here (for example, Florentine, Buus, & Mason, 1987; Jesteadt, Wier, & Green, 1977), nor is the Weber fraction always found to drop off so smoothly with increasing intensity (Long & Cullen, 1985). For moderate stimulus intensities and frequencies, however, the Weber fraction is rather constant. Some studies have found even less change in the Weber fraction (even at the lowest intensities) for tones at intermediate frequencies (Green, Nachmias, Kearny, & Jeffress, 1979; Hanna, von Gierke, & Green, 1986). Figure 7-5 shows that the auditory system can detect changes of 10% to 20% in stimulus intensity (and perhaps as low as 5% under optimal conditions). This level of discrimination holds across a broad range of frequencies and intensities, covering the stimulus range where most of our everyday hearing takes place.

You might expect that, as is true with detection, it would be easier to discriminate intensities of sounds presented to both ears

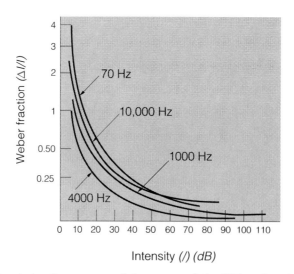

Figure 7-5 *Intensity discrimination measured in terms of the Weber fraction for various intensities and frequencies of standard stimuli (based on Riesz, 1928).*

(binaural presentation) than those presented to a single ear (monaural presentation). In fact, intensity difference thresholds are about 33% smaller when the stimuli are presented simultaneously to both ears than when they are presented to either ear alone (Jesteadt & Weir, 1977). This is probably because the binaural presentation gives the observer two chances to hear the difference (one in each ear) rather than just the single chance available when monaural presentation is used. Similarly, the intensity difference threshold is smaller the longer the duration of the stimuli, over a range of 2 msec to 2 seconds (Florentine, 1986). The longer stimulus durations give more information about the stimulus difference and thus more opportunity to detect it.

A similar, but special, case of intensity discrimination arises in what has been called **profile analysis** (Green, 1987). In this situation, a listener is presented with a complex sound made up of many different frequencies (often more than 20 of them) and is asked to discriminate a slight change in the intensity of one of the component sounds. For example, a complex sound (a standard "flat" profile) might consist of pure tones with frequencies of 250, 500, 1000, 2000, and 4000 Hz, all with amplitudes of 60 dB. A comparison sound could consist of tones with the same frequencies and amplitudes except, for instance, the 1000-Hz tone (the signal frequency), which is raised to an amplitude of 65 dB. A listener would be asked to say which of two successive intervals contained the more intense 1000-Hz component (this is called a 2-interval forced choice technique).

Under these conditions, intensity difference thresholds can be much smaller than for single tones. Thresholds for signal frequencies between 500 and 2000 Hz can decrease by nearly 10 dB as the number of other component frequencies is increased from 3 to 21 (Kidd, Mason, Uchanski, Brantley, & Shah, 1991; Robinson & Green, 1988). The auditory system seems to carry out a profile analysis in which the intensity of the tone at the signal frequency is compared with a weighted average of the intensities of the other components (Berg & Green, 1990). The more component frequencies there are, the more stable, and thus the more useful such an average would be, and therefore the more a "bump" in the profile (change in a single component) would stand out. Of course, if the profile is very "bumpy" already (for example, has tones of many different intensities), it is more difficult to detect any particular bump (Robinson & Green, 1988). It is not surprising that listeners must practice for many trials before they can detect these profile differences. Once they can, however, the thresholds obtained are robust and consistent with thresholds obtained with older methods. For example, profile discrimination is best when the intensity increment is added to components of intermediate frequencies, as in the example above (Bernstein & Green, 1987).

We also may ask, "By how much must two tones differ in frequency for the difference to be noticed?" Again, the classic study was done at the Bell Telephone Laboratories, this time by Shower and Biddulph (1931). (You might guess that the telephone company would have an interest in discovering the limits of our ability to discriminate sounds.) Again, we may express the limits of frequency discrimination using the Weber fraction. In this case, however, the fraction consists of $\Delta f/f$, where f represents the frequency of the standard tone and Δf represents the modulation (brief change) in frequency of the continuous standard that can just be detected.

Figure 7-6 shows Shower and Biddulph's measurements of the Weber fraction for frequency for several different intensity levels and a broad range of frequencies. Notice that above 1000 Hz the Weber fraction is fairly constant and quite small (around 0.005). This means that if we presented a listener with tones of 1000 Hz and 1005 Hz, this small difference in

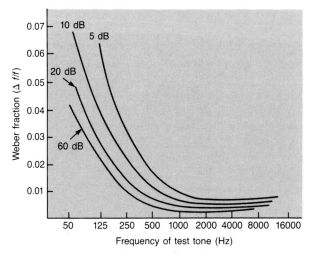

Figure 7-6 *Frequency discrimination measured in terms of the Weber fraction for various intensities and frequencies of standard stimuli (based on Shower & Biddulph, 1931).*

frequency (0.5%) would be detected half the time. At lower intensity levels our discrimination of frequency differences is not quite this good. The most comprehensive modern study of frequency discrimination was done by Wier, Jesteadt, and Green (1977). Their results were similar to those of Shower and Biddulph (1931), that is, the Weber fraction for frequency depended on both frequency and intensity in a way similar to that shown in Figure 7-6.

An interesting recent technique to measure frequency discrimination is to present sounds that may or may not change in frequency (*glide*) while they are on and ask observers to discriminate which of two such sounds changed, or which direction the change was in. Weber fractions for discriminating increases versus decreases in frequency (up versus down glides) are about the same as for static differences in frequency (0.002 to 0.005), but discriminating which of two tones glided from one that didn't glide is significantly more difficult (0.005 to 0.009) (Dooley & Moore, 1988). Under special conditions, when two tones are presented to the same ear, and

they interact as described in Chapter 6 to produce distortion-product otoacoustic emissions, the Weber fraction for frequency modulation can be as low as 0.0005 (meaning that a difference of only 1.50 Hz at 3000 Hz can reach threshold (McAnally & Calford, 1990). Finally, as was the case for intensity discrimination, binaural frequency difference thresholds are about 33% smaller than are monaural ones (Jesteadt & Wier, 1977).

Sound Localization

Sounds are usually perceived as having a location in space—as emanating from sources to the right or left of, in front of or behind, above or below our bodies. Some sounds appear to come from close by, others from a distance. Our auditory systems use a variety of aspects of sound to construct a sort of auditory space, with our bodies at the center, within which sounds can be localized and their sources approached ("Hey Jan, nice to see you!") or avoided ("Grrrrooowwwlll").

Direction Cues: Simple Tones

When a sound comes from some distance away and from a particular angle to the listener, a number of cues indicate the direction to the right or left—the **azimuth**—of the sound source. Figure 7-7 shows a typical situation when a sound is coming from a source positioned at about 45 deg azimuth. Notice that one ear receives the sound directly from the source while the other ear is in what could be called a **sound shadow.** The shadowed ear receives only those sounds from the source that are *bent* around the head, or *diffracted* by the

edge of the head. The presence of a sound shadow means that the sound intensity at one ear is less than the intensity at the other ear.

Measurements have been made of **intensity differences** between the ears as both the azimuth of the sound source and the frequency of the emitted sound is varied (for example, Middlebrooks, Makous, & Green, 1989). These show that the intensity difference between the ears increases as a sound source is moved toward one side. In addition, although low-frequency sound waves (those less than 3000 Hz) bend around the head readily, high-frequency sound waves tend to rush right past

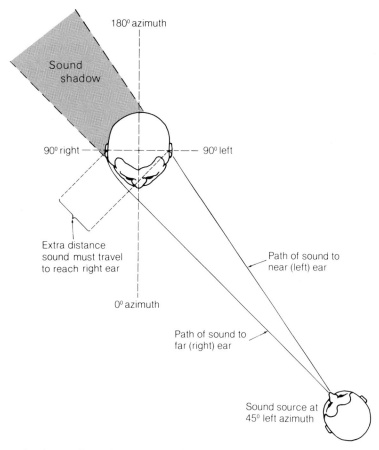

Figure 7-7 *The path of sound to the two ears for a sound source at 45 deg left azimuth (based on Lindsay & Norman, 1977).*

the hidden ear unless deflected into it. This ex-aggerates the intensity differences caused by the sound shadow for higher-frequency sounds. The changes in intensity difference as the angle of the sound source changes can serve as a cue to direction. A large intensity difference be-tween the two ears suggests that the source of the sound is positioned to one side; the greatest intensity difference occurs when the sound source is at 90 deg azimuth. The ear receiving the most intense input is closest to the sound source and is perceived to be so.

When a sound source is at an angle, sound must travel different distances to reach the two ears. This is always the case unless the sound source is positioned at either 0 or 180 deg,

when the ears are at equal distances from the source. Because sound takes time to travel through space, there is a **time difference** in the arrival of the sound at the two ears except for a sound at 0 or 180 deg azimuth. For a sound at 90 deg azimuth in either direction, the ear closer to the sound is stimulated approximately 0.80 msec earlier than the hidden ear. Interme-diate azimuths result in intermediate values for this time difference (see Figure 7-7). Such a time difference can be a cue to the location of a sound source and can result in the experience of an apparent direction for it. You can dem-onstrate the effects of this time difference on direction perception using Demonstration Box 7-4.

DEMONSTRATION BOX 7-4   Time Differences and Auditory Direction

For this demonstration you will need a length of rubber hose or flexible plastic tube. Hold one end up to each ear as shown in the figure. Now, have a friend tap the tube using a pencil. At the point where she taps, a sound wave starts moving in both directions down the tube. If she taps so that there is a

longer section of tube on one side, the sound must travel farther before reaching one of your ears. This delay is perceived as a shift in direction of the sound. Notice how the sound seems to change direction as different parts of the tube are tapped, causing differ-ent patterns of sound delays.

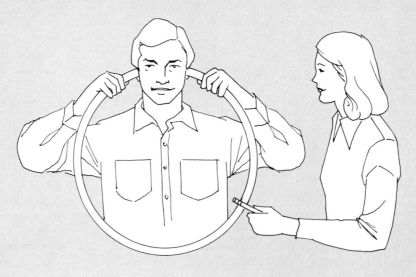

Under certain circumstances, the time difference between the stimulation of the two ears results in a **phase difference.** If a sound is arriving earlier at one ear it will be in a different portion of its cycle of compression and rarefaction of the air molecules than the sound arriving at the other ear (see Chapter 6). This is especially true for low-frequency sounds, where the time taken to complete one cycle is more than the maximum time difference of the arrival of sound at the two ears. For example, it takes a 1000-Hz tone exactly 1 msec to complete one cycle. If such a tone arrived 0.50 msec earlier at the closer ear (as it would if the sound source were positioned at about 62 deg azimuth), it would always be 0.50/1 or 1/2 cycle ahead of the sound arriving at the opposite ear.

Although phase difference could be a cue to sound direction, it provides ambiguous information when we consider the full range of sound frequencies. For instance, with a tone of 10,000 Hz at 62 deg azimuth, the time difference between the arrival of the sound at the two ears would once again be 0.50 msec. However, a 10,000-Hz tone takes only 0.10 msec to complete 1 cycle. This implies a phase difference of 0.50/0.10 or 5 cycles. Thus the sound at the ear closest to the source is 5 cycles ahead of the sound arriving at the more distant ear. However, every cycle is identical. Therefore, how can the observer tell just what the phase difference might be? It could range from 5 cycles to 1 cycle. Even at the lower frequencies, where potentially the phase difference cue could be more useful, the same phase difference is characteristic of sounds positioned directly opposite to one another (in reference to a line drawn through the head in any direction).

Finally, it has also been argued that the *pinnae* (the fleshy parts of the ears outside of the head) delay (Batteau, 1967) or amplify (Butler, 1987; Flannery & Butler, 1981) sounds of different frequencies by different amounts.

Such differential delays and amplifications apparently provide cues as to the location of complex sound sources, especially their elevation (Oldfield & Parker, 1984; Asano, Suzuki, & Sone, 1990). This is because the pinnae are asymmetrically shaped and shadow some frequencies more than others depending on their direction, therefore altering the sound spectra (frequency composition) of complex sounds at each of the two ears (Middlebrooks et al., 1989; Oldfield & Parker, 1986). These differences in spectra can serve as learned cues to the directions of the sounds.

In 1907, Lord Raleigh proposed a dual, or two-process, theory of sound localization. He suggested that we localize low-frequency sounds by using time or phase differences, or both, at the two ears, and that we localize high-frequency sounds by using the intensity differences at the two ears caused by the sound shadow and differences in their distance from the sound source. This notion has been confirmed by later research. For example, Stevens and Newman (1934) had observers with their eyes closed make judgments as to the azimuth of a sound source. The researchers played sounds of different frequencies from a variety of azimuths and recorded the listeners' errors of localization for each sound. Their data are shown in Figure 7-8.

The solid line in this graph represents a summary of the data they collected, with errors averaged over all the locations at a particular frequency. As you can see, most errors occurred in the region of 2000–4000 Hz. There were fewer errors above and below this frequency range. We can interpret this as indicating the efficient use of at least one cue in the low- and high-frequency ranges. Performance is worst in the midrange, however, where neither cue to localization is particularly useful. This interpretation has been confirmed by work on the **minimum audible angle,** which is the smallest amount of movement of a sound source that can be detected (Mills, 1958).

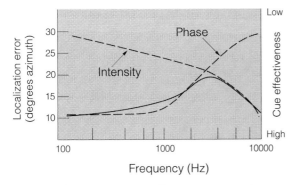

Figure 7-8 Relative cue effectiveness in arbitrary units for interaural intensity and phase differences (dashed lines) as a function of frequency. The solid line shows mean localization errors as a function of frequency (from Gulick, 1971. Copyright 1971 by Oxford University Press, Inc. Reprinted by permission. Data from Stevens & Newman, 1934).

The minimum audible angle varies as a function of frequency and location of a sound source. We are most sensitive to horizontal position changes when a sound source is centered in front of our nose (near 0 deg azimuth) but most sensitive to vertical positions when the sound is located directly at the side (90 deg azimuth) (Makous & Middlebrooks, 1990; Perrot & Saberi, 1990). Minimum audible angle also varies as a function of how fast a sound source is moving, being smallest when movement is in the horizontal or oblique direction at moderate velocities (Saberi & Perrott, 1990). On average, movements of a sound source of only 0.90 deg can be reliably detected under most conditions (Hartmann & Rakerd, 1989).

Direction and Distance Cues: Complex Sounds

When we are in an ordinary room, the sound from any source may bounce around the room, reflecting from the walls, ceiling, and floor many times before it reaches our ears. Figure 7-9 illustrates this phenomenon. Why do we not experience an overwhelming auditory confusion as these sounds ricochet around us?

Typically, we respond only to the *first* of the many replicas of a particular complex sound in echo-producing surroundings. We do not respond to the echoes that arrive several milliseconds later. In fact, we do not even experience echoes until the reflecting surface is far enough away so the echoes take a substantial time to reach us (more than 35 msec or so). Groups of sounds that arrive at intervals of less than 35 msec are fused into one sound. The first arrival appears to be the major determinant of where in space we perceive the sound source to be.

This phenomenon, called the **precedence effect,** has been extensively studied (see Rakerd & Hartmann, 1985; Wallach, Newman, & Rosenzweig, 1949; Zurek, 1980). The experiments of Wallach et al. (1949) indicated that the earliest of a pair of fused sounds (separated by 2 msec) was 6–10 times more important than the later of the pair in determining the perceived direction of the sound source. The study also showed that the precedence effect is

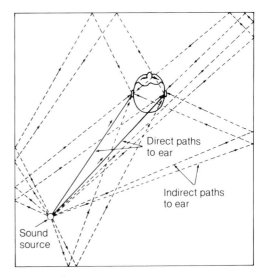

Figure 7-9 Some of the echoes produced by sound reflecting from the walls of a room. Unless the walls are quite far away, the echoes are not perceived (from Lindsay & Norman, 1977).

DEMONSTRATION BOX 7-5   Precedence and the One-Speaker Stereo Illusion

For this demonstration you will need a radio, phonograph, or tape recorder that has stereo speakers located about 2 m apart. Turn on some music and stand about midway between the two speakers, facing a point between them. You will notice that the sound seems to envelop you. It comes from both sides, and you can clearly identify sounds coming from one speaker or the other. Take a few steps (you need not go very far) toward one side where a speaker is located. After only a step or two you will suddenly find that all the sound seems to be coming from the speaker nearest you. You no longer get any sensation of sound coming from the more distant speaker (although it still affects sound quality as you can demonstrate by turning it off). A few steps to the other side will reverse this effect, making it appear as though all the sound is coming from the other speaker. As you move toward a speaker, you alter the time it takes for the sound to reach your ears. The precedence process then takes the sound arriving first and emphasizes it, giving you the impression that all the sound emanates from that source.

---

an important part of our ability to listen selectively to one source of sound out of a larger group of competing sounds (see the discussion of the cocktail party problem in Chapter 15). You can experience the effects of precedence on the localization of sound by using Demonstration Box 7-5.

Under appropriate conditions, echoes can be important to the judgment of the location of sounds. For example, blind individuals apparently use echoes to help them locate and avoid obstacles (Supra, Cotzin, & Dallenbach, 1944; Worchel & Dallenbach, 1947). Animals such as bats and whales have highly developed **echolocation systems,** similar to sonar, which they use to locate objects with the same facility with which we use our eyes (Simmons, 1989). They may even have special auditory brain pathways analogous to the tecto-pulvinar visual pathway (serving visual localization; see Chapter 3) to control scanning head movements, which in turn may help to build up a representation of the immediate environment (Kobler, Isbey, & Casseday, 1987), especially complex auditory images of prey (Simmons, 1989). We might call this representation *auditory space* to distinguish it from our more familiar perception of space based on vision.

There are several other cues to the spatial location of complex sounds. As we have suggested, head movements are important in building up our representation of auditory space. They serve to resolve ambiguities of location, such as whether the sound is in front of or behind the observer (Noble & Gates, 1985; Wallach, 1939). They also provide information showing that a sound is really "out there," as opposed to one generated inside the head, such as the ringing in the ears, called *tinnitus*, that some people experience if they take too much aspirin, have a bad head cold, or have permanent damage to a part of the inner ear. Internally generated noise does not change as you rotate your head, whereas sounds from the environment appear to.

Distance information is also carried by complex sounds. One major source of this information is the relative intensity of a sound, with nearer sources being more intense. Changes in sound distance are thus reliably coded by changes in sound intensity (Ashmead, LeRoy, & Odom, 1990; Mershon & King, 1975). Of course, it is always possible that the more distant source is emitting a stronger intensity signal, making this cue unreliable in deciding the absolute distance of a sound source unless the sound is a familiar one. Through experience we build up memories of what a phone bell or a car engine sounds like when these sounds are made at different distances from us. In later encounters we can use this knowledge to judge the distance of a sound source based on the remembered loudness of other similar sounds.

Another important source of distance information is the relative amount of **reverberation** in the impinging sound. As we stated earlier, sound reaches our ears both directly from a source and after being reflected from (*reverberating* from) various surfaces such as walls (see Figure 7-9). In general, as a sound source gets further away from an observer, the amount of sound that directly reaches the ears decreases more rapidly than the amount reaching the ears after reverberation. Thus, the relative amount of *reverberation sound* (which has a distinct quality, like an echo) is a cue to the distance of a sound source from an observer. Bekesy was one of the first to investigate this cue systematically. In 1938, he showed that altering the proportion of reverberant sound alters judgments of perceived distances of sounds (Bekesy, 1960). More recent work (Butler, Levy, & Neff, 1980; Mershon, Ballenger, Little, McMurtry, & Buchanan, 1989; Mershon & Bowers, 1979) has confirmed and extended this earlier work.

Another cue to distance that seems as compelling as the amount of reverberation is the frequency makeup, or *spectrum*, of a complex sound. Sounds composed mostly of high frequencies seem to come from quite nearby, and the more the sound is dominated by low-frequency components the farther away its source appears to be. Butler et al. (1980) sug-

gested that this is because more distant sounds typically are more dominated by low-frequency components, perhaps because the high-frequency components are so easily blocked by intervening obstructions. Again, our previous experiences may play a role in determining how far away we judge a sound to be based on the frequency spectrum.

A final important cue to the distance of a sound source is the presence of a compelling visual object that *could* be the source. Thus, the ventriloquist's dummy seems to be talking because its mouth moves and the ventriloquist's does not (if the ventriloquist is a good one). Echoes and reverberation play no role in this effect (Mershon, Desaulniers, & Amerson, 1980). The illusion that a sound is coming from a likely visual object can be so compelling that it can affect the perceived loudness of the sound. If the sound seems to emanate from far away, it sounds louder than if it seems to emanate from close by (Mershon, Desaulniers, Kiefer, & Amerson, 1981). Observers seem to correct for the fact that sound intensity diminishes rapidly as the distance from the sound source increases, a phenomenon termed *loudness constancy* (see Chapter 14 for a discussion of constancies).

Physiological Mechanisms

The auditory system contains neural units that respond to both time and intensity differences between the two ears, which may, in turn, signal the location of a sound source. For instance, some neurons in the superior olives, inferior colliculi (Semple & Kitzes, 1987), and auditory cortex of various birds and mammals respond best to binaural stimuli that reach the two ears at slightly different times or intensities (see Erulkar, 1972, and Phillips & Brugge, 1985, for reviews). Different neurons have different "best" interaural time differences, or different "best" interaural intensity differences. In other words, different neurons are "tuned" to different time or intensity differences between the two ears. Some neurons are also tuned to spectral differences that indicate elevation of the sound source (Aitkin & Martin, 1990). Since these differences are cues to the location of sounds, we could say that these tuned neurons encode sound location much as neurons tuned to sounds of different frequencies encode frequency. It is possible that such neurons constitute a kind of map of auditory space, with each neuron having a region of auditory space to which it responds best, a sort of "auditory receptive field" much like the visual receptive fields discussed in Chapter 3.

This idea has some problems, however. The major one is that the tuning of the neurons is too gross to account for the accuracy with which animals, including humans, can localize sounds. In other words the auditory receptive fields of these neurons are too large to account for the accuracy shown in behavioral data. In some species, such as the barn owl, neurons with much smaller, more intricately organized auditory receptive fields have been found using electrophysiological recording techniques (Knudsen & Konishi, 1978a). In the barn owl the receptive fields of these neurons have a center-surround organization (Knudsen & Konishi, 1978b). That is, not only do these neurons fire above their background rate to stimuli in their "best" areas of space, but also they are inhibited in their response by sounds in areas outside their best areas, thus resembling, in many ways, the center-surround organization of neurons at various levels of the visual system (see Chapter 3) and other parts of the auditory system (see Chapter 6). So far no direct evidence has been found that such center-surround neurons exist in the auditory systems of mammals, but it is possible that the time and intensity difference detectors are preliminary stages leading to such neurons.

Some researchers have speculated that interaction of time and intensity difference detectors might give rise to higher-level neurons that have relatively restricted receptive fields and might allow a fairly accurate auditory mapping of auditory space. One way this could happen is that *change* in time or intensity difference cues could be coded more precisely than the absolute values of the time difference between the ears or stimulus intensities. It has been shown psychophysically that the localization mechanism adapts very quickly to sounds that do not change. On the other hand, the localization mechanism seems to cancel this adaptation and responds vigorously again as soon as a stimulus change occurs (Hafter & Buell, 1990). In cats and gerbils, the inferior colliculi neurons respond more accurately to *changes* in interaural phase than to interaural phase itself (Spitzer & Semple, 1991). Another possibility is that the auditory map of space is based on or calibrated by the more precise map of visual space by assigning spatial coordinates to particular auditory neurons. Visual maps of space clearly calibrate auditory maps in the barn owl, both in terms of performance (Knudsen & Knudsen, 1989) and in the superior colliculus of the brain (Knudsen & Brainerd, 1991).

SUBJECTIVE DIMENSIONS OF SOUND

The analyses of detection and discrimination of sounds we have described so far may seem somewhat divorced from our subjective experiences of sounds. In the past, experimenters believed that a direct correspondence existed between subjective experiences of sounds and physical properties of sounds. It was taken for granted that every *qualitatively different psychological variable* would reflect almost perfectly some corresponding *quantifiable physical variable*. For example, it was believed that the subjective dimension of **loudness** was a direct reflection of the physical dimension of *amplitude* (or intensity of the sound-wave stimulus. In similar fashion, it was believed that the subjective dimension of **pitch** (whether a sound is high or low in tone) simply reflected the *frequency* of the sound wave. This mechanistic viewpoint has been opposed by many investigators, who have pointed out that we should separate concepts and expressions that describe our conscious or phenomenal experience from those that describe the physical stimulus. The subjective qualities of loudness and pitch are complex perceptions that depend on the interaction of several physical characteristics of the stimulus, as well as the physical and psychological state of the observer.

The deeply rooted older view maintained that at best a person could be expected to distinguish only two phenomenal dimensions of sound (loudness and pitch) because there are two predominant physical dimensions of sound (intensity and frequency). Actually, we can differentiate many qualitatively different experiences arising from sound stimuli. These include not only pitch and loudness, but also the **perceived location** of a sound (where it seems to come from), its **perceived duration** (how extended in time it appears to be), its **timbre** (that complex quality that allows us to distinguish a note played on a clarinet from the same note played on a violin), its **volume** (the sense in which it fills space and seems large or small), and its **density** (a complex feeling of the compactness or hardness of the sound), as well as **consonance** or **dissonance** (how two sounds seem to "go together" or "clash"). Our auditory experience is rich with these and other sensory qualities—it is not simply a crude device to register the frequency and intensity of sounds.

Recent work has emphasized the interaction of these subjective dimensions of sound rather than their separateness. For example, pitch and loudness are indeed "privileged" dimensions, since people can classify sounds faster on the basis of pitch and loudness than on the basis of volume or other subjective qualities (Grau & Nelson, 1988). However, pitch and loudness do interfere with one another in such tasks, and each also interferes with timbre (Grau & Nelson, 1988; Melara & Marks, 1990). Our subjective experiences of sounds not only provide additional richness to our conscious experience of sound, but also interact with one another to produce complex effects. In the sections that follow, we will discuss a few of these subjective experiences of sound in more detail.

Loudness

The experienced loudness of a sound is greatly affected by the stimulus intensity. If everything else is held constant, it is fair to say that the greater the amplitude of a sound the greater its apparent loudness. The experience of loudness, however, is *not* identical with stimulus intensity, and other factors influence our experience of the loudness of a sound. Thus decibels are *not* measures of loudness.

To study loudness we use psychophysical scaling procedures such as those discussed in Chapter 2. Stevens (1956) did a classic study of this type using magnitude estimation. In his study, observers listened to 1000-Hz tones of different intensities and assigned a number to each one in such a way that the number was proportional to its perceived loudness relative to a standard intensity that was given the number 100. Thus, a tone that sounded twice as loud as the standard would be called 200 and a tone that sounded half as loud would be called 50. Stevens found that the perception of loudness varied according to the simple equation $L = aI^{0.6}$ where L is the perceived loudness, I is the physical intensity of the sound (in units of pressure amplitude), and a is a constant. Loudness increased as approximately the 0.6 power of the pressure amplitude, meaning that changes in weaker stimuli produce more of a change in loudness than changes in stronger stimuli. The precise value of the exponent depends on the specific stimuli used and the test conditions employed (Marks, 1974). For example, the exponent of the power function varies with stimulus frequency, being somewhat larger for frequencies lower than 400 Hz (Hellman & Zwislocki, 1968; Ward, 1990).

Based on his own and others' work, Stevens suggested a new unit by which to measure loudness based on comparison of loudness to the apparent loudness of a standard sound. For this standard sound, he chose a 40 dB, 1000-Hz pure tone. Any sound that matches this in loudness is said to have a loudness value of 1 **sone.** For most of the stimulus range, a linear relationship exists between the loudness measured by the logarithm of the number of sones and the sound pressure level measured in decibels. To double the loudness (for instance, from 1 to 2 sones), we must increase the sound pressure level of the sound by about 10 dB. For very weak sounds (below 30 dB), however, the change in apparent loudness is much more rapid with increases in sound pressure level (for example, Canevet, Hellman, & Scharf, 1986). This relationship is shown in Figure 7-10, which also shows the loudness in sones of some typical sounds. Table 7-1 summarizes essential aspects of sones and other audiometric units discussed in this chapter.

Our perception of the loudness of a tone is also affected by its frequency. One way to measure this relationship is to present an observer

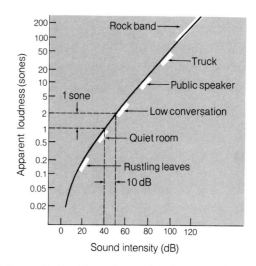

Figure 7-10 *The relationship between loudness (measured in sones) and stimulus intensity (measured in decibels).*

with a standard tone of a given frequency and intensity and ask the person to adjust the intensity of a tone with a different frequency until its loudness matches that of the standard tone. This procedure is repeated for tones of various frequencies. A curve that describes the intensities at which tones of varying frequencies appear to be equally loud as the standard tone is called an **equal loudness contour.**

A series of equal loudness contours is shown in Figure 7-11. Each curve represents a

Table 7-1 Audiometric Units

AUDIOMETRIC TERM	UNIT	WHAT IS MEASURED	HOW MEASURED
Pressure amplitude	Dyne/cm^2	Variation of sound pressure from atmospheric	Measure peak compressive force per 1 cm^2 area
Sound pressure level	Decibel (dB)	Ratio of pressure amplitudes of two sounds	$20 \log (P/P_0)$
Frequency	Hertz (Hz)	Number of cycles of compression/rarefaction	Count cycles per second
Loudness	Sone	Subjective impression of sound intensity	1 sone=loudness of 1000-Hz tone at 40 dB
Pitch	Mel	Subjective impression of sound frequency	Pitch of 1000-Hz tone at 40 db is 1000 mels

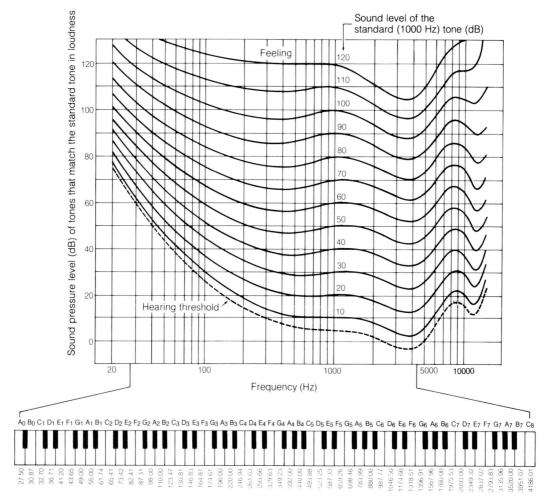

Figure 7-11 *Equal loudness contours (from Lindsay & Norman, 1977. Data from Robinson & Dadson, 1956).*

different sound pressure level of the standard tone in decibels. Notice that the lines are not flat. If tones of various frequencies sounded equally loud when they were the same intensity, all of the curves would be horizontal straight lines. The fact that the contours rise and fall with frequency (much as the graph of absolute threshold for sound varies with frequency) means that tones of equal intensity but of different frequencies appear to differ in loudness. Tones of less than 1000 Hz, or greater than 6000 Hz, must be considerably more intense to match the loudnesses of tones between 1000 and 6000 Hz. Thus, tones in the middle range of frequencies sound considerably louder than equally intense tones outside this range.

Duration also influences the apparent loudness of a tone. For tones briefer than about 200 msec, we must increase intensity to match the loudness of a longer tone. An equal-

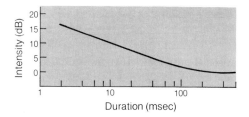

Figure 7-12 *Equal loudness contour showing the changes in intensity needed to maintain a constant loudness as the duration of the standard is varied (from Gulick, 1971. Copyright 1971 by Oxford University Press, Inc. Reprinted by permission).*

loudness contour for tones of various durations is shown in Figure 7-12. According to this curve, a 2-msec burst of sound must have a sound pressure level of about 16 dB in order to sound as loud as a 10-msec burst at 10 dB. This suggests that the auditory system may sum all of the inputs arriving over a 200-msec window of time (Gulick, 1971).

Presentation of the same stimulus to both ears causes the subjective impressions of loudness from each ear to add together (Algom, Ben-Aharon, & Cohen-Raz, 1989; Levelt, Riemersma, & Bunt, 1972; Marks, 1979b). Thus, a binaural presentation will sound about twice as loud as a monaural presentation of the same tone. If you have a sound source nearby such as a radio or a television, you can demonstrate this for yourself by assessing the loudness when you hear the source with two ears and then by covering one ear and noting how the apparent loudness diminishes. The mechanism that sums loudnesses from the two ears appears to be separate from the one that sums loudnesses over time (Algom, Rubin, & Cohen-Raz, 1989).

Other sounds occurring at the same time, or just before, a sound to be judged also can affect apparent loudness. For example, if a continuous tone is played to one ear and an intermittent one to the other, the loudness of the continuous tone appears to diminish with time

(Botte, Canevet, & Scharf, 1982). The reduction in apparent intensity for a continuously presented stimulus is called **auditory adaptation.** Adaptation is weak for a continuous tone alone but can be quite dramatic when different tones are presented to the two ears. The apparent loudness of the continuous tone actually diminishes to zero if the intermittent tone in the other ear is close to it in frequency and is presented for 40 seconds (Botte, Baruch, & Scharf, 1986).

A related phenomenon, called **auditory fatigue,** is caused by exposing the ear to very intense sounds. The resultant reduction of loudness of other stimuli presented after the intense sound stops may persist for a considerable time. For instance, Postman and Egan (1949) exposed observers to an intense sound (115 dB) for 20 minutes. They then measured the sensitivity of their observers over a period of several days. The results are shown in Figure 7-13. The horizontal line represents preexposure sensitivity, and the other curves represent the hearing loss, which could be interpreted as a reduction in loudness, for varying periods of time following exposure to the stimulus. As you can see, the largest hearing loss immediately follows the exposure to the intense noise; however, it persists to measurable extent over a period of 24 hours. You can experience an interesting analog to this experiment using Demonstration Box 7-6.

Another factor that influences our perception of loudness is the complexity of the stimulus. Most of the sounds we hear in our everyday environment are mixtures of many different frequencies of sound. We can create a new kind of equal loudness contour by asking listeners to adjust the intensity of a pure tone of 1000 Hz until its loudness matches that of some complex sound. Suppose we take a complex sound composed of a group of frequencies clustered around 1000 Hz. We can systematically increase or decrease the range of frequencies in-

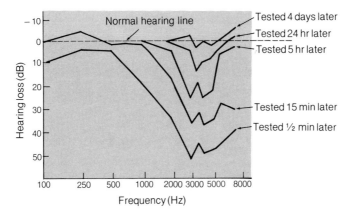

Figure 7-13 *Prolonged reduction of loudness following exposure to an intense (115 dB) sound for 20 minutes (based on Postman & Egan, 1949).*

cluded, changing the highest or lowest frequencies in the mixture, or both. We usually refer to the range of frequencies as the **bandwidth.** As the bandwidth of the sound is increased, the intensity of each of the component frequencies is decreased in order to keep the overall intensity of the sound the same. Figure 7-14 displays an equal loudness contour for such a complex sound. Notice that when only a small band of frequencies makes up the complex sound, increasing the bandwidth does not affect our per-

ception of the loudness of the stimulus. This is reasonable, since the total intensity of the sound is not changing but only the number of different frequencies included in it. Notice, however, what happens when the frequencies reach a critical bandwidth of about 160 Hz. From this bandwidth onward, loudness begins to increase as we include a greater number of frequencies, although the total intensity of the sound is unchanged (Cacace & Margolis, 1985; Scharf, 1978).

DEMONSTRATION BOX 7-6   Auditory Fatigue

During an average day you are exposed to many noises and sounds, from individuals who talk with you, from stereos, televisions, radios, and numerous other sources. Set a radio or a stereo to an intensity level where the sound seems comfortable for listening in the evening before you go to bed. At the day's end, your auditory system has become fatigued by the ongoing, persistent noise of the day. When you awaken in the morning, however, you may find that the radio, set to

the same sound level, will appear to be too loud. During the night your ears have recovered from the auditory fatigue caused by exposure to the sounds you heard during the previous day. The quiet of the night has given you a chance to recover your sensitivity; hence all sounds now seem louder. This may explain why an alarm clock, whose bell seems low and pleasant when bought one evening in a department store, will seem so jarring and loud the following morning.

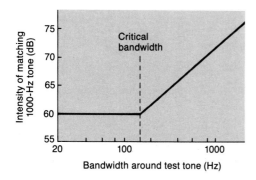

Figure 7-14 *The effect on loudness of increasing the bandwidth of frequencies in a complex tone (based on Gulick, 1971).*

Pitch

Every time you sing or play a musical scale, you are varying the subjective experience of **pitch.** The *do, re,* and *mi* you sing differ in pitch. The most important physical determinant of our perception of pitch is the frequency of the sound stimulus. The high notes on the piano have higher frequencies than the low notes. For instance, the dominant frequency of A_4 (the 49th key on the extended piano keyboard pictured in Figure 7-11, counting from the left—A_0 the lowest note on the standard piano—to the right) is 440 Hz. The dominant frequency of the A note one octave higher (A_5 or the 61st key from the left) is 880 Hz.

An important demonstration of the relationship between frequency and pitch was performed by Robert Hooke in 1681. Hooke placed a card against a wheel that had teeth notched in it, and then spun the wheel. The spinning wheel's teeth hit the card and the resultant vibrations sent out a sound wave—a sort of rough, buzzing musical note. When the speed of rotation was increased, the frequency of vibration of the card increased, and so did the pitch of the note. For centuries thereafter, the terms *pitch* and *frequency* were used interchangeably on the assumption that pitch rises and falls in exact step with frequency. However, this turns out not to be so.

The most commonly used measure of the pitch of a sound is probably the musical scale. Any note one octave higher than another note of the same name has exactly twice the frequency of the lower note, resulting in equal spacing of the logarithms of the frequencies. Thus, the note A_3 (the 37th key from the left in Figure 7-11) has a frequency of 220 Hz, whereas A_4 (the 49th key from the left) is one octave higher and has a frequency of 440 Hz. The musical scale has undergone very little change over the years, although some attempts have been made to adjust the spacing between the notes in an attempt to represent more accurately the pitches of different musical notes. One example, is a version of the musical scale called the **equal temperament scale** (W. D. Ward, 1970). Here each octave is divided into 12 standard intervals (representing equal logarithmic steps) between the musical notes. These intervals are called *semitones*, and each semitone can be further divided into 100 *cents.* Thus, an octave consists of 1200 cents, and the pitch of any tone can be precisely described in terms of what octave it is in and how many cents it lies above the lowest tone in that octave.

The most useful psychological scale for pitch so far is the **mel** scale proposed by Stevens, Volkman, and Newman (1937). Like the sone scale of loudness, the mel scale can be created by various psychophysical scaling techniques. For instance, in one experiment the researchers created a sort of electronic piano with 20 keys and 20 corresponding knobs set above the keyboard. Turning a knob varied the tone produced by the corresponding key through a wide range of frequencies. Listeners tuned the "piano" to produce pitch intervals that appeared to be equally wide. The results were surprising. Subjects did not tune the piano to equal steps on the frequency scale, nor did they tune them to equal steps on a scale of musical intervals.

To specify pitch, as in the case of loudness, we select a standard stimulus for purposes of comparison. The standard stimulus is the same as that used for sones, namely a sound with a frequency of 1000 Hz and an intensity of 40 dB. This tone has been assigned a pitch of 1000 mels (see Table 7-1 for a summary of measures of frequency and pitch). This frequency lies between the notes B_5 and C_6 on the extended piano keyboard in Figure 7-11 (the 63rd and the 64th keys from the left). When we compare the mel scale with the musical scale, we find several large discrepancies. For instance, the one-octave difference between C_3 (Key 28) and C_4 (Key 46) is 167 mels, whereas the one-octave difference between C_6 (Key 64) and C_7 (Key 76) is 508 mels. Such measurements confirm the feeling, often expressed by musicians, that the higher musical octaves sound "larger" than the lower ones. It is as if

more "psychological distance" exists between the keys at the high end of the piano than between those at the low end. The linear relationship between the musical scale and the logarithm of sound frequency is shown in Figure 7-15A. The nonlinear relationship between perceived pitch (in mels) and the logarithm of sound frequency is shown in Figure 7-15B.

Just as factors other than sound intensity affect the loudness of a sound, factors other than frequency affect its pitch. A glance at Figure 7-15B shows that pitch is not identical with frequency. This is verified by the fact that when a listener is asked to find a sound that is half the pitch of a standard sound, the individual does not produce a sound that is half the frequency of the standard. Perhaps the major physical factor, other than frequency, that affects the perceived pitch of a pure tone is its intensity. In a classic demonstration of this, a tuning fork tuned to middle C (C_4 or 262 Hz) was struck a few feet from the ear of a trained

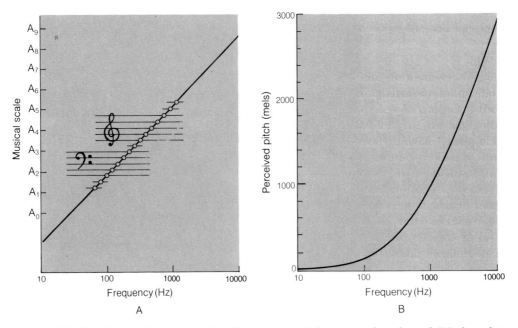

Figure 7-15 (A) *The relationship between log frequency and the musical scale and* (B) *the relationship between mels and log frequency (from Lindsay & Norman, 1977).*

singer. She was asked to sing the note she heard, and she reproduced the sound with reasonable accuracy. Next, the investigator held the same tuning fork a few inches from her ear. This increased the intensity of the sound reaching her ear, but it left the frequency unchanged since a tuning fork (when properly struck) produces sounds of only a single frequency. Nonetheless, the pitch the singer heard did change. She now sang a note that was considerably lower in pitch than middle C, clearly demonstrating that sound intensity affects pitch.

Using an experimental technique similar to that used in producing equal loudness contours, we can produce equal **pitch contours.** The listener can be asked either to adjust the intensity of one of two tones that differ in frequency until the two tones match in pitch (Stevens, 1935) or to adjust the frequency of one of two tones that differ in intensity until it matches the other in pitch (Gulick, 1971). Figure 7-16 shows the results from one listener measured by Stevens (1935). The graph shows the percentage change in the frequency necessary to keep the pitch constant as intensity is changed. The ordinate was chosen so that lines

curving upward mean that the pitch is increasing (sounds higher) and lines curving downward mean that the pitch is decreasing (sounds lower). As the figure shows, varying the intensity of the tone alters its perceived pitch. For higher-frequency tones the pitch tends to rise as intensity increases, whereas for lower-frequency tones an increase in intensity tends to lower the pitch.

Another factor that affects our perception of pitch is the duration of the stimulus. A pure tone that lasts for only a few milliseconds is always heard as a click, whatever the frequency. Before a tone is perceived to have the quality of pitch, one of two conditions must be met. For high-frequency tones (greater than 1000 Hz), the minimum length of time the stimulus must be sounded is around 10 msec. For low-frequency tones (less than 1000 Hz), at least 6–9 cycles of the sound wave must reach the ear before it is perceived to have pitch, meaning that most lower-frequency tones must last for considerably longer than 10 msec before they have pitch (Gulick, 1971). Even for tones that exceed the minimum duration for number of cycles, the tonal quality continues to improve as the duration is increased up to about

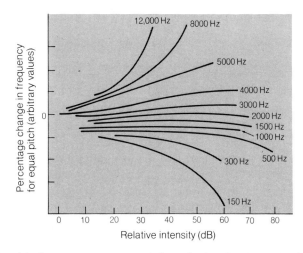

Figure 7-16 *The relationship between apparent pitch and stimulus intensity for one listener (based on Stevens, 1935).*

250 msec. Listeners are better able to discriminate between tones of different frequencies when their duration is longer. You may recall that the loudness of a tone also increases as we increase stimulus duration up to around 200–250 msec. Perhaps a quarter of a second represents some sort of fundamental time period for sensory systems such as the ear. Our phenomenal impressions of the world in many modalities seem to be based on averages or sums of energy changes taken over this small window of time (see also Chapter 13).

Theories of Pitch Perception

We now have some inkling of *where* in the cortex pitch is encoded. Studies with patients with parts of their temporal lobes removed (to control epilepsy) suggest that a part of the right temporal lobe called *Heschl's gyrus* (in area A1 of the brain; see Figure 6-18) might be where pitch is computed (Zatorre, 1988). The issue of *how* pitch is computed, and what information from the ear is used to do this, is a bit more complex. To explore this issue, let us first introduce you to an auditory "illusion."

Suppose we create a complex sound by adding several different sinusoidal sound waves (pure tones). The auditory system conducts its own waveform analysis of the complex sound, and we are able to perceive the pitch of the various components separately. For instance, if two tones are played simultaneously, you perceive a musical chord containing two distinct pitches—you do not hear a single, unitary sound (as you discovered in Demonstration Box 6-2).

When we are considering a complex stimulus composed of several sound-wave frequencies, the lowest (usually most intense) frequency sound wave is called the **fundamental.** Musical instruments tend to produce complex sounds in which **harmonics** (frequencies higher than the fundamental) occur at wholenumber multiples of the fundamental frequency. For example, we have already noted that a sound wave of 220 Hz corresponds to a musical note that we call A (it would be A_3, or the 37th key from the left, in Figure 7-11). When a musical instrument sounds this note, the complex waveform produced also will contain some sound energy at frequencies of 440 Hz, 880 Hz, 1320 Hz, and so on. These would be called *high even harmonics* (because they represent frequencies of 2, 4, and 6 times the fundamental frequency). The characteristic sound of a particular instrument depends on the specific harmonics it produces, a quality called its **timbre.** Different instruments emphasize different higher harmonics (sometimes called *overtones*). The number of higher harmonics and their strength determine the complex perception that allows us to distinguish between a note played on a piano and the same note (with the same pitch) played by plucking a violin or a guitar string. The pitch of a sound is largely determined by the frequency of the fundamental, whereas the timbre is determined by the harmonics. Helmholtz's (1863/1930) summary of the various subjective feelings pertaining to the composition of a complex tone is shown in Table 7-2.

Because the fundamental frequency is the greatest common factor of all the harmonics present in a complex sound, we could correctly determine the fundamental from our knowledge of the way in which harmonics work. For example, if we had harmonics of 600, 900, and 1200 Hz, the fundamental frequency would be 300 Hz. As just noted, a complex waveform normally contains both a fundamental frequency and several higher harmonics. For experimental purposes it is possible to present together a set of pure tones that have a particular fundamental without presenting the fundamental (for example, 600-, 900-, and 1200-Hz tones without the 300-Hz fundamental). Such an artificial sound complex, from which the

Table 7-2   Sound Composition and Timbre (based on Helmholtz, 1863/1930)

MAKEUP OF COMPLEX TONE	SUBJECTIVE IMPRESSION
Fundamental alone	Soft
Fundamental plus first harmonic	Mellow
Fundamental plus several harmonics	Broad or full
Fundamental plus high harmonics	Sharp
Fundamental intense, harmonics less intense	Full
Harmonics intense, fundamental less intense	Hollow
Odd harmonics (for example, 1, 3, 5,) dominating	Nasal
Frequency ratios of 16:15, 9:8, 15:8, 7:5, or 7:6	Rough or screeching

fundamental frequency is missing, is called a stimulus with a **missing fundamental.**

An interesting and puzzling problem comes from a particular illusion associated with the missing fundamental. Suppose you are presented with two complex sounds. One contains the fundamental along with the higher harmonics and the other contains only the higher harmonics. The illusion lies in the fact that the pitch of both sounds appears to be that of the fundamental frequency, and thus the same, even though the fundamental frequency is not physically present in the waveform of the second sound (it has a missing fundamental). This phenomenon is fairly universal, since several lower animals, including cats, birds, and monkeys, have been shown to perceive the missing fundamental in the same way as humans (Tomlinson & Schwarz, 1988). Furthermore, magnetic recordings of brain response of humans show that in the primary auditory cortex the same response is produced when a complex sound with a missing fundamental is presented as when the sound complex contains the fundamental tone (Pantev, Hoke, Lutkenhoner, & Lehnertz, 1989).

While this auditory illusion seems of only passing interest, it actually has an important role in testing the two major theories of pitch. The first theory of pitch perception is based on the **place principle** and the second is based on the **frequency principle.** The place principle states that different pitches are encoded at different places along the basilar membrane; the frequency principle states that pitch is encoded by the frequency of neural activity in the auditory nerve.

To be more specific, the place principle began more than 100 years ago, when Helmholtz became intrigued by the fact that the ear could separate a complex sound stimulus into its component simple frequencies. He suggested that some parts of the basilar membrane resonate to (that is, vibrate in sympathy with) lower-frequency tones, whereas other parts resonate to tones of higher frequency. Thus, if we sounded a complex tone, it would be automatically decomposed into its component frequencies on the basilar membrane. Each different tone would cause a different *place* on the membrane to vibrate.

This basic idea was later supported and modified by Bekesy in a series of precise experiments (see Bekesy, 1960). He discovered that high-frequency tones maximally displace the narrow end of the basilar membrane near the oval window, and tones of lower frequencies cause displacement farther toward the other (wider) end of the basilar membrane. The action of the basilar membrane was not quite as simple as Helmholtz's resonance notion, however, since waves of activation were found to travel down the membrane. Moreover, as we discussed in Chapter 6, complex interactions occur between outer hair cells and the basilar membrane that sharpen the mechanical tuning of the basilar membrane (the active process).

The place theory has difficulty in explaining the phenomenon of the missing fundamental. Hemholtz attempted to deal with this by suggesting that the conduction process in the middle ear distorts the sound waves before they affect the cochlea. This distortion creates the fundamental frequency, so the fundamental is present inside the cochlea even though it is missing in the stimulus that contacts the outer ear. Bekesy (1960) modified this notion somewhat so the distortion became part of the response of the basilar membrane, which was said to respond "as if" the fundamental were also physically present.

Unfortunately, several experimental results throw doubt on this distortion hypothesis for the missing fundamental. The basic form of such experiments (Patterson, 1969) involves the presentation of pairs of tones, such as 2000 Hz and 2400 Hz, which would produce a missing fundamental of 400 Hz. If a low-frequency band of noise, centered at 400 Hz, is now added to the complex wave, we would expect that when the noise is sufficiently intense it would be very effective in masking the fundamental tone, since it is stimulating approximately the place on the basilar membrane that is, according to the place theory, vibrating. Nevertheless, despite the presence of this noise, the pitch of the complex wave is still perceived to be that of the fundamental frequency. This rules out the suggested place theory distortion mechanism for the missing fundamental phenomenon.

The second major class of theory is based on the *frequency principle*, where a sound wave of, for example, 100 Hz, which has 100 pressure peaks per second, will be transduced into a neural signal that gives 100 bursts of activity per second down the auditory nerve. The frequency principle also has a long history,

having been championed by August Seeback in the 1840s (Green, 1976) and then carried forward to the present by Wever (1970) and in a modified form by J. L. Goldstein (1973). Specifically, this theory argues that the vibrations of the basilar membrane reproduce at least partially the vibrations of the incoming sounds. The frequency of the sound is transmitted by the pattern of neural excitation resulting from this vibration. This situation is analogous to the microphone end of a telephone transducing the pattern of vibrations into variations of electrical signals as it vibrates in unison with your voice. According to this theory, pitch is determined by the frequency of impulses traveling up the auditory nerve. The greater the frequency, the higher the pitch. Some studies have shown that for tones of up to about 4000 Hz, the electrical response of the auditory nerve tracks the frequency of the tone (see Chapter 6). A tone of 500 Hz produces a pattern of response that contains some 500 bursts of electrical responses per second in the nerve, and a tone of 1000 Hz produces twice as many responses.

Such a theoretical position could explain the missing fundamental. Since there are many harmonics but only one fundamental frequency, masking the region of the fundamental should not appreciably change the general pattern of sound excitation. The low frequency of the fundamental may actually be signaled by the neurons that respond to the higher harmonics, since these neurons convey most of the information about the pattern of excitation. This may seem topsy-turvy in that we are saying that the fundamental is *not* fundamental, yet consider the example we used earlier in our discussion. Given a sound wave with harmonics of 600, 900, and 1200 Hz, the fundamental is inferred to be 300 Hz. In much the same way that we *infer* the fundamental from knowledge of the harmonic structure, a higher auditory center ("pitch processor") could infer the fundamental from the pattern of excitation reported by neurons that respond to higher frequencies (see Goldstein, 1973; Javel, 1981; Srulovicz & Goldstein, 1983).

This phenomenon can be verified to a certain extent by the following experiment. We again present an individual with a pair of tones, such as 2000 and 2400 Hz, to produce a missing fundamental of 400 Hz. If we now introduce a high-frequency band of noise, centered at 2200 Hz and extending for several hundred Hertz on either side of it (which should mask the higher harmonics), the missing fundamental is no longer heard (Patterson, 1969).

Additional experiments give a similar picture. If we present one component of a complex tone, say 600 Hz, to one ear, and another, say 800 Hz, to the other, a missing fundamental corresponding to 200 Hz is perceived (Houtsma & Goldstein, 1972). Here no activity on either basilar membrane could correspond to that created when a 200-Hz pure tone stimulates it, since each membrane was stimulated only by a single tone far from 200 Hz. Missing fundamental pitches seem to be perceived using a different mechanism than that used for the pitch of pure tones.

Problems also exist with the frequency theory for pitch perception. One difficulty is that an individual neuron cannot fire at high enough rates to account for the perception of high-frequency signals. An individual neuron can conduct only about 1000 impulses per second. Thus, the ability of the auditory nerve to track frequencies above this point (up to about 4000 Hz; see the discussion of phase-locking in Chapter 6) has to be explained in terms of a **volley principle** (Wever, 1970), which describes how neural fibers fire in groups or squads. While one neuron is "reloading" (actually resting between impulses), its neighbour might be firing. The overall effect down the auditory nerve is still a burst of activity for each pressure peak in the sound input, although different neurons are firing at different times. An example of how this can work is shown in Figure 7-17. The use of this volley mechanism may be sharpened or supported by an individual's learning and experience (Hall & Peters, 1982; Terheardt, 1974).

A major problem with a volley principle of pitch perception is that it requires the frequency of neural firing to encode both the intensity and the frequency of the sound. Although at first this seems impossible, one way to resolve the problem is to differentiate a concept involving the *total density* of neural activity from one based on the *number of volleys* (or bursts of firing) per unit time. The density of neural firing is the total number of neurons responding in each volley, or the number of "shots" being fired in each volley down the auditory nerve. An increase in the intensity of the sound, although not changing the volley frequency, could increase the number of neurons joining in the firing, or cause the rate of each individual neuron to increase somewhat. If all the neurons were connected to some higher center (the pitch processor) that computes pitch based on the frequency of volleys, and loudness based on the number of responses per volley, the problem would be solved. An example of how this could work is also shown in Figure 7-17.

Since both the place principle and the frequency principle seem to be supported by some data, it seems likely, as Wever (1970) has suggested, that the ultimate explanation of pitch will include some aspects of both theories. Wever has proposed that in humans pitch is coded by the frequency principle for frequencies lower than about 4000 Hz (the theoretical upper limit for volleying). For frequencies from 500 to 20,000 Hz, the place principle can explain pitch perception. Below 500 Hz, however, the vibration pattern on the basilar membrane seems too broad to explain our excellent pitch discrimination by the place

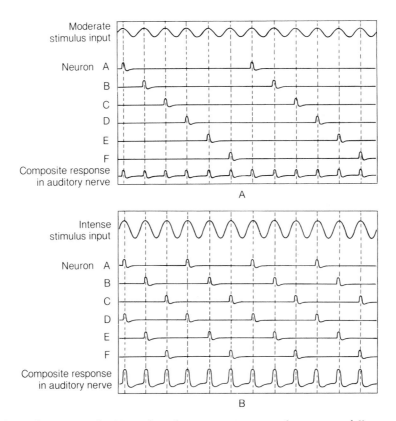

Figure 7-17   *The volley principle. Note that the composite neural response follows the frequency of the stimulus. However, for the weaker stimulus* (A) *fewer neurons are firing in each volley than for the stronger stimulus* (B).

theory, so the frequency theory is needed to explain performance in this frequency range. Notice that for frequencies between 500 and 4000 Hz, both principles are operating. This could explain the superior performance of the ear for sounds in this range as compared to sounds of higher or lower frequencies. For frequencies outside this range we must rely on only one mechanism; therefore performance is poorer.

The place–frequency compromise is supported by a good deal of research (for example, Srulovicz & Goldstein, 1983). In one study, Simmons et al. (1965) placed electrodes in the auditory nerve corresponding to different parts of the basilar membrane of a subject's deaf ear. They found that electrical stimulation produced an auditory sensation for this person, as expected. More importantly, stimulation at different locations produced the perception of different pitches. Similarly, modern cochlear implants (see Chapter 6) produce perceptions of pitch differences by electrically stimulating different places in the cochlea (Townshend et al., 1987). This, of course, supports the place principle. In another stimulation study, Simmons et al. (1965) varied the frequency of the electrical stimulus from about 20 to 300 Hz in a subject. These various rates of stimulation produced the appropriate changes in pitch perception regardless of the specific place where the stimulating electrode was located. This supports the frequency principle. Clearly both mechanisms are needed to explain all of the data.

Auditory Scene Analysis

Everyday sounds are not simple, isolated, and meaningless pure tones or noise bursts. We are surrounded most of the time by a multitude of complex hisses, squeaks, booms, chirps, and roars, not to mention the constant streams of words or music that pour out of our social gatherings. All of these sounds are rich sources of diagnostic information about important events happening in our world. How do our auditory systems and the rest of our brains deal with this enormous flow of sound to produce the rich auditory world, filled with sounding objects, events, and locations, that we experience?

The most general way to view our auditory surroundings is as an **auditory scene** (Bregman, 1990). At any moment, the auditory scene may consist of any number of sound-producing events. The sound from each source or event varies in spectrum (the amplitude of sound at each frequency), duration, location, and time. Sounds from various events are all mixed together in the pattern of acoustic energy received by the ear. The problem we are faced with is to build separate mental representations of the various sound sources from the mixture received. This is called **auditory scene analysis.** To analyze the auditory scene into its components, we must infer backwards from the mixture of sound we receive to the events that generated them. To complicate matters further, in order to build a coherent picture of the world, we must integrate the mental representation of the auditory scene with the representation of the world extracted by our visual analyses of the scene. It is likely that the auditory and the visual maps of the world are "calibrated" against each other as we grow and develop, through multisensory experience with various objects and events. It is also affected by processes such as visual capture, which we discussed earlier in this chapter. Figure 7-18 illustrates the problem, where all of the sounds from a trio of musicians mix at the ear, but must be sorted out both as to identity and location to create the auditory scene.

The actual construction of the auditory scene in consciousness appears to involve at least two mechanisms. The first is a fast, involuntary process of auditory grouping. The second involves using *schemas* to guide the grouping and listening process. Schemas are higher-level hypotheses or expectations based upon our knowledge of familiar sounds (Bregman, 1990).

The more primitive auditory grouping mechanism uses several sources of information. First it analyses the continuous flow of sound received by the ear into separate time chunks and tries to group sounds together according to shared frequency ranges. Each time/frequency segment is described in terms of intensity, temporal change, frequency change, location, and other variables, which also include some of the variables that give rise to our perception of sound location (such as time delays between arrival at the two ears, and so forth). Finally it groups together sounds that have similar patterns over time **(sequential integration)** or have similar frequency spectra **(simultaneous integration)** into separate **auditory streams** (groups of sounds that "belong together" because they appear to emanate from the same source). These processes

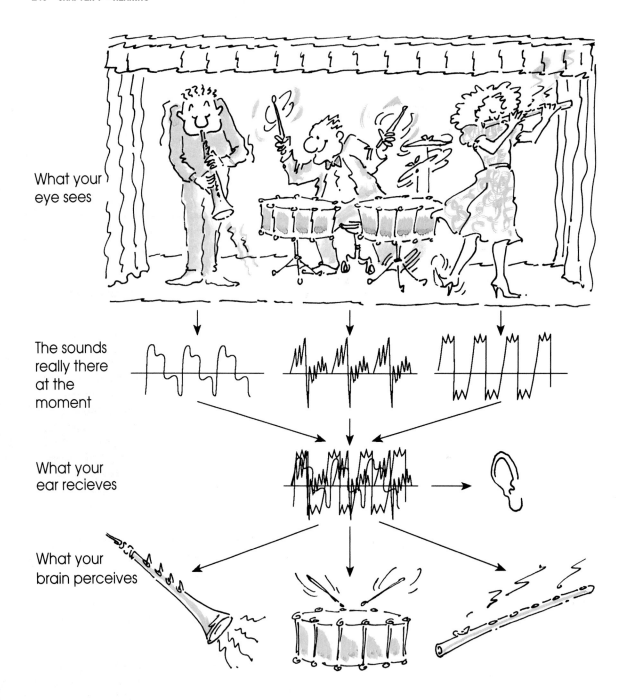

Figure 7-18 *The problem of auditory scene analysis.*

What your
eye sees

The sounds
really there
at the
moment

What your
ear recieves

What your
brain perceives

operate according to general rules, probably specified innately, based on patterns of time and frequency similarity. For example, the low-pitched, continuous but relatively brief roar of a lion differs in many ways from the high-pitched, intermittent but long-lasting chirp of a bird. Similar rules are followed in the grouping of visual stimuli, as we shall see in Chapter 11.

These basic auditory grouping processes have been extensively studied in the laboratory (see Bregman, 1990), and we know a lot about what affects their operation. For example, the faster a series of sounds is presented, the easier it is to separate out the different streams. Similarly, the more different the locations from which two sounds come, the easier it is to hear them as separate streams. Once separated, perception of the information in each auditory stream is much easier (Barsz, 1990). This low-level grouping process can create some interesting illusions. For example, when a longer pure tone is repeatedly alternated with a short noise burst, the pure tone is heard as continuing *through* the train of noise bursts, although it is really turned off while each noise burst is on (D. H. Warren, 1984). Apparently the auditory system is interpreting this auditory scene as if a continuous pure tone, representing one environmental event, is repeatedly being masked by short noise bursts representing another (much as we hear a sustained trumpet note from a radio as continuous, even though parts of it are masked by the clanking of pots or plates in the kitchen as we fix dinner). This illusion of continuity appears to arise from the same processes that produce auditory streaming in different contexts (Bregman, 1990; Tougas & Bregman, 1990). Demonstration Box 7-7 allows you to experience the influence of differences in physical location on the ease of separating a sound mixture into separate streams.

We also depend on the use of learned schemas to help interpret the auditory scene. These schemas contain detailed knowledge about regular patterns of sound that have certain meanings in our lives. For example, a skilled auto mechanic can listen to an ailing engine and separate out the squeaking noise made by a degenerating water pump from the many roars, hisses, clanks, and buzzes made by the other components of the engine. Interestingly, although the mechanic might be able to tell you how long your water pump will continue to function as a result of paying attention to its sound, if the motor suddenly died, the mechanic could not tell you anything about why the generator stopped working, since he was not attending to the sound stream that it emitted. The schema-based process allows a selected sound source to be processed better, but it does not aid processing of the rejected sounds (Bregman, 1990). Schema-based scene analysis takes longer to operate than the more primitive grouping processes, but also integrates sounds over longer time. Schemas appear to be activated by detecting all or part of a known pattern in the sound input. Attention can then be paid to the remainder of the pattern, aiding in its analysis. The schema appears to preempt the sounds appearing in "its" pattern for use in constructing "its" event, and this process then contributes to the final interpretation of the auditory scene. Each person's schemas might be different, because they depend on each person's unique learning history. However, the schema-based process and the grouping process work with other perceptual and cognitive processes (such as those of vision) to create our world of perceptual objects from the "booming, buzzing confusion" confronted by our sensory systems. We will discuss some of the most sophisticated examples of the operations of auditory grouping and schema analysis (those associated with music and speech perception) in Chapter 12.

DEMONSTRATION BOX 7-7   Auditory Streaming

One of the most powerful factors in allowing us to create auditory or visual groupings of stimuli involves differences in spatial location. For instance, in the figure accompanying this box you will see an example of a problem involving visual scene analysis. The line of print in the top part of the figure contains a mixture of two messages. They are very difficult to separate. However, when they are separated slightly in location the two messages are easily understood.

An analogous process operates in interpreting separate but similar sound sources. You can experience this by using two portable tape players or radios with earphones. First tune each so you can hear only static. Now change the tone control so that one of the sounds is a high-pitched static and the other is low-pitched and turn the volume up on each. Place one earphone from each radio set next to each other (you might use a rubber band to hold them close) and hold the pair of sounding earphones near and slightly in front of one ear. Notice how difficult it is to separate the mixture of sounds into two high- and low-pitched streams. Next, remove the rubber band and hold one earphone near, but slightly in front of one ear, and the other earphone in the same relative position near your other ear. Notice how much easier it is to separate out the two streams. The intensity differences of the two sounds at the two ears allows them easily to be assigned to different locations, and thus to different streams, and you hear a higher-pitched and a lower-pitched noise separately, each emanating from a different sound source.

YWOEU   TSAMSETLEL   SLMIOMKEE

YWOEU   TSAMSETLEL   SLMIOMKEE

GLOSSARY

The following definitions are specific to their use in this book.

Auditory adaptation   Transient reduction in auditory sensitivity due to prior or concurrent exposure to sound stimuli.

Auditory fatigue   Prolonged reduction in auditory sensitivity following exposure to very intense sounds.

Auditory scene   The array of sounds produced by the events in our environment; these sounds are mixed together at the ear.

Auditory scene analysis   The process of building separate mental representations of sound-producing events in the auditory scene based on the mixture of sound received from those events.

Auditory stream   A perception of a group of sounds as belonging together or coming from a single source.

Azimuth   The direction of a sound source indicated as degrees right or left around a horizontal circle, with 0 deg straight ahead of and 180 deg directly behind an observer.

Backward masking   Masking of a sound by another sound presented later in time. *See* Masking.

When auditory scene analysis fails

Bandwidth The range of frequencies (frequency *band*) making up a complex sound.

Binaural Sound presentation to both ears simultaneously.

Central masking Masking resulting from presentation of target sound and masking sound to different ears. *See* Masking.

Consonance The quality of two tones blending or "going together."

Density The quality of compactness or hardness of a sound.

Dissonance The quality of two sounds being discordant or "clashing."

Dynamic range For a particular frequency, the difference between the absolute threshold and the pain threshold, measured in decibels.

Echolocation system A system used by some animals, such as bats and whales, to locate objects by analyzing self-emitted sound waves reflected from them.

Equal loudness contour A curve describing the intensities at which tones of varying frequencies appear to be equally loud.

Equal pitch contour   A curve describing the frequencies at which tones of varying intensities appear to have the same pitch.

Equal temperament scale   A version of the musical scale where each octave is divided into 12 equal parts, called *semitones,* which are further divided into 100 *cents.*

Forward masking   Masking of a sound by another sound presented before it in time. *See* Masking.

Frequency principle   Asserts that sound frequency is encoded by the overall frequency of firing in the auditory nerve.

Fundamental   The lowest, usually most intense, frequency sound wave in a complex stimulus.

Harmonics   Frequencies that are whole-number multiples of the fundamental frequency in complex sounds.

Informational masking   Simultaneous masking of a pure tone by a complex sound made up of several frequencies that vary randomly from trial to trial. *See* Masking.

Intensity difference   A difference in sound intensity at the two ears caused by the presence of a sound shadow; cue to localization of higher-frequency sounds.

Interstimulus interval   The time span between the end of one stimulus and the beginning of the next.

Loudness   The subjective experience of the magnitude or intensity of sound.

Masker   A sound that, when presented, makes perception of another sound more difficult.

Masking   When a usually audible sound can no longer be heard because of the presentation of another sound close to it in time.

Mel   A scale used to measure pitch; also the unit of that scale—a 1000-Hz tone at 40 dB has a pitch of 1000 mels.

Minimum audible angle   The smallest amount of movement of a sound source that can be detected.

Minimum audible field   The threshold intensity for a sound stimulus presented and measured in a free field.

Minimum audible pressure   The threshold intensity for a sound stimulus presented through earphones and measured at the eardrum.

Missing fundamental   When a complex sound has a fundamental frequency that is not actually present in the sound.

Monaural   Sound presentation to one ear.

Perceived duration   The length of time a sound appears to last.

Perceived location   Where in space a sound seems to come from.

Phase difference   The difference in the phase of a sound wave between the two ears caused by the different distances the sound wave has to travel to reach each ear; cue to localization of lower-frequency sounds.

Pitch   The psychological attribute of sound most closely associated with sound frequency, described by the words *high* or *low.*

Place principle   Asserts that sound frequency is encoded by what *place* on the basilar membrane vibrates most to each frequency.

Precedence effect   A phenomenon in which the first of a group of sounds (for example, a sound and its echoes) to arrive at the ear is the major determinant of where in space the sound source is perceived to be.

Profile analysis   Detection of an intensity increment ("bump") or other difference between complex sounds that differ in their profiles (amplitudes at the various frequencies making them up).

Reverberation   A cue to perception of the distance of a sound source; reverberant sound is sound that reaches the ears after having bounced off some surface.

Sequential integration   Integration of a group of sounds into a single auditory stream by virtue of their temporal proximity.

Simultaneous integration   Integration of a group of sounds into a single auditory stream by virtue of the similarity of their frequency spectra.

Simultaneous masking   When a sound is masked by another sound presented at the same time.

Sone   A scale used to measure the loudness of a sound; also the unit of that scale—a tone of 1000 Hz at 40 dB has a loudness of 1 sone.

Sound shadow   An area in which only sounds diffracted by the edge of the head are received by the ear, resulting in lower intensity especially for sounds of higher frequencies.

Target   The sound to be detected in a masking situation.

Temporal summation   A phenomenon by which the auditory system adds the sound energy received over about 200 msec for near-threshold stimuli, giving rise to the relationship $T = I \times D$.

Timbre   A sound attribute associated with the harmonics or overtones of a complex sound.

Time difference   The difference between the time taken by a sound wave to travel to the two ears when starting from an azimuth other than 0 or 180 degrees; a cue to the direction of a lower-frequency sound source.

Volley principle   The theory that neural fibers fire in groups, with one group of neurons firing while another group "recharges."

Volume   The sound quality associated with the degree to which a sound fills space and seems large or small.

Chapter ...

TASTE AND SMELL

The Gustatory (Taste) Sense
  Taste Stimuli
  Taste Receptors
  Neural Responses in Taste
  Taste Thresholds
  Taste Adaptation
  Taste Intensity and Qualities
The Olfactory (Smell) Sense
  Smell Stimuli and Receptors
  Neural Responses in Smell
  Smell Thresholds
  Smell Adaptation
  Smell Intensity and Qualities
  Pheromones

A properly trained police dog can follow the track of a single individual even when it has been entangled with the tracks of many others. The dog is smelling the fatty acids that seep through the shoes of the suspect, even though these are present in incredibly small amounts. For example, each human footprint contains only about 0.00000000004 grams of valeric acid, a typical fatty acid secreted by glands in the sole of the foot. This is only about one one-hundredth the amount in a single fingerprint (R. H. Wright, 1982). No wonder criminals fear such dogs and often confess voluntarily when tracked and caught through the dogs' astounding "nose work."

We humans are somewhat inferior to police dogs and many other animals in our abilities to taste and smell; we rely more heavily on sight and hearing. Nonetheless, chemical sensitivities are important in many ways. The flavor of your favorite dessert; the acrid taste of a broken aspirin on your tongue; the smell of fresh coffee, cut grass, or roses all can evoke intense feelings and guide our behaviors in many ways.

More important than esthetics, chemical senses serve a survival function. A reasonable rule of thumb, at least for natural substances, is that things that taste bad are likely to be harmful, indigestible, or poisonous, whereas things that taste good are apt to be digestible and contain substances the body can metabolize. When you eat a hot pepper, you usually experience a "burning" sensation in addition to (or masking completely) the flavor of the pepper. Some cultures, such as Mexican, Indian, or Szechuan, use this effect as a major flavor ingredient, and most people, whatever their native culture, appreciate "hot" foods. Humans are nearly unique in the animal kingdom in ignoring the warnings (the burning sensation) of the *common chemical sense* and continuing to ingest, even finding enjoyable, foods that burn (Rozin, Ebert, & Schull, 1982).

Smell has similar survival functions, since foul odors often signify danger in the sense of putrefied or spoiled substances that are no longer safely edible. Smell also helps species survive by conveying sexual and social information. Although often we are not consciously aware that we are responding to smells, some odors serve to identify individuals and to convey information between members of the same species, even in humans.

Certain short-term changes in how things taste and smell also are important for well-being. The pleasantness and the intensity of sweet and salty tastes are less when we are sated (full) than when we are hungry (for example, Scott, 1990). If we have experienced nausea after eating a distinctive food, we often acquire a *conditioned taste aversion* to that food, based especially on how it smells, that will make us avoid that food in the future (for example, Bartoshuk, 1990). In general, taste and smell help us obtain the nutrients our bodies need while helping us to avoid harmful substances (see Capaldi & Powley, 1990, for more on this).

THE GUSTATORY (TASTE) SENSE

Presumably, life began in the giant bowl of chemical soup we call the sea. Various substances suspended or dissolved in water were important to the survival of primitive living things. Some substances provided food, some gave warning, some caused destruction. The most primitive, one-celled organisms clearly could not use anything like visual or auditory sensory systems, which require large numbers of specialized cells. They relied on chemical or mechanical interactions with their environment mediated by the cell's outer membrane. As life evolved, multicelled animals could afford a "division of labor" among the many cells composing their bodies. Groups of specialized cells picked up chemical information from the surroundings. For example, fish have pits lined with cells responsive to a variety of chemical and mechanical stimuli. Insects and other invertebrates have such cells located on their antennae.

Although two anatomically separate systems developed, in the sea there was little differentiation between taste and smell. All important chemical stimuli were dissolved or suspended in the same substance, water. When life moved on to land, the two existing chemical receptor systems came to serve different functions. The taste system became a "close-up" sense, which provided the last check on the acceptability of food. Smell turned out to be useful as a distance sense, although it also retained an important function in dealing with food (see Rozin, 1982, and the discussion of smell later in this chapter).

Taste Stimuli

The physical stimuli for the taste system are substances that can be dissolved in water. As is usual for physical stimuli, the amount of a chemical substance present is related to the intensity of the taste we experience. Which property (or collection of properties) of the stimulus gives rise to the various different taste qualities is still somewhat of a mystery, although new biochemical studies are making progress at least for the most basic taste qualities.

Scientists generally agree on the existence of at least four primary taste qualities: *sweet, salty, sour,* and *bitter.* These taste qualities are associated with some general types of molecules. A sweet taste is generally associated with so-called *organic molecules,* which are made up mostly of carbon, hydrogen, and oxygen in different combinations. These organic molecules are commonly called sugars, alcohols, and so forth. Other sweet substances, like saccharide, are also organic chemicals, but they

are quite different from "natural" sweeteners, such as sugars, in their molecular structure. Many sweet-tasting substances have a particular structure in common, termed the **AB,H system,** which consists of two negatively charged atoms (represented by the letters *A* and *B*) and a positively charged hydrogen atom (*H*) arranged in a special way. It is thought that this molecular structure selectively interacts with special parts of some taste receptors to cause them to respond (see Bartoshuk, 1979).

Bitter taste is related to sweet taste. Many substances that taste sweet in small amounts taste bitter in large amounts (for example, saccharide). Also, a number of chemicals containing nitrogen (such as strychnine, caffeine, quinine, and nicotine) taste bitter. The relationship between sweet and bitter is further strengthened by the fact that bitter-tasting molecules also often contain an AB,H system. In bitter substances, however, the components have a different spatial arrangement than they do in sugars.

A salty taste is elicited by molecules that, when dissolved in water, break into two electrically charged parts called *ions.* For example, common table salt is composed of two atoms: one sodium (Na) and one chlorine (Cl).When dissolved in water, the atoms break apart. The sodium atom is now a positively charged ion, and the chlorine atom is a negatively charged ion. The size and weight of the negatively charged ions helps determine how salty a substance tastes. Substances with small negative ions, such as chlorine, taste saltier than those with larger negative ions, such as acetate or gluconate. This is because the smaller negative ions can penetrate more easily to the space around the taste receptors, making it more electrically neutral and thus making it easier for the taste cell to signal the presence of the positive ion (Ye, Heck, & DeSimone, 1991). Salts with very large negative ions tend to taste bitter as well as less salty, especially in high concentrations. In very low concentrations, salts tend to taste sweet, explaining why a dash of salt is often part of many sweet dessert recipes.

Sour substances also break up into two parts when in solution, but they are usually acids (such as hydrochloric, sulphuric, acetic, and nitric) rather than salts. In all these substances, hydrogen is the positively charged ion. The behavior of the hydrogen seems to be directly related to the sourness of such acids, but other properties must also be important because most acids taste sweet or bitter instead of sour. Thus, although we can relate some aspects of chemical stimuli to the tastes they produce, this relationship is not simple.

Taste Receptors

The tongue is covered with little bumps called **papillae.** The major receptors for taste are groups of cells called **taste buds** that are found in three types of papillae (see Figure 8-1). *Fungiform papillae,* which are shaped like little mushrooms (*fungi*), are found at the tip and the sides of the tongue. *Foliate papillae* make up a series of folds (*folia*) along the sides of the rear portion of the tongue. *Circumvallate papillae* are shaped like a flattened hill with a circular trench or valley surrounding it, and are located at the back of the tongue. A fourth type, the *filiform papillae,* contain no taste buds. Filiform papillae are shaped like rough, tapered arrowheads or blades of grass that abrade food into smaller bits that will dissolve more easily. Some taste receptors are also scattered over parts of the mouth other than the tongue, such as on the *soft palate* (which is the back portion of the roof of your mouth). Figure 8-2A shows how the taste buds are distributed within a circumvallate papilla. Each taste bud consists of several receptor cells (perhaps up to 30) arranged like the closed petals of a flower (Figure 8-2B). Your mouth contains about 10,000 taste buds when you are young, although their number decreases with age.

Within each taste bud, the individual cells are continually developing. Each taste cell has a life span of only a few days, so the composition of the taste bud is always changing, with some immature cells (around the outside), some mature cells (near the inside), and some dying cells always present (Beidler & Smallman, 1965). The taste cells in the taste bud seem to be a specialized evolution of skin cells. This probably explains their short life span, since all skin cells are periodically replaced. A slender projection from the top end of each cell lies near an opening onto the surface of the tongue called a **taste pore.** It is thought that the actual reception mechanism for taste is located in these slender processes (called *microvilli*).

Several theories have been proposed for how the receptors interact with the stimulating molecules to generate an electrical current that ultimately results in action potentials in the taste nerves. Probably several different transduction mechanisms exist, and it has been suggested that different transduction mechanisms are involved for different classes of taste stim-

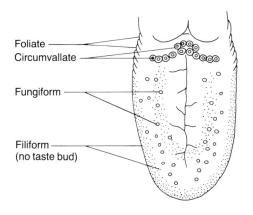

Figure 8-1 A diagram of the human tongue showing the locations of the different types of papillae.

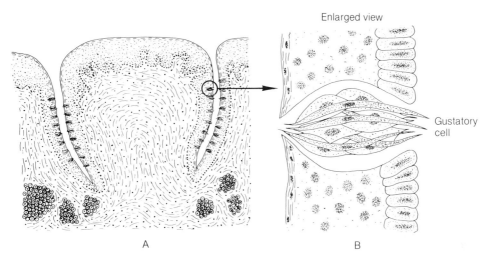

Figure 8-2 (A) *A typical papilla with taste buds (one is circled); (B) Enlarged picture of a single taste bud (from Wyburn, Pickford, & Hurst, 1964).*

uli (Brand, Teeter, Cagan, & Kare, 1989; Teeter & Brand, 1987). In one proposed mechanism, salt ions, such as sodium or lithium, directly penetrate the cell membrane of the microvilli, causing an electrical current to flow across the membrane. Another theory suggests that reversible chemical bonds form between specific parts of the taste stimulus molecule (for example, the AB,H system) and receptor molecules in the cell membrane. These bonds, either directly or through causing chemical reactions inside the receptor cell, change the flow of ions across the cell membrane, thus generating an electrical current. For example, some taste cells respond to the presence of calcium salts because such salts cause the cells' permeability to potassium to change (Bigiani & Roper, 1991). On the other hand, some taste cells respond to a bitter substance called denatonium, because denatonium causes calcium stored inside the cell to be released into the cell in an ionic form, thus changing the potential across the cell membrane (Akabas, Dodd, & Al-Awqati,

1988). Finally, it is possible that some stimulus molecules alter the electrical properties of the cell membrane directly, causing an electrical current. In all of these mechanisms, the final result is the release of a neurotransmitter across the synapse of the receptor cell with a taste nerve cell, causing spike potentials to travel up the taste nerves. (See the Appendix for more about spike potentials.)

Neural Responses in Taste

Three large nerves (the *chorda tympani, vagus,* and *glossopharyngeal*) carry fibers from the taste buds. They run from the tongue to the several nuclei in the **solitary tract,** which is located in the medulla (the place where the spinal chord widens to form the brainstem). In addition, information is carried from the *common chemical sense.* This system is separate from the taste system and in humans consists mostly of the *trigeminal nerve* of the head and its free nerve endings in the mouth and nasal cavity. The common chemical sense is sensitive to a wide variety of different stimuli; of particular interest to humans are several popular spices, including peppers and ginger (see Silver, 1987).

From the nuclei in the solitary tract, taste information is carried via a set of pathways called the **medial lemnisci** to the taste center of the **thalamus,** which is situated at the top of the rear central portion of the thalamus (*ventral posterior nuclei*). The thalamic taste area projects to three areas in the brain. Two are regions at the base of the primary somatosensory cortex (near where information from touch for the face is projected), and the third is the **anterior-insular cortex,** which is a part of the frontal cortex under the front end of the temporal cortex.

As in vision and audition, most of our knowledge of the electrical activity of the taste system has come from studies of nonhuman animals. Several studies have shown that taste fibers respond to increasing intensity (concentration) of the stimulus by increasing their overall rate of firing. One of the few studies that actually used human subjects for direct recording (Diamant, Funakoshi, Strom, & Zotterman, 1963) capitalized on the fact that taste pathways from the front of the tongue must be cut during a certain kind of ear operation. Electrical activity in response to taste stimuli was recorded from this nerve during the operation. The data from these patients show that the amount of neural response grows as the logarithm of the intensity of the stimulus (in this case, table salt). In other words, a small increase in a weaker taste stimulus has a greater effect than a similar increase in a stronger taste stimulus, much like the responses in vision and audition to increasing stimulus intensity (see Chapters 3 and 6). As in other modalities, the neural code for intensity seems to be the overall amount of firing of all the sensory fibers.

How is taste *quality* encoded? At first it was thought that certain taste cells would respond only to sweet stimuli, or only to salty stimuli, and so forth, one for each taste quality, perhaps even corresponding to the different categories of papillae. However, most receptor cells seem to respond to all of the four basic kinds of taste stimuli, although with different sensitivity (Arvidson & Friberg, 1980; Kimura & Beidler, 1961). Given the several different transducer mechanisms described above, it seems possible that each taste cell might respond to several different types of taste stimuli and thus to several different taste qualities. The same sort of responsiveness to most stimulus types has been found in the solitary nucleus and in the thalamus as well (Doetsch, Ganchrow, Nelson, & Erickson, 1969; Scott & Erickson, 1971).

We have no theoretical need for specialized taste receptor cells so long as the various neural units have different stimulus-specific response rates. If this condition is met, then the code for taste quality could be an **across-fiber pattern** of neural activity (Erikson, 1985; Erickson & Schiffman, 1975; Pfaffman, 1955). Figure 8-3 shows how this might work. Notice that although all of the fibers respond to all taste inputs to some extent, the pattern of firing across the four diagramed fibers is different for each quality. Thus, for a sugar stimulus (S), we find fiber *A* responding vigorously, *B* moderately, and *C* and *D* only weakly. For salt (NaCl), *A* and *D* respond weakly, whereas *B* responds strongly and *C* nearly as vigorously. Erickson (1963) was able to show such distinct across-fiber pattern differences. These patterns become somewhat less distinct in the thalamus (Doetsch et al., 1969; Scott & Erickson, 1971).

Although no taste receptor cells seem to exist that respond only to one of the four basic taste qualities, different gustatory nerve fibers do seem to be "tuned" to certain taste stimuli, much as auditory nerve fibers are tuned to cer-

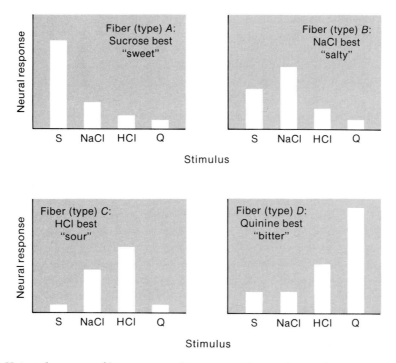

Figure 8-3 *Using the across-fiber pattern theory, consider each graph to represent the response of a unique taste fiber to the various stimuli. Using the labeled-line theory, consider each graph to represent the average response of a group of more-or-less equivalent taste fibers.*

tain frequencies of sound (see Chapter 6). Such fibers respond most vigorously to their "best" substances and less vigorously to others. Eventually, it may be possible to classify such fibers into a few classes, corresponding to the basic taste qualities (Frank, 1975, 1985; Pfaffman, Frank, & Norgren, 1979). The response patterns shown in Figure 8-3 could thus also be interpreted as those characteristic of such tuned fiber types. On the basis of such data, Pfaffman (1974) proposed the **labeled-line theory** of taste quality encoding. The basic idea is that each taste fiber encodes the intensity of a single basic taste quality, that associated with its best stimulus. To the extent that a stimulus activates the "sweet" fibers, it tastes sweet; to the extent it activates the "bitter" fibers, it tastes bitter. This means that a "simple" stimu-

lus, such as table salt (NaCl), could have a complex taste if it activates several types of fibers. This does appear to happen, such as when salts at particular concentrations taste both salty and sour (Bartoshuk, 1978). This theory is compatible with the across-fiber pattern approach, except that here the code for taste quality is a profile across a few fiber types, rather than a pattern across many thousands of unique fibers (see also Scott, 1987; Smith, 1985).

Although it is unknown whether labeled lines exist along the entire taste pathway, neurons in the solitary nucleus of rats can be categorized into four groups corresponding to the four basic tastes. The response profiles of the different neuron groups are differentially affected by blocking the flow of sodium across receptor cell membranes (Scott & Giza, 1990), indicating that saltiness, at least, is independently coded. Also, neurons most responsive to the four basic tastes seem to be localized in different parts of the taste cortex (Yamamoto, Yayama, & Kawamura, 1981). Furthermore, it is likely that some recoding of the taste information takes place in the cortex. Specific cortical cells may give an "on" response to some taste stimuli and an "off" response to others, similar to the feature-specific cells in the visual cortex discussed in Chapter 3 (Funakoshi, Kasahara, Yamamoto, & Kawamura, 1972).

Taste Thresholds

What are the limits of a human's sensitivity to taste? It is difficult to study the thresholds for taste stimuli, since we have so many different stimuli to consider. Also, we find that thresholds vary with the viscosity of the mixture to be tasted (Paulus & Haas, 1980) or with its temperature (Paulus & Reisch, 1980). The study is further complicated by the fact that the various parts of the tongue and mouth are not equally sensitive to different stimuli.

First we must decide how to measure physically the amount of a taste stimulus present at any moment. Probably the most useful (and used) measure is the **molar concentration** of a substance (Pfaffman, Bartoshuk, & McBurney, 1971). Molar concentration is based on the weight of a substance dissolved in a given amount of a solvent (usually water when we deal with taste). A solution is said to have a concentration of 1 *mole* if the molecular weight of the substance (in grams) is added to enough water to make one liter of solution. Different solutions with the same molar concentrations have the same number of stimulus molecules in a given volume of liquid.

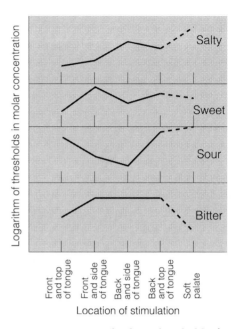

Figure 8-4 *Average absolute thresholds for four different taste stimuli at four locations on the tongue and at a location on the soft palate (based on Collings, 1974).*

Once we have decided how to specify the stimulus concentrations, we can measure thresholds. Since the surface of the tongue is large and contains various types of papillae, we should not be surprised to find that the absolute sensitivity depends on the region of the mouth or tongue stimulated. Figure 8-4 shows a summary of the results of Collings (1974) for four different parts of the tongue and the soft palate. For the bitter substance, the lowest absolute threshold on the tongue is at the front. For this substance, however, an even lower threshold occurs on the palate. The tip and back of the tongue are most sensitive to sweet, while the front and sides are most sensitive to salt. The sensitivity of parts of the mouth to "hot" tastes, such as those associated with chili peppers, also differs from place to place.

DEMONSTRATION BOX 8-1   Variations in Taste Sensitivity

Although you have all probably experienced spicy "hot" foods on numerous occasions, you may not know that sensitivy to hot spices varies over the mouth. For example, the tip of the tongue is most sensitive to red and black peppers, and the anterior (hard) palate and cheek are least sensitive (Lawless & Stevens, 1988). You could demonstrate this for yourself by placing several drops of Tabasco sauce or other hot sauce (which contain hot red peppers) on the tip of a cotton swab or a bit of paper napkin twirled around a pencil or toothpick. Touch this "taste stimulator" to different parts of your mouth and tongue, and notice how the sensations differ in strength for different locations.

Demonstration Box 8-1 helps you explore these differences.

Individuals often differ in marked ways in their absolute sensitivity to certain tastes. For example, Blakeslee and Salmon (1935) measured the absolute thresholds of 47 people for 17 different substances. Figure 8-5 summarizes some of their results. Most substances, such as table salt or saccharide, have a narrow range of thresholds for different people. For others, however, such as vanillin or **PTC** (phenylthiocarbamide), large individual differences in sensitivity exist. These latter two substances are interesting because some people are apparently "taste-blind" to them. That is, at ordinary concentrations many people cannot taste these substances at all. PTC produces a bitter taste for those who are sensitive to it. If the concentration is high enough, however, even the taste-blind can taste PTC, as Figure 8-5 shows. Taste blindness for PTC is similar to color blindness (discussed in Chapter 5) in that both appear to have a genetic component and tend to run in families.

Another substance associated with taste blindness is caffeine (Hall, Bartoshuk, Cain, & Stevens, 1975). For caffeine, the taster and nontaster groups are not as distinct as they are with PTC, but the range of thresholds is still

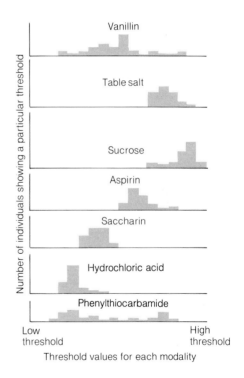

Figure 8-5 Frequency distributions of absolute thresholds of 47 observers to various taste stimuli. Phenylthiocarbamide (PTC) and vanillin have particularly wide ranges of thresholds, and PTC clearly shows two modes—tasters with low thresholds and nontasters with high thresholds (based on Blakeslee & Salmon, 1935).

quite large and two groups clearly appear. Tasters of PTC tend to be tasters of caffeine and vice versa. Similarly, tasters of PTC also find the bitter taste in a common salt substitute, potassium chloride (KCl), and that of a preservative found in many foods, sodium benzoate, to be more intense than do nontasters (Bartoshuk, Rifkin, Marks, & Hooper, 1988). A common mechanism may be responsible for the relatively greater sensitivity of PTC tasters to these bitter tastes. This is not simply a general "bitter" taste mechanism, however, for Hall et al. (1975) also found that thresholds to two other bitter-tasting substances were unrelated to thresholds for PTC and caffeine. Moreover, Bartoshuk et al. (1988) found that the bitter taste of KCl is caused by the K^+ ion, whereas the bitter taste of sodium benzoate is caused by the negative benzoate ion. Similar results have been found for the bitter and sweet tastes of saccharide (Bartoshuk, 1979). In general, the attempt to explain taste blindnesses by attributing them to deficiencies in some particular taste system (as is often possible for color blindness) has not succeeded very well.

Taste Adaptation

Taste thresholds can also be affected by stimuli that have reached the tongue prior to the threshold test. The taste system adapts very readily to continued stimulation of the same type, and this adaptation temporarily raises the absolute threshold for the particular substance to which it has been adapted. Figure 8-6 shows an example of the effects of previous stimulation on absolute threshold. Here both the adapting stimulus and the test stimulus were table salt (NaCl). As you can see from the figure, the absolute threshold varied both with how long the tongue had been exposed to the

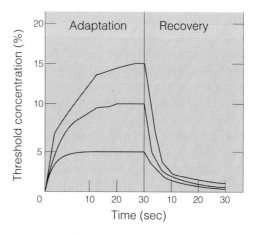

Figure 8-6 *Adaptation and recovery from adaptation to continued stimulation of the tongue with table salt (NaCl). The three curves represent three different adapting concentrations. The time axis represents the amount of exposure to the adapting concentration, or recovery time, before determination of absolute threshold. Note the resemblance to dark adaptation curves (see Chapter 4; based on Hahn, 1934).*

adapting stimulus and the strength of the stimulus (Hahn, 1934; O'Mahoney, 1979). Similar results can be demonstrated for the effects of adaptation on sensory intensity (Gent, 1979). This sort of adaptation explains why at dinner some people resalt their food again and again. As they eat, they adapt to the salty taste and come to need more salt to experience the taste at the same level. You can avoid resalting your food if you eat something that is not salty between bites of salty food (see Halpern & Meiselman, 1980). As Figure 8-6 shows, recovery from adaptation of the threshold sensitivity is virtually complete in about 10 seconds, no matter how much salt was tasted previously. On the other hand, to experience the same level of taste intensity as you started with, you may need more time. For example, the sensory intensity experience for a given taste stimulus is only about 50% recovered by 10 seconds after complete adaptation (Bujas, Szabo, Adjukovic, & Mayer, 1991). Complete recovery can take up to 2 minutes. Taken together, these results suggest that to experience the full flavor of a meal one should eat slowly, with many interpolated pauses between bites of food.

Adaptation to one substance can also have an effect on the threshold for (and the subsequent taste of) different substances. This is called **cross-adaptation.** For example, adaptation to one salt will raise the threshold to other salts. Similarly, exposure to a sour substance will raise the threshold to other sour stimuli. In some cases, exposure of the tongue to one stimulus may actually *lower* the threshold to another taste stimulus (or make its taste more intense). This special case of cross-adaptation is called **potentiation.** Thus, adaptation to an acid, while reducing the sourness of another acid, may increase the sweetness of a sugar. Adaptation to urea (the bitter substance contained in human urine) will increase the inten-

sity of salty sensations (McBurney, 1969). You can experience a dramatic example of potentiation and cross-adaptation by trying Demonstration Box 8-2.

Perhaps the most striking phenomenon associated with cross-adaptation is the variability of the taste of ordinary tap water with adaptation to various substances. In fact, all four of the basic tastes can be induced in water by previous adaptation to a suitable taste stimulus (McBurney & Bartoshuk, 1972). For example, human saliva has a substantial concentration of NaCl in it, so you are always somewhat adapted to its salty taste, making water taste slightly bitter. Interestingly, "off" responses to pure water have been recorded in the human chorda tympani nerve (Oakley, 1985); such neural responses may partly mediate our experience of the taste of water. You can experience some of these tastes for yourself by trying Demonstration Box 8-3.

DEMONSTRATION BOX 8-2   Potentiation and Cross-Adaptation

Have you ever drunk some orange juice right after brushing your teeth in the morning and noticed that it tasted terrible? If so, you were experiencing the effects of sodium laurel sulphate, the detergent in toothpaste, on your taste system's response to citric acid. Citric acid, which is what makes orange juice or lemon juice taste sour, tastes only slightly bitter at very high concentrations. However, stimulation of the taste cells with sodium laurel sulphate causes this bitter taste to increase greatly in intensity, making it noticeable at lower concentrations such as those found in orange or lemon juice (Bartoshuk, 1988). If you have never experienced this, try the following. Wash your mouth out by swishing with pure water.

Then taste some orange (or lemon) juice. Notice that the bitter taste is very faint if it is there at all. Now brush your teeth and rinse thoroughly to get rid of the other toothpaste tastes such as mint, which tastes sweet. Again taste the orange or lemon juice. Notice how the bitter taste has increased in intensity, but the sourness has not changed much as all. Sodium laurel sulphate also decreases the intensity of sweet, salty, and bitter tastes somewhat. You can try to experience these effects by repeating the orange juice experiment just described with sugar water, salt water, and cold coffee. It would be best to do these other experiments on different days so that adaptation effects do not confound your taste sensations.

DEMONSTRATION BOX 8-3   The Taste of Water

Water has a distinctive taste, especially when you have been eating or drinking some other substance before you taste the water. In this demonstration, you will be able to make water taste sweet, bitter, sour, or salty. Although you may not be able to (or want to) try all of the demonstrations, be assured that all of them work under the carefully controlled conditions of the laboratory (Bartoshuk. 1974).

The most pleasant of the demonstrations requires that you eat a few cooked artichokes of any variety (canned, fresh, or frozen) and then taste a sip of water. Be sure to mash the artichoke thoroughly onto your tongue and palate while eating it. Water tasted after eating the artichoke usually tastes sweet. Another way to obtain the sweet taste is to swish a mouthful of strong (caffeinated) coffee on the tongue for 30 seconds before tasting tap water. To make water taste bitter or sour, take some very salty water and swish it around in your mouth for 30 seconds and then spit it out. Afterward, taste some tap water. Something that has been tried in the laboratory but that you may not want to try is to swish some urea (a major component of urine) on the tongue for 30 seconds. Tap water tasted after this treatment tastes salty.

Taste Intensity and Qualities

Our ability to discriminate intensity differences in taste, regardless of the stimulus tested, is really not too good. The Weber fraction (the proportional amount by which the more intense of two stimuli must be larger than the less intense for them to be discriminated, as discussed in Chapter 2) ranges from a fair 0.10 to an awful 1.00, making taste the least sensitive of the senses by this criterion (Pfaffman et al., 1971). Moreover, the Weber fraction for the bitter taste increases as we age, especially for higher concentrations of tastant. For example, for high concentrations of caffeine, the Weber fraction is about 0.40 for young people and around 2.30 for the elderly (Gilmore & Murphy, 1989). For sucrose (common table sugar), however, Weber fractions are unaffected by age, remaining at a more respectable value of about 0.15 for both groups.

The intensity of the taste sensation increases with the stimulus intensity. For example, magnitude estimations (see Chapter 2) of taste intensity are a power function of stimulus intensity: $ME = aI^n$, where ME is the average magnitude estimation, I is the intensity of the stimulus, a is a constant, and n is an exponent that characterizes the shape of the function. The exponent n is usually approximately 1 (that is, for table salt it is 0.91, for quinine hydrochloride it is 0.85, for hydrochloric acid it is 0.99, and for sucrose it is 0.93; Meiselman, Bose, & Nykvist, 1972; Norwich, 1984). An exponent of 1 means that sensation is linear with stimulus intensity; that is, changes in stimulus intensity of the same size cause changes in sensation intensity of the same size no matter how intense the stimulus. Contrast this with vision and hearing, where the corresponding exponents are less than one and changes in weaker stimuli are perceived as greater than changes in more intense stimuli. An important caution here is that we must be careful to specify exactly the conditions under which such exponents are measured, for they are greatly affected by adaptation. For example, O'Mahoney and Heintz (1981) found an exponent for NaCl of only about 0.70 under conditions somewhat different from those used by other investigators (see also Meiselman et al., 1972). Also, the exponent may change with age, being somewhat smaller for sour and bitter substances for the elderly (see Bartoshuk, 1988).

Several studies have compared the changes in the rate of neural response with changes in stimulus intensity to the psychophysical data. They have shown that both neural and psychophysical responses vary with stimulus intensity in a similar fashion (Borg, Diamant, Oakley, Strom, & Zotterman, 1967; Diamant & Zotterman, 1969). It seems likely that our sensation of the intensity of a taste is directly related to the overall amount of neural activity evoked by the stimulus, which in turn depends on the intensity (molar concentration) of the stimulus (see McBride, 1987, and Norwich, 1984, for recent theoretical discussions of this

relationship). However, the situation is rather complex, since our sensation of the intensity of any one taste stimulus may be affected by the presence of other taste stimuli (taste mixtures), or even by the same taste stimuli elsewhere on the tongue or in the mouth (probably because taste nerves mutually inhibit one another; see Bartoshuk, 1988). Demonstration Box 8-4 provides one way you can explore this complex interaction between tastes.

Modern psychophysical scaling techniques have also been used to look at the relationships among taste *qualities*. In 1916, Henning proposed that the qualities of all tastes could be described as a form in a three-dimensional geometrical space, in much the same way that colors can be described (see Chapter 5). The form he proposed was that of a pyramid, with the primary tastes at the corners. Mixtures of the primary tastes would be represented by points on the surface of (or within) this space, as shown in Figure 8-7A. Schiffman and Erikson

---

DEMONSTRATION BOX 8-4   Putting out the Fire

You may have had the experience of putting too much pepper or other hot spice in your mouth and finding the burning too much to bear. Or you may have been prevented from eating some tasty dish because it was "too hot." These are circumstances in which you want to reduce the intensity of sensations arising from stimulation of your common chemical sense. Surprisingly, the effectiveness of swishing various liquids in your mouth to put out the fire depends to some extent on how they taste (Stevens & Lawless, 1986). The most effective liquid has a sweet (for example, soda pop) or sour (for example, lemon or other citrus juice) taste, and is at a cool temperature. Bitter-tasting

substances (for example, quinine, or possibly beer) do not seem to help any more than simply waiting for the burning to cease, and salty substances are intermediate in effect. The cool temperature explains some but not all of the cooling effect, since different tastants at the same temperature have different effects. If you are daring, you might try swishing some *diluted* Tabasco sauce around in your mouth until it begins to burn and then experimenting with different quenching substances to see whether you can confirm these results. Remember to leave plenty of time between trials for the burning sensation to fade completely.

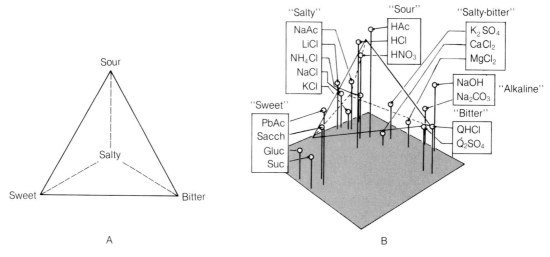

Figure 8-7 (A) *Henning's taste pyramid;* (B) *Multidimensional scaling results for similarity judgments of taste stimuli. Henning's taste pyramid is superimposed on the three-dimensional space to show the correspondence (from Schiffman & Erikson, 1971).*

(1971) used multidimensional scaling to test whether this notion actually describes how people perceive taste stimuli. In multidimensional scaling, observers' dissimilarity judgments for pairs of taste stimuli are represented as distances between points in a geometric space (see Chapter 2 for a more complete discussion). Figure 8-7B shows their results. Henning's taste pyramid fits reasonably well into the stimulus configuration uncovered by multidimensional scaling. This has been verified in another study using a larger set of stimuli (Schiffman & Dackis, 1975).

Such techniques have also been used to explore the relationships between the tastes of more similar substances, such as sodium salts (Schiffman, McElroy, & Erikson, 1980) and sweeteners (Schiffman, Reilly, & Clark, 1979) and to try to discover the physical and psychological properties that underlie these relationships. In general, multidimensional scaling yields results consistent with the existence of the four primaries: sweet, salty, sour, and bit-

ter, as shown in Figure 8-7. Other approaches give similar results. For example, reaction times to identify various taste stimuli of equal relative intensity are highly similar for substances that have the same primary taste but are very different for substances with different tastes. Saltiness is identified fastest and bitterness slowest, with sourness and sweetness intermediate, regardless of which salts, acids, and so on are used (Bujas, Szabo, Ajdukovic, & Mayer, 1989). Although some controversy exists over other relevant facts (see Erikson, 1985; Erikson & Covey, 1980; McBurney & Gent, 1979), it seems likely that investigators will continue to refer to four basic taste qualities because they provide a useful summary of most research findings in taste. However, their interpretation may change. For example, it has been suggested that each of the basic tastes should be considered to be a separate sensory modality, much as the skin senses can be separated into touch, warmth, cold, and pain (McBurney & Gent, 1979).

THE OLFACTORY (SMELL) SENSE

All of us are familiar with the sight of a dog or a cat sniffing at some object, clearly processing information provided by its sense of smell. Since we seldom see a human being sniffing the ground to find out who has been there recently, or exploring a new room by sniffing the furniture, we tend to think that smell is unimportant; it is often referred to as a "minor" sense. Although much of our perceptual processing of odors is unconscious, our sense of smell plays a role that is far from minor. For example, it is very difficult to recall smells, or to name them, but the experience of a particular smell at a particular moment can stimulate a flood of memories of episodes in which that smell was present (Engen, 1987). These memories of our past are often rich in emotional tones. Thus, the scent of cinnamon might evoke feelings of joy associated with your mother baking apple pies, or the scent of ether might evoke the memory and fears associated with a childhood visit to the hospital. Moreover, such smell-invoked memories are often necessary for normal biological functioning. For example, if a recently mated female mouse is exposed to a strange male's urine before the egg implants in the uterus, implantation will likely fail. This will also happen if she "forgets" what her mate smells like, either because she was separated from him for 50 days, or because a part of the olfactory system responsible for these memories was interfered with (Brennan, Kaba, & Keverne, 1990).

In many common situations, smell works together with taste. When we have a bad head cold, food seems flavorless, yet our nasal passages are most affected by the cold, not our mouths where the taste receptors are located. When our nasal passages are clogged with extra mucus our olfactory receptors cannot function properly. This affects both our ability to smell and to experience flavor, since much of the richness and subtlety of our experiences of the flavors of food and drink come from their odors (Brillat-Savarin, 1825/1971; Hyman, Mentyer, & Calderone, 1979; Murphy & Cain, 1980). When we cannot smell, our ability to identify foods by taste alone is significantly inferior, as Figure 8-8 shows. And this happens often. In an informal survey conducted by *National Geographic* magazine, it was found that in more than two-thirds of the analyzed returns, respondents reported occasional loss of the sense of smell, many of them quite often—for example, every time a head cold occurred (Gilbert & Wysocki, 1987). Many people over 70 years of age also experience major loss of the smell sense (Gilbert & Wysocki, 1987; Rabin & Cain, 1986) with similar consequences for the experience of flavor (see Chapter 16). Demonstration Box 8-5 allows you to experience this for yourself in a controlled way (so that you do not have to wait for a head cold).

Smell acts as if it has two separate modes of action that may result in different perceptual experiences and different forms of information extraction (for example, Rozin, 1978). One mode, which we have already mentioned, is associated with the experience of the flavors of food. The second is a distance sense, responding to molecules that float about in the air, carrying information about the objects or organisms from which they have become detached. For instance, we leave molecules of ourselves on the ground and in the air near the ground whenever we take a walk. Insects and some higher animals secrete volatile chemicals (*pheromones*) whose molecules waft through the air to other members of the species. The specific molecules secreted can carry messages about fear or sexual availability, among other things. Species that possess sensory systems that respond to these low concentrations of molecules in the air can take advantage of this information, hence improving their ability to

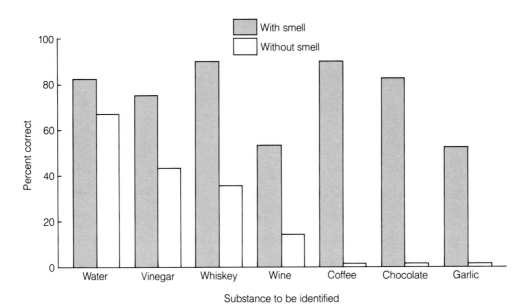

Figure 8-8 *Identification of some common foods with and without smell (based on Mozel, Smith, Smith, Sullivan, & Swender, 1969).*

DEMONSTRATION BOX 8-5   Flavor without Smell

The simplest way to experience flavor without smell is to pinch your nostrils closed before coming near to the substance to be tasted, and then put some of that substance into your mouth and swish it around while paying attention to its flavor. Then release your nostrils, open your mouth slightly, and breathe in gently through both mouth and nose. You should experience a significant change in the flavor when you do this. Try it for the various substances listed in Figure 8-8 and any others you can think of. Your experiences with nose pinched approximate those of elderly people who have experienced large deficits in their sense of smell.

It is rather easy to show that food identification is impaired when the sense of smell is absent. You simply need to get a friend to help you. First prepare several different substances to be identified—the ones listed in Figure 8-8 will do. They should be in a liquid state (mash up the garlic and mix it with water). Then seat your friend at some distance from the solutions and blindfold him or her. For each substance, first ask him to pinch his nose and when he has done that, put some of the solution in his mouth and ask for its name. After he has tried that, tell him to release his nostrils and again attempt to name the substance. Repeat this for each substance, and several friends if you can, and see how closely the results match those of Figure 8-8.

reproduce (see Gibbons, 1986, for a popular review). It is interesting to note that at times the "distant smell" and "food smell" functions give different perceptual experiences. For instance, Limburger cheese has a long distance smell that is quite strong and, most people think, offensive, but this "smell" when in the mouth contributes in a positive way to the flavor of the cheese, which many people find quite pleasing.

Smell Stimuli and Receptors

Which aspects of a molecule give it the quality of evoking the sensation of smell? First, it must come from a volatile substance (one that has a gaseous state at ordinary temperatures—in other words, something that can evaporate), since air currents carry the molecules to the smell receptors in the nose. However, the most volatile substances do not necessarily smell the strongest. Water, which has a high volatility, has no smell at all (if it is pure). In fact, the extent to which a smell stimulus separates itself chemically from water *(hydrophobicity)* is highly correlated with the perceived intensity of that stimulus (Greenberg, 1981). Conversely, musk (a secretion obtained from some deer and beavers) has a low volatility, yet is a very powerful odorant and is used in making some of our most expensive perfumes.

In general, any molecules may be described as having a specific size, weight, shape, and vibration frequency. The last property has to do with the fact that atoms in a given molecule are often not held firmly in place but move around in a characteristic pattern, at predictable speeds that are different for different substances (R. H. Wright, 1977, 1982). In addition, the particular atoms that make up a molecule, and the number of electrons available for chemical bonding with other molecules on the

smell receptors, are probably important components of smell stimuli. As yet no consensus exists as to which of these properties are critical; given the large number of molecules that can be smelled, it is likely that several of them are important.

The receptor cells that interact with the smell stimuli are located in a relatively small area in the upper nasal passages (see Figure 8-9) called the **olfactory epithelium,** which translates to "smell skin." Each oval-shaped receptor cell sends a long extension (called the **olfactory rod**) to the surface of the olfactory epithelium, and in addition sends its axons toward the brain. Thus, the receptors are actually specialized neurons. Remarkably, the receptor cells only function for about four to eight weeks before deteriorating; new receptor cells are continually being produced by the basal cells (see Figure 8-9 and Costanzo & Graziadei, 1987). These are one of the few types of neurons in adult mammals that can regenerate.

From a knob at the end of the olfactory rod protrude a number of **olfactory cilia**—hairlike structures embedded in a special type of watery mucus secreted by a set of glands found nowhere else in the nasal passages. The mucus contains many molecules of a special protein called **olfactory binding protein** (or **OBP**), which can attach to hydrophobic odorant molecules that would ordinarily be repelled from the watery mucus. It is thought that odorant molecules bound to OBP are transported from the surface of the mucus to the olfactory receptors and then detached from the receptors again by the continually moving stream of mucus sweeping across the cilia (Pelosi & Tirindelli, 1989; Pevsner, Sklar, Hwang, & Snyder, 1989).

The olfactory cilia contain the receptor molecules that actually make contact with the smell stimulus (Cagan & Rein, 1980). Both the number of cilia per receptor and the total number of receptors are correlated with olfactory

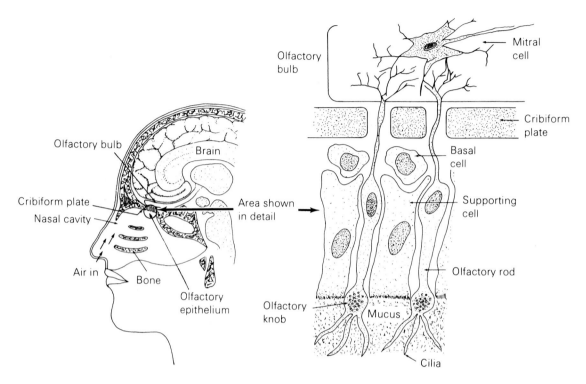

Figure 8-9 *Anatomy of the olfactory system and a detail of the structure of the olfactory epithelium and olfactory bulb.*

sensitivity. Animals that have more receptors and more cilia per receptor have much keener senses of smell. Humans are at the lower end of the scale of smell sensitivity. For example, a dog has about 200 million olfactory receptors as opposed to only about 10 million in humans. Also a dog has 100–150 cilia per receptor as opposed to a paltry 6–8 cilia in humans (T. S. Brown, 1975).

As is the case with the other senses, the mechanism by which the stimulus molecules cause an electrical response in the receptors of the olfactory epithelium is still not completely known. Probably at least two classes of transduction mechanisms exist (Gesteland, 1986; Getchell & Getchell, 1987). One is made up of highly selective processes in which specific re-

ceptor cell proteins form reversible chemical bonds with specific parts of odorant molecules. These then cause depolarization of the receptor cell either directly or through other biochemical processes inside the cell. The depolarization of course produces the action potentials that travel up the axons of the receptor cells. Notice that in this theoretical formulation the specific receptors are *specialists* for a specific odorant. Such selective processes may be distributed unevenly over the epithelium in addition to being located on specific parts of the cilia.

Figure 8-10 shows how one of these mechanisms might work. Numerous studies have suggested that a substance called *cyclic adenosine monophosphate (cAMP)* is produced when an

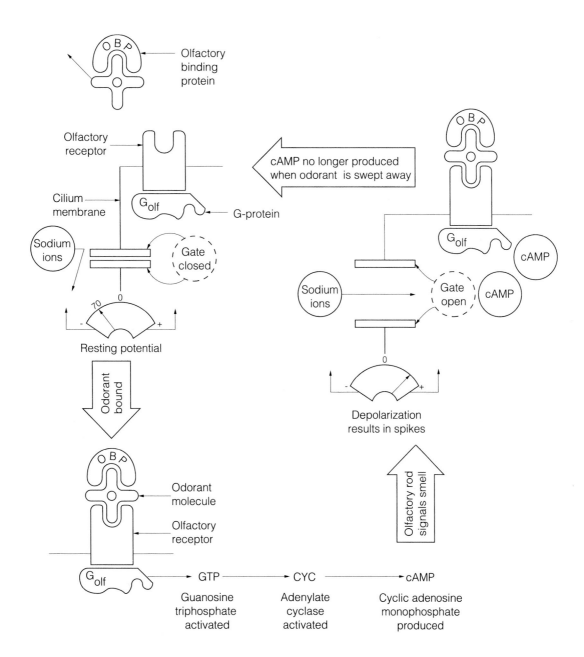

Figure 8-10   *One of the ways in which olfactory receptors respond to odorant molecules.*

odorant molecule stimulates an olfactory receptor (see Brand et al., 1989). Recent biochemical studies (Jones & Reed, 1989) have identified a specific protein, called G_{olf}, that is activated by odorant reception and in turn activates a specific enzyme called *adenylate cyclase* (Bakalyar & Reed, 1990), which causes cAMP to be produced. The presence of cAMP causes the cell membrane to allow positively charged sodium ions to enter, depolarizing the cell and causing spike potentials to travel up the axon. Direct recording of the effect of odorants on the flow of electrical current across the membrane of the cilium are consistent with this scheme (Firestein & Werblin, 1989). This mechanism is reminiscent of the mechanism used in vision for rod responses to light inputs. The major differences lie in the particular molecules involved, and the fact that the reception of the stimulus opens a gate for sodium to flow through the cell membrane in smell, whereas it closes a sodium gate to produce the response in vision (see Figure 3-8).

The second class of mechanism consists of less selective processes, in which various chemicals directly affect the receptor cell membrane anywhere they contact it, causing ions to leak in or out, thus producing depolarization. These processes are the same for all receptor cells and may constitute what may be called *generalist* smell receptors. Some insects seem to possess both specialist and generalist receptors in their olfactory systems (D. Schneider, 1969), and it is likely that mammals do too.

Two particular theories of which properties of odorant molecules make them "fit" with a receptor molecule have been popular among psychologists. The **lock and key theory** maintains that variously shaped molecules fit into special sites on the receptor membrane like a key into a lock. When a molecule fits into a receptor site, then the processes outlined earlier cause depolarization and subsequent action potentials (Amoore, 1970). The **vibration theory** maintains that the stimulus molecule ruptures certain chemical bonds in molecules making up the cell membrane, causing the release of stored-up energy, which in turn may trigger ion flow across the cell membrane either directly or via a process like the one outlined in Figure 8-10. Which bonds are ruptured in which cells depends on the unique vibration frequency of each stimulus molecule (R. H. Wright, 1977, 1982).

Neural Responses in Smell

The olfactory receptor cells send their axons through tiny holes in a bone at the top of the nasal cavity (the cribiform plate) to form the **olfactory nerve.** The nerve goes straight to the **olfactory bulb,** which is located in front of and below the main mass of the brain (see Figure 8-9). The passage of the olfactory nerve through the cribiform plate makes it very vulnerable to being severed by shearing forces generated when the head suddenly starts or stops moving in a particular direction. Many people who have had head injuries, for example in automobile accidents, have lost their sense of smell for this reason.

The axons of the receptors and the dendrites of cells from the olfactory bulb form complex clusters of connections (called *glomeruli*) in the bulb. These clusters may be grouped according to the type of receptor or type of stimulus molecule involved (Kauer, 1980, 1987). One type of olfactory bulb cell seems to send axons directly to the primary sensory cortex for smell, which is located in the temporal lobe of the cortex. Another type of cell sends axons to a variety of lower brain centers, especially the limbic system (which is involved in our experience of emotion and memory), as well as to the smell cortex. The number of fibers leaving the olfactory bulb is *much* smaller (about a thousand times smaller) than the number entering it, so presumably many receptor cells contribute to the activity of each of the cells in the olfactory bulb and later centers (Allison, 1953). The major route of information from the olfactory bulb to the smell cortex is called the **lateral olfactory tract.** After the primary smell cortex the neural pathways become extremely complex, including projections to the thalamus and several other cortical areas (see Price, 1987).

The study of the electrophysiology of the smell system is still in its infancy. As we mentioned earlier, however, a number of studies have found that the intensity of the neural response varies directly with the intensity of the stimulus. Most contemporary investigators have focused on the more subtle problem of how different smell qualities are signaled to the brain. They have tried to find evidence of specific types of receptors for different types of stimuli. One major early study was that of Ottoson (1956), who measured the electrical response of the entire olfactory epithelium to various stimuli. He discovered that passing a puff of odor-laden air across the epithelium resulted in a unique type of electrical response, a slow change in the electrical charge of the receptor cells. This change is thought to generate spike potentials in the axons of these cells.

With improved experimental techniques, Gesteland, Lettvin, Pitts, and Rojas (1963) were able to record the responses of single receptors in the olfactory epithelium. They recorded both the slow potential response to stimuli and the spike potentials generated in the axons of the receptors by the same stimuli. These two types of electrical responses are shown one on top of the other in Figure 8-11. As you can see in the figure, this particular receptor responded vigorously to a musky odor, less to nitrobenzene, hardly at all to benzoni-

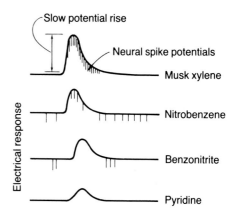

Figure 8-11 *Slow potential and spike potential responses of olfactory receptor cells to four different smell stimuli (based on Gesteland et al., 1963).*

trite, and not at all to pyridine. Gesteland et al. (1963) thought these responses indicated the existence of the sought-after receptor types, although they were cautious in making this interpretation. Such caution seems to have been well founded, since later recordings from single cells in the epithelium, olfactory bulb, and cortical and lower brain centers that receive olfactory information have found that each neural unit responds to a broad range of stimuli (Cain & Bindra, 1972; Giachetti & MacLeod, 1975; Kauer, 1987; O'Connell & Mozell, 1969).

The same sort of across-fiber patterns found in taste seem to be present in the olfactory system, and it is possible the "code" for smell qualities will be found in these patterns (Erickson & Schiffman, 1975; Kauer, 1987). At present we have no evidence of olfactory fibers falling into groups like the taste fibers seem to, although some investigators have proposed that receptors sensitive to the same stimuli send their axons to the same part of the olfactory bulb (see Kauer, 1987). Some evidence has also indicated that odorant quality is coded as a pattern of activity across the entire olfactory bulb (Skarda & Freeman, 1987). However, a *labeled-line theory,* such as the one we discussed for taste, would be somewhat cumbersome for olfaction, since the much greater number of "primary" smells would require many more types of labeled lines than for taste.

Smell Thresholds

A dog's sense of smell can be amazingly acute. Droscher (1971) tells the story of an experienced dog trainer who brought his dog to a university professor for testing, claiming that the dog's ability was "supernatural" since it could track people by scent even if they were wearing rubber boots. Actually, the dog was simply using its acute sense of smell to detect the millions of sweat molecules that leaked through the rubber boots. Why can't we humans smell such things?

In the early 1960s, Stuiver studied the absolute sensitivity of human smell receptors by making a model of the nasal passages around the olfactory epithelium. He used this model to calculate just how much of an olfactory stimulus actually arrived at the surface of the epithelium (see Figure 8-12). When threshold stimuli were considered, he found that it takes 8 molecules at most to stimulate a single receptor cell in the human. Considering all aspects of the manner in which molecules of odor stimuli are distributed in the nose, it can be argued that a single receptor cell can respond to contact by one stimulus molecule (De Vries & Stuiver, 1961). Quite clearly this is the greatest sensitivity that any single olfactory receptor cell could have. Thus, at the level of an individual receptor, a dog (or any other animal) cannot be more sensitive than a human. However, dogs have 200 times more cilia than humans have. Thus, the likelihood that a very weak stimulus will stimulate an olfactory receptor and pro-

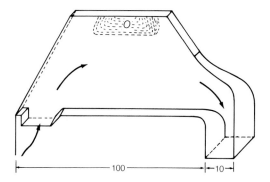

Figure 8-12 *A model of the nasal passage used by Stuiver to calculate the proportion of molecules in a smell stimulus that reaches the olfactory epithelium (O). Air follows the path indicated by the arrows (measurements of distances are in millimeters). Stimulus molecules reach O via eddy currents (like the eddies in a stream) (from De Vries & Stuiver, 1961. Copyright 1961 by the MIT Press).*

duce a noticeable sensation is greater for the dog (see Marshall & Moulton, 1981).

More traditional attempts to determine the absolute thresholds for various odors encounter problems similar to those found when measuring taste sensitivity. Thresholds vary across psychophysical methods (for example, Burgland, Hogman, & Johansson, 1988). They depend on the purity of the odorant, the way it is delivered to the olfactory epithelium, and how the stimulus intensity is measured. Moreover, an individual's thresholds for the same substance vary dramatically from moment to moment (Stevens, Cain, & Burke, 1988). Different substances also have different average thresholds.

In much the same way that we found individual differences in taste sensitivity, such differences are also present in smell sensitivity (Rabin & Cain, 1986; Stevens et al., 1988), with some individuals relatively "odor-blind" to certain substances (see Engen, 1982). Amoore (1969, 1975; Amoore, Pelosi, & Forrester,

1977) has reported the results of an extensive search for instances of odor blindnesses as a part of his plan to identify the primary odors. By 1975 he was able to report 76 different **anosmias** (odor blindnesses), ranging from the smell of skunk to the smell of vanilla. Some of these are quite common; for example, about 1 out of 3 individuals cannot smell a strong stimulus of 1,8 cineole, which produces a camphorous odor (Pelosi & Pisanelli, 1981). Conversely, some anosmias are quite rare, as when only 4 people out of 4030 could not smell a strong stimulus of n-butyl mercaptan, which has a foul, putrid odor. Amoore was able to divide these 76 anosmias into about 31 classes, each of which might represent a primary odor quality. Such specific anosmias are consistent with the idea that humans have two classes of olfactory receptors, the specialists and the generalists we mentioned earlier (R. H. Wright, 1978a).

Smell Adaptation

As in most sensory systems, adaptation (from prolonged exposure to a particular stimulus) affects smell thresholds and the perceived intensity of an odor. It even affects the pleasantness of odors (Cain & Johnson, 1978). One of the great disappointments of wine tasting is that the aroma and the bouquet of the wine seem to last only for a few sniffs. The rich complexity of a great wine soon fades into a bland, featureless odor, even for the most experienced "smeller," unless frequent breaks of about 15 seconds are taken. Luckily, the odors of sweaty bodies, rotten eggs, and the sulphurous smell of air pollution also soon fade away, if you continue to sniff.

An important early study of adaptation of the smell sense was that of Moncrieff (1956).

He studied the effects of previous exposure to an odorant on the threshold for that odorant **(self-adaptation).** He also studied how exposure to one odorant affected the threshold for different odorants **(cross-adaptation).** As you might expect, the largest loss of sensitivity was found for conditions of self-adaptation. Cross-adaptation effects varied with the similarity of the smells of the two stimuli. Stimuli with similar smells gave large cross-adaptation effects; those that differed in smell gave smaller effects. Surprisingly, all of the adapting odors had some effect on observers' sensitivity for the others. This means that it was not possible to classify the various stimuli into a small number of primary classes based on adaptation data, which is similar to Amoore's conclusions based on anosmias. You can experience self- and cross-adaptation by trying Demonstration Box 8-6.

Cain and Engen (1969) looked at the effects of adapting stimuli on the perceived intensity of odorants. They found that the higher the concentration of the adapting stimulus the greater the reduction in the apparent intensity of the test stimuli presented afterward. This relationship does not hold for extreme test stimulus values, however, since *very* intense test stimuli all appeared to arouse about the same sensory response, regardless of the state of adaptation.

Smell Intensity and Qualities

When we consider how the intensity of an odor depends on the stimulus intensity, we again find it useful to refer to the exponent of the psychophysical power function to describe this relationship. The exponents of power functions fitted to magnitude estimations of odor intensity differ across the various odors scaled. Cain (1969) found that exponents ranged from

---

DEMONSTRATION BOX 8-6   Smell Adaptation

You experience self-adaptation of odorants every day. The next time you notice a strong odor, take several deep sniffs and then take a more usual sniff and pay close attention to the intensity of the odor as compared to what you at first experienced. You should notice a significant decrease in sensation intensity. Alternatively, prepare yourself a cup of coffee or aromatic tea, keeping your nostrils pinched while you do. When the steaming cup is in front of you, release your nostrils and take a gentle sniff, noting the intensity of the odor. Then take several deep sniffs followed by another gentle sniff and compare the odor intensity during the final gentle sniff to that during the first gentle sniff.

It is a bit more difficult to demonstrate cross-adaptation, since the effects are weaker and not systematic. You should use your own judgment and explore a range of odorants using the general method described here. When two odorants you wish to test have been obtained, first step into another room, where you cannot smell them, and take several deep sniffs. Then approach the odorants with pinched nose. Release your nostrils near the first (test) odorant, and take a gentle sniff, noting the intensity of the odor. Then take several deep sniffs of the other (adapting) odorant, and return to the test odorant and take another gentle sniff. Compare the odor intensity on this sniff to the first one. If it is less intense, you have experienced cross-adaptation; if it is more intense you have experienced facilitation, as sometimes happens with biologically significant odors (see Engen, 1982).

---

about 0.70 to a low of about 0.15. Cain reported that the size of the exponent is directly related to the degree of water solubility of the odorant, with exponents for completely water-soluble odorants about 2.5 times as large as those for non-water-soluble odorants. R. H. Wright (1978b, 1978c) showed that the exponents for various odorants can be predicted from specific ways the odorant molecules interact with receptor cell membranes. Perceived odor intensity can also be affected by seemingly extraneous things, such as the color of the thing sniffed. For example, a strawberry odor smells more intense when the solution in which it is presented is colored red than when it is colorless (Zellner & Kautz, 1990).

In *absolute* terms the sense of smell is remarkably acute, but for a long time it was thought that humans could not *discriminate* between different odor intensities very well. Most recent measurements, however, indicate that the olfactory system is actually more sensitive than the taste system in this regard. In fact, the olfactory system may be as sensitive as the visual or auditory system in discriminating changes in intensity, with Weber fractions as low as 0.05, meaning that a change in intensity of only 5% can be detected about half of the time (Cain, 1977). Interestingly, smell intensities can be discriminated better if the odorants enter the right nostril than if they enter the left nostril (Zatorre & Jones-Gotman, 1990). Since the olfactory pathways stay on the same side of the brain as where they begin, this, along with other evidence, may indicate that the right hemisphere of the brain is more specialized for olfactory processing (Zatorre & Jones-Gotman, 1990).

As in all of the other sensory modalities, attempts have been made to isolate a small set of "primary" smell qualities. If such could be found, then all olfactory sensations could be predicted as the result of a combination of these primary responses. As we have already seen, the data from adaptation and anosmias do not support such a small set of primaries for smell. The classical attempt to describe smell primaries was that of Henning (1915). Figure 8-13 shows his "smell prism," which had six primary qualities arranged at its corners.

Although it was a standard representation of the "smell primaries" for quite some time, Henning's prism apparently does a poor job of describing the perceived relationships among odorants. When multidimensional scaling techniques are used to provide a geometrical representation of odor similarity judgments, in much the same way as for taste judgments, neither Henning's smell prism nor any other readily identifiable classification scheme emerges. Figure 8-14 displays some representative results from this kind of study. This type of result has led some investigators (for example, Erickson & Schiffman, 1975; Southwick & Schiffman, 1980) to speculate that only a complex set of physicochemical considerations could account for the interrelationships shown in the qualities of smell stimuli. Such results seem consistent with Amoore's (1975) suggestion that there may be as many as 31 primary odors. Of particular interest is that some of these suggested primaries seem to be associated with receptor systems that respond to odors produced by the human body. These are the same types of odors emitted by most animals in various situations relevant to the survival of the species, such as danger and sexual contact, and humans seem to respond to this class of stimuli as well.

Pheromones

Some smells have been said to have a special biological significance for humans. Ellis (1905) pointed out that both men and women often emit strong odors during sexual excitement, and some researchers contend that human behavior can be strongly influenced by such olfactory stimuli (for example, Comfort, 1971). Chemicals secreted by animals that transmit information to other animals (usually of the same species) are called **pheromones.** Many studies have shown that pheromones strongly influence behavior in many animal species. However, the possibility that pheromones strongly affect human behavior has been entertained only recently. As you might expect, manufacturers of colognes and perfumes, ever searching for ways to enhance the sales of their products, have immediately responded to this suggestion. For example, for a while a number of products on the market contained *alpha androstenol,* which is known to be an effective sex-attractant pheromone for pigs and also occurs in some human secretions.

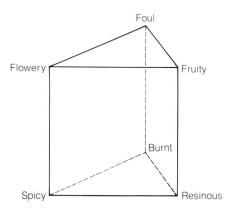

Figure 8-13 Henning's smell prism. Six "primary" odors are at the corners; the surfaces represent stimuli that resemble more than one primary.

Figure 8-14 *A composite replotting of selected odors from multidimensional scaling of similarity judgments of odor pairs (Schiffman, 1974). Dimension I is thought to be "pleasantness." This mapping bears little resemblance to Henning's smell prism (Figure 8-13).*

To put the possible effects of pheromones on human behavior in perspective, we will describe some of the work done on nonhuman animals. Pheromones were first studied, indeed discovered and named, in insects (see E. O. Wilson, 1971). Insects have a fairly evolved sense of smell, with their smell receptors mounted on their antennae. Most animals respond to two major types of pheromones: **releasers,** which on reception by an animal "release," or automatically trigger, a specific behavioral response; and **primers,** which trigger glandular and other physiological activities in the recipient. Most aspects of the lives of insects, particularly social insects such as ants, bees, and termites, are regulated via communication by pheromones. Insects attract their mates, recruit fellows for food gathering or fighting, and recognize each other and their own species via releasers. Queen ants, bees, and termites control swarming, new queen production, proportion of types of workers, and so on, using primers. The important thing to remember about insect pheromones is that usually a *specific chemical,* produced by a *specific gland,* and detected and recognized by a *specific (or specialist) receptor* is involved in such communication. Insect behavior is directly under the control of these pheromones.

Mammals, of course, are much more complex than insects, and the effects of pheromones on their behavior are more subtle. Many pheromone-related effects have been found, however, in several species, including rodents,

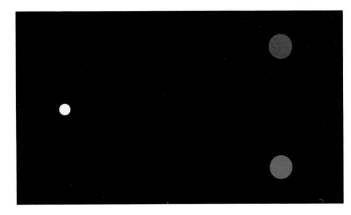

Color Plate 1

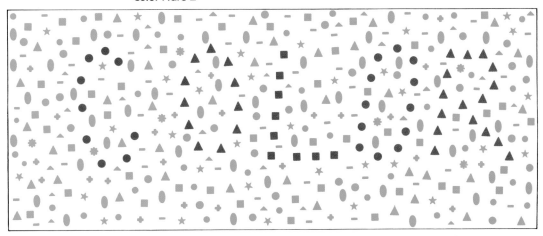

Color Plate 2

Color Plate 3

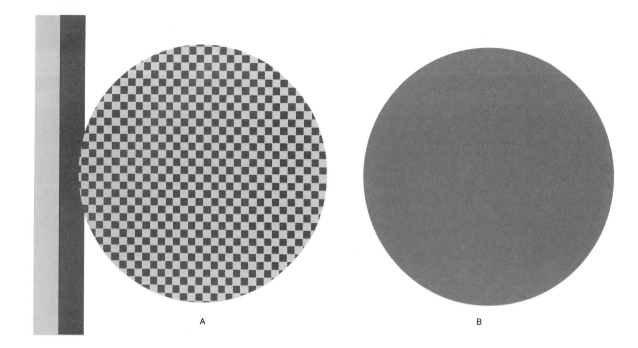

A   B

Color Plate 4

Color Plate 5

Color Plate 6

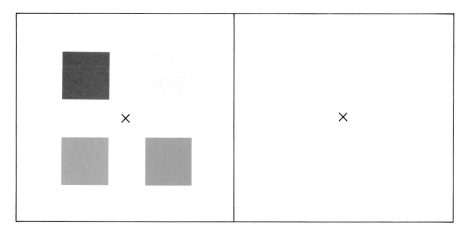

Color Plate 7

A   Read through this list of color names as quickly as possible.
    Read from right to left across each line.

RED	YELLOW	BLUE	GREEN
RED	GREEN	YELLOW	BLUE
YELLOW	GREEN	BLUE	RED
BLUE	RED	GREEN	YELLOW
RED	GREEN	BLUE	YELLOW

B   Name each of these color patches as quickly as possible.
    Name from left to right across each line.

C   Name the color of ink in which each word is printed as quickly as possible.
    Name from left to right across each line.

RED	BLUE	GREEN	YELLOW
YELLOW	BLUE	RED	GREEN
BLUE	YELLOW	GREEN	RED
GREEN	BLUE	YELLOW	RED
BLUE	YELLOW	RED	GREEN

Color Plate 8

Color Plate 9

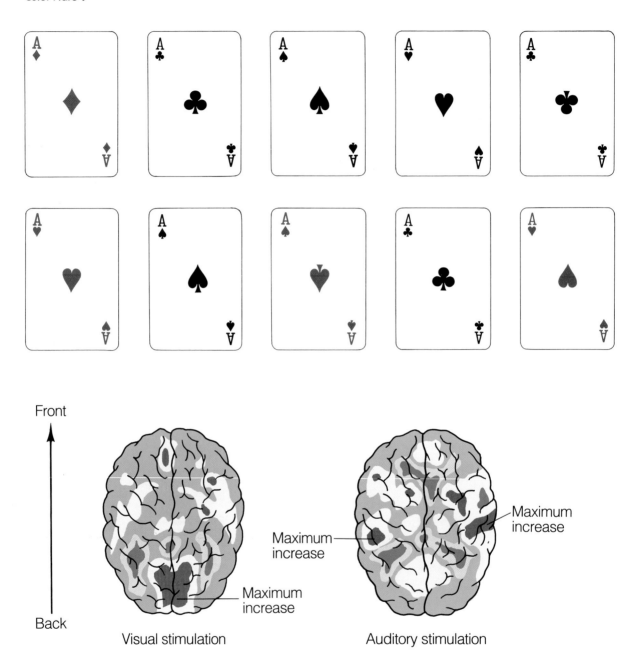

Color Plate 10   *A typical colorized map of the brain resulting from measurements of neural activity via a PET scan. Areas of highest activity are indicated by the reds and yellows; areas of lowest activity are indicated by the blues. Arrows point to the region of highest specific activity when an individual is stimulated visually (looking at a change pattern of colors) or auditorially (hearing a complex sequence of tones).*

dogs, and monkeys (see Brown & MacDonald, 1985a, 1985b, for a review). Mammalian releaserlike effects include the mutual recognition of mother and young offspring. Male and female sexual attraction is also affected by pheromones. A salient example is the effect of the odor of a female dog in heat on the male (Goodwin, Gooding, & Regnier, 1979). Other pheromones elicit aggression in males, inhibit aggression in females, and are used for signaling purposes, such as trail marking or defining territorial boundaries. Primerlike effects include control of the estrus cycle of females, the age at which puberty is attained, and even the likelihood of becoming pregnant.

Some effects of pheromones have been observed in species rather close to humans on the evolutionary scale, namely monkeys. However, here the story becomes even more complex. Some early research studied the effect of vaginal secretions from female monkeys in estrus (that is, those that are sexually receptive) on the copulating behavior of males. Early work seemed to indicate that a powerful pheromone was involved. Normally, male monkeys seldom attempt to engage nonestrus females sexually. Such behavior could be elicited, however, if the females' sexual skins had been rubbed with the secretions of the sexual skins of females who were in estrus. These secretions, presumably containing pheromones, were dubbed *copulins* (Michael & Keverne, 1968; Michael, Keverne, & Bonsall, 1971). Later work indicated that the suspected releaser pheromone was not as powerful as had been thought, and that monkey sexual behavior was under the control of many interacting factors, only one of which was the smell of the partner's sexual skin (Goldfoot, 1981; Goldfoot, Kravetz, Goy, & Freeman, 1976; Keverne, 1978). In fact, odor cues are not necessary at all, for anosmic male monkeys show normal mating behavior (Goldfoot, Essock-Vitale, Asa, Thornton, & Leshner, 1978). In all of the pheromonelike effects studied with

mammals, communications delivered by chemical means, although often very important, have not been found to be as imperative as they are with insects. Mammals have more complex brains and their behavior is influenced by many different environmental factors, only one of which is odorants (see MacDonald & Brown, 1985).

When we consider humans, the behavioral effects of pheromones are most subtle, since social and learning factors influence our behavior even more than they do that of other mammals. Some very interesting results, however, indicate that smells may play an important, although probably subordinate, role in many aspects of human social behavior. First, several studies (Lord & Kasprzak, 1989; McBurney, Levine, & Cavanaugh, 1977; Russell, 1976; Schleidt, Hold, & Attili, 1981) have demonstrated that people can reliably detect their own body odor from among a set of similar stimuli contributed by other people. In a typical study, the actual stimuli were collected by having people wear T-shirts for several days. When asked to rate the pleasantness of the body odors and to describe the individual whose odor they were smelling, remarkable degree of consistency was found across people. In general, the individuals having unpleasant odors were usually described as if they also would be likely to have socially undesirable traits. They were supposedly dumb, ugly, fat, and unhealthy. The more pleasant odors were described as coming from people with more desirable traits (McBurney et al., 1977).

People seem to be able to discriminate reliably the sex of an odor donor. In one study, the odors of males were characterized as "musky" while female odors were described as "sweet" (Russell, 1976); other studies have found that the stronger (and more unpleasant) odors are more likely to be attributed (correctly) to males (Doty, 1985; Doty, Green, Ram, & Yankell, 1982; Doty, Kligman, Leyden, & Orndorff, 1978).

Similar results are found in different cultures (Schleidt et al., 1981). Males and females can also be discriminated on the basis of hand odor (Wallace, 1977) and breath odor (Doty et al., 1982). Females do better at this (Doty et al., 1982; Wallace, 1977) and in fact do better than males at odor identification in general (Doty, Applebaum, Zusho, & Settle, 1985; Lord & Kasprzak, 1989). You can try your nose at some of these tasks using Demonstration Box 8–7.

Human sensitivity to human odors seems to be present from an early age. For instance, Russell (1976) found that a small sample of 2-week-old babies reliably responded to the odor of their own mother's breast and not to that of a strange mother; this ability may exist as early as 6 days after birth (MacFarlane, 1975). Breast-feeding babies (but not bottle-feeding babies) of the same age can also recognize their mothers' armpit odor (Cernoch & Porter, 1985). Actually, female (but not male) neonates (less than 2 days old) can develop a preference for an artificial odorant simply by being exposed to it, which clearly indicates that these very young infants can make odor discriminations (Balogh & Porter, 1986).

One of the necessary conditions for accurate odor identification, at least in adults, seems to be a lot of experience with the odor and its source (Cain, 1979; Rabin, 1988; Rabin & Cain, 1984; Schab, 1991). Certainly the relationship between parents and children contains much such experience. We might thus expect that parents could recognize the odors of their own offspring, and that perhaps siblings could recognize each others' odors as distinct from those of other children. This seems to be the case, raising the possibility that smell plays an important role in interactions among humans from the same family (Porter, Balogh, Cernoch, & Franchi, 1986; Porter & Moore, 1981).

A second line of research with humans has been aimed at finding a sex attractant based on releaserlike pheromone action. The most

---

DEMONSTRATION BOX 8-7   Social Significance of Human Odor

This demonstration is a bit complex, but is worth the effort. It is designed to see whether you or your friends can discriminate male from female body odors. The most important factor here is to eliminate the effects of perfumes and deodorants, which is difficult since almost all commercial products now contain scents. Ivory soap is one product that does not, so it is advisable to have odor-donors wash themselves with this soap before contributing the odor, or simply to soak for a period of time in clear water. The same should apply for the clothing mentioned below. The simplest experiment involves having a group of friends put on scent-free T-shirts and wear them for at least 24 hours. At the end of the time period, put the T-shirts (with paper labels under them to indicate the sex and identity of the donor) into clean plastic bags. You now have your odor stimuli. Have each friend sniff at the opening of each bag and indicate whether the sample came from a male or a female. You might also want to have them try to guess whose T-shirt it is, and which one is their own, and you might even want to ask for a rank order in terms of pleasantness. When all have done this, tabulate the results and see how well everyone did.

promising candidate is the substance alpha androstenol mentioned above, which causes a sow to become immobile, and thus receptive to a boar's sexual advances, when the boar secretes it in his saliva. Since alpha androstenol is also present in human apocrine (a gland in the underarm region) sweat, it may play a role in human sexual attraction, especially since humans have been shown to discriminate reliably among axillary (underarm) odors. A few published studies have found positive effects. For example, androstenol affects ratings of various social characteristics of hypothetical applicants for a job, and affects male and female ratings differently (Cowley, Johnson, & Brooksbank, 1977). Similarly, women in photographs were rated as more sexually attractive by both men and women wearing surgical masks impregnated with androstenol than by those wearing control masks (Kirk-Smith, Booth, Carroll, & Davies, 1978). More women and fewer men (than in a control condition) used a seat in a dentist's waiting room that had been sprayed with androstenone (Kirk-Smith & Booth, 1980). Finally, overnight contact with alpha androstenol may increase the willingness of females to initiate social interactions with males but not with females; it seems to have no effect on males' social interactions (Cowley & Brooksbank, 1991).

Such results are exciting to perfume manufacturers (and, perhaps, to the sexually deprived), but they may not be easy to interpret.

Rogel (1978) critically reviewed a number of the older studies along with those of monkeys, and concluded that although it is possible that olfaction does influence many aspects of social behavior, it would be wrong to believe that human behavior could be *controlled,* to the extent seen in lower mammals and insects, by such pheromones. This means that human sexual choice, contrary to the claims of some perfume manufacturers, is apt to be more a matter of higher mental processes than of primitive responses to sexual odors.

Work on primerlike effects in humans has also been done. It has been found that regular (weekly) intimate contact with a male, or even with male underarm secretions, might cause the female menstrual cycle to become more regular in length (Cutler et al., 1986; but see Wilson, 1988 for a critique). Regular contact with another female, or with her underarm secretions might cause the female smelling this pheromone to synchronize her menstrual cycle with that of the woman providing the odorant (McClintock, 1971; Preti, Cutler, Garcia, Huggins, & Lawley, 1986; but see Wilson, 1987 for a critique). These are primerlike effects since they involve physiological changes and not specific behaviors. They can be important—for example, menstrual regularity is associated with healthy reproductive functioning and fertility—but they are not direct and powerful immediate influences on human behavior.

GLOSSARY

The following definitions are specific to their use in this book.

AB,H system A chemical structure consisting of two negatively charged atoms (A,B) and a positively charged hydrogen atom (H) arranged in a special way; involved in sweet and possibly bitter tastes.

Across-fiber pattern A pattern of neural activity in which various neural units have different stimulus-specific response rates.

Anosmia Relative insensitivity to an odor.

Anterior-insular cortex A cortical center for taste information.

Early attempts at scientific birth control for animals

Cross-adaptation   A phenomenon in which exposure to one tastant (or odorant) affects the absolute threshold or sensation intensity of other tastants (or odorants).

Labeled-line theory   A theory of taste in which each taste fiber encodes the intensity of a single basic taste quality.

Lateral olfactory tract   The main route, composed of axons, from the olfactory bulb to the smell cortex.

Lock and key theory   A theory of smell mechanism in which variously shaped molecules fit into holes in the walls of olfactory receptor cells like a key into a lock, causing an electrochemical change that in turn causes an action potential in the axon.

Medial lemnisci   The pathways that convey taste information from the solitary nucleus to the thalamus.

Molar concentration   A measure of the amount of a tastant present; 1 *mole* equals the molecular weight of a substance in grams added to enough water to make 1 liter of solution.

Olfactory binding protein (OBP)   A type of protein molecule found in the watery mucus covering the olfactory epithelium; it may transport hydrophobic odorant molecules to and from olfactory receptors.

Olfactory bulb   A complex brain nucleus where the axons of olfactory receptor cells terminate; sends axons to various brain centers including the olfactory cortex and limbic system.

Olfactory cilia   Hairlike projections extending from the knoblike end of the olfactory rod, protruding through the surface of the olfactory epithelium.

Olfactory epithelium   The small area of oval-shaped cells in the upper nasal passages that respond to smell stimuli.

Olfactory nerve   The bundle of axons of smell receptor cells that passes through the top of the nasal cavity and terminates in the olfactory bulb.

Olfactory rod   A long extension from smell receptor cells toward the surface of the olfactory epithelium.

Papillae   Small bumps on the tongue in which taste buds are located.

Pheromones   Secreted by animals, these chemicals transmit information to other animals, usually of the same species.

Potentiation   A case of cross-adaptation in which exposure to one taste stimulus lowers the threshold to another taste stimulus.

Primers   Pheromones that trigger glandular and other physiological responses.

PTC   Phenythiocarbamide, a substance that shows large variations in absolute threshold across different individuals; some people are "taste-blind" to it.

Releasers   Pheromones that trigger specific behavioral responses.

Self-adaptation   A phenomenon in which exposure to a tastant (or odorant) raises the absolute threshold or decreases the sensory intensity of the same tastant (or odorant).

Solitary tract   Region of the brain stem that receives information from cranial nerves about taste.

Taste buds   The group of cells in which the major receptors for taste are located, on the tongue and parts of the mouth.

Taste pore   An opening in the surface of the tongue leading to the taste cells extending from the taste bud.

Thalamus   The region of the lower brain that relays impulses to the cortex.

Vibration theory   A theory of smell mechanism in which a stimulus molecule ruptures chemical bonds in the cell membrane of olfactory receptor cells, causing a release of stored energy that generates an electrical current and action potentials.

TOUCH AND PAIN

Chapter ...

9

The Skin Senses

Skin Stimuli and Receptors

Neural Pathways

Touch

Touch Thresholds

Touch Adaptation

Touch Intensity

Tactile Pattern Perception

Kinesthesis

Kinesthetic Stimuli and Receptors

Neural Responses in Kinesthesis

Perception of Weight and Force

Haptic Perception

Warmth and Cold

Neural Coding of Temperature

Thermal Thresholds and Adaptation

Thermal Intensity and Qualities

Pain

Pain Stimuli and Receptors

Neural Responses to Pain Stimuli

Pain Thresholds, Intensity, and Adaptation

Analgesia and Endogenous Opiates

*P*eople who are both blind and deaf (Helen Keller is one famous example) exist in a perceptual world restricted to smells, tastes, touches, and feelings of warmth and cold and pain. Although such a world may be difficult to imagine for those who can see and hear, the so-called "minor senses" do provide a rich and varied perceptual life. Even linguistic communication is possible, as Helen Keller's teacher demonstrated when she taught her to communicate by finger taps on one another's palms. Moreover, many species of animals rely almost exclusively on the so-called "minor senses" (touch, taste, and smell) for survival-related information about the world. We have already described the chemical senses, taste and smell, in Chapter 8. Here we deal with the mechanical senses—touch, kinesthesis, and pain—which can be sensed anywhere in the body but are most clearly understood in relationship to the skin.

THE SKIN SENSES

All living things have a "skin" of some kind. Probably the most important function of the skin is to *define* the organism, that is, to set boundaries in space, inside of which exists the organism and outside of which exists the environment. The skin is an *interface* (a place where two systems meet) between the organism and the environment, and it is in intimate contact with the outside world. In the most primitive one-celled organisms, the skin is the cell membrane, and it is responsible for all of the organism's contacts with its environment. These contacts include such functions as taking in food, excreting waste, isolating the inside of the cell from damaging outside substances, and responding to all sorts of external stimuli. Although more advanced organisms, such as mammals (including humans), have more specialized sensory organs to handle these tasks, their skins are also important and complex organs. The skin plays a role in respiration, temperature regulation, and protection. It also has a wide variety of sensory functions, and produces the sensations of touch, warmth or cold, and pain.

Skin Stimuli and Receptors

The skin responds to a variety of physical stimuli. When we press an object against the skin, it deforms the surface and we experience the sensation of touch, or pressure. When an object makes contact with a hair, causing it to bend, we also experience touch. The temperature of the object with which we touch the skin also elicits a sensation. Whether it is warmth or cold depends both on the temperature of the stimulus and on the temperature of the skin. Finally, the skin responds to electrical stimulation. For mild electrical stimuli, a type of touch sensation is usually felt, although temperature can also be experienced. When electrical stimulation becomes intense, the sensation usually becomes painful.

In humans the skin has a very complex structure. Figure 9-1 is a diagram of the most important structures in **hairy skin,** which covers most of the human body. A different kind of skin, found on the palms of the hands, soles of the feet, parts of fingers and toes, lips, and other places, has no hairs protruding from it and is called **glabrous skin.** Although a thick outer layer of dead cells is present in glabrous skin, many free nerve endings are also embedded in this layer. This makes such skin effective protection but also extremely sensitive to stimulation. All skin consists of two basic layers. The outer layer, called the **epidermis,** consists of several layers of tough dead cells on top of a single layer of living cells. The living layer divides constantly to generate the dead protective layers above. The inner layer, called the **dermis,** contains most of the nerve endings in the skin. Under these two layers is usually a layer of fat cells. In addition to these layers, the

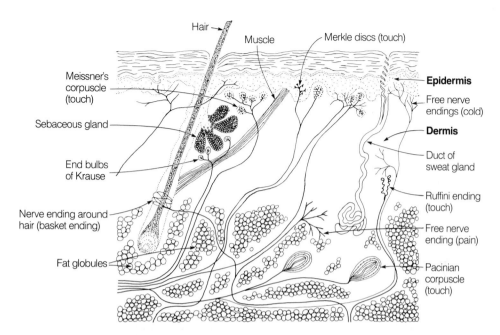

Figure 9-1 A piece of hairy skin in cross section (based on Woolard, Weddell, and Harpman, 1940).

skin contains a variety of hairs, muscles, glands, arteries, veins, and capillaries. Some of these are shown in Figure 9-1.

Figure 9-1 also shows some of the most common nerve endings in the skin. It has been difficult to specify exactly which ending is responsible for which of the skin sensations. In fact, all of the endings seem to respond somewhat to all of the different types of stimulation. Recently, some progress has been made in associating various receptor types with nerve fibers that have different response characteristics (for example, receptors that respond selectively to mechanical, thermal, or painful stimuli). In particular, most "corpuscular" endings—nerve endings with small bodies or swellings on the dendrites, including the *Pacinian corpuscles, Meissner corpuscles, Merkle disks,* and *Ruffini endings*—seem to be associated with various types of fibers that are particularly responsive to touch stimuli, whereas "noncorpuscular" or so-called **free nerve endings** in subcutaneous fat are associated with

pain fibers (see Vierck, 1978). Free nerve endings projecting into the epidermis may be associated with cold fibers (Hensel, 1981) or pain fibers (Perl, 1984). Modern electrophysiological and histological techniques may eventually succeed in identifying the nerve endings associated with the several types of nerve fibers that exist further along in the neural pathways (for example, Torebjork, Ochoa, & Schady, 1983). Much progress has already been made with regard to Merkle disks and Pacinian corpuscles (Gottschaldt & Vahle-Hinz, 1981).

As an example of how a skin receptor responds to stimulation, consider the **Pacinian corpuscle** (see Figures 9-1 and 9-2). It has been well studied because it is large, easily accessible, and occurs in nearly all animals that have complex nervous systems. The elegant work of Loewenstein and his colleagues (see Loewenstein, 1960) involved peeling away the surrounding layers of the cell (much as we would peel an onion) to allow the researchers to touch the axon itself. They were able to

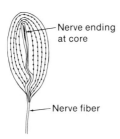

- Nerve ending at core
- Nerve fiber

Figure 9-2   A Pacinian corpuscle.

show that a mechanical stimulus operates directly on the axon of the nerve by deforming its membrane. This mechanical action causes numerous tiny holes in the membrane to open, allowing electrically charged particles (ions) to flow from one side of the membrane to the other, which in turn causes an electrical current to flow between the point of stimulation and another point on the axon. Finally, this electrical current generates a *spike potential* that jumps along the myelinated axon and carries the message of stimulation to the brain (see the Appendix for more information about ion flow and spike potentials). The surrounding layers of material in the Pacinian corpuscle seem to be present simply to make the effect of the stimulus less intense. Temperature could act in a similar way, perhaps by controlling chemical reactions that would affect the ability of electrically charged particles to cross the cell's membrane. Electrical stimuli probably trigger spike potentials directly. We do not know whether all of the cutaneous nerve endings operate in a similar fashion, but it is reasonable to suppose that they do. It is also possible that each nerve ending may utilize more than one of the several possible transduction mechanisms, as seems to be the case in taste (see Chapter 8).

Neural Pathways and Responses

Because the skin contains so many different types of nerve endings, you might think that the nerve pathways to the brain would be hopelessly complex. They *are* complex, but they follow an organizational plan we can understand. The plan depends on two major principles associated with the *type of nerve fiber* and *the place of termination* of the pathway in the cortex.

The *type of nerve fiber* is important because different types of nerve fibers carry different types of information to the brain. Fibers can be classified in at least three ways: (1) according to the type of stimulus that most easily excites them (mechanical, temperature, or noxious), (2) according to the way they respond to those stimuli (slow- or fast-adapting), and (3) according to whether they have large, ill-defined receptive fields or small, well-defined ones. By *receptive field* here, we mean much the same thing we did for vision (see Chapter 3), but here it refers to that region of the *skin* that, when stimulated, causes responses in a particular neural fiber. The receptive fields in the skin also possess the same sort of excitatory-center, inhibitory-surround organization found in the visual system (Bekesy, 1967; Gardner, 1983). Demonstration Box 9-1 shows how you can demonstrate this organization for yourself with touch stimuli.

Using the three classification criteria just described, humans have been shown to have at least four different types of fibers that respond to mechanical deformation of glabrous skin: fibers with small, well-defined receptive fields that adapt either rapidly or slowly, and fibers with large, ill-defined receptive fields that adapt either rapidly or slowly (Vallbo, 1981). Such fiber types are reminiscent of the parvo and magno pathways associated with the nerve fibers that leave the retina of the eye (see Chapter 3).

The second major principle is that *where on the skin* a particular nerve ending is found determines *where its information goes in the brain*, regardless of the type of fiber it represents. All of the sensory information from the skin is passed on to the spinal cord through 31 pairs of nerves (1 member of each pair for each

DEMONSTRATION BOX 9-1   Inhibitory Interactions on the Skin

In this demonstration you will see how skin sensations interact. You will need two fairly sharply pointed objects such as two toothpicks or two bristles from a hairbrush. The demonstration will work better if you ask a friend to control the stimuli. Do not use anything like a knife, for you will be pushing the point quite strongly against your skin. First, try pressing one point against the skin of your palm. Notice the spread of sensation around the stimulated point. Now put the two points as close together as you possibly can. Push them together on the same place on your palm. Notice that you feel only one point, although two are present. Now move the two stimulating points slightly apart. You should *still* feel only one point. Repeat this procedure several times, moving the points apart by a little more each time and paying careful attention to whether the sensation

feels like two points or one on your skin. If you are pushing hard enough and paying close attention to your sensations, at just about the separation where the two points begin to feel like two distinct points on the skin, you should have a surprising experience. The magnitude of the sensation from the two points should diminish greatly, perhaps vanish altogether for a short time. The sensation should be very faint, even though two toothpicks (or brush bristles) are pushing with some force against the skin. As you then move the points even farther apart, you will perceive two distinct, full-strength sensations, appropriately separate on the skin. This phenomenon is explained by the overlapping of regions of excitation and inhibition in adjacent receptive fields of the skin, as shown in the accompanying figure.

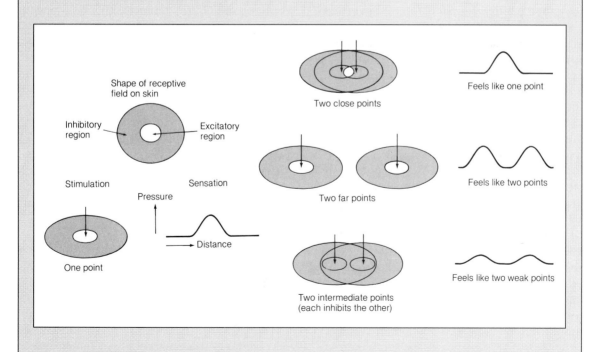

side of the body). There are also 4 cranial nerves that collect cutaneous information from the head region. These inputs are gathered into 2 main pathways to the brain, each of which seems to carry different types of information. Figure 9-3 shows various aspects of these pathways.

The first pathway is called the **dorsal column.** The nerve fibers that comprise it are large, conduct information quickly, and mostly receive inputs from the large, myelinated, fast-conducting Aβ (A-beta) fibers terminating in corpuscular endings in the skin. The pathway ascends the spinal cord on the same side of the body until it reaches the brain stem, where most of the nerve fibers cross over to the other side. The pathway then continues to the **thalamus** and finally arrives at the **somatosensory cortex,** which is located in the **parietal** region of the brain (the upper central region, shown in Figure 9-4). Thus, the pathway terminates in the somatosensory cortex on the opposite side of the body from where it started. This system has fibers that respond mostly to touch and movement, although temperature fibers have also been found (Hensel, 1981).

The second major pathway is called the **spinothalamic pathway.** This pathway is made up of many short fibers instead of a few long axons. At the brain stem, its two branches, the **paleospinothalamic** (*paleo* means "old") and the **neospinothalamic** (*neo* means "new"), join with the dorsal column to form the **medial lemniscus.** The paleospinothalamic pathway is older in an evolutionary sense, and seems specialized for signaling dull or burning pain—it probably receives most of its input from the small, unmyelinated, slow-conducting, C fibers that terminate in the skin. The neospinothalamic pathway seems specialized for signaling sharp or pricking pain and probably receives most of its input from the small, myelinated, but slower-conducting Aδ (A-delta) fibers that terminate in the skin. It also receives some input from the large, fast-conducting Aβ fibers. (Aβ, Aδ, and C fibers are described in more de-

tail in the "Pain" section of this chapter.) The two spinothalamic pathways ascend on the opposite side of the spinal cord from where their input fibers terminate in the skin and then innervate several areas of the brain, the most important being the thalamus and the **limbic system** (responsible for emotion and memory). Fibers from these areas then go to the somatosensory cortex. This pathway seems to carry information about temperature and touch as well as pain.

The somatosensory cortex is divided into two main parts, labeled *SI* and *SII,* and SI has several identifiable layers, labeled *1, 2, 3a,* and *3b* (see Kaas, 1983). Thalamic neurons project mainly to one or more layers in SI, depending where they came from. SI neurons then project to SII (Pons, Garraghty, Friedman, & Mishkin, 1987). This organization is very similar to that of the visual cortex (see Chapter 3).

The relationship between where a stimulus is applied to the skin and where neural activity occurs in the somatosensory cortex is quite regular. One classic "map" of this relationship was created by Penfield and Rasmussen (1950). These investigators electrically stimulated the somatosensory cortex of patients during brain operations. As various points on the cortex were stimulated, the patients reported the sensations they felt, which might be the tingling of one leg and so forth. The resulting somatosensory map of the body is shown in Figure 9-4. Notice that the spatial location of stimulation on the skin is preserved in the spatial location of activity in the cortex. Such maps may be subject to revision if afferent input is lost from some region of the skin, even in adulthood. For example, in monkeys who have lost innervation from an arm, the region of SI that previously encoded touch and pain information from that arm comes after several years to encode information from adjacent regions of the skin (Pons et al., 1991). Also, details of just how the cells in the somatosensory cortex encode information about touch stimuli

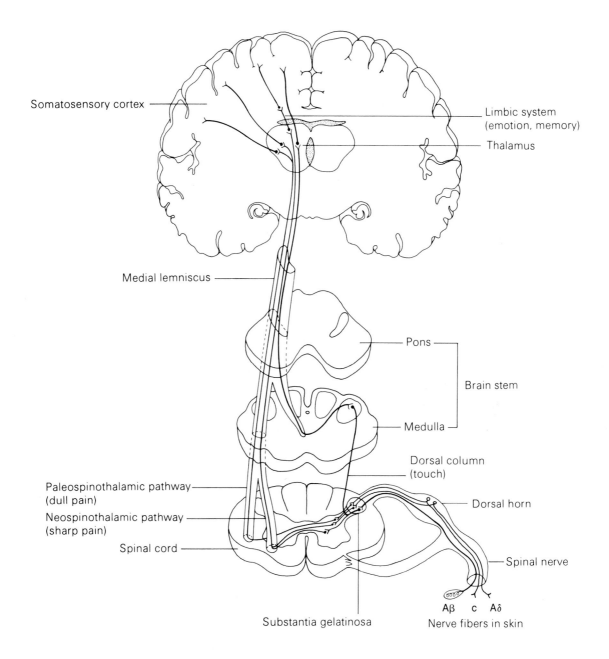

Figure 9-3 *Schematic drawing of some of the important neural pathways from the skin to the brain. The sections of the spinal cord and brain stem are horizontal; that of the brain is vertical.*

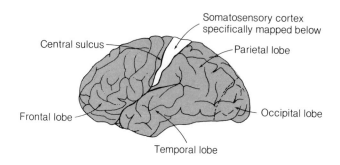

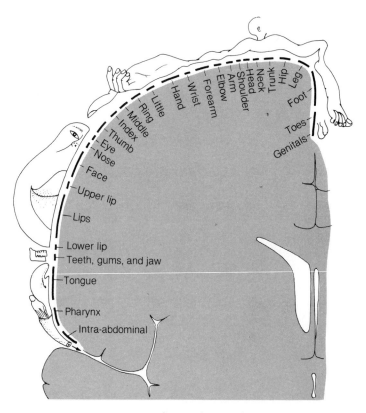

Sensory homunculus

Figure 9-4 *Penfield and Rasmussen's (1950) topographic map of projections of "touch" nerve fibers on the somatosensory cortex. The length of the line next to the drawing of each body part is proportional to the area of somatosensory cortex subserving that body part (from* The Cerebral Cortex of Man *by W. Penfield and T. Rasmussen. Copyright 1950 by Macmillan Publishing Co., Inc., renewed 1978 by Theodore Rasmussen).*

have become clearer. For example, these cells respond to movement of ridges across the skin in much the same way that cells in the visual cortex respond to moving edges in the visual field (Darian-Smith, Sugitani, Heywood, Karita, & Goodwin, 1982; Gardner, 1983; Leinonen, 1983; Whitsel, Dreyer, Hollins, & Young, 1979). You can experience one of the consequences of a cortical map that encodes the stimulation of adjacent regions of the skin into adjacent regions of cortical activity by trying Demonstration Box 9-2.

TOUCH

Given the fact that stimulation of any point on our body's surface can evoke the sensation of touch, it is surprising how often this modality is ignored. For instance, we seldom consider that major components of most sexual experiences are touch sensations. The very act of touching another person, in Western society, is considered to be an act of considerable intimacy, whether it is the gentle touch of a friend or lover or the violent punch of an aggressor.

Touch Thresholds

One of the most striking aspects of our sense of touch is how our sensitivity varies from one region of the body to another. Figure 9-5 shows the absolute touch thresholds for several different regions of the body. Such thresholds are obtained by applying a small rod or hair (pig bristles were used in some of the earliest work) to the surface of the skin with differing amounts of force per unit area, which changes the tension of the skin. An abrupt change in skin tension is the stimulus for touch (Frey & Kiesow, 1899), much as an abrupt change in light intensity is the stimulus for vision (see Chapter 4). When the same hair is used for all skin loci, these thresholds can be expressed simply in terms of the amount of force applied to the hair, since the area over which the force is applied (the tip of the hair) remains constant. This has been done in Figure 9-5, where the higher the bar, the greater the force needed for absolute threshold, and the lower the sensitivity.

Even more dramatic variations of threshold exist within a relatively small area of skin, say, the surface of the arm. If you explore a 2 x 2 cm area on your forearm with a toothpick or hairbrush bristle, pressing with the same light pressure every time you touch the skin (just enough to make the bristle bend slightly), you will discover a number of spots that respond to this stimulus with a distinct sensation of touch. You will also find a number of places that will give only a faint sensation, or none at all.

The sensitivity of the skin is often tested using a *vibrating* stimulus, which alternately applies and releases a force to the same small surface region at frequencies ranging from 20 to 20,000 Hz. Generally, vibrating the touch stimulus results in a lower absolute threshold; that is, when the stimulation is intermittent (on again, off again), the skin is more sensitive. The absolute threshold for a touch sensation caused by a vibrotactile stimulator on the skin depends on the frequency of vibration much as the threshold of hearing depends on the frequency of a sound wave. Also, similar to responses of the ear, the skin is sensitive only to a limited range of vibration frequencies. The range most investigators agree on is from about 40 to about 2500 Hz. However, some researchers have claimed that under special conditions sensations can result from stimuli of frequencies up to 20,000 Hz (Verrillo, 1975). Absolute thresholds for vibration also depend on skin temperature; the higher the temperature, the lower they usually are. This effect is restricted to vibration frequencies over 100 Hz for glabrous skin, but occurs at all frequencies for hairy skin, for example, that of the forearm

DEMONSTRATION BOX 9-2   Aristotle's Illusion

The famous Greek philosopher-scientist Aristotle noticed an interesting illusion of touch that is quite easy to demonstrate. Hold your fingers as shown in Figure A and touch the point between them with a pencil, as shown. Notice that you feel one item touching you and the sensation of one single touch. Now cross your fingers as shown in Figure B, touching yourself again with a pencil in the place indicated between the fingers. Notice that you feel two distinct touches. The effect may be stronger if you close your eyes during the touches. The simplest and most plausible explanation of the illusion is that when the pencil is stimulating the inside of the two fingers (Figure A), the touch information is being sent to overlapping or adjacent areas of the touch cortex, resulting in the sensation of one touch. When the pencil is stimulating the outsides of the two fingers because of your finger contortions, the information is being sent to two separate areas of the touch cortex, allowing you to experience two distinct touches. Such a cortical mapping is quite reasonable, since commonly a single object between two fingers would be expected to stimulate adjacent skin surfaces, and hence should be encoded as a single touch source. It is normally not possible, however, for a single object to stimulate the outsides of two different fingers, and so two different touches should be experienced in these circumstances. The cortical mapping reflects these common situations. It seems that whether the fingers are actually crossed or not, all processing makes the assumption that they are uncrossed (Benedetti, 1985).

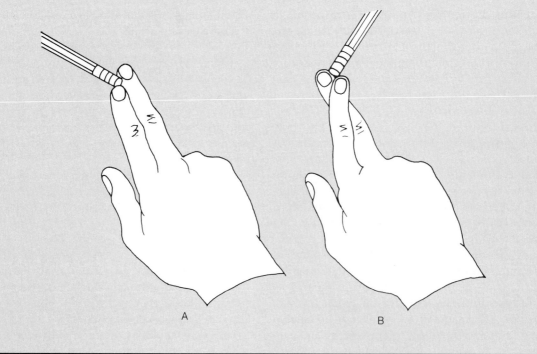

A   B

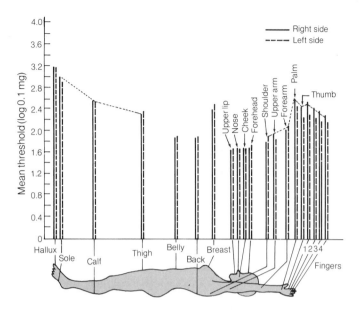

Figure 9-5 *Average absolute thresholds for different regions of the female skin. Relative values for males are similar but higher overall (from S. Weinstein, in D. R. Kenshalo, ed.,* The Skin Senses, *1968. Courtesy of Charles C. Thomas, Publisher, Springfield, Illinois).*

(Verrillo & Bolanowski, 1986). Cooling increases absolute threshold on the tongue, at least for intermediate vibration frequencies (B. G. Green, 1987).

A minimum absolute threshold seems to be measurable for touch, similar to the vision threshold. Vallbo (1983) reported experiments that determined that one nerve impulse in one rapidly adapting fiber from the hand could be detected (he was recording the nerve impulse from a subcutaneous electrode inserted into the nerve of an awake human volunteer). This single impulse was stimulated in this case by a 10-μm movement of a tiny probe placed on the skin. This is a very small movement indeed. Certainly, we can expect no greater sensitivity at the neural level than the detection of a single spike potential as a touch sensation.

One aspect of all tactual stimuli is that each touch sensation seems to be located at a particular place on the skin. Our ability to localize a touch sensation accurately varies across different regions of the skin, but seems to be directly related to the amount of neural representation each area has in the touch cortex. In general, the greater the representation of a particular area, the smaller are the errors of localization for that area (the relative cortical representation of areas of the body was shown in Figure 9-4.

One way of measuring our sensitivity for localization is to introduce a second stimulus and to measure the **two-point threshold.** This refers to a fact discovered by Weber in the 1830s, that two-touch stimuli (such as the points of a drawing compass) will be felt as a single touch if they are close enough together. The two-point threshold is a measure of how far apart the stimuli must be before they are felt as two separately localizable touches. It was during investigations of this kind that Bekesy (1967) discovered inhibitory interaction in the skin (see Demonstration Box 9-1). A comprehensive determination of two-point

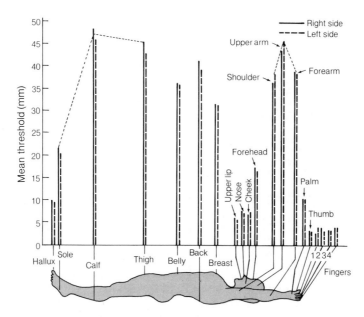

Figure 9-6 *Average two-point thresholds for different regions of the male skin. Relative values for females are similar but lower overall (from S. Weinstein, in D. R. Kenshalo, ed.,* The Skin Senses, *1968. Courtesy of Charles C. Thomas, Publisher, Springfield, Illinois).*

threshold was provided by Weinstein (1968), and a summary of his results is shown in Figure 9-6. Notice the remarkable differential sensitivity of the lower face and the hands, and even the feet. Presumably this reflects the use of these areas in manipulation of objects. The high sensitivity of the feet may be a leftover from our primate ancestors, who could manipulate objects with their feet. Also, two-point threshold is smaller the more the temperature of the stimulating objects departs from that of the skin, in either direction, and even when one is warmer and the other colder (J. C. Stevens, 1989). Yet another interesting aspect of touch localization is studied in Demonstration Box 9-3.

Touch Adaptation

Touch sensations adapt, as do all other sensations. This can be shown by simply applying a

stimulus to the skin and observing the gradual disappearance of the sensation. For example, when you first get dressed in the morning you may be (uncomfortably) aware of your belt or waistband, but after a while you no longer are consciously aware of the sensation from it. Zigler (1932) measured touch adaptation for several different areas of the body. He reported that the heavier the stimulus, the longer it took for the sensation to disappear, but that the larger the area covered by the stimulus, the less time it took for the sensation to disappear. You can demonstrate this result using Demonstration Box 9-4.

Another technique for measuring adaptation is to present a stimulus for some period of time and then introduce a second stimulus. The observer is asked to adjust the intensity of the second stimulus until the sensation associated with it matches that associated with the first. Since adaptation has reduced the sensation intensity of the first stimulus, the differ-

DEMONSTRATION BOX 9-3   Touch Localization

Bekesy has studied localization in all the major sensory modalities and has discovered similar phenomena in all of them. One of the most striking is the discovery that a touch can be localized as being outside of the body under the appropriate circumstances (Bekesy, 1967). We will demonstrate a somewhat simpler phenomenon that apparently depends on the difference in arrival times of neural impulses from different parts of the skin surface to the primary sensory areas of the brain.

Touch your two index fingers together. Try to concentrate on experiencing *where* the sensations of touch are felt, that is, on which of the two fingers. Most people report sensations of about equal intensity from both fingertips. Now touch your fingertip (either one) repeatedly to your lower lip with light, quick touches. When asked to say where the sensation is, most people report that they feel it mostly on the lip and little or not at all on the fingertip, even though both are of about equal sensitivity and are being

stimulated approximately equally. Now use the same finger to touch, with the same light, quick touches, your little toe or your ankle. Most people now report that the sensation seems to be located mostly in the finger, rather than in the toe or the ankle, even though both are being equally stimulated. As it turns out, it takes somewhat more than 1 msec longer for the nerve impulses to travel from the fingertip to the brain than for them to travel from the lip to the brain. Similarly, it takes more than 1 msec longer for impulses to travel from the foot to the brain than from the finger to the brain. The impulses that arrive at the brain first (providing the difference is more than 1 msec) seem to dictate where the sensation will be experienced, even though the two places on the skin are being stimulated equally. The various other parts of the body fall in between these extremes, but in all cases the localization depends on the relative lengths of the pathways from the touching parts to the brain.

ence between the magnitudes of the two stimuli is a measure of the amount of adaptation that has taken place. Using this technique, Frey and Goldman (1915) determined that

adaptation to touch stimuli is similar to that for other modalities. Adaptation is very rapid for the first second or so and then gradually slows down. After 3 seconds, the sensation level has

DEMONSTRATION BOX 9-4   Touch Adaptation

For this demonstration, you will need a watch with a sweep second hand, two pieces of cardboard (cut into small circles with diameters of about 1 cm and about 4 cm), and a friend. Lay one piece of cardboard on the skin of your friend's back and record the amount of time before the sensation of

touch disappears. Repeat this with the other piece of cardboard. Try the experiment again, only this time press gently on each cardboard. Notice that the lighter touches and the larger surface area stimulations disappear faster from consciousness. Thus, they show faster adaptation.

decreased to about one-quarter of the beginning value.

Bekesy (1959) used this same technique to measure the time course of adaptation for vibratory stimuli, which generally takes longer than adaptation for static stimuli. Again, different parts of the body respond differently. On the lip, adaptation is complete after about 20 seconds. For the forearm, however, loss of sensation is more gradual, and adaptation is not completed even after 60 seconds. These longer adaptation times are consistent with the greater effectiveness of the vibratory stimulus.

Touch Intensity

When measuring the subjective intensity of touch stimuli, vibrating stimuli are often used because, as we just noted above, they do not adapt as quickly. Magnitude estimations of the intensity of a 60-Hz vibratory stimulus on the fingertip follow the standard psychophysical power function with an exponent of about 0.95 (S. S. Stevens, 1959), suggesting an almost one-to-one relationship between the sensation magnitude and the magnitude of the stimulus. More recent measurements using single mechanical pulses applied to the skin of the hand found that magnitude estimates for both hairy and glabrous skin are a power function of stimulus intensity, but that exponents were somewhat lower for glabrous skin (about 0.70) than for hairy skin (about 1.05) (Hamalainen & Jarvilehto, 1981).

We mentioned earlier that the action of a vibratory stimulus on the skin is quite similar to that of sound on the ear in that sensitivity is greatest for certain stimulus frequencies (see also, for example, Gescheider & Verrillo, 1982; Marks, 1979a). This means that for a given physical pressure, some vibration frequencies give a more intense touch sensation than others. This can be seen in Figure 9-7, which shows a set of equal-sensation curves for a vi-

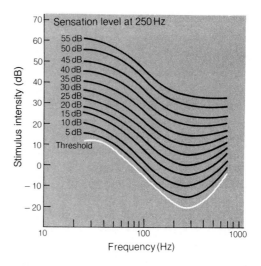

Figure 9-7 *Equal-sensation contours for a vibrating stimulus. These contours are quite similar to equal-loudness contours over the same range of frequencies—see Figure 7-12 (from Verrillo, Fraioli, & Smith, 1969).*

brating stimulus on the skin that are highly similar to the equal-loudness contours presented in Figure 7-12. Here, maximum sensitivity seems to be in the region of 200–400 Hz, with sensitivity decreasing dramatically as frequency declines. Notice that stimulus intensity in Figure 9-7 is measured in decibels (compared to a displacement of the vibrator surface by one millionth of a meter, which represents 0 dB). This makes the vertical scale a logarithmic scale similar to the logarithmic decibel scale used in hearing (see Chapter 6).

Many other similarities exist between vibrotaction and hearing, both because of the similarity of the vibrotactile stimulus to sound (both are mechanical vibrations) and because of the evolutionary origins of the cochlea of the auditory system in hairy skin (see Chapter 6). For example, discrimination of vibratory amplitudes follows Weber's law as closely as discrimination of sound amplitudes does (Gescheider, Bolanowski, Verrillo, Arpajian, & Ryan, 1990).

Channel capacity is similar for vibratory amplitude and sound amplitude at about 2 bits maximum (Rabinowitz, Houtsma, Durlach, & Delhorne, 1987). Forward, backward, and simultaneous masking of vibratory stimuli all occur in the presence of another vibratory stimulus, and the amount of masking decreases with increases in the temporal gap between target and mask (Gescheider, Bolanowski, & Verrillo, 1989).

However, the skin is different from the ear in that the skin seems to have two distinct receptor systems, termed *Pacinian* and *non-Pacinian*, rather than the single system represented by the cochlea of the ear. The Pacinian system (composed of Pacinian corpuscles and their nerves) seems to be most sensitive to higher-frequency vibrations, in the region around 250 Hz., while the non-Pacinian system (composed of Meissner disks and other corpuscular endings) is more sensitive to lower-frequency vibrations, in the region below 200 Hz (Verrillo, 1968). More recently, the non-Pacinian system has been further differentiated into three channels, each with its own operating range of frequencies (for example, Bolanowski, Gescheider, Verrillo, & Checkosky, 1988). Current work promises to identify these three different non-Pacinian channels with specific receptor systems and the mechanical properties of the skin (for example, Lamore & Keemink, 1988; Van Doren, 1989).

In addition to passively perceiving vibrating stimuli, we can perceive changes in pressure from textured surfaces as they move relative to our skin surface. The perception of "roughness" varies over the body, with greatest sensitivity on the lips, fingers, and forearm, and least sensitivity on the heel, back, and thigh (J. C. Stevens, 1990). These relative sensitivities are similar to those for sensitivity to the pressure of a single point (see Figure 9-5). Roughness is perceived similarly whether the surface or the body part moves (Heller, 1989).

Moreover, although vision and touch perform similarly in discriminating relatively rough textures, touch is superior for smoother textures (Heller, 1989).

Tactile Pattern Perception

The sense of touch has the ability to discriminate and recognize complex stimulus patterns (see, for example, Klatzky, Lederman, & Metzger, 1985), although it tends to respond best to different aspects of stimulus patterns than, for example, the visual system does (Klatzky, Lederman, & Reed, 1987). You have probably heard about Louis Braille's tactile pattern alphabet, by which blind people can read any suitably translated text. In this alphabet, patterns of raised dots on paper play the role of the patterns of ink on paper that constitute written language for sighted people. The speed with which an experienced blind person can read with the Braille alphabet is a testimony not only to long hours of practice (as is any form of reading) but also to the remarkable sensitivity of the touch system. Of course, the final interpretation of these patterns of touch stimuli involves a number of complicated cognitive processes (Krueger, 1982).

Braille is not the only method by which tactile patterns are used to convey information by way of touch. Alternate methods have been invented by those who wanted to more directly substitute patterns of touch for those of vision. White, Saunders, Scadden, Bach-y-Rita, and Collins (1970) developed a **vision substitution system** in which a television camera is used to scan a visual pattern. The information gathered by the television camera is then converted into a pattern of vibrating points on the skin of the back of an observer (see Figure 9-8). The observer can move the camera to view different parts of the visual scene. When visual stimuli are presented tactually in this way, observers

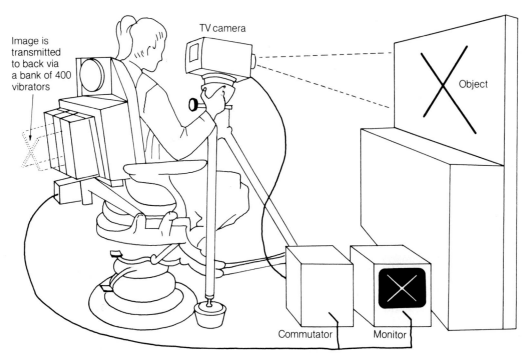

Figure 9-8 *The vision substitution system (from White, Saunders, Scadden, Bach-y-Rita, & Collins, 1970).*

can recognize a wide variety of different stimulus patterns (up to 25). Remarkably, the relative distance of several visual objects in a scene can be perceived from the tactile pattern, and even visual illusions can be experienced. These types of findings raise questions similar to those raised by visual and auditory pattern perception. For example, we might ask if feature detectors also exist for touch. These and other findings (for example, Horner, 1991) also point to the importance of higher-level cognitive processes in even the simplest types of perceptual experiences.

Reading in Braille requires that the paper or book be translated into Braille. This is especially difficult to do with newspapers and magazines, which are published in large numbers. The **optacon** (Bliss, Katcher, Rogers, & Shepard, 1970) works similarly to the vision substi-

tution system except that the size of the visual field scanned is about 1 printed letter, and the pattern of vibrations corresponding to each letter is formed on the fingertip instead of the back. After approximately 50 hours of training, blind users can read untreated material at about 20 words per minute. Experienced users attain rates as high as 60 words per minute.

Another relatively recent development is the utilization of tactile perceptual systems to aid the hearing impaired. Several devices have been developed in which an array of electrodes or vibrators is used to transmit speech information to the skin of hearing impaired people. In these devices, the prominent frequency components in speech are recoded into stimulation at different places on the skin, and people can learn to recognize the electrotactile or vibratory patterns as words. Devices such as the

"Tickle Talker" (Cowan, Alcantara, Blamey, & Clark, 1988), the Queens vocoder (for example, Brooks & Frost, 1983), and the Tacticon (for example, Weisenberger, Broadstone, & Saunders, 1989) all have been shown to be useful, especially in conjunction with lip-reading.

The Optacon and similar devices are now being used for research into the mechanisms of tactile pattern perception (see, for example, J. C. Craig, 1981, 1983b; Loomis, 1981; Schneider, Hughes, Epstein, & Bach-y-Rita, 1986). One particularly active area involves the interaction between successively presented patterns. When the presentation of one pattern on the skin makes it more difficult to recognize another pattern, we refer to this as *masking* (see J. C. Craig, 1978). For example, when a letter pattern is presented on the Optacon and then followed immediately by a rectangular pattern, observers have a harder time identifying the letter than when no masking pattern is presented. This is called **backward masking,** since the masking pattern seems to act backward in time to interfere with the perception of the earlier target. **Forward masking** also occurs with tactile patterns; here, the masking pattern is presented first, followed by the target. As in audition and vision (see Chapters 7 and 11), masking studies often reveal basic mechanisms of tactile perception. For example, more backward masking usually occurs when the time interval between target and mask is short, and more forward masking occurs when the time interval is longer (J. C. Craig, 1983a). This is consistent with the idea that the perceptual representations of tactile features persist for about 1200 msec (Craig & Evans, 1987; Evans & Craig, 1986), and it reveals something about how those representations are integrated over time (P. M. Evans, 1987). These masking effects do not depend very much on where on the body the patterns are presented, although pattern discrimination and recognition in the absence of masking does vary with location on the body (Cholewiak & Craig, 1984). The ability to localize tactile stimuli is similarly subject to backward, forward, and simultaneous masking and depends on the time interval between mask and target (J. C. Craig, 1989). However, masking of identification is most effective when the mask and target occur at the same location, whereas masking of localizability is most effective when mask and target occur at different locations (J. C. Craig, 1989).

KINESTHESIS

We have been talking about receptors that respond to mechanically encoded information from the world around us when contact is made with our skin. A vast amount of mechanically encoded information is also available from within our own bodies. This information indicates whether our bodies are moving or stationary (see also the "Motion" section of Chapter 13), and informs us of the position and movement of our body parts. The neural processing of this information, and the sensations we feel, called collectively **kinesthesis,** bear striking resemblances to touch.

One of the things that distinguishes animal from plant life is the ability to move about in the world. In higher organisms, specialized receptor systems inform the brain about the position of the limbs or the orientation of the body. The bodies of such organisms (including humans) are literally enmeshed in a web of sensory receptors, which accurately monitor the positions of various parts so appropriate action can be initiated. In many cases the signals of these sensory systems are not consciously perceived, but rather are used in controlling reflex actions that maintain an upright posture. When these signals are perceived, they give rise to the sensations of force or weight, which are often used to help guide our voluntary movements, as in sports or other skilled motor performance.

Kinesthetic Stimuli and Receptors

The overt physical stimulus to which the kinesthetic system responds is *movement* (the root *kine* is from the Greek word for "movement"). Some information about position is available, however, even when no movement is taking place. This information is generated by our continual battle against gravity. Both movement and postural responses involve tension, compression, or twisting forces on the muscles, tendons, or joints of limbs. These physical forces are the stimuli for kinesthesis. Any position of the body, even supine and fully relaxed, results in a complex pattern of muscular tensions and compressions and consequent mechanical forces acting on tendons and joints. The relative intensities of the various forces, or changes in those intensities over time, signal body movement and posture.

A great many touch and stretch receptors are scattered throughout the body in addition to those in the surface layers of the skin. First, at least two types of nerve endings exist in the deeper layers of tissue beneath the skin: free nerve endings and Pacinian corpuscles. The free nerve endings are thought to be responsible for pain sensations. The Pacinian corpuscles provide our sense of deep pressure (which can be felt even when the overlying skin has been anesthetized). Although the visceral organs themselves are rather insensitive to touch, temperature, or pain stimuli (with the obvious exception of stretching or twisting forces that cause, for example, gas pains), these organs are surrounded by muscle. This muscle is supplied with a variety of nerve endings responsive to the movements of the viscera. Finally, several types of nerve endings are located in and around our joints in the muscles that move our limbs.

Matthews (1933) divided the receptors in the muscles into three major types, two of which are important in kinethesis (shown in Figure 9-9). His first type is called the *A endings*, which have two subtypes. The A_1 endings

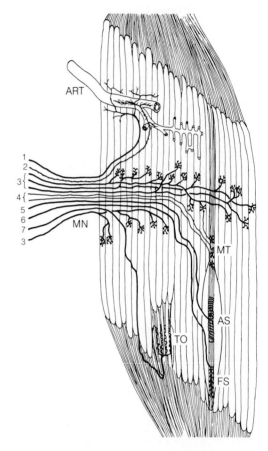

Figure 9-9 Nerve endings in muscle. (1) Free nerve endings around an artery (ART); (2) efferent nerves that regulate the size of the artery; (3) motor nerves (MN) that cause the muscle to contract; (4) more motor nerves; (5) Matthews type A_2, or annulospiral (AS), nerve endings on a muscle spindle; (6) Matthews type A_1, or flower-spray (FS), nerve endings on the same muscle spindle; (7) Matthews type B, or Golgi tendon organs (TO), nerve endings on a muscle tendon (MT). Matthews type C endings, or Pacinian corpuscles, are not shown (from Creed, Denny-Brown, Eccles, Liddell, & Sherrington, 1932).

are often called "flower-spray" endings because they look like a bouquet of flowers against the muscles where they synapse. Endings of the A₂ type are wound around strands of muscle fibers called *muscle spindles.* Both subtypes respond to stretching of the muscle and therefore have been called **stretch receptors** or **spindle organs,** since they both attach to muscle spindles. This type of nerve ending is found also in great numbers in the joints between limbs. Matthews's second type, the *B endings,* look much like the flower-spray endings but are attached to the tendons that connect the muscles to the bones. B endings are also called **golgi tendon organs.** They seem to respond to both stretching and contracting of the muscle, whereas the spindle organs respond only to stretching. In addition to the spindle and tendon organs, muscles and joints are well supplied with free nerve endings that may be responsible for pain sensations in these areas.

Neural Responses in Kinesthesis

The various receptors we have described send their messages to the brain via the two major neural pathways described previously for touch: the dorsal column and spinothalamic pathways. Most of the fibers follow the dorsal column pathway, except for the free nerve endings, many of which follow the spinothalamic pathway. There are also a great many branchings and interactions of these two pathways with others of less importance. The nerves that terminate on muscles or tendons and in joints also project to the somatosensory cortex. Thus, information about stimuli touching the skin of the arm and about the position and movement of the arm are both projected onto the same general area of the cortex. However, the cutaneous information is kept separate (in different layers) from the position and movement information even at the cortical level (see Vierck, 1978).

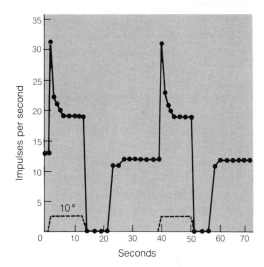

Figure 9-10 *The response of a single nerve fiber that terminates in the knee joint of a cat. The dotted lines represent bendings of the knee joint by 10 deg. The slow-adapting fiber gives a large initial burst of impulses to the bending, which then gradually declines to a stable rate of firing above background (no bending). When the limb is "unbent," an inhibition of responses occurs, so nerve firing is below background rate, and then firing climbs back to the background rate (from Boyd & Roberts, 1953).*

Figure 9-10 shows an electrophysiological recording from a nerve fiber that terminated in the knee joint of a cat. The limb was repeatedly bent and returned to its original position. The movement of the limb is signaled by a sudden change in neural response rate, the size of the change indicating the speed of movement. The static position of the limb is signaled by the resting level of neural response. These are slow-adapting fibers, because after a limb movement it takes several seconds for them to find a new resting rate of firing corresponding to a new limb position. Cells with similar response characteristics are also found higher up in the kinesthetic system at sites in the thalamus and cortex (Mountcastle, Poggio, & Werner, 1963; Mountcastle & Powell, 1959). In addition, more rapidly adapting fibers and "postural neurons" (which respond only when a joint is in a particular position) have been found in the monkey somatosensory cortex, along with neurons that act much like feature detectors for the different limb components of particular postures (Costanzo & Gardner, 1981; Gardner & Costanzo, 1981). Virtually all positional and movement information comes from the receptors located in the joints (J. A. Adams, 1977). The other kinesthetic receptors may give us the sensation of strain when lifting something, or of pain. Their major role seems to be to provide information to control our postural reflexes, automatically adjusting our muscle tension to the requirements of whatever load we are carrying. However, under some conditions they can give us erroneous information, resulting in illusions. For example, vibrating the biceps tendon in an immobile arm produces the illusion that the elbow is moving into extension (see Jones, 1988, for a review).

Perception of Weight and Force

The sensations of weight and force can be described psychophysically, much as other sensations have been (see Jones, 1986, for a review). In fact, the discrimination of lifted weights was the first and the most generally used task in the early days of psychophysics. Weber was the first to study it experimentally, and Fechner did an enormous number of experiments testing Weber's law with lifted weights (see Chapter 2). Weight discrimination is about as good as discrimination of sound intensity or light intensity, with a typical Weber fraction of about 0.07 (for example, Pang, Tan, & Durlach, 1991), meaning that a 7% change in stimulus magnitude can just be detected.

Force and weight can be scaled by direct scaling methods. Judgments are affected by many factors, for example the size–weight illusion in which a larger object feels lighter than a smaller object of the same weight (for example, Masin & Crestoni, 1988). Physiological factors also play a role, such as fatigue, which makes everything feel heavier. Because of this, scientists disagree about the exact form of the psychophysical function. Sensations of force or weight seem to increase as a power function of stimulus intensity, but increase differently for lifted weights with a moderate range (exponents near 1.00) versus grip or squeezing force generated on a dynamometer (exponents of 1.50–2.00).

Gravity also affects the perception of weight. During parabolic flight, which provides periods of 0 gravity at the apex and about 1.80 gravity at the nadir, magnitude estimates of weights were lowest during 0 gravity, next lowest during 1.00 (ordinary) gravity, and highest during 1.80 gravity (Ross & Reschke, 1982). Interestingly, the value of the Weber fraction approximately doubled under conditions of prolonged weightlessness (or 0 gravity) in the U.S. Spacelab (Ross, Brodie, & Benson, 1984). Of course, everything weighs nothing under such conditions, but objects still have mass and, therefore, momentum. The Weber fraction obtained in 0 gravity was really a Weber fraction for mass, obtained by having the astronauts shake the stimulus objects in order to generate forces that could be perceived.

You can demonstrate some of these effects for yourself by trying Demonstration Box 2-2 again while riding in an elevator. The starting and stopping of an elevator, especially one of the fast ones now in use in large hotels, also generates short periods of lessened and greater than normal gravity (or vice versa depending on the direction of movement). As you ride the elevator, pay attention to the sensation of weight of the objects you are trying to discriminate. Do they feel heavier as the elevator comes to a stop after a drop from the 10th to the 1st floor? Did they feel lighter as the drop began?

Haptic Perception

When we move our limbs about actively through the world, we perceive objects through a combination of cutaneous and kinesthetic sensations caused by our mechanical interaction with them. Such experiences play an important role in perceptual development as vision and touch calibrate each other (see Chapter 16), and they can also be important under conditions in which visual and auditory information about the world are missing or impoverished, such as when stumbling about in a dark bedroom. Our experience of the world based on a combination of cutaneous and kinesthetic sensation is called **haptic perception** (for example, Gibson, 1966).

People are very good at identifying ordinary objects presented haptically (for example, Klatzky, Lederman, & Metzger, 1985). We are beginning to understand how this is accomplished, although the study of haptics is still young. One important piece of haptic information is object size (extension in space). We now know that our ability to discriminate lengths haptically is quite good. For example the difference threshold for length for objects between 10 and 20 mm is about 1 mm, indicating a Weber fraction of 5% to 10% (Durlach et al., 1989). Haptic length discrimination does not follow Weber's law very well, however, since the Weber fraction tends to decrease for larger objects. Nonetheless, channel capacity is about 2 bits for haptic length, similar to visually perceived length (Durlach et al., 1989). Another important aspect of haptic information appears to be texture, which may be a feature that is registered automatically from objects perceived haptically, much as color is registered automatically for objects perceived visually (Lederman, Browse, & Klatzky, 1988). The perception of hardness seems to be integrated with texture in haptic perception (Klatzky, Lederman, & Reed, 1989). Sometimes the cues to haptic shape perception are quite subtle. Figure 9-11 illustrates an intriguing experimental setup that shows that the shape of solid objects can often be identified when they are merely wielded by a handle and their edges and contours are not seen or touched. This appears to occur because observers can sense haptically the moments of inertia and resistance to rotation around various axes of the objects. It also indicates that the distribution of mass of an object can play a role in the perception of its shape (Burton, Turvey, & Solomon, 1990).

Haptics is closely related to vision in some ways, as might be expected from the importance of the coordination of vision and active touch in perceptual development. Indeed, Gibson (1966) proposed that there was at least partial equivalence between visual and haptic representations of objects. In testing this notion, Garbin (1988) developed a measure of visual–haptic dissimilarity of objects based on their relative positions in multidimensional scaling similarity spaces (see Chapter 2 for more on multidimensional scaling). Garbin (1988) found that when haptic and visual representations of objects were similar (higher equivalence), they could be identified more easily cross-modally than if their representations were dissimilar (lower equivalence).

Another example of the close visual–haptic relationship is that many of the visual-optical illusions also occur when the stimulus shapes are explored by touch. One such case is the Bourdon illusion, which has been extensively studied in visual modality (e.g. Walker & Shank, 1988; Wenderoth, Criss, & van der Zwan, 1990). This illusion is shown in Figure 9-12A. Notice that the line XYZ appears to be bent at Y. Actually the line is straight, which you can confirm with a ruler or by holding the book at a slant and sighting down the line. This same illusion also occurs in "haptic space" (Day, 1990). When blindfolded observers explore a solid object resembling the visual stimulus

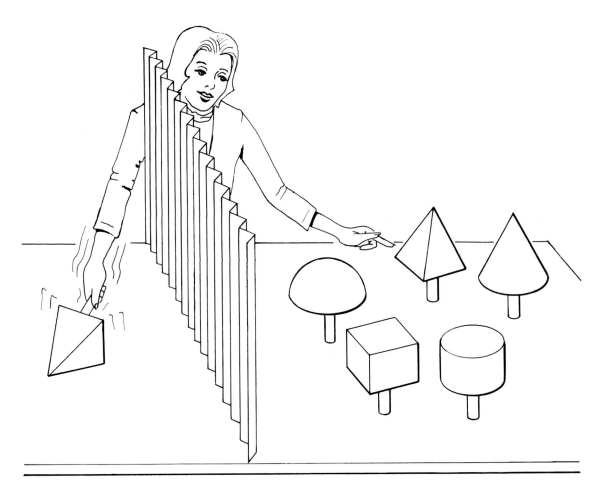

Figure 9-11 *Experimental setup for recognition of objects based on haptic information, especially the distribution of mass in the object (based on Burton, Turvey, & Solomon, 1990).*

(Figure 9-12B) it is felt to be bent at the place where the two triangles meet, although the surface is really straight.

Understanding haptic perception can also be practically useful. For example, a method of assisting speech perception by people who are both blind and hearing impaired, called **Tadoma,** is based on haptic perception. In Tadoma, an observer haptically monitors the speech articulators (the parts of the face and neck that produce speech sounds—e.g., lips, jaw, etc.). From the motions of the articulators perceived

by the "listener" the words said by the speaker can be deduced, with results that are superior to any other artificial speech display known (Norton, Schultz, Reed, Braida, Durlach, Rabinowitz, & Chomsky, 1977). Similar to the perception of visual patterns (see Chapter 11), perception of each dimension of articulator movement is in the usual range of about 2 bits of information transmission, making it somewhat of a mystery why Tadoma works so well (Tan, Rabinowitz, & Durlach, 1989). You can try Tadoma for yourself in Demonstration Box 9-5.

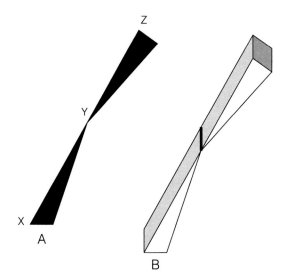

Figure 9-12 *Visual (A) and haptic (B) versions of the Bourdon illusion. The line XYZ is actually straight but appears to be bent inward to form an angle at Y (based on Day, 1990).*

WARMTH AND COLD

Are you cold right now? Are you warm? Probably you are feeling rather neutral, that is, comfortably unaware of any temperature sensations. Our bodies contain a remarkable system of thermal sensors that trigger reflexes to regulate the flow in the blood vessels in our skin, the activity of the sweat glands, and the tiny muscles located around the roots of hairs in the skin. When our internal body temperature is too high (above 37 deg C), the blood vessels of the skin dilate, allowing more blood to flow and thus radiating more heat into the air. We also begin to sweat, losing heat both by the conduction of the overheated sweat to the surface of the skin, where it can radiate more efficiently, and by the cooling of the skin surface through evaporation. When we are too cold, the blood vessels in the skin contract, thereby slowing heat loss, and we begin to shiver, which gener-

ates more heat from our muscles. The thermal sensitivity of the skin plays a major part in this complex, mostly reflex-operated temperature-regulating system that keeps our internal body temperatures around 37 deg C or 98.6 deg F (see Hensel, 1981). Usually the system functions so well that we do not notice any temperature sensations, at least in temperate environments. The ability of this system to regulate body temperature is limited, however, and when the limits are exceeded the body needs to take more dramatic steps, such as changing clothing or starting a fire. Such actions bring the temperature of the skin's environment within its safe limits again. Such necessities are signaled by the conscious sensations of warmth and cold.

Neural Coding of Temperature

Temperature is sensed in the skin by nerve endings quite similar in appearance to those sensitive to mechanical contacts. Two types of nerve fibers respond when the skin is cooled or warmed. **Cold fibers** respond to cooling of the skin with an increase in firing relative to their resting rate, and to warming with a firing decrease. **Warm fibers** respond to warming with an increase in firing rate and to cooling with decreased firing (see Hensel, 1981). Also, after an initial change in firing rate in the direction appropriate to the type of stimulus and the type of receptor, both types of fibers gradually adopt a steady rate of firing. This "resting" rate is related to the *absolute* temperature of the skin (and thus of the receptor).

Cold and warm fibers have different patterns of response over a broad range of skin temperatures (Zotterman, 1959). As you can see in Figure 9-13, the cold fibers respond in the range from about 13 to 35 deg C (55 to 95 deg F) with a maximum at about 25 deg C (77 F), and also from about 45 to 50 deg C (113

DEMONSTRATION BOX 9-5   Tadoma with Your Friends

When perceiving speech using Tadoma, the perceiver places his or her hand on the face and neck of the speaker, with the thumb across the middle of the lips and the fingers fanned out across the face and neck as in the figure in this box. To try this for yourself, get a friend to whisper the words listed below while you monitor the person's articulators as shown in the figure. Pay attention to the in-and-out movements of the lips, the up-and-down movements of the jaw, and the flow of air from the mouth (the cure of larynx vibration is abolished by the need to whisper if you have normal hearing). You should have your eyes closed and put earplugs or cotton in your ears so visual and auditory information are absent. Your friend should read the words very slowly, in an irregular order, and (since you are new at this method of perceiving speech) with exaggerated movements. There should be a pause after each word for you to guess what the word was. For an even more difficult test, your friend should choose words you have not seen, and use normal movements of the articulators, although he or she should still speak slowly. Some words that are relatively easy to discriminate are: *you, me, yes, why, but, candy, tree, push.* Reverse roles so your friend can try it too.

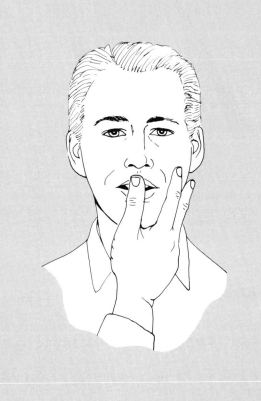

to 122 deg F) with the maximum at about 50 deg C. Above this limit the receptors become damaged and the response ceases. Warm fibers respond from about 23 to 46 deg C (73 to 117 deg F) with a maximum at about 38 deg C (100 deg F—just above body temperature). These *steady-state* responses provide us with information about the absolute temperature of the skin. This information is quite important since internal body temperature must be maintained within a narrow range of values around 37 deg C or 98.6 deg F (see Hensel, 1981). Demonstration Box 9-6 allows you to experience the consequences of having both cold and warm fibers stimulated optimally, something that would not happen under normal conditions.

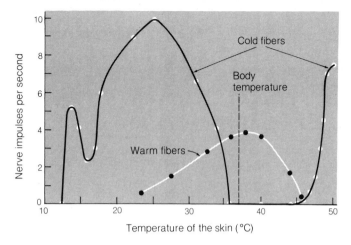

Figure 9-13 *Steady-state discharge of cold and warm fibers in the cat as it varies with skin temperature (based on Zotterman, 1959).*

Thermal Thresholds and Adaptation

Because the skin works to maintain a constant internal body temperature, sensations of warmth or cold are generally caused by departures from a reference skin temperature called **physiological zero.** Thus, when we talk about feeling "cold," we mean a stimulus has caused the *skin temperature* to drop below physiological zero. This reference temperature is a floating neutral point, based on the temperature to which the thermal receptors in the skin have adapted. A **neutral zone** is present at around physiological zero, within which no sensation will be felt if a stimulus within that temperature range is applied to the skin. This zone is seldom more than a couple of degrees on either side of physiological zero, but it varies in width depending on what the physiological zero is, where on the body the change occurs, and what kind of stimulus is applied. A good average value for physiological zero in a temperate environment (room temperature—about 20 deg C) would be around 33 deg C (91 deg F). At room temperature such a skin temperature

maintains the internal body temperature at about 37 deg C.

The measurement of absolute thresholds for warm and cold sensations is complicated by the fact that relatively complete adaptation to thermal stimuli takes place over a range of temperatures, and that thermal sensations are relative to the temperature to which the skin has become adapted. For instance, Kenshalo and Scott (1966) had observers change the temperature of a sophisticated thermal stimulator just enough to maintain a detectable sensation, while they adapted the skin to a given thermal level. The stimulator started at the previously measured temperature of the observer's skin. Adjustments were made every minute at first and then every 5 minutes for up to 40 minutes. Figure 9-14 shows the results obtained for four observers. Using this technique, Kenshalo and Scott (1966) found that complete adaptation occurred over a range of about 4 to 8 deg C centered at the average skin temperature. This then serves as an experimental measurement of the neutral zone around the physiological zero set by adaptation. Notice that when

DEMONSTRATION BOX 9-6   The Heat Grill

For this demonstration you will need two pipe cleaners bent as shown in Figure A. Be careful to bend the pipe cleaners so that they fit together closely when both are laid on a table, as shown in Figure B. Place one pipe cleaner in a glass of cool water and the other in a glass of very warm (not unpleasantly hot) water. Take the pipe cleaner out of the glass of cool water and place it on a flat surface. Working quickly, take the pipe cleaner out of the glass of warm water and arrange it to form the configuration shown as Figure B. As soon as this is done, place your forearm over the set of pipe cleaners and press down as shown in Figure C. The temperature sensation you receive will probably be quite surprising. Although the stimulus consists of alternately cool and warm surfaces, you will feel no coolness. Observers usually get a sensation of an intense stinging heat. Some people may find the heat sensation sufficiently intense to cause them to withdraw their arms. The temperatures of the pipe cleaners are such (if you followed directions faithfully) that receptors of both cold and warm fibers in the same general area of the skin are being stimulated near their optimum. Usually this does not happen. When it does, you mislead your brain by making both the cold and the warm fibers fire near their maxima. The brain processes this information as emanating from a single, very hot stimulus.

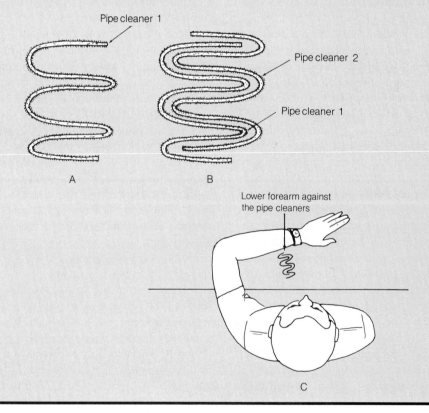

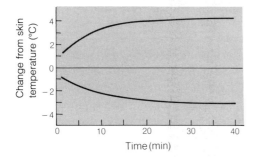

Figure 9-14 *Adaptation to thermal stimuli. Each curve represents the average amount of adjustment by four observers to maintain a just-noticeable warm or cool sensation with a thermal stimulator. Thermal changes closer to the 0 line than the curves are felt as having neutral temperature (based on Kenshalo & Scott, 1966).*

adaptation has not fully occurred (early in the period), the neutral zone is actually quite narrow (perhaps about 2 deg), but it widens as the adaptation becomes more complete.

Overall, the sensation of warmth or coldness caused by stimuli with temperatures near 33 deg C is determined largely by the temperature to which the skin has been adapted before the stimulus is applied. You can experience this by using Demonstration Box 9-7. Absolute thresholds for these sensations can be defined as the amount of temperature change (from the adapting temperature) necessary to cause a report of warmth or cold. Absolute thresholds differ for upward and downward changes in temperature depending on the adapting temperature (Kenshalo, Nafe, & Brooks, 1961). Sensitivity to lowering of temperature is greater when skin temperature is colder, but it is greater to raising of temperature when skin temperature is warmer, as can be seen in Figure 9-15. Thus, at relatively high or low temperatures we are more sensitive to fluctuations in temperature, especially those changes that indicate greater deviation from our normal body temperature. This makes sense, since very low or very high temperatures can be dangerous for the body, so the detection of thermal

changes is more important when the stimuli are more extreme. The minimum threshold values obtained seem to be about 0.10 deg C of temperature change from the adapting temperature.

As in touch, the place on the body surface to which the stimulus is applied also affects our sensitivity to warmth and cold. The head is the most sensitive to warm stimuli, with the limbs least and the trunk intermediate. Conversely, the trunk, particularly the back, is the most sensitive to cold stimuli, with the limbs intermediate and the head least (J. C. Stevens, 1979). This is easy to demonstrate for yourself using pieces of metal that have been dipped in water of different temperatures (pay attention to the intensity of the sensations aroused by the stimuli on the various parts of your body). The mouth seems to be more sensitive to increases in temperature than to decreases (B. G. Green, 1986).

Significant differences in sensitivity to warmth and cold exist even over a small patch of skin. If the thermal stimulus has a small area (perhaps the size of a pin head), it is possible to find some spots that yield only sensations of warmth and others that produce only sensations of cold (try using a pin head as the thermal stimulus on your forearm). Some regions produce no temperature sensations at all (although they may respond to touch). Figure 9-16 shows a set of maps of such warm and cold spots from an area of 1 cm² on the skin of the upper arm (Dallenbach, 1927). The spots were mapped on four successive days so the permanence of the spots could be determined. As you can see from the figure, the spots tend to be in the same places from day to day. Since all these spots are innervated only by free nerve endings, the difference between the cold and warm spots probably has to do with the type of nerve fiber generating these nerve endings. Cold fibers are typically larger in diameter and myelinated, whereas warm fibers are smaller and unmyelinated (Hensel, 1981).

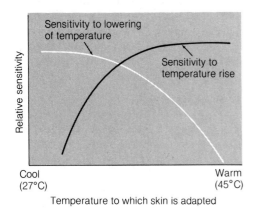

Figure 9-15 Sensitivity to increases and decreases in temperature varies as a function of the adaptation temperature of the skin.

Thermal Intensity and Qualities

Intensities of warmth and cold sensations can be measured directly using the scaling techniques discussed in Chapter 2. For instance, Stevens and Stevens (1960) had observers make magnitude estimations of the thermal sensations caused by the application of warm (above-average skin temperature) or cool (below-average skin temperature) pieces of aluminum to the skin of the forearm. They found that warmth and cold sensations follow the psychophysical power law when measured in this way, with exponents of the power function for warmth about 1.60 and for cold about 1.00. Similar results have been found for the skin of

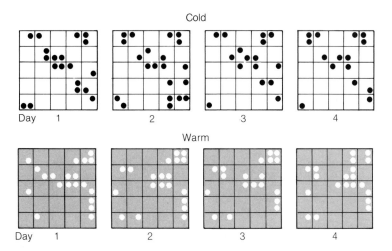

Figure 9-16 *Maps of cold and warm spots on a 1 cm² area of the skin of the upper arm of a single observer on four successive days. Notice how the spots tend to be in the same places from day to day (from "The Temperature Spots and End-Organs" by K. M. Dallenbach, 1927,* American Journal of Psychology, 39, pp. 402–407. *Copyright by the University of Illinois Press).*

the lips and tongue, although the power function exponents differ under different conditions and locations, especially for cold (B. G. Green, 1984). Exponents also differ dramatically across people, even when everything in the experimental situation is the same and differences in age, gender, and body temperature are accounted for (Refinetti, 1989). In general, however, the sensation of warmth grows somewhat more rapidly with stimulus intensity than does that of cold.

Because of the close relationship between the sensations of warmth and cold, some very interesting and somewhat paradoxical phenomena are associated with thermal stimuli. One of these, called **paradoxical cold,** was discovered by Max von Frey in 1895. He found that if cold spots (such as those illustrated in Figure 9-16) are touched with a very warm stimulus above 45 deg C (113 deg F), a sensation of cold will result. The opposite phenomenon, *paradoxical warmth,* has been much sought after but never convincingly demonstrated. This asymmetry is consistent with the fact that cold fibers respond both between

about 12 and 35 deg C (54–95 deg F) and between 46 and 50 deg C (113–122 deg F). Warm fibers respond only in the range between about 25 and 46 deg C (77–117 deg F). When the skin temperature rises above 46 deg C (117 deg F), only the cold fibers respond (see Figure 9-13). Therefore, very high temperatures actually result in neural activity equivalent to that given rise to by very cold temperatures, and both are felt subjectively as cold.

PAIN

The shrill squeal of the siren seemed to pierce his head like a knife. The pain was exquisite. Then came a brilliant flash of light; he blinked, trying somehow to relieve the savage pain flooding in through his eyes. He stumbled, barking his shin on a log, and another bright, fierce pain penetrated his consciousness. On top of all this, the old World War II shrapnel wound in his hip began to throb with a dull, sickening ache. Finally, he found the water, diving into a dark, cool world that promised to soothe his battered body. But something was wrong with the water; instead of cooling, it was burning. His head seemed to explode as the caustic liquid burned its way along his nasal passages and forced its way between his lips. Finally, and almost gratefully, he lost consciousness, his body succumbing to an assault it was never meant to experience.

Pain comes in many varieties, and each is a complex experience, as illustrated by the preceding fictional passage. It is usually associated with damage to the body of an animal, and, in humans, it is usually accompanied by myriad emotions and thoughts. Some sensory psychologists consider it to be a sensation in its own right; other psychologists argue that pain is not a sensation at all, but rather an emotion, or even a bodily state akin to hunger or thirst (for example, Wall, 1979). Perhaps the best view is a compromise. There certainly seem to be identifiable sensory characteristics in the experience of pain. Pain apparently has absolute and differential thresholds; it adapts and has definable and separate physiological pathways and projection areas in the brain. Furthermore, its intensity dimension is separable from the intensity dimension of nonpainful stimuli in the same modality (Janal, Clark, & Carroll, 1991). In these ways pain acts much like a sensory system, and we will treat it as a unique sensory modality. We must be aware, however, that to more completely understand many pain phenomena we must consider interactions of pain with other sensations and with more complex cognitive and emotional processes.

Pain Stimuli and Receptors

The evolutionary significance of pain is at least twofold. First, it is essential that an animal be able to respond appropriately to environmental situations that could destroy it. It must respond by terminating the ongoing dangerous stimulus and avoiding these situations in the future. Light, sound, touch, and temperature, when they occur at very high intensities or for prolonged durations, can destroy the receptors that are specialized to receive them. If such potentially harmful intensities are not signaled quickly to the brain, the organism will be damaged beyond repair. Second, pain seems to have the effect of requiring a person to cope appropriately with an injury if it does happen. Many people who receive serious injuries do not feel pain until quite a while, sometimes several hours, after they occur (see Melzack, Wall, & Ty, 1982). Their pain seems to have the function of inducing them to be still in order that healing may occur, or to seek treatment for the injury. When an injury first occurs, more important responses than pain may be appropriate, such as escape or fighting for life. In this view, the biological significance of pain lies in its ability to promote healing (see Wall, 1979). During the recovery phase, the stimulus for pain is the injury itself, and the function of the pain is not to warn but to promote recovery. Without the pain sense to warn and immobilize, we would have a hard time living long enough to reproduce. This is often the unfortunate fate of those humans who are born without a well-functioning pain sense (see Sternbach, 1963). In a famous case of this type, a woman called Miss C died at the young age of 29 of massive infections caused by extensive damage to her skin and bones from a (short) lifetime of abrasion and unhealed injury, especially to her joints (Melzack & Wall, 1982).

All pain does not arise from overstimulation or serious injuries. Certain kinds of painful experiences arise from only moderately intense stimulation, such as a pin prick or salt touching an open wound. On the other hand, overstimulation can sometimes occur without eliciting pain. For instance, pain is not experienced as one increases the concentration of sugar stimulating the tongue. At present it is difficult to say exactly what stimulus properties are responsible for the experience of pain. Intense stimulation and tissue damage are certainly only part of the story.

The best candidates for pain receptors are the free nerve endings with which the skin and the rest of the body are particularly well supplied. As we mentioned earlier in this chapter, free nerve endings in the subcutaneous fat under the dermis of the skin have been found to be connected to nerve fibers associated with pain (see Vierck, 1978). The position of these endings in the subcutaneous fat makes them respond only to higher-intensity stimuli, whether mechanical or temperature. Other pain fibers terminate in the epidermis; these endings are wrapped in a Schwann cell sheath (see Appendix), which allows them to retain a high stimulation threshold even in this more exposed location (Perl, 1984).

Another view puts less emphasis on the receptors than on the nerve fibers that carry information away from the stimulated site on the body. At least three major classes of such nerve fibers exist. Large, myelinated fibers, called *Aβ fibers*, seem to respond especially well to light touch stimuli. These fibers conduct nerve impulses at high speed (as fast as any in the nervous system, at least 40 m/sec) and connect with both the dorsal column and spinothalamic pathways. Smaller myelinated fibers *(Aδ)* and small, unmyelinated fibers *(C)* are much slower conducting (about 5–20 m/sec for Aδ and less than 2.50 m/sec for C), have higher thresholds, and respond only to noxious stimuli such as pinches, pin pricks, or extreme temperatures (Willis, 1985). The Aδ fibers seem especially sensitive to noxious mechanical stimuli, whereas the C fibers respond to all kinds of noxious stimuli (they are often called *polymodal nociceptors*). Aδ and C fibers typically terminate in free nerve endings, either in the subcutaneous fat or epidermis of the skin or deep in muscles and joints, and the Aβ fibers typically terminate in corpuscular endings. Aδ and C fibers connect mainly with the spinothalamic pathway, and are now generally acknowledged to be "the" pain fibers (see Figure 9-3). Apparently the fast fibers and their pathway (Aβ fibers and dorsal column pathway) are specialized for highly discriminative, complicated processing of touch information, whereas the slower fibers and pathways (Aδ and C fibers and spinothalamic pathways), which are also the more primitive ones, carry less complicated information such as pain, temperature, and rudimentary touch, as Henry Head (1920) first suggested.

This view is appealing on physiological grounds and is consistent with some interesting psychological phenomena. For example, **double pain** is the experience of two distinct peaks of pain, differing in quality and separated in time, arising from a single pain stimulus. It is now generally accepted that the first, sharp or pricking pain arises from the response of the somewhat faster Aβ fibers to the noxious stimulus, whereas the second, dull or burning pain arises from the slower-conducting C fibers (Cooper, Vierck, & Yeomans, 1986; Torebjork & Hallin, 1973; Willis, 1985). You can experience this for yourself if you try Demonstration Box 9-8.

Neural Responses to Pain Stimuli

The electrophysiology of the pain systems has been studied by applying noxious stimuli (such as electric shock, pinching, or pricking) to animals and recording the responses of neurons at various levels of the nervous system. It is assumed that these stimuli cause pain for the animals, as they usually do for humans, but this may not always be the case. Unfortunately, simply knowing that a particular stimulus was present cannot guarantee that a particular sensation was present. Thus, injured humans, particularly those engaged in some demanding activity such as war or athletics, often do not

DEMONSTRATION BOX 9-8   The Production of Double Pain

This demonstration uses the method of Sinclair and Stokes (1964) to generate two pains for the price of one. Double pain is experienced only under certain conditions. When these conditions are met, people report a first, sharp, stinging sensation, followed about 1 second later by a more intense burning pain that may spread to a wider area and fades more gradually. Although most people, under the appropriate conditions, experience this sequence without being told what to expect, we are telling you now so that you will have a good chance to experience it. For this demonstration you will need to find a source of hot water, something to measure its temperature, and two medium-sized bowls to hold it in. You need to produce two water baths: one at 35 deg C (95 deg F) and one at 57 deg C (135 deg F). If you have access to a thermometer (a meat thermometer is fine for this demonstration), this would obviously be the best way to measure the temperatures of the baths. If you do not have a thermometer, simply mix $3\frac{1}{2}$ cups of very hot tap water with $3\frac{1}{2}$ cups of cold tap water for the 35 deg C bath. To keep it at about this temperature, add a little hot water every minute or so. To create the 57 deg C bath, combine $6\frac{2}{3}$ cups of hot tap water with $\frac{1}{3}$ cup of cold tap water.

Immerse your entire hand in the 35 deg C bath for about 10 minutes. When this time has elapsed, mix the 57 deg C bath, and carefully insert your finger into it until the water comes up past the second joint of the finger. Count "one-thousand-one" to yourself, and then withdraw your finger. Pay careful attention to the sensations you experience. Notice that first you feel a sharp stinging and then about a second later a burning feeling. You may try the experiment again and again without fear of any damage if you immerse your hand in the 35 deg C bath between trials, and always limit your immersion in the 57 deg C bath to 1 second. If you wish, you can try varying the temperatures of the two baths to find the limits of the conditions under which the phenomenon will occur. Also, in calculating the formulas for the two baths, we assumed that the cold tap water in your area has a temperature of about 10 deg C (50 deg F), and the hot tap water a temperature of about 60 deg C (140 deg F). If your water temperatures vary significantly from these, you will have to adjust the proportions of each to make up the baths.

feel pain although horribly wounded, presumably because of conflicting and more urgent responses (Melzack & Wall, 1982). We do know, however, that certain nerve fibers appear to fire only when their receptive fields are stimulated by noxious stimuli. For example, Poggio and Mountcastle (1960) found such neurons in the cat's thalamus, and Casey and Morrow (1983) and Bushnell and Duncan (1989) found them in the thalamus of awake monkeys. Such neurons also have been found in area SI of the somatosensory cortex of rats (Lamour, Willer, & Guilbaud, 1983) and monkeys (Kenshalo & Isensee, 1983), and may also occur in area SII (see Willis, 1985). Using PET (a noninvasive technique—see Appendix), Talbot et al. (1991) have discovered three different areas in the human cerebral cortex that respond when painful heat is applied to the skin of the arm: the anterior cingulate gyrus (Brodman's area 24), and SI and SII. The relevant sites are all contralateral to the arm that was stimulated. It is clear that both the thalamus and the cortex play roles in pain perception. Just what these roles are, however, is not completely clear. Probably several brain areas each participate in various ways in the pain experience (see Casey, 1978; Willis, 1985). For example, the medial thalamus may mediate both sensory discriminative and emotional aspects (Bushnell & Duncan, 1989).

Perhaps the most interesting electrophysiological fact about pain is that the several types of nerve fibers involved in pain and in other cutaneous and kinesthetic sensations interact, sometimes in opposition to each other. Melzack and Wall (1965, 1982) devised an ingenious conceptual model of pain, called the **gate-control theory,** based on the interaction of two of these fiber types. This theory provides the foundation for most modern accounts of a variety of pain phenomena, so it is important to understand it thoroughly at this point. Figure 9-17 presents the theory diagrammatically.

First, notice in Figure 9-17 that both fast (Aβ) and slow (Aδ and C) fibers are said to have connections with the **substantia gelatinosa** (a group of neurons in the spinal cord; see also Figure 9-3) and with the **transmission cells** (T cells). These T cells are part of the set of slow fibers that make up the spinothalamic pathways and send pain information up the spinal cord to the brain. The fast fibers also have a direct connection (the dorsal column) to the brain, which can in turn send information back down the spinal cord to the gate-control system. Notice in Figure 9-17 that the connections of both the fast and the slow fibers to the T cells are marked with a plus sign, meaning that they increase neural activity in, or excite, those cells. The actions of these fibers on the substantia gelatinosa cells are different, however. The fast fibers excite the neurons in the substantia gelatinosa (+), whereas the slow fibers inhibit their action (−). When the T cells are sufficiently active, we experience pain. A normal stimulus, say a touch, would mostly

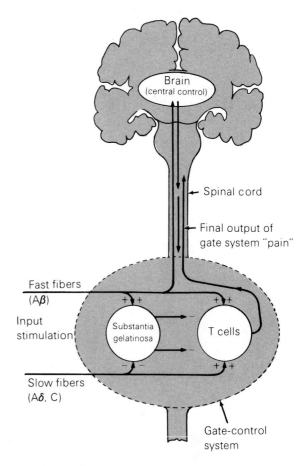

Figure 9-17 *An illustration of the* gate-control theory *of pain.*

stimulate the fast fibers, which have lower thresholds. This would excite the substantia gelatinosa neurons, causing them to inhibit the T cells, thus canceling the excitation of the T cells by the fast fibers and keeping them below the activity level sensed as pain. A noxious stimulus, however, would stimulate the higher-threshold slow fibers as well as the fast fibers. Because the slow fibers inhibit the substantia gelatinosa cells, canceling their excitation by the fast fibers, the substantia gelatinosa neurons no longer inhibit the T cells, which can fire more vigorously in response to input from both fast and slow fibers, and pain is experienced. The substantia gelatinosa is the "gate" for the activity of the T cells—the fast fibers close this gate and the slow fibers open it.

Generally speaking, chemical analgesics act to inhibit the slow fibers, but do not affect the fast fibers. This allows the substantia gelatinosa to inhibit the T cells and close the pain gate. Another way to close the pain gate (at least somewhat) is to rub around an area where you have hurt yourself, thus stimulating the fast fibers in the surrounding skin which will stimulate the substantia gelatinosa. Melzack and Casey (1968) suggested that the central pathway to the gate can also be responsible for closing it, so other perceptions, cognitions, and emotions could be responsible for changing the nature of a potentially painful experience. Evidence has indicated that the descending pathways do inhibit responses of spinal cord neurons to noxious stimuli (for example, Dickhaus, Pauser, & Zimmerman, 1985; Willis, 1983; Zimmerman, 1983).

Pain Thresholds, Intensity, and Adaptation

To treat pain as a sensation, it is useful to define a pain threshold. Usually this is taken to be the intensity of a stimulus that will just barely produce a sensation of pain. Obviously, thresholds will vary across the different conditions under which they are measured, since pain can be aroused in so many different ways. As in the case of touch and thermal sensitivity, specific tiny points on the skin respond selectively to pain. These points give the sensation of pain for stimuli that do not produce painful sensations when applied to places other than "pain points." In general, pain points seem to correspond to receptive fields of the small, slow-conducting pain fibers (see Willis, 1985). The distribution of such pain points over the body

Table 9-1   Distribution of Pain Sensitivity[a]

SKIN REGION	PAIN POINTS/CM^2
Back of knee	232
Neck region	228
Bend of elbow	224
Shoulder blade	212
Inside of forearm	203
Back of hand	188
Forehead	184
Buttocks	180
Eyelid	172
Scalp	144
Ball of thumb	60
Sole of foot	48
Tip of nose	44

[a]Based on Geldard, 1972.

seems quite variable, as can be seen from Table 9-1. Pain thresholds vary in the oral-facial regions as well, with the tongue and inside of the lip being less sensitive than other parts to heat-induced pain (Green, 1985).

A major advance in the standardization of conditions for measuring pain thresholds was made by Hardy, Wolff, and Goodell (1943). They used a device that focused an intense beam of light on the ink-blackened forehead of a subject in order to produce a painful heat stimulus. Since the device used radiant heat as a stimulus, the stimulus could be precisely controlled and measured. They called the device a **dolorimeter,** from the Latin *dolor*, "pain," and *meter*, "to measure." This development permitted the investigation of the various conditions that affect the pain threshold. The exact thresholds measured in this way are of little importance to us here, since the units of any pain threshold stimulus vary with the pain-producing device or stimulus modality. However, Hardy et al. (1943) were able to show that pain thresholds acted very much like the thresholds for other sensations. Pain thresholds were shown to be relatively stable as long as the conditions were stable, but they varied systematically with changes in the neurological, pharmacological (drugs), or psychological state of the individual. These results have been replicated many times, and more recently even social situations have been shown to affect pain thresholds (K. D. Craig, 1978).

Whether two pains are the same or different in intensity can be discriminated, indicating that pain has a difference threshold. The first good measurement of the difference threshold was done by Hardy, Wolff, and Goodell (1947) using a modification of the dolorimeter. Since the authors felt the knowledge was important, they served as their own subjects and as a result experienced both a large amount of pain and considerable tissue damage. They even moved the site of the painful stimulation from the forehead to the forearm because the latter was more easily cared for when blistered by the pain stimuli. These rather extreme measures resulted in some very important results. Hardy et al. (1947) found that the difference threshold could be measured for pain, and that it is reproducible under constant conditions. Moreover, they also found that the Weber fraction remains remarkably constant (as Weber's law would assert) at about 0.04 (a mere 4% stimulus difference) over quite a large range of stimulus intensities. This indicates that we are quite sensitive to differences in pain intensity. Weber fractions begin to increase dramatically at only the highest stimulus intensities. At the extremes, however, the data were not very reliable, because the skin damage sustained made it difficult for the observers (the authors themselves) to concentrate on the pain intensities. More recently, signal detection theory has been successfully applied to the study of pain discrimination, although great care must be taken in doing this (see Irwin & Whitehead, 1991, and references there).

Hardy et al. (1947) also created the first scale of pain intensity. Since they had established the validity of Weber's law for pain, they merely added up *jnds*, as Fechner had done (see Chapter 2), to create a scale of pain intensity based on the discriminability of painful stimuli. They appropriately called this scale the **dol scale** (again based on the Latin *dolor*). Later scales of pain intensity were created by more direct methods (see Chapman et al., 1985, for a review of pain measurement). For example, S. S. Stevens (1961) obtained magnitude estimations of the intensity of pain produced by electric shocks. He found that the magnitude estimations were a power function of the stimulus intensity with an exponent of about 3.50, making pain produced by electric shock the sensory modality with the largest power function exponent (see Chapter 2). The size of the exponent varies as a function of a variety of stimulus and even social factors (Craig, Best, & Ward, 1975; Sternbach & Tursky, 1964), and more recent studies have obtained somewhat lower exponents, usually under 2.00 (for example, Rollman & Harris, 1987).

Being able to measure pain is important to understanding pain phenomena. For example, it has recently been observed that pain summates; that is, different pains add together to produce a higher intensity of experienced pain than either one alone. This is true both within modalities and across modalities. Thus, stimulating two teeth at the same time lowers the pain threshold compared to stimulating a single tooth, and turns mild discomfort into pain (Brown, Beeler, Kloka, & Fields, 1985). Also, pain from shock and loud noise experienced together is roughly the linear sum of the pains experienced separately (Algom, Raphaeli, & Cohen-Raz, 1986).

Does pain adapt? Dallenbach (1939) demonstrated that pain caused by needles, heat, and cold does adapt. Heat-induced pain was studied by Hardy, Stolwijk, and Hoffman (1968) by having observers judge the degree of experienced pain as they sat with their hands in hot water over a period of time. As can be

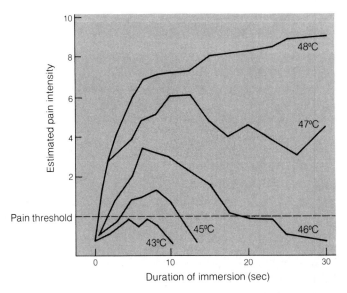

Figure 9-18   *Average estimations of pain intensity from hot-water immersions of different temperatures at different durations.*

seen from Figure 9-18, adaptation was complete for the lower-temperature pain stimuli, which were only mildly painful, and less complete for the more painful stimuli. Adaptation may not take place at all for extremely painful stimuli, although even dental pain adapts (Ernst, Lee, Dworkin, & Zaretsky, 1986).

Analgesia and Endogenous Opiates

Because pain is unpleasant we seek to minimize it. Yet strong pain signals often persist, or indeed may occur for the first time, well after a damaging stimulus is gone. This pain induces us to remain relatively immobile, which aids healing under primitive conditions (Wall, 1979). However, modern humans are not content simply to accept this immobilizing pain, nor do they desire to experience the pain from surgery or illness. Thus, we have assembled an impressive array of analgesics (reduce pain but leave touch, and so on) and anesthetics (elimi-

nate all sensation) to rid ourselves of pain. The major focus of much pain research is the discovery of new ways to alleviate pain. The most potent and reliable method of pain alleviation involves chemicals that are ingested (such as aspirin) or are injected into nerves or muscles (such as the novocaine used by dentists). We can even buy sprays or tubes of salve that contain substances that cause a temporary anesthesia on cut or burned skin. For more severe pain we resort to narcotic drugs (such as morphine, an opium derivative) or opt for unconsciousness (as with ether or chloroform).

While studying how some of the more powerful opium-based drugs produce analgesia, researchers made a discovery that helped advance our understanding of how our bodies control pain naturally. Opiates interact with specific receptors in the brain to produce their analgesic and intoxicating effects. Since the brain has receptors for this family of chemicals already, it seemed likely that a class of chemicals naturally present in the body also interact with these receptors. Presumably, these **en-**

dogenous opiates (meaning opiates generated from within) should exhibit analgesic properties similar to those of opium derivatives. Several such substances were discovered by biochemists in the early 1970s (see Kosterlitz & McKnight, 1981; Snyder, 1977). At least two major classes of endogenous opiates, the **enkephalins** and the **endorphins,** have significant analgesic effects, and seem to react with the same sites that opiates do (see Millan, 1986; Yaksh, 1984). When bodily levels are artificially raised (by administration of extra amounts of these substances), the endorphins seem to be the more potent and longer lasting. The opiumlike action of these endogenous substances is further demonstrated by the fact that their analgesic effect can be blocked by the administration of *naloxone*, a potent antagonist of opiates such as morphine and heroin, which is often administered to those who have taken overdoses. Administration of naloxone by itself makes people who are under stress more sensitive to pain, presumably because it blocks the effectiveness of endogenous opiates released naturally under these circumstances (Schull, Kaplan, & O'Brien, 1981).

Specific sites in the brain seem to be responsible for both the generation of endogenous opiates and for their analgesic effect. For example, electrical stimulation of certain parts of the thalamus can produce strong analgesic effects. This analgesia is reversible by naloxone and is less strong for individuals who have developed a tolerance or relative insensitivity to morphine, thus suggesting that this part of the brain may be one site where endogenous opiates are produced (see Akil & Watson, 1980). It is interesting to note that sufferers of chronic pain have lower than normal levels of some endogenous opiates in their spinal fluid, and electrical stimulation of the brains of such people produces both analgesia and dramatic increases in the levels of endorphins in their spinal fluid (Akil & Watson, 1980; Terenius & Wahlstrom, 1975).

Our conscious experience of pain intensity is affected not only by the magnitude of the pain stimulus but also by these chemical regulators, generated internally and acting directly on specific areas of the central nervous system. Study of endogenous opiate systems may also provide clues as to the mechanisms involved in the nonchemical methods for the reduction of pain. For example, in many instances purely psychological factors seem to cause reduced sensitivity to pain. Willer, Dehen, and Cambier (1981) found that the psychological stress caused by the anticipation of a painful shock resulted in analgesic effects. Presumably the stress triggered the endogenous opiate system (see also Lewis, Terman, Shavit, Nelson, & Liebeskind, 1984). Similarly, women during the last two weeks of pregnancy experience significant increases in pain thresholds, which reduces their discomfort (Cogan & Spinnato, 1986). Since pregnant rats experience the same threshold increases, and since the effect is much reduced when the rats are given naltrexone, another opiate antagonist (Gintzler, 1980), it is likely that the endogenous opiate system is involved.

Similar factors seem to be involved in some of the more "mysterious" reports of reduced pain sensitivity. For example, placebo effects (such as pain reduction caused by ingestion of a substance that is believed to be a powerful analgesic but that is really an ineffective inert substance) are sometimes reversible by naloxone, suggesting that some opiate system is involved. Perhaps even more mysterious is the traditional Chinese technique for alleviating pain called *acupuncture* (from the Latin *acus* meaning "needle" and *pungere* meaning "to sting"). In this technique, long, thin needles are inserted at various sites on the body (see Figure 9-19). These needles may be twirled, heated, or have electrical current passed through them. Although Western doctors have been cautious about accepting acupuncture as a valid means of reducing pain, most studies

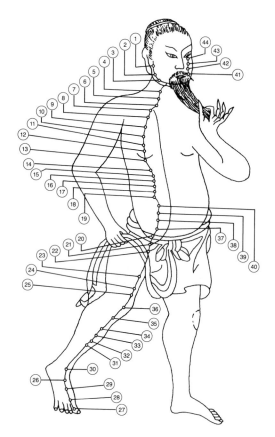

Figure 9-19 A typical acupuncture chart. The numbers indicate sites at which needles can be inserted and then either twisted, electrified, or heated. An impressive analgesia results in many cases.

support its effectiveness (see P. E. Brown, 1972; Chapman, 1978; T. O. Cheng, 1973; Clark & Yang, 1974). Many studies have now established that pain reduction achieved through acupuncture is mediated by release of endogenous opiates (Akil & Watson, 1980; He, 1987; He, Lu, Zhuang, Zhang, & Pan, 1985; Kosterlitz & McKnight, 1981).

The brain–chemical interaction we have been discussing provides only an incomplete picture of the factors influencing our perception of pain. For instance, many forms of pain reduction, such as that achieved via hypnosis,

do *not* appear to be mediated by endogenous opiates (Akil & Watson, 1980; Kosterlitz & McKnight, 1981). It is therefore not the case that all forms of "mysterious" analgesia can be explained by endogenous opiates. The most recent evidence suggests that humans have at least two pain control systems, and that only one of them involves endogenous opiates (Akil & Watson, 1980; Mayer & Watkins, 1984; Watkins & Mayer, 1982).

Some of the most interesting analgesic procedures involve cognitive processes. These include such techniques as suggestion, attitude, concentration of attention, and social modeling (see Craig, 1978; Weisenberg, 1984; Wolff & Goodell, 1943). The efficacy and interpretation of these techniques vary, but there is no doubt that they are real—pain thresholds can be affected dramatically. For instance, social modeling, where observers see another person's reactions to painful stimuli before judging the painfulness of the same stimuli for themselves, has been reported to affect both *d'* and physiological reactivity to painful electric shocks (Craig & Coren, 1975; Craig & Prkachin, 1978). Similarly, when people are attending to a stimulus modality different from the one a painful stimulus appears in, they experience significantly less pain and can less accurately and quickly discriminate levels of the painful stimulus, indicating that sensory processing of noxious stimuli is affected by manipulating attention (Miron, Duncan, & Bushnell, 1989). Demonstration Box 9-9 allows you to assess the effectiveness of one form of cognitive control of the perceived intensity of pain.

The perception of pain is complex, involving a number of different levels of control. These many levels may be integrated by considering the gate-control theory of pain discussed earlier. According to this theory, pain is experienced when the T cells are firing at a high enough rate. The theory describes not only a spinal gate controlled by fast and slow conducting fibers, but also allows inputs from

---

DEMONSTRATION BOX 9-9   Cognitive Effects on Pain: The Lamaze Technique

A cognitive technique to alleviate the pain of childbirth is taught in many places in North America and Europe (see Beck & Siegel, 1980). The basic idea was that of a French medical doctor named Fernand Lamaze. One demonstration of how this technique works requires a friend to assist you.

Have your friend grasp your leg just above the knee with a hand. Have your friend squeeze gently at first, then with steadily increasing force until you can feel a fairly severe pain. This should convince you that the stimulus is actually painful. Now you have three things to practice simultaneously. First, you have to breathe in a particular way. To do this you must take five short panting breaths in a row, followed by a strong blow outward (pant-pant-pant-pant-pant-*blow*). Repeat this pattern during the entire period during which the painful stimulus might occur. Do not breathe too quickly for you might hyperventilate and get dizzy. If you do get dizzy, stop for a moment and then start up again at a slower place. Second, you must count the breaths (1-2-3-4-5-

blow) or say a short poem or nonsense sentence over and over again to the rhythm of your breathing ("Am I a bird or *plant*?"). Third, you must concentrate your visual attention on (look intently at) some clearly visible object during this entire period. Practice these behaviors until you feel fairly confident of your ability to maintain them for a couple of minutes. Then have your friend give you the gradually increasing pressure on the leg, while you do your breathing. Under these conditions, if your concentration is really intense, you might not feel the pain (or the pressure) at all, or at least it will be of much less intensity. According to the Melzack-Wall-Casey (Melzack & Casey, 1968; Melzack & Wall, 1965) approach to pain, what is happening here is that your central control system is closing the pain gate. Thousands of mothers claim that this basic technique of concentrating on something removed from the source of the pain effectively alleviates the pain and distress of childbirth.

---

higher levels of the nervous system to open or close the gate. Thus, cognitive factors, motivational states, attentional factors, or other stimulation such as high-intensity hissing noises, electricity, or music could all be responsible for controlling the gate via the pathway *descending* from the brain to the spinal cord gate (Willis, 1983, 1985). These descending pathways seem to be strongly implicated in analgesia caused by release of endogenous opiates. Perhaps activation of the descending pathways causes release of endogenous opiates into the spinal cord, thus decreasing firing of the T cells (Watkins & Mayer, 1982). However, the mechanism involving the substantia gelatinosa does

not seem to use endogenous opiates to produce its effects.

We do not understand fully the story of the perception of pain. However, we now have a hint of why the second-century physician Galen prescribed the shock from an electric fish for a headache, a twelfth-century English doctor prescribed the wearing of a copper bracelet on the left hand to relieve a pain in the right hand, and a modern Chinese doctor twirls needles stuck through the skin of an appendectomy patient—all claiming successful analgesic results. Perhaps each was stimulating one of the several pain control systems we possess, rather than simply engaging in "empty superstition."

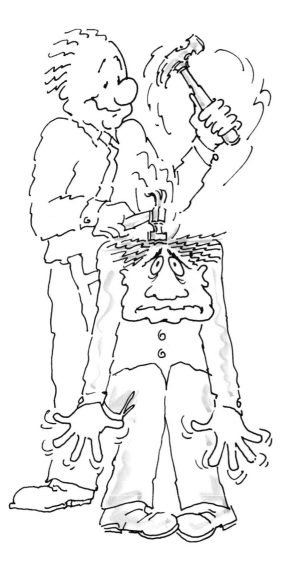

A slight misunderstanding of the double-pain demonstration

GLOSSARY

The following definitions are specific to their use in this book.

Backward masking   When a masking pattern interferes with the perception of a target presented earlier in time.

Cold fibers   Neurons that respond to cooling by firing more rapidly and to warming by firing more slowly.

Dermis   The inner layer of skin, containing most of the nerve endings.

Dol scale   A scale of pain intensity based on the discriminability of painful stimuli.

Dolorimeter   A device that delivers precise quantities of radiant heat; used to measure pain thresholds.

Dorsal column   One of the two major nerve pathways in the spinal cord; it receives input mostly from Aβ fibers and carries mostly touch information.

Double pain   The phenomenon of two distinct peaks of pain, differing in quality and separated in time, from a single pain stimulus.

Endogenous opiates   Analgesia-inducing opiates produced naturally in the brain and other areas of the body.

Endorphins   One of the major groups of endogenous opiates.

Enkephalins   One of the major groups of endogenous opiates.

Epidermis   The outer layer of skin.

Forward masking   When a masking pattern interferes with the perception of a target presented later in time.

Free nerve endings   Noncorpuscular, branching nerve endings in skin, joints, and so on, which may be receptors for pain and temperature.

Gate-control theory   A conceptual model of pain based on the interaction of slow, high-threshold nerve fibers and fast, low-threshold nerve fibers via the substantia gelatinosa (the "pain gate").

Glabrous skin   A type of skin that has no hairs (for example, on lips); it is highly sensitive to stimulation.

Golgi tendon organs   Nerve endings attached to tendons that respond to both stretching and contraction of muscle.

Hairy skin   Covering of the human body from which numerous hairs protrude; it is both a protective and stimulus-sensitive covering. *See* Glabrous skin.

Haptic perception Experience of the world based on a combination of cutaneous and kinesthetic sensations.

Kinesthesis Sensations of force, weight, and limb position and movement.

Limbic system A part of the brain, old in an evolutionary sense, involved in emotion and memory.

Medial lemniscus A part of the spinal cord composed of large, rapidly conducting nerve fibers that conduct touch information from the skin to the brain.

Neospinothalamic pathway A part of the spinal cord, evolutionarily more recent, that conducts information representing sharp, pricking pain, temperature, and rudimentary touch from the skin, muscles, and joints to the brain.

Neutral zone A temperature range surrounding physiological zero. Stimuli within this range feel neither warm nor cold.

Optacon A system, similar to the vision substitution system, that converts printed letters into vibration patterns on the fingertip.

Pacinian corpuscle A corpuscular nerve ending found in skin and joints, sensitive to mechanical deformation.

Paleospinothalamic pathway A part of the spinal cord, evolutionarily older, that conducts information (representing dull, burning pain, temperature, and rudimentary touch) from the skin, muscles, and joints to the brain.

Paradoxical cold The phenomenon of cold spots in the skin responding to very warm stimuli with a sensation of cold.

Parietal cortex The upper central region of the brain housing the somatosensory cortex.

Physiological zero A neutral point in the perception of heat and cold, usually taken to be the skin temperature.

Somatosensory cortex The part of the cerebral cortex, located in the parietal lobe, that receives input from the thalamus and other brain regions representing touch, temperature, pain, and kinesthesis.

Spindle organs *See* Stretch receptors.

Spinothalamic pathway A slow pathway of short fibers in the spinal cord that conducts information (representing pain, temperature, and rudimentary touch) to the brain from the skin, muscles, tendons, and organs.

Stretch receptors Nerve endings attached to muscle spindles that respond to stretching of the muscle.

Substantia gelatinosa The part of the spinal cord implicated in pain transmission through the gate-control theory.

Tadoma A method of assistance to speech perception in which the "listener" places his or her hand on the face and neck of the speaker and deduces what is said from the haptically perceived actions of the articulators.

Thalamus The region of the lower brain that relays nerve impulses to the somatosensory cortex.

Transmission (T) cells In the gate-control theory of pain, these transmit pain impulses to the brain.

Two-point threshold The minimum distance necessary between two pointed touch stimuli (such as two toothpicks) so that they will be felt as two distinct sensations.

Vision substitution system An instrument that converts a visual pattern from a television camera into a pattern of vibrating points on the skin of the back; used for the visually impaired.

Warm fibers Neurons that respond to warming by firing more rapidly and to cooling by firing more slowly.

Chapter ...

SPACE

Types of Depth Perception
Pictorial Depth Cues
    Interposition or Occlusion
    Shading and Shadows
    Aerial Perspective
    Retinal and Familiar Size
    Linear Perspective
    Texture Gradients
    Height in the Plane
Physiological Cues for Depth
    Accommodation
    Convergence and Divergence
Motion and Motion Parallax
Binocular Depth Perception
    Cues for Stereopsis
    The Process of Stereopsis
Interaction of Depth Cues
Perception of Direction
    Eye Movements and Direction
    Eye Dominance and Perceived Direction
Development of Space Perception
    Species Differences
    Experience and Depth Perception

*I*n 1621 Robert Burton noted, "All places are distant from heaven alike." Perhaps for a clergyman-philosopher such a description of spatial relations was sufficient. Yet for you, a simple mortal trying to pick up a cup of coffee from the tabletop, much more precision is needed. You must be able to judge how far the cup is from your hand with a good deal of accuracy, lest you end up with a messy puddle of hot fluid. Your very life may depend on your precision in judging depth and distance, as when you sense you are near the edge of a cliff. You must know how close you are to avoid falling, and you must also know the direction of the edge from your body lest you step toward it rather than away from it. We cannot get cut by a knife edge pictured in a flat photograph, but a real blade extending toward us in space can produce a nasty gash. Thus, safely performing our daily tasks depends on the accuracy of our spatial perception.

TYPES OF DEPTH PERCEPTION

Your perception of depth consists of at least two different aspects. One aspect involves the perception of the distance of an object from you, such as how far away a pencil is on your desk. This is an estimate of **absolute distance,** which involves a process called **egocentric localization.** Most of us are familiar with the word *egocentric* in its everyday use—you are egocentric if you are concerned only about your own activities and their effect on yourself. In the context of space perception, *egocentric* means we have a good sense of where our bodies are positioned relative to other objects in the external environment. We encounter a different aspect of space perception when we ask whether the pencil is lying nearer to the book or to the coffee cup, which are also on the desk. This is the judgment of **relative distance,** requiring the observer to make **object-relative localizations,** which are estimates of the *distances between objects* in the environment. The judgment of relative distance is also involved in the perception of whether an object is flat (as in a two-dimensional picture) or solid (three-dimensional), in that this requires estimation of the spatial relationships between parts of an object.

The accomplishment involved in seeing objects in depth is quite amazing considering that the basic information available to the nervous system is just a flat image on the retina. The question of how we convert this two-dimensional image into our three-dimensional conscious impression of the world has stimulated a number of different theoretical approaches. Before discussing the research on this problem, we will briefly summarize these approaches. (Recall that we introduced them in Chapter 1.)

One approach, called **direct perception** (Michaels & Carello, 1981), is characterized by the work of J. J. Gibson (for example, 1979). Three assumptions are central to direct perception. The first is that all the information you need to see three-dimensionally is present in the retinal image, or in relationships among parts of the retinal image. The second is the concept that the visual scene is analyzed in terms of whole objects and surfaces, rather than in terms of elementary stimulus attributes such as edges, colors, and specific locations that together make up objects. Finally, direct perception assumes that the impression of depth or distance arises immediately in the observer and needs no further computation or any additional information based on inferences or experience.

An alternative approach is given by scientists who view visual processing as being similar to information processing done by a computer. These scientists have been influenced by developments in *artificial intelligence,* which is a part of computer science that attempts to design machines to interpret visual information. There are actually two different types of these scientists. The first is interested in designing robots that can perform tasks for humans based on visual input. The second group is interested in designing computer programs that will duplicate the processing steps actually used by a human observer when viewing visual stimuli such as pictures. For this second group the computer program actually serves the same function as a theory, in that it can be used to predict what a person might see in particular circumstances. Because of this, the computer programs, or the description of the processes implemented by the programs, are often referred to as **computational theories** of vision. One of the most well-known of the computational theorists was David Marr (1982). He began with one of the assumptions made in direct perception, namely, that all the information you need to derive three-dimensionality is present in the visual inputs. However, he departed from the direct perception view, in the manner of all computational theorists, when he suggested that accurate interpretation of three-dimensionality required a number of complex computations and several stages of analysis. (See Chapter 11 for more on computational theories.)

Another major approach to perceptual theory is based on the assumption that our perceptual representation of the world is much richer and more accurate than might be expected on the basis of the information contained in the visual image alone. This approach, which might be called **intelligent perception,** originated with Helmholtz in 1867 and is today best exemplified by Gregory (1978) and Rock (1983). It suggests that perception is like other logical processes in that, in addition to the information available at the moment, we can also use information derived from our previous experience, our expectations, and so forth. In other words, our visual perception of space may involve "going beyond" the information given in the visual

image. Some of this information may be nonvisual in nature, such as that from our history and habitual cognitive processing strategies. Because this approach emphasizes the combining of several sources of information, these theories have also been called **constructive theories** of perception.

Although it is quite likely that each of these approaches is valid for some aspects of the perceptual process (compare Coren & Girgus, 1978; Uttal, 1981), theorists who favor particular approaches will tend to try to isolate different factors when they consider the perception of depth or distance. Some will concentrate on isolating structures within the sensory systems themselves, others on the properties of the physical world and the way our sensory systems interact with it, and still others on the cognitive processes called into play when we interpret the three-dimensional nature of the world. All of these approaches, however, usually begin by attempting to isolate the **cues** for depth. These are stimulus characteristics of which we are often not consciously aware, but that function to shape our perceptual responses.

PICTORIAL DEPTH CUES

When you look at a realistic painting or a photograph, you find it quite easy to perceive the spatial relationship among the various items portrayed. Your impression of the relative distances in such scenes is based on a set of cues, appropriately called **pictorial depth cues.** These cues are also called **monocular cues,** since they do not only appear in pictures but are also relevant to our perception of depth when only one eye is used. Remember that the image on the retina is two-dimensional (we will have more to say about this in Chapter 11). To understand these depth cues, we must first recognize that our visual experience usually depends on the transfer of light reflected from an object in the external world to the eye of the observer. A number of depth cues depend on characteristic ways in which light travels to the eye, and on ways in which it is affected by the medium (usually air) through which it passes. Other depth cues arise from how light interacts with objects, and also from the geometry of images.

Interposition or Occlusion

The vast majority of objects in the world are not transparent. Since light reflected from distant objects cannot pass through opaque objects that stand between them and the observer, a nearer object tends to block the view of a more distant one. This depth cue is called **interposition** or **occlusion.** It is easy to see that the cat in Figure 10-1 is nearer to you than the man's leg because your view of the leg is partially covered by the image of the cat. Notice that interposition is a cue for relative depth only—it indicates that the cat is nearer than the man's leg, but not how far the cat or the man is away from you.

One of the most interesting findings with regard to interposition is that the absence in the image of the part of the man's leg hidden by the cat is only rarely brought into your consciousness. Instead, the visual system usually "fills in" the occluded portion of an object rapidly and automatically (Nakayama, Shimojo, & Silverman, 1989; Weisstein, Montalvo, & Ozog, 1972). For example, several studies have shown that subjects are able to make a speeded "same–different" response to pairs of shapes just as rapidly when one member of the pair is partly occluded as when both members of the pair are completely visible (Gerbino & Salmaso, 1987; Sekuler & Palmer, 1992). Careful investigation of the amount of time needed for the "filling in" to be complete suggests that it occurs within the first 200 ms of processing (Sekuler & Palmer, 1992).

Figure 10-1 Interposition as a depth cue is illustrated by the fact that the cat is seen as closer than the man's leg since it partially blocks your view of the leg.

Shading and Shadows

The fact that light cannot pass through most objects gives rise to the interposition cue. The fact that light usually travels in straight lines gives us another cue for relative depth. This means that surfaces facing the light source will be relatively bright, whereas surfaces away from the light source will be in shadow. Particular patterns of shadow can provide information about the shape of solid objects. Thus if light comes from above an in-going dent or "dimple," the lower part will catch more of the light, while the upper part will be in relative shadow. For an outgoing protrusion or "pim-

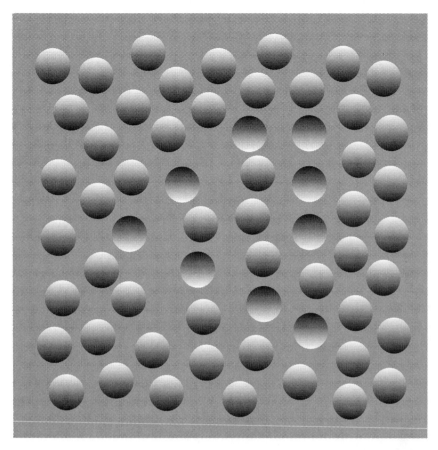

Figure 10-2 *Shading makes it clear that we are looking at a picture of spherical "pimples" and "dimples." Turning the figure upside-down reverses the shadow pattern and now makes it appear that what used to be "dimples" are now "pimples," and vice versa.*

ple," the top part will be bright and the lower part in shadow. This is illustrated in the picture of "pimples and dimples" shown in Figure 10-2. Obviously, if you turn this book upside down, the light and shadow patterns in the figure reverse, and now the "pimples" become "dimples" and vice versa (compare Berbaum, Bever, & Chung, 1984; Ramachandran, 1988). Clearly, for this shading cue to work consistently in this example, we must assume that the light is coming from above (which it does in most everyday situations). If the light were coming from another direction, the shading

pattern would be different. Observers do seem to use their knowledge or presumptions about the location of the light source to help them accurately perceive the three-dimensional nature of objects using the shading cue (Berbaum, Bever, & Chung, 1983; Enns & Rensink, 1990; Ramachandran, 1988).

The shading pattern on an object or surface is only one of the cues associated with shadows. The shading that defines the shape of an object can be called an **attached shadow,** because the pattern of light that serves as a cue to its three-dimensional shape is distributed

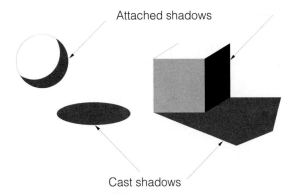

Attached shadows

Cast shadows

*Figure 10-3   Two types of shadows that give us different information about depth. **Attached shadows** help to indicate the intrinsic shape of an object, and **cast shadows** indicate the relative distance of an object from another object or surface.*

over the object itself (see Figure 10-3). However, another factor that can affect the shading pattern is the presence of a second object or surface lying in the path of the light source. Such an object will give rise to a **cast shadow,** as shown in Figure 10-3. Observers are able to use cast shadows as well as attached shadows to determine the relative depth of objects (Berbaum, Bever, & Chung, 1984; Cavanagh & Leclerc, 1989). Specifically, the more separated the object is from its cast shadow, the greater will be the perceived distance between the object and the shadowed surface. However, it appears that the visual system does not analyze cast shadows in as much detail as attached shadows, and certain patterns of "shadows" that cannot occur under natural conditions in the real world are still processed as if they were acceptable as cues (Cavanagh & Leclerc, 1989).

Aerial Perspective

The partial or complete blockage of light provides pictorial cues for relative depth. A cue for *absolute* depth emerges from the fact that the

air is filled with light-absorbing and light-scattering molecules even on the clearest of days. As light passes through the air, it tends to be absorbed and somewhat scattered by these particles of dust and moisture. Larger particles (such as dust) scatter light uniformly, causing a uniform distribution of light or a blurring of the image. For particles that are small in comparison to the various wavelengths of light (such as minute bits of water vapor), the degree of scatter depends on the specific wavelength. Shorter wavelengths (blue) are scattered more than longer wavelengths (Uttal, 1981). The combined effect of these phenomena produces the cue called **aerial perspective,** in which the image of a very distant object, such as a distant mountain, will be slightly bluer in hue and hazier or less distinct in appearance than the images of nearer objects that are physically the same. Such changes in appearance can provide information about the absolute distance of relatively faraway objects. In some geographic regions (such as the prairies of the United States and Canada), this can lead to considerable errors in distance judgments, since clear, dry air reduces aerial perspective. Thus, a plateau that appears to be only 1 or 2 miles away on a clear day, when looking across a dry sector of Wyoming, may actually be 20 or 30 miles from the observer. Conversely, this explains why objects seen in the morning fog or a mist appear to be farther away than when seen in bright midday sun (Ross, 1975).

An interesting variant of the aerial perspective cue is usually referred to as **relative brightness.** The luminance of a lighted surface or object does not decrease with distance, but the light from more distant objects must travel through the atmosphere for a greater distance. Therefore, increased absorption or scattering of the light by the particles in the air could account for the perception of a diminished brightness with increasing object distance, even though the distances may not be as great

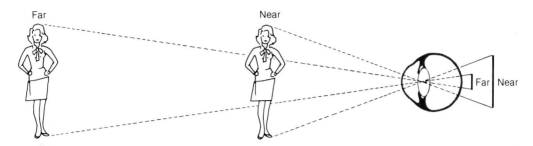

Figure 10-4 *Objects of the same physical size produce smaller retinal angle sizes with increasing distance from the observer. Thus, relatively speaking, smaller images are perceived to be more distant.*

as those described in the context of the usual aerial perspective cue (Uttal, 1981). In the absence of any other cues, we tend to see the brighter of two identical objects as closer (Ittelson, 1960).

Retinal and Familiar Size

As an object moves farther away from you, its **retinal image size** begins to diminish. One country song captured this effect in its lyric, "If you see me getting smaller I'm leaving." The geometry of this situation is shown in Figure 10-4, where the more distant person is casting a smaller retinal image. We use these differ-

ences in retinal image size as a cue for relative distance, as in Figure 10-5, where we see a row of puppies that seem to recede in distance because of their decreasing image size. Thus, the comparison of the sizes of objects in the visual field is an important part of the process of perceiving relative distance.

Retinal image size is a cue used by both direct perception and computational theories of perception. Another size cue exists that is important in constructive theories. This has nothing to do with image size, but rather with previous experience with the usual or **familiar size** of the object. For example, we know that playing cards all tend to be around the same size. Ittleson (1951) presented to observers

Figure 10-5 *Relative size differences are interpreted as cues for relative distance. Thus, we see a row of puppies that seems to recede in distance because of their decreasing image size.*

three playing cards, under **reduction condi-tions** (a darkened room with all other depth cues removed). One of the playing cards was normal in size, a second was twice normal size, and a third was one-half normal size. The ob-servers tended to judge the double-sized play-ing cards as being much closer to them and the half-sized cards as much more distant than the normal-sized cards. This is the same process that causes you to see the dogs in Figure 10-5 as receding into the distance. These images are assumed to be all about the same "dog size" and this familiar-size information, in conjunc-tion with the differences in retinal size, gives rise to the impression of differences in relative distance.

As long as the objects are commonplace, and the distances not too extreme, familiar size can give you absolute, not merely relative, depth information (Epstein & Baratz, 1964; Fitzpatrick, Pasnak, & Tyer, 1982). Thus, if we see a very tiny elephant, we can use our knowl-edge that elephants are relatively large crea-tures to deduce that the elephant has not shrunk in size but rather has moved away from us and is now more distant. You may demon-strate the effect of familiar size for yourself by following the instructions in Demonstration Box 10-1.

Linear Perspective

One well-known pictorial depth cue may be seen as an extension of the retinal image size cue to distance. This cue is **linear perspective.** For example, look at Figure 10-6, which is adapted from a book on how to depict perspec-tive in drawings authored by Jan Vredman de Vries in 1604 (de Vries, 1604/1968). In this schematic scene we notice that physically par-allel lines, such as those defining the paving blocks making up the floor, seem to converge as objects become more distant. So do the hy-pothetical lines that connect all the tops and all the bottoms of the pillars, all of which are phys-ically the same size. This means that parallel lines in the real world, such as railroad tracks, appear to converge and objects appear to get smaller in a systematic fashion as their dis-tance from you increases. Eventually they will reach a **vanishing point,** where all the per-spective lines will converge and objects will diminish to invisibility. This point is usually on the horizon, as shown in the figure. This is a simple geometric effect that occurs in the real world and when we project a three-dimensional scene onto a two-dimensional sur-face. It provides a powerful relative depth cue. Hence, it is easy to determine that pillar *B* is

---

DEMONSTRATION BOX 10-1   Familiar size and distance

Look at Figure 10-4. Notice that the row of puppies seems to recede into the distance. Off to the right is a ball. If we told you that it is a tennis ball or a baseball, you would have no difficulty in deciding which dog is at the same distance away from you as the ball. After you decide this, return to this box.

Now, suppose we told you that the ball is really a volleyball or a basketball. Which dog

is the same distance as the basketball? No-tice that the ball apparently "moved back-ward" in depth when you assumed it was a larger object. This shows how knowledge of the size of an object can affect our judgment of the distance of the object, giving us the *fa-miliar size* cue to distance.

Figure 10-6 *An example of linear perspective, in which physically parallel lines seem to converge as they grow more distant. Notice that the lines have been extrapolated to show a vanishing point on the horizon.*

farther away from you than pillar *A* by utilizing the perspective cue.

Texture Gradients

J. J. Gibson (1950) suggested an interesting way of combining both linear perspective and relative size information into one cue, which he referred to as **texture gradient.** A visual texture is loosely defined as any collection of objects in the visual image (Caelli, 1982), and the gradient (continuous change) is the change in the relative size and compactness of these object elements. The more distant parts of a texture have smaller elements that are more densely packed together (Gibson, 1950). The depth impression associated with texture gradients is sometimes called *detail perspective.* Figure 10-7A shows a texture of lines. Since the texture is uniform, it shows little depth and looks much like a flat wall or garage door. If we introduce a gradient, however, as is done in 10-7B, with the lines becoming more compact as we move toward the top, we now get an impression of depth. An even stronger impression of depth appears if we allow the gradient to appear in the horizontal placing of elements as well as the vertical, as can be seen in the texture of dots in 10-7C. One important type of information contained in texture gradients

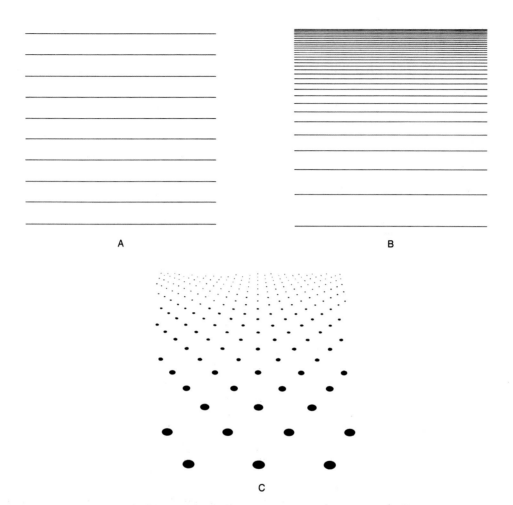

A

B

C

Figure 10-7 *Examples of texture gradients are shown in B and C, which appear as surfaces receding in depth. In A there are no decreases in element size or spacing, and thus the perception is of a flat surface.*

emerges from the fact that sudden changes in texture usually signal a change in the direction or distance of a surface. Thus, Figure 10-8A shows how the gradient changes when we shift from floor to wall, and 10-8B shows how the gradient changes at a cliff or step down. The perception of depth obtained from texture gradients can be quite striking. Texture helps define the shapes of solid objects (Todd & Akerstrom, 1987; see also Chapter 11) as well

as to reveal delicate variations in distance, as shown in the undulating surface depicted by texture cues alone in Figure 10-9.

Height in the Plane

Another cue to distance depends on the relationships between objects as their images are projected onto our retinas. This cue, known as

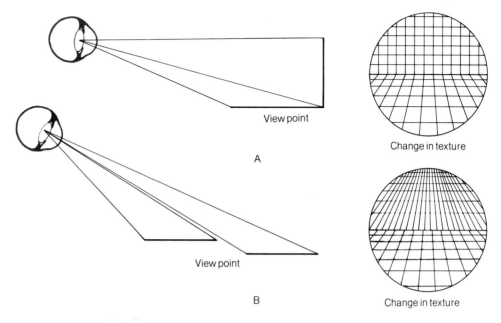

Figure 10-8 *How texture changes at a corner* (A) *and an edge next to a sharp drop in depth* (B).

Figure 10-9 *This rippling or undulating surface is defined completely on the basis of variations in texture density.*

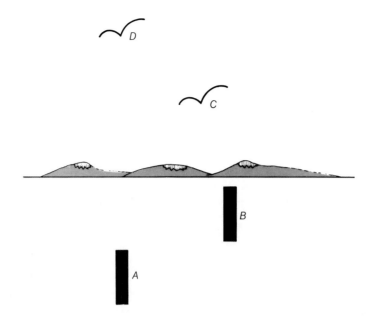

Figure 10-10 *Height in the plane and proximity to the horizon will determine which elements in the diagram are perceived as being more distant. In this case, B and C are seen as being farther away because they are closer to the horizon.*

height in the plane, or *relative height*, refers to the location of an object relative to the horizon line. In Figure 10-10, post *B* seems farther away than post *A* because the base of post *B* is closer to the horizon line. Hence it is said to be "higher in the plane," or "higher in the picture plane," if we consider this as a two-dimensional representation. The reverse holds for targets above the horizon. Bird *C* seems farther away than bird *D* because *C* is "lower in the picture plane." In other words, proximity to the horizon line signals greater distance.

PHYSIOLOGICAL CUES FOR DEPTH

Until now we have only considered cues for depth that can be found in the retinal image itself. Other cues for distance come about because of the way the visual system responds to or interacts with the visual stimulus. These may be called **structural** or **physiological cues,** since they tend to arise from muscular responses and adjustments of the eye.

Accommodation

When we discussed the physiology of the eye in Chapter 3, we described how the crystalline lens system responds to targets at different distances from us. Basically, we noted that shape of the lens must be changed (its curvature must be changed) to focus the retinal images of objects at different distances (Dalziel & Egan, 1982). This process is called **accommodation.** Only one particular curvature will clearly focus the retinal image of an object viewed at a particular distance from the eye. *Relaxed accommodation*, where the lens is relatively flattened, is necessary if distant objects are to be clearly focused on the retina, whereas a strongly curved lens is needed to image closer objects on the retinal surface. Feedback from changes in the tension on the ciliary muscles, which control the lens shape, can provide us with some additional, nonvisual, information about the distance of the object we are looking at.

In addition to feedback from the act of accommodation, the presence or absence of blur due to an object's image being out of focus can serve as a cue for relative distance. It has been shown that in the absence of all other depth information, observers can judge that two spots of light presented in complete darkness are at different distances. This is probably because accommodation cannot be correct for two stimuli at different distances at the same time; hence, one of the lights will be slightly out of focus, suggesting that the targets are not equidistant (Kaufman, 1974).

Some controversy exists over the utility of accommodation as a cue to depth in everyday situations. Accommodation is rather slow in its effects and is also limited in the range of observer-to-object distances over which it is useful (Graham, 1965). For example, at a distance of around 3 m, the lens has fully relaxed accommodation and does not flatten out any further, regardless of how far away an object is. A similar limit exists for close objects. If a target is within 20 cm of your face, your lens has reached its point of maximum curvature. Within the range of 20 to 300 cm, however, accommodation may provide a useful, if not very precise or rapid, auxiliary cue for distance (Hochberg, 1971; Iida, 1983).

Convergence and Divergence

Another potential distance cue comes from the fact that we have two eyes. Two-eyed perception is referred to as **binocular,** from *bi,* meaning "two," and *ocula,* meaning "eye." Since (as we learned in Chapter 3) the best visual acuity is obtained when the image of an object is focused on the two foveae, eye movements are executed to bring the image to this region of each eye. If the eyes move in different directions, these are called **vergence movements.** If an object is close to you, you must rotate your eyes inward (toward the nose) in order to focus its image on the fovea. Such movements are called **convergence** (the root *con* means "toward"). When a target is farther away, the eyes must move away from each other in an outward rotation (toward the temples); hence, these movements are called **divergence** (from the root *di* meaning "apart"). Different degrees of convergence and divergence are shown in Figure 10-11.

Each target distance, up to about 6 m, is associated with a unique angle between the eyes called the *convergence angle,* as indicated in Figure 10-11. To achieve each eye position, a unique pattern of muscular contractions must occur. Feedback from such vergence movements could be useful in determining the distances of objects, although there has been some controversy about how useful and reliable such information is as a depth cue (Gogel, Gregg, & Wainwright, 1961; Hochberg, 1971). Recent evidence, however, suggests that convergence and accommodation together may provide quite accurate absolute depth information, even when the only visible stimulus is a single point of light whose distance observers are asked to judge (Morrison & Whiteside, 1984). Some evidence also has indicated that the eyes converge and accommodate as if they were looking at objects at various distances in response to the pictorial depth cues found in paintings and line drawings (Enright, 1987a, 1987b).

MOTION AND MOTION PARALLAX

Except for the physiological cues, all the cues to depth we have discussed so far can be defined with respect to a single static image, such

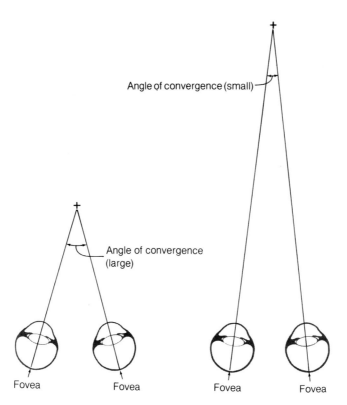

Figure 10-11 *Convergence angle changes as a function of fixation distance. This may provide some information about target distance.*

as a photograph or a painting. However, most of our perception of depth occurs in an environment where the observer is in motion (because of body, head, or eye movements) and very often one where objects are in motion as well. This gives the visual system the opportunity to compare multiple images over time, each slightly different depending on the speed of movement. Therefore, it should not be surprising that when we add motion to the incoming visual pattern, we acquire some additional depth cues.

One of these movement-derived cues concerns the motion pattern of an object as you travel past it. Suppose you are traveling in a car or bus and looking at the scene in Figure 10-12.

Suppose also that your direction of movement is from right to left and you are gazing at the spot marked *fixation point.* Under these conditions, all the objects closer to you than the fixation point will appear to move in a direction opposite to your movement, whereas objects that are farther away will appear to move in the same direction you are moving. Not only the direction but also the speed of movement varies with the objects' proximity to you and to your point of fixation—the nearer the object is to the retina, the faster will be its motion across the retina relative to other objects. This cue to distance is called **motion parallax.** Motion parallax can also be generated by swinging your head back and forth while your body is

Figure 10-12 *Motion parallax. When an observer moves, objects at varying distances from the observer will move in different directions at differing speeds. These differences can serve as cues for the relative distances of the objects.*

stationary, giving you very good information about the depth of objects if they are not too distant from you (Ono, Rivest, & Ono, 1986; Ono & Rogers, 1988; Rogers & Graham, 1979).

A special form of motion parallax occurs when an object moves or rotates. The relative pattern of movement of parts of the object can give us information about its three-dimensional shape (for example, Carpenter & Dugan, 1983; Doner, Lappin, & Perfetto, 1984). The fact that motion cues can give us information about the relative depth of parts of an object has been called the **kinetic depth effect** (Gibson, 1966; Kaufman, 1974; Rock, 1975). Demonstration Box 10-2 allows you to see this phenomenon for yourself. In Chapter 13 you will also learn how motion parallax can give you information

about the direction of your movements through space.

BINOCULAR DEPTH PERCEPTION

Just as motion provides the visual system with multiple images to compare, thereby giving it additional cues to depth, the fact that we have two eyes confers a great advantage in trying to estimate relative depth. For example, in many common tasks involving judgments of relative depth, such as threading a needle, inserting items into slots, or even placing cards behind alphabetic dividers in a box, people perform up to 30% faster and more accurately when using

DEMONSTRATION BOX 10-2   The Kinetic Depth Effect

To see how subtle motion parallax effects can create the impression of a three-dimensional form in a two-dimensional pattern, you will need a candle and a piece of stiff wire (a coat hanger or a long pipe cleaner will do). Bend the wire into a random three-dimensional shape. Now light the candle and darken the room. Place the bent wire so it casts a shadow on a blank wall as shown in the figure. Notice that when the shape is absolutely motionless, the shadow is seen as a flat pattern of lines. Now if you rotate the shape with your hand, the shadow suddenly changes perceptually, becoming a three-dimensional object that cannot be seen as flat, despite the fact that you are viewing a two-dimensional shadow.

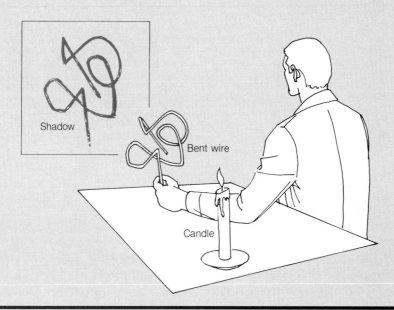

DEMONSTRATION BOX 10-3   Binocular versus Monocular Depth Perception

For this demonstration, which was suggested by Sekuler and Blake (1985), you will need two sharp pencils. Hold one in each hand at a relaxed arm's length, so their tips are pointed toward each other but are separated by about 10 cm. Now close one eye, and slowly bring the two pencils together so the two points touch each other. Now try this with both eyes open. You will probably find that you were much more accurate with both eyes open than with one eye alone. However, not all of you will show this improvement with binocular viewing, since between 5% and 10% of the population do not have **stereopsis,** which is the term used to describe the ability to see depth based on binocular disparity.

both eyes than they do with one eye alone (Sheedy, Bailey, Burl, & Bass, 1986). Demonstration Box 10-3 allows you to see how much better your depth perception is under binocular (two-eyed) conditions, as compared to monocular (one-eyed) viewing.

Cues for Stereopsis

The cues for binocular depth perception *(stereopsis)* depend on the fact that, in humans and other animals, the two eyes are horizontally separated. In humans, the distance between the two pupils may be up to 6.5 cm. Because of this separation, each eye has a different direction of view and, hence, a different image of the world. We call the differences between the two eyes' images **binocular disparity.** You can see how different the images can be by following the instructions in Demonstration Box 10-4.

The process by which we merge these disparate images into a single unified percept is

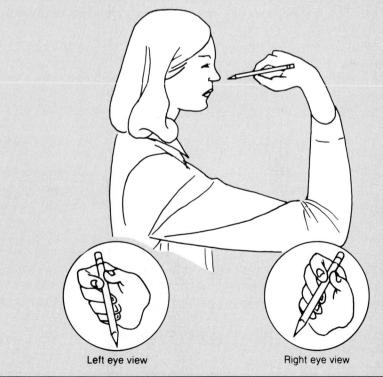

DEMONSTRATION BOX 10-4   Binocular Disparity

You can see the difference between the views of your eyes by holding a pencil up near your nose, as shown. The tip of the pencil should be toward you and angled slightly downward. Now alternately close each eye. The pencil seems to swing back and forth. With your right eye open, it appears angled toward the left; with the left eye open, it appears angled toward the right. With both eyes open, the fused view is of a pencil straight ahead of your nose.

Left eye view

Right eye view

called **fusion.** However, fusion is fairly limited in its range of operation, and many parts of the total visual image do not fuse. This failure of the two eyes' views to merge completely gives rise to double vision, or **diplopia.** Under normal viewing conditions, you are usually not consciously aware of this diplopia; however, you can readily learn to see the double images in the unfused portion of the visual field. Demonstration Box 10-5 shows how this is done.

In Demonstration 10-5, you should have noticed that the pattern of double images is different depending on whether the unfused image is in front of or in back of the target you fixated. In the demonstration we defined these

---

DEMONSTRATION BOX 10-5   Double Images and Disparity

Find a piece of transparent colored material such as cellophane (any hue will work). Place it before your right eye. If you wear glasses, you can affix it to the frame over the lens in front of your right eye; if not, use a piece of tape to hold it to your forehead. Now align two index fingers directly in front of your nose with the closer finger about 10–20 cm from your nose and the farther finger about 8 cm behind the closer one.

Now that you have arranged the appropriate situation, fixate your nearer finger. However, simultaneously try to pay attention to what the far finger looks like. This is a pretty difficult feat to accomplish at first, but with practice you should be able to fixate one target while simultaneously paying attention to what is going on beyond the fixated area. When you fixate the near target, you will notice that two images of the far target will be seen. The fact that one eye is viewing the image through a colored filter should help make the presence of double images beyond the fixation point more apparent. If you switch your fixation to the farther object, the closer of the two targets will appear as a double image. Targets that lie away from the area surrounding the point of fixation are not fused into a single image. They produce *disparate* retinal images. Disparate, unfused images are always present in the visual field; however, we are usually not aware of them unless forced to attend to them as in this demonstration.

Once you have become comfortable with this procedure, fixate the near target and then close your right eye. You should notice that the image of the far target (the uncolored image) appears to lie to the left of the nearer, fixated object. Now close the left eye and open the right and you will notice the opposite. The image of the far target (the colored image) now appears to lie to the right of the closer, fixated target. The fact that the right eye is seeing the right disparate image and the left eye is seeing the left disparate image means that, when both eyes are open, the far target is seen in *uncrossed disparity*. The opposite will happen if you change your fixation to the far target. Now the closer object appears as *diplopic* (double). If you once again alternately close each eye, you will notice that the right eye is now seeing the image that lies to the left of the fixated target (the colored image), while the left eye is viewing the image that lies to the right. In the case of double images that lie closer to us than the point of fixation, we have a situation of *crossed disparity*. As the text explains, these differences in disparity may be a cue to distance.

patterns as **crossed** versus **uncrossed disparity.** Objects more distant than the point of fixation are seen in uncrossed disparity, whereas closer objects are seen with crossed disparity. Hence, we can use the type of double image as a cue to relative distance. Only objects at about the same distance as the target we are fixating will be fused and seen singly. When we map out all the points where targets are at about the same convergence or fixation distance in visual space, we trace out an imaginary curved plane called the **horopter.** A narrow region on either side of this hypothetical plane includes all points in visual space that are fused into single images. It is called **Panum's area.** Figure 10-13 contains a diagram of the horopter and

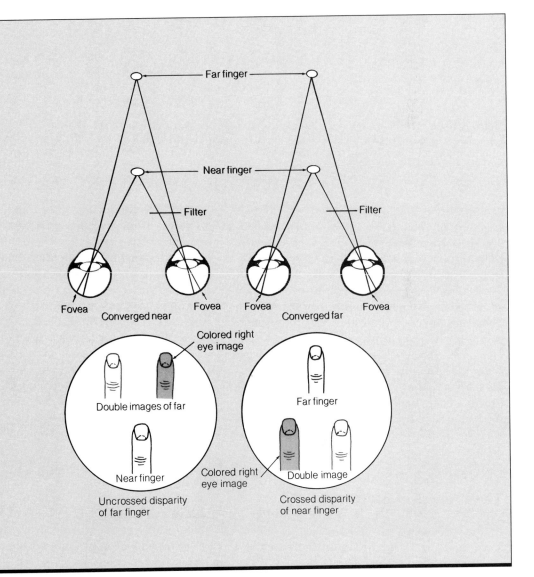

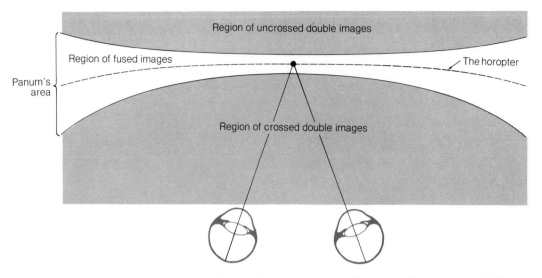

Figure 10-13 *The horopter and Panum's area for one fixation distance. The regions of fusion and disparate images are shown. Crossed disparity is present at distances closer to the observer than the fixation distance; uncrossed disparity is present beyond the fixation distance. The presence of disparate images may provide a cue to distance.*

Panum's area. The size and shape of Panum's area actually changes a bit with varying fixation distances. However, it always remains the zone in the visual field where the disparate images are seen as fused into a single object.

The process of fusion has also been looked at in terms of **corresponding retinal points.** These are areas on the retina that represent a common direction or location according to the map of the visual field represented in the visual areas of the brain. The foveae of the two eyes are corresponding retinal points, and according to this conceptualization, the horopter represents the zone in visual space that stimulates corresponding retinal points for one fixation distance.

The Process of Stereopsis

In the 1830s two physicists, Charles Wheatstone and Sir David Brewster, independently created a technique to recreate the impression of depth from flat pictures using only the binocular disparity cue (see Wade, 1984). Basically, this involves recreating the disparate views each eye would see and representing them to the eyes in the form of drawings or photographs. Thus, in Figure 10-14A, we have two rods at different distances from the observer. If we drew the image each eye sees, we would get something like Figure 10-14B. Notice that the images are disparate, since the rods are more widely separated in the right eye's image than in the image in the left eye. The resulting images are viewed in an optical instrument known as a **stereoscope,** which places different stimuli into the two eyes simultaneously, as shown in Figure 10-14C. When this is done, the disparate images fuse, and the objects are seen as if they were an actual three-dimensional scene. For a period of time, every Victorian living room had a stereoscope and a set of travel pictures of famous places that had

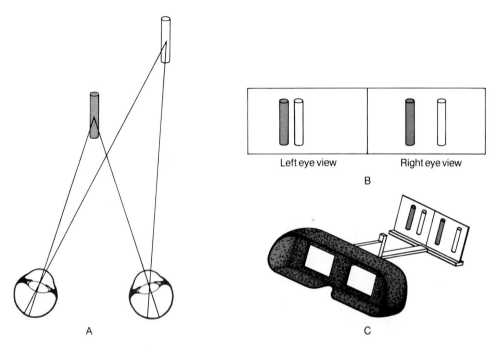

Left eye view   Right eye view

B

A   C

Figure 10-14 *Disparate retinal images.* (A) *The two retinal images of a scene are different because the two eyes view the world from slightly different directions.* (B) *A stereogram is a flat representation that mimics the differences between the two retinal images.* (C) *A stereogram is viewed in a stereoscope that allows for the separate but simultaneous stimulation of the two eyes. The phenomenon is called* stereopsis.

been taken using a two-lensed camera. This produced the "visual magic" of depth from flat images.

Understanding how stereopsis is achieved is more difficult than setting up the conditions that allow us to see binocular depth. Several computational approaches have been used for this problem, most of which involve selecting a particular location in space and then comparing and computing the relative positions of parts of the images. From such computations, it was hoped that the relative depth of the objects being viewed could be derived (for example, Marr & Poggio, 1979; Mayhew & Frisby, 1980). Although these approaches are interesting, they have not yet provided a "breakthrough" conceptualization. However, as will

be seen later, they do provide some descriptively useful suggestions.

The most provocative findings about stereopsis have come from direct physiological measurement. The first important results appeared in the late 1960s, when investigators began to find disparity-tuned detectors in the visual cortex of the cat (Bishop & Pettigrew, 1986). These detectors are neurons that are finely tuned to small differences in the relative horizontal placement of images in the two eyes (Bishop, 1981). For example, suppose no disparity is present in the images of the two eyes and a particular cell responds maximally to this condition. This neuron would represent a spatial position that lies on the horopter, or the zone of fused images in external space. In a like manner, other neurons may be tuned to particular disparities that represent locations in space that lie in front of or behind the horopter. This means that rather large populations of cortical neurons would be needed to represent all the possible disparity values in the visual scene.

It is now clear that the mere existence of disparity-tuned detectors is not enough to explain stereoscopic depth perception. The problem is illustrated in Demonstration Box 10-6, which contains a random-dot stereoscopic display. These displays were first introduced by Julesz (1964, 1971), who used them to demonstrate the notion of **global stereopsis,** or the perception of depth in the absence of monocular shape or form. If you follow the instructions in Demonstration Box 10-6, you will see a dotted square floating in front of the background of random dots. This perception comes about because of disparity cues built into the dot patterns. Figure 10-15 shows how this disparity, which consists of a horizontal shift in a group of these random dots, is created.

You might suppose that since disparity is built into the random-dot stimulus, neurons tuned for such information should be capable of detecting depth from these arrays. However, it is not that simple, mainly because the stimulus is composed of identical dot elements rather than discrete and identifiable contours. If stereopsis is based on the action of disparity-tuned detectors, each of which responds to one disparity value in the array, any dot potentially could be combined with any other dot. Each of the many possible combinations would produce a different depth perception. The task of the visual system is to find the dots in one eye that correspond to the same dots in the other eye—computational researchers call this solving the **correspondence problem.** To solve this problem, we must have a method of eliminating or avoiding false combinations and selecting only correct disparity pairs.

Computational theorists have proposed very sophisticated computer programs to do exactly this. Many of these are based on the idea that disparity detectors tuned to the same disparity mutually facilitate one another, whereas those of different disparities inhibit one another (Burt & Julesz, 1980; Marr, 1982; Mayhew & Frisby, 1980). Mathematically it can be shown that with a population of detectors working together in this fashion, only one depth solution would be common to this facilitory-inhibitory process and only one global stereoscopic view would be seen (Julesz & Schumer, 1981). Together, these programs have come to be called **cooperative algorithms** for achieving stereopsis in the absence of familiar shapes and forms.

In this instance, computational theorists seem to have reached a solution similar to that suggested by physiological investigators. Both attempt to explain the random-dot stereo problem by assuming that neurons tuned to the same disparity cooperate, whereas those tuned to different disparities inhibit each other. For many years this idea was only a theoretical possibility, based on Hubel & Weisel's (1962) observation that the receptive fields of most cells in the striate cortex (V1) could be stimulated through either eye (Mustillo, 1985). Since the 1970s, however, this idea has received increasing support from electrophysiological recordings made on alert, behaving monkeys. Gian Poggio and his colleagues (Poggio & Fischer, 1977; Poggio & Poggio, 1984; Poggio & Talbot, 1981) have been able to identify two classes of disparity-sensitive neurons in the striate cortex. One type of neuron is sensitive to disparities tuned over a narrow range about the fixation point; the other type is sensitive to crossed (signaling "near") and uncrossed (signaling "far") disparities. Within each of these classes, cells can be further subdivided into those with excitatory responses and those with inhibitory responses. For instance, a cell with

DEMONSTRATION BOX 10-6   Random-Dot Stereograms and Global Stereopsis

You may demonstrate how depth cues can bring about the perception of binocular form by using the accompanying figure. You will need a pocket mirror, which should be placed on the dotted center line of Figure B while you hold your head as shown in Figure A. Adjust the images until the two views seem to overlap and the frames around the outside seem to be at the same distance. Viewing it in this way, you will see a square form emerge, floating above the background, created completely by the depth cue of binocular disparity. Notice that this square cannot be seen in either monocular view alone.

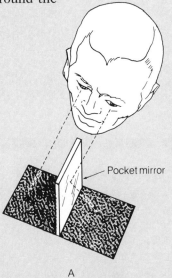

Pocket mirror

A

B

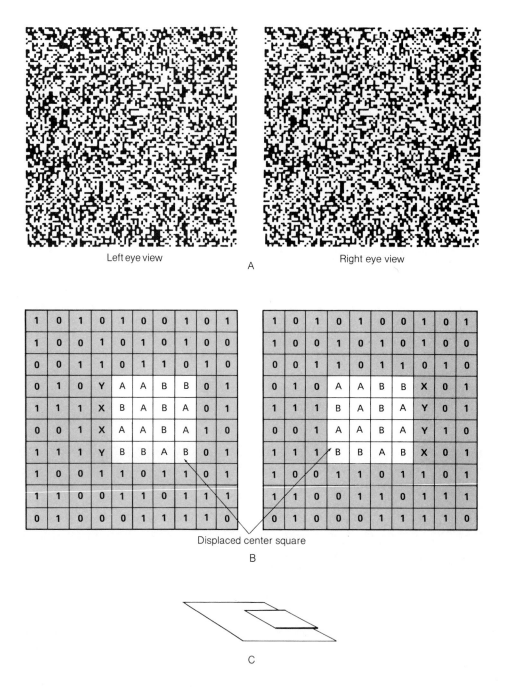

Figure 10-15 *Figure* A *is a random-dot stereogram. Figure* B *shows how* A *is constructed, and* C *illustrates that a central square is seen floating above the background when the two views are combined in a stereoscope (from* Foundations of Cyclopean Perception *by B. Julesz, Copyright 1971 by the University of Chicago Press).*

an excitatory response to crossed disparity will give an inhibitory response to uncrossed disparities, and vice versa. Thus, all of the components for a cooperative algorithm for stereo depth appear to be present already in the first cortical region of visual processing (Aslin & Dumais, 1980; DeValois & DeValois, 1980).

Since the introduction of the random-dot stereo display, most of the research on stereo depth has focused on this form of stimulus (Regan, Frisby, Poggio, Schor, & Tyler, 1990). One of its main advantages over more traditional stimuli is that it completely bypasses the need for monocular form perception. The process of stereo fusion can be understood without first having to explain shape and form identification processes (Julesz, 1986). Another very important advantage of this stimulus is that it ensures that all perceived forms are being assembled in the visual cortex after information from the two eyes has been combined. (Recall from Chapter 3 that information from the two eyes is still in separate layers at the lateral geniculate nucleus but is combined in the primary visual cortex, V1.) This same random-dot stimulus allows researchers to determine whether perceptual phenomena other than depth perception are occurring prior to, or only after, visual information has reached the cortex. Among the phenomena that have been studied in this way are visual illusions (Papert, 1961), visual aftereffects (Julesz, 1986; Regan & Beverly, 1973; Tyler, 1975), and apparent motion (Julesz & Payne, 1968).

INTERACTION OF DEPTH CUES

Although each of the cues for depth that we have discussed is sufficient to give the conscious impression of a three-dimensional arrangement in space, the accuracy of our perception of distance often depends on the interaction of a number of cues. Under normal conditions, if a cue such as interposition suggests that your friend Fred is standing closer to you than your friend Maria, other cues, such as relative size, height in the plane, and binocular disparity, will tend to confirm this relationship. Chaotic and conflicting cues, such as those shown in William Hogarth's 1754 engraving *False Perspective* (Figure 10-16), virtually never occur in "real world" settings.

How do cues for depth combine? Jameson and Hurvich (1959) suggested that an observer's sensitivity to a difference in distance when several cues are available is approximately the arithmetic sum of the sensitivities obtained with each cue alone. This has now been demonstrated experimentally by several investigators. For example, one study showed that information from binocular disparity and linear perspective added together in the final judgment of perceived depth (van der Meer, 1979). Another found consistently additive relations among depth specified by relative size, height in the plane, occlusion, and motion parallax (Bruno & Cutting, 1988). Still another study found additive relations between motion parallax and binocular disparity (Rogers & Collett, 1989). Although the exact form of the addition rule has yet to be determined (Massaro, 1988), it is certain that the more cues are available, and the more consistent they are, the stronger is the perception of depth (Berbaum, Tharp, & Mroczek, 1983).

One important consequence of the interaction of depth cues is their ability to provide unique information about dynamic events. For example, consider what happens to the image on your retina as you watch an automobile pass by a house that lies on the other side of the highway from you. One cue to the relative depths of these objects is, of course, occlusion—parts of the more distant house will be only partially visible for some period of time and perhaps entirely occluded by the car for a brief period. Another cue is given by motion—the car will be moving at a faster speed on your

Figure 10-16 *Ambiguity of depth cues gives a confusing, difficult interpretation to a scene, as shown in Hogarth's 1754 engraving* False Perspective. *The more you study this figure, the more contradictory depth cues you find.*

retina than the house as you move your head. However, the combination of these two cues produces an important emergent property with regard to the visible contours of the automobile and the house. Portions of the surface of the house will disappear behind the auto as it moves past the house (*deletion*), and then portions of the surface will again become visible when it passes (*accretion*). This emergent property of **surface deletion** and **surface accretion** can itself be a powerful cue to depth, even when defined only with random-dot displays. The stimuli that are deleted or accreted over time are perceived to lie in a plane behind the dots that may move but remain visible (Craton & Yonas, 1990; Kaplan, 1969).

Another depth cue that emerges from a combination of simpler cues is that of **stereo-motion,** or a difference in the relative rates of motion in the two eyes (Regan & Beverley, 1973, 1979; Regan et al., 1990). If an object such as a baseball is hurtling toward you on a direct collision course with your head, the edge of the ball that projects onto your left eye will be moving across the retina at exactly the same rate, albeit in the opposite direction, as the edge of the ball that projects to your right eye. On the other hand, if the ball is coming toward you at an angle, such as might happen if it were to miss your head narrowly, then the rate of motion in one eye will be faster than that in the other. Thus, this cue involves a comparison between motion in the two eyes. Interestingly, investigators have found neurons in the striate cortex of cats and monkeys that are sensitive to leftward motion in one eye at the same time that they are sensitive to rightward motion in the other eye (Cynader & Regan, 1978; Poggio & Talbot, 1981). In fact, some neurons are tuned sharply enough to be able to detect objects on a "near miss" collision course, while others are tuned to detect "a hit in the head" (Regan et al., 1990).

A final consideration regarding the interaction of depth cues is the possibility that absolute and relative depth cues may help calibrate each other. For example, binocular disparity is most effective as a relative depth cue, indicating whether one target is nearer or farther than another, rather than how close either is to an observer. The geometry of the situation, however, is complicated by the fact that if we keep the relative distance between two targets constant but move both targets farther away from the observer, the amount of disparity in the image grows smaller. Nonetheless, our perception of the relative difference in the depth of these targets remains the same, a phenomenon sometimes called *stereoscopic depth constancy* (Ono & Comerford, 1977; Wallach, Gillam, & Cardillo, 1979). Apparently, this adjustment of the relative depth obtained from binocular disparity comes about as a consequence of using other cues for absolute distance. In other words, we recalibrate our interpretation of the magnitude of depth difference signaled by a particular amount of binocular disparity by using other information about absolute depth (Cormack, 1984).

The phenomenon of stereoscopic depth constancy reveals a problem with depth perception originally noticed by Brunswick (1952, 1956). He argued that each separate distance and depth cue is ambiguous under certain conditions, such as those depicted in Figure 10-16, and that sometimes any single cue may lead us to an incorrect interpretation of depth or distance within a scene. The importance we assign to a particular cue will be determined by its reliability and our past experience with its accuracy. Simply shifting our attention to a given depth cue seems to increase its power in determining how we perceive three-dimensional space (Kawabata, 1986). If we accept such an argument, we are, in effect, accepting a constructive theory of depth perception, in which our ability to decipher and to combine depth cues may be a learned ability that becomes more efficient with experience. It is on the issue of whether there is a learned component in the perception of depth that direct and constructive theories of perception have focused much of their argument. In the older literature this has been referred to as the *nativist versus empiricist* question (Hochberg, 1972). The nativists argue that these perceptual abilities and our capacity to use them are inborn and automatically invoked by stimulation, whereas the empiricists maintain that interaction with the world, through which we learn about its properties and organization, is crucial to our spatial awareness and abilities. We will consider this issue briefly in the last section of this chapter.

PERCEPTION OF DIRECTION

Three-dimensional depth is only one aspect of our perception of space. The perception of the location of an object will also include its direction relative to our bodies. We integrate two types of directional judgments in a complex fashion to give us our sense of up, down, right, and left (Howard, 1982). The first, called **bodycentric** direction, uses as a reference location the midline of the body, an imaginary vertical line parallel to the spine passing vertically through the navel. This can be contrasted to **headcentric** direction, where the midline of the head is used as another reference location for right and left. This is an imaginary vertical line running up and down, centered on the nose. Of course, bodycentric and headcentric directions are potentially different, since it is possible to rotate your head independently of your body. The distinction between these two aspects of direction is shown in Figure 10-17.

Most of the research on direction has concentrated on one aspect of headcentric perception we can refer to as the *visual straight ahead.* Generally speaking, we tend to define our notion of "straight ahead" as a direction in

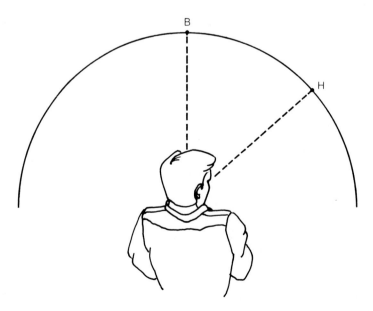

Figure 10-17 *The distinction between bodycentric and headcentric directions. Point B is straight ahead of the body midline, whereas H is straight ahead of the midline of the head. Notice, however, that these two straight ahead directions can be two different points in visual space.*

front of us, oriented around the midline of the head, regardless of eye position. The visual **egocenter** is the position in the head that serves as our reference point for the determination of headcentric straight ahead. In some respects, this is a very complex judgment, since we seem to ignore the directions in which the eyes are pointing and to compute a straight ahead that seems to be located in front of the middle of the head. Researchers often refer to this compromise direction as the location pointed to by a hypothetical **Cyclopean eye,** a name derived from the mythical Greek giant Cyclops who had a single eye in the middle of his forehead. Demonstration Box 10-7 shows

how you can experience for yourself the referring of the visual direction of the two eyes to this common egocenter.

Eye Movements and Direction

A number of variables affect our sense of the direction of objects. Stimulus factors are, of course, important; the more stimuli available, the more stable our directional judgments, which accounts for the fact that our ability to judge direction is much less stable in the dark. Also, specific visual configurations influence the judgment of direction. For example, if you

---

DEMONSTRATION BOX 10-7   The Common Visual Direction of the Two Eyes

You can experience how the visual directions of the two eyes are referred to one common direction in the center of the head. First, take a sheet of stiff cardboard (20×27 cm will do) and place it in front of the eyes as shown in the figure. Put a dot in the middle of the far end of the cardboard and stare at it while a friend marks the exact center position of each of your pupils on the end of the cardboard closest to your face. Next, draw lines from these marked points until they form an angle, or V (as pictured). Finally, reposition the cardboard in front of your face at a point slightly below your eyes. Now, stare at the far point where the two drawn lines intersect, and you should see, in addition to the two lines you have drawn, an additional, somewhat more shadowy line running between them. This "new" line is the fusion of the views of the two eyes and should appear to point directly at a spot close to the midline of the head. This demonstrates that, although the direction of each eye's view is different (as shown by the

spatial separation between the two drawn lines converging on the far point on which you are fixating), the visual direction of the combined binocular view is referred to a common point between the eyes. This point is called the *egocenter,* or the *Cyclopean eye.*

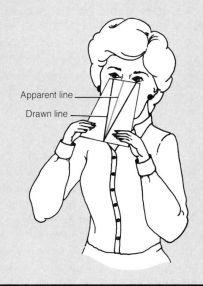

Apparent line

Drawn line

are looking at a square or rectangle that is not exactly centered in your visual field, you will tend to judge the straight-ahead direction in terms of the center of this displaced square or rectangle. It is as if the perceptual system confuses what is straight ahead of the observer with what is centered with respect to the other contents in the visual field (Roelofs, 1935). However, nonvisual factors also play a role in directional localization.

In the previous section, we saw how eye movements, in the form of convergence and divergence, conveyed information about the distances of objects. It would also seem reasonable that feedback from eye movements could help in determining the visual direction of an object. At least two sources of eye movement information could be used to compute the direction of an object in space. The first arises from the movement commands sent to the eye muscles (the **efference copy**); the second (the **afference copy**) arises from feedback from the eye movement itself. One study examined the influence of the efference copy by having subjects judge "straight ahead" while pressing a finger lightly against the side of their eyeball—hence having the eye moved without efference from the eye muscles (Bridgeman & Graziano, 1989). Observers showed very little influence of this manipulation when judging "straight ahead" in a normal visual environment, but their judgments were considerably biased in the direction of the finger press when the judgments were made viewing a blank field with no landmarks. Although controversy exists about whether efferent or afferent information is more important (for example, Matin, 1982; Shebilske, 1976; Stark & Bridgeman, 1983), it seems clear that eye movement information does play a role in localizing targets in space.

Many examples demonstrate how eye movements affect our localization of targets. Target localization seems to be associated with information about where the eyes are pointing at any given moment. Imagine that the fovea of

the eye serves as a reference point. In the absence of other information, you localize a target as being in the direction your fovea is pointing when you try to look at the target. This means that if you accurately image the target on your fovea, you will accurately perceive the direction of the target. If, on the contrary, you inaccurately point your eyes, such as when the eyes lag behind a moving target you are trying to track (see Chapter 13), you will inaccurately localize the target. A good deal of evidence indicates that this is exactly what happens (for example, Coren, Bradley, Hoenig, & Girgus, 1975; Festinger & Easton, 1974; Honda, 1984; Mack & Herman, 1972).

The role of eye movements in target localization can be quite subtle. For example, there is a suggestion that the eye movement does not actually have to be made; the eye movement you compute in order to move the eye at some later time may bias your perception of direction (for example, Coren, 1986; Hershberger, 1987). Furthermore, eye movement information both influences and is influenced by other aspects of localization behavior. Thus, Mather and Fisk (1985) were able to show that the information obtained from looking at a target can aid in accurately pointing to the target. Conversely, information obtained from pointing can assist in accurately looking at other targets.

Eye Dominance and Perceived Direction

We have considered movements of either eye to be interchangeable, but some data suggest that the two eyes are not used equivalently in the computation of visual direction. Before we consider this evidence, it is important to understand that we habitually do some tasks with one eye. In sighting tasks where only one eye can be used at a time (such as in looking through a telescope), 65% of all observers con-

DEMONSTRATION BOX 10-8   Sighting Dominance and the Straight-Ahead Direction

The visual straight ahead may depend on a single eye (Porac & Coren, 1976, 1981; Walls, 1951). Try the following demonstration to see how this works. Stand in front of a wall at a distance of about 3 m. Pick a point on the wall that is directly in front of you (a small crack or bump will do). Now, with both eyes open, *quickly* stretch out your arm and align your fingertip with the point on the distant wall. When the alignment has been completed, alternately close each eye. You will find that the point on the distant wall will shift out of alignment for one of the eyes. However, the other eye will seem to be aligned with the point on the wall whether one or both eyes are opened. The eye that maintains the alignment is called the *sighting-dominant eye.* You will notice that regardless of which hand you use to perform the alignment, you will tend to line up a near (your fingertip) and a distant (the point on the wall) target in terms of the same eye. The presence of a sighting-dominant eye, and our tendency to make a straight-ahead alignment in terms of this eye, indicates that the locus of the egocentric straight-ahead direction may be shifted toward the side of the sighting-dominant eye.

sistently use their right eye, whereas the remainder consistently use their left (Coren, Porac, & Duncan, 1981). The preferred eye for such tasks is usually called the **sighting-dominant eye** (Porac and Coren, 1981; Ruggieri, Cei, Ceridono, & Bergerone, 1980). Demonstration Box 10-8 shows how you can determine which eye is your sighting-dominant eye.

For the purposes of our discussion of the perception of direction, sighting dominance is important because the visual direction associated with straight ahead is more strongly influenced by the dominant eye (Porac & Coren, 1976, 1981). This does not mean that only one eye is used to determine visual direction (Ono & Weber, 1981). Rather, it means that the location of the egocenter, or Cyclopean eye, is biased toward the side of the sighting-dominant eye (Barbeito, 1981). For instance, Porac and Coren (1986) tested observers in a totally darkened room and had them set a point of light so it appeared to be visually straight ahead. Whether observers used only one or both eyes they tended to set the point so it was closer to the side of the dominant eye, rather than midway between the two eyes.

DEVELOPMENT OF SPACE PERCEPTION

One of the most common ways to assess whether there is a constructive aspect to space perception is to observe the behavior of young organisms when they are placed in situations that call on their abilities to perceive distance or direction. Since infants and young animals have limited experience with the world, their abilities to deal with such situations should shed some light on the role of inborn versus learned components in the perception of visual space.

Species' Differences

The evidence is quite clear that in certain simpler animals, the perception of direction and distance is inborn. For example, in salamanders it is possible to rotate the eye 180 deg, thus inverting the retina. When this is done, the salamanders consistently swim and snap in the opposite direction when presented with a food lure (Sperry, 1943). Since the same results occur when similar operations are performed during the animals' embryonic stage, it is clear that visual direction is related innately to the location of retinal stimulation in this species (Stone, 1960). Similarly, immediately after birth chicks peck at small objects with reasonable accuracy. When experimenters optically displaced the images of the targets to one side (using special lenses attached to hoods), the chicks proceeded to peck systematically to one side. This pattern of inaccuracy showed little improvement over time, suggesting that this response to the apparent direction of stimuli was not changeable by experience (Hess, 1950). In higher animals, such as mammals, experience may play a larger role.

To allow more exact determination of which factors may be influenced by experience, investigators frequently use controlled-rearing procedures, such as rearing an animal in total darkness from birth until testing. Such dark-rearing eliminates all externally generated visual experience. If experience with various visual depth cues is necessary for the development of normal depth perception, these dark-reared animals should have measurable deficits when required to respond to distance cues. If depth perception simply matures as the animal ages, then restricting the animal's visual experience should not affect its behavior, and the only important variable should be its chronological age.

A simple and popular procedure for measuring depth perception in young animals uses an apparatus called the **visual cliff** (Walk and Gibson, 1961). A diagram of a typical visual cliff arrangement is shown in Figure 10-18. Basically it consists of two sections, divided by a *start platform*. Each section provides a different depth impression. The *shallow* side is a piece of glass that lies directly over a patterned surface. The *deep* side has the same type of patterned surface but looks like a sharp drop since the surface is placed at some distance

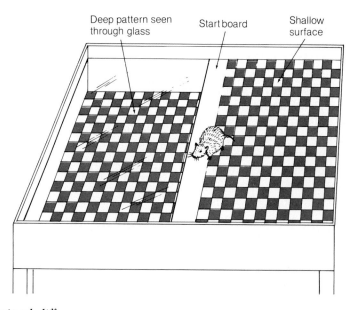

Deep pattern seen through glass   Start board   Shallow surface

Figure 10-18   *The visual cliff.*

below the glass. For testing, a young animal is placed on the central starting platform that separates the apparently shallow and deep surfaces. It is assumed that from this position the subject can see that the shallow side is safe, whereas the deep side, with its simulated cliff-like drop-off, would be perceived as being dangerous. Investigators make the presumption that if the animal consistently chooses the shallow over the deep side, then it can perceive the difference in apparent depth and is attempting to avoid a fall.

A number of different types of animals have been tested on the visual cliff, including rats, chickens, turtles, goats, sheep, pigs, cats, dogs, monkeys, and humans (Walk & Gibson, 1961). In all cases, even when testing very young animals, subjects showed a preference for the shallow over the deep side of the cliff. There were some interesting species differences, however, which seemed to be related to the habitat features of the natural environment for the various species (Sloane, Shea, Procter, & Dewsbury, 1978). For instance, aquatic animals, such as certain turtles, did not show the marked preference for the shallow side that the other, more landbound species displayed. Perhaps the survival value of cliff avoidance may not be as pronounced in animals that spend much of their lives swimming, since changes in depth of water are not as perilous as sudden sharp drops on land.

Experience and Depth Perception

Although the cross-species differences observed in depth perception are of interest, the visual cliff apparatus has been used primarily to generate data concerning the development of depth perception. A combination of controlled rearing followed by observations of behavior on the visual cliff has been the experimental technique most commonly used in animal studies. In general, the findings have suggested that experience and innate factors interact to produce an animal's ability to perceive depth. For example, when cats or rats are reared in the dark, they show little depth discrimination on the visual cliff when first tested. However, as they receive more and more experience in a lighted world, their depth discrimination rapidly improves until they are indistinguishable from normally reared animals (Walk & Gibson, 1961; Tees & Midgley, 1978).

When the visual experience takes place also seems important. There seem to be **sensitive periods** in an animal's development, meaning that there is an age range during which depriving an animal of a particular type of visual experience will produce the largest perceptual deficits (Aslin, 1981b; Mitchell, 1981; Timney, 1985). For instance, a study by Tees (1974) shows how deprivation of visual experience during a sensitive period can affect later depth perception. Dark-reared rats were compared to light-reared rats on their preference for the deep versus the shallow side of the visual cliff. The amount of time the animals were dark-reared was varied, and in addition, the strength of the depth information was varied by changing the distance to the bottom of the deep side of the visual cliff. In this study, the age of the animal, the amount of distance information, and the amount of visual experience all interacted. It was only among the animals that had been dark-reared for a comparatively long time (60 to 90 days) that the effects of rearing conditions revealed themselves. For these animals, although depth could be discriminated when the drop-off was large, there was an insensitivity to weaker distance cues. These data indicate that there might be inborn components in the ability of rats to discriminate depth on the visual cliff. These are probably sharpened through experience with depth cues in the environment, a finding that has been supported by other research as well (for example, Kaye, Mitchell, & Cynader, 1982).

The developmental time course and the effects of experience seem to be different for the various depth cues. Binocular depth perception develops quite early, since evidence for the use of binocular disparity for a depth cue may be found in 3- or 4-month-old infants (Birch, Shimojo, & Held, 1985; Braddick et al., 1980; Hutz & Bechtoldt, 1980; Petrig, Julesz, Kropfl, Baumartner, & Anliker, 1981). Infants at this age are too young to crawl and cannot be tested on the visual cliff, so other techniques must be used. For example, Fox, Aslin, Shea, and Dumais (1980) presented random-dot stereograms, similar to those in Figure 10-15, to infants between 2 and 5 months of age. When these patterns were viewed with special glasses, these infants saw a square floating in front of a background only if they could combine the disparate information from the two eyes' views. (You saw in Demonstration Box 10-6 that such patterns are meaningless unless you can make use of the disparity cues hidden in each monocular view.) This square was then moved. When infants could see the square in depth, they tended to follow it with their eyes.

An alternative technique for measuring depth perception in somewhat older infants capitalizes on the fact that infants older than 4 months tend to reach for objects that appear to be near them (Granrud, Yonas, & Petterson, 1984). Results using this technique verified other findings that binocular depth perception is present by 4 months of age (Granrud, 1986), suggesting either an innate or a rapidly learned process. This is consistent with earlier animal work, which suggested that the use of monocular cues for depth is much more dependent on specific experience than is binocular depth perception (Eichengreen, Coren, & Nachmias, 1966).

The ability to use kinetic depth information seems to develop at about the same time the ability to use binocular depth information appears, at roughly 3 to 5 months of age (Kell-

man, 1984; Owsley, 1983; Yonas & Granrud, 1985b). One biologically important aspect of depth perception—sensitivity to information about object motion toward the body (which may indicate an impending collision)—seems to be present at an even earlier age. It has been measured at ages as young as 2 to 3 weeks (Ball & Vurpillot, 1976; Yonas, 1981). Even at this young age, infants will blink their eyes when presented with an object that seems to be moving close enough to hit them in the head.

Studies that have looked at sensitivity to pictorial depth cues have shown a slower developmental process; it lags by about 3 to 4 months. For example, several studies have shown that 6- to 7-month-old infants respond to linear perspective information (Arterberry & Yonas, 1989; Kaufman, Maland, & Yonas, 1981; Yonas, Cleaves, & Pettersen, 1978), familiar size (Granrud, Haake, & Yonas, 1985), texture gradients (Arterberry & Yonas, 1989; Yonas & Granrud, 1986) and concavity–convexity specified by shading (Granrud & Yonas, 1985). Use of more complex cues, such as the perception of relative depth in a picture based on the direction of shadows cast in the pictorial representation, may not appear until the age of 3 years (Yonas, Goldsmith, & Hallstrom, 1978).

Developmental studies indicate that the perception of depth and distance cannot be fully understood unless some components can be explained by inborn factors, whereas others may require active experience to emerge. These studies suggest that adhering strictly to either a direct perception or constructive perception viewpoint might be too limiting. Innate components of perception must mature, and certain types of experience can help or hinder the achievement of a high level of perceptual functioning. Some aspects of depth perception seem to be given directly, and others require memory and experience to allow them to function properly.

The railroad passes through Panum's area

GLOSSARY

The following definitions are specific to their use in this book.

Absolute distance   The distance of an object from the observer.

Accommodation   The change in focus of the lens of the eye, which may serve as a depth cue.

Aerial perspective   A distance cue in which objects appear hazy, less distinct, and bluer the farther away they are, because of the interaction of light with dust and moisture particles in the air.

Afference copy   Information about eye movement arising from the contractions of the muscles that move the eye.

Attached shadow   A shading pattern on an object that is determined by the shape of the object itself. For example, a ball that is illuminated from above will appear to be lighter on top and darker on the bottom.

Binocular   Pertaining to two eyes.

Binocular disparity   The difference in the monocular views of the two eyes.

Bodycentric Direction with the midline of the body used as a reference point.

Cast shadow A shading pattern that is produced when one object falls between the light source and another object or surface. For example, a ball that lies between the light and a surface will cast an elliptical shadow on the surface.

Computational theories Theories involving the presumption that certain perceived qualities must be computed from stimulus information and that these computations can be precisely described mathematically.

Constructive theories Theories maintaining that perception may involve the integration of several sources of information, and may be affected by cognitive factors and experience.

Convergence The inward rotation of both eyes toward the nose as a fixated object becomes closer.

Cooperative algorithm A method for solving the correspondence problem, based on the idea that disparity detectors tuned to the same disparity will cooperatively excite one another, whereas those with different disparities will inhibit one another.

Correspondence problem The task of identifying the elements in one eye that correspond to the same elements in the other eye, when each eye is given a slightly different view of the world.

Corresponding retinal points Areas in the two retinas that share a common visual direction when the two monocular inputs are processed in the brain.

Crossed disparity A cue for relative distance, where, when double images are present, the unfused image in the right eye appears on the left and that in the left eye on the right.

Cues Features of visual stimuli that prompt the perception of depth or distance.

Cyclopean eye An imaginary point midway between the eyes thought to be used as a reference point for the straight ahead direction.

Diplopia Double vision.

Direct perception The idea that all of the information needed for the final conscious percept is in the stimulus array and is apprehended without the need for computation.

Divergence The outward rotation of both eyes away from the nose as a fixated object becomes more distant.

Efference copy Information about eye movement arising from the commands issued to the ocular musculature to rotate the eye.

Egocenter The position in the head that serves as the reference point for the determination of head-centered straight ahead.

Egocentric localization The awareness of where our bodies are positioned relative to other objects in the external environment.

Familiar size The known or remembered size of an object.

Fusion The process by which disparate views are synthesized into one percept.

Global stereopsis Stereopsis that is not dependent on local contour elements (as in random-dot stereograms).

Headcentric Direction judged using the midline of the head as a reference point.

Height in the (picture) plane A cue for distance referring to the location of an object relative to the horizon.

Horopter An imaginary plane in external space used to describe the region of fused images.

Intelligent perception The presumption that cognitive processes and experience can affect perception.

Interposition The depth cue based on the blocking of an object from view by another closer object. Also called *occlusion*.

Kinetic depth effect The perception of the three-dimensional shape of an object based on cues generated by the object's motion.

Linear perspective The apparent convergence of physically parallel lines as they recede into the distance.

Monocular cues Depth cues requiring only one eye to be used.

Motion parallax The apparent relative motion of objects in the visual field as the observer moves the head or body.

Object-relative localizations The estimation of the relative positions of objects (other than the observer) within the environment.

Occlusion *See* Interposition.

Panum's area The region around the horopter where all images in space are fused.

Physiological cues *See* Structural cues.

Pictorial depth cues Cues for distance that can be found in photographs and pictures.

Reduction conditions An experimental procedure in which an attempt is made to eliminate or reduce most depth cues.

Relative brightness   A depth cue in which the brighter of two otherwise identical objects will be seen as closer.

Relative distance   Distances of objects relative to one another.

Retinal image size   A potential depth cue based on the size of the image on the retina.

Sensitive period   An age range during which the development of a perceptual ability may be strongly influenced by the presence or absence of relevant stimulation or experience.

Sighting-dominant eye   The eye whose use is preferred in monocular tasks such as looking through a telescope.

Stereomotion   A dynamic cue to depth based on the relative rates of motion in the two eyes.

Stereopsis   The ability to see depth based solely on the disparity of the two retinal images.

Stereoscope   An optical instrument enabling two different images to stimulate the two eyes simultaneously to produce an effect of depth.

Structural cues   Depth and distance cues arising from adjustments of the eye in interaction with the visual stimulus. Also called *physiological cues.*

Surface deletion and **surface accretion**   An emergent property signaling relative depth between two objects. Portions of a more distant object's surface will be deleted (disappear) and then be accreted (reappear) as the nearer object moves past the more distant one.

Texture gradient   Distance cue based on variations in surface texture as a function of distance from the observer.

Uncrossed disparity   A cue for relative distance in which, when double images are present, the unfused image in the right eye appears on the right and that in the left eye on the left.

Vanishing point   In linear perspective, a point on the horizon at which converging parallel lines seem to meet.

Vergence movements   Movements of the eyes in which the two eyes move together but in opposite directions, either converging or diverging.

Visual cliff   A table with shallow and deep sides overlaid by a sheet of glass; used for measuring depth perception in young animals.

FORM

The Problem of Visual Form Perception

Contour Detection and Feature Extraction

Contour and Change

Contour Emergence

Feature Extraction

Perceptual Organization

Figure and Ground

Figural Grouping

• Figural Grouping by Texture

• Spatial Frequencies and Figural Grouping

Information, Symmetry, and Good Figures

Feature Integration Theory

Object Recognition and Identification

Recognition versus Identification

Data-Driven versus Conceptually Driven Processing

• Global versus Local Processing

• Integral versus Separable Stimuli

• Context and Identification

Theories of Object Identification

Pandemonium

Model-Based Identification

Identification-by-Components

Computational Theories

Chapter ... 11

When I lift my eyes from the paper on which I am writing I see the chairs and tables and walls of my room . . . I see, from my window, trees and meadows, and horses and oxen, and distant hills. I see each of its proper size, of its proper form, and at its proper distance; and these particulars appear as immediate transformations of the eye . . . How, then, is it that we receive accurate information, by the eye, of size and shape and distance?

John Stuart Mill (1829, p. 97)

*L*ook around you, as John Stuart Mill did. You will be struck, as he was, with how filled the perceptual world is with *objects*. When you enter your room, you see a desk, a chair, some books and so forth, not patches of light, brown, gray, red, and green, which make up the actual stimulus on your retina. You not only *see* these patches as objects, but also identify them as members of particular classes of objects, and can recall whether you have seen them before.

In this chapter, we tell you something of what we know about the perception of form. (Mill's other questions, about size and distance, are dealt with in Chapters 10 and 14, respectively.) First we will describe the information about the world that is present in the distribution of light on our retinas, and then we will describe how the visual system transforms that stimulation into perceptual objects. Finally, we will discuss how you recognize and identify these perceptual objects. In several places in this chapter, we will demonstrate the differences between the traditional psychological approach to the perception of form and the newer "computational" approach.

THE PROBLEM OF VISUAL FORM PERCEPTION

The eye receives information in the form of light reflected from objects and surfaces in the environment. The total of all the light from the environment that stimulates your eyes at any given moment is called the **visual field.** Figure 11-1 portrays the visual field as seen by the left eye of the physicist/psychologist Ernst Mach as he lay on the couch in his study in Prague, Czechoslovakia, sometime around 1885. Reflected light from the visual field forms a **retinal image,** consisting of a two-dimensional distribution of light of various intensities and wavelengths on the retina. The intensity and wavelength of each point of light in this image is determined by the combination of four general aspects of the environment and its relationship to the viewer, as is shown in Figure 11-2.

Figure 11-1 *The visual field as imaged in the left eye of Ernst Mach (based on Mach, 1959/1886).*

The first of these aspects, the **light source,** refers to the direction and intensity of the light-producing regions in the environment. For example, in a natural outdoor scene, there is only one primary source—the sun. All light reflected from the various objects in the environment originates from this source, although reflections of light from one surface to another may provide *secondary sources* of illumination. The light reflected to earth on a moonlit night is an example of such secondary light. An indoor scene, of course, may have more than one primary light source (for example, several light bulbs) and many secondary sources (such as reflecting walls).

A second factor that determines the nature of the retinal image is the **reflectance** properties of the various surfaces that come in contact with the light. As discussed in Chapter 5, some surfaces absorb light from one region of the spectrum more than from other regions, leading to the perception of differently colored surfaces. Thus, if one surface absorbs the short and middle wavelengths and reflects only the longer wavelengths, the portion of the retinal image that corresponds to this surface will contain only red-appearing light. In addition to these wavelength reflectance characteristics, surfaces differ in the total amount of light they absorb. Some surfaces are highly reflectant and thus look glossy or mirrorlike; others absorb much of the light and thus are matte or dull.

A third aspect is the **surface orientation** (relative to the light source and the viewer) of the various reflecting surfaces in the scene. Surface orientation is determined with reference to an imaginary line perpendicular to the surface, which is called the *surface normal.* For instance, a surface oriented for optimal light reflection would be one in which the angle

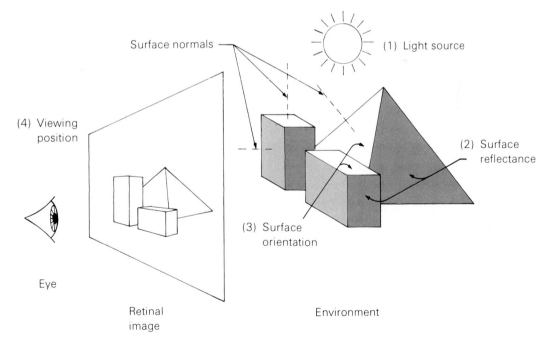

Figure 11-2 *Four properties of the visual environment that together determine the intensity and wavelength of each point in the retinal image:* (1) *Light source,* (2) *Reflectances,* (3) *Surface Orientations, and* (4) *Viewing Position. The surface normals are also noted for some surfaces.*

between the direction of the light source and the surface was exactly the same as the angle between the direction of the viewer and the surface normal. As these two angles be come more unequal, less and less light will be reflected from the objects onto the image. For example, the surface of the pyramid facing the eye in Figure 11-2 is reflecting more light to the eye than are the block surfaces facing the same way. This is because the angle between this surface and the light source is approximately equal to the angle between the surface and the eye.

The fourth aspect is the **viewing position,** specifically the relationship between the viewer and the scene. If Ernst Mach had left his couch and walked to the bookshelf on the side of the room, the retinal image projected from the room would have changed dramatically from that shown in Figure 11-1. This would occur despite the fact that the light sources, surface reflectance characteristics, and surface orientations had not changed at all relative to one another. Similarly, your own viewing position on the scene depicted in Figure 11-2 is quite different than that for the eye shown in the figure.

These four aspects of the viewing situation, then, determine the distribution of light in the retinal image of the viewer. It is at this place in the discussion that many people, including even some perception researchers, have been fooled into thinking that the problem of form perception is fairly straightforward. Their false reasoning goes something like this: If the two-dimensional retinal image is completely determined by the four features describing the three-dimensional world and the viewer's relationship to it that we have listed, then it should be possible to examine the image and decompose it in a way that will tell us the exact contribution of each of these properties to the final image. What this reasoning fails to take into account is that for any given retinal image, potentially an infinite number of scenes exist that could have produced it.

The ambiguity of the form information in the retinal image is shown in Figure 11-3. Suppose a viewer is looking at a wire hoop and that the image it casts in his eye is circular. On the basis of this information alone he really cannot say what the shape of the hoop is, since the same image would be cast by circular hoop viewed straight on; a tall, thin hoop tilted back; or a short, fat hoop tilted to the side. The orientation of the hoop relative to the viewing position combines with the shape of the object to determine the shape of the retinal image. Unless the viewer knows something about the orientation of the hoop relative to himself, the retinal image does not contain enough information to tell the difference between a glimpse of a circular or an oval hoop. This illustrates that the perception of an object's shape and the assumed viewing position are intertwined aspects of the observer's perceptual experience.

This process of getting from the flat patches of light that make up the retinal image to the world of objects about us is the major problem in the perception of visual form. What makes this problem so fascinating to study is that it is solved by our visual systems every moment that our eyes are open, without even a hint of effort on our part. It is only when attempts have been made to understand the visual system with mathematical equations (Grossberg, 1987; Tsotsos, 1988) or to build a functioning visual system by machine (Horn, 1977, 1986; Marr, 1982; Nevatia, 1982) that the enormous complexity of this problem becomes apparent. Because of its complexity, perception researchers now tend to work on the problem by dividing it up into several smaller subproblems, which we will now examine in turn.

CONTOUR DETECTION AND FEATURE EXTRACTION

At the most basic level, the visual system divides the visual field into **shapes,** sometimes called *blobs,* separated by **contours.** A contour

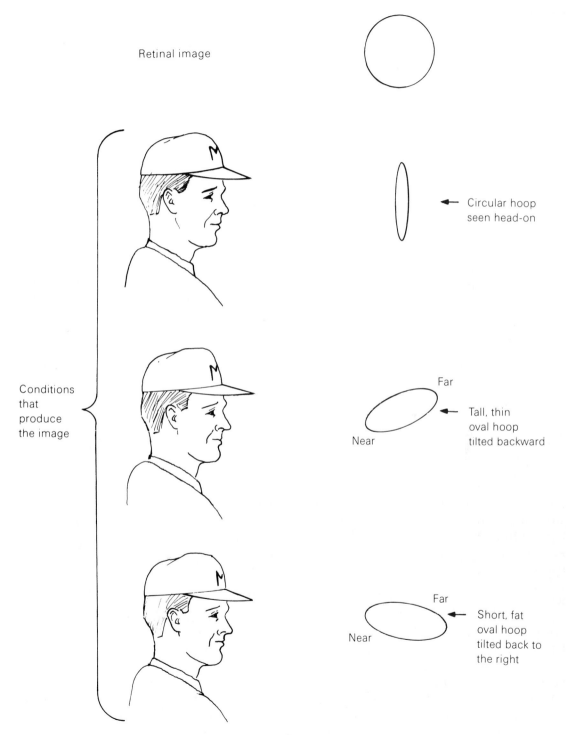

Retinal image

Conditions
that
produce
the image

← Circular hoop
seen head-on

Far

Near

← Tall, thin
oval hoop
tilted backward

Far

Near

← Short, fat
oval hoop
tilted back to
the right

Figure 11-3 *The inherent ambiguity of the shape of objects in the retinal image.*

is a place in the retinal image where the light intensity (or wavelength composition) changes abruptly. Examples of contours include a black line on a sheet of white paper, the edge of a blackboard, and the outline of the moon against the night sky. Generally speaking, shapes are regions in the retinal image that are surrounded by contours. In addition to the spatial dimensions of these regions, shapes may have other attributes such as color, texture, or even motion. We will refer to these attributes as **features.** Under appropriate circumstances, we may interpret the shapes in the retinal image as objects in the real world; however, since this is an interpretation, at times we will find that it can be wrong.

Contour and Change

Contours are the basic building blocks of visual perception; in their absence we actually lose our ability to see. We can demonstrate this by looking into a **Ganzfeld** (German for "whole field"). A Ganzfeld is a visual field that contains no abrupt luminance changes and thus no contours. When observers look into a Ganzfeld, they usually report seeing "a shapeless fog that goes on forever." Any hint of color soon fades to gray, even if the entire field is illuminated with, say, green or blue or red light (W. Cohen, 1958). Many observers even experience perceptual *blank out,* a feeling that they *cannot see,* after prolonged viewing. This feeling quickly disappears the instant any kind of luminance change is introduced into the visual field (Avant, 1965; W. Cohen, 1958).

Blank out can occur in natural environments as well. For instance, *snow blindness* is a kind of natural blank out, caused by the lack of contour in the retinal image when the visual field contains a lot of snow and ice. The snow and ice scatter much of the light in all directions and together are often very uniform in texture, which creates a kind of natural Ganzfeld. You can experience some of these sensations by trying Demonstration Box 11-1.

For vision to occur, not only local variations in the intensity of light, such as contours, must be present, but also variations in the pattern of illumination on the retina over time. This can be demonstrated using a **stabilized retinal image.** In this technique, the retinal image is made to stay in one place on the retina, in spite of where or how the eye moves. Normally, the retinal image is continually in motion because of saccadic eye movements made as we look around the environment, smooth-tracking movements of the eye as it follows moving objects, and spontaneous drifting eye movements. **Microsaccades** (tiny, involuntary eye movements) also occur, which keep our eyes shivering in their sockets. These microsaccades occur many times a second and cause the retinal image to shift from place to place on the retina, even when we are trying to hold our eyes completely still. The effect of the microsaccades, combined with other forms of eye movement, is constantly to move any contours across a number of different retinal receptors. This causes variations over time in the stimulation of any given receptor (in the form of "on" times followed by "off" times) as contours are swept across the retina.

When we do manage to stabilize the retinal image, usually by having an observer wear a special contact lens that moves with the eye and has a mirror or a tiny projector mounted on it, the stabilized image soon fades from view (for example, Pritchard, Heron, & Hebb, 1960; Riggs, Ratliff, Cornsweet, & Cornsweet, 1953; Yarbus, 1967). The contours disappear in chunks, and the color fades away. If we now flicker the stabilized image on and off, it will reappear and, if the flicker rate is high enough, it will not fade (Cornsweet, 1956). Flickering the image has reintroduced the temporal changes in light intensity usually caused by the eye's movements. The disappearance of our perception of patterns when the retinal image is stabilized, and its reappearance when the retinal image is flickered supports the idea that constant temporal change in the stimulation of the individual receptors is a necessary condition for vision. Without this constant change, receptors soon cease to respond differently from neighboring receptors, and hence we lose the signal that should be present if a contour is in the image (compare Norwich, 1983). In the absence of signals indicating that a contour

DEMONSTRATION BOX 11-1   The Ganzfeld

Although Ganzfeld situations have been produced with elaborate laboratory equipment, there are several simple ways to produce a Ganzfeld that will allow you to experience this contourless field for yourself. You can take a table tennis ball and cut it in half, placing one half over each eye, or you can use two white plastic spoons (like those probably available in any campus cafeteria) to produce a Ganzfeld by placing the bowl of a spoon over each eye as shown in the accompanying figure. Direct your gaze toward a light source (a fluorescent lamp, say) prior to placing the objects before your eyes, so your field of view will be flooded with diffuse, contourless light. Stay in this position for a few minutes and monitor any changes or alterations in your conscious perceptual experience. If the light originally had a tint, you will soon notice that the color will fade into a gray. After a while you will suddenly feel that you cannot see. This feeling of blindness is called *blank out*. It seems that in the absence of contours in the field, vision ceases. If a friend now casts a shadow over part of the field (say, with a pencil across the spoons), vision will immediately return with the introduction of this contour.

Spoon

is present, much like our experience in the Ganzfeld, our perception of patterns will fade and disappear from consciousness.

You may experience the reappearance of a stabilized image that has disappeared by trying Demonstration Box 3-3 (see Chapter 3) again. In that demonstration, you mapped the pattern of blood vessels that lie above your retina. Ordinarily you do not see these blood vessels because they create a stabilized image on your retina as light passes through them. They are always in the same place, so they create no temporal changes in stimulation of the receptors. By moving a flashlight placed at the corner of the eye, however, you cause their shadows to move across the retina, making them visible. You will note that as soon as you stop moving the flashlight (thus stopping the temporal change), the blood vessels disappear, since their image is stabilized again.

Contour Emergence

Temporal factors are important to our perception of contours in another way. We are not immediately aware of a contour when it appears on the retina. It takes some time for the contour information to be processed and for the perceived contour to emerge into our consciousness. If anything interferes with that processing before we see the contour, it may never become visible. The first demonstration of this, performed by Werner (1935), created an experimental technique that is now used to investigate many other phenomena. Werner presented observers with a brief view of a black disk on a white background (the *target*) and then, after a variable amount of time (called the *interstimulus interval*), presented a brief view of a black ring (the *mask*) in the same place in the visual field. The inner contour of the ring was exactly the same size as the outer contour of the disk, so the procedure resulted in two opposite contours appearing in the same place on the retina separated by different inter-

vals of time. Figure 11-4 contains a diagram of this situation and summarizes the results of the experiment, which were quite striking.

For very short interstimulus intervals, less than 100 msec, observers tended to see only a large black disk (really a combination of the disk and the ring seen together). It was as if the two had merged, or added together. For long interstimulus intervals, greater than 200 msec, observers saw both of the stimuli clearly, the disk before the ring. But for interstimulus intervals between 100 and 200 msec, observers tended to see only the ring. It was as if the disk had not been presented at all, although it stimulated the retina exactly as it had at other interstimulus intervals. Werner interpreted this *masking* of the disk by the ring to mean that the later-appearing contour had interfered with the processing of the earlier one, preventing its appearance in consciousness. This kind of masking is called **backward masking,** since the mask appeared *after* the target and seemed to be acting backward in time. A more general term, used to refer to any situation in which contours on adjacent parts of the retina interfere with one another, is **metacontrast.**

Studies of masking have helped shed light on several aspects of form perception, such as how contours interact in the visual system (for example, Kahneman, 1968; Lefton, 1973). One interesting suggestion is that, for each contour detected, the visual system produces both *excitation,* to indicate the existence of the contour, and *inhibition* of contours detected nearby. This idea is based on the receptive fields of visual cells with a center-surround organization discussed in Chapter 3. If two contours are detected closely enough in time and are spatially close to each other, then the inhibition produced for one (the ring) may cancel the excitation produced for the other (the disk; see Weisstein, 1968; Weisstein, Ozog, & Szoc, 1975). Another suggestion is that if the visual system does indeed decompose the retinal image into spatial frequency components (as

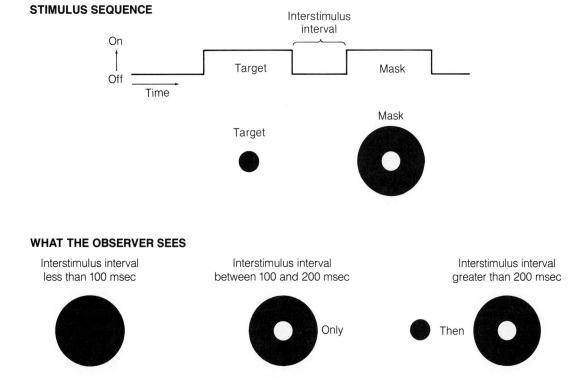

STIMULUS SEQUENCE

Interstimulus interval

On

Target

Mask

Off

Time

Target

Mask

WHAT THE OBSERVER SEES

Interstimulus interval less than 100 msec

Interstimulus interval between 100 and 200 msec

Interstimulus interval greater than 200 msec

Only

Then

Figure 11-4 A typical metacontrast experiment. Notice that when the interstimulus interval is of the appropriate length, the target is often not seen at all.

suggested in Chapter 4), different components may be processed in different channels (see Graham, 1981). Because of this separation, contours composed of similar spatial frequency components will mask one another, whereas those composed of different components will not (Weisstein, Harris, Berbaum, Tangney, & Williams, 1977).

Feature Extraction

The shapes that emerge into our consciousness from the retinal image can be said to possess **features** that differentiate them from other shapes. For example, if you have ever picked raspberries or blackberries, you will recall that the image of a ripe berry consists of a curved and roughly oval shape. Sometimes these

shapes overlap the leaves of the plant, and sometimes they are themselves overlapped by leaves or other berries. A ripe berry will tend to be larger than the others, will have a texture of bumps that is coarser than the others, and will reflect a darker "reddish" or "purplish" color. The so-called **relevant features** of the ripe berries are those that help you differentiate it from the others (Garner, 1974)—in this case these features are size, texture, and color.

Perception researchers use several different experimental methods to help them determine what the basic features of objects are for the human visual system. One of these is a **visual search** task, in which the subject looks for the presence of a single target item, and the experimenter varies the total number of items to be searched among in the display from trial to trial. An example of two of these displays is shown in Figures 11-5A and 11-5B. If the time it takes the subject to find the target stays approximately the same as the number of items is increased, the target is said to *pop out,* and the feature that differentiates the target item from the distractor items is thought to constitute a basic visual feature.

In a related task, subjects are asked to identify the presence or the location of an "odd" region in a briefly flashed display consisting of tiny figural elements. Two examples of displays from such a **texture segregation**

task are shown in Figures 11-5C and 11-5D. If subjects are able to find the "odd" region in a display shown for less than 100 msec, the region is again said to pop out, and the feature that differentiates the elements in the "odd" region from background elements is believed to be a basic visual feature.

These two tasks, and others, tend to agree in their identification of a number of basic visual features of shape, including color, brightness, orientation, length, and curvature (Beck, 1982; Cavanagh, 1988; Julesz, 1984; Neisser, 1967; Ramachandran & Anstis, 1986; Treis-

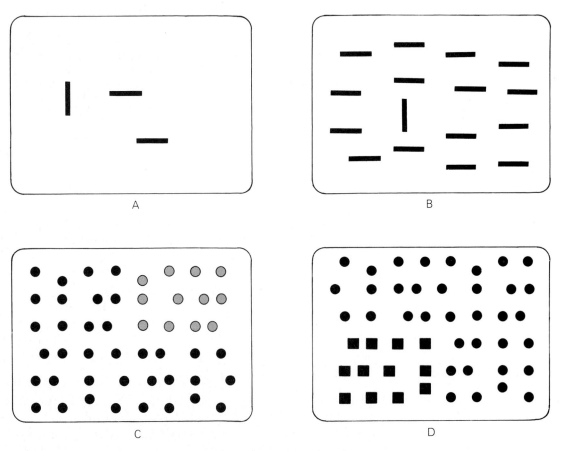

Figure 11-5 (A) and (B) Displays from a typical visual search experiment in which the target is a vertical bar. This target is easy to find, regardless of the number of horizontal bars present. (C) and (D) Displays from a typical texture segregation experiment in which the elements in the "odd" region differ in brightness or in shape from the elements in the "background" region.

man, 1986b; Treisman, Cavanagh, Fischer, Ramachandran, & von der Heydt, 1990). Some of the features identified are also more complex interactions between shapes such as line intersections, line endings, and line closure (Julesz, 1984; Treisman & Souther, 1985). The strength of using these perceptual tasks to define a set of basic image features is that the features can be seen directly; thus they appear in our consciousness and can be talked about easily. The weakness in this approach is that the total feature set is to some degree arbitrary and the tasks seem to be under constant revision, with new features appearing and others dropping out as each new set of data is collected (for example, Enns, 1990).

An alternative way to characterize visual features is to trace them to a physiological base, as, for example, the line or angle detectors of the visual cortex discussed in Chapter 3. A related approach, dealt with in Chapter 4, involves specifying the spatial frequency components that make up a shape as its features. As was pointed out in Chapter 4, the two-dimensional distribution of light on the retina can be completely described in terms of simple sine wave gratings. Through the process of Fourier analysis, we can determine which sine wave gratings, at which spatial frequencies, need to be combined to create any pattern. One suggestion has been that these sine wave frequencies (called *Fourier components* once they are determined by the appropriate mathematical calculations) are the features used to identify perceptual objects (for example, Campbell & Robson, 1968; Pollen, Lee, & Taylor, 1971). It has now been shown that this approach cannot work if the Fourier analysis is applied over the entire visual field (for example, Caelli, 1984; Cavanagh, 1984; DeValois & DeValois, 1987), but it still appears to be useful if the analysis is done over smaller regions, around the size of cortical receptive fields (Fogel & Sagi, 1989; Gurnsey & Browse, 1989; Sutter, Beck, & Graham, 1989).

Unfortunately, the spatial frequency approach is different from other forms of feature analysis in more ways than simply being describable in terms of mathematical equations. First, the spatial frequency components are not apparent to consciousness and thus are not useful in describing what we see. Second, they are not always related to texture segregation, since regions of the visual array that are clearly different in their Fourier components sometimes cannot be seen (Caelli, 1988; Julesz, 1981; Julesz & Bergen, 1983). However, this approach does have the advantage that the set of possible Fourier components is not as arbitrary as the feature list seems to be and does not change with the set of shapes. Some researchers therefore feel that it may ultimately still prove to be useful for the description of our perception of forms.

We will gain a greater appreciation of the complexity of the feature approach to form perception when we examine the principles of figural grouping in the next section. For example, Figure 11-6 shows that when several smaller shapes are placed together to create a larger whole, an **emergent feature** can be created that cannot be predicted by examining the smaller parts in isolation. These emergent features sometimes behave just like simpler features in visual search and other feature detection tasks (Enns, 1990; Enns & Prinzmetal, 1984; Pomerantz, 1986).

PERCEPTUAL ORGANIZATION

The quotation from Mill beginning this chapter emphasizes that the visual world is filled with *objects*. That is, under normal viewing conditions, our visual systems operate to produce **perceptual objects** from the array of blobs and contours contained in the distribution of light on the retina. No perceptual objects are present on the retina; they exist only in our

Component A	+	Component B	=	Whole figure	Emergent property

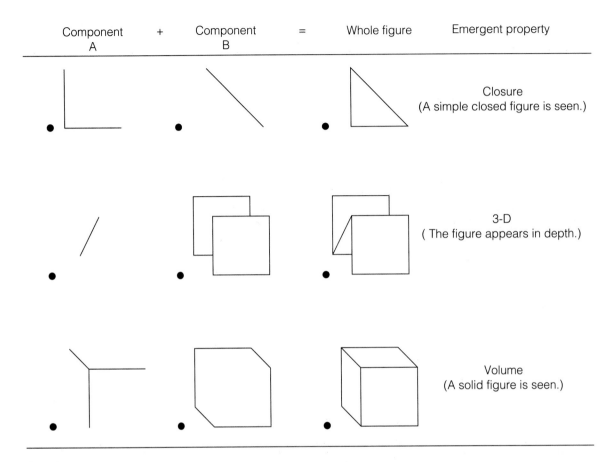

Closure
(A simple closed figure is seen.)

3-D
(The figure appears in depth.)

Volume
(A solid figure is seen.)

Figure 11-6 When several component figures are added together, emergent features are sometimes created that cannot be explained by examining the smaller parts (based on Enns, 1990; Pomerantz, 1986).

minds, and only as the result of many levels of processing and interpretation applied to the retinal image. The miraculous thing is that the perceptual objects so closely resemble what physics tells us is the nature of the "real" objects "out there" in the world. An apple to our consciousness is very like an apple "out there." How does this come about? Our best guess at this time is that the perceptual object is *constructed* from a group of features (or attributes) detected at a particular spatial location.

Figure and Ground

The simplest perceptual object is a two-dimensional **figure** on a two-dimensional **ground.** A figure is simply an integrated group of contours. A shape can be a figure, but shapes can also form part of the background (or *ground*) from which the figure emerges. Thus, a ball resting on a field of grass is a figure (here a round shape) resting on a ground consisting of many elongated shapes (the blades of grass).

How can we tell the difference between a figure and its ground? For example, how can you distinguish the book you are reading from the table on which it rests, or the printed words from the page? On your retina the blobs of contours that make up figures and grounds are all run together, intersecting and overlapping, but somehow the visual system separates the book from the table and the words from the page.

To begin with, this separation is a psychological achievement, as can be seen in Figure 11-7B. This is the famous Rubin (1915, 1921) face–vase ambiguous figure. When you look at this figure you might see a pair of silhouette faces gazing at each other or you might see an ornate vase. The vase appears white against a black ground, whereas the faces are black against a white ground. Notice that as you look at 11-3B for a few moments the two pattern organizations alternate in consciousness, demonstrating that the organization into figure and ground is in your mind, not in the stimulus. Notice also that the faces and the vase never appear together. You "know" that both are possible but you cannot "see" both at the same time. It is impossible for a given part of a visual pattern to be simultaneously interpreted as both figure and ground. Generally speaking, the smaller an area or a shape is, the more likely it is to be seen as figure (see Weisstein & Wong, 1986). This is demonstrated in Figure

11-7, where it is easier to see the vase when the white area is smaller (11-7A) and easier to see the faces when the black area is smaller (11-7C).

Once a particular interpretation has been arrived at (for example, the vase), figure and ground take on distinct properties. When the white area is seen as the vase, it appears to be "in front of" the black area seen as the ground, and the contours in the pattern seem to "belong" to the vase. However, when the interpretation changes, the contours are seen to belong to the faces, and the faces seem closer than, and in front of, the white background. Furthermore, figures appear to be more "thinglike" and appear to have a shape, whereas the ground appears formless. Figures are seen as "richer" and more meaningful and are remembered more easily. Figures also contrast more than the ground, appearing brighter or darker than equivalent patches of light that form part of the background (Coren, 1969). Finally, the stimuli seen as figures are registered in greater detail than stimuli seen as ground (Weisstein & Wong, 1986).

Of course, in natural visual scenes, the distinction between figure and ground is rarely as arbitrary as in Rubin's face–vase figure. However, in some natural conditions ambiguity exists as to what constitutes a figure. For instance, we are often confronted with scenes

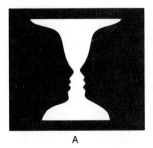
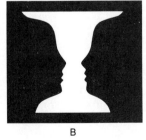
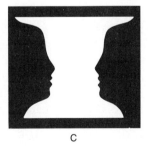

A   B   C

Figure 11-7 (B) *A reversible figure-ground stimulus in which a pair of black faces or a white vase (or perhaps a bird bath or goblet) are seen alternately. When the white area is smaller* (A) *the vase is easier to see; when the black area is smaller* (C) *the faces are more easily seen.*

in which our view of one figure is partially
blocked by the shape of another object. (*Interposition,* or the partial occlusion of one object
by another, was discussed in Chapter 10). Look
at Figure 11-8A. Despite the large amount of
black interposed in front of the gray figures,
our visual system is effortlessly able to group
together the correct portions of the image. In
this figure, several copies of a familiar letter of
the alphabet (*B*) can be seen lying in various
orientations underneath some spilled ink. How
are these various letter fragments grouped so
effortlessly? Familiarity with the occluded objects is clearly *not* a sufficient condition for this
to occur, as is shown in Figure 11-8B. This figure contains the same letter fragments, but the
occluding spots of black ink have been removed—subjects find these letters almost impossible to decipher even when they know
which letters to look for (Bregman, 1981;
Kanisza, 1979). Thus, the grouping in Figure
11-8A must be following some rules that work
regardless of the meaning of the objects.

One suggestion is that shape contours are
"labeled" very early in the grouping process as
either **intrinsic contours** (meaning they belong to the figure) or **extrinsic contours** (meaning
they are simply a consequence of one object
occluding another) (Nakayama, Shimojo, & Silverman, 1989). The intrinsic contours of the
ink spilled in Figure 11-8A can be traced to
form continuous shapes. Extrinsic contours
(where the ink crosses the underlying letters)
serve as a signal that allows the intrinsic contours of the letter *B* to be "filled in" underneath
the occluding black ink. In Figure 11-8B the
shape fragments that have been drawn are a
combination of intrinsic contours of the letter
B and extrinsic contours caused by the ink
spill. In this case the visual system has no way
of knowing which is which, since the interposing figure is not visible, and hence the "filling-
in process" is not evoked. Now examine Figure
11-8C. Here only the intrinsic contours of the
letter *B* have been retained and so the letters

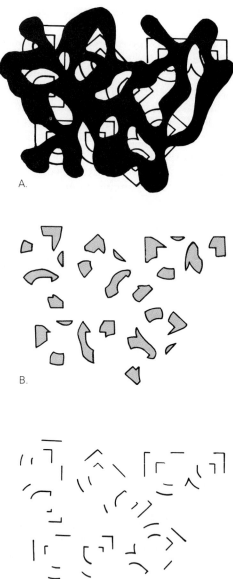

A.

B.

C.

Figure 11-8 (A) *Several copies of the letter* B *are
lying beneath some spilled ink, but they are easy to
read.* (B) *The same letter fragments, without the
ink as an occluding object, are very difficult to
read.* (C) *When only the* intrinsic *contours of the letters are shown, the letters are easy to read, despite
the absence of any ink to act as an occluding object
(based on Brown & Koch, 1991).*

are once again quite readable (Brown & Koch, 1991). It appears that correct contour labeling can be achieved in a number of ways, including the assignment of contours to different depth planes—such as the ink being seen in front of the *B*s (Nakayama et al., 1989). Sometimes the characteristics of the contours determine the labels. For instance, at approximately T-shaped intersections between contours, the stem of a T-intersection is labeled intrinsic and is seen as part of the more distant figure, whereas the crossbar is labeled extrinsic and is seen as part of the nearer, interposing figure (Enns & Rensink, 1991; Kellman & Shipley, 1990).

Contours that are not physically present on the retina but that still affect our perception of figure and ground are called **subjective contours** or **illusory contours** (Petry & Meyer, 1987; Purghé & Coren, 1992). Figure 11-9A illustrates how a figure can emerge from a two-dimensional array without the contribution of any intrinsic contours. The only contours that are used to define the rectangle in Figure 11-9A and the triangle in 11-9B are extrinsic contours that occur when these figures occlude the shapes underneath them. The implicit depth cues derived from these contours cause you to conclude that such a figure must be present, and you then reorganize the perception of the array to perceive a figure (the white rectangle) that actually is not present (Coren, 1972).

Although many factors can contribute to the formation of subjective contours (see, for example, Coren, 1991; Halpern, 1981; Ware, 1981), the presence of depth cues seems to provide a powerful impetus to organize parts of the field into simple figures. This is consistent with observers' reports that the figures created by subjective contours appear to lie in front of their backgrounds, even when all other depth cues are carefully removed (Coren & Porac, 1983b). Interestingly, subjective contours act very much like real contours, in that they can mask real contours (Lehmkuhle & Fox, 1980; Weisstein, Matthews, & Berbaum, 1974), can improve judgments of the position of a dot (Pomerantz, Goldberg, Golder, & Tetewsky, 1981), and can cause motion aftereffects (Smith & Over, 1979). If subjective contours are moved across the retina, they can even make real stationary contours, such as dots or stripes, appear to move with them. This illusion has playfully been called *motion capture* by Ramachandran (1986).

Figural Grouping

Most forms or objects we see are composed of a number of elements. We have already found that the organization of elements into perceptual objects involves an active constructive

A   B

Figure 11-9 *The white rectangle across the word* STOP *in* A *and the white triangle in* B *are bounded by subjective contours. They actually do not exist in the stimulus (from Coren, 1972. Copyright 1972 by the American Psychological Association. Reprinted by permission).*

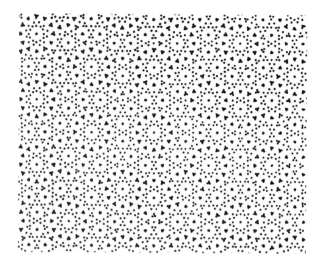

Figure 11-10 *A stimulus revealing the "urge to organize." Many organizations of the various small elements are possible, and the visual pattern you see is continually changing as you shift from one organization to another.*

process. We can see the action of this "urge to organize" in Figure 11-10, where the many possible organizations of the elements seem to alternate in a rapid, unstable manner.

The general question of how all perception comes to be organized into patterns, shapes, and forms was central to a group of psychologists (including Max Wertheimer, Kurt Koffka, and Wolfgang Kohler) who formed the **Gestalt** school of psychology. *Gestalt* is a German word that can be translated to mean "form," "whole," or even "whole form." These psychologists were interested in processes that cause certain elements to seem to be part of the same figure or grouping and others to seem to belong to other figures or groups. They formulated several laws of perceptual organization that govern the emergence of a visual figure (Wertheimer, 1923). Their basic observation was that elements within a pattern do not seem to operate independently. At the phenomenal level, there appear to be attractive "forces" among the various elements that cause them to form a meaningful and coherent figure, much

as gravity organizes the planets, sun, and moons of our solar system. They described how certain regular properties of elements within a pattern bring about the emergence of stable figures.

A Gestalt principle is illustrated in Figure 11-11A, which is usually seen as two clusters of dots. Although the array actually contains 12 individual dots, we experience them as two distinct groups of 6 dots. This is an example of the **law of proximity,** which states that elements close to one another tend to be perceived as a unit or figure. Figure 11-11B is normally seen as a triangle composed of black dots on a background of (or surrounded by a swarm of) *X*'s. This is an example of the **law of similarity,** which maintains that similar objects tend to be grouped together. Another example of this law is seen in Figure 11-11C, where the two halves of the circular field appear quite separate because of grouping by similarity (for a more advanced analysis of such effects see Julesz, 1981). Figure 11-11D is usually viewed as a spiral of dots with one standing outside. This is an example of the **law of good continuation,** which states that elements that appear to follow in the same direction (as in a straight line or simple curve) tend to be grouped together. Figure 11-11E is an example of the **law of closure,** which states that when a space is enclosed by a contour it tends to be perceived as a figure. Most people see a diamond between two vertical lines here. Actually, Figure 11-11E also could be seen as a letter *W* stacked on a letter *M,* or a normal *K* and a mirror-image *K* facing each other, were it not for the compelling nature of closure. Closure also allows us to complete broken contours as in Figure 11-11F, which is seen as a triangle rather than as simply three separated acute angles.

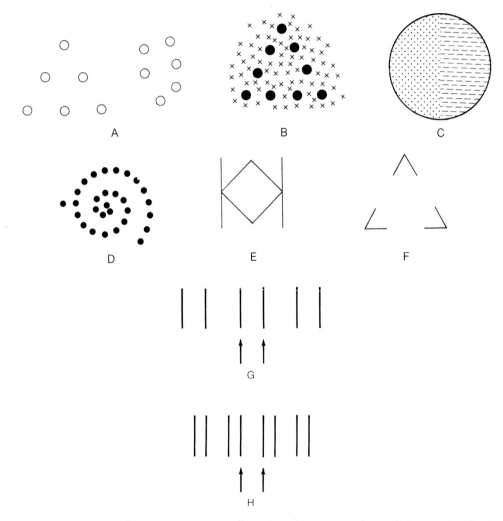

Figure 11-11 Examples of the Gestalt principles of figural organization: (A) grouping by proximity; (B) and (C) grouping by similarity; (D) good continuation; (E) an extreme example of closure in which two common figures are hidden; (F) closure; (G) and (H) the distortion of the distance between elements (the distances marked by arrows are the same) by the principle of proximity.

The Gestalt principles are so powerful that they may even be responsible for visual illusions. For example, distances between parts of a pattern organized into the same group, or figure, are underestimated relative to the same distances when the same parts belong to different groups (Coren & Girgus, 1980; Enns & Girgus, 1985). Figures 11-10G and 11-10H illustrate this effect. The figures show two different groupings formed by operation of the law of proximity. The distance between the two lines pointed to by the arrows in each figure is identical, yet that distance seems larger in the lower figure, where the lines are parts of two different groups. Such distortions support and enhance the operation of the Gestalt laws to form perceptual objects from discrete parts of the visual array.

All of the Gestalt laws operate to create the most stable, consistent, and simple forms possible within a given visual array. The Gestalt psychologists called this process the **law of Pragnanz,** which states that the organization of the visual array into perceptual objects will always be as "good" as the prevailing conditions allow. Here the meaning of *good* encompasses concepts such as *regularity, simplicity,* and *symmetry.* The law of Pragnanz is also a way of saying that the perceptual systems work to produce a perceptual world that conveys the "essence" of the real world, that is, to ensure that information about the real world is correctly interpreted. In fact, the German word *Pragnanz* means approximately "conveying the essence of something." Because prevailing conditions are sometimes not ideal, as in line drawings or on a foggy night, the essence can be "better" than the reality. Seeing complex patterns of contours as perceptual objects makes further processing of the vast array of information in the retinal image simpler and faster. For example, it would take you less time to count 12 dots if they were organized into two triangles of the sort shown in the left half of 11-10A, than if the 12 dots were randomly

grouped in a single cluster (Oyama, 1986). Demonstration Box 11-2 allows you to explore the concept of Pragnanz further.

Figural Grouping by Texture

Shapes and figures can be formed by changes in the stimulus pattern other than intensity or wavelength. For instance, object boundaries may be defined by regions of the retinal image that differ only in **visual texture.** Visual textures are collections of tiny contour elements or shapes that do not differ in average brightness or color. For example, if you look back at Figure 11-11C you will see two regions defined by different textures—one a texture of dots, the other a texture of dashes. Notice that there is apparently a boundary, or contour, between these regions. This **textural contour** is a form of subjective contour, since it is not actually present in the stimulation.

The ease with which we can make out shapes defined only by textures depends on the nature of the textural elements. It has often been suggested that the segregation of parts of the field on the basis of textural elements **(texture segregation)** is really an example of grouping by similarity, which we discussed earlier. Although the number of dimensions in which groups of textural elements differ from one another is indeed quite important, the situation is quite complicated and predictions based on a simple definition of grouping by similarity are sometimes not confirmed. A good example is shown in Figures 11-12A and 11-12B. Although people judge a single upright *T* to be more similar to a single tilted *T* than to a single upright *L*, these judgments do not predict what happens when entire regions of a texture are made up of these shapes (Beck, 1966, 1982). The square shape created by the tilted-*T*/upright-*T* boundary is much more apparent in Figure 11-12B than is the shape created by the *L/T* boundary in Figure 11-12A. Apparently the orientation of small contours is an impor-

DEMONSTRATION BOX 11-2   Pragnanz

Look at the accompanying figures for a moment and (without looking back again) draw them on a separate piece of paper. When you have finished, return to this box.

Now carefully compare the figures you drew to the actual figures. Did you pick up the fact that the "circle" is actually a tilted ellipse? that the "square" contains no right angles? that the "triangle" has two rounded corners and an open one? that the "X" is actually made up of curved lines? Look back at your reproductions. If you drew (or remembered) just a good circle, square, triangle, and X, your percepts have been "cleaned up" by the action of Pragnanz.

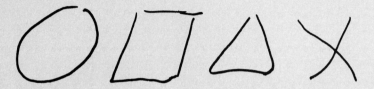

---

tant aspect of their contribution to borders defined by texture.

Texture segregation is usually easy and automatic when there are differences in the number, density, or type of a few classes of local elements generically called **textons** (Julesz, 1981; Julesz & Bergen, 1983). Textons include elongated blobs of a particular color, length, width, or orientation; line ends (called *terminators*); and line crossings (*inter-sections*). For example, the central square shape that appears in Figure 11-12F is defined by a boundary between elements that have no terminators and elements that have three terminators. Notice that all of the elements are made up of the same parts, a slanted line in two different orientations, and a "corner" shape in four different orientations. The local texture elements differ only in how these parts are put together.

Although Julesz's theory and demonstrations are convincing, careful experiments have shown that they must be modified somewhat. To begin with, all textons are not equally powerful in their ability to define textural contours.

This is demonstrated in Figures 11-12C and 11-12D. In *C* the central square is formed by a shape difference, whereas in *D* it is formed by a color difference. Notice that the color difference seems much more dramatic and that color differences between elements actually make the shape boundary harder to see in *C*. Color differences are clearly dominant over shape differences in forming textures, and this differential salience strongly affects texture segregation (Callaghan, 1989; Callaghan, Lasaga, & Garner, 1986; Gurnsey & Browse, 1987). Certain higher-level factors, such as closed versus open figures, can often act as a texton when the closed figures are very different from the background figures (Enns, 1986). The best suggestion seems to be that texture segregation is determined by the degree to which textons unique to a particular region of the visual field are salient in the context of textons in other, surrounding, regions (Beck, 1982; Enns, 1986; Olson & Attneave, 1970).

In addition, the number of stimulus dimensions involved is important. Treisman and Gelade (1980) showed that although texture

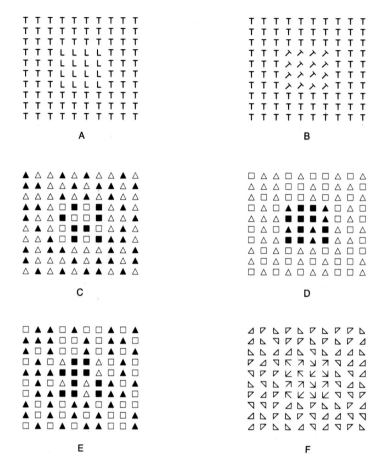

Figure 11-12 *Examples of shapes defined by textural contours of varying strength.*

segregation was easy and automatic when either the shape or the color of elements differed, forming a boundary, it was impossible when particular conjunctions (pairings) of shape and color differed. For example, look at Figure 11-10E. Is there a central square here? Actually there is, but only *conceptually,* not *perceptually*. It is formed where the outside elements are only empty squares *or* filled triangles and the inside elements are only empty triangles *or* filled squares. But because the element boundary is defined only by differences in *conjunctions* (combinations) of basic properties, the textural contour does not emerge. To find the boundary you must scrutinize the shapes one by one. Apparently the form of grouping by similarity that results in textural contours depends on elements that differ in only a single dimension, and does not work for combinations of dimensions or properties (Humphreys, Quinlan, & Riddoch, 1989; Treisman, 1986b).

Spatial Frequencies and Figural Grouping

Several investigators have tried to combine certain aspects of figural grouping with a consideration of spatial frequency analysis such as we discussed in Chapter 4. Their aim is to develop a multiprocess, multilevel explanation of how the perceptual object is formed. In the context of figure and ground, for example, Julesz (1978) argued that texture segregation was a kind of "early warning" mechanism that drew attention to regions requiring finer analysis. This was all accomplished by background processes, whereas the finer, more detailed analysis of important shapes was accomplished by figural processes. This argument has been interpreted as meaning that regions that are defined by *higher spatial frequencies* (e.g., smaller-sized details or sharper contours) are more likely to be seen as being figure.

A demonstration of the relationship between spatial frequency analysis and the perception of figures comes from Klymenko and Weisstein (1986). They found that when regions of a visual field were defined by different spatial frequency gratings, the regions containing the higher spatial frequency grating were more likely to be seen as figure. Regions containing lower frequency gratings were more likely to be seen as ground. This is demonstrated in Figure 11-13, where the faces are much easier to see as figure because they are filled with high-spatial-frequency gratings.

Figure 11-13   A reversible figure–ground stimulus in which the faces are easier to see than the vase because they are filled with relatively high spatial frequency gratings (based on Klymenko & Weisstein, 1986).

There is one important implication of these results linking spatial frequency to figure perception. Analyses of higher-spatial-frequency regions are more likely to be accomplished by the parvocellular system (see Chapter 3), which also has higher visual acuity for finer details. Thus figure perception may be more intimately associated with the parvocellular system than with the low-spatial-resolution magnocellular system.

Information, Symmetry, and Good Figures

When we spoke about the law of Prägnanz, we introduced the notion of "figural goodness." Although we referred to "good" figures as being regular and symmetrical, this definition is too imprecise and limited for many situations and stimuli. For example, can we determine whether the letter *F* and the letter *R* differ in terms of figural goodness given that neither demonstrates regularity or symmetry? Several suggested solutions to this problem have been offered, but still no consensus seems to have been reached. One reasonable scheme involves defining figural goodness in terms of the amount and complexity of the information needed to describe a particular stimulus or perceptual organization (Hochberg & Brooks, 1960; Leeuwenburg, 1971, 1988). Hochberg and Brooks (1960) used a formula to compute figural complexity based on the number of angles in the figure, the number of different sized angles in the figure, and the number of separate line segments. This computation was supposed to represent the amount of information needed to identify the figure when perceived in a particular way. Thus Figure 11-14 shows figures varying in complexity from *A* (most complex) to *D* (least complex). Figures with the lowest complexity are apt to be seen as two-dimensional; thus 11-14D is seen as a flat pattern made up of interlocking triangles. Seeing

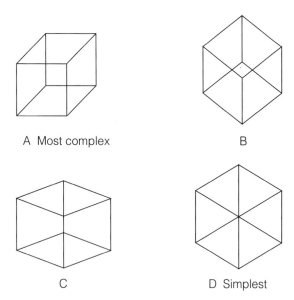

A Most complex   B

C   D Simplest

Figure 11-14   Various projections of a cube. The figures are more likely to be seen as two dimensional as we move from the most complex (A) to the least complex (D).

figures as three-dimensional involves more information. Thus, it is possible to see 11- 14D as a three-dimensional cube (sort of a variation of 11-14A, but tilted a bit), but to do so you must consider 24 angles (4 on each cube face) instead of the 18 angles (3 from each triangle) needed to describe the figure as flat. Generally it is the organization with the least figural complexity that is most likely to be seen, as if the visual system is biased toward expending the least amount of processing effort possible when viewing any stimulus.

Closely related to the Hochberg and Brooks computations is an alternative way of looking at the amount of information in a figure and the resulting consequences for perception. This method was proposed by Attneave (1955), who tried to quantify the figural goodness of patterns using *information theory* (discussed in Chapter 2). To see how information theory applies to patterns, consider Figure 11-15, which is an image of a woman's right eye as it

Figure 11-15   An example of a figure made up of dots that can be either black or white.

might appear in an enlargement of a newspaper photo. Notice that the picture is made up of a number of dots, each of which can be either black or white. We can analyze any figure into such an array of *pixels,* each of which is a dot that will be "on" (black) or "off" (white).

Consider Figure 11-16, where we have broken up square visual fields into separate, smaller squares called *cells,* which represent something like big pixels. We will call the whole stimulus array a *matrix.* Notice that we can construct a variety of patterns by filling in various cells (like turning pixels on or off in Figure 11-15). Suppose we asked you to guess the figure present, without actually seeing it, by simply guessing whether each cell was black or white. Since each guess deals with two alternatives, the answer to each contains one *bit* of information, as we pointed out in Chapter 2. If we filled in the pattern randomly, in order to guess the complete pattern you would need 64 guesses (1 for each cell) or 64 bits of information (1 for each guess needed). If we told you that the left side was the mirror image of the right side, called a *vertically symmetrical* pattern since the mirror images are symmetrical around a vertical line, you would need to guess only 32 cells either on the right or on the left in order to guess the pattern, thus reducing the amount of information to 32 bits. Therefore, a

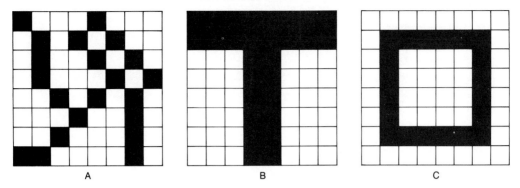

Figure 11-16 *Examples of symmetry in patterns:* (A) *no symmetry;* (B) *symmetry around a vertical axis;* (C) *symmetry around both horizontal and vertical axes.*

vertically symmetrical figure, such as 11-16B, contains less information than an asymmetrical figure such as 11-16A. Figure 11-16C, which is symmetrical around both the vertical and horizontal axes, contains even less information than the other two patterns (16 bits), since only one corner (16 cells) must be known before the entire pattern can be derived.

Since good figures are generally symmetrical and regular, we can now see that they also contain less information. This means they should be easier to remember and easier to recognize. Studies show that groupings of simple linear features that form closed, good figures or symmetrical, low-information patterns are much easier to recognize than those composed of the same features in a different arrangement (Attneave, 1955; Pomerantz, Sager, & Stoever, 1977). These data seem to indicate some kind of advantage (faster or earlier) for the perception of good figures. Yodogawa (1982) has given a mathematically rigorous measure of pattern symmetry, based on information theory, that nicely predicts perceptions of pattern symmetry and pattern complexity in such situations.

There appears to be a general bias in perception toward symmetry or figural goodness. Freyd and Tversky (1984) found that symmetrical forms were often matched to even more symmetrical forms. They argued that detection of overall symmetry in a form leads to the observer's assumption that it is symmetric in its details as well, which might explain the results you got when you tried Demonstration Box 11-2.

A final suggestion about goodness that has been influential was made by Garner (1962, 1974), whose definition of the amount of information in a pattern is somewhat different. According to Garner, the amount of information depends on the number of possible alternatives that a given figure could be one of, much like the definition for the difficulty of recognition that we used in Chapter 2 when we first introduced the concept of information. Garner argued that the smaller the set of possible alternatives that could be created from a figure by rotation and reflection, the less the information and the better the figure. Figure 11-17 shows the set of alternative patterns for three different dot patterns. Clearly, Figure 11-17A is the "best" and 11-17C the "worst" under Garner's definition. Since Figure 11-17A is unique, it is the least informative about its set of alternatives (which has no members); Figure 11-17C, in contrast, is one of eight patterns that can be created by reflection and rotation. Seeing it indicates that the other seven alternatives did not appear and thus conveys three bits of information (since, as you learned in

Set of all possible unique rotations and reflections

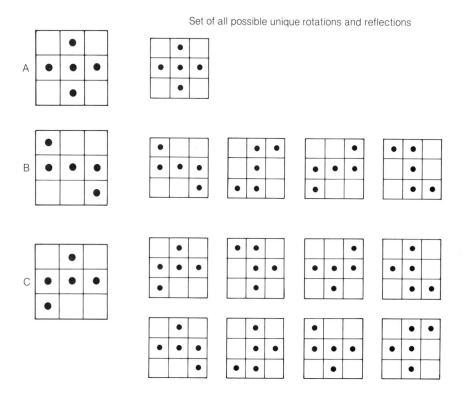

Figure 11-17 *Relationships between figural goodness and the set of possible alternative stimuli that can be created by rotations and reflections:* (A) *is the "best" figure and* (C) *is the "worst" (based on Handel & Garner, 1965).*

Chapter 2, the amount of information is equal to $\log_2$ of the number of equally likely stimulus alternatives). Garner and his colleagues (Garner & Clement, 1963; Handel & Garner, 1965) found that the smaller the set of possible alternatives, the more likely an observer was to rate a pattern as "good" (the observers did not see the set of alternatives). This approach, and the others described earlier, all support the conclusion that good figures are simple and contain less information. In this sense it does not matter which approach we prefer—the law of Pragnanz is the same in all of them.

Feature Integration Theory

In our discussion so far, although we have referred to the perceptual object being *constructed* from the information available in the retinal image, we have perhaps given the impression that all the constructive activity happens automatically, without any effort and for all parts of the visual field at once. This is probably not the case. Quite a bit of evidence is accumulating that we can construct only one perceptual object at a time (as noticed in a reversible figure) and that usually we must focus our attention on a particular location in "visual space" to synthesize a perceptual object from all the information coming from that location.

A particularly attractive version of this viewpoint is Treisman's **feature integration theory** (Treisman, 1986a, 1986b; Treisman & Gormican, 1988). This theory asserts that two major stages are involved in the construction of a perceptual object. First, **preattentive processes** (those that happen without active attention playing a part) operate on the information in the retinal image to extract the contours and their features and then to group these contours into preliminary figures. A crucial assumption about this stage is that features such as color, the various features of edges (for example, line orientation, closure), and three-dimensional location are registered separately from one another in special processing systems (for example, carried separately in the parvocellular or magnocellular system or registered in different "maps" of the visual field in different places in the cortex; see Chapter 3). The second stage of the process consists of active **focal attention** (see Chapter 15) selecting a spatial location and integrating the features registered at that location into a perceptual object. This perceptual object, or *object file,* to use Treisman and Kahneman's label (see Kahneman & Treisman, 1984), consists of a temporary representation of the current appearance of the object that is constantly updated as new information is obtained. This representation may also be compared with those stored in long-term memory for identification and categorization.

When attention shifts to another object, either because the current one disappears from view or because in the process of scanning the observer was distracted by another collection of features, the old object file vanishes and is replaced by a new one at a different location. This view explains how objects in the "real world" can be seen as enduring and solid, even though the information about them that we receive changes drastically from moment to moment. The "glue" that holds each object together is the process of attention being focused on a particular location in space. This is somewhat reminiscent of earlier speculations by Ames (1955) that the minimum properties of any perceived stimulus are its *thereness,* referring to its location in space, and its *thatness,* referring to its object properties.

A lot of data have accumulated to test these ideas. One of the most intriguing findings is the discovery of **illusory conjunctions.** Feature in-

tegration theory predicts that if attention is overloaded so it is difficult to integrate separable features into a perceptual object, the features might combine incorrectly, giving rise to the perception of an object that is not really there (an illusory conjunction). For example, an observer may be presented with a briefly flashed red *O* and blue *X,* but may see a red *X,* which was not really there (Treisman & Schmidt, 1982). A simple analogy to this is meeting a man named Fred, who is an architect, and another named George, who is an accountant, then in recounting your experiences to a friend recalling Fred, the accountant. The name and the occupation are features that you assign to the particular stimulus (the person) separately. In the perceptual synthesis, however, the objects do not even have to be similar for their properties to be exchanged in this way. For example, color is exchanged among dissimilar-shaped objects (such as a triangle and a circle) just as easily as it is among similar-shaped objects, such as two small outline triangles (Treisman, 1986a). This is possible because the individual features are processed separately and then synthesized with reference to a given place in space via a different process.

Just how the Gestalt principles interact with the feature integration process is an interesting, and still controversial, question. Prinzmetal (1981) found evidence that illusory conjunctions were less likely when the components came from different Gestalt groupings of visual contours than when they came from the same grouping. He argued that perceptual organization prevented the illusory conjunction of features from groups of contours that were likely to be parts of different objects (see also Butler & Kring, 1987). Also, Prinzmetal and Millis-Wright (1984) found that illusory conjunctions were more likely to occur within letter strings that formed pronounceable words than in random, unpronounceable letter strings. Again, the preattentive analysis of the contours in the retinal image into shapes that may signify objects in the real world seems to constrain feature integration. Since we learn through experience which features are likely to go together, feature integration is less subject to error when we know which objects to expect (Treisman, 1986a). One role played by the feature integration process seems to be to maintain the continuity and coherence of the perceptual object in the face of constantly changing visual information about it. Demonstration Box 11-3 allows you to experience the coherence of the perceptual object in a somewhat different way.

OBJECT RECOGNITION AND IDENTIFICATION

Study Figure 11-18 for a minute or so. You have never seen it before, because it was especially constructed for this book. It is clearly an object, but what is it? Now look at it again. You

will recognize it because you have seen it before (just a minute or so ago), although you still are not able to identify it (it is not a "real" object). You experience familiarity, but the object makes no sense. Now study it a little longer. Eventually you may begin to be able to classify it into some object class or other—perhaps it resembles a distorted version of a streetside hot dog vendor's cart, or perhaps a child's toy. The longer you look at it, the more associations it generates, although it still does not have a name. If we told you it was a "horned wheeler," the name might suggest it is an apparatus for conveying or transporting things, although how or why still might be a puzzle.

Every day, practically every moment, you recognize and identify perceptual objects like the one in Figure 11-18, although they are seldom as novel. Actually, the ability to see a stimulus as an object is often not sufficient. Our very survival may depend on our recognition of an object as something we have seen be-

---

DEMONSTRATION BOX 11-3   Figural Integration

It is rare that we see an object in its entirety. Either we or the object are moving about, resulting in glimpses that are partially occluded by other objects (for example, a dog running through some trees). Yet we have no difficulty identifying the object. Parks (1965) studied this phenomenon by moving a shape behind a narrow window, or slit. His surprising result was that a wide variety of shapes could be easily recognized, even though the shape was never seen except as a series of fragments. Because of one of the shapes Parks used, the phenomenon of easy identification of shapes presented by moving them behind a slit has come to be called *Park's camel.*

In order to experience Park's camel for yourself, have a friend pass various objects

(including himself or herself) behind a narrow slit created by a door that is slightly ajar (Shimojo & Richards, 1986). Try varying the size of the slit and the speed with which the object passes across it. You will find that over a surprisingly wide range of size and speed conditions the object will be identifiable. Also, pay attention to the strength of the feeling you will have that the *entire* object is present, even though at any moment you are only receiving a fragmentary view of it. When the conditions are optimal, that impression is very strong. This demonstrates the importance of the integration over time required to create the perceptual object out of a chaotic and constantly changing retinal image.

Figure 11-18 *An object you have never seen before (based on Biederman, 1987).*

fore, and on our labeling (really *categorizing*) that object so we can retrieve information about its likely behavior or the behavior we should perform in its presence. How do we go about identifying objects?

Recognition versus Identification

The first thing we must do is make our terminology clear. In what follows, when we refer to object **recognition,** we mean the experience of "perceiving something as previously known" (Mandler, 1980). Object **identification** means naming an object, correctly classifying it in some categorization scheme, knowing in what context it is usually encountered, knowing its relation to other concepts, and so on—in short, remembering something more about it than merely having seen it before. According to Mandler (1980), the experience of familiarity comes about because the more exposure we have to a perceptual object, the more we have organized the various processes that create and maintain that object out of a particular combination of critical features. The process of fea-

ture integration leaves memory traces, which are then experienced as familiarity the next time that particular conjunction of features is encountered. The more times an object file is constructed for an object or event, the more detailed that file can become, and the more familiar it will seem when it is next encountered.

Identification, however, clearly requires some sort of memory and retrieval process. The representation of the perceptual object created for the moment, the object file, must be compared to other representations in memory, along with the connections these other representations have to other information stored in memory. Most investigators agree on this much. What they do not agree on is the nature of the representations that are compared—whether they are composed of features of some sort, or of spatial frequency components, or of some other type of basic elements.

Data-Driven versus Conceptually Driven Processing

Feature integration theory and most modern theories of visual object recognition and identification assume at least two major types of psychological processes. One type, referred to as **data-driven processing,** begins with the arrival of sensory information at the receptors. This type of processing is characterized by the processing of information, or data, in terms of some fixed set of rules or procedures. In a sense, the data themselves *drive* the processing, since the rules usually concern the registration of particular patterns in the data. In terms of visual object identification, data-driven processing would include the registration of distinctive features in the image (the data), such as luminance differences, line orientations, and other attributes that distinguish the pattern from others. To some extent, figural grouping processes can also be data-driven, as we saw in the case of subjective contours and the Gestalt laws. For example, our perception of Figure 11-18 was largely determined by data-driven processes, in that we were able to determine its shape and the relations between its various parts without having a previously stored representation with which to compare it.

The second type of processing is called **conceptually driven processing,** and its importance is illustrated in Demonstration Box 11-4. In this type of processing, higher-level *conceptual* processes, such as memories of past experiences, general organizational strategies, and expectations based on knowledge of the world and previous events or the surrounding context, guide an active search for certain patterns in the stimulus input. An example of conceptually driven processing is the feature integration stage of feature integration theory, where focal attention selects a locus in space and integrates the features there into a perceptual object, perhaps in conjunction with prior hypotheses as to what to expect. Thus, a dark thing flashing through the air on a playground might be seen as a ball someone has thrown, whereas in a quiet park it might be seen as a bird flying by, because of prior expectations. Both conceptually driven and data-driven types of processing may occur together, or in sequence, but both must occur. If only conceptually driven processing occurred, we would see only what we expected to see, and we would make too many mistakes to survive. If only data-driven processing occurred, we would not be able to take advantage of our tremendous amount of experience with the visual world to enhance our perceptual functioning, especially in information-poor environments, and to distinguish the relevant from the irrelevant in the flux of information on our retinas.

Global versus Local Processing

Because considerable evidence for physiological feature detectors exists, most approaches to data-driven processing emphasize the role of **local** features in object recognition and identification. Local features may be viewed as the small-scale or detailed aspects of a figure, in contrast to the overall or **global** aspect that gives the whole form its apparent shape. In Figure 11-19B, we see the global shape of a letter *H* made up of small *S*'s. Each small *S* is made up in turn of local features (the curved line segments), and each of these features could be subdivided into even smaller local features (such as microdots of ink) if we had a large enough magnifying glass. Thus, the terms local and global are relative; we must specify what level of detail we are referring to when we use them. You can see the importance of local features in object identification by trying Demonstration Box 11-5.

An interesting issue arises with respect to global and local levels of detail in visual forms. Navon (1977) argued that the detection of global (larger-scale) aspects of a form with several levels of detail would always be faster than the detection of the more local details **(global precedence).** This position resembles the Gestalt position, in that whole forms grouped by Gestalt processes seem more immediately available to our consciousness than do the more local constituents that have been so grouped, but is not identical with it (see Kimchi, 1992, for a detailed argument). Navon (1977) did several experiments to test the hypothesis of global precedence, and one in particular was provocative. In this experiment, observers were asked to name forms like those in Figures 11-19A and 11-19B at either the global level (*H*) or the local level (*H* for 11-19A, *S* for 11-19B) as fast as they could. Sometimes the name of the global form was the same as that of its more local constituents (11-19A), and sometimes the names at the two levels were different (11-19B). The first result was that regardless of the nature of the stimuli, observers were always faster in naming the global level than the local level. Moreover, when naming the global level form, it did not matter whether the local constituents had the same name as the global form or not; observers were

DEMONSTRATION BOX 11-4   Conceptually Driven Processing

The figure in this box is a drawing of an animal you have seen many times before. Do you know what it is? If not, turn the page and look at the hint given in the figure there.

In the figure on the next page, the cow's head is outlined. Now look back at the figure here. Having once "seen" the cow, you may wonder how you missed recognizing it in your first glance at this picture.

The difference between your experience during the first look at the figure and your experience during the second look (after you knew what it was a picture of) illustrates the distinction between data-driven and conceptually driven visual processing. In the first

viewing, the data-driven processes extracted shapes of various sizes and with various features. You then tried to match this collection of features with objects in your long-term memory. Perhaps you thought it was an aerial photograph of the Great Lakes or some other familiar scene. In the second viewing, your memory representations of a cow influenced the way you grouped the shapes in the picture. From now on, your memory will contain a record of this picture and you will probably be unable to look at the figure below (even weeks from now) without seeing the cow immediately.

equally fast. However, when naming the local constituents, observers were greatly slowed down if the global form had a different name. This empirical finding of a *global advantage* (Kimchi, 1992), or *global processing dominance* (Ward, 1983), provided a strong argument that global precedence occurs, and

stimulated many others to investigate this problem.

Although Navon (1977) did demonstrate one set of conditions under which global dominance occurred, other studies suggest that local and global features are detected simultaneously (in parallel) and at approximately

Demonstration Box 11-4

equal speed (Boer & Keuss, 1982; Hughes, Layton, Baird, & Lester, 1984; Paquet & Merikle, 1984) so that global dominance does not imply global precedence in this case. More specifi-

```
H         H           S           S
H         H           S           S
H         H           S           S
H         H           S           S
H H H H H H       S S S S S
H         H           S           S
H         H           S           S
H         H           S           S
H         H           S           S

      A                        B


H         H           S           S

H         H           S           S

H    H    H       S    S    S

H         H           S           S

H         H           S           S

      C                        D
```

Figure 11-19 *Examples of stimuli that have two distinct levels of detail.*

cally, it seems that global dominance for visual forms seems to hold only for a specific set of conditions. When the global form is made a bit harder to see, for example, by spacing out the local features as in Figures 11-19C and 11-19D, the results are reversed (Martin, 1979). Now the smaller letters are named more quickly, and the naming of the larger letter is slowed down when the smaller constituents have different names, as in Figure 11-19D. The *absolute* size of the figure is also important in determining whether global or local features are processed more easily. When the stimulus is much larger (for instance, when you hold Figures *A* or *B* close to your eyes), you will notice that now the smaller letters are much more salient and easier to see and the larger letter is more difficult to see. In the laboratory, observers can tell which of two smaller letters is present in such a display more quickly than which of two larger letters is present when the display is larger than about 7 deg of visual angle. When the display is smaller than this (try holding the book at arm's length to view *A* or *B*), the larger letters are more quickly discriminated (Kinchla & Wolfe, 1979). Although

DEMONSTRATION BOX 11-5   The Role of Local Features in Pattern Recognition

Harmon (1973) and Harmon and Julesz (1973) have presented an interesting set of demonstrations that illustrate how local features can interfere with a more global percept. One of their demonstrations is presented in the figure shown in this box—a computer-processed block representation of a photograph. The brightness information from this scan has been locally averaged, so the brightness value in each of the squares is an average of a number of brightness samples taken in that area of the picture. This technique can be used to see if such local brightness information can elicit the percept of the original photograph. To try this, look at the figure at normal reading distance. Do you recognize the person? Try again, viewing from 2 m this time. (It will also help if you squint your eyes.) If you follow these instructions, you should be able to identify this block portrait as a very famous historical person. If not, the name of the individual is printed upside down in the bottom right-hand corner of this page (from Harmon & Julesz, 1973. Copyright 1973 by the American Association for the Advancement of Science. Used by permission).

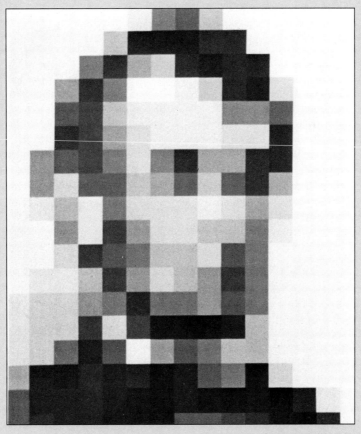

Abraham Lincoln

this demonstration seems convincing, it does confound globality with distance from the fovea—when very large the global forms in Figure 11-9 have much of their structure outside the fovea while at least some of the smaller constituents are entirely within the fovea. Navon and Norman (1983) showed that when eccentricity on the retina is controlled for, the *relatively* larger forms always have a processing advantage.

All of the factors just discussed, and others, (see Kimchi, 1992, for a review) are affected by how an observer distributes attention to the figure. Observers are able to direct their attention voluntarily either to global or local aspects of the figure and thus give that level processing dominance (Hoffman, 1980; Kinchla, Solis-Macias, & Hoffman, 1983). If they are forced to switch attention from one level to the other, however, this tends to slow and interfere with their ability to process either level of features (L. M. Ward, 1982b, 1985).

Integral versus Separable Stimuli

Certain aspects of good figures seem to make them perceptually special. For instance, they have a certain unitary wholeness; that is, they appear to be coherent and not easily broken into components. One analysis of processing dominance that incorporates this idea introduces the concept of an **integral stimulus,** which is seen in all of its aspects simultaneously (Lockhead, 1966). A light bulb is such a stimulus, since it is seen to have shape and color all at once. Subjectively, integral stimuli have many characteristics reminiscent of good figures. In scientific, or operational, terms they are often defined as stimuli for which visual attention can be given to two different features simultaneously (Garner, 1974).

In contrast to the integral stimulus, we have the **separable stimulus,** which has features that cannot be easily integrated. An example of a separable stimulus would be one of

the matrices in Figure 11-17, in which the dots and the lines forming the grid do not seem to be parts of a coherent figure. Most operational definitions of separable stimuli include the idea of being unable to attend to two of its features simultaneously (Garner, 1974).

It has been argued that integral stimuli are processed first as *blobs* at a global level before they are analyzed into their component parts (Lockhead, 1972, 1979; Lockhead & King, 1977; Monahan & Lockhead, 1977). Some separable stimuli, however, hang together better than others. These are said to contain a **configural feature,** which is usually something like the Gestalt qualities of closure or symmetry. Thus, a pair of parentheses like () is seen as more like a figure than one like ((and is processed more quickly, even though it still remains a separable configuration of two components (Garner, 1978).

In our discussion of global versus local processing, we noted that processing dominance may be affected by attentional factors. Attention also seems to interact with figural goodness in determining how well we process certain patterns and pattern components. Many patterns are not really very good and are certainly not very integral. These include the compound letter stimuli shown in Figure 11-19 (see Pomerantz, 1983). Such stimuli tend to be synthesized into perceptual objects by attentional factors, as well as by the Gestalt principles. According to feature integration theory, we need to pay attention to a particular place in visual space in order to join the separately extracted features of a pattern into a proper perceptual object. This would explain why dividing attention between aspects of a pattern slows identification at all levels. The less attention paid to features at a given level, the more difficult (and slower) it would be to combine those aspects into a perceptual object. Since much evidence has suggested that our attention is usually "caught" by good figures, or the best aspects of figures, this would also explain why better features are more easily and quickly joined into perceptual objects. Gestalt processes operating on the entire pattern would produce groups of elements that would be easy to join together into a perceptual unit (Prinzmetal, 1981; Treisman, 1982). The relationship between attention and the Gestalt principles of perceptual organization is like that of a train engine to its track. Although the force and movement is provided by the engine (attention), the path it must follow, if it is to go anywhere at all, is determined by the pattern of the track (the principles of organization). Of course, the fuel that powers the engine is data-driven feature extraction.

Context and Identification

As you have seen in the discussion above, we could not talk about data-driven processing without mentioning attention, an aspect of conceptually driven processing. Many other examples show the importance of conceptually driven processing in the formation, recognition, and identification of perceptual objects. Look at Figure 11-20. Most people would see there two lines of characters, the top line being *A, B, C, D, E, F* and the bottom one being *10, 11, 12, 13, 14*. Now look closely at the forms you saw as *B* and *13*. They are identical; the same form was interpreted as a letter *B* in the context of other letters, and as a number *13* in the context of other numbers. Notice that the

data (the actual stimulus input) are identical for both the perceptual organizations representing the *B* and the *13*. Your identification of those perceptual objects, however, has been affected by a conceptually driven processing based on knowledge and assumptions, mostly obtained here from the other stimuli that form the context.

Another example of the effect of context on identification comes from a study by Palmer (1975a). Palmer asked observers to identify objects presented after they had seen either an appropriate context or an inappropriate context for that object. For example, in Figure 11-21, the loaf of bread (A) would be appropriate in the context of the kitchen counter displayed there, but the mailbox (B) and the drum (C) would be inappropriate. Objects presented after an appropriate scene were more readily identified than were the same objects presented after an inappropriate scene. It seems that what we see immediately before the presentation of a stimulus evokes a series of expectations about objects likely to be present. When the next object seen matches these expectations, identification is easier, whereas incongruous or unexpected items become harder to identify.

It should be clear by now that the final interpretation of a visual scene depends on both data-driven and conceptually driven processing (Norman, 1976; Palmer, 1975b). Palmer (1975b) demonstrated this notion in relation to face perception. Look at Figure 11-22. Notice that when seen as part of a face (as in 11-22A), any bump or line will suffice to depict a feature. When we take these features out of context (as in 11-22B), they do not really portray the objects very well. We actually require more of a detailed presentation (such as those in 11-22C) to identify facial features unambiguously when presented in isolation. Thus, in this situation the conceptually driven contextual expectations compensate for lack of detail in the data-driven feature extraction.

A, B, C, D, E, F
10, 11, 12, 13, 14

Figure 11-20 The effect of context on pattern recognition. The B and the 13 are identical figures.

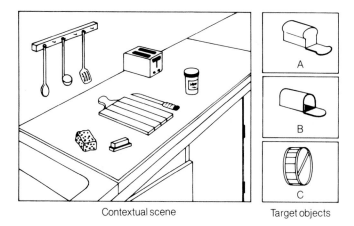

Figure 11-21   *Context and target stimuli used by S. E. Palmer (1975a).*

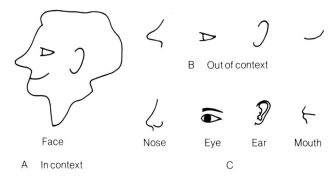

Figure 11-22   *Facial components are easily recognized in context (A), but out of context they are much less identifiable (B) unless they are made more detailed (C) (S. E. Palmer, 1975b). (From Norman, Rumelhart, & the LNR Research Group 1975. Copyright 1975 by W. H. Freeman and Co. Used by permission.)*

THEORIES OF OBJECT IDENTIFICATION

Many different types of theories have been offered to explain how perceptual objects are identified. We have already encountered parts of a few of them in our discussion. One recurring theme in these theories is the presumption that, during the first stage of perception, information in the retinal image is processed to detect contours and simple features, which are then grouped into figures and regions at a sec- ond stage and finally compared to memories of perceptual objects at a third stage to determine the identity of the stimulus. Expectations and context play their most important role at the stage of comparing the input to memories; the match required for identification does not need to be as good if a particular object is expected either because of the context or because it is being searched for. The major disagreements between theories arise in specifying just what aspects of the perceptual object are used in the comparison process. This question is often stated as, "What are the fundamental units of object perception?"

Pandemonium

One very successful theory of this type emphasizes the data-driven feature extraction processes. It is called **pandemonium,** because each stage of the analysis of an input pattern was originally conceived of as a group of *demons* shouting out the results of their analyses (Selfridge, 1959). Figure 11-23 shows how the theory works. In the first stage, an *image demon* passes on the contents of the retinal image to each of a set of *feature demons.* These feature demons shout when they detect "their" feature in the input pattern. These shouts are listened to by the *cognitive demons,* each of which is listening for a particular combination of shouts from feature demons. As the information is analyzed by the feature demons, the cognitive demons start "yelling" when they find a feature appropriate to their own pattern, and the more features they find, the louder they yell. A *decision demon* listens to the "pandemonium" caused by the yelling of the various cognitive demons. It chooses the cognitive demon that is making the most noise as the one most likely to be the pattern presented to the sensory system.

Pandemonium is one of many similar models that depend on data-driven analysis of simple features much like those to which cortical cells are tuned (see Chapter 3). In general, such models can account for many aspects of object identification, such as the mistakes people make when trying to identify alphabetic characters (see Ashby & Perrin, 1988; Keren & Baggen, 1981; Townsend & Ashby, 1982). Variations of the basic theory can be constructed to account for between-letter confusions that depend on minute details of the letters such as size, type style, and the like (Friedman, 1980; Sanocki, 1987).

Model-Based Identification

A second type of theory deliberately avoids the use of any features such as specific shapes or line arrangements. These theories rely instead on detailed conceptual knowledge of the objects expected in a scene, and so are called **model-based** (for example, Brooks, 1981; Lowe, 1987). Earlier and simpler versions of this theory were often called *template theories.* Object identification occurs by comparing the projection of the real object on the retinal image with a projection of a model stored in memory (that is, the template). The projection of the model is adjusted for viewing position until it matches the object in the scene exactly. From this information, the position and distance of the viewer from the object can be determined.

Model-based identification is therefore an example of a completely conceptually-driven theory. The only objects that can be "seen" are those for which models have been stored in memory. This theory has been successfully used to design machines that can pick up single objects (for example, razor blades) from a jumbled bin of objects using only an artificial camera as a guide to action. This success in "artificially intelligent" machines has caused vision researchers to consider it carefully. However, its complete inability to process novel objects means that, at best, it can be only one-half of the story for human object perception.

Identification-by-Components

Although Pandemonium is a successful theory, we have seen that one of its shortcomings is that the set of features used to characterize perceptual objects is really quite arbitrary. This gives the theory very little generality. For example, a theory designed to account for letter perception will have a great deal of difficulty

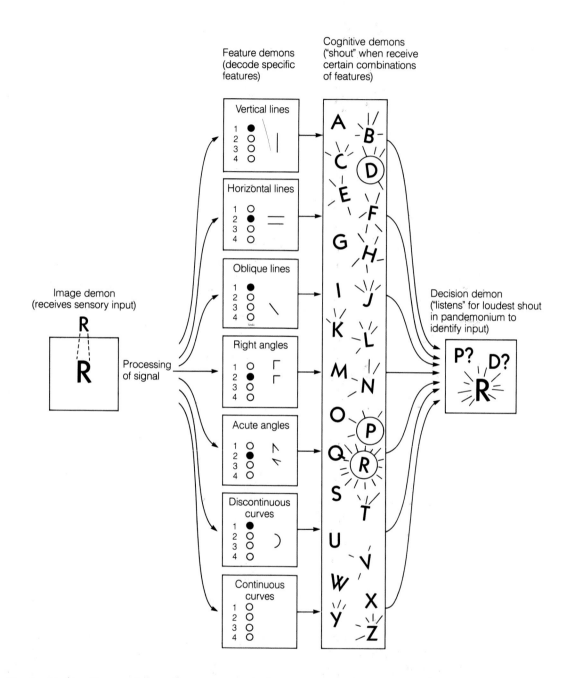

Figure 11-23 *The pandemonium model in action. The number of each type of feature registered by the feature demons is indicated by which circle is blackened in each box and by the number of times the feature is printed in the box.*

explaining how landscape scenes are perceived. Model-based theories overcome this problem by "building in" views of all possible objects that might be encountered. Of course, this causes a new problem—novel objects are not perceived.

These two problems have been addressed by a more recent approach based on the idea that objects can be represented by what some feel is a less arbitrary, primitive set of parts or modules (Guzman, 1971; Leeuwenburg, 1988; Marr, 1982; Pentland, 1986). According to this theory, some simple properties of visual geometry generally remain constant even though the image and the observer are moving and changing in various ways. From these properties, the researchers derived a set of simple components of which perceptual objects are said to be composed (Biederman, 1987). All of the components, called **geons,** are variations of a generalized cylinder. Figure 11-24A displays some of these geons and something of the variety of shapes that can be derived from one of them. Figure 11-24B shows how various combinations of the simple geons give rise to various perceptual objects (see also Figure 11-18). Biederman (1987) calculated that a very small set of such geons (no more than 36) could generate more than 150 million 3-geon objects, ample to describe the richness of human object perception.

Not only does this theory provide a set of primitive features (the geons) with which to describe an object, but it also accounts for some of the major phenomena of object identification. The importance of geons can be seen in that, if you degrade a pattern but still permit an arrangement of as few as two or three geons to be seen, it does not hinder object identification (Biederman, 1987). The idea is that the description of an object in terms of its geon components is compared to other remembered geon-based descriptions. Moreover, even if you have never seen the form before, as in Figure 11-18, it can still be analyzed into its geon components, and even tentatively placed into a

category. Finally, this approach also emphasizes that the law of Pragnanz applies to the geons that make up an object and not to the whole object. We tend to see the best *geons,* which will then give rise to the best object.

Computational Theories

Most modern theories of object perception and identification have been influenced by the attempts of computer scientists and engineers to develop machines that can "see" and identify patterns. Pandemonium models have been used to design machines that can read the account numbers on your bank checks; model-based theories have been used to assist in the sorting and handling tasks needed on a manufacturing assembly line; and identification-by-components theories have been used to design robots that can roam around an office picking up empty soda cans. It did not take perception researchers long to recognize that this line of endeavor might lead to some useful insights about alternative ways biological organisms see forms, since, at the very least, in order to program a machine to perform this function, we must be very specific about the way information is selected and processed.

Probably the most influential version of this approach has been that of Marr (1982), who first analyzed the problem of creating such a "seeing machine" into three levels. These three levels should not be confused with the levels of feature extraction, grouping, and object identification that are required for object perception and that we have already discussed. Instead, these are three levels at which the problem of form perception can be studied. They are arranged hierarchically from most abstract to most concrete. However, it is important to realize that none of these levels can be reduced to another; they are each essential for a complete understanding.

The first level consists of specifying the *computational theory* behind the visual task to

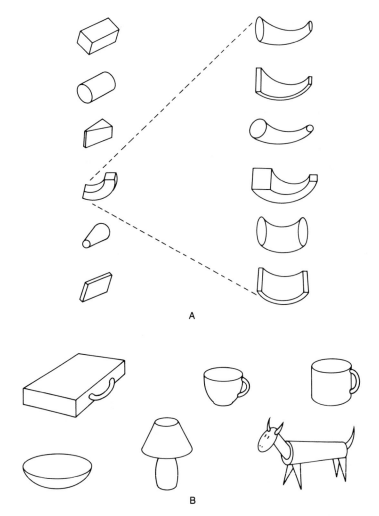

A

B

Figure 11-24 (A) *On the left is a partial set of geons, from any one of which many variants can be created (as on the right for one of them) by varying the basic parameters. (B) Some of the objects that can be created from geons (based on Biederman, 1987).*

be solved. This usually consists of an attempt to state the exact nature of the visual problem, the information that may be available in the retinal image, and the information required ultimately to achieve the correct solution. The second level, called *representation and algorithm,* has to do with the various ways the required information could be represented and the necessary calculations made. Often at this level, several different algorithms are specified that each perform the same computational steps. Finally, the third level, *hardware implementation,* describes the actual implementation of a given algorithm in some device. The device can either be a computer, for which the term *hardware* is appropriate, or it can be a brain, in which case some researchers prefer the term *wetware* (Zucker, 1987).

This *computational approach* is quite different from the behavioral approach of traditional psychology. For example, perception psychologists typically deal only with the second level (representation and algorithm), and even then usually do not use mathematical language to specify their theories. A good example of the psychological approach is that of Treisman (1986b). She defines the task of object perception in terms of three domains: the physical domain (physics' description of the real world), the phenomenological domain (what we experience, the perceptual object), and the functional domain (the various processes that connect the other two domains). Really, all of Treisman's domains are within Level 2 of the computational approach, as shown in Figure 11-25.

Not all computational theories to object identification follow Marr, but all have in common the emphasis on being able to compute the solution to an identification problem, at least in principle, on a machine. In Marr's own approach, the object identification process is broken down into computable problems. First, a set of routines computes from the retinal image what Marr called a *primal sketch*. This is an abstract representation (described mathematically) of the location of various contours, along with a rough grouping of contours into shapes (blobs) that may belong together. From the primal sketch is computed the $2\frac{1}{2}$-D

sketch, which contains a description of the orientation and approximate depth relationships of potential surfaces in relation to the viewer. Finally, a *3-D model* is computed from the $2\frac{1}{2}$-D sketch. This model, corresponding to what we have called the perceptual object, represents shapes and their spatial organization in terms of their relationship to each other and in terms of volumetric primitives similar to geons. This set of descriptions constitutes the computational theory of object representation, although we do not provide you here with the mathematical procedures for accomplishing these computations. Many investigators are still working both to refine the computational theory and to construct representations and algorithms that will do the computations (for example, Horn, 1986; Pentland, 1986; Ullman, 1986). Ultimately, however, the usefulness to psychology of such approaches will depend on whether they provide us with any insights as to how the brain actually processes the visual information in a biological system, such as in humans. It is truly humbling to realize that understanding the simple act of recognizing that you are looking at a pencil, and that the pencil is not part of the desk on which it rests, remains a problem about which we have many theories but still no firm answer.

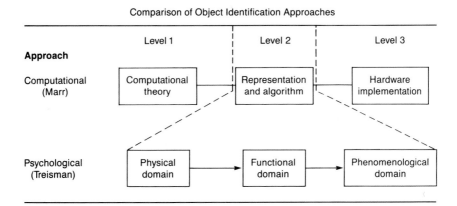

Figure 11-25 *An indication of the different concerns, and levels of analysis, of computational and psychological approaches to object perception.*

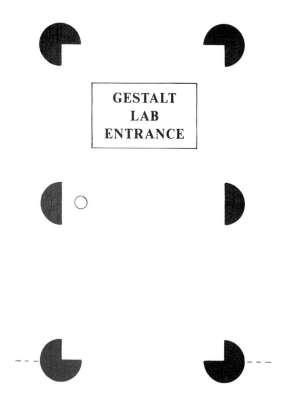

GESTALT
LAB
ENTRANCE

GLOSSARY

The following definitions are specific to their use in this book.

Backward masking The phenomenon whereby exposure to a second stimulus interferes with the perception of an initial stimulus presented previously at a critical interval.

Conceptually driven processing Perceptual information processing that is guided by conceptual processes, such as memories and expectations concerning the nature of the incoming stimulation.

Configural feature A stimulus whose aspects can be seen separately but still produce an emergent feature, such as closure, that dominates processing.

Contour Any place in the retinal image where the light intensity changes abruptly.

Data-driven processing Perceptual information processing that responds directly to properties of the incoming stimuli according to fixed procedures and without influence from memories, expectations, or the like.

Emergent feature A feature that characterizes a particular configuration of parts and is at least as perceptually salient as any of the parts.

Extrinsic contour A contour in the retinal image that occurs as a consequence of one object occluding another.

Feature integration theory A theory of how features are integrated to form perceptual objects; it assumes that features are detected in parallel and automatically, but that attention must be paid to a particular spatial locus in order for perceptual objects to be formed from the features.

Features Attributes of a shape that distinguish it from other shapes.

Figure An integrated visual experience that "stands out" in the center of attention.

Focal attention Active attention focused on a particular spatial location.

Ganzfeld A visual field that contains no abrupt luminance changes and thus no visible contours.

Geon One of the primitive components from which perceptual objects are constructed in identification-by-components theory.

Gestalt A concept and school of psychology emphasizing the notion of meaningful and coherent form, or "whole."

Global The overall arrangement of parts of a figure, as opposed to the local details.

Global precedence The hypothesis that detection of the more global aspects of a visual form is always faster than detection of the more local aspects.

Ground The background against which figures appear.

Identification Naming a perceptual object and knowing something about it.

Illusory conjunction A percept consisting of an incorrect integration of features from separate objects into a single perceptual object (for example, seeing a red *X* when only a red *O* and a green *X* are present).

Illusory contours *See* Subjective contours.

Integral stimulus A stimulus that is experienced in all of its aspects at once and inseparably.

Intrinsic contour A contour in the retinal image that is part of the true shape of an object.

Law of closure The Gestalt law stating that contours that form a closed region tend to be attracted to each other and form a figure.

Law of good continuation The Gestalt law stating that figural elements that form smooth curves tend to be grouped together.

Law of Pragnanz The Gestalt law stating that the psychological organization of the percept will always be as "good" as prevailing conditions allow.

Law of proximity The Gestalt law stating that elements close to one another tend to be grouped together.

Law of similarity The Gestalt law stating that the more similar figural elements are, the more likely they are to be grouped together.

Light source The direction and intensity of the one or more light sources in the visual environment. This property, together with the reflectance, surface orientations, and viewing position of the observer, completely determines the retinal image.

Local The detailed aspects of a figure as opposed to the global aspects.

Metacontrast Interference (for example, masking) between two contours that are adjacent but not necessarily overlapping.

Microsaccades Small, involuntary eye movements that cause the retinal image to shift from place to place on the retina.

Model-based Theory of object identification in which the image of a real object is compared with the image of a model object.

Pandemonium A computer model of pattern identification based on a series of successive stages of feature analysis and recombination.

Perceptual object The perceptual experience of a part of the retinal image forming a whole entity—an *object*—that usually corresponds to a real-world object.

Preattentive processes Perceptual processes that operate to produce shapes and to register their features without the need for focal attention.

Recognition The experience of perceiving something as previously known.

Reflectance Light-reflecting property of the surfaces in the visual environment. This property, together with the light source(s), surface orientations, and viewing position of the observer, completely determines the retinal image.

Relevant features Attributes such as color, size, and texture that differentiate one shape from another.

Retinal image The two-dimensional distribution of light of various intensities and wavelengths on the retina.

Separable stimulus A stimulus that has features that cannot be easily integrated.

Shape A region of the retinal image surrounded by contours.

Stabilized retinal image An image whose retinal position remains constant regardless of eye movements.

Subjective contours Contours that are consciously experienced, but not associated with physical stimulus change. Also called illusory contours.

Surface orientation The orientation of the light-reflecting surfaces in the visual environment. This property, together with the light source(s), reflectances, and viewing position of the observer, completely determines the retinal image.

Textons Elongated blobs of a particular color, length, width, or orientation; line ends; or line crossings. Differences between regions of the visual array in the textons they contain define textural contours.

Textural contour A contour created by a boundary between two areas differing in visual texture.

Texture segregation A perceptual task in which subjects must find an "odd" region of form elements amongst a larger region of "background" form elements.

Viewing position The position of the viewer with respect to the objects in the visual environment. This property, together with the light source(s), reflectances, and surface orientations in the visual environment, completely determines the retinal image.

Visual field All the parts of the environment that are sending photons to the eyes at any moment.

Visual search A perceptual task in which the subject looks for the presence of a *target* item amidst a number of other *distractor* items.

Visual texture Aggregates of many small elements in the retinal image that do not differ in average brightness or color from one another.

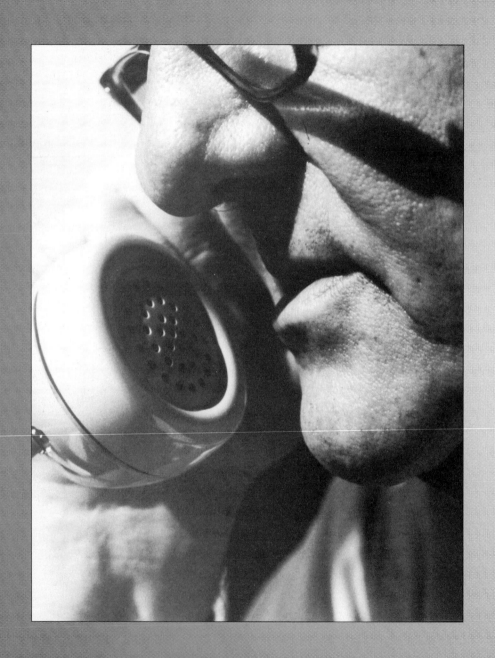

Chapter ...

SPEECH AND MUSIC

Music
  Musical Pitch versus Acoustical Pitch
  Musical Tones and Chords
  Musical Forms
Speech
  The Speech Stimulus
    • Consonants and Vowels
    • Phonemes
    • Acoustic Properties of Speech
  Issues in Speech Perception
    • Ambiguity and Invariance
    • Is Speech Special?
        Categorical Perception
        Duplex Perception
        Cross-Modal Integration
    • Development
    • Context
  Theories of Speech Perception

MUSIC

*I*f a classical pianist sits down to the piano to play a concerto by Bach, the result is undoubtedly music. If a small child sits down at the piano, having never studied the instrument, the child's best efforts at playing produce auditory stimuli politely describable as *random sounds* but perhaps more accurately called *noise.* This is in spite of the fact that a standard piano has only 88 notes for professionals such as Arthur Rubinstein to work with. It is also in spite of the fact that almost anyone can sound each note, although not necessarily in the sequence suggested by Bach.

What, then, distinguishes between a mere collection of sounds, varying in intensity, pitch, timbre, and duration, and the stimuli we experience as music? The answer seems to be that music is created by the context—the relationship of each sound to those preceding and following it. A child's random striking of the keys on the piano, or your experience when presented with single stimuli in a pitch-judgment experiment, lack the relationships that would transform the stimuli into music. Once you perceive a sequence of sounds as music, however, an entirely new set of phenomena emerges, and even the perception of individual sounds will be different (Krumhansl, 1990).

Musical Pitch versus Acoustical Pitch

One of the most striking examples of the perceptual phenomena that differentiate musical perception from other forms of auditory perception is the difference between *musical pitch* and *acoustical pitch.* In Chapter 7 we introduce the *mel scale* for acoustical pitch. This scale shows that when subjects are asked to adjust a set of pure tones differing in frequency so that the intervals between "notes" are equal

steps, the results are not the same frequency intervals that correspond to our common (equal tempered) musical scale. For both the mel scale and the musical scale, sounds vary along the dimension musicians call **tone height,** which is simply whether a sound appears to be of higher or lower pitch. In musical scales, however, other relations between the pitches of sounds help to describe what we hear.

One relationship that is important for musical perception involves the concept of the *octave.* In the common scale—*do, re, me, fa, so, la, ti, do*—the second *do* is one octave higher than the first *do.* To get a tone one octave higher than another, you simply double the frequency of the first sound. Thus, middle C on a piano has a frequency of 261.6 Hz and the C one octave higher is 523.2 Hz. Sounds separated by an octave seem more similar than sounds separated by less than an octave (such as C and G, or *do* and *so*). In other words, as you ascend the musical scale all of the *dos* sound similar to each other, as do the *res,* and so forth regardless of how many octaves apart they are.

This tendency for tones separated by octaves to sound musically similar means that a simple one-dimensional scale (with low notes at the bottom and high at the top) will not suffice to describe our sensation of musical pitch. As we ascend the scale, each note seems to reappear periodically, cycling through again but with a different height each time. This is reminiscent of the situation we discussed in Chapter 5 for color. There, when dealing with the dimension of hue, we found that we seemed to be moving around a circle, from red through yellow, green, blue, and purple, then back to red. In color we could independently vary the brightness dimension linearly, without changing the identity of the hue. In music we can vary the tone height without changing the identity of the tone. Thus we can have a high *do* and a low *do* that sound similar, although one is clearly of a higher pitch. To represent this relationship graphically, we have to use a three-dimensional scheme, much as we did for color. In 1846, Drobisch proposed that musical pitch might be represented as a helix, an idea that has persisted until the present (see Krumhansl, 1990; Shepard, 1982). Figure 12-1 shows this representation of tonal qualities.

The additional aspect of musical pitch represented in the figure is called **tone chroma,** a name that shows its similarity to hue in the realm of color perception. Thus, all *dos* have the same chroma, as do all *res*, and so forth. More precisely, all tones with the same name (for example, C or G) share the same chroma. Like hue, tone chroma is represented by a circle. It can be seen in Figure 12-1 as the circular component of the helix, whereas tone height is represented by the vertical component. One complete turn of the helix (a 360-degree rotation in the horizontal plane) represents a single octave. All notes with the same name fall on a line drawn down the helix onto the same point on the chroma circle at the bottom, and all sound similar. For convenience, we have labeled the spiral with some names of musical scale notes corresponding to the white keys on the piano rather than use tone frequencies. Thus, A_1 is the lowest A note on the piano, A_2 is one octave above it, and so on.

Although the usual laboratory experiment in pitch perception is able to isolate tones that seem to vary only in tone height, it is also possible to produce a series of sounds that vary only in tone chroma (move around the chroma circle in Figure 12-1) yet seem to ascend in height (Shepard, 1964; but see also Burns, 1981; Pollack, 1978). You can try this for yourself in Demonstration Box 12-1. An interesting variant of this illusion was reported by Deutsch (1986, 1987; Deutsch & Kuyper, 1987). She found a circular pattern of tones that is heard as ascending when played in one musical key but descending when played in another, which is contrary to the usual experience that a

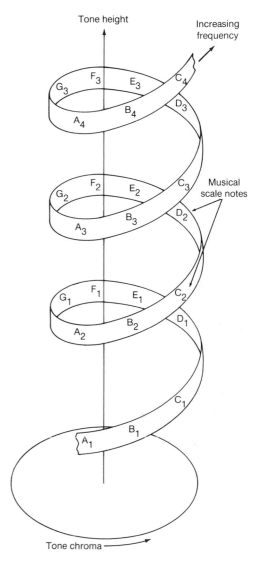

Figure 12-1 *A regular helix represents the two aspects of musical pitch: height and chroma.*

melody sounds the same when transposed to another key.

Although the musical helix represents the major aspects of musical pitch, it does not tell the whole story. Although research has confirmed the importance of the tone chroma circle, much work has indicated that other

DEMONSTRATION BOX 12-1   The Tonal Staircase

Shepard (1964) invented a series of complex tones generated by a computer that when listened to in sequence seemed continually to increase in pitch. That is, each step between tones was perceived as being a step upward in pitch. Shepard, however, used a trick in generating this series of sounds, and in fact the series ended where it had begun, completing a journey around the chroma circle (see Figure 12-1). The continuing rise in pitch was an illusion. It is rather difficult to produce Shepard's series of sounds without complex equipment, but it may be possible for you to hear the illusion anyway. First, fill a glass partially full of water; a crystal glass would be best, perhaps a wine glass, but any glass with a "ring" should do. Now tap the glass gently with a knife or other implement to make it ring. Continue tapping gently to produce a series of complex sounds. Each sound will be slightly different from the others in its frequency components because of variation in the way the knife strikes the glass. The series of sounds produced this way can often be heard to ascend or descend in pitch continuously, much in

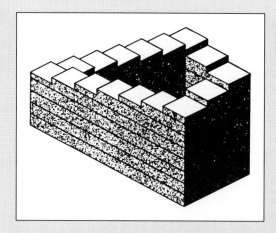

the way Shepard's sounds did, even though the sounds are highly similar and the fundamental frequency probably does not change. In Shepard's demonstration, this illusion is quite similar to the visual staircase illusion shown here. The stairs seem to climb endlessly but never get anywhere. This is probably the most striking demonstration of the reality of the quality of tone chroma in musical sounds.

relations between musical tones are also quite important (see Krumhansl & Kessler, 1982; Shepard, 1982). For example, when one tone is exactly 1.5 times the frequency of the other (a 3-to-2 ratio, or a *perfect fifth* to a musician), the two tones seem to "go together" or sound better together than when the tones are separated by other frequency steps (save for the octave step where tones sound similar). This and other relations between tones and between musical keys (for example, the key of C or F# or any particular group of tones that comprise

the musical scale used for a particular melody) require a much more complicated representation, and researchers are still working on this problem (see Bregman, 1990; Krumhansl, 1990; Krumhansl & Kessler, 1982; Shepard, 1982). What is certain, however, is that such relations play an important role in music theory and do have a perceptual reality, at least for the musically inclined. Since these relations must be taken into consideration in any description of music perception, it is much more difficult to generate a *musical space* than it was to generate a color space to represent our perceptions (see Chapter 5).

Musical Tones and Chords

How well can people identify musical notes? In music contexts, we frequently hear of individuals who have *perfect pitch.* Such musicians are able to identify a musical note that is played on an instrument even when it is presented in complete isolation from other notes (although they do occasionally misidentify the octave where it is located because of the perceptual similarity we have already discussed). However, when these musicians are presented with pure, sine-wave tones, they can identify the notes correctly only about half the time (Lockhead & Byrd, 1981). This is still much better than those without perfect pitch, who tend to be correct on only about 8% of the trials, but it is nowhere near "perfect." Remember from Chapter 7 that the perception of the pitch of a set of tones is predominantly determined by the frequency of the *fundamental,* or lowest tone, in the set. When a note is played on a musical instrument, though, different harmonic frequencies (multiples of the fundamental) are also sounded, giving the *timbre,* or complexity, to the sound. Clearly, the musicians who have perfect pitch are using more than the fundamental frequency of the musical notes to identify them; they are probably using these higher harmonics (the same ones that allow us to determine whether a note was struck on a piano or a guitar) to aid in identification. From their self-reports these musicians judge chroma by comparing the test note with an internal (remembered) standard for each note, whereas people without perfect pitch simply seem to guess at chroma.

The spacing between notes is called a **musical interval.** In music of the Western world, scales have been arranged with logarithmic musical intervals. This is because frequency intervals that are equal on a logarithmic scale are perceived as being approximately equal intervals of musical pitch. For example, if, in a musical context, you heard an interval generated by a pair of notes with fundamental frequencies of 200 and 400 Hz and another generated by a pair with fundamental frequencies of 2000 and 4000 Hz, they would seem to be about equally large (since $\log 400 - \log 200 = \log 4000 - \log 2000 = 0.3$). One implication of this is that any pair of steps between notes of the musical scale that are separated by the same number of intervening notes will appear to be the same size. The preceding example dealt with octaves, a separation of eight notes (from *do* to *do,* excluding sharps and flats), which are actually separated by 0.3 log units. When you subtract logarithms of frequencies, you are performing the mathematical equivalent of division on the original numbers representing the frequencies. This means that when we talk about the logarithmic intervals between musical notes, we are also talking about the ratios between the fundamental frequencies of those notes.

When three or more musical notes are played at the same time, we have a **chord.** Chords give much of the characteristic sound to what we call music (see, for example, Krumhansl, Bharucha, & Kessler, 1982). Formal music theory provides a somewhat complicated system for naming chords, which we will not go into here. Suffice it to say that chords are also defined in terms of the ratios of the fundamental frequencies of the notes that constitute them. Chords whose respective components stand in the same frequency relationship are given the same name, no matter what octave they are from. For example, an E major chord is composed of the notes E, G#, and B regardless of whether the notes are 3 octaves up from the lowest on the piano (E_4, $G\#_4$, and B_4) or 6 octaves up (E_7, $G\#_7$, and B_7). This aspect of musical pitch also is consistent with the helix shown in Figure 12-1, if spacings between the notes are logarithmic, since the intervals between the notes remain the same regardless of tonal height or absolute frequency.

Musical Forms

So far we have described a few of the most important local, or individual-component, aspects of musical sequences or combinations of notes. That is, we have described music at the level of the particular frequencies of the notes that make up the music. Any sequence of notes also has important global properties, however, that give it an overall pattern. These properties, which comprise the aspect of music called *melody,* include the sequence of pitch changes, the proportion and sizes of the various ascending and descending intervals, and so on. They are global properties because they are perceived in relationship to one another, rather than as individual features (Cuddy, Cohen, & Mewhort, 1981; Deutsch, 1978). Together, these global cues are often called the **contour** of a piece of music. *Contour* means much the same thing here as it does in visual form perception. It is the general shape of the musical sequence of sounds, defined in terms of rises and drops in frequency instead of in terms of changes in direction of a line in space. Figure

Figure 12-2 When a melodic sequence is transposed to different positions on the musical scale (A), it still retains the same contour (B).

12-2 shows some examples of musical passages that share a contour even though they are in different positions on the musical scale. Even trained musicians often fail to detect a distortion in the particular notes that make up a piece of music, provided that the contour remains intact (Krumhansl, 1990). The same subjects, on the other hand, are extremely sensitive to changes in contour. In fact, melodies can even be recognized on the basis of such global properties alone, although performance is better when the local cues are also available.

A typical piece of music consists of a rather long sequence of different notes and chords, similar to a long string of sounds uttered by a person making a speech. Just as we perceive a complicated hierarchy of words, phrases, and sentences as we listen to someone speaking, we also organize music in a hierarchical fashion (Palmer & Krumhansl, 1990; Serafine & Glassman, 1989). Combinations of notes form *motifs* (sometimes written as *motive* but still pronounced "mo-teef"), combinations of motifs form *phrases,* and so on (Deutsch, 1978).

How are these combinations formed perceptually? It turns out that notes, motifs, and phrases are grouped together according to principles that strongly resemble those of visual form perception. As in vision, on the one hand, unlearned and primitive processes operate automatically to group auditory events into unified "streams." On the other hand, there are also *schema-based* rules for organizing musical events, which are really learned strategies based on musical conventions (Bregman, 1990). Thus, we can consider the perception of music and melody as a form of auditory pattern perception that follows the general rules of perceptual organization.

We will begin by discussing the application of the Gestalt laws of grouping for visual form that we encountered in Chapter 11. Three major principles tend to group notes or chords together in a listener's consciousness (see Deutsch, 1978). The first of these is based on

pitch range. This principle says that notes that are close together in pitch are perceived as part of the same perceptual unit, whereas notes that are far apart in pitch are perceived to be in separate groups. This principle is related to the Gestalt law of *proximity,* and its visual equivalent can be seen in Figure 11-11A. A striking example of this principle was given in an experiment by Bregman (1990). He began by playing two familiar melodies to subjects, one to each ear, in a similar pitch. The notes for each melody were alternated in sequence to the two ears (for example, note 1 of melody 1 was played in the right ear followed by note 2 of melody 1 in the left ear, then back to the right ear, and so on, while note 1 of melody 2 was played in the left ear followed by note 2 of melody 2 in the right ear and so forth). As you might expect, subjects heard only a mishmash of sound and were unable to identify the two tunes. As the two melodies were separated gradually in pitch—one becoming progressively higher, the other progressively lower—subjects were able to identify the two familiar melodies even though they were "split" across the two ears. This auditory grouping based on *pitch proximity* is implicitly taken into account by musicians. Whenever the same instrument plays both a melody and an accompaniment, they are played in different pitch or frequency ranges so the melody will be the *figure* (the part that stands out perceptually) and the accompaniment will be the *ground* (or background against which the melody is imaged). An example is in folk-guitar playing, where the performer often keeps a steady accompaniment going on the bass strings of the guitar while playing a melody on the treble strings.

Another principle of grouping is based on timbre (see Chapter 7). Different types of musical instruments play the same notes with different timbres, which gives them their characteristic sounds and allows you to identify which instrument is playing any given note.

When several instruments are playing simultaneously, the observer tends to group those of similar timbre into units, in a way analogous to the Gestalt law of *similarity* (see Figure 11-11B or *C*). In symphonic music, this principle is used to separate phrases that have a similar fundamental frequency range but a different musical message. Also, timbre provides an additional principle of grouping to that of pitch range when different instruments play different parts of a piece (as in the lead and rhythm guitar parts of a piece of modern rock music).

The third principle is based on the concept of *good continuation,* in direct analogy to the Gestalt principle of that name (again, Figure 11-11D provides a visual analogue of this principle). Sequences of frequency changes in the same direction (for example, rising up the scale) tend to be perceived as part of the same sequence, whereas changes in direction between sequences of notes tend to act as bound-

Figure 12-3 *Three examples of the Deutsch illusion. In all cases, the left part of the figure shows what is played, and the right shows what is usually heard. (A) The original, from Deutsch, 1975. (B) From Tchaikovsky, Sixth Symphony, last movement. (C) From Rachmaninov, Suite for Two Pianos, Opus 17, second movement.*

aries between segments (Deutsch & Feroe, 1981). A good illustration of this is the illusion shown in Figure 12-3, first described by Deutsch (1975). Two different sequences of tones are presented, one to each ear, as in the left panel of A. Seventy percent of Deutsch's listeners heard the sound sequences represented in the right panel of A; apparently good continuation created an illusory "stream" of notes in each ear (see Bregman, 1978). Later data indicated that such sequences are ambiguous figures, as in Figure 11-7, that have competing organizations (Smith, Hausfeld, Power, & Gorta, 1982). However, some cases are compelling enough to be used by composers of music, as in Figures 12-3B and 12-3C. In B, two violin sections play the phrases of music shown on the left, but the audience hears the notes as if the phrases on the right were being played. A similar phenomenon occurs for the music in Figure C, in which the parts are played by two pianos. If you would like to hear this effect, you might wish to look in the library for Dowling and Harwood's (1986) book, which includes a taped demonstration of this and many other musical phenomena.

So far we have concentrated on variations in the frequency of musical notes or combinations of notes, neglecting the other major dimension of musical sounds: duration. You probably learned in grade school that written sequences of musical notes indicate not only tone height (frequency) but also tone length—a quarter note is held for half the duration of a half note, and so forth. Both the duration and height of notes are vital in determining our perception of melody. You can clearly see this in Figure 12-4, which presents three musical excerpts. All have the same tonal contour. They differ only in the time that the notes are held, but this causes a tremendous difference in the melody you perceive. The first is the beginning of the familiar American folk song "Red River Valley," the second is the opening of Mozart's Serenade in D, and the third is the beginning of the second movement of Beethoven's Symphony No. 5. If you play a musical instrument or can sing, you may want to try these phrases for yourself, just to hear how different they sound.

A sequence of sounds of various durations possesses **rhythm** and **tempo.** Tempo is the perceived speed associated with the presentation of the sounds, and rhythm is their perceived organization in time. When listeners are presented with a sequence of sounds, they spontaneously organize it into subsets consisting of an accented sound followed by at least

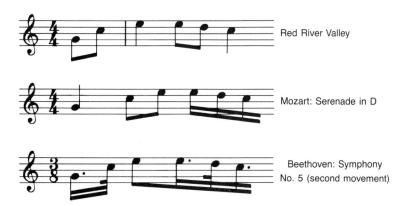

Figure 12-4   *Three musical phrases in which the contour is the same, and the notes differ only in duration.*

one and sometimes several unaccented sounds (Bolton, 1894). This is why the ticking of a clock seems to go "*tick,* tock, *tick,* tock," despite the fact that every ticking sound emitted by the clock is identical. This spontaneous organization happens when the sounds are presented at rates between 10 per second and 1 every 2 seconds and seems to be optimal at rates of 2 to 3 sounds per second. Under some circumstances, the percept may vary in the degree of accenting of sounds so a fairly complex rhythmic structure is perceived despite a physical stimulus that is absolutely regular. In the perception of music, these perceptual rhythms are superimposed on a deliberately manipulated rhythmic structure according to principles of grouping similar to the Gestalt-like principles mentioned above. This rhythmic organization interacts with the organization induced by the variations in pitch of the musical notes, making it easier to perceive the melodic structure of the music (Deutsch, 1978; Handel & Oshinsky, 1981). Actually, the most recent evidence indicates that the principles associated with determining an apparent melody and those determining perception of rhythmic structure combine to produce a coherent musical pattern (Palmer & Krumhansl, 1987).

DEMONSTRATION BOX 12-2   Rhythmic Grouping

In this demonstration you will produce a series of tapping sound as stimuli. In order to indicate how your taps should be distributed in time, let us establish a sort of rhythmic notation. Whenever we present a *V* it indicates a tap, whereas a hyphen indicates a brief pause. First, tap this simple sequence *VV-V.* Listen carefully, and notice that the first two taps seem to "go together" or form a unit, but the last seems to stand alone. Now, repeat this sequence of taps several times and try to mentally change this organization so you have two groups with the first tap *(V)* forming one and the last two taps *(V-V)* forming the other. Notice that no effort of will allows you to do this. The two taps that are close together in time seem to go together and the other does not. This is analogous to the Gestalt principle of grouping by proximity that we discuss in Chapter 11.

Next, try the sequence VVV-V-V-VVV-V-V-VVV, and so on. Notice that this is a repetition of three quick taps, followed by two slow taps. Notice that now the three taps form one group, and the two slow taps form another, perceptually. It is virtually impossible to hear this any other way. This is analogous to the Gestalt principle of similarity (the visual analogue is shown in Figure 11-11).

While you are tapping, you can see that perceptual groups or clusters can be formed by frequency or timbre differences despite the absence of rhythmic differences. Begin by steadily tapping a surface with your pencil. Make sure the tapping rhythm is steady and unchanging. Now take a piece of paper and slip it between the surface and your pencil and notice that the sound quality changes. Without changing your rhythm, slip the paper in and out so that you are tapping *table, table, paper, paper, table, table,* and so on. Notice that the sounds seem to take on a grouping, with the table taps together and the paper taps together, and it seems, despite the fact that you are tapping quite steadily and monotonously, that the sounds have a rhythm that goes *table, table,* pause, *paper, paper,* pause, *table, table,* and so forth. Here, grouping by perceived similarity has imposed an apparent rhythm on the sound sequence.

Demonstration Box 12-2 shows how sounds may be grouped together by varying the rhythm or timing between them.

To follow the analogy of vision once again, not all perceptual grouping is based on automatic, and perhaps unlearned, organizational principles. There is plenty of evidence that music listeners rely on their experience to "fill in" aspects of the melody and impose structure on the musical stream. One study showed that musical "filling in" was influenced by several levels of structure, ranging from expectations based on musical key structure to predictions based on Western music styles, to familiarity with specific melodies (DeWitt & Samuel, 1990). In another study, when both musically trained and untrained listeners were asked to rate the subjective goodness of various tones within a larger melodic sequence, their responses followed quite closely the statistical predictions made from the types of music they had had most exposure to, even when this violated a Gestalt law such as good continuation (Krumhansl, 1985).

The "learned" aspect of musical organization can also be seen in developmental studies. For example, one group of researchers studied the ability of 6-month-old infants and adults to detect "mistakes" in new melodies based on their native musical scales (Lynch & Eilers, 1990). North American infants were equally able to detect "mistakes" in a traditional Western major scale and a Javanese *pelog* scale that was not part of their birth culture. Adults, on the other hand, were much better able to detect "mistakes" in their native Western scale. This suggests that infants are born with an equal ability to perceive music from all cultures but that the music perception system becomes "tuned" by experience. We will see a similar story for language learning later in this chapter.

Music is an important part of every culture, and it has many more aspects than those few we have space to cover here. Several recent books (Bregman, 1990; Dowling & Harwood, 1986; Howell, Cross, & West, 1985; Krumhansl, 1990; Pierce, 1983; Sloboda, 1985) and a special issue of the journal *Perception & Psychophysics* (Dowling & Carterette, 1987) cover these other aspects in some detail. In the future, comparisons between the music of different cultures may yield some insight into which aspects of music depend on learning the musical vocabulary of a particular culture and which depend on mechanisms that characterize all human beings (Deutsch, 1982). Similarly, comparisons between species that produce music (for example, among varieties of songbirds, or between songbirds and humans) may shed light on the neural mechanisms that are critical to various aspects of music perception (for example, Brenowitz, 1991; Hulse & Page, 1988).

SPEECH

"I just can't understand it," Consuela muttered to herself as she strolled down the Champs Élysée at dusk. "I've given myself practically a Berlitz course in French. I can read French fluently. Signs and papers are no problem at all. Yet every time I try to talk to someone in a store, or on the street, and especially when I go to a student party to try to find out where the excitement is, I can't understand a word anyone is saying. It all sounds like noise." She sighed as she turned into the street where her hotel was located. "I guess I just don't have an *ear* for French."

Consuela's problem is not unique among those learning a second language. We seldom think about how remarkable an accomplishment speech perception is until we are in a situation like hers, where we must listen to a stream of nearly continuous speech without understanding it. In our native language we can understand speech at rates of up to about 50 discrete sound units per second, although speech usually proceeds at about 12 units per second (Foulke & Sticht, 1969). This is quite amazing, since listeners can determine the order of nonspeech sounds only when they occur at rates of less than 1 unit every 1.5 seconds (2/3 unit per second) (Warren, Obusek, Farmer, & Warren, 1969). Remember, we are discriminating not only various units of sound but also their order of occurrence (as when we discriminate between the words *tab* and *bat*). Advertisers often take advantage of our ability to process rapidly occurring speech sounds by having announcers in commercials speak much faster than usual. Our ability to interpret speech sounds much more quickly than the identity or order of nonspeech sounds suggests to some researchers that speech may involve some special form of perceptual processing.

Knowledge of the nature of sound signals may not be enough to allow us to understand how people interpret speech sounds so accurately, since we can understand speech even when the signal is grossly distorted or transformed (see Remez, Rubin, Pisoni, & Carrell, 1981). Examples of distorted but understandable speech are found when individuals speak with an accent, with a mouthful of food, or while holding their nose. Devices such as telephones and radios also produce distortions of the sound signal that do not greatly affect the intelligibility of speech. Telephones allow only a limited range of frequencies to pass along the wire, and yet normal conversation is possible over the telephone (but try it in a foreign language that you do not know very well, and you will see how this distortion may render the conversation difficult to understand). Other transmission systems can severely *clip* the speech signal (turn it into a series of *on* or *off* pulses) yet still only marginally affect its intelligibility (although it *will* sound different). You can also easily understand conversations despite a background of noise, even when the noise level is only 6 decibels less than the speech intensity. In fact, even if the utterances

and noise are the same intensity, we can identify about 50% of single words, and we can understand speech even when it is less intense than the noise if it is about a familiar subject.

As a first guess, you might think that speech perception is merely another form of auditory pattern perception and as such should follow principles similar to those of music perception. To a certain extent this is true. However, because its function is to convey information, and because speech plays such an important role in so many aspects of human behavior, the way we conceptualize speech identification problems and mechanisms will be quite different from the way we treated simple sound stimuli or music. Also, we should warn you in advance that no final answers will be presented here. Speech is one of the most controversial areas of perception research, and we are moving only slowly toward the best way to think about the difficult problems that exist.

The Speech Stimulus

When we dealt with visual form perception in Chapter 11, we suggested that the major task for the observer centered around the construction of perceptual objects that in turn carry information about the environment. Speech perception is similar, but in this case the objects are words, or phrases, that carry linguistic information. As Liberman and Mattingly (1985) put it, "[T]he objects of speech perception are the intended phonetic gestures of the speaker" (page 2). This simply means that the ultimate goal of the speech perception process is to put into consciousness an accurate representation of what the speaker *intended to say.*

Given the intimate association between speech and language, it was probably inevitable that linguists were the first to set up procedures to describe the speech stimulus. Their description depends on the analysis of speech sounds in terms of how they are produced *(phonetics)* and how specific sounds distinguish words *(phonemics).* Such descriptions are universal, in the sense that speech production and the methods of distinguishing linguistic units follow the same rules in every human language, although the specific sounds and the rules for combining them may be quite different (see Clark & Clark, 1977; Ladefoged, 1975). Although our discussion will be limited to the English language, you should be aware that a similar analysis can be conducted in any language.

Consonants and Vowels

In the English language, the vocal apparatus produces two basic types of speech sounds: **vowels** and **consonants.** They are produced by alternating sequences of opening and closing the vocal tract (the air passages in the throat, mouth, and nasal areas) while air from the lungs flows through it. Typically, closing movements produce consonants whereas opening movements produce vowels.

Consonants can be classified along three major dimensions, corresponding to the ways in which they are produced. First, consonants can be *voiced* or *unvoiced.* Voiced consonants consist of a constriction of the flow of air out of the mouth followed very closely in time (less than 30 msec) by vibration of the vocal folds (vocal cords). For an unvoiced consonant, the vocal folds do not begin vibrating until a longer time after the constriction, usually more than 40 msec. Demonstration Box 12-3 allows you to experience an exaggerated version of voiced and unvoiced consonants for yourself.

The other two classifications are by how *(manner)* and where *(place)* in the vocal tract the constriction of the airflow occurs. The constriction can be produced in one of three ways. *Stop consonants* are formed by completely stopping the flow of air from the lungs and then suddenly releasing the flow. The *p* in "pea," the *t* in "tea," and the *k* in "keep" are examples of stop consonants. *Fricatives* are formed by stopping the flow through the nasal passages but leaving a small opening in the mouth and forcing air through it, producing some variety

---

DEMONSTRATION BOX 12-3   Voiced and Voiceless Fricatives

Consonants in the English language are produced by a combination of vocal-fold vibration and variations in the passage of air through the oral cavity. *Fricatives* are a class of consonants formed when the mouth moves to a position that nearly blocks the flow of air, so air is forced through the tiny hole. However, fricatives also differ in whether they are voiced (accompanied by vocal-fold vibration) or voiceless (have no vocal-fold vibration). To illustrate this interaction between the flow of air and the quality of voicing, try the following demonstration suggested by Brown and Deffenbacher (1979). Make the sound of a *z*, such as in the

word "zip." Now try producing a tune (for example, "Oh, Susannah") while you sound the *z.* You should be able to do this easily; in fact, it will sound something like a kazoo. However, now try the same thing while making the sound of an *f,* such as in the word "fat." *F* is a voiceless fricative; therefore, the lack of vocal-fold vibration should make it impossible for you to produce a melody (remember, just produce the sound of *f,* do not hum simultaneously). The quality of voicing, or vocal-fold vibration, allows one type of fricative to be "melodic," whereas the other is lacking in that quality.

of "hissing" sound. Examples are the *s* in "best," the *z* in "buzz," and, as is only proper, the *f* in "fricative". *Nasal consonants* are produced through the nose, as you might have guessed. For these sounds the mouth is closed and the air from the lungs flows through the nasal passages. Examples are the *m* in "mean" and, of course, the *n* in "nasal."

Most of the constrictions occur in two areas in the vocal tract. In one, the lips or the lips against the teeth control the flow of air from the lungs; consonants produced by such constrictions are called *labial* (*labium* is Latin for "lip"). Examples of labial consonants are the *b* in "bat" (voiced, stop), the *v* in "vat" (voiced, fricative), and the *m* in "mat" (voiced, nasal). The other area of constriction is inside the mouth. Here the tongue is positioned at various places, most often either at the ridge behind the teeth *(alveolar),* against the hard palate *(palatal),* or against the velum (the soft palate at the top of the throat, *velar*). Examples are the *t* in "tin" (unvoiced, stop, alveolar), the *n* in "gnat" (voiced, nasal, palatal), and the *c* in "cot" (unvoiced, stop, velar). Try producing these sounds and paying attention to where your **articulators** (the parts of the vocal tract used to produce speech sounds, such as teeth, tongue, lips, and palates) are while you are doing it.

Vowels are produced in a very different way from consonants. In general, as we mentioned above, vowels are produced by vibrating the vocal folds as air moves out of the lungs through the open mouth. Here also, which vowel is produced depends on the relative positions of various parts of the vocal tract. First, the position of the tongue in the mouth is important, whether front, center, or back, and so is its relative height. Changes in tongue position and height change the shape of the resonating chamber in your mouth, resulting in the various vowels. For example, the *ee* in "beet" is produced with the tongue at the front and quite high up in the mouth, the *a* in "sofa"

is produced with the tongue central and of middle height in the mouth, and the *o* in "pot" is produced with the tongue at the back and low down in the mouth. Try saying these sounds and pay attention to where your tongue is. Second, the degree of rounding of the lips is important in vowel production. The *o* in "who" is called a *rounded* vowel since the lips must be rounded in order to produce it, while the *e* in "he" is *unrounded* since the lips are flat when it is produced.

Phonemes

Linguists have also worked out a descriptive system of speech units that is sufficient to describe any utterance in any language. In this system, the basic unit of speech sound is the **phone.** A phone that is used in a language to distinguish one word from another is called a **phoneme.** Every language has its own group of necessary phonemes; some have only a few (Hawaiian has 11), whereas others require as many as 60 (some African dialects) in order to distinguish all of the words. North American English has 40 basic phonemes (excluding regional dialects such as drawls and nasal twangs). Table 12-1 lists the major phonemes of American English and the symbols used by The International Phonetic Association (IPA) to refer to them. Phonemes are usually set off from text by a pair of slashes (for example, /p/ or /θ/), but to make things more natural we will simply italicize phonemes and give an example word in quotes (for example, the *p* in "pod"). You should try saying the various example words in Table 12-1, paying attention to how the sounds of the phonemes correspond to the way the sounds are produced (their phonetic features).

Every phoneme has a unique description in terms of its articulatory features (for example, the *b* in "bat" is a voiced, bilabial, stop), so a one-to-one correspondence exists between the articulatory and phonemic descriptions of words.

Table 12-1   The Major Phonemes of North American English

CONSONANTS				VOWELS		
p	pea	θ	thigh	i	beet	o	go
b	beet	ð	thy	ɪ	bit	ɔ	ought
m	man	s	see	e	ate	a	dot
t	toy	ʒ	measure	ε	bet	ə	sofa
d	dog	tʃ	chip	æ	bat	ɜ	urn
n	neat	dʒ	jet	u	boot	ai	bite
k	kill	l	lap	U	put	aU	out
ǵ	good	r	rope	ʌ	but	ɔi	toy
f	foot	y	year	ɒ	odd	ou	own
ç	huge	w	wet				
h	hot	ŋ	sing				
v	vote	z	zip				
ʍ	when	ʃ	show				

Note: The phonetic symbol is to the left of each column and its sound corresponds to the part of the word represented in bold type. Some vowel and consonant combinations are also shown.

Unfortunately, if we look at the acoustic properties of the speech signal itself, it is sometimes impossible to isolate the sound features that correspond to a particular phone in a particular uttered phrase. This is due to the fact that when we speak we often move our articulators to produce sounds that provide information about several different phones simultaneously (this is called *coarticulation*). It is therefore difficult (some say impossible) to find a clear correspondence between acoustic features and perceived phonemes except in fairly specific, often simplified, instances.

Acoustic Properties of Speech

Since phones refer to speech *sounds*, it would seem useful to have a means of displaying the speech sound signal so we can better analyze it, perhaps with an idea of trying to determine some aspects of the relationship between articulatory and acoustic features and the final perceived speech units. One popular way is based on the fact that any complex sound wave can be represented as the combination of a set of simple sine waves of different amplitudes and frequencies (see Chapter 6). For speech we must add the dimension of time, since the speech waveform is not periodic (repeating) over space, but instead varies over time. The result of analyzing a sequence of speech sounds into its sine-wave components on a moment-to-moment basis is displayed as a **speech spectrogram.** An example is shown in Figure 12-5. In all such spectrograms, the horizontal axis shows time in milliseconds from the onset of the speech signal, and the vertical axis shows the frequency (in Hz) of the sine-wave components at a given moment. The intensity of the sine-wave components is represented by the darkness of the smudges on the spectrogram: The darker the smudge the more intense the component. Notice in Figure 12-5 that there are very intense components from about 300 to 700 Hz in all of the syllables. These components last about 200 msec for the "bab" syllable and about 300 msec for the "gag" syllable.

The dark smudges in a speech spectrogram are called **formants.** Formants are bands of especially intense components that arise because the complex sound waves created by the passage of air from the lungs across the vocal folds and out through the mouth or nose are affected by the positions of the various parts of the vocal tract. For each mouth posture and air flow pattern, certain ranges of nearby frequencies are enhanced and others are diminished. These show up as the pattern of smudges on the spectrogram. At least four formants can be distinguished for each of the syllables in Figure 12-5. The one at the lowest frequency (around 500 Hz in the figure) is called the *first formant* and is produced by the shape of the pharynx (wall of the throat). Any change in the shape of the pharynx produces a change in the frequency at which the first formant happens. The *second formant*, at about 1400 to 1500 Hz in the different parts of Figure 12-5, is produced by the shape of the oral cavity. Higher

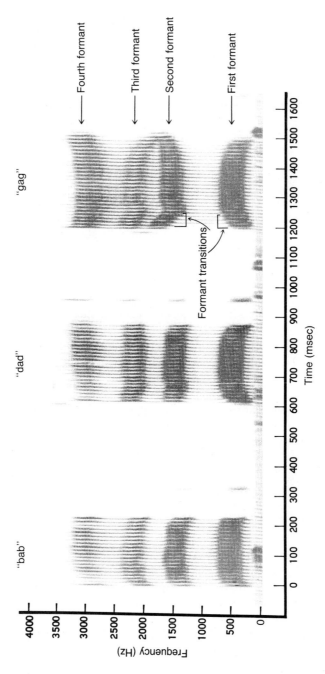

Figure 12-5 *Speech spectrograms of the words "bab," "dad," and "gag," spoken with a British accent (based on Ladefoged, 1975).*

formants are produced by complex resonances of the vocal tract, including the nasal passages.

In general, vowels and consonants can be distinguished in speech spectrograms. The relative positions of the various formants roughly correspond to the different vowel sounds. A special apparatus, called a *vocoder*, provides a sort of reverse spectrograph, recreating the sounds for any pattern it has been fed and even creating artificial speechlike sounds. Using artificial speech stimuli, it has been shown that only the first two formants are needed to create sounds that listeners readily identify as vowels; hence in our presentation we will indicate only the first two formants. Figure 12-6 shows the first two formants for a set of vowel sounds spoken by an adult male. Since people have different-sized mouths, noses, and throat passages, they have different ranges of possible shape changes. This means that the first and second formants will appear at a range of different frequencies across different speakers. Figure 12-6 also shows, for comparison, one vowel spoken by a child. Notice that both formants are centered on higher frequencies for the child than for the adult.

Consonants are generally indicated by changes of formants over short intervals of time (usually less than 100 msec), called **formant transitions.** A typical formant transition is highlighted in Figure 12-5 and depicted schematically in Figure 12-7. Notice in Figure 12-7 that as the formant transition changes the consonant changes from *b* to *d* to *g*, although the vowel (defined as the two formants) remains the *o* as in "sod."

The rate of change in the formant transition is also quite important in the perception of the phoneme. Figure 12-8 shows that for the *e* vowel as in "let," a short formant transition is heard as the consonant *b* and a slightly longer one as the consonant *w;* however, when it is made longer yet, it does not sound like a consonant at all, but rather like a *diphthong*, which is a change between two vowels, as the *ue* in "duet."

Simple sounds of the sort described here do produce systematic perceptual responses, yet in natural speech the signal is not so regular. The theoretically expected components are often missing or distorted. Some individuals (such as Victor Zue) seem to be able to "read"

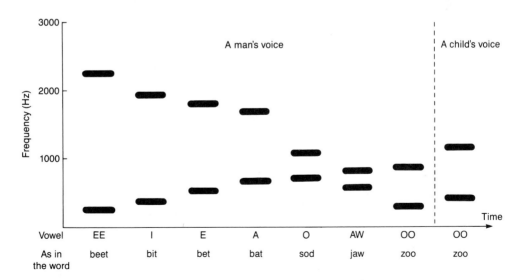

Figure 12-6 *The first two formants for a series of vowel sounds made by an adult male voice. For comparison, the last vowel sound is shown also as it would be made by a child's voice.*

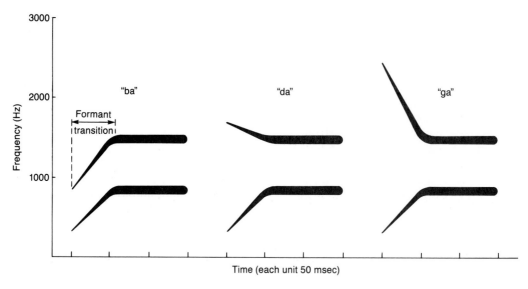

Figure 12-7 *Changes in the formant transition cause a systematic change in the consonant sound heard for the same vowel. The vowel sound is the o in "sod."*

speech spectrograms with an accuracy of about 90% (Cole, Rudnicky, Zue, & Reddy, 1980), but this is a rare quality. In our usual conversational exchanges, a precise correspondence seldom exists between the acoustic properties of the stimulus and the speech signal as it is heard. As we will soon see, whereas it is possible to obtain a precise acoustic description of any utterance in terms of a speech spectrogram, it is not always possible to say exactly what aspects of that spectrogram are meaningfully related to speech perception. In some respects this is quite reasonable, suggesting that we should be looking for relationships or patterns rather than individual speech units. In music we can recognize a melody played on a

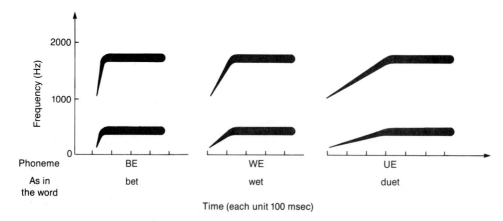

Figure 12-8 *The duration of the formant transition affects what is heard. When it is short a consonant is heard; when it is long a shift between two vowels is heard.*

piano in one key as being the same melody when played on the clarinet in another key, even though no two acoustic signals corresponding to parts of the melody are ever the same. The melody is carried in the relationships among the individual sounds rather than in the sounds themselves. Such a global analysis based on relationships instead of individual acoustic components must certainly be needed in speech perception as well, considering that we are able to comprehend the same message from such a wide variety of speakers.

Issues in Speech Perception

Our orientation thus far has been to view speech perception as a form of auditory pattern perception in which the listener's immediate task is to isolate phonemic units and integrate them into a meaningful whole, much like the visual-perceptual object task we discussed in Chapter 11. To this end, we have been looking at some features of the speech signal and their characteristics. However, because speech perception is studied by investigators from so many different disciplines—linguists, electrical engineers, and computer scientists, as well as psychologists and speech and hearing scientists—approaches to the field are extremely diverse. One way to integrate these different views is to focus on the major problems, or issues, common to most approaches. We have chosen a few of these for discussion here.

Ambiguity and Invariance

Although we suggested earlier that we can find consistent features of the speech signal that correspond to our conscious perception of the speech elements, this is actually an oversimplification that only holds under certain controlled circumstances. In natural speech we do not simply add together the various simple vowel and consonant components to produce the final complex utterance. Conversely, when

we are listening to normal speech, we may perceive a consonant in the absence of the expected formant transition, or hear a vowel that is not the one predicted by the actual formants present. Put simply, the problem is that specific features in the acoustic signal do not always predict specific perceptual experiences associated with the speech stimulus.

Our perception of the speech signal differs from its acoustic properties in a number of ways. For instance, we hear speech in segments we interpret as phonemes, words, or phrases separated by pauses. Actually, the acoustic signal is often a continuous stream, without any obvious breaks or other "markers" corresponding to these perceived subdivisions (for example, Chomsky & Miller, 1963). Another feature the speech signal lacks is **linearity.** In terms of phonemes, linearity means that for each phoneme in an utterance, we should be able to find a corresponding segment of the physical speech signal. Furthermore, linearity requires that the order of the segments in the physical signal must correspond to the order of phonemes. Neither of these criteria is met in the natural speech signal. One example to illustrate this lack of correspondence is the children's ditty, "Mares eat oats and does eat oats and little lambs eat ivy." If you are unfamiliar with this poem, and you hear someone read it for the first time, it will probably sound something like this: "Maresee doats and dosee doats . . ." After you know what it means, you will begin to hear "breaks" in the acoustical stream where none physically exist.

Another source of ambiguity comes from the fact that the speech signal lacks **acoustic–phonetic invariance.** Invariance refers to the notion that each phoneme must have some *constant set* of acoustic features associated with it whenever it is heard. In concrete terms this might mean that some specific feature, say the formant transition representing a particular consonant, must be present if we are to hear this consonant in the utterance. If this acoustic feature is present, it means that the associated phoneme was intended, whereas its absence means that the phoneme was not intended. Unfortunately, such invariance is not found in the speech signal. The actual state of affairs is much more complex.

Figure 12-9 illustrates how very different acoustic signals can be perceived as the same phoneme. In this case the phoneme is *d* (as in "date"). As we discussed earlier, formant transitions usually convey information about consonants; the formants themselves contain information about the vowels. Here we have a set of consonant–vowel combinations in which the consonant remains *d*. As we saw in Figure 12-7, it was the change in the formant transition of the second formant that determined which consonant we heard. If that is the case, then at the acoustic level something strange is going on here: When we hear *d* in combination with the vowel *ee*, to form the complex *dee* as in "deep," the formant transition in the second formant is a rise; when we hear *d* in combination with *o*, to form the sound *do* as in "dope," the second formant transition is a sharp drop; and when we hear the *d* in combination with *e*, forming the *de* in "deck," no second formant transition occurs at all. This situation seems to violate linearity, since the information about *d* does not correspond to a specific segment of the speech signal. It also violates invariance, since the acoustic cue for *d* depends on the context (here the vowel it is paired with) rather than a specific set of invariant acoustic features. This lack of clear correspondence between phonemes and acoustic features makes it quite difficult to determine exactly what you will perceive given only the information present in the acoustic input. At the very least, such examples indicate that the relations between several acoustical properties, such as both the formant transition *and* the formant frequency, must be the basis for acoustic-phonetic invariance. Some recent work has confirmed that such relations derived from speech spectrograms can be used to correctly classify phonemes in natural utterances (Sussman, 1991a, 1991b). You can see how difficult it is to segment the speech signal in Demonstration Box 12-4.

Is Speech Special?

In some respects, we must recognize that speech is quite different from other stimuli.

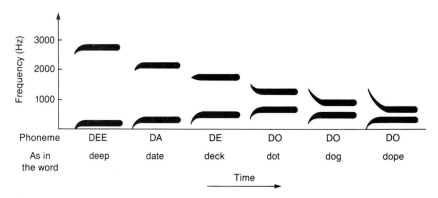

Figure 12-9 *Despite the fact that the formant transition in the second formant changes from a rise to a drop, depending on the vowel, the same consonant phoneme* d *is heard. The fact that the first formant is largely irrelevant to the perception of a consonant suggests that no single feature corresponds to this phoneme; hence it demonstrates the lack of acoustic–phonetic invariance in the speech signal.*

DEMONSTRATION BOX 12-4   Segmenting the Speech Signal

To see how difficult it is to segment the nearly continuous speech signal into words purely on the basis of acoustic criteria, look at the two speech spectrograms in this box, both of which are adapted from Pisoni and Luce (1986). Before reading the next paragraph, look at each segment and try to figure out how many words or syllables are in phrase A.

Phrase A has five words and six syllables. It was made from a recording of the sentence "I owe you a yoyo." How successful were you? Even knowing the phrase in advance doesn't seem to help very much does it?

Now look at phrase B. It represents the spectrogram of the phrase "Peter buttered the burnt toast." There are five occurrences of the phoneme *t* as in "toy" in this phrase. If there is invariance and linearity in the speech signal you should be able to find five repetitions of the same signal representing this phoneme *t*. Can you find them? It may be of some comfort to know that speech researchers have the same difficulties, and they have not solved them yet. A recent book devoted to this problem illustrates the variety of approaches that is being tried and provides an excellent summary of the current state of knowledge on this subject (Perkell & Klatt, 1986).

Frequency (Hz) →

Time (msec) →   A   B

The speech stimulus is produced by humans to communicate linguistic information, something only humans do naturally. Speech even sounds special in that there is a distinct difference between our perception of speech and of other sounds. However, speech researchers usually mean something else by the question of whether speech is special. They refer to the proposal by a group of researchers that the perception of speech is accomplished by a specialized set of neural mechanisms in the brain (for example, Liberman, 1982; Liberman & Mat-tingly, 1989). This a major point of controversy within the speech research community, and researchers often classify each other by where they stand on this issue. Several lines of research have been used to argue for or against the special quality of speech processing. We will discuss only a few of them here. The arguments usually take the form of the "speech-is-special" forces obtaining a dramatic finding that appears to demonstrate a special "speech mode" of processing, followed by the "speech-is-just-a-form-of-auditory-pattern-perception" forces showing that the same finding can be obtained using nonspeech stimuli and proposing a purely acoustic explanation for the phenomenon with both speech and nonspeech stimuli. The results have thus been much like a tennis match, with players lobbing research findings and interpretations back and forth.

At the physiological level, there is a reason to suggest that speech is different from other aspects of auditory processing. It has long been known that in most humans the two hemispheres of the brain show some degree of specialization in their functioning (see Coren, 1992). Damage to the left side of the brain is more likely to produce disruption in speech comprehension or production (for example, Kolb & Wishaw, 1985), and a series of behavioral studies has also confirmed that speech processing is predominantly left hemisphere in nature. Such studies have either used *dichotic listening* procedures (where different messages are simultaneously presented to the two ears, and hence differentially activate the two hemispheres) or direct recording of brain activity while individuals are presented with various speech and nonspeech stimuli. The general pattern of data obtained shows that specific parts of the left hemisphere are most strongly involved in speech processing, whereas the right hemisphere is most strongly activated when musical or other patterned auditory stimuli are presented or when acoustical judgments such as pitch are made about speech stimuli (Bryden, 1982; Springer & Deutsch, 1985; Zatorre, Evans, Meyer, & Gjedde, 1992). Although this specialization is not exclusive—some language processing is also undertaken in the right hemisphere (Millar & Whitaker, 1983), and simple auditory stimulus processing seems to be bilateral—such specialization of function in different areas of the brain suggests that speech might require a different form of perceptual processing than other forms of auditory pattern perception. We will now discuss three lines of evidence that are often marshaled in support of the view that "speech is special."

Categorical Perception   One of the first phenomena to suggest a special speech mode of auditory processing was that of **categorical perception** (Liberman, Harris, Hoffman, & Griffith, 1957). An example of categorical perception uses the continuum of **voice onset time** for stop consonants discussed above. If voicing occurs shortly (say 20 msec) after a constriction of the airflow from the lungs is released, a *voiced* consonant (such as the *b* in "bad") is heard. If the voicing is delayed somewhat after the constriction is released, an *unvoiced* consonant (such as the *p* in "pad") is heard. The time at which the onset of voicing occurs can be viewed as a stimulus continuum, ranging from about 0 to 70 msec or so after the constriction is released. This might lead you to expect that if we varied the voice onset time we should get a gradual change of the consonant from *b* to *p*, with perhaps some region in which the identity of the phoneme was ambiguous or a combination of the two. Perceptually, such a gradual change does not occur.

In studies using artificial speech sounds, we find that for every voice onset time from 0 msec up to some particular value, listeners report hearing only the voiced consonant (for example, *b* in "ba"), as shown in Figure 12-10A. When the voice onset time is just a little longer than this, they suddenly start hearing the unvoiced consonant (such as the *p* in "pa"), as is also seen in Figure 12-10A, and hear only that for all longer voice onset times. The value at which this change in the phoneme occurs, called the **phonemic boundary,** is around 35 msec in the curve in Figure 12-10A. In other words, a sudden shift in percept occurs from the phoneme *b* to the phoneme *p* at the phonemic boundary. Moreover, if listeners are presented with pairs of sounds with voice onset times on the same side of the phonemic boundary (say 10 versus 20 msec before voice onset), they have a very hard time discriminating them at all, whereas if the stimuli come from opposite sides of the boundary (say 30 and 40 msec) discrimination is very good. Conso-

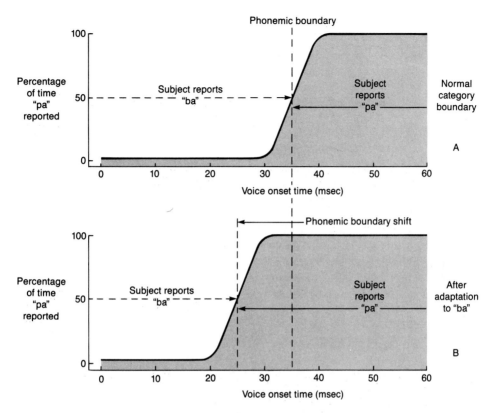

Figure 12-10 *Typical results of an experiment on categorical perception of phonemes. Before adaptation, the phonemic boundary is at about 35 msec voice onset time. After listening to "ba" for 2 minutes, the phonemic boundary is shifted to about 25 msec voice onset time.*

nants show this categorical perception, but vowels do not.

When these findings were first presented, it was thought that nonspeech stimuli did not segregate into perceptual categories but rather produced much more gradual perceptual transitions as the stimulus changed along some single dimension. This led many researchers to assume that some special kind of mechanism must exist to process and categorize acoustic cues defining the various consonants. The data are not so clear now, however (see Pisoni & Luce, 1986, for a review). Several studies have shown that similar dramatic categorization effects can occur for nonspeech stimuli. For example, Cutting (1976) found a fairly sharp categorical boundary for "plucked" versus "bowed" sounds (like those of violins), which differed only in their onset times. Other studies have found similar results for nonspeech "chirps" and "bleats" (Pastore & Li, 1990) and for simple temporal rhythms (Schulze, 1989).

Another group of researchers, critical of the "speech-is-special" view, have shown that phoneme boundaries are perceived in a categorical way in nonhuman species such as macaque monkeys (May & Moody, 1989; Morse & Molfese, 1987), Japanese quail (Kluender, Diehl, & Killeen, 1987; Kuhl & Padden, 1983), and border collies (Adams & Molfese, 1987), none of which should be expected to have a special mechanism for human speech processing. Such data, although still quite controversial, seem more consistent with the notion that speech perception is a special case of auditory pattern perception, rather than a special perceptual process.

Categorical perception effects can actually be obtained for any perceptual continuum. The trick seems to be to use the *adaptation level* as the category boundary. You should recall from Chapter 2 that the adaptation level represents a sort of neutral point on any perceptual continuum that serves as a subjective reference point for judgments. Stimuli above the adaptation level seem to be qualitatively different from those below the adaptation level (for example, hot versus cold, loud versus soft). For a variety of stimulus continua, discrimination of stimuli is considerably worse when stimuli are selected either all from below or all from above the adaptation level. This pattern of data is much like that observed in categorical speech perception (Streitfeld & Wilson, 1986).

Just as the adaptation level can be made to change because of previous experience with particular sets of stimuli, the phonemic boundary can be made to shift around. You may have had some informal experience with such a shift if you have spent time listening to someone speak English with a strong foreign accent. At first, you may have had a difficult time understanding what was being said. However, after some time you may have been startled at the realization that you no longer were "hearing" an accent. Although you may have suspected that the speaker's English had improved over time, you can prove that this is not so by being apart from the person for several weeks. What changed was your adaptation level for certain phonemic boundaries.

This informal observation can be studied systematically by presenting listeners repeatedly with a good example of a phoneme at one end of a continuum such as voice onset time—say, the syllable *ba* with a voice onset time of 10 msec. After 2 minutes or so of listening to *ba*, listeners are now presented with the other voice onset time stimuli as before, such as

those used to generate the curve in Figure 12-10A. This results in a category shift, as though the effectiveness of the original stimulus has been weakened. Thus, some stimuli that previously were heard as *ba* are now classified as *pa*. The boundary has been shifted in the direction of the adapting stimulus *(ba)* so now a stronger (shorter voice onset time) stimulus is necessary to perceive *ba* as shown in Figure 12-10B. Similar results have been obtained with other characteristics of speech stimuli, such as place of articulation and vowel pronunciation (see Diehl, 1981).

Originally, these findings were interpreted by proponents of the "speech-is-special" view as meaning that speech feature detectors were present that were being fatigued or adapted (Abbs & Sussman, 1971; Eimas & Corbit, 1973; Lisker & Abramson, 1970). As a counter to this argument, the "speech-is-just-auditory-pattern-perception" group obtained similar shifts in categorical boundaries with nonspeech stimuli, depending on the acoustic similarity of the nonspeech stimulus used for adaptation to the speech stimulus used for testing (Samuel, 1986; Sawusch, 1986). These results have been taken to suggest that no special speech feature detectors, or special speech processing, need to be postulated to explain the data. However, researchers are now engaged in fine-grained analyses of both categorical perception and adaptation effects, and the only certainty is that the controversy is far from over (for example, Hary & Massaro, 1982; Massaro & Cohen, 1990; Samuel, 1986).

Duplex Perception   Yet another finding that has been interpreted as evidence for a special speech processing mode is a phenomenon called **duplex perception,** in which the same sound can be perceived as having both speech and nonspeech qualities (Rand, 1974). The most common technique used to demonstrate duplex perception is to present a group of synthetically generated formants, called the *base stimulus,* to one ear and present an isolated formant transition to the other ear. Typically, the base stimulus is heard as a particular syllable, say *da,* which either is heard this way or modified by the presence of the formant transition in the other ear (for example, it might now be heard as *ga*). Duplex perception manifests itself when, in addition to hearing the speech sound, most observers also hear a nonspeech "chirp." This chirp is actually the same sound you would hear if the isolated formant transition were presented alone. If observers are attending to the speech sound they show many of the phenomena usually associated with speech processing, such as categorical perception. If they are attending to the nonspeech chirp, they do not show these phenomena. Studies of auditory masking show that the speech percept and the chirp are influenced differently when the stimulus or presentation is modified, arguing further for the separation between speech and acoustic feature perception (Bentin & Mann, 1990). Results such as these are used to argue that, when you attend to speech stimuli, you invoke a different mode of perceptual processing than you do for nonspeech stimuli (Liberman, 1982; Liberman & Mattingly, 1989).

It is also possible to produce duplex perception by presenting the same specifically constructed stimulus to both ears (Whalen & Liberman, 1987). In this case, the speech percept alone is heard at lower intensities, whereas at higher intensities both speech sounds and nonspeech chirps are heard. Interestingly, the *duplexity threshold*, at which both sounds are heard, is about 20 dB higher than the threshold for discriminating speech sounds in the same stimuli. At the least this indicates that speech processing dominates nonspeech processing, and this is consistent with the idea of a separate speech processing mode. However, duplex perception has also been shown to occur for some nonspeech stimuli such as musical chords (Collins, 1985; Pastore, Schmeckler, Rosenblum, & Szczesiul, 1983) and the sound

of a door slamming (Fowler & Rosenblum, 1990), providing evidence that is inconsistent with the interpretation of these phenomena as due to a special speech processing mode.

Cross-modal Integration A final phenomenon that has implications for the "Is speech special?" controversy is the **McGurk effect** (McGurk & MacDonald, 1976). This involves a form of cross-modal integration in which nonacoustic stimuli affect what the listener hears when listening to speech. In this effect, you listen to a string of speech sounds, for example, *da,* and at the same time look at a movie or video of a face articulating speech sounds in synchrony with the actual speech stimuli. Everything is fine as long as the sounds and the facial movements refer to the same syllable. Suppose, however, the sound reaching your ear is *ba* but the face is making the articulatory and mouth movements associated with saying *ga.* The visual input seems to alter your interpretation of the sound, and you hear a compromise sound, *da.* This suggests that in some fashion nonauditory information is used to aid in our interpretation of speech, and perhaps to resolve some of the ambiguities inherent in the acoustic signal. Some evidence has indicated that the McGurk effect is stronger for syllables than for complete words (Easton & Basala, 1982). This has been taken to mean that if a great deal of auditory and semantic information is available about what is being said, the visual cue is not powerful enough to overcome it. Only when about an equal amount of information is gained from each cue does the conflict produce the "in between" percept.

Of course, in normal speech, the visual and auditory cues are usually consistent, hence sight may be a useful means of augmenting the intelligibility of the sound. It is reasonable to suppose that speech perception would involve such a mechanism, since most linguistic communication takes place, and is learned by the child, in a face-to-face mode where both types of cues are available. However, we do not *need* visual cues to understand speech. For example, we understand speech on the radio, even at higher-than-normal presentation rates as in commercials. Also, other theories can account for such cue integration (for example, Massaro, 1987). You can experience a similar effect caused by the cross-modal integration of speech cues by trying Demonstration Box 12-5.

The McGurk effect has been interpreted as evidence that visual and auditory cues about what is being said converge at some special brain site of speech processing. Some data seem to be inconsistent with this interpretation, however. For instance, Roberts and Summerfield (1981) set up conditions like those we have described (the sound was *ba*, the visual image mouthed *ga*, and the subject heard *da*) and then repeated the presentation until subjects had adapted. Next the phonemic bound-

ary was measured, as we illustrated in Figure 12-10. The question was: Does the phonemic boundary shift in a manner consistent with the phoneme that the subject perceives (as a special process might predict) or in a manner consistent with the actual acoustic signal (as auditory pattern theory might predict)? The answer was that the phonemic boundary seems to shift according to the acoustic signal *ba*, rather than the perceived signal *da*.

Let us now reiterate our original question, "Is speech perception a special process?" As you can see from the give-and-take nature of the data we have presented, a special process is a possibility, but an extension of auditory pattern perception processes cannot be rejected. Hence, this question is far from decided, and the controversy will probably continue for a while yet.

DEMONSTRATION BOX 12-5   Cross-Modal Integration of Cues

For this demonstration you need access to a television set and a radio. Bring the radio into the same room as the television set and turn them both on. Tune the radio to a point between channels so a hissing or roaring sound comes from the speaker. Tune the television set to a newscast or other show where a person is talking steadily, looking directly into the camera. Set the volume of the television set to a medium setting, so you can comfortably understand what is being said, but low enough so when the radio noise is turned to a high level you can't hear the television. Now, close your eyes and turn up the radio noise until you can't understand what the speaker on the television is saying, then lower the radio noise until you can just barely understand the speaker, and finally raise it a bit so you can't again. Now, open your eyes. In the presence of the visual cues as to what is being said, you will find that you now can understand the television speaker when you see his or her face. The effect will be similar to turning down the noise slightly, except that all you did was add the visual cues. When you close your eyes again, you should find it again impossible to understand the television speaker's speech. The additional information you are obtaining visually by watching the speaker talk is clearly having an effect on the intelligibility of the speech. These visual cues are particularly important anywhere the intelligibility of speech is reduced by the presence of noise, such as at a noisy party or on a noisy downtown street, or if your hearing is not very acute. Thus, many hearing-impaired people find it easier to understand speech when they are looking at a speaker's face.

Development

Infants are born with a remarkable ability to respond to human speech in a special way (see Jusczyk, 1986; Kuhl, 1987). At birth, infants move their limbs in synchrony with connected adult speech but not with other sounds, such as tapping sounds or disconnected vowel sounds (Condon & Sander, 1974). In addition, infants show much the same patterns of responses to spoken phonemes that adults do. Eimas, Siqueland, Jusczyk, and Vigorito (1971) found that infants as young as 1 month of age discriminated speech stimuli better across phonemic boundaries than within phonemic categories, showing categorical perception in the way adults do. Since, at 1 month of age, infants have had only a little bit of exposure to speech sounds, and their utterances consist only of cries, screams, and babbles, they clearly have not yet learned language. Their ability to make speech discriminations similar to those of adults has thus been taken as evidence of some innate mechanism for speech processing.

Other developmental evidence for an innate language system comes from studies of children's babbling (Lenneberg, 1967; Locke, 1983). By 7 to 10 months of age, infants normally engage in vocalizations that are characterized as repetitive (for example, saying *dadada*), syllabic in structure (that is, consonant-vowel clusters), without apparent reference or meaning, and progressing through a well-defined series of stages. Although some critics have tried to dismiss babbling as nothing more than evidence that motoric aspects of the vocal speech apparatus are developing, recent evidence from hearing-impaired infants suggests that babbling points directly to an early *amodal* language system (Petitto & Marentette, 1991). Petitto and Marentette studied the manual babbling of severely hearing-impaired infants raised by parents whose only form of linguistic communication was American Sign Language (ASL). The babbling pro-

duced by these infants, although it was made with the hands and fingers, was indistinguishable in its time course, structure, and function from the vocal babbling of hearing infants. Interestingly, the hand and finger movements of the hearing infants bore no resemblance to those of the young ASL "signers."

Another very impressive demonstration of infants' speech perception ability was made by Kuhl and Meltzoff (1982). They presented 4-month-old infants with two video displays of the same person's face speaking two different vowel sounds, as illustrated in Figure 12-11. At the same time, the baby was presented (from a loudspeaker midway between the faces) with the sound of the person's voice producing one or the other of the vowel sounds. The voice and the two faces were all in synchrony with each other, but the voice corresponded to only one of the face's articulatory movements. From video recordings of where the baby looked during the tests, it was determined that the baby spent more time (about 73% of the total looking time) looking at the face that was articulating the vowel sound it was hearing. Thus, very young infants also demonstrate cross-modal integration of speech cues, just like adults do (for example, the McGurk effect), even though they have had only limited experience with such cues and do not yet speak. Moreover, this ability is apparently a function of the left hemisphere of the brain in infants, just as speech production is a function of that hemisphere in adults (MacKain, Studdert-Kennedy, Spieker, & Stern, 1983).

Although a good deal of evidence suggests that from birth infants can discriminate the entire set of possible phonemes that the human vocal apparatus is capable of making, adults cannot. Thus, a native Japanese speaker may say "ararm crock" when he actually means "alarm clock," not because of sloppy speech but because the Japanese language does not have the two separate phonemes *r* as in "run" versus *l* as in "look." Instead Japanese has a

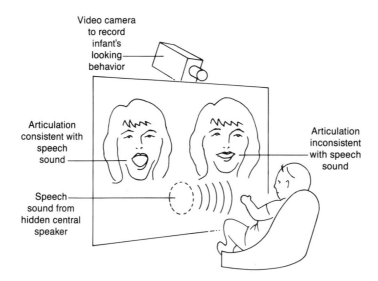

Figure 12-11   Illustration of the setup of an experiment showing that infants can integrate phonemic information across auditory and visual modalities (based on Kuhl & Meltzoff, 1982).

sound that is intermediate to these two consonants in English, one that will often sound like an *r* to the English speaker when *l* is intended, and vice versa.

As infants develop, they maintain the ability to make subtle discriminations between the phonemes present in their own language environment, but they soon lose the capacity to discriminate contrasting phonemes that they are not regularly hearing (Werker, 1989, 1992). For instance, 6-month-old infants can still make discriminations in languages other than the one their parents speak, but by the time they are 1 year old they have lost much of this ability. One study demonstrated this with two different *t* sounds, taken from the Hindi language, that are not discriminated in English. Nearly all 6- to 8-month-old infants, regardless of their language background, were able to discriminate the two sounds as accurately as adult Hindi speakers. However, by 1 year of age, only infants from Hindi speaking families had retained this ability (Werker & Tees, 1984). Conversely, infants also quickly learn to accept a broad range of sounds within a phoneme cate-

gory as representative of their language. In one study, 6-month-old American babies were better able to detect slight deviations from the ideal Swedish *y* sound (which is not found in English) than were their 6-month-old Swedish counterparts. The Swedish babies, not to be outdone, were better able than American babies to detect slight departures from the English *ee* sound, which is not found in Swedish (Kuhl, Williams, Lacerda, Stevens, & Lindbloom, 1992). Both of these types of studies demonstrate that an infant's linguistic surroundings tune the mechanisms that will later be used to discriminate speech. The end result is that adults lose the ability to perceive phonemes found only in other tongues and develop a greater tolerance for deviations from the prototypical sounds of their own language. Thus we might say that infants have a "language-general" discrimination ability, whereas adults have a "language-specific" discrimination ability (compare Best, 1992).

Language-specific discrimination may arise from the fact that different languages have different phonemic boundaries. Phonemes that sound different in one language might then be heard as the same phoneme in another, and our experience may alter our placement of this boundary and hence our categorization of the phoneme. For instance, if you make a continuous *z* sound as in "zzzzz" and then bring the tip of your tongue close to your teeth, the sound will change into an extended *th* as in "that." The distinction between *z* and *th* is determined by the tongue position that sets the phonemic boundary conditions. This boundary is different for different languages. Thus, adult native French speakers will make sounds that their ears tell them have crossed the boundary from *z* to *th*, but that to native English speakers still appear to be on the *z* side. That is why a French speaker may be perceived by an English speaker as saying that she is going out to "walk ze dog."

Context

We mentioned earlier that a major problem in speech perception is the ambiguity of the speech signal due to the lack of an invariant set of acoustic features that correspond to the perceived speech units. We encountered this fairly graphically in Demonstration Box 12-4. One factor that helps interpret patterns, whether visual, auditory, or speech, is the context in which these patterns appear. The other stimuli in the environment assist our identification of the present stimulus. We saw this for visual patterns in Figure 11-20, where the same pattern elements were seen as either a letter or a number, depending on the context formed by the surrounding stimuli. In terms of the ultimate function of speech, which is to convey meaning, context is vital, since the same sound unit may signify different things. This occurs in the case of **homophones,** which are words that sound alike when spoken—such as *be* and *bee, rain* and *reign, no* and *know*—but convey different meanings. Although certain acoustic cues may differentiate these words, most often

the surrounding context helps us tell which word was meant by the speaker.

Interestingly, certain other words sound quite different to us, such as *married* and *buried*, but are produced using nearly identical movements of the mouth and lips. These are called **homophenes,** and are difficult for lip readers to discriminate out of context. Clearly, if we are watching a speaker's face for some cross-modal information in a difficult listening context and if the word uttered is a homophene, we will not get much help from the visual image, but we may get help from the context provided by other words in the sentence. Demonstration Box 12-6 gives an example that demonstrates how context affects our ability to extract the meaning of speech stimuli.

The context effect in Demonstration Box 12-6 was based on identifying the general topic an utterance was concerned with. A great many other context effects are involved in speech perception, many of them depending on the meaning attached to the speech sounds (see also Liberman & Mattingly, 1985; Sawusch, 1986). One interesting demonstration of this type of effect was provided by Day (1968, 1970). She presented sound sequences simultaneously to both ears of listeners. For example, if the left ear received *b-a-n-k-e-t*, the right ear received *l-a-n-k-e-t*. Many of the listeners fused the two sequences into the word *blanket*, even when *lanket* preceded *banket* by several milliseconds; other listeners heard only the separate sound sequences. But no one heard *lbanket,* which is a sequence of phonemes that does not occur in English. The expectations as to which sounds *can* occur in speech clearly provide a context that influences what is perceived.

The importance of context in speech perception is demonstrated by the fact that if trained listeners are asked to provide a phonetic transcription of spoken passages in an exotic language, they do quite poorly, despite

---

DEMONSTRATION BOX 12-6   Context and Speech Perception

In the absence of an appropriate context, even common words are often difficult to identify. To see how context interacts with speech perception, read the following phrase in a smooth, rapid, conversational style to a friend: "In mud eels are, in clay none are." Ask your friend to write down the phrase exactly as he or she heard it. Now you should provide a context by telling your listener that you are going to read a sentence from a book that describes where various types of amphibians can be found. Then read the above sentence again at the same speed you did before. After your listener writes down

what was heard this time, you can compare the sentences (or nonsentences) that were heard with and without the context. Without the context you might find responses such as "In middies, sar, in clay nanar" or "In may deals are, en clainanar" (Reddy, 1976). Here the words in the sentence are difficult to identify when presented rapidly, and a strange and largely meaningless set of segments is generated. When the proper context is supplied, however, the same speech sounds are correctly segmented into words, and are interpreted as meaningful elements.

---

their training, simply because of the absence of an adequate semantic and syntactic context (Shockey & Reddy, 1974). Even if we know the language, our ability to identify isolated words taken from a stream of recorded speech is quite poor. Generally in such tests, listeners are capable of identifying less than half of the items presented in isolation (Pollack & Picket, 1964). If the same words are presented surrounded by longer strings of the words in the original recorded utterance, identification is much better. Thus the more acoustic, syntactic, or semantic context is provided, the better the observers are at identifying the words.

The context of a sentence can actually induce a listener to supply missing parts of the stimulus to fill in a gap in continuous speech. R. M. Warren (1970) presented listeners with a taped sentence: "The state governors met with their respective legislatures convening in the capital city." The acoustic information corresponding to the first *s* in "legislatures" was deleted and replaced by the sound of a cough. Nineteen of 20 listeners reported nothing un-

usual about the sentence. They restored the missing phoneme; hence the effect was named the **phonemic restoration effect.** Again, the context of the sentence determined the speech sequence actually perceived. Apparently both meaning and acoustic cues play a role in such restoration of missing or obliterated components (Bashford & Warren, 1987; Samuel, 1981). Linking this effect with our previous discussion, one study found that the degree of phonemic restoration was related to whether or not visual cues were available as well as to the place and manner of articulation (Trout & Williams, 1990). Another study found that restoration was more likely for words that had a larger number of possible completions in the phrase (for example, *l*egion or *r*egion) than for those that were unique (for example, *l*esion) (Samuel, 1987). This means that if we delete portions of common words or phrases, or present only the distinctive parts of words, the listener is more likely to "hear" the speech as being continuous if the context makes the missing part more predictable. In effect, we hear the speech units that the immediate context suggests should be in the phrase, even if they are not physically present.

Theories of Speech Perception

Many different theories have been proposed to explain various subsets of the phenomena we have discussed. It is probably safe to say that no one theory has been universally recognized among researchers as being the most useful. In fact, many researchers feel that theory is an area of significant weakness in speech perception research (for example, Pisoni & Luce, 1986). The many theories of speech perception can be subdivided on the basis of their level of analysis, whether they are oriented toward the identification of phonemes or words, and whether they utilize **active** or **passive processing** (Nusbaum & Schwab, 1986). Passive processing, like the data-driven processing we discussed for visual form in Chapter 11, involves a filtering or feature detection sequence of events that is relatively fixed in nature. After the message is sensed and filtered, it is then mapped fairly directly onto the acoustic or articulatory features of the language. Active processing involves a much more interactive sequence, in which the acoustic features are sensed, and then a series of higher-level processes involving analysis of the context (either meaning or phonetic) is considered. Expectations or even knowledge of speech production and articulation may also play a role. This is reminiscent of the conceptually driven processes of form perception we discussed in Chapter 11, in that the sequence of processing steps may not be fixed but may vary depending on the results of earlier computations. Both active and passive models may use general acoustic processing rules or invoke "special" speech analysis units.

Many passive theories incorporate the notions of *feature detectors* or *template matching*. Feature detectors for speech are usually conceptualized as neurons specialized for the detection of specific aspects of the speech signal, much the way specific neurons in the visual cortex selectively respond to aspects of the visual stimulus such as line orientation (see Chapter 3). The concept of an auditory template may be viewed as a stored abstract representation of certain aspects of speech that develops as a function of experience and serves the same function as a feature detector. The use of feature detectors or templates in speech identification is often viewed as a process similar to the visual feature extraction model called *pandemonium* (discussed in Chapter 11), in that the signal is perceived on the basis of the template that it most closely matches or the phoneme or word that has the most features in common with it.

Some theories that are predominantly passive in nature stress that ordinary auditory processes are sufficient to explain speech perception at the level of phonemes (for example, Fant, 1967; Massaro, 1987). These *auditory theories* usually postulate several stages of processing of speech sounds. The first stage consists of "ordinary" auditory processing, including analysis of a complex sound into its simple sine wave components, auditory feature analysis, and auditory pattern processing. For some theorists feature analysis occurs first, then pattern analysis, whereas for others they occur at the same time (in parallel). The next stage applies more specialized (but not "special") rules to the outputs of the first stages, integrating them to produce perception of phonemes. A good example of this approach that uses words, rather than phonemes, as the unit is Klatt's (1980) Lexical Access From Spectra (**LAFS**) model. In this model the listener does a spectral analysis of the input signal, matching the results of this analysis to a set of templates of features stored in memory. Words are then identified from the set of features detected in the input. In this model, it is unnecessary to describe segments or phonemes or other linguistic entities; the speech input is directly matched to words in memory by a fixed process.

It is possible also to have a passive model that uses "special" speech units (for example, Eimas & Corbit, 1973). In such a model, the first stages would consist of detection of speech features by "special" feature detectors followed by integration of these features into percepts by (possibly) "special" rules. Figure 12-12A

gives a schematic representation of a general passive speech perception theory that contains elements similar to many current models.

Active models of speech perception are somewhat more variable, since they often involve analysis of the context in which the speech is occurring, the expectations of the listener, the distribution of attentional resources, and memory components. Since different researchers place different degrees of emphasis on these various mechanisms, active theories often differ dramatically from one another.

For example, Marslen-Wilson (1980) offered an active model of word identification

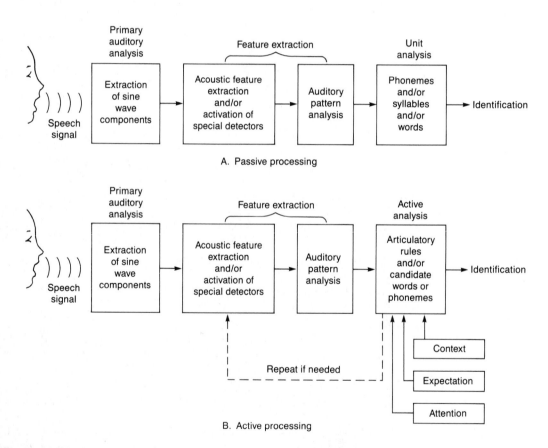

Figure 12-12 *Diagrammatic representation of the difference between a typical passive model of speech processing (A) and a generalized active model of speech processing (B).*

called *cohort theory*. In this model, the early passive stages of analysis initially extract the first phoneme (or phonemes) of a word. On the basis of this information, all the words in memory that have the same beginning (for example, all words beginning with *st,* such as "stop," "stall," or "stride") are activated. These words constitute the *cohort,* or group of possibilities to be considered. After the cohort is activated, other acoustic or phonetic information and higher-level expectations operate to eliminate all the candidates except one, which is the perceived identity of the word.

Phonetic refinement theory (Pisoni, Nusbaum, Luce, & Slowiaczek, 1985) is also concerned with word identification. It resembles cohort theory in its belief that initial feature processing activates candidate words that all sound alike along some dimensions (not just the first phoneme) and form a *phonetic space.* The set of candidates is narrowed down through the application of additional information, both phonetic and contextual, until a single word is identified because it best satisfies all the available constraints and is hence most strongly activated. In this model, words can be identified even if only partial information is available, since even that partial information may activate the correct word more than it does any other words.

Another active theory, which has been implemented as a computer model, is McClelland and Elman's (1986) **trace** model. This model begins with passive feature detection in three levels: (1) acoustic feature detectors whose output is the input to (2) phoneme detectors whose output is the input to (3) word detectors. The unique aspect of this model is that the various detectors and other processors, referred to in the computer model as *nodes,* are highly interconnected. Activating one node tends to activate all the nodes to which it is connected, both at the same level and at other higher or lower levels. This is actually quite a complex model in which various levels may interact with one another in a looping fashion, with higher levels "tuning" or altering the weighting given to specific features.

All active theories have one thing in common: They all have higher-level decisional processes superimposed on the initial feature extraction results. Thus, the speech you "hear" may be determined by factors other than the acoustic signal you receive. A diagram of a general active speech processing theory is shown as Figure 12-12B.

One of the first, and most influential, theories of speech perception is difficult to classify as active or passive because it seems to have elements of both approaches. This is the *motor theory* proposed by Liberman, Cooper, Shankweiler, and Studdert-Kennedy (1967) and recently revised by Liberman and Mattingly (1985, 1989). It is oriented toward the identification of phonemes considered as the intended phonetic *gestures* of a speaker, that is, what the speaker intends to say. In this theory, speech is clearly "special," in the sense that perception of speech sounds is accomplished by a specialized processing mode that is both innate and part of the more general specialization for language that humans possess. In particular, the theory assumes that the same adaptations of the mammalian motor system that made speech possible for humans also made possible a system for perceiving the sounds produced by the speech motor system based on the actual movement commands issued to produce the speech sounds. This system uses complex calculations to deduce the intended speech gestures from the acoustic signal based on an abstract representation of the articulatory movements the listener would have used to produce just such a speech signal.

An example of how this system might work can be seen by looking back at Figure 12-9 and noting that the *d* in the composite *dee* as in "deep" is perceived as the same *d* as in *do* (in "dope"), although they are quite different acoustically. According to motor theory, both are heard as *d* because the listener would use equivalent articulatory movements to produce the *d* phoneme for both utterances. The fact that the actual sounds of the two *d*'s are not the same is irrelevant, just as the pitch of voice, speed of speech, and other sound-distorting factors are irrelevant.

A recent further development of this approach emphasizes the *modular* nature of the special and distinct system proposed to process speech sounds (Liberman & Mattingly, 1985, 1989). A module consists of neural circuits that perform special processing to provide higher cognitive processes with representations of events that have particular biological, ecological, or behavioral significance (see Fodor, 1983). We may have little awareness of what a module is doing, and its processing is automatic and dominates other processing of the same stimuli. In this sense the theory is a passive one because it holds that speech perception cannot be greatly influenced by conscious analysis. However, the processing involved is complex and flexible, taking into account the effects of expectations, context, and other important factors, just as the more active theories do.

No one theory or level of analysis has come to dominate speech perception. In fact, some of the distinctions appear to be gradually blurring. For instance, we have seen that active processing models begin with a passive processing, feature-extraction component; some of the passive processing models may well allow active processing when the signal is degraded or conditions are difficult (for example, Fant, 1967; Massaro, 1987); and motor theory does not fit especially well into either the active or the passive category. In addition, some investigators have proposed that both general auditory processes and special speech processes are necessary to account for all the data (for example, Pisoni, 1973; Werker & Logan, 1985). Certainly there can be no argument as to whether an auditory mode of processing exists. The problem speech theorists still must contend with is just how "special" speech perception is and how much of what is heard is in the signal and how much is constructed in the mind of the listener.

Stimulus arrangement to test the limits of the McGurk effect

GLOSSARY

The following definitions are specific to their use in this book.

Acoustic–phonetic invariance The idea that some set of acoustic features must be associated with each phoneme in all contexts.

Active processing Models of speech perception that incorporate the effects of expectations, context, memory, and attention. Processing may vary depending on previous computations.

Articulators Parts of the vocal tract that are used to produce speech, such as teeth, tongue, lips, and palates.

Categorical perception A phenomenon in which discrimination of stimuli within a perceptual category is worse than that across a category boundary.

Chord Simultaneous presentation of three or more musical tones.

Consonant A basic speech sound produced by closing the vocal tract.

Contour The general "shape" of a musical sequence of sounds defined by the rises and drops in frequency of the notes.

Duplex perception Perception of both speech and nonspeech sounds simultaneously from a single auditory stimulus.

Formant transitions Changes in formants over relatively short intervals of time (less than 100 msec) that are related to consonant sounds.

Formants Bands of especially intense components of a speech signal, seen as dark smudges on a spectrogram.

Homophenes Different words that are produced by almost identical patterns of lip movements.

Homophones Words that are pronounced similarly, but spelled differently.

LAFS Acronym for Klatt's (1980) theory of word recognition: Lexical Access From Spectra.

Linearity The idea that for each phoneme in an utterance there must correspond a segment of the physical speech signal.

McGurk effect The perception of an "intermediate" phoneme when auditory and visual speech cues conflict.

Musical interval The perception of the separation in musical pitch between two musical sounds.

Passive processing A model of speech perception based on filtering the signal for features only, with no higher-level interactions.

Phone The basic sound unit used by linguists to describe speech.

Phoneme A phone used in a language to distinguish one word from another.

Phonemic boundary The point on a speech feature continuum where the perception of the phoneme changes from one category to another (for example, from "ba" to "pa" as voice onset time increases past 25–35 msec).

Phonemic restoration effect When listener hearing a spoken sentence fills in a missing phoneme based on the context.

Rhythm The perceived organization in time of a sequence of sounds.

Speech spectrogram A representation of the speech signal in terms of the frequencies and amplitudes of its sine wave components as these change over time.

Tempo The perceived speed with which the sequence of sounds is proceeding.

Tone chroma A "circular" dimension of musical pitch that connects similar notes of different octaves.

Tone height The simple "vertical" dimension of pitch in musical scales.

Trace McClelland and Elman's (1986) theory of word identification.

Voice onset time The latency in producing a vowel sound following a stop-consonant sound.

Vowel A basic speech sound produced by opening the vocal tract and vibrating the vocal folds.

Chapter ...

TIME AND MOTION

Time
  Biological Clocks
    • Circadian Rhythms
    • Short-Term Timers
    • Biological Pacemakers
  Cognitive Clocks
    • Change
    • Processing Effort
    • Temporal versus Nontemporal Attention
Motion
  Physiological Motion Detectors
  Stimulus Factors in Motion Perception
  Apparent Motion
  Biological Motion
  Eye Movements and Motion Perception
  The Vestibular Sense
    • The Vestibular Stimuli and Receptors
    • Neural Responses in the Vestibular Sense
  Self Motion

Nobel-prize-winning physicist Albert Einstein often thought about the meaning of time, ultimately to conclude that "the distinction between past, present and future is only an illusion, however persistent" (Einstein & Besso, 1972). From the psychological point of view, a better conclusion might be that time is an aspect of our perception of the world, rather than a physical condition that we register like light or sound.

People do have a conscious sense of the passage of time; hence it is clearly a perceptual experience. Up to now we have seen that most perceptual experiences are more or less related to some physical stimulus continuum. However, in the case of time the situation is less clear. There certainly is no readily visible "time organ" for such stimuli to impinge on. Our notion of time may be associated with some form of internal clock that we consult like a wristwatch to determine the span of an event, but it also seems tied to our experience of successive change (Fraisse, 1963). It is through the concept of change that time and motion become intertwined. Changes that occur in a sequence are often associated with a perception of time passing, whereas changes in location may, under the proper conditions, be perceived as movement. Time and motion thus represent dynamic qualities of perceptual experience.

TIME

The concept of time is fundamental to human beings. For example, every language thus far analyzed has separate tenses for past, present, and future, plus innumerable modifiers to specify *when* more precisely—*yesterday*, *today*, *recently*, *in an hour*, *while*, *during*, *after*, and hundreds more (Bentham, 1985). Despite its position as a fundamental experience, the study of time is complex. It has even been sug-

gested that "time is not a thing that, like an apple, may be perceived" (Woodrow, 1951). At the very least, time involves two qualities of our perception that seem to be added to our consciousness and that do not seem to correspond to simple physical dimensions: an awareness of a present moment and the impression that time passes. Let us call these the concepts of **now** and **flow** respectively (Michon, 1985).

The concept of *now* is fairly unitary and was described by William James (1890) as the "saddle-back of time with a certain length of its own, on which we sit perched, and from which we look in two directions into time." Sometimes called the *subjective present*, it is the few seconds of our current experience of ongoing consciousness; all else is either past or future. While *flow* is an equally fundamental perceptual attribute of time, it can be further subdivided into several measurable aspects of experience (compare J. W. Brown, 1990; Poppel, 1978). Each of these additional aspects of time perception may be different from the others and may be maintained by different physiological or information-processing mechanisms. First we have *duration estimation*, which is a report of the experience of how much time has elapsed between two events (for example, between when you turn on the heating element under a pot of water and when the water boils). We usually use units such as seconds or minutes to describe duration. Next, we have the perception of *order* or *sequence*, which involves the determination of which event came first, second, and so forth (such as the sequence of digits in a phone number someone has just read to you). A special case of the perception of sequence involves determining the minimum time interval that must separate two events before they are perceived as occurring one after the other, rather than at the same moment. This judgment involves the discrimination between the experience of *simultaneity* versus *successiveness*. The last aspect of flow is somewhat less perceptual but still requires time estimation: the anticipation or planning of an ordered sequence of events before they occur. This is especially important in playing musical instruments, or in actions such as speech production where we automatically plan and execute an ordered sequence of sounds to produce meaningful utterances.

When we look for the mechanisms by which we perceive time, we find that two general processes have been suggested. We may call these *clock theories*, since each involves a mechanism that determines how we monitor the passage of time. The first, which involves a **biological clock,** assumes that our perception of time has a biological or physiological basis. Just as we have a sense organ that is sensitive to light (the eye), we also have a sense organ that accounts for our ability to keep track of time. The second involves a **cognitive clock,** where time is viewed as a purely cognitive process that is not tied to any objective or "clock" time but is based on how much sensory information is processed, how many events occur within a given interval, or how much attention is paid to ongoing cognitive events. In this latter viewpoint time is constructed rather than simply monitored. Both types of clocks may exist, and each may be used for different types of time perception.

Biological Clocks

Many physical phenomena have their own rhythms or timing—there are day–night cycles, cycles of the moon, cycles of the seasons, and many others. Living organisms often display similar rhythmic activities—many flowers open and close at particular times of the day, and animals have physiological and behavioral processes that cycle regularly. One proposal

about the way time is perceived is based on the idea that the *flow* of subjective time is related to some body mechanism that acts in a periodic manner, with each period serving as one "tick" of the biological timer. Anything that alters the speed of our physiological processes would then be expected to alter our perception of the speed at which time passes.

Circadian Rhythms

One of the most obvious examples of an apparently timed behavior is the sleep–wakefulness cycle that runs through a regular daily rhythm. Another is the return of hunting and foraging animals to a particular area 24 hours after a successful hunt or food find there (Groos & Daan, 1985; Rijnsdorp, Daan, & Dijkstra, 1981). There are also more subtle physiological processes that have their own periodic changes. For example, the pulse, blood pressure, and temperature of the body show day–night variations in humans as well as in many other animals. There is a difference of more than 1 deg C in body temperature between the coolest point, which occurs during the night, and the warmest point, which occurs during the afternoon. These are all examples of a **circadian rhythm** (from the Latin *circa*, meaning "approximately," and *dies*, meaning "day"). Thus, a circadian rhythm is one that varies with a cycle of roughly 24 hours.

So much rhythmic activity in behavior suggests control by some internal *biological clock*. Alternatively, these repetitive 24-hour changes may be simply a function of the regular changes in light and temperature that occur in the day–night cycle. Thus, an animal might become active in the presence of daylight, when it can see more clearly and the temperature is a bit higher, and it is this activity that then alters the physiological function. The "built-in" approximately 24-hour cycle, however, can be demonstrated experimentally in the absence of light or temperature changes. For example, suppose we find ourselves in a constant-light environment, where no changing cues show the passage of time. Under these conditions our biological clock will "run free," gaining or losing time like a not-too-accurate clock. Although different people will have different cycle lengths, most of us will begin to live a "day" that is approximately 25 hours long (for example, Aschoff, 1981; Wever, 1979).

If the internal biological clock is set for about 25 hours, why do our internal and behavioral rhythms continue on a 24-hour cycle? Why doesn't our daily activity cycle drift out of phase with local time? This is because of a mechanism that synchronizes the internal timer with local time. From the behavioral point of view, the most salient aspect of local time is the alternation of light and dark cycles. To be an accurate reference against local time, a biological clock must be synchronized with the local day–night cycle, and it must have a stable period that is relatively free of unpredictable environmental fluctuation. This process of synchronization is called **entrainment.** If no such mechanism existed, and you were traveling across the continent, where the sun might rise 3 hours earlier relative to the current setting of your biological clock, you would be 3 hours "out of step" with your new environment. Of course, some disruption of your time sense does occur from such trips in the form of *jet lag*, which accounts for the sight of newly arrived Europeans wandering through the lobbies of New York hotels at 4 or 5 A.M., looking for an open restaurant to have breakfast in. Because of the great speed of travel, their circadian rhythms are still set to Paris, Moscow, or some other European time. Body time does eventually adapt to the new time zone at a rate of $\frac{1}{2}$ to 1 hour per day. This adaptation comes about through entrainment of the biological clock to the local environmental sunlight-to-darkness cycle.

To use the scientific term, we would say that light is the primary **Zeitgeber** (German for "time giver"). There is much evidence, based on several species of animals including humans, that shows the internal clock is synchronized to light (for example, Johnson & Hastings, 1986). A brief flash of light will reset the biological clocks of animals reared in constant darkness, either advancing it or retarding it, depending on when the flash occurs (Aschoff, 1979). If there is no regular light cycle, however, other environmental stimuli, such as daily fluctuations in temperature, may serve as Zeitgebers to set the internal timer.

Might a single structure serve as the biological clock? Researchers have isolated several regions in the hypothalamus that seem to be important in maintaining the circadian rhythm (Gerkema & Groos, 1990; Rusak & Zucker, 1979). The most important of these, called the **suprachiasmatic nucleus** (or **SCN**), is located very near the optic chiasm, as can be seen in Figure 13-1. The timing function of this brain structure is easily demonstrated. For example, rats are nocturnal animals, sleeping during the day and foraging at night. Destroying the SCN abolishes this pattern. The animal still sleeps the same amount of time, but the circadian pattern is gone and it sleeps in random periods throughout the day and night (Stephan & Nunez, 1977). Tumours in this region have the same effect in humans (Fulton & Bailey, 1929). Furthermore, electrical stimulation of the SCN in animals will reset the biological clock, in much the same way brief flashes of light do for dark-reared animals (Rusak & Groos, 1982). Because light is the primary Zeitgeber for the circadian clock, we would expect that the SCN would receive inputs from the visual system, and it does (for example, Groos & Meijer, 1985). It also may be affected by a hormone secreted by the pineal gland (which is also light-sensitive). This hormone, called *melatonin*, is normally secreted at night (or after a period of

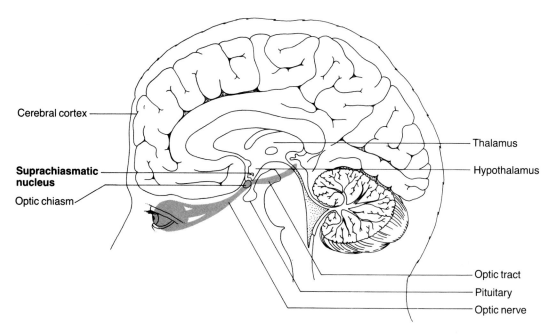

Cerebral cortex

Thalamus

Hypothalamus

Suprachiasmatic nucleus

Optic chiasm

Optic tract

Pituitary

Optic nerve

Figure 13-1   The location of the suprachiasmatic nucleus of the hypothalamus, which is thought to be the basis of the biological clock that maintains circadian rhythms.

light exposure) and appears to reset the circadian clock in the SCN (Cassone, 1990; E. G. Wever, 1990).

Short-Term Timers

It seems clear that, although our circadian rhythms are maintained by an internal biological clock, we often make estimates of times that are considerably shorter than 24 hours. We can even accurately determine which of two time intervals was longer, when each was less than a second in duration. The circadian clock, calibrated to monitor activities separated by a full day, probably would be quite useless for this task. This suggests that animals probably have several biological clocks. For example, destroying the SCN does not affect the cyclic change in body temperature (Fuller et al., 1981), nor does it seem to affect some shorter-cycling biological rhythms. In much

the same way we might use a stopwatch to measure short intervals, our wristwatch to measure longer ones, and a calender to measure even longer periods of time, there seem to be different biological clocks for different aspects of behavior. Heartbeats, electrical activity in the brain, breathing, hormonal and metabolic activities, and even walking steps have at one time or another been suggested as candidates for an internal biological timing mechanism (Aschoff, 1981; Ornstein, 1969; Poppel, 1978; M. Treisman, 1963). Some of these might be useful as biological clocks to measure intervals shorter than the 24-hour circadian period. Therefore, we might view the perception of time as occurring in a "clock shop" rather than in a single biological timer.

Rather than look at long time intervals, some researchers have gone to the other extreme and asked what is the shortest time interval we can sense. Experimentally they asked the question, "What is the minimum time separation needed for two events to be perceived as occurring at different times (successively) rather than at the same time (simultaneously)?" In effect, they were searching for the basic time unit in perception. This idea was discussed in some detail by Stroud (1955), who suggested that psychological time is not a continuous dimension but consists of discrete chunks. These **perceptual moments** are the psychological unit of time. Based on several research findings, Stroud estimated that each moment is about 100 msec in duration, which would be the shortest perceived duration a stimulus can have. In addition, stimuli presented within the same moment either would be perceived as occurring simultaneously, or, depending on the nature of the stimulus, would not be distinguishable from each other. Stimuli presented in different moments would be perceived as being successive. Efron (1967, 1973) demonstrated this aspect of the perceptual moment by looking at *micropatterns*, which are variations in a stimulus that occur so quickly that no corresponding change in the perception occurs. For instance, a 20-msec stimulus composed of 10 msec of red light followed by 10 msec of green light is not perceptibly different from one in which the green comes before the red—both appear yellow. This is true even when visual persistence is eliminated (Yund, Morgan, & Efron, 1983).

White (1963) attempted to measure the perceptual moment by having observers estimate the number of clicks they heard. He presented the clicks at different rates of up to 25 per second. Observers were fairly accurate at rates of up to 5 per second; at the highest click rates, however, observers still estimated a presentation rate of about 6–7 clicks per second. This corresponds to a perceived rate of one stimulus every 150 msec. Thus, information could not be processed in "chunks" smaller than 150 msec, which would be the resolution limit of the internal timer. In another study,

Efron (1967) presented two brief pulses of light and asked observers to say which one was longer. One of the flashes was always 1 msec in duration; the other was of a variable duration. Both flashes were always seen as being of the same length until the exposure time of the variable flash exceeded a value of 60 or 70 msec. At this duration, the variable flash was seen as being longer than the 1-msec flash. Efron concluded that the minimum duration of a stimulus in consciousness (which should be one perceptual moment) was around 60 or 70 msec.

It seems likely that the perceptual moment is different for different tasks and, perhaps, for different sensory modalities (for example, Kolers & Brewster, 1985). For instance, reaction time studies (where observers are asked to react as quickly as possible to a stimulus input) have indicated that short-term memory can be scanned at about the rate of 25–30 msec per item (for example, Sternberg, 1975). The timing of well-trained motor tasks, such as typing or piano playing, also seems to support a 30-msec internal timing organization (Augenstine, 1962; Shaffer, 1985). Eriksen and Collins (1968) used a set of patterns that, if seen by themselves, seemed random. If, however, two patterns were superimposed, either physically or psychologically, they contained a word. They found that when observers were shown patterns sequentially, recognition for the word was highest when the interval between the presentations was about 25 msec. This implies that the perception of simultaneity is maintained over only a 25-msec interval rather than one that approaches 100 msec. There is also some suggestion that the perceptual moment becomes unstable when judgments involve more than one sensory modality, such as judging the order of presentation of a sound and a light (Ulrich, 1987).

An interesting demonstration of the perceptual moment using a different method comes from Intraub (1985). She presented a series of pictures to subjects at a rate of one every 111 msec. One of these pictures always had a frame around it, and observers were simply asked to indicate which picture had the frame. On 54% of the trials, subjects reported that the frame was around the picture that appeared before or after the correct one, probably because the two pictures fell within the same perceptual moment. All these data suggest that, depending on the specific task, the minimum perceptual duration (or the time between ticks of the fastest biological clock) is probably between 25 and 150 msec.

Biological Pacemaker

To the extent that a biological timer exists that serves as a sort of **pacemaker,** ticking away internal time, we would expect that it would speed up or slow down along with other physiological processes in the body. Hoagland (1933) verified this when his wife became ill with a high fever. He asked her to estimate the duration of 1 minute by counting to 60 at a rate of one number per second. When her body temperature was approximately 39 deg C (103 deg

F), her perceived minute was only 37.5 seconds by objective clock time. This suggests that at higher body temperatures the speed of physiological activities increases, and this causes the pacemaker to tick more rapidly than usual. Thus, when asked to reproduce a given physical time interval, a person with a high body temperature produces an interval that is too short. Similar results have been obtained in rats, using natural daily variations in body temperature (Shurtleff, Raslear, & Simmons, 1990). An alternative way of looking at these results is to note how our perception of physical (clock) time seems to change when psychological time is running quickly. A given physical duration will appear to be too long if the psychological clock is ticking faster than the physical clock, therefore giving more ticks per unit time than normally occur (see Figure 13-2).

If an increase in body temperature increases apparent duration, then lowering body temperature may have the opposite effect. This was found by Baddeley (1966), who tested scuba divers diving in cold water off the coast of Wales. Like Hoagland, he asked his subjects

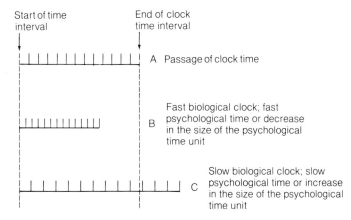

Figure 13-2 Each tick mark on these lines represents a unit of time. Those in A are clock time; those in B and C are ticks of the biological clock. Notice that in B the internal clock is faster, so that the same amount of clock time seems psychologically longer and time "drags by." For C the internal clock is slower, so the same amount of clock time seems much shorter psychologically.

to count to 60 at a rate of one number per second. After the dive, when their body temperature was approximately 1 deg C lower than it had been before entering the water, his subjects required approximately 70 seconds to count to 60. This indicates that their pacemakers were ticking at a slower rate than the external clock. Counting time using the slower ticking rate of their internal timer led them to underestimate the passage of time. In other words, when your internal clock is too slow, physical time seems to whiz by (see Figure 13-2). You may demonstrate the effects of temperature on your own time sense by trying Demonstration Box 13-1.

If we have an internal biological clock, then anything that affects the rate of physiological function might also affect our estimates of time. For instance, fatigue usually slows physiological functioning. Thus, the longer you are awake (or the greater the pressure for sleep), the slower your biological clock and the more likely that, when asked to estimate the passage of an hour, your estimate will be longer than a physical clock hour because of shortened time experience (Aschoff, 1984; Daan, Beersma, & Borbely, 1984). Similarly, general anesthetics lead to a shortening of time experience (Adam, Rosner, Hosick, & Clark, 1971; Steinberg, 1955). Conversely, many investigations have found that drugs such as amphetamines and caffeine (both of which are stimulants) lead to a lengthening of time experience (Frankenhauser, 1959; Goldstone, Boardman, & Lhamon, 1958). Drugs such as marijuana, mescaline, psilocybin, and LSD also seem to produce a lengthening of perceived time relative to a nondrug state (Fisher, 1967; Weil, Zinberg, & Nelson, 1968). It has been argued that all these changes in time perception are caused by acceleration or deceleration of the pacemaker that serves as our internal timer.

Cognitive Clocks

When you say that two minutes watching a pot on a hot stove feels like two hours, but two hours sitting with your loved one seems like two minutes, you actually are expressing the central aspect of most cognitive clock theories of time perception. These theories are based on the presumption that the perception of the pas-

---

DEMONSTRATION BOX 13-1   Body Temperature and Time Perception

This demonstration is based on an experiment performed by Pfaff (1968). We know our body temperature can fluctuate as much as 1 deg C during the course of a day. It is at its lowest point early in the day and tends to rise throughout the afternoon. Given this, try the following observations. On rising in the morning, try counting to 60 at the rate of what you perceive to be one number per second. You will probably need a friend to keep track of clock time for you so that you can relate your perceived minute to a clock minute. Then take your temperature. (Do not take your temperature before you count; otherwise it may bias your counting rate.) Do this several times throughout the day, and keep a record of your results. If the theory is supported, you should find that your counting time will shorten (relative to a clock minute) as your body temperature increases. Thus, as the body clock speeds up, the passage of time tends to be overestimated and "clock" time seems to pass more slowly.

sage of time is based not on physical time but rather on the mental processes that occur during an interval. In effect, time is not directly perceived but rather "constructed" or "inferred" (Fraisse, 1963; Woodrow, 1951). This suggests that the tasks a person engages in will influence that person's perception of the passage of time. Given the variety of potential cognitive activities, it is perhaps not surprising that a number of different variables affect the cognitive clock. Among the variables that have been shown to increase the subjective perception of duration are (1) increases in the number of events occurring during the interval (for example, R. D. Adams, 1977; Block, 1974), (2) increases in the complexity of the stimulus events (for example, Block, 1978), (3) increases in the effort required for cognitive processing (for example, Hicks, Miller, & Kinsbourne, 1976; Thomas & Weaver, 1975), and (4) increases in the attention paid to the passage of time (for example, S. W. Brown, 1985; McClain, 1983). All of these affect the perception of the *flow* or passage of time, and all are consistent with the idea that the rate at which the cognitive clock ticks is affected by how internal events are processed.

Change

One notion is that the ticking rate of the cognitive clock is dependent on **event processing** or **change monitoring.** The greater the number of events or the more changes that occur during an interval, the faster your cognitive clock ticks, and thus the longer is your estimate of the amount of time that has passed. Several studies seem to support this idea. A duration filled with stimulus events is perceived as longer than an identical time period empty of any external events, a phenomenon known as the **filled duration illusion.** For example, if we fill a time interval with brief tones, this interval will be perceived as longer than an identical

time period in which no tones (or fewer tones) are presented. This is also true for such events as light flashes, words, or drawings (for example, Avant, Lyman, & Antes, 1975; Hicks, Miller, Gaes, & Bierman, 1977; Ornstein, 1969; Poynter & Holma, 1985). Conversely, observers engaging in **restricted environmental stimulation technique** studies (where they remain up to 24 hours or more, reclining in a soundproof, darkened chamber with essentially all typical environmental stimulation removed) tend to underestimate drastically the amount of time they have spent in the chamber (Suedfeld, 1980). This underestimation occurs, presumably, because so few stimulus events have transpired during the interval.

Processing Effort

How difficult stimuli are to process and the amount of memory storage they require have also been shown to affect our perception of the duration of a time interval. For example, we tend to judge the brief presentation of a word to be longer in duration than a blank interval of the same length (Thomas & Weaver, 1975). Furthermore, the presentation interval of familiar words is judged to be shorter than the presentation interval of meaningless verbal stimuli (Avant & Lyman, 1975; Avant, Lyman, & Antes, 1975), and presentations of nonfamiliar words appear to take longer than familiar words (Warm & McCray, 1969). In both instances, an increase in the amount of information processing required during the interval (a word versus a blank and a meaningless group of letters versus a word) leads to an increase in the estimated duration of the interval. This is consistent with a **processing effort model** of time perception. Similarly, the more items we store in memory during an interval of time, the longer we judge the time to be (Block, 1974; Mulligan & Schiffman, 1979), a notion sometimes called the **storage size model** of time perception. Both are based on the presumption that the ticking rate of the cognitive clock is dependent on the amount of cognitive activity actually engaged in.

Temporal versus Nontemporal Attention

Both the *event processing* and *processing effort* mechanisms seem to affect our cognitive clock time, but the results are complicated by the way the observer is attending to the task. A simple example of this is given by the old homily, "A watched pot never boils," which suggests that the more attention you pay to the passage of time, the longer the time interval appears to be (for example, Block, George, & Reed, 1980; Cahoon & Edmonds, 1980). This is called the **temporal processing model** of time perception.

One of the best examples of the temporal processing model is the fact that, when we are told in advance that we will have to judge the time that a task takes, we tend to judge the duration as longer than if we are unexpectedly asked to judge the time after the task is com-

pleted (for example, S. W. Brown, 1985; McClain, 1983). Telling observers that they will later have to estimate the time that has passed causes them to pay attention to, and perhaps to order, internal events and external physical events in a way that increases the perceived duration of the task.

Conversely, anything that draws our attention away from actually monitoring the passage of time should shorten our sense of "time passing." For instance, making the task we are working on more difficult makes it harder to attend to time directly. For this reason, we find that estimates of the duration of difficult tasks are usually shorter than estimates of the duration of easy tasks (for example, Arlin, 1986; S. W. Brown, 1985; McClain, 1983). Sometimes directing attention toward or away from the passage of time may even reverse the *filled duration illusion*, which we discussed earlier, since it is more difficult to process many events in an interval while at the same time attending to the flow of time itself (for example, Miller, Hicks, & Willette, 1978; Zakay, Nitzan, & Glicksohn, 1983). Demonstration Box 13-2 shows how attention to time and task difficulty

---

DEMONSTRATION BOX 13-2   Time Perception and Attentional Factors

For this demonstration you will need a stopwatch or a watch with a sweep second hand. Do each step *before* you read the instructions for the next one.

1. Sitting quietly, note the time and then, with your eyes closed and with no counting, estimate the passage of 30 seconds. Then open your eyes and note the actual amount of time that has passed.

2. Next, note the time, look away from the watch, and start to count backwards from 571

by threes (e.g., 571, 568, 565, etc.). Be sure to count out loud. When you feel that 30 seconds has passed, stop counting and note the amount of time that has elapsed.

3. Compare the two time estimates. The first one should be shorter than the second one, because your cognitive clock was moving slower when you were attending only to the passage of time and faster when you were dividing your attention between the counting task and the monitoring of time (see Figure 13-2).

interact to affect our perception of the passage of time.

It should be clear from our discussion that, just as a number of biological clocks can interact in complex ways to give us a sense of the *flow* of time, there are also a number of cognitive clocks, or at least a number of ways to set the speed of a single cognitive clock. One interesting aspect of the effects of cognitive processes on the estimation of time is the effect of age. We all remember how, as children, the time between birthdays seemed endless. There is now a good deal of evidence that as people age, the passage of larger units of time (such as days, months, or even years) seems to be much faster (Joubert, 1990; Lemlich, 1975). One possible explanation for this is that the total amount of time you have experienced serves as a reference level, and the perceived duration of any time interval is compared to this baseline (Joubert, 1983; J. L. Walker, 1977). Thus, when you are 5 years old, the passage of a year represents the passage of an interval equivalent to 20% of your life span, so it seems to drag by. When you are 50, however, a year represents only 2% of your elapsed time experience, and therefore it seems to zip past more quickly.

MOTION

Perception is not static but changes continually over time. Some of these changes are like successive "snap shots," such as glancing from one page to another or shifting your gaze from one building to another as you stand in the street. Other changes are more continuous in nature, such as the sight of a car moving in the street beside you or a bird flying through the air. These latter perceptual experiences have the added quality of *perceived motion.*

Your initial feeling might be that the perception of motion is really quite trivial. You might expect that all you need for motion to be perceived is the image of a visual stimulus moving across your retina. Actually, motion perception involves some fairly complex interactions among a number of different systems (compare Sekuler, Ball, Tynan, & Machmer, 1982). For instance, it is possible for us to perceive movement when the image of the stimulus is not moving across our retina at all, such as when we follow a moving car with our eyes and the image of the car remains fixed on the same retinal location. There are also times when we should see movement but do not. When your eyes move from one location to another, the images of objects that are stationary in the environment are sliding across our retinal receptors, yet we perceive the world as remaining stationary. Thus, movement of the retinal image does not fully account for the perception of motion. Although it is important to understand the visual stimulus conditions that elicit the perception of motion, you will soon see that important nonvisual factors must also be considered.

Physiological Motion Detectors

We begin our discussion by asking whether specific neural units detect motion, much as some detect colors. The existence of such physiological mechanisms is supported by clinical cases where patients have lost the ability to perceive motion. Consider one case of bilateral brain damage, where a woman reported that, although she could still recognize cars when she saw one, she could no longer judge their speed. The simple act of pouring a cup of coffee became virtually impossible since she could not see the dynamic flow of the fluid, nor the rise of the liquid level (Zihl, von Cramon, & Mai, 1983). One region of the brain that appears to be vital to motion perception is Area 7, in the parietal lobe (Hess, Baker, & Zihl, 1989),

Central sulcus

Postcentral sulcus

Area 7

Lateral fissure

Superior temporal sulcus

Medial temporal and
Medial superior temporal
areas

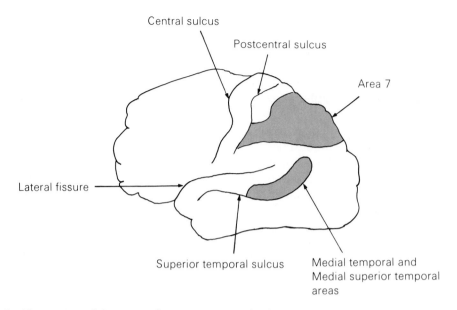

Figure 13-3 *The regions of the cortex that are most involved in motion perception.*

although regions in the temporal lobe also play a role (Newsome & Pare, 1988). These motion processing regions of the cortex are shown in Figure 13-3.

In Chapter 3, we considered evidence from anatomy, physiology, and clinical neuropsychology suggesting that different pathways in the visual system process various kinds of information (for example, Livingstone & Hubel, 1988; Maunsell & Newsome, 1987; Ungerleider & Mishkin, 1982). Apparently, different pathways process *what* an object is (that is, its visual form) and *where* an object is (which includes the analysis of visual motion). Although many researchers speak as if these pathways are quite distinct, which would suggest that the perception of form and motion involve independent physiological mechanisms, probably the functions of these two systems overlap somewhat (compare DeYoe & Van Essen, 1988).

If we consider the two general visual pathways, the geniculostriate seems less involved in motion perception than the tectopulvinar. There are some suggestions that the entire tec-

topulvinar pathway in vision may be specialized for the perception of movement and for controlling the direction of responses, such as eye movements, toward moving stimuli (Flandrin & Jeannerod, 1981; Guitton, Crommelink, & Roucoux, 1980; Van Essen, 1979). Some parts of the geniculostriate system are, however, involved with motion analysis. Specifically, the magnocellular system seems to be more involved in motion perception than the parvocellular system. Both the tectopulvinar system and the magnocellular part of the geniculostriate system contain many more neurons that have transient rather than sustained responses (see Chapter 3). Transient response neurons seem better suited to the perception of rapid rates of movement since they respond to any change in stimulation. Sustained response neurons seem better suited for the detection of details and hence might be better at the perception of form, or very slow movement.

These two types of ganglion cells are not distributed equally across the retina. Ganglion cells with transient response patterns are more abundant in the peripheral retina. This fact helps to explain why the apparent speed of a moving target depends on where in the visual field it is (Campbell & Maffei, 1981). Our ability to detect slow target movements (up to about 1.5 deg per second) *decreases* with distance from the fovea (Choudhurt & Crossey, 1981; Lichtenstein, 1963; McColgin, 1960). For higher target velocities, however, this relationship reverses. At moderate to fast velocities, the peripheral retina seems better able to detect movement (because of the increased proportion of transient response cells), even though the decrease in acuity can be so great the observer may not be able to identify what is moving (Bhatia, 1975; B. Brown, 1972).

The involvement of the magnocellular system in motion perception has been shown recently using a technique involving **isoluminant stimuli.** These stimuli contain lines or forms that are distinguished from their backgrounds on the basis of color only, and all brightness differences have been eliminated (hence the terms *iso,* meaning "same," and *luminant,* referring to lightness). These stimuli are useful because the magnocellular system responds much better to brightness differences than to color, whereas the parvocellular system detects color differences quite well. Therefore isoluminant stimuli are less effective stimuli for the magnocellular system than for the parvocellular system. Using such stimuli, it has been shown that the perception of motion is much more difficult (Ramachandran & Gregory, 1978). Not only do moving isoluminant stimuli appear to move more slowly (Cavanagh, Tyler, & Fareau, 1984; Troscianko & Fahle, 1988), but it is even difficult to tell in which direction they are moving (Lindsey & Teller, 1990). These findings are consistent with the notion that the magnocellular system is more involved in motion perception than the parvocellular system.

At the level of the visual cortex, we find clear evidence for specialized cells tuned to stimulus motion. Specifically, many complex cells in the cortex of mammals respond only to moving targets. Not only do these cells respond to motion, but they are tuned to the direction of stimulus movement, discharging strongly when a properly oriented stimulus drifts in one direction across the visual field and responding less strongly (or not at all) when the same stimulus moves through the field in the opposite direction (see Hubel & Wiesel, 1979). The degree of specificity of response to moving stimuli may be quite strong. Thus, certain cells respond not only to particular directions of movement but also to particular speeds of the moving targets (Maunsell & Van Essen, 1983; Orban, Kennedy, & Maes, 1981a, 1981b).

Computational models or theories have often been applied to motion perception. One such model, which fits well with what we know about physiological mechanisms for the detection of motion, is shown in Figure 13-4 (Marr & Ullman, 1981; Reichardt, 1961; van Santen & Sperling, 1985). This model requires at least three different neuronal units to make it work. The two cells at the top of the diagram (A and B) behave like the simple cortical cells we discussed in Chapter 3; their receptive fields are both tuned to edges of a particular orientation. The neural signals from these two cells are compared with one another by the third cell (C) shown in the lower part of the diagram, but only after the signal from cell A has been delayed by some small amount of time. The purpose of the delay is to compensate for the movement of the stimulus, which will cause successive neural receptive fields to be stimulated. If the two signals (A and B) arrive at C at about the same time, then the comparator cell (C) will fire vigorously. This particular system will signal the presence of motion in a particular direction (here a rightward motion) since movement from B to A (leftward) will produce signals that do not arrive at C at the same time. The system is also tuned for a particular speed, and this tuning depends on the length of time

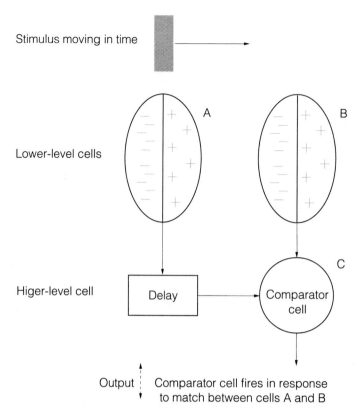

Stimulus moving in time

Lower-level cells

Higer-level cell

Delay

Comparator cell

C

A

B

Output ⁞ Comparator cell fires in response to match between cells A and B

Figure 13-4 *A computational model of motion detection that is consistent with physiological evidence (based on Reichardt, 1961).*

that the signal from A is delayed. Shorter delays are needed to synchronize the signals corresponding to a faster-moving stimulus. The region of the cortex that contains many cells with the characteristics of comparator cells (specific speed tuning and directional selectivity) is located in the temporal lobe of the brain in adjacent regions called the *medial temporal* and *medial superior temporal* areas (Allman, Miezin, & McGuinness, 1985; Maunsell & Van Essen, 1983). This region of the cortex is indicated in Figure 13-3.

Some of the information about the nature of motion-specific cells in humans comes from use of a psychophysical technique called **selective adaptation** (Sekuler, 1975). The rationale

of this technique is the same as that of the adaptation procedures discussed in the spatial frequency section of Chapter 4. It involves exposing the eye to a moving pattern such as a field of stripes. Prolonged viewing of such a stimulus causes the motion-specific cells that have been responding to the direction of the pattern's movement to become less sensitive (for example, Hunzelmann & Spillmann, 1984). When this happens, an observer's ability to detect the movement of other patterns, moving in the same direction and at the same speed as the previously exposed adapting pattern, is reduced. However, this drop in sensitivity does not carry over to faster or slower movements, nor does it generalize to movements in the opposite direction (Dawson & Di Lollo, 1990; Sekuler, 1975; Sekuler & Ganz, 1963; Wright & Johnston, 1985). Thus, the selective adaptation procedure gives results consistent with the idea that our brains contain movement-sensitive cells tuned to a particular direction and speed. To experience an interesting illusion that researchers believe is caused by the fatigue of motion-sensitive cells, try Demonstration Box 13-3.

Stimulus Factors in Motion Perception

Generally speaking, we perceive motion through two principal mechanisms. The first involves detecting shifts in the relative position of parts of the visual image; the second involves using our eyes to follow a moving target. Presumably these involve different perceptual systems, and for convenience we call the system that responds to image changes the **image-retina system** and the one that interprets motion from our eye and head movements the **eye-head system** (compare Gregory, 1978). Since the image-retina system involves stimulus relationships, let us consider it first.

Perhaps the first question to ask is how much movement in the image is needed before we can perceive motion. To answer this question, we usually measure a movement threshold, just as we measured thresholds for the minimum amount of light or sound needed for sensation (see Chapter 2). Our sensitivity to the movement of an external target depends on several variables. In experimental settings, movement thresholds have usually been studied using a small point of light that moves against some sort of stationary background, as in one of the earliest studies by Hermann Aubert (1886). He found that observers could detect the movement of a luminous dot in the dark, 50 cm from the eye, when it was moving at about 2.50 mm per second (which is about 1/5 of a degree of visual angle per second).

Target movement alone, however, is not enough to allow us to describe the motion thresholds, since motion perception often involves the recognition that relationships are changing between visual stimuli. The interaction among visual targets, such as *edge transitions* (where parts of a moving surface systematically block or expose our view of other elements), can assist the perception of motion (Kaiser & Calderone, 1991; J. T. Walker, 1975). Perhaps the best situation for detecting when a target has moved is when some motionless reference point is present, such as a stationary feature nearby or on the background, which forms the **visual context.** An example might be a stationary square frame surrounding the target. Under these circumstances we find that observers are much more sensitive to motion (for example, J. Palmer, 1986). The minimum movement that can be detected in the presence of a stationary visual context is about 0.25 mm per second (or 3/100 of a degree of visual angle per second). This is an incredible degree of movement sensitivity. If a snail were to crawl across a desk 1.50 m wide at this rate, it would take it 1 hour and 40 minutes to go from end to end.

Our ability to judge the difference between two velocities is similarly facilitated by the presence of other stimuli that are stationary (Bonnet, 1984). Some researchers contend that the image-retina system responds to two different types of motion information. The first, **subject-relative change,** is the movement of a target relative to the observer's position in space. The second, called **object-relative change,** is the movement of one target relative to others. It creates a sort of "configurational change" in the visible pattern and therefore may involve processes similar to form perception (for example, Mack, Heuer, Fendrich, Vilardi, & Chambers, 1985; Wallach, Becklen, &

DEMONSTRATION BOX 13-3   Motion Aftereffect

The form of **motion aftereffect** demonstrated in this box is often called the *spiral aftereffect* because the stimulus used to induce it is a rotating spiral. Cut out (or trace) the accompanying stimulus and place it on the turntable of a record player as if it were a record. Let the stimulus rotate for about a minute, while you stare at the center. Stop the turntable and hold it so that it is completely stationary. While the turntable was moving, the spiral appeared to expand. Now it should appear to be (paradoxically) shrinking. This shrinking (without any apparent change in size) is an illusory movement, since the stimulus is no longer in motion. It is probably caused by fatiguing, or selective adaptation, of physiological motion detectors, produced by prolonged stimulation in one direction of movement. The 60 seconds of viewing will give you an aftereffect (the paradoxical contraction) that will last about 10 to 15 seconds (compare Hershenson & Bader, 1990). You can demonstrate that the cells are tuned for different stimulus velocities by changing the speed of your turntable and repeating the demonstration. You will notice that this will change the rate of shrinking in the aftereffect.

Nitzberg, 1985). In terms of the detection and discrimination of motion, we appear to be much more sensitive to object-relative change. Furthermore, our ability to detect object-relative motion is present quite early in development, perhaps as early as 8 weeks of age in human infants (Dannemiller & Freeland, 1991).

We have just seen how the addition of a visual context or background, in the form of stationary stimuli in the visual field, can increase our sensitivity to motion. Under certain conditions the relationship between the visual context and a target stimulus also can distort our perception of movement. For instance, Duncker (1929) displayed a bright dot in a dark room. When the dot was moved very slowly, observers were not certain whether or not it was moving. However, when a stationary dot was placed near the moving dot (in effect becoming the visual context), it became quite clear that one of the dots was in motion (due to the object-relative changes). Curiously, observers could not identify which of the two dots was moving. Duncker next changed the context stimulus by making it a rectangular luminous frame that was stationary and surrounded the dot. Under these circumstances there was no ambiguity, and observers were able to tell that the dot rather than the frame was in motion.

Duncker next varied the conditions so the dot was stationary and the surrounding rectangular frame was moving. Under these circumstances an illusion appeared, in that observers reported that the stationary dot was moving rather than the frame. Duncker called this **induced motion,** since the perceived movement of the dot was induced or brought about by the real movement of the surrounding context. This is similar to the perception that the moon is moving behind the clouds, when actually the clouds are moving quickly while the moon moves much more slowly (relative to the earth) than we can detect. The clouds provide a surrounding context that is in motion and, consistent with the principle that Duncker discovered in the laboratory, they induce an apparent motion of the not-detectably-moving moon.

Induced movement effects are most dramatic when the context is moving slowly rather than quickly (Wallach & Becklen, 1983). Square frame shapes are more effective than circular frames, and large surrounds are more effective than small ones (Michael & Sherrick, 1986). Whether you look at the target or the background also makes a difference in the amount of motion induced (Heckmann, Post, & Deering, 1991). Furthermore, the target and the background should be at the same distance from the observer (that is, apparently near each other). If the frame that supplies the context is too far in front of or behind the target, no motion will be induced (Gogel & Koslow, 1972). Actually, the appearance of induced motion seems to be controlled by the part of the visual context or frame that is closest to the target (Schulman, 1979). You can produce induced motion yourself by following the instructions in Demonstration Box 13-4.

Apparent Motion

Illusions of movement, such as induced motion, might seem to be interesting but not very useful curiosities. Yet every time you go to the movies, you are paying to see two hours of a motion illusion. Each frame in the film you watch is actually stationary, being exchanged for a new frame about 24 times per second; television works in much the same way, with static frames changing about 30 times per second.

One of the early psychological researchers who systematically studied this phenomenon was Max Wertheimer (1912). Beginning with

---

DEMONSTRATION BOX 13-4   Induced Movement

To induce movement in a stationary target, all you need is a sheet of clear cellophane or glass, and a sheet of white paper. In the middle of the white paper draw a small dot. On the clear cellophane draw a large rectangle, about 10 by 16 cm (4 by 6 in), using a felt-tip marker or a grease pencil. Now lay the clear sheet over the paper so the dot is enclosed by the rectangle and is near one of its sides.

Look steadily at the dot and *slowly* move the cellophane across the paper. You will notice that the dot appears to move in the direction opposite the motion of the rectangle. The effect is strongest when the dot is near the sides of the rectangle, where object-relative change plays a role. Increasing the speed of movement should reduce the amount of induced motion you perceive. Why?

---

two lines separated in space, which could be flashed on and off sequentially, he varied the time interval between the offset of the first line and the onset of the second (we call this variable period the **interstimulus interval**). When the interstimulus interval was very brief, observers saw two lines appear simultaneously. If the interval was long, the observers saw a line appear, followed by a second line in a different location. However, for some intermediate interstimulus intervals, Wertheimer's observers reported that they saw a line appear and then *move* from the first position in space to the second. Although this was initially called *phi movement*, we now refer to this experience of movement between successively presented stationary stimuli as **apparent movement,** to distinguish it from **real movement,** where the stimulus actually moves in space. You can demonstrate this type of apparent movement by following the instructions in Demonstration Box 13-5.

The magnitude of the apparent movement experience is dependent on the interstimulus interval and on the distance between the positions of the stimuli. Generally speaking, when the stimuli are separated by larger distances, longer time intervals between the stimuli are needed for apparent motion to be perceived (Farrell, 1983).

Several researchers have suggested that two separate perceptual systems bring about apparent movement: the **short-range process** and the **long-range process** (Anstis, 1978; Braddick, 1980; Nakayama; 1985; Petersik, 1989). The short-range process encodes only small spatial target jumps as motion, perhaps 15 minutes of visual angle or less. It also responds only to fairly short interstimulus intervals, usually less than 100 msec (for example, Baker & Braddick, 1985). This perceptual process probably detects only simple shifts of a luminance contour and probably is mediated by activity of some of the physiological motion detectors discussed earlier. This is supported by the observation that if we expose an observer to such short-range apparent motion in one direction for a while, a motion aftereffect much like the one produced in Demonstration Box 13-3 will appear (Vautin & Berkley, 1977).

The second system, the long-range process, responds to stimuli that are spatially separated by distances greater than 15 minutes of visual angle; this may include separations of many degrees across the visual field. The interstimulus interval needed to produce the perception of motion is also much longer; sometimes this interval can be as long as 500 msec. The long-range process also seems to be based on more complex inferential procedures—for instance,

DEMONSTRATION BOX 13-5   Apparent Movement

To see apparent movement similar to that described by Wertheimer, simply hold your index finger vertically a short distance in front of your nose. Look at any distant target (such as a mark on the far wall of the room). Relax your eyes and alternately wink each eye. You should see your finger in a different place with each eye. Now, begin to rhythmi- cally open and close each eye in turn (remembering to keep your eyes relaxed). At slow rates you should see your finger "jump" from side to side; however, at some moderate rate of winking you should see the finger appear to actually "move" from one position to the other.

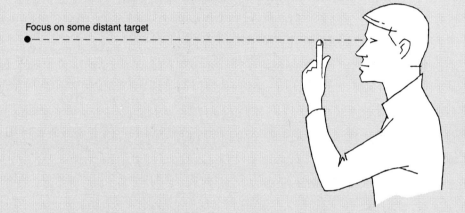

Focus on some distant target

the brain "deciding" it is improbable that the disappearance of one stimulus should be followed so quickly by the sudden and independent appearance of an identical stimulus nearby and therefore concluding that the original stimulus must have moved to this new location. In some ways this process seems to involve a form of "logic" or simplifying principle, which derives apparent motion as a reasonable interpretation of the stimulus changes observed (Hatfield & Epstein, 1985; Rock, 1983).

The degree of higher-level interpretation involved in the perception of apparent motion can be seen by considering what has been called the **motion correspondence problem.** Consider the stimulus situation shown in Fig- ure 13-5. At the start (Time 1), three spots of light appear at one side of a screen. They disappear and are replaced a fraction of a second later by three identical spots of light on the other side of the screen (Time 2). What the observer sees is apparent motion, where the three spots move across the screen as shown. However, this is not the only logically possible motion. Since all of the spots are identical, a large number of different patterns of movement might have been seen, and two examples (which observers never actually see) are shown in Figure 13-5.

The reason some paths of apparent motion are seen and others are not has to do with the fact that apparent motion seems to be derived by following certain rules in a computational

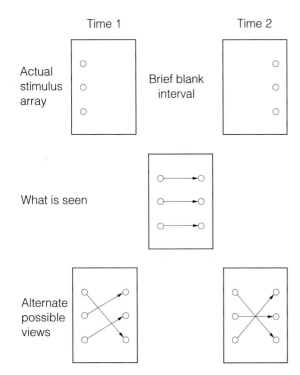

Figure 13-5 *A stimulus involving three spots of light that are flashed on one side of a screen, and then are flashed on the other side a moment later, is seen as the simple apparent movement of the three spots of light as shown in the central frame. Logically, however, many other forms of motion could be seen, including those shown in the bottom frames.*

manner (see M. R. W. Dawson, 1991). These rules include a preference for the smallest possible movement (for example, Burt & Sperling, 1981), preference for the motion that requires the slowest speed (for example, Dawson & Pylyshyn, 1988), and preference for motion that preserves the rigidity of three-dimensional objects (Ullman, 1979). Thus apparent motion is most often seen as following the tracks between the nearest neighboring stimuli in the two time intervals.

However, the apparent motion obtained from the long-range process demonstrates a good deal of "tolerance" in its interpretation of movement in the way the correspondence problem is solved. For example, suppose we present an apparent movement display, alternately flashing spatially separated stimuli at a rate we know produces the sensation of motion. Now suppose the target on the right is red and the one on the left is green. Will we still see motion? The answer is that we will see a target both moving *and* changing color as it moves. We can get apparent motion not only between targets of different colors but between targets with different shapes, sizes, brightnesses, and orientations, and in most of these situations the target seems to be transformed while it is moving (Anstis & Mather, 1985; Bundesen, Larsen, & Farrell, 1983; Kolers & Green, 1984; Kolers & von Grunau, 1976).

The stimulus inputs to the long-range motion process can also be considerably more abstract than stimuli for the short-range process (Cavanagh & Mather, 1989). Figure 13-6 illustrates this point in two ways. When Figure 13-6A is alternated with 13-6B every 200 msec or so, observers see a dot-covered square jumping back and forth with its corners resting on the quartets of large black disks (Ramachandran & Anstis, 1986). To appreciate how much interpretation is involved in this perception, note that the "jumping square" is defined by subjective contours alone (see Chapter 11). Physically, the dots covering the subjective square do not move at all (this means that the retinal images of the dots are fixed in the same place, regardless of whether the square is seen at the right or left). Yet in our perception the dots apparently move. It appears as though the square not only jumps back and forth, but also takes the dots covering it with it. Thus all of the dots are also seen jumping right and left, despite the fact that nothing is actually moving across the retina.

Long-range apparent motion adapts flexibly to other conditions in the visual field. If you

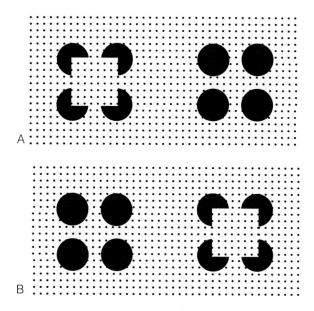

Figure 13-6 *Two stimulus displays* (A *and* B) *that are alternated to produce the apparent motion of subjective squares (based on Ramachandran & Anstis, 1986).*

place an object in the pathway of the apparent movement, the perceived path of motion will seem to deflect around the object (Berbaum & Lenel, 1983). If a particular pathway is suggested by, for instance, briefly flashing a curved path between the two flickering stimuli, the apparent motion will seem to follow that pathway (Shepard & Zare, 1983). If the stimulus looks like a solid object, the path the apparent motion follows can be quite complex and even involve motions that appear to be three-dimensional (rather than simply side to side) (for example Hecht & Proffitt, 1991). It is as if the observer is trying to "figure out" how the object could have gotten from the position and orientation it had at Time 1 to the position and orientation at Time 2, while still remaining a solid and real object. All these factors suggest that higher-level cognitive processing mechanisms play a role in the perception of apparent motion, at least when we are dealing with the long-range process (Rock, 1983).

Biological Motion

All the experiments we have thus far described have tended to use rather simple stimuli, and we have mostly been concerned with the process by which we see motion in these stimuli. Movement patterns themselves, however, serve an important function in helping us identify objects in our environment. In a series of studies, Gunnar Johansson and his co-workers have shown how various perspective transformations can predict the motion of differing objects, and how individuals can later identify these objects based on schematic movement patterns.

Perhaps the most interesting work is with **biological motion** (for example, Johansson, 1976a). This refers to the intricate and coordinated set of movement patterns accomplished by the skeletal structure of the human body, for example when walking across the room. Johansson began by asking, "Will an observer be able to identify these motions as the act of walking even in the absence of any other information, such as sight of the person?" To answer this question Johansson and his co-workers used the following technique. They attached small flashlight bulbs to the shoulders, elbows, wrists, hips, knees, and ankles of an individual (see Figure 13-7A). They then made a motion picture film of the person as he moved around in a darkened room. When observers later watched the film, they only saw a pattern of lights moving about in total darkness. Nonetheless, observers were able to iden-

tify the pattern as a person walking or running, even when they only got to see the motion for as short an exposure as 200 msec (Johansson, von Hofsten, & Jansson, 1980). Observers were also easily able to detect abnormalities, such as the simulation of a small limp. In another experiment, two people with similar arrays of lights were filmed while performing a spirited folk dance. Figure 13-7B shows a series of positions from the folk dance in which the black dots mark the positions of the lights. Once again, even with only a moving pattern of lights, observers had no difficulty identifying

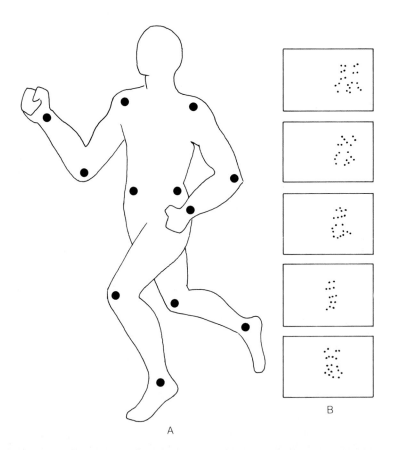

Figure 13-7 An example of the type of displays used by investigators to study patterns of humans in motion. A indicates the portions of lights affixed to individuals and B shows a sequence of movement positions made by a dancing couple.

the motion as a dancing couple (Johansson, 1976b). Infants as young as 4 months of age seem to notice that biological motion is different from other forms of motion and prefer to watch patterns of the sort we have been discussing, rather than random patterns of lights moving (Fox & McDaniel, 1982).

Our precision in recognizing individuals based only on their biological motion patterns is really quite striking. For example, in one study researchers photographed a group of people who were acquainted with one another. These people were photographed with only lighted portions of several joints visible. Several months later these same individuals were invited to watch the films and attempt to identify themselves and their friends in the motion picture. People were able to identify themselves and others correctly on many trials, although their performance was not perfect. The investigators also asked the observers how they went about making their identifications of various individuals in the film. People tended to mention a variety of motion components, such as the speed, bounciness, and rhythm of the walker; the amount of arm swing; or the length of steps as features that allowed them to make their identification. In other studies, these same investigators found that observers could tell, even under these conditions, whether a person was a male or a female, despite seeing only a moving pattern of dots. In fact, it was not necessary for all the body joints to be represented in the light display for people to make correct identifications. Even when only the ankles were represented, observers could detect the sex of the walker. They could also make these gender identifications within about five seconds of viewing (Barclay, Cutting, & Kozlowski, 1978; Cutting & Kozlowski, 1977; Cutting & Proffitt, 1981; Kozlowski & Cutting, 1977). Thus, different motion patterns characterize each sex and each individual.

Much work has been done to determine the nature of the information used to identify individuals. While some of this has been in terms of a theory of direct perception (simply searching for the specific stimuli, or relationships among stimuli, that support our identification of individuals from their motion patterns), other theories are more computational in nature. In the context of these computational theories, some fairly sophisticated computer programs have been developed to create simulated biological motion patterns (for example, Cutting, 1978; Runeson & Frykholm, 1983; Todd, 1983). For instance, Cutting, Proffitt, and Kozlowski (1978) proposed that the torso of the body acts like a flat spring with the limbs in symmetrical motion around it. This, along with certain individual differences in bodily dimensions (such as the relative widths of the shoulders and hips), provides a center of movement that is not necessarily associated with any body part; however, it organizes the coherent motion of the body parts in an individual fashion making identification possible. Perhaps patterns of biological motion such as this enable us to identify people in light too dim to allow us to see their faces. It also probably explains how we can identify people walking down the street, even though they may be too far away for us to make out their features or they may have their backs to us.

Eye Movements and Motion Perception

Up to now we have focused our discussion mainly on the visual stimulus factors that contribute to our perception of motion, such as movement within the image on the retina. To that extent we have been concerned with the image-retina movement system (see Figure 13-8A). However, some aspects of motion perception are based on information from sources other than the visual image. The most well-researched of these alternative modes of motion perception involves the *eye-head movement system*, which we mentioned earlier.

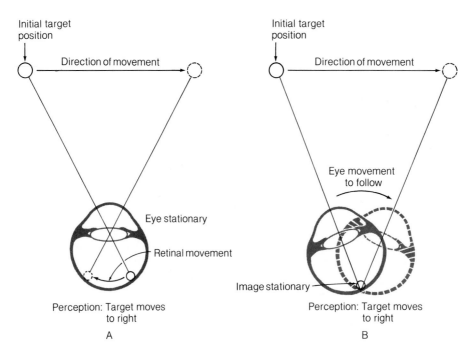

Figure 13-8 (A) *The image-retina movement system. The image of the moving object stimulates the retina when the eyes are held stationary. This gives information about object motion, possibly as a result of the involvement of movement-detecting cells.* (B) *One of the functions of the eye-head movement system. When the eye pursues a moving target, the image remains stationary on the fovea of the eye, but we still perceive the movement of the object.*

This system enables us to detect the movement of external objects even when the image remains in a fixed position on the retina. This most commonly occurs when we move our eyes to follow the path of a physically moving object, as when we track an automobile moving down the highway. Such eye movement, called **smooth pursuit movement** and illustrated in Figure 13-8B, functions to keep the image of the target on the fovea (the part of the retina with greatest acuity). Suppose the image of the target remains on the fovea and there is no patterned background to provide object-relative information as to movement. This means that the only way the observer can know the path or the speed of an object is to monitor the path or

the speed of the tracking eye movements (e.g., Epstein & Hanson, 1977; Rock & Halper, 1969). Since we have previously (see Chapter 10) discussed how eye movements can provide us with information as to the size and location of objects (e.g., Coren, 1986), it should not surprise us to learn that spatial and movement information is provided by eye movement signals as well as the flow of objects behind the tracked object (Pola & Wyatt, 1988).

Actually, there are two forms of smooth pursuit eye movements. The first is the **reflex pursuit movement,** which keeps images of objects relatively fixed in one place on the retina despite the fact that the head may be moving. An example of this is shown in Figure 13-9, where the individual is maintaining fixation on the lens of the camera. Notice that the eyes seem to remain stationary while the head seems to rotate around them, whereas actually the eyes are tracking in the direction opposite to the head movement. This automatic reflex movement is controlled by the *vestibular system* (see Parker, 1980), which we will discuss later in this chapter. The second type of smooth eye movement is **voluntary pursuit movement.** This type of eye movement (the one shown in Figure 13-8B) tries to keep the image of the object fixed on the fovea, despite physical movement of the image across the visual field. This system is found only in animals that have foveae. It now seems clear that voluntary pursuit eye movements provide most of the information about target movements (Post & Leibowitz, 1985; Raymond, Shapiro, & Rose, 1984).

To the extent that our perception of the motion of an object depends on information about the movements our eye has used to track the object, it seems reasonable that anything that alters the direction or speed of motion of the eye also might alter our perception of the movement of an object. This routinely occurs, since the eye does not pursue moving targets with perfect accuracy, but rather tends to follow some distance behind the target. The degree to which the eye lags behind is dependent on the speed of the target (Fender, 1971; Puckett & Steinman, 1969), and under some circumstances the eye never really catches up to the stimulus (Young, 1971). This may cause distortions in the size or the shape of the path the eye follows (for example, Festinger & Easton, 1974). For instance, Coren, Bradley, Hoenig, and Girgus (1975) have shown that the size of the circular path traced out by a rotating spot of light seems to shrink as the speed of the target increases. At slow speeds, where the eye can track accurately, or at speeds much too fast for even an attempt at tracking, the judgments are reasonably accurate.

Another example of the effect of tracking lag is the **Aubert-Fleischl effect** (named for the two researchers who explored the effect). Aubert and Fleischl noted that when we track a target with our eyes while it moves relative to a stationary background, it appears to move more slowly than it would if we were to fixate

Figure 13-9 Reflex pursuit eye movements are used to keep the image of an object fixed on the retina in spite of head movements. Here the individual is looking at the camera while rotating her head. Notice how these vestibularly controlled movements keep the eyes fixed while the head seems to rotate around them.

steadily on the stationary background. This phenomenon is associated with several predictable perceptual distortions. Because of the lag in tracking, an observer will not only underestimate the velocity of a target tracked with the eye, but also will tend to underestimate the distance the target has moved (Mack & Herman, 1972). Demonstration Box 13-6 allows you to see this effect.

In some circumstances, our own eye or head movements produce movements of the visual image across our retina that are very similar to those that might occur if the scene were actually in motion. One important function of the eye-head movement system is to compensate for such movements, so we continue to see the world as being stationary even though we are moving. This process of compensating for eye movements is called **position constancy,** and the fact that objects seem to maintain a fixed position relative to us, despite rotations of both our head and eyes, is called **direction constancy.** We are quite accurate in our ability to distinguish image movements caused by target movements from those caused by our own movements (see Wallach, 1987). Although we do not know exactly how this movement compensation system works, it must include a system that monitors the changing position of the eye relative to the position of the head, either when we are tracking a moving target or when we are making eye movements to scan a sta-

---

DEMONSTRATION BOX 13-6   The Aubert-Fleischl Effect

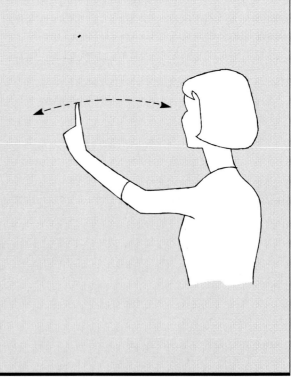

To experience the underestimation of both speed and distance moved when you track a target, begin by practicing a movement that will serve as your tracking target. With your eyes closed, swing your hand back and forth in front of you at a moderate speed and in a rhythmic fashion as shown in the figure. When you are moving with a nice regular tempo, open your eyes, look straight ahead, and judge the speed and the distance your hand is moving. Now look directly at your finger and track it. Notice that your hand seems to be moving more slowly, and the size of the back-and-forth movement (the path length) appears to be shorter. The apparent path length seems shorter probably because when you are tracking the target, information about the extent of the motion comes from the eye-head system, and your tracking movements lag behind the physical target, resulting in a slower overall velocity and a shorter eye-movement path length.

tionary scene (Howard, 1982). Two classes of theory have been proposed to explain how the eye-head movement system accomplishes this.

Sir Charles Sherrington (1906) suggested that motion is detected via feedback information from the six extraocular muscles that control the eye movements. This feedback information, called *proprioceptive* or *position information*, enables the observer to monitor eye position. The proprioceptive information tells the brain that the eyes have moved, and in turn this information allows the brain to interpret movement across the retina as being observer-generated rather than object-generated. In support of this theory, there is evidence that the superior colliculus and visual cortex of the cat contain cells that monitor eye position (Berkley, 1982; Kurtz & Butter, 1980). These cells fire at different rates, depending on the extent and direction of eye movement (Donaldson & Long, 1980; Kasamatsu, 1976; Noda, Freeman, & Creutzfeldt, 1972). Sherrington's theory is often called an **inflow theory,** because the information "flowing in" from the eye muscles to the brain is the crucial message for the interpretation of movement.

A different theory about how the eye-head system compensates for self-generated movements of the visual image was offered by Hermann von Helmholtz (1909/1962). He suggested that when the brain initiates an eye movement, efferent (motor) signals are sent out commanding the eyes to move. Copies of these signals, sent to central regions of the visual system, cancel the movement information coming from the retina as the eyes move. Since the interpretation of the origin of movement is based on information from the message sent out from the brain that initiates an eye movement, this is called an **outflow theory.** This theory is supported by the fact that certain cells in the cerebellum and the cortex of monkeys seem to represent information about eye position. Since these cells respond before the

actual movement takes place, they could represent the source of outflow information registering the *intention to move,* rather than the movements themselves (Miles & Fuller, 1975; Wurtz & Goldberg, 1971).

To see how outflow information might compensate for eye movements, try this little experiment suggested by Helmholtz. Place your hand over one eye and try tapping or pushing (through the eyelid) the side of your other (uncovered) eye very gently with your fingertip. This rotates the eye in a movement similar to one that could be initiated by the brain. However, in this case the brain has not sent a signal to the eye muscles to move the eye. When the eye is rotated in this passive fashion, the visual field will be seen to swing around in the direction opposite to the movement of the eye and to the same extent that the eye actually moved (for example, Miller, Moore, & Wooten, 1984). Thus, the stability of the visual field holds only for eye movements initiated by signals from the brain. Passive eye movements result in an apparent movement of the visual field. It seems as though the action of the eye-head system requires that the signals to or from the eye muscles be compared to signals arriving from the retina indicating changes in retinal image position (Matin, 1982). Figure 13-10 illustrates the difference between the inflow and outflow theories; it seems likely that both inflow and outflow are needed to provide a full explanation of the eye-head movement system. Table 13-1 gives a summary of the relationship between the image-retina and eye-head movement systems. Demonstration Boxes 13-7 and 13-8 (pp. 472–73) give other interesting examples that illustrate the relationships between eye movements, visual stability, and the perception of motion.

The Vestibular Sense

Another sensory system primarily concerned with motion and motion-related matters tends

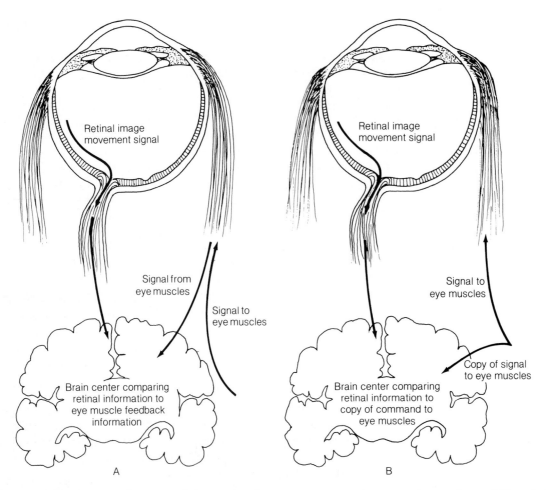

Figure 13-10 A major function of the eye-head movement system is to maintain the stability of the visual world during eye movements, thus achieving position or direction constancy. The inflow theory (A) states that this is accomplished by comparing movement signals from the retina with proprioceptive feedback from the eye muscles, which indicate that the eye has moved. The outflow theory (B) maintains that commands from the brain to initiate voluntary eye movements cancel the movement information coming from the retina as the eyes move.

to interact with visual stimulation to separate bodily motion from stimulus motion. The **vestibular system** functions to inform us about the motion of our body through space, assists in the maintenance of an upright posture, and controls eye position as we move our heads while viewing various stimuli. For the most part, these operations take place outside of consciousness. Before we consider the higher-level interactions that involve this system, we will describe its basic structure and physiology.

Some of the most primitive organisms have organs sensitive to changes in motion of the body. In primitive invertebrates such as the crayfish these are called **statocysts.** Each consists of a fluid-filled cavity lined with hair cells.

Table 13-1   The Effect of Retinal Image Change and
Voluntary Eye Movements on the Perception of Motion

PHYSICAL TARGET	ACTION OF EYE	RETINAL IMAGE	COMMANDS TO EYE (head)	PERCEPTION
Image-Retina				
Moving	Stationary	Moves	None	Movement
Eye-Head				
Moving	Tracks target	Stationary on fovea	Yes	Movement
Stationary	Moves	Moves	Yes	No movement
Stationary	Passively pushed	Moves	None	Movement in direction opposite to eye motion
Image stabilized on retina	Moves	Stationary on retina	Yes	Movement in same direction as eye motion

In the cavity is a tiny stone, called a **statolith** or "still stone," which rests on the hairs. When the animal accelerates, the stone tends to lag behind because of its inertia, thus bending the hairs on which it rests. This action generates a neural response to the movement. If the animal is tilted, the stone rolls along over a number of different hairs, bending them and generating a different response indicating tilt. The function of such organs is to signal the animal's orientation with respect to gravity. More advanced invertebrates, such as the squid or octopus, have statocysts that approach vertebrate vestibular organs in complexity, with multichambered statocysts and the ability to detect acceleration in several planes (Stephens & Young, 1982).

Primitive vertebrates have organs that have a similar function; they are called **otocysts,** and the bones they contain are called **otoliths.** Notice that these terms each contain the root *oto,* meaning "ear." These organs are usually closely associated with the ears, since both the auditory receptors and the vestibular organs probably evolved from pits on the surface of hairy skin. In mammals, these organs are protected by the skull from possibly damaging outside forces. In humans, the **bony labyrinth** in the head contains the cochlea (which is the auditory organ), and the **semicircular canals,** the **utricle,** and the **saccule,** which comprise the vestibular organs (see Figure 13-11 and look back at Figure 6-4).

Vestibular Stimuli and Receptors

The effective physical stimulus for any vestibular organ is change of rate of motion, or **acceleration,** which occurs whenever we move through space, whether we jump up and down, take off in a jet plane, or simply stand up and walk. The semicircular canals and their associated receptor organs seem particularly well-suited for monitoring rotary acceleration (as when we turn around or fall down). The other two organs, the utricle and the saccule, seem mainly to respond to linear acceleration (as when we take off in a plane).

The movement-receptive portion of the semicircular canals is called the **crista,** which is found in a swelling (called an **ampulla**) at the base of each semicircular canal (see Figure 13-11, p. 474). The crista consists of an array of sensory cells from which tiny hairs protrude, as shown in Figure 13-12A (p. 474). These hairs are embedded in a jellylike material called the **cupola.** When the head accelerates, the inertia of the cupola and the fluid in the canals causes the cupola to move in the opposite direction. This in turn causes the hairs to bend, generating neural responses. As the head continues to move at a particular rate of speed, the cupola gradually comes back to its resting position, no longer bending the hairs and no longer causing a response in the sensory cells. This is why the effective stimulus is acceleration rather than steady movement.

The receptor organ found in the utricle and the saccule, called the **macula,** is shown in Figure 13-12B. It functions much like the statocyst we discussed before. As in the crista, tiny hairs protrude from the sensory cells in the macula. These hairs are embedded in a jellylike substance covered by a membrane containing otoliths, which lags behind when the head is accelerated, bending the hair cells and generating an electrical response. When the jelly and hairs catch up to the rest of the head, which would happen if the acceleration ceased and motion became steady, the hairs are no longer bent. This means no response would be generated, even though the head could be traveling

---

DEMONSTRATION BOX 13-7   Afterimages and Apparent Movement

You can readily experience one of the ways the eye-head movement system differentiates external from observer movement. The first thing needed is to generate a *stabilized retinal image.* Ordinarily, the retinal image is in constant motion and stimulates varying groups of receptors at a rapid rate. However, by quickly satiating or fatiguing a single group of retinal receptors, we can generate an image that maintains its position regardless of eye movements. Many of you are probably familiar with the technique used to give rise to such an image if you have ever had your picture taken with a flashbulb attached to the camera. If you looked at the light while it flashed, you may have noticed a purple dot that tended to linger in your field of view for some time after the picture was taken. This purple dot is called an *afterimage.* It is one example of a stabilized retinal image. The afterimage does not shift position on the retina. It stays in a constant position regardless of how we move our eyes. We can use the afterimage to demonstrate the operation of the eye-head movement system.

Perhaps the easiest way to generate an afterimage is to look at a rather bright but small source of light for a brief period of time. Make a 1-cm hole in an index card and hold it up in front of a light bulb. Look at the hole for a few moments, and this should provide a clearly visible afterimage when you look away from the light. Now notice that each time you move your eyes the afterimage seems to jump in the same direction. This apparent movement is due to the action of the eye-head system.

Commands have been issued to the eye to move, yet the image remains on the same place on the retina. This could only occur if the image had moved as much as the eye (see Table 13-1). You may also notice that the image sometimes seems to drift smoothly from place to place. Again, the image never moves; the movement is signaled from the movements of your eyes. This is one example of how the action of the eye-head movement system can lead to illusions of motion.

DEMONSTRATION BOX 13-8   The Autokinetic Effect

There is an interesting phenomenon in which movement is seen in the absence of any physical motion of the target. The word used to describe the occurrence is *autokinesis,* which means "self-moving." For this experiment, you will need a *very* dark room. No stray light of any sort should be visible. In addition, you will need a small, dim point of light (a lighted cigarette works fine). Place the point of light about 2 m away from you and look at it steadily. After a few minutes it should appear to move, perhaps slowly drifting in one direction or another. Of course the light is still stationary; hence the movement is an illusion, which is called the **autokinetic effect.**

The autokinetic effect demonstrates the outflow principle that operates in the eye-head movement system. The visual system only monitors commands to initiate voluntary eye movements. However, these are not the only types of eye movements possible.

Our eyes also exhibit involuntary movements. As you may have guessed, these are not monitored by the visual system. One type of involuntary eye movement is *eye drift,* and this is the mechanism implicated in the autokinetic effect (Matin & MacKinnon, 1964). When we steadily fixate or stare at a target, it is difficult for the eyes to maintain steady and accurate fixation on that one point in space (Ditchburn, 1973). The eyes will tend to drift off of the fixation point; however, the visual system does not monitor this movement until it exceeds a critical point. In the autokinetic situation, retinal image movement has been signaled in the absence of commands to initiate voluntary eye movements. This is the situation under which the movement of the retinal image is attributed to an externally moving object (see Table 13-1). There is no information that the eyes have moved, so illusory movement of the dim spot of light is seen.

at thousands of kilometers per hour relative to the earth.

Neural Responses in the Vestibular Sense

The hair cells from both the crista and the macula send their information to the brainstem via the eighth cranial nerve. From there most of the nerve fibers go to the **vestibular nuclei** (still in the brainstem). After this the sensory pathways become complicated and somewhat obscure. There are projections to the cerebellum and to the cortex, but they vary in different animals (see Correia & Guedry, 1978). It is important to note that most of the fibers leaving the vestibular nuclei are motor or

efferent fibers. One major group of these fibers forms a pathway to the muscles that move the eyes. Szentagothai (1950) discovered that each pair of eye muscles receives fibers from a different semicircular canal. The arrangement indicates that muscles that move the eye in a particular plane are controlled by nerve fibers originating in the semicircular canal that responds to acceleration in that plane. Acceleration in a particular direction causes compensatory eye movements in the opposite direction. This allows the eyes to remain fixed on an object even though the head is turning in various directions. The relationship between eye movements and vestibular stimulation is shown in Demonstration Box 13-9.

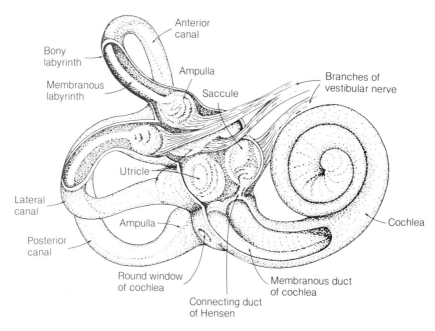

Figure 13-11 *A diagram of the right inner ear showing the cochlea (which houses the auditory receptor), the semicircular canals, the utricle, and the saccule (from Geldard, 1972).*

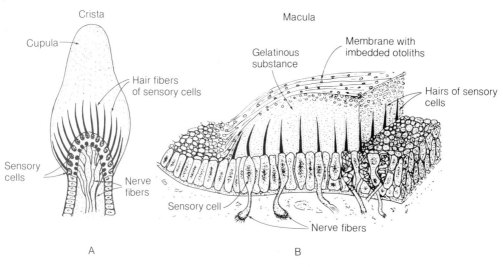

Figure 13-12 *(A) Diagram of the crista, the receptor found in the ampulla of each semicircular canal. (B) Diagram of the macula, the receptor found in the utricle and the saccule (from Geldard, 1972).*

DEMONSTRATION BOX 13-9 Vestibular Stimulation and Eye Movements

For this demonstration you will need a friend and a little space. Have your friend hold her arms out and spin around (like a whirling ice skater) until she becomes dizzy. This continuous rotation sets up currents in the semicircular canals that trigger the compensatory eye-movement system. Now stop your friend from turning and look into her eyes. You will notice that the eyes drift steadily in one direction, and then snap back and start to drift again. This type of repetitive eye movement is called **nystagmus.** It is a reflex movement evoked automatically by the vestibular stimulation caused by fluid currents in the semicircular canals.

Lowenstein and Sand (1940) performed a classic study that illustrates the electrophysiology of the vestibular system. They recorded the electrical activity of single nerve fibers from the crista of a ray (a kind of fish) while the entire labyrinth was rotated on a turntable. They found that as long as the head was accelerating, the fibers responded. The fibers increased their firing rate above the resting rate for acceleration in one direction and decreased it below the resting rate when the acceleration was in the opposite direction. Thus, as in other sensory systems, both excitatory and inhibitory responses to physical stimuli occur. Lowenstein and Sand also showed that the magnitude of the response (impulses per second in single fibers) varies directly with the magnitude of the stimulating acceleration. So stimulus intensity seems to be encoded in a manner similar to that in other sensory systems. There are at least two other types of nerve fibers: One always responds to acceleration (regardless of direction) with an increase in firing rate, and the other only responds with a decrease in firing rate.

The fibers connected to the hair cells of the macula respond to their stimuli somewhat more simply. Two types of responses have been described. The first is an increase in the rate of neural firing when the head is tilted; the second is a rate increase when the head is returned to its original position (Wyburn et al., 1964). Although there have been some studies of cortical responses to acceleration of the head, little is known in detail about these responses. One fact that has emerged is that inputs from vestibular, kinesthetic, and visual systems converge in the cortex, so our sensations of "turning" and the like depend in a complex way on all of these inputs (Mergner, Anastasopoulos, Becker, & Deecke, 1981; Parker, 1980). One striking example of this complex interaction is the phenomenon of motion sickness, often caused by a mismatch between visual and vestibular or kinesthetic inputs. A great deal of effort is being put into studying this aspect of human reaction, especially because of its importance in space travel, which involves zero-gravity conditions.

Self-Motion

Back in the nineteenth century there was a fairground ride called the Haunted Swing. In this ride, people entered a boat-shaped enclosure and artificial scenery was slowly swung backward and forward outside the windows. This resulted in an incredibly strong illusion that the chamber was rocking, and people felt all of the bodily sensations of real motion, including vertigo and a feeling of loss of their postural stability that made them sway (Howard, 1982; Wood, 1985). There is an everyday example of this effect. Probably most of you have had the experience of sitting in a bus or a train parked next to another vehicle. All at once the adjacent vehicle starts to move. However, instead of correctly attributing the movement to the vehicle beside you, you have a powerful sensation of yourself in motion. This is a case of induced movement, such as we discussed earlier, but it is an *induced movement of the self*. It is important since it reflects the interchangeability of visual and vestibular factors in the perception of body motion.

If we were not aware of dynamic changes in the visual image as we moved, we probably would bump into things much more often as we walked around, or not notice that our body had swayed or leaned until we actually inclined too far and toppled over. Our perception of **self motion** depends on an analysis of the continually changing aspects of the retinal image as we move. Consider our most typical motion, which is forward in depth. Although a number of sources of information are important in this situation (see Larish & Flach, 1990), some features of the visual array seem to be particularly useful. As we move forward, the visual array in front of us displays a radially expanding pattern in the center of our visual field and a laterally translating pattern in our periphery.

For example, consider the pattern shown in Figure 13-13A. Here the arrows represent the flow of the visual array as if you were moving toward the door marked *A*. Images of objects around door *A*, that is those stimuli to its sides or above or below it, expand radially outward and into the periphery as we move forward. This flow of stimuli has been called **streaming perspective** (Gibson, 1979). If our path were angled so we were going toward the door marked *B*, the optical transformation pattern would be similar to that in Figure 13-13B. In both cases, the center of this outward flow, called the **focus of expansion,** indicates the direction of movement. Although the specific patterns shown by the streaming perspective of targets in the field will vary as you move your eyes (Andersen, 1986; Cutting, 1986; Regan & Beverly, 1982), it is still easy to direct your movements by keeping the door you wish to reach in the center of the outward flow of stimuli (compare Warren & Hannon, 1988).

If we present you with a steadily moving pattern that is the equivalent of a natural streaming-perspective pattern, you will feel as though you are moving. If the pattern is radially expanding, as in Figure 13-13, you will feel as though your body is moving forward. If the pattern is moved steadily to the side, you will feel that you are moving (or starting to lean or tilt) sideways, or even rotating if the pattern surrounds you. Such induced motion of the self is usually called **vection** (Dichgans & Brandt, 1978). Generally speaking, the consensus is that the central visual field is more specialized for object motion, whereas stimulation of the peripheral visual field is necessary to induce the feeling of self motion. Thus, patterns that extend into the periphery tend to produce strong feelings of vection (for example, Delorme & Martin, 1986; Held, Dichgans, & Bauer, 1975). If the speed of flow is not too fast, and the pattern is correct, visually induced self motion can be experienced even for smaller central patterns (Andersen & Braunstein, 1985; Stoffregen, 1985). Demonstration Box 13-10 shows how you may experience a form of induced self motion.

The relatively greater contribution of the peripheral retina to vection may explain why the feelings of self motion can be so strong when you view motion pictures with an oversized or wraparound screen. In fact, a modern version of the "haunted swing" illusion can be found in some fairs and amusement parks,

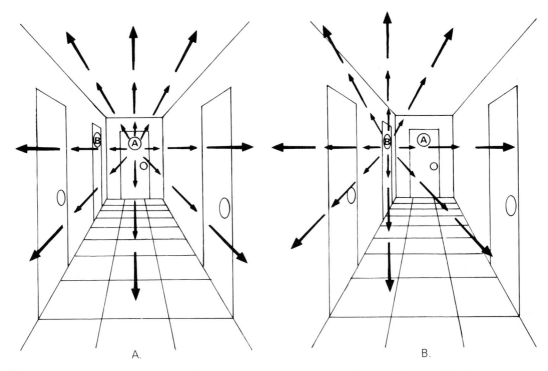

Figure 13-13 *Streaming perspective. Figure A shows the pattern of flow or expansion of stimuli as it would appear if you were moving toward door A. The length of the arrows indicates the rate of change or speed of expansion, with longer arrows meaning faster change. Figure B shows how the pattern of stimulus flow changes if you were now moving toward door B, rather than straight down the hallway.*

where viewers are surrounded by projected pictures associated with riding down a roller coaster, flying in a helicopter, or hurtling down a raceway at high speed. Most viewers feel all the bodily effects normally associated with the equivalent self-motion, and they are sufficiently indistinguishable from actual movement to suggest that the visual and vestibular inputs must have some common neural pathways and centers. This would be a sensible arrangement since the vestibular system only responds to accelerations or decelerations of body motions. As we saw in the previous section, after any prolonged period of constant velocity the vestibular system would cease to

respond, and the only remaining indication of movement would be the motion in the visual array.

To the extent that vestibular and visual information can each produce similar feelings of self motion, it should not be surprising to find that cells are present in the vestibular nuclei whose rates of firing are influenced by signals suggesting bodily motion, whether such signals come from the vestibular organs themselves or from visual motion (for example, Henn, Young, & Finley, 1974; Waespe & Henn, 1977). A complex interaction between the visual and the nonvisual inputs seems to give us this feeling of self motion (DiZio & Lackner, 1986; Henn,

DEMONSTRATION BOX 13-10   Induced Self-Motion

For this demonstration you should have two small light sources (lighted candles will work fine) and a darkened room. Hold the candles out at arm's length and about at eye level, as shown in the figure. Look straight forward (remove your glasses or squint your eyes a bit so that you don't see the surrounding room too clearly). Now slowly move the candles back toward the sides of your head (not too close!). As you do so, you should experience an induced motion of your body so you now feel that you are leaning forward slightly. If you move the candles slowly forward, you should get the impression that you have straightened up, or are now leaning backward somewhat. Next, try the same arm movements with your eyes closed to see that this effect does not occur in the absence of the visual stimulation. This means that the feeling of body tilt produced in this situ-

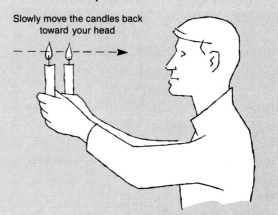

Slowly move the candles back toward your head

ation is a form of vection caused by the streaming perspective simulated by the movements of the lights, which suggested that at least the upper portion of your body was moving forward.

Cohen, & Young, 1980). However, the situation is really very complicated. In some of the situations we have described, where the illusion of self motion is produced, the mismatch between visual and vestibular signals can produce unpleasant feelings. Some individuals experience symptoms of motion sickness (complete with nausea and vomiting) because of the lack of agreement between visual and vestibular signals (Reason & Brand, 1975; Stern et al., 1985). With continued exposure, individuals become used to this situation, and the symptoms then disappear (Hu, Grant, Stern, & Koch, 1991).

The perception of motion and to some extent the perception of time are good examples of a process we will call **sensory convergence.** This is a process by which several inputs combine to produce a single coherent perception,

in which you may not be conscious of all of the components that have gone into the computation. Thus, we have seen that the apparently *visual* experience of motion may contain proprioceptive inputs from eye movements and the vestibular sense, or copies of efferent commands issued to the eye muscles, even though your conscious impression remains strictly visual. The mechanism of sensory convergence may be quite simple, with various peripheral sources of information converging on a single group of neurons, or it may involve higher-level, central or cognitive integration, as we saw in our consideration of the factors influencing our perception of the passage of time. The final percept, as experienced in our consciousness, may be an amalgam of many sources, though to us it seems quite simple and pure.

I hate hot summers because the commercials take so long

GLOSSARY

The following definitions are specific to their use in this book.

Acceleration   Change in rate of motion.

Ampulla   Swelling at the base of the semicircular canal containing the crista.

Apparent movement   Perceived movement of spatially separated static stimuli flashed successively at appropriate interstimulus intervals.

Aubert-Fleischl effect   A phenomenon in which a moving target being tracked with the eyes seems to move more slowly than when the eyes fixate on a stationary background behind the moving target.

Autokinetic effect   The illusion of movement of a stationary point of light viewed in an otherwise totally dark field.

Biological clock   A physiological mechanism that underlies our experience of time.

Biological motion   The movement patterns of the skeletal structure of a human engaged in activities such as walking or running.

Bony labyrinth   The structure inside the head that contains the cochlea and the vestibular organs. It is made of very hard bone.

Change monitoring   The theory that the tick rate of the cognitive clock reflects the number of events, or changes, that occur in an interval. Also called *event processing*.

Circadian rhythm   A rhythmic biological cycle occurring over an approximately 24-hour period.

Cognitive clock   A cognitive mechanism that determines our experience of time.

Crista   Movement-perceptive organ found in the ampulla of the semicircular canal of the ear.

Cupola   Jellylike material in which the hairs of the crista are embedded.

Direction constancy   The stability of an object's perceived direction despite changes in eye position.

Efferent fibers   Neural fibers that carry outgoing commands from the brain to muscles or other action systems.

Entrainment   The process by which the biological clock is synchronized to physical time cycles.

Event processing   *See* Change monitoring.

Eye-head system   A movement-perception system that monitors and differentiates eye- or head-generated from object-generated movement of the visual image on the retina.

Filled duration illusion   A phenomenon in which an interval filled with stimulus events is perceived as being longer than an identical interval without stimulus events.

Flow   The perception of time passing.

Focus of expansion   A point in space around which all other stimuli seem to expand. If you are moving forward, it represents the place toward which you are moving.

Image-retina system   A movement-perception system that detects movement within the retinal image.

Induced motion   An illusion of movement of a stationary object created by movement of the background or surrounding context.

Inflow theory   The suggestion that motion is detected via feedback information from the six extraocular muscles controlling eye movement.

Interstimulus interval   The time span between the end of one stimulus presentation and beginning of the next.

Isoluminant stimuli   Stimuli that contain lines or forms of equal brightness and are distinguished from their backgrounds on the basis of color only.

Long-range process   The perceptual system responsible for apparent motion when stimuli are separated by more than 100 msec in time and more than 15 minutes of visual angle in space.

Macula   The receptor organ of the utricle and saccule. It is responsive to linear acceleration.

Motion aftereffect   An illusion of movement that occurs in the direction opposite to a moving stimulus that an observer has viewed for an extended time.

Motion correspondence problem   In apparent motion the visual system must first identify which elements shown at Time 1 correspond to which elements shown in a different position at Time 2, in order to determine the path of the apparent motion.

Now   The interval of time that we interpret as "the present."

Nystagmus   A reflexive, jerky eye movement caused by stimulation of the vestibular organs (cristas) in the semicircular canals.

Object-relative change   The movement of objects in relation to one another.

Otocysts   In primitive vertebrates, fluid-filled cavities functioning to maintain balance and attitude to gravity. *See* Statocysts.

Otoliths   Bony bodies in otocysts.

Outflow theory   The suggestion that brain commands initiating eye movements enable the eye-head movement system to differentiate object-generated from observer-generated movement of the retinal image.

Pacemaker   The mechanism that sets the speed of the biological clock.

Perceptual moment   The hypothetical basic psychological unit of time, between 25 and 150 msec in duration (depending on how it is measured).

Position constancy   The stable perceived position of objects despite body, eye, or head movements.

Processing effort model   A theory that time is measured internally by the amount of cognitive work or processing an individual does during an interval.

Real movement   Physical movement of a stimulus.

Reflex pursuit movements   Smooth eye movements, under vestibular control, that are made to keep the image of a target on the fovea despite head movements.

Restricted environmental stimulation technique A procedure in which a subject remains in a dark sound-deadened room for specified intervals of time.

Saccule A vestibular organ contained in the bony labyrinth.

Selective adaptation A psychophysical technique in which prolonged exposure to a particular motion stimulus causes reduced sensitivity to other visual stimuli moving in the same direction and at the same speed.

Self motion The perception that the body is moving through space.

Semicircular canals Vestibular organs contained in the bony labyrinth, next to the cochlea of the ear.

Sensory convergence The notion that several different sensory inputs, from different modalities and sources, combine to form an apparently simple perceptual experience.

Short-range process The perceptual system responsible for apparent movement when stimuli are separated by less than 100 msec in time and less than 15 minutes of visual angle in space.

Smooth pursuit movement The continuous eye movement involved in following a smoothly and steadily moving object.

Statocysts In invertebrates, motion-sensitive cavities lined with hair cells.

Statolith A tiny stonelike body resting on the hairs of statocytsts and causing them to bend in response to the motion or change of position of an animal.

Storage size model A model that contends that time is measured internally by the number of items processed and stored in memory during an interval.

Streaming perspective The optical flow of stimuli as we move through space, centered on the direction of movement.

Subject-relative change The movement of objects relative to the body.

Suprachiasmatic nucleus (SCN) A center in the hypothalamus that is believed to be responsible for circadian rhythms.

Temporal processing model The theory that experience of the passage of time depends on the amount of attention directed toward monitoring time.

Utricle A vestibular organ contained in the bony labyrinth.

Vection An illusion of induced motion, in which the body is experienced as moving through space or tilting because of changes in the optical flow.

Vestibular nuclei In the brainstem, way stations along the route of nerve fibers from the crista and macula to the cerebellum and cortex.

Vestibular system The system that monitors the body's movement and orientation in space. Its receptors are located in the bony labyrinth.

Visual context Visual stimuli that surround or accompany other stimuli.

Voluntary pursuit movements The eye movements by which you voluntarily track a moving target.

Zeitgeber The stimulus used to calibrate, or entrain, the biological clock.

Chapter ...

THE CONSTANCIES

The Task of Perception

Perceptual Constancies

Size Constancy

   Size Constancy and Distance Cues

   Direct and Constructive Aspects of Size Constancy

   Size Constancy and Illusion

Shape Constancy

Lightness or Whiteness Constancy

Color or Hue Constancy

Other Constancies

When we look around at the world, our perception is of objects and surfaces. Each of these has a relatively enduring set of properties, such as size, shape, and color. Now consider a very simple problem. Suppose you are presented with two rectangles made of cardboard and asked to say which is larger. If the difference in their physical size is not too small, you would probably have little trouble giving the correct answer. Now consider a second problem. How did you reach your conclusion? Many people would probably give an answer like this: "The larger rectangle produces a larger image in my eye." However, this answer would be quite wrong, as can be seen from Figure 14-1. There we have three different rectangles; the image of each is the same size on your retina, yet each is a representation of a different-sized cardboard rectangle "out there" in "the real world." The smallest of these pictured objects would be only a few centimeters on each side "out there," whereas the largest would be over a meter in width and length.

To paraphrase Albert Einstein, "We like to keep things simple, but not too simple." Often in this book we have treated perception in a fairly simple fashion, in that we have adopted the general position that for every distinct kind of perceptual experience—color, brightness, distance, size, or the like—there is some unique stimulus or type of stimulus information that affects our sense organs. Although we may not fully understand what that stimulus is, we believe that we could potentially discover it. We also have often assumed that our perception is related directly to the stimulus information that reaches us, with, perhaps, room for some minor adjustments caused by interactions with or limitations imposed by the nature of our sensory receptors or by the neural processes used to encode the information they receive. However, this assumption that a given identifiable stimulus dimension (such as the size of a retinal image) is related uniquely to a corresponding perceptual dimension (such as

Figure 14-1 Three rectangles whose retinal images are all the same size, although each appears to be different in size from the others.

the apparent size of the object we are looking at) is "too simple."

THE TASK OF PERCEPTION

Before we go any further in our discussion, we must make some distinctions. To begin with, stimuli can be divided into two general classes:

a **distal stimulus** is an actual object or event "out there" in the world; a **proximal stimulus** is the information our sensory receptors receive about that object. For example, a tree falling in the forest would be a distal stimulus, whereas the sound of its fall at our ears and the changing light reflected from it to our eyes would be proximal stimuli. The task of perception is to characterize accurately the distal stimulus, since that corresponds to an actual object or event in the real world (Brunswick, 1956). The problems associated with doing this come from the fact that the proximal stimulus is, by itself, not always an ideal source of information about the distal stimulus, as we saw when we judged the size of the real-world objects depicted in Figure 14-1. Other factors, such as the context in which the distal stimulus occurs, must be taken into account. In this sense, our perception of objects may be viewed as being a form of **multidimensional interaction** (Uttal, 1981).

Controversy exists about the nature of the multidimensional interactions that allow us to perceive the properties of objects. One approach, known as **direct perception,** is identified with the work of J. J. Gibson (1979). This theory has an implicit evolutionary background, in that it contends that the importance of any object rests in how an animal may respond to it. These response opportunities are called **affordances** (since the object *affords* certain types of action). These affordances depend on the actual size and shape of the object in the real world. According to direct perception, the proximal stimulus contains enough information to derive these affordances. The trick is to isolate stimulus **invariants,** which are features of the stimulus that are always good predictors of the nature of the object. These stimulus invariants may actually be higher-level features of the stimulus, such as the comparison of the size of the image of the object to the sizes of images of other objects that form its visual context (Bruce & Green, 1985; Gibson, 1979; Michaels & Carello, 1981). Presumably, if we

are considering any aspect of our perception of an object, such as its size, all the researcher needs to do is look carefully enough, and he or she should be able to isolate a set of *purely optical* stimulus factors that determines our perception of the size of that item. The whole process is automatic and should not involve any complex computation, or any inferential or cognitive processing.

An alternative viewpoint can be traced to the works of Helmholtz (1909/1962). It has many active supporters (for example, Epstein, 1973; Rock, 1983; Uttal, 1981) and presents a **constructive theory** of perception, sometimes referred to as **intelligent perception,** since thinking processes, as well as perceptual processes, are involved. In constructive theories, perception arises as a form of **unconscious inference,** which is to say that information from the stimulus may be unconsciously combined with other information in an inferential or problem-solving manner to "derive" the perceived object. The nonstimulus information used in this process may come from other sensory inputs, such as feedback from eye movements, from prior experience that has given us a concept as to the usual size or shape of an object, or even from expectations and guesses as to the nature of the distal stimulus. In other words, our visual perception of an object's properties may depend on some completely nonvisual sources of information, plus some complex cognitive processes that treat the current perceptual situation as if it were a puzzle to be solved.

Somewhere between the direct and the constructive theories of perception are the **computational theories,** which are often presented as mathematical or computer program models of perceptual processes. These agree with direct perception in that they try to explain as much of perception as possible by analyzing only the optical stimulus. They also agree with constructive theories in their assumption that the perception of objects does require some form of computation. What is unique about computational theories is their multilayered analysis of the perceptual task to be solved and their careful attention to the details of the computations needed (Marr, 1982). A typical computational theory would begin by answering the question, "What function does a particular perceptual process play in the life of the organism?" It would then undertake an analysis of the information available in the stimulus to perform this function. Finally, the theory would describe precisely all the steps needed to go from the optical stimulus to the necessary perceptual experience.

Perceptual Constancies

If the only information we had about nature were the proximal stimulus, such as the retinal image of an object, our world would be as chaotic as the Wonderland that Alice found at the bottom of the rabbit hole. Since the retinal image is larger the closer an object is, an approaching friend would appear to grow larger as she grew nearer. A piece of white paper would appear black when viewed in the moonlight, since the amount of light in the retinal image is no greater under these conditions than in the image of a piece of coal viewed in normal room light. This same piece of paper would appear to change shape continually—the retinal image changing from rectangular to trapezoidal as the paper's angle of tilt was varied—and its color would appear to be blue under fluorescent lighting and yellow under incandescent lighting. Fortunately our perception of objects is much more *constant* than would be expected if the only information available were the proximal stimulus. Your friend remains the same size but changes her distance from you. The piece of paper remains a white rectangle, although you might sense that the color or intensity of the light falling on it, or its angle of tilt

relative to you, has changed. This illustrates a very basic aspect of perception, which is that *the properties of objects tend to remain constant in consciousness although our perception of the viewing conditions may change.* The fact that our perception of the world does not vary as much as fluctuations in the proximal stimulus would lead us to expect is what we mean by the *perceptual constancies.*

Although there are many varieties of perceptual constancies, they fall into three general classes. The first pertains to object properties, such as an object's size and shape; the second to certain qualities, such as the whiteness or color of surfaces; and the third to the locations of objects in space relative to the observer.

Each constancy has two major perceptual phases. The first phase involves **registration,** the process by which changes in proximal stimuli are encoded for processing. The individual is not consciously aware of this registration process. The second phase involves **apprehension,** the actual subjective experience. This is the conscious component available for you to describe. Normally, registration is oriented toward a **focal stimulus,** which is the object you are paying attention to. In addition, you also register a set of stimuli that are nearby, or occurring at the same time, and form the **context stimuli.** During apprehension you become aware of two classes of properties: the **object properties** of the focal stimulus, which tend to remain constant, and the **situation properties,** which indicate more changeable aspects of the environment (such as your position relative to the focal object or the amount or color of the available light) and which are derived from cues found in the context. The way these categories interact is shown in Table 14-1, which describes these variables for a number of constancies. If all this appears a bit complicated in theory, in practice it is really quite straightforward. Let us look at some of the more common constancies to see how they work.

Table 14-1 The Relationships between the Registered and Apprehended
Variables in Some of the More Common Perceptual Constancies.

| Constancy | REGISTERED STIMULUS (may be unconscious) | | APPREHENDED STIMULUS (conscious) | |
	Focal Stimulus	Context	Constant	Changes
Size constancy	retinal image size	distance cues	object size	object distance
Shape constancy	retinal image shape	orientation cues	object shape	object orientation
Lightness constancy	intensity of light on the retina	illumination cues	surface whiteness	apparent illumination
Color constancy	color of retinal image	illumination cues	surface colors	apparent illumination color
Position constancy	retinal location of image	sensed head or eye position	object position in space	head or eye position
Loudness constancy	intensity of sound at the ear	distance cues	loudness of sound	distance from sound
Odor constancy	amount of odorant in the nose	proprioception from sniff	intensity of smell	strength of sniff

SIZE CONSTANCY

Before you can understand size constancy, you must understand what happens to the retinal images of objects as our distance from them varies. As the distance between the eye and the object grows larger, the size of the retinal image grows smaller (see Figure 14-2). As you proba-

bly recall from Chapter 4, retinal image size is usually expressed and measured in terms of visual angle. The visual angle for S_1 (stimulus 1) is α_1, and for S_2 is α_2. Like other angles, these are expressed in degrees, minutes, and seconds of arc. As an example, the image size of a quarter (25-cent piece) held at arm's length is about 2 deg, whereas at a distance of about 80 m the

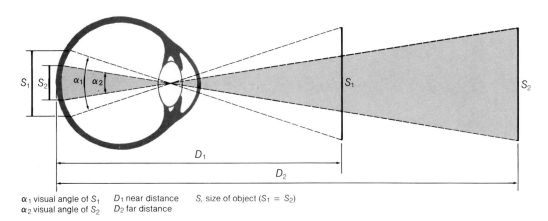

α_1 visual angle of S_1 D_1 near distance S, size of object ($S_1 = S_2$)
α_2 visual angle of S_2 D_2 far distance

Figure 14-2 *The visual angle. Although the physical size (S) of the object does not change, changes in distance (D) will result in changes in the size of the visual angle (α). Here α_1 (the image of object S_1 close to the eye) is larger than α_2 (the image of object S_2 farther from the eye).*

quarter would have a visual angle of 1 minute of arc. At a distance of 5 km (around 3 miles), it would have the tiny retinal image size of only 1 second of arc. Thus, as the quarter's distance from an observer increases, its retinal image size decreases.

Consider what happens as you watch someone walk down the street. Suppose we perceived size only in terms of retinal image size. If such were the case, a man who is 180 cm (about 6 ft) tall would look like a small child when he was at a reasonable distance but would appear to "grow" as he approached us. Of course this does not happen. Instead, we perceive him to be "man size" regardless of his distance from us. This stability of perceived size despite changes in objective distance and retinal image size is called **size constancy.** In essence, it involves assigning a constant size to an object in consciousness, no matter what its distance or retinal size may be.

Size Constancy and Distance Cues

Size constancy, we have seen, is a process by which we "take into account" the apparent distance of an object in order to "adjust" the perceived size to represent more accurately the actual physical size of the object. For example, in Figure 14-3A, we see three men standing in a courtyard. All appear to be about the same size, even though the retinal image size of the apparently most distant individual is only about one-third that of the apparently nearest one. In other words, we estimate distance and size together and adjust our perception of size in accordance with our distance judgment, perceptually "enlarging" more distant objects. You can see how this **constancy scaling** works by looking at 14-3B, where all the images of men are exactly the same size. Here the constancy scaling correction becomes more obvious when it makes the apparently farthest appear much

A

B

Figure 14-3 (A) *Three men, whose retinal image grows smaller as they appear to be more distant; however, because of size constancy they appear to be the same size.* (B) *Here, when the images remain the same size, the more distant man appears to be larger.*

DEMONSTRATION BOX 14-1   Size Constancy and Apparent Distance

An easy way to demonstrate how apparent distance affects apparent size requires that you carefully fixate the point marked X in the accompanying white square while holding the book under a strong light. After a minute or so, you will form an afterimage (see Chapter 5) of the square. If you now transfer your gaze to a blank piece of paper on your desk, you will see a ghostly dark square floating there. This is the afterimage, which will appear to be several centimeters long on each side. Now shift your gaze so that you are looking at a more distant, light-colored wall. Again you will see the dark square projected against the wall, but now it will appear to be much larger in size. Because of the nature of an afterimage, its visual angle does not change. But as you project it against surfaces at varying distances from you, its apparent size changes. It appears to be larger when it is projected on a distant surface. This is an example of how size and distance perception interact by means of the size constancy mechanism. The quantitative expression of the relationship is often called **Emmert's law.**

larger than we would usually expect a man to be. This demonstrates that changes in apparent distance alter our perception of apparent size. A more direct example of this process is shown in Demonstration Box 14-1.

How does the perceptual system take depth into account? The simplest answer is that we utilize cues to the distance of the target that are available as part of the visual context. This would suggest that when we increase the number of distance cues constancy should be bet-ter, whereas reducing the number of cues should reduce our tendency toward constancy. Many experiments have demonstrated how the availability of cues in the visual array contributes to the maintenance of size constancy, beginning with the early work by Holway and Boring (1941). Simply stated, the more cues, the better the size constancy (for example, Chevrier & Delorme, 1983). For instance, Harvey and Leibowitz (1967) asked observers to choose a size match for a standard target that was placed at various distances. Two viewing conditions were used. One corresponded to natural situations with many distance cues, and the second involved the removal of the surrounding context by having the observers view the standard target through a small opening that blocked the view of everything but the target to be observed. Under natural viewing conditions, size matches conformed very well to the predictions based on the efficient operation of the size constancy mechanism. This was the case for all the observer–target distances used in this experiment. However, when the context was removed, size matches conformed to constancy predictions only at viewing distances up to about 120 cm (about 4 ft). After that, size matches began to deviate from the predictions based on size constancy. This experiment shows that depth cues are needed to maintain size constancy and our accurate perception of the size of objects around us.

Why was there still constancy at the closer distances even though the depth cues were removed? Probably because viewing through a small hole only removes the *visible* distance cues. As we discussed in Chapters 3 and 10, when we fixate objects at different distances, the lens of the eye changes shape to accommodate for changes in fixation distance. Simultaneously, the eyes either converge for near objects or diverge for distant objects to produce stable binocular foveal fixation. When targets are relatively close, information about their distance can be gotten from feedback from the accommodation and convergence actions of the eyes. This suggests that these physiological cues to distance have been incorporated into the multidimensional mix of information resulting in size constancy.

One important thing to notice in this example is that the source of the distance cues is not really important. The cues do not have to come from the visual array per se, but can come from other sources. We can show this by demonstrating that in the absence of any other information about the distance of the target (such as the pictorial cues to distance catalogued in Chapter 10), changes in accommodation and convergence result in changes in perceived size (Roscoe, 1989). A demonstration of this is found in Leibowitz and Moore (1966). Their observers viewed a white triangle in an otherwise completely dark field. They matched the size of this stimulus by making size adjustments in a similar triangle. Accommodation and convergence were varied by inserting prisms and lenses before the eyes. This forced the subjects to adjust their convergence and accommodation to closer or farther distances when viewing the target, although the retinal size remained constant. If these depth cues help to stabilize the perception of size, this experimental manipulation should have resulted in changes in perceived size.

The prediction of these investigators was confirmed. The size of the target judged to be equal to that of the standard triangle increased as accommodation and convergence changes were manipulated to indicate increasing target distance (much as the size of the man increased with increasing apparent distance in Figure 14-3B). Hence, it seems that the state of the oculomotor (eye muscle) system, which varies with the distance of the distal stimulus, conveys information that helps to stabilize size perception. Since the perception of size seems to be linked to the perception of distance somehow, this is one way structures within the visual system "take distance into account" in computing the size constancy correction.

Actually any source of distance information can be used to obtain accurate size constancy. We have seen that visual depth cues trigger size constancy, as do accommodation and convergence. Adding binocular disparity, the depth cue involved in stereopsis (see Chapter 10), can also strengthen size constancy, as shown in Demonstration Box 14-2.

DEMONSTRATION BOX 14-2   Additional Depth Cues Strengthen Size Constancy

Hold out both of your hands with their backs toward you. One hand should be relatively near you (about 20 cm or 8 in should do), and the other should be out at arm's length. At first glance, both hands should appear to be about the same size. Now, remove the binocular disparity depth cue by closing one eye. Keeping your hands at these different distances and your head very steady (to prevent motion parallax as a further depth cue), move your distant hand to the side until its image appears to be just next to the near one. Now when you compare the size of the two hands it should be clear to you that the more distant one appears smaller than the near one, showing a clear weakening of size constancy. You can restore the size constancy by adding additional depth cues—open both eyes and swing your head from side to side, and your hands will again appear to be the same size.

Direct and Constructive Aspects of Size Constancy

Earlier in this chapter we contrasted the *direct* and the *constructive* theories of perception. Direct theories of perception are based on the presumption that all the information we need for such things as constancy can be found in the proximal stimulus. Geometric regularities, such as the convergence of parallel lines with increasing distance (linear perspective) or the increasing textural density of more distant fields of elements, serve as reliable cues for distance. Such cues may be sufficient to maintain size constancy (Bruce & Green, 1985; Gibson, 1979; Michaels & Carello, 1981).

For example, we can imagine two objects of the same size sitting on a surface at different distances from the observer. As you know from Chapter 10, the fact that textured surfaces show denser gradations of coarseness as they recede into the distance is a very powerful distance cue. If two objects at different distances appear to cover the same number of texture elements (in other words, their relationship to the textured surface remains constant), they will remain perceptually the same size. This principle was first described in detail in 1604 by the artist Jan de Vries and was reintroduced by Gibson (1979) within a more modern framework. In Figure 14-4 we have modified one of the drawings used by de Vries. You will notice that here we have two rectangular structures (*A* and *B*) that appear to be about the same size, but that appear to vary in distance. Despite the fact that their retinal image size differs, notice that, regardless of its distance, each rectangular object is 3 texture-elements long and 3 wide (here the texture-elements are the square "tiles"). Notice that this relationship holds even when the viewing angle is different, as for object *D*. Different sizes are associated with different ratios between the textures and the objects themselves. Thus *A*, *B*, and *D* appear to be the same height (about one texture element), whereas *C* (whose height in the picture is actually smaller than *A*) appears to be a much taller object since it is about 4 texture elements high. Thus, according to direct perception, the observer could extract the physical size of the objects by comparing the relative size of the objects to the size of the surrounding texture elements, and this extracted information results in size constancy.

Figure 14-4 *Rectangles A, B, and D all appear to be the same size, since each covers the same number of texture elements (based on de Vries, 1604/1968).*

Constructive theories of perception allow for sources of information other than the proximal stimulus to shape the final percept. We have already seen how feedback from the accommodative and convergence movements of the eye might serve such a function. More important than this type of information for constructive theories, however, is information generated by cognitive judgments and operations or from learned factors and expectations (for example, Epstein, 1973; Rock, 1983; Uttal, 1981). In this type of theorizing it is probably inappropriate to speak of *cues*. Rather, any factor that results in a change in one aspect of perception (here the distance of the target) can bring about a change in another aspect of perception (here the size of the object), regard-

less of the source of that information (see Hochberg, 1974). Let us see how some nonvisual sources of information can affect our perception of size.

Our experience with the world has already provided us with much information that assists us in maintaining size constancy. For example, we learn that particular objects have typical physical sizes. This *familiar size* information can be used in the absence of any other information to judge the size of the object once it has been identified or to judge the distance of the object based on its retinal and familiar size, similarly to the situation in Demonstration Box 10-1. For example, we have an expectation that playing cards have a customary size. If we were presented with a very tiny image of a playing card, we would maintain our size constancy by seeing this as a normal-sized playing card viewed from a long distance rather than a playing card that is much smaller than usual (compare Gogel & DaSilva, 1987b; Higashiyama, 1985; Ono, 1969).

Our experience and expectations also explain an interesting breakdown of size constancy that occurs at very large target–observer distances. If you stand at the top of a tall building, you will note that people below appear to be tiny dolls and cars appear to be little toys. It seems likely that the unusual viewing conditions and exceptional distances are so unfamiliar that they simply do not trigger the size constancy mechanism in this instance (Day, Stuart, & Dickinson, 1980). This is supported by the fact that the range of distances over which size constancy works is greater for adults than for children (for example, Zeigler & Leibowitz, 1957), presumably because adults have had more experience with a greater variety of environmental viewing conditions.

A number of other considerations seem to support some constructive factors in size constancy. Some evidence suggests that you do not actually have to *perceive* the distance. Simply *knowing* the distance, such as being told how far an object is from you, seems to be enough to elicit the size constancy adjustment (Pasnak, Tyer, & Allen, 1985). Furthermore, if your attention is directed elsewhere, so the full measure of cognitive processing is not available, your size constancy processing begins to break down (Epstein & Broota, 1986). Demonstration Box 14-3 allows you to see how attention interacts with size constancy.

Neither direct nor constructive theories of perception seem adequate to explain all aspects of size constancy (nor any constancy, for that matter). It is more likely that both processes combine to produce the final perception of size and distance (for example, Gogel & DaSilva, 1987a).

Size Constancy and Illusion

Size constancy provides stability in our perception of the world by giving our conception of particular objects a consistent set of properties despite variations in the retinal image size. This is usually useful, but under special circumstances it can lead to errors or illusion. To see how this comes about, consider a variation of Figure 14-3: In Figure 14-5A we see two logs lying in the middle of a road. Although they have been drawn to be two different sizes on the paper, the distance cues in the context (perspective, texture, and others) indicate that the upper log is more distant. Because of size constancy, we see it as being the same size as the closer log. In Figure 14-5B we have two logs that appear to be different in size, with the more distant one seemingly longer than the closer one, although they have been drawn to be exactly the same physical size on the page. Once again, this merely represents the operation of size constancy. To the extent that the picture mimics conditions in the real world, the upper log appears to be more distant. In the real world, the upper log could cause the same-sized retinal image as the lower log only under conditions where it was physically longer. Since in the picture the logs have been drawn the same size, the constancy scaling mechanism has correctly adjusted our perception.

The perceptual problem arises with Figure 14-5C, where we see two converging lines and two horizontal lines. Notice that the upper line appears to be sightly longer. Because, like the logs in Figure 14-5B, the two lines are physically equal in length, this perceptual difference is called a visual-geometric illusion (this particular version is usually called the **Ponzo illusion**). Actually, this is an illusion only in the sense that no context for depth or distance has been drawn into the figure. It is caused by the fact that there are *registered* cues for distance here (the converging perspective lines) that are

DEMONSTRATION BOX 14-3   Attention and Size Constancy

Begin with your right hand in front of you at arm's length. Now look directly at your hand and move it toward your face and away again several times. Although the retinal image size is changing, your hand appears to be the same size because of the operation of size constancy.

Next hold the index finger of your other hand up in front of your face (at about 20 cm) as shown in the figure. Look steadily at the finger. Now, while maintaining fixation on your fingertip, bring you right hand toward and away from your face. Try not to move your eyes from your finger, but try also to pay some attention to the image of your hand as you move it closer and farther from your face. Under these conditions, where your attention is divided and pulled away from simply viewing the target, your size constancy should break down. Now the hand seems smaller when farther and larger when nearer to you, demonstrating that when attention is somewhat diverted, we are more apt to experience the proximal (retinal) stimulus changes rather than apply the constancy correction.

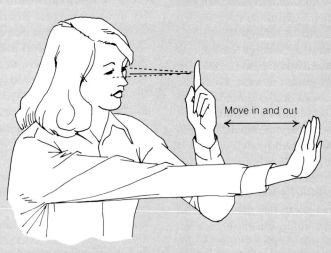

Move in and out

sufficiently strong to evoke the size constancy mechanism yet are not sufficiently strong to evoke the conscious *apprehension* of distance (Coren & Girgus, 1977; Gillam, 1980; Gregory, 1966). Thus, at one level we are treating the stimuli as if they were three-dimensional, while we are still representing the stimulus in consciousness as a flat, two-dimensional array. If this seems difficult to imagine, note that in some instances a very fine distinction exists between a picture (representing a three-dimensional arrangement where constancy scaling is appro-priate) and a simple array of lines that produces a visual illusion. It is possible to imagine someone with poor drawing ability producing a figure like 14-5C when asked to draw 14-5B, where the converging lines were really meant to be depth cues.

Cues that are registered in sufficient strength to elicit size constancy inappropriately are often quite subtle. Consider Figure 14-6, where the vertical line in *A* appears to be shorter than the vertical line in *B* although they are equal in length. This distortion, called

Figure 14-5 (A) *The two logs lying on the road appear to be at different distances. Therefore, their apparent size is the same despite the fact that the apparently more distant log is physically smaller (on the page) than the other one. (B) The logs are identical in size; however, the one that appears to be more distant looks larger. The application of size constancy can lead to illusions of size, as seen in (C), which is the Ponzo illusion and is similar to (B), except that the context indicating distance and depth has been greatly reduced (based on Coren & Girgus, 1978).*

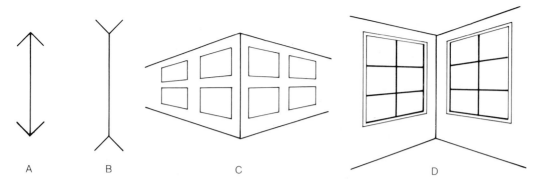

Figure 14-6 (A) *The underestimated segment of the Mueller-Lyer illusion.* (B) *The overestimated segment.* (C) *and* (D) *The corresponding perspective configurations.*

the **Mueller-Lyer illusion,** probably involves several different mechanisms (Coren, Porac, Aks, & Morikawa, 1988; McClellan & Bernstein, 1984), with one of the most important being size constancy (Coren & Girgus, 1978; Eijkman, Jongsma, & Vincent, 1981; Gregory, 1966; Madden & Burt, 1981; Nijhawan, 1991). For example, the wings turned toward the vertical line might mimic the perspective cues of the outside of a building (shown in dark lines in C), whereas the wings turned away from the vertical line might mimic an interior corner of a room (shown in D). Since the closest point in the array is the plane of the paper, it is easy to see that if the wings imply increases or decreases in distance away from that plane, the vertical shaft in B is more distant than that pictured in A. Hence, the operation of size constancy would enlarge the apparent length of B relative to A. Notice again that this is an illusion of size only in the sense that no depth or distance was intended; therefore, the application of size constancy is inappropriate in this situation.

If we deliberately add or emphasize the depth cues to the basic Mueller-Lyer figure elements, we can get a particularly powerful illusion effect. This is shown in Figure 14-7, where the depth effects shown in Figure 14-6 are accentuated. Here the two heavy vertical lines are the same physical length but appear to be very different in length because of the action of

size constancy. Conversely, if the depth cues at each end of the line are made to contradict one another, the size of the illusion is greatly reduced (Nijhawan, 1991).

Several other illusion distortions also seem to result, at least in part, from observers' responding to implied depth cues in the configuration (Coren & Girgus, 1978; Ward, Porac, Coren, & Girgus, 1977). Perhaps the most spectacular of these is the **moon illusion,** where the moon on the horizon appears to be larger than the moon when it is high in the sky, despite the fact that it is optically always the same-sized disk (Hershenson, 1989). One explanation of this phenomenon is based on size constancy (Kaufman & Rock, 1989). The notion is that the moon is registered as if it were on the "surface" of the sky. If the sky were a uniform hemisphere, no illusion would occur. However, the sky actually appears to be a flattened bowl, with the horizon farther away than the zenith, as shown in Figure 14-8. This is because the distance of the horizon is registered in relation to many depth cues (such as texture gradients and familiar objects), whereas the distance of the zenith sky must be registered in the absence of such cues. This means that the moon is registered as farther away when on the horizon than when at zenith, and hence, by the action of size constancy, its apparent size is apprehended as being larger. This is verified by the fact that the moon illusion occurs in pic-

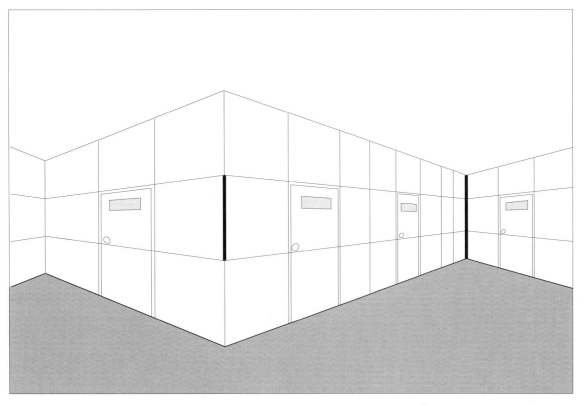

Figure 14-7 *A version of the Mueller-Lyer illusion in which the depth relationships are accentuated. The two heavy vertical lines are identical in length.*

tures, and its strength seems to be directly related to the number and strength of depth cues in the drawing (Coren & Aks, 1990). Although size constancy does not account for all the effects in the moon illusion (see Coren, 1989; Hershenson, 1989; McCready, 1986; Reed, 1989), it does appear to play a role in producing this and several other illusions of size.

SHAPE CONSTANCY

We have spent a good deal of time describing size constancy, mainly because the other constancies have much in common with it. Each involves the registration of either environmental cues or cues about our relationship to an object in the environment and the apprehension of the object properties as being constant while the environment changes or our own relative condition changes. Thus, Epstein and Park (1964) have defined **shape constancy** as the relative constancy of the perceived shape of an object despite variations in its orientation. To see why such a constancy correction is necessary, consider what happens when you view a rectangular card from different angles, as in Figure 14-9. As the tilt of the card is increased, the retinal image becomes more like a trapezoid with the formerly vertical sides tapering outward. Yet the object still "looks" rectangular. The same thing happens when we swing a door outward. The large changes in the shape of retinal image are ignored, and the

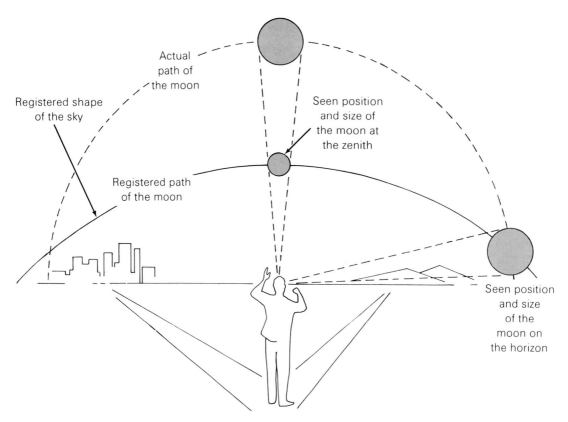

Actual
path of
the moon

Registered shape
of the sky

Seen position
and size of
the moon at
the zenith

Registered path
of the moon

Seen position
and size
of the
moon on
the horizon

Figure 14-8 *The fact that the moon is registered to be more distant when it is at the horizon than when it is overhead helps to explain the moon illusion.*

door still appears to be rectangular. In achieving shape constancy, the perceptual system appears to compensate for changes in slant in a way analogous to the compensation for distance changes in size constancy. Follow the instructions in Demonstration Box 14-4 to see the operation of shape constancy for yourself.

There is an intimate relationship between size and shape constancy—both are related to distance perception. However, for shape constancy the distance information pertains to the *relative distance* of different parts of the object from the observer—in other words, to its orientation in space or its slant. The relationship between size and shape constancy is shown more clearly in Demonstration Box 14-5.

In unrestricted viewing, with many contextual cues available, observers tend to perceive the shape and slant of objects with remarkable accuracy (Lappin & Preble, 1975). As in the size constancy situation, if the number of depth cues available is reduced or observers are prevented from using contextual information that would indicate the degree of slant, the operation of shape constancy becomes less effective and the precept comes to reflect the retinal situation rather than the actual object (Leibowitz, Wilcox, & Post, 1978; Niall, 1990).

Observers use several strategies to assist in the judgment of orientation and to supplement contextual information. For example, in Figure 14-10A we have a shape (the letter *E*) that has

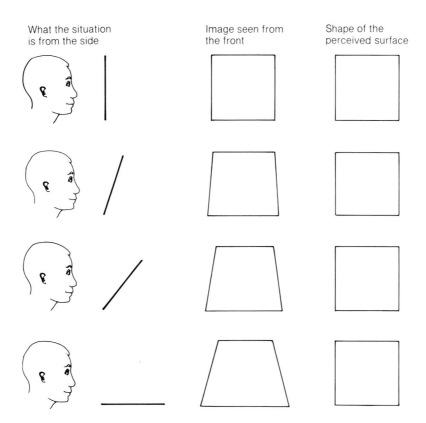

What the situation is from the side

Image seen from the front

Shape of the perceived surface

Figure 14-9 *Changes in the tilt or slant of objects will cause changes in the shape of the retinal image; however, because of shape constancy, perceived shape remains constant (based on Lindsay & Norman, 1977).*

DEMONSTRATION BOX 14-4   Shape Constancy

Look at the box in the accompanying figure. Most people believe that a dime will fit inside the top of this box. Try placing a dime (flat on one face) into the box. Does it fit?

The reason that the top surface of this box appeared to be large enough to accommodate the dime is because you made a shape (and size) constancy correction. The shape constancy correction changed the appearance of the top of the box into a square; the size constancy correction made the sides of the box top appear equal. Look back at the box and notice that its real physical shape is a parallelogram, not a square.

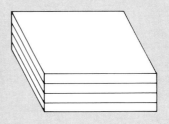

DEMONSTRATION BOX 14-5   Size and Shape Constancy Interactions

To see how size and shape constancy interact, first consider the two light-gray box tops in the figure below. Are they the same shape? Next look at the sides marked *A, B,* and *C.* Which side is the longest, and which is the shortest?

Actually (as a ruler will confirm), all three marked sides are the same length. If you trace the light-gray top of one box and superimpose it on the light-gray top of the other (you will have to rotate it 90 deg, of course), you will also find that the shapes of the two gray areas are exactly the same.

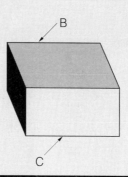

---

a common or a *normative* orientation based on our experiences with this form. We can use such normative information to infer whether the shape is upright, rotated, or tilted (for example, Braine, Plastow, & Greene, 1987; Rock, 1973). In the absence of such prior experience, we make certain presumptions about shapes. For example, we presume that the longest dimension (sometimes called the *principle axis*) represents the upright dimension. Thus, we are apt to consider the rectangle shown in Figure 14-10C as more tilted than that shown in Figure 14-10B (compare Humphreys, 1983, 1984).

The way we approach the task of looking at objects may also affect the degree of constancy we obtain. For example, some researchers have systematically varied the way observers are asked to judge the stimuli by directing them either to report the sizes and shapes of the objects they were viewing (the **objective instruction)** or to report the sizes and shapes of their retinal images (the **projective instruc-**

tion). The objective instruction is closest to normal viewing, where the perceptual task is to derive what is "out there." The projective instruction is similar to what an artist must do in trying to translate the scene being viewed onto a canvas consisting of sizes and shapes of colored regions that will represent objects in space when viewed by an observer. It has been shown many times (for example, Carlson, 1977; Gilinsky, 1989; Kaess, 1980) that when observers are asked to adopt the projective viewing set they show less size and shape constancy, although it appears that they cannot completely turn off the constancy correction. Observers continue to make constancy corrections, although the judgments become more like the retinal image (Lappin & Preble, 1975; Lichte & Borresen, 1967).

Other viewing factors also affect the degree of constancy obtained. For instance, Epstein, Hatfield, and Muise (1977) showed that, much like any cognitive task, the more processing

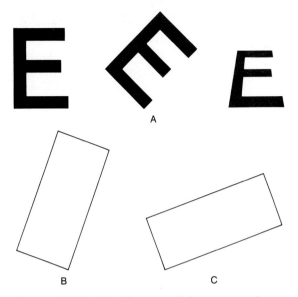

Figure 14-10 (A) *We can tell how some shapes are tilted in space because of our familiarity with them. For less common shapes, we assume that the longest axis indicates "upright"; hence, we will see* (C) *as more tilted than* (B), *although they are both tilted the same amount from the horizontal.*

time is available), the more shape constancy is found. Epstein and Lovitts (1985) showed that, much like in size constancy, the more attention you pay to the task, the better the shape constancy correction.

LIGHTNESS OR WHITENESS CONSTANCY

How light or white an object appears to be is also affected by a constancy mechanism. The amount of light at different points in our retinal image coming from an object (the **retinal illuminance**) is determined by two things. The first is the amount of light from any source, such as the sun or a light bulb, that falls on the object. This is called **external illuminance.** The second is the **reflectance** (sometimes called the *albedo*), which is the proportion of light falling on the object that is reflected to the eye of the observer. The reflectance is the object property that most closely corresponds to how light or white a surface appears. For example, a white surface will reflect most (perhaps 80–90%) of the light that falls on it. In contrast, a black surface will absorb a great deal of light, and the proportion reflected will be quite small (often less than 4–5%). Roughly speaking, the amount of light reaching the eye can be obtained from the simple formula

light at eye = reflectance × external illuminance

Thus, if a surface that reflects 90% (or 0.90) of the incident light receives that light from a source with a physical intensity of 100 units, we would calculate a "light at eye" value of 90 units. Although not all of the light reaching the eye from a surface actually reaches the retina itself, since some is absorbed or reflected by the cornea, lens, and the like, the proportion of the "light at eye" that does reach the retina is a constant.

Brightness refers to the apparent intensity of the light source illuminating a region of the visual field (for example, a brightly lit versus a dimly lit part of a room). **Lightness,** on the other hand, refers to the apparent reflectance of a surface, with black objects reflecting little light, white objects reflecting a lot, and gray reflecting intermediate amounts (Jacobsen & Gilchrist, 1988). Because *lightness* actually determines the color of the object on a scale from white through black, this property is sometimes referred to as **whiteness.** Your impression of how white an object is, however, is relatively independent of the amount of light reaching your eye. A piece of white paper will change its *brightness* depending on whether it is viewed in dim light or bright light. On the other hand, it will always appear to be the same shade of white, thus maintaining a constant *whiteness*. A piece of coal viewed in bright sunlight will still appear black, even though it may be reflecting a greater amount of light to the eye than would a piece of white paper viewed in ordinary room light (that is, 5% reflected to your eye from the 1000 units of sunlight falling on the coal equals 50 units of light reaching the eye from the coal, which is greater than the 90% of 50 units of room light falling on the paper, which equals only 45 units of light reaching the eye from the paper). These are examples of **lightness** or **whiteness constancy.**

Two types of explanation have been given for lightness constancy. The first fits well with direct perception and computational theories, because it maintains that constancy is computed or derived from stimulus relationships. Remember that the direct perception explanation of size constancy involved looking at the ratio or relationship between the size of a visual object and the texture elements around it. In lightness constancy, a similar ratio is considered, but instead of a size ratio, it is a ratio or comparison between regions of illuminance on the retina.

This **ratio principle** works as follows. Consider Figure 14-11. Suppose you are looking at a white table top with a reflectance of 80% on which is resting a gray piece of paper with a reflectance of 40%. They are illuminated by a light source of 100 units of intensity. The amount of light reaching your eye would then be 80 units from the table and 40 units from the paper. Suppose an identical piece of paper is seen in shadow so the intensity of the light in the shadow is only half of the original 100 units (50 units). Now the amount of light reaching your eye from the table and paper is 40 and 20 units, respectively. On the basis of the amount of light reaching your eye, we might now predict that the shadowed white table top would

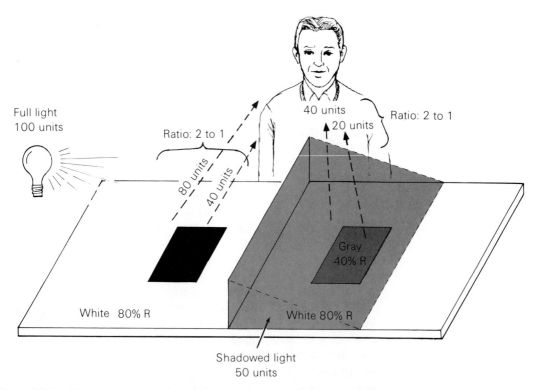

Figure 14-11 *The ratio principle in lightness constancy. Notice that the ratio of the amount of light reaching the eye of the observer from the background and the target remains constant regardless of the amount of light falling on the two surfaces.*

appear to be gray, and would be similar in lightness to the gray paper viewed under the intense illumination. This, however, is not the case—the white still appears white and the gray appears gray. It is not the total retinal illumination that matters, but rather the ratio of the intensities of the two patches of light on the retina, which remains constant (Wallach, 1972). In this situation, the light from the white surface is twice as intense as that from the gray surface, regardless of the intensity of the external illumination; hence the ratio remains 2 to 1 here. Lightness constancy based on predictions from the ratio principle seems to hold over a million-to-one range of illumination (Jacobsen & Gilchrist, 1988).

There have also been a number of elaborations of the ratio principle. One of the more well-known is a computational model called the **retinex theory** (Land, 1986; Land & McCann, 1971). The retinex theory provides a specific set of conditions under which the ratio principle comes into play. According to this theory, brightness ratios are only computed from sharp edges where brightness differences occur. Small or gradual changes in brightness tend to be ignored in the computations. Items separated by a wide distance in visual field can be compared by computing the ratios of all the boundaries between them. At the computational level, this theory has been very successful in allowing the ratio principle to be extended to lightness constancy situations where there are gradual and complex changes in the illumination falling on a number of regions with different reflectance levels.

To explain how a ratio principle might work at the physiological level, some investigators have suggested that lateral inhibition (which we discussed in Chapter 4 as an explanation for brightness contrast) might play a role in maintaining lightness constancy (compare Cornsweet, 1985; Gilchrist, 1988; Richards, 1977; Shapley, 1986). Lateral inhibition could work if we assume that the amount of inhibition increases as we increase the intensity of retinal illumination. The idea is that increased stimulus intensity not only increases the level of neural response in the excited areas, but also increases the level of inhibition generated by adjacent areas. Since the increased inhibition would subtract from the increased excitation, it could offset the increased response of the eye to more intense illumination. This would leave the overall neural response of the eye relatively unchanged regardless of the average intensity of the light input. If the change in inhibition and excitation are balanced, it can be shown computationally that changes in the intensity of overall illumination will leave the difference in the neural responses to dark and light areas relatively unchanged. Thus, according to this theoretical notion, lightness constancy is the result of neural interactions taking place at the retinal level.

One prediction made by the ratio theory is that lightness constancy should depend on having several different levels of reflectance under the same illumination in close proximity in the visual field. This prediction is confirmed in the results of a classic experiment by Gelb (1929). He used a concealed light source to illuminate an object placed in a dimly lit field, as shown in Figure 14-12. The illuminated object was a black disk. However, observers reported seeing a white disk in dim light, rather than a very brightly lit black disk. Of course, this represents a complete failure of constancy. If constancy were operating, the observers would see the black disk as black even though it was very brightly lit. Gelb then tried a second manipulation. He placed a piece of white paper in front of the brightly lit black disk. As soon as this was done, observers reported that the disk looked black. In other words, with the addition of the reference white paper, constancy returned. However, as soon as the piece of white paper was removed, the black disk returned to its former white appearance. Although these results appear to support strongly the direct perception notion of constant intensity ratios as the

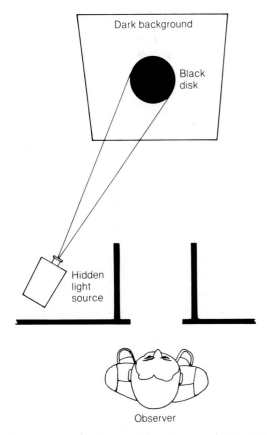

Figure 14-12 Experimental situation used by Gelb (1929) to test for lightness constancy when a light source was hidden from view.

basis for lightness constancy, Gilchrist and Jacobsen (1984) have shown that still other factors must play a role, since we do maintain lightness constancy even in a world of one reflectance level, such as an all-white room.

A second explanation based on a constructive theory of perception would add a number of factors to the constant ratio explanation of lightness constancy. Such a theory would argue that the observer responds to cues indicating the nature of the illumination falling on the object and adjusts the apprehended lightness of the object in consciousness accordingly. Thus, in the Gelb experiment, it could be argued that the introduction of the white piece of paper provides a cue indicating the presence of an in-

tense, hidden light source. This information evokes the formerly inoperative constancy correction.

Several such cues seem to be important in triggering lightness constancy. For instance, the presence of visible shadows produces a lightness correction (Gilchrist & Jacobsen, 1984; MacLeod, 1947). Also, cues as to the location of the object relative to the light source provide information to allow us to correct our perception of the whiteness or lightness of the object, despite the retinal illumination intensity (for example, Beck, 1965; Flock & Freedberg, 1970; Hochberg & Beck, 1954). Even information about the relative spatial relationships among objects seems to contribute to this effect (Gilchrist, 1980; Mershon & Gogel, 1970). Demonstration Box 14-6 shows how presumptions about the illumination falling on a surface can affect its apparent lightness.

COLOR OR HUE CONSTANCY

Similar to the size and intensity changes of the retinal image, systematic changes occur in the spectral composition of the retinal image that could be registered as color or hue changes. Nonetheless, within limits, we can identify red as red, whether it is viewed under fluorescent lights, whose output is dominated by blue-appearing light, or incandescent lights, whose output is dominated by yellow-appearing light. **Color constancy** refers to our ability to maintain the percept of a particular hue regardless of variations in the quality of the illuminance and the reflectance properties of an object's surface pigment. An example of color constancy is shown in Demonstration Box 14-7.

Obviously, changes in the wavelength composition of the illumination will change the wavelength composition of the retinal image. Color constancy is maintained by a number of different processes, however. If, for instance, we shine reddish light on an object, the surface

DEMONSTRATION BOX 14-6   Lightness Constancy

To a certain extent, lightness constancy depends on assumptions that the observer makes about the nature of the world. Consider the gray tube shown here. Notice that the gray of the interior of the tube appears to be lighter than the gray of the exterior. In fact, they are the same gray. Coren and Komoda (1973) suggested that this apparent lightness difference involves a cognitive adjustment based on presumptions that we make about the environment. If the tube were real, its interior would be likely to receive less light than its exterior. In the tube pictured here, however, the same amount of light reaches the eye from both the apparent interior and the apparent exterior surfaces. This could only happen if the interior surface reflects a greater proportion of the light that reaches it; in other words, the internal surface must have a greater reflectance. This demonstration shows one way lightness constancy operates. The visual system makes presumptions about the amount of light reaching surfaces and adjusts the perceptual experience so the apparent lightness corresponds to the assumed relative reflectances,

rather than to the actual distribution of light reaching the eye.

Also notice one other interesting aspect of the tube shown here, namely that either the right- or the left-hand portion can be viewed as the interior or the exterior surface. A figure that can assume several different orientations depending on one's point of view is called a *reversible figure*. Notice how the apparent lightness difference between the two sides changes, depending on whether you see the right or the left side as the interior surface. The apparent inner surface, regardless of whether it is the right or the left, appears to be the lighter one.

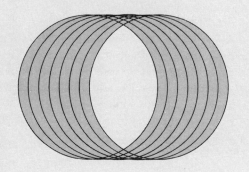

appears redder because of the increased activity of the red-responsive cones. However, this increased activity leads to faster *chromatic adaptation* (see Chapter 5), which is the process through which a cone's response to a particular colored stimulus is weakened with continuous exposure. The greater red response leads to more vigorous activity, which in turn leads to faster adaptation in the red cones, which then makes the object seem less red than it otherwise would, thus canceling out the effect of the colored illumination (Uchikawa, Uchicawa, & Boynton, 1989; Werner & Walraven, 1982).

Just as in lightness constancy, our perception of color is not based completely on an object's image on the retina but also depends on its relationship to surrounding stimuli (for example, Brou, Sciancia, Linden, & Lettvin, 1986; Land, 1986). There is a certain similarity in the theories used for lightness constancy and color constancy. For instance, the direct perception and computational approaches are represented by several very elaborate and often mathematically complex models based on comparison of color and lightness changes occurring at boundaries. These bear much in common with the kind of reasoning that led to the ratio principle and

---

DEMONSTRATION BOX 14-7   Color Constancy

Although people have color constancy and compensate for the hue of the illumination falling on objects, camera film does not. Look at Color Plate 5. In *A*, we have a person under normal daylight illumination, and the skin tones and white areas in the scene appear quite normal. In *B*, using the same film, we have the same person under standard tungsten illumination. Here a yellowish cast (due to the yellowish color of standard incandescent light) is quite visible on the skin and the white areas. Photographers must compensate for this by using different films for indoors (tungsten illumination) and daylight or by using filters or auxiliary lights (such as daylight-balanced photoflashes). Our own color constancy compensation is automatic.

---

the retinex theory for lightness constancy (Bainard & Wandell 1986; Dannemiller, 1989; Land, 1986; Worthey & Brill, 1986). Finally, constructive theories assert that color constancy draws upon other sources of information. For instance, cues about the nature of illumination falling on a surface would allow us to correct for color shifts. Our prior knowledge about the identity of the object being viewed can also be used to maintain constancy. Thus a banana may appear yellow in red light, in part, simply because we know that it is a banana (see also Jameson & Hurvich, 1989).

OTHER CONSTANCIES

There are many other constancies, some well-known, some less obvious. For example, an auditory version of size constancy is called **loudness constancy.** In this situation, the perceived loudness of a sound source remains constant, even when the sound level at the ear is diminished because it is moving farther away from the listener.

There are also several other visual constancies. We already encountered one class of these in Chapter 13. There we saw that, despite the fact that the retinal image moves, we do not experience the world as moving but recognize that this change is due to our eye movements.

This phenomenon is known as **position constancy,** which we saw is controlled by feedback from our eye and head movements combined with the actual movements of the visual image across the retina. Similar, but not the same, is **direction constancy,** in which, despite our head and eye movements, the egocentric direction of objects (where they lie relative to our bodies) remains constant.

Position and direction constancy can be distinguished from each other because eye movements do not change egocentric direction, but head and body movements can. For example, look at an object that is straight ahead of your body. Now shift your head to one side. Since we tend to use the head as the reference for egocentric direction (see Chapter 10), the object no longer seems to be directly straight ahead. Although the object is now perceived to lie in a different direction, its position in space is the same as it was before the head movement. Position and direction constancy are related but still separable phenomena (Shebilske, 1977).

There is even a kind of **odor constancy.** When you are sniffing an object, a deep sniff will tend to pull more of the odorous molecules into your nose. We know that if we artificially give a large puff of vapors to an observer, it will smell more intense than a smaller puff (for example, Rehn, 1978). Yet when we actually sniff something, its "smelliness" remains constant despite the strength of the sniff, hence demonstrating odor constancy (Teghtsoonian, Teghtsoonian, Berglund, & Berglund, 1978).

As we go through this list of constancies, a pattern ought to be emerging. The purpose of perception is to derive information about the nature of the external environment and the objects that inhabit it. The viewing conditions, our relationship to objects, and our own exploratory behaviors will frequently change the pattern of the proximal stimuli at our receptor surfaces. The constancies, then, are a complex set of "corrections" that take into account the ongoing conditions and allow us to extract a relatively stable set of object properties from the continuous flow of sensory inputs at our receptors. Were it not for such constancy corrections, objects would have no permanent properties in consciousness at all. They would continually change size, shape, lightness, color, and direction, with every move we make. Consciousness and sanity would be difficult to sustain in a world of such sudden changes.

Size constancy breaks down on Maple Road

GLOSSARY

The following definitions are specific to their use in this book.

Affordances   A set of actions that a specific object or environmental situation *affords* or makes available to the perceiver.

Apprehension   The conscious representation of a perceptual experience.

Brightness   The perceptual impression of the amount of light falling on a surface or a part of the visual field (for example, a brightly lit versus a dimly lit hallway).

Color constancy   The phenomenon whereby the color of an object does not appear to change despite changes in the spectral composition of the light falling on it.

Computational theories   Theories that attempt to specify the computations needed to go from the optical stimulus to the perceptual experience. These theories are often presented as mathematical models or computer programs.

Constancy scaling   The process by which the size of a target is changed in consciousness to correct for registered viewing distance.

Constructive theory   An approach to constancy contending that perception may be altered by experience or by other factors not in the proximal stimulus.

Context stimuli   Stimuli that are near to, or occur at the same time as, the stimulus being perceived.

Direct perception   An approach to constancy maintaining that all aspects of the percept must be directly derived from components of the proximal stimulus.

Direction constancy   The stability of an object's perceived egocentric direction despite changes in eye or head position.

Distal stimulus   An object or event in the environment.

Emmert's law   The quantitative expression of the relationship between apparent size and apparent distance; objects appear larger when projected on a more distant surface.

External illuminance   The amount of light falling on an object.

Focal stimulus   The stimulus on which attention is focused.

Intelligent perception   The theoretical presumption that cognitive processes and experience can affect perception.

Invariants   Aspects of the stimulus situation that are always present in the stimulus and are good predictors of object properties such as size, shape, or distance.

Lightness   An aspect of an object's color that is based on its ability to reflect light. Thus a gray object has more lightness than a black object. Also called *whiteness*.

Lightness constancy   The process by which the apparent lightness of a surface remains unchanged, despite changes in physical illumination. Also called *whiteness constancy.*

Loudness constancy   The process by which the apparent loudness of a sound source remains unchanged despite changes in its distance from the observer.

Moon illusion   An illusion in which the moon appears larger when near the horizon than when high in the sky.

Mueller-Lyer illusion   An illusion of length caused by placing inward or outward facing wings on the ends of lines.

Multidimensional interaction   Interaction between several stimulus channels or sources of information.

Object properties   The physical properties characterizing an object, such as size or shape.

Objective instruction   Instruction directing an observer to report the sizes and shapes of real-world objects.

Odor constancy   The process by which odor intensity appears to be unchanged, despite variations in the strength of sniffing.

Ponzo illusion   A length illusion produced by registration of converging lines as distance cues.

Position constancy   Stable perceived position of objects despite body, eye, or head movements.

Projective instruction   Instruction directing an observer to report the sizes and shapes of parts of his or her retinal image.

Proximal stimulus   Information about a distal stimulus that reaches the receptors, such as visual image on the retina, or sound at the ears.

Ratio principle   The principle that the lightness of an object is determined by the ratio of the light reaching the eye from the object and its background, which is always the same regardless of the illumination.

Reflectance   The percentage of light reflected from a surface.

Registration   Information extracted from the proximal stimulus, but not necessarily consciously apprehended.

Retinal illuminance   The amount of light falling on the retina.

Retinex theory   A computational elaboration of the ratio theory of lightness and color constancy, based on multiple comparisons of illumination and color differences at various boundaries across the visual field.

Shape constancy   The process by which the apparent shape of an object remains constant despite changes in the shape of the retinal image.

Situation properties   The conditions affecting the way objects are viewed, such as distance from them or the amount of ambient light.

Size constancy   The stability of perceived size despite changes in objective distance and retinal image size.

Unconscious inference   A process by which information from a number of sources is unconsciously put together to create a perception.

Whiteness   *See* Lightness.

Whiteness constancy   *See* Lightness constancy.

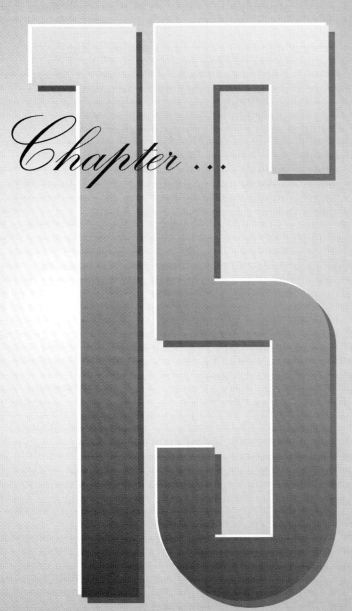

Chapter ...

ATTENTION

Varieties of Attention

Orienting

    Orienting Reflex

    Covert Orienting

    The Attentional Gaze

    The Neurophysiology of Orienting

Filtering

    The Cocktail Party Phenomenon

    The Video Overlap Phenomenon

    The Neurophysiology of Filtering

    Divided Attention

Searching

    Eye Movements and Visual Searching

    Feature versus Conjunction Searching

    Automatic versus Controlled Searching

    Vigilance and Arousal

Expecting

    Costs and Benefits of Information Cues

    The Neurophysiology of Expecting

Theories of Attention

My experience is what I agree to attend to. Only those items which I notice, shape my mind.

William James (1890, p. 402)

Our ability to perceive, process, and interpret the numerous and diverse stimuli that continually bombard our receptors is limited. For this reason, we are forced to choose among all that is there to be looked at, listened to, felt, smelled, or tasted. The various ways by which we select among stimuli as we sense our world are often grouped together under the general label of *attention.*

VARIETIES OF ATTENTION

Attention has several different aspects. For example, think back to the last time you were reading this book and the various extraneous events that distracted you. You got a cramp in your foot and initiated a stretching movement; a fire engine screamed by outside, and you listened until the siren stopped somewhere down the block; a flicker of movement in the periphery of your visual field caused you to look toward the door to the room where your roommate was bringing you a midnight snack. In all of these cases, important environmental events demanded an **orienting** response. That is, your attention was drawn to the source of a sudden change in your sensory world. Some events you gave only brief attention, as when you initiated the foot-stretch. Other events you listened to (the fire siren) or looked at (your roommate bringing the snack) for longer periods of time. While you attended to some stimuli you were also excluding many others; hence you were probably unaware of the goldfish swimming in its bowl or the humming of the refrigerator in the next room. Technically we would say that you were **filtering** out the extra-

neous events—attending to only one, or perhaps a few distinct and separable sources of stimuli, which we will refer to as **information channels.**

As you continued to study this book, perhaps your attention wandered for a moment and you thought of the exam scheduled for tomorrow in calculus. You wondered where your notes were and looked up, scanning your room for the green binder you would be poring over in a few minutes. You were **searching** for a relevant stimulus in the environment, scanning your sensory world for particular features or combinations of features. Finally, just as you were about to start studying your math notes, you paused, realizing that it was at about this time every night that the wolves in the zoo next door began to howl at the moon. You listened for a few moments. Yes, there they were, right on time. You were **expecting** something to happen and momentarily attended to "empty space" until it did. In all of these situations, different forms of attention were called on, and each played a major role in determining your conscious perceptual experience.

In what follows, we describe in more detail some of what is known about how attention operates in these four tasks: *orienting, filtering, searching,* and *expecting.* Our discussion will be restricted to the visual and auditory modalities, since the most work has been done on these, but our conclusions apply to the other modalities as well. By way of definition, it must be clear that each of the tasks can involve a single target or event **(focused attention)** or several **(divided attention).** Figure 15-1 is a summary of all of the situations we discuss in this chapter.

ORIENTING

The simplest form of selecting among the stimulus inputs is to *orient* the sensory receptors toward one set of stimuli and away from an-

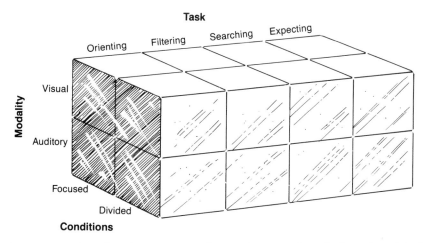

Figure 15-1 *A representation of various perceptual attention situations dealt with in this chapter.*

other. In this sense we might say that we do not passively see or hear, but rather we actively look or listen.

Orienting Reflex

Whenever a sudden movement or loud sound happens in the environment, attention tends to be drawn toward that event. We have all seen a dog or a cat prick up its ears and turn its head toward a sudden sound. The animal is performing the most primitive form of **orienting response,** which involves adjusting the sense organs so they can optimally pick up information about the event. Responses such as flicking the eye in the direction of a sound or peripheral movement occur automatically and are collectively referred to as the **orienting reflex.** This is such a reliable reflex (for example, Butterworth, 1981; Muir & Field, 1979) that eye- and head-turns toward sounds have been used to test the hearing of newborn infants. The best stimuli to elicit the orienting reflex are loud sounds, suddenly appearing bright lights, changes in contours, or movements in the peripheral visual field that are not regular or predictable occurrences. Interestingly, the

sudden offset of a light or sound that has been on continuously can also elicit the orienting reflex. When these stimuli happen, the animal, or human, turns its eyes so as to fixate the visual object or sound source, and often orients the head and body to face toward the event as well.

Normally, there are two types of eye movements. Smooth pursuit eye movements occur when you follow a slowly moving target such as a swinging pendulum. The eye movements most closely associated with orienting, however, occur in sharp, steplike movements known as **saccades** (from the French word for "jerk," since the eye moves as if it were jerked by a sharp tug on a string). When we are voluntarily looking at stimuli, such as inspecting a photograph, the fastest we can initiate an eye movement to a new stimulus is about 200–250 msec. The eye movements that are made to a suddenly occurring stimulus, however, can begin with lightning speed. These so-called **express saccades** have been measured to begin as early as 75 msec after the onset of the stimulus. The circumstance required to generate these rapid eye movements is that the viewer must not already be attending to anything in the visual field (Fischer & Boch, 1983; Fischer & Breitmeyer, 1987; Mayfrank & Mobashery,

1986). It appears that the visual system is designed always to be attending to something. In the absence of an object of attention, it becomes especially sensitive to new events.

A variety of other behaviors also follow a sudden event, such as postural adjustments, skin conductance changes, pupil dilation, decrease in heart rate, a pause in breathing, and constriction of the peripheral blood vessels (see Rohrbaugh, 1984, for more details). It is as though we have an internal "model" of the immediate world of stimuli around us. When we notice a departure of stimulus input from that model, we reflexively attend to that stimulus in order to update that model as quickly as possible (Donchin, 1981; Sokolov, 1975). If the same stimulus occurs repeatedly, it becomes an expected part of our model of the world and our orienting reflex toward it becomes weaker, even if the stimulus is quite strong. With any change in the nature of the stimulus, however, the reflex recovers to full strength.

Covert Orienting

Up to now we have been dealing only with *overt orienting* responses, which actually involve looking at or turning toward a stimulus. Although this is one of the most direct signs that we are attending to something, a number of researchers have pointed out that it is possible to attend to an event or stimulus without making any overt sign that we are doing so. For example, Helmholtz (1909/1962) observed that he could direct his attention without the necessity of an eye movement or change in accommodation or convergence. This shift of attentional focus, which is dissociated from any visible change in overt eye/head/body orientation, is called *covert attention*.

A common example of covert attention is when you become aware of a familiar voice in a conversation somewhere else at a party even while looking at the person in front of you. Most modern research on attention takes for granted that overt orienting is not necessary

for paying attention. Typically, in attentional experiments, eye/head/body movements are strictly controlled, or they are made irrelevant by using headphones or by using such short stimulus presentations that the eyes have no time to move. Such controlled presentations allow researchers to separate the effects of overt orienting from more covert shifts of attention. When your attention is involuntarily drawn to a stimulus, without any overt orienting response, we refer to this as **covert orienting.**

Your attention can be seized by certain stimuli in many ways. A dramatic example capitalizes on the fact that visual stimuli seem to be more capable of drawing our attention to particular locations in space than auditory stimuli. This is the phenomenon ventriloquists depend on, called **visual capture.** Demonstration Box 15-1 allows you to experience this for yourself.

An interesting demonstration of how attention can be drawn to a stimulus was made by Yantis and Jonides (1984; Jonides & Yantis, 1988). They showed that the abrupt appearance of a stimulus in the visual field captures visual attention and gives that stimulus an advantage in terms of how quickly or accurately it can be responded to. They asked observers to say whether a letter target, whose identity was indicated at the beginning of each trial, was present in a field of other distracter letters. On each trial, one letter appeared abruptly in the visual field, while either one or three others appeared gradually by the fading of selected lines in figures displayed previously, as shown in Figure 15-2. Sometimes the target letter was the abruptly appearing one; at other times it was one of the gradually appearing letters. When the target appeared abruptly, observers detected it significantly more quickly than when it faded on. The abruptly appearing stimulus seems to have drawn attention to itself. If it was the target, a positive response could immediately be made; if it was not the target, then the other figures had to be checked to see whether the target was among them before a response could be made, slowing the response. Even if the abruptly appearing figure was not the target, observers still covertly oriented toward it first, before they checked any of the other figures.

Recently other studies have confirmed the ability of an abruptly appearing stimulus to attract attention (for example, Muller & Findlay, 1988). Researchers found that when such a stimulus preceded the occurrence of a target by about 100 msec, the target information was

DEMONSTRATION BOX 15-1   Visual Capture

Visual capture is a phenomenon in which attention is caught by a visual stimulus in a way that results in an illusion of auditory localization. Whenever you are listening to a sound, such as a voice talking, there is a tendency to try to identify visual events, or objects, that could be causing the sound. When the ventriloquist's dummy is moving its mouth and limbs, and the ventriloquist is talking without moving *his* mouth, then your visual attention is "captured" by the dummy's movements and you *hear* the ventriloquist's voice coming from its mouth, even though it is really the ventriloquist speaking.

You can demonstrate this effect for yourself by obtaining two television sets (or going to a store that sells them and asking to use two of theirs for a "scientific demonstration"). Place them side by side, about 500 centimeters apart, and tune both sets to the same newscast, talk show, or other show in which the sound is highly correlated with the picture. (You could also use a radio and a television set, tuning in to a simulcast show like some concerts.) Now turn off the sound on one of the sets and turn off the picture on the other. Move back a short distance and look at a place between the two sets while paying attention to the picture-displaying set. The sound seems to come from that set, even though its sound is turned off. It actually doesn't matter where you look, the sound will seem to come from the set with the picture. You could also try moving the sets apart to see how powerful the phenomenon is. You will be surprised at how far apart these sets can be before the actual sound source dominates. By the way, this also explains why when you are watching a film the sound seems to come from the actors' mouths, even though the speakers may be located at the side of the film screen, or even in the back of the room.

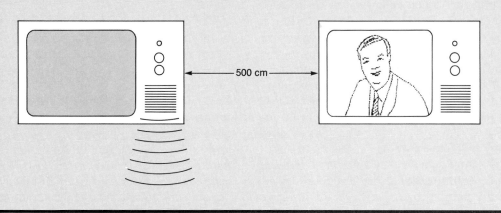

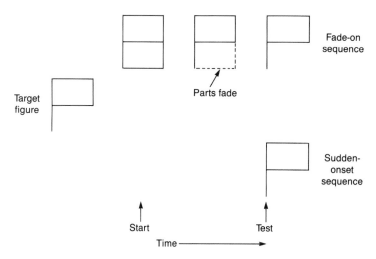

Figure 15-2   The upper sequence shows how a stimulus is gradually presented by fading lines as opposed to sudden onset of the stimulus in the Yantis and Jonides (1984) study. Sudden-onset stimuli were more easily detected.

processed optimally. It seems that attention is attracted to the spatial location of the abruptly appearing stimulus within about 100 msec of its appearance. At that time attention is optimally prepared to deal with any other information appearing in the same location. It has been suggested that such alignments of attention occur automatically, without conscious control, in contrast to what happens when we voluntarily attend to some stimulus in the visual field (Jonides, 1981; Muller & Humphries, 1991).

A similar phenomenon happens in the auditory modality. For example, in the early experiments on divided attention, subjects were given a different message in each ear by means of headphones. They were asked to pay attention to and repeat the message they were hearing in one ear (this procedure is called **shadowing**) while another message was delivered to the other ear. When an abrupt or distinctive sound was presented, or an unexpected change, such as a switch from a male to a female voice, occurred in the nonshadowed ear, subjects tended to "stumble" or lose the continuity of their shadowing (see, for exam-

ple, Kahneman, 1973). Apparently, their attention was drawn involuntarily to the nonshadowed message, causing them to fail to hear what they were supposed to be attending to and thus to interrupt the smooth flow of the shadowing. More recent experiments have confirmed the ability of an abrupt sound to trigger automatically a reorientation of attention (Mori & Ward, 1991; Scharf, 1989; Schlauch & Hafter, 1991).

In both of the examples above, attention was drawn to some conspicuous stimulus somewhere in the visual or auditory field. We refer to such a stimulus as a **stimulus cue.** Orienting, filtering, and searching all depend on the presence of one or more stimulus cues toward which attention is either automatically drawn (orienting) or voluntarily directed (filtering or searching). When we receive information in advance about where or when something is likely to happen (we call this an **information cue**), attentional phenomena appear to be somewhat different. This suggests that our expectations interact with how we direct our attention, a matter discussed later, in the section on "expecting."

The Attentional Gaze

A useful way of conceptualizing some of the findings in covert visual orienting and visual search is a metaphor that we will call the **attentional gaze.** Other terms have been suggested for this concept (for example, a *zoom lens* by Eriksen & Hoffman, 1972; Eriksen & St. James, 1986; and Eriksen & Murphy, 1987; a *spotlight* by Hernandez-Peon, 1964, and Treisman, 1982; the *mind's eye* by Jonides, 1980), but attentional gaze is the most general. In this metaphor, we imagine that your attention can "gaze" about independently of where your eyes are looking. In the case of orienting, attention can be drawn to a stimulus cue anywhere in the visual field where acuity and sensitivity are adequate to register it, either by an abrupt onset or by other conspicuous differences in movement, shape, or color (Julesz, 1981; Nakayama & Silverman, 1986; Treisman, 1982).

Covert shifts in the attentional gaze seem to behave in a similar way to physical movements of the eye. In order to move from point *A* to point *B*, your attentional gaze may move through all the intermediate positions like a smooth pursuit eye movement (Shulman, Remington, & McLean, 1979) or might jump from *A* to *B* like a saccade (Tsal, 1983), depending on the stimulus conditions (although some researchers disagree, for example, Murphy & Eriksen, 1987, and Yantis, 1988). One study estimated that these shifts of attentional gaze move through space with a fixed velocity of about 125 deg per second—that is only 8 msec to move 1 deg (Tsal, 1983). Another similarity between attentional gaze and physical eye movements is that your attention usually cannot be drawn to more than one location in the visual field at any instant in time (Eriksen & Yeh, 1985; Muller & Humphries, 1991; van der Heijden, Wolters, Groep, & Hagenaar, 1987; Yantis & Jonides, 1984).

Auditory attention also acts as if it has a direction of gaze. It can be drawn to particular spatial locations in a way similar to that of visual attention. However, auditory attention moves at about 233 deg per second, almost twice as fast as the shift of visual attention (Rhodes, 1987). For shifts greater than 90 deg, the time it takes to move attention no longer increases with increasing distance; instead, auditory attention seems to "pop up" at the new location as if the ear had made an "auditory saccade" to the new location.

The fact that the attentional gaze can be shifted without accompanying eye (or head) movements raises the interesting question of how these two systems are coordinated. Under normal circumstances a stimulus cue will attract both a shift in attentional gaze and an eye movement to the location of the stimulus. However, as you may have noted in listening to a boring conversation, an eye movement to a location of greater interest can be prevented by sheer force of will (Klein, 1980; Posner, 1980), although it is almost impossible for attention not to be attracted by a conspicuous event, at least momentarily. Experimental studies of the attentional gaze show that it can shift much faster than the eye—it reaches a stimulus location before the eye does and seems to help to guide the eye to the proper location (Fischer & Breitmeyer, 1987; Henderson & Pollatsek, 1989; Posner, 1988; Remington, 1980). These experiments suggest that the attentional gaze and the eye are related much like the eye and hand are related in the everyday act of reaching. Under normal circumstances the eye will first move to the object of interest and then help guide the hand to the correct location. However, an eye movement can occur without a hand movement necessarily following, and hand movements can be made even with one's eyes closed.

Three aspects of the attentional gaze are important in the processing of sensory information. At any one moment attention may be described as having a *locus*, an *extent*, and a *detail set*. As we have noted, the attention gaze shifts around much as your eyes move to take in visual information. Once attention is located at a particular place, or **locus,** in the visual field, processing of stimuli occurring at or near that locus is improved. It is improved more if the locus is near the fovea than if it is in the more peripheral regions of the retina (Shulman, Sheehy, & Wilson, 1986). The **extent** of the area over which attention is spread can be controlled by making the stimulus cue larger or smaller (LaBerge & Brown, 1989; Podgorny & Shepard, 1983). The greater the extent, the less the processing efficiency. Processing also becomes less efficient for stimuli that are farther away from the center of the attended region (Eriksen & St. James, 1986).

Finally, there is some evidence that the attentional gaze is set or calibrated for a particular level of detail at any one time. In the visual modality, for example, this **detail set** tends to direct the focus of attention to elements of a particular relative size. Several studies have shown that observers can focus selectively on either the more global (relatively larger) aspects or the more local (relatively smaller) features in a visual form. Thus, if we have a large figure made up of smaller distinct components (such as the large letter made up of smaller letters that we saw in Figure 11-19), we may be set to attend to either the larger figure or its smaller elements. When we are set to attend to one level of detail, our processing of features at the other level is poorer (J. E. Hoffman, 1980; Kinchla, Solis-Macias, & Hoffman, 1983; L. M. Ward, 1985). An example of the effects of detail set is given in Demonstration Box 15-2.

The Neurophysiology of Orienting

Over the past 15 years, researchers studying the physiology of the brain have begun to examine some of the neural mechanisms of orienting. Several areas of the monkey brain contain single nerve cells that fire more vigorously when the monkey's attention is directed to target stimuli in their receptive fields (Mountcastle, Motter, Steinmetz, & Sestokas, 1987; Wurtz, Goldberg, & Robinson, 1980). (Recall from Chapter 3 that the *receptive field* of a particular cell is that region of the visual field in which a stimulus can produce a response from that cell.) Several of the areas of the brain involved in orienting attention are shown in Figure 15-3.

DEMONSTRATION BOX 15-2   Level of Detail and Attention

How many times in your life have you looked at a penny? Probably thousands of times. Take a piece of paper and, from memory, draw both sides of a penny. There is no need to be artistic, just try to represent all the figures, all the words, numbers, and dates on a penny, each in its proper place. Next, compare your drawings to an actual penny. It is likely that you will find at least one, and probably several, errors in the material you include and your placement of it. The reason for this is that it is possible to recognize a penny based on a fairly global set of characteristics, namely its size, shape, and color. So your *detail set* when attending to pennies has probably seldom been small enough to pick out the local characteristics, regardless of the thousands of times you have looked at one.

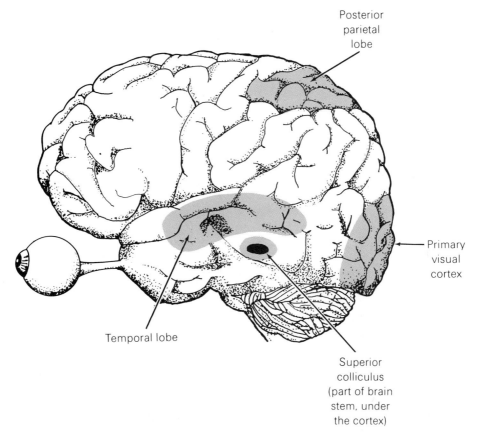

Figure 15-3 *Areas of the brain involved in attention to visual stimuli. The* superior colliculus *is involved in making overt eye movements to stimuli; the* posterior parietal lobe *is involved in covert orienting; and the* temporal lobe *is involved in filtering objects on the basis of color and shape.*

One of these areas, called the **superior colliculus,** sits at the top of the brain stem in mammals. (It is not visible from the vantage point of Figure 15-3, unless the cortex and overlying structures are removed.) The superior colliculus contains many cells that fire only when stimuli appear in specific locations in the visual field. However, these cells fire even more vigorously when the monkey makes an overt eye movement toward the stimulus location that the cell is responsive to (Wurtz, Goldberg, & Robinson, 1980). These cells are not simply recording eye movements, however,

since they do not respond when eye movements are made in complete darkness. Rather, they seem to reflect the shift in attention toward the target, with the increased firing rate of the cells beginning 50 msec after the target is flashed onto the screen, while the eye movement that follows might actually begin 200 msec later.

To determine whether we are dealing with overt or covert orienting, we can use an experimental situation like the one shown in Figure 15-4. This involves a screen for a visual stimulus and a lever that the monkey can press to in-

No orienting

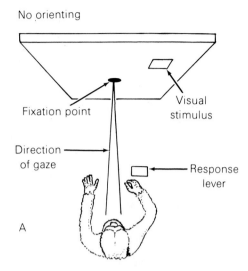

Overt orienting

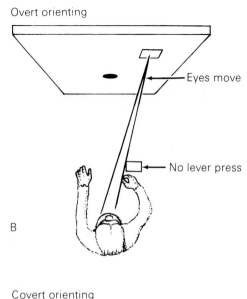

Figure 15-4   Conditions used to test for various attention functions in the brains of monkeys. (A) No eye movement or response (no orienting). (B) Eye movement only (overt orienting). (C) Lever press with no eye movement (covert orienting).

Covert orienting

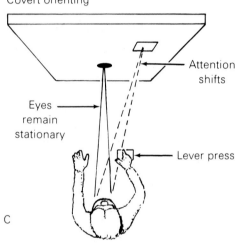

dicate that it has seen a particular stimulus. In part *A*, the monkey is looking at a point in the center of the screen, and not attending to the stimulus that has just flashed on to its right; hence we have neither overt nor covert orienting here. In *B* the monkey shifts its eyes to the stimulus, demonstrating overt orienting. In *C* the monkey responds to the stimulus with a lever press indicating covert orienting but does not move its eyes, showing that there is no overt orienting. That the superior colliculus cells are specifically responsive to *overt* orienting is suggested by the fact that if the monkey responds to the stimulus with a lever press but does not actually move its eyes, these cells do not increase their firing rate.

A second brain area that has been studied is the **posterior parietal lobe,** a part of the cortex that lies toward the back of the brain and above the occipital lobes. Cells in this area become more active both when the monkey makes an eye movement toward the target and when the monkey keeps its eyes fixed but responds to the target stimulus with a button press (Mountcastle et al., 1987; Wurtz et al., 1980), as in Figure 15-4C. This suggests that the parietal lobe is an important brain area for directing the *covert* attentional gaze. Since each hemisphere of the brain receives direct inputs from only one side of the visual field, this may explain why damage to the posterior parietal lobe can result in **hemifield** neglect, which is the inability to pay attention to and to notice stimuli from one-half of the visual field (De Renzi, 1982; Posner, Inhoff, Friedrich, & Cohen, 1987; see also Chapter 18).

Of equal importance to the finding that cells in some regions of the brain respond selectively when the individual orients or pays attention to certain stimuli in the visual field is the finding that other regions in the brain, which we might expect to be related to visual processing, show no changes in firing associated with shifts in attention. For instance, cells in the *primary visual cortex* (area V1) do not show a differential response when the stimulus is the target for an eye movement or for a covert orientation of attention. You may recall from Chapter 3 that this is the first cortical area of the brain that receives information about visual shape and color. This lack of responsiveness to shifts in attention suggests that the analysis or *registration* of visual form and color occurs independently from the processes associated with actually paying attention to the stimulus.

FILTERING

Once we have oriented, either covertly or overtly, to a source of stimulation, we may continue to attend to (look at, listen to) that source to the exclusion of other things happening in our environment. Specifically, we are filtering out all stimuli except those that come from the region or channel we are attending to. How well can we do this? What factors affect how well we can select one information source and filter out others? What happens to information we do not attend to? Everyday experience asserts that things we attend to seem sharp and clear and are easy to recall, whereas unattended stimuli are less distinct and more difficult to remember. It turns out that research confirms these informal impressions.

The Cocktail Party Phenomenon

Consider a noisy cocktail party. This is a good example of many possible sources of stimulation occurring at one time, which require attentional filtering for you to make any sense out of the proceedings. For example, often many conversations are going on simultaneously, including the one in which you are involved. If you hear a significant or familiar voice, you may covertly orient toward a conversation off to the side of you, even while you nod occasionally to the person standing in front of you who thinks you are paying attention to him. You may also suddenly be startled when the person to whom you had been "talking" gives a sniff and walks away rapidly, obviously angry with you. You are puzzled, because you cannot remember a thing that person has said in the last five minutes. However, you remember perfectly what your former sweetheart said in the conversation beside you to which you *were* listening. Apparently you very effectively filtered out everything else, including whatever it was that caused your conversational partner to walk away.

Colin Cherry (1953), in a now-classic article, investigated some of the problems exemplified in the behavior we described above. He introduced the experimental technique called **shadowing** in order to control how his observers oriented their auditory attention. In this technique, an observer is presented with two messages through two different information channels. For example, the two channels could be the two ears (one message to each ear, a technique called **dichotic listening**), or one message could be presented visually and the other auditorially, or the two messages could be presented at different locations in space. The observer must repeat aloud (that is, follow along with, or shadow) one of the messages as it is presented. If the observer is allowed to lag slightly behind the message and repeat entire phrases at once, the technique is called **phrase shadowing.** If the requirement is to repeat each syllable as it is presented, it is called **phonemic shadowing.** Cherry demonstrated that observers could orient to one message and filter out the other.

It is not equally easy to shadow all messages. For example, using the dichotic listening technique, it has been shown that if the selected message is prose, such as a selection from a story, shadowing is relatively easy. Shadowing random lists of words is more difficult, and shadowing nonsense syllables (for example, *orp*, *vak*, *bij*) is the most difficult of all. Clearly meaning and grammatical structure help us to attend to one message and filter out others. Shadowing is also easier if the messages come from two different places in space, are different in pitch (for example, one male voice and one female voice), or are presented at different speeds. For an example of how this works, try Demonstration Box 15-3.

What happens to the inputs we do not attend to, which we earlier suggested were "filtered out"? Cherry (1953) found that listeners could remember very little of the rejected message in the shadowing task. Moray (1959) found that in difficult shadowing tasks, even though listeners knew they would later be asked about it, they were unable to remember words that had been repeatedly presented in the unshadowed message. Did the listeners simply not hear the unshadowed message, or did the shadowed message somehow interfere with their memory of the unshadowed message? Both Cherry and Moray had waited a little while after the shadowing task was completed to ask about the unshadowed message. Perhaps the unshadowed message was heard, and maybe the words were actually recognized, but they were forgotten quickly because they were not entered into a long-lasting memory. Perhaps we must pay attention to an input in order to remember it for longer than a few seconds. This idea was tested by interrupting listeners' shadowing to ask them to report what had just been presented to the unshadowed ear (Glucksberg & Cowen, 1970; Norman, 1969). When this happens, listeners can usually recall the last five to seven words, numbers, or whatever units are being shadowed. It seems that material in the unshadowed ear is actually perceived at some level and is available for processing and attention for a short while after it occurs, but unless it is attended to, it is not entered into a long-lasting memory.

The Video Overlap Phenomenon

Although it happens rarely in this electronically sophisticated age, sometimes two powerful TV stations may be geographically near enough that their signals encroach on each other, making it impossible to tune a television set to a single channel. When this happens, there will be an overlap of video broadcast of two different programs, with one usually looking somewhat ghostly or like a negative picture. If you have ever experienced this but wanted to watch one of the channels enough (your favorite soap opera), you may have experienced a video phenomenon similar to the cocktail party phenomenon for sound. What you probably found was that it was possible to watch "your" program and filter out the other one, although of course if was not pleasant because you had to make an unaccustomed effort to do so.

An analog of the shadowing task described earlier has been used to study this kind of visual filtering (Neisser & Becklin, 1975). Overlapping video programs, one of a hand game and the other of a ball game, were presented to

DEMONSTRATION BOX 15-3 Selective Attention and the Precedence Effect

You may remember our discussion of the precedence effect from Chapter 7, where we listed some variables that affect our ability to localize the position of sound sources in space. When sounds are emitted in enclosed spaces, they tend to cause echoes as they bounce from walls, ceilings, and floors. However, we can still make a correct localization of the sound source, because the sound emanating directly from this source will reach our ears before its echoes. The auditory system is sensitive to these time differences and can use this information in the localization of sound-producing sources. The direction of the sound emanating directly from the sound source, takes precedence over other sounds in localization; hence the name *precedence effect*.

The precedence effect can also be helpful in selective attention, when we are attempting to process one of many simultaneously occurring stimulus events. A good example of this is found in cocktail party situations, where you may try to follow one of many competing conversations. This aspect of selective attention is helped by the spatial and temporal separations of the auditory inputs. You can demonstrate this for yourself with the aid of two friends (preferably of the same sex) and a doorway. First have your friends stand as shown in Figure *A*, while each reads passages from a book or newspaper simultaneously. Notice that even with your eyes closed you can easily separate and locate the two messages. Now stand out of the direct line of sight (and sound) of each friend, as shown in Figure *B*. In this situation the messages must travel indirectly out through the open door. This means that they will tend to reach you at the same time and come from the same direction. Now, again with your eyes closed, notice how difficult it is to locate the voices and to separate their messages.

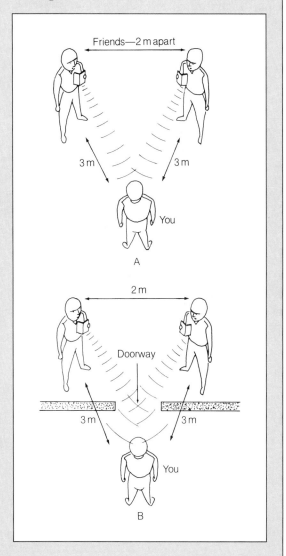

observers. In the hand game, the players tried to slap each other's hands, and observers who "shadowed" this game had to report each attacking stroke (but not feints). In the ball game, players threw a basketball to one another while moving about irregularly. Observers who shadowed the ball game had to report each throw of the ball from one player to another (but not fakes and dribbles). "Odd" events were also sometimes inserted in the programs (for example the hand-game players shook hands then resumed play, or the ball-game players threw the ball out of the picture, played with an imaginary ball for a few seconds, then resumed playing with the real ball). Figure 15-5 shows examples of single frames from each game and the two frames superimposed.

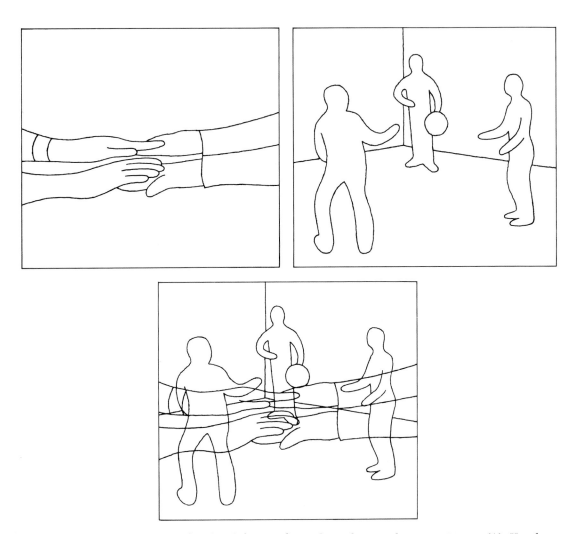

Figure 15-5 *Outline tracings of isolated frames from the video overlap experiment.* (A) *Hand game only.* (B) *Ball game only.* (C) *Hand game and ball game superimposed (from Neisser & Becklin, 1975).*

The results of this study were remarkably similar to those from auditory shadowing experiments. Observers could easily follow the events in one program presented alone, as would be expected. They also had little difficulty following the events of one program when the other one was superimposed upon it, although they did make a few more errors in this condition. Moreover, the odd events in the shadowed programs were almost always noticed, whereas the odd events in the unshadowed programs were rarely noticed. For example, only 1 of 24 subjects noticed the handshake in the hand game while shadowing the ball game; no subjects noticed the ball disappear in the ball game while they were watching the hand game. The reports that did occur were vague and uncertain, and usually not correct. Generally, those few subjects felt that there might be something unusual about the unshadowed program but they did not know what it was. Most subjects noticed nothing unusual at all. This indicates that, like auditory filtering, visual filtering allows little of the filtered-out information to make a lasting impression, a result that has been verified in many different situations (for example, Rock & Guttman, 1981). You can experience a similar type of visual shadowing, and its effect on memory of the unshadowed message, by trying Demonstration Box 15-4.

The Neurophysiology of Filtering

Where in the brain might filtering of this sort occur? For the orienting aspect of attention, we saw that the brain regions known as the *superior colliculus* and the *posterior parietal lobe* were involved in shifting our attention to various regions of the visual field. However, filtering involves more than simply attending to

---

DEMONSTRATION BOX 15-4   Visual Shadowing and Memory

In the accompanying passage, the relevant message is shaded and the irrelevant message is printed in the normal fashion. You are to read the shaded passage aloud as rapidly as possible, ignoring the irrelevant (unshaded) message. Now without cheating and looking back, write down all the words you remember from the irrelevant message. Go back and read the shaded passage again, but this time stop after each line to write down the words you recall from the irrelevant message (without looking back at it). You should find that the list of remembered words is longer when your reading is interrupted and you are not asked to recall all the irrelevant message at once (from Lindsay & Norman, 1977).

In performing an experiment like this one on man attention car it house is boy critically hat important shoe that candy the old material horse that tree is pen being phone read cow by book the hot subject tape for pin the stand relevant view task sky be read cohesive man and car grammatically house complete boy but hat without shoe either candy being horse so tree easy pen that phone full cow attention book is hot not tape required pin in stand order view to sky read red it not too difficult

one region of space and ignoring others. As we have seen, it can involve choosing to attend to one of several stimuli that appear in the same spatial location. We can also choose to focus on the color rather than the shape of an object, or on its texture rather than its size. To study the physiological bases of filtering, researchers have begun to study those regions of the brain involved in the analysis of form and color.

One area in which the behavior of single cells has been examined is in the **temporal lobe** of the cortex (Desimone & Ungerleider, 1989; Moran & Desimone, 1985; Spitzer, Desimone, & Moran, 1988). A representation of this area can be seen in Figure 15-3. You may recall from Chapter 3 that the temporal lobe is involved in the analysis of shape and form. To study this area, researchers first trained monkeys to attend to one of two stimuli. For example, a monkey might be rewarded with food to press a button every time a red rectangle appeared on the screen.This was called the *attended stimulus*. Responses to other stimuli such as a green rectangle were not rewarded, and soon the monkey learned to ignore them. They were called the *unattended stimuli*. The researchers then recorded from a single cell in the temporal lobe that responded best to one of the stimuli. Suppose we have a cell in the temporal lobe that has a fairly large receptive field and will normally respond to a red rectangle anywhere in that region. If the monkey is paying attention to the red rectangle, we find that the cell responds vigorously. Not only that, but the cell seems to become insensitive to other stimuli in that region, as if the receptive field had shrunk to fit the boundaries of the rectangular stimulus that is attracting all of the monkey's attention. When the red rectangle was not being attended to, because the reinforced stimuli had changed, the cell's rate of firing decreased dramatically—it was as though withdrawal of attention had made the cell unable to recognize the stimulus to which it was usually tuned to respond.

Divided Attention

An important question relevant to perception is whether it is possible to pay attention to more than one source of information at the same time, and if so, whether performance suffers. In the visual filtering experiment (the hand game and ball game) discussed earlier, observers were also asked to try to *divide* their attention and to shadow both programs simultaneously. That is, they had to report both attacks in the hand game and throws in the ball game. When they tried to do this, their performance deteriorated dramatically. Observers missed many more events and typically said the task was "demanding" or even "impossible" (Neisser & Becklin,1975). Moreover, presenting the two programs to different eyes (*dichoptic presentation*) made the divided attention task no easier. The conclusion is that dividing visual attention between two (or more) sources is very difficult; we can look at only one thing at a time. Another example of what happens when we must divide our attention visually is demonstrated by the phenomenon of **binocular rivalry.** When the views presented to the two eyes are different enough, it is virtually impossible to hold both views in consciousness simultaneously. The two views *rival* each other for our attention. Thus we first see one eye's image while suppressing the other, and then the view alternates to that of the other eye. Demonstration Box 15-5 allows you to experience this failure of divided visual attention.

Attempts to divide attention between two auditory information channels are similarly difficult. Of course, it is impossible to verbally shadow two messages at once because we cannot say two things at once. Experiments have been done, however, in which people were asked to listen to messages (in this case word lists) in both ears and later distinguish words they had heard from distracters (Levy, 1971, cited in Kahneman, 1973). Recognition performance was far poorer when people were trying

DEMONSTRATION BOX 15-5   Binocular Rivalry

You may demonstrate binocular rivalry by using the accompanying figure and a pocket mirror. Place the mirror on the center line of Figure B and hold your head relatively close as shown in Figure A. Adjust the mirror, and your head, so the half of the figure seen in it appears to be at the same distance as when seen directly. The two halves of the figure should overlap, with one eye viewing the vertical and the other the horizontal stripes. Now look at the superimposed lines for few moments. At first you will see one set of lines. Then they will be replaced by the other set as they rival each other, alternating in and out of your consciousness.

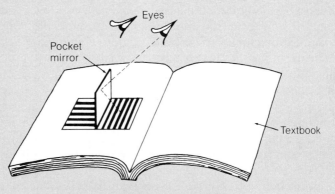

A   How to view the stimulus given below
     in order to experience binocular rivalry

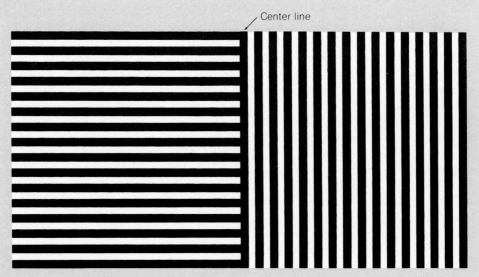

B   Binocular rivalry stimulus

to pay attention to both ears than when they listened to only one ear and filtered out the other. You may have had similar experiences at a party when trying to listen to two interesting conversations at once. It is possible to switch back and forth between them, but if they are at all demanding, a great deal of the information of each one will be lost.

Divided attention is easier if the information channels are in different modalities, such as vision and audition, although performance still suffers in comparison to attention focused on only one channel whenever the filtering task is at all difficult (for example, Treisman & Davies, 1972). Only when the task is very easy, such as responding to a simple signal as soon as it occurs in either of two modalities, is there no decline in performance under divided attention conditions (for example, Miller, 1982). An apparent exception to this rule is a study by Allport, Antonis, and Reynolds (1972) in which musicians sight-read music and shadowed a message at the same time without loss of efficiency compared to doing either task alone. This seems to imply that there may be attentional resources that are unique to certain sensory modalities or perhaps even particular tasks, allowing better performance in dividing across modalities or tasks. However, in the vast majority of cases, divided-attention performance is considerably worse than focused-attention performance.

Finally, it is worth mentioning that dividing attention between two demanding tasks does become easier with extensive practice. We all have experienced doing two or more things at once, such as driving a car and carrying on a conversation, or reading a book, chewing on a sandwich, and scratching our head. It has been shown that a skilled typist can type at a high rate and shadow a message at the same time with almost no loss of efficiency at either task (H. L. Shaffer, 1975). What seems to be happening here is that extensive practice in typing has made that skill somewhat automatic for the typist. **Automatic processing** does not require conscious effort, thus allowing more attention

to be allocated to the less-automatic skill (shadowing, in this case). We discuss *automaticity* more fully in the next section.

SEARCHING

Imagine you are waiting in an airport for a loved one to arrive from a trip abroad. The plane arrives and a flood of people surges through the exit door. Your eyes flick back and forth across the mass of faces, searching for that familiar face. You don't bother looking at the people's clothes because you know she is wearing a new outfit, and you do not know what it looks like. You are looking for the peculiar combination of longish, coal-black hair, large nose, and close-set eyes that you remember so well. Someone near you suddenly shouts to a large man in a bright orange suit, who waves in reply. The shouter confides to you that she always has an easy time finding her husband at the airport because he always wears that silly suit and "stands out like a sore thumb." We have been describing a typical circumstance where we know what we are looking for or listening for and must search a field of "distracters" to find it. This task has become one of the most commonly used for studying attention, partly because it is easy to implement in the laboratory and partly because it has important implications for everyday life.

Eye Movements and Visual Searching

It is much easier to study looking-for than listening-for, since eye movements provide an obvious external indicator of visual searching. Our eyes are constantly exploring the visual field with high-speed ballistic movements called *saccades*. Demonstration Box 15-6 will show you an easy way to observe saccades directly in someone who is reading.

The path taken by our eyes as they move (or more correctly, jerk) over the visual field is

DEMONSTRATION BOX 15-6   Saccadic Eye Movements

For this demonstration you will need a volunteer to help you. The materials you will need are a stiff piece of paper with a small hole punched in it and a piece of reading material for your partner. Sit facing your partner at a distance of 2 ft to 3 ft. Ask your partner to read the passage silently and to move his or her eyes as smoothly as possible. While your partner is reading, look at one of the eyes through the peephole in the stiff piece of paper. Adjust the viewing distance so only your partner's eye is in view. You should now be able to see each small jerking movement (saccade) as the eye moves across the page. Note that you can identify the end of a line in the passage by the long saccade that is made every so often. You may also be able to tell when your partner goes back to reread some words that were not understood on the first scan.

determined by our intentions, by our previous experience, and by the way the eye-movement system is designed. We will consider each of these influences in turn. There is much evidence that meaning and expectation help to direct where we look in a visual scene (Antes & Penland, 1981; Findlay, 1981; Stark & Ellis, 1981). For example, Yarbus (1967) recorded eye-movement patterns while observers looked at pictures with different intentions in mind. Figure 15-6 shows the eye-movement patterns observers made for a typical picture (A) when

Figure 15-6 *Eye-movement patterns made when viewing the picture* (A) *vary depending on whether the viewer was asked the ages of the individuals in the picture (scan pattern B) or their wealth (scan pattern C; from Yarbus,* Eye movements in vision. *Copyright 1967 by Plenum Publishing Company. Reprinted by permission).*

Figure 15-7 *It is easier to find a target object in a coherent, natural scene* (above) *than in the same scene randomly jumbled* (opposite page; *from Biederman et al., 1973).*

asked to estimate either the ages of the individuals in the picture (B) or their wealth (C). Clearly, people looked at different places in order to find information relevant to the different questions.

People rapidly learn to inspect spatial locations in systematic order to detect targets that may be present. Although this is a fairly automatic process for adults, it does not appear to be fully developed (for some tasks) until children are about 6 or 7 years of age (for example, K. Cohen, 1981; Green, Hammond, & Supramaniam, 1983) and becomes much more difficult for the elderly (P. M. A. Rabbitt, 1984). People also use their knowledge of the world to guide their searching. If a scene has been jumbled by randomly interchanging different areas, as has been done in Figure 15-7, people

have a harder time locating a target object, such as a store sign (Biederman, Glass, & Stacey, 1973). We also look at unusual objects in a visual scene longer when we find them (Antes & Penland, 1981; A. Friedman, 1979; Friedman & Liebelt, 1981). Perhaps because of this, unexpected objects tend to be remembered and recognized more easily, and exchanges of one unusual object for another (a cow for a car in a living room) are noticed far more often than are exchanges of one usual object for another (a chair for a table in a living room) (A. Friedman, 1979).

There is also evidence of an important involuntary process that contributes to the constant search for novelty in our looking patterns. This process has been called **inhibition of return** because it refers to a decreased

likelihood that people will move their eyes and their attentional gaze back to a location they have recently attended to (Posner & Cohen, 1984; Maylor & Hockey, 1985). Inhibition of return can be studied with an experiment in which subjects are asked repeatedly to identify visual targets. Some targets occur in locations previously occupied by targets presented earlier while others occur in previously empty locations. The tendency to avoid returning attention to objects that have been looked at before seems to last for several seconds and seems to be related to specific locations in the visual world (Maylor & Hockey, 1985) or to previously identified objects (Tipper, Driver, & Weaver, 1991). It has even been observed in infants as young as 6 months of age (Rothbart, Posner, & Boylan, 1990). This mechanism

maximizes the amount of information the person picks up, since it is more likely that new information will be found in new locations in the visual field that have not yet been searched and attended to (Klein, 1988; Posner, Rafal, Choate, & Vaughan, 1985).

Feature versus Conjunction Searching

A common laboratory task to study visual search involves asking an observer to scan a collection of letters (or other forms) in order to find a specified target letter (or form). One early study of this type was conducted by Neisser (1967). Observers scanned, from top to bottom, a group of letters arranged in 50 lines of 6 letters each, looking for particular targets.

With practice they came to perform this search at great speed (as fast as 60 letters per second). A number of factors, however, affected their search speed. For instance, when the target was an angular letter (W, Z, X) and the other letters (distracters) were roundish (O, Q, C), observers searched much more quickly than when the target was more similar to the distracters (for example, a W when distracters were K, Z, X, Y). When the target differs from all of the distracters by possessing a feature they do not have (for example, an angled line), we call this a **feature search.** When the only way to detect the target is to detect a conjunction (or particular combination) of features (such as the particular angles and their orientation that distinguish between a W and an M), we call this a **conjunction search.** In general, feature searches are much easier than conjunction searches. Thus, Neisser's subjects typically reported that when they were searching the list, particularly when the target was very different from the distracters, the nontarget letters were just a blur and they did not "see" individual letters. In fact the target often just "popped out" of the array.

Neisser (1967) argued that there was a *preattentive* level of processing that segregates a visual scene into figure and ground, a distinction we discussed in Chapter 11. When clear feature differences exist between the target and the distracter items, the target becomes readily visible because the distracters are lumped together as ground, and the target stands out as a figure by the action of this preattentive process alone. The notion is that similar elements are grouped together automatically and the ones that do not fit seem to leap into consciousness. This is not possible when the target and background items closely resemble each other as in a conjunction search (Duncan & Humphreys, 1989). Here, closer attention and scrutiny are needed to detect specific elements (for example, Julesz, 1980).

The differences between feature and conjunction searching have been extensively explored (for example, Pashler, 1987; Treisman, 1982, 1986a; Wolfe, Franzel, & Cave, 1989). The really striking result is that when feature search is possible the number of distracter items does not seem to affect searching speed. The target simply pops out of the display. This is called **parallel search** to indicate that all of the items are effectively processed at the same time. However, when conjunction search is required, the number of distracters does affect search speed. This can be seen clearly in some prototypical data illustrated in Figure 15-8. In conjunction search we seem to be comparing each of the distracters, one at a time, with the image of the target and responding only when they match. Such an orderly and sequential set of comparisons is often referred to as a **serial search.**

To explain this kind of data, Treisman offered a **feature integration theory.** It suggests that each feature of a stimulus (such as color, size, or shape) is registered separately. When an object must be identified from a combination of features, a correct analysis can only be achieved if attention is focused on one location at a time. Recalling our discussion of the attentional gaze, we might say that features occurring in a single attentional "glance" are combined to form an object. This combination and comparison takes time and effort. If attention is diverted or overloaded, errors may occur, and we may attribute the wrong features to a particular item and either miss the target or select a wrong target (Prinzmetal, 1981; Prinzmetal, Presti, & Posner, 1986; Treisman & Schmidt, 1982). Demonstration Box 15-7 gives you an opportunity to try feature and conjunction searches.

Sometimes conjunctions of simple features also result in very rapid search—even in "popout." Examples of such displays are shown in Figure 15-9. Demonstrations such as these

Conjunction
search

Feature search

2   4   6   8   10   12   14

Number of distractors

Response latency (msec)

Figure 15-8 *The relation between response latency to report the presence of a target and the number of distracter items that must be checked. The function is almost flat for feature search and much steeper for conjunction search (based on Treisman, 1982).*

have been used to argue that the elementary features of forms with respect to attention are not *situation properties*, but rather *object properties* (Enns & Rensink, 1990, 1991; Ramachandran, 1988). We saw in Chapter 14 that situation properties are the relatively variable features of a picture, such as the shapes and colors that change with viewpoint and lighting. In contrast, object properties, such as the orientation of an object relative to other objects

---

DEMONSTRATION BOX 15-7 Feature and Conjunction Search

In each of these arrays of visual forms there are targets to find. The target is a white *0*. Scan each array quickly, only once, and write down how many targets you see. Notice in each array how difficult or easy it is to find the targets. Do this before reading further.

Now you can know that arrays *A* and *B* required a feature search (in *A* the feature was brightness; in *B* it was shape), whereas array *C* required a conjunction search (for both brightness and shape). There were three targets in each array. Did you get them all? Most people find the conjunction search to be the most difficult of these tasks, and if they are apt to miss any targets it will be in array *C*.

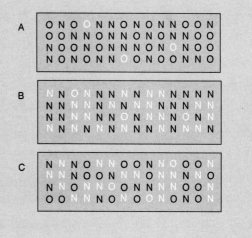

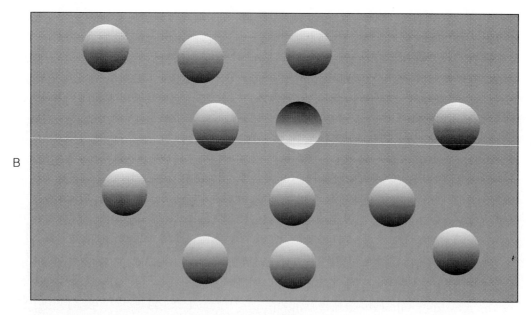

Figure 15-9 *Examples of conjunctions of simple features that pop out in visual search. In A each item consists of three diamond shapes—only their spatial relations distinguish the target item from the distracter items (based on Enns & Rensink, 1990). In B each item consists of a shaded circle— only the direction of the shading distinguishes the target item from the distracter items (based on Ramachandran, 1988).*

and surface curvature, tend to remain constant over changes in the observer's viewpoint and scene lighting.

Automatic versus Controlled Searching

Searching can be improved by particular strategies that an observer adopts, and by practice. For example, a conjunction search may be treated as two simple feature searches under some circumstances (Egeth, Virzi, & Garbart, 1984; Wolfe, Franzel, & Cave, 1989). This has been called **guided search.** It means that in Demonstration Box 15-7 you might be able to look only at the white letters in array C, ignoring the black letters, while searching for the white O. In a sense, the figure–ground preattentive process is used to reject as ground all distracters that can be ruled out on the basis of a simple feature difference from the target, leaving you with only a second simple feature search to complete.

Another strategy that sometimes helps is to group items together into smaller sets of stimuli. If stimulus sets are small enough (say two to eight items), attention operates as if all items are checked at the same time (parallel search), rather than sequentially as in serial search. Using such a grouping strategy, the smaller arrays may be searched in parallel for both features and conjunctions (Pashler, 1987).

When observers have been able to practice for a long time on a task that always demands the same response under the same conditions, the nature of the search process seems to change—search time gradually becomes independent of the number of distracters present. In a typical study of this kind, some observers searched for a fixed set of targets (such as the letters H, S, and T) among a fixed set of distracters (such as the digits 1 to 9). At first, the more distracters in the display, the longer it took to find the target. However, after 14 days of practice (more than 4000 searches) on the same task, the number of distracters in the display ceased to matter. It took the same amount of time to find the target regardless of the number of distracters (Schneider & Shiffrin, 1977; Shiffrin & Schneider, 1977). Figure 15-10 shows this result graphically. It seems that before much practice the search is typical of conjunction searches and is serial in nature (this is often called **controlled processing**). After a lot of practice in a consistent environment, the search is said to be *automatic*, rather like simple feature search. A similar result has been obtained for an auditory detection task (Poltrock, Lansman, & Hunt, 1982), which indicates that automatic and controlled processing are not limited to vision but occur in other modalities as well.

The shift from controlled to automatic processing that occurs with practice is accompanied by several other changes (Schneider, Dumais, & Shiffrin, 1984). On the negative side, for example, it becomes more difficult to inhibit response to targets we are automatically set to search for, even if we wish to ignore them. We also do not remember as well the things we found and responded to under automatic control. On the positive side, however, we are able to do other tasks at the same time as engaging in an automatic search, and the added tasks do not interfere with the automatic processing. Actually, many lapses of attention in everyday life can be traced to such automatic processes and their inevitable effects (see Reason, 1984). You can experience the powerfully automatic nature of reading words, and how this can interfere with other tasks, by trying the demonstration of the **Stroop effect** in Demonstration Box 15-8.

Is it possible that when a process is truly automatic it requires no attentional resources at all? If we answer "yes" to this question, we have taken a position called *strong automatic-*

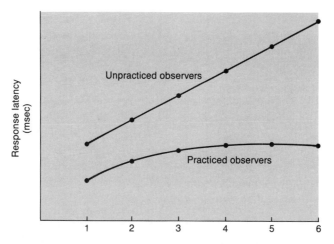

Figure 15-10 *The relation between response latency to report the presence of a target and the number of distracters to be checked. This function is steeper for unpracticed than practiced observers (based on Glass & Holyoak, 1986).*

ity (Schneider et al., 1984). This extreme position is appealingly simple, but a number of results are in disagreement with it. For example, in the Stroop effect demonstrated in Demonstration Box 15-8 reading is supposed to be automatic. However, the Stroop effect is much weaker when the colored ink and the incompatible color name are spatially separated than when they occur in the same place (Kahneman & Treisman, 1984). Strong automaticity would require that as long as the word could be read automatically it would not matter where it was, yet it seems that it is possible to filter out the incompatible color word if it is not part of the same perceptual object, but not if it is. This and other similar results favor a weaker notion of automatic processing (Cooke, Breen, & Schvaneveldt, 1987; Fisher, Duffy, Young, & Pollatsek, 1988; Hoffman, Nelson, & Houck, 1983).

A somewhat different approach to these same data emphasizes the acquisition of knowledge (Logan, 1988) or the development of **skill** in accomplishing various perceptual tasks (Neisser, 1976). Here the suggestion is that the effects of practice do not simply involve a switch from controlled to automatic processing, but rather that a different *strategy* is being used to accomplish the same task (Cheng, 1985). A nonperceptual example would be adding a group of identical numbers, such as $2 + 2 + 2 + 2 + 2$. This could be accomplished by adding each of the numbers to a running sum, by learning the multiplication rule and calculating 5×2, or by simply committing to memory the answer to the question, "What is 5 times 2?" In this view, extensive practice allows a new strategy to be learned or new knowledge to be used—for example, a switch from addition to memory retrieval—instead of causing a transition from controlled to automatic processing.

Vigilance and Arousal

Sometimes we are asked to search for targets that appear very rarely. Therefore, we must

---

DEMONSTRATION BOX 15-8   The Stroop Effect

The *Stroop effect* is an interesting example of how well-learned material can interfere with our ability to attend to the demands of a task. In 1935, Stroop found that observers had difficulty screening out meaningful information even when it was irrelevant to the task. He devised three situations. In the first he recorded how long it took individuals to read a list of color names, such as *red* and *green*, printed in black ink. He then took an equal number of color patches and recorded how long it took observers to name each one of the series. Then he took a color name and printed it in a color of ink that did not coincide with the linguistic information (for example, the word *blue* printed in red ink). When he had observers name the ink color in this last series, he found that they often erroneously read the printed color name rather than the ink color name; therefore, it took them much longer to read through this last series. The Stroop effect demonstrates that meaningful linguistic information is difficult to ignore, and the automatic expectations that have come to be associated with the presence of words often take over, resulting in difficulties in focusing attention.

Color Plate 8 is an example of the Stroop Color Word Test, so you can try this for yourself. Have a friend time you either with the second hand of a watch or with a stopwatch as you read each group. Start timing with the command "Go" and read across the lines in exactly the same fashion for each group. When the last response is made in each group, stop timing and note your response time. You should find that reading the color names will take the least amount of time, whereas naming the colors of the ink when the printed word names a different color will take you the most time. Naming the color patches will fall in between these two.

---

sustain a high level of readiness for an indefinite, sometimes long, period of time. Some examples include a radar technician who is watching for the signal of a particular type of aircraft that flies by only occasionally, or a quality control inspector on an assembly line where damaged or substandard items seldom appear. In these cases the observer is said to be performing a **vigilance** task. Research into vigilance began after it was noticed that radar operators during World War II tended to become fatigued after a time on duty, resulting in a decrease in their ability to detect enemy planes. After the war, experiments began in an attempt to understand how attention sustained itself, particularly in boring search tasks with infrequent stimuli.

The original experiments on vigilance required observers to watch a display similar to a clock face around which a clock hand moved in steps. They had to press a key each time the hand took a double step. After only 30 minutes of watching, observers began to report fewer and fewer double steps, missing almost 25% of them (Mackworth, 1948). Physical fatigue did not seem to be a reasonable explanation of the drop in performance since the work load was very light. Perhaps the visual system itself was becoming fatigued and thus less sensitive, or perhaps the observer was just as sensitive to the double steps but simply failed to respond on some occasions. It was important to decide whether one or the other or both of these explanations were correct.

The scene was set for the application of signal detection theory (see Chapter 2). If the visual system was becoming less sensitive, it would be reflected in a decrease in d', the measure of the observer's sensitivity. If there was some change in how willing the observer was to report the double step, it would be reflected in a change in β, the observer's criterion that indicates response bias. With this type of analysis, it was found that sensitivity, or d', did not change over time but β did. Observers were becoming less willing to admit to themselves that the rare event they searched for had actually occurred, the longer they had to maintain vigilance (Broadbent & Gregory, 1963, 1965). More recent research has indicated that extensive training can decrease or eliminate such vigilance decrements (Fisk & Schneider, 1981; Parasuraman, 1984). Apparently the setting of a criterion for responding in such tasks is a function of alertness, or the way available attention is allocated to the task at hand (Parasuraman, 1984).

Does sensitivity ever change in a vigilance task? Yes it does, for the worse, but only when the numbers of events per unit of time that must be monitored is very high and the targets are difficult to discriminate from the nontargets (Parasuraman & Mouloua, 1987). Declines in sensitivity seem to be associated with prolonged high demand on attentional resources and do indeed result from a kind of fatigue.

A major part of maintaining attention seems to be a certain degree of physiological arousal. We adopt certain body positions, tense specific muscle groups, and have the feeling of "concentrating" whenever we are vigilant. Apparently most of us believe that if we are highly aroused physiologically, we will be better able to sustain attention, since we often attempt to raise our arousal level in vigilance situations with stimulants such as the caffeine in coffee. In order to understand how arousal affects vigilance, we should look at how arousal affects performance in general.

The relation between arousal and performance is perhaps most elegantly expressed in the well-known **Yerkes-Dodson law** (Yerkes & Dodson, 1908). Figure 15-11 shows this relation graphically. Contrary to what common sense might tell us, performance does not always improve the more highly aroused we are. In fact, overall performance of any task peaks at an intermediate level of arousal. This intermediate level is lower for difficult tasks than for easy tasks, suggesting that very difficult tasks are best performed under quite low levels of arousal (Easterbrook, 1959; Hockey, 1970).

An increased level of arousal can also have a strong influence on the way attention is allocated. This has been studied by artificially inducing arousal through the administration of mild electrical shocks to the subject's fingers (Johnson & Shapiro, 1989; Shapiro & Johnson, 1987) or by playing anxiety-inducing music (Shapiro & Lim, 1989). Subjects who are moderately aroused in this way were more likely to detect brief tones than they were to detect brief flashes of light, even though these signals were equally detectable when the subjects were not aroused (Shapiro & Egerman, 1984). Moderately aroused subjects were also more likely to detect brief visual flashes in the visual

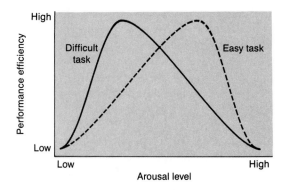

Figure 15-11 Yerkes-Dodson law. Performance is best at intermediate levels of arousal, and performance peaks at lower levels of arousal for difficult than for easy tasks.

periphery than in the center of the visual field (Johnson & Shapiro, 1989; Shapiro & Lim, 1989). These findings suggest that arousal associated with negative outcomes assists our "early-warning" mechanisms. When confronted with danger, humans are probably better off being more vigilant to sounds than to sights (alerting them to dangers they cannot even see) and to visual events in the periphery rather than those at fixation (alerting them to new dangers entering the visual field).

EXPECTING

Knowing exactly when or where an important signal will occur is often difficult. For this reason we have orienting mechanisms that draw our attention to conspicuous stimuli. We also have search strategies that allow us to investigate likely locations where important stimuli might be. However, sometimes we get an advance cue about where or when something will happen. We call such a cue an information cue. For example, imagine you are back in the airport, this time trying to monitor two doors at once, through one of which your beloved will arrive. Suddenly the loudspeaker announces that most of the passengers disembarking from that flight will arrive through Gate 21 (the left one of the two doors). Although you know this still does not *guarantee* it will be *the* door, you find yourself more often shifting your attention to the left door. You are actively *expecting* something to happen there, and it has affected your attentional state.

Costs and Benefits of Information Cues

Probably the most effective demonstration of the effects of information cues on performance was done for another reason. Posner (1980) was trying to demonstrate covert orienting by asking observers to press a key when they detected a flash of light either to the right or to the left of a fixation point. On half of the trials (the *neutral* trials), observers fixated a plus sign in the middle of the visual field and the flash occurred randomly on one side or the other. On the other trials, observers received an information cue in the form of an arrow pointing either right or left and located where the plus was located on the neutral trials. These were the *cued* trials. On 80% of the cued trials the flash occurred on the side to which the arrow pointed (*valid* trials), and on the other 20% it occurred on the opposite side (*invalid* trials). The observers were not allowed to move their eyes away from either the plus or the arrow; they could only orient their attention. Figure 15-12A shows a summary of these conditions.

Figure 15-12B shows the results of Posner's experiment. Using the neutral trials as a baseline to indicate what performance level we would expect without any information cue, you can see that it took about 30 msec less to respond to the flash on valid trials (a **benefit** of the valid information cue) but it took more than 50 msec longer to respond to the flash on invalid trials (a **cost** of the information cue being invalid). The costs and benefits of information cues have been interpreted by Posner (1980) and others as indicating that attention can be covertly oriented by an information cue, even in the absence of a stimulus on which to focus the attentional gaze.

The effects of expectation and information cues on attention depend upon a number of factors. One test situation involved a visual field that contained a set of stimulus cues in the form of several small empty boxes to which attention could be covertly oriented in response to an information cue. Under these conditions it was found that the maximum costs and benefits of information cues do not occur

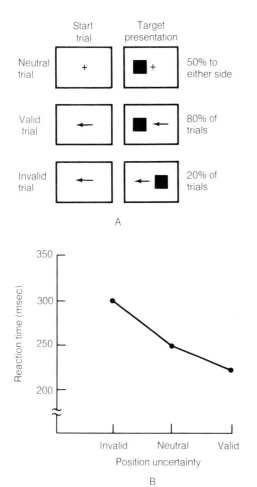

Figure 15-12 (A) *Stimulus presentations used to study the effects of expectation on detection.* (B) *Results of reaction-time study of expectation showing the costs (invalid cue reaction time minus neutral cue reaction time) and benefits (valid cue minus neutral cue) of advance knowledge of stimulus location (based on Posner, 1980).*

immediately, but take at least 300 to 500 msec after the appearance of the cue to produce their full effect (Shepard & Muller, 1989). Thus, attentional alignments in response to an information cue take much longer than does orienting in response to an abruptly appearing stimulus cue (about 50 to 100 msec). Part of

this extra time must be the time necessary to decode the meaning of the information cue and to initiate the indicated covert shift of attention voluntarily. The voluntary nature of such attention shifts is supported by the fact that information cues can be ignored easily, especially if the subject discovers that, in a particular situation, the available information cues are often wrong (Jonides, 1981). The slow, voluntary alignment of attention in response to an information cue is not automatic. Thus response to an information cue can be interrupted by the occurrence of another, attention-grabbing, stimulus (Muller & Rabbitt, 1989). However, the costs and benefits associated with information cues do affect a broad range of tasks, including detection, identification, and discrimination (Downing, 1988).

Our expectations do not only help or hinder our detection of visual stimuli. They affect audition as well. For instance, imagine you are expecting your mother to come home any minute now. You are expecting to hear her cheery "Hello" in her usual, high-pitched voice. At this moment your father shouts to you to come help him in the basement. You do not hear him calling and a minute later he storms into the room, demanding to know why you were not responding to him. You might explain that you were listening for your mother's voice and simply did not hear his much-lower-frequency voice. (If he does not believe you, you can always show him this book). Much evidence has shown that detection of sounds is more difficult; that is, there is a cost, when they are of uncertain frequency (for example, Scharf, Quigley, Aoki, Peachly, & Reeves, 1987; Swets, 1963). However, if observers are told which frequency to listen for by an information cue, their discrimination of certain aspects of the stimulus (such as its intensity) is improved (Mori & Ward, 1991). Thus expectations can help to "tune in" or "tune out" aspects of a stimulus.

The Neurophysiology of Expecting

In addition to the effects that expectancies have on behavior, such as the ability to respond more rapidly to expected stimuli than to unexpected ones, researchers have now found expectancies to be related to patterns of brain activity. One way to examine brain activity is through the measurement of **event-related potentials** (Mangun & Hillyard, 1990), a technique that allows the researcher to measure tiny changes in the brain's electrical activity by recording from the scalp of the subject (see Appendix). As shown in Figure 15-13A, recording electrodes are attached to various locations on the surface of the head with a small amount of paste. Recording is synchronized to start with the stimulus event, and many trials are averaged to produce an indication of the time course of the brain activity (as in *B*). By monitoring the size of the voltage changes at the various electrode placements, the precise location of maximum activity can be determined. In *C* the darker areas indicate stronger responses. An intriguing finding has resulted from measurements of event-related potentials related to expectation: When an individual sees a target at an expected location, a greater amount of electrical brain activity is recorded than when the same target falls on the same retinal location but is unexpected (Hillyard & Kutas, 1983; Van Voorhis & Hillyard, 1977). The differences in brain response associated with expectation are most pronounced in the posterior parietal region of the brain.

A second technique that is sensitive to brain activity that accompanies changes in attention is **positron-emission tomography,** usually called *PET scans* (Posner & Petersen, 1990; see Appendix). This method involves injecting a weakly radioactive dye into the bloodstream. Areas of the brain with active blood flow tend to collect more of the dye and thus

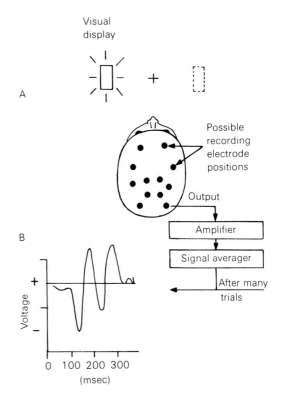

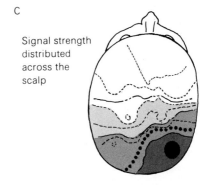

Figure 15-13 Event-related potentials measured from the scalp of a human subject. (A) A display is viewed while electrical responses of the brain are recorded from scalp electrodes. (B) Averages over many trials show the time course of the responses. (C) A comparison of responses from several locations shows the location of the most vigorous brain response (dark areas).

are more radioactive. The results can be imaged on a color computer screen, with the brain regions of high blood flow coded in a distinctive color such as red. By comparing the *hotspots* associated with different tasks, researchers are able to locate the brain regions most important for a given task (Petersen, Fox, Posner, Mintum, & Raichle, 1988). As with event-related potentials, PET studies tend to associate the posterior parietal cortex with the perception of target stimuli in expected locations (Posner & Petersen, 1990).

THEORIES OF ATTENTION

Since the first studies on attention, investigators have attempted to construct a coherent theoretical account of the major phenomena. As you have seen in this chapter, however, the concept of attention can mean several different things and it has been studied in several different ways. Therefore, the goal of a coherent and widely accepted theory is still out of reach. At present there are several different approaches to understanding attention. We will try to give you the flavor of a few of them here, but you must remember that no one of these approaches is adequate to explain all of the data described above, let alone the vast array of other data we do not have space to describe.

All of these theories attempt to explain how attention functions so that some information reaches consciousness while other information is filtered out. Probably the oldest surviving theoretical approach is the group of **structural theories.** As pointed out by Kahneman and Treisman (1984), the studies of stimulus filtering that were popular in the 1950s and 1960s seemed to imply that perceptual attention was *structurally* limited. The notion was that a bottleneck or filter is present somewhere in the information processing system beyond which

only one, or at most a few, stimulus inputs can pass at one time. The first studies suggested that this bottleneck occurs very early in the perceptual process, just after registration by the sensory system and before the meaning of an input can be determined (for example, Broadbent, 1958). This is called an **early selection** model and is depicted schematically in Figure 15-14. Suppose you are trying to listen to only one person in a room filled with talking people. According to an early selection model, you would isolate that person's voice based on the physical characteristics (such as frequency, intensity, and location) that distinguish it from the others, rather than try to isolate what the various speakers are saying. Whereas the physical qualities are registered for all of the voices, only the words associated with the particular physical characteristics admitted by this early filter (such as *low* frequency and *very* intense) are processed for content and understanding.

The early selection models had difficulty with evidence that at least some analysis is done on information coming through unattended perceptual channels. This processing may affect our responses even if we are unaware of it (Cheeseman & Merikle, 1985; Holender, 1986; Marcel, 1983). A striking example is when someone, in a conversation you are not paying direct attention to, mentions your name. In this instance you often immediately become aware of that fact and may even switch your attention to that conversation. This kind of evidence led to a set of structural theories that emphasized **late selection.** They hypothesized that *all* information entering sensory systems gets some preliminary analysis. The bottleneck is believed to occur at a stage of more or less conscious processing, when material is being entered into a longer lasting memory (for example, Deutsch & Deutsch, 1963; Norman, 1968). A schematic representation of this kind of model is shown in Figure 15-14. The debate between early and late selection

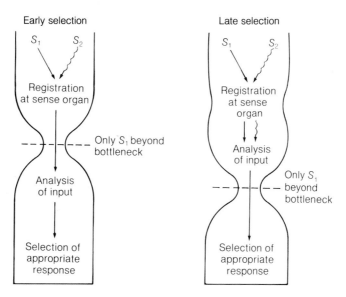

Figure 15-14 *Schematic diagrams of two types of bottleneck models of attention. Both models assume that perceptual selectivity stems from a structural limitation on our capacity to process all the incoming stimulation (stimuli are indicated by S_1 and S_2). The early selection models see the limitation as occurring at the earliest stages; only limited amounts of stimulation are allowed past for further processing. The late selection models conceptualize stimulus selection as occurring at later stages of information processing.*

still rages and has spilled over to other approaches as well (compare Pashler, 1984).

A second general approach to attention has grown mostly from studies of search and expectation (see Kahneman & Treisman, 1984), especially studies involving comparisons of focused and divided attention. The general finding that dividing attention between two tasks or searching for more than one target usually is more difficult than focusing on one task or target has led to the notion of **attentional resources** that can be "used up" by a task. If there is more demand than resources available, then performance suffers. The first theories of a limited attentional capacity viewed attention as a single "pool" of capacity (for example, Kahneman, 1973). The operation of such a model is shown in Figure 15-15A and B. All of the available capacity is used for one

task in *A*, whereas in *B*, which involves divided attention, the capacity must be shared, leaving less processing resources for each task. This would predict that both of the processing tasks in a divided attention condition would be less efficiently done, since fewer resources are available.

Recently the attentional resource models have had to be revised. There have been some demonstrations of near-perfect division of attention, for instance, when sight-reading music and shadowing at the same time. This has led some theorists to suggest that we may have multiple resources, as shown in Figure 15-15C (Navon & Gopher, 1979; Wickens, 1984). Some of these resources are probably specific to a particular modality, whereas others may be attributable to an "executive" that monitors inputs from the various modalities and that

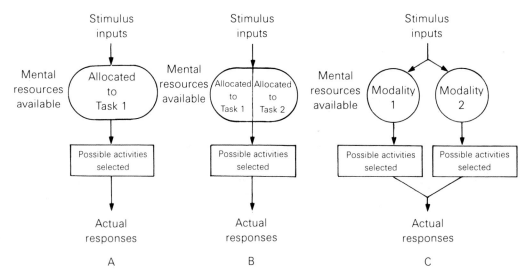

Figure 15-15 *Attentional resource models. These models suggest that attention is limited by the mental resources available. Parts A and B show a single resource model. Notice that in B, where attention must be divided between two tasks, fewer resources are available for Task 1 than in A, where attention is undivided. This would suggest decreased performance for Task 1 under divided attention. Model C shows separate resources available for different modalities or task types. Whether tasks interfere with each other thus depends on whether they require the same or different resources.*

controls access to response selection. Whether attention to one task interferes with attention to another would then depend on the characteristics of the tasks and the processing required. For example, monitoring and analyzing two prose passages read into the two ears will probably require that the same set of resources and analyzers be utilized. This is like *B*; hence these two tasks would interfere with each other. In contrast, drawing a picture or doodling while monitoring someone speaking probably involves different types of mental capacity, and one task will not compete with the other for mental resources (more like *C*). Recent research suggests that the bottleneck

and capacity models can be combined, and it may make sense to think of selectivity and capacity limitations at both early and late processing stages (Dark, Johnston, Myles-Worsley, & Farah, 1985).

Can we draw any conclusions about the role of attention in perception? Yes. Simply put, that to which we do not attend, or which does not force us to orient toward it, has no more effect on us than a subthreshold stimulus. Attention is the gateway through which only selected stimuli, a few out of endless hordes impinging on our receptors, enter into the limited realm we call consciousness.

I think that the reason it is so difficult to find a person who wants to be a politician and who is honest is that it is a conjunction search

GLOSSARY

The following definitions are specific to their use in this book.

Attentional gaze A metaphor for how attention is drawn to or directed to stimulus cues.

Attentional resources The capacity for processing stimulus inputs. These can be "used up" by a task, resulting in poorer performance in divided-attention situations.

Automatic processing A type of information processing characterized by parallel, capacity-free, and involuntary comparison of stimulus items with target representations.

Benefit When a valid information cue results in improved perceptual performance.

Binocular rivalry A phenomenon through which, if the views presented to the two eyes are different enough, we see only one or the other of them but not both.

Conjunction search A type of search for a target defined by a conjunction, or particular combination, of features each of which is also possessed by some distracters.

Controlled processing A type of information processing characterized by a serial, capacity-limited, voluntary comparison of stimulus items with target representations.

Cost When an invalid information cue results in poorer perceptual performance.

Covert orienting When attention is focused on a stimulus in the absence of an overt orienting response.

Detail set The level of detail, for example the relative size of elements, for which the attentional gaze is set.

Dichotic listening A technique in which two different messages are simultaneously played through earphones, with a different message to each ear.

Divided attention Attention directed toward more than one source of stimulus information or more than one perceptual task.

Early selection An attentional selection that occurs immediately following sensory registration, before the meaning of an input can be determined.

Event-related potentials A technique for measuring tiny changes in the brain's electrical activity using electrodes placed on the scalp of the subject.

Expecting When an observer is in possession of advance information about where or when a stimulus event will happen.

Express saccades Very rapid eye movements that happen in response to a sudden stimulus. These occur when the viewer is not attending to anything in the visual field.

Extent The area of the visual or auditory field over which the attentional gaze is spread.

Feature integration theory The theory that features are detected in parallel and preattentively, but that perceptual objects formed from a conjunction of features require attention to a locus in space.

Feature search A type of search for a target when the target differs from all distracters by possessing a feature they do not have.

Filtering Attending to a single information channel and attempting to ignore others.

Focused attention Attention directed toward only a single source of stimulus information or a single perceptual task.

Guided search A strategy for increasing the speed of a conjunction search. Some of the display items are rejected first by looking only at those with one of the target features. This leaves only a second simple feature search.

Hemifield One-half of the visual field, usually as divided vertically through the fovea.

Information channel A separable source of stimulus information, such as each of the two ears or a particular spatial location in the visual field.

Information cue Advance information about where or when a stimulus event will happen.

Inhibition of return The tendency to avoid moving one's attentional gaze back to a location of recent attention. This biases the visual system to process novel information.

Late selection A sensory system in which all information entering gets preliminary analysis; the selection occurs at the stage where material is entered into longer-lasting memory.

Locus A particular spatial location to which the attentional gaze has been drawn or directed.

Orienting When attention is drawn toward a sudden change in the environment. Often accompanied by an orienting reflex.

Orienting reflex A constellation of responses to a novel or dramatic stimulus, including the orienting response and various physiological changes such as pupil dilation or heart rate decrease.

Orienting response When an observer turns toward and orients sensory receptors toward a novel or dramatic stimulus.

Parallel search A pattern of visual search in which all the items in an array can be compared to a target representation at the same time.

Phonemic shadowing When a listener must repeat each syllable of a shadowed message as it occurs.

Phrase shadowing When a listener is allowed to lag somewhat behind a shadowed message and to repeat entire phrases at once.

Positron emission tomography A technique for detecting brain activity that accompanies changes in attention in which radioactivity from an injected substance is greatest where blood flow (indicating brain activity) is greatest.

Posterior parietal lobe Area of cortex toward the back of the brain and above the occipital lobes involved in both the orienting of attention and the formation of expectations.

Saccades High-speed ballistic eye movements that facilitate exploration of the visual field.

Searching Scanning the environment for particular features or combinations of features.

Serial search A pattern of visual search in which items in an array are compared one at a time with a target representation.

Shadowing When listeners are asked to repeat the verbal input they are receiving, usually in a particular ear; used to study filtering and divided attention.

Skill An approach to attention that emphasizes learning how to process stimuli optimally, rather than shifting between modes of processing, as an explanation for good divided-attention performance.

Stimulus cue A conspicuous stimulus somewhere in the visual or auditory field toward which attention is drawn or directed.

Stroop effect The difficulty observers have in eliminating meaningful but conflicting information from a task even when that information is irrelevant to the task.

Structural theories Theories of attention that emphasize a structural limitation on the ability to attend to multiple perceptual inputs.

Superior colliculus A bundle of neurons at the top of the brain stem in mammals, involved in the overt orienting of attention.

Temporal lobe An area of the cortex toward the bottom of the brain and in front of the occipital lobes, involved in the analysis of shape and form. Neurons in this area are sensitive to the intentions of the subject to filter out unwanted stimuli.

Vigilance Maintaining overt attention to a perceptual task, often with infrequent stimulus events, for prolonged time periods.

Visual capture When sound seems to be originating from a spatial location where visual movement is occurring, as in ventriloquism.

Yerkes-Dodson law The principle that arousal and performance are related, with the best performance occurring for a medium amount of arousal.

Chapter... 16

DEVELOPMENT

Perception in Infants
Development of the Visual System
Psychophysical Methods for Testing Infants
Eye Movements and Visual Attention
Visual Acuity
Brightness and Color
Pattern Discrimination
Object Perception
Infant Hearing
Touch, Pain, Taste, and Smell
Perceptual Change through Childhood
Eye Movements and Attention
Orienting and Filtering
Encoding and Memory
Perceptual Change in Adults
Visual Function and Aging
Age Effects on the Other Senses
Global Changes in Perceptual Performance

*T*he camp counselor turned to the newest arrival and asked, "And how old are you, son?"

"Well," said the boy, "it all depends. According to my latest set of anatomical tests I'm 7. According to my physical dexterity test I'm 10. I've got a mental age of 11, a moral age of 9, and a social age of 10. If you are referring to my chronological age though, that's 8, but nobody pays any attention to that these days."

Although you might not relish the thought of spending a summer with this child, his comments point out significant changes in many of our physical and psychological characteristics as we age. Each of these changes has its own time course. Some changes simply represent physiological transformations occurring as the body matures (such as a person's anatomical age). Others represent patterns of behavior that are learned as the individual grows older (such as social or moral age). Still others may represent a combination of both learning and maturation (such as mental age). Although no one refers to a perceptual age, changes in perceptual characteristics also occur as an individual develops and matures. These changes are usually improvements, producing perceptual experiences that more accurately represent the physical environment. However, some perceptual capacities deteriorate with age.

In considering how an individual's perceptual functioning changes, we can adopt two different perspectives. The first is long-term, viewing people over their entire life span. This is the **developmental approach,** which assumes that knowledge of a person's chronological age will allow us to predict many aspects of perceptual behavior. The other approach is short-term, viewing the changes that occur in perceptual responses as a result of a circumscribed set of experiences. This is the **perceptual learning approach.** It is based on the presumption that our interactions with the world can shape our percepts.

These two approaches are not mutually exclusive; understanding the nature of perception often requires us to use both. Common to both viewpoints is the conclusion that, despite the fact that we may not be aware of it, our perceptual behavior is continually changing. Your experience of the world differs from individuals who are 10 years older or 10 years younger than you. Because the developmental and perceptual learning approaches use different techniques and often address somewhat different theoretical issues, we deal with these areas in separate chapters. Here we begin with the developmental approach, and we proceed to the effects of learning and experience in Chapter 17.

PERCEPTION IN INFANTS

Before speaking about how perception changes as we age and develop, we must first know what perceptual capacities we had at the moment of birth. Unfortunately, newborn infants **(neonates)** are difficult to test. They sleep most of the time, and they do not respond to instructions or answer our questions in any direct verbal fashion. They also produce only a limited range of observable behaviors. These problems require experimenters to be quite creative in devising measures of the perceptual abilities of the very young. However, the use of these different techniques sometimes results in findings that do not agree with one another (Teghtsoonian, 1987; Trehub & Schneider, 1987). In an attempt to resolve these inconsistencies, researchers are sometimes forced to use animal subjects rather than humans, especially if direct physiological measures of functioning are desired.

Development of the Visual System

Let us begin by looking at the physiology of the infant's visual system. In comparison to the rest of the body, the size of the eye changes very little after birth. The body may increase in size about 20 times, but the eye merely doubles in volume, with the length from the cornea to the retina growing from about 16 mm to about 24 mm (Hickey & Peduzzi, 1987). The infant's retina contains rods and cones, as does the adult's. Electrical measures indicate that these receptors are functioning from birth, although the responses do not exactly match those of older children or adults (Aantaa, 1970; Maurer, 1975). Anatomically, however, the retina still seems immature (Banks & Salapatek, 1983; Johnson, 1990). For instance, the region of the central fovea is not well defined in a 1-week-old infant—the cones in this region are stubby in appearance and much more sparsely packed than they will be eventually (Abramov et al., 1982). Visual functioning of the retinal receptors is somewhat more developed at birth in the periphery of the eye than in the central re-

gion (Banks & Salapatek, 1983). By 11 to 12 months, however, the receptors in all regions of the retina have an adultlike appearance (Russoff, 1979). The optic nerve fibers that carry information from the retina to the brain become myelinated quite rapidly during the first 4 months of life, reaching adult levels by about 2 years of age (see Appendix for a discussion of myelinization).

Our knowledge of the status of the visual pathways in newborns and infants comes mostly from animal studies, with the cat providing most of the data. If we measure the physiological functions of the various sites in the visual pathways of the cat at the time when the animal first opens its eyes, we get the results shown in Table 16-1 (see Hickey & Peduzzi, 1987; Imbert, 1985; Norton, 1981a). The table shows that a number of adultlike and immature response patterns coexist in the newborn cat. Thus, in the retinal ganglion cell, we

Table 16-1   The Functional Condition of Various Sites in the Visual Pathways of the Newborn Cat

ADULTLIKE RESPONSES	IMMATURE RESPONSES
Retinal Ganglion Cells	
Center-surround organization of receptive fields Adult percentage of on/off center	Low activity level Overly large receptive fields Slow responses to light and weak inhibition Parvo vs. magno responses not clear
Lateral Geniculate Nucleus	
Normal visual-field mapping Binocular separation of inputs	Low activity and silent areas Large receptive field diameter Slow, sluggish, fatigable responding
Superior Colliculus	
Normal visual-field mapping Center-surround receptive fields Adult percentage of on/off center	Slow, sluggish fatigable responses Large receptive fields No movement direction sensitivity
Striate Cortex	
Normal visual-field mapping Adult separation of responses by eye of input	Sluggish, fatigable responses Many silent cells Fewer or absent orientation and direction-selective cells with broader tuning No binocular disparity cells

find the expected center-surround arrangement of excitatory and inhibitory responses; however, the receptive fields differ in size from those of the adult and there is a general sluggishness in the response (for example, Russoff & Dubin, 1977).

In Chapter 3 we discussed two different visual pathways, one originating from the small ganglion cells in the retina, called the *parvocellular* pathway, and the other originating from the larger ganglion cells, called the *magnocellular* pathway. These pathways appear to process different types of information in parallel, with the parvocellular pathway associated principally with color and detailed form vision and the magnocellular pathway specialized for movement and depth perception. These two systems are also characterized by response pattern differences—parvo cells give a sustained response, magno cells a transient response. In the cat and monkey, however, at the retinal level, these two response types are not well-defined at birth (Hamasaki & Sutija, 1979; Mooney, Dubin, & Russoff, 1979; Shiller, 1986).

Farther along in the visual pathways, at the lateral geniculate nucleus, we do find the adult division of two magnocellular layers and four parvocellular layers in the neonate. Here we also can observe the separation of the inputs from the two eyes into clearly defined layers that are interleaved. However, many of the cells in the geniculate do not seem to respond to any sort of visual input, and the responses that can be measured are often slow and easily fatigued (Daniels, Pettigrew, & Norman, 1978). The parvo cells in the lateral geniculate reach their adult size first, by about 12 months of age, whereas the magno cells are much slower to develop, only reaching full size by 2 years of age (Hickey, 1977). A somewhat similar pattern emerges for the superior colliculus, with the general organization of cell layers and the center-surround organization of receptive fields resembling those of an adult by 3 to 6 months. However, at birth the receptive field size of these cells is much larger than that of adults, and the responses are relatively slow, weak, and insensitive to direction (Norton, 1981a).

Finally, at the level of the primary visual cortex (V1), we find that the inputs from the two eyes separate into the expected columnar arrangement discussed in Chapter 3, and that directional and orientation-sensitive cells (both simple and complex) are sometimes present. In infant monkeys, single-cell recordings show that some cells are orientation-selective (Weisel & Hubel, 1974), although they are fewer in number and their responses are slow and easily fatigued (Imbert, 1985). In human newborns, using behavioral measures, orientation-selective responses have not been observed until 5 to 6 months (Braddick, Wattam-Bell, & Atkinson, 1986). In addition, binocular-disparity–sensitive cells seem to be almost absent until several weeks of age in both monkeys and humans (Braddick et al., 1980; Held, 1985). Overall, many of the characteristics of the adult system seem to be present in the newborn visual system, but the full adult response pattern is not present (Banks & Salapatek, 1983). Of course, many of these statements are species specific, and humans appear to develop somewhat more slowly than cats and monkeys do. Thus, whereas those animals show separation of the inputs from the two eyes into separate ocular dominance columns from birth, humans may take 4 to 6 months to develop similar complex neural structures (Hickey & Peduzzi, 1987).

It should be clear from this discussion that the various characteristics of the visual system mature at different rates. The parvocellular pathway to the cortex matures in some respects more quickly than the magnocellular pathway (Maurer & Lewis, 1979). The cells in V1 that are associated with more peripheral retina (for both of these pathways) mature more quickly than the cells in V1 that are more related to central or foveal vision. Within the primary visual cortex, the layers of cortex that receive inputs directly from the eye reach their mature size and complete the myelinization process before the layers that process information to or from other brain centers (Rabinowicz, 1979). Also, even when neonatal cells are relatively mature in appearance, their responses are slower and less vigorous than those of the adult. Taken together, these observations suggest that the quality of information reaching the higher visual centers of the newborn's brain may be relatively poor and that different perceptual functions will emerge at different times during development.

In humans, we can determine how well the visual cortex of the infant is functioning by measuring what is called the **visually evoked potential** (often abbreviated **VEP**). This is a change in the electrical activity of the brain in response to a visual stimulus. The VEP has been shown to be related to some aspects of visual detection and pattern identification (Cannon, 1983). The VEP is usually recorded by pasting or taping electrodes (generally flat pieces of silver) to the scalp and connecting them to very sensitive amplifiers (See Appendix).

Almost all newborn infants (even most premature infants) show some VEP, although it differs somewhat from the adult response in its pattern, size, and speed (Atkinson, 1984; Ellingson, 1968; Umezaki & Morrell, 1970). For instance, VEP measures from subcortical regions of the brain are always present at birth, but only some of the measures from cortical regions can be seen (Vaughan & Kurtzberg, 1989). Over a period of about 3 to 6 months, the infant's electrical responses to visual stimuli come to look more and more like those of adults (Banks & Salapatek, 1983; Braddick, Wattam-Bell, & Atkinson, 1986; Harter & Suitt, 1970). It is generally agreed that during the first year of life the visual system matures rapidly, and that, although the system shows many adult capabilities by the end of the sec-

ond year (Ellingson, Lathrop, Nelson, & Donahy, 1972; Movshon & van Sluyters, 1981), some brain centers continue to develop until the child is 10 to 12 years of age or older (Huttenlocher, de Courten, Garey, & Van der Loos, 1982; Imbert, 1985).

Psychophysical Methods for Testing Infants

Methods of testing infant's visual capacities must be very carefully devised, since we cannot use verbal instructions or obtain verbal responses from them. The researcher's only recourse is to use existing behaviors, which, for perceptual research, usually involve some form of attentional orientation. These include eye movements, head turns, visual following behavior, and other subtle indicators (Banks & Dannemiller, 1987). Given the limited response repertoire available to a young baby, we can appreciate the methodological breakthrough accomplished by Fantz (1961). His procedure, called **preferential looking,** involves first placing a baby in a special chamber (either on its back or in an infant chair). Visual stimuli are then placed on the walls or the roof of the chamber. Through a tiny hole, the experimenter can watch the baby looking at the stimuli. An apparatus similar to Fantz's is shown in Figure 16-1. When the baby views one of a pair of stimulus patterns placed in the chamber, the experimenter determines which one is being looked at by simply noting the side to which the baby's eyes turn. A timer is used to record how long the infant views each of the two stimuli. If the baby looks at one target longer than the other, this is taken to indicate a preference for that target. The existence of a preference for a pattern implies that the infant can discriminate between the patterns. Unfortunately, this result alone does not tell us *why* the baby preferred to look at one stimulus rather than the other, nor can we be sure that the absence

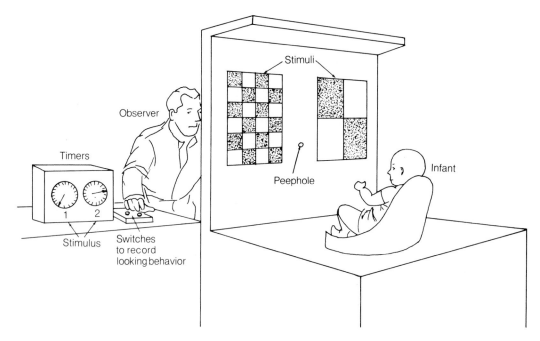

Figure 16-1 *An apparatus for monitoring how long infants view particular stimuli.*

of a viewing preference means that the baby cannot discriminate between the two stimuli.

Many elaborations of this technique have been developed, such as one by Teller (1981) called the **forced-choice preferential looking** technique. Her procedure allows the study of stimulus detection as well as discrimination between stimuli. Here, the infant is presented with only a single stimulus, while its response is monitored by a hidden observer or television camera. If, on the basis of the infant's head and eye movements alone, an observer can reliably determine whether the test target was presented to the left or to the right side of the screen, it is presumed that the information concerning the position of the target has been transmitted from the screen, through the infant's visual system and behavior, to the observer. At the minimum, this suggests that the infant can see the stimulus.

A further variation of this method allows researchers to determine whether an infant can notice any difference between stimuli. Again, only one stimulus is presented and the viewing behavior is monitored. At first the infant will spend a good deal of time looking at the stimulus, but as time passes it will begin to look at it less and less. Researchers often informally say that the infant is becoming "bored" with the stimulus. The technical name for this process is **habituation.** If a different stimulus is now presented, often the baby will again look at it. The presence of this renewed interest in the stimulus suggests that the infant has recognized that something has changed, and that the present stimulus is different from the former one (for example, Kellman & Spelke, 1983; McCall, 1979).

Eye Movements and Visual Attention

In Chapter 10 we saw that certain aspects of spatial vision, such as the binocular perception of depth or distance, are not present at birth but develop as the baby grows (for example, Held, 1985; Yonas & Granrud, 1985a). The perception of direction, however, is much better at birth. Newborn infants can move their eyes so as to bring visual targets onto or close to their foveas. Thus, if we present a young infant (about 2 weeks of age) with a target that suddenly appears 20 deg from the fovea, it will slowly turn its eyes toward that target (Aslin, 1987; Harris & MacFarlane, 1974). Furthermore, 3-month-old infants seem to be able to identify targets in the periphery of their visual field well enough to guide their eyes to selected or preferred stimuli (Maurer & Lewis, 1991).

Although infants will look at a target that suddenly appears or moves, infants' eye movements are not exactly like those of adults. Each of the two main types of voluntary eye movements takes some time to develop fully. The first type, called **saccadic eye movements,** are fast, ballistic movements that occur when you direct your attention toward a target. In adults,

a saccade will start the eye moving toward a target some distance from the current fixation point within 200 to 250 msec. The time taken by the movement itself can be as short as 4 to 10 msec (for example, Komoda, Festinger, Phillips, Duckman, & Young, 1973; Kowler & Martin, 1980; Rayner, 1978). Saccades are also accurate in positioning the eye so the new target is centered on the fovea. A typical long saccade would bring the eye to the desired position with an error of only 5% to 10% of the distance moved. A representative adult eye movement to a target 30 deg from the current fixation point is shown in Figure 16-2. Infants are much slower to begin the saccade and tend to make a series of small saccades, often not reaching the target for well over a second (Aslin, 1987; Regal, Ashmead, & Salapatek, 1983). However, even the immature saccadic eye movements of infants can reveal something of their perceptual capacities. For example, expectation (see Chapter 15) can be studied in

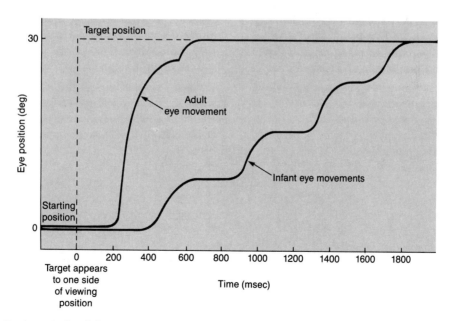

Figure 16-2 A typical adult eye movement to a target appearing 30 deg to one side of fixation will involve a single, fast, large saccade and a small, corrective flick, whereas an infant will have a longer delay before moving, and the movement will involve a series of shorter saccades.

infants by showing them a light that either consistently alternates between two locations (so its "next" location can be anticipated) or simply appears randomly at various locations. Newborn infants' eye movements are similar in both conditions, indicating that they probably are not able to anticipate where the light will be next even when it alternates consistently. However, by 3 to 4 months of age infants move their eyes toward the "next" location when the light alternates consistently, indicating that they are expecting it to appear there (Haith, Hazan, & Goodman, 1988).

The other type of eye movement is the **smooth-pursuit eye movement.** Here the eyes track a steadily moving object, such as a ball flying through the air or a person on a swing, with a uniform and even motion. Smooth-pursuit eye movements do not appear in newborns—they use short, jumpy, saccadic eye movements to track even smoothly moving objects. Thus, instead of keeping pace with a moving target, an infant grabs a glimpse of it, waits till it drifts from view, and then attempts to look at it again. As with saccades, newborns are unable to anticipate the path of an object that moves smoothly back and forth. Instead they seem always to be "catching up" with small stepwise movements that are the same size regardless of the speed of the object. This pattern does not simply reflect an immature motor system since infants can be shown to make much larger saccades under other circumstances (Aslin, 1981a). The adult pattern of smooth anticipatory movements begins to emerge at 8 to 10 weeks of age.

The fact that infants move their eyes in response to moving or suddenly appearing stimuli can be used to measure other capacities in the newborn. For instance, if we show an adult observer a continuously moving pattern (such as a screen full of stripes all moving in one direction), we get a characteristic eye-movement pattern. The eye will smoothly track in the direction of the movement for some distance and

then will flick back in the opposite direction. After this return movement, the observer's eyes fixate another stripe and follow it, and this process repeats itself while the observer views the array. This repetitive eye movement sequence in the presence of a moving pattern is called **optokinetic nystagmus.** A similar (but not as smooth) pattern of eye movements is found in infants younger than 5 days (Kremenitzer, Vaughan, Kurtzberg, & Dowling, 1979). In fact its appearance is so reliable that the absence of optokinetic nystagmus is used as an indication of possible neurological problems (Brazelton, Scholl, & Robey, 1966). This eye-movement pattern seems to be automatic or reflexive in nature, rather than voluntary, and is probably controlled by the tectopulvinar system described in Chapter 3 (Atkinson & Braddick, 1981; K. P. Hoffmann, 1979). If an infant cannot see a pattern of moving stripes (because they are not large enough or lack sufficient contrast), optokinetic nystagmus will be absent. This technique has been used to study brightness discrimination, visual acuity, and motion perception in infants (Banks & Salapatek, 1983).

Although newborns will move their eyes to suddenly appearing stimuli, they show a much more consistent response to stimuli in the **temporal visual field** (the half of the visual field toward the temple) than to those in the **nasal visual field** (the half of the visual field toward the nose) (M. H. Johnson, 1990; Lewis, Maurer, & Mileski, 1979). By 2 months of age, this asymmetry has diminished greatly, although it can still be observed to some extent in adults (Posner, 1980). Interestingly, eye movements toward stimuli in the temporal visual field can be elicited by the superior colliculus, a part of the tectopulvinar system, without any contribution from the visual cortex. However, movements toward the nasal field require activation of the visual cortex in addition to the superior colliculus (M. H. Johnson, 1990). This suggests that this movement asymmetry is due to an immaturity in the control over eye movements exerted by the visual cortex (Maurer & Lewis, 1991).

The eye movements of young infants are also easily disrupted by the appearance of more than one stimulus in the visual field. "Competing" stimuli increase the time required to complete an eye movement and decrease the accuracy with which a saccade will cause a target to be fixated (Atkinson, Hood, Braddick, & Wattam-Bell, 1988). When infants up to 3 months of age are faced with the choice between looking again at a previously fixated stimulus or a new one that is presented simultaneously, they tend to look again at the original stimulus (Hood & Atkinson, 1991; Rothbart, Posner, & Boylan, 1990). However, 6-month-olds will choose to fixate the novel stimulus instead. This is similar to the *inhibition of return* phenomenon seen in adults (see Chapter 15) in that it biases the infant observer to take in new information.

Visual Acuity

The visual acuity of infants is rather poor, but improves steadily with age. This fact has been established in several ways. For instance, the optokinetic response that we described earlier can be used to test the visual acuity of infants. This is done by finding the narrowest width of stripes that will still produce the tracking response. Other methods, such preferential looking procedures, can be used to measure infant visual acuity. Although the level of acuity found for infants varies with the technique (Teller & Movshon, 1986), and with the specific acuity stimulus used (Shimoho & Held, 1987), there is a general agreement that visual acuity is around 20/800 (6/240 in metric units) at birth. This is less acuity than is needed to see the single big E on a standard Snellen acuity chart (which is a Snellen acuity of 20/200).

Newborns also act as if they have limited ability to change focus through lens accommodation. They act as if their lenses are fixed in focus to see something about 20 cm away (White, 1971). This is about the distance of the mother's face for a nursing baby. A rapid increase in visual acuity occurs during the first 3 months of age (e.g. Courage & Adams, 1990), and as shown in Figure 16-3, the child's acuity increases steadily with age up to 3 years (see Gwiazda & Bauer, 1989). Some tests show, however, that the improvement continues for

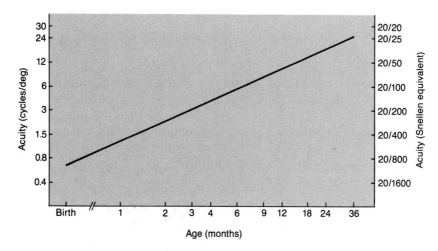

Figure 16-3   *Steady improvement in visual acuity from birth to 3 years of age.*

DEMONSTRATION BOX 16-1   Infant Accommodation

To demonstrate that an infant's accommodation is limited to close objects, you will, of course, need an infant, preferably 2 months of age or younger. If you can find one, catch its attention and then slowly move a pencil from side to side near the infant's face. Use a distance of about 20 cm, or around 8 in. Watch the child's head and eyes and notice that the infant will track, or at least try to track, the pencil. Now repeat this, only vary the distance to 1 or 2 m away from the child. At this distance you should have exceeded the ability of the infant to accommodate and you should notice that little, if any, tracking occurs.

---

quite a while, and the child may not finally reach average adult levels until more than 7 years of age (Scharre, Cotter, Block, & Kelly, 1990). If you have access to a young infant, you can see the effect of this limited accommodation by trying Demonstration Box 16-1.

Brightness and Color

A variety of techniques has been used to assess the basic sensitivity of infants to brightness and color. One-month-old infants are about 1/50th as sensitive to light as adults are, while three-month-old infants are 1/10th as sensitive to light, both under dark-adapted (scotopic) and light-adapted (photopic) conditions (Peeples & Teller, 1978; Powers, Schneck, & Teller, 1981). However, despite these differences infants are still very sensitive to light. For example, in Chapter 4, we found that an adult can detect as few as 6 quanta of light hitting anywhere in a patch of 1300 rod receptors. In comparison, a 3-month-old infant would need to receive about 60 quanta of light over the same region, and a 1-month-old infant would require about 300 quanta of light (Teller & Bornstein, 1987). Although this amount is substantially greater than that required by adults, it is still a very small amount of light.

Several studies show that despite differences in absolute sensitivity, the relative sensitivity of infants and adults to different wavelengths of light is about the same. Both are most sensitive to middle wavelengths and exhibit a gradual decrease in sensitivity to longer and shorter wavelengths (Dobson, 1976; Moskowitz-Cook, 1979; Werner, 1979). This does not mean, however, that infants have color vision equivalent to that of adults. In general, young infants do show some ability to discriminate between colors (Bornstein, 1985; Werner & Wooten, 1979). Infants have good color discrimination between the long and middle wavelengths of light (red and green), and, at least for large stimuli, this may be present as early as the first week of life (J. Adams, 1989). However, for the 1-month-old infant the short-wavelength (blue) discriminating mechanism seems still to be immature (Teller & Bornstein, 1987). Most 1-month-old infants have poor discrimination among the various short-wavelength stimuli. In fact their discrimination appears much like tritanopic color-blind individuals (see Chapter 5). By the age of 2 months, however, most infants can make such short-wavelength discriminations (Varner, Cook, Schneck, McDonald, & Teller, 1985).

Pattern Discrimination

The preferential looking technique has been used extensively to explore pattern perception in infants. This procedure has been used to show that even premature infants, born 1 to 2 months prior to a full-term gestation, often preferentially look at patterned stimuli rather than plain ones of equal average brightness and also sometimes discriminate between different patterns (Fantz & Miranda, 1977). This means that the optical and neural bases of pattern vision do not abruptly become functional at the end of the full term of pregnancy, which is the age at which babies can first be ordinarily observed. Rather, these mechanisms have already matured to a reasonable degree of function prior to the normal birth time.

Preferential looking studies have also shown that young infants can discriminate among a variety of different types of patterns. For instance, in one experiment newborn infants were shown pairs of targets. These neonates showed a clear preference for viewing patterns of stripes over a simple square and also preferred patterns with high contrast between the figures and the background. They showed a preference for larger patterns, indicating they could discriminate size, and also preferred patterns containing many rather

than few elements. In addition, they showed some ability to discriminate certain aspects defining contours, such as curvature, by preferring curved to straight-line elements. Figure 16-4 shows some representative forms. In the figure, the star indicates those most preferred by newborns for each pair (Fantz & Yeh, 1979).

Generally, infants prefer moderately complex stimuli over those that are very simple or very complex, although preferences do change with age (Karmel & Maisel, 1975). Younger infants prefer simple patterns with highly contrasting elements, whereas 5-month-olds can make more subtle distinctions in contrast and configuration (Fantz & Yeh, 1979). Banks and Salapatek (1983) suggested that pattern perception in infants reflects the developing ability to discriminate various spatial frequencies (see Chapter 4).

Preferences in viewing also show that some higher-level aspects of pattern perception are possible for the young infant. Infants can discriminate the orientation of patterns within the first few weeks (Maurer & Martello, 1980) and perhaps even on the first day of life (Kessen, Salapatek, & Haith, 1972). Furthermore, they

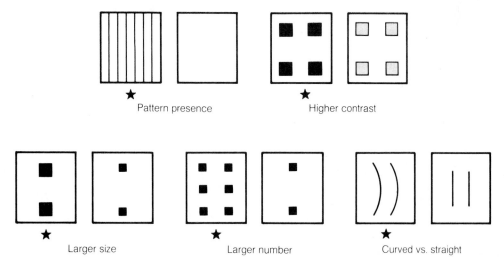

Figure 16-4 *Patterns most looked at by newborns are indicated with a star for each pair of stimuli (based on Fantz & Yeh, 1979).*

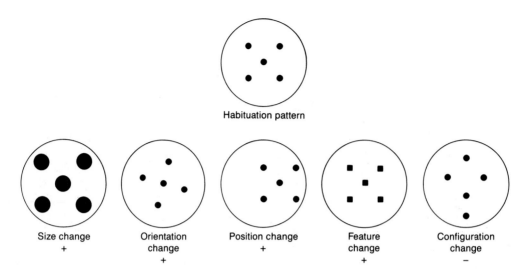

Figure 16-5 *When 4-month-old infants habituate to the top pattern, they act as if they recognize changes in the pattern indicated by a plus (+) sign, but do not recognize the change indicated by the minus (−) sign.*

seem to be aware of certain forms of symmetry, or its absence (Bornstein, 1981). Although infants respond to both the size and position of stimuli, at age 4 months they are relatively insensitive to changes in the configuration of stimuli (Humphrey, Humphrey, Muir, & Dodwell, 1986). Furthermore, 3-to-4-month-old infants seem to pay attention to specific features (such as whether the dots making up a pattern are square rather than round) instead of to the global configuration (such as the pattern the dots make). By 6 or 7 months they are responding to these global aspects of the pattern as well (Dineen & Meyer, 1980). Figure 16-5 summarizes the sensitivity of the 4-month-old infant to various aspects of visual patterns. It shows a pattern to which the infant is habituated and then some test patterns. The patterns accompanied by a plus sign exemplify changes that the infant would be expected to notice; the one with a minus sign shows a change that would not be noticed (Dodwell, Humphrey, & Muir, 1987).

Object Perception

Certain meaningful patterns receive special attention, even from neonates. A number of researchers have studied the response of infants to patterns that resemble the human face (Nelson & Ludemann, 1989). One common procedure is to use some stimuli that are only head-shaped, others containing only some facial features (such as a hairline or eyes), some containing scrambled facial features, and others that actually look like faces. Samples of such stimuli are shown in Figure 16-6. In general, it is found that by 2 months of age infants prefer to look at stimuli that contain facial features arranged in the normal configuration rather than scrambled, whereas children younger than 1 month of age do not make this discrimination (Carey, 1981; Haaf, 1977; Maurer & Barrera, 1981). Between 1 and 4 months of age infants begin to take note of certain features in the facelike stimulus. By about 10 or 12 weeks of age, infants notice and recognize

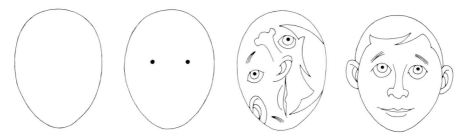

Figure 16-6 *Schematic and scrambled facelike stimuli.*

changes in hairline and eyes, although changes in mouth and nose configurations go unnoticed (Caron, Caron, Caldwell, & Weiss, 1973). However, the configurational and specific features picked up by infants only 1 month of age do seem to be sufficient to permit the infant to discriminate its own mother's face from that of a stranger (Maurer & Salapatek, 1976), which suggests that young infants can discriminate among certain classes of fairly complex patterns.

One group of researchers has looked at the ability of infants to integrate fragments of an object that are physically separated from each other in the visual image, as for instance, when a nearer object blocks part of a farther object from view. In one study 4-month-olds were repeatedly shown a rod that moved back and forth but was partially occluded by a brick that lay in front of it. After the infants had habituated to this display, they were either shown a connected rod moving back and forth or two short rods that moved back and forth in synchrony. These displays are shown in Figure 16-7. The infants looked longer at the broken-rod display, indicating that they perceived this display as different from the occluded rod display (Kellman & Spelke, 1983). This suggests that the infant was perceptually completing the object when it was partially occluded from sight. This result has been shown under a number of conditions (Kellman & Short, 1987; Kellman, Spelke, & Short, 1986) and apparently

also includes correction of certain shape distortions that occur when a moving object passes behind a nearer object (Craton & Yonas, 1990).

Figure 16-8 summarizes how the child's visual competence develops over the first few months of life.

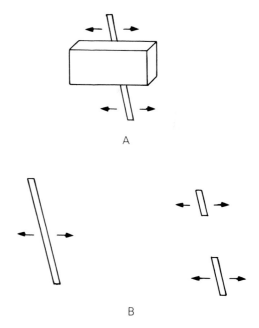

Figure 16-7 *Stimuli to test whether objects are perceptually completed when they are partially obscured by other objects: (A) the original habituation stimulus; (B) two possible test stimuli (based on Kellman & Spelke, 1983).*

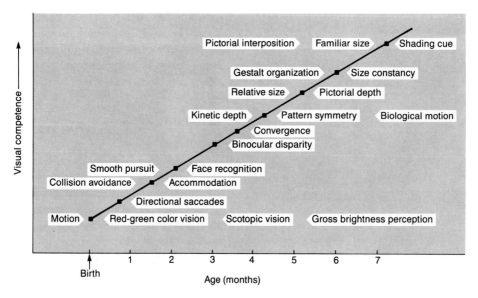

Figure 16-8 *Various visual abilities, and sensitivity to various environmental or stimulus dimensions, appear at different ages.*

Infant Hearing

The ears of infants are functional at birth, but the auditory cortex is still rather immature and continues to develop over the first year (Kuhl, 1987). Several studies have suggested that infants less than 6 months of age have higher absolute thresholds than adults (Berg & Smith, 1983; Trehub, Schneider, & Endman, 1980). An interesting feature of these data is that the differences are most noticeable in the frequency range below 10,000 Hz. The ability of adults to detect tones in this range is nearly twice as good as that of infants (Olsho, 1984). At the higher frequencies, however, infants show more adultlike sensitivity (Kuhl, 1987).

Newborns are able to indicate their ability to localize the direction of a sound source by turning either their head or eyes toward the sound (Butterworth, 1981; Muir & Field, 1979). Longer stimulus durations and frequent stimulus repetitions increase the likelihood of head movement in the direction of the sound (Clark-son, Swain, Clifton, & Cohen, 1991). Probably the youngest child tested for this ability was studied by Wertheimer (1961). A mere 3 minutes after birth, with the infant lying on his or her back, a loud click was sounded next to the right ear or left ear. Two observers noted whether the eyes moved to the infant's right or left, or not at all. On 18 out of the 22 occasions when the child's eyes moved, they moved in the direction of the click. When the experiment was completed the child was still only 10 minutes old. Hence these data allow us to conclude that some directional aspects of auditory stimuli are accurately processed and may influence behavior from birth.

Recall from Chapter 7 that several binaural cues help to indicate the direction of a sound relative to the listener. The two most important of these are the time differences in the arrival of low-frequency sounds to the two ears (earlier to the closer ear) and the intensity differences between the two ears caused by the lack of bending of higher frequencies of sound around the head (more intense to the closer ear—see D. M. Green, 1976; Moore, 1977). Which of these cues is most effective for the infant? By directly controlling both the time differences between the ears and the intensity of sound reaching the two ears, Clifton, Morrongiello, and Dowd (1984) demonstrated that newborn infants, and those up to about 9 weeks of age, respond to intensity differences between the two ears by turning in the direction of the sound. At these younger ages, the more complex time discrimination cue is not adequate to induce the child to turn its head in the appropriate direction. However, by age 5 months both cues are effective and cause the child to look in the direction of the sound source (Muir, Clifton, & Clarkson, 1989). If you have access to an infant, Demonstration Box 16-2 will show you how to demonstrate auditory localization.

One of the more interesting biases that newborns exhibit is a preference to orient their head and eyes toward the location of a relatively high-pitched speaking voice. This bias seems to coincide very conveniently with the tendency on the part of adults to speak in high-pitched and exaggerated voices to young infants. This kind of "baby talk" was once called *motherese*, but is now referred to as **infant directed talk** because it can be heard when both men and women speak to infants and young children (Werker & McLeod, 1989). Infants of 4 to 6 months respond to such talk by increased smiling and vocalization (Fernald, 1985; Tre-

hub & Trainor, 1990; Wolff, 1987) and by engaging in a "conversational" exchange of vowel-like sounds (a sort of cooing) with the adult talker (Bloom, 1990).

There is now also growing evidence that infants perceptually group sounds in systematic ways, similar to the ways they (and adults) perceptually group visual patterns (Trehub & Trainor, 1990). In one study, infants of 6 to 9 months of age listened to sequences of tones separated by equal time intervals, in which the first three tones were the same high frequency and the last three tones were the same lower frequency (Thorpe & Trehub, 1989). Such sequences can be represented as *HHHLLL*, where *H* is the high tone and *L* the low. Following habituation to this tone sequence the infants listened to a modified tone sequence. In one such sequence there was a longer silent interval (indicated by ') at the boundary between the two frequencies (*HHH'LLL*), which is the place where adults will tend to perceptually separate the series into two groups. Alternatively, the silent interval could be placed in another place (for example, *HHHL'LL*). The infants payed more attention to the latter sequence, showing that they had grouped the tones in the original sequence on the basis of their frequency much the way that adults do. Other studies have shown that this kind of **auditory grouping,** or perceptual organization of sounds on the basis of their temporal and frequency relationships, also occurs for infants' perceptions of classical music (Krumhansl & Jusczyk, 1990) and their

---

DEMONSTRATION BOX 16-2   Auditory Localization in Infants

If you have access to an infant, auditory localization is easily demonstrated. Simply look squarely at the child and then make a sharp sound near one ear. Good sound sources are a rattle, a snap of the fingers, or a toy "clicker." Watch the infant's head and eyes. You should see the eyes flick in the direction of the sound, or you may see the head turn in the direction of the stimulus.

perceptions of infant directed talk (Kemler-Nelson, Hirsh-Pasek, Juscyk, & Wright-Cassidy, 1989).

Touch, Pain, Taste, and Smell

Touch and heat sensitivity appear to be among the first sensory modalities to emerge during the course of fetal development (Hall & Oppenheim, 1987). This can be demonstrated through the reflexes of the infant, which show the ability to feel and to localize touch stimuli immediately after birth. One example is the **rooting response,** in which a child will reflexively turn its head in the direction of a touch to its cheek. This response helps the child to locate the mother's breast for nursing. Demonstration Box 16-3 shows you how to elicit this directional response.

There has been a widespread belief among many clinicians and other investigators that because the cortex is not fully developed in the neonate, infants do not experience pain as severely as adults, and its impact does not persist as long (for example, Eland & Anderson, 1977). This has led to the practice of giving little treatment for pain to babies, even during or after major medical procedures and operations (Liebeskind & Melzack, 1987; Owens, 1984). However, recent evidence (for example, Grunau & Craig, 1987) suggests that this belief is wrong. Infants appear to be just as susceptible to the perception of pain as adults are.

Taste receptors start to form early in fetal life and are apparent as early as 13 weeks after conception (Bradley & Stern, 1967). Neonates appear to be as well equipped with taste receptors as adults. However, they respond to the taste primaries differently (Crook, 1987). Using sucking responses as an indicator, Lipsett (1977) found a preference for sweet stimuli in newborns. Even small differences in the concentration of sweetness produce differences in neonatal reactions. However, infants less than about 4 months of age seem to be insensitive to the taste of salt (Beauchamp & Cowert, 1985). And only strong concentrations of sour and bitter stimuli elicit facial expressions of disgust in young infants (Ganchrow, Steiner, & Daher, 1983).

Much work on infant olfactory ability has involved presenting newborns with cotton swabs saturated with various smell stimuli. A swab is placed under the infant's nose, and responses such as heart rate, respiration, and general bodily activity are monitored using a polygraph (Engen, Lipsitt, & Kaye, 1963). These studies have shown that infants can detect a number of strong odorants, such as anise oil, asafoetida (rotten smell), alcohol, and vinegar. Moreover, even newborn infants turn away from noxious odors and toward pleasant ones (Rieser, Yonas, & Wikner, 1976). This turning response has been used to show that infants respond to odorants of human body origin. Babies less than 2 weeks old will orient toward an object carrying their mother's scent, such as a

---

DEMONSTRATION BOX 16-3   The Rooting Response

The easiest method to show tactile sensitivity and localization in infants is to elicit the reflex called the *rooting response*. To see how early this ability exists, a very young baby of less than 2 months of age should be used (although the response can be elicited in older infants). To demonstrate tactile localization ability, you should stroke the infant's cheek lightly with your finger. If you stroke the right cheek, the infant should turn to the right. If you stroke the left cheek, the infant should turn to the left.

breast pad (Cernoch & Porter, 1985; Russell, 1976). There is even the suggestion that, in contrast to some of the limitations on infant sensory capacities, children actually may be more responsive than adults to human body odors (Filsinger & Fabes, 1985).

PERCEPTUAL CHANGE THROUGH CHILDHOOD

Throughout childhood a general improvement takes place in perceptual discrimination, identification, and information processing. Many of these changes occur fairly rapidly within the first year or two of life, while others continue over much longer time spans. The most dramatic changes seem to occur at around the age of 2 to 3 months (Atkinson & Braddick, 1981; Maurer & Lewis, 1979), when the child's visual abilities suddenly improve. Acuity increases markedly (Braddick & Atkinson, 1979; Courage & Adams, 1990), tracking behavior becomes more adultlike (Atkinson, 1979), the ability to recognize individual elements surrounded by an enclosing contour appears (Milewski, 1976), and infants begin to show more adultlike eye-movement patterns when viewing figures (Hainline, 1978). By 3 months of age stereoscopic depth perception appears (Shea, Fox, Aslin, & Dumais, 1980), and this ability continues to improve over the first 2 years (Fox, Aslin, Shea, & Dumais, 1980; Held, 1985). Although the most rapid period of improvement in the ability to discriminate depth based on binocular disparity seems to have been completed by about 30 months of age (Ciner, Schanel-Klitsch, & Scheiman, 1991), binocular depth perception seems to improve throughout childhood and into early adolescence (Romano, Romano, & Puklin, 1975).

Other basic visual processes also seem to develop rapidly over the first 2 years. Thus, visual acuity, which is originally quite poor, improves steadily into early childhood (Gwiazda, Brill, Mohindra, & Held, 1980), and early astig-

matic problems (lens flattening), which lower visual resolution in infants, also usually disappear (Atkinson, Braddick, & French, 1979; Ingram & Barr, 1979). By 5 years of age children seem to have fully developed scotopic and photopic visual systems, which show adaptation effects and sensitivities equivalent to those of adults.

A similar pattern is found for the other senses. Consider hearing as an example. Infants begin with a substantial low-frequency hearing deficit and a lesser high-frequency deficit. Over the first 2 years hearing improves quickly, especially for the low frequencies, and the improvement then continues more gradually until about 10 years of age (Kuhl, 1987; Trehub et al., 1980; Yoneshige & Elliott, 1981).

Eye Movements and Attention

In addition to changes in basic sensory processes, changes occur in the patterns of attention and information encoding, which appear as developmental changes in perception. Theorists such as Hochberg (1981, 1982) have suggested that the way information is integrated over time changes as the child develops. The notion of **integration** involves the child's constructing mental models (such as pictures or images), called **schemata,** to help make sense of the perceptual information available in a given situation. In addition, integration involves the child's selecting new information from the perceptual array through the process of **encoding.** Once information is encoded, it has been modified into a form suitable for remembering. In this form it can be compared to other new information as well as to information from existing schemata. This means that attention and memory play a major role in the perceptual process.

As we learned in Chapter 15, one of the ways we can observe the pattern of overt attention is to monitor eye movements. Developmental theorists, such as Piaget (1969), have argued that patterns of eye movements provide some clues as to which stimuli are being selected and compared by individuals of different ages. For instance, we know that adults display a strong tendency to look at forms that are informative, unusual, or of particular functional value (Antes, 1974; Friedman & Liebelt, 1981; Loftus & Mackworth, 1978). Thus, by monitoring eye-movement patterns in children, we can observe the **search** component of visual attention. Information about search should be helpful in determining how children are viewing, and hence constructing, their visual world.

We have already seen that infants from birth to 2 months of age do make a variety of eye movements (such as fixating stationary stimuli, tracking moving stimuli, or moving their eyes toward stimuli in the periphery of the visual field), although not as precisely as adults do. More importantly, they often do not move their eyes to the most informative parts of the stimulus (at least by adult standards), but rather seem to view only limited parts of the stimulus, usually around a border or corner (Day, 1975; Mackworth & Bruner, 1970). For instance, when a distinct contour is present within the visual field of an infant, its eye is drawn toward it. Infants of around 1 month of age tend to direct their eyes toward one distinctive feature of a visual stimulus, such as the corner of a triangle (Bronson, 1990; Haith, Bergman, & Moore, 1977). Their eyes seem to be "captured" by the feature, since they dwell on it for prolonged periods (Salapatek & Kessen, 1973).

Because the gaze of a 1-month-old infant is caught by the first contour encountered, most viewing time is spent focused on the external contours of a form. If the stimulus has internal features, they are ignored or missed. This changes by the age of 2 months. Now the infant scans the contours a little more, and shorter periods are spent on each feature (Banks & Salapatek, 1983; Hainline, 1978; Salapatek, 1975). In addition, the infant dwells almost exclusively on the internal features of the stimulus, seeming to ignore the overall pattern. These differences are shown in Figure 16-9. If the stimulus is unstable (such as when it is flickering), however, the eye movements revert to patterns typical of younger ages (Bronson, 1990).

The eye-movement patterns of 3- and 4-year-olds are similar to those of a 2-month-old infant. Children of this age spend most of their time dwelling on the internal details of a figure, with only an occasional eye movement beyond the contour boundary. The 4- or 5-year-old child begins to make eye-movement excursions toward the surrounding contour. At 6 and 7 years of age, the child systematically scans the outer portions of the stimulus with occasional

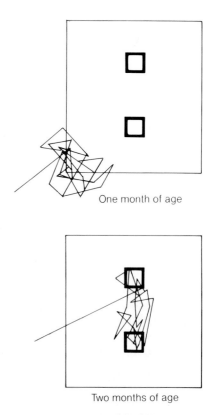

One month of age

Two months of age

Figure 16-9 *Eye movements typical of 1- and 2-month-old infants.*

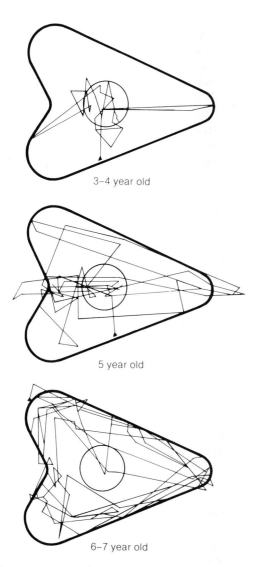

Figure 16-10 *Changes in eye movements from ages 3 to 6 (from Zaporozhets, 1965. Copyright The Society for Research in Child Development, Inc.).*

eye movements into the interior. This development is shown in Figure 16-10 (Zaporozhets, 1965).

Eye-movement patterns have important consequences for certain perceptual discrimination tasks. Vurpillot (1968) monitored the eye movements of children between the ages of 2 and 9 years. They were presented with pictures of houses with different kinds of windows and were asked to indicate whether or not the houses appeared to be the same, a task that required systematic comparison of the windows. She found that the youngest children did not conduct a systematic search. Rather, they often continued searching through the houses even after looking at a pair of windows that were quite different. This lack of systematic viewing was accompanied by a low degree of accuracy in the discrimination judgments of the younger children. Older children, with more regular and systematic viewing patterns, were much more accurate. Similarly, Cohen (1981) found in a figure-matching task that 5- and 8-year-old children take longer to decide where to move their eyes than adults do in the same task. In addition, they make more eye movements and are less likely than adults to look directly at the matching target in their first eye movements. It is likely that these differences reflect differences in strategies of attention and information pickup, rather than differences in visual capacity, since eye movements seem to be strongly affected by task demands, meaning, context, and expectations (Antes & Penland, 1981; Findlay, 1981; Stark & Ellis, 1981).

Such differences in observing strategy may explain why as children become older, they gradually change the way they view patterns and the elements that make them up (Elkind, 1978). For instance, consider Figure 16-11. It consists of several objects (fruits and vegetables) organized into a larger figure (a bird). Children 4 and 5 years old report seeing only the parts ("carrots and a pear and an orange"). By the age of 7, children report seeing both the parts and the global organization ("fruits and carrots and a bird"). By 8 or 9 years of age, most children respond in terms of both the parts and the global organization ("a bird made of fruits and vegetables").

Figure 16-11 *A vegetable-fruit-bird figure used to measure part-versus-whole perception in children.*

Orienting and Filtering

Attention involves more than simply searching for targets and scanning the environment with eye movements. Several other aspects have also been shown to change systematically with age (Enns, 1990; Enns & Cameron, 1987). For instance, the aspect we called **covert orienting** in Chapter 15 (a shift in attention without accompanying physical movement of the eye) shows changes with age for both *stimulus* and *information* cues. It is possible to measure covert orienting in response to a stimulus that suddenly appears in the visual periphery in children as young as 3 and 4 years of age (Enns, 1990). However, when this ability has been studied systematically in 6- to 7-year-olds, it is still apparent that these children do not shift their visual attention as efficiently as adults do (Akhtar & Enns, 1989; Enns & Brodeur, 1989). Even larger developmental differences can be seen when attention must be reoriented voluntarily by a child in response to an information cue. Children as old as 11 years require more time than adults to shift their attention between information in the two ears

(Pearson & Lane, 1991a) and between information from two visual locations (Pearson & Lane, 1991b).

Selective attention also involves the component we called **filtering** in Chapter 15. This refers to the ability to ignore irrelevant stimuli in the environment while more task-relevant stimuli are being processed. Several studies have shown that children are more easily distracted by irrelevant stimuli (for example, Day & Stone, 1980). Thus, in a card-sorting task, both children and adults show poorer performance if irrelevant as well as relevant features are present; however, children show a much greater reduction in efficiency than adults (Well, Lorch, & Anderson, 1980).

An interesting set of phenomena may show age changes in stimulus filtering more graphically. These are responses to **visual-geometric illusions,** which are simple line drawings in which the *actual* size, shape, or direction of some elements differs from the *perceived* size, shape, or direction (see Coren & Girgus, 1978). We have already encountered some of these illusions in Chapters 1 and 14; two of them are shown in Figure 16-12. Figure 16-12A shows the **Mueller-Lyer illusion,** in which the line marked *x* appears to be longer than the line marked *y*. Figure 16-12B shows the **Ponzo illusion,** in which the line marked *w* appears to be longer than the line marked *z*. This is the case in spite of the fact that *x* and *y* are physically equal in length and *w* and *z* are also physically equal to each other.

One explanation for certain visual-geometric illusions is that the lines that induce the illusion become confused with the test lines, thus causing the distortion (Coren & Girgus, 1978). For instance, in the Mueller-Lyer illusion (16-12A), the upper figure *is* longer if you measure from wing tip to wing tip. Thus, confusing the wings with the horizontal line might add to the distortion. This idea is supported by the fact that focusing attention on the lines, and ignoring the wings, reduces the strength of the illusion (Coren & Girgus, 1972b), whereas

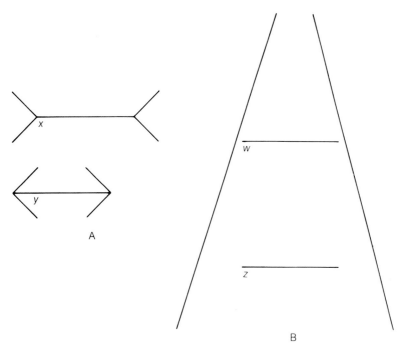

Figure 16-12 *Two illusions that show age-related differences in perception:* (A) *the Mueller-Lyer;* (B) *the Ponzo.*

directing attention to certain parts of a figure can produce illusions (Coren & Porac, 1983a). If we accept this explanation, and if children are poorer at filtering out extraneous stimuli, then we would expect children to show stronger visual illusions than adults. In general, we do find that visual illusions are larger for children and decrease with age, suggesting that children are less able to ignore the inducing lines when making their judgments (Coren & Girgus, 1978; Enns & Girgus, 1985; Pick & Pick, 1970). In one study, illusion magnitude was found to decrease until about the age of 25 years, after which it did not change further (Porac & Coren, 1981).

Encoding and Memory

Another factor that can affect perceptual development is the change in encoding ability. For a child to integrate and compare stimuli, he or she must first have the ability to register the information obtained in a glance, as well as the ability to remember information from other glances and the schemata associated with a particular class of stimuli. Thus, it is not surprising that a number of studies have shown that the ability to discriminate between visual patterns improves with age (for example, Cratty, 1979).

Studies that have directly compared the ability of children to encode versus the ability to remember visual stimuli indicate that the largest developmental changes lie in the memory component. For instance, when children are presented with a brief (100 msec) visual display of eight items arranged in an imaginary circle, they can report the identity of the items with adultlike accuracy under some conditions (Morrison, Holmes, & Haith, 1974; Sheingold, 1973). Specifically, this is possible when a stimulus marker, indicating the item to be reported, appears within 50 to 200 msec of the onset of the display. When the delay between the display and the marker is longer than 200 msec, the children's accuracy is worse than adults'. This suggests that children differ from adults mainly in the memory processes associated with object identification, not in the initial stimulus encoding processes. Other studies have come to this same conclusion by varying the spatial and temporal distance between pieces of information that must be integrated before a response can be made (Enns & Girgus, 1986; Enns & King, 1990) and by varying the degree of symmetry in patterns that must only be encoded versus those that must be encoded and remembered (Enns, 1987).

An interesting example of how pattern discrimination improves with age can be seen in the recognition of human faces. The impressive achievements we noted earlier for 5- to 7-month-old infants in discriminating face from nonface stimuli should not be interpreted to mean that these infants have full adult abilities in this area. The development of the ability to recognize faces continues for many years (Carey, 1981; Flin, 1980). For example, a dramatic increase in the ability of children to recognize unfamiliar faces occurs between the ages of 6 and 10 years. Under conditions where a 6-year-old will recognize about 60% of previously viewed faces, a 10-year-old will recognize nearly all of them (95%). Furthermore, improvement in this ability can be observed even through adolescence to the age of 16 (Carey, Diamond, & Woods, 1980).

One particular form of pattern discrimination error seems to be characteristic of young children: mirror reversals. Children confuse lateral mirror-image pairs, such as p and q, or b and d, more frequently than up-down mirror-image pairs such as p and b, or q and d (Springer & Deutsch, 1985). These confusions are quite common in young children (around 3 years old) and gradually decrease until about

the age of 10 or 11 (Gaddes, 1985; Serpell, 1971). Some of the improvement seems to be associated with educational processes, since between the ages of $5\frac{1}{2}$ and $6\frac{1}{2}$, the ability to make these discriminations suddenly increases. It is likely that the improvement is caused by the formal instruction in reading and writing that usually begins at about that age. With appropriate training, kindergarten-aged children can learn the left-right discrimination quite well, although it still seems to be more difficult than the up-down discrimination (Clark & Whitehurst, 1974).

Children who continue to have difficulties with left-right confusions can experience problems later with reading. The specific term used for such reading disability (when it is not associated with other disturbances such as mental retardation, sensory impairment, or emotional problems) is **dyslexia.** Estimates of the incidence of dyslexia vary widely, but it seems that the problem affects at least 2% of all children in Western countries, with the incidence perhaps being as high as 10% (Bannatyne, 1971; Gaddes, 1985; Spreen, 1976). This problem seems to have a perceptual rather than an intellectual basis. A dyslexic individual may be highly talented in many other respects. There are many case histories of exceptional people who have been dyslexic, including Thomas A. Edison, the surgeon Harvey Gushing, Auguste Rodin, Woodrow Wilson, and Hans Christian Andersen. One characteristic of all children who have been diagnosed as dyslexic is that they show confusions between the left-right mirror images of targets, although they have no problem with up-down mirror images (Gaddes, 1985; Newland, 1972; Sidman & Kirk, 1974).

Children's inability to discriminate letter reversals suggests that they are relatively insensitive to the orientation of a stimulus. An interesting phenomenon is associated with this issue. Consider a stimulus, such as a human face, that has familiar orientation. When a face is inverted it seems to lose much of its facelike quality, and even very familiar individuals are difficult to recognize when their photographs are turned upside down (Rock, 1973). Thus, it is not surprising to find that adult observers, who have had thousands of exposures to upright faces, show greater accuracy of identification when faces are upright than when they are inverted (Yin, 1970). However, the ability of 6-year-olds to identify faces is about the same whether the face is presented in a normal or in an inverted position. By the age of 10 years, children's ability to identify faces is disrupted when the faces are inverted (Carey & Diamond, 1977; Carey, Diamond, & Woods, 1980). It seems that the adults' sensitivity to orientation differences makes it more difficult for them to identify inverted familiar faces than for 6-year-olds tested on the same task. You can explore the adult sensitivity to orientation by trying Demonstration Box 16-4.

PERCEPTUAL CHANGE IN ADULTS

Perceptual and sensory functions continue to change throughout the life span, although the rate of change is usually slower in adults than during infancy and childhood. Also, the earlier changes are toward increasing efficiency in perceptual processing, whereas the later changes, beginning around age 40, are toward decreased functioning, as sensory receptors age and neural efficiency drops (Corso, 1981; Werner, Peterzell, & Scheetz, 1990).

Visual Function and Aging

We have all seen individuals who, upon reaching their mid- to late forties, suddenly begin to wear reading glasses or bifocals in order to see

---

DEMONSTRATION BOX 16-4   Orientation and Stimulus Recognition

Adults are more rigid in their reliance on normal orientations than are children. Look at the two figures here, and you will probably find them quite difficult to identify, but if you invert the page you will see them suddenly become identifiable. This effect is especially striking for faces and for handwritten script.

A

B

the details of objects within arms' reach. This reduction in the accommodative range of the eye, called *presbyopia,* was discussed in Chapter 3. However, a number of other, less obvious, changes occur in the aging individual that reduce visual sensitivity. For instance, the aged eye generally has a smaller pupil size; hence less light enters the eye (Corso, 1981; Weale, 1982). The optics of the eye also become less efficient with increasing age, because the crystalline lens continues to become yellower and darker (Coren, 1987; Coren & Girgus, 1972a), and the cornea yellows somewhat (Lerman, 1984). Of course, we would expect a decrease in sensitivity because of the resulting decrease in the amount of light reaching the retina. Between 20 and 70 years of age, we find a consistent increase in threshold sensitivities for the detection of spots of light (Fozard, Wolf, Bell, McFarland, & Podolsky, 1977). This is particularly evident in dark adaptation. Although the time to reach minimum threshold remains the same, the maximum sensitivity eventually achieved decreases with age. This is shown in Figure 16-13 (McFarland, Domey, Warren, & Ward, 1960).

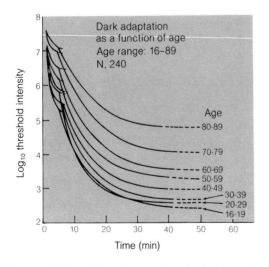

Figure 16-13 *Age changes in dark-adaptation (from McFarland et al., 1960).*

Some deterioration in vision may be due to a progressive decrease in the number of functioning rods and cones in the retina (Werner et al., 1990). For example, loss of cones sensitive to short-wavelength light may account for the gradual deterioration in color vision with age (Knoblauch et al., 1987). Sensitivity to the shorter wavelengths of light (those that appear bluish) continually diminishes from early childhood until death (Bornstein, 1977; Lakowski, 1962). Also, some reduced function may be due to an age-related loss of neurons in the visual cortex. This neuron loss can be quite extensive. Consider, for instance, the area of the cortex receiving foveal projections. In the average 20-year-old this area contains about 46 million neurons per gram of tissue, whereas in one 80-year-old the neuronal density was reduced by nearly one-half, to only 24 million neurons per gram of tissue (Devaney & Johnson, 1980).

Although the number of remaining neurons is adequate for most visual tasks, we might expect a dramatic reduction in their number to cause a reduction in visual acuity and in absolute sensitivity (Weale, 1986). Many studies have shown that visual acuity decreases with age; at age 40 nearly 94% of individuals have 20/20 visual acuity or better, whereas by age 80 only 6% of the population has this level of acuity (Richards, 1977; Woo & Bader, 1978). The relationship between age and visual acuity can be seen in Figure 16-14.

The pattern of the acuity loss with age is quite interesting. Older observers are still able to resolve visual details, but the light level necessary for them to do so is greatly increased. In terms of our discussion in Chapter 4, we would say that the contrast threshold is higher for the older observers (Crassini, Brown, & Bowman, 1988; Leibowitz, Post, & Ginsburg, 1980). Furthermore, it appears that the neural system that processes depth and movement information (remember the magnocellular pathway discussed in Chapter 3) shows the greatest loss

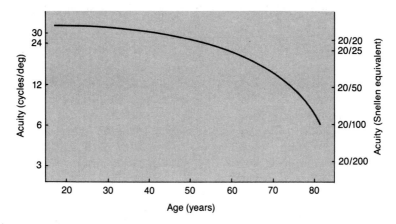

Figure 16-14 *Age-related decrease in visual acuity.*

of sensitivity (Sekuler & Hutman, 1980). These findings suggest that in tasks such as night driving, where good acuity and response to relatively fast-moving stimuli are required, yet illumination conditions are low, older individuals might be quite inefficient, and may even be at risk.

How do healthy older adults perform on the standard tests used to assess attentional functioning? On tests of covert orienting and filtering, they often perform in a very similar way to college-age adults (D'Aloisio & Klein, 1990; Nissen & Corkin, 1985; Plude & Hoyer, 1986). Like the children we discussed earlier, they tend to diverge from the performance of college-age adults on orienting tasks that involve informational cues. So long as visual attention is shifted involuntarily for them, as by a stimulus cue suddenly appearing in the visual field, attention shifts are quite efficient (Madden, 1986). However, if the cue is informational only, thus requiring a voluntary effort to reorient attention, it appears that shifts in visual orientation can be quite slow for elderly adults (Hartley, Keiley, & Slabach, 1990; Madden, 1983; Nissen & Corkin, 1985). On tests of visual filtering, elderly adults also perform similarly to college-age observers (D'Aloisio & Klein, 1990), so long as no uncertainty exists

about where the to-be-identified target will appear (Plude & Hoyer, 1986) and stimuli are not presented too far into the visual periphery (Cerella, 1985). Under the more taxing conditions performance drops in the elderly.

The attentional aspect in which older adults do show a consistent and substantial performance difference from younger adults is that of visual search (D'Aloisio & Klein, 1990; Plude, 1990; P. M. A. Rabbitt, 1965). We discussed several examples of such tasks in Chapter 15, all of which involve scanning for the presence of a particular target stimulus. One possible explanation for this result is that the visual field of older observers might be smaller because of loss of acuity in the periphery of the retina, where fewer receptors are present. Although this is certainly true at the furthest edges of the visual field, within approximately 70 deg on either side of the center of gaze, the acuity variation with age is not as pronounced (Burg, 1968; Scialfa, 1990). Since all visual search tasks involve displays that fall well within this range, the loss in peripheral acuity would not seem to be the major cause of the poorer performance. An additional fact that seems to argue against the decreased search efficiency arising from contraction of the visual field from acuity losses in the periphery with age is the finding that older subjects do not appear to have any difficulty identifying isolated stimuli in the peripheral visual field (Cerella, 1985; Sekuler & Ball, 1986).

Another possible explanation for poorer search performance with age is that older observers are slower in moving their eyes across the various items in the display. However, this possibility is eliminated by the observation that the difference in search speeds between older and younger adults remains even after eye movements are not a factor, such as in briefly flashed stimulus presentations (D'Aloisio & Klein, 1990).

In order to distinguish these attentional aging effects from the receptor-related and muscular effects we have already discussed, some researchers refer to the **useful field of view** (or simply **UFOV**) in their descriptions of aging (Ball, Roenker, & Bruni, 1990; Sanders, 1970). The UFOV is defined as the area of the visual field that is functional for an observer at a given time and for a given task. Thus, for tasks involving the detection of bright light flashes and identification of briefly presented targets, we can say that the UFOV does not differ greatly between younger and older adults. In contrast, for the task of finding a specific target amidst many distracters, the UFOV is much

smaller for older observers. It is of interest, then, that studies looking for relations between traffic accident records and the UFOV indicate no relation between the two when the UFOV is measured with tasks involving simple detection and identification (Allen, 1970; Shinar, 1977). However, a significant relation exists between the number of traffic accidents a person has and the size of the UFOV when it is measured in a situation where the individual must identify targets in the presence of visual distracters (Avolio, Kroeck, & Panek, 1986).

Age Effects on the Other Senses

Hearing ability declines with age. Generally speaking, hearing impairments begin to appear during middle age and occur with increasing frequency after age 60. About 15% of all people over 65 could be classified as hearing impaired, and as many as 75% of all 70-year-olds have some hearing problems (Schaie & Geiwitz, 1982). The loss of hearing ability is much more marked for high-frequency stimuli (Corso, 1981). As can be seen from Figure 16-15, at age 70 there is still very little decrease in threshold sensitivity for a 1000-Hz tone, but an 8000-Hz

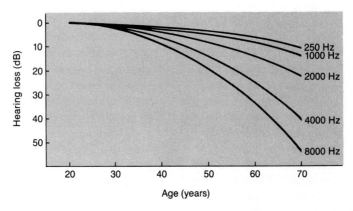

Figure 16-15 *The age-related decrease in auditory sensitivity is particularly noticeable for the higher frequencies.*

tone might show a reduction in threshold sensitivity of nearly 50 db.

Absolute sensitivity in a number of other modalities also decreases with advancing age. The pattern of change, however, is not always consistent. Thus, although older observers show lower sensitivity to touch (Thornbury & Mistretta, 1981), they do not show any decrease in their sensitivity to pain (Harkins & Chapman, 1977).

Some of the most noticeable changes with age occur in the realm of taste and small. Odor sensitivity is greatly diminished, although the reduction is not uniform across all stimuli or individuals (Cain & Stevens, 1989). For instance, elderly subjects seem best able to discriminate among fruity odors, as compared to other classes of scents (Schiffman & Pasternak, 1979). However, they adapt more quickly than younger adults to a particular odor and, once adapted, require considerably more time to return to their original level of sensitivity (Stevens, Cain, & Oatley, 1989; Stevens, Cain, Shiet, & Oatley, 1989). Odor memory also shows large age differences in adulthood. In one study many of the young adults tested were able to recognize odors they had smelled one week earlier, whereas many of the older adults failed to recognize such odors only several minutes after the initial exposure (Stevens, Cain, & Demarque, 1990).

A diminished sensitivity to some tastes can also be seen in the elderly. For instance, thresholds for the taste primaries of both salt and sugar rise measurably, although not dramatically, with age (Grzegorczyk, Jones, & Mistretta, 1979; Moore, Nielson, & Mistretta, 1982). Recovery from adaptation to these tastes is also slowed (Stevens & Wellen, 1989). This combination of diminished sensitivity to odor and taste in the elderly can reduce their ability to identify foods, especially when the foods are blended or pureed so that they are not identifiable by sight (Cain, Reid, & Stevens, 1990; Schiffman, 1977; Stevens, Cain, De-

Table 16-2   The Percentage of 20-Year-Olds versus the Percentage of Elderly Individuals (Mean Age of 73 Years) Correctly Identifying Some Common Foods in Pureed Form (Based on Schiffman, 1977)

FOOD	20-YEAR-OLDS	ELDERLY
Apple	81	55
Lemon	52	24
Strawberry	78	33
Broccoli	30	0
Carrot	63	7
Corn	67	38
Beef	41	28
Coffee	89	70
Sugar	63	57

marque, & Ruthruff, 1991). This could potentially put the elderly at risk for ingesting dangerous substances and overlooking important ingredients in their diet. Just how large a deficit is experienced by the elderly can be seen by comparing the performance of a group of 20-year-olds at identifying foods by taste and smell alone with a group whose average age is 73 years. As can be seen in Table 16-2, in most instances the younger individuals do twice as well as the elderly, although on some common items, such as coffee, performance is about the same for both age groups.

Global Changes in Perceptual Performance

Several types of change seem to affect all of the sensory modalities. The most important of these is a general slowing of neural responses, accompanied by an increasing persistence of the stimulus (actually slower recovery or clearing time) in the neural representation (Salthouse, 1985). This means that older individuals have more trouble with briefly presented stimuli (Hoyer & Plude, 1980), show slower reaction times to stimulus onsets (Stern, Oster, & Newport, 1980), cannot readily identify stimuli arriving in a rapid sequence (Birren, Woods, & Williams, 1980), and retrieve information more slowly from memory (Salthouse & Kail, 1983). This slowing of processing in the elderly individual becomes most apparent when the perceptual tasks are complex (Cerella, Poon, & Williams, 1980; Cunningham, 1980).

Another general change that accompanies aging involves the distribution of attention to perceptual tasks (Botwinick, 1984). Much of this can be traced to the idea that a fixed amount of attentional resources can be divided among various tasks (see Chapter 15 and Kahneman, 1973). Older individuals seem to have more difficulty dividing their attention between various stimuli or input channels (Craik & Simon, 1980). In addition, they seem to have more difficulty filtering or extracting relevant from irrelevant targets in search or recognition tasks (Rabbitt, P.M.A., 1977; Wright & Elias, 1979). The more similar the irrelevant stimuli are to the target stimuli, the greater the difficulty all observers have in detecting targets in a search task. However, elderly observers have their performance disrupted at levels of difficulty that do not seem to affect younger observers (Farkas & Hoyer, 1980).

This would taste a lot better if it had less pepper or if I were 80 years old

GLOSSARY

The following definitions are specific to their use in this book.

Auditory grouping   The perceptual organization of sound on the basis of temporal and frequency relationships.

Covert orienting   A part of selective attention that involves shifting attention from one source of information to another, without any accompanying movements of the eyes, ears, or head.

Developmental approach   An approach to perception that presumes that chronological age is the best predictor of perceptual ability.

Dyslexia   A form of impaired reading ability characterized by confusion of letters that are left-right mirror images.

Encoding   Entering the perceptual information in a glance into some form of memory storage to allow identification and comparison with other stimuli.

Filtering   A part of selective attention that involves screening out irrelevant stimuli while attending to relevant stimuli.

Forced-choice preferential looking   An experimental method in which observers watch infants and attempt to determine, solely on the basis of their orienting responses, on which side of the visual field a stimulus was presented.

Habituation   The process by which an observer ceases to respond to a repeated stimulus.

Infant directed talk   The tendency on the part of adults to speak in a high-pitched and exaggerated voice to young infants.

Integration   The process by which an observer builds an internal model of perceptual objects based on incoming stimulation and knowledge from previous perceptions.

Mueller-Lyer illusion   An illusion of size in which the apparent length of a line is affected by the direction of its contextual wings.

Nasal visual field   The half of each eye's visual field that lies toward the nose.

Optokinetic nystagmus   An eye-movement sequence in which smooth-tracking eye movements alternate with saccades in the opposite direction in the presence of a moving pattern.

Perceptual learning approach   An approach to perception that maintains that the primary determinant of our perceptual abilities is our previous experience with certain environmental stimuli.

Ponzo illusion   An illusion of size in which the perceived length of a line is affected by its place in the context of surrounding converging lines.

Preferential looking   A behavioral measure of infant discrimination in which target fixation time is assumed to be positively related to stimulus preference.

Rooting response   An infant reflex consisting of the head's turning in the direction of a touch to the face.

Saccadic eye movements   Fast, ballistic eye movements that place the images of objects that observers are attending to on the fovea.

Schemata   Internal models or hypotheses about the external world that help organize perceptual information.

Search   The process of scanning a scene or a display for a particular target stimulus.

Smooth-pursuit eye movement   Smooth eye movements used to track a moving target, as opposed to saccadic eye movements.

Temporal visual field   The half of each eye's visual field that lies toward the temple.

UFOV   *See* Useful field of view.

Useful field of view (UFOV)   The area of the visual field that is functional for an observer performing a given task. In general, the more difficult a task, the smaller the useful field of view.

VEP   *See* Visually evoked potential.

Visual-geometric illusions   Simple line drawings in which the actual physical characteristics of certain elements differ from the perceived characteristics of those elements.

Visually evoked potential (VEP)   The change in the electrical activity of the brain produced in response to a visual stimulus.

Chapter ... 17

LEARNING AND EXPERIENCE

Experience and Development

Restricted and Selective Rearing

Neurophysiological Effects

Perceptual Effects

Human Studies

Sensory-Motor Learning

Perceptual Rearrangement

Illusion Decrement

Context and Meaning

Eyewitness Testimony

Environmental and Life History Differences

Picture Perception

Illusion and Constancy

Speech

Effects of Occupation

Perceptual Set

An article in the *New York Times* spoke of a tea expert who was called in to determine the components of a blend of tea that an American company was about to market. A small cup of it was poured for him. He sniffed it gently, sipped a bit, swished it around in his mouth a little, then looked up.

"I detect," he said crisply, "a rather good Assam, a run-of-the-mill Darjeeling, a mediocre Ceylon, and, of course, the tea bag" (Root, 1974).

Although we might be amazed at performances such as these, or similar ones of expert wine tasters, we must realize that this degree of perceptual discrimination has come about through years of training and experience. In other words, this expert had to *learn* to taste and identify these flavors.

In some of the previous chapters we have mentioned some ways in which our past history, experience, knowledge, and hypotheses affect our perception. Most people are willing to admit that some aspects of perception may be susceptible to the influences of experience, but they are often unaware of the magnitude of these effects. Our past can even influence whether we perceive anything at all in certain circumstances. For example, imagine we briefly flash a visual stimulus (such as a word) in front of you. If we have chosen the duration and intensity of the stimulus carefully, you may be unaware of any aspect of the stimulus. If we flash the same stimulus again, we would expect that, again, you would see nothing. However, with repeated presentations something about its appearance would begin to change. Soon you would be able to make out fragments of this stimulus, and after a while these fragments would become more complex. Eventually the entire stimulus pattern would be identified on every trial (that is, you would be able to read the word), even though the luminance and exposure durations are the same as for the very first trials when you saw and identified nothing (Haber & Hershenson, 1965;

Uhlarik & Johnson, 1978). Your prior experience with this stimulus would have changed your perceptual abilities in some manner, and now you would be able to see what was formerly invisible. In other words, during the course of this experiment you would have learned to see this pattern.

EXPERIENCE AND DEVELOPMENT

As an organism develops, its nervous system matures, and over the years many changes in physiology and perceptual ability also come about simply due to physiological maturation. Of course, as the months and years pass, the organism is also accumulating new experiences with the environment and is encountering many chances to learn new perceptual coordinations. It is important for us to understand how the natural course of development interacts with an individual's life history to shape that individual's perception of the world.

Experience can affect the development of the individual's perceptual processes in several different ways. We have outlined these in Figure 17-1 (see Aslin, 1985; Gottlieb, 1981).

The strongest form of interaction between experience and development is **induction.** Here, the presence of some sort of relevant experience actually determines both the presence and final level of the ability (Figure 17-1A). The weakest form of effect we will call **maturation.** This actually represents no effect at all, and the ability might be expected to develop regardless of the individual's experience or lack of it (B). Another possible interaction is **enhancement.** Here the final level of an ability, which is already present or developing, is improved because of experiential factors (C). **Facilitation** increases the rate at which an ability develops, but not its final level, providing earlier acquisition of the skill but not greater proficiency (D). Finally, **maintenance**

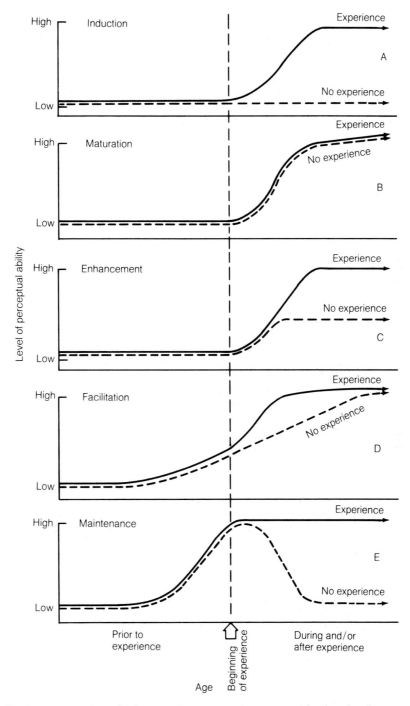

Figure 17-1 *Various ways in which experience can interact with the development of perceptual abilities.*

serves to stabilize, or to keep, an ability that is already present (E). Of course, different mechanisms might be expected to produce each of these patterns of interaction between development and experience.

Restricted and Selective Rearing

The most direct method for assessing the relationship between development and experience is to deprive the observer of the opportunity to use a particular sensory modality from the moment of birth. After the individual has fully matured, we test the perceptual capacities in the deprived modality. If the observer has developed poorly, we have demonstrated the need for experience in the development of normal functions. This technique is called **restricted rearing.** (We previously encountered this procedure in Chapter 10 when we discussed the development of depth perception.) A somewhat more elegant technique involves deliberately altering the pattern of experience that the developing organism is exposed to from birth. For example, an animal may be exposed only to diffuse light, vertical stripes, the color red, and so forth. Such a procedure should selectively bias, rather than eliminate, certain perceptual abilities, if experience plays a role in their development. This procedure is known as **selective rearing.**

Neurophysiological Effects

Recent research indicates that experience may play a role in the development of sensory physiological structures themselves. For instance, as discussed in Chapter 16, the visual pathways and visual cortex of the newborn differ from that of the adult; fewer responsive cells are present, and these show lesser degrees of directional and orientational sensitivity (see also Hickey & Peduzzi, 1987; Norton, 1981a). Visual experience, in addition to the growth and maturation of the nervous system, seems to be necessary for the development of normal visual functioning. This has been demonstrated though restricted-rearing studies.

Let us consider what happens if we completely deprive an animal of any visual input by rearing it in the dark from birth. This animal will have a visual cortex that shows reduced overall responsiveness, when tested using the electrode implantation techniques discussed in Chapter 3. Furthermore, those cells that are found will not show the usual degree of orientation and movement selectivity (Blakemore, 1978; Leventhal & Hirsch, 1980), nor will the usual separation of responses according to eye of input be as clear (Swindale, 1988). The visual cortex of such animals appears to be very immature because of the absence of the usual history of visual experience.

Such neurophysiological disruption caused by the absence of visual experience can be found all along the visual pathways. Some effects are as peripheral as the retina, but they appear as well at other places, such as the superior colliculus, the lateral geniculate nucleus, and the visual cortex (Movshon & Van Sluyters, 1981; Riesen & Zilbert, 1975). Different aspects of the visual pathways seem to be more or less susceptible to such damage. Thus, we find that parvo ganglion cells are relatively unaffected by dark rearing, whereas magno ganglion cells are readily lost if no visual experience is available (Hoffman & Sherman, 1975; Rothblat & Schwartz, 1978). These effects are not irreversible, since even animals who have been raised for a year following birth in total darkness show some recovery after several months of exposure to illuminated surroundings, although recovery is never complete (Cynader, Berman, & Hein, 1976).

Much subtler neurophysiological changes come about through selective-rearing practices. For instance, in Chapter 3 we stated that cells in the visual cortex tend to show ocular dominance. This means that although most cells in the cortex can be activated by stimulation of either eye, they tend to respond more vigorously to one eye than to the other. The fact that most cells respond somewhat to each eye's input probably has to do with the depth cue of binocular disparity (see Chapter 10). Suppose we rear an animal from birth so it only views the world through one eye. Later we test separately the ability of the two eyes to produce a response in the visual cortex. We would find that the majority of the cells are activated by the experienced eye, and often less than 10% of the cells can be driven by the deprived eye (LeVay, Wiesel, & Hubel, 1980).

The degree of disruption of normal functioning seems to depend on when the period of deprivation begins. If the animal is deprived of binocular viewing during the period of 3 weeks to 3 months after birth, large disruptions of the normal pattern of binocular response occur. However, if the monocular viewing period is instituted after 3 months of age, even for periods of up to a year, virtually no effect is found (Cynader, Timney, & Mitchel, 1980; Held, 1985; Pettigrew, 1978). This means that there is a particular time period during which the visual experience is most required and most effective. Such an interval, called a **critical period,** characterizes many aspects of the interaction between experience and development (Mitchell, 1981). Critical periods may correspond to periods of maximal growth and development in the nervous system (Aslin, 1985; Hickey, 1977). Any disruption of normal visual experience during the critical period, even for periods as short as 3 days, produces measurable changes in the responses of cells in the visual system (Freeman, Mallach, & Hartley, 1981).

Perhaps the most subtle form of selective visual rearing involves limiting an animal to a world containing only contours oriented in one direction. Thus, an animal might be exposed to only vertically oriented lines from birth. This is

Figure 17-2 An apparatus for selectively rearing a kitten so its only visual experience will be with vertical lines.

accomplished by either affixing to the animal goggles that only contain lines of one orientation, or giving the animal experience for a few hours each day in an apparatus similar to that shown in Figure 17-2. This is simply a large cylinder containing nothing but vertical stripes and a clear plastic floor on which the animal stands. Notice that the animal is wearing a special collar that prevents it from seeing its own limbs.

What happens in the nervous system after exposure to this kind of selective rearing and stimulation might be called *environmental surgery*. Such surgery drastically alters the response characteristics of neurons in the visual cortex. Normally, when we insert an electrode into the visual cortex in order to map receptive fields, we find large numbers of cells that respond most strongly to lines in a particular orientation, as we saw in Chapter 3, and the particular preferred orientations are rather evenly distributed. The left side of Figure 17-3

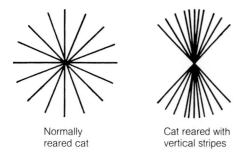

Normally
reared cat

Cat reared with
vertical stripes

Figure 17-3 *Distribution of the preferred orientation of cortical receptive fields in a normally reared cat versus that for a cat reared with selective exposure to vertical lines. Each line indicates the preferred orientation of one cell.*

depicts this distribution as a set of lines, each of which represents a neuron responding best to that orientation. However, recording from an animal that has never seen horizontal stripes produces quite a different result. In this animal, virtually no cells are responsive to horizontally oriented lines, resulting in a distribution of preferred stimulus orientations much like that shown on the right in Figure 17-3 (Hirsch & Spinelli, 1970; Movshon & Van Sluyters, 1981). It is as if the absence of horizontally oriented stimuli in the environment has served as a (figurative) scalpel that has systematically cut off any responding to stimuli other than the vertical stimuli to which the animal was exposed. Again, this sort of selective stimulation seems to be most effective during a critical period between 3 weeks and 3 months (Mitchell, 1981; Rothblat & Schwartz, 1978).

Blake (1981) has summarized the evidence from such selective rearing studies, saying, "In effect, the neurophysiologists have compiled a set of recipes for creating animals with specific kinds of neural deficits at sites along the visual pathways" (page 97). The ingredients that go into these recipes are particular experiences, or the lack of certain normal experiences, with visual stimuli.

Perceptual Effects

How do all these unusual environmental experiences affect what the organism perceives? We find a slight divergence between the physiological and the behavioral data when we answer this question. Consider a kitten reared in total darkness until the age of 6 months. When we remove this kitten from darkness, it at first appears to be completely blind; however, within about 48 hours of exposure to illuminated surroundings the kitten begins to show some visual responsiveness. Various forms of sensory motor coordination begin to appear in a piecemeal fashion, and after a 6-week period of normal experience a great deal of recovery has occurred. Direct measures of visual acuity show a gradual improvement. If the animal had been dark-reared for only about 4 months, the acuity gradually would return to that of a normally reared cat; however, visual acuity never reaches normal levels for animals that have been dark-reared for longer periods (Timney, Mitchel, & Griffin, 1978). Although many of the physiological changes appear to be permanent, the animal seems to have enough plasticity to allow for considerable behavioral recovery of function after the initial period of deprivation. Still, the animal will show measurable deficits in many visual tasks, including obstacle avoidance, tracking, jumping under visual guidance, and eye blinks to oncoming objects, even after 2 years of normal experience (Mitchell, 1978; Rothblat & Schwartz, 1978). Dark-reared animals also seem less responsive to visual information and use it less efficiently in tasks such as maze or spatial learning (Tees & Buhrmann, 1990; Tees & Symons, 1987).

Since selective rearing is a more subtle procedure than restricted rearing, it should not be surprising to find that its behavioral effects are often somewhat indirect and elusive. For instance, the most dramatic behavioral effects of rearing animals with one eye occluded is a reduction in the visual acuity of the deprived eye (Mitchell, 1981). However, there are a number of interesting visual field effects as well. **Visual field** refers to the region of the outside world to which an eye will respond, measured in degrees around the head. For instance Figure 17-4 shows the visual fields for the right and left eyes of a cat. There is a rather large region of overlap between the two eyes in the frontal part of the field. This is the region of binocular vision, where either or both eyes of the cat should be able to see an object. Generally, if an interesting stimulus appears in the visual field of a cat, it will immediately turn its eyes and head toward it, displaying an orienting response (see Chapter 15). We can use this response to measure the effectiveness of stimuli in the visual field of the cat, and if we cover one eye at a time, we can measure each visual field separately.

Let us first consider an animal that has been completely dark-reared. This animal shows a severe loss of response in the region of binocular overlap. Each eye seems to respond only to objects on its side of the head as shown in the middle view of Figure 17-4. An animal reared with one eye occluded also does not show a binocularly responsive region of the visual field. The eye that had normal visual experience shows a normal visual field, overlapping well to the opposite side. However, the eye that did not receive visual experience acts as if it only responds to targets far to the side of the head and excludes all of the visual field that the normally exposed eye covers, as shown in the bottom view of Figure 17-4 (Sherman, 1973). A similar effect has been reported in humans. A young man was born with a cataract that prevented any patterned vision in his left eye, so his visual experience was similar to the monocularly reared animals we have been discussing. When this cataract was removed at age 19, the normal eye had its usual visual field size, but the patient simply could not detect any stimuli

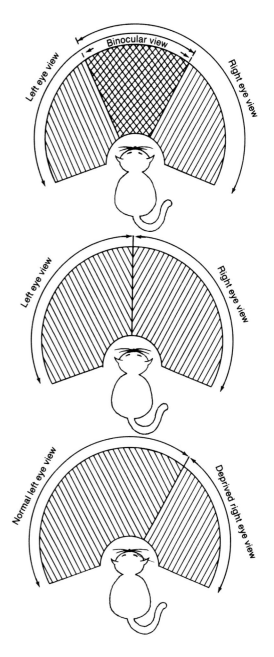

Figure 17-4 *Regions of the visual field in which a cat will respond to visual stimuli presented to the right or left eye are altered by depriving one or both eyes of visual experience from birth (based on Sherman, 1973).*

in a large portion of the region where the two eyes' views overlapped (the binocular region) with the deprived (cataract) eye. Although some recovery occurred over the next 10 months, the visual field of the deprived eye never became as large as that of the normal eye (Moran & Gordon, 1982). Some recent evidence has suggested that depriving one eye of visual input may also reduce the visual field of the undeprived eye as well (Maire-Lepoivre & Przybyslawski, 1988).

The other form of selective rearing, where an animal is reared under conditions of exposure to horizontal or vertical stripes alone, also produces a behavioral deficit, in addition to the change in the distribution of cells in the cortex with a specific set of preferred orientations. Here the results are not as dramatic as one might expect. Animals that have been reared only with vertical stripes are not blind to horizontal stripes; rather they have measurably lower visual acuity for stripes in an orientation never seen during their rearing (Blasdel, Mitchell, Muir, & Pettigrew, 1977; Hirsch, 1972).

Human Studies

Restricted-rearing studies cannot be conducted with human observers because of the possibility of producing long-lasting perceptual deficits. However, some clinical conditions reproduce the circumstances needed to study the effects of experience on perception. For example, Senden (1960) collected case reports of individuals who had suffered from lifelong blindness due to the presence of cataracts; these individuals later had vision restored through a surgical procedure. After the removal of the cataracts, these adults were unable to identify familiar objects by sight, although they were capable of identifying them if they were allowed to touch the objects. For instance, when asked to discriminate between a square and a triangle, these individuals had to undertake the painstaking procedure of seeking out and counting the corners of the figure before the forms could be distinguished from each other.

These newly sighted observers were able to detect the presence or absence of an object in the visual field, but this was the extent of their abilities. For example, one patient was shown a watch and was asked whether it was round or square. When he seemed unable to answer, he was asked whether or not he knew the shape of a square or a circle. He was able to position his hands to form both a square and a circular shape, but he could not visually identify the shape of the watch. When the watch was placed in his hands, he immediately recognized it as being round. It appears that his sense of touch, although not more sensitive than that of a sighted person, had come through long experience to be a more reliable source of information about the world than his untrained sense of vision (see D. H. Warren, 1984).

There is an interesting naturally occurring analogy to selective rearing in which cats see only contours in a single orientation. This analogy arises from a common visual problem known as **astigmatism.** Astigmatism usually occurs if the cornea of the eye is not perfectly spherical, perhaps being flatter in some places and more curved in others. This deviation from perfect sphericity brings contours of some orientations into sharper focus than those in other orientations. Thus, with a vertical astigmatism, horizontal lines will be clear and vertical lines will be blurry, and so forth. The fact that this condition can mimic selective-rearing effects was shown by Freeman and Pettigrew (1973), who reared cats wearing cylindrical lenses that artificially created an astigmatism. They were able to show that such selective rearing can also alter the distribution of preferred orientations of visual cortical neurons, causing a reduction of the number of cells preferring the blurred orientation. Severe astigmatism at an early age in humans results in a permanent loss of visual acuity in the direction of the astigmatism. This is an acuity loss due to neural changes, because it remains even after correcting for any optical errors, and is probably the result of selective restriction of exposure to contours in the astigmatic direction (Mitchell, 1980).

A variation of this same selective-rearing effect is caused by living in an urbanized environment. The nature of our carpentered cities means that we have frequent exposure to vertical lines (defining walls, corners, furniture legs, and so forth) and to horizontal lines (defining floors, ceilings, table edges, and so forth). Proportionally we have much less exposure to oblique lines. Therefore, as inhabitants of such a selectively stimulating environment, it might be expected that we would show reduced acuity for diagonal lines relative to horizontal and vertical lines. In fact, the human visual system is *anisotropic*, meaning that it often reacts differently to stimuli depending on their orientation. In general, the normal visual system shows a slight, but well-defined, preference for horizontal or vertical stimuli over diagonal stimuli. This is demonstrated in a number of acuity-related tasks, where resolution acuity and vernier acuity seem to be poorer for stimuli oriented diagonally (Bowker & Mandler, 1981; Corwin, Moskowitz-Cook, & Green, 1977; Jenkins, 1985; Vogels & Orban, 1986). This phenomenon, known as the **oblique effect,** can be demonstrated using Demonstration Box 17-1.

Some investigators feel that at least part of the oblique effect is caused by genetic factors (Leehey, Moskowitz-Cook, Brill, & Held, 1975; Timney & Muir, 1976), but Annis and Frost (1973) provided some interesting data that are compatible with selective environmental effects. They compared the variations in acuity as a function of the orientation of lines in a group of students from Queens University in Kingston, Ontario, with that observed in a group of Cree Indians from James Bay, Quebec. The students had all grown up in typical nonnative North American buildings. The Cree Indians, however, were among the last to be raised in traditional housing, consisting of a cook tent (or *meechwop*) in summer and a winter lodge (or *matoocan*) during the rest of the year. Both the insides and outsides of these structures consist of a rich array of contours, with no obvious preponderance of verticals and horizontals. In

---

DEMONSTRATION BOX 17-1   The Oblique Effect

To demonstrate that visual acuity is better for horizontal or vertical stimuli than for obliquely oriented stimuli, prop this book up on a table so you can see the three stimulus patterns. Now slowly walk backward from the book until you can no longer resolve clearly the oblique lines in the center circle.

It will appear uniform gray at this point, as your resolution acuity fails. Notice, however, that at this distance you still can see that the left circle contains vertical lines, and the right contains horizontal lines, thus indicating your greater visual acuity for these orientations.

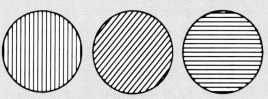

addition, the natural environment of the Cree shows no excesses of verticals and horizontals, in contrast to the urbanized environment of the students. In line with the selective exposure hypothesis, the students showed the expected reduction in acuity for obliquely oriented contours, whereas the Cree, without this selective exposure, did not.

Although we have emphasized the visual modality in our discussions thus far, it is important to recognize that selective and restricted rearing in other senses also has measurable effects in humans and animals. In hearing, for example, it has been found that individuals who are deaf in one ear, or who are congenitally deaf, tend to have different brain organizations from those of normal-hearing subjects (Neville, 1985; Neville, Schmidt, & Kutas, 1983). Parts of the brain normally reserved for auditory processing now appear to be available for visual functions.

SENSORY-MOTOR LEARNING

One variable that seems to be essential for the development of normal visual functioning involves not only the eyes but also the entire body. It seems that normal perceptual development depends on active bodily movement under visual guidance. Holst and Mittelsteadt (1950) proposed a distinction between stimulus input that simply acts on a passive observer, which they called **exafference,** and stimulation that changes as a result of an individual's own movements, called **reafference.**

Reafference has been suggested as being necessary for the development of accurate visually guided spatial behavior (Hein, 1980). An experiment by Hein and Held (1963) elegantly demonstrates this notion. They reared kittens in the dark until they were 8 to 12 weeks old. From that age on, the kittens received 3 hours of patterned visual exposure in a "carousel" ap-

paratus, shown in Figure 17-5. As you can see from the figure, one of the animals is active and can walk around freely. The other animal is passive and is carried around in a gondola that moves in exactly the same direction and at exactly the same speed as the movements of the active animal. Thus, the moving animal experiences changing visual stimuli as a result of its own movements (reafference); the passive animal experiences the same stimulation, but it is not the result of self-generated movements (exafference).

The animals were later tested on a series of behaviors involving depth perception. These included dodging or blinking when presented with a rapidly approaching object and the avoidance of the deep side of the visual cliff (see Chapter 10). They were also tested for the visual placing response, a paw extension (as if to avoid collision) when the animal is moved quickly toward a surface. In all three measures, the active animals performed like normal kittens, and the passive animals showed little evidence of depth perception.

An interesting extension of this work, which shows the specificity of experiential effects, was done by Hein, Held, and Gower (1970). They repeated the carousel experiment; however, each animal received both active and passive exposure. One eye was used when the visual exposure was active, and the other eye was used when the visual exposure was passive. They reported that when the kittens were tested on the actively exposed eye, they seemed to have normal depth perception, whereas when tested on the passively exposed eye, they acted as if they did not.

How much of the development of our visually guided behavior requires practice and exposure? Consider the simple tasks of reaching out and picking up an object with one hand. This involves not only the accurate assessment of the distance and the size of the object but also the ability to guide your limb on the basis of the perceptual information. Held and Hein

Figure 17-5 *Kitten carousel for active or passive exposure to visual stimulation (from "Movement-Produced Stimulation in the Development of Visually Guided Behavior" by R. Held and A. Hein, 1963,* Journal of Comparative and Physiological Psychology, 56. *Copyright © 1963 by the American Psychological Association. Reprinted by permission).*

(1967) reared kittens in the dark until they were 4 weeks old. After this period, they were allowed 6 hours of free movement each day in a lighted and patterned environment. However, during the time when the cats received their exposure to patterned stimuli, they wore lightweight opaque collars that prevented them from seeing their bodies or paws while they moved about (see Figure 17-6). The remainder of the time, the kittens were placed in a dark room. After 12 days of such exposure, these animals showed normal depth perception, but their ability to place their paws accurately by visually directing them toward targets was quite poor. Nonetheless, after 18 hours of free movement in a lighted environment, with their paws visible, all directional confusions seemed to have disappeared.

Hein and Diamond (1971) conducted a similar experiment in which each of the cat's

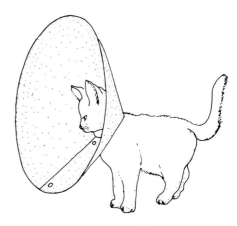

Figure 17-6 *Kitten in collar that prevents view of paws (from "Dissociation of the Visual Placing Response into Elicited and Guided Components" by A. Hein and R. Held, 1967,* Science, 158, *pp. 390–392. Copyright 1967 by the American Association for the Advancement of Science).*

front paws was placed in a separate cone instead of using a collar. One cone was opaque, and the other one was transparent so the animal could see its limb. When tested using the limb they could see, cats accurately placed their paws, but the unseen limb could not be accurately directed toward the targets. In another experiment, Held and Bauer (1967) reared a monkey for 34 days without sight of its limbs. When the animal was first able to see its arm, it acted startled and spent much time looking at its hand. The animal's behavior was awkward and inaccurate at first but improved rapidly with practice. When the other hand (which had not been previously exposed) was tested, it also showed inaccurate reaching until some experience had been gained.

Certain reports of behaviors in human infants seem similar to the responses of the deprived monkey. White (1971) reports that after the first month of life (during which infants are alert about 5% of the time), infants spend many hours watching their hands. Their reaching is quite inaccurate at first but improves steadily. Actually, practice can speed up this process of perceptual development. If conditions are arranged so many objects are available to reach for and to play with, infants develop accurate reaching behavior several weeks earlier than children who have not received this type of enriched experience. Experience with the sight of actively moving parts of the body seems to be a necessary condition for the successful development of visually guided behavior (Hein, 1980).

Perceptual Rearrangement

In 1896 George Stratton reasoned that if some aspects of the perception of space and direction were learned, then it ought to be possible to learn a new set of spatial percepts. To test this, Stratton used a technique that altered spatial relations in the visual world (Stratton,

1897a, 1897b). His technique involved wearing a set of goggles that optically rotated the field of view by 180 deg, so everything appeared to be upside down. Such a procedure is called optical **rearrangement** (Welch, 1978).

More recently, Kohler (1962, 1964) elaborated on this procedure. Kohler's observers often wore optically distorting devices for several weeks. Observers reported that at first the world seemed very unstable, with the visual field appearing to swing as the head was turned. During this stage of the experiment, observers often had difficulty walking and needed help to perform very simple tasks. However, after about 3 days one observer was able to ride a bicycle, and after only a few weeks he was able to ski. The observers reported that they sporadically experienced the world as being upright. If they observed common events that had definite directional components, such as smoke rising from a cigarette or water pouring from a pitcher, they reported that the world appeared to be upright. This suggests that their ability to adapt to the optically rearranged visual input was facilitated by the notion of gravitational direction, along with interaction with familiar events and objects. Kohler suggested that a real perceptual change had taken place, because when the inverting lenses were removed, observers experienced a sense of discomfort. The world suddenly appeared to be inverted again, and they had difficulty moving about. However, the readaptation to the normal upright world was accomplished within a period of about 1 hour. Demonstration Box 17-2 shows how you can experience this inverted visual stimulation.

Most rearrangement studies involve a less dramatic change of optical input. A common technique is to use a wedge prism, which is a wedge-shaped piece of glass that bends, or refracts, light. The locations of objects viewed through the prism seem to be shifted in the direction of the apex (the pointed edge of the wedge). If an observer viewed the world

DEMONSTRATION BOX 17-2   Optical Inversion

You can experience some of the effects associated with inverted optical stimulation by holding a mirror as shown in the accompanying figure. Walk around and view the world by looking up at the mirror. Notice that the world seems inverted, and also notice how the world swings as you turn. Now pour some water from a glass. Does the water pour up or down? Are you sure?

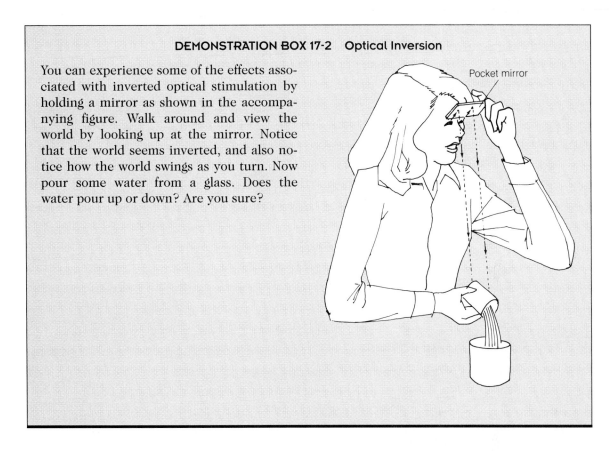

Pocket mirror

through goggles containing such prisms and reached for an object, she would find herself missing it. After only a few minutes of practice, however, the observer's reaching would become quite accurate. We would say that she has adapted to the prismatic distortion; in other words, she has compensated for the optical distortion. If the observer is consciously correcting for the distortion (for instance, saying to herself, "I must reach 10 degrees to the right of where the object appears"), when the goggles are removed she will, of course, know that the distortion is no longer present. Being rational, she should then drop this conscious correction and reach for seen stimuli with her usual accuracy. However, suppose some perceptual change has occurred. In this case we would expect that when the distorting prism is

removed, the visual world would appear to be shifted several degrees to one side. When reaching for an object, the observer should err in the direction opposite to that of the initial distortion. This is what actually does occur. These errors are called **aftereffects.** The occurrence of aftereffects in prism adaptation is evidence that some perceptual rearrangement has occurred (Harris, 1980). This process is outlined in Figure 17-7.

Several investigators have attempted to specify what conditions are necessary for adaptation to rearranged stimulation (Welch, 1978). Held and Hein (1958) argued that adaptation depends on active movements, as does the development of visually guided behavior discussed earlier. They tested this notion by having an observer view his hand through a prism under

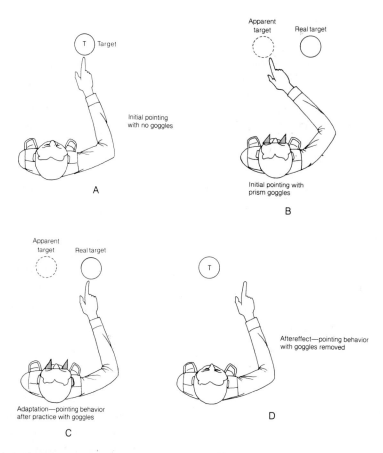

Figure 17-7   *Prism adaptation and aftereffect.*

one of three conditions. One was a no-movement condition, in which the observer viewed only his stationary hand. The second was a passive-movement condition, in which the observer's arm was swung back and forth by the experimenter. The third was an active-movement condition, in which the observer saw his hand through the prism while he actively moved it from side to side. There was considerable adaptation to the distortion produced by the prism under the active-movement condition, whereas in the other conditions there was not. These results have been verified several times (Pick & Hay, 1965).

Another series of experiments used conditions similar to the kitten carousel discussed earlier. Observers wearing displacing prism goggles either walked around for about 1 hour (active exposure) or were wheeled around in a wheelchair over the same path for about 1 hour (passive exposure). They were then measured to see if any perceptual change had taken place. Adaptation to the prismatic distortion occurred in the active condition but not during the passive exposure condition (Held & Bossom, 1961; Mikaelian & Held, 1964).

One important aspect of active movement under optically distorted conditions seems to be that it provides observers with error feedback that informs them of the direction and the extent of the distortion. This information provides a basis for learning a new correlation between the incoming stimuli and the conscious percept. The more information we give observers about the nature of their errors, the greater is the adaptation to the distortion (Coren, 1966; Welch, 1969, 1971), and the timing and amount of information from feedback is an important factor in adaptation (Redding & Wallace, 1990).

Some investigators suggest that error information in the absence of active movement is sufficient to produce prism adaptation. Howard, Craske, and Templeton (1965) had observers watch a rotating rod through an optical system that displaced it to the side. For some observers the rod appeared to be displaced to the side, and they merely watched it rotate. For another group the rod appeared displaced to the same degree; however, as the rod swung about it brushed each observer across the lips, indicating that it was directly in front of the observer rather than off to the side as it appeared. Although both groups were passive, the groups receiving the information that their percept was erroneous (being touched by a stimulus that looked like it would pass them by) showed perceptual adaptation, whereas the other group did not.

Another study involved a more subtle manipulation. O'Leary and McMahon (1991) used cylindrical lenses, which make stimuli appear too wide or too tall. When observers view photographs of faces distorted in this way, even though the observers are not engaged in movement, they still show some adaptation to the distortion. When they view line drawings of simple figures (for example, circles or squares), no adaptation occurs. Presumably, their familiarity with the normal dimensions of faces provides the cue that a distortion is present and triggers the perceptual recalibration. Thus, information indicating how our percepts are in error may be sufficient to produce adaptation (Howard, Anstis, & Lucia, 1974).

What actually changes during the adaptation process? This issue is still being debated. Some researchers believe that adaptation simply alters the felt position of various parts of the body. This is based on the observation that after prism adaptation, when observers are asked to point to a straight-ahead position (by feel alone), they tend to point off to the side. This indicates some proprioceptive or "felt" component in the aftereffect (Harris, 1980). Other data indicate that this may be only part of the process (Mikaelian, 1974; Redding & Wallace, 1976). For example, animals can still adapt to visual displacement when the nerves that provide information about the position of the arm are severed (Bossom & Ommaya, 1968; Taub & Berman, 1968). The consensus is that a change is taking place in both proprioceptive and visual perception, which is the result of recalibration of the higher brain centers used to interpret perceptual input (Howard, 1982; Welch, 1978).

Some direct evidence for this perceptual recalibration comes from an interesting experiment by Foley (1970, 1974). She placed wedge prisms in front of the eyes of observers so the direction of displacement was different for each eye. Either one eye saw an upward displacement and the other a downward displacement, or one eye saw a displacement to the right and the other to the left. After several hours of exposure, the two eyes were tested separately. The results indicated that each eye had adapted to its own particular distortion. This implies a perceptual recalibration. It seems likely that adaptation to optically rearranged stimuli involves a form of perceptual learning that alters the appearance of visual space, which, like many other forms of learning, is sensitive to what the observer is paying attention to (Redding, Clark, & Wallace, 1985).

However, whether learning to deal with re-arranged spatial stimuli involves the same mechanisms that may have gone into the original development of our perception of space is not clear.

Illusion Decrement

Another form of perceptual learning is similar to rearrangement in that it involves learning to compensate for a perceptual error. It differs from the situations we have been discussing in that the error is not optical in nature, and the observer usually is not conscious either of the erroneous perception or of any perceptual change. The situation involves visual geometric illusions, which are simple line drawings that evoke percepts differing in size or shape from those expected on the basis of physical measurements of the stimuli. We have encountered several of these already in Chapters 1, 11, 14, and 16, including the Mueller-Lyer illusion (Figure 17-8), in which the horizontal line with the outward-turned wings appears longer than the line with the inward-turned wings, despite the fact that they are physically equal in length. Suppose we present the Mueller-Lyer figure to an observer and measure the individual's susceptibility to the line-length distortion. Next we instruct the observer to begin moving the eyes across the figure, scanning from one end of the horizontal line to the other on both portions of the figure. We ask the observer to be as accurate as possible with the eye movements. At 1-minute intervals we stop the scanning process and take measurements of illusion magnitude until a total of 5 minutes of viewing time has elapsed. This simple process of inspection leads to a 40% reduction in the original illusion magnitude (Coren & Porac, 1984). This decrease, known as **illusion decrement,** has been demonstrated many times and for many different types of illusions, not just

A

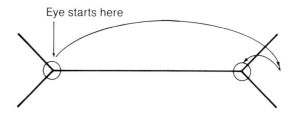

B

Eye starts here

Eye starts here

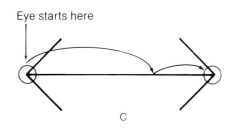

C

Figure 17-8 *The overestimated* (A) *and underestimated* (B) *portions of the Mueller-Lyer illusion, and* (C) *typical eye movements obtained when viewing them.*

the Mueller-Lyer figure (for example, Beckett, 1989; Coren & Girgus, 1978; Porac & Coren, 1985; Predebon, 1990).

What is happening in this situation? Some researchers have suggested that continuously inspecting the illusion figure fatigues or adapts some of the neural units that register or distort the pattern, and thus the illusion is weakened (Long, 1988; Porac, 1989). Although this may contribute to the process, it cannot be a full explanation, since inspection of fields of lines that have been designed to fatigue the same neural units does not result in a reduction of the illusion when the figure is viewed afterward (Coren, Girgus, & Schiano, 1986). If neural fatigue is not the answer, then it seems likely that we are looking at a form of perceptual learning (Coren & Girgus, 1978; Long, 1988).

Perceptual learning requires some information processing that will later affect how a stimulus is perceived. In this situation observers must somehow learn that an illusion is present so they can begin to correct their perception and eliminate the illusory distortion. Observers get this information not via rulers or measuring tapes, but rather through information from their eye movements (see Coren, 1986). If we measure the actual pattern of eye movements an observer makes over an illusion figure, we find that the eyes are directed to move as if the distorted percept were actually correct. In other words, if the eyes were resting on the end of the line in the perceptually elongated portion of the Mueller-Lyer figure (Figure 17-8A), an attempt to look at the far end of the line would produce an eye movement that is too long. This eye-movement error is in agreement with the percept, which tends to overestimate the length of the line. A corrective adjustment in the eye movement must be made if the fovea is to come to rest on the exact end of the line. The opposite happens for the underestimated portion of the Mueller-Lyer figure (Figure 17-8B). Here the eye movements are too short (again in agreement with the perceptual underestimation of the line length), and a corrective adjustment must be made. The eye-movement patterns over the two portions of the figure are shown in *C*.

In Chapters 15 and 16 we saw instances where patterns of eye movements could be used to tell us something about the information-processing abilities of an observer. The same reasoning can be applied to the study of eye-movement patterns across illusion configurations. As the observer views the illusory array, eye movements and eye-movement errors provide information about the existence (as well as the direction and the strength) of the illusory distortion. This error information can be used by the observer to correct the percept. This point of view is supported by the fact that an illusion decrement does not occur unless the observer is allowed to scan the figure (Coren, Girgus, & Schiano, 1986; Coren & Hoenig, 1972; Festinger, White, & Allyn, 1968).

The phenomenon of illusion decrement implies that perceptual learning is taking place. The information obtained from the eye movements is being used to reduce a perceptual error, and the direction of this change (from greater to lesser illusion susceptibility) mimics that associated with perceptual rearrangement studies. The most interesting aspect of this form of perceptual adjustment, however, is the fact that nothing about it appears to be available to consciousness. Unless observers are provided with a ruler or a direct explanation, they do not consciously know that the original perception is in error, nor do they know that illusory error has been reduced as a result of their active interactions with the illusion figure. The percept simply becomes more accurate with no change in the observers' own awareness.

CONTEXT AND MEANING

Basically, all percepts are ambiguous. Consider a target that casts a square image on the retinal surface. The object the image represents could

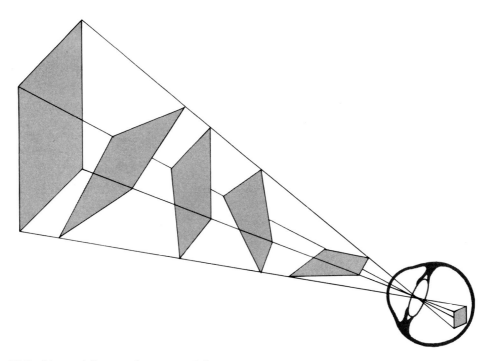

Figure 17-9 Many different objects at different distances and slants, all of which cast the same square retinal image (from Coren & Girgus, 1978).

actually be one of an infinite number of different shapes at any distance or inclination relative to the observer, as is shown in Figure 17-9. Since any retinal image can be caused by a variety of different physical targets in the world, it is surprising that our normal perceptual experiences are generally so unambiguous. Actually, what we perceive is the result of a decision-making process in which we "deduce," on the basis of all available information, what the stimulus object is. This **transactional viewpoint** maintains that any current perceptual experience consists of a complex evaluation of the significance of stimuli reaching our receptors. Through our life experience we learn that certain objects or conditions have a high probability of being related to each other. On this basis we derive our "best bet" as to what we are viewing. In a sense, the world we

experience is more the *result* of perceptual processing than the *cause* of the perception (Coren, 1983; Ittelson, 1962). The transactional approach implies that if our expectations change, or our analysis of the situation changes, then our perceptual experience will also change (Ames, 1951; Brunswick, 1955). A simple example of the effect of context and expectations can be seen in Demonstration Box 17-3.

Many of our percepts are constructed from incomplete stimuli. Look at Figure 17-10A. It is clear that this represents a dog, yet it should also be clear that no dog is actually present. The figure is completely constructed in the mind's eye of the observer. The elephant in Figure 17-10B will probably be somewhat more difficult to identify. The less familiar the object, the more difficult is the identification. Further-

DEMONSTRATION BOX 17-3 A Context Effect on Perception

Read the accompanying handwritten message. You probably read it as, "My phone number is area code 604, 876-1569. Please call!" If you did, you were being affected by several contextual influences on perception. Go back to the message and look carefully at the script. You will see that the two pairs of characters you read as the word *is* and the numbers *15* are identical. In addition, the *h* in the word *phone* and the *b* in the word *number* are identical, as are the *d* in the word *code* and the *l* in the word *please*. You saw each letter or number within a context, when you first read the message, and this context determined how you interpreted the script character.

My phone number 15 area code 604, 876-1569. Please call!

more, you must begin with the initial hypothesis that some object is there in the first place, or you may never see any pattern at all (Reynolds, 1985). However, once you have seen (or "constructed") the figure, the meaningful organization will be apparent immediately when you look at it again. Our ability to perceive such stimuli as objects depends on our prior experience. This was shown by Steinfield (1967), who found that when observers

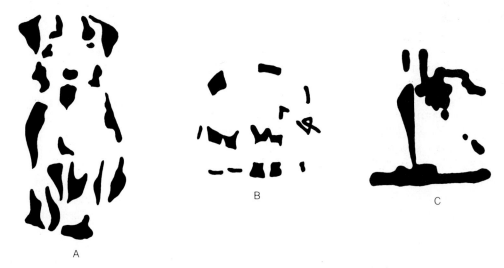

A B C

Figure 17-10 *Some degraded stimuli that may be seen as objects (based on Street, 1931).*

were told a story about an ocean cruise, they identified Figure 17-10C as a steamship in less than 5 seconds. Observers who were told an irrelevant story took six times longer to identify the figure.

In Chapter 14 we talked about the difference between stimuli that are *registered* and those that are *apprehended.* Apprehended stimuli are present in our conscious experience whereas registered stimuli may only be strong enough to trigger some form of perceptual processing, without actually being strong enough to make us consciously aware of their presence. This means that some of the experiences that affect perception may take place without any conscious awareness. For instance, earlier in the chapter we spoke of an experiment in which researchers presented a word for so brief a time period that it could not be identified. They found that if the word was presented several times, even though the length of time of each presentation was not increased, the word was eventually identified (Haber & Hershenson, 1965; Uhlarik & Johnson, 1978). If the word was not identified on the first presentation, why should an observer be able to identify it after repeated exposures? It may be that very fast presentations of stimuli do not give the brain sufficient time to do the necessary computations required for recognition but still allow some low-level subjective awareness of the stimulus (Cheesman & Merikle, 1986; Dodwell, 1971). The partially processed stimulus is held in memory, and as the information extraction continues, hypotheses are formed and checked until the stimulus appears to make sense. At this point, the conscious identification response may take place (Doherty & Keeley, 1972). Even when the stimulus is still not fully identified, sufficient information may be present to "prime" (make easier) the recognition of other stimuli that are related to it or that fall in the same general class, because relevant perceptual hypotheses are now already

activated and set up a context for new incoming stimuli (Bernstein, Bissonnette, Vyas, & Barclay, 1989; Dark, 1988).

These same perceptual hypotheses, which allow us eventually to formulate a percept from minimal or degraded input, can also modify our perception so it no longer accurately represents the stimulus. For example, Ross and Schilder (1934) presented observers with a series of briefly flashed line drawings. Some of the drawings were incomplete or distorted, such as three-armed people and faces with a mouth missing. A look at some of the observers' comments is informative. When presented with the side view of a dog with the left hind leg missing, the subject reported: "It's a dog, a wolf, two ears stand upright, a round mouth, a long tail." The experimenter then instructed the observer: "Look at his legs." Observer: "He has five toes on each leg." Experimenter: "Look at the hind legs." Observer: "I saw two; the tail goes up." Despite continued urging from the experimenter, the observer continued to correct the percept, filling in the missing leg on the hypothesis that dogs have four legs.

These researchers also used a drawing of a woman's head facing forward. She had the usual two eyes as well as a large third eye on her forehead. One observer described the picture as "a woman with long hair, black, two eyes, one nose, one mouth, two ears." The stimulus was presented again briefly, and the observer was asked if the forehead was in order, to which he replied, "Yes." After several other stimuli were presented again, the observer now reported: "The same woman I saw before. She is funny—big eyes, a big nose, and a big mouth." Experimenter: "Look at the forehead." Observer: "She has a small curl in the middle."

Even with more brief presentations, this observer still insisted that all that appeared on the forehead was a curl of hair. Third eyes do

---

DEMONSTRATION BOX 17-4   An Expectancy Effect on Perception

Turn to Color Plate 9 and *quickly* count the number of aces of spades you see. Then return to this demonstration box. Although you probably only saw two aces of spades, three are actually there. One of the aces of spades is printed in red ink, rather than black. Since you "expect" spades to be black, your identification process for incongruent or unexpected stimuli is impaired.

---

not occur normally, so we apparently correct our percept on the basis of our expectations—we see extra hair, not extra eyes. You may see how expectations alter our perception in Demonstration Box 17-4.

Language as well as expectations may modify percepts. This view was advanced by Whorf (1956) and Sapir (1939), who suggested that specific language labels for certain types of stimuli increase the accuracy of perceptual recognition. They maintained, for example, that the Eskimo, whose language has a wide variety of different names for different kinds of snow, may be able to make better discriminations among types of snow than those of us who speak English and have only the single label *snow*.

An example of how language can affect perception is seen in a classic experiment conducted by Gottschaldt (1926, 1929), who gave observers from 3 to 520 presentations of a simple target. He then asked them to find this target in a more complex figure. Such a target is shown in Figure 17-11, where Figure A is embedded in Figure B. He reported that prolonged experience with the simple figure did not make it any easier to find when it was hidden in the more complex stimulus. Djang (1937) repeated this experiment. However, her observers did not just look at the simple stimulus; they were required to draw it. She reported that when such active practice was combined with exposure, there was an improvement in later identification of the simple component embedded in the more complex figure. Schwartz (1961) then added a language component. He had observers learn distinctive verbal labels to attach to each of the simple figures. This modification of the

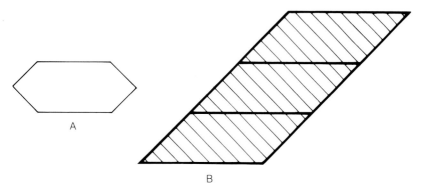

Figure 17-11   *Figure* A *may be found embedded in Figure* B.

experiment resulted in an improved ability to find and identify the named stimuli.

Verbal labeling, though, can either help or hinder identification. Ellis and Muller (1964) trained subjects using either a narrow labeling system (one label for each shape) or a wide labeling system (one label for four shapes). In later tests of identification for these forms, the group using the narrow labeling approach performed better than the group that simply observed the shapes without labeling; the group that used the wide labeling system had the fewest correct identifications. Thus the wide labeling seemed to emphasize the learning of similarities between the stimuli, which later resulted in poorer discrimination and identification.

Eyewitness Testimony

Language and expectation can also modify our reports of what we have seen. Carmichael, Hogan, and Walter (1932) presented observers with simple line drawings and associated each with a label. Observers were then asked to reproduce these drawings. In general, their reproductions were biased in the direction of the verbal label. When presented with Figure 17-12A and told that it was a broom, observers tended to reproduce patterns similar to B. When told that it was a rifle, observers tended to reproduce patterns similar to that in C. In this experiment the reproductions occurred only a few moments after the stimulus

was taken away. Such distortions in our recollections of what we have seen may have important consequences for many behaviors. Our memory of scientific data presented in a graph or our ability to reproduce contours drawn on a map may be distorted by the context provided from someone's verbal description of it (Tversky & Shiano, 1989). It also may explain why eyewitness reports of events that occurred during a crime tend to be remarkably unreliable, even when obtained immediately after the event. Observers have a tendency to include details that they could not have seen. Such details are often provided on the basis of the observer's expectations or biases (Buckhout, 1976; Wells & Loftus, 1984; Yarmey, 1979).

Information received after a stimulus is seen can distort the way it is encoded (see, for example, Loftus & Donders, 1989). For instance in one experiment Loftus (1974) showed observers a brief videotape of an automobile accident and then asked them some questions about what they had just observed. For one group of observers one of the questions was, "How fast was the white sports car going while traveling along the country road?" For the other group the question was, "How fast was the white sports car going when it passed the barn while traveling along the country road?" In fact, there was no barn present. Yet when the observers were questioned about the incident a week later, more than 17% of the group exposed to the false suggestion about a barn answered the question, "Did you see a barn?" by saying "Yes," as opposed to only 3% of the group that did not get such a suggestion.

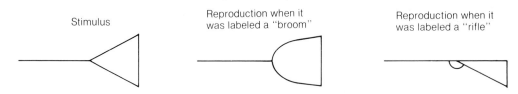

Figure 17-12 *The effects of labels on later perceptual recall.*

There are limitations to how much perception (or a remembered perception) can be affected by later inputs (see McCloskey & Egeth, 1983; Zaragoza & McCloskey, 1989). For instance, some data suggest that when we have clearly perceived something, the perceptual memory resists any later change. It seems that the suggestions from later (possibly false) context provided after the actual perceptual event acts only to fill in gaps in the perception (Loftus, 1979; Yuille, 1984). This is much like the experiment discussed earlier, in which the observer's expectation that dogs have four legs caused the missing leg to be added perceptually. Structuring the questioning to fit the actual sequence of events may help to prevent such eyewitness errors, perhaps by restoring the original context that was present during the actual viewing of the event (Geiselman, Fisher, MacKinnon, & Holland, 1986; Morris & Morris, 1985).

ENVIRONMENTAL AND LIFE HISTORY DIFFERENCES

We have seen earlier what effect the availability, or nonavailability, of particular environmental stimuli can have on the development of sensory systems, and hence on the observer's later perceptual abilities. Certain aspects of our environment and culture may also teach us different perceptual strategies and may alter the internal set of expectations and analyses we bring to each new perceptual situation. Thus, if we live in the desert or on the pampas or the plains, we are exposed to broad vistas of open space that are never experienced by a forest dweller. If we live in a technologically advanced country, we are exposed to sets of visual stimuli (such as photographs and television) that are usually not available to someone dwelling in the African bush or the Australian outback. Such differences, especially when experienced over an entire lifetime, may have dramatic consequences for perceptual processes.

Picture Perception

In our civilized, urbanized, and media-intensive culture, we are inundated with images. Not just the images of our immediate environment, but images representing environments or objects that are not present. Some of these latter images are in the form of patterns of color, or black and white, shown on televisions and in cinemas. We also encounter photographs in magazines and newspapers, where we might "see" a baby elephant peaceably grazing a few feet in front of its gigantic mother, all in a 5-cm-square smudge of black ink on a perfectly flat surface. If you have some artistic talent, you may be able to represent such a scene with a few strokes of a pen on a sheet of paper and thus be able to let your friends "see for themselves" what you have seen. This seems like a perfectly natural fact of life.

Pictures of the sort that we encounter daily are often viewed as simply "windows" through which we see other worlds (Haber, 1980). Certainly these images must follow all of the same optical laws as the real world. Certainly every observer must follow these laws to interpret such stimuli in the same way we do. Unfortunately, neither statement is completely "certain." Pictures do contain much information that mimics the optical patterns encountered in natural viewing (Gibson, 1979; Sedgwick, 1980), but many discrepancies exist between the pictured and the real image. For instance, the sizes of the images are usually too large or too small, which in turn ruins the geometric correspondence between the image and the actual scene (Lumsden, 1980). Furthermore, even if we could make the geometry of perspective perfect, it would only be correct for one single viewing angle, and viewing any pictured image from a vantage point other than the viewpoint adopted by the camera or artist who produced the picture ought to lead to distorted percepts (Kennedy & Ostry, 1976). However, such distortions do not appear (Rosinski & Farber, 1980). We could enlarge this list of discrepancies between the real scene and a picture of it. For instance, the picture is flat, whereas the real world is three dimensional; the picture is interpreted correctly even if its colors are all wrong, or even if there are no colors at all; and so forth. Such considerations have led some theorists to conclude that pictures may be statements in a sort of visual language that are created and interpreted according to the agreed-on set of conventions in any given culture. Thus, they are not simple representations of reality at all (Gombrich, 1972; Goodman, 1968). At the very least, they must be interpreted as hypotheses shared among individuals growing up with a common heritage (Gregory, 1971). By either of these two theories, however, the perception of pictures must be learned in some manner.

Before we investigate whether we must learn to interpret pictures, it is important for us to specify that we are really talking about two separate skills. The first is the ability to identify objects depicted in a picture, and the second is the ability to interpret the three-dimensional arrangement implied in the flat image.

Hochberg & Brooks (1962) conducted a heroic experiment, using one of their children as the subject. The child was reared to the age of 19 months carefully shielded from any sort of pictorial representation. This meant that the television was never used in the child's presence, nor were there magazines or picture books. Even the labels on cans and boxes of food were removed or covered. When the child was tested after this restricted rearing, he had no difficulty identifying pictures of common

items. This implies that we need not learn to interpret patterns or drawings as representations of real world objects.

The unlearned nature of picture identification seems to be supported by the fact that color photos are interpreted readily when shown to individuals who have lived in cultures where they have never experienced pictures (Hagen & Jones, 1978). However, when black-and-white photos or drawings are used, individuals reared in isolated cultures sometimes have difficulties that are strange to those who have been reared with the continuous company of graphic images. Deregowski (1980) has collected a number of such reports, including one from a Scottish missionary working in Malawi (a country in southwestern Africa between northern Rhodesia and Mozambique) nearly 75 years ago:

Take a picture in black and white, and the natives cannot see it. You may tell the natives: "This is a picture of an ox and a dog"; and the people will look at it and look at you, and that look says that they consider you a liar. Perhaps you say again, "Yes, this is a picture of an ox and a dog. Look at the horn of the ox, and there is his tail!" And the boy will say, "Oh, yes and there is the dog's nose and eyes and ears!" Then the old people will look again and clap their hands and say, "Oh yes, it is a dog."

Clearly, such a report indicates that the individuals involved did not respond to the photo with the immediate spontaneous object identification characteristic of our viewing of pictures. Still, when their attention was directed to the relevant aspects of the pattern they did have an "Aha!" experience, indicating that the ability to identify the pattern was there, although they lacked training to direct their attention appropriately.

Although humans may have a general ability to identify objects depicted in pictures, interpreting the implied spatial relationships seems to be more subject to cultural and educational influences. Identifying depth in a flat image requires a certain amount of selection among the perceptual cues available. For instance, the photograph might include such cues for depth as *linear perspective, interposition,* and *texture gradients,* among others mentioned in Chapter 10. However, other cues indicate that the picture is flat: no *binocular disparity* is present between items in the picture, and all the elements in the photo require the same degree of *accommodation* and *convergence* (see Chapter 10). Thus, to see a drawing or a photograph as representing an arrangement of objects in three dimensions, rather than as a flat surface with different shadings of dark and light, we must attend to some depth cues and ignore others (Pick, 1987). An observer's particular perceptual strategy may depend on the individual's life history and the relative frequency with which certain cues are encountered in the immediate environment.

Hudson (1960, 1962) attempted to identify cultural factors associated with the use of pictorial depth information. His technique consisted of using a series of pictures that depicted certain combinations of pictorial depth cues. Figure 17-13 shows one picture similar to those used by Hudson; as you can see, it depicts a hunting scene containing two pictorial depth cues. The first is **interposition,** in which objects closer to the observer block the view of portions of more distant objects. Since the hunter and the antelope are covering portions of the rocks, they appear closer to the observer than the rocks.

The second pictorial depth cue contained in this drawing is **familiar size.** We know the relative sizes of familiar objects; therefore, if an object is depicted as relatively small or large, we will judge its distance from us in a way consistent with our expectations based on its known size. For example, an elephant is a very large animal. However, in Figure 17-13 the elephant is one of the smaller items in the picture. If we are responding to the cue of familiar size, we would tend to see the elephant as being the most distant object in this hunting scene. When something as large as an elephant casts a

Figure 17-13 A figure used to test ability to respond to pictorial depth cues (based on Hudson, 1962).

smaller image than an antelope, the elephant must be farther away, since we know it is physically larger than the antelope.

Hudson used these stimuli because they are uniquely constructed to allow for both **two-dimensional** (no use of pictorial depth) and **three-dimensional** (full use of pictorial depth) types of responses. Suppose we asked an observer to describe this picture. First we would expect the individual to identify correctly all the component objects in the picture. However, suppose we also asked for a description of the actions taking place. A correct three-dimensional response would indicate that the hunter was attempting to spear the antelope (which is, of course, nearer to him than the elephant if pictorial depth is correctly perceived). A two-dimensional response would state that the hunter is attempting to spear the elephant, which is closer to the tip of the spear in the picture. Such a response would indicate that the observer had not responded to either the interposition or the familiar size cues that place the elephant at a greater pictorial distance from the hunter than the antelope.

Stimuli similar to these have been used in a number of studies conducted throughout Africa to test observers from a number of tribal and linguistic groups (Deregowski, 1980). The results indicate that the African observers have difficulty seeing pictorial depth within these pictures relative to Western observers, a fact that has been verified using other types of pictures (Jahoda & McGurk, 1974). Presumably this is due to the fact that they have been rela-

tively isolated from the sort of formal exposure and training with drawings that Western-style education and exposure to the mass media provide. The ability to perceive three-dimensionality in pictures is improved if more depth cues are added (Hagen & Jones, 1978; Killbride & Leibowitz, 1975), or if formal education, involving the use of picture books, drawings, and so forth, has been experienced (Killbride & Robbins, 1968; Leibowitz & Pick, 1972; Pick, 1987). You can explore your own tendencies to use certain depth cues but not others by trying Demonstration Box 17-5.

Culturally determined conventions associated with the interpretation of pictures can be shown best in situations where the flat, stationary picture is supposed to depict not only three-dimensionality but also motion. For instance, Figure 17-14 depicts three different forms of motion. From left to right, we see a speeding car, a boy rapidly whipping his head around, and a dog with a wagging tail. Of course, we see no actual motion, yet we "read" such motion into the picture. Within Western cultures, such interpretation of motion in pictorial arrays may appear as early as 4 years of age (Friedman & Stevenson, 1975). Non-Western cultures, without pictorial experience, however, virtually never "see" movement in such representations. The likelihood that movement will be seen in such an array increases with education, urbanization, and exposure to pictorial materials (Duncan, Gourlay, & Hudson, 1973; Friedman & Stevenson, 1980).

Figure 17-14 Scenes conventionally recognized as depicting motion by Western observers, but not necessarily by non-Western observers.

DEMONSTRATION BOX 17-5   Cross-Cultural Differences in Perception

The figure accompanying this box is sometimes called the "Devil's tuning fork." Look at the figure for about 30 seconds or so; then close the book and try to draw it from memory. Return to this box when you have done this.

Most of you probably found this task to be quite difficult. The source of your difficulty comes from the fact that your cultural experience with graphic representations has caused you to interpret this two-dimensional stimulus as a three-dimensional object. Unfortunately, such an interpretation leads to problems since the depth cues implied in this figure are ambiguous. It is interesting to note that Africans who have not received formal education have no difficulty reproducing the figure. Since they do not interpret the figure as three-dimensional, they merely see a pattern of flat lines, which is easy to reproduce.

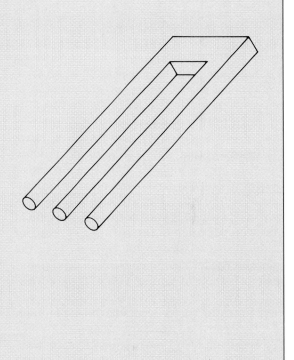

Illusion and Constancy

Certain facets of the environment make us more or less responsive to certain patterns of depth cues appearing in pictures. For instance, the **carpentered world hypothesis** begins with the observation that in the urbanized Western world, rooms and buildings are usually rectangular, many objects in the environment have right-angled corners, city streets have straight sides, and so forth. (See also the earlier discussion of the oblique effect.) Surrounded by such an environment, we may learn to depend more heavily on depth cues based on linear perspective than would people who live in less "carpentered" and more rural environments (Coren & Girgus, 1978; Gregory, 1966; Segall, Campbell, & Herskovits, 1966). For example, rural, isolated Zulus have been described as surrounded by a circular culture. They live in round huts with round doors. They do not plough their land in straight lines but tend to use curved furrows. Individuals living in such a world would not be expected to rely on linear perspective as heavily as those of us living in a more linear environment.

In a classic study, Segall, Campbell, and Herskovits (1966) compared the responsiveness of individuals in carpentered versus non-carpentered environments to certain types of depth cues. However, instead of using pictures as stimulus materials, they chose a more subtle class of patterns, namely the visual-geometric illusions. Some of these configurations have already been discussed in Chapter 14, where we pointed out how susceptibility to size distortions in some figures, such as the Mueller-Lyer illusion, may be dependent on a three-dimensional interpretation of the pattern (to refresh your memory, refer to Figure 14-6). As we discussed then, the apparently longer portion of the Mueller-Lyer figure may be interpreted as a corner of a room receding in depth because the wings of the illusion act as linear perspective cues. The inappropriate application of size constancy based on this interpretation of the wings as perspective cues results in our overestimation of the size of this segment of the figure relative to the segment with the inward-turned wings. Since pictorial depth information is thought to play a role in the formation of these illusory percepts, these types of configurations are well-suited to an exploration of the carpentered world hypothesis.

Segall et al. (1966) gathered data from throughout Africa and also from several groups of people living in Evanston, Illinois. Although variations occurred within the noncarpentered samples, the average Mueller-Lyer illusion was greater for the more urban groups. Similar re-sults have been reported for other perspective-related illusions (Coren & Girgus, 1978; Deregowski, 1980; Killbride & Leibowitz, 1975).

Although the observed differences in illusion susceptibility for different cultural groups may be partially caused by factors other than experience with a carpentered world (Berry, 1971; Coren & Porac, 1978; Pollack & Silvar, 1967), ample evidence has shown that the absence of experience with certain types of depth cues impairs other perceptual functions (such as size constancy) dependent on depth perception. One of the most striking examples of this

was provided by the anthropologist Turnbull (1961). He observed the behavior of the Bambuti Pygmies, who live in the Ituri Forest in the Congo. Since they live in the dense rain forest, their vision is generally limited to short distances with vistas that only extend for, at most, 30 m. Therefore they seem to lack the visual experience needed to learn to use the depth cues responsible for the maintenance of size constancy at greater viewing distances. Turnbull noted one instance when he had taken his Bambuti guide, Kenge, out of the forest for the first time in his life. They were crossing over a broad plain and happened to spot a herd of buffalo:

Kenge looked over the plains and down to where a herd of about a hundred buffalo was grazing some miles away. He asked me what kind of insects they were, and I told him they were buffalo, twice as big as the forest buffalo known to him. He laughed loudly and told me not to tell such stupid stories. . . . We got into the car and drove down to where the animals were grazing. He watched them getting larger and larger, and though he was as courageous as any Pygmy, he moved over and sat close to me and muttered that it was witchcraft. . . . Finally, when he realized that they were real buffalo he was no longer afraid, but what puzzled him still was why they had been so small, and whether they really had been small and suddenly grown larger, or whether it had been some kind of trickery. (From "Some Observations Regarding the Experiences and Behavior of the Bambuti Pygmies" by C. Turnbull, 1961, American Journal of Psychology, 74. Copyright 1961 by the University of Illinois Press.)

Turnbull's description of Kenge's perceptual impressions suggests that our experience with particular stimuli prevalent in our immediate environment can result in differences in how we perceive new stimuli and situations. It seems that we learn to utilize stimulus information we encounter frequently but fail to learn to utilize stimulus information that is rare. This holds for the auditory as well as the visual environment.

Speech

The most dominant feature in our auditory environment is the constant flow of language sounds. As discussed in Chapter 12, each language uses a small set of word-differentiating *phonemes*, which are the functionally characteristic sounds of that language. Since different languages use different subsets and combinations of these phonemes, experiments on people reared in different linguistic settings offer a unique opportunity to observe the effects of specific kinds of experience on perception (see Kuhl, 1987). Because some sounds may be treated as distinctively different in some languages and not in others—for instance, the sounds r as in "rope" and l as in "lope" are different phonemes in English but not in Japanese—we would expect a bias in the auditory experience of individuals brought up surrounded by one or the other of these two languages. Numerous studies have shown that adults who have grown up with exposure to only one language often have difficulty discriminating certain linguistic contrasts characteristic of other languages (Strange & Jenkins, 1978; Werker & Tees, 1984). This type of difficulty may persist even if the adult has learned the other language and appears to be fluent in it. For example, Goto (1971) recorded pairs of words that contrasted the r and l sounds (such

as "lead" versus "read," or "play" versus "pray"). Several native Japanese speakers, who were bilingual in Japanese and English, could produce these sounds so native English-speaking listeners could differentiate them without error. However, this seems to be a learned ability to *produce* rather than to perceive the phonemic difference, since, when asked to listen to recordings of pairs of words that contrasted these phonemes, the native Japanese speakers could not do so, even when listening to their own speech productions.

The mechanism responsible for our ability to discriminate some speech sounds but not others is still somewhat mysterious. Surprisingly, infants seem to be born with the ability to discriminate sound pairs not used in their native tongue and appear to lose this ability as adults (Trehub, 1976; Werker & Tees, 1984). A striking example was provided by Werker, Gilbert, Humphrey, and Tees (1981), who presented English-speaking and Hindi-speaking adults with pairs of sounds that are differentiated as different phonemes in Hindi but not in English. As we might expect, the adult Hindi speakers could make the discrimination, but the adult English speakers could not. The interesting result, however, is that 6-month-old infants could make the discrimination. It seems that at some time during the first year of exposure to the language, infants begin to respond selectively to certain aspects in their linguistic environment and to lose selectively their ability to respond to phonemic dimensions not used in their native language.

This is not to say that we cannot learn to make certain phonemic distinctions. Evidence suggests that learning through exposure and experience plays a role in the ability to discriminate between various linguistic sounds, and some linguistic discriminations seem to be learned during the childhood years (Eilers, Wilson, & Moore, 1979). However, this appears to be limited to certain dimensions of the sound.

Tees and Werker (1984) showed that short-term, intensive training improved the ability of native English speakers to make certain nonnative (Hindi) speech discriminations, although after 5 years of language study, the ability to make these discriminations was already apparent. An interesting additional finding pertained to individuals who spent their early years in a setting where Hindi was spoken (perhaps by a live-in relative). Even though these individuals had never studied the language and as adults were unable to speak, understand, or write more than a few words of Hindi, they could make the phonemic discriminations that non-native Hindi speakers found impossible. Thus their early experience seems to have "tuned" their speech-sound decoding capacity for certain phonemes even though they were not actually speaking the language.

In terms of our earlier discussion about the relationship between experience and development, these results suggest that different aspects of the perception of speechlike sounds follow different courses. Whereas some auditory discriminations are facilitated through contact with particular sounds in the linguistic environment, others are lost through their absence or rarity, thus showing that experience is necessary for their maintenance (compare Walley, Pisoni, & Aslin, 1981). Overall, this confirms that much of what we perceive and many of the perceptual distinctions we make are strongly influenced by the culture and environment in which we were reared.

Effects of Occupation

Even within a given culture, selective exposure occurs to different sets of environmental stimuli. We are exposed to our occupational settings during about one-fifth of our adult working life, and specific sets of occupational experiences can affect our perceptual abilities both at the physiological and at higher cognitive levels. One aspect of an occupation that may have effects at the physiological level on a sensory system is the magnitude of sound, light, or chemical stimulation to which we are exposed.

Consider, for example, the amount of auditory input you receive in your occupational setting. Some work environments are relatively quiet (such as offices and small stores); others are associated with continuous, high-intensity noise (for example, factories, mills, or rock-music bands). Figure 17-15 illustrates the effects of noise on hearing for different occupations. The horizontal axis represents the frequencies at which hearing was tested in a sample of male office, farm, and factory workers. The 0-decibel point on the vertical axis represents the average minimum threshold for an auditory experience. The three curves on the graph plot the average threshold sound intensity at each of the frequencies used in the test. As you can see, the group of factory workers has lowered sensitivity (higher average thresholds). Fortunately, many factory workers

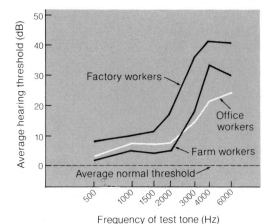

Figure 17-15 *The effect of occupation on hearing (based on Glorig, Wheeler, Quigle, Grings, & Summerfield, 1970).*

have begun to wear ear plugs while working; these help protect them from the destructive effects of continual noise exposure.

According to Kryter (1985), factory workers are not the only group that should be concerned about exposure to very loud sounds. For instance, soldiers exposed to the sound of gunfire and airline pilots exposed to engine noises have been shown to have hearing deficits. The loss tends to be greatest in the higher frequency ranges and seems to increase in severity as the length of the exposure increases. Thus, airline pilots who had from 1,000 to 2,000 hours of flying time on the noisy planes of the 1960s had an average auditory threshold of approximately 0 dB at a sound frequency of 4000 Hz, whereas more experienced pilots, with 10,000 to 16,000 hours of flying time, had an average auditory threshold of 10 dB at that sound frequency.

Rice et al. (1968) have shown that performers of rock music may also suffer hearing losses. In Figure 17-16, average auditory thresholds are again plotted for various test frequencies. The lowest curve represents the thresholds of the control group of nonperformers. Notice that relative to nonperformers of the same age, the rock performers have elevated auditory thresholds (lower sensitivity). At 4000 Hz, the thresholds of the performers and the controls differ by about 20 dB. To give you a reference point, a 20-dB difference would be roughly equivalent to being able to hear a normal conversational tone as opposed to a shout. Figure 17-16 also shows the immediate effects of prolonged exposure to very loud sounds. The top curve on this graph plots the measured thresholds immediately after 85 minutes of exposure to very loud music; as you can see, the threshold at 4000 Hz has risen to 25 dB.

In a similar vein, some occupations expose the eyes to high-intensity lights (such as welding arcs and furnace blazes). In the same man-

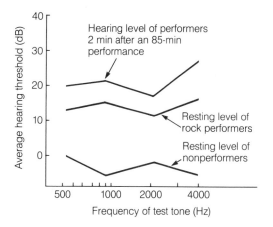

Figure 17-16 *A comparison of the hearing of rock musicians to that of nonperformers (based on Rice et al., 1968).*

ner that exposure to prolonged high-intensity sound can impair hearing, exposure to prolonged high-intensity light can permanently impair vision (Noell, 1980).

Perhaps the most interesting occupational effect on vision pertains to **myopia,** or nearsightedness. This is a condition where the length of the eye is somewhat too great, and the parallel rays of light from distant objects come to a focus in front of the retina, thus resulting in poor distance acuity. Myopia is the most prevalent visual disorder in the world, affecting more than 2 billion individuals. Over the past 40 years, several studies have established that one of the major causes of myopia has to do with a life history of exposure to "near work," which would include reading and other activities restricted to close distances (see Birnbaum, 1981; Grosvenor & Flom, 1991). It is believed that trying hard to see at close distances leads to overaccommodation of the crystalline lens and increased internal pressure in the eye. Over a long period of time, this may lengthen the eye and lead to myopia. It has been demonstrated that after only a short span of near work (such as 3 hours of editing text on a visual display terminal), a person may become temporarily myopic (Jaschinski-Kruza, 1984). It is also possible to induce myopia in animals by using certain environmental and visual exposure conditions (for example, Sivak et al., 1990). In monkeys this has been done by rearing them under conditions where the maximum visual distance they could see was about 50 cm (20 in) for extended periods (for example, F. A. Young, 1981).

The most common way to correct for myopia is, of course, to prescribe eyeglasses. In fact, with the high prevalence of myopia, we are very used to seeing people with glasses. Wearing glasses is so common that we seldom think about it, which must have been the case with the artist C. Schoneus, who depicted the circumcision of Jesus shown in Figure 17-17. Notice that the rabbi performing the operation is using *pince-nez* or "nose-clip" eyeglasses that permit the use of both hands, even though these were not to be invented for another 1500 years.

Glasses, however, are not the only solution to myopia that has been suggested. One attempted remedy is based on the assumption that if myopia comes about through a particular pattern of eye use, then it should be possible to develop a set of exercises that might reverse the process causing nearsightedness. Vision training to correct myopia has been discussed and debated extensively since 1920, when William Bates wrote his controversial book *Better Eyesight Without Glasses*. He and his successors emphasized relaxation-type exercises and discouraged the use of corrective spectacles. Since that time several different training techniques have been developed. Some use recognition training; some focus on exercises to accommodate to more distant targets; and some have even used biofeedback techniques where complex oculometers monitor the individual's state of lens accommodation (Freidman, 1981; Roscoe & Couchman,

1987; Woo & Wilson, 1990).

How well does vision training work? There have been some reports of success, with at least some individuals showing measurable improvement in their ability to recognize familiar targets and letters (for example, Lundervold, Lewin, & Irvin, 1987). Unfortunately, this success seems to be due to attentional changes, which allow individuals to recognize blurred stimuli better, rather than any actual improvement in the refractive state of the eye (Goodson & Rahe, 1981). The most recent studies have shown that vision training does not really change the state of myopia at all, nor does it allow individuals better distance vision in situations where the targets have few recognition clues when they are blurred or are much different from the ones the observers trained with (for example, Koslowe, Spierer, Rosner, & Belkin, 1991; Woo & Wilson, 1990). Thus, although an individual's viewing practices and close work habits are capable of causing myopia, simple training and exercise procedures do not seem to be able to reverse the condition once it has developed.

Perceptual Set

Experiences in an occupational or other setting may bias our perception and interpretation of various stimuli. This seems to be because specific past experiences produce a sensitization or predisposition to "see" a situation in a certain way, especially when several alternative perceptual experiences are possible (as when the stimulus is ambiguous or degraded because of poor viewing conditions). The expectancies or predispositions an observer brings to the perceptual situation are known as a **perceptual set** (Coren, 1984b). In many respect, perceptual set can be thought of as another example of selective attention (as we discussed in Chapter 15), in which the observer is set to process some but not all incoming information or to organize it in a specific manner. To get a better feeling as to how perceptual set operates, try Demonstration Box 17-6.

As an example, let us consider police as observers and eyewitnesses, since this is an occupation in which observation is an important part of the job. Some findings suggest that perceptual set may influence the observations of

Figure 17-17 *Part of an engraving by C. Shoneus, depicting the circumcision of Jesus by a rabbi wearing glasses, despite the fact that these were invented 1,500 years after Jesus's birth.*

DEMONSTRATION BOX 17-6   Perceptual Set

Something of the flavor of perceptual set can be experienced by simply reading the set of words below out loud:

MACBETH   MACARTHUR   MACWILLIAMS MACNAMARA MACDILLON MACDONALD MACMASTER MACDOWELL MACHINES MACKENZIE

Now look back at the next to the last word. Did you pronounce it as if it were or-

ganized as the name *Mac Hines*, or did you pronounce it as if it were organized as the more familiar and natural form that makes the common word *machines*? If you pronounced it as the name, organizing the prefix *Mac* into a separate unit, you were demonstrating the effects of perceptual set.

---

police in certain situations. In one study, police officers and civilians were shown films of a street scene over a period of several hours. Their task was to watch for various people (whose photos were on display below the screen) and for certain types of actions (normal exchanges of goods versus theft, and so forth). The police tended to report more alleged thefts than the nonpolice, although there was no significant difference between the police and civilians in their detection of people and actions (Clifford & Bull, 1978).

A more subtle demonstration of this effect of perceptual set was provided by Toch and Schulte (1961), who studied perception of violence and crime in ambiguous visual scenes. They simultaneously presented different pictures to each eye in a stereoscope (see Chapter 10). One eye was shown a violent scene and the other a nonviolent one, as in the pair of stimuli in Figure 17-18. If these two views are seen simultaneously by the two eyes, perceptual confusion should result. Observers tend to resolve this ambiguous situation in favor of one scene or the other; that scene then dominates the percept. Toch and Schulte were interested in exploring the notion that police

students would be predisposed to interpret this particular ambiguous situation in terms of the violent as opposed to the nonviolent scene. They compared the performance of advanced police administration students with two control groups: beginning police students and university students. In general they found that the advanced police students interpreted the stereograms as depicting violence approximately twice as many times as the other two groups. Thus, these data provide some evidence that certain occupations, especially those requiring intensive training, may set an

Figure 17-18   A stereogram used to test for occupational influences on the perception of violence (from "Readiness to Perceive Violence as a Result of Police Training" by H. H. Toch, and R. Schulte, 1961, British Journal of Psychology, 52, pp. 389–393).

individual to interpret ambiguous stimulation in a particular way.

We are not singling out the police for particular scrutiny. Perceptual set associated with occupational training and experience and education can affect all groups of individuals. An example of how our educational background can bias our perception can be seen by looking at Figure 17-19A. Most Western observers will see a complex pattern of black shapes, which,

by some stretching of the imagination, might appear to cohere into some sort of boot. Conversely, Figure 17-19B is quite different. Here the white spaces clearly shape the word *FLY*, and the black spaces serve as the background. Our familiarity with the English language helps to focus our attention on this region of the figure, and we supply the missing contours, subjectively, to complete the percept (see Chapter 11). Actually, if you were an educated native Chinese, you might be more captured by Figure 17-19A, since it outlines in the white spaces between the black shapes the calligraphic character for the Chinese word *FLY*, and Figure 17-19B might appear to be merely five meaningless black shapes (See Coren, Porac, & Theodor, 1987).

Another interesting example of perceptual set based on language (here written language) has been provided by Diener (1990). Look at the two words printed in Figure 17-20. Pay particular attention to the letter *P* in both. In the word on the left the letter *P* appears to be lowercase, and on the right it appears to be a capital letter. Now look at the size of both of these letters. Notice that the capital *P* appears to be physically larger than its lowercase counterpart. Actually both are the same size. Our set and expectations based on our knowledge that capital letters are usually larger than lowercase letters has distorted our perception in this case. Thus, much of what we see is determined by what our experience, culture, and education set us to see.

A

B

Figure 17-19 *Although* A *may appear to be a relatively random collection of black shapes, perhaps depicting some sort of boot, it is actually similar to* B *in that it contains the word FLY depicted in the white areas, but in* A *the word is in Chinese calligraphy.*

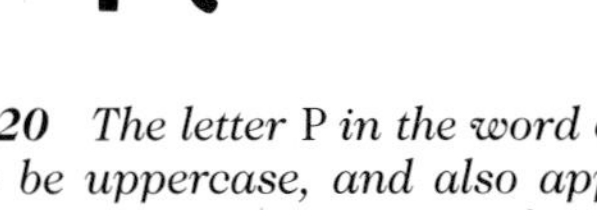

apt APt

Figure 17-20 *The letter* P *in the word on the right appears to be uppercase, and also appears to be larger than in the word on the left. Both letters, however, are physically identical (based on Diener, 1990).*

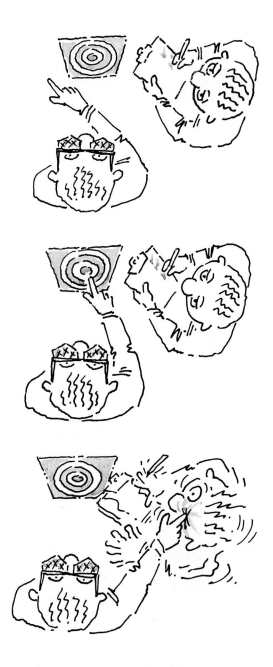

Fred overadapts to prism goggles

GLOSSARY

The following definitions are specific to their use in this book.

Aftereffects Errors in hand-eye coordination that follow adaptation to wedge-prism distortion.

Astigmatism A selective visual bias caused by physical distortion of the cornea.

Carpentered world hypothesis States that individuals living in urban environments characterized by straight lines and angles will tend to depend more on depth cues based on linear perspective than people living in more primitive rural environments characterized by curved lines.

Critical period An interval during which sensory experience is essential if perceptual development is to proceed normally.

Enhancement An improvement in the final level of an existing ability caused by a relevant experience.

Exafference Stimulus input that acts on a passive observer.

Facilitation An increase in the rate at which an ability develops, but not in its final level.

Familiar size A cue to depth based on the known or remembered size of objects.

Illusion decrement The decrease in the strength of a visual illusion with prolonged viewing.

Induction A process in development whereby experience determines the presence and final level of an ability.

Interposition The depth cue based on the blocking of an object or part of an object from view by another closer object.

Maintenance Preservation of a developed ability by relevant experience.

Maturation Development of an ability independent of experience.

Myopia Nearsightedness resulting in poor acuity for distant targets.

Oblique effect The phenomenon whereby acuity for diagonally oriented stimuli is poorer than for horizontally or vertically oriented stimuli.

Perceptual set The expectancies or predispositions that an observer brings to a perceptual situation.

Reafference Stimulus input that results from an observer's own movements.

Rearrangement An experimental technique that alters spatial relations in the visual world.

Restricted rearing An experimental technique in which an animal is reared without exposure to a particular class of sensory inputs.

Selective Rearing An experimental technique in which an animal is reared under conditions that bias the stimulus input it receives toward a particular class of stimuli (for example, it sees only vertical stripes).

Set *See* Perceptual set.

Three-dimensional Possessing pictorial depth.

Transactional viewpoint An approach that maintains that any perceptual experience consists of a complex evaluation of the significance of available stimuli based on expectations and experience.

Two-dimensional Lacking pictorial depth.

Visual field The portion of the visual environment to which an eye will respond, measured in degrees around the head.

Chapter ...

18

INDIVIDUAL DIFFERENCES

Physiological Differences
  The Effects of Drugs
  The Effects of Physical Pathology
Gender Differences
  Visual-Spatial Abilities
    • Physiological Factors
    • Psychosocial Factors
Personality and Cognitive Style Differences

*H*ow often have you heard people arguing over whether a color is green or blue, whether the room was too hot or too cold, or whether the coffee is too weak or too strong? Such arguments may represent real differences in the perceptions of the individuals involved. Remember that perception is not simply a process by which the qualities of the world get transferred from "out there" to "in here." Rather, your final conscious experience of a stimulus involves many levels of processing. Not only must the peripheral sensory receptors be stimulated, but also stimuli must be interpreted and encoded. As one ancient philosopher said, "The eyes are blind; only the mind sees." If this premise is true, it is quite probable that individuals differ in the way they perceive their worlds, since it is certainly true that no two minds are identical.

Many factors can cause individuals to have different perceptions even when encountering identical stimuli. For instance, consider Figure 18-1, which shows a common visual distortion called the **Poggendorff illusion.** For most people, it appears that if the line marked *A* were extended it would pass below the line marked *B*

by several millimeters. Actually, *A* and *B* are directly in line with each other. The magnitude of this illusion differs among individuals depending on their age, their education, whether they are male or female, and even how well they do on spatial skills tests, such as those that form part of many intelligence scales (Coren & Girgus, 1978; Coren & Porac, 1987; Girgus & Coren, 1987). Some of these factors are probably not surprising to you, since we have already discussed how age and past experience can affect perception (in Chapters 16 and 17). However, many other variables operate to make each person's perceptual experiences unique. These include physiological factors, such as changes in the sensory receptors themselves or the neural apparatus that decodes the sensory information. Perception is also affected by an individual's cognitive or perceptual style, which is actually a reflection of personality differences and different approaches to gathering information from the environment. Even an individual's gender seems to cause differences in the way sensory information is processed. All of these factors lead to individual differences in perception.

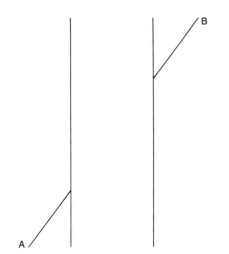

Figure 18-1 The Poggendorff illusion, in which line A appears as if it would pass below line B if extended, even though both are exactly aligned.

PHYSIOLOGICAL DIFFERENCES

Each of us can be seen as a complex physiological machine, and we certainly have seen how factors that alter the structure and function of our sensory apparatus alter what we perceive. For example, nonfunctional retinal cones will cause color-vision deficits. Calcium deposits on the bones of the inner ear will lessen the intensity of sounds transmitted to the inner ear while making your own voice seem very loud to you. In addition to such specific factors, certain other physiological factors affect the body generally and also affect perception as a side effect.

The Effects of Drugs

Many drugs can cause marked changes in sensory capacities. For instance, smokers are continually ingesting several active chemicals. The most important of these is the poison nicotine; next in importance is the gas carbon monoxide. Since these chemicals enter the body predominantly via the mouth, it is not surprising that the major sensory effects of smoking tobacco are on the sense of taste. Absolute taste thresholds are higher for smokers than for nonsmokers, with smokers being especially insensitive to bitter tastes such as quinine (Kaplan & Glanville, 1964; Sinnot & Rauth, 1937). However, you may be surprised to learn that smoking also affects vision. Most of these effects are probably due to the inhalation of carbon monoxide, a substance that has been shown to produce alterations in some visual tasks, particularly those involving sustained visual attention (Gliner, Horvath, & Mihevic, 1983) or smoothly tracking targets with the eyes (Sibony, Evinger, & Manning, 1987). In addition, habitual smokers tend to have somewhat poorer contrast sensitivity (Fine & Kobrick, 1987) and reduced ability to make light-intensity discriminations, especially under scotopic illumination conditions (Rhee, Kim, & Kim, 1965). This latter fact might explain why smokers tend to have more nighttime driving accidents than nonsmokers. Evidence also has indicated that ingestion of nicotine slows the rate of recovery from certain visual aftereffects (such as the afterimages associated with viewing bright targets or the fatigue effects of prolonged staring at certain types of patterns, as we discussed in Chapters 4 and 5). It has been hypothesized that nicotine slows recovery from aftereffects, because it affects the balance of neural excitation and inhibition within the visual system (Amure, 1978).

One general theme that characterizes the data describing the effects of drugs on perception is that drugs that depress neural activity—such as sedatives, barbiturates, tranquilizers, or alcohol—also decrease sensory acuity. For example, Hellekant (1965) measured the effect of alcohol on taste sensitivity by recording directly from the chorda tympani nerve of a cat. This nerve conveys taste information from most of the tongue. Alcohol reduced responsiveness to sweet (sucrose), acid (acetic acid), salt (sodium chloride), and bitter (quinine) stimuli. The strongest reduction of taste response was for the bitter stimuli. Alcohol also may affect other sensory systems, and recent studies suggest that these effects may be cumulative. One study found that chronic alcoholics show delays in the neural response to auditory signals when compared to nonalcoholics (Begleiter, Porjesz, & Chou, 1981) and slower recognition responses to auditory signals (Gustafson, 1986). Studies of the effect of alcohol on visual abilities have produced similar findings. Research with chronic alcoholics has found that they have a higher incidence of color-vision deficiencies than nonalcoholic observers (Granger & Ikeda, 1968; D. C. Reynolds, 1979).

You do not have to be an alcoholic or a habitual drinker to experience the effects of alcohol on visual perception. Some studies of nonalcoholic observers have indicated that high doses of alcohol decrease an individual's ability to follow a moving target with the eyes (Flom, Brown, Adams, & Jones, 1976; Levy, Lipton, & Holzman, 1981) and also decrease the ability of the eye to accommodate or change focus of the lens (Miller, Pigion, & Martin, 1985). Even small amounts of alcohol can decrease an observer's ability to detect the onset of a moving stimulus (Bates, 1989; MacArthur & Sekuler, 1982). Alcohol also affects some more complex perceptual processes, such as size constancy (Farrimond, 1990). The breakdown of size constancy with alcohol is particularly dangerous when driving. If individuals under the influence of alcohol do not apply the size-constancy scaling mechanism as usual, problems can arise, since perceived size and distance interact (see Chapter 14). After an individual has drunk enough alcohol, objects such as pedestrians or other vehicles seem smaller and more distant than they do under conditions where the driver is completely sober. This means that the intoxicated driver is less likely to think it is necessary to apply the brakes or to slow down to avoid collisions even when such actions are called for.

The overall sensitivity of the visual and auditory systems is also affected by many depressant drugs. A popular technique for measuring visual responsiveness is the **critical flicker fusion frequency** task (usually abbreviated **CFF**). This task requires an observer to view a flickering light. As the flicker rate is increased, the observer will eventually no longer see the successive on-and-off cycles, but rather will see them fused into a steady, continuous light. The flicker speed at which the shift from an apparently flickering to an apparently steady light takes place is the CFF. The more sensitive the eye is to changes in illumination level, the faster the light must be cycled on and off to cause the perception of flicker to disappear. A similar task used in hearing is called the **auditory flutter fusion (AFF)** task. In measuring AFF, a tone, rather than a light, is switched on and off repeatedly. The AFF is the rate at which the tone must be cycled on and off for the listener to hear the signal as a continuous sound. Depressant drugs, such as alcohol and tranquilizers, tend to lower both the CFF and the AFF, thus indicating that the visual and auditory systems are acting sluggishly and with less sensitivity under the influence of such drugs (Besser, 1966; Holland, 1960). It is interesting to note that fasting, which increases fatigue and makes individuals sluggish, also tends to lower the CFF (Ali & Amir, 1989).

Drugs that increase the arousal level of the observer, including stimulants such as caffeine or amphetamines (and even some of the B vitamins), may sometimes improve the sensitivity of the observer. For instance, the high-level stimulant cocaine may enhance identification performance (Higgens & Bickel, 1990). However, the effects of stimulants do not seem as widespread or as reproducible as those obtained with depressant drugs. We do find that amphetamines and caffeine seem to increase the responsiveness of the visual and auditory systems and even the olfactory system (Turner, 1968). There are hints that some aspects of the superior perceptual performance with stimulants may be due to improved attention rather than changes in threshold level (Fagen & Swift, 1988; Swift & Tiplady, 1988).

Another technique used to monitor drug effects involves reversible figures, such as the one shown as Figure 18-2. When you look steadily at this figure (called the **Necker Cube**), you will notice that it seems to reverse its apparent orientation from time to time. Sometimes the face with the corner labeled *A* appears closer than the face with the corner labeled *B*, and at other times *B* seems closer. Most people have a fairly constant rate of reversal for this figure. Many factors can affect the reversal rate, such as the way you attend to it (Reisberg & O'Shaughnessy, 1984; Wallace & Priebe, 1985). Depressive drugs, such as some

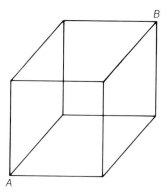

Figure 18-2 *The Necker Cube, in which the face with corner A sometimes appears nearer than the face with corner B and sometimes is perceived to reverse so the face with corner B appears nearer.*

DEMONSTRATION BOX 18-1   The Effects of Stimulants on Figure Reversals

For this demonstration you will need a friend and a watch. Have your friend monitor you while you look at Figure 18-2 for 1 minute. Call out each time the figure reverses its orientation and have your friend keep count. Next, drink a cup of coffee. Don't use decaffeinated coffee, since we want you to receive a dose of caffeine. Since caffeine is a stimulant, it should increase your visual responsiveness (as well as keep you awake for the rest of the chapter). The effects take about 15 minutes to appear; after this interval, repeat the viewing process. Look at Figure 18-2 again for 1 minute while your friend records the number of reversals. You should find that the stimulant has increased the number of perceptual shifts that you experience.

---

tranquilizers, slow the reversal rate (Phillipson & Harris, 1984). Demonstration Box 18-1 provides a procedure for testing the effects of a stimulant on this phenomenon.

The hallucinogenic and psychoactive drugs—including LSD, mescaline, psilocybin, and marijuana—are often reported to have profound perceptual effects. For instance, Aldous Huxley (1963) described his visual experiences after taking mescaline, saying, "First and most important is the experience of light . . . . All colors are intensified to a pitch far beyond anything seen in the normal state, and at the same time the mind's capacity for recognizing fine distinctions of tone and hue is notably heightened." Unfortunately, although some aspects of the subjective experience seem to be heightened, actual measurements do not always show increased sensory sensitivity. For instance, Hartman and Hollister (1963) found that LSD, mescaline, and psilocybin all reduced the accuracy of color discriminations. V. R. Carlson (1958) showed that LSD reduced visual sensitivity in a threshold task, and there are reports of blurred vision (Hoffer & Osmond, 1967) and slower-than-normal dark adaptation for observers under the influence of LSD (Ostfeld, 1961). Even if individuals begin to abstain from LSD use, these negative visual effects may persist for periods of 2 years or more (Abraham & Wolf, 1988). Susceptibility to at least one visual geometric illusion, the Mueller-Lyer, increases under the influence of LSD (Edwards & Cohen, 1961). However, LSD does seem to improve auditory acuity and seems to enhance the CFF (Hoffer & Osmond, 1967; J. M. Williams, 1979).

Similarly, when observers are asked to describe their experiences after smoking moderate doses of marijuana (cannabis), they often report improved visual clarity and acuity. However, the experimental results indicate that, as with LSD, the actual perceptual effects involve losses in sensitivity (in some respects very similar to those of alcohol). For instance, in a vigilance task where observers were asked to fixate a target and report stimuli appearing in the periphery of vision, those who had smoked marijuana produced fewer accurate reports (Moskowitz, Sharma, & McGlothin, 1972). Such an effect could be due to a narrowing of attention induced by the drug, which also could interfere with the perceptual motor skills needed when driving a car or flying a plane (Murray, 1986). Intake of marijuana has also been shown to increase the interstimulus interval at which visual masking occurs (visual masking is discussed in Chapter 11), suggesting that it acts like a sedative and decreases the speed of visual-information processing (Braff, Silverton, Saccuzzo, & Janowsky, 1981). As with alcohol, prolonged use of marijuana seems to have a cumulative effect, causing slower reaction times in perceptual-motor tasks (Varma & Malhotra, 1988). Evidence also has indicated that color discrimination, particularly for short wavelengths (blues), is much poorer in habitual marijuana users (Adams, Brown, Haegerstrom-Portnoy, & Flom, 1976).

Some more complex sensory effects have also been reported after the smoking of marijuana. Some observers experience changes in depth perception and distortions in the perception of size (Tart, 1971). In addition, the autokinetic effect, which is the illusory movement of a stationary light viewed in total darkness (illustrated in Demonstration Box 13-8), may become exaggerated. This last observation has led one group of experimenters to caution against night driving while under the influence of marijuana (Sharma & Moskowitz, 1972). Yet marijuana, even at relatively high intake levels, does not seem to impair eye-movement facility, since neither saccadic eye movements nor the ability to pursue a moving visual stimulus with the eyes is affected by its ingestion (Flom, Brown, Adams, & Jones, 1976).

Although contact with hallucinogenic drugs involves a departure from everyday behavior for most people, many of the stimulants (such as caffeine) and depressants (such as tobacco and alcohol) that alter perception are used commonly. Everyday drugs, including antihistamines and aspirin, can cause the perceptual responses of individuals to differ. For instance, aspirin may cause dimness of vision or ringing in the ears (Allen, 1985; Goodman & Gilman, 1965). The auditory effects of aspirin can reduce threshold sensitivity (Bennett & Morgan, 1978) and even interfere with speech perception (Young & Wilson, 1982). Another common drug, the antiseasickness compound scopolamine, can cause blurred vision and alter the ability of the lens of the eye to accommodate to near targets (Parrott, 1988). Thus, an individual who has just had a cup of coffee or a martini or who has tried to alleviate a headache or nausea may differ from other individuals in perceptual responses because of the actions of the ingested drugs.

The Effects of Physical Pathology

Many pathological conditions affect perception. The most obvious of these are maladies that directly damage a particular receptor organ. Glaucoma, which causes a pressure increase inside the eye, can produce blindness if left untreated, and otosclerosis, which causes the bones of the middle ear to become immobile, will impair hearing. Other pathological conditions cause disturbances in more complex aspects of perception, rather than a loss of sensitivity to a given stimulus dimension. Such effects are often caused by severe toxic conditions, such as carbon monoxide poisoning, as well as diseases or injuries that damage or reduce the functioning in some parts of the brain (Critchley, 1964; Davidoff, 1975; Luria, 1973). These can affect such complex functions as the ability to identify objects or to place them in space and also the ability to distribute attention. In general, such a problem is called an **agnosia,** from the Greek *a* meaning "not" and *gnosis* meaning "intuitive knowledge." People suffering from agnosias seem to perceive but are not capable of understanding the information presented to them.

Freud (1953) noticed a form of perceptual disturbance that he called **visual object agnosia.** Some of his patients were unable to identify familiar objects, although they seemed to have no psychopathological disturbance or readily detectable elementary damage to the visual apparatus. Later, Luria (1973) suggested that agnosias might arise from lesions in the secondary visual areas of the cortex. These lesions do not cause blindness, nor to they seem to diminish visual acuity. Rather, they make it difficult for a person to combine parts of an object to identify it. Some of these effects might be quite subtle, such as not being able to see both aspects of a reversible figure, such as Figure 11-19 (Ricci & Blundo, 1990). Other errors are more dramatic. For instance, Luria (1973) gave a patient a line drawing of a pair of eyeglasses. The patient examined the picture carefully in a manner indicating that he was confused and did not know exactly what it represented. He then started to guess. "There is a circle . . . and another circle . . . a cross bar . . . why, it must be a bicycle?"

Such patients also have problems separating the parts of the figure from the overall context. Thus, if the patient is shown a drawing of a clock (see Figure 18-3A), the person can usually identify it correctly. However, if the clock is crossed out with a couple of lines, as in Figure 18-3B, the patient can no longer identify what the picture represents. Such a patient may identify a telephone with a dial as a clock or perceive a sofa, upholstered in brown fabric, as a trunk. Such difficulties seem to be even more pronounced when the stimuli are presented for less than 500 msec.

What sort of underlying mechanisms are involved in these perceptual disturbances? As long ago as 1909, the Hungarian neurologist Balint made some observations that suggest a problem with visual attention. Thus researchers find patients have a decrease in attention span, being able to see only one object at a time, regardless of its size (for example, Rizzo & Robin, 1990). For instance, such a person could not place a dot in the center of a circle, since this would require paying attention to both the circle and the dot simultaneously. This type of patient is said to be suffering from **simultagnosia.** Thus, a patient who is shown a series of overlapping objects, such as those in Figure 18-4, might report a single object, for example, the hammer, and deny seeing any of the others (M. Williams, 1970). If such individuals are asked to copy a simple drawing, such as the specimen in Figure 18-5, they depict only its individual parts. Essentially, they give a visual list of most of the details. Despite the fact that their ability to localize objects in space is still functional, they seem unable to meld the parts into an integrated and unified figure (Goodale & Milner, 1991). Visual object agnosia and simultagnosia are often found in the same patients and are sometimes grouped together under the label **visual integrative agnosia** (for example, Grailet & Seron, 1990). A drawing typical of such a patient is shown as the copy in Figure 18-5.

Evidence from several physiological experiments implies that this defect is caused by disturbances in the temporal and sometimes the upper occipital regions of the cortex. It also

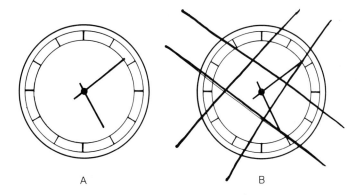

A   B

Figure 18-3   (A) *A figure identified as a clock.* (B) *A figure no longer identifiable to a visual agnosic.*

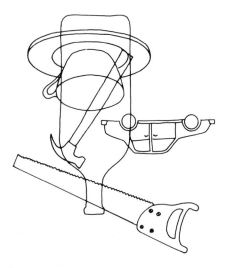

Figure 18-4 *A test figure for simultagnosia.*

seems to be specific to the way attention is distributed to the visual targets (Butters, Barton, & Brody, 1970; Gerbrandt, Spinelli, & Pribram, 1970). Luria (1973) claimed that injections of caffeine (to stimulate the appropriate region of the cortex) can reduce some of the symptoms, thus allowing the patient to attend to two or three objects in the visual field simultaneously.

Unfortunately, this improvement lasts only as long as the drug is active.

Some of the agnosia effects are quite general in scope and may involve more than one sensory modality. Patients with diseases of the parietal lobe of the brain may show a **spatial agnosia.** They have difficulty negotiating their way through the world. They make wrong turns even in familiar surroundings, do not easily recognize landmarks, and can become lost in their own homes. This problem does not appear to be caused by a defect in a single, sensory modality. These patients seem to be just as impaired using their tactile or kinesthetic senses as their visual (Heaton, 1968; Weinstein, Cole, Mitchell, & Lyerly, 1964). Such patients often also show a tendency to ignore one side in space and are therefore said to be suffering from **visual hemineglect,** where the term *hemi* means "half" (see Chamorro & Sacco, 1990; Ladavas & Petronio, 1990). For example, if asked to draw symmetrical objects, they will usually produce some sort of imperfection on one side. Thus, an individual with left-sided spatial agnosia would reproduce Figure 18-6 as the copy shown.

Specimen

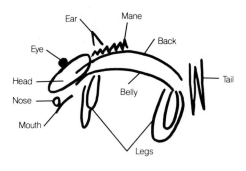

Copy

Figure 18-5 *A target figure to be copied, and a reproduction typical of a person suffering from visual integrative agnosia.*

Specimen   Copy

Figure 18-6 A target figure to be copied, and a reproduction typical of a person with visual hemineglect.

While some of these perceptual effects are quite general, others are very specific, such as the rare disorder called **prosopagnosia.** In this type of agnosia, the patient has difficulty perceiving and identifying human faces (Damasio & Tranel, 1990; Levine & Calvanio, 1989). In extreme cases the patient may not even know his or her own face in a mirror. Prosopagnosia is of interest because the human face is a very important stimulus. Your mother's face was probably one of the first visual forms to which you attended as an infant. When children draw, the face is usually the first part of the body to be depicted. So we find that facial perception is one of the aspects of form perception that is lost only in cases of serious brain injury, usually involving the right temporal lobe. The loss of the ability to identify faces is often quite specific, leaving the ability to identify emotional expressions, gender, or age unaffected (Damasio & Tranel, 1990). Unfortunately, since the problem of face identification is perceptual in nature, training and practice on identifying faces seem to produce no improvement in prosopagnosic patients (Ellis & Young, 1988).

A related disorder, called **autotopagnosia,** is the distorted perception of body image and body parts (see Semenza, 1988). For example,

one patient, when asked to point to her ear, looked around for it and replied that she must have lost it. Finger agnosias and finger-naming difficulties are the most widely known forms of specific autotopagnosias, and these are thought to be associated with lesions in the left parietal portion of the brain (Pirozzolo, 1978).

Although we have concentrated on the visual sense in this discussion, similar difficulties are found in speech and sound perception. These are usually grouped under the overall heading of **aphasia** (from *a* meaning "not" and *phasis* meaning "utterance"). Aphasia sufferers have an inability to name common objects and often fail to recall the meanings of words designating common objects (Luria, 1972; Tsvetkova, 1972). In addition, some people suffer from specific *auditory agnosias*, resulting from damage to the auditory pathways. There are many varieties of these auditory agnosias. For instance, some types lead to the selective loss of the perception of words (for example, Buchtel & Stewart, 1989), sometimes called pure word deafness. Loss of the perception of nonlinguistic sounds is called *sound agnosia*; deficient perception of music is called *sensory amusia* (Pizorrolo, 1978); and loss of the ability to recognize familiar voices is called phonagnosia (Van Lancker & Kreiman, 1989). Thus, it should be clear that there are a large number of different forms of agnosia, or higher perceptual disruption. A number of the more common of these agnosias are listed and named in Table 18-1.

Most agnosias seem to have been caused by physiological damage, usually of the higher brain centers involved in the interpretation of stimuli. Thus, when we find agnosias, we tend often to find damage of particular brain sites. However, these are usually not the primary receiving areas of the cortex for that particular sensory modality. Visual agnosias often are associated with damage to the more forward portions of the occipital cortex, generally areas 18

Table 18-1   Some of the More Common Forms of Agnosia That Manifest Themselves As Complex Perceptual Deficits

TYPE OF AGNOSIA	SENSORY MODALITY	PERCEPTUAL DEFICIT
Object agnosia	Visual	Inability to name, recognize, or use objects
Simultagnosia	Visual	Inability to attend to more than one visual object at a time
Integrative agnosia	Visual	Inability to combine parts of an object into a whole (often symptoms of both Object agnosia and Simultagnosia are combined with this)
Color agnosia	Visual	Inability to associate colors with objects.
Drawing agnosia	Visual	Inability to recognize drawn stimuli
Spatial agnosia	Visual	Deficits in stereoscopic vision and ability to relate objects in space
Prosopagnosia	Visual	Inability to recognize faces
Unilateral neglect	Visual	Apparent deficit in processing stimuli on one side
Amusia	Auditory	Inability to recognize melodies, often accompanied by inability to reproduce rhythm or tempo
Sound agnosia	Auditory	Inability to identify the meaning of nonverbal sounds (such as bells, dog bark)
Phonagnosia	Auditory	Inability to recognize familiar voices
Sensory aphasia	Auditory	Inability to comprehend speech, although verbal (Wernicke's aphasia) production is unimpaired (as opposed to motor or Broca's aphasia, which affects production but not comprehension)
Astereagnosia	Somatosensory	Inability to recognize objects by touch
Autotopagnosia	Somatosensory	Inability to name or localize body parts
Asomatagnosia	Somatosensory	Inability to recognize bodily states
Asymbolia for pain	Somatosensory	Inability to localize or properly react to pain

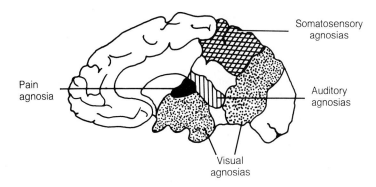

Figure 18-7 Damage to particular portions of the brain is often associated with the indicated agnosias.

and 19, which are the secondary visual areas, and to the temporal lobes, which are tertiary visual processing areas and seem to be associated with complex visual analysis, as we saw in Chapter 3. Similarly, for the other sensory modalities, the various forms of agnosia are associated with secondary and tertiary areas of the cortex, rather than the primary receiving areas. A map of areas often found to be damaged when an individual demonstrates various agnosias is shown as Figure 18-7.

Specifiable physiological differences are not the only source of individual differences in perception, however. In the next sections, we will consider factors affecting perception that may or may not have a physiological basis, or that may be the result of a combination of physiological and experiential processes. Unlike drug and specific sensory damage, the causes of gender and personality differences in perception are harder to specify, although both appear to exist.

GENDER DIFFERENCES

The gender of an individual (whether a person is male or female) may partially determine what is perceived in any given stimulus situation. Gender, of course, carries with it many

physiological implications. One of the most important of these is the chemical differences between the bodies of men and women due to the presence of specific male or female hormones. Hormones are carried in the blood, which infuses and supplies all our sensory receptors, and are found in many parts of the brain. Thus, it would not be surprising to find that men and women might differ in certain sensory and perceptual capacities.

Examples of gender differences in perception are found in both taste and olfaction (Velle, 1987). For instance, women, on average, have more acute senses of smell than men (Money, 1965), and this difference holds over the entire life span (Doty, Shaman, & Applebaum, 1984). This difference seems to be directly attributable to hormonal influences, since the acuity of a female's sense of smell varies over the course of the menstrual cycle, reaching its peak at midcycle when estrogen (one of the major female hormones) levels are at their highest (Mair, Bouffard, Engen, & Morton, 1978; Parlee, 1983). Women whose ovaries are less active than normal have decreased smell sensitivity, but this can be remedied by the administration of estrogen. Conversely, doses of androgen (such as the male hormone testosterone) make the sense of smell less sensitive (Schneider, Costiloe, Howard, & Wolf,

1958). Additionally, although men and women seem to remember visual and acoustic stimuli equally well, women seem to have a better memory for odors (Klutky, 1990).

Gender-related differences are also found in taste. Women tend to have higher taste sensitivity, and the differences between men and women increase with age (Weiffenbach, Baum, & Burghauser, 1982). A more subtle difference between the sexes involves taste preference rather than taste sensitivity: Females prefer the sweet taste more than males do, and this preference varies with the menstrual cycle (Aaron, 1975). This is true for rats as well as humans. When the ovaries of female rats are removed, their preference for the sweet taste diminishes; therapeutic doses of estrogen restore the preference (Zucker, Wade, & Ziegler, 1972). This may also help us to understand why women using contraceptive pills (which contain estrogen as a component) often complain that they have a tendency to overeat sweets and, as a consequence, gain weight.

Male-female differences in sensory sensitivity are found in other modalities as well (Velle, 1987; McGuinness, 1976a). For example, women usually show greater touch sensitivity than do men (Ippolitov, 1973; Weinstein & Sersen, 1961). They also show superior hearing sensitivity, especially at higher frequencies and in older people (Corso, 1959; McGuinness, 1972; Royster, Royster, & Thomas, 1980). Women generally are more sensitive than men to pain produced by electric shock, and women's pain thresholds also seem to vary over the menstrual cycle (Goolkasian, 1980; Tedford, Warren, & Flynn, 1977).

Gender differences in vision seem to be more complex. Males generally appear to have better visual acuity under photopic conditions (Burg, 1966; Roberts, 1964), whereas females have lower absolute thresholds under scotopic conditions (McGuinness & Lewis, 1976). This difference seems to be present from childhood (see Brabyn & McGuinness, 1979). Addition-

ally, men seem to have faster reaction times to visual stimuli over all ages tested (Bleecker & Bolla-Wilson, 1987). As for taste and smell, some evidence has indicated that the visual abilities vary because of hormonal factors. For example, the visual acuity of women varies with their menstrual cycle (Parlee, 1983; Scher, Pionk, & Purcell, 1981), being poorest just prior to and during menstruation. The hormone progesterone (another predominately female hormone) is often prescribed for women who suffer from severe anxiety or depression during menstruation. Progesterone relieves these symptoms and also restores visual acuity to its normal level in most patients (Dalton, 1964). When visual sensitivity is measured at different spatial frequencies (Chapter 4), females have lower contrast thresholds in the low spatial frequency ranges and males have lower contrast thresholds for the high spatial frequencies (Brabyn & McGuinness, 1979). Also, some data have suggested that females dark-adapt more rapidly than males do (McGuinness, 1976b).

Men and women also differ in their perception of time and motion. Men tend to be more accurate than women in their discrimination of time durations (Rammsayer & Lustnauer, 1989). An interesting study by Schiff & Oldak (1990) combined time and motion estimates. Observers looked at a film of an oncoming vehicle. The view of the scene was then interrupted, and the observers had to estimate how long it would take from the moment when the view of the car was lost until the moment when the car would reach (or collide) with them. All observers tended to underestimate the time needed for collision. For the women, however, the underestimates of the time before impact were some 10% to 20% shorter than those of the men. This suggests that women judge the motion as faster or tend to underestimate the distance relative to men. It may also provide a perceptual explanation for why many women complain that men are "more risk-taking" drivers and seem to "cut things too close" or do not apply the brake soon enough in many traffic situations. This belief could come about simply because women judge the time to collision to be much shorter than men do, rather than because of any social or personality differences as a function of gender.

Visual-Spatial Abilities

An interesting and complex gender difference concerns visual-spatial abilities. These are tasks that involve nonverbal cognitive manipulations of objects and include the ability to visualize how objects will appear when they are rotated, to detect the orientations of and relationships between different stimuli, and to correctly perceive complex visual patterns (McGee, 1979). Such tasks seem to produce consistent sex differences favoring males (Halpern, 1986). One of these involves **disembedding,** or the ability to disentangle a target object from a surrounding, and often confusing, context. For example, in Figure 18-8A, you see a figure marked *Target* that is hidden, or embedded, in the more complex figure beside it. The observer's task is to find the simple shape as quickly as possible. Such a task is usually called the **embedded figures test** or the **hidden figures test.** A different spatial task involves the ability to recognize targets when they have been rotated. An example of this **mental rotation task** is shown in Figure 18-8B. The observer has to recognize the shape marked *Target* from among the three figures next to it. It is often difficult to recognize which shape is exactly the same as the target, since the correct shape has been rotated into a different spatial orientation.

Both disembedding and mental rotation tasks produce performance differences that favor males (Halpern, 1986; Wilson et al., 1975), and the differences hold up whether we are dealing with simple or complex patterns

(Bryden & George, 1990). Sometimes the size of the performance difference is quite large, amounting to 16% or more, depending on the tests involved (Sanders, Soares, & D'Aquila, 1982). Males either are more accurate in their responses or show greater speed when completing such tasks (Blough & Slavin, 1987; Harris, 1981; Lohman, 1986). The male advantage in a task such as mental rotation seems to be established by about 10 years of age (Johnson & Meade, 1987). In addition, McGlone (1981) has shown that females approach these tasks differently from males. Females appear to make more rotational hand movements while completing cognitive rotations; in other words, they more frequently need concrete aids or verbal strategies to complete the task successfully (Clarkson-Smith & Halpern, 1983). Demonstration Box 18-2 provides an opportunity for you to test this gender difference in spatial ability.

Physiological Factors

Disembedding a figure, or recognizing it when it has been rotated in space, is a complex task that would seem to involve many learned skills and would seen to be affected by a familiarity with such things as maps and blueprints, which might involve the use of similar skills. So it is somewhat surprising to find that evidence has suggested that some of the same physiological factors distinguishing males from females might be partially responsible for these effects. J. L. Dawson (1967) used a series of these tests on a number of West African males who suffered from a disease that results in estrogen levels higher than those usually found in males. When tested on a series of spatial tasks, these males showed reduced spatial ability relative to a sample of nonaffected males. Similar effects were found in certain South American tribes, where the males habitually chew the leaves of the coca shrub, thus releasing cocaine, which when ingested decreases the secretion of the male hormone testosterone. Such males tend to show typical signs of feminization (including enlarged breasts, widened hips, softened skin texture, and the like) and also show reduced spatial abilities, similar to those of females. Male hormones influence these spatial abilities in the opposite way. Thus, males who produce little or are insensitive to androgens (for exam- ple, testosterone) also show reduced spatial abilities, whereas females with high androgen (for example, androstenedione) levels show greater spatial abilities (Hier & Crowley, 1982; Masica, Money, Ehrhardt, & Lewis, 1969; Peter- son, 1976). Hormonal effects in these complex spatial abilities have also been implicated by the finding that the spatial abilities of pregnant

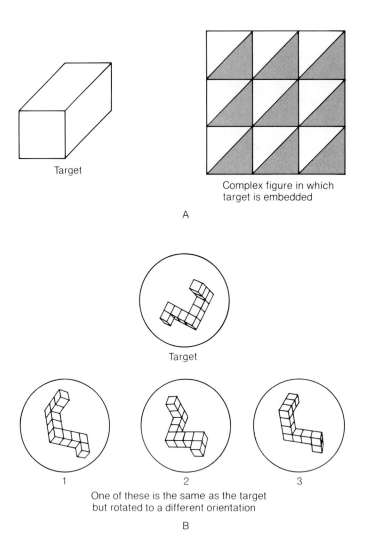

Target

Complex figure in which
target is embedded

A

Target

1   2   3

One of these is the same as the target
but rotated to a different orientation

B

Figure 18-8 (A) *An embedded-figures test in which the target is found in the more complex array.* (B) *A mental rotation test in which the target is found as one of the three test figures, but in a different orientation.*

DEMONSTRATION BOX 18-2   Gender Differences in Mental Rotation

For this demonstration, you will need a stopwatch or a wristwatch that allows you to read seconds (either with a sweep hand or digitally). You will also need a couple of male and female friends. Test them one at a time. First show them what is meant by a mental rotation task by using Figure 18-8B. If they have difficulty, point out that only Stimulus 3 can be rotated to be identical to the target, whereas the other 2 are differently shaped figures. Next, tell your observers that they will see another target figure and a set of 12 test figures. Five of the test figures are identical in shape to the target figures, and their

task is to pick out those 5 as quickly as possible. Start your watch, show them the figure, and time how long it takes for them to find the 5 correct ones. If they get any wrong, tell them, but keep the time going until all 5 are found. The correct answers are on the bottom of page 637.

You should notice that, on average, females will take longer at this task than males. Another interesting observation should be that females are more likely to perceive the task as being difficult, as indicated by comments like "I can never do this sort of thing" or "I'm terrible at this," and so forth.

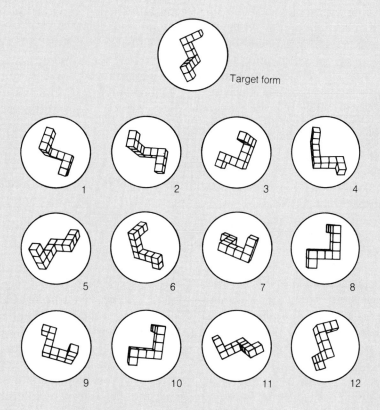

Target form

women (who have higher-than-usual levels of estrogen are decreased relative to those who are not pregnant (Woodfield, 1984).

Other factors are also consistent with physiological determination of spatial ability. For instance, the rate at which individuals mature seems to predict spatial performance. In this case, "maturing" means developing secondary sexual characteristics. Typically, late-maturing individuals are better at such spatial tasks than early-maturing individuals (Gilger & Ho, 1989; Petersen & Crockett, 1985; Waber, 1976, 1977). This is consistent with the usually observed gender differences, since males tend to mature later than females.

Psychosocial Factors

We have been dealing with some of the physiological variables that seem to produce different patterns of perceptual abilities in males and females. Of course, many factors relating to experience, life history, and cultural influences will also affect perceptual behaviors. This is because many aspects of perception are subject to learning influences, as we discussed in Chapter 17. Research has shown that even at an early age, males and females may differ in the types of tasks and activities they engage in and also in the tools, implements, or utensils they use in their everyday activities (see Harris, 1981). These factors can also influence some aspects of perception. Demonstration Box 18-3 provides an object-identification task that occasionally produces different responses from males and females. The task shows differences that are most likely to have an experiential basis rather than the kind of physiological basis we have already discussed.

Perhaps the strongest data in favor of psychosocial factors contributing to gender differences in spatial skills come from studies in which specific training was given to boys and girls using toys and games that have a spatial component and that are typically preferred by boys (such as blocks, Tinkertoys, or paper cut in geometric shapes). Individuals who received such training tended to do better on spatial-skills tests, such as the embedded-figures task, suggesting that a learned component is involved in spatial ability (Smith, Frazier, Ward, & Webb, 1983; Sprafkin, Serbin, Denier, & Conner, 1983). However, improvement does not occur with training for all of the spatial skills that usually show gender differences (Thomas, Jamison, & Hammel, 1973).

It seems likely that differences in spatial skills arise from the interaction between biological and psychosocial factors (Gilger & Ho, 1989; Halpern, 1986). Such interactions may explain why identification behavior differs for individuals who are more strongly sex-typed, that is, who identify themselves to be "a typical male or female," versus those who are "androgynous," showing a mixture of typical male and female behaviors (Bem, 1981). They may also help to explain why homosexual males resemble heterosexual females more than they resemble heterosexual males in terms of their performance on spatial tasks (Sanders & Ross-Field, 1986).

PERSONALITY AND COGNITIVE STYLE DIFFERENCES

Individuals differ from one another in myriad nonperceptual ways. Some are outgoing and sociable; others are withdrawn and prefer to be alone. Some are careful and methodical in everything; others are haphazard and unsystematic. The total of all these behavior traits composes the individual's personality. People with different personalities tend to behave differently in many social situations and tend to respond differently to information of various sorts. Do they also perceive the world differently?

DEMONSTRATION BOX 18-3   Sex Differences and Object Identification

Look at the three accompanying figures and decide what each looks like. Do this before reading any further.

Responses to patterns similar to these show differences depending on the sex of the observer. Most males view the top figure as a brush or a centipede, whereas females tend to view it as a comb or teeth. Most men view the middle figure as a target, whereas women tend to view it as a dinner plate (but both respond equally with "ring" and "tire"). Most men see the bottom figure as a head, whereas women tend to view it as a cup.

Many attempts have been made to link individual differences in personality to individual differences in perception. Often the perceptual responses themselves are used to classify individuals as belonging to one personality type or another. A large amount of evidence has suggested that individuals differ in their ability to disembed figures from one another in tasks such as the one illustrated in Figure 18-8A (for example, T. B. Ward, 1985). Some investigators have suggested that these tests separate individuals not only according to their spatial abilities but also according to underlying personality type. Observers who have difficulty with this task are called **field dependent.** They have been classified by personality tests as being socially dependent, eager to make a good impression, conforming, and sensitive to their social surroundings (Konstadt & Forman, 1965; Linton & Graham, 1959; Ruble & Nakamura, 1972). Individuals who have little difficulty with such perceptual disembedding tasks are called **field independent.** They have been characterized by the same tests as being self-reliant, inner-directed, and individualistic (Alexander & Gudeman, 1965; Crutchfield, Woodworth, & Albrecht, 1958; Klein, 1970). Witkin has been one of the major proponents of this approach. He and his associates look upon both the personality and perceptual effects as examples of an individual's **cognitive style** (Witkin & Berry, 1975). They maintain that perceptual, cognitive, personality, and social interactions all are affected by the same set of processes that determine how a person approaches the world. In effect, cognitive style is part of what we call in everyday language "life style," affecting not only our habitual interpersonal and task-oriented behaviors but also the way we process information and, in effect, the way we perceive the world. Thus, by measuring how someone normally responds in complex perceptual situations, we can predict to some extent how that person will approach many other, nonperceptual aspects of life.

Some investigators use perception as the starting point and then move into predictions about personality; others have attempted to go in the opposite direction, predicting individual differences in perception from prior considerations of personality theory. Characteristic of this approach is the work of Eysenck (1967). He divided individuals into two groups on the basis of certain theoretical and physiological considerations. We can describe one of these groups as outgoing and sociable **(extrovert),** whereas the second group is more withdrawn and self-contained **(introvert).** Eysenck found that he could classify individuals along this dimension on the basis of a simple questionnaire, and he speculated on some physiological differences that might account for the differences in personality traits. He suggested that extroverts have a neural system that is slower to respond and more weakly aroused by stimuli than that of introverts. In addition, extroverts generate neural inhibition more quickly. If this physio-

logical speculation is correct, then introverts should be more perceptually sensitive than extroverts. Several studies have investigated the effect of introversion–extroversion on perception. Introverts do seem to have more sensitive perceptual systems as predicted by the theory. They show lower average thresholds for vision (Siddle, Morish, White, & Mangen, 1969), hearing (Stelmack & Campbell, 1974), touch (Coles, Gale, & Kline, 1971), and pain (Halsam, 1967). In addition, introverts are better at tasks requiring sustained attention or vigilance (Harkins & Green, 1975).

When we are studying the effects of personality factors on perception, it is important to be sure we are measuring perceptual sensitivity rather than simply detecting differences in how observers respond. It could be the case that introverts simply say, "Yes, I detected the stimulus" more often than extroverts. Signal detection theory (discussed in Chapter 2) allows us to separate these possibilities. When Stelmack and Campbell (1974) analyzed their data from this viewpoint, they found that introverts have more sensitive hearing than extroverts, even though extroverts are also more biased toward saying "yes."

Another way to ascertain sensitivity independent of the observer's response bias is to use direct physiological measurements. One technique is called **evoked response** recording. An electrode is placed on an observer's head over the region of the cortex receiving the primary sensory information for the sense modality being tested. Another electrode, elsewhere on the body, serves as a reference electrode. Any changes in the electrical activity of this brain region can be picked up by sensitive recording devices, and such activity presumably means that the sensory information has, at least, been registered in the brain. In this way, Stelmack, Achorn, and Michaud (1977) demonstrated that introverts seem to have greater auditory sensitivity than extroverts. Unfortunately, not all researchers have been able to verify these findings (Campbell, Baribeau-Braun, & Braun, 1981). This may mean that non-sensory factors, such as motivation or distribution of attention, or even the sort of cognitive style just discussed, rather than neurological differences, may account for the differences between introverts and extroverts on sensory tasks.

It is surprising nonetheless that the answers to a few questions about how a person interacts with other individuals can be used to predict how one person's perceptual responses may differ from those of another. Demonstration Box 18-4 allows you to estimate your own degree of introversion and extroversion and to test a typical perceptual preference for yourself.

Since personality factors that differ among those in the general population are related to differences in processing of sensory information, it is not surprising that dramatic perceptual effects are associated with certain severe personality disorders. The perceptual responses that differentiate schizophrenic from nonschizophrenic observers is one area that has received a large amount of research attention. **Schizophrenia** (from the Greek for "split mind") is the most frequent diagnosis of a

severe or psychotic personality disorder. It is usually characterized by a withdrawal (or "splitting off") from the environment, reduced levels of emotional response, a reduction in abstract thinking, and a general diminishing of daily activity. In other words, schizophrenia is a disorder that affects all aspects of the sufferer's social and cognitive life. Studies of the perceptual responses of schizophrenics have shown that they differ from control groups in their performance on time estimation (Wahl & Sieg, 1980), attentional tasks (Cegalis & Deptula, 1981), and even the perception of visual aftereffects (Tress & Kugler, 1979). Several studies have shown also that schizophrenics display eye-movement patterns that differ from those of control groups; they perform poorly when they are asked to track a moving target with their eyes (Rea & Sweeney, 1989; Levin, Lipton, & Holzman, 1981). Since poor eye-tracking behavior is also found in the close relatives of schizophrenics (who are not affected with the disorder), it has been suggested that eye-movement behavior may be a genetic marker for the disorder (Iacono, Peloquin, Lumry, Valentine, & Tuason, 1982). Other psychological disorders show different patterns of perceptual involvement. For example, patients

---

DEMONSTRATION BOX 18-4   Introversion–Extroversion and Taste Perception

It is easy to determine your own standing on introversion versus extroversion by answering the following questions with a "Yes" or a "No."

Do you often wish for more excitement in life?

Do you often say things without stopping to think?

Do you like going out a lot?

Do other people think of you as being lively?

Do you like interacting with people?

If you answered all the questions "Yes," you are rather extroverted; if you answered them all "No," you are rather introverted.

Have some friends or relatives answer these questions, but add one additional item to the list:

Do you like spicy foods?

What answer do you expect extroverts versus introverts to give? What *sensory data* would lead you to expect that answer?

suffering from depression may show increased sensitivity to light (Seggie & Canny, 1989).

Some investigators feel that these perceptual problems may be part of the cause of some personality disorders. For example, when infants with difficult temperaments were examined, well over half of them showed perceptual disturbances. Their sensory problems included poorly coordinated eye movements, excessive touch sensitivity, vestibular problems, and difficulty coordinating vision with touch (De-Gangi & Greenspan, 1988). Similarly, 62% of schizophrenics report visual distortions (including distortions in sensory processes as basic as brightness contrast), and 44% report distortions in their auditory processing (Phillipson & Harris, 1985). The close associa-

tion between perceptual difficulties and personality problems is intriguing. It has led to the speculation that alterations in sensory abilities, especially those that occur during the early phases of an individual's development, may play a key role in the later development of personality problems and even in the development of certain forms of psychopathology.

Overall, who you are, the kind of person you are, and the life history that you have had all affect what you perceive in any stimulus situation. Since you differ along many dimensions from those around you, your perception of the world has a unique flavor. What you perceive in any situation is not necessarily the same as what is perceived by the person next to you.

A family with visual hemineglect solves the pet selection problem

GLOSSARY

The following definitions are specific to their use in this book.

Agnosia   A pathological condition in which an individual can no longer attach meaning to a sensory impression.

Aphasia   A disorder characterized by difficulties involving speech and sound perception.

Auditory flutter fusion (AFF)   The rate of interruption of a continuous tone at which an observer first hears the tone as continuous.

Autotopagnosia   The distorted perception of body image and body parts.

Cognitive style   The overall personality and perceptual predispositions that are characteristics of a particular individual.

Critical flicker fusion frequency (CFF)   The minimum rate of a flickering light at which the light is perceived as continuous.

Disembedding   The ability to disentangle a target object from a surrounding, and often confusing, context.

Embedded figures test   A task used to determine spatial abilities, in which a subject is asked to find a simple shape hidden in a more complex figure.

Evoked response   Electrical response of a specific region of the brain to presentation of a stimulus.

Extrovert   An outgoing and sociable person.

Field dependent   Descriptive of individuals exhibiting difficulty with embedded-figures tasks.

Field independent   Descriptive of individuals exhibiting little difficulty with embedded-figures tasks.

Hidden figures test   *See* Embedded figures test.

Introvert   A withdrawn and self-contained person.

Mental rotation task   A task in which observers are asked to recognize a visual target in different spatial orientations (rotations).

Necker Cube   A drawing in which the three-dimensional interpretation alternates between two equally compelling possibilities (see Figure 18-2).

Poggendorff illusion   An illusion of direction that shows both age and sex differences.

Prosopagnosia   A perceptual disorder in which an individual cannot identify human faces.

Schizophrenia   A psychotic disorder characterized by withdrawal from the environment, reduced levels of emotional response, a reduction in abstract thinking, and a general diminishing of daily activity.

Simultagnosia   An attentional disorder in which an individual cannot pay attention to more than one stimulus at a time.

Spatial agnosia   A perceptual disorder in which individuals cannot accurately localize objects or themselves.

Visual hemineglect   A form of spatial agnosia in which one side of all objects and the visual field is not processed.

Visual integrative agnosia   An inability to integrate parts of a figure into a whole (usually combines symptoms of visual object agnosia and simultagnosia).

Visual object agnosia   An inability to recognize familiar objects in the absence of psychopathological or organic damage to the visual apparatus.

Answers to Demonstration Box 18-2: 3, 6, 7, 9, 11

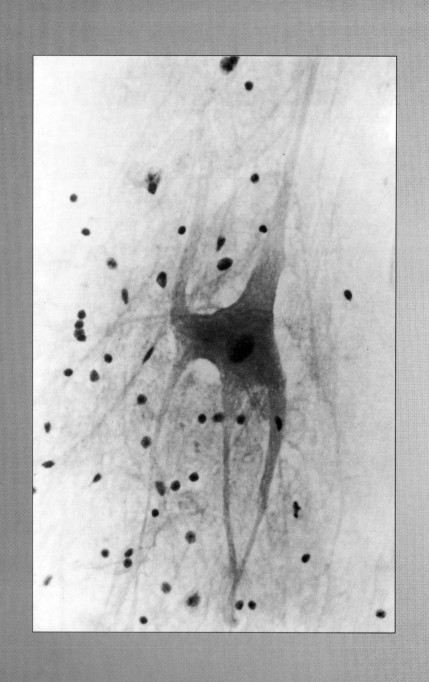

PRIMER OF NEUROPHYSIOLOGY

Appendix...

Neurons and the Nervous System

The Nature of Neural Activity

Techniques to Measure Neural Function

Individual Neural Response Techniques

Measurement of Brain Activity

Several discussions in this book assume you know some neurophysiology. Specifically, you need to know some of the terminology used for parts of the nervous system, how a neuron functions, and how we investigate neural activity in sensory systems. This appendix provides you with that information in a condensed form. More details are available from most basic texts in biopsychology (for example, N. R. Carlson, 1988; Kalat, 1992; Pinel, 1990).

NEURONS AND THE NERVOUS SYSTEM

The human nervous system contains approximately 10 to 14 billion neurons. Figure A-1 shows some aspects of several types of neurons. A **sensory neuron** conducts information from sensory receptors (either part of the neuron itself or a separate cell) toward the brain, an **interneuron** conducts information between other neurons, and a **motor neuron** conducts nerve impulses outward to the muscles. Each of these neurons is a separate cell, generally composed of three distinct parts: a **cell body,** an **axon,** and **dendrites.** The cell body contains the nucleus (which contains the genetic material) and a large variety of the molecules that govern the functioning of the neuron. The dendrites are branching structures that receive information from incoming nerve fibers from many other neurons. The axons are usually long fibers that conduct nerve impulses toward the many other neurons (or muscle fibers) with which each neuron connects. Axons typically terminate near dendrites of other neurons. Many, but not all, neurons have axons covered by protective and nutritive cells called **glial cells.** Some glial cells (including a variety called **Schwann cells)** form the **myelin sheath** around the axon, which, as you will see later, helps to increase the speed at which electrical changes travel. The myelin sheath is inter-

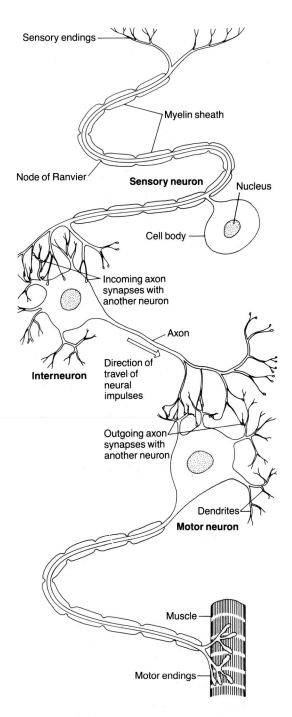

Figure A-1 Neurons of various types and their important parts and connections with each other.

rupted about every millimeter by **nodes of Ranvier,** which are the gaps between successive glial cells. Most sensory and motor nerves have a myelin sheath.

When many axons gather together into a pathway to carry information from one part of the body to the other, that pathway is called a **nerve.** Sensory information usually is carried by nerves to the **central nervous system (CNS),** which consists of the brain and the spinal cord. In the central nervous system, a pathway is no longer called a nerve, but rather a **tract,** although the terms *fasciculus* or *peduncle* are sometimes used for certain pathways. A bundle of nerve fibers ascending the spinal cord is quite often referred to as a **lemniscus.** In addition to pathways in the central nervous system, which appear as *white matter* because the myelin sheath is white, certain distinct regions containing cell bodies of many neurons grouped together appear as *gray matter*. Distinct islands of gray matter are referred to as **nuclei.** Much of the sensory information processing and complex channeling of information takes place in nuclei of the brain and spinal cord.

THE NATURE OF NEURAL ACTIVITY

Information is passed along neurons, and from one to another, by electrochemical changes in the neuron. When unstimulated, the inside of a neuron is electrically negative with respect to the outside, with a **resting potential** of about −70 millivolts (mV), mostly because of the presence of large, negatively charged proteins inside the cell. In addition, millions of *ions* (atoms that have gained or lost an electron and hence are electrically charged) occur inside and outside the neuron. The most important ions for neural action are sodium (Na^+), potassium (K^+), and chloride (Cl^-). These ions are not distributed equally on both sides of the cell membrane. The negative chloride ion is many times more common outside. The positive sodium ion is more common outside, and the positive potassium ion more common inside, mainly because of the **sodium-potassium pump,** a biochemical process that ejects 3 sodium ions for every 2 potassium ions it allows in. The resting state of the neuron represents a dynamic chemical equilibrium resulting from the flow of these and other ions across the membrane.

When a neuron is stimulated, either by a physical stimulus or by another neuron, the difference in electrical potential across the cell membrane either becomes less negative by moving toward 0 mV **(depolarization)** or more negative **(hyperpolarization).** This happens because the stimulation causes changes in the permeability of the cell membrane to various ions. Typically, when sodium is blocked from its usual flow across the membrane into the cell, the negative charge inside the cell increases (hyperpolarization). Conversely, if sodium ions are allowed to flow more rapidly into the cell, the charge becomes less negative (depolarization).

Such stimulation occurs in several different ways. Different sensory cells use different methods to transduce or change the received environmental stimulation into a depolarization or a hyperpolarization. We discuss some of these processes in the chapters devoted to particular sensory systems, since they are rather specialized. For neurons stimulated by other neurons, however, the changes in permeability are fairly standard. They are caused by release of a **transmitter substance** across the **synapse,** which is a small gap separating two cells. Figure A-2 shows the most important parts of a synaptic connection. The transmitter substance is stored in the **synaptic vesicle,** located in the **synaptic knob** near the **presynaptic membrane,** and is released across the **synaptic cleft** in amounts determined by the

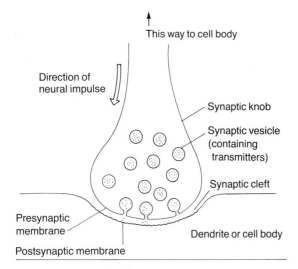

Figure A-2 A typical synapse. Transmitter substances are stored in the synaptic vesicles and released across the synaptic cleft.

amount of electrical activity in the neuron. Another positive ion, calcium (Ca^{2+}), that is present outside the cell begins the process of transmitter substance release when it enters through tiny channels opened by an electrical change in the cell membrane. Although there are many types of neurotransmitters, and some are selectively located and may be used to define particular neural circuits or systems in the central nervous system, at the functional level they can be grouped into two types. **Excitatory transmitters** *depolarize* the **postsynaptic membrane** making it more likely that the adjacent neural cell will trigger a neural impulse, whereas **inhibitory transmitters** *hyperpolarize* the postsynaptic membrane, making it less likely that a neural impulse will be sent by the receiving cell. Transmitter substances are active for only a short time after release and are either quickly neutralized by enzymes that are always present in the synaptic cleft or collected back into the emitting neuron. Typically, a given neuron will itself possess only one type of neurotransmitter in its vesicles, although it

may receive inputs from neurons that emit either type.

Usually, the stronger the excitatory stimulus to a neuron is, the greater the change in electrical potential that results. Such changes are called **graded potentials.** The neural responses in several sensory systems, such as parts of the retina that respond first (including rods, cones, and bipolar and horizontal cells), involve only a continuous graded change in electrical potential. For more central sensory neurons (such as retinal amacrine and ganglion cells), and for virtually all nonsensory neurons, the graded response is not the only response to stimulation. If a depolarization reaches a critical level, a more dramatic and rapid change in the electrical state of the neuron follows. It is referred to as the **action potential** or **spike potential.** In the action potential, the initial small depolarization is suddenly followed by a much larger and more rapid depolarization as sodium ions flow into the axon through tiny channels. This rapid depolarization, which occurs within about 1 msec, is quickly reversed and followed by a period of hyperpolarization as the sodium channels are closed and potassium ions flow out through other tiny channels. After this sudden swing in electrical charge, the potential returns to the resting level of –70 mV. During the time of hyperpolarization following a spike, called the **refractory period,** the neuron is much more difficult to excite.

These changes in electrical potentials in the neuron can be recorded by various devices, and one such recording is shown as Figure A-3. Increased stimulation does not change the degree of depolarization in the spike potential, but rather increases the number of such neural spike potentials produced by the neuron in any unit of time. This is often called the *firing rate* of the neuron. You might imagine that each neural response is a bark from a dog, and the excitement of the dog is measured by the speed at which he is barking. Thus, the frequency of responses shows the level of stimulation. Be-

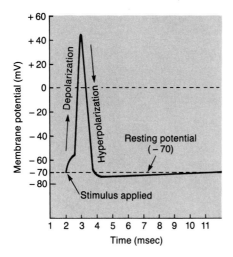

Figure A-3 *Voltage changes over time that describe a typical spike or action potential.*

cause of the refractory period, the maximum rate at which spikes can occur is about 1000 per second. Most of the information carried to the central nervous system is in the form of a series of spike potentials.

The spike potential moves as a wave of sudden depolarization along the axon of the neuron until it stimulates the release of transmitter substance where the neuron makes synapses with the dendrites or cell bodies of other neurons. The wave of depolarization moves more quickly along thicker axons than along thin ones, with a maximum speed of about 35 m per second in squid "giant" axons, which are about 500 micrometers in diameter. However, even the thickest axons in humans and other animals require help in getting conduction speeds up to levels where they are useful for quick sensing and muscular action. This help is provided by the myelin sheath worn by many axons (see Figure A-1). In myelinated axons, spikes travel from one node of Ranvier to the next at the speed of electrical conduction, which is about 300 million m per second. However, the spike occurs anew by the usual ion-exchange process at each node of Ranvier. The

slower ion-exchange process of conduction through the nodes of Ranvier limits the speed with which spike potentials can travel down a myelinated axon to a rate far less than that of electricity in a wire. However, speeds may still reach 120 m per second in myelinated axons only 20 micrometers in diameter.

TECHNIQUES TO MEASURE NEURAL FUNCTION

Investigation of the brain and neural function has tended to be conducted at two different levels. At the micro level, individual neurons have been isolated in known sensory pathways or processing centers. At the macro level, the function of neural systems or larger brain regions is studied. Each of these requires its own technology and study methods.

Individual Neural Response Techniques

Neural responses, mainly in the form of spikes, are measured using *microelectrodes*. These consist of tiny glass tubes (the tip might be 0.01 mm in size or smaller) filled with salt water. The electrode is inserted into the cell body or the axon, and the potential difference between the test electrode and a comparison or reference electrode located outside the cell is amplified and then recorded by a computer, which converts the continuous voltages to digital numbers and stores them many times per second. The continuous changes in electrical activity can also be displayed visually on an **oscilloscope,** which is a sensitive voltmeter that displays voltage changes over time by tracing them out on a screen. Oscilloscope recordings of typical spike responses are shown in Figure A-4, which shows two neurons responding at different rates.

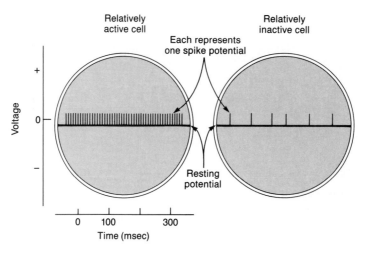

Figure A-4 Oscilloscope records of spikes generated by two neurons penetrated by recording microelectrodes.

The use of microelectrode techniques to record the activity of single neurons has produced some of the most exciting data in the field of sensory physiology. Generally, the procedure involves the application of a muscle relaxant combined with local anaesthetics to eliminate the discomfort from the restraining device used to hold an animal, in accordance with strict ethical guidelines. A **stereotaxic instrument** is used to allow the researcher to accurately place electrodes in the brain. Figure A-5 shows a cat with its head in a stereotaxic instrument. Note that the cat is viewing a screen on which visual stimuli may be presented. The electrode is attached through a set of amplifiers to the computer, to the oscilloscope, and also often to a speaker. The loudspeaker transforms the amplified neural response into a series of pops or clicks, each click caused by a single neural spike potential.

Researchers can then listen to the neural response, keeping their eyes free to attend to other matters. An increase in the rate of clicking means an increase in the frequency of cell firing, and a decrease means a reduction. An increase in firing rate when a stimulus is applied means that the neuron is being excited by the stimulus or by whatever other neurons it is connected to that are responding to the stimulus. A decrease in the firing rate indicates that the stimulus or other neurons are inhibiting the neuron from which the recordings are being made. Typically, the records of neural activity, along with the conditions under which they occurred, are analyzed by the computer for patterns that indicate their functional significance.

Measurement of Brain Activity

The earliest attempts to study the function of larger areas of the nervous system involved **lesions** (places where neural tissue is destroyed) or **ablations** (where part of the brain is removed). By observing the relation between where a lesion or ablation was made and which functions were affected, much information was gained about sensory processing. Unfortunately, the results of lesion or ablation experiments are often difficult to interpret, since the loss of function may be due to many factors. A somewhat crude example is that it is possible to stop an animal from further visual process-

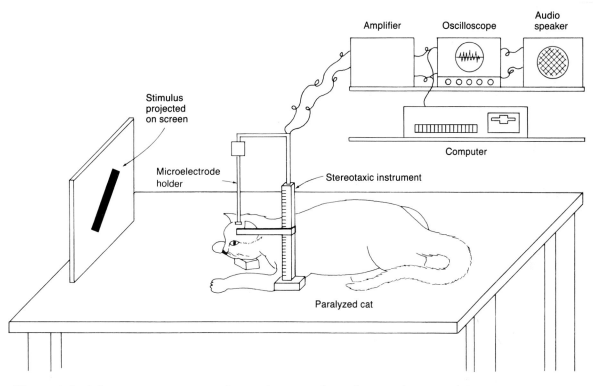

Figure A-5 Schematic setup to record neural activity from the visual cortex of the cat (actual apparatus is designed for maximal comfort and safety of the animal).

ing by destroying the centers in the brain stem that control breathing, since an animal that cannot breathe dies, and a dead animal cannot see. We would *not* want to conclude from this lesion study that the brainstem is directly involved in processing visual stimuli.

Electrical recordings have also been used to study the function of brain regions by attaching electrodes to the scalp. This produces the familiar **electroencephalogram** or **EEG,** which measures the average activity of thousands of cells in a particular region. Locating a number of electrodes over various regions of the skull allows precise pinpointing of the areas of the brain that are most active (for example, John, Prichep, Fridman, & Easton, 1988). Localized EEGs measured in response to brief sensory stimuli, which are called *evoked po-*

tentials, are now routinely used in studies of vision, audition, and speech perception and are the main tool of a new field called *cognitive psychophysiology*. Recent variations of electrical recordings involve the measurement of magnetic fields produced as a side effect of the electrical changes caused by neural activity in regions of the brain. This technique, called **magnetoencephalography** or **MEG,** allows more precise localization of regions of neural activity (for example, Hari & Lounasmaa, 1989).

Other techniques for measuring the dynamic functioning of the brain take advantage of normal metabolic functioning. One of the most exciting is **positron emission tomography (PET)** scans. Basically, it involves the injection of a radioactive form of glucose

(2-deoxyglucose, or 2-DG) that is the major fuel for brain activity. This substance is picked up by the active energy-consuming brain areas that are seeking fuel to sustain their continued activity. However, the 2-DG is slow to metabolize and accumulates in the active neurons. Thus, if a person were viewing a picture, we would expect 2-DG to accumulate in the visually active areas. The radioactive glucose in the brain regions is detectable by sensitive recorders that detect the gamma ray bursts that result as positrons (subatomic antiparticles emitted by the decay of the radioactive 2-DG) collide with normal matter and mutually annihilate. Maps of the active regions of the brain can then be made (for example, Fox, Mintun, Reiman, & Raichle, 1988). Two such maps (one for visual and another for auditory activities) are shown in Color Plate 10.

Two other techniques for measuring brain activity also depend on metabolic changes (Andreasen, 1988). Specifically, they rely on the fact that there is increased blood flow to active brain areas. Since this change in blood flow occurs fairly quickly, it can allow the measurement of rapid changes in the pattern of brain activity. The original method for monitoring these activity changes is called the **regional cerebral blood flow** method, or **rCBF.** The technique involves injecting into a person a relatively inert, radioactively tagged substance that goes where the blood goes without being absorbed. Detectors placed around the head determine the blood flow by detecting the radioactive emissions, hence indicating the most active regions (Berman, Zec, & Weinberger, 1986).

The second method for determining function based on blood flow is **magnetic resonance imaging (MRI),** also called **nuclear magnetic resonance (NMR).** This technique does not involve any added radioactive substances. Rather, it depends on the fact that the ordinarily randomly oriented axes of rotation of the hydrogen atoms bound in blood can be aligned by an outside magnetic field and then made to spin like tiny gyroscopes by a radio-frequency electromagnetic field. When the radio-frequency field is turned off, the hydrogen atoms release electromagnetic energy as their spinning slows. The released energy can be measured, and from it can be deduced the concentration of hydrogen atoms in the region being monitored. This can tell us about the blood flow and volume in any region of the brain, and it thus helps to pinpoint the most active regions of neural activity during sensory activity (for example, Belliveau, et al., 1991; Moonen, van Zijl, Frank, Le Bihan, & Becker, 1990).

These new methods are beginning to expand our knowledge of how the brain processes sensory information. They are particularly exciting because, like the older EEG, they allow us comfortably to test human beings, who are conscious and responding to the stimuli in the world around them, without any surgical interventions or pain.

GLOSSARY

The following definitions are specific to their use in this book.

Ablation   Surgical removal of neural tissue.

Action potential   The large depolarization of a neuron, 1 msec in duration, that occurs when a graded depolarization exceeds a certain threshold. Also called *spike potential*.

Axon   The long, slender part of a neuron that conducts membrane potential changes away from the cell body and makes synapses with other neurons or their dendrites or with muscle fibers.

Cell body   The part of a neuron that contains the nucleus.

Central nervous system (**CNS**)   The brain and spinal cord.

Dendrites The branching parts of a neuron that make synapses with other neurons and serve as receivers of excitatory or inhibitory neural stimulation.

Depolarization A change from the resting level of −70 mV toward 0 mV of electrical potential across the cell membrane of a neuron.

Electroencephalogram (EEG) Recordings of the activity of brain neurons by measuring electrical potentials between electrodes affixed to the scalp and reference electrodes on the body.

Excitatory transmitter A substance released across a synapse that causes the postsynaptic membrane to depolarize.

Glial cells Cells that protect and feed neurons; some types form the myelin sheath as well.

Graded potential A change in electrical potential across the cell membrane of a neuron that varies in magnitude with the intensity of the stimulation.

Hyperpolarization An increase in the negative electrical potential across the cell membrane.

Inhibitory transmitter A substance released across a synapse that causes the postsynaptic membrane to hyperpolarize.

Interneuron A neuron that conducts information from one neuron to another.

Lemniscus A bundle of neural fibers ascending the spinal cord.

Lesion The destruction or functional disruption of neural pathways or nuclei.

Magnetic resonance imaging (MRI) Mapping brain activity by measuring blood flow and volume by monitoring changes in a magnetic field that occur after hydrogen atoms in the brain are exposed to a strong radio frequency signal. Also called nuclear magnetic resonance (NMR).

Magnetoencephalography (MEG) Mapping of brain activity from changes in the brain's magnetic field caused by the electrical activity of neurons.

Motor neuron A neuron that conducts activity from the central nervous system outward toward the muscles.

Myelin sheath A covering of glial cells on the axons of neurons that allows an increase in the speed of transmission of neural activity.

Nerve A bundle of axons that carries information from one part of the body to another.

Nodes of Ranvier Interruptions in the myelin sheath (about every millimeter) that increase the speed of neural spike transmission.

Nuclear magnetic resonance (NMR) See Magnetic resonance imaging (MRI).

Nuclei Groups of cell bodies of neurons found in the spinal cord and brain.

Oscilloscope A sensitive voltmeter that displays voltage changes over time as a tracing on a screen.

Positron emission tomography (PET) Mapping of brain activity by detecting the metabolic uptake of a radioactively tagged form of glucose molecule.

Postsynaptic membrane The cell membrane of a neuron that is *receiving* transmitter substance across a synapse.

Presynaptic membrane The cell membrane of a neuron that is *sending* transmitter substance across a synapse.

Refractory period A period of time shortly after a spike, during which it is difficult to stimulate the neuron sufficiently to produce another spike.

Regional cerebral blood flow (rCBF) Mapping of brain activity by monitoring blood flow with a relatively inert but radioactively tagged material dissolved in the blood.

Resting potential The usual electrical potential difference across the cell wall of a neuron, typically with the inside about −70 mV with respect to the outside.

Schwann cells One type of glial cell forming the myelin sheath around axons.

Sensory neuron A neuron that carries information from a sensory receptor toward the brain or spinal cord.

Sodium-potassium pump A mechanism that ejects 3 sodium ions from inside the neuron for every 2 potassium ions it lets in, thus helping to maintain the −70 mV resting potential.

Spike potential *See* Action potential.

Stereotaxic instrument A device that allows accurate placement of electrodes in the brains of experimental animals.

Synapse The place where two neurons almost touch each other.

Synaptic cleft The gap between two neurons at a synapse, into which neural transmitters are released.

Synaptic knob Swelling at the ends of an axon. It contains the synaptic vesicles.

Synaptic vesicles Small reservoirs in the synaptic knobs that contain neural transmitters.

Tract The most common name for a nerve in the central nervous system.

Transmitter substance Chemicals released into the synaptic cleft that polarize or hyperpolarize the postsynaptic membrane.

References

Aantaa, E. (1970). Light-induced and spontaneous variations in the amplitude of the electro-oculogram. *Acta Otolaryngologica, Supplementum, 267.*

Aaron, M. (1975). Effect of the menstrual cycle on subjective ratings of sweetness. *Perceptual and Motor Skills, 40,* 974.

Abbs, J. H., & Sussman, H. M. (1971). Neurophysiological feature detectors and speech perception: Discussion of theoretical implications. *Journal of Speech and Hearing Research, 14,* 23–36.

Abraham, H. D., & Wolf, E. (1988). Visual function in past users of LSD: Psychophysical findings. *Journal of Abnormal Psychology, 97,* 443–447.

Abramov, I., Gordon, J., Henderson, A., Hainline, L., Dobson, V., & La Brossiere, E. (1982). The retina of the newborn human infant. *Science, 217,* 265–267.

Adam, N., Rosner, B. S., Hosick, E. C., & Clark, D. L. (1971). Effect of anesthetic drugs on time production and alpha rhythm. *Perception & Psychophysics, 10,* 133–136.

Adams, A. S., Brown, B., Haegerstrom-Portnoy, G., & Flom, M. C. (1976). Evidence for acute effect of alcohol and marijuana on color discrimination. *Perception & Psychophysics, 20,* 119–124.

Adams, C. L., & Molfese, D. L. (1987). Electrophysiological correlates of categorical speech perception for voicing contrasts in dogs. *Developmental Neuropsychology, 3,* 175–189.

Adams, J. (1989). Newborns' discrimination among mid- and long-wavelength stimuli. *Journal of Experimental Child Psychology, 47,* 130–141.

Adams, J. A. (1977). Feedback theory of how joint receptors regulate the timing and positioning of a limb. *Psychological Review, 84,* 503–523.

Adams, R. D. (1977). Intervening stimulus effects on category judgments of duration. *Perception & Psychophysics, 21,* 527–534.

Aitkin, L., & Martin, R. (1990). Neurons in the inferior colliculus of cats sensitive to sound-source elevation. *Hearing Research, 50,* 97–106.

Akabas, M. H., Dodd, J., & Al-Awqati, Q. (1988). A bitter substance induces a rise in intracellular calcium in a subpopulation of rat taste cells. *Science, 242,* 1047–1050.

Akhtar, N., & Enns, J. T. (1989). Relations between covert orienting and filtering in the development of visual attention. *Journal of Experimental Child Psychology, 48,* 315–334.

Akil, H., & Watson S. J. (1980). The role of endogenous opiates in pain control. In H. W. Kosterlitz & L. Y. Terenius (Eds.), *Pain and Society* (pp. 201–222). Weinheim: Verlag Chemie Gmblt.

Alexander, J. B., & Gudeman, H. E. (1965). Personal and interpersonal measures of field dependence. *Perceptual and Motor Skills, 20,* 70–86.

Alexander, K. R., & Shansky, M. S. (1976). Influence of hue, value, and chrom on the perceived heaviness of colours. *Perception & Psychophysics, 19,* 72–74.

Algom, D., Ben-Aharon, B., & Cohen-Raz, L. (1989). Dichotic, diotic, and monaural summation of loudness: A comprehensive analysis of composition and psychophysical functions. *Perception & Psychophysics, 46,* 567–578.

Algom, D., & Marks, L. E. (1990). Range and regression, loudness scales, and loudness processing: Toward a context-bound psychophysics. *Journal of Experimental Psychology: Human Perception and Performance, 16,* 706–727.

Algom, D., Raphaeli, N., & Cohen-Raz, L. (1986). Integration of noxious stimulation across separate somatosensory communications systems: A functional theory of pain. *Journal of Experimental Psychology: Human Perception and Performance, 12,* 92–102.

Algom, D., Rubin, A., & Cohen-Raz, L. (1989). Binaural and temporal integration of the loudness of tones and noises. *Perception & Psychophysics, 46,* 155–166.

Ali, M. R., & Amir, T. (1989). Effects of fasting on visual flicker fusion. *Perceptual and Motor Skills, 69,* 627–631.

Allan, L. G., & Siegel, S. (1986). McCollough effects as conditioned responses: Reply to Skowbo. *Psychological Bulletin, 100,* 388–393.

Allen, J. R. (1985). Salicylate-induced musical perceptions. *New England Journal of Medicine, 313,* 642–643.

Allen, M. (1970). *Vision and highway safety.* Radnor, PA: Chilton Books.

Allison, A. C. (1953). The structure of the olfactory bulb and its relation to the olfactory pathways in the rabbit and the rat. *Journal of Comparative Neurology, 98,* 309–348.

Allman, J., Miezin, F., & McGuinness, E. (1985). Direction- and velocity-specific responses from beyond the classical receptive field in the middle temporal visual area (MT). *Perception, 14,* 105–126.

Allport, D. A., Antonis, B., & Reynolds, P. (1972). On the division of attention: A disproof of the single channel hypothesis. *Quarterly Journal of Psychology, 24,* 225–235.

Alpern, M. (1979). Lack of uniformity in color matching. *Journal of Physiology, 288,* 85–105.

Ames, A., Jr. (1951). Visual perception and the rotating trapezoid window. *Psychological Monographs, 65* (14, Whole No. 324).

Ames, A., Jr. (1955). *The nature of our perception, apprehensions and behavior.* Princeton, NJ: Princeton University Press.

Amoore, J. E. (1969). A plan to identify most of the primary odors. In C. Pfaffman (Ed.), *Olfaction and taste III* (pp. 158–171). New York: Rockefeller University Press.

Amoore, J. E. (1970). *Molecular basis of odor.* Springfield, IL: Thomas.

Amoore, J. E. (1975). Four primary odor modalities of man: Experimental evidence and possible significance. In D. A. Denton & J. P. Coghlan (Eds.), *Olfaction and Taste V* (pp. 283–289). New York: Academic Press.

Amoore, J. E., Pelosi, P., & Forrester, L. J. (1977). Specific anosmias to 5α-androst-16 en-3one and w-pentadecalone: The urinous and musky odors. *Chemical Senses and Flavor, 5,* 401–425.

Amure, B. O. (1978). Nicotine and decay of the McCullough effect. *Vision Research, 18,* 1449–1451.

Andersen, G. J. (1986). Perception of self-motion: Psychophysical and computational approaches. *Psychological Bulletin, 99,* 52–65.

Andersen, G. J., & Braunstein, M. L. (1985). Induced self-motion in central vision. *Journal of Experimental Psychology: Human Perception and Performance, 11,* 122–132.

Anderson, N. H. (1975). On the role of context effects in psychophysical judgment. *Psychological Review, 82,* 462–482.

Anderson, N. S., & Fitts, P. M. (1958). Amount of information gained during brief exposures of numerals and colors. *Journal of Experimental Psychology, 56,* 362–369.

Andreasen, N. C. (1988). Brain imaging: Applications in psychiatry. *Science, 239,* 1381–1388.

Andrews, B. W., & Pollen, D. A. (1979). Relationship between spatial frequency selectivity and receptive field profile of simple cells. *Journal of Physiology, 287,* 163–176.

Annis, R. C., & Frost, B. (1973). Human visual ecology and orientation anisotropies in acuity. *Science, 182,* 729–731.

Anstis, S. M. (1975). What does visual perception tell us about visual coding? In M. S. Gazzaniga & C. Blakemore (Eds.), *Handbook of psychobiology* (pp. 267–234). New York: Academic Press.

Anstis, S. M. (1978). Apparent movement. In R. Held, H. W. Leibowitz, & H. L. Teuber (Eds.), *Handbook of sensory physiology* (pp. 655–673). New York: Springer Verlag.

Anstis, S. M., & Mather, G. (1985) Effects of luminance and contrast on direction of ambiguous motion. *Perception, 14,* 167–179.

Anstis, S. M., Rogers, B., & Henry, J. (1978) Interactions between simultaneous contrast and colored afterimages. *Vision Research, 18,* 899–911.

Antes, J. R., & Penland, J. (1981). Picture context effects on eye movement patterns. In D. Fisher, R. Monty, & J. Senders (Eds.), *Eye movements: Cognition and visual perception* (pp. 157–170). New Jersey: Erlbaum.

Antes, J. R. (1974). The time course of picture viewing. *Journal of Experimental Psychology, 103,* 62–70.

Arend, L. E., & Goldstein, R. (1987). Lightness models, gradient illusions, and curl. *Perception & Psychophysics, 42,* 65–80.

Arlin, M. (1986). The effects of quantity, complexity, and attentional demand on children's time perception. *Perception & Psychophysics, 40,* 177–182.

Arterberry, M., & Yonas, A. (1989). Self-produced locomotion and the development of responsiveness to linear perspective and texture gradients. *Developmental Psychology, 25,* 976–982.

Arvidson, K., & Friberg, U. (1980). Human taste response and taste bud number in fungiform papillae. *Science, 209,* 807–808.

Asano, F., Suzuki, Y., & Sone, T. (1990). Role of spectral cues in median plane localization. *Journal of the Acoustical Society of America, 88,* 159–168.

Aschoff, J. (1979). Circadian rhythms: General features and endocrinological aspects. In D. T. Krieger (Ed.), *Endocrine rhythms* (pp. 1–61). New York: Raven Press.

Aschoff, J. (1981). *Handbook of behavioral neurobiology: Vol. 4.* New York: Plenum Press.

Aschoff, J. (1984). Circadian timing. *Annals of the New York Academy of Sciences, 423,* 442–468.

Ashby, F. G., & Perrin, N. A. (1988). Toward a unified theory of similarity and recognition. *Psychological Review, 95,* 124–150.

Ashmead, D. H., LeRoy, D., & Odom, R. D. (1990). Perception of the relative distances of nearby sound sources. *Perception & Psychophysics, 47,* 326–331.

Aslin, R. N. (1981a). Development of smooth pursuit in human infants. In D. Fisher, R. Monty, & J. Senders (Eds.) *Eye movements: Cognition and visual perception,* (pp. 31–52). Hillsdale, NJ: Erlbaum.

Aslin, R. N. (1981b). Experiential influences and sensitive periods in perceptual development: A unified model. In R. N. Aslin, J. R. Alberts, & M. R. Peterson (Eds.), *Development of perception* (pp. 45–93). New York: Academic Press.

Aslin, R. N. (1985). Effects of experience on sensory and perceptual development: Implications for infant cognition. In J. Mehler & R. Fox (Eds.), *Neonate cognition: Beyond the blooming buzzing confusion* (pp. 157–184). Hillsdale, NJ: Erlbaum.

Aslin, R. N. (1987). Motor aspects of visual development in infancy. In P. Salapatek & L. Cohen (Eds.), *Handbook of infant perception: Vol. 1. From sensation to perception* (pp. 43–113). Orlando: Academic Press.

Aslin, R. N., & Dumais, S. (1980). Binocular vision in infants: A review and a theoretical framework. In H. Reese & L. Lipsett (Eds.) *Advances in child development and behavior: Vol. 15* (pp. 54–95). New York: Academic Press.

Aslin, R. N., & Smith, L. B. (1988). Perceptual development. *Annual Review of Psychology, 39,* 435–473.

Atkinson, J. (1979). Development of optokinetic nystagmus in the human infant and monkey infant: An analogue to development in kittens. In R.D. Freeman (Ed.), *Developmental neurobiology of vision* (pp. 277–288). New York: Plenum Press.

Atkinson, J. (1984). Human visual development over the first six months of life: A review and a hypothesis. *Human Neurobiology, 3,* 61–74.

Atkinson, J., & Braddick, O. (1981). Acuity, contrast, sensitivity, and accommodation in infancy. In R. Aslin, J. Alberts, & M. Petersen (Eds.), *Development of perception: Psychobiological perspectives: Vol.2. The visual system* (pp. 243–278). New York: Academic Press.

Atkinson, J., Braddick, O., & French, J. (1979). Contrast sensitivity of the human neonate measured by the visual evoked potential. *Investigative Ophthalmology and Visual Sciences, 18,* 210–213.

Atkinson, J., Hood, B., Braddick, O. J., & Wattam-Bell, J. (1988). Infants' control of fixation shifts with single and competing targets: Mechanisms for shifting attention. *Perception, 17,* 367–368.

Attneave, F. (1954). Some informational aspects of visual perception. *Psychological Review, 61,* 183–193.

Attneave, F. (1955). Symmetry, information and memory for patterns. *American Journal of Psychology, 68,* 209–222.

Aubert, H. (1886). Die Bewegungsempfindung. *Archiv fuer die Gesamte Physiologie des Menschen and der Tiere, 39,* 347–370.

Augenstine, L. G. (1962). A model of how humans process information. *Biometrics, 18,* 420–421.

Avant, L. L. (1965). Vision in the Ganzfeld. *Psychological Bulletin, 64,* 246–258.

Avant, L. L., & Lyman, P. J. (1975). Stimulus familiarity modifies perceived duration in prerecognition visual processing. *Journal of Experimental Psychology: Human Perception and Performance, 1,* 205–213.

Avant, L. L., Lyman, P. J., & Antes, J. R. (1975). Effects of stimulus familiarity upon judged visual duration. *Per-*

ception & Psychophysics, 17, 253–262.

Avolio, B., Kroeck, K., & Panek, P. (1986) Individual differences in information processing ability as a predictor of motor vehicle accidents. *Human Factors, 27,* 577–588.

Baddeley, A. D. (1966). Time estimation at reduced body temperature. *American Journal of Psychology, 79,* 475–479.

Bainard, D. H., & Wandell, B. A. (1986). Analysis of the retinex theory of color vision. *Journal of the Optical Society of America A, 3,* 1651–1661.

Baird, J. C. (1975). Psychophysical study of numbers: IV. Generalized preferred state theory. *Psychological Research, 38,* 175–187.

Baird, J. C., Green, D. M., & Luce, R. D. (1980). Variability and sequential effect in cross modality matching of area and loudness. *Journal of Experimental Psychology: Human Perception and Psychophysics, 6,* 277–289.

Baird, J. C., & Noma, E. (1978). *Fundamentals of scaling and psychophysics.* New York: Wiley.

Bakalyar, H. A., & Reed, R. R. (1990). Identification of specialized adenylyl cyclase that may mediate odorant detection. *Science, 250,* 1403–1406.

Baker, C. L., & Braddick, O. J. (1985). Temporal properties of the short-range process in apparent motion. *Perception, 14,* 181–192.

Balint, R. (1909). Seelenlahmung des "Schauens," optische Ataxie, raumliche Storung der Aufmerksamkeit. *Monatsschr. Psychiatr. Neurol., 25,* 51–81.

Ball, K. K., Roenker, D. L., & Bruni, J. R. (1990). Developmental changes in attention and visual search throughout adulthood. In J. T. Enns (Ed.), *The development of attention: Research and theory* (pp. 489–508). Amsterdam: Elsevier.

Ball, W., & Vurpillot, E. (1976). La perception du mouvement en profondur chez le nourrisson. *L'Annee Psychologique, 67,* 393–400.

Ballard, D. H., Hinton, G. E., & Sejnowski, T. J. (1983). Parallel visual computation. *Nature, 306,* 21–26.

Balogh, R. D., & Porter, R. H. (1986). Olfactory preferences resulting from mere exposure in human neonates. *Infant Behavior and Development, 9,* 395–401.

Banks, M. S., & Dannemiller, J. L. (1987). Infant visual psychophysics. In P. Salapatek & L. Cohen (Eds.), *Handbook of infant perception: Vol. 1. From sensation to perception* (pp. 115–184). Orlando: Academic Press.

Banks, M. S., & Salapatek, P. (1983). Infant visual perception. In M. M. Haith & J. J. Campos (Eds.), *Handbook of child psychology* (pp. 435–571). New York: Wiley.

Bannatyne, A. (1971). *Language, reading and learning disabilities.* Springfield, IL: Thomas.

Barbeito, R. (1981). Sighting dominance: An explanation

based on the processing of visual direction in tests of sighting dominance. *Vision Research, 21,* 855–860.

Barclay, C. D., Cutting, J. E., & Kozlowski, L. T. (1978). Temporal and spatial factors in gait perception that influence gender recognition. *Perception & Psychophysics, 23,* 145–152.

Barlow, H. B. (1985). The role of single neurons in the psychology of perception. *Quarterly Journal of Experimental Psychology, 37A,* 121–145.

Barsz, K. (1991). Auditory pattern perception: The effect of tone location on the discrimination of tonal sequences. *Perception & Psychophysics, 50,* 290–296.

Bartleson, C. J. (1960). Memory colors of familiar objects. *Journal of the Optical Society of America, 50,* 73–77.

Bartoshuk, L. M. (1974). Taste illusions: Some demonstrations. *Annals of the New York Academy of Sciences, 237,* 279–285.

Bartoshuk, L. M (1978). Gustatory system. In R. B. Masterton (Ed.), *Handbook of behaviorial neurobiology: Vol. I. Sensory integration* (pp. 503–567). New York: Plenum Press.

Bartoshuk, L. M. (1979). Bitter taste of saccharine related to the genetic ability to taste the bitter substance 6-n-propylthiouracil. *Science, 205,* 934–935.

Bartoshuk, L. M. (1988). Clinical psychophysics of taste. *Gerodontics, 4,* 249–255.

Bartoshuk, L. M. (1990). Distinctions between taste and smell relevant to the role of experience. In E. Capaldi & T. L. Powley (Eds.), *Taste, experience, and feeding* (pp. 62–72). Washington, DC: American Psychological Association.

Bartoshuk, L. M., Rifkin, B., Marks, L. E., & Hooper, J. E. (1988). Bitterness of KCl and benzoate: Related to genetic status for sensitivity to PTC/PROP. *Chemical Senses, 13,* 517–528.

Bashford, J. A. & Warren, R. M. (1987). Multiple phonemic restorations follow the rules for auditory induction. *Perception & Psychophysics, 42,* 114–121.

Bates, M. E. (1989). The effect of repeated occasions of alcohol intoxication on two processes involved in the visual discrimination of movement. *Journal of Studies on Alcohol, 50,* 143–154.

Batteau, D. W. (1967). The role of the pinna in human localization. *Proceedings of the Royal Society of London, Series B, 168,* 158–180.

Beauchamp, G. K., & Cowart, B. J. (1985). Congenital and experiential factors in the development of human flavor preferences. *Appetite, 6,* 357–372.

Beck, J. (1965). Apparent spatial position and the perception of lightness. *Journal of Experimental Psychology, 69,* 170–179.

Beck, J. (1966). Effects of orientation and of shape similarity on perceptual grouping. *Perception & Psychophysics, 1,* 300–302.

Beck, J. (1982). Textural segmentation. In J. Beck (Ed.), *Organization and representation in perception* (pp. 285–317). Hillsdale, NJ: Erlbaum.

Beck, J., & Schwartz, T. (1979). Verner acuity with dot test objects. *Vision Research, 19,* 313–319.

Beck, N. C., & Siegel, L. J. (1980). Preparation for childbirth and contemporary research on pain, anxiety, and stress reduction: A review and critique. *Psychosomatic Medicine, 42,* 429–447.

Beckett, P. A. (1989). Illusion decrement and transfer of illusion decrement in real- and subjective-contour Poggendorff figures. *Perception & Psychophysics, 45,* 550–556.

Begleiter, H., Porjesz, B., & Chou, C. L. (1981). Auditory brain-stem potentials in chronic alcoholics. *Science, 211,* 1064–1066.

Beidler, L. M., & Smallman, R. L. (1965). Renewal of cells within taste buds. *Journal of Cell Biology, 27,* 263–272.

Bekesy, G. von. (1947). A new audiometer. *Acta oto–laryngologica, 35,* 411–422.

Bekesy, G. von. (1959). Synchronism of neural discharges and their demultiplication in pitch perception on the skin and in learning. *Journal of the Acoustical Society of America, 31,* 338–349.

Bekesy, G. von. (1960). *Experiments in hearing.* New York: McGraw-Hill.

Bekesy, G. von. (1967). *Sensory inhibition.* Princeton, NJ: Princeton University Press.

Belliveau, J. W., Kennedy, D. N., McKinstry, R. C., Buchbinder, R. R., Weisskipff, R. M., Cohen, M. S., Vevea, J. M., Brady, T. J., & Rosen, B. R. (1991). Functional mapping of the human visual cortex by magnetic resonance imaging. *Science, 254,* 716–719.

Bem, S. L. (1981). Gender schema theory: A cognitive account of sex typing. *Psychological Review, 88,* 354–364.

Benedetti, F. (1985). Processing of tactile spatial information with crossed fingers. *Journal of Experimental Psychology: Human Perception and Performance, 11,* 517–525.

Bennett, T. L., & Morgan, R. J. (1978). Temporary threshold shifts in auditory sensitivity produced by the combined effects of noise and sodium salicylate. *Bulletin of the Psychonomic Society, 12,* 95–98.

Bentham, J. van (1985). Semantics of time. In J.A. Michon & J.L. Jackson (Eds.), *Time, mind and behavior* (pp. 266–278). Berlin: Springer-Verlag.

Bentin, S., & Mann, V. A. (1990). Masking and stimulus intensity effects on duplex perception: A confirmation of the dissociation between speech and nonspeech modes. *Journal of the Acoustical Society of America, 88,* 64–74.

Berbaum, K., Bever, T., & Chung, C. S. (1983). Light

source position in the perception of object shape. *Perception, 12,* 411–416.

Berbaum, K., Bever, T., & Chung, C. S. (1984). Extending the perception of shape from known to unknown shading. *Perception, 13,* 479–488.

Berbaum, K., Lenel, J. C. (1983). Objects in the path of apparent motion. *American Journal of Psychology, 96,* 491–501.

Berbaum K., Tharp, D., & Mroczek, K. (1983). Depth perception of surfaces in pictures: Looking for conventions of depiction in Pandora's box. *Perception, 12,* 5–20.

Berg, B. G., & Green, D. M. (1990). Spectral weights in profile listening. *Journal of the Acoustical Society of America, 88,* 758–766.

Berg, K. M., & Smith, M. C. (1983). Behavioral thresholds for tones during infancy. *Journal of Experimental Child Psychology, 35,* 409–425.

Bergeijk, W.A. van (1967). The evolution of vertebrate hearing. In W. D. Neff (Ed.), *Contributions to sensory physiology: Vol. 2* (pp. 1–49). New York: Academic Press.

Berger, G. O. (1896). Uber den Einfluss der Reizstarke auf die Dauer einfacher psychischer Vorgange mit besonderer Rucksicht auf Lichtreize. *Philosophische Studien, (Wundt), 3,* 38–93.

Berglund, M. B. (1991). Quality assurance in environmental psychophysics. In S. J. Bolanowski & G. A. Gescheider (Eds.), *Ratio scaling of Psychological Magnitude* (pp. 140–162). Hillsdale, NJ: Erlbaum.

Berkley, M. A. (1982). Neural substrates of the visual perception of movement. In A. H. Wertheim, W. A. Wagenaar, & H. W. Leibowitz (Eds.), *Tutorials on motion perception* (pp. 201–229). New York: Plenum Press.

Berlin, B., & Kay, P. (1969). *Basic color terms.* Berkeley: University of California Press.

Berman, E. R. (1991). *Biochemistry of the eye.* New York: Plenum Press.

Berman, K. F., Zec, R. F., & Weinberger, D. R. (1986). Physiologic dysfunction of dorsolateral prefrontal cortex in schizophrenia: II. Role of neuroleptic treatment, attention and mental effort. *Archives of General Psychiatry, 43,* 126–135.

Bernstein, I. H., Bissonnette, V., Vyas, A., & Barclay, P. (1989). Semantic priming: Subliminal perception or context. *Perception & Psychophysics, 45,* 153–161.

Bernstein, L. R., & Green, D. M. (1987). Detection of simple and complex changes of spectral shape. *Journal of the Acoustical Society of America, 82,* 1587–1592.

Berry, J. W. (1971). Mueller-Lyer susceptibility: Culture, ecology, race? *International Journal of Psychology, 7,* 193–196.

Besser, G. (1966). Centrally acting drugs and auditory flutter. In A. Herxheimer (Ed.), *Proceedings of the Symposium on Drugs and Sensory Functions* (pp. 199–200). London: SS Churchill, Ltd.

Best, C. T. (1992). The emergence of language-specific phonemic influences in infant speech perception. In J. Goodman & H. C. Nusbaum (Eds.), *Speech perception and word recognition.* Cambridge, MA: MIT Press.

Betke, K. (1991). New hearing threshold measurements for pure tones under free-field listening conditions. *Journal of the Acoustical Society of America, 89,* 2400–2403.

Bhatia, B. (1975). Minimum separable as function of speed of a moving object. *Vision Research, 15,* 23–33.

Biederman, I. (1987). Recognition-by-components: A theory of human image understanding. *Psychological Review, 94,* 115–147.

Biederman, I., Glass, A. L., & Stacey, E. W. Jr. (1973). Searching for objects in real-world scenes. *Journal of Experimental Psychology, 97,* 22–27.

Bigiani, A. R., & Roper, S. D. (1991). Mediation of responses to calcium in taste cells by modulation of a potassium conductance. *Science, 252,* 126–128.

Billings, B. L., & Stokinger, T. E. (1977). Investigation of several aspects of low-frequency (200 Hz) central masking. *Journal of the Acoustical Society of America, 61,* 1260–1263.

Birch, E. E., Shimojo, S., & Held, R. (1985). Preferential-looking assessment of fusion and stereopsis in infants aged 1–6 months. *Investigative Ophthalmology and Visual Science, 26,* 366–370.

Birnbaum, M. H. (1981). Clinical management of myopia. *American Journal of Optometry and Physiological Optics, 58,* 554–559.

Birren, J. E., Woods, A., & Williams, M. (1980). Behavioral slowing with age: Causes, organization, and consequences. In L. Poon (Ed.), *Aging in the 1980s* (pp. 293–308). Washington, DC: American Psychological Association.

Birren, J. E., Casperson, R. C., & Botwinick, J. (1950). Age changes in pupil size. *Journal of Gerontology, 5,* 267–271.

Bishop, P .O. (1981). Binocular vision. In R. A. Moses (Ed.), *Adler's physiology of the eye: Clinical applications* (7th ed.) (pp. 575–649). St. Louis, MO: Mosby.

Bishop, P. O. (1984). Processing of visual information within the retinostriate system. In I. Darian-Smith (Ed.), *Handbook of physiology: Section I. The nervous system. Volume III: Sensory Processes* (pp. 340–424). Bethesda, MD: American Physiological Society.

Bishop, P. O., & Pettigrew, J. D. (1986). Neural mechanisms of binocular vision. *Vision Research, 26,* 1587–1600.

Blake, R. (1981). Strategies for assessing visual deficits in animals with selective neural deficits. In R. N. Aslin, J. R. Alberts, & M. R. Petersen (Eds.), *Development of perception: Vol. 2. The visual system* (pp. 95–110). New York: Academic Press.

Blakemore, C. (1978). Maturation and modification in the developing visual system. In R. Held, M. W. Leibowitz, & H. L. Teuber (Eds.), *Handbook of sensory physiology: Vol. VIII. Perception* (pp. 377–436). New York: Springer-Verlag.

Blakemore, C., & Nachmias, J. (1971). Orientation specificity on two visual aftereffects. *Journal of Physiology, 171,* 286–288.

Blakeslee, A. F., & Salmon, T. H. (1935). Genetics of sensory thresholds: Individual taste reactions for different substances. *Proceedings of the National Academy of Sciences of the U.S.A., 21,* 84–90.

Blamey, P. J., Dowell R. C., Brown, A. M., Clark, G. M., & Seligman, P. M. (1987). Vowel and consonant recognition of cochlear implant patients using formant–estimating speech processors. *Journal of the Acoustical Society of America, 82,* 48–57.

Blasdel, G. G., Mitchell, D. E., Muir, D. W., & Pettigrew, J. D. (1977). A combined physiological and behavioral study of the effect of early visual experience with contours of a single orientation. *Journal of Physiology, 265,* 615–636.

Blazynski, C. & Ostroy, S. E. (1981). Dual pathways in the photolysis of rhodopsin: Studies using a direct chemical method. *Vision Research, 21,* 833–841.

Bleeker, M. L., & Bolla-Wilson, K. (1987). Simple visual reaction time: Sex and age differences. *Developmental Neuropsychology, 3,* 165–172.

Bliss, J. C., Katcher, M. H., Rogers, C. H., & Shepard, R. P. (1970). Optical-to-tactile image conversion for the blind. *IEEE Transactions on Man–Machine Systems, 11,* 58–65.

Block, R. A., (1974). Memory and the experience of duration in retrospect. *Memory and Cognition, 2,* 153–160.

Block, R. A. (1978). Remembered duration: Effects of event and sequence complexity. *Memory and Cognition, 6,* 320–326.

Block, R. A., George, E. J., & Reed, M. A. (1980). A watched pot sometimes boils: A study of duration experience. *Acta Psychologica, 46,* 81–94.

Bloom, K. (1990). Selectivity and early infant vocalization. In J. T. Enns (Ed.), *The development of attention: Research and theory* (pp. 121–136). Amsterdam: Elsevier.

Blough, P. M., & Slavin, K. (1987). Reaction time assessments of gender differences in visual-spatial performance. *Perception & Psychophysics, 41,* 276–281.

Boer, K., & Keuss, P. (1982). Global precedence as a postperceptual effect: An analysis of speed accuracy trade off functions. *Perception & Psychophysics, 31,* 358–366.

Bolanowski, S. J. Jr., Gescheider, G. A., Verrillo, R. T., & Checkosky, C.M. (1988). Four channels mediate the mechanical aspects of touch. *Journal of the Acoustical Society of America, 84,* 1680–1694.

Bolton, T. L. (1894). Rhythm. *American Journal of Psychology, 6,* 145–238.

Bonnet, C. (1984). Discrimination of velocities and mechanisms of motion perception. *Perception, 13,* 275–282.

Borg, G., Diamant, H., Oakley, B., Strom, L., & Zotterman, Y. (1967). A comparative study of neural and psychophysical responses to gustatory stimuli. In T. Hayashi (Ed.), *Olfaction and taste II* (pp. 253–264). Oxford: Pergamon Press.

Borg, G. A. V. (1982). Psychophysical bases of perceived exertion. *Medicine and Science in Sports and Exercise, 14,* 377–381.

Bornstein, M. H. (1973). Color vision and color naming: A psychophysiological hypothesis of cultural difference. *Psychological Bulletin, 80,* 257–285.

Bornstein, M. H. (1975). The influence of visual perception on culture. *American Anthropologist, 77,* 774–798.

Bornstein, M. H. (1977). Developmental pseudocyanapsia: Ontogenetic change in human color vision. *American Journal of Optometry and Physiological Optics, 54,* 464–469.

Bornstein, M. H. (1981). Two kinds of perceptual organization near the beginning of life. In W. Collins (Ed.), *Aspects of the development of competence* (pp. 39–91). Hillsdale, NJ: Erlbaum.

Bornstein, M. H. (1985). Infant into adult: Unity to diversity in the development of visual categorization. In J. Mehler & R. Fox (Eds.), *Neonate cognition: Beyond the blooming buzzing confusion* (pp. 115–138). Hillsdale, NJ: Erlbaum.

Bornstein, M. H., Kessen, W., & Weiskopf, S. (1976). Color vision and hue categorization in young human infants. *Journal of Experimental Psychology: Human Perception and Performance, 2,*115–129.

Bornstein, M. H., & Monroe, M. D. (1978). Color-naming evidence for tritan vision in the fovea. *American Journal of Optometry and Physiological Optics, 55,* 627–630.

Bossom, J., & Ommaya, A. K. (1968). Visuo-motor adaptation (to prismatic transformation of the retinal image) in monkeys with bilateral dorsal rhizotomy. *Brain, 91,* 161–172.

Botstein, D. (1986). The molecular biology of color vision. *Science, 232,* 142–143.

Botte, M. C., Baruch, C., & Scharf, B. (1986). Loudness reduction and adaptation induced by a contralateral tone. *Journal of the Acoustical Society of America, 80,* 73–81.

Botte, M. C., Canavet, G., & Scharf, B. (1982). Loudness adaptation induced by an intermittent tone. *Journal of the Acoustical Society of America, 72,* 727–739.

Botwinick, J. (1984). *Aging and behavior: A comprehensive integration of research findings* (3rd ed.). New York: Springer.

Bowen, R. W. (1981). Latencies for chromatic and achromatic visual mechanisms. *Vision Research, 2,* 1457–1466.

Bowker, D. O., & Mandler, M. B. (1981). Apparent contrast of suprathreshold gratings varies with stimulus orientation. *Perception & Psychophysics, 29,* 585–588.

Bowmaker, J. K., & Dartnall, H. J. A. (1980). Visual pigments of rods and cones in a human retina. *Journal of Physiology, 298,* 501–511.

Boycott, B. B., & Waessle, H. (1974). The morphological types of ganglion cells of the domestic cat's retina. *Journal of Physiology, 240,* 397–419.

Boyd, I. A., & Roberts, T. D. M. (1953). Proprioceptive discharges from the stretch receptors in the knee–joint of the cat. *Journal of Physiology* (London), *122,* 38–58.

Boynton, R. M. (1971). Color vision. In J. W. King & L. A. Riggs (Eds.), *Woodworth and Schlossberg's experimental psychology.* (3rd ed.) (pp. 315–368). New York: Holt, Rinehart & Winston.

Boynton, R. M. (1979). Human color vision. New York: Holt, Rinehart & Winston.

Boynton, R. M. (1988). Color vision. *Annual Review of Psychology, 39,* 69–100.

Boynton, R. M., & Gordon, J. (1965). Bezold-Brucke hue shift measured by color-naming technique. *Journal of the Optical Society of America, 55,* 78–86.

Braddick, O. J. (1980). Low-level and high-level processes in apparent motion. *Philosophical Transactions of the Royal Society of London, Series B, 290,* 137–151.

Braddick, O. J., & Atkinson, J. (1979). Accommodation and acuity in the human infant. In R. D. Freeman (Ed.), *Developmental neurobiology of vision* (pp. 289–300). New York: Plenum Press.

Braddick, O. J., Atkinson, J., Julesz, B., Kropfl, W., Bodis–Wollner, I., & Raab, E. (1980). Cortical binocularity in infants. *Nature, 288,* 363–385.

Braddick, O. J., Wattam-Bell, J., & Atkinson, J. (1986). Orientation-specific cortical responses develop in early infancy. *Nature, 320,* 617–619.

Bradley, A., & Skottun B. C. (1987). Effects of contrast and spatial frequency on vernier acuity. *Vision Research, 27,* 1817–1824.

Bradley, R. M., & Stern I. B. (1967). The development of the human taste bud during the foetal period. *Journal of Anatomy, 101,* 743–752.

Braff, D. L., Silverton, L., Saccuzzo, D. P., & Janowsky, D. S. (1981). Impaired speed of visual information processing in marihuana intoxication. *American Journal of Psychiatry, 138 (5),* 613–617.

Braida, L. D., & Durlach, N. D. (1988). Peripheral and central factors in intensity perception. In G. M. Edelman, W. E. Gall, & M. W. Cowan (Eds.), *Auditory function: Neurobiological bases of hearing* (pp. 559–583). New York: Wiley.

Braine L. G., Plastow, E., & Greene, S. I. (1987). Judgments of shape orientation: A matter of contrasts. *Perception & Psychophysics, 41,* 335–344.

Brand, J. G., Teeter, J. H., Cagan, R. H., & Kare, M. R. (Eds.). (1989). *Chemical senses: Vol. 1. Receptor events and transduction in taste and olfaction.* New York: Marcel, Dekker, Inc.

Braun, C. M., & Daigneault, S. (1989). Color discrimination testing reveals early printshop solvent neurotoxicity better than a neuropsychological test battery. *Archives of Clinical Neuropsychology,* 4–13.

Braybyn, L. B., & McGuinness, D. (1979). Gender differences in response to spatial frequency and stimulus orientation. *Perception & Psychophysics, 26,* 319–324.

Brazelton, T., Scholl, M., & Robey, J. (1966). Visual responses in the newborn. *Pediatrics, 37,* 284–290.

Bregman, A. S. (1978). Auditory streaming: Competition among alternative organizations. *Perception & Psychophysics, 23,* 391–398.

Bregman, A. S. (1981). Asking the "What for?" question in auditory perception. In M. Kubovy & J. R. Pometrantz (Eds.), *Perceptual organization* (pp. 99–118). Hillsdale, NJ: Erlbaum.

Bregman, A. S. (1990). *Auditory scene analysis.* Cambridge, MA: Bradford/MIT Press.

Brennan, P., Kaba, H., & Keverne, E. B. (1990). Olfactory recognition: A simple memory system. *Science, 250,* 1223–1226.

Brenowitz, E. A. (1991). Altered perceptions of species-specific song by female birds after lesions of a forebrain nucleus. *Science, 251,* 303–305.

Bridgeman, B., Graziano, J. A. (1989). Effect of context and efference copy on visual straight ahead. *Vision Research, 29,* 1729–1736.

Bridges, C. D. B. (1986). Biochemistry of vision—A perspective. *Vision Research, 26,* 1317–1337.

Brillat-Savarin, J. A. (1971). *The physiology of taste: Or meditations on transcendental gastronomy.* (M. K. F. Fisher, Trans.). New York: Knopf. (Original work published 1825)

Broadbent, D. (1958). *Perception and communication.* Oxford: Pergamon.

Broadbent, D. E., & Gregory, M. (1963). Vigilance considered as a statistical decision. *British Journal of Psychology, 54,* 309–323.

Broadbent, D. E., & Gregory, M. (1965). Effects of noise and of signal rate upon vigilance analyzed by means of decision theory. *Human Factors, 7,* 155–162.

Brodmann, K. (1914). Physiologie des gehirng. In F. Krause (Ed.), *Allsemaie chirurgie der gehirnkankheiten.* Stuttgart: F. Enke.

Bronson, G. W. (1990). Changes in infants' scanning across the 2- to 14-week age period. *Journal of*

Experimental Child Psychology, 49, 101–125.

Brooks, P. L., & Frost, B. J. (1983). Evaluation of a tactile vocoder for word recognition. *Journal of the Acoustical Society of America, 74,* 34–39.

Brooks, R. A. (1981). Symbolic reasoning among 3-D models and 2-D images. *Artificial Intelligence, 17,* 205–244.

Brou, P., Sciancia, T. R., Linden, L., & Lettvin, J. Y. (1986). The colors of things. *Scientific American, 255 (3),* 84–91.

Brown, A. C., Beeler, W. J., Kloka, A. C., & Fields, R. W. (1985). Spatial summation of pre-pain and pain in human teeth. *Pain, 21,* 1–16.

Brown, B. (1972). Resolution thresholds for moving targets at the fovea and in the peripheral retina. *Vision Research, 12,* 293–304.

Brown, E. L., & Deffenbacher, K. (1979). *Perception and the senses.* New York: Oxford University Press.

Brown, J. M., & Koch, C. J. (1991). *Influences of closure and occlusion on the perception of fragmented pictures.* Paper presented at ARVO, Sarasota, FL.

Brown, J. W. (1990). Psychology of time awareness. *Brain and Cognition, 14,* 144–164.

Brown, P. E. (1972). Use of acupuncture in major surgery. *Lancet, 1,* 1328–1330.

Brown, P. K., & Wald, G. (1964). Visual pigments in single rods and cones of the human retina. *Science, 144,* 45–52.

Brown, R. E., & MacDonald, D. W. (Eds.). (1985a). *Social odours in mammals: Vol. 1.* Oxford: Clarendon Press.

Brown, R. E., & MacDonald D. W. (Eds). (1985b). *Social odours in mammals: Vol. 2.* Oxford: Clarendon Press.

Brown, S. W. (1985). Time perception and attention: The effects of prospective versus retrospective paradigms and task demands on perceived duration. *Perception & Psychophysics, 38,* 115–124.

Brown, T. S. (1975). General biology of sensory systems. In B. Scharf (Ed.), *Experimental sensory psychology* (pp. 69–111). Glenview, IL: Scott–Foresman.

Brown, W. (1910). The judgment of difference. *University of California, Berkeley, Publications in Psychology, 1,* 1–71.

Brownell, W. E., Bader, C. R., Bertrand, D., & de Ribaupierre, Y. (1985). Evoked mechanical responses of isolated cochlear outer hair cells. *Science, 227,* 194–196.

Bruce, C., Desimone, R., & Gross, C. G. (1981). Visual properties of neurons in a polysensory area in superior temporal sulcus of the macaque. *Journal of Neurophysiology, 46,* 369–384.

Bruce, V., & Green, P. (1985). *Visual perception physiology, psychology and ecology.* Hillsdale, NJ: Erlbaum.

Bruner, J. S., Postman, L., & Rodrigues, J. (1951). Expectations and the perception of color. *American Journal of Psychology, 64,* 216–227.

Bruno, N., & Cutting, J. E. (1988). Minimodularity and the perception of layout. *Journal of Experimental Psychology: General, 117,* 161–170.

Brunswick, E. (1952). The conceptual framework of psychology. *International Encyclopedia of Unified Science, 1,* No. 10.

Brunswick, E. (1955). Representative design and probabilistic theory in a functional psychology. *Psychological Review, 62,* 193–217.

Brunswick, E. (1956). *Perception as a representative design of psychological experiments.* Berkeley: University of California Press.

Brussell, E. M., & Festinger, L. (1973). The Gelb effect: Brightness contrast plus attention. *American Journal of Psychology, 86,* 225–235.

Bryden, M. P. (1982). *Laterality: Functional asymmetry in the intact brain.* New York: Academic Press.

Bryden, M. P., & George, J. (1990). Sex differences and the role of figural complexity in determining the rate of mental rotation. *Perceptual and Motor Skills, 70,* 467–477.

Buchtel, H. A., & Stewart, J. D. (1989). Auditory agnosia: Apperceptive or associative disorder? *Brain and Language, 37,* 12–25.

Buckhout, R. (1976). Eyewitness testimony. In R. Held & W. Richards (Eds.), *Recent progress in perception* (pp. 205–213). San Francisco: Freeman.

Bujas, Z., Szabo, S., Ajdukovic, D., & Mayer, D. (1989). Individual gustatory reaction times to various groups of chemicals that provoke basic taste qualities. *Perception & Psychophysics, 45,* 385–390.

Bujas, Z., Szabo, S., Ajdukovic, D., & Mayer, D. (1991). Time course of recovery from gustatory adaptation to NaCl. *Perception & Psychophysics, 49,* 517–521.

Bundesen, C., Larsen, A., & Farrell, J. E. (1983). Visual apparent movement: Transformations of size and orientation. *Perception, 12,* 549–568.

Burg, A. (1966). Visual acuity as measured by dynamic and static tests: A comparative evaluation. *Journal of Applied Psychology, 50,* 460–466.

Burg, A. (1968). Lateral visual field as related to age and sex. *Journal of Applied Psychology, 52,* 10–15.

Burgland, B., Hogman, L., & Johansson, I. (1988). Reliability of odor measurements near threshold. *Reports from the Department of Psychology.* Stockholm: The University of Stockholm.

Burns, E. M. (1981). Circularity in relative pitch judgments for inharmonic complex tones: The Shepard demonstration revisited, again. *Perception & Psychophysics, 30,* 467–472.

Burt, P., & Julesz, B. (1980). A disparity gradient limit for binocular fusion. *Science, 208,* 615–617.

Burt, P., & Sperling, G. (1981). Time, distance and feature trade-offs in visual apparent motion. *Psychological Review, 88,* 137–151.

Burton, G., Turvey, M. T., & Solomon, H. Y. (1990). Can shape be perceived by dynamic touch? *Perception & Psychophysics, 48,* 477–487.

Burton, G. J., Nagshineh, S., & Ruddock, K. H. (1977). Processing by the human visual system of the light and dark contrast components of the retinal image. *Biological Cybernetics, 27,* 189–197.

Bushnell, M. C., & Duncan, G. H. (1989). Sensory and affective aspects of pain perception: Is medial thalamus restricted to emotional issues? *Experimental Brain Research, 78,* 415–418.

Butler, D. L., & Kring, A. M. (1987). Integration of features in depictions as a function of size. *Perception & Psychophysics, 41,*159–164.

Butler, R. A. (1987). An analysis of the monaural displacement of sound in space. *Perception & Psychophysics, 41,* 1–7.

Butler, R. A., Levy, E. T., & Neff, W. D. (1980). Apparent distance of sounds recorded in echoic and anechoic chambers. *Journal of Experimental Psychology: Human Perception and Physiology, 6,* 745–750.

Butters, N., Barton, M., & Brody, B. A. (1970). Right parietal lobe and cross–model associations. *Cortex, 6,* 19–46.

Butterworth, G. (1981). The origins of auditory-visual perception and visual proprioception in human development. In R. D. Walk & H. L. Pick, Jr. (Eds.), *Intersensory perception and sensory integration* (pp. 37–70). New York: Plenum Press.

Cacace, A. T., & Margolis, R. H. (1985). On the loudness of complex stimuli and its relationship to cochlear excitation. *Journal of the Acoustical Society of America, 78,* 1568–1573.

Caelli, T. (1982). On discriminating visual textures and images. *Perception & Psychophysics, 31,* 149–159.

Caelli, T. (1984). On the specification of coding principles for visual image processing. In P. C. Dodwell & T. Caelli (Eds.), *Figural synthesis* (pp. 153–184). Hillsdale, NJ: Erlbaum.

Caelli, T. (1988). An adaptive computational model for texture segregation. *IEEE transactions on systems, man, and cybernetics, 18,* 9–17.

Cagen, R. H., & Rhein, L. D. (1980). Biochemical basis of recognition of taste and olfactory stimuli. In H. van der Starre (Ed.), *Olfaction and taste VII* (pp. 35–44). London: IRL Press.

Cahoon, D., & Edmonds, E. M. (1980). The watched pot still won't boil: Expectancy as a variable in estimating the passage of time. *Bulletin of the Psychonomic Society, 16,* 115–116.

Cain, D. P., & Bindra, D. (1972). Response of amygdala single units to odors in the rat. *Experimental Neurology, 35,* 98–110.

Cain, W. S. (1969). Odor intensity: Differences in the exponent of the psychophysical function. *Perception &*

Psychophysics, 6, 349–354.

Cain, W. S. (1977). Differential sensitivity for smell: "Noise" at the nose. *Science, 195,* 796–798.

Cain, W. S. (1979). To know with the nose: Keys to odor identification. *Science, 203,* 467–470.

Cain, W. S., & Engen, T. (1969). Olfactory adaptation and the scaling of odor intensity. In C. Pfaffman (Ed.), *Olfaction and taste III* (pp. 127–141). New York: Rockefeller University Press.

Cain, W. S., & Johnson, F., Jr. (1978). Lability of odor-pleasantness: Influence of mere exposure. *Perception, 7,* 459–465.

Cain, W. S., Reid, F., & Stevens, J. C. (1990). Missing ingredients: Aging and the discrimination of flavor. *Journal of Nutrition for the Elderly, 9,* 3–15.

Cain, W. S., & Stevens, J. C. (1989). Uniformity of olfactory loss in aging. *Annals of the New York Academy of Sciences, 561,* 29–38.

Cajal, S. R. (1893). La retine des vertebres. *Cellule, 9,* 17–257.

Calis, G., & Leeuwenberg, E. (1981). Grounding the figure. *Journal of Experimental Psychology: Human Perception and Performance, 7,* 1386–1397.

Callaghan, T. C. (1989). Interference and dominance in texture segregation: Hue, geometric form, and line orientation. *Perception & Psychophysics, 46,* 299–311.

Callaghan, T. C., Lasaga, M. L., & Garner, W. R. (1986). Visual texture segregation based on orientation and hue. *Perception & Psychophysics, 39,* 32–38.

Campbell, F. W., & Maffei, L. (1981). The influence of spatial frequency and contrast on the perception of moving patterns. *Vision Research, 21,* 713–721.

Campbell, F. W., & Robson, J. G. (1968). Application of Fourier analysis to the visibility of gratings. *Journal of Physiology, 197,* 551–566.

Campbell, K. B., Baribeau-Braun, J., & Braun, C. (1981). Neuroanatomical and physiological foundations of extraversion. *Psychophysiology, 18,* 263–267.

Canevet, G., Hellman, R., & Scharf, B. (1986). Group estimation of loudness in sound fields. *Acustica, 60,* 277–282.

Cannon, M. W., Jr. (1983). Contrast sensitivity: Psychophysical and evoked potential methods compared. *Vision Research, 23,* 87–95.

Capaldi, E., & Powley, T. L. (Eds.). (1990). *Taste, experience, and feeding.* Washington, DC: American Psychological Association.

Carey, S. (1981). The development of face perception. In G. Davies, H. Ellis, & J. Shepherd (Eds.), *Perceiving and remembering faces* (pp. 9–38). London: Academic Press.

Carey, S., & Diamond, R. (1977). From piecemeal to configurational representation of faces. *Science, 195,* 312–314.

Carey, S., Diamond, R., & Woods, B. (1980). The development of face recognition: A maturational component. *Developmental Psychology, 16,* 257–269.

Carlson, C. R. (1983). A simple model for vernier acuity. *Investigations in Ophthalmology and Visual Science, 24* (Suppl. 276).

Carlson, N. R. (1988). *Foundations of physiological psychology.* Boston: Allyn & Bacon.

Carlson, V. R. (1958). Effect of lysergic acid diethylamide (LSD-25) on the absolute visual threshold. *Journal of Comparative and Physiological Psychology, 51,* 528–531.

Carlson, V. R. (1977). Instructions and perceptual constancy judgments. In W. Epstein (Ed.), *Stability and constancy in visual perception: Mechanisms and processes* (pp. 217–254). New York: Wiley.

Carlyon, R.P. (1988). The development and decline of forward masking. *Hearing Research,* 65–80.

Carmichael, L., Hogan, H. P., & Walter, A. A. (1932). An experimental study of the effect of language on the reproduction of visually perceived forms. *Journal of Experimental Psychology, 15,* 73–86.

Caron, A., Caron, R., Caldwell, R., & Weiss, S. (1973). Infant perception of the structural properties of the face. *Developmental Psychology, 9,* 385–399.

Carpenter, D. L., & Dugan, M. P. (1983). Motion parallax information for direction of rotation in depth: Order and direction components. *Perception, 12,* 559–569.

Carroll, J. D., & Chang, J. J. (1970). Analysis of individual differences in multidimensional scaling via an N-way generalization of Ekhart-Young decomposition. *Psychometrika, 48,* 157–169.

Carson, C. R. (1983). A simple model for vernier acuity. *Investigative Ophthalmology and Visual Science, 24* (Suppl. 276).

Casey, K. L. (1978). Neural mechanisms of pain. In E. C. Carterette & M. P. Friedman (Eds.), *Handbook of perception: Vol. VIB. Feeling and hurting* (pp. 183–230). New York: Academic Press.

Casey, K. L., & Morrow, T. J. (1983). Ventral posterior thalamic neurons differentially responsive to noxious stimulation of the awake monkey. *Science, 221,* 675–677.

Cassone, V. M. (1990). Effects of melatonin on vertebrate circadian systems. *Trends in Neurosciences, 13,* 457–464.

Cattell, J. M. (1886). The influence of the intensity of the stimulus on the length of the reaction time. *Brain, 9,* 512–514.

Cavanagh, P. (1984). Image transforms in the visual system. In P. C. Dodwell & T. Caelli (Eds.), *Figural synthesis* (pp. 185–218). Hillsdale, NJ: Erlbaum.

Cavanagh, P. (1988). Pathways in early vision. In Z. Pylyshyn (Ed.), *Computational processes in human vision* (pp. 239–261). Norwood, NJ: Ablex.

Cavanagh, P., & Leclerc, Y. G. (1989). Shape from shadows. *Journal of Experimental Psychology: Human Perception and Performance, 15,* 3–27.

Cavanagh, P., & Mather, G. (1989). Motion: The long and short of it. *Spatial Vision, 4,* 103–129.

Cavanagh, P., Tyler, C. W., & Favreau, O. E. (1984). Perceived velocity of moving chromatic gratings. *Journal of the Optical Society of America A, 1,* 893–899.

Cegalis, J. A., & Deptula, D. (1981). Attention in schizophrenia: Signal detection in the visual periphery. *Journal of Nervous and Mental Health Diseases, 169,* 751–760.

Ceralla, J. (1985). Age-related decline in extra–foveal letter perception. *Journal of Gerontology, 40,* 727–736.

Cerella, J., Poon, L., & Williams, D. (1980). Age and the complexity hypothesis. In L. Poon (Ed.), *Aging in the 1980s* (pp. 332–345). Washington, DC: American Psychological Association.

Cernoch, J. M., & Porter, R. H. (1985). Recognition of maternal axillary odors by infants. *Child Development, 56,* 1593–1598.

Chamorro, A. & Sacco, R. L. (1990). Visual hemineglect and hemihallucinations in a patient with subcortical infarction. *Neurology, 40,* 1463–1464.

Chapman, C. R. (1978). The hurtful world: Pathological pain and its control. In E. C. Carterette & M. P. Friedman (Eds.), *Handbook of perception: Vol. VIB. Feeling and hurting* (pp. 264–301). New York: Academic Press.

Chapman, C. R., Casey, K. L., Dubner, R., Foley, K. M., Gracely, R. H., & Reading, A. E. (1985). Pain measurement: An overview. *Pain, 22,* 1–31.

Cheeseman, J., & Merikle, P. M. (1984). Priming with and without awareness. *Perception & Psychophysics, 36,* 387–395.

Cheeseman, J., & Merikle, P. M. (1985). Word recognition and consciousness. *Reading Research: Advances in Theory and Practice, 5,* 311–352.

Cheeseman, J., & Merikle, P. M. (1986). Distinguishing conscious from unconscious perceptual processes. *Canadian Journal of Psychology, 40,* 343–367.

Cheng, P. W. (1985) Restructuring versus automaticity: Alternative accounts of skill acquisition. *Psychological Review, 92,* 414–423.

Cheng, T. O. (1973). Acupuncture anesthesia. *Science, 179,* 521.

Cherry, E. C. (1953). Some experiments on the recognition of speech, with one and with two ears. *Journal of the Acoustical Society of America, 25,* 975–979.

Chevrier, J., & Delorme, A. (1983). Depth perception in Pandora's box and size illusion: Evolution with age. *Perception, 12,* 177–185.

Chocolle, R. (1940). Variations des temps de réaction auditifs en fonction de l'intensité à diverses frequences. Année *Psychologique, 41,* 65–124.

Chocolle, R. (1962). Les effets des interactions interaurales dans l'audition. *Journale de psychologie, 3,* 255–282.

Cholewiak, R. W., & Craig, J. C. (1984). Vibrotactile pattern recognition and discrimination at several body sites. *Perception & Psychophysics, 35,* 503–514.

Chomsky, N., & Miller, G. A. (1963). Introduction to the formal analysis of natural languages. In R. D. Luce, R. Bush, & E. Galanter (Eds.), *Handbook of mathematical psychology: Vol. 2* (pp. 269–231). New York: Wiley.

Choudhurt, B. P., & Crossey, A. D. (1981). Slow-movement sensitivity in the human field of vision. *Physiology and Behavior, 26,* 125–128.

Cicerone, C. M., & Nerger, J. L. (1989). The density of cones in the fovea centralis of the human dichromat. *Vision Research, 29,* 1587–1595.

Ciner, E. B., Schanel-Klitsch, E., & Scheiman, M. (1991). Stereoacuity development in young children. *Optometry & Vision Science, 68,* 533–536.

Clark, H. H., & Clark, E. V. (1977). *Psychology and language: An introduction to psycholinguistics.* New York: Harcourt.

Clark, J. C., & Whitehurst, G. S. (1974). Asymmetrical stimulus control and the mirror-image problem. *Journal of Experimental Child Psychology, 17,* 147–166.

Clark, W. C., & Yang, J. C. (1974). Acupunctural analgesia? Evaluation by signal detection theory. *Science, 184,* 1096–1098.

Clarkson, M. G., Swain, I. U., Clifton, R. K., & Cohen, K. (1991). Newborns' head orientation toward trains of brief sounds. *Journal of the Acoustical Society of America, 89,* 2411–2420.

Clarkson-Smith, L., & Halpern, D. F. (1983). Can age-related deficits in spatial memory be attenuated through the use of verbal coding? *Experimental Aging Research, 9,* 179–184.

Clifford, B. R., & Bull, R. (1978). *The psychology of person identification.* London: Routledge & Kegan Paul.

Clifton, R. K., Morrongiello, B. A., & Dowd, J. M. (1984). A developmental look at an auditory illusion: The precedence effect. *Developmental Biology, 17,* 519–536.

Coffield, K. E., & Buckalew, L. W. (1988). A study of color preferences for drugs and implications for compliance and drug-taking. *Journal of Alcohol and Drug Education, 34,* 28–36.

Cogan, R., & Spinnato, J. A. (1986). Pain and discomfort thresholds in late pregnancy. *Pain, 27,* 63–68.

Cohen, K. (1981). The development of strategies of visual search. In D. Fisher, R. Monty, & J. Senders (Eds.), *Eye movements: Cognition and visual perception.* Hillsdale, NJ: Erlbaum.

Cohen, W. (1958). Color-perception in the chromatic Ganzfeld. *American Journal of Psychology, 71,* 390–394.

Cole, R. A., Rudnicky, A. I., Zue, V. W., & Reddy, D. R. (1980). Speech as patterns on paper. In R. A. Cole (Ed.) *Perception and production of fluent speech* (pp. 3–50). Hillsdale, NJ: Erlbaum.

Coles, M. G., Gale, A., & Kline, P. (1971). Personality and habituation of the orienting reaction: Tonic and response measures of electrodermal activity. *Psychophysiology, 8,* 54–63.

Collings, V. B. (1974). Human taste response as a function of locus of stimulation on the tongue and soft palate. *Perception & Psychophysics, 16,* 169–174.

Collins, S. C. (1985). Duplex perception with musical stimuli: A further investigation. *Perception & Psychophysics, 38,* 172–177.

Comfort, A. (1971). Likelihood of human pheromones. *Nature, 230,* 432–433.

Condon, W. S., & Sander, L. W. (1974). Neonate movement is synchronized with adult speech: Interactional participation and language acquisition. *Science, 183,* 99–101.

Cooke, N. M., Breen, T. J., & Schvaneveldt, R. W. (1987). Is consistent mapping necessary for high-speed search? *Journal of Experimental Psychology: Learning, Memory, and Cognition, 13,* 223–229.

Cooper, B. Y., Vierck, C. J., Jr., & Yeomans, D. C. (1986). Selective reduction of second pain sensations by systemic morphine in humans. *Pain, 24,* 93–116.

Coren, S. (1966). Adaptation to prismatic displacement as a function of the amount of available information. *Psychonomic Science, 4,* 407–408.

Coren, S. (1969). Brightness contrast as a function of figure-ground relations. *Journal of Experimental Psychology, 80,* 517–524.

Coren, S. (1972). Subjective contours and apparent depth. *Psychological Review, 79,* 359–367.

Coren, S. (1984). Set. In R. J. Corsini (Ed.), *The Encyclopedia of Psychology: Vol. 3* (pp. 296–298). New York: Wiley.

Coren, S., (1986). An efferent component in the visual perception of direction and extent. *Psychological Review, 93,* 391–410.

Coren, S. (1987). In vivo measures of the density of human lens pigmentation: A rapid and simple psychophysical procedure. *Acta Ophthalmologica, 65,* 575–578.

Coren, S. (1989). The many moon illusions: An integration through analysis. In M. Hershenson (Ed.), *The moon illusion* (pp. 351–370). Hillsdale, NJ: Erlbaum.

Coren, S. (1991). Retinal mechanisms in the perception of subjective contours: The contribution of lateral inhibition. *Perception, 20,* 181–191.

Coren, S. (1992). *The left-hander syndrome: Causes and consequences of left-handedness.* New York: Free Press.

Coren, S., & Aks, D. J. (1990). Moon illusion in pictures: A multimechanism approach. *Journal of Experimental Psychology: Human Perception and Performance, 16,* 365–380.

Coren, S., Bradley, D. R., Hoenig, P., & Girgus, J. S. (1975). The effect of smooth tracking and saccadic eye movements on the perception of SIE: The shrinking circle illusion. *Vision Research, 15,* 49–55.

Coren, S., & Girgus, J. S. (1972a). Density of human lens pigmentation: In vivo measures over an extended age range. *Vision Research, 12,* 343–346.

Coren, S., & Girgus J. S. (1972b). Differentiation and decrement in the Mueller-Lyer illusion. *Perception & Psychophysics, 12,* 466–470.

Coren, S., & Girgus, J. S. (1977). Illusions and constancies. In W. Epstein (Ed.), *Stability and constancy in visual perception: Mechanisms and processes* (pp. 255–284). New York: Wiley.

Coren, S., & Girgus, J. S. (1978). *Seeing is deceiving: The psychology of visual illusions.* Hillsdale, NJ: Erlbaum.

Coren, S., & Girgus, J. S. (1980). Principles of perceptual organization and spatial distortion: The Gestalt illusions. *Journal of Experimental Psychology: Human Perception and Performance, 6,* 404–412.

Coren, S., Girgus, J. S., & Schiano, D. (1986). Is adaptation of orientation-specific cortical cells a possible explanation of illusion decrement? *Bulletin of the Psychonomic Society, 24,* 207–210.

Coren, S., & Hakstian, A. R. (1987). Visual screening without the use of technical equipment: Preliminary development of a behaviorally validated questionnaire. *Applied Optics, 26,* 1468–1472.

Coren, S., & Hakstian, A. R. (1988). Color vision screening without the use of technical equipment: Scale development and cross-validation. *Perception & Psychophysics, 43,* 115–120.

Coren, S., & Hoenig, P. (1972). Eye movements and decrement in the Oppel-Kundt illusion. *Perception & Psychophysics, 12,* 224–225.

Coren, S., & Keith, B. (1970). Bezold-Brucke effect: Pigment or neural locus? *Journal of the Optical Society of America, 60,* 559–562.

Coren, S., & Komoda, M. K. (1973). Apparent lightness as a function of perceived direction of incident illumination. *American Journal of Psychology, 86,* 345–349.

Coren, S., & Porac, C. (1978). Iris pigmentation and visual-geometric illusions. *Perception, 7,* 473–478.

Coren, S., & Porac, C. (1983a). The creation and reversal of the Mueller-Lyer illusion through attentional manipulation. *Perception, 12,* 49–54.

Coren, S., & Porac, C. (1983b). Subjective contours and apparent depth: A direct test. *Perception & Psychophysics, 33,* 197–200.

Coren, S., & Porac, C. (1984). Structural and cognitive components in the Mueller-Lyer illusion assessed via cyclopean presentation. *Perception & Psychophysics, 35,* 313–318.

Coren, S., & Porac, C. (1987). Individual differences in visual-geometric illusions: Predictions from measures of spatial cognitive abilities. *Perception & Psychophysics, 41,* 211–219.

Coren, S., Porac, C., Aks, D. J., & Morikawa, K. (1988). A method to assess the relative contribution of lateral inhibition to the magnitude of visual-geometric illusions. *Perception & Psychophysics, 43,* 551–558.

Coren, S., Porac C., & Duncan, P. (1981). Lateral preference in pre-school children and young adults. *Child Development, 52,* 443–450.

Coren, S., Porac, C., & Theodor, L. H. (1987). Set and subjective contour. In S. Petry & G. E. Meyer (Eds.), *The perception of illusory contours* (pp. 237–245). New York: Springer-Verlag.

Cormack, R. H. (1984). Stereoscopic depth perception at far viewing distances. *Perception & Psychophysics, 35,* 423–428.

Cornsweet, T. N. (1956). Determination of the stimuli for involuntary drifts and saccadic eye movements. *Journal of the Optical Society of America, 46,* 987–993.

Cornsweet, T. N. (1970). *Visual perception.* New York: Academic Press.

Cornsweet, T. N. (1985). Prentice Award Lecture: A simple retinal mechanism that has complex and profound effects on perception. *American Journal of Optometry and Physiological Optics, 62,* 427–438.

Correia, M. J., & Guedry, F. E. (1978). The vestibular system: Basic biophysical and physiological mechanisms. In R. B. Masterton (Ed.), *Handbook of sensory neurobiology: Vol. I. Sensory integration.* New York: Plenum Press.

Corso, J. F. (1959). Age and sex differences in thresholds. *Journal of the Acoustical Society of America, 31,* 498–509.

Corso, J. F. (1981). *Aging sensory systems and perception.* New York: Praeger.

Corwin, T. R., Moskowitz-Cook, A., & Green, M.A. (1977). The oblique effect in a vernier acuity situation. *Perception & Psychophysics, 21,* 445–449.

Costanzo, R. M., & Gardner, E. P. (1981). Multiple-joint neurons in somatosensory cortex of awake monkeys. *Brain Research, 24,* 321–333.

Costanzo, R. M., & Graziadei, P. P. C. (1987). Development and plasticity of the olfactory system. In T. E. Finger & W. L. Silver (Eds.), *Neurobiology of Taste and Smell* (pp. 233–250). New York: Wiley.

Courage, M. L., & Adams, J. (1990). The early development of visual acuity in the binocular and monocular peripheral fields. *Infant Behavioral Development, 13,* 123–128.

Cowan, R. S. C., Alcantara, J. I., Blamey, P. J., & Clark, G. M. (1988). Preliminary evaluation of a multichannel electrotactile speech processor. *Journal of the Acoustical Society of America, 83,* 2328–2338.

Cowey, A. (1981). Why are there so many visual areas? In F. O. Schmitt, F. G. Worden, G. Adelman, and S. G. Dennis (Eds.), *The organization of the cerebral cortex.* (pp. 395–413). Cambridge, MA: MIT Press.

Cowley, J. J., & Broolsbank, B. W. L. (1991). Human exposure to putative pheremones and changes in aspects of social behavior. *Journal of Steroid Biochemistry and Molecular Biology, 39,* 647–659.

Cowley, J. J., Johnson, A. L., & Brooksbank, B.W. L. (1977). The effect of two odorous compounds on performance in an assessment-of-people test. *Psychoneuroendocrinology, 2,* 159–172.

Craig, J. C. (1978). Vibrotactile pattern recognition and masking. In G. Gordon (Ed.), *Active touch: The mechanism of recognition of objects by manipulation* (pp. 229–242). Oxford: Pergamon Press.

Craig, J. C. (1981). Tactile letter recognition: Pattern duration and modes of pattern generation. *Perception & Psychophysics, 30,* 540–546.

Craig, J. C. (1983a). The role of onset in the perception of sequentially presented vibrotactile patterns. *Perception & Psychophysics, 34,* 421–432.

Craig, J. C. (1983b). Some factors affecting tactile pattern recognition. *International Journal of Neuroscience, 19,* 47–58.

Craig, J. C. (1989). Interference in localizing tactile stimuli. *Perception & Psychophysics, 45,* 343–355.

Craig, J. C., & Evans, P. M. (1987). Vibrotactile masking and the persistence of tactual features. *Perception & Psychophysics, 42,* 309–317.

Craig, K. D. (1978). Social modeling influences on pain. In R. A. Sternbach (Ed.), *The psychology of pain.* New York: Raven Press.

Craig, K. D., Best, H., & Ward, L. M. (1975). Social modelling influences on psychophysical judgments of electrical stimulation. *Journal of Abnormal Psychology, 84,* 366–373.

Craig, K. D., & Coren, S. (1975). Signal detection analysis of social modelling influences on pain expressions. *Journal of Psychosomatic Research, 19,* 105–112.

Craig K. D., & Prkachin, K. M. (1978). Social modeling influences on sensory decision theory and psychophysiological indexes of pain. *Journal of Personality and Social Psychology, 36,* 805–815.

Craik, F., & Simon, E. (1980). The roles of attention and depth of processing in understanding age differences in memory. In L. Poon, J. Fozard, L. Cermak, and L. Thompson (Eds.), *New directions in memory and aging: Proceedings of the George A. Talland Memorial Conference* (pp. 95–112). Hillsdale, NJ: Erlbaum.

Crassini, B., Brown, B., & Bowman, K. (1988). Age-related changes in contrast sensitivity in central and peripheral retina. *Perception, 17,* 315–332.

Craton, L. G., & Yonas, A. (1990). The role of motion in infants' perception of occlusion. In J. T. Enns (Ed.), *The development of attention: Research and theory* (pp. 21–46). Amsterdam: Elsevier.

Cratty, B. (1979). *Perceptual and motor development in infants and children.* New Jersey: Prentice-Hall.

Creed, R. S., Denny-Brown, D., Eccles, J. C., Liddell, E. G. T., & Sherrington, C. S. (1972). *Reflex activity of the spinal cord* (reprint). London & New York: Oxford University Press, Clarendon. (Original work published 1932)

Critchley, M. (1964). The problem of visual agnosia. *Journal of Neurological Science, 1,* 274.

Crook, C. (1987). Taste and olfaction. In P. Salapatek & L. Cohen (Eds.), *Handbook of infant perception: Vol. 2. From perception to cognition* (pp. 237–264). Orlando: Academic Press.

Crossman, E. R. F. W. (1953). Entropy and choice time: The effect of frequency unbalance on choice response. *Quarterly Journal of Experimental Psychology, 5,* 41–51.

Crutchfield, R. S., Woodworth, D. G., & Albrecht, R. E. (1958). *Perceptual performance and the effective person.* (WADC-TN-58-60). Lackland Air Force Base, TX: Wright Air Development Center. (NTIS No. AD-151-039).

Cuddy, L. L., Cohen, A. J., & Mewhort, D. J. K. (1981). Perception of structure in short melodic sequences. *Journal of Experimental Psychology: Human Perception and Performance, 7,* 869–883.

Cunningham, W. (1980). Speed, age and qualitative differences in cognitive functioning. In L. Poon (Ed.), *Aging in the 1980s* (pp. 327–331). Washington, DC: American Psychological Association.

Curcio, C. A., Sloan, K. R., Packer, O., Hendrickson, A. E., & Kalina, R. E. (1987). Distribution of cones in human and monkey retina: Individual variability and radial asymmetry. *Science, 236,* 579–582.

Cutler, W. B., Preti, G., Krieger, A., Huggins, G. R., Garcia, C. R., & Lawley, H. J. (1986). Human axillary secretions influence women's menstrual cycles: The role of donor extract from men. *Hormones and Behavior, 20,* 463–473.

Cutting, J. E. (1976). Auditory and linguistic processes in speech perception: Inferences from six fusions in dichotic listening. *Psychological Review, 83,* 114–140.

Cutting, J. E. (1978). Generation of synthetic male and female walkers through manipulation of a biomechanical invariant. *Perception, 7,* 393–405.

Cutting, J. E. (1986). *Perception with an eye for motion.* Cambridge, MA: MIT Press.

Cutting, J. E. (1987). Perception and information. *Annual Review of Psychology, 38,* 61–90.

Cutting, J. E., & Kozlowski, L. T. (1977). Recognizing friends by their walk: Gait perception without familiarity cues. *Bulletin of the Psychonomic Society, 9,* 353–356.

Cutting, J. E., Proffitt, D. R. (1981). Gait perception as an example of how we may perceive events. In R. Walk & H. L. Pick, Jr. (Eds.), *Intersensory perception and sensory integration* (pp. 249–273). New York: Plenum Press.

Cutting, J. E., Proffitt, D. R., & Kozlowski, L. T. (1978). A biomechanical invariant for gait perception. *Journal of Experimental Psychology: Human Perception and Performance, 4,* 357–372.

Cynader, M., Berman, N., & Hein, A. (1976). Recovery of function in cat visual cortex following prolonged deprivation. *Experimental Brain Research, 25,* 139–156.

Cynader, M., & Regan, D. (1978). Neurons in cat parastriate cortex sensitive to the direction of motion in three-dimensional space. *Journal of Physiology, 274,* 549–569.

Cynader, M., Timney, B. N., & Mitchell, D. E. (1980). Period of susceptibility of kitten visual cortex to the effects of monocular deprivation extends beyond 6 months of age. *Brain Research, 191,* 545–550.

Daan, S., Beersma, D. G. M., & Borbely, A. A. (1984). Timing of human sleep: Recovery process gated by a circadian pacemaker. *American Journal of Physiology, 246,* 161–178.

Dacey, D. M. (1988). Dopamine-accumulating retinal neurons revealed by in vitro fluorescence display a unique morphology. *Science, 240,* 1196–1198.

Dallenbach, K. M. (1927). The temperature spots and end-organs. *American Journal of Psychology, 39,* 402–427.

Dallenbach, K. M. (1939). Pain: History and present status. *American Journal of Psychology, 52,* 331–347.

D'Aloisio, A., & Klein, R. M. (1990). Aging and the deployment of attention. In J. T. Enns (Ed.), *The development of attention: Research and theory* (pp. 447–466). Amsterdam: Elsevier.

Dallos, P. (1978). Biophysics of the cochlea. In E. C. Friedman & M. P. Carterette (Eds.), *Handbook of perception: Vol. IV. Hearing* (pp. 125–162). New York: Academic Press.

Dallos, P., Santos-Sacchi, J., & Flock, A. (1982). Intracellular recordings from cochlear outer hair cells. *Science, 18,* 582–584.

Dalton, K. (1964). The premenstrual syndrome. Springfield, IL: Thomas.

Dalziel, C. C., & Egan, D. J. (1982). Crystalline lens thickness changes as observed by pachometry. *American Journal of Optometry and Physiological Optics, 59,* 442–447.

Damasio, A. R., & Tranel, D. (1990). Face agnosia and the neural substrates of memory. *Annual Review of Neuroscience, 13,* 89–109.

Daniels, J. D., Pettigrew, J. D., & Norman, J. L. (1978). Development of single-neuron responses in kittens' lateral geniculate nucleus. *Journal of Neurophysiology, 41,* 1373–1393.

Dannemiller, J. L. (1989). Computational approaches to color constancy: Adaptive and ontogenetic considerations. *Psychological Review, 96,* 225–266.

Dannemiller, J. L., & Freedland, R. L. (1991). Detection of relative motion by human infants. *Developmental Psychology, 27,* 67–78.

Darian-Smith, I., Sugitani, M., Heywood, J., Karita, K., & Goodwin, A. (1982). Touching textured surfaces: Cells in somatosensory cortex respond both to finger movement and to surface features. *Science, 218,* 906–909.

Dark, V., Johnston, W., Myles-Worsley, M., & Farah, M. (1985). Levels of selection and capacity limits. *Journal of Experimental Psychology: General, 114,* 472–497.

Dark, V. J. (1988). Semantic priming, prime reportability, and retroactive priming are interdependent. *Memory and Cognition, 16,* 299–308.

Dartnall, H. M. A. (1957). *The visual pigments.* London: Methuen.

Daugman, J. G. (1980). Two-dimensional spectral analysis of cortical receptive field profiles. *Vision Research, 20,* 847–856.

Davidoff, J. B. (1975). *Differences in visual perception: The individual eye.* New York: Academic Press.

Dawson, J. L. (1967). Cultural and physiological influences upon spatial processes in West Africa: I. *International Journal of Psychology, 2,* 115–128.

Dawson, M. R. W. (1991). The how and why of what went where in apparent motion: Modelling solutions to the motion correspondence problem. *Psychological Review, 98,* 569–603.

Dawson, M. R. W., & Di Lollo, V. (1990). Effects of adapting luminance and stimulus contrast on the temporal and spatial limits of short-range motion. *Vision Research, 30,* 415–429.

Dawson, M. R. W., & Pylyshyn, Z. W. (1988). Natural constraints on apparent motion. In Z.W. Pylyshyn (Ed.), *Computational processes in human vision* (pp. 99–120). Norwood, NJ: Ablex.

Day, M. C. (1975). Developmental trends in visual scanning. In H. W. Reese (Ed.), *Advances in Child Development and Behavior: Vol. 10* (pp. 154–193). New York: Academic Press.

Day, M. C., & Stone, C. A. (1980). Children's use of perceptual set. *Journal of Experimental Child Psychology, 29,* 428–445.

Day, R. H. (1990). The Bourdon illusion in haptic space. *Perception & Psychophysics, 47,* 400–404.

Day, R. H., Stuart G. W., & Dickinson, R. G. (1980). Size constancy does not fail below half a degree. *Perception & Psychophysics, 28,* 263–265.

Day, R. H., & Webster, W. R. (1989). Negative afterimages and the McCollough effect. *Perception & Psychophysics, 46,* 419–424.

Day, R. S. (1968). *Fusion in dichotic listening.* Unpublished doctoral dissertation, Stanford University, Stanford, CA.

Day, R. S. (1970). Temporal order judgments in speech: Are individuals language-bound or stimulus-bound? *Haskins Laboratories Status Report* (SR-21/22), 71–87.

DeGangi, G. A., & Greenspan, S. I. (1988). The development of sensory functions in infants. *Physical & Occupational Therapy in Pediatrics, 8,* 21–33.

Delgutte, B. (1990). Physiological mechanisms of psychophysical masking: Observations from auditory-nerve fibers. *Journal of the Acoustical Society of America, 87,* 791–809.

Delk, J. L., & Fillenbaum, S. (1965). Differences in perceived color as a function of characteristic color. *American Journal of Psychology, 78,* 290–293.

Delorne, A., & Martin, C. (1986). Roles of retinal periphery and depth periphery in linear vection and visual control of standing in humans. *Canadian Journal of Psychology, 40,* 176–187.

De Monasterio, F. M. (1978). Center and surround mechanisms of opponent-color X and Y ganglion cells of retina of macaques. *Journal of Neurophysiology, 41,* 1418–1434.

Deregowski, J. (1980). *Illusions, patterns and pictures: A cross-cultural perspective.* London: Academic Press.

De Renzi, D. E. (1982). *Disorders of space exploration and cognition.* New York: Wiley.

Derrington, A. M., & Fuchs, A. F. (1981). The development of spatial-frequency selectivity in kitten striate cortex. *Journal of Physiology, 316,* 1–10.

Desimone, R., Albright, T. D., Gross, C. G., & Bruce, C. (1980). Responses of inferior temporal neurons to complex visual stimuli. *Society of Neurosciences. Abstracts, 6,* 581.

Desimone, R., & Gross, C. G. (1979). Visual areas in the temporal cortex of the macaque. *Brain Research, 178,* 363–380.

Desimone, R., Schein, S. J., Moran, J., & Ungerleider, L. G. (1985). Contour, color and shape analysis beyond the striate cortex. *Vision Research, 25,* 441–452.

Desimone, R., & Ungerleider, L. G. (1989). Neural mechanisms of visual processing in monkeys. In I. Boller &

J. Grafman (Eds.), *Handbook of neuropsychology: Vol. 2* (pp. 267–299). Amsterdam: Elsevier.

Deutsch, D. (1975). Two channel listening to musical scales. *Journal of the Acoustical Society of America, 57,* 1156–1160.

Deutsch, D. (1978). The psychology of music. In E. C. Carterette & M. P. Friedman (Eds.), *Handbook of perception: Vol. X. Perceptual ecology* (pp. 191–224). New York: Academic Press.

Deutsch, D. (Ed.). (1982). *The psychology of music.* New York: Academic Press.

Deutsch, D. (1986). A musical paradox. *Music Perception, 3,* 275–280.

Deutsch, D. (1987). The tritone paradox: Effects of spectral variables. *Perception & Psychophysics, 41,* 563–575.

Deutsch, D., & Feroe, J. (1981). The internal representation of pitch sequences in tonal music. *Psychological Review, 88,* 503–522.

Deutsch, D., & Kuyper, W. L. (1987). The tritone paradox: Its presence and form of distribution in a general population. *Music Perception, 5,* 79–92.

Deutsch, J. A., & Deutsch, D. (1963). Attention: Some theoretical considerations. *Psychological Review, 70,* 80–90.

DeValois, K. K. (1977). Independence of black and white: Phase specific adaptation. *Vision Research, 17,* 209–215.

DeValois, R. L., Albrecht D. G., & Thorell, L. G. (1982). Spatial frequency selectivity of cells in the macaque visual cortex. *Vision Research, 22,* 545–559.

DeValois, R. L., & DeValois, K. K. (1975). Neural coding of color. In E. C. Carterette & M. P. Friedman (Eds.), *Handbook of perception: Vol. V. Seeing* (pp.117–168). New York: Academic Press.

DeValois, R. L., & DeValois, K. K. (1980). Spatial vision. *Annual Review of Psychology, 31,* 309–341.

DeValois, R. L., & DeValois, K. K. (1987). *Spatial vision.* New York: Oxford University Press.

DeValois, R. L., Yund, E. W., & Hepler, N. (1982). The orientation and direction selectivity of cells in macaque visual cortex. *Vision Research, 22,* 531–544.

Devaney, K. O., & Johnson, H. A. (1980). Neuron loss in the aging visual cortex of man. *Journal of Gerontology, 35,* 836–841.

De Vries, H., & Stuiver, M. (1961). The absolute sensitivity of the human sense of smell. In W. A. Rosenblith (Ed.), *Communication processes* (pp. 159–167). New York: Wiley.

De Vries, J. V. (1968). *Perspective.* New York: Dover. (Original work published 1604)

DeWitt, L. A., & Samuel, A. G. (1990). The role of knowledge-based expectations in music perception: Evidence from musical restoration. *Journal of Memory & Language, 26,* 36–56.

DeYoe, E. A., & van Essen, D. C. (1988). Concurrent processing streams in monkey visual cortex. *Trends in Neuroscience, 11,* 219–226.

Diamant, H., Funakoshi, M., Strom, L., & Zotterman, Y. (1963). Electrophysiological studies on human taste nerves. In Y. Zotterman (Ed.), *Olfaction and taste* (pp. 191–203). Oxford: Pergamon Press.

Diamant, H., & Zotterman, Y. (1969). A comparative study on the neural and psychophysical response to taste stimuli. In C. Pfaffman (Ed.), *Olfaction and taste III.* (pp. 428–435). New York: Rockefeller University Press.

DiCarlo, L. T., & Cross, D. V. (1990). Sequential effects in magnitude scaling: Models and theory. *Journal of Experimental Psychology: General, 119,* 375–396.

Dichgans, J., & Brandt, T. (1978). Visual-vestibular interaction: Effects on self-motion perception and postural control. In R. Held, H. W. Leibowitz, & H. L. Teuber (Eds.), *Handbook of sensory physiology: Vol. 7. Perception* (pp. 755–804). New York: Springer-Verlag.

Dickhaus, H., Pauser, G., & Zimmerman, M. (1985). Tonic descending inhibition affects intensity coding of nociceptive responses of spinal dorsal horn neurones in the cat. *Pain, 23,* 145–158.

Diehl, R. L. (1981). Feature detectors for speech: A critical reappraisal. *Psychological Bulletin, 89,* 1–18.

Diener, D. (1990). The P&p illusion. *Perception & Psychophysics, 47,* 65–67.

Dineen, I. T., & Meyer, W. J. (1980). Developmental changes in visual orienting behavior to featural versus structural information in the human infant. *Developmental Psychology, 13,* 123–130.

Ditchburn, R. W. (1973). *Eye movements and perception.* Oxford: Clarendon Press.

DiZio, P. A., & Lackner, J. R. (1986). Perceived orientation, motion, and configuration of the body during viewing of an off-vertical rotating surface. *Perception & Psychophysics, 39,* 39–46.

Djang, S. (1937). The role of past experience in the visual apprehension of masked forms. *Journal of Experimental Psychology, 20,* 29–59.

Dobson, V. (1976). Spectral sensitivity of the 2-month-old infant as measured by the visual evoked cortical potential. *Vision Research, 16,* 367–374.

Dobson, V., & Teller, D.Y. (1978). Visual acuity in human infants: A review and comparison of behavioral and electrophysiological studies. *Vision Research, 18,* 1469–1483.

Dodwell, P. C. (1971). On perceptual clarity. *Psychological Review, 78,* 275–279.

Dodwell, P. C., & Humphrey, G. K. (1990). A functional theory of the McCollough effect. *Psychological Review, 97,* 78–89.

Dodwell, P. C., Humphrey, G. K., & Muir, D. W. (1987). Shape and pattern perception. In P. Salapatek & L. Cohen (Eds.), *Handbook of infant perception: Vol. 2. From perception to cognition* (pp. 1–80). Orlando: Academic Press.

Doetsch, G. S., Ganchrow, J. J., Nelson, L. M., & Erickson, R. P. (1969). Information processing in the taste system of the rat. In C. Pfaffman (Ed.), *Olfaction and taste III* (pp. 492–511). New York: Rockefeller University Press.

Doherty, M. E., & Keeley, S. M. (1972). On the identification of repeatedly presented visual stimuli. *Psychological Bulletin, 78,* 142–154.

Donaldson, I. M. L., & Long, A. C. (1980). Interactions between extraocular proprioceptive and visual signals in the superior colliculus of the cat. *Journal of Physiology, 298,* 85–110.

Donchin, E. (1981). Surprise! . . . Surprise? *Psychophysiology, 18,* 493–513.

Doner, J., Lappin, J. S., & Perfetto, G. (1984). Detection of three-dimensional structure in moving optical patterns. *Journal of Experimental Psychology: Human Perception and Performance, 10,* 1–11.

Dooley, G. J., & Moore, B. C. J. (1988). Detection of linear frequency glides as a function of frequency and duration. *Journal of the Acoustical Society of America, 84,* 2045–2057.

Doty, R. L. (1985). The primates: III. Humans. In R. E. Brown & D. W. MacDonald (Eds.), Social odours in mammals: Vol. 2 (pp. 804–832) Oxford: Clarendon Press.

Doty, R. L., Applebaum, S., Zusho, H., & Settle, R. G. (1985). Sex differences in odor identification ability: A cross-cultural analysis. *Neuropsychologia, 23,* 667–672.

Doty, R. L., Green, P. A., Ram, C., & Yankell, S. L. (1982). Communication of gender from human breath odors: Relationship to perceived intensity and pleasantness. *Hormones and Behavior, 16,* 13–22.

Doty, R. L., Kligman, A., Leyden, J., & Orndorff, M. M. (1978). Communication of gender from human axillary odors: Relationship to perceived intensity and hedonicity. *Behavioral Biology, 23,* 373–380.

Doty, R. L., Shaman, P., & Applebaum, S. L. (1984). Smell identification ability: Changes with age. *Science, 226,* 1441–1443.

Dowling, W. J., & Carterette, E. C. (Eds). (1987). The understanding of melody and rhythm. *Perception & Psychophysics, 41* [Special Issue], 482–656.

Dowling, W. J., & Harwood, D. L. (1986). *Music cognition.* Orlando: Academic Press.

Downing, C. J. (1988). Expectancy and visual-spatial attention: Effects on perceptual quality. *Journal of*

Experimental Psychology: Human Perception and Performance, 14, 188–202.

Droscher, V. B. (1971). *The magic of the senses: New discoveries in animal perception.* New York: Harper.

Drum, B. (1980). Relation of brightness to threshold for light-adapted and dark-adapted rods and cones: Effects of retinal eccentricity and target size. *Perception, 9,* 633–650.

Drum, B. (1981). Brightness interactions between rods and cones. *Perception & Psychophysics, 29,* 505–510.

Duncan, H. F., Gourlay, N., & Hudson, W. (1973). A study of pictorial perception among the Bantu and white primary school children in South Africa. Johannesburg: Witwatersrand University Press.

Duncan, J., & Humphreys, G. W. (1989). Visual search and stimulus similarity. *Psychological Review, 96,* 433–458.

Duncker, K. (1929). Uber induzierte Bewegung (ein Beitrag zur Theorie optisch warigenommener Bewegung). *Psychologische Forschung, 2,* 180–259.

Durlach, N. I., Delhorne, L. A., Wong, A., Ko, W. Y., Rabinowitz, W. M., & Hollerbach, J. (1989). Manual discrimination and identification of length by the finger-span method. *Perception & Psychophysics, 46,* 29–38.

Easterbrook, J. A. (1959). The effect of emotion on cue utilization and the organization of behavior. *Psychological Review, 66,* 183–201.

Easton, R. D., & Basala, M. (1982). Perceptual dominance during lipreading. *Perception & Psychophysics, 32,* 562–570.

Edwards, A., & Cohen, S. (1961). Visual illusions, tactile sensibility and reaction time under LSD-25. *Psychopharmacologia, 2,* 297–303.

Efron, R. (1967). The duration of the present. *Annals of the New York Academy of Sciences, 138,* 713–729.

Efron, R. (1973). Conservation of temporal information by perceptual systems. *Perception & Psychophysics, 14,* 518–530.

Egan, J. P. (1975). *Signal detection theory and ROC-analysis.* New York: Academic Press.

Egeth, H. E., Virzi, R. A., & Garbart, H. (1984). Searching for conjunctively defined targets. *Journal of Experimental Psychology: Human Perception and Performance, 10,* 32–39.

Eichengreen, J. M., Coren, S., & Nachmias, J. (1966). Visual-cliff preference by infant rats: Effects of rearing and test conditions. *Science, 151,* 830–831.

Eijkman, E. G. J., Jongsma, H. J., & Vincent, J. (1981). Two dimensional filtering, oriented line detectors and figural aspects as determinants of visual illusions. *Perception & Psychophysics, 29,* 352–358.

Eilers, R., Wilson, W., & Moore, T. (1979). Speech perception in the language innocent and the language wise: A study in the perception of voice onset time. *Journal of Child Language, 6,* 1–18.

Eimas, P. D., & Corbit, J. D. (1973). Selective adaptation of linguistic feature detectors. *Cognitive Psychology, 4,* 99–109.

Eimas, P. D., & Miller, J. D. (1980). Contextual effects in infant speech perception. *Science, 209,* 1140–1141.

Eimas, P. D., Siqueland, E. R., Jusczyk, P., & Vigorito, J. (1971). Speech perception in infants. *Science, 171,* 303–306.

Einstein, A., & Besso, M. (1972). *Correspondence 1903–1955.* Paris: Hermann.

Ekman, G. (1954). Dimensions of color vision. *Journal of Psychology, 38,* 467–474.

Eland, J. M., & Anderson, J. E. (1977). The experience of pain in children. In A. Jacox (Ed.), *Pain: A sourcebook for nurses and other professionals.* Boston: Little Brown.

Elkind, D. (1978). The child's reality: Three developmental themes. Hillsdale, NJ: Erlbaum.

Ellingson, R. (1968). Clinical applications of evoked potential techniques in infants and children. *Electroencephalography and Clinical Neurophysiology, 24,* 293.

Ellingson, R., Lathrop, G., Nelson, G., & Donahy, T. (1972). Visual evoked potentials of infants. *Revue d'Electroencéphalographie et de Neurophysiologie Clinique, 2,* 395–400.

Ellis, H. (1905). *Sexual selection in man.* New York: Davis.

Ellis, H. C., & Muller, D. G. (1964). Transfer in perceptual learning following stimulus predifferentiation. *Journal of Experimental Psychology, 68,* 388–395.

Ellis, H. D., & Young, A. W. (1988). Training in face-processing skills for a child with acquired prosopagnosia. *Developmental Neuropsychology, 4,* 283–294.

Emmerson, P. G., & Ross, H. E. (1986). The effect of brightness on colour recognition under water. *Ergonomics, 29,* 1647–1658.

Emmerton, J. (1983). Pattern discrimination in the near-ultraviolet by pigeons. *Perception & Psychophysics, 34,* 555–559.

Engen, T. (1982). *Perception of odors.* New York: Academic Press.

Engen, T. (1987). Remembering odors and their names. *American Scientist, 75,* 497–503.

Engen, T., Lipsitt, L. P., & Kaye, H. (1963). Olfactory responses and adaptation in the human neonate. *Journal of Comparative and Physiological Psychology, 56,* 73–77.

Enns, J. T. (1986). Seeing textons in context. *Perception & Psychophysics, 39,* 143–147.

Enns, J. T. (1987). A developmental look at pattern symmetry in perception and memory. *Developmental Psychology, 23,* 839–850.

Enns, J. T. (1990a). Relations between components of visual attention. In J. T. Enns (Ed.), *The development of attention: Research and theory* (pp. 447–466). Amsterdam: Elsevier.

Enns, J. T. (1990b). Three dimensional features that pop out in visual search. In D. Brogan (Ed.), *Visual search* (pp. 37–45). London: Taylor & Francis.

Enns, J. T., & Brodeur, D. A. (1989). A developmental study of covert orienting to peripheral visual cues. *Journal of Experimental Child Psychology, 48,* 171–189.

Enns, J. T., & Cameron, S. (1987). Selective attention in young children: The relations between visual search, filtering and priming. *Journal of Experimental Child Psychology, 44,* 38–63.

Enns, J. T., & Girgus, J. S. (1985). Perceptual grouping and spatial distortion: A developmental study. *Developmental Psychology, 21,* 241–246.

Enns, J. T., & Girgus, J. S. (1986). A developmental study of shape integration over space and time. *Developmental Psychology, 22,* 491–499.

Enns, J. T., & King, K. A. (1990). Components of line-drawing interpretation: A developmental study. *Developmental Psychology, 26,* 469–479.

Enns, J. T., & Prinzmetal, W. (1984). The role of redundancy in the object-line effect. *Perception & Psychophysics, 35,* 22–32.

Enns, J. T., & Rensink, R. A. (1990). Influence of scene-based properties on visual search. *Science, 247,* 721–723.

Enns, J. T., & Rensink, R. A. (1991). Preattentive recovery of three-dimensional orientation from line drawings. *Psychological Review, 98,* 335–351.

Enright, J. T. (1987a). Art and the oculomotor system: Perspective illustrations evoke vergence changes. *Perception, 16,* 731–746.

Enright, J. T. (1987b). Perspective vergence: Oculomotor responses to line drawings. *Vision Research, 27,* 1513–1526.

Epstein, W. (1973). The process of taking into account in visual perception. *Perception, 2,* 267–285.

Epstein, W., & Baratz, S. S. (1964). Relative size in isolation as a stimulus for relative perceived distance. *Journal of Experimental Psychology, 67,* 507–513.

Epstein, W., & Broota, K. D. (1986). Automatic and attentional components in perception of size-at-a-distance. *Perception & Psychophysics, 40,* 256–262.

Epstein, W., & Hanson, S. (1977). Discrimination of unique motion-path length. *Perception & Psychophysics, 22,* 152–158.

Epstein, W., Hatfield, G., & Muise, G. (1977). Perceived shape at a slant as a function of processing time and processing load. *Journal of Experimental Psychology: Human Perception and Performance, 3,* 473–483.

Epstein, W., & Lovitts, B. E. (1985). Automatic and attentional components in perception of shape-at-a-slant. *Journal of Experimental Psychology: Human Perception and Performance, 11,* 355–366.

Epstein, W., & Park, J. N. (1964). Shape constancy: Functional relationships and theoretical formulations. *Psychological Bulletin, 62,* 180–196.

Erickson, R. P. (1963). Sensory neural patterns and gustation. In Y. Zotterman (Ed.), *Olfaction and taste* (pp. 205–213). Oxford: Pergamon Press.

Erickson, R. P. (1985). Definitions: A matter of taste. In D. W. Pfaff (Ed.), *Taste, olfaction, and the central nervous system* (pp. 129–150). New York: Rockefeller University Press.

Erickson, R. P., & Covey, E. (1980). On the singularity of taste sensations: What is a taste primary? *Physiology and Behavior, 25,* 527–533.

Erickson, R. P., & Schiffman, S. S. (1975). The chemical senses: A systematic approach. In M. S. Gazzaniga & C. Blakemore (Eds.), *Handbook of psychobiology* (pp. 393–425). New York: Academic Press.

Eriksen, C. W., & Collins, J. F. (1968). Sensory traces versus the psychological movement in the temporal organization of form. *Journal of Experimental Psychology, 77,* 376–382.

Eriksen, C. W., & Hake, H. W. (1955). Absolute judgments as a function of stimulus range and number of stimulus and reponse categories. *Journal of Experimental Psychology, 49,* 323–332.

Eriksen, C. W., & Hoffman, J. E. (1972). Some characteristics of selective attention in visual perception determined by vocal reaction time. *Perception & Psychophysics, 11,* 169–171.

Eriksen, C. W., & Murphy, T. D. (1987). Movement of attentional focus across the visual field: A critical look at the evidence. *Perception & Psychophysics, 42,* 299–305.

Eriksen, C. W., & St. James, J. D. (1986). Visual attention within and around the field of focal attention: A zoom lens model. *Perception & Psychophysics, 40,* 225–240.

Eriksen, C. W., & Yeh, Y. (1985). Allocation of attention in the visual field. *Journal of Experimental Psychology: Human Perception and Performance, 11,* 583–597.

Ernst, M., Lee, M. H. M., Dworkin, B., & Zaretsky, H. H. (1986). Pain perception decrement produced through repeated stimulation. *Pain, 26,* 221–231.

Erulkar, S. C. (1972). Comparative aspects of spatial localization of sound. *Physiological Review, 52,* 237–360.

Evans, E. F. (1975). Cochlear nerve and cochlear nucleus. In W. D. Keidel & W. D. Neff (Eds.), *Handbook of sensory physiology: Vol. V/2. Auditory system: Physiol-*

ogy (CNS). *Behavioral Studies. Psychoacoustics* (pp. 1–108). New York: Springer-Verlag.

Evans, P. M. (1987). Vibrotactile masking: Temporal integration, persistence, and strengths of representation. *Perception & Psychophysics, 42,* 515–525.

Evans, P. M., & Craig, J. C. (1986). Temporal integration and vibrotactile backward masking. *Journal of Experimental Psychology: Human Perception and Performance, 12,* 160–168.

Eysenck, H. J. (1967). *The biological basis of personality.* Springfield, IL: Thomas.

Fagen, D., & Swift, C. G. (1988). Effects of caffeine on vigilance and other performance tests in normal subjects. *Journal of Psychopharmacology, 2,* 19–25.

Falmagne, J. C. (1985). *Elements of psychophysical theory.* New York: Oxford University Press.

Fant, G. (1967). Auditory patterns of speech. In W. Wathen-Dunn (Ed.), *Models for the perception of speech and visual form* (pp. 111–125). Cambridge, MA: MIT Press.

Fantz, R. L. (1961). The origin of form perception. *Scientific American, 204,* 66–72.

Fantz, R. L., (1965). Ontogeny of perception. In A. M. Schrier, H. F. Harlow, & F. Stollnitz (Eds.), *Behavior of nonhuman primates* (Vol. 2, pp. 365–403). New York: Academic Press.

Fantz, R. L., & Miranda, S. B. (1977). Visual processing in the newborn preterm, and mentally high-risk infant. In L. Gluck (Ed.), *Intrauterine asphyxia and the developing fetal brain* (pp. 453–471). Chicago: Year Book Medical Publishers.

Fantz, R. L., & Yeh, J. (1979). Configurational selectives: Critical for development of visual perception and attention. *Canadian Journal of Psychology, 33,* 277–287.

Farkas, M., & Hoyer, W. (1980). Processing consequences of perceptual grouping in selective attention. *Journal of Gerontology, 35,* 27–216.

Farrell, J. E. (1983). Visual transformations underlying apparent movement. *Perception & Psychophysics, 33,* 85–92.

Farrimond, T. (1990). Effect of alcohol on visual constancy values and possible relation to driving performance. *Perceptual and Motor Skills, 70,* 291–295.

Favreau, O. E., & Cavanagh, P. (1981). Color and luminance: Independent frequency shifts. *Science, 212,* 831–832.

Fechner, G. T. (1966). *Elements of psychophysics.* (H. E. Alder, Trans.). New York: Holt, Rinehart & Winston. (Original work published 1860)

Fender, D. H. (1971). Time delays in the human eye-tracking system. In P. Bach-y-Rita, C. C. Collins, & J. E. Hyde (Eds.), *The control of eye movements* (pp. 539–543). New York: Academic Press.

Fernald, A. (1985). Four-month-old infants prefer to listen to motherese. *Infant Behavior and Development, 8,* 181–195.

Festinger, L., Allyn, M. R., & White, C. W. (1971). The perception of color with achromatic stimulation. *Vision Research, 11,* 591–612.

Festinger, L., Coren, S., & Rivers, G. (1970). The effect of attention on brightness contrast and assimilation. *American Journal of Psychology, 83,* 189–207.

Festinger, L., & Easton, M. (1974). Inference about the efferent system based on a perceptual illusion produced by eye movements. *Psychological Review, 81,* 44–58.

Festinger, L., White, C. W., & Allyn, M. R. (1968). Eye movements and decrement in the Mueller-Lyer illusion. *Perception & Psychophysics, 3,* 376–382.

Filsinger, E. E., & Fabes, R. A. (1985). Odor communication, pheromones, and human families. *Journal of Marriage and the Family, 47,* 349–360.

Findlay, J. (1981). Local and global influences on saccadic eye movements. In D. Fisher, R. Monty, & J. Senders (Eds.), *Eye movements: Cognition and visual perception* (pp. 171–179). Hillsdale, NJ: Erlbaum.

Fine, B. J., & Kobrick, J. L. (1987). Cigarette smoking, field-dependence and contrast sensitivity. *Aviation, Space and Environmental Medicine, 58,* 777–782.

Fiorentini, A., Baumgartner, G., Magnussen, S., Shiller, P. H., & Thomas, J. P. (1990). The perception of brightness and darkness. In L. Spillman & J. S. Werner (Eds.), *Visual perception: The neurophysiological foundations* (pp. 129–161). New York: Academic Press.

Firestein, S., & Werblin, F. (1989). Odor-induced membrane currents in vertebrate-olfactory receptor neurons. *Science, 244,* 79–82.

Fischer, B., & Boch, R. (1983). Saccadic eye movements after extremely short reaction times in the monkey. *Brain Research, 260,* 21–26.

Fischer, B., & Breitmeyer, B. (1987). Mechanisms of visual attention revealed by saccadic eye movements. *Neuropsychologia, 25,* 73–83.

Fisher, D. L., Duffy, S. A., Young, C., & Pollatsek, A. (1988). Understanding the central processing limit in consistent-mapping visual search tasks. *Journal of Experimental Psychology: Human Perception and Performance, 14,* 253–266.

Fisher, R. (1967). The biological fabric of time. In *Interdisciplinary perspectives of time, Annals of the New York Academy of Sciences, 138,* 451–465.

Fisk, A. D., & Schneider, W. (1981). Control and automatic processing during tasks requiring sustained attention: A new approach to vigilance. *Human Factors, 23,* 737–750.

Fitzpatrick, V., Pasnak, R., & Tyer, Z. E. (1982). The effect of familiar size at familiar distances. *Perception, 11,* 85–91.

Flandrin, J. M., & Jeannerod, M. (1981). Effects of unilateral superior colliculus ablation on oculomotor and vistibulo-ocular responses in the cat. *Experimental Brain Research, 42,* 73–80.

Flannery, R., & Butler, R. A. (1981). Spectral cues provided in the pinna for monaural localization in the horizontal plane. *Perception & Psychophysics, 29,* 438–444.

Flin, R. H. (1980). Age effects in children's memory for unfamiliar faces. *Developmental Psychology, 16,* 373–374.

Flock, H. R., & Freedberg, E. (1970). Perceived angle of incidence and achromatic surface color. *Perception & Psychophysics, 8,* 251–256.

Flock, H. R., & Nusinowitz, S. (1984). Visual structures for achromatic color perceptions. *Perception & Psychophysics, 36,* 111–130.

Flom, M. C., Brown, B., Adams, A. J., & Jones, R. T. (1976). Alcohol and marihuana effects on ocular tracking. *American Journal of Optometry and Physiological Optics, 53,* 764–773.

Florentine, M. (1986). Level discrimination of tones as a function of duration. *Journal of the Acoustical Society of America, 79,* 792–798.

Florentine, M., Buus, S., & Mason, C. R. (1987). Level discrimination as a function of level for tones from 0.25 to 16 kHz. *Journal of the Acoustical Society of America, 81,* 1528–1541.

Fodor, J. (1983). *The modularity of mind.* Cambridge, MA: MIT Press.

Fogel, I., & Sagi, D. (1989). Gabor filters as texture discriminator. *Biological Cybernetics, 61,* 103–113.

Foley, J. E. (1970). Prism adaptation with opposed base orientation: The weighting of direction information from the two eyes. *Perception & Psychophysics, 8,* 23–25.

Foley, J. E. (1974). Factors governing interocular transfer of prism adaptation. *Psychological Review, 81,* 183–186.

Foulke, E., & Sticht, T. (1969). Review of research on the intelligibility and comprehension of accelerated speech. *Psychological Bulletin, 72,* 50–62.

Fowler, C. A., & Rosenblum, L. D. (1990). Duplex perception: A comparison of monosyllables and slamming doors. *Journal of Experimental Psychology: Human Perception & Performance, 16,* 742–754.

Fox, P. T., Mintun, M. A., Reiman, E. M., & Raichle, M. E. (1988). Enhanced detection of focal brain responses using intersubject averaging and change-distribution analysis of subtracted PET images. *Journal of Cerebral Blood Flow and Metabolism, 8,* 642–653.

Fox, R., Aslin, R. N., Shea, S. L., & Dumais, S. T. (1980). Stereopsis in infants. *Science, 207,* 323–324.

Fox, R., & McDaniel, C. (1982). The perception of biological motion by human infants. *Science, 486–487.*

Fozard, J., Wolf, E., Bell, B., McFarland, R., & Podolsky, S. (1977). Visual perception and communication. In J. Birren & K. Schaie (Eds.), *Handbook of the psychology of aging* (pp. 497–534). New York: Van Nostrand Reinhold.

Fraisse, P. (1963). The psychology of time. New York: Harper & Row.

Frank, M. E. (1975). Response patterns of rat glossopharyngeal taste neurons. In D. A. Denton & P. Coghlan (Eds.), *Olfaction and taste V* (pp. 59–64). New York: Academic Press.

Frank, M. E. (1985). On the neural code for sweet and salty taste. In D. W. Pfaff (Ed.), *Taste, olfaction, and the central nervous system* (pp. 107–128). New York: Rockefeller University Press.

Frankenhauser, M. (1959). *The estimation of time.* Stockholm: Almqvist & Wiksell.

Fraser. J. (1908). A new illusion of direction. *British Journal of Psychology, 8,* 49–54.

Freeman, D. M., & Weiss, T. F. (1990). Hydrodynamic analysis of a two-dimensional model for micromechanical resonance of free-standing hair bundles. *Hearing Research, 48,* 37–68.

Freeman, R., Mallach, R., & Hartley, S. (1981). Responsivity of normal kitten striate cortex deteriorates after brief binocular deprivation. *Journal of Neurophysiology, 45,* 1074–1084.

Freeman, R., & Pettigrew, J. (1973). Alteration of visual cortex from environmental asymmetries. *Nature, 246,* 359–360.

Freidman, E. (1981). Vision training program for myopia management. *American Journal of Optometry and Physiological Optics, 58,* 546–553.

Freud, S. (1953). *An aphasia.* London: Imago.

Frey, M. von, & Kiesow, F. (1899). Uber die Function der Tastkorperchen. *Zeitschrift feur Psychologie, 20,* 126–163.

Frey, M. von, & Goldman, A. (1915). Der zeitliche Verlauf det Einstellung bei den Druckempfindungen. *Zeitschrift feur Biologie, 65,* 183–202.

Freyd, J., & Tversky, B. (1984). Force of symmetry in form perception. *American Journal of Psychology, 97,* 109–126.

Friedman, A. (1979). Framing pictures: The role of knowledge in automatized encoding and memory for gist. *Journal of Experimental Psychology: General, 108,* 316–355.

Friedman, A., & Liebelt, L. (1981). On the time course of viewing pictures with a view towards remembering. In D. Fisher, R. Monty, & J. Senders (Eds.), *Eye movements: Cognition and visual perception* (pp. 137–155). Hillsdale, NJ: Erlbaum.

Friedman, R. B. (1980). Identity without form: Abstract representations of letters. *Perception & Psychophysics, 28,* 53–60.

Friedman, S. L., & Stevenson, M. (1975). Developmental changes in the understanding of implied motion in two-dimensional pictures. *Child Development, 46,* 773–778.

Friedman, S. L., & Stevenson, M. (1980). Perception of movements in pictures. In M. Hagen (Ed.), *Perception of pictures; Vol. I. Alberti's window: The projective model of pictural information* (pp. 225–255). New York: Academic Press.

Frisby, J. P. (1980). *Seeing: Illusion, brain and mind.* Oxford: Oxford University Press.

Fuld, K., Wooten, B. R., & Whalen, J. J. (1981). The elemental hues of short-wave and extraspectral lights. *Perception & Psychophysics, 29,* 317–322.

Fuller, C. A., Lydic, R., Sulzman, F. M., Albers, H. E., Tepper, B., & Moore-Ede, M. C. (1981). Circadian rhythm of body temperature persists after suprachiamatic lesions in the squirrel monkey. *American Journal of Physiology, 241,* R385–R391.

Fulton, J. F., & Bailey, P. (1929). Tumors in the region of the third ventricle: Their diagnosis and relation to pathological sleep. *Journal of Nervous and Mental Disorders, 69,* 1–25,145–164, 261–277.

Funakoshi, M., Kasahara, Y., Yamamoto, T., & Kawamura, Y. (1972). Taste coding and central perception. In D. Schneider (Ed.), *Olfaction and taste IV* (pp. 336–342). Stuttgart: Wissenshaftliche Verlagsgesellschaft MBH.

Funkenstein, H. H., Nelson, P. G., Winter, P. L., Wolberg, Z., & Newman, J. D. (1971). Unit responses in auditory cortex of awake squirrel monkeys to vocal stimulation. In M. B. Saschs (Ed.), *Physiology of the auditory system* (pp. 307–326). Baltimore: National Educational Consultants, Inc.

Gaddes, W. H. (1985). *Learning disabilities and brain function: A neuropsychological approach* (2nd ed.). New York: Springer-Verlag.

Gagne, J. P. (1988). Excess masking among listeners with a sensorineural hearing loss. *Journal of the Acoustical Society of America, 83,* 2311–2321.

Galanter, E. (1962). Contemporary psychophysics. In R. Brown, E. Galanter, E., Hess, E., & Mandler, G. (Eds.), *New Directions in Psychology* (pp. 87–157). New York: Holt, Rinehart & Winston.

Ganchrow, J. R., Steiner, J. E., & Daher, M. (1983). Neonatal facial expressions in response to different qualities and intensities of gustatory stimuli. *Infant Behavior and Development, 6,* 189–200.

Garbin, C. P. (1988). Visual-haptic perceptual nonequivalence for shape information and its impact upon cross-modal performance. *Journal of Experimental Psychology: Human Perception and Performance, 14,* 547–553.

Gardner, E. B., & Costanzo, R. H. (1981). Properties of kinesthetic neurons in somatosensory cortex of awake monkeys. *Brain Research, 214,* 301–319.

Gardner, E. P. (1983). Cortical neuronal mechanisms underlying the perception of motion across the skin. In C. von Euler, O. Franzen, U. Lindblom, & D. Ottoson (Eds.), *Somatosensory mechanisms* (pp. 93–112). New York: Plenum Press.

Garner, W. R. (1953). An informational analysis of absolute judgments of loudness. *Journal of Experimental Psychology, 46,* 373–380.

Garner, W. R. (1962). *Uncertainty and structure as psychological concepts.* New York: Wiley.

Garner, W. R. (1974). The processing of information and structure. Potomac, MD: Erlbaum.

Garner, W. R. (1978). Aspects of a stimulus: Features, dimensions and configurations. In E. H. Rosch & B. B. Lloyd (Eds.), *Cognition and categorization* (pp. 99–139). Hillsdale, NJ: Erlbaum.

Garner, W. R., & Clement, D. E. (1963). Goodness of pattern and pattern uncertainty. *Journal of Verbal Learning and Verbal Behavior, 2,* 446–452.

Garner, W. R., & Hake, H. W. (1951). The amount of information in absolute judgments. *Psychological Review, 58,* 446–459.

Geiselman, R. E., Fisher, R. P., MacKinnon, D. P., & Holland, H. L. (1986). Enhancement of eyewitness memory with the cognitive interview. *American Journal of Psychology, 99,* 385–401.

Geisler, C. D. (1991). A cochlear model using feedback from motile outer hair cells. *Hearing Research, 54,* 105–117.

Geisler, C. D., Yates, G. K., Patuzzi, R. B., & Johnstone, B. M. (1990). Saturation of outer hair cell receptor currents causes two-tone suppression. *Hearing Research, 44,* 241–256.

Gelb, A. (1929). Die "Farbenkonstanz" der Sehdinge. *Handbuch der normalen und pathologische physiologie, 12,* 549–678.

Geldard, F. A. (1972). *The human senses.* (2nd ed.). New York: Wiley.

Gent, J. F. (1979). An exponential model for adaptation in taste. *Sensory Processes, 3,* 303–316.

Gerbino, W., & Salmaso, D. (1987). The effect of amodal completion on visual matching. *Acta Psychologia, 65,* 25–46.

Gerbrandt, L. K., Spinelli, D. N., & Pribram, K. H. (1970). Interaction of visual attention and temporal cortex stimulation on electrical activity evoked in striate cortex. *Electroencephalography and Clinical Neurology, 29,* 146.

Gerkema, M. P., & Groos, G. A. (1990). Differential elimination of circadian and ultradian rhythmicity by hypothalamic lesions in the common vole, Microtus arvalis. *Journal of Biological Rhythms, 5,* 81–95.

Gescheider, G. A. (1985). *Psychophysics: Method, theory, and application.* Hillsdale, NJ: Erlbaum.

Gescheider, G. A. (1988). Psychophysical scaling. *Annual Review of Psychology, 39,* 169–200.

Gescheider, G. A., & Bolanowski, S. J. (1991). Final comments on ratio scaling of psychological magnitudes. In S. J. Bolanowski & G. A. Gescheider (Eds.), *Ratio scaling of psychological magnitude* (pp. 295–311). Hillsdale, NJ: Erlbaum.

Gescheider, G. A., Bolanowski, S. J., Jr., & Verrillo, R. T. (1989). Vibrotactile masking: Effects of stimulus onset asynchrony and stimulus frequency. *Journal of the Acoustical Society of America, 85,* 2059–2064.

Gescheider, G. A., Bolanowski, S. J., Verrillo, R. T., Arpajian, D. J., & Ryan, T. F. (1990). Vibrotadile intensity discrimination measured by three methods. *Journal of the Acoustical Society of America, 87,* 330–338.

Gescheider, G. A., & Verrillo, R. T. (1982). Contralateral enhancement and suppression of vibrotactile sensation. *Perception & Psychophysics, 32,* 69–74.

Gesteland, R. C. (1986). Speculations on receptor cells as analyzers and filters. *Experientia, 42,* 287–291.

Gesteland, R. C., Lettvin, J. Y., Pitts, W. H., & Rojas, A. (1963). Odor specificities of the frog's olfactory receptors. In Y. Zotterman (Ed.), *Olfaction and taste* (pp. 19–34). Oxford: Pergamon Press.

Getchell, T. V., & Getchell, M. L. (1987). Peripheral mechanisms of olfaction: Biochemistry and neurophysiology. In T. E. Finger & W. L. Silver (Eds.), *Neurobiology of taste and smell* (pp. 91–124). New York: Wiley.

Giachetti, I., & MacLeod, P. (1975). Cortical neuron responses to odours in the rat. In D. A. Denton & J. P. Coghlan (Eds.), *Olfaction and taste V* (pp. 303–307). New York: Academic Press.

Gibbons, B. (1986). The intimate sense of smell. *National Geographic, 170,* 324–361.

Gibson, J. J. (1950). *Perception of the visual world.* Boston: Houghton Mifflin.

Gibson, J. J. (1966). *The senses considered as perceptual systems.* Boston: Houghton Mifflin.

Gibson, J. J. (1979). *The ecological approach to visual perception.* Boston: Houghton Mifflin.

Gibson, R. H., & Tomko, D. L. (1972). The relation between category and magnitude estimates of tactile intensity. *Perception & Psychophysics, 12,* 135–138.

Gilbert, A. N., & Wysocki, C. J. (1987). The smell survey: Results. *National Geographic, 172,* 514–525.

Gilchrist, A. L. (1980). When does perceived lightness depend on perceived spatial arrangement? *Perception & Psychophysics, 28,* 527–538.

Gilchrist, A. L. (1988). Lightness contrast and failures of constancy: A common explanation. *Perception & Psychophysics, 43,* 415–424.

Gilchrist, A. L., Delman, S., & Jacobsen, A. (1983). The classification and integration of edges as critical to the perception of reflectance and illumination. *Perception & Psychophysics, 33,* 425–436.

Gilchrist, A. L., & Jacobsen, A. (1984). Perception of lightness and illumination in a world of one reflectance. *Perception, 13,* 5–19.

Gilger, J. W., & Ho, H. (1989). Gender differences in adult spatial information processing: Their relationship to pubertal timing, adolescent activities and sex-typing of personality. *Cognitive Development, 4,* 197–214.

Gilinsky, A. S. (1989). The moon illusion in a unified theory of visual space. In M. Hershenson (Ed.), *The moon illusion,* (pp. 167–192). Hillsdale, NJ: Erlbaum.

Gillam, B. (1980). Geometrical illusions. *Scientific American, 242,* 102–111.

Gilmore, M. M., & Murphy, C. (1989). Aging is associated with increased Weber ratios for caffeine, but not for sucrose. *Perception & Psychophysics, 46,* 555–559.

Gintzler, A. R. (1980). Endorphin-mediated increases in pain threshold during pregnancy. *Science, 210,* 193–195.

Girgus, J. S., & Coren, S. (1987). The interaction between stimulus variations and age trends in the Poggendorff illusion. *Perception & Psychophysics. 41,* 60–66.

Glass, A. L., & Holyoak, K. J. (1986). *Cognition.* New York: Random House.

Gliner, J. A., Horvath, S. M., & Mihevic, P. M. (1983). Carbon monoxide and human performance in a single and dual task methodology. *Aviation, Space and Environmental Medicine, 54,* 714–717.

Glorig, A., Wheeler, D., Quigle, R., Grings, W., & Summerfield, A. (1970). 1954 Wisconsin State Fair hearing survey: Statistical treatment of clinical and audiometric data. Cited in D. D. Kryter, *The effects of noise on man* (p. 116). New York: Academic Press.

Glucksberg, S., & Cowen, G. N., Jr. (1970). Memory for nonattended auditory material. *Cognitive Psychology, 1,* 149–156.

Gogel, W. C., & DaSilva, J. A. (1987a). A two-process theory of the response to size and distance. *Perception & Psychophysics, 41,* 220–238.

Gogel, W. C., & DaSilva, J. A. (1987b). Familiar size and the theory of off-sized perceptions. *Perception & Psychophysics, 41,* 318–328.

Gogel, W. C., Gregg, J. M., & Wainwright, A. (1961). Convergence as a cue to absolute distance. (Report No. 467, pp. 1–16). Fort Knox, KY: U.S. Army Medical Research Laboratory.

Gogel, W. C., & Koslow, M. (1972). The adjacency principle and induced movement. *Perception & Psychophysics, 11,* 309–324.

Goldfoot, D. A. (1981). Olfaction, sexual behavior and the pheromone hypothesis in the rhesus monkey: A critique. *American Zoologist, 21,* 153–164.

Goldfoot, D. A., Essock-Vitale, S. M., Asa, C. S., Thornton, J. E., & Leshner, A. I. (1978). Anosmia in male rhesus monkeys does not alter copulatory activity with cycling females. *Science, 199,* 1095–1096.

Goldfoot, D. A., Kravetz, M. A., Goy, R. W., & Freeman, S. K. (1976). Lack of effect of vaginal lavages and aliphatic acids on ejaculatory responses in rhesus monkeys: Behavioral and chemical analyses. *Hormones and Behavior, 7,* 1–27.

Goldstein, E. B. (1980). *Sensation and perception.* Belmont, CA: Wadsworth.

Goldstein, J. L. (1973). An optimum processor theory for the central formation of the pitch of complex tones. *Journal of the Acoustical Society of America, 54,* 1496–1516.

Goldstone, S., Boardman, W. K., & Lhamon, W. T. (1958). Effect of quinal barbitone dextro-amphetamine, and placebo on apparent time. *British Journal of Psychology, 49,* 324–328.

Gombrich, E. H. (1972). The mask and the face: The perception of physiognomic likeness in life and in art. In E. H. Gombrich, J. Hochberg, & M. Black (Eds.) *Art, perception and reality* (pp. 1–46). Baltimore: Johns Hopkins Press.

Goodale, M. A., & Milner, A. D. (1991). A neurological dissociation between perceiving objects and grasping them. *Nature, 349,* 154–156.

Goodman, L., & Gilman, A. (Eds.). (1965). *The pharmacological basis of therapeutics.* New York: Macmillan.

Goodman, N. (1968). *Languages of art.* New York: Bobbs-Merrill.

Goodson, R., & Rahe, A. (1981). Visual training effects on normal vision. *American Journal of Optometry and Physiological Optics, 58,* 787–791.

Goodwin, M., Gooding, K. M., & Regnier, F. (1979). Sex pheromone in the dog. *Science, 203,* 559–561.

Goolkasian, P. (1980). Cyclic changes in pain perception: A ROC analysis. *Perception & Psychophysics, 27,* 499–504.

Goto, H. (1971). Auditory perception by normal Japanese adults of the sounds "L" or "R." *Neuropsychologia, 9,* 317–323.

Gottlieb, G. (1981). Roles of early experience in species-specific perceptual development. In R. Aslin, J. Alberts, & M. Petersen (Eds.), *Development of perception: Psychobiological perspectives, Vol. 1. Audition, somatic perception and the chemical senses* (pp. 5–44). New York: Academic Press.

Gottleib, M. D., Kietzman, M. I., & Bernhaus, I. J. (1985). Two-pulse measures of temporal integration in the fovea and peripheral retina. *Perception & Psychophysics, 37,* 135–138.

Gottschaldt, K. (1926). Uber den Einfluss der Erfahrung auf die Wahrnehmung von Figuren: I. *Psychologische Forschung, 8,* 261–317.

Gottschaldt, K. (1929). Uber den Einfluss der Erfahrung auf die Wahrenhmung von Figuren: II. *Psychologische Forschung, 12,* 1–87.

Gottschaldt, K. M., & Vahle-Hinz, C. (1981). Merkle cell receptors: Structure and transducer function. *Science, 214,* 183–185.

Gouras, P., & Zrenner, E. (1981). Color coding in primate retina. *Vision Research, 21,* 1591–1598.

Graham, C. H. (1965). Visual space perception. In C. H. Graham (Ed.), *Vision and visual perception* (pp. 504–547). New York: Wiley.

Graham, C. H., & Hisa, Y. (1958). Color defect and color theory. *Science, 127,* 657–682.

Graham, N. (1980). Spatial-frequency channels in human vision: Detecting edges without edge detectors. In C. S. Harris (Ed.), *Visual coding and adaptability* (pp. 215–262). New York: Erlbaum.

Graham, N. (1981). Psychophysics of spatial-frequency channels. In M. Kubovy & J. Pomerantz (Eds.), *Perceptual organization* (pp. 1–26). Hillsdale, NJ: Erlbaum.

Graham, N. V. S. (1989). *Vision pattern analyzers.* New York: Oxford University Press.

Grailet, J. M., & Seron, X. (1990). Case report of a visual integrative agnosia. *Cognitive Neuropsychology, 7,* 275–309.

Granger, G. W., & Ikeda, H. (1976). Drugs and visual thresholds. In A. Herxheimer (Ed.), *Drugs and sensory functions* (pp. 299–344). London: Churchill.

Granrud, C. E. (1986). Binocular vision and spatial perception in 4- and 5-month-old infants. *Journal of Experimental Psychology: Human Perception and Performance, 12,* 36–49.

Granrud, C. E., Haake, R. J., & Yonas, A. (1985). Infants' sensitivity to familiar size: The effect of memory on spatial perception. *Perception & Psychophysics, 37,* 459–466.

Granrud, C. E., & Yonas, A. (1985). Infants' sensitivity to the depth cue of shading. *Perception & Psychophysics, 37,* 415–419.

Granrud, C. E., Yonas, A., & Pettersen, L. (1984). A comparison of monocular and binocular depth perception in 5- and 7-month-old infants. *Journal of Experimental Child Psychology, 38,* 19–32.

Grau, J. W., & Nelson, D. G. K. (1988). The distinction between integral and separable dimensions: Evidence for the integrality of pitch and loudness. *Journal of Experimental Psychology: General, 117,* 347–370.

Gravetter, F., & Lockhead, G. R. (1973). Criterial range as a frame of reference for stimulus judgment. *Psychological Review, 80,* 203–216.

Green, B. G. (1984). Thermal perception on lingual and labial skin. *Perception & Psychophysics, 36,* 209–220.

Green, B. G. (1985). Heat pain thresholds in the oral-facial region. *Perception & Psychophysics, 38,* 110–114.

Green, B. G. (1986). Oral perception of the temperature of liquids. *Perception & Psychophysics, 39,* 19–24.

Green, B. G. (1987). The effect of cooling on the

vibrotactile sensitivity of the tongue. *Perception & Psychophysics, 42,* 423–430.

Green, D. G., & Powers, M. K. (1982). Mechanisms of light adaptation in rat retina. *Vision Research, 22,* 209–216.

Green, D. M. (1976). *An introduction to hearing.* New York: Academic Press.

Green, D. M. (1987). *Profile analysis: Auditory intensity discrimination.* New York: Oxford University Press.

Green, D. M., Nachmias, J., Kearny, J. K., & Jeffress, L. A. (1979). Intensity discrimination with gated and continuous sinusoids. *Journal of the Acoustical Society of America, 66,* 1051–1056.

Green, D. M., & Swets, J. A. (1974). Signal detection theory and psychophysics (reprint). New York: Krieger. (Original work published 1966)

Green, D. W., Hammond, E. J., & Supramaniam, S. (1983). Letters and shapes: Developmental changes in search strategies. *British Journal of Psychology, 74,* 11–16.

Greene, H. A., & Madden, D. J. (1987). Adult age differences in visual acuity, stereopsis, and contrast sensitivity. *American Journal of Optometry and Physiological Optics, 64,* 749–753.

Greenberg, M. J. (1981). The dependence of odor intensity on the hydrophobic properties of molecules. In H. R. Moskowitz & C. B. Warren (Eds.), *Odor quality and chemical structure* (pp. 177–194). Washington, DC: American Chemical Society.

Greenwood, D. D. (1990). A cochlear frequency-position function for several species—29 years later. *Journal of the Acoustical Society of America, 87,* 2592–2605.

Gregory, R. L. (1966). *Eye and brain.* New York: World University Library.

Gregory, R. L. (1971). *Concepts and mechanisms of perception.* London: Duckworth.

Gregory, R. L. (1978). *Eye and brain* (3rd ed.). New York: McGraw-Hill.

Grice, G. R., Nullmeyer, R., & Schnizlein, J. M. (1979). Variable criterion analysis of brightness effects in simple reaction time. *Journal of Experimental Psychology: Human Performance and Perception, 5,* 303–314.

Groos, G., & Daan, S. (1985). The use of the biological clocks in time perception. In J. A. Michon & J. L. Jackson (Eds.), *Time, mind and behavior* (pp. 65–74). Berlin: Springer-Verlag.

Groos, G., & Meijer, J. H. (1985). The effects of illumination on suprachiasmatic nucleus electrical discharge. *Annals of the New York Academy of Sciences, 453,* 134–146.

Gross, C. G., Rocha-Miranda, E. C., & Bender, D. B. (1972). Visual properties of neurons in inferotemporal cortex of the macaque. *Journal of Neurophysiology, 35,* 96–111.

Grossberg, J. M., & Grant, B. F. (1978). Clinical psychophysics. *Psychological Bulletin, 85,* 1154–1176.

Grossberg, S. (1983). The quantized geometry of visual space: The coherent computation of depth, form, and lightness. *Behavioral and Brain Sciences, 6,* 625–692.

Grossberg, S. (1987). Cortical dynamics of three-dimensional form, color, and brightness perception: I. Monocular theory. *Perception & Psychophysics, 41,* 87–116.

Grosvenor, T., & Flom, M. C. (Eds.). (1991). *Refractive anomalies: Research and clinical applications.* Boston: Butterworth-Heineman.

Grunau, R. V. E., & Craig, K. D. (1987). Pain expression in neonates: Facial action and cry. *Pain, 28,* 395–410.

Grzegorczyk, P. B., Jones, S. W., & Mistretta, C. M. (1979). Age-related differences in salt taste acuity. *Journal of Gerontology, 34,* 834–940.

Guirao, M. (1991). A single scale based on ratio and partition estimates. In S. J. Bolanowski & G. A. Gescheider (Eds.), *Ratio scaling of psychological magnitude* (pp. 59–78). Hillsdale, NJ: Erlbaum.

Guitton, D., Crommelink, M., & Roucoux, A. (1980). Stimulation of the superior colliculus in the alert cat: Eye movement and neck EMG activity evoked when the head is restrained. *Experimental Brain Research, 39,* 63–74.

Gulick, W. L. (1971). *Hearing: Physiology and psychophysics.* London and New York: Oxford University Press.

Gurnsey, R., & Browse, R. A. (1987). Micropattern properties and presentation conditions influencing visual texture discrimination. *Perception & Psychophysics, 41,* 239–252.

Gurnsey, R., & Browse, R. A. (1989). Asymmetries in visual texture discrimination. *Spatial Vision, 4,* 31–44.

Gustafson, R. (1986). Effect of moderate doses of alcohol on simple auditory reaction time in a vigilance setting. *Perceptual and Motor Skills, 62,* 683–690.

Guzman, A. (1971). Analysis of curved line drawings using context and global information. *Machine Intelligence, 6,* 325–375. Edinburgh: Edinburgh University Press.

Gwiazda, J., & Bauer, J. (1989). From visual acuity to hyperacuity: A 10-year update. *Canadian Journal of Psychology, 43,* 109–120.

Gwiazda, J., Brill, S., Mohindra, I., & Held, R. (1980). Preferential looking acuity in infants from 2 to 58 weeks of age. *American Journal of Optometry and Physiological Optics, 57,* 428–432.

Haaf, R. (1977). Visual responses to complex facelike patterns by 15 and 20 week old infants. *Developmental Psychology, 38,* 893–899.

Haber, R. N. (1980). Perceiving space from pictures: A theoretical analysis. In M. Hagen (Ed.), *Perception of pictures. Vol. 1. Alberti's window: The projective model of pictorial information* (pp. 3–31). New York: Academic Press.

Haber, R. N., & Hershenson, M. (1965). The effects of repeated brief exposures on the growth of a percept. *Journal of Experimental Psychology, 69,* 40–46.

Hafter, E. R., & Buell, T. (1990). Restarting the adapted binaural system. *Journal of the Acoustical Society of America, 88,* 806–812.

Hagen, M., & Jones, R. (1978). Cultural effects on pictorial perception: How many words is one picture really worth? In R. Walk and H. Pick (Eds.), *Perception and experience* (pp. 171–212). New York: Plenum Press.

Hahn, H. (1934). Die Adaptation des Geschmackssinnes. *Zeitschrift fuer Sinnesphysiologie, 65,* 105–145.

Hainline, L. (1978). Developmental changes in the scanning of face and nonface patterns by infants. *Journal of Experimental Child Psychology, 25,* 90–115.

Haith, M. M., Bergman, T., & Moore, M. J. (1977). Eye contact and face scanning in early infancy. *Science, 198,* 853–855.

Haith, M. M., Hazan, C., & Goodman, G. S. (1988). Expectation and anticipation of dynamic visual events by 3.5-month-old babies. *Child Development, 59,* 467–479.

Hall, J. W., III, & Peters, R. W. (1982). Change in the pitch of a complex tone following its association with a second complex tone. *Journal of the Acoustical Society of America, 71,* 142–146.

Hall, M. J., Bartoshuk, L. M., Cain, W. S., & Stevens, J. C. (1975). PTC taste blindness and the taste of caffeine. *Nature (London), 253,* 442–443.

Hall, W. G., & Oppenheim, R. W. (1987). Developmental psychobiology: Prenatal, perinatal and early postnatal aspects of behavioral development. *Annual Review of Psychology, 38,* 91–128.

Halpern, B. P., & Meiselman, H. L. (1980). Taste psychophysics based on a simulation of human drinking. *Chemical Senses, 5,* 279–294.

Halpern, D. F. (1981). The determinants of illusory-contour perception. *Perception, 10,* 191–213.

Halpern, D. F. (1986). *Sex differences in cognitive abilities.* Hillsdale, NJ: Erlbaum.

Halpern, D. L., Blake, R., & Hillenbrand, J. (1986). Psychoacoustics of a chilling sound. *Perception & Psychophysics, 39,* 77–80.

Halsam, D. (1967). Individual differences in pain threshold and level of arousal. *British Journal of Psychology, 58,* 139–142.

Hamalainen, H., & Jarvilehto, T. (1981). Peripheral neural basis of tactile sensations in man: I. Effect of frequency and probe area on sensations elicited by single mechanical pulses on hairy and glabrous skin of the hand. *Brain Research, 219,* 1–12.

Hamasaki, D. J., & Sutija, V. G. (1979). Development of X- and Y-cells in kittens. *Experimental Brain Research, 35,* 9–23.

Hamid, P N., & Newport, A. G. (1989). Effect of colour on physical strength and mood in children. *Perceptual and Motor Skills, 69,* 179–185.

Handel, S., & Garner, W. R. (1965). The structure of visual pattern associates and pattern goodness. *Perception & Psychophysics, 1,* 33–38.

Handel, S., & Oshinsky, J. S. (1981). The meter of syncopated auditory polyrhythms. *Perception & Psychophysics, 30,* 1–9.

Hanna, T. E., von Gierke, S. M., & Green, D. M. (1986). Detection and intensity discrimination of a sinusoid. *Journal of the Acoustical Society of America, 80,* 1335–1340.

Hardie, R. C., & Kirschfeld, K. (1983). Ultraviolet sensitivity of fly photoreceptors R7 and R8: Evidence for a sensitizing function. *Biophysics of Structure and Mechanism, 9,* 171–180.

Hardy, J. D., Stolwijk, J. A. J., & Hoffman, D. (1968). Pain following step increase in skin temperature. In D. R. Kenshalo (Ed.), *The skin senses* (pp. 444–457). Springfield, IL: Thomas.

Hardy, J. D., Wolff, H. G., & Goodell, B. S. (1943). The pain threshold in man. *Research Publications Association for Research in Nervous and Mental Disease, 23,* 1–15.

Hardy, J. D., Wolff, H. G., & Goodell, H. (1947). Studies on pain: Discrimination of differences in intensity of a pain stimulus as a basis of a scale of pain intensity. *Journal of Clinical Investigation, 26,* 1152–1158.

Hari, R., & Lounasmaa, O. V. (1989). Recording and interpretation of cerebral magnetic fields. *Science, 244,* 432–436.

Harkins, S., & Green, R. G. (1975). Discriminability and criterion differences between extraverts and introverts during vigilance. *Journal of Research in Personality, 9,* 335–340.

Harkins, S. W., & Chapman, C. R. (1977). The perception of induced dental pain in young and elderly women. *Journal of Gerontology, 32,* 428–435.

Harmon, L. D. (1973). The recognition of faces. *Scientific American, 229,* 70–82.

Harmon, L. D., & Julesz, B. (1973). Masking in visual recognition: Effects of two dimensional filtered noise. *Science, 180,* 1194–1197.

Harper, R. S. (1953). The perceptual modification of coloured figures. *American Journal of Psychology, 66,* 86–89.

Harris, C. S. (1980). Insight or out of sight?: Two examples of perceptual plasticity in the human adult. In C. S. Harris (Ed.), *Visual coding and adaptability* (pp. 95–149). Hillsdale, NJ: Erlbaum.

Harris, L. J. (1981). Sex related variations in spatial skill.

In L. S. Liben, A. H. Patterson, & N. Newcombe (Eds.), *Spatial representation and behavior across the lifespan: Theory and application* (pp. 83–128). New York: Academic Press.

Harris, P., & MacFarlane, A. (1974). The growth of the effective visual field from birth to seven weeks. *Journal of Experimental Child Psychology, 18,* 340–348.

Harrison, R. V., Nagasawa, A., Smith, D. W., Stanton, S., & Mount, R. J. (1991). Reorganization of auditory cortex after neonatal high frequency cochlear hearing loss. *Hearing Research, 54,* 11–19.

Harter, M., & Suitt, C. (1970). Visually-evoked cortical responses and pattern vision in the infant: A longitudinal study. *Psychonomic Science, 18,* 235–237.

Hartley, A. A., Keiley, J. M., & Slabach, E. H. (1990). Age differences and similarities in the effects of cues and prompts. *Journal of Experimental Psychology: Human Perception and Performance, 16,* 523–537.

Hartline, H. K. (1940). The receptive fields of optic nerve fibers. *American Journal of Physiology, 130,* 690–699.

Hartline, H. K., & Ratliff, F. (1957). Inhibitory interaction of receptor units in the eye of Limulus. *Journal of General Physiology, 40,* 357–376.

Hartman, A., & Hollister, L. (1963). Effect of mescaline, Lysergic acid diethylamide and psilocybin on color perception. *Psychopharmacologia, 4,* 441–451.

Hartmann, W. M., & Rakerd, B. (1989). On the minimum audible angle—a decision theory approach. *Journal of the Acoustical Society of America, 85,* 2031–2141.

Harvey, L.O., Jr., & Leibowitz, H. (1967). Effects of exposure duration, cue reduction, and temporary monocularity on size matching at short distances. *Journal of the Optical Society of America, 57,* 249–253.

Hary, J. M., & Massaro, D. W. (1982). Categorical results do not imply categorical perception. *Perception & Psychophysics, 32,* 409–418.

Hatfield, G., & Epstein, W. (1985). The status of the minimum principle in the theoretical analysis of visual perception. *Psychological Bulletin, 97,* 155–186.

He, L. (1987). Involvement of endogenous opioid peptides in acupuncture analgesia. *Pain, 31,* 99–122.

He, L., Lu, R., Zhuang, S., Zhang, X., & Pan, X. (1985). Possible involvement of opioid peptides of caudate nucleus in acupuncture analgesia. *Pain, 23,* 83–93.

Head, H. (1920). *Studies in neurology.* London & New York: Oxford University Press.

Heaton, J. M. (1968). *The eye: Phenomenology and psychology of function and disorder.* London: Tavistock.

Hecht, H., & Proffitt, D. (1991). Apparent extended body motions in depth. *Journal of Experimental Psychology: Human Perception and Performance, 17,* 1090–1103.

Hecht, S., & Mandelbaum, M. (1938). Rod-cone dark adap-

tation and vitamin A. *Science, 88,* 219–221.

Hecht, S., Shlaer, S., & Pirenne, M. H. (1942). Energy quanta and vision. *Journal of General Physiology, 25,* 819–840.

Heckmann, T., Post, R. B., & Deering, L. (1991). Induced motion of a fixated target: Influence of voluntary eye deviation. *Perception & Psychophysics, 50,* 230–236.

Heffner, H. E., & Heffner, R. S. (1984). Temporal lobe lesions and perception of species-specific vocalizations by macaques. *Science, 226,* 75–76.

Heggelund, P. (1981a). Receptive field organization of simple cells in cat striate cortex. *Experimental Brain Research, 42,* 89–98.

Heggelund, P. (1981b). Receptive field organization of complex cells in cat striate cortex. *Experimental Brain Research, 42,* 99–107.

Hein, A. (1980). The development of visually guided behaviour. In C. Harris (Ed.), *Visual coding and adaptability* (pp. 51–68). Hillsdale, NJ: Erlbaum.

Hein, A., & Held, R. (1967). Dissociation of the visual placing response into elicited and guided components. *Science, 158,* 390–392.

Hein, A., Held, R., & Gower, E. C. (1970). Development and segmentation of visually controlled movement by selective exposure during rearing. *Journal of Comparative and Physiological Psychology, 73,* 181–187.

Hein, A., & Diamond, R. M. (1971). Contrasting development of visually triggered and guided movements in kittens with respect to interocular and interline equivalence. *Journal of Comparative and Physiological Psychology, 76,* 219–224.

Held, R. (1985). Binocular vision—behavioral and neuronal development. In J. Mehler & R. Fox (Eds.), *Neonate cognition: Beyond the blooming buzzing confusion* (pp. 37–44). Hillsdale, NJ: Erlbaum.

Held, R., & Bauer, J. A. (1967). Visually guided reaching in infant monkeys after restricted rearing. *Science, 155,* 718–720.

Held, R., & Bossom, J. (1961). Neonatal deprivation and adult rearrangement: Complementary techniques for analyzing plastic sensory-motor coordinations. *Journal of Comparative and Physiological Psychology, 54,* 33–37.

Held, R., Dichgans, J., & Bauer, J. (1975). Characteristics of moving visual scenes influencing spatial orientation. *Vision Research, 15,* 357–365.

Held, R., & Hein, A. (1958). Adaptation of disarranged hand-eye coordination contingent upon re-afferent stimulation. *Perceptual and Motor Skills, 8,* 87–90.

Held, R., & Hein, A. (1963). Movement-produced stimulation in the development of visually guided behavior. *Journal of Comparative and Physiological Psychology, 56,* 872–876.

Held, R., & Hein, A. (1967). On the modifiability of form

perception. In W. Wathen-Dunn (Ed.), *Models for the perception of speech and visual form* (pp. 296–304). Cambridge, MA: MIT Press.

Hellekant, G. (1965). Electrophysiological investigation of the gustatory effect of ethyl alcohol: The summated response of the chorda tympani in the cat, dog and rat. *Acta Physiologica Scandinavica, 64,* 392–397.

Heller, M. A. (1989). Texture perception in sighted and blind observers. *Perception & Psychophysics, 45,* 49–54.

Hellman, R. P., & Zwislocki, J. J. (1968). Loudness determination at low sound frequencies. *Journal of the Acoustical Society of America, 43,* 60–64.

Hellstrom, A. (1979). Time errors and differential sensation weighting. *Journal of Experimental Psychology: Human Perception and Performance, 5,* 460–477.

Hellstrom, A. (1985). The time-order error and its relatives: Mirrors of cognitive processes in comparing. *Psychological Bulletin, 97,* 35–61.

Helmholtz, H. E. F. von (1930). *The sensations of tone* (A. J. Ellis, Trans.). New York: Longmans, Green. (Original work published 1863)

Helmholtz, H. E. F. von (1962). *Treatise on physiological optics* (J. P. C. Southall, Ed. and Trans.). New York: Dover. (Original work published 1909)

Helson, H. (1964). *Adaptation level theory: An experimental and systematic approach to behavior.* New York: Harper.

Henderson, J. M., & Pollatsek, A. (1989). Covert visual attention and extrafoveal information use during object identification. *Perception & Psychophysics, 45,* 196–208.

Henmon, V. A. C. (1906). The time of perception as a measure of differences in sensations. *Archives of Philosophy, Psychology and Scientific Methods,* No. 8.

Henn, V., Cohen, B., & Young, L. (1980). Visual-vestibular interaction in motion perception and the generation of nystagmus. *Neurosciences Research Program Bulletin, 18,* 459–651.

Henn, V., Young, L. R., & Finley, C. (1974). Vestibular nucleus units in alert monkeys are also influenced by moving visual field. *Brain Research, 71,* 144–149.

Henning, H. (1915) Der Geruch: I. *Zietschrift fuer Psychologie, 73,* 161–257.

Henning, H. (1916). Die Qualitatenreihe des Geschmaks. *Zeitschrift fuer Psychologie, 74,* 203–219.

Hensel, H. (1981). *Thermoreception and temperature regulation.* New York: Academic Press.

Hernandez-Peon, R. (1964). Psychiatric implications of neurophysiological research. *Bulletin of the Meninger Clinic, 28,* 165–185.

Hershberger, W. (1987). Saccadic eye movements and the perception of visual direction. *Perception & Psychophysics, 41,* 35–44.

Hershenson, M. (1989). *The moon illusion.* Hillsdale, NJ: Erlbaum.

Hershenson, M., & Bader, P. (1990). Development of the spiral aftereffect. *Bulletin of the Psychonomic Society, 28,* 300–301.

Hess, E. H. (1950). Development of the chick's response to light and shade cues of depth. *Journal of Comparative and Physiological Psychology, 43,* 112–122.

Hess, R. H., Baker, C. L., & Zihl, J. (1989). The "motion-blind" patient: Low-level spatial and temporal filters. *Journal of Neuroscience, 9,* 1628–1640.

Heywood, C. A., Wilson, B., & Cowey, A. (1987). A case study of cortical colour "blindness" with relatively intact achromatic discrimination. *Journal of Neurology, Neurosurgery, and Psychiatry, 50,* 22–29.

Hick, W. E. (1952). On the rate of gain of information. *Quarterly Journal of Experimental Psychology, 4,* 11–26.

Hickey, T. L. (1977). Postnatal development of the human lateral geniculate nucleus: Relationship to a critcal period for the visual system. *Science, 198,* 836–838.

Hickey, T. L., & Peduzzi, J. D. (1987). Structure and development of the visual system. In P. Salapatek & L. Cohen (Eds.), *Handbook of infant perception: Vol. 1. From sensation to perception* (pp.1–43). Orlando: Academic Press.

Hicks, R. E., Miller, G. W., Gaes, G., & Bierman, K. (1977). Concurrent processing demands and the experience of time in passing. *American Journal of Psychology, 90,* 431–446.

Hicks, R. E., Miller, G. W., & Kinsbourne, M. (1976). Prospective and retrospective judgments of time as a function of amount of information processed. *American Journal of Psychology, 89,* 719–730.

Hier, D. B., & Crowley, W. F., Jr. (1982). Spatial ability in androgen-deficient men. *New England Journal of Medicine, 306,* 1202–1205.

Higashiyama, A. (1985). The effects of familiar size on judgments of size and distance: An interaction of viewing attitude with spatial cues. *Perception & Psychophysics, 35,* 305–312.

Higgins, S. T., & Bickel, W. K. (1990). Effects of intranasal cocaine on human learning, performance and physiology. *Psychopharmacology, 102,* 451–458.

Hillyard, S. A., & Kutas, M. (1983). Electrophysiology of cognitive processing. *Annual Review of Psychology, 34,* 33–61.

Hirsch, H. V. (1972). Visual perception in cats after environmental surgery. *Experimental Brain Research, 15,* 409–423.

Hirsch, H. V., & Spinelli, D. N. (1970). Visual experience modifies distribution of horizontally and vertically oriented receptive fields in cats. *Science, 168,* 869–871.

Hoagland, H. (1933). The physiological control of judgment of duration: Evidence for a chemical clock. *Journal of General Psychology, 9,* 267–287.

Hochberg, J. (1971). Perception: II. Space and movement. In J. W. Kling & L. A. Riggs (Eds.), *Woodworth and Schlossberg's experimental psychology* (3rd ed., pp. 475–550). New York: Holt, Rinehart & Winston.

Hochberg, J. (1972). Nativism and empiricism in perception. In L. Postman (Ed.), *Psychology in the making* (pp. 255–330). New York: Knopf.

Hochberg, J. (1974). Higher-order stimuli and interresponse coupling in the perception of the visual world. In R. B. Macleod & H. L. Pick (Eds.), *Perception: Essays in honor of James J. Gibson* (pp. 17–39). Ithaca: Cornell University Press.

Hochberg, J. (1981). On cognition in perception: Perceptual coupling and unconscious inference. *Cognition, 10,* 127–134.

Hochberg, J. (1982). How big is a stimulus? In J. Beck (Ed.), *Organization and representation in perception* (pp. 191–218). Hillsdale, NJ: Erlbaum.

Hochberg, J., & Beck, J. (1954). Apparent spatial arrangement and perceived brightness. *Journal of Experimental Psychology, 47,* 263–266.

Hochberg, J., & Brooks, V. (1960). The psychophysics of form: Reversible-perspective drawings of spatial objects. *American Journal of Psychology, 73,* 337–354.

Hochberg, J., & Brooks, V. (1962). Pictorial recognition as an unlearned ability: A study of one child's performance. *American Journal of Psychology, 75,* 624–628.

Hockey, G. R. (1970). Effect of loud noise on attentional selectivity. *Quarterly Journal of Experimental Psychology, 22,* 28–36.

Hoffer, A., & Osmond, H. (1967). *The hallucinogens.* New York: Academic Press.

Hoffman, J. E. (1980). Interaction between global and local levels of form. *Journal of Experimental Psychology: Human Perception and Performance, 6,* 222–234.

Hoffman, J. E., Nelson, B., & Houck, M. R. (1983). The role of attentional resources in automatic detection. *Cognitive Psychology, 51,* 379–410.

Hoffman, K. P. (1979). Optokinetic nystagmus and single cell responses in the nucleus tractus opticus after early monocular deprivation in the cat. In R. D. Freeman (Ed.), *Developmental neurobiology of vision* (pp. 63–72). New York: Plenum Press.

Hoffmann, K. P., & Sherman, S. (1975). Effects of early binocular deprivation on visual input to cat superior colliculus. *Journal of Neurophysiology, 38,* 1049–1059.

Holender, D. (1986). Semantic activation without conscious identification in dichotic listening, parafoveal vision, and visual masking: A survey and appraisal. *The Behavioral and Brain Sciences, 9,* 1–23.

Holland, H. (1960). Drugs and personality: XII. A comparison of several drugs by the flicker-fusion method. *Journal of Mental Science, 106,* 858–861.

Holst, E. von, & Mittelstaedt, H. (1950). Das Reafferenzprincip (wechselwirkungen zeischen zentral Nervensystem und Peripherie). *Naturwissenschaften, 37,* 464–476.

Holway, A. F., & Boring, E. G. (1941). Determinants of apparent visual size with distance variant. *American Journal of Psychology, 54,* 21–37.

Honda, H. (1984). Functional between-hand differences and outflow eye position information. *Quarterly Journal of Experimental Psychology, 36A,* 75–88.

Hood, B., & Atkinson, J. (1991). Sensory visual loss and cognitive deficits in the selective attentional system of normal infants and neurologically impaired children. *Developmental Medicine and Child Neurology, 32,* 1067–1077.

Horn, B. K. P. (1977). Understanding image intensities. *Artificial Intelligence, 8,* 201–231.

Horn, B. K. P. (1986). *Robot vision.* Cambridge, MA: MIT Press.

Horner, D. T. (1991). The effects of complexity on the perception of vibrotactile patterns. *Perception & Psychophysics, 49,* 551–562.

Horton, J. C., & Sherk, H. (1984). Receptive field properties in the cat's lateral geniculate nucleus in the absence of ON-center retinal input. *Journal of Neuroscience, 4,* 374–380.

Houck, M. R., & Hoffman, J. E. (1986). Conjunction of color and form without attention: Evidence from an orientation-contingent color aftereffect. *Journal of Experimental Psychology: Human Perception and Performance, 12,* 186–199.

Houtsma, A. J. M., & Goldstein, J. L. (1972). The central origin of the pitch of complex tones: Evidence from musical interval recognition. *Journal of the Acoustical Society of America, 51,* 520–529.

Howard, I. P. (1982). *Human visual orientation.* Chichester: Wiley.

Howard, I. P., Anstis, T., & Lucia, H. C. (1974). The relative lability of mobile and stationary components in a visual-motor adaptation task. *Quarterly Journal of Experimental Psychology, 26,* 293–300.

Howard, I. P., Craske, B., & Templeton, W. B. (1965). Visuomotor adaptation to discordant exafferent stimulation. *Journal of Experimental Psychology, 70,* 189–191.

Howell, P., Cross, I., & West, R. (Eds.). (1985). *Musical structure and cognition.* London: Academic Press.

Hoyer, W., & Plude, D. (1980). Attentional and perceptual processes in the study of cognitive aging. In L. Poon (Ed.), *Aging in the 1980s* (pp. 227–238). Washington, DC: American Psychological Association.

Hu, S., Grant, W. F., Stern, R. M., & Koch, K. (1991). Motion sickness severity and physiological correlates during repeated exposures to a rotating optokinetic drum. *Aviation, Space and Environmental Medicine, 62,* 308–314.

Hubbell, W. L., & Bownds, M. D. (1979). Visual transduction in vertebrate photoreceptors. *Annual Review of Neurosciences, 2,* 17–34.

Hubel, D. H., & Wiesel, T. N. (1962). Receptive fields, binocular interaction and functional architecture in the cat's visual cortex. *Journal of Physiology (London), 160,* 106–154.

Hubel, D. H., & Wiesel, T. N. (1968). Receptive fields and functional architecture of monkey striate cortex. *Journal of Physiology (London), 195,* 215–243.

Hubel, D. H., & Wiesel, T. N. (1979). Brain mechanisms of vision. *Scientific American, 82,* 84–97.

Hudson, W. (1960). Pictorial depth perception in subcultural groups in Africa. *Journal of Social Psychology, 52,* 183–208.

Hudson, W. (1962). Pictorial perception and educational adaptation in Africa. *Psychologia, Africana, 9,* 226–239.

Hudspeth, A. J. (1985). The cellular basis of hearing: The biophysics of hair cells. *Science, 230,* 745–752.

Hughes, H. C. (1986). Asymmetric interference between components of suprathreshold compound gratings. *Perception & Psychophysics, 40,* 241–250.

Hughes, H. C., Layton, W. M., Baird, J. C., & Lester, L. S. (1984). Global precedence in visual pattern recognition. *Perception & Psychophysics, 35,* 361–371.

Hulse, S. H., & Page, S. C. (1988). Toward a comparative psychology of music perception. *Music Perception, 5,* 427–452.

Humphrey, G. K., Humphrey, D. E., Muir, D. W., & Dodwell, P. C. (1986). Pattern perception in infants: Effects of structure and transformation. *Journal of Experimental Child Psychology, 41,* 128–148.

Humphreys, G. W. (1983). Reference frames and shape perception. *Cognitive Psychology, 15,* 151–196.

Humphreys, G. W (1984). Shape constancy: The effects of changing shape orientation and the effects of changing the position of focal features. *Perception & Psychophysics, 36,* 50–64.

Humphreys, G. W., Quinlan, P. T., & Riddoch, M. J. (1989). Grouping processes in visual search: Effects with single- and combined-feature targets. *Journal of Experimental Psychology: General, 118,* 258–279.

Hunzelmann, N., & Spillman, L. (1984). Movement adaptation in the peripheral retina. *Vision Research, 24,* 1765–1769.

Hurlbert, A. C., & Poggio, T. A. (1988). Synthesizing a color algorithm from examples. *Science, 239,* 482–485.

Hurvich, L. M. (1981). *Color vision.* Sunderland, MA: Sinauer Associates.

Hurvich, L. M., & Jameson, D. (1974). Opponent processes as a model of neural organization. *American Psychologist, 29,* 88–102.

Huttenlocher, P. R., DeCourten, C., Garey, L. J., & Van der Loos, H. (1982). Synaptic development in human cerebral cortex. *International Journal of Neurology, 16,* 144–154.

Hutz, C. S., & Bechtoldt, H. P. (1980). The development of binocular discrimination in infants. *Bulletin of the Psychonomic Society, 16,* 83–86.

Huxley, A. (1963). *The doors of perception and heaven and hell.* New York: Harper.

Hyman, A., Mentyer, T., & Calderone, L. (1979). The contribution of olfaction to taste discrimination. *Bulletin of the Psychonomic Society, 13,* 359–362.

Iacono, W. G., Pelouin, L. J., Lumry, A. E., Valentine, R. H., & Tuason, V. B. (1982). Eye tracking in patients with unipolar and bipolar affective disorders in remission. *Journal of Abnormal Psychology, 91,* 35–44.

Iida, T. (1983). Accommodative response under reduced visual conditions. *Japanese Psychological Research, 25,* 222–227.

Imbert, M. (1985). Physiological underpinnings of perceptual development. In J. Mehler & R. Fox (Eds.), *Neonate cognition: Beyond the blooming buzzing confusion* (pp. 69–88). Hillsdale, NJ: Erlbaum.

Ingram, R. M., & Barr, A. (1979). Changes in refraction between the ages of 1 and 3 1/2 years. *British Journal of Opthalmology, 63,* 39–342.

Intraub, H. (1985). Visual dissociation: An illusory conjunction of pictures and forms. *Journal of Experimental Psychology: Human Perception and Performance, 11,* 431–442.

Ippolitov, F. W. (1973). Interanalyser differences in the sensitivity-strength parameter for vision, hearing and cutaneous modalities. In V. D. Nebylitsyn & J. A. Gray (Eds.), *Biological bases of individual behavior* (pp. 43–61). New York: Academic Press.

Irwin, R. J., & Whitehead, P. R. (1991). Towards an objective psychophysics of pain. *Psychological Science, 2,* 230–235.

Ittelson, W. H. (1951). Size as a cue to distance: Static localization. *American Journal of Psychology, 64,* 54–67.

Ittelson, W. H. (1960). *Visual space perception.* Berlin and New York: Springer-Verlag.

Ittelson, W. H. (1962). Perception and transactional psychology. In S. Koch (Ed.), *Psychology: A study of a science: Vol. 4* (pp. 660–704). New York: McGraw-Hill.

Jacobs, G. H. (1976). Color vision. *Annual Review of Psychology, 27,* 63–89.

Jacobs, G. H. (1986). Cones and opponency. *Vision Research, 26,* 1533–1541.

Jacobsen, A., & Gilchrist, A. (1988). The ratio principle holds over a million-to-one range of illumination. *Perception & Psychophysics, 43,* 1–6.

Jahoda, G., & McGurk, H. (1974). Pictorial depth perception: A developmental study. *British Journal of Psychology, 65,* 141–149.

James, W. (1890). *The principles of psychology.* New York: Holt, Rinehart & Winston.

Jameson, D., & Hurvich, L. M. (1959). Note on factors influencing the relation between stereoscopic acuity and observation distance. *Journal of the Optical Society of America, 49,* 639.

Jameson, D., & Hurvich, L. M. (1964). Theory of brightness and color contrast in human vision. *Vision Research, 4,* 135–154.

Jameson, D., & Hurvich, L. M. (1989). Essay concerning color constancy. *Annual Review of Psychology, 40,* 1–22.

Janal, M. N., Clark, W. C., & Carroll, J. D. (1991). Multidimensional scaling of painful and innocuous electrocutaneous stimuli: Reliability and individual differences. *Perception & Psychophysics, 50,* 108–116.

Jarvis, J. R. (1977). On Fechner-Benham subjective colour. *Vision Research, 17,* 445–451.

Jaschinski-Kruza, W. (1984). Transient myopia after visual work. *Ergonomics, 27,* 1181–1189.

Javel, E. (1981). Suppression of auditory nerve responses I: Temporal analysis, intensity effects and suppression contours. *Journal of the Acoustical Society of America, 69,* 1735–1745.

Jenkins, B. (1985). Orientational anisotropy in the human visual system. *Perception & Psychophysics, 37,* 125–134.

Jennings, J. A. M., & Charman, W. N. (1981). Off-axis image quality in the human eye. *Vision Research, 21,* 445–455.

Jesteadt, W. (1980). An adaptive procedure for subjective judgments. *Perception & Psychophysics, 28,* 85–88.

Jesteadt, W., Bacon, S. P., & Lehman, J. R. (1982). Forward masking as a function of frequency, masker level, and signal delay. *Journal of the Acoustical Society of America, 71,* 950–962.

Jesteadt, W., & Wier, C. C. (1977). Comparison of monaural and binaural discrimination of intensity and frequency. *Journal of the Acoustical Society of America, 61,* 1599–1603.

Jesteadt, W., Wier, C. C., & Green, D. M. (1977). Intensity discrimination as a function of frequency and sensation level. *Journal of the Acoustical Society of America, 61,* 169–177.

Johansson, G. (1976a.) Visual motion perception. In R. Held & W. Richards (Eds.), *Recent progress in perception: Readings from* Scientific American (pp. 67–75). San Francisco: Freeman.

Johansson, G. (1976b). Spatio-temporal differentiation and integration in visual motion perception. *Psychological Research, 38,* 379–393.

Johansson, G., von Hofsten, C., & Jansson, G. (1980). Event perception. *Annual Review of Psychology, 31,* 27–63.

John, E. R., Prichep, L. S., Fridman, J., & Easton, P. (1988). Neurometrics: Computer-assisted differential diagnosis of brain dysfunctions. *Science, 239,* 162–169.

Johnson, C. H., & Hastings, J. W. (1986). The elusive mechanism of the circadian clock. *American Scientist, 74*(1), 29–36.

Johnson, D. H. (1980). The relationship between spike rate and synchrony in responses of auditory-nerve fibers to single tones. *Journal of the Acoustical Society of America, 68,* 1115–1122.

Johnson, E. S., & Meade, A. C. (1987). Developmental patterns of spatial ability: An early sex difference. *Child Development, 58,* 725–740.

Johnson, M. A. (1986). Color vision in the peripheral retina. *American Journal of Optometry and Physiological Optics, 63,* 97–103.

Johnson, M. H. (1990). Cortical maturation and the development of visual attention in early infancy. *Journal of Cognitive Neuroscience, 2,* 81–95.

Johnson, S. C. (1967). Hierarchical clustering schemes. *Psychometrika, 32,* 241–254.

Johnson, T. L., & Shapiro, K. L. (1989). Attention to auditory and peripheral visual stimuli: Effects of arousal and predictability. *Acta Psychologica, 72,* 233–245.

Jones, D. T., & Reed, R. R. (1989). G_{olf}: An olfactory neuron specific-G protein involved in odorant signal transduction. *Science, 244,* 790–795.

Jones, L. A. (1986). Perception of force and weight: Theory and research. *Psychological Bulletin, 100,* 29–42.

Jones, L. A. (1988). Motor illusions: What do they reveal about proprioception? *Psychological Bulletin, 103,* 72–86.

Jonides, J. (1980). Towards a model of the mind's eye's movements. *Canadian Journal of Psychology, 34,* 103–112.

Jonides, J. (1981). Voluntary versus automatic control over the mind's eye's movement. In J. B. Long & A. D. Baddeley (Eds.), *Attention & performance: Vol. 9* (pp. 187–203). Hillsdale, NJ: Erlbaum.

Jonides, J., & Yantis, S. (1988). Uniqueness of abrupt visual onset in capturing attention. *Perception & Psychophysics, 43,* 346–355.

Joubert, C. E. (1983). Subjective acceleration of time: Death anxiety and sex differences. *Perceptual and Motor Skills, 57,* 49–50.

Joubert, C. E. (1990). Subjective expectations of the acceleration of time with aging. *Perceptual and Motor Skills, 70,* 334.

Julesz, B. (1964). Binocular depth perception without familiarity cues. *Science, 145,* 356–362.

Julesz, B. (1971). *Foundations of cyclopean perception.* Chicago: University of Chicago Press.

Julesz, B. (1978). Perceptual limits of texture discrimination and their implications to figure-ground separation. In E. Leeuwenberg & H. Buffart (Eds.), *Formal theories of perception* (pp. 205–216). New York: Wiley.

Julesz, B. (1980). Spatial nonlinearities in the instantaneous perception of textures with identical power spectra. In C. Longuet-Higgins & N. S. Sutherland (Eds.), *The psychology of vision. Philosophical transactions of the Royal Society, London, 290,* 83–94.

Julesz, B. (1981). Textons, the elements of texture perception and their interactions. *Nature, 290,* 91–97.

Julesz, B. (1984). A brief outline of the texton theory of human vision. *Trends in Neuroscience, 7,* 41–45.

Julesz, B. (1986). Stereoscopic vision. *Vision Research, 26,* 1601–1612.

Julesz, B., & Bergen, J. R. (1983). Textons, the fundamental elements in preattentive vision and perception of textures. *The Bell System Technical Journal, 62,* 1619–1645.

Julesz, B., & Payne, R. A. (1968). Differences between monocular and binocular stroboscopic movement perception. *Vision Research, 8,* 433–444.

Julesz, B., & Schumer, R. A. (1981). Early visual perception. *Annual Review of Psychology, 32,* 575–627.

Jung, R. (1961). Korrelationen von Neuronentaetigkeit und Sehen. In R. Jung & H. H. Kornhuber (Eds.), *Neurophysiologie und Psychophysik des visuellen Systems* (pp. 410–435). New York: Springer-Verlag.

Jusczyk, P. W. (1986). Toward a model of the development of speech perception. In J. S. Perkell & D. H. Klatt (Eds.), *Invariance and variability in speech processes* (pp. 1–19). Hillsdale, NJ: Erlbaum.

Kaas, J. H. (1983). The organization of somatosensory cortex in primates and other mammals. In C. von Euler, O. Franzen, U. Lindblom, & D. Ottoson (Eds.), *Somatosensory mechanisms* (pp. 51–60). New York: Plenum Press.

Kaernbach, C. (1990). A single-interval adjustment-matrix (SIAM) procedure for unbiased adaptive testing. *Journal of the Acoustical Society of America, 88,* 2645–2655.

Kaernbach, C. (1991). Simple adaptive testing with the weighted up-down method. *Perception & Psychophysics, 49,* 227–229.

Kaess, D. W. (1980). Instructions and decision times of size-constancy responses. *Perception & Psychophysics, 27,* 477–482.

Kahneman, D. (1966). Time-intensity reciprocity in acuity as a function of luminance and figure-ground contrast. *Vision Research, 6,* 207–215.

Kahneman, D. (1968). Method, findings, and theory in studies of visual masking. *Psychological Bulletin, 70,* 404–425.

Kahneman, D. (1973). *Attention and effort.* Englewood Cliffs, NJ: Prentice-Hall.

Kahneman, D., Norman, J., & Kubovy, M. (1967). Critical duration for the resolution of form: Centrally or peripherally determined? *Journal of Experimental Psychology, 73,* 323–327.

Kahneman, D., & Treisman, A. (1984). Changing views of attention and automaticity. In R. Parasuraman & D. R. Davies (Eds.), *Varieties of attention.* (pp. 29–61). Orlando: Academic Press.

Kaiser, M., & Calderone, J. B. (1991). Factors influencing perceived angular velocity. *Perception & Psychophysics, 50,* 428–434.

Kaiser, P. K., & Boynton, R. M. (1985). Role of the blue mechanism in wavelength discrimination. *Vision Research, 25,* 523–529.

Kalat, J. W. (1992). *Biological psychology.* Belmont, CA: Wadsworth.

Kaneko, A., Nishimura, Y., Tachibana, M., Tauchi, M., & Shimai, K. (1981). Physiological and morphological studies of signal pathways in the carp retina. *Vision Research, 21,* 1519–1526.

Kanisza, G. (1979). *Organization in vision: Essays on Gestalt perception.* New York: Praeger.

Kaplan, A., & Glanville, E. (1964). Taste thresholds for bitterness and cigarette smoking. *Nature (London), 202,* 1366.

Kaplan, G. (1969). Kinetic disruption of optical texture: The perception of depth at an edge. *Perception & Psychophysics, 6,* 193–198.

Karmel, B. Z., & Maisel, E. B. (1975). A neuronal activity model for infant visual attention. In L. B. Cohen & P. Salapatek (Eds.), *Infant perception: From sensation to cognition: Vol. 1. Basic visual processes* (pp. 78–133). New York: Academic Press.

Kasamatsu, T. (1976). Visual cortical neurons influenced by the oculomotor input: Characterization of their receptive field properties. *Brain Research, 113,* 271–292.

Kauer, J. S. (1980). Some spatial characteristics of central information processing in the vertebrate olfactory pathway. In H. van der Starre (Ed.), *Olfaction and taste VII* (pp. 227–236). London: IRL Press.

Kauer, J. S. (1987). Coding in the olfactory system. In T. E. Finger & W. L. Silver (Eds.), *Neurobiology of taste and smell* (pp. 205–232). New York: Wiley.

Kaufman, L. (1974). *Sight and mind: An introduction to visual perception.* London and New York: Oxford University Press.

Kaufman, L., & Rock, I. (1989). The moon illusion thirty years later. In M. Hershenson (Ed.), *The moon illusion,* (pp. 193–234). Hillsdale, NJ: Erlbaum.

Kaufmann, R., Maland, J., & Yonas, A. (1981). Sensitivity of 5- and 7-month-old infants to pictorial depth information. *Journal of Experimental Child Psychology, 32,* 162–168.

Kawabata, N. (1986). Attention and depth perception. *Perception, 15,* 563–572.

Kaye, M., Mitchell, D.E., & Cynader, M. (1982). Depth perception, eye dominance and cortical binocularity of dark-reared cats. *Developmental Brain Research, 2,* 37–53.

Kellman, P. J. (1984). Perception of three-dimensional form by human infants. *Perception & Psychophysics, 36,* 353–358.

Kellman, P. J., & Shipley, T. F. (1990). A theory of visual interpolation in object perception. *Cognition, 23,* 141–221.

Kellman, P. J., & Short, K. R. (1987). Development of three-dimensional form perception. *Journal of Experimental Psychology: Human Perception and Performance, 13,* 545–557.

Kellman, P. J., & Spelke, E. S. (1983). Perception of partly occluded objects in infancy. *Cognitive Psychology, 15,* 483–524.

Kellman, P. J., Spelke, E. S., & Short, K. R. (1986). Infant perception of object unity from translatory motion in depth and vertical translation. *Child Development, 57,* 72–86.

Kemler-Nelson, D. G., Hirsh-Pasek, K., Jusczyk, P. W., & Wright-Cassidy, K. (1989). How the prosodic cues in motherese might assist language learning. *Journal of Child Language, 16,* 66–68.

Kemp, D. T. (1978). Stimulated acoustic emissions from within the human auditory system. *Journal of the Acoustical Society of America, 64,* 1386–1391.

Kendrick, K. M., & Baldwin, B. A. (1987). Cells in the temporal cortex of conscious sheep can respond preferentially to the sight of faces. *Science, 236,* 448–450.

Kennedy, J. M., & Domander, R. (1985). Shape and contour: The points of maximum change least useful for recognition. *Perception, 14,* 367–370.

Kennedy, J. M., & Ostry, D. (1976). Approaches to picture perception: Perceptual experience and ecological optics. *Canadian Journal of Psychology, 30,* 90–98.

Kenshalo, D. R., & Isensee, O. (1983). Responses of primate SI cortical neurons to noxious stimuli. *Journal of Neurophysiology, 50,* 1479–1496.

Kenshalo, D. R., Nafe, J. P., & Brooks, B. (1961). Variations in thermal sensitivity. *Science, 134,* 104–105.

Kenshalo, D. R., & Scott, H. A., Jr. (1966). Temporal course of thermal adaptation. *Science, 151,* 1095–1096.

Keren, G., & Baggen, S. (1981). Recognition models of alphanumeric characters. *Perception & Psychophysics, 29,* 234–245.

Kessen, W., Salapatek, P., & Haith, M. M. (1972). The vi-

sual response of the human newborn to linear contour. *Journal of Experimental Child Psychology, 13,* 9–20.

Keverne, E. B. (1978). Olfactory cues in mammalian behavior. In J. E. Hutchinson (Ed.), *Biological determinants of sexual behavior* (pp.727–763). Chichester: Wiley.

Khanna, S. M., & Leonard, D. G. B. (1982). Basilar membrane tuning in the cat cochlea. *Science, 215,* 305–306.

Kiang, K. Y. S., Rho, J. M., Northrop, C. C., Liberman, M. C., & Ryugo, D. K. (1982). Hair-cell innervation by spiral ganglion cells in adult cats. *Science, 217,* 175–177.

Kidd, G., Jr., Mason, C. R., Uchanski, R. M., Brantley, M. A., & Shah, P. (1991). Evaluation of simple models of auditory profile analysis using random reference spectra. *Journal of the Acoustical Society of America, 90,* 1340–1354.

Kilbride, P. E., Hutman, L. P., Fishman, M., & Read, J. S. (1986). Foveal cone pigment density difference in the aging human eye. *Vision Research, 26,* 321–325.

Killbride, P. L., & Leibowitz, H. W. (1975). Factors affecting the magnitude of the Ponzo illusion among the Baganda. *Perception & Psychophysics, 17,* 543–548.

Killbride, P. L., & Robbins, M. (1968). Linear perspective pictorial depth perception and education among the Baganda. *Perception and Motor Skills, 27,* 601–602.

Kim, D. O. (1985). Functional roles of the inner- and outer-hair-cell subsystems in the cochlea and brainstem. In C. J. Berlin (Ed.), *Hearing science: Recent advances* (pp. 241–262). San Diego: College Hill.

Kimchi, R. (1992). Primacy of wholistic processing and global/local paradigm: A critical review. *Psychological Bulletin, 112,* 24–38.

Kimura, K., & Beidler, L. M. (1961). Microelectrode study of taste receptors of rat and hamster. *Journal of Cellular and Comparative Physiology, 58,* 131–140.

Kinchla, R. A., Solis-Macias, V., & Hoffman, J. E. (1983). Attending to different levels of structure in a visual image. *Perception & Psychophysics, 33,* 1–10.

Kinchla, R. A., & Wolfe, J. (1979). The order of visual processing: "Top-down," "bottom-up," or "middle-out." *Perception & Psychophysics, 25,* 225–231.

Kirk-Smith, M. D., & Booth, D. A. (1980). Effects of androstenone on choice of location in other's presence. In H. van der Starre (Ed.), *Olfaction and taste VII* (pp. 397–400). London: IRL Press.

Kirk-Smith, M. D., Booth, D. A., Caroll, D., & Davies, P. (1978). Human social attitudes affected by androstenol. *Research Communications in Psychology, Psychiatry and Behavior, 3,* 379–384.

Kitzes, L. M., Gibson, M. M., Rose, J. E., & Hind, J. E. (1978). Initial discharge latency and threshold considerations for some neurons in cochlear nucleus complex of the cat. *Journal of Neurophysiology, 41,* 1165–1182.

Klatt, D. H. (1980). Speech perception: A model of acoustic-phonetic analysis and lexical access. In R. Cole (Ed.), *Perception and production of fluent speech* (pp. 243–288). Hillsdale, NJ: Erlbaum.

Klatzky, R.L., Lederman, S. J., & Reed, C. (1987). There's more to touch than meets the eye: The salience of object attributes for haptics with and without vision. *Journal of Experimental Psychology: General, 116,* 356–369.

Klatzky, R. L., Lederman, S. J., & Reed, C. (1989). Haptic integration of object properties: Texture, hardness and planar contour. *Journal of Experimental Psychology: Human Perception and Performance, 15,* 45–57.

Klatzky, R. L., Lederman S. J., & Metzger, V. A. (1985). Identifying objects by touch: An "expert system." *Perception & Psychophysics, 37,* 299–302.

Klein, G. S. (1970). *Perception, motives and personality.* New York: Knopf.

Klein, R. (1980). Does oculomotor readiness mediate cognitive control of visual attention? In R. S. Nickerson (Ed.), *Attention and performance VIII* (pp. 259–276). Hillsdale, NJ: Lawrence Erlbaum.

Klein, R. (1988). Inhibitory tagging system facilitates visual search. *Nature, 334,* 430–431.

Klein, S. A., & Levi, D. M. (1985). Hyperacuity threshold of 1.0 second: Theoretical predictions and empirical validation. *Journal of the Optical Society of America A2,* 1170–1190.

Kluender, K. R., Diehl, R. L., & Killeen, P. R. (1987). Japanese quail can learn phonetic categories. *Science, 237,* 1195–1197.

Klutky, N. (1990). Geschlechtsunterschiede in der Gedachtnisleistung fur Geruche, Tonfolgen und Farben. *Zeitschrift fur Experimentelle und Angewandte Psychologie, 37,* 437–446.

Kluver, H., & Bucy, P. C. (1937). "Psychic blindness" and other symptoms following bilateral temporal lobectomy in rhesus monkeys. *American Journal of Physiology, 119,* 352–353.

Klymenko, V., & Weisstein, N. (1986.) Spatial frequency differences can determine figure–ground organization. *Journal of Experimental Psychology: Human Perception and Performance, 12,* 324–330.

Knoblauch, K., Saunders, F., Kusuda, M., Hynes, R., Podgor, M., Higgins, K. E., & deMonasteriod, F. M. (1987). Age and illuminance effects in the Farnsworth-Munsell 100-hue test. *Applied Optics, 26,* 1441–1448.

Knudsen, E. I., & Brainard, M. S. (1991). Visual instruction of the neural map of auditory space in the developing optic tectum. *Science, 253,* 85–87.

Knudsen, E. I., & Knudsen, P. F. (1989). Vision calibrates

sound localization in developing barn owls. *The Journal of Neuroscience, 9,* 3306–3313.

Knudsen, E. I., & Konishi, M. (1978a). A neural map of auditory space in the owl. *Science, 200,* 795–797.

Knudsen, E. I., & Konishi, M. (1978b). Center-surround organization of auditory receptive fields in the owl. *Science, 202,* 778–780.

Kobler, J. B., Isbey, S. F., & Casseday, J. H. (1987). Auditory pathways to the frontal cortex of the mustache bat, Pteronotus parnelli. *Science, 236,* 824–826.

Koffka, K. (1935). *Principles of Gestalt psychology.* New York: Harcourt, Brace & World.

Kohler, I. (1962). Experiments with goggles. *Scientific American, 206,* 62–86.

Kohler, I. (1964). The formation and transformation of the perceptual world. *Psychological Issues, 3*(Whole No. 4).

Kohler, W. (1923). Zur Theories des Sukzessivvergleichs und der Zeitfehler. *Psychologische Forschung, 4,* 115–175.

Kohlston, P. J. (1988). Sharp mechanical tuning in a cochlear model without negative damping. *Journal of the Acoustical Society of America, 83,* 1481–1487.

Kolb, B., & Whishaw, I. O. (1985). Fundamentals of human neuropsychology (2nd ed.), New York: Freeman.

Kolb, H., Nelson, R., & Mariani, A. (1981). Amacrine cells, bipolar cells and ganglion cells of the cat retina: A Golgi study. *Vision Research, 21,* 1081–1114.

Kolers, P. A., & Brewster, J. M. (1985). Rhythms and responses. *Journal of Experimental Psychology: Human Perception and Performance, 11,* 150–167.

Kolers, P. A., & Green, M. (1984). Color logic of apparent motion. *Perception, 13,* 249–254.

Kolers, P. A., & von Grunau, M. (1976). Shape and color in apparent motion. *Vision Research, 16,* 329–335.

Komoda, M. K., Festinger, L., Phillips, L. J., Duckman, R. H., & Young, R. A. (1973). Some observations concerning saccadic eye movement. *Vision Research, 13,* 1009–1020.

Konstadt, N., & Forman, E. (1965). Field dependence and external directedness. *Journal of Personality and Social Psychology, 1,* 490–493.

Koslowe, K. C., Spierer, A., Rosner, M., & Belkin, M. (1991). Evaluation of accommotrac biofeedback training for myopia control. *Optometry and Vision Science, 68,* 338–343.

Kosterlitz, H. W., & McKnight, A. T. (1981). Opioid peptides and sensory function. In D. Ottoson (Ed.), *Progress in sensory physiology: Vol. 1* (pp. 31–95). Heidelberg: Springer-Verlag.

Kowler, E., & Martin, A. J. (1980). Eye movements in preschool children. *Science, 215,* 997–999.

Kozlowski, L. T., & Cutting, J. E. (1977). Recognizing the sex of a walker from a dynamic point-light display. *Perception and Psychophysics, 21,* 575–580.

Krauskopf, J., & Reeves, A. (1980). Measurement of the effect of photon noise on detection. *Vision Research, 20,* 193–196.

Kremenitzer, J. P., Vaughan, H. G., Kurtzberg, D., & Dowling, K. (1979). Smooth-pursuit eye movements in the newborn infant. *Child Development, 50,* 442–448.

Kries, J. von. (1895). Uber die Natur gewisser mit den spychischen Vorgangen verknupfter Ghirnzustande. *Zeitschrift fur Psychologie, 8,* 1–33.

Krueger, L. E. (1982). A word superiority effect with print and Braille characters. *Perception & Psychophysics, 31,* 345–352.

Krueger, L. E. (1989). Reconciling Fechner and Stevens: Toward a unified psychophysical law. *Behavioral and Brain Sciences, 12,* 277–281.

Kruger, J. (1981). The difference between x- and y-type responses in ganglion cells of the cat's retina. *Vision Research, 21,* 1685–1687.

Krumhansl, C. L. (1985). Perceiving tonal structure in music. *American Scientist, 73,* 371–378.

Krumhansl, C. L. (1990). *Cognitive foundations of musical pitch.* Oxford: Oxford University Press.

Krumhansl, C. L., Bharucha, J. J., & Kessler, E. J. (1982). Perceived harmonic structure of chords in three related musical keys. *Journal of Experimental Psychology: Human Perception and Performance, 8,* 24–36.

Krumhansl, C. L., & Jusczyk, P. W. (1990). Infants' perception of phrase structure in music. *Psychological Science, 1,* 70–73.

Krumhansl, C. L., & Kessler, E. J. (1982). Tracing the dynamic changes in perceived tonal organization in a spatial representation of musical keys. *Psychological Review, 89,* 334–368.

Krumhansl, C. L., & Shepard, R. N. (1979). Quantification of the hierarchy of tonal functions within a diatonic context. *Journal of Experimental Psychology: Human Perception and Performance, 5,* 579–594.

Kruskal, J.B. (1964). Multidimensional scaling by optimizing goodness of fit to a nonmetric hypothesis. *Psychometrika, 29,* 1–27.

Kryter, K. D. (1985). *The effects of noise on man* (2nd ed.). Orlando: Academic Press.

Kuffler, S. W. (1953). Discharge patterns and functional organization of mammalian retina. *Journal of Neurophysiology, 16,* 37–68.

Kuhl, P. K. (1987). Perception of speech and sound in early infancy. In P. Salapatek & L. Cohen (Eds.), *Handbook of infant perception: Vol. 2: From perception to cognition* (pp. 275–382). Orlando: Academic Press.

Kuhl, P. K., & Meltzoff, A. N. (1982). The bimodal perception of speech in infancy. *Science, 218,* 1138–1141.

Kuhl, P. K., & Padden, D. M. (1983). Enhanced discriminability at the phonetic boundaries for the place feature in macaques. *Journal of the Acoustical Society of America, 73,* 1003–1010.

Kuhl, P. K., Williams, K. A., Lacerda, F., Stevens, K. N., & Lindbloom, B. (1992). Linguistic experience alters phonetic perception in infants by 6 months of age. *Science, 255,* 606–608.

Kupchella, C. (1976). *Sights and sounds.* Indianapolis: Bobbs-Merrill.

Kurtz, D., & Butter, C. M. (1980). Impairments in visual discrimination performance and gaze shifts in monkeys with superior colliculus lesions. *Brain Research, 196,* 109–124.

Kuyk, T., Veres, J. G., III, Lahey, M. A., & Clark, D. J. (1986). The ability of protan color defectives to perform color-dependent air traffic control tasks. *American Journal of Optometry and Physiological Optics, 63,* 582–586.

LaBerge, D., & Brown, V. (1989). Theory of attentional operations in shape identification. *Psychological Review, 96,* 101–124.

Ladavas, E., & Petronio, A. (1990). The deployment of visual attention in the intact field of hemineglect patients. *Cortex, 26,* 307–317.

Ladefoged, P. (1975). *A course in phonetics.* New York: Harcourt Brace Jovanovich.

Lakowski, R. (1962). Is the deterioration of colour discrimination with age due to lens or retinal changes? *Farbe, 11,* 69–86.

Lakowski, R., Aspinall, P. A., & Kinnear, P. R. (1972). Association between colour vision losses and diabetes mellitus. *Ophthalmic Research, 4,* 145–159.

Lakowski, R., & Drance, S. M. (1979). Acquired dyschromatopsias: The earliest functional losses in glaucoma. *Documenta Ophthalmologica,* Proceedings Series 19, 159–165.

Lakowski, R., & Morton, B. A. (1977). The effect of oral contraceptives on colour vision in diabetic women. *Canadian Journal of Opthalmology, 12,* 89–97.

Laming, D. (1986). *Sensory analysis.* Orlando: Academic Press.

Lamore, P. J. J., & Keemink, C. J. (1988). Evidence for different types of mechanoreceptors from measurements of the psychophysical threshold for vibrations under different stimulus conditions. *Journal of the Acoustical Society of America, 83,* 2339–2351.

Lamour, Y., Willer, J. C., & Guilbaud, G. (1983). Rat somatosensory (SmI) cortex: I. Characteristics of neuronal responses to noxious stimulation and comparison with responses to non-noxious stimulation. *Experimental Brain Research, 49,* 35–45.

Land, E. H. (1986). Recent advances in retinex theory. *Vision Research, 26,* 7–21.

Land, E. H., & McCann, J. J. (1971). Lightness and retinex theory. *Journal of the Optical Society of America, 61,* 1–11.

Landolt, E. (1889). Tableau d'optotypes pour la determination de l'acuité visuelle. *Societé Francais d'Opthalmologie, 1,* 385ff.

Lappin, J. S., & Preble, L. D. (1975). A demonstration of shape constancy. *Perception & Psychophysics, 17,* 439–444.

Larish, J. F., & Flach, J. M. (1990). Sources of optical information useful for the perception of speed of rectilinear self–motion. *Journal of Experimental Psychology: Human Perception and Performance, 16,* 295–302.

Lauter, J. L., Herscovitch, P., Formby, C., & Raichle, M. E. (1985). Tonotopic organization in human auditory cortex revealed by positron emission tomography. *Hearing Research, 20,* 199–205.

Lawless, H. T., & Stevens, D. A. (1988). Responses by humans to oral chemical irritants as a function of locus of stimulation. *Perception & Psychophysics, 43,* 72–78.

Lea, S. E. G. (1984). *Instinct, environment, and behaviour.* London: Methuen.

Lederman, S. J., Browse, R. A., & Klatzky, R. L. (1988). Haptic processing of spatially distributed information. *Perception & Psychophysics, 44,* 222–232.

Leehey, S. C., Moskowitz-Cook, A., Brill, S., & Held, R. (1975). Orientational anisotropy in infant vision. *Science, 190,* 900–902.

Leek, M. R., Brown, M. E., & Dorman, M. F. (1991). Informational masking and auditory attention. *Perception & Psychophysics, 50,* 205–214.

Leeuwenberg, E. L. J. (1971). A perceptual coding language for visual and auditory patterns. *American Journal of Psychology, 84,* 307–346.

Leeuwenberg, E. L. J. (1988). *On geon and global precedence in form perception.* Paper presented at the meetings of the Psychonomic Society, Chicago, IL.

Lefton, L. A. (1973). Metacontrast: A review. *Perception & Psychophysics, 13,* 161–171.

Lehmkuhle, S., & Fox, R. (1980). Effect of depth separation of metacontrast masking. *Journal of Experimental Psychology: Human Perception and Performance, 6,* 605–621.

Lehmkuhle, S., Kratz, K. E., Mangel, S. C., & Sherman, S. M. (1980). Spatial and temporal sensitivity of x- and y-cells in dorsal lateral geniculate nucleus of the cat. *Journal of Neurophysiology, 43,* 520–541.

Lehmkuhle, S., Kratz, K. E., & Sherman, S. M. (1982). Spatial and temporal sensitivity of normal and amblyopic cats. *Journal of Neurophysiology, 48,* 372–387.

Leibowitz, H. W., & Moore, D. (1966). Role of changes in accommodations and convergence in the perception of size. *Journal of the Optical Society of America, 56,* 1120–1123.

Leibowitz, H. W., & Owens, D. A. (1977). Nighttime accidents and selective visual degradation. *Science, 197,* 422–423.

Leibowitz, H. W., & Pick, H. (1972). Cross-cultural and educational aspects of the Ponzo perspective illusion. *Perception & Psychophysics, 12,* 430–432.

Leibowitz, H. W., Post, R. B., Brandt, T., & Dichgans, J. (1982). Implications of recent developments in dynamic spatial orientation and visual resolution for vehicle guidance. In A. H. Wertheim, W. A. Wagenaar, & H. W. Leibowitz (Eds.), *Tutorials on motion perception* (pp. 231–260). New York: Plenum Press.

Leibowitz, H. W., Post, R. B., & Ginsburg, A. (1980). The role of fine detail in visually controlled behavior. *Investigative Ophthalmology and Visual Science, 19,* 846–848.

Leibowitz, H. W., Shupert, C. L., Post, R. B., & Dichgans, J. (1983). Autokinetic drifts and gaze deviation. *Perception & Psychophysics, 33,* 455–459.

Leibowitz, H. W., Wilcox, S. B., & Post, R. B. (1978). The effect of refractive error on size constancy and shape constancy. *Perception, 7,* 557–562.

Leinonen, L. (1983). Integration of somatosensory events in the posterior parietal cortex of the monkey. In C. von Euler, O. Franzen, U. Lindblom, & D. Ottoson (Eds.), *Somatosensory mechanisms* (pp. 113–124). New York: Plenum Press.

Lemlich, R. N. (1975). Subjective acceleration of time with aging. *Perceptual and Motor Skills, 41,* 235–238.

Lenneberg, E. H. (1967). *Biological foundations of language.* New York: Wiley.

Lennie, P., Trevarthen, C., Van Essen, D., & Waessle, H. (1990). Parallel processing of visual information. In L. Spillman & J. S. Werner (Eds.), *Visual perception: The neurophysiological foundations* (pp. 103–128). Orlando: Academic Press.

LePage, E. L. (1987). A spatial template for the shape of tuning curves in the mammalian cochlea. *Journal of the Acoustical Society of America, 82,* 155–164.

LePage, E. L. (1989). Functional role of the olivo-cochlear bundle: A motor unit control system in the mammalian cochlea. *Hearing Research, 38,* 177–198.

Lerdahl, F., & Jackendoff, R. (1983). *A generative theory of tonal music.* Cambridge, MA: MIT Press.

Lerman, S. (1984). Biophysical aspects of corneal and lenticular transparency. *Current Eye Research, 3,* 3–14.

LeVay, S., Wiesel, T. N., & Hubel, D. H. (1980). The development of ocular dominance columns in normal and visually deprived monkeys. *Journal of Comparative Neurology, 191,* 1–51.

Levelt, W. J. M., Riemersma, J. B., & Bunt, A. A. (1972). Binaural additivity of loudness. *British Journal of Mathematical and Statistical Psychology, 25,* 51–68.

Leventhal, A., & Hirsch, H. (1980). Receptive-field

properties of different classes of neurons in visual cortex of normal and dark-reared cats. *Journal of Neurophysiology, 43,* 1111–1132.

Levin, A., Lipton, R. B., & Holzman, P. S. (1981). Pursuit eye movements in psychopathology: Effects of target characteristics. *Biological Psychiatry, 16,* 255–267.

Levine, D. N., & Calvanio, R. (1989). Prosopagnosia: A defect in visual configural processing. *Brain and Cognition, 10,* 149–170.

Levine, M. W., & Shefner, J. M. (1981). *Fundamentals of sensation and perception.* Reading, MA: Addison-Wesley.

Levy, D. L., Lipton, R. B., & Holzman, P. S. (1981). Smooth pursuit eye movements: Effects of alcohol and chloral hydrate. *Journal of Psychiatric Research, 16,* 1–11.

Lewis, J. W., Terman, G. W., Shavit, Y., Nelson, L. R., & Liebeskind, J. C. (1984). Neural, neurochemical, and hormonal bases of stress-induced analgesia. In L. Kruger & J. C. Liebeskind (Eds.), *Neural mechanisms of pain* (pp. 277–288). New York: Raven Press.

Lewis, T. L., Maurer, D., & Milewski, A. (1979). The development of nasal detection in young infants. *Investigating Ophthalmology and Visual Science Supplement,* 271.

Liberman, A. M. (1982). On finding that speech is special. *American Psychologist, 37,* 148–167.

Liberman, A. M., Cooper, F. S., Shankweiler, D. P., & Studdert-Kennedy, M. (1967). Perception of the speech code. *Psychological Review, 74,* 431–461.

Liberman, A. M., Harris, K. S., Hoffman, H. A., & Griffith, B. C. (1957). The discrimination of sounds within and across phoneme boundaries. *Journal of Experimental Psychology, 54,* 358–368.

Liberman, A. M., & Mattingly, I. G. (1985). The motor theory of speech perception revised. *Cognition, 21,* 1–36.

Liberman, A. M., & Mattingly, I. G. (1989). A specialization for speech perception. *Science, 243,* 489–494.

Liberman, M. C. (1982). Single-neuron labeling in the cat auditory nerve. *Science, 216,* 1239–1241.

Lichte, W. H., & Borresen, C. R. (1967). Influence of instructions on degree of shape constancy. *Journal of Experimental Psychology, 74,* 538–542.

Lichtenstein, M. (1963). Spatio-temporal factors in cessation of smooth apparent motion. *Journal of the Optical Society of America, 53,* 302–306.

Lie, I. (1980.) Visual detection and resolution as a function of retinal locus. *Vision Research, 20,* 967–974.

Liebeskind, J. C., & Melzack, R. (1987). The International Pain Foundation: Meeting a need for education in pain management. *Pain, 30,* 1.

Lim, D. J. (1980). Cochlear anatomy related to cochlear micromechanics: A review. *Journal of the Acoustical Society of America, 67,* 1686–1695.

Lindsay, P. H., & Norman, D. A. (1977). Human information processing (2nd ed.). New York: Academic Press.

Lindsey, D. T., & Teller, D. Y. (1990). Motion at isoluminance: Discrimination detection ratios for moving isoluminant gratings. *Vision Research, 30,* 1751–1761.

Linton, H., & Graham, E. (1959). Personality correlates of persuasibility. In I. Janis (Ed.), *Personality and persuasibility.* New Haven, CT: Yale University Press.

Lipsett, L. P. (1977). Taste in human neonates: Its effect on sucking and heart rate. In J. M. Weiffenbach (Ed.), *Taste and development: The ontogeny of sweet preference* (pp. 125–140). Washington, DC: U.S. Government Printing Office.

Lisker, L., & Abramson, A. (1970). The voicing dimension: Some experiments in comparative phonetics. *Proceedings of the 6th International Congress of Phonetic Sciences* (pp. 563–567).

Livingstone, M. S., & Hubel, D. H. (1988). Segregation of form, color, movement and depth: Anatomy, physiology, and perception. *Science, 240,* 740–749.

Locke, J. L. (1983). *Phonological acquisition and change.* New York: Academic Press.

Lockhead, G. R. (1966). Effects of dimensional redundancy on visual discrimination. *Journal of Experimental Psychology, 72,* 95–104.

Lockhead, G. R. (1970). Identification and the form of multidimensional discrimination space. *Journal of Experimental Psychology, 85,* 1–10.

Lockhead, G. R. (1972). Processing dimensional stimuli: A note. *Psychological Review, 79,* 410–419.

Lockhead, G. R. (1979). Holistic versus analytic process models: A reply. *Journal of Experimental Psychology: Human Perception and Performance, 5,* 746–755.

Lockhead, G. R., & Byrd, R. (1981). Practically perfect pitch. *Journal of the Acoustical Society of America, 70,* 387–389.

Lockhead, G. R., & King, M. C. (1977). Classifying integral stimuli. *Journal of Experimental Psychology: Human Perception and Performance, 3,* 436–443.

Loewenstein, W. R. (1960). Biological transducers. *Scientific American, 203,* 98–108.

Loftus, E. (1974). Reconstructing memory: The incredible eye witness. *Psychology Today, 8,* 116–119.

Loftus, E. (1979). *Eyewitness testimony.* Cambridge, MA: Harvard University Press.

Loftus, E. F., & Donders, K. (1989). Creating new memories that are quickly accessed and confidently held. *Memory and Cognition, 17,* 607–616.

Loftus, G., & Mackworth, N. (1978). Cognitive determinants of fixation location during picture viewing. *Journal of Experimental Psychology: Human Perception and Performance, 4,* 565–572.

Logan, G. D. (1988). Toward an instance theory of automatization. *Psychological Review, 95,* 492–527.

Lohman, D. F. (1986). The effect of speed–accuracy trade-off on sex differences in mental rotation. *Perception & Psychophysics, 39,* 427–436.

Long, G. M. (1988). Selective adaptation vs. transfer of decrement: The conjoint effects of neural fatigue and perceptual learning. *Perception & Psychophysics, 43,* 207–209.

Long, G. R., & Cullen, J. K., Jr. (1985). Intensity difference limens at high frequencies. *Journal of the Acoustical Society of America, 78,* 507–513.

Longstreth, L. E. (1987). Hick's law: Its limit is 3 bits. *Bulletin of the Psychonomic Society, 26,* 8–10.

Lonsbury-Martin, B. L., Harris, F. P., Stagner, B. B., Hawkins, M. D., & Martin, G. K. (1990). Distortion product emissions in humans: I. Basic properties in normally hearing subjects. *Annals of Otology, Rhinology and Laryngology, 99,* 3–14.

Loomis, J. M. (1981). Tactile pattern perception. *Perception, 10,* 5–27.

Loop, M. S. (1984). Effect of duration on detection by the chromatic and achromatic systems. *Perception & Psychophysics, 36,* 65–67.

Lord, T., & Kasprzak, M. (1989). Identification of self through olfaction. *Perceptual and Motor Skills, 69,* 219–224.

Lovegrove, W. J., & Over, R. (1973). Color selectivity in orientation masking and aftereffect. *Vision Research, 13,* 895–902.

Lowe, D. (1987). Three-dimensional object recognition from single two-dimensional images. *Artificial Intelligence, 31,* 355–395.

Lowenstein, O., & Sand, A. (1940). The mechanism of the semicircular canal: A study of the responses of single-fibre preparations to angular accelerations and to rotation at constant speed. *Proceedings of the Royal Society of London, Series B, 129,* 256–275.

Luce, R. D. (1990). "On the possible psychophysical laws" revisited: Remarks on cross-modality matching. *Psychological Review, 97,* 66–77.

Luce, R. D., Green, D. M., & Weber, D. L. (1976). Attention bands in absolute identification. *Perception & Psychophysics, 20,* 49–54.

Luce, R. D., & Narens, L. (1987). Measurement scales on the continuum. *Science, 236,* 1527–1532.

Lueck, C. J., Zeki, S., Friston, K. J., Deiber, M. P., Cope, P., Cunningham, V. J., Lammertsma, A. A., Kennard, C., & Frackowiak, R. S. J. (1989). The colour centre in the cerebral cortex of man. *Nature, 340,* 386–389.

Lufti, R. A. (1990). How much masking is informational masking? *Journal of the Acoustical Society of America, 88,* 2607–2610.

Lumsden, E. (1980). Problems of magnification and minification: An explanation of the distortions of distance, slant, shape, and velocity. In M. Hagen (Ed.), *Perception of pictures: Vol. I, Alberti's window: The projective model of pictorial information* on (pp. 91–135). New York: Academic Press.

Lundervold, D., Lewin, L. M., & Irvin, L. K. (1987). Rehabilitation of visual impairments: A critical review. *Clinical Psychology Review, 7,* 169–185.

Luria, A. R. (1972). Memory disturbances in local brain lesions. *Neuropsychologia, 9,* 367–375.

Luria, A. R. (1973). *The working brain.* London: Penguin.

Lynch, M. P., & Eilers, R. E. (1990). Innateness, experience, and music perception. *Psychological Science, 1,* 272–276.

Lynn, P. A., & Sayers, B. M. A. (1970). Cochlear innervation, signal processing, and their relation to auditory time–intensity effects. *Journal of the Acoustical Society of America, 47,* 523–533.

MacArthur, R. O., & Sekuler, R. (1982). Alcohol and motion perception. *Perception & Psychophysics, 31,* 502–505.

MacDonald, D. W., & Brown, R. E. (1985). Introduction: The pheromone concept in mammalian chemical communication. In R. E. Brown & D. W. MacDonald (Eds.), *Social odours in mammals: Vol. 1* (pp. 1–18). Oxford: Clarendon Press.

MacFarlane, A. (1975). Olfaction in the development of social preferences in the human neonate. In *Ciba Foundation Symposium 33: The human neonate in parent–infant interaction* (pp. 103–177). Amsterdam: Elsevier.

Mach, E. (1959). The analysis of sensations and the relation of the physical to the psychical. New York: Dover. (Originally published 1886)

Mack, A., & Herman, E. (1972). A new illusion: The underestimation of a distance during pursuit eye movements. *Perception & Psychophysics, 12,* 471–473.

Mack, A., Heuer, F., Fendrich, R., Vilardi, K., & Chambers, D. (1985). Induced motion and oculomotor capture. *Journal of Experimental Psychology: Human Perception and Performance, 11,* 329–345.

MacKain, K., Studdert-Kennedy, M., Spieker, S., & Stern, D. (1983). Infant intermodal speech perception is a left hemisphere function. *Science, 219,* 1347–1349.

Mackworth, N. H. (1948). The breakdown of vigilance during prolonged visual search. *Quarterly Journal of Experimental Psychology, 1,* 6–21.

Mackworth, N. H., & Bruner, J. S. (1970). How adults and children search and recognize pictures. *Human Development, 13,* 149–177.

MacLeod, D. I. (1978). Visual sensitivity. *Annual Review of Psychology, 29,* 613–645.

MacLeod, P. (1971). An experimental approach to the peripheral mechanisms of olfactory discrimination. In

G. Ohloff & A. F. Thomas (Eds.), *Gustation and olfaction* (pp. 28–44). New York: Academic Press.

MacLeod, R. (1947). The effects of "artificial penumbra" on the brightness of included areas. In A. Michotte (Ed.), *Miscellanea psychologica* (pp. 1–22). Paris: Librairie Philosophique.

MacNichol, E. F., Jr. (1986). A unifying presentation of photopigment spectra. *Vision Research, 29,* 543–546.

Madden, D. J. (1983). Aging and distraction by highly familiar stimuli during visual search. *Developmental Psychology, 19,* 499–507.

Madden, D. J. (1986). Adult age differences in the attentional capacity demands of visual search. *Cognitive Development, 2,* 100–107.

Madden, T. M., & Burt, G. S. (1981). Inappropriate constancy scaling theory and the Meuller-Lyer illusion. *Perceptual and Motor Skills, 52,* 211–218.

Mair, R. G., Bouffard, J. A., Engen, T., & Morton, T. (1978). Olfactory sensitivity during the menstrual cycle. *Sensory Process, 2,* 90–98.

Maire-Lepoivre, E., & Przybyslawski, J. (1988). Visual field in dark-reared cats after an extended period of recovery. *Behavioural Brain Research, 28,* 245–251.

Makous, J. C., & Middlebrooks, J. C. (1990). Two-dimensional sound localization by human listeners. *Journal of the Acoustical Society of America, 87,* 2188–2200.

Mandler, G. (1980). Recognizing: The judgment of previous occurrence. *Psychological Review, 87,* 252–271.

Mangun, G. R., & Hillyard, S. A. (1990). Electrophysiological studies of visual selective attention in humans. In A. B. Scheibel & A. F. Wechsler (Eds.), *Neurobiology of higher cognitive function* (pp. 271–295). New York: Guildford Press.

Marcel, A. J. (1983). Conscious and unconscious perception: Experiments on visual masking and word recognition. *Cognitive Psychology, 15,* 197–237.

Marks, L. E. (1968). Stimulus range, number of categories, and form of the category scale. *American Journal of Psychology, 81,* 467–479.

Marks, L. E. (1974). On scales of sensation: Prolegomena to any future psychophysics that will be able to come forth as science. *Perception and Psychophysics, 16,* 358–376.

Marks, L. E. (1979a). Summation of vibrotactile intensity: An analogy to auditory critical bands? *Sensory Processes, 3,* 188–203.

Marks, L. E. (1979b): A theory of loudness and loudness judgments. *Psychological Review, 86,* 256–285.

Marks, L. E. (1988). Magnitude estimation and sensory matching. *Perception & Psychophysics, 43,* 511–525.

Marks, L. E., Szczesiul, R., & Ohlott, P. (1986). On the cross-modal perception of intensity. *Journal of Experimental Psychology: Human Perception and Performance, 12,* 517–534.

Marks, W. B., Dobelle, W. H., & MacNichol, E. F. (1964). Visual pigments of single primate cones. *Science, 143,* 1181–1183.

Marley, A. A. J., & Cook, V. T. (1984). A fixed rehearsal capacity interpretation of limits on absolute identification performance. *British Journal of Mathematical and Statistical Psychology, 37,* 136–151.

Marr, D. (1982). *Vision.* San Francisco: W. H. Freeman.

Marr, D., & Poggio, T. (1979). A computational theory of human stereo vision. *Proceedings of the Royal Society (London), Series B, 204,* 301–328.

Marr, D., & Ullman, S. (1981). Directional selectivity and its use in early visual processing. *Proceedings of the Royal Society of London, Series B, 211,* 151–180.

Marshall, D. A., & Moulton, D. G. (1981). Olfactory sensitivity to α-ionine in humans and dogs. *Chemical Senses, 6,* 53–61.

Marslen-Wilson, W. D. (1980). Speech understanding as a psychological process. In J. C. Simon (Ed.), *Spoken language generation and understanding* (pp. 39–67). Dordrecht, The Netherlands: Reidel.

Martin, D. K., & Holden, B. A. (1982). A new method for measuring the diameter of the in vivo human cornea. *American Journal of Optometry and Physiological Optics, 59,* 436–441.

Martin, G. K., Lonsbury-Martin, B. L., Probst, R., & Coats, A. C. (1988). Spontaneous otoacoustic emissions in a nonhuman primate: I. Basic features and relations to other emissions. *Hearing Research, 33,* 49–68.

Martin, M. (1979). Local and global processing: The role of sparsity. *Memory and Cognition, 7,* 476–484.

Martin, R. L., Webster, W. R., & Service, J. (1988). The frequency organization of the inferior colliculus of the guinea pig: A [^{14}C]-2-deoxyglucose study. *Hearing Research, 33,* 245–256.

Masica, D. N., Money, J., Ehrhardt, A. A., & Lewis, V. G. (1969). IQ, fetal sex hormones and cognitive patterns-studies in testicular feminizing syndrome of androgen insensitivity. *Johns Hopkins Medical Journal, 124,* 34.

Masin, S. C., & Crestoni, L. (1988). Experimental demonstration of the sensory basis of the size-weight illusion. *Perception & Psychophysics, 44,* 309–312.

Masland, R. H. (1986). The functional architecture of the retina. *Scientific American, 255,* 102–111.

Massaro, D. (1988). Ambiguity in perception and experimentation. *Journal of Experimental Psychology: General, 117,* 417–421.

Massaro, D. W. (1987). *Speech perception by ear and eye: a paradigm for psychological inquiry.* Hillsdale, NJ: Erlbaum.

Massaro, D. W., & Cohen, M. M. (1990). Perception of synthesized audible and visible speech. *Psychological Science, 1,* 55–63.

Mather, J. A., & Fisk, J. D. (1985). Orienting to targets by looking and pointing: Parallels and interactions in ocular and manual performance. *Quarterly Journal of Experimental Psychology, 37A,* 315–338.

Matin, L. (1982). Visual localization and eye movements. In A. H. Wertheim, W. A. Wagenaar, & H. W. Leibowitz (Eds.), *Tutorials on Motion Perception* (pp. 101–156). New York: Plenum Press.

Matin, L., & MacKinnon, G. E. (1964). Autokinetic movement: Selective manipulation of directional components by image stabilization. *Science, 143,* 147–148.

Matthews, B. H. C. (1933). Nerve endings in mammalian muscle. *Journal of Physiology (London), 78,* 1–53.

Maunsell, J. H. R., & Newsome, W. T. (1987). Visual processing in monkey extrastriate cortex. *Annual Review of Neuroscience, 10,* 363–401.

Maunsell, J. H. R., & Van Essen, D. C. (1983). Functional properties of neurons in middle temporal visual area of the macaque monkey: I. Selectivity for stimulus direction, speed, and orientation. *Journal of Neurophysiology, 49,* 1127–1147.

Maurer, D. (1975). Infant visual perception: Methods of study. In L. B. Cohen & P. Salapatek (Eds.), *Infant perception: From sensation to cognition, basic visual processes: Vol. 1* (pp. 1–77). New York: Academic Press.

Maurer, D., & Barrera, M. (1981). Infant's perception of natural and distorted arrangements of a schematic face. *Child Development, 52,* 196–202.

Maurer, D., & Lewis, T. L. (1979). A physiological explanation of infants' early visual development. *Canadian Journal of Psychology, 33,* 232–251.

Maurer, D., & Lewis, T. L. (1991). The development of peripheral vision and its physiological underpinnings. In M. J. Weiss & P. R. Zelazo (Eds.), *Newborn attention* (pp. 218–255). Norwood, NJ: Ablex.

Maurer, D., & Martello, M. (1980). The discrimination of orientation by young infants. *Vision Research, 20,* 201–204.

Maurer, D., & Salapatek, P. (1976). Development changes in the scanning of faces by young infants. *Child Development, 47,* 523–527.

Maxwell, J. C. (1873). *Treatise on electricity and magnetism.* Oxford: Clarendon Press.

May, B., & Moody, D. B. (1989). Categorical perception of conspecific communication sounds by Japanese macaques, Macaca fuscata. *Journal of the Acoustical Society of America, 85,* 837–847.

Mayer, D. J., & Watkins, L. R. (1984). Multiple endogenous opiate and nonopiate analgesia systems. In L. Kruger & J. C. Liebeskind (Eds.), *Neural mechanisms of pain* (pp. 253–276). New York: Raven Press.

Mayfrank, L., & Mobashery, M. (1986). The role of fixation and visual attention in the occurrence of express saccades in man. *European Archives of Psychiatry & Neurological Sciences, 235,* 269–275.

Mayhew, J. E. W., & Frisby, J. P. (1979). Convergent disparity discriminations in narrow-band-filtered random-dot stereograms. *Vision Research, 19,* 63–71.

Mayhew, J. E. W., & Frisby, J. P. (1980). The computation of binocular edges. *Perception, 9,* 69–86.

Maylor, E. A., & Hockey, R. (1985). Inhibitory component of externally controlled covert orienting in visual space. *Journal of Experimental Psychology: Human Perception and Performance, 11,* 777–787.

McAnally, K. I., & Calford, M. B. (1990). A psychophysical study of spectral hyperacuity. *Hearing Research, 44,* 93–96.

McBride, R. L. (1987). Taste psychophysics and the Beidler equation. *Chemical Senses, 12,* 323–332.

McBurney, D. H. (1969). Effects of adaptation on human taste function. In C. Pfaffman (Ed.), *Olfaction and taste III* (pp. 407–419). New York: Rockefeller University Press.

McBurney, D. H., & Bartoshuk, L. M. (1972). Water taste in mammals. In D. Schneider (Ed.), *Olfaction and taste IV* (pp. 329–335). Wissenshafliche Verlagsgesellschaft MBH.

McBurney, D. H., & Gent, J. F. (1979). On the nature of taste qualities. *Psychological Bulletin, 86,* 151–167.

McBurney, D. H., Levine, J. M., & Cavanaugh, P. H. (1977). Psychophysical and social ratings of human body odor. *Personality and Social Psychology Bulletin, 3,* 135–138.

McCall, R. B. (1979). Individual differences in the pattern of habituation at five and 10 months of age. *Developmental Psychology, 15,* 559–569.

McClain, L. (1983). Interval estimation: Effect of processing demands on prospective and retrospective reports. *Perception & Psychophysics, 34,* 185–189.

McClellan, P. G., & Bernstein, I. H. (1984). What makes the Mueller a liar: A multiple-cue approach. *Perception & Psychophysics, 36,* 234–244.

McClelland, J. L., & Elman, J. L. (1986). The TRACE model of speech perception. *Cognitive Psychology, 18,* 1–86.

McClintock, M. K. (1971). Menstrual synchrony and suppression. *Nature (London), 229,* 244–245.

McCloskey, M., & Egeth, H. E. (1983). Eyewitness identification: What can a psychologist tell a jury? *American Psychologist, 38,* 550–553.

McColgin, F. H. (1960). Movement threshold in peripheral vision. *Journal of the Optical Society of America, 50,* 774–779.

McCready, D. (1986). Moon illusions redescribed. *Perception & Psychophysics, 39,* 64–72.

McFarland, R. A., Domey, R. G., Warren, A. B., & Ward, D. C. (1960). Dark-adaptation as a function of age: I. A statistical analysis. *Journal of Gerontology, 15,* 149–154.

McGee, M. G. (1979). Human spatial abilities: Psychometric studies and environmental, genetic, hormonal, and neurological influences. *Psychological Bulletin, 86,* 889–918.

McGlone, J. (1981). Sexual variations in behavior during spatial and verbal tasks. *Canadian Journal of Psychology, 35,* 277–282.

McGuinness, D. (1972). Hearing: Individual differences in perceiving. *Perception, 1,* 465–473.

McGuinness, D. (1976a). Away from a unisex psychology: Individual differences in visual sensory and perceptual processes. *Perception, 5,* 279–294.

McGuinness, D. (1976b). Sex differences in the organization of perception and cognition. In B. Lloyd & U. Archer (Eds.), *Exploring sex differences* (pp. 123–156). New York: Academic Press.

McGuinness, D., & Lewis, I. (1976). Sex differences in visual persistence: Experiments on the Ganzfeld and the after-image. *Perception, 5,* 295–301.

McGurk, H., & MacDonald, J. (1976). Hearing lips and seeing voices. *Nature, 264,* 746–748.

Meddis, R. (1988). Simulation of auditory-neural transduction: Further studies. *Journal of the Acoustical Society of America, 83,* 1056–1063.

Meiselman, H. L., Bose, H. E., & Nykvist, W. F. (1972). Magnitude production and magnitude estimation of taste intensity. *Perception & Psychophysics, 12,* 249–252.

Melara, R. D., & Marks, L. E. (1990). Interaction among auditory dimensions: Timbre, pitch, and loudness. *Perception & Psychophysics, 48,* 169–178.

Melzack, R., & Casey, K. L. (1968). Sensory, motivational, and central control determinants of pain. In D. R. Kenshalo (Ed.), *The skin senses* (pp. 423–443). Springfield, IL: Thomas.

Melzack, R., & Wall, P. D. (1965). Pain mechanisms: A new theory. *Science, 150,* 971–979.

Melzack, R., & Wall, P. D. (1982). *The challenge of pain.* Harmondsworth, England: Penguin.

Melzack, R., Wall, P. D., & Ty, T. C. (1982). Acute pain in an emergency clinic: Latency of onset and descriptor patterns related to different injuries. *Pain, 14,* 33–43.

Mercer, M. E., Courage, M. L., & Adams, R. J. (1991). Contrast/color card procedure: A new test of young infants' color vision. *Optometry and Vision Science, 68,* 522–532.

Mergler, D., Bowler, R., & Cone, J. (1990). Colour vision loss among disabled workers with neuropsychological impairment. *Neurotoxicology and Teratology, 12,* 669–672.

Mergner, T., Anastasopoulos, D., Becker, W., & Deecke, L. (1981). Discrimination between trunk and head rotation: A study comparing neuronal data from the cat with human psychophysics. *Acta Psychologica, 48,* 291–302.

Merkel, J. (1885). Die zeitlichen Verhaltnisse der Willensthatigkeit. *Philosophische Studien (Wundt), 2,* 73–127.

Mershon, D. H., Ballenger, W. L., Little, A. D., McMurtry, P. L., & Buchanan, J. L. (1989). Effects of room reflectance and background noise on perceived auditory distance. *Perception, 18,* 403–416.

Mershon, D. H., & Bowers, J. N. (1979). Absolute and relative cues for the auditory perception of egocentric distance. *Perception, 8,* 311–322.

Mershon, D. H., Desaulniers, D. H., & Amerson, T. L., Jr. (1980). Visual capture in auditory distance perception: Proximity image effect reconsidered. *Journal of Auditory Research, 20,* 129–136.

Mershon, D. H., Desaulniers, D. H., Kiefer, S. A., & Amerson, T. L., Jr. (1981). Perceived loudness and visually determined auditory distance. *Perception, 10,* 531–543.

Mershon, D. H., & Gogel, W. C. (1970). Effect of stereoscopic cues on perceived whiteness. *American Journal of Psychology, 83,* 55–67.

Mershon, D. H., & King, L. E. (1975). Intensity and reverberation as factors in the auditory perception of egocentric distance. *Perception & Psychophysics, 18,* 409–415.

Merzenich, M. M., Knight, P. L., & Roth, G. L. (1975). Representation of cochlea within primary auditory cortex in the cat. *Journal of Neurophysiology, 38,* 231–249.

Metzler, D. E., & Harris, C. M. (1978). Shapes of spectral bands of visual pigments. *Vision Research, 18,* 1417–1420.

Michael, C. R. (1985). Laminar segregation of color cells in the monkey's striate cortex. *Vision Research, 25,* 415–423.

Michael, R. P., & Keverne, E. B. (1968). Pheromones in the communication of sexual status in primates. *Nature, 218,* 746–749.

Michael, R. P., Keverne, E. B., & Bonsall, R. W. (1971). Pheromones: Isolation of male sex attractants from a female primate. *Science, 172,* 964–966.

Michael, S., & Sherrick, M. F. (1986). Perception of induced visual motion: Effects of relative position, shape and size of the surround. *Canadian Journal of Psychology, 40,* 122–125.

Michaels, C. F., & Carello, C. (1981). *Direct perception.* Englewood Cliffs, NJ: Prentice-Hall.

Michell, J. (1986). Measurement scales and statistics: A clash of paradigms. *Psychological Bulletin, 100,* 398–407.

Michon, J. (1985). The compleat time experiencer. In J. A. Michon & J. L. Jackson (Eds.), *Time, mind and behavior* (pp. 20–52). Berlin: Springer-Verlag.

Middlebrooks, J. C., Makous, J. C., & Green, D. M. (1989). Directional sensitivity of sound-pressure levels in the human ear canal. *Journal of the Acoustical Society of America, 86,* 89–108.

Mikaelian, H. (1974). Adaptation to displaced hearing: A nonproprioceptive change. *Journal of Experimental Psychology, 103,* 326–330.

Mikaelian, H., & Held, R. (1964). Two types of adaptation to an optically-rotated visual field. *American Journal of Psychology, 77,* 257–263.

Miles, F. A., & Fuller, J. E. (1975). Visual tracking and the primate flocculus. *Science, 189,* 1000–1002.

Milewski, A. E. (1976). Infant's discrimination of internal and external pattern elements. *Journal of Experimental Child Psychology, 22,* 229–246.

Mill, J. (1829). *Analysis of the phenomena of the human mind.* London.

Millan, M. J. (1986). Multiple opioid systems and pain. *Pain, 27,* 303–347.

Millar, J. M., & Whitaker, H. A. (1983). The right hemisphere's contribution to language: A review of the evidence from brain-damaged subjects. In S. Sagalowitz (Ed.), *Language function and brain organization* (pp. 87–114). New York: Academic Press.

Miller, D. L., Moore, R. K., & Wooten, B. R. (1984). When push comes to pull: Impressions of visual direction. *Perception & Psychophysics, 36,* 396–397.

Miller, G. A. (1956). The magical number seven, plus or minus two: Some limits on our capacity for processing information. *Psychological Review, 63,* 81–97.

Miller, G. W., Hicks, R. E., & Willette, M. (1978). Effects of concurrent verbal rehearsal and temporal set upon judgments of temporal duration. *Acta Psychologica, 42,* 173–179.

Miller, J. (1982). Divided attention: Evidence for coactivation with redundant signals. *Cognitive Psychology, 14,* 247–279.

Miller, J. L., & Liberman, A. M. (1979). Some effects of later-occurring information on the perception of stop consonants and semivowel. *Perception & Psychophysics, 25,* 457–465.

Miller, J. M., & Spelman, F. A. (1990). *Cochlear implants: Models of the electrically stimulated ear.* New York: Springer-Verlag.

Miller, N. D. (1965). Visual recovery from brief exposures to high luminance. *Journal of the Optical Society of America, 55,* 1661–1669.

Miller, R. J., Pigion, R. G., & Martin, K. D. (1985). The effects of ingested alcohol on accommodation. *Perception & Psychophysics, 37,* 407–414.

Mills, A. W. (1958). On the minimum audible angle. *Journal of the Acoustical Society of America, 30,* 127–246.

Mills, A. W. (1960). Lateralization of high-frequency tones. *Journal of the Acoustical Society of America, 32,* 132–134.

Milne, J., & Milne, M. (1967). *The senses of animals and men.* New York: Atheneum.

Miron, D., Duncan, G. H., & Bushnell, M. C. (1989). Effects of attention on the intensity and unpleasantness of thermal pain. *Pain, 39,* 345–352.

Mishkin, M., & Lewis, M. E. (1982). Equivalence of parieto-preoccipital subareas for visuospatial ability in monkeys. *Journal of Brain and Behavioral Sciences, 6,* 41–55.

Mishkin, M., & Ungerleider, L. G. (1982). Contribution of striate inputs to the visuospatial functions of parieto-preoccipital cortex in monkeys. *Journal of Brain and Behavioral Sciences, 6,* 57–77.

Mishkin, M., Ungerleider, L. G., & Macko, K. A. (1983). Object vision and spatial vision: Two cortical pathways. *Trends in Neuroscience, 6,* 414–417.

Mitchell, D. (1978). Effect of early visual experience on the development of certain perceptual abilities in animals and man. In R. Walk & H. Pick (Eds.), *Perception and experience.* New York: Plenum Press.

Mitchell, D. (1980). The influence of early visual experience on visual perception. In C. Harris (Ed.), *Visual coding and adaptability* (pp. 1–50). Hillsdale, NJ: Erlbaum.

Mitchell, D. (1981). Sensitive periods in visual development. In R. Aslin, J. Alberts, & M. Petersen (Eds.), *Development of Perception* (pp. 1–43). New York: Academic Press.

Monahan, J. S., & Lockhead, G. R. (1977). Identification of integral stimuli. *Journal of Experimental Psychology: General, 106,* 94–110.

Moncrieff, R. W. (1956). Olfactory adaptation and colour likeness. *Journal of Physiology (London), 133,* 301–316.

Money, J. (1965). Psychosexual differentiation. In J. Money (Ed.), *Sex research: New developments* (pp. 3–23). New York: Holt.

Montellese, S., Sharpe, L. T., & Brown, J. L. (1979). Changes in critical duration during dark-adaptation. *Vision Research, 19,* 1147–1153.

Montgomery, J. C., & MacDonald, J. A. (1987). Sensory tuning of lateral line receptors in Antarctic fish to the movements of planktonic prey. *Science, 235,* 195–196.

Moonen, C. T. W., van Zijl, P. C. M., Frank, J. A., Le Bihan, D., & Becker, E. D. (1990). Functional magnetic resonance imaging in medicine and physiology. *Science, 250,* 53–61.

Mooney, R. D., Dubin, M. W., & Rusoff, A. C. (1979). Interneuron circuits in the lateral geniculate nucleus of monocularly deprived cats. *Journal of Comparative Neurology, 187*(3), 533–544.

Moore, B. (1977). *Introduction to the psychology of hearing.* Baltimore: University Park Press.

Moore, L. M., Nielson, C. R., & Mistretta, C. M. (1982). Sucrose taste thresholds: Age-related differences. *Journal of Gerontology, 37,* 64–69.

Moran, J., & Desimone, R. (1985). Selective attention gates visual processing in the extrastriate cortex. *Science, 229,* 782–784.

Moran, J., & Gordon, B. (1982). Long term visual deprivation in a human. *Vision Research, 22,* 27–36.

Moray, N. (1959). Attention in dichotic listening: Affective cues and the influence of instructions. *Quarterly Journal of Experimental Psychology, 11,* 56–60.

Moray, N. (1969). *Attention: Selective processes in vision and hearing.* London: Hutchinson Educational.

Mori, S., & Ward, L. M. (1991). Listening versus hearing: Attentional effects on intensity discrimination. *Technical Report on Hearing: The Acoustical Society of Japan,* No. H-91-36.

Mori, S., & Ward, L. M. (1992). Listening versus hearing II: Attentional effects on intensity discrimination by musicians. *Technical Report on Hearing: The Acoustical Society of Japan,* No. H-92-48.

Morris, V., & Morris, P. E. (1985). The influence of question order on eyewitness accuracy. *British Journal of Psychology, 76,* 365–371.

Morrison, F. J., Holmes, D. L., & Haith, M. M. (1974). A developmental study of the effect of familiarity on short-term visual memory. *Journal of Experimental Child Psychology, 18,* 412–425.

Morrison, J. D., & Whiteside, T. C. D. (1984). Binocular cues in the perception of distance of a point source of light. *Perception, 13,* 555–566.

Morse, P. A., & Molfese, D. L. (1987). Categorical perception for voicing contrasts in normal and lead-treated rhesus monkeys: Electrophysiological indices. *Brain and Language, 30,* 63–80.

Moskowitz, H., Sharma, S., & McGlothlin, W. (1972). Effect of marijuana upon peripheral vision as a function of the information processing demands in central vision. *Perceptual and Motor Skills, 35,* 875.

Moskowitz-Cook, A. (1979). The development of photopic spectral sensitivity in human infants. *Vision Research, 9,* 113–1142.

Mountcastle, V. B., Motter, B. C., Steinmetz, M. A., & Sestokas, A. K. (1987). Common and differential effects of attentive fixation on the excitability of parietal and prestriate (V4) cortical visual neurons in the macaque monkey. *Journal of Neuroscience, 7,* 2239–2255.

Mountcastle, V. B., Poggio, G. F., & Werner, G. (1963). The relation of thalamic cell response to peripheral stimuli varied over an intensive continuum. *Journal of Neurophysiology, 26,* 807–834.

Mountcastle, V. B., & Powell, T. P. S. (1959). Central nervous mechanisms subserving position sense and kinesthesis. *Bulletin of the Johns Hopkins Hospital, 105,* 173–200.

Movshon, J. A., & Van Sluyters, R. C. (1981). Visual neural development. *Annual Review of Psychology, 32,* 477–522.

Mozel, M. M., Smith, B., Smith, P., Sullivan, R., & Swender, P. (1969). Nasal chemoreception in flavor identification. *Archives of Otolaryngology, 90,* 367–373.

Muir, D., & Field, J. (1979). Newborn infants orient to sounds. *Child Development, 50,* 431–436.

Muir, D. W., Clifton, R. K., & Clarkson, M. G. (1989). The development of a human auditory localization response: A U-shaped function. *Canadian Journal of Psychology, 43,* 199–216.

Mullen, K. T. (1990). The chromatic coding of space. In C. Blakemore, (Ed.), *Vision: Coding and efficiency* (pp. 150–158). New York: Cambridge University Press.

Muller, H. J., & Findlay, J. M. (1988). The effect of visual attention on peripheral discrimination thresholds in single and multiple element displays. *Acta Psychologica, 69,* 129–155.

Muller, H. J., & Humphreys, G. W. (1991). Luminance-increment detection: Capacity-limited or not? *Journal of Experimental Psychology: Human Perception and Performance, 17,*107–124.

Muller, H. J., & Rabbitt, P. M. A. (1989). Reflexive and voluntary orienting of visual attention: Time course of activation and resistance to interruption. *Journal of Experimental Psychology: Human Perception and Performance, 15,* 315–330.

Mulligan, R. M., & Schiffman, H. R. (1979). Temporal experience as a function of organization in memory. *Bulletin of the Psychonomic Society, 14,* 417–420.

Munsell, A. H. (1915). *Atlas of the Munsell color system.* Maldin, MA: Wadsworth, Howland.

Murphy, C., & Cain, W. S. (1980). Taste and olfaction: Independence vs. interaction. *Physiology and Behavior, 24,* 601–605.

Murphy, T. D., & Eriksen, C. W. (1987). Temporal changes in the distribution of attention in the visual field in response to precues. *Perception & Psychophysics, 42,* 576–586.

Murray, J. B. (1986). Marijuana's effects on human cognitive functions, psychomotor functions, and personality. *Journal of General Psychology, 113,* 23–55.

Mustillo, P. (1985). Binocular mechanisms mediating crossed and uncrossed stereopsis. *Psychological Bulletin, 97,* 187–201.

Myers, A. K. (1982). Psychophysical scaling and scales of physical stimulus measurement. *Psychological Bulletin, 92,* 203–214.

Nagy, A. L. (1980). Short-flash Bezold-Brucke hue shifts. *Vision Research, 20,* 361–368.

Naka, Ken-Ichi. (1982). The cells horizontal cells talk to. *Vision Research, 22,* 653–660.

Nakayama, K. (1985). Biological image motion processing: A review. *Vision Research, 25,* 625–660.

Nakayama, K., Shimojo, S., & Silverman, G. H. (1989). Stereoscopic depth: Its relation to image segmentation, grouping, and the recognition of occluded objects. *Perception, 18,* 55–68.

Nakayama, K., & Silverman, G. H. (1986). Serial and parallel processing of visual feature conjunctions. *Nature, 320,* 264–265.

Narens, L., & Luce, R. D. (1986). Measurement: The theory of numerical assignments. *Psychological Bulletin, 99,* 166–180.

Nathans, J. (1987). Molecular biology of visual pigments. *Annual Review of Neuroscience, 10,* 163–164.

Nathans, J., Piantanida, T. P., Eddy, R. L., Shows, T. B., & Hogness, D. S. (1986). Molecular genetics of inherited variation in human color vision. *Science, 232,* 203–210.

Navon, D. (1977). Forest before trees: The precedence of global features in visual perception. *Cognitive Psychology, 9,* 353–383.

Navon, D., & Gopher, D. (1979). On the economy of the human-processing system. *Psychological Review, 86,* 214–255.

Navon, D., & Norman, J. (1983). Does global precedence really depend on visual angle? *Journal of Experimental Psychology: Human Perception and Performance, 9,* 955–965.

Neff, D. L. (1991). Forward masking by maskers of uncertain frequency content. *Journal of the Acoustical Society of America, 89,* 1314–1323.

Neff, D. L., & Green, D. M. (1987). Masking produced by spectral uncertainty with multicomponent maskers. *Perception & Psychophysics, 41,* 409–415.

Neisser, U. (1967). *Cognitive psychology.* New York: Appleton.

Neisser, U. (1976). *Cognition and reality: Principles and implications of cognitive psychology.* San Francisco: Freeman.

Neisser, U., & Becklin, R. (1975). Selective looking: Attending to visually specified events. *Cognitive Psychology, 7,* 480–494.

Neitz, J., & Jacobs, G. H. (1986). Polymorphism of the long-wavelength cone in normal human colour vision. *Nature, 323,* 623–625.

Nelson, C. A., & Ludemann, P. M. (1989). Past, current, and future trends in infant face perception research. *Canadian Journal of Psychology, 43,* 183–198.

Nelson, R., Kolb, H., Robinson, M. M., & Mariani, A. P. (1981). Neural circuitry of the cat retina: Cone pathways to ganglion cells. *Vision Research, 21,* 1527–1537.

Nevatia, R. (1982). *Machine perception.* Englewood Cliffs, NJ: Prentice–Hall.

Neville, H. J. (1985). Effects of early sensory and language experience on the development of the human brain. In J. Mehler & R. Fox (Eds.), *Neonate cognition: Beyond the bloom buzzing confusion* (pp. 349–364). Hillsdale, NJ: Erlbaum.

Neville, H. J., Schmidt, A., & Kutas, M. (1983). Altered visual evoked potentials in congenitally deaf adults. *Brain Research, 266,* 127–132.

Newhall, S. M., Burnham, R. W., & Clark, J. R. (1957). Comparison of successive with simultaneous color matching. *Journal of the Optical Society of America, 47,* 43–56.

Newhall, S. M., Nickerson, D., & Judd, D. B. (1943). Final report of the O.S.A. subcommittee on spacing of the Munsell colors. *Journal of the Optical Society of America, 33,* 385–418.

Newland, J. (1972). *Children's knowledge of left and right.* Unpublished master's thesis, University of Auckland. Cited in M. C. Corballis & J. L. Beale (1976). The psychology of left and right (p. 167). Hillsdale, NJ: Erlbaum.

Newsome, W. T., & Pare, E. B. (1988). A selective impairment of motion processing following lesions of the middle temporal visual area (MT). *Journal of Neuroscience, 8,* 2201–2211.

Niall, K. K. (1990). Projective invariance and picture perception. *Perception, 19,* 637–660.

Nijhawan, R. (1991). Three-dimensional Mueller-Lyer illusion. *Perception & Psychophysics, 49,* 333–341.

Nissen, M. J., & Corkin, S. (1985). Effectiveness of attentional cueing in older and younger adults. *Journal of Gerontology, 40,* 185–191.

Noble, W., & Gates, A. (1985). Accuracy, latency, and listener-search behavior in localization in the horizontal and vertical planes. *Journal of the Acoustical Society of America, 78,* 2005–2012.

Noda, H., Freeman, R. B., & Creutzfeldt, O. D. (1972). Neuronal correlates of eye movements in the cat visual cortex. *Science, 175,* 661–664.

Noell, W. (1980). Possible mechanisms of photoreceptor damage by light in mammalian eyes. *Vision Research, 20,* 1163–1172.

Norman, D. A. (1968). Toward a theory of memory and

attention. *Psychological Review, 75,* 522–536.

Norman, D. A. (1969). Memory while shadowing. *Quarterly Journal of Experiental Psychology, 21,* 85–93.

Norman, D. A. (1976). *Memory and attention* (2nd ed.). New York: Wiley.

Norman, D. A., Rumelhart, D. E., and the LNR Research Group. (1975). *Explorations in cognition.* San Francisco: Freeman.

Norton, S. J., Schultz, M. C., Reed, C. M., Braida, L. D., Durlach, N. I., Rabinowitz, W. M., & Chomsky, C. (1977). Analytic study of the Tadoma method: Background and preliminary results. *Journal of Speech and Hearing Research, 20,* 574–595.

Norton, T. T. (1981a). Development of the visual system and visually guided behavior. In R. Aslin, J. Alberts, & M. Petersen (Eds.), *Development of perception: Psychobiological perspectives: Vol. 2. The visual system* (pp. 113–156). New York: Academic Press.

Norton, T. T. (1981b). Geniculate and extrageniculate visual systems in the tree shrew. In A. R. Morrison and P. L. Strick (Eds.), *Changing concepts of the nervous system* (pp. 377–410). New York: Academic Press.

Norwich, K. H. (1981). The magical number seven: Making a "bit" of "sense." *Perception & Psychophysics, 29,* 409–422.

Norwich, K. H. (1983). To perceive is to doubt: The relativity of perception. *Journal of Theoretical Biology, 102,* 175–190.

Norwich, K. H. (1984). The psychophysics of taste from the entropy of the stimulus. *Perception & Psychophysics, 35,* 269–278.

Norwich, K. H. (1987). On the theory of Weber fractions. *Perception & Psychophysics, 42,* 286–298.

Nusbaum, H. C., & Schwab, E. C. (1986). The role of attention and active processing in speech perception. In E. C. Schwab & H. C. Nusbaum (Eds.), *Pattern recognition by humans and machines: Vol. 1. Speech perception* (pp. 113–157). Orlando: Academic Press.

Oakley, B. (1985). Taste responses of human chorda tympani nerve. *Chemical Senses, 10,* 469–481.

O'Connell, R. J., & Mozell, M. M. (1969). Quantitative stimulation of frog olfactory receptors. *Journal of Neurophysiology, 32,* 51–63.

Ogasawara, K., McHaftie, J. G., and Stein, B. E. (1984). Two visual corticotectal systems in the cat. *Journal of Neurophysiology, 52,* 1226–1245.

Ohala, J. J. (1986). Phonological evidence for top-down processing in speech perception. In J. S. Perkell and D. H. Klatt (Eds.), *Invariance and variability in speech processes* (pp. 386–397). Hillsdale, NJ: Erlbaum.

Oldfield, S. R., & Parker, S. P. A. (1984). Acuity of sound localisation: A topography of auditory space: II. Pinna cues absent. *Perception, 13,* 601–617.

Oldfield, S. R., & Parker, S. P. A. (1986). Acuity of sound localisation: A topography of auditory space: III. Monaural hearing conditions. *Perception, 15,* 67–81.

O'Leary, A., & McMahon, M. (1991). Adaptation to form distortion of a familiar shape. *Perception & Psychophysics, 49,* 328–332.

Olsho, L. W. (1984). Infant frequency discrimination. *Infant Behavior and Development, 7,* 27–35.

Olson, R., & Attneave, F. (1970). What variables produce similarity grouping? *American Journal of Psychology, 83,* 1–21.

Olzak, L. (1986). Widely separated spatial frequencies: Mechanism interactions. *Vision Research, 26,* 1143–1154.

O'Mahony, M. (1979). Salt taste adaptation: The psychophysical effects of adapting solutions and residual stimuli from prior tastings on the taste of sodium chloride. *Perception, 8,* 441–476.

O'Mahony, M., & Heintz, C. (1981). Direct magnitude estimation of salt taste intensity with continuous correction for salivary adaptation. *Chemical Senses, 6,* 101–112.

Ono, H. (1969). Apparent distance as a function of familiar size. *Journal of Experimental Psychology, 79,* 109–115.

Ono, H., & Comerford, T. (1977). Stereoscopic depth constancy. In W. Epstein (Ed.), *Stability and constancy in visual perception: Mechanisms and processes.* New York: Wiley.

Ono, H., & Rogers, B. J. (1988). Dynamic occlusion and motion parallax in depth perception. *Perception, 17,* 255–256.

Ono, H., & Weber, E. U. (1981). Nonveridical visual direction produced by monocular viewing. *Journal of Experimental Psychology: Human Perception and Performance, 7,* 937–947.

Ono, M. E., Rivest, J., & Ono, H. (1986). Depth perception as a function of motion parallax and absolute-distance information. *Journal of Experimental Psychology: Human Perception and Performance, 12,* 331–337.

Orban, G. A. (1984). *Neuronal operations in the visual cortex.* Berlin: Springer-Verlag.

Orban, G. A., Kennedy, H., & Maes, H. (1981a). Response to movement of neurons in areas 17 and 18 of the cat: Velocity sensitivity. *Journal of Neurophysiology, 45,* 1043–1058.

Orban, G. A., Kennedy, H., & Maes, H. (1981b). Response to movement of neurons in areas 17 and 18 of the cat: Direction sensitivity. *Journal of Neurophysiology, 45,* 1059–1073.

Ornstein, R. E. (1969). *On the experience of time.* London: Penguin.

Osaka, N. (1981). Brightness exponent as a function of flash duration and retinal eccentricity. *Perception & Psychophysics, 30,* 144–148.

Osborne, M. P., Comis, S. D., & Pickles, J. O. (1988). Further observations on the fine structure of tip links between stereocilia of the guinea pig cochlea. *Hearing Research, 35,* 99–108.

Osterberg, G. (1935). Topography of the layer of rods and cones in the human retina. *Acta Ophthalmologica,* (Suppl. 6).

Ostfeld, A. (1961). Effects of LSD-25 and JB318 on tests of visual and perceptual functions in man. *Federation Proceedings, Federation of American Societies for Experimental Biology, 20,* 876–883.

Ottoson, D. (1956). Analysis of the electrical activity of the olfactory epithelium. *Acta Physiologica Scandinavica, 35*(Suppl. 122), 1–83.

Owens, M. E. (1984). Pain in infancy: Conceptual and methodological issues. *Pain, 20,* 213–220.

Owsley, C. (1983). The role of motion in infants' perception of solid shape. *Perception, 12,* 707–717.

Owsley, C. J., Sekuler, R., & Siemensen, D. (1983). Contrast sensitivity throughout adulthood. *Vision Research, 23,* 689–699.

Oyama, T. (1968). A behavioristic analysis of Stevens's magnitude estimation method. *Perception & Psychophysics,* 317–320.

Oyama, T. (1986). The effect of stimulus organization on numerosity discrimination. *Japanese Psychological Research, 28,* 77–86.

Palmer, A. R., Winter, I. M., & Darwin, C. J. (1986). The representation of steady-state vowel sounds in the temporal discharge pattern of the guinea pig cochlear nerve and primarylike cochlear nucleus neurons. *Journal of the Acoustical Society of America, 79,* 100–113.

Palmer, C., & Krumhansl, C. L. (1987). Independent temporal and pitch structures in determination of musical phrases. *Journal of Experimental Psychology: Human Perception and Performance, 13,* 116–126.

Palmer, C., & Krumhansl, C. L. (1990). Mental representations for musical meter. *Journal of Experimental Psychology: Human Perception and Performance, 16,* 728–741.

Palmer, J. (1986). Mechanisms of displacement discrimination with and without perceived movement. *Journal of Experimental Psychology: Human Perception and Performance, 12,* 411–421.

Palmer, S. E. (1975a). The effects of contextual scenes on the identification of objects. *Memory and Cognition, 3,* 519–526.

Palmer, S. E. (1975b). Visual perception and world knowledge: Notes on a model of sensory-cognitive interaction. In D. A. Norman & D. E. Rumelhart (Eds.), *Explorations in cognition* (pp. 297–307). San Francisco: Freeman.

Pang, X. D., Tan, H. Z., & Durlach, N. I. (1991). Manual discrimination of force using active finger motion.

Perception & Psychophysics, 49, 531–540.

Pantev, C., Hoke, M., Lutkenhoner, B., & Lehnertz, K. (1989). Tonotopic organization of the auditory cortex: Pitch versus frequency representation. *Science, 246,* 486–488.

Papert, S. (1961). Centrally produced geometric illusions. *Nature, 191,* 733.

Paquet, L., & Merikle, P. M. (1984). Global precedence: The effect of exposure duration. *Canadian Journal of Psychology, 38,* 45–53.

Parasuraman, R. (1984). Sustained attention in detection and discrimination. In R. Parasuraman & D. R. Davies (Eds.), *Varieties of attention* (pp. 243–271). Orlando: Academic Press.

Parasuraman, R., & Mouloua, M. (1987). Interaction of signal discriminability and task type in vigilance decrement. *Perception & Psychophysics, 41,* 17–22.

Parducci, A. (1965). Category judgment: A range-frequency model. *Psychological Review, 72,* 407–418.

Parker, D. E. (1980). The vestibular apparatus. *Scientific American, 243,* 118–135.

Parks, T. E. (1965). Post-retinal visual storage. *American Journal of Psychology, 78,* 145–147.

Parlee, M. B. (1983). Menstrual rhythms in sensory processes: A review of fluctuations in vision, olfaction, audition, taste and touch. *Psychological Bulletin, 93,* 539–548.

Parrott, A. C. (1988). Transdermal scopolamine: Effects upon psychological performance and visual functioning at sea. *Human Psychopharmacology Clinical & Experimental, 3,* 119–125.

Pashler, H. (1984). Evidence against late selection: Stimulus quality effects in previewed displays. *Journal of Experimental Psychology: Human Perception and Performance, 10,* 429–448.

Pashler, H. (1987). Detecting conjunctions of color and form: Reassessing the serial search hypothesis. *Perception & Psychophysics, 41,* 191–201.

Pasnak, R., Tyer, Z. A., & Allen, J. A. (1985). Effect of distance instructions on size judgements. *American Journal of Psychology, 98,* 297–304.

Pastore, R. E., & Li, X. F. (1990). Categorical perception of nonspeech chirps and bleats. *Perception & Psychophysics, 48,* 151–156.

Pastore, R. E., Schmeckler, M. A., Rosenblum, L., & Szczesiul, R. (1983). Duplex perception with musical stimuli. *Perception & Psychophysics, 33,* 469–474.

Patterson, R. D. (1969). Noise masking of a change in residue pitch. *Journal of the Acoustical Society of America, 45,* 1520–1524.

Paulus, K., & Haas, E. M. (1980). The influence of solvent viscosity on the threshold values of primary tastes. *Chemical Senses, 5,* 23–32.

Paulus, K., & Reisch, A. M. (1980). The influence of

temperature on the threshold values of primary tastes. *Chemical Senses, 5,* 11–21.

Pearson, D. A., & Lane, D. M. (1991a). Auditory attention switching: A developmental study. *Journal of Experimental Child Psychology, 51,* 320–334.

Pearson, D. A., & Lane, D. M. (1991b). Visual attention movements: A developmental study. *Child Development, 61,* 1779–1795.

Peeples, D. R., & Teller, D. Y. (1978). White-adapted photopic spectral sensitivity in human infants. *Vision Research, 18,* 39–53.

Peichl, L., & Wassle, H. (1979). Size, scatter and coverage of ganglion-cell receptive-field centers in the cat retina. *Journal of Physiology (London), 291,* 117.

Pelosi, P., & Pisanelli, A. M. (1981). Specific anosmia to 1,8-cineole: The camphor primary odor. *Chemical Senses, 6,* 87–93.

Pelosi, P., & Tirindelli, R. (1989). Structure/activity studies and characterization of an odorant-binding protein. In J. G. Brand, J. H. Teeter, R. H. Cagan, & M. R. Kare (Eds.), *Chemical senses. Vol. 1: Receptor events and transduction in taste and olfaction* (pp. 207–226). New York: Marcel Dekker, Inc.

Penfield, W., & Rasmussen, T. (1950). *The cerebral cortex of man.* New York: Macmillan.

Pentland, A. P. (1986). Perceptual organization and the representation of natural form. *Artificial Intelligence, 28,* 293–331.

Perkell, J. S., & Klatt, D. H. (Eds.), (1986). *Invariance and variability in speech processes.* Hillsdale, NJ: Erlbaum.

Perl, E. R. (1984). Characterization of nociceptors and their activation of neurons in the superficial dorsal horn: First steps for the sensation of pain. In L. Kruger & J. C. Liebeskind (Eds.), *Neural mechanisms of pain* (pp. 23–52). New York: Raven Press.

Perrett, D. I., & Mistlin, A. M. (1987). Visual neurones responsive to faces. *Trends in Neuroscience, 10,* 358–364.

Perrot, D. R., & Saberi, K. (1990). Minimum audible angle thresholds for sources varying in both elevation and azimuth. *Journal of the Acoustical Society of America, 87,* 1728–1731.

Perry, V. H., & Silveira, L. C. (1988). Functional lamination in the ganglion cell layer of the macaque's retina. *Neuroscience, 12,* 1101–1123.

Petersen, A. C., & Crockett, L. (1985, August). Factors influencing sex differences in spatial ability during adolescence. In S. L. Willis (Chair), *Sex differences in spatial ability across the lifespan.* Symposium conducted at the Ninety-third Annual Convention of the American Psychological Association, Los Angeles, CA.

Petersik, J. T. (1989). The two-process distinction in apparent motion. *Psychological Bulletin, 106,* 107–127.

Peterson, A. C. (1976). Physical androgyny and cognitive functioning in adolescence. *Developmental Psychology, 12,* 524–533.

Petitto, L. A., & Marentette, P. F. (1991). Babbling in the manual mode: Evidence for the ontogeny of language. *Science, 251,* 1493–1496.

Petrig, B., Julesz, B., Kropfl, W., Baumgartner, G., & Anliker, M. (1981). Development of stereopsis and cortical binocularity in human infants: Electrophysiological evidence. *Science, 213,* 1402–2405.

Petry, S., & Meyer, G. E. (1987). *The perception of illusory contours.* New York: Springer-Verlag.

Pettigrew, J. (1978). The paradox of the critical period for striate cortex. In C. W. Cotman (Ed.), *Neuronal plasticity* (pp. 311–330). New York: Raven Press.

Pevsner, J., Sklar, P. B., Hwang, P. M., & Snyder, S. H. (1989). Odorant binding protein: Sequence analysis and localization suggest an odorant transport function. In J. G. Brand, J. H. Teeter, R. H. Cagan, & M. R. Kare (Eds.), *Chemical senses. Vol. 1: Receptor events and transduction in taste and olfaction (pp. 227–242)* New York: Marcel Dekker, Inc.

Pfaff, D. (1968). Effects of temperature and time of day on judgment. *Journal of Experimental Psychology, 76,* 419–422.

Pfaffman, C. (1955). Gustatory nerve impulses in rat, cat, and rabbit. *Journal of Neurophysiology, 18,* 429–440.

Pfaffman, C. (1974). Specificity of the sweet receptors of the squirrel monkey. *Chemical Senses and Flavor, 1,* 61–67.

Pfaffman, C., Bartoshuk, L., & McBurney, D. H. (1971). Taste psychophysics. *Handbook of Sensory Physiology, 1,* 75–101.

Pfaffman, C., Frank, M., & Norgren, R. (1979). Neural mechanisms and behavioral aspects of taste. *Annual Review of Psychology, 30,* 283–325.

Pfeiffer, R. R. (1966). Classification of response patterns of spike discharges for units in the cochlear nucleus: Tone-burst stimulation. *Experimental Brain Research, 1,* 220–235.

Phillips, C. G., Zeki, S., & Barlow, H. B. (1984). Localization of function in the cerebral cortex. *Brain, 107,* 328–360.

Phillips, D. P., & Brugge, J. F. (1985). Progress in neurophysiology of sound localization. *Annual Review of Psychology, 36,* 245–274.

Phillipson, O. T., & Harris, J. P. (1984). Effects of cloropromazine and promazine on the perception of some multi-stable visual figures. *Quarterly Journal of Experimental Psychology, 36A,* 291–308.

Phillipson, O. T., & Harris, J. P. (1985). Perceptual changes in schizophrenia: A questionnaire survey. *Psychological Medicine, 15,* 859–866.

Piaget, J. (1969). *The mechanisms of perception.* (G. N. Seagrine, Trans.). New York: Oxford University Press.

Pick, H. L., Jr. (1987). Information and the effects of early perceptual experience. In N. Eisenberg (Ed.), *Contemporary topics in developmental psychology* (pp. 59–76). New York: Wiley.

Pick, H. L., Jr., & Hay, J. C. (1965). A passive test of the Held reafference hypothesis. *Perceptual and Motor Skills, 20,* 1070–1072.

Pick, H. L., Jr., & Pick, A. D. (1970). Sensory and perceptual development. In P. H. Mussen (Ed.), *Carmichael's manual of child development* (pp. 773–848). New York: Wiley.

Pickles, J. O. (1988). *An introduction to the physiology of hearing* (2nd ed.). San Diego: Academic Press.

Pickles, J. O., Comis, S. D., & Osborne, M. P. (1984). Cross-links between stereocilia in the guinea pig organ of Corti, and their possible relation to sensory transduction. *Hearing Research, 15,* 103–112.

Pierce, J. R. (1983). *The science of musical sound.* New York: Scientific American Books.

Piggins, D. J., Kingham, J. R., & Holmes, S. M. (1972). Colour, colour saturation and pattern induced by intermittent illumination: An initial study. *British Journal of Physiological Optics, 27,* 120–125.

Pinel, J. P. J. (1990). *Biopsychology.* Boston: Allyn & Bacon.

Pinkers, A., & Marre, M. (1983). Basic phenomena in acquired colour vision deficiency. *Documenta Ophthalmologica, 55,* 251–271.

Pirozzolo, F. J. (1978). *The neuropsychology of developmental reading disorders.* New York: Praeger.

Pisoni, D. B. (1973). Auditory and phonetic codes in the discrimination of consonants and vowels. *Perception & Psychophysics, 13,* 253–260.

Pisoni, D. B., & Luce, P. A. (1986). Speech perception: Research, theory, and the principal issues. In E. C. Schwab & H. C. Nusbaum (Eds.), *Pattern recognition by humans and machines: Vol. 1. Speech perception* (pp. 1–50). Orlando: Academic Press.

Pisoni, D. B., Nusbaum, H. C., Luce, P. A., & Slowiaczek, L.M. (1985). Speech perception, word recognition and the structure of the lexicon. *Speech Communication, 4,* 75–95.

Plateau, M. H. (1872). Sur la mesure des sensations physiques, et sur la loi qui lie l'intensité de la cause excitante. *Bulletin de l'Academie Royale de Belgique, 33,* 376–388.

Plude, D. J. (1990). Aging, feature integration, and visual attention. In J. T. Enns (Ed.), *The development of attention: Research and theory* (pp. 467–487). Amsterdam: Elsevier.

Plude, D. J., & Hoyer, W. J. (1986). Age and the selectivity of visual information processing. *Psychology and Aging, 1,* 4–10.

Podgorny, P., & Shepard, R. N. (1983). Distribution of visual attention over space. *Journal of Experimental Psychology: Human Perception and Performance, 9,* 380–393.

Poggio, G. F., & Fischer, B. (1977). Binocular interaction and depth sensitivity in striate cortical neurons of behaving rhesus monkeys. *Journal of Neurophysiology, 40,* 1392–1405.

Poggio, G. F., & Mountcastle, V. B. (1960). A study of the functional contributions of the lemniscal and spinothalamic systems to somatic sensibility: Central nervous mechanisms in pain. *Bulletin of the Johns Hopkins Hospital, 106,* 266–316.

Poggio, G. F., & Poggio, T. (1984). The analysis of stereopsis. *Annual Review of Neuroscience, 7,* 379–412.

Poggio, G. F., & Talbot, W. H. (1981). Mechanisms of static and dynamic stereopsis in foveal cortex of rhesus monkey. *Journal of Physiology, 315,* 469–492.

Pohl, W. (1973). Dissociation of spatial discrimination deficits following frontal and parietal lesions in monkeys. *Journal of Comparative Physiology and Psychology, 82,* 227–239.

Pokorny, J., & Smith, V. C. (1986). Eye disease and color defects. *Vision Research, 26,* 1573–1584.

Pola, J., & Wyatt, H. J. (1989). The perception of target motion during smooth pursuit eye movements in the open-loop condition: Characteristics of retinal and extraretinal signals. *Vision Research, 29,* 471–483.

Pollack, I. (1952). The information of elementary auditory displays. *Journal of the Acoustical Society of America, 24,* 745–749.

Pollack, I. (1953). The information of elementary auditory displays: II. *Journal of the Acoustical Society of America, 25,* 765–769.

Pollack, I. (1975). Auditory informational masking. *Journal of the Acoustical Society of America, 57,* S5.

Pollack, I. (1978). Decoupling of auditory pitch and stimulus frequency: The Shepard demonstration revisited. *Journal of the Acoustical Society of America, 63,* 202–206.

Pollack, I., & Pickett, J. M. (1964). Intelligibility of excerpts from fluent speech: Auditory vs. structural context. *Journal of Verbal Learning and Verbal Behavior, 3,* 79–84.

Pollack, R. H., & Silvar, S. D. (1967). Magnitude of the Mueller-Lyer illusion in children as a function of pigmentation of fundus oculi. *Psychonomic Science, 8,* 83–84.

Pollen, D. A., Lee, J. R., & Taylor, J. H. (1971). How does the visual cortex begin the reconstruction of the visual world? *Science, 173,* 74–77.

Poltrock, S. E., Lansman, M., & Hunt, E. (1982). Automatic and controlled attention processes in auditory target detection. *Journal of Experimental Psychology: Human Perception and Performance, 8,* 37–45.

Pomerantz, J. R. (1983). Global and local precedence: Selective attention in form and motion perception.

Journal of Experimental Psychology: General, 112, 511–535.

Pomerantz, J. R. (1986). Visual form perception: An overview. In E. C. Schwab & H. C. Nusbaum (Eds.), *Pattern Recognition by Humans and Machines: Vol. 2. Visual Perception* (pp. 1–30). Orlando: Academic Press.

Pomerantz, J. R., Goldberg, D., Golder, P., & Tetewsky, S. (1981). Subjective contours can facilitate performance in a reaction-time task. *Perception & Psychophysics, 29,* 605–611.

Pomerantz, J. R., Sager, L. C., & Stoever, R. J. (1977). Perception of wholes and of their component parts: Some configural superiority effects. *Journal of Experimental Psychology: Human Perception and Performance, 1,* 422–435.

Pons, T. P., Garraghty, P. E., Friedman, D. P., & Mishkin, M. (1987). Physiological evidence for serial processing in somatosensory cortex. *Science, 237,* 417–420.

Pons, T. P., Garraghty, P. E., Ommaya, A. K., Kaas, J. H., Taub, E., & Mishkin, M. (1991). Massive cortical reorganization after sensory deafferentation in adult macaques. *Science, 252,* 1857–1860.

Poppel, E. (1978). Time perception. In R. Held, H. W. Leibowitz, & H. L. Teuber (Eds.), *Handbook of sensory physiology: Vol. VIII. Perception* (pp. 713–729). New York: Springer-Verlag.

Popper, R., Parker, S., & Galanter, E. (1986). Dual loudness scales in individual subjects. *Journal of Experimental Psychology: Human Perception and Performance, 12,* 61–69.

Porac, C. (1989). Is visual illusion decrement based on selective adaptation? *Perception & Psychophysics, 46,* 279–283.

Porac, C., & Coren, S. (1976). The dominant eye. *Psychological Bulletin, 83,* 880–897.

Porac, C., & Coren, S. (1981). Life-span age trends in the perception of the Mueller-Lyer: An additional evidence for the existence of two illusions. *Canadian Journal of Psychology, 35,* 58–62.

Porac, C., & Coren, S. (1985). Transfer of illusion decrement: The effects of global versus local figural variations. *Perception & Psychophysics, 37,* 515–522.

Porac, C., & Coren, S. (1986). Sighting dominance and egocentric localization. *Vision Research, 26,* 1709–1713.

Porter, R. H., Balogh, R. D., Cernoch, J. M., & Franchi, C. (1986). Recognition of kin through characteristic body odors. *Chemical Senses, 11,* 389–395.

Porter, R. H., & Moore, J. D. (1981). Human kin recognition by olfactory cues. *Physiology & Behavior, 27,* 493–495.

Posner, M. I. (1978). *Chronometric exploration of mind.* Hillsdale, NJ: Erlbaum.

Posner, M. I. (1980). Orienting of attention. *Quarterly Journal of Experimental Psychology, 32,* 3–25.

Posner, M. I. (1988). Structures and functions of selective attention. In T. Boll & B. Bryant (Eds.), *Master Lectures in Clinical Neuropsychology* (pp. 173–202). Washington, DC: American Psychological Association.

Posner, M. I., & Cohen, Y. (1984). Components of visual attention. In H. Bouma & D. G. Bouhuis (Eds.), *Attention and performance X.* Hillsdale, NJ: Erlbaum.

Posner, M. I., Inhoff, A., Friedrich, F. J., & Cohen, A. (1987). Isolating attentional systems: A cognitive–anatomical analysis. *Psychobiology, 15,* 107–121.

Posner, M. I., & Petersen, S. E. (1990). The attention system of the human brain. *Annual Review of Neuroscience, 13,* 25–42.

Posner, M. I., Rafal, R. D., Choate, L. S., & Vaughan, J. (1985). Inhibition of return: Neural basis and function. *Cognitive Neuropsychology, 2,* 211–228.

Post, B., & Leibowitz, H. W. (1985). A revised analysis of the role of efference in motion perception. *Perception, 14,* 631–643.

Postman, L., & Egan, J. P. (1949). *Experimental psychology.* New York: Harper.

Poulton, E. C. (1989). *Bias in quantifying judgments.* Hillsdale, NJ: Erlbaum.

Powers, M. K., Schneck, M., & Teller, D. Y. (1981). Spectral sensitivity of human infants at absolute visual threshold. *Vision Research, 21,* 1005–1016.

Poynter, W. D., & Holma, D. (1985). Duration judgment and the experience of change. *Perception & Psychophysics, 33,* 548–560.

Predebon, J. (1990). Illusion decrement and transfer of illusion decrement in obtuse- and acute-angle variants of the Poggendorff illusion. *Perception & Psychophysics, 48,* 467–476.

Preti, G., Cutler, W. B., Garcia, C. R., Huggins, G. R., & Lawley, H. J. (1986). Human axillary secretions influence women's menstrual cycles: The role of donor extract of females. *Hormones and Behavior, 20,* 474–482.

Price, J. L. (1987). The central and accessory olfactory systems. In T. E. Finger & W. L. Silver (Eds.), *Neurobiology of taste and smell* (pp. 179–204). New York: Wiley.

Prinzmetal, W. (1981). Principles of feature integration in visual perception. *Perception & Psychophysics, 30,* 330–340.

Prinzmetal, W., & Millis-Wright, M. (1984). Cognitive and linguistic factors affect visual feature integration. *Cognitive Psychology, 16,* 305–340.

Prinzmetal, W., Presti, D. E., & Posner, M. I. (1986). Does attention affect visual feature integration? *Journal of Experimental Psychology: Human Perception and Performance, 12,* 361–369.

Pritchard, R. M., Heron, W., & Hebb, D. O. (1960). Visual perception approached by the method of stabilized images. *Canadian Journal of Psychology, 14,* 67–77.

Puckett, J. de W., & Steinman, R. M. (1969). Tracking eye movements with and without saccadic correction. *Vision Research, 9,* 295–303.

Puel, J. L., Bobbin, R. P., & Fallon, M. (1988). An ipsilateral cochlear efferent loop protects the cochlea during intense sound exposure. *Hearing Research, 37,* 65–70.

Purghé, F., & Coren, S. (1992). Subjective contours 1900–1990: Research trends and bibliography. *Perception & Psychophysics, 51,* 291–304.

Quinn, P. C., Wooten, B. R., & Ludman, E. J. (1985). Achromatic color categories. *Perception & Psychophysics, 37,* 198–204.

Rabbitt, P. M. A. (1965). An age decrement in the ability to ignore irrelevant information. *Journal of Gerontology, 20,* 233–238.

Rabbit, P. M. A. (1977). Changes in problem solving ability in old age. In J. Birren & K. Schaie (Eds.), *Handbook of the psychology of aging.* New York: Van Nostrand Reinhold.

Rabbitt, P. M. A. (1984). The control of attention in visual search. In R. Parasuraman & D. R. Davies (Eds.), *Varieties of attention* (pp. 273–291). Orlando: Academic Press.

Rabbitt, R. D. (1990). A hierarchy of examples illustrating the acoustic coupling of the eardrum. *Journal of the Acoustical Society of America, 87,* 2566–2582.

Rabin, M. D. (1988). Experience facilitates olfactory quality discrimination. *Perception & Psychophysics, 44,* 532–540.

Rabin, M. D., & Cain, W. S. (1984). Odor recognition: Familiarity, identifiability, and encoding consistency. *Journal of Experimental Psychology: Learning, Memory, and Cognition, 10,* 316–325.

Rabin, M. D., & Cain, W. S. (1986). Determinants of measured olfactory sensitivity. *Perception & Psychophysics, 39,* 281–286.

Rabinowicz, T. (1979). The differential maturation of the human visual cortex. In F. Faulkner & J. M. Tanner (Eds.), *Human Growth: Vol. 3. Neurobiology and Nutrition* (pp. 97–123). New York: Plenum Press.

Rabinowitz, W. M., Houtsma, A. J. M., Durlach, N. I., & Delhorne, L. A. (1987). Multidimensional tactile displays: Identification of vibratory intensity, frequency, and contactor area. *Journal of the Acoustical Society of America, 82,* 1243–1252.

Raftenberg, M. N. (1990). Flow of endolymph in the inner spiral sulcus and the subtectorial space. *Journal of the Acoustical Society of America, 87,* 2606–2620.

Rakerd, B., & Hartmann, W. M. (1985). Localization of sound in rooms: II. The effects of a single reflecting surface. *Journal of the Acoustical Society of America,* 78, 524–533.

Ramachandran, V. S. (1986). Capture of stereopsis and apparent motion by illusory contours. *Perception & Psychophysics, 39,* 361–373.

Ramachandran, V. S. (1988). Perceiving shape from shading. *Scientific American, 259,* 76–83.

Ramachandran, V. S., & Anstis, S. M. (1986). The perception of apparent motion. *Scientific American, 254,* 80–87.

Ramachandran, V. S., & Gregory, R. L. (1978). Does colour provide an input to human motion perception? *Nature, 275,* 55–56.

Rammsayer, T., & Lustnauer, S. (1989). Sex differences in time perception. *Perceptual and Motor Skills, 68,* 195–198.

Rand, T. C. (1974). Dichotic release from masking for speech. *Journal of the Acoustical Society of America, 55,* 678–680.

Randsom-Hogg, A., & Spillman, L. (1980). Perceptive field size in fovea of the light and dark adapted. *Vision Research, 20,* 221–228.

Ratliff, F. (1965). *Mach bands: Quantitative studies on neural networks in the retina.* San Francisco: Holden-Day.

Rayleigh, Lord. (1907). On our perception of sound direction. *Philosophical Magazine, 13* (6), 214–232.

Raymond, J. E., Shapiro, K. L., & Rose, D. J. (1984). Optokinetic backgrounds affect perceived velocity during ocular tracking. *Perception & Psychophysics, 36,* 221–224.

Rayner, K. (1978). Eye movements in reading and information processing. *Psychological Bulletin, 85,* 618–660.

Rea, M. M., & Sweeney, J. A. (1989). Changes in eye tracking during clinical stabilization in schizophrenia. *Psychiatry Research, 28,* 31–39.

Reason, J. (1984). Lapses of attention in everyday life. In R. Parasuraman & D. R. Davies (Eds.), *Varieties of attention* (pp. 515–549). Orlando: Academic Press.

Reason, J., & Brand, J. (1975). *Motion sickness.* London: Academic Press.

Redding, G. M., Clark, S. E., & Wallace, B. (1985). Attention and prism adaptation. *Cognitive Psychology, 17,* 1–25.

Redding, G. M., & Wallace, B. (1976). Components of displacement adaptation in acquisition and decay as a function of hard and hall exposure. *Perception & Psychophysics, 20,* 453–459.

Redding, G. M., & Wallace, B. (1990). Effects on prism adaptation of duration and timing of visual feedback during pointing. *Journal of Motor Behavior, 22,* 209–224.

Reddy, D. R. (1976). Speech recognition by machine: A review. *Proceedings of the IEEE, 64,* 501–531.

Reed, C. F. (1989). Terrestrial and celestial passage. In M.

Hershenson (Ed.), The moon illusion (pp. 267–280). Hillsdale, NJ: Erlbaum.

Refinetti, R. (1989). Magnitude estimation of warmth: Intra- and intersubject variability. *Perception & Psychophysics, 46,* 81–84.

Regal, D. M., Ashmead, D. H., & Salapatek, P. (1983). The coordination of eye and head movements during early infancy: A selective review. *Behavioral and Brain Research, 10,* 125–132.

Regan, D. M., & Beverley, K. (1973). Disparity detectors in human depth perception: Evidence for directional selectivity. *Science, 181,* 877–879.

Regan, D. M., & Beverley, K. (1979). The visual perception of motion in depth. *Scientific American, 241,* 136–151.

Regan, D. M., & Beverly, K. (1982). How do we avoid confounding the direction we are looking and the direction we are moving? *Science, 215,* 194–196.

Regan, D. M., Frisby, J. P., Poggio, G. F., Schor, C. M., & Tyler, C. W. (1990). The perception of stereodepth and stereomotion: Cortical mechanisms. In L. Spillman & J. S. Werner (Eds.), *Visual perception* (pp. 317–347). New York: Academic Press.

Rehn, T. (1978). Perceived odor intensity as a function of airflow through the nose. *Sensory Processes, 2,* 198–205.

Reichardt, W. (1961). Autocorrelation: A principle for the evaluation of sensory information by the central nervous system. In W. A. Rosenblith (Ed.), *Principles of sensory communication.* New York: Wiley.

Reisberg, D., & O'Shaughnessy, M. (1984). Diverting subjects' concentration slows figural reversals. *Perception, 13,* 461–468.

Remez, R. E., Rubin, P. E., Pisoni, D. B., & Carrell, T. D. (1981). Speech perception without traditional speech cues. *Science, 212,* 947–950.

Remington, R. (1980). Attention and saccadic eye movements. *Journal of Experimental Psychology: Human Perception and Performance, 6,* 726–744.

Repp, B. H. (1987). The sound of two hands clapping: An exploratory study. *Journal of the Acoustical Society of America, 81,* 1100–1109.

Reuter, G., & Zenner, H. P. (1990). Active radial and transverse motile responses of outer hair cells in the organ of Corti. *Hearing Research, 43,* 219–230.

Reynolds, D. C. (1979). A visual profile of the alcoholic driver. *American Journal of Optometry and Physiological Optics, 56,* 241–251.

Reynolds, R. I. (1985). The role of object-hypotheses in the organization of fragmented figures. *Perception, 14,* 49–52.

Rhee, K., Kim, D., & Kim, Y. (1965). The effects of smoking on night vision. *14th Pacific Medical Conference (Professional papers).*

Rhodes, G. (1987). Auditory attention and the representation of spatial information. *Perception & Psychophysics, 42,* 1–14.

Ricci, C., & Blundo, C. (1990). Perception of ambiguous figures after focal brain lesions. *Neuropsychologia, 28,* 1163–1173.

Rice, C. G., Ayley, J. B., Bartlett, B., Bedford, W., Gregory, W., & Hallum, G. (1968). A pilot study on the effects of pop group music on hearing. Cited in K. D. Kryter (1970). *The effects of noise on man* (p. 203). New York: Academic Press.

Richards, W. (1977). Lessons in constancy from neurophysiology. In W. W. Epstein (Ed.), *Stability and constancy in visual perception: Mechanisms and processes* (pp. 421–436). New York: Wiley.

Riesen, A., & Zilbert, D. (1975). Behavioral consequences of variations in early sensory environments. In A. Riesen (Ed.), *The developmental neuropsychology of sensory deprivation* (pp. 211–252). New York: Academic Press.

Rieser, J., Yonas, A., & Wikner, K. (1976). Radial localization of odors by human newborns. *Child Development, 47,* 856–859.

Riesz, R. R. (1928). Differential intensity sensitivity of the ear for pure tones. *Physical Review, 31,* 867–875.

Riggs, L. A., Ratliff, F., Cornsweet, J. C., & Cornsweet, T. N. (1953). The disappearance of steadily fixated visual test objects. *Journal of the Optical Society of America, 43,* 495–501.

Rijnsdorp, A., Daan, S., & Dijkstra, C. (1981). Hunting in the kestrel (Falco tinnunculus) and the adaptive significance of daily habits. *Oecologia, 50,* 391–406.

Rizzo, M., & Robin, D. (1990). Simultanagnosia: A defect of sustained attention yields insights on visual information processing. *Neurology, 40,* 447–455.

Roberts, J. (1964). *Binocular visual acuity of adults.* Washington, DC: U. S. Department of Health, Education and Welfare.

Roberts, M., & Summerfield, A. Q. (1981). Audio-visual adaptation in speech perception. *Perception & Psychophysics, 30,* 309–314.

Robertson, P. W. (1967). Color words and colour vision. *Biology and Human Affairs, 33,* 28–33.

Robinson, D. W., & Dadson, R. S. (1956). A redetermination of the equal-loudness relations for pure tones. *British Journal of Applied Physics, 7,* 166–181.

Robinson, L. R., & Green, D. M. (1988). Detection of changes in spectral shape: Uniform vs. non-uniform background spectra. *Hearing Research, 32,* 157–166.

Robson, J. G. (1980). Neural images: The physiological basis of spatial vision. In C. S. Harris (Ed.), *Visual coding and adaptability* (pp. 177–214). Hillsdale, NJ: Erlbaum.

Rock, I. (1973). *Orientation and form.* New York: Academic Press.

Rock, I. (1975). *An introduction to perception.* New York: Macmillan.

Rock, I. (1983). *The logic of perception.* Cambridge, MA: MIT Press.

Rock, I., & Guttman, D. (1981). The effect of inattention on form perception. *Journal of Experimental Psychology: Human Perception and Performance, 7,* 275–285.

Rock, I., & Halper, F. (1969). Form perception without a retinal image. *American Journal of Psychology, 82,* 425–440.

Rockland, K. S., & Pandya, P. N. (1981). Cortical connections of the occipital lobe in the rhesus monkey: Interconnections between areas 17, 18, 19 and the superior temporal sulcus. *Brain Research, 212,* 249–270.

Rodieck, R. W. (1965). Quantitative analysis of the cat retinal ganglion cell response to visual stimuli. *Vision Research, 5,* 583–601.

Rodieck, R. W. (1973). *The vertebrate retina: Principles of structure and function.* San Francisco: Freeman.

Roelofs, C. O. (1935). Optische Lokalisation, *Archiv fuer Augenheilkunde, 109,* 395–415.

Rogel, M. J. (1978). A critical evaluation of the possibility of higher primate reproductive and sexual pheromones. *Psychological Bulletin, 85,* 810–830.

Rogers, B. J., & Collett, T. S. (1989). The appearance of surfaces specified by motion parallax and binocular disparity. *Quarterly Journal of Experimental Psychology: Human Experimental Psychology, 41,* 697–717.

Rogers, B. J., & Graham, M. (1979). Motion parallax as an independent cue for depth perception. *Perception, 8,* 125–134.

Rohrbaugh, J. W. (1984). The orienting reflex: Performance and central nervous system manifestations. In R. Parasuraman & D. R. Davies (Eds.), *Varieties of attention.* (pp. 323–373). Orlando: Academic Press.

Rollman, G. B., & Harris, G. (1987). The detectability, discriminability, and perceived magnitude of painful electric shock. *Perception & Psychophysics, 42,* 257–268.

Romani, G. L., Williamson, S. J., & Kaufman, L. (1982). Tonotopic organization of the human auditory cortex. *Science, 216,* 1339–1340.

Romano, P. E., Romano, J. A., & Puklin, J. E. (1975). Stereoactivity development in children with normal single vision. *American Journal of Ophthalmology, 79,* 966–971.

Root, W. (1974, December 22). Of wine and noses. *New York Times Magazine,* pp. 14 et seq.

Roscoe, S. N. (1989). The zoom-lens hypothesis. In M. Hershenson (Ed.), *The moon illusion* (pp. 31–58).

Hillsdale, NJ: Erlbaum.

Roscoe, S. N., & Couchman, D. H. (1987). Improving visual performance through volitional focus control. *Human Factors, 29,* 311–325.

Rose, J. E., Brugge, J. F., Anderson, D. J., & Hind, J. E. (1967). Phase-locked response to low frequency tones in single auditory nerve fibers of the squirrel monkey. *Journal of Neurophysiology, 30,* 769–793.

Rose, J. E., Galambos, R., & Hughes, J. (1959). Microelectrode studies of the cochlear nuclei of the cat. *Johns Hopkins Hospital Bulletin, 14,* 211–251.

Rose, J. E., Galambos, R., & Hughes, J. (1960). Organization of frequency sensitive neurons in the cochlear nuclear complex of the cat. In G. L. Rasmussen & W.F. Windle (Eds.), *Neural mechanisms of the auditory and vestibular systems* (pp. 116–136). Springfield, IL: Thomas.

Rosinski, R., & Farber, J. (1980). Compensation for viewing point in the perception of pictured space. In M. Hagen (Ed.), *Perception of Pictures: Vol. 1. Albert's window: The projective model of pictorial information.* New York: Academic Press.

Ross, H. (1975, June 19). Mist, murk and visual perception. *New Scientist,* pp. 658–660.

Ross, H. E., Brodie, E., & Benson, A. (1984). Mass discrimination during prolonged weightlessness. *Science, 225,* 219–221.

Ross, H. E., & Reschke, M. F. (1982). Mass estimation and discrimination during brief periods of zero gravity. *Perception & Psychophysics, 31,* 429–436.

Ross, N., & Schilder, P. (1934). Tachistoscopic experiments on the perception of the human figure. *Journal of General Psychology, 10,* 152–172.

Rothbart, M. K., Posner, M. I., & Boylan, A. (1990). Regulatory mechanisms in infant development. In J. T. Enns (Ed.), *The development of attention: Research and theory* (pp. 47–66). Amsterdam: Elsevier.

Rothblat, L., & Schwartz, M. (1978). Altered early environment: Effects on the brain and visual behavior. In R. Walk & H. Pick (Eds.), *Perception and Experience* (pp. 7–36). New York: Plenum Press.

Rouiller, E. M., Rodrigues-Dagaeff, C., Simm, G., De Ribaipierre, Y., Villa, A., & De Ribaupierre, F. (1989). Functional organization of the medial division of the medial geniculate body of the cat: Tonotopic organization, spatial distribution of response properties and cortical connections. *Hearing Research, 39,* 127–142.

Royster, L. H., Royster, J. D., & Thomas, W. G. (1980). Representative hearing levels by race and sex in North Carolina industry. *Journal of the Acoustical Society of America, 68,* 551–566.

Rozin, P. (1978). The use of characteristic flavorings in human culinary practice. In C. M. Apt (Ed.), *Flavor: Its chemical, behavioral, and commercial aspects* (pp. 101–127). Boulder, CO: Westview Press.

Rozin, P. (1982). "Taste-smell confusions" and the duality of the olfactory sense. *Perception & Psychophysics, 31,* 397–401.

Rozin, R., Ebert, L., & Schull, J. (1982). Some like it hot: A temporal analysis of hedonic responses to chili pepper. *Appetite, 3,* 13–22.

Rubin, E. (1915). *Synoplevede Figuren.* Copenhagen: Gyldendalske.

Rubin, E. (1921). *Visuell wahrgenommene Figuren.* Copenhagen: Glydendalske.

Ruble, D. N., & Nakamura, C. Y. (1972). Task orientation versus social orientation in young children and their attention to relevant social cues. *Child Development, 43,* 471–480.

Ruggieri, V., Cei, A., Ceridono, D., & Bergerone, C. (1980). Dimensional approach to the study of sighting dominance. *Perceptual and Motor Skills, 51,* 247–251.

Runeson, S., & Frykholm, G. (1983). Kinematic specifications of dynamics as an informational basis for person-and-action perception: Expectation, gender recognition, and deceptive intention. *Journal of Experimental Psychology: General, 112,* 585–615.

Rusak, B., & Groos, G. (1982). Suprachiasmatic stimulation phase shifts rodent circadian rhythms. *Science, 215,* 1407–1409.

Rusak, B., & Zucker, I. (1979). Neural regulation of circadian rhythms. *Physiological Review, 59,* 449–526.

Rushton, W. A. H. (1962). Visual pigments in man. *Scientific American, 205,* 120–132.

Rushton, W. A. H. (1965). Cone pigment dynamics in the deuteranope. *Journal of Physiology (London), 176,* 38–45.

Russell, M. J. (1976). Human olfactory communication. *Nature (London), 260,* 520–522.

Russoff, A. C. (1979). Development of ganglion cells in the retina of the cat. In R. D. Freeman (Ed.), *Developmental neurobiology of vision* (pp. 19–30). New York: Plenum Press.

Russoff, A. C., & Dubin, M. W. (1977). Development of receptive-field properties of retinal ganglion cells in kittens. *Journal of Neurophysiology, 40,* 1188–1198.

Saberi, K. & Perrott, D. R. (1990). Minimum audible movement angles as a function of sound source trajectory. *Journal of the Acoustical Society of America, 88,* 2639–2644.

Sachs, M. B., & Kiang, N. Y. S. (1968). Two-tone inhibition in auditory nerve fibers. *Journal of the Acoustical Society of America, 43,* 1120–1128.

Sacks, O. (1987). *The man who mistook his wife for a hat.* New York: Summit.

Salapatek, P. (1975). Pattern perception in early infancy. In L. B. Cohen & P. Salapatek (Eds.), *Infant perception: From sensation to cognition: Vol. 1* (pp. 133–248). New York: Academic Press.

Salapatek, P., & Kessen, W. (1973). Prolonged investigation of a plane geometric triangle by the human newborn. *Journal of Experimental Child Psychology, 15,* 22–29.

Salthouse, T. A. (1985). A theory of cognitive aging. Amsterdam: North-Holland.

Salthouse, T. A., & Kail, R. (1983). Memory development throughout the life span: The role of processing rate. In P. B. Baltes & O. G. Brim (Eds.), *Life-span development and behavior: Vol. 5* (pp. 90–116). New York: Academic Press.

Samuel, A. G. (1981). Phonemic restoration: Insights from a new methodology. *Journal of Experimental Psychology: General, 110,* 474–494.

Samuel, A. G. (1986). Red herring detectors and speech perception: In defense of selective adaptation. *Cognitive Psychology, 18,* 452–499.

Samuel, A. G. (1987). Lexical uniqueness effects on phonemic restoration. *Journal of Experimental Psychology: General, 119,* 123–144.

Sanders, A. (1970). Some aspects of the selective process in the functional field of view. *Ergonomics, 13,* 101–107.

Sanders, B., Soares, M. P., & D'Aquila, J. M. (1982). Sex difference on one test of spatial visualization: A nontrivial difference. *Child Development, 53,* 1106–1110.

Sanders, G., & Ross-Field, L. (1986). Sexual orientation and visuospatial ability. *Brain and Cognition, 5,* 280–290.

Sanocki, T. (1987). Visual knowledge underlying letter perception: Font-specific, schematic tuning. *Journal of Experimental Psychology: Human Perception and Performance, 13,* 267–278.

Sapir, E. (1939). *Language.* New York: Harcourt, Brace & World.

Sawusch, J. R. (1986). Auditory and phonetic coding of speech. In E. C. Schwab & H. C. Nusbaum (Eds.), *Pattern recognition by humans and machines: Vol. 1. Speech perception* (pp. 51–88). Orlando: Academic Press.

Schab, F. R. (1991). Odor memory: Taking stock. *Psychological Bulletin, 109,* 242–251.

Schaie, K. W., & Geiwitz, J. (1982). *Adult development and aging.* Boston: Little, Brown.

Scharf, B. (1964). Partial masking. *Acustica, 14,* 16–23.

Scharf, B. (1975). Audition. In B. Scharf (Ed.), *Experimental sensory psychology* (pp. 112–149). Glenview, IL: Scott, Foresman.

Scharf, B. (1978). Loudness. In E. C. Carterette & M. P. Friedman (Eds.), *Handbook of perception: Vol. IV. Hearing.* New York: Academic Press.

Scharf, B. (1989). Spectral specificity in auditory detection: The effect of listening on hearing. *Journal of the Acoustical Society of Japan, 10,* 309–317.

Scharf, B., Quigley, S., Aoki, C., Peachey, N., & Reeves, A.

(1987). Focused auditory attention and frequency selectivity. *Perception & Psychophysics, 42,* 215–223.

Scharre, J. E., Cotter, S. A., Block, S. S., & Kelly, S. A. (1990). Normative contrast sensitivity data for young children. *Optometry and Vision Science, 67,* 826–832.

Schefrin, B. E., & Werner, J. S. (1990). Loci of spectral unique hues throughout the life span. *Journal of the Optical Society of America A, 7,* 305–311.

Schenkel, K. D. (1967). Die beidohrigen Mithorschoellen von Impulsen. *Acustica, 18,* 38–46.

Scher, D., Pionk, M., & Purcell, D. G. (1981). Visual sensitivity fluctuations during the menstrual cycle under dark and light adaptation. *Bulletin of the Psychonomic Society, 18,* 159–160.

Schiff, W., & Oldak, R. (1990). Accuracy of judging time to arrival: Effects of modality, trajectory, and gender. *Journal of Experimental Psychology: Human Perception and Performance, 16,* 303–316.

Schiffman, S. S. (1974). Physiochemical correlates of olfactory quality. *Science, 185,* 112–117.

Schiffman, S. S. (1977). Food recognition by the elderly. *Journal of Gerontology, 32,* 586–592.

Schiffman, S. S., & Dackis, C. (1975). Taste of nutrients: Amino acids, vitamins, and fatty acids. *Perception & Psychophysics, 17,* 140–146.

Schiffman, S. S., & Erikson, R. P. (1971). A theoretical review: A psychophysical model for gustatory quality. *Physiology and Behavior, 1,* 617–633.

Schiffman, S. S., McElroy, A. E., & Erikson, R. F. (1980). The range of taste quality of sodium salts. *Physiology and Behavior, 24,* 217–224.

Schiffman, S. S., & Pasternak, M. (1979). Decreased discrimination of food odors in the elderly. *Journal of Gerontology, 84,* 73–79.

Schiffman, S. S., Reilly, D. A., & Clark, T. B., III. (1979). Qualitative differences among sweeteners. *Physiology and Behavior, 23,* 1–9.

Schiller, P. H. (1986). The central visual system. *Vision Research, 26,* 1351–1386.

Schiller, P. H., & Logothetis, N. K. (1990). The color-opponent and broad-band channels of the primate visual system. *Trends in Neurosciences, 13,* 392–398.

Schindler, R. A., & Merzenich, M. M. (Eds.). (1985). *Cochlear implants.* New York: Raven Press.

Schlauch, R. S., & Hafter, E. R. (1991). Listening bandwidths and frequency uncertainty in pure-tone signal detection. *Journal of the Acoustical Society of America, 90,* 1332–1339.

Schleidt, M., Hold, B., & Attili, G. (1981). A cross-cultural study on the attitude towards personal odors. *Journal of Chemical Ecology, 7,* 19–31.

Schmiedt, R. A., Zwislocki, J. J., & Hamernik, R. P. (1980). Effects of hair cell lesions on responses of cochlear nerve fibers: I. Lesions, tuning curves, two-tone inhibition, and responses to trapezoidal-wave patterns. *Journal of Neurophysiology, 43,* 1367–1389.

Schnapf, J. L., & Baylor, D. A. (1987). How photoreceptor cells respond to light. *Scientific American, 256,* 40–47.

Schneider, B., & Parker, S. (1990). Does stimulus context affect loudness or only loudness judgments? *Perception & Psychophysics, 48,* 409–418.

Schneider, B. A., & Bissett, R. J. (1981). The dimensions of tonal experience: A nonmetric scaling approach. *Perception and Psychophysics, 30,* 39–48.

Schneider, D. (1969). Insect olfaction: Deciphering system for chemical messages. *Science, 163,* 1031–1037.

Schneider, G. E. (1969). Two visual systems. *Science, 163,* 895–902.

Schneider, R., Costiloe, J., Howard, R., & Wolf, S. (1958). Olfactory perception thresholds in hypogonadal women: Changes accompanying administration of androgen and estrogen. *Journal of Clinical Endocrinology, 18,* 379–390.

Schneider, S. L., Hughes, B., Epstein, W., & Bach-y-Rita, P. (1986). The detection of length and orientation changes in dynamic vibrotactile patterns. *Perception & Psychophysics, 40,* 290–300.

Schneider, W., Dumais, S. T., & Shiffrin, R. M. (1984). Automatic and control processing and attention. In R. Parasuraman & D. R. Davies (Eds.), *Varieties of attention* (pp. 1–27). Orlando: Academic Press.

Schneider, W., & Schiffrin, R. M. (1977). Controlled and automatic human information processing: I. Detection, search and attention. *Psychological Review, 84,* 1–66.

Schoenlein, R. W., Peteanu, L. A., Mathies, R. A., & Shank, C. V. (1991). The first step in vision: Femtosecond isomerization of rhodopsin. *Science, 254,* 412–415.

Schouten, M. E. H. (1980). The case against a speech mode of perception. *Acta Psychologica, 44,* 71–98.

Schubert, E. D. (1978). History of research on hearing. In E. C. Carterette & M. P. Friedman (Eds.), *Handbook of Perception: Vol. IV. Hearing* (pp. 41–80). New York: Academic Press.

Schull, J., Kaplan, H., & O'Brien, C. P. (1981). Naloxone can alter experimental pain and mood in humans. *Physiological Psychology, 9,* 245–250.

Schulman, P. H. (1979). Eye movements do not cause induced motion. *Perception & Psychophysics, 26,* 381–383.

Schulze, H. H. (1989). Categorical perception of rhythmic patterns. *Psychological Research, 51,* 10–15.

Schwartz, C. B. (1961). *Visual discrimination of camouflaged figures.* Unpublished doctoral dissertation, University of California at Berkeley.

Schwartz, S. H., & Loop, M. S. (1984). Effect of duration on detection by the chromatic and achromatic systems. *Perception & Psychophysics, 36,* 65–67.

Scialfa, C. T. (1990). Adult age differences in visual search: The role of non-attentional processes. In J. T. Enns (Ed.), *The development of attention: Research and theory* (pp. 509–526). Amsterdam: Elsevier.

Scott, T. R. (1987). Coding in the gustatory system. In T. E. Finger & W. L. Silver (Eds.), *Neurobiology of taste and smell* (pp. 355–378). New York: Wiley.

Scott, T. R. (1990). The effect of physiological need on taste. In E. Capaldi & L. T. Powley (Eds.), *Taste, experience, and feeding* (pp. 45–61). Washington, DC: American Psychological Association.

Scott, T. R., & Erickson, R. P. (1971). Synaptic processing of taste-quality information in the thalamus of the rat. *Journal of Neurophysiology, 34,* 868–884.

Scott, T. R., & Giza, B. K. (1990). Coding channels in the taste system of the rat. *Science, 249,* 1585–1587.

Sedgwick, H. (1980). The geometry of spatial layout in pictorial representation. In M. Hagen (Ed.), *Perception of pictures: Vol. I. Alberti's window: The projective model of pictorial information* (pp. 33–90). New York: Academic Press.

Segall, M. H., Campbell, D. T., & Herskovits, M. J. (1966). The influence of culture on visual perception. Indianapolis: Bobbs-Merrill.

Seggie, J., & Canny, C. (1989). Antidepressant medication reverses increased sensitivity to light in depression: Preliminary report. *Progress in Neuro-Psychopharmacology and Biological Psychiatry, 13,* 537–541.

Sekuler, A. B., & Palmer, S. E. (1992). Perception of partly occluded objects: A microgenetic analysis. *Journal of Experimental Psychology: General, 121,* 95–111.

Sekuler, R. (1975). Visual motion perception. In E. C. Carterette & M. P. Friedman (Eds.), *Handbook of perception: Vol. 5* (pp. 387–433). New York: Academic Press.

Sekuler, R., & Ball, K. (1986). Visual localization: Age and practice. *Journal of the Optical Society of America A, 3,* 864–867.

Sekuler, R., Ball, K., Tynan, P., & Machmer, J. (1982). Psychophysics of motion perception. In A. H. Wertheim, W. A. Wagenaar, & H. W. Leibowitz (Eds.), *Tutorials on motion perception* (pp. 81–100). New York: Plenum Press.

Sekuler, R., & Blake, R. (1985). *Perception*. New York: Knopf.

Sekuler, R., & Ganz, L. (1963). A new aftereffect of seen movement with a stabilized retinal image. *Science, 139,* 419–420.

Sekuler, R., & Hutman, L. P. (1980). Spatial vision and aging: I. Contrast sensitivity. *Journal of Gerontology, 35,* 692–699.

Selfridge, O. G. (1959). Pandemonium: A paradigm for learning. In D. V. Blake & A. M. Uttley (Eds.), *Proceedings of the Symposium on the Mechanisation of Thought Processes* (pp. 511–529). London: HM Stationery Office.

Sellick, P. M., Patuzzi, R., & Johnstone, B. M. (1982). Measurement of basilar membrane motion in the guinea pig using the Mössbauer technique. *Journal of the Acoustical Society of America, 72,* 131–141.

Semenza, C. (1988). Impairment in localization of body parts. *Cortex, 24,* 443–449.

Semple, M. N., & Kitzes, L. M. (1987). Binaural processing of sound pressure level in the inferior colliculus. *Journal of Neurophysiology, 57,* 1130–1147.

Senden, M. von. (1960). *Space and sight: The perception of space and shape in congenitally blind patients before and after operation.* London: Methuen.

Serafine, M. L., & Glassman, N. (1989). The cognitive reality of hierarchic structure in music. *Music Perception, 6,* 397–430.

Serpell, R. (1971). Discrimination of orientation by Zambian children. *Journal of Comparative Physiology, 75,* 312.

Shaffer, H. L. (1975). Multiple attention in continuous verbal tasks. In P. M. A. Rabbitt & S. Dornic (Eds.), *Attention and Performance V.* London: Academic Press.

Shaffer, L. H. (1985). Timing in action. In J. A. Michon & J. L. Jackson (Eds.), *Time, mind and behavior* (pp. 226–242). Berlin: Springer-Verlag.

Shallice, T., & Vickers, D. (1964). Theories and experiments on discrimination times. *Ergonomics, 7,* 37–49.

Shannon, C. E., & Weaver, W. (1949). *The mathematical theory of communication.* Urbana: University of Illinois Press.

Shannon, R. V., & Otto, S. R. (1990). Psychophysical measures from electrical stimulation of the human cochlear nucleus. *Hearing Research, 47,* 159–168.

Shapiro, K. L., & Egerman, B. (1984). Effects of arousal on human visual dominance. *Perception & Psychophysics, 35,* 547–552.

Shapiro, K. L., & Johnson, T. L. (1987). Effects of arousal on attention to central and peripheral visual stimuli. *Acta Psychologica, 66,* 157–172.

Shapiro, K. L., & Lim, A. (1989). The impact of anxiety on visual attention to central and peripheral events. *Behaviour Research & Therapy, 27,* 345–351.

Shapley, R. (1986). The importance of contrast for the activity of single neurons, the VEP and perception. *Vision Research, 26,* 45–61.

Shapley, R. (1990). Visual sensitivity and parallel retinocortical channels. *Annual Review of Psychology, 41,* 635–658.

Shapley, R., & Enroth-Cugell, C. (1984). Visual adaptation and retinal gain controls. *Progress in Retinal Research, 3,* 263–346.

Shapley, R., & Kaplan, E. (1989). Responses of magnocellular LGN neurons and M retinal ganglion cells to drifting heterochromatic gratings. *Investigative Ophthalmology and Visual Science, 30* (Suppl.), 323.

Shapley, R., & Reid, R. C. (1985). Contrast and assimilation in the perception of brightness. *Proceedings of the National Academy of Science, USA, 82,* 5983–5986.

Sharma, S., & Moskowitz, H. (1972). Effect of marijuana on the visual autokinetic phenomenon. *Perceptual and Motor Skills, 35,* 891.

Sharpe, L. T., & Nordby, K. (1989). Total color-blindness: An introduction. In R. F. Hess, L. T. Sharpe, & K. Nordby (Eds.), *Night vision: Basic, clinical and applied aspects.* Cambridge: Cambridge University Press.

Shea, S. L., Fox, R., Aslin, R. N., & Dumais, S. T. (1980). Assessment of stereopsis in human infants. *Investigative Ophthalmology, 19,* 1400–1404.

Shebilske, W. L. (1976). Extraretinal information in corrective saccades and inflow vs. outflow theories of visual direction constancy. *Vision Research, 16,* 621–628.

Shebilske, W. L. (1977). Visuomotor coordination in visual direction and position constancies. In W. Epstein (Ed.), *Stability and constancy in visual perception: Mechanisms and processes* (pp. 23–70). New York: Wiley.

Sheedy, J. E., Bailey, I. L., Buri, M., & Bass, E. (1986). Binocular vs. monocular task performance. *American Journal of Optometry and Physiological Optics, 63,* 839–846.

Sheingold, K. (1973). Developmental differences in the uptake and storage of visual information. *Journal of Experimental Child Psychology, 16,* 1–11.

Shepard, M., & Muller, H. J. (1989). Movement versus focusing of attention. *Perception & Psychophysics, 46,* 146–154.

Shepard, R. N. (1962). The analysis of proximities: Multidimensional scaling with an unknown distance function: I & II. *Psychometrika, 27,* 125–246.

Shepard, R. N. (1964). Circularity in judgments of relative pitch. *Journal of the Acoustical Society of America, 36,* 2346–2353.

Shepard, R. N. (1974). Representation of structure in similarity data: Problems and prospects. *Psychometrika, 39,* 373–421.

Shepard, R. N. (1980). Multi-dimensional data, tree-fitting, and clustering. *Science, 210,* 290–298.

Shepard, R. N. (1982). Geometrical approximations to the structure of musical pitch. *Psychological Review, 89,* 305–333.

Shepard, R. N., & Zare, S. L. (1983). Path-guided apparent motion. *Science, 220,* 632–634.

Shera, C. A., & Zweig, G. (1991). Asymmetry suppresses the cochlear catastrophe. *Journal of the Acoustical Society of America, 89,* 1276–1289.

Sherk, H., & Horton, J. C. (1984). Receptive field properties in the cat's area 17 in the absence of ON-center geniculate input. *Journal of Neuroscience, 4,* 381–393.

Sherman, S. M. (1973). Visual field defects in monocularly and binocularly deprived cats. *Brain Research, 49,* 25–45.

Sherman, S. M. (1985). Parallel W-, X- and Y-cell pathways in the cat: A model for visual function. In D. Rose & V. G. Dobson (Eds.), *Models of the visual cortex* (pp. 71–84). Chichester: Wiley.

Sherrington, C. S. (1906). Integrative action of the nervous sytem. New Haven, CT: Yale University Press.

Shiffman, S. S., Reynolds, M. L., & Young, F. W. (1981). *Introduction to multidimensional scaling.* New York: Academic Press.

Shiffrin, R. M., & Schneider, W. (1977). Controlled and automatic human information processing: II. Perceptual learning, automatic attending and a general theory. *Psychological Review, 84,* 127–190.

Shiller, P. H. (1984). Central connections on the retinal ON- and OFF-pathways. *Nature, 297,* 580–583.

Shiller, P. H., Sandell, J. H., & Maunsell, J. H. R. (1986). Functions of the ON and OFF channels of the visual system. *Nature, 322,* 824–825.

Shimojo, S., & Held, R. (1987). Vernier acuity is less than grating acuity in 2- and 3 month olds. *Vision Research, 27,* 77–86.

Shimojo, S., & Richards, W. (1986). "Seeing" shapes that are almost totally occluded: A new look at Park's camel. *Perception & Psychophysics, 39,* 418–426.

Shinar, D. (1977). *Driver visual limitations: Diagnosis and treatment.* Institute for Research in Public Safety, DOT-HS-5-1275, Indiana University.

Shockey, L., & Reddy, R. (1974, August). *Quantitative analysis of speech perception: Results from transcription of connected speech from unfamiliar languages.* Paper presented at the Speech Communications Seminar, Stockholm.

Shower, E. G., & Biddulph, R. (1931). Differential pitch sensitivity of the ear. *Journal of Acoustical Society of America, 3,* 275–287.

Shulman, G. L., Remington, R. W., & McLean, J. P. (1979). Moving attention through visual space. *Journal of Experimental Psychology: Human Perception and Performance, 5,* 522–526.

Shulman, G. L., Sheehy, J. B., & Wilson, J. (1986). Gradients of spatial attention. *Acta Psychologica, 61,* 167–181.

Shulman, G. L., Wilson, J., & Sheehy, J. B. (1985). Spatial determinants of the distribution of attention. *Perception & Psychophysics, 37,* 59–65.

Shurtleff, D., Raslear, T. G., & Simmons, L. (1990). Circadian variations in time perception in rats. *Physiology and Behavior, 47,* 931–939.

Sibony, P. A., Evinger, C., & Manning, K. A. (1987). Effects of tobacco on pursuit eye movements and blinks. *Investigative Ophthalmology and Visual Science, 28,* 316.

Siddle, D. A., Morish, R. B., White, K. D., & Mangen, G. L. (1969). Relation of visual sensitivity to extraversion. *Journal of Experimental Research in Personality, 3,* 264–267.

Sidman, M., & Kirk, B. (1974). Letter reversals in naming, writing, and matching to sample. *Child Development, 45,* 616–625.

Silver, W. L. (1987). The common chemical sense. In T. E. Finger & W. L. Silver (Eds.), *Neurobiology of taste and smell* (pp. 65–87). New York: Wiley.

Simmons, F. B., Epley, J. M., Lummis, R. C., Guttman, N., Frishkopf, L. S., Harmon, L. D., & Zwicker, E. (1965). Auditory nerve: Electrical stimulation in man. *Science, 148,* 104–106.

Simmons, J. A. (1989). A view of the world through the bat's ear: The formation of acoustic images in echolocation. *Cognition, 33,* 155–199.

Simpson, W. A. (1988). The method of constant stimuli is efficient. *Perception & Psychophysics, 44,* 433–436.

Sinclair, D. C., & Stokes, B. A. R. (1964). The production and characteristics of "second pain." *Brain, 87,* 609–618.

Sinnot, J., & Rauth, J. (1937). Effect of smoking on taste thresholds. *Journal of General Psychology, 17,* 155–162.

Sivak, J. G., Barrie, D. L., Callender, M. G., Doughty, M. J., Seltner, R. L., & West, J. A. (1990). Optical causes of experimental myopia. In *Myopia and the control of eye growth. Ciba Foundation Symposium 155.* (pp. 160–177). Chichester: Wiley.

Sivian, L. S., & White, S. D. (1933). On minimum audible sound fields. *Journal of the Acoustical Society of America, 4,* 288–321.

Skarda, C. A., & Freeman, W. J. (1987). How brains make chaos in order to make sense of the world. *Behavioral and Brain Sciences, 10,* 161–195.

Skowbo, D. (1984). Are McCollough effects conditioned responses? *Psychological Bulletin, 96,* 215–226.

Slaughter, M. M., & Miller, R. F. (1981). 2-Amino-4-phosphonobutyric acid: A new pharmacological tool for retina research. *Science, 211,* 182–184.

Sloane, M. E., Ost, J. W., Etheriedge, D. B., & Henderlite, S. E. (1989). Overprediction and blocking in the McCollough effect. *Perception & Psychophysics, 45,* 110–120.

Sloane, S. A., Shea, S. L., Proctor, M. M., & Dewsbury, D. A. (1978). Visual cliff performance in 10 species of muroid rodents. *Animal Learning and Behavior, 6,* 244–248.

Sloboda, J. A. (1985). *The musical mind: The cognitive psychology of music.* Oxford: Oxford University Press.

Small, L. H., & Bond, Z. S. (1986). Distortions and deletions: Word-initial consonant specificity in fluent speech. *Perception & Psychophysics, 40,* 20–26.

Smith, A., & Over, R. (1979). Motor aftereffect with subjective contours. *Perception & Psychophysics, 25,* 95–98.

Smith, D. V. (1985). Brainstem processing of gustatory information. In D. W. Pfaff (Ed.), *Taste, olfaction, and the central nervous system.* (pp. 151–177). New York: Rockefeller University Press.

Smith, J., Hausfeld, S., Power, R. P., & Gorta, A. (1982). Ambiguous musical figures and auditory streaming. *Perception & Psychophysics, 32,* 454–464.

Smith, W. S., Frazier, N. I., Ward, S., & Webb, F. (1983). Early adolescent girls' and boys' learning of spatial visualization skill-replications. *Journal of Education, 67,* 239–243.

Snellen, H. (1862). *Probebuchstaben zur Bestimmung der Sehscharfe.* Utrecht: Weijer.

Snodgrass, J. G., & Corwin, J. (1988). Pragmatics of measuring recognition memory: Applications to dementia and amnesia. *Journal of Experimental Psychology: Human Perception and Performance, 117,* 34–50.

Snyder, S. H. (1977). Opiate receptors and internal opiates. *Scientific American, 236,* 44–56.

Sokolov, E. N. (1975). The neuronal mechanisms of the orienting reflex. In E. N. Sokolov & O. S. Vinogradova (Eds.), *Neuronal mechanisms of the orienting reflex* (pp. 217–238). New York: Wiley.

Southwick, E., & Schiffman, S. S. (1980). Odor quality of pyridyl ketones. *Chemical Senses, 5,* 343–357.

Sperling, H. G. (1986). Spectral sensitivity, intense spectral light studies and the color receptor mosaic of primates. *Vision Research, 26,* 1557–1571.

Sperry, R. W. (1943). Effect of 180 degree rotation of the retinal field on visuomotor coordination. *Journal of Experimental Zoology, 92,* 263–277.

Spillman, L., Ransom-Hogg, A., & Oehler, R. (1987). A comparison of perceptive and receptive fields in man and monkey. *Human Neurobiology, 6,* 51–62.

Spitzer, H., Desimone, R., & Moran, J. (1988). Increased attention enhances both behavioral and neuronal performance. *Science, 240,* 338–340.

Spitzer, M. W., & Semple, M. N. (1991). Interaural phase coding in auditory midbrain: Influence of dynamic stimulus features. *Science, 254,* 721–724.

Spoendlin, H. H. (1978). The afferent innervation of the cochlea. In R. F. Naunton & C. Fernandey (Eds.), *Evoked electrical activity in the auditory nervous system* (pp. 21–42). New York: Academic Press.

Spoendlin, H. H., & Schrott, A. (1989). Analysis of the human auditory nerve. *Hearing Research, 43,* 25–38.

Sprafkin, C., Serbin, L. A., Denier, C., & Conner, J. M. (1983). Sex-differentiated play: Cognitive consequences and early interventions. In M. B. Liss (Ed.), *Social and cognitive skills* (pp. 167–192). New York: Academic Press.

Spreen, O. (1976). Neuropsychology of learning disorders: Post conference review. In R. M. Knights & D. J. Bakker (Eds.), *The neuropsychology of learning disorders* (pp. 445–467). Baltimore: University Park Press.

Springer, S. P., & Deutsch, G. (1985). *Left brain, right brain* (rev. ed.). San Francisco: Freeman.

Srulovicz, P., & Goldstein, J. L. (1983). A central spectrum model: A synthesis of auditory-nerve timing and place cues in monaural communication of frequency spectrum. *Journal of the Acoustical Society of America, 73,* 1266–1276.

Stark, L., & Bridgeman, B. (1983). Role of corollary discharge in space constancy. *Perception & Psychophysics, 34,* 371–380.

Stark, L., & Ellis, S. (1981). Scanpaths revisited: Cognitive models direct active looking. In D. Fisher, R. Monty, & I. Senders (Eds.), *Eye movements: Cognition and visual perception* (pp. 193–226). Hillsdale, NJ: Erlbaum.

Stebbins, W. C. (1980). The evolution of hearing in the mammals. In A. N. Popper & R. R. Fay (Eds.), *Comparative studies of hearing in vertebrates* (pp. 421–436). New York: Springer-Verlag.

Steinberg, A. (1955). Changes in time perception induced by an anaesthetic drug. *British Journal of Psychology, 46,* 273–279.

Steinfield, G. J. (1967). Concepts of set and availability and their relation to the reorganization of ambiguous pictorial stimuli. *Psychological Review, 74,* 505–525.

Stelmack, R. M., Achorn, E., & Michaud, A. (1977). Extravision and individual differences in auditory evoked response. *Psychophysiology, 14,* 368–374.

Stelmack, R. M., & Campbell, K. B. (1974). Extraversion and auditory sensitivity to high and low frequency. *Perceptual and Motor Skills, 38,* 875–879.

Stephan, F. K., & Nunez, A. A. (1977). Elimination of circadian rhythms in drinking activity, sleep, and temperature by isolation of suprachaismatic nuclei. *Behavioral Biology, 20,* 1–16.

Stephens, P. R., & Young, J. Z. (1982). The stacocyst of the squid Loligo. *Journal of Zoology, London, 197,* 241–266.

Stern, J. A., Oster, P. J., & Newport, K. (1980). Reaction time measures, hemispheric specialization, and age. In L. Poon (Ed.), *Aging in the 1980's* (pp. 309–326).

Washington, DC: American Psychological Association.

Stern, R. M., Koch, K. L., Leibowitz, H. W., Lindblad, I. M., Shupert, C. L., & Stewart, W. R. (1985). Tachygastria and motion sickness. *Aviation, Space and Environmental Medicine, 56,* 1074–1077.

Sternbach, R. A. (1963). Congenital insensitivity to pain: A review. *Psychological Bulletin, 60,* 252–264.

Sternbach, R. A., & Tursky, B. (1964). On the psychophysical power function in electric shock. *Psychonomic Science, 1,* 247–248.

Sternberg, S. (1975). Memory scanning: New findings and current controversies. *Quarterly Journal of Experimental Psychology, 27,* 1–32.

Stevens, D. A., & Lawless, H. T. (1986). Putting out the fire: Effects of tastants on oral chemical irritation. *Perception & Psychophysics, 39,* 346–350.

Stevens, J. C. (1979). Variation of cold sensitivity over the body surface. *Sensory Processes, 3,* 317–326.

Stevens, J. C. (1989). Temperature and the two-point threshold. *Somatosensory and Motor Research, 6,* 275–284.

Stevens, J. C. (1990). Perceived roughness as a function of body locus. *Perception & Psychophysics, 47,* 298–304.

Stevens, J. C., & Cain, W. S. (1986). Smelling via the mouth: Effects of aging. *Perception & Psychophysics, 40,* 142–146.

Stevens, J. C., Cain, W. S., & Burke, R. J. (1988). Variability of olfactory thresholds. *Chemical Senses, 13,* 643–653.

Stevens, J. C., Cain, W. S., & Demarque, A. (1990). Memory and identification of simulated odors in elderly and young persons. *Bulletin of the Psychonomic Society, 28,* 293–296.

Stevens, J. C., Cain, W. S., Demarque, A., & Ruthruff, A. M. (1991). On the discrimination of missing ingredients: Aging and salt flavor. *Appetite, 16,* 129–140.

Stevens, J. C., Cain, W. S., & Oatley, M. W. (1989). Aging speeds olfactory adaptation and slows recovery. *Annals of the New York Academy of Sciences, 562,* 323–325.

Stevens, J. C., Cain, W. S., Shiet, F. T., & Oatley, M. W. (1989). Olfactory adaptation and recovery in old age. *Perception, 18,* 265–276.

Stevens, J. C., & Marks, L. E. (1980). Cross-modality matching functions generated by magnitude estimation. *Perception & Psychophysics, 27,* 379–389.

Stevens, J. C., & Stevens, S. S. (1960). Warmth and cold: Dynamics of sensory intensity. *Journal of Experimental Psychology, 60,* 183–192.

Stevens, J. C., & Wellen, D. G. (1989). Recovery from adaptation to NaCl in young and elderly. *Chemical Senses, 14,* 633–635.

Stevens, K. N., & House, A. S. (1972). Speech perception. In J.V. Tobias (Ed.), *Foundations of modern auditory theory: Vol. 2* (pp. 3–62). New York: Academic Press.

Stevens, S. S. (1935). The relation of pitch to intensity. *Journal of the Acoustical Society of America, 6,* 150–154.

Stevens, S. S. (1946). On the theory of scales of measurement. *Science, 103,* 677–680.

Stevens, S. S. (1956). The direct estimation of sensory magnitudes—loudness. *American Journal of Psychology, 69,* 1–25.

Stevens, S. S. (1959). Tactile vibration: Dynamics of sensory intensity. *Journal of Experimental Psychology, 57,* 210–218.

Stevens, S. S. (1961). The psychophysics of sensory function. In W. A. Rosenblith (Ed.), *Sensory communication* (pp. 1–33). Cambridge, MA: MIT Press.

Stevens, S. S. (1975). *Psychophysics: Introduction to its perceptual, neural, and social prospects.* New York: Wiley.

Stevens, S. S., & Galanter, E. (1957). Ratio scales and category scales for a dozen perceptual continua. *Journal of Experimental Psychology, 54,* 377–411.

Stevens, S. S., & Newman, E. B. (1934). The localization of pure tones. *Proceedings of the National Academy of Sciences of the USA, 20,* 593–596.

Stevens, S. S., Volkman, J., & Newman, E. B. (1937). A scale for the measurement of the psychological magnitude of pitch. *Journal of the Acoustical Society of America, 8,* 185–190.

Stevens, S. S., & Warshovsky, F. (1965). *Sound and hearing.* New York: Time-Life Books.

Stinson, M. R., & Khanna, S. M. (1989). Sound propagation in the ear canal and coupling to the eardrum, with measurements on model systems. *Journal of the Acoustical Society of America, 85,* 2481–2491.

Stoffregen, T. A. (1985). Flow structure versus retinal location in the optical control of stance. *Journal of Experimental Psychology: Human Perception and Performance, 11,* 554–565.

Stone, L. S. (1960). Polarization of the retina and development of vision. *Journal of Experimental Zoology, 145,* 85–93.

Strange, W., & Jenkins, J. (1978). Role of linguistic experience in the perception of speech. In R. Walk & H. Pick (Eds.), *Perception and experience* (pp. 125–169). New York: Plenum Press.

Stratton, G. M. (1896). Some preliminary experiments on vision without inversion of the retinal image. *Psychological Review, 3,* 611–617.

Stratton, G. M. (1897a). Upright vision and the retinal image. *Psychological Review, 4,* 182–187.

Stratton, G. M. (1897b). Vision without inversion of the retinal image. *Psychological Review, 4,* 341–360.

Street, R. F. (1931). A Gestalt completion test: A study of a cross section of intellect. New York: Bureau of Publication, Columbia University.

Streitfeld, B., & Wilson, M. (1986). The ABCs of categorical perception. *Cognitive Psychology, 18,* 432–451.

Stromeyer, C. F., III. (1978). Form-color aftereffects in human vision. In R. Held, H. Leibowitz, & H. L. Teuber (Eds.), *Handbook of sensory physiology: Vol. 8* (pp. 97–142). New York: Springer-Verlag.

Stroop, J. (1935). Studies of interference in serial verbal reactions. *Journal of Experimental Psychology, 18,* 624–643.

Stroud, J. M. (1955). The fine structure of psychological time. In H. Quastler (Ed.), *Information theory in psychology: Problems and methods* (pp. 174–207). Glencoe, IL: Free Press.

Stryer, L. (1987). The molecules of visual excitation. *Scientific American, 257,* 42–50.

Stuart, G. W. & Day, R. H. (1988). The Fraser illusion: Simple figures. *Perception & Psychophysics, 44,* 409–420.

Suedfeld, P. (1980). *Restricted environmental stimulation: Research and clinical applications.* New York: Wiley.

Supra, M., Cotzin, M. E., & Dallenbach, K. M. (1944). "Facial vision": The perception of obstacles by the blind. *American Journal of Psychology, 57,* 133–183.

Sussman, H. M. (1991a). The representation of stop consonants in three-dimensional acoustic space. *Phonetica, 48,* 18–31.

Sussman, H. M. (1991b). An investigation of locus equations as a source of relational invariance for stop place categorization. *Journal of the Acoustical Society of America, 90,* 1309–1325.

Sutter, A., Beck, J., & Graham, N. (1989). Contrast and spatial variables in texture segregation: Testing a simple spatial-frequency channels model. *Perception & Psychophysics, 46,* 312–332.

Svaetichin, G. (1956). Spectral response curves of single cones. *Acta Physiologica Scandinavica, 1,* 93–101.

Svaetichin, G., & MacNichol, E. F., Jr. (1958). Retinal mechanisms for achromatic vision. *Annals of the New York Academy of Sciences, 74,* 385–404.

Swarbrick, L., & Whitfield, I. C. (1972). Auditory cortical units selectively responsive to stimulus "shape." *Journal of Physiology (London), 224,* 68–69.

Swensson, R. G. (1980). A two-stage detection model applied to skilled visual search by radiologists. *Perception & Psychophysics, 27,* 11–16.

Swets, J. A. (1963). Central factors in auditory frequency selectivity. *Psychological Bulletin, 60,* 429–441.

Swift, C. G., & Tiplady, B. (1988). The effects of age on the response to caffeine. *Psychopharmacology, 94,* 29–31.

Swindale, N. V. (1988). Role of visual experience in promoting segregation of eye dominance patches in the visual cortex of the cat. *Journal of Comparative Neurology, 267,* 472–488.

Swindale, N. V., & Cynader, M. S. (1986). Vernier acuity of neurones in cat visual cortex. *Nature, 319,* 591–593.

Szentagothai, J. (1950). The elementary vestibulo-ocular reflex arc. *Journal of Neurophysiology, 13,* 395–407.

Talbot, J. D., Marrett, S., Evans, A. C., Meyer, E., Bushnell, M. C., & Duncan, G. H. (1991). Multiple representations of pain in human cerebral cortex. *Science, 251,* 1355–1358.

Talmadge, C. L., Tubis, A., Wit, H. P., & Long, G. (1991). Are spontaneous otoacoustic emissions generated by self-sustained cochlear oscillators? *Journal of the Acoustical Society of America, 89,* 2391–2399.

Tan, H. Z., Rabinowitz, W. M., & Durlach, N. I. (1989). Analysis of a synthetic Tadoma system as a multidimensional tactile display. *Journal of the Acoustical Society of America, 86,* 981–988.

Tart, C. (1971). *On being stoned.* Palo Alto: Science and Behavior Books.

Taub, E., & Berman, A. J. (1968). Movement and learning in the absence of sensory feedback. In S. J. Freedman (Ed.), *The neuropsychology of spatially oriented behavior* (pp. 173–192). Homewood, IL: Dorsey.

Taylor, S. P., & Woodhouse, J. M. (1980). A new illusion and possible links with the Munsterberg and Fraser illions of direction. *Perception & Psychophysics, 9,* 479–481.

Tedford, W. H., Warren, D. E., & Flynn, W. E. (1977). Alternation of shock aversion thresholds during menstrual cycle. *Perception & Psychophysics, 21,* 193–196.

Tees, R. C. (1974). Effect of visual deprivation on development of depth perception in the rat. *Journal of Comparative and Physiological Psychology, 86,* 300–308.

Tees, R. C., & Buhrmann, K. (1990). The effect of early experience on water maze spatial learning and memory in rats. *Developmental Psychobiology, 23,* 427–439.

Tees, R. C., & Midgley, G. (1978). Extent of recovery of function after early sensory deprivation in the rat. *Journal of Comparative and Physiological Psychology, 92,* 768–777.

Tees, R. C., & Symons, L. A. (1987). Intersensory coordination and the effects of early sensory deprivation. *Developmental Psychobiology, 20,* 497–507.

Tees, R. C., & Werker, J. F. (1984). Perceptual flexibility: Maintenance or recovery of the ability to discriminate non-native speech sounds. *Canadian Journal of Psychology, 38,* 579–590.

Teeter, J. H., & Brand, J. G. (1987). Peripheral mechanisms of gustation: Physiology and biochemistry. In T. E. Finger & W. L. Silver (Eds.), *Neurobiology of taste and smell.* (p.299–330). New York: Wiley.

Teghtsoonian, M. (1987). The structure of an experiment.

In M. Teghtsoonian & R. Teghtsoonian (Eds.), *Fechner Day '87* (pp. 49–52). Northampton, MA: International Society for Psychophysics.

Teghtsoonian, R. (1971). On the exponents in Stevens' law and the constant in Ekman's law. *Psychological Review, 78,* 71–80.

Teghtsoonian, R. (1975). Review of Psychophysics by S. S. Stevens. *American Journal of Psychology, 88,* 677–684.

Teghtsoonian, R., Teghtsoonian, M., Bergulund, B., & Berglund, U. (1978). Invariance of odor strength with sniff vigor: An olfactory analogue to size constancy. *Journal of Experimental Psychology: Human Perception and Performance, 4,* 144–152.

Teller, D. Y. (1980). Locus questions in visual science. In C. S. Harris (Ed.), *Visual coding and adaptability* (pp. 151–176). Hillsdale, NJ: Erlbaum.

Teller, D. Y. (1981). Color vision in infants. In R. Aslin, J. Alberts, & M. Petersen (Eds.), *Development of perception, physiological perspectives: Vol. 2* (pp. 298–312). New York: Academic Press.

Teller, D. Y., & Bornstein, M. H. (1987). Infant color vision and color perception. In P. Salapatek & L. Cohen (Eds.), *Handbook of infant perception: Vol. 1. From sensation to perception* (pp. 185–237). Orlando: Academic Press.

Teller, D. Y., & Movshon, J. A. (1986). Visual development. *Vision Research, 26,* 1483–1506.

Terenius, L., & Wahlstrom, A. (1975). Morphine-like ligand for opiate receptors in human CSF. *Life Sciences, 16,* 1759–1764.

Terheardt, E. (1974). Pitch, consonance and harmony. *Journal of the Acoustical Society of America, 55,* 1061–1069.

Thomas, E. A. C., & Weaver, W. B. (1975). Cognitive processing and time perception. *Perception & Psychophysics, 17,* 363–367.

Thomas, H. (1983). Parameter estimation in simple psychophysical models. *Psychological Bulletin, 93,* 396–403.

Thomas, H., Jamison, W., & Hammel, D. D. (1973). Observation is insufficient for discovering that the surface of still water is invariantly horizontal. *Science, 181,* 173–174.

Thornbury, J. M., & Mistretta, C. M. (1981). Tactile sensitivity as a function of age. *Journal of Gerontology, 36,* 34–39.

Thorpe, L. A., & Trehub, S. E. (1989). Duration illusion and auditory grouping in infancy. *Developmental Psychology, 24,* 484–491.

Timney, B. (1985). Visual experience and the development of depth perception. In D. J. Ingle, M. Jeannerod, & D. N. Lee (Eds.), *Brain mechanisms and spatial vision* (pp. 147–174). Dordrecht: Martinus Nijhoff.

Timney, B., Mitchel, D. E., & Griffin, F. (1978). The development of vision in cats after extended periods of dark rearing. *Experimental Brain Research, 31,* 547–560.

Timney, B., & Muir, D. W. (1976). Orientation anisotropy: Incidence and magnitude in Caucasian & Chinese subjects. *Science, 193,* 699–700.

Tipper, S. P., Driver, J., & Weaver, B. (1991). Object-centered inhibition of return of visual attention. *Quarterly Journal of Experimental Psychology, 43A,* 289–298.

Toch, H. H., & Schulte, R. (1961). Readiness to perceive violence as a result of police training. *British Journal of Psychology, 52,* 389–393.

Todd, J. T. (1983). Perception of gait. *Journal of Experimental Psychology: Human Perception and Performance, 9,* 31–42.

Todd, J. T., & Akerstrom, R. A. (1987). Perception of three-dimensional form from patterns of optical texture. *Journal of Experimental Psychology: Human Perception and Performance, 13,* 242–255.

Tomlinson, R. W. W., & Schwarz, D. W. F. (1988). Perception of the missing fundamental in nonhuman primates. *Journal of the Acoustical Society of America, 84,* 560–565.

Tootell, R. B. H., Silverman, M. S., Hamilton, S. L., DeValois, R. L., & Switkes, E. (1988). Functional anatomy of the macaque striate cortex: III. Color. *Journal of Neuroscience, 8,* 1569–1593.

Torebjork, H. E., & Hallin, R. G. (1973). Perceptual changes accompanying controlled, preferential blocking of A and C fibre responses in intact human skin nerves. *Experimental Brain Research, 16,* 321–332.

Torebjork, H. E., Ochoa, J. L., & Schady, W. J. L. (1983). Role of single mechanoreceptor units in tactile sensation. In C. von Euler, O. Franzen, U. Lindblom, & D. Ottoson (Eds.), *Somatosensory mechanisms* (pp. 173–184). New York: Plenum Press.

Torgerson, W. S. (1958). *Theory and methods of scaling.* New York: Wiley.

Torgerson, W. S. (1961). Distances and ratios in psychophysical scaling. *Acta Psychologica, 19,* 201–205.

Tougas, Y., & Bregman, A. S. (1990). Auditory streaming and the continuity illusion. *Perception & Psychophysics, 47,* 121–126.

Townshend, B., Cotter, N., Van Compernolle, D., & White, R. L. (1987). Pitch perception by cochlear implant subjects. *Journal of the Acoustical Society of America, 82,* 106–115.

Townsend, J., & Ashby, F. G. (1982). Experimental test of contemporary mathematical models of visual letter recognition. *Journal of Experimental Psychology: Human Perception and Performance, 8,* 834–864.

Trehub, S. (1976). The discrimination of foreign speech contrasts by infants and adults. *Child Development, 47,* 466–472.

Trehub, S. E., & Schneider, B. A. (1987). Problems and promises of developmental psychophysics: Throw out the bath water but keep the baby. In M. Teghtsoonian & R. Teghtsoonian (Eds.), *Fechner Day '87* (pp. 43–47). Northampton, MA: International Society for Psychophysics.

Trehub, S. E., Schneider, B. A., & Endman, M. (1980). Developmental changes in infants sensitivity to octave-band noises. *Journal of Experimental Child Psychology, 29,* 282–293.

Trehub, S. E., & Trainor, L. J. (1990). Rules for listening in infancy. In J. T. Enns (Ed.), *The development of attention: Research and theory* (pp. 87–119). Amsterdam: Elsevier.

Treisman, A. M. (1982). Perceptual groupings and attention in visual search for features and for objects. *Journal of Experimental Psychology: Human Perception and Performance, 8,* 194–214.

Treisman, A. M. (1986a). Features and objects in visual processing. *Scientific American, 255,* 114B–125.

Treisman, A. M. (1986b). Properties, parts, and objects. In K. R. Boff, L. Kaufman, & J. P. Thomas (Eds.), *Handbook of Perception and Human Performance* (pp. 35-1– 35-70). New York: Wiley.

Treisman, A. M., Cavanagh, P., Fischer, B., Ramachandran, V. S., & von der Heydt, R. (1990). Form perception and attention: Striate cortex and beyond. In L. Spillman & J. S. Werner (Eds.), *Visual perception* (pp. 273–316). New York: Academic Press.

Treisman, A. M., & Davies, A. (1972). Divided attention to ear and eye. In S. Kornblum (Ed.), *Attention and performance IV* (pp. 101–118). New York: Academic Press.

Treisman, A. M., & Gelade, G. (1980). A feature-integration theory of attention. *Cognitive Psychology, 12,* 97–136.

Treisman, A. M., & Gormican, S. (1988). Feature analysis in early vision: Evidence from search asymmetries. *Psychological Review, 95,* 15–48.

Treisman, A. M., & Schmidt, H. (1982). Illusory conjunctions in the perception of objects. *Cognitive Psychology, 14,* 107–141.

Treisman, A. M., & Souther, J. (1985). Search asymmetry: A diagnostic for preattentive processing of separable features. *Journal of Experimental Psychology: General, 114,* 285–310.

Treisman, M. (1963). Temporal discrimination and the indifference interval: Implications for the model of an internal clock. *Psychological Monographs, 77* (1–31, Whole No. 576).

Treisman, M. (1976). On the use and misuse of psychophysical terms. *Psychological Review, 83,*

246–256.

Tress, K. H., & Kugler, B. T. (1979). Interocular transfer of movement after-effects in schizophrenia. *British Journal of Psychology, 70,* 389–392.

Tronick, E. (1972). Stimulus control and the growth of the infant's effective visual field. *Perception & Psychophysics, 11,* 373–376.

Troscianko, T., & Fahle, M. (1988). Why do isoluminant stimuli appear slower? *Journal of the Optical Society of America A, 5,* 871–880.

Trout, J. D., & Poser, W. J. (1990). Auditory and phonemic influences on phonemic restoration. *Language & Speech, 33,* 121–135.

Tsal, Y. (1983). Movements of attention across the visual field. *Journal of Experimental Psychology: Human Perception and Performance, 9,* 523–530.

Tsotsos, J. K. (1988). A "complexity level" analysis of immediate vision. *International Journal of Computer Vision, 1,* 303–320.

Tsvetkova, L. S. (1972). *Rehabilitative training in local brain lesions.* Moscow: Pedagogika.

Tuck, J. P., & Long, G. M. (1990). The role of small-field tritanopia in two measures of color vision. *Ophthalmic and Physiological Optics, 10,* 195–199.

Turnbull, C. (1961). Some observations regarding the experiences and behavior of the Bambuti pygmies. *American Journal of Psychology, 74,* 304–308.

Turner, P. (1968). Amphetamines and smell threshold in man. In A. Herxheimer (Ed.), *Drugs and sensory functions* (pp. 91–100). Boston: Little, Brown.

Tversky, A. (1977). Features of similarity. *Psychological Review, 84,* 327–352.

Tversky, B., & Schiano, D. J. (1989). Perceptual and conceptual factors in distortions in memory for graphs and maps. *Journal of Experimental Psychology: General, 118,* 387–398.

Tyler, C. W., (1975). Stereoscopic tilt and size aftereffects. *Perception, 4,* 187–192.

Uchikawa, K., Uchicawa, H., & Boynton, R. M. (1989). Partial color constancy of isolated surface colors examined by a color-naming method. *Perception, 18,* 83–91.

Uhlarik, J., & Johnson, R. (1978). Development of form perception in repeated brief exposures to visual stimuli. In R. Walk & L. Pick, Jr. (Eds.), *Perception and experience.* New York: Plenum.

Ullman, S. (1979). The interpretation of structure from motion. *Proceedings of the Royal Society of London, Series B, 203,* 405–426.

Ulrich, R. (1987). Threshold models of temporal-order judgments evaluated by a ternary response task. *Perception & Psychophysics, 42,* 224–239.

Umezaki, H., & Morrell, F. (1970). Developmental study of photic evoked responses in premature infants. *Electroencephalography and Clinical Neurophysiology, 28,* 55–63.

Ungerleider, L. G., Mishkin, M. (1982). Two cortical visual systems. In D. J. Ingle, M. A. Goodale, & R. J. W. Mansfield (Eds.), *Analysis of visual behavior* (pp. 549–586). Cambridge, MA: MIT Press.

Uttal, W. (1981). *A taxonomy of visual processes.* Hillsdale, NJ: Erlbaum.

Vallbo, A. B. (1981). Sensations evoked from the glabrous skin of the human hand by electrical stimulation of unitary mechano-sensitive afferents. *British Research, 215,* 359–363.

Vallbo, A. B. (1983). Tactile sensation related to activity in primary afferents with special reference to detection problems. In C. von Euler, O. Franzen, U. Lindblom, & D. Ottoson (Eds.), *Somatosensory mechanisms* (pp. 163–172). New York, Plenum Press.

van Dijk, P., & Wit, H. P. (1990). Amplitude and frequency fluctuations of spontaneous otoacoustic emissions. *Journal of the Acoustical Society of America, 88,* 1779–1793.

Van Doren, C. L. (1989). A model of spatiotemporal sensitivity linking psychophysics to tissue mechanics. *Journal of the Acoustical Society of America, 85,* 2065–2080.

van der Heijden, A. H. C., Wolters, G., Groep, J. C., & Hagenaar, R. (1987). Single-letter recognition accuracy benefits from advance cuing of location. *Perception & Psychophysics, 42,* 503–509.

van der Meer, H. C. (1979). Interrelation of the effects of binocular disparity and perspective cues on judgments of depth and height. *Perception & Psychophysics, 26,* 481–488.

Van Essen, D. C. (1979). Visual areas of the mammalian cerebral cortex. *Annual Review of Neurosciences, 2,* 227–263.

Van Essen, D. C. (1984). Functional organization of primate visual cortex. In A. Peters & E. G. Jones (Eds.), *Cerebral cortex: Vol. 3* (pp. 259–329). New York: Plenum Press.

Van Essen, D. C., Anderson, C. H., & Felleman, D. J. (1992). Information processing in the primate visual system: An integrated systems perspective. *Science, 255,* 419–423.

Van Lancker, D. R., & Kreiman, J. (1989). Voice perception deficits: Neuroanatomical correlates of phonagnosia. *Journal of Clinical and Experimental Neuropsychology, 11,* 665–674.

van Santen, J. P. H., & Sperling, G. (1985). Elaborated Reichardt detectors. *Journal of the Optical Society of America A, 2,* 300–321.

Van Voorhis, S., & Hillyard, S. A. (1977). Visual evoked potentials and selective attention to points in space. *Perception & Psychophysics, 22,* 54–62.

Varma, V. K., & Malhotra, A. K. (1988). Cannabis and cognitive functions: A prospective study. *Drug & Alcohol Dependence, 21,* 147–152.

Varner, D., Cook, J. E., Schneck, M. E., McDonald, M., & Teller, D. (1985). Tritan discriminations by 1- and 2-month-old human infants. *Vision Research, 6,* 821–831.

Vaughan, H. G., & Kurtzberg, D. (1989). Electrophysiologic indices of normal and aberrant cortical maturation. In P. Kelaway & J. Noebels (Eds.), *Problems and concepts of developmental neurophysiology* (pp.263–287). Baltimore: Johns Hopkins University Press.

Vautin, R. G., & Berkley, M. A. (1977). Responses of single cells in cat visual cortex to stimulus movement: Neural correlates of visual after-effects. *Journal of Neurophysiology, 40,* 1051–1065.

Velle, W. (1987). Sex differences in sensory functions. *Perspectives in Biology and Medicine, 30,* 490–522.

Verriest, G. (1974). Recent advances in the study of the acquired deficiences of color vision. *Fondazione "Gorgio Ranchi," 24,* 1–80.

Verrillo, R. T. (1968). A duplex mechanism of mechanoreception. In D. R. Kenshalo (Ed.), *The skin senses* (pp. 139–159). Springfield, IL: Thomas.

Verrillo, R. T. (1975). Cutaneous sensation. In B. Scharf (Ed.), *Experimental sensory psychology* (pp. 150–184). Glenview, IL: Scott, Foresman.

Verrillo, R. T., & Bolanowski, S. J., Jr. (1986). The effects of skin temperature on the psychophysical responses to vibration on glabrous and hairy skin. *Journal of the Acoustical Society of America, 80,* 528–532.

Verrillo, R. T., Fraioli, A. J., & Smith, R. L. (1969). Sensation magnitude of vibrotactile stimuli. *Perception & Psychophysics, 6,* 366–372.

Viemeister, N. F. (1988). Intensity coding and the dynamic range problem. *Hearing Research, 34,* 267–274.

Vierck, C. (1978). Somatosensory system. In R. B. Masterston (Ed.), *Handbook of sensory neurobiology: Vol. I. Sensory integration* (pp. 249–310). New York: Plenum Press.

Vimal, R. L. P., Pokorny, J., & Smith, V. C. (1987). Appearance of steadily viewed lights. *Vision Research, 27,* 1309–1318.

Vogels, R., & Orban, G. A. (1986). Decision factors affecting line orientation judgments in the method of single stimuli. *Perception & Psychophysics, 40,* 74–84.

Vurpillot, E. (1968). The development of scanning strategies and their relation to visual differentiation. *Journal of Experimental Child Psychology, 6,* 632–650.

Waber, D. P. (1976). Sex differences in cognition: A function of maturation rate? *Science, 192,* 572–574.

Waber, D. P. (1977). Sex differences in mental abilities, hemispheric lateralization and rate of physical growth at adolescence. *Developmental Psychology, 13,* 29–38.

Wade, N. J. (1984). *Brewster & Wheatstone on vision.* New York: Academic Press.

Waespe, W., & Henn, V. (1977). Neuronal activity in the vestibular nuclei of the alert monkey during vestibular and optokinetic stimulation. *Experimental Brain Research, 27,* 523–538.

Wahl, O. F., & Sieg, D. (1980). Time estimation among schizophrenics. *Perceptual and Motor Skills, 50,* 535–541.

Wald, G. (1968). The molecular basis of visual excitation. *Nature (London), 219,* 800–807.

Walk, R. D., & Gibson, E. J. (1961). A comparative and analytic study of visual depth perception. *Psychological Monographs, 75,* 1–44.

Walker, J. L. (1977). Time estimation and total subjective time. *Perceptual and Motor Skills, 44,* 527–532.

Walker, J. T. (1975). Visual texture as a factor in the apparent velocity of objective motion and motion after-effects. *Perception & Psychophysics, 18,* 175–180.

Walker, J. T., & Shank, M. D. (1988). Real and subjective lines and edges in the Bourdon illusion. *Perception & Psychophysics, 43,* 475–484.

Wall, P. D. (1979). On the relation of injury to pain. *Pain, 6,* 253–264.

Wallace, B., & Priebe, F. A. (1985). Hypnotic susceptibility, interference and alternation frequency to the Necker cube illusion. *Journal of General Psychology, 112,* 271–277.

Wallace, P. (1977). Individual discrimination of humans by odor. *Physiology and Behavior, 19,* 577–579.

Wallach, H. (1939). On sound localization. *Journal of the Acoustical Society of America, 10,* 270–274.

Wallach, H. (1972). The perception of neutral colors. In R. Held & W. Richards (Eds.), *Perception: mechanisms and models: Readings from Scientific American* (pp. 278–285). San Francisco: Freeman. (Originally published in *Scientific American,* 1963)

Wallach, H. (1987). Perceiving a stable environment when one moves. *Annual Review of Psychology, 38,* 1–27.

Wallach, H., & Becklen, R. (1983). An effect of speed on induced motion. *Perception & Psychophysics, 34,* 237–242.

Wallach, H., Becklen, R., & Nitzberg, D. (1985). Vector analysis and process combination in motion perception. *Journal of Experimental Psychology: Human Perception and Performance, 11,* 93–102.

Wallach, H., Gillam, B., & Cardillo, L. (1979). Some consequences of stereoscopic depth constancy. *Perception & Psychophysics, 26,* 235–240.

Wallach, H., Newman, E. B., & Rosenzweig, M. R. (1949). The precedence effect in sound localization. *American Journal of Psychology, 62,* 315–336.

Walley, A., Pisoni, D., & Aslin, R. (1981). The role of early experience in the development of speech perception. In R. Aslin, J. Alberts, & M. Petersen (Eds.), *Develop-*

ment of perception: Psychobiological perspectives: Vol. 1. Audition, somatic perceptions, and the chemical senses (pp. 219–256). New York: Academic Press.

Walls, G. L. (1951). A theory of ocular dominance. AMA Archives of Ophthalmology, 45, 387–412.

Walraven, J., Enroth-Cugell, C., Hood, D. C., McLeod, D. I., & Schnapf, J. L. (1990). The control of visual sensitivity: Receptoral and postreceptoral processes. In L. Spillman & J. S. Werner (Eds.), Visual perception: The neurophysiological foundations (pp. 53–101). New York: Academic Press.

Ward, L. M. (1971). Some psychophysical properties of category judgments and magnitude estimations. Unplished doctoral dissertation, Duke University, Durham, NC.

Ward, L. M. (1972). Category judgments of loudness in the absence of an experimenter-induced identification function: Sequential effects and power function fit. Journal of Experimental Psychology, 94, 179–184.

Ward, L. M. (1973). Repeated magnitude estimations with a variable standard: Sequential effects and other properties. Perception & Psychophysics, 13, 193–200.

Ward, L. M. (1974). Power functions for category judgments of duration and line length. Perceptual and Motor Skills, 38, 1182.

Ward, L. M. (1975). Sequential dependencies and response range in cross-modality matches of duration to loudness. Perception & Psychophysics, 18, 217–223.

Ward, L. M. (1979). Stimulus information and sequential dependencies in magnitude estimation and cross-modality matching. Journal of Experimental Psychology: Human Perception and Performance, 5, 444–459.

Ward, L. M. (1982a). Mixed-modality psychophysical scaling: Sequential dependencies and other properties. Perception & Psychophysics, 31, 53–62.

Ward, L. M. (1982b). Determinants of attention to local and global features of visual forms. Journal of Experimental Psychology: Human Perception and Performance, 8, 562–581.

Ward, L. M. (1983). On processing dominance: Comment on Pomerantz. Journal of Experimental Psychology: General, 112, 541–546.

Ward, L. M. (1985). Covert focussing of the attentional gaze. Canadian Journal of Psychology, 39, 546–563.

Ward, L. M. (1986). Mixed-modality psychophysical scaling: Double cross-modality matching for "difficult" continua. Perception & Psychophysics, 39, 407–417.

Ward, L. M. (1987). Remembrance of sounds past: Memory and psychophysical scaling. Journal of Experimental Psychology: Human Perception and Performance, 13, 216–227.

Ward, L. M. (1990). Critical bands and mixed-frequency scaling: Sequential dependencies, equal-loudness contours, and power function exponents. Perception & Psychophysics, 47, 551–562.

Ward, L. M. (1991). Associative measurement of psychological magnitude. In S. J. Bolanowski & G. A. Gescheider (Eds.), Ratio scaling of psychological magnitude (pp. 79–100). Hillsdale, NJ: Erlbaum.

Ward, L. M. (1992). Mind in psychophysics. In D. Algom (Ed.), Psychophysical approaches to cognition. (pp. 187–249). Amsterdam: North-Holland (Elsevier).

Ward, L. M., & Lockhead, G. R. (1970). Sequential effects and memory in category judgments. Journal of Experimental Psychology, 854, 27–34.

Ward, L. M., Porac, P., Coren, S., & Girgus, J. S. (1977). The case for misapplied constancy scaling: Depth associations elicited by illusion configurations. American Journal of Psychology, 90, 609–620.

Ward, T. B. (1985). Individual differences in processing stimulus dimensions: Relation to selective processing ability. Perception & Psychophysics, 37, 471–482.

Ward, W. D. (1970). Musical perception. In J. V. Tobias (Ed.), Foundations of modern auditory theory. Vol. 1 (pp. 407–47). New York: Academic Press.

Ware, C., (1981). Subjective contours independent of subjective brighteners. Perception & Psychophysics, 29, 500–504.

Ware, C., & Cowan, W. B. (1987). Chromatic Mach bands: Behavioral evidence for lateral inhibition in human color vision. Perception & Psychophysics, 41, 173–178.

Warm, J. S., & McCray, R. E. (1969). Influence of word frequency and length on the apparent duration of tachistoscopic presentations. Journal of Experimental Psychology, 79, 56–58.

Warren, D. H. (1984). Blindness and early childhood development. New York: American Foundation for the Blind.

Warren, R. M. (1970). Perceptual restoration of missing speech sounds. Science, 167, 392–393.

Warren, R. M. (1984). Perceptual restoration of obliterated sounds. Psychological Bulletin, 96, 371–383.

Warren, R. M., Obusek, C. J., Farmer, R. M., & Warren, R. P. (1969). Auditory sequence: Confusion of patterns other than speech or music. Science, 164, 586–587.

Warren, W. H., & Hannon, D. J. (1988). Direction of self-motion is perceived from optical flow. Nature, 336, 162–163.

Wassle, H., Peichl, L., & Boycott, B. B. (1983). A spatial analysis of on- and off-ganglion cells in the cat retina. Vision Research, 23, 1151–1160.

Watanabe, T., & Katsuki, Y. (1974). Response patterns of single auditory neurons of the cat to species-specific vocalization. Japanese Journal of Physiology, 24, 135–155.

Watkins, L. R., & Mayer, D. J. (1982). Organization of endogenous opiate and nonopiate pain control systems. Science, 216, 1185–1192.

Watson, A. B. (1983). Detection and recognition of simple spatial forms. In O. J. Braddick & A. C. Sleigh (Eds.), *Physical and biological processing of images* (pp. 100–114). New York: Springer-Verlag.

Watson, A. B., & Fitzhugh, A. (1990). The method of constant stimuli is inefficient. *Perception & Psychophysics, 47,* 87–91.

Watson, C. S., Kelly, W. J., & Wroten, H. W. (1976). Factors in the discrimination of tonal patterns: II. Selective attention and learning under various levels of stimulus uncertainty. *Journal of the Acoustical Society of America, 60,* 1176–1185.

Weale, R. A. (1979). Discoverers of Mach-bands. *Investigative Ophthalmology and Visual Sciences, 18,* 652–654.

Weale, R. A. (1982). *Focus on vision.* Cambridge, MA: Harvard University Press.

Weale, R. A. (1986). Aging and vision. *Vision Research, 26,* 1507–1512.

Weber, E. H. (1834). *De pulen, resorptione, auditu et tactu: Annotationes anatomicae et physiologicae.* Leipzig: Koehler.

Webster, M., & DeValois, R. (1985). Relationship between spatial frequency and orientation tuning of striate cortex cells. *Journal of the Optical Society of America A, 2,* 1124–1132.

Webster, W. R., & Atkin, L. M. (1975). Central auditory processing. In M. S. Gazzaniga & C. Blakemore (Eds.), *Handbook of sensory psychobiology* (pp. 325–364). New York: Academic Press.

Wegener, B. (Ed.). (1982). *Social attitudes and psychophysical measurement.* Hillsdale, NJ: Erlbaum.

Weiffenbach, J. M., Baum, B. J., & Burghauser, B. (1982). Taste thresholds: Quality specific variation with human aging. *Journal of Gerontology, 37,* 372–377.

Weil, A. T., Zinberg, E., & Nelson, J. N. (1968). Clinical and psychological effects of marijuana in man. *Science, 162,* 1234–1242.

Weinstein, E. A., Cole, M., Mitchell, M. S., & Lyerly, O. G. (1964). Anosagnosia and aphasia. *Archives of Neurology, 10,* 376–386.

Weinstein, S. (1968). Intensive and extensive aspects of tactile sensitivity as a function of body part, sex, and laterality. In D. R. Kenshalo (Ed.), *The skin senses* (pp. 195–218). Springfield, IL: Thomas.

Weinstein, S., & Sersen, E. A. (1961). Tactual sensitivity as a function of handedness and laterality. *Journal of Comparative and Physiological Psychology, 54,* 665–669.

Weisel, T. N., & Hubel, D. H. (1974). Ordered arrangement of orientation columns in monkeys lacking visual experience. *Journal of Comparative Neurology, 158,* 307–318.

Weisenberg, M. (1984). Cognitive aspects of pain. In P. D. Wall & R. Melzack (Eds.), *Textbook of pain* (pp. 162–172). Edinburgh: Churchill Livingstone.

Weisenberger, J. M., Broadstone, S. M., & Saunders, F. A. (1989). Evaluation of two multichannel tactile aids for the hearing impaired. *Journal of the Acoustical Society of America, 86,* 1764–1775.

Weisstein, N. A. (1968). Rashevsky-Landahl neural net: Simulation of metacontrast. *Psychological Review, 75,* 494–521.

Weisstein, N. A. (1980). Tutorial: The joy of Fourier analysis. In C. S. Harris (Ed.), *Visual coding and adaptability* (pp. 365–380). Hillsdale, NJ: Erlbaum.

Weisstein, N. A., Harris, C., Berbaum, K., Tangney, J., & Williams, A. (1977). Contrast reduction by small localized stimuli: Extensive spatial spread of above-threshold orientation-selective masking. *Vision Research, 17,* 341–350.

Weisstein, N. A., Mantalvo, F. S., & Ozog, G. (1972). Differential adaptation to gratings blocked by cubes and gratings blocked by hexagons: A test of the neural symbolic activity hypothesis. *Psychonomic Science, 27,* 89–91.

Weisstein, N. A., Matthews, M., & Berbaum, K. (1974, November). *Illusory contours can mask real contours.* Paper presented at the meeting of the Psychonomic Society, Boston.

Weisstein, N. A., Ozog, G., & Szoc, R. (1975). A comparison and elaboration of two models of metacontrast. *Psychological Review, 82,* 325–343.

Weisstein, N. A., & Wong, E. (1986). Figure-ground organization and the spatial and temporal responses of the visual system. In E. C. Schwab & H. C. Nusbaum (Eds.), *Pattern recognition by humans and machines: Vol. 2. Visual perception* (pp. 31–64). Orlando: Academic Press.

Welch, R. B. (1969). Adaptation to prism-displaced vision: The importance of target pointing. *Perception & Psychophysics, 5,* 305–309.

Welch, R. B. (1971). Prism adaptation: The "target pointing effect" as a function of exposure trials. *Perception & Psychophysics, 5,* 102–104.

Welch, R. B. (1978). *Perceptual modification, adapting to altered sensory environments.* New York: Academic Press.

Welford, A. T. (1980). *Reaction times.* London: Academic Press.

Well, A. D., Lorch, E. P., & Anderson, D. R. (1980). Developmental trends in distractability: Is absolute or proportional decrement the appropriate measure of interference? *Journal of Experimental Child Psychology, 30,* 109–124.

Wells, G. L., & Loftus, E. (1984). *Eyewitness testimony: Psychological perspectives.* Cambridge: Cambridge University Press.

Wenderoth, P., Criss, G., & van der Zwan, R. (1990). Determinants of subjective contour: Bourdon illusions and "unbending" effects. *Perception & Psychophysics, 48,* 497–508.

Werker, J. F. (1989). Becoming a native listener. *American Scientist, 77,* 54–59.

Werker, J. F. (1992). Cross–language speech perception: Developmental change does not involve loss. In J. Goodman & H. C. Nusbaum (Eds.), *Speech perception and word recognition.* Cambridge, MA: MIT Press.

Werker, J. F., Gilbert, J., Humphrey, K., & Tees, R. (1981). Developmental aspects of cross-language speech perception. *Child Development, 52,* 349–355.

Werker, J. F., & Logan, J. S. (1985), Cross-language evidence for three factors in speech perception. *Perception & Psychophysics, 37,* 35–44.

Werker, J. F., & McLeod, P. J. (1989). Infant preference for both male and female infant directed talk: A development of attention and affective responsiveness. *Canadian Journal of Psychology, 43,* 230–246.

Werker, J. F., & Tees, R. C. (1984). Cross-language speech perception: Evidence for perceptual reorganization during the first year of life. *Infant Behavior and Development, 7,* 49–63.

Werner, H. (1935). Studies on contour. *American Journal of Psychology, 47,* 40–64.

Werner, J. S. (1979). *Developmental change in scotopic sensitivity and the absorption spectrum of the human ocular media.* Unpublished doctoral dissertation, Brown University, Providence, RI.

Werner, J. S., Peterzell, D. H., & Sheetz, A. J. (1990). Light, vision and aging. *Optometry and Vision Science, 67,* 214–229.

Werner, J. S., & Walraven, J. (1982). Effect of chromatic adaptation on the achromatic locus: The role of contrast, luminance and background color. *Vision Research, 22,* 929–943.

Werner, J. S., & Wooten, B. R. (1979). Human infant color vision and color perception. *Infant Behavior and Development, 2,* 241–274.

Wertheimer, M. (1912). Experimentelle Studien uber das Sehen von Bewegung. *Zeitschrift fur Psychologie, 61,* 161–265.

Wertheimer, M. (1923). Principles of perceptual organization (Abridged trans. by M. Wertheimer). In D. S. Beardslee & M. Wertheimer (Eds.), *Readings in perception* (pp. 115–137). Princeton, NJ: Van Nostrand-Reinhold. (Original work published 1923, *Psychologishe Forschung, 41,* 301–350)

Wertheimer, M. (1961). Psychomotor coordination of auditory and visual space at birth. *Science, 134,* 1692.

Westerman, L. A., & Smith, R. L. (1988). A diffusion model of the transient response of the cochlear inner hair cell synapse. *Journal of the Acoustical Society of America, 83,* 2266–2276.

Westheimer, G. (1965). Spatial interaction in the human retina during scotopic vision. *Journal of Physiology, 181,* 812–894.

Westheimer, G. (1967). Spatial interaction in human cone vision. *Journal of Physiology, 190,* 139–154.

Westheimer, G. (1979). Spatial sense of the eye. *Investigative Ophthalmology and Visual Science, 18,* 893–912.

Wever, E. G. (1970). *Theory of hearing.* New York: Wiley.

Wever, R. A. (1979). *The circadian system of man.* New York: Springer-Verlag.

Wever, R. A. (1989). Light effects on human circadian rhythms: A review of recent Andechs experiments. *Journal of Biological Rhythms, 4,* 161–185.

Whalen, D. H., & Liberman, A. M. (1987). Speech perception takes precedence over nonspeech perception. *Science, 237,* 169–171.

White, B. L. (1971). *Human infants.* Englewood Cliffs, NJ: Prentice-Hall.

White, B. W., Saunders, F. A., Scadden, L., Bach-y-Rita, P., & Collins, C. C. (1970). Seeing with the skin. *Perception & Psychophysics, 7,* 23–27.

White, C. (1963). Temporal numerosity and the psychological unit of duration. *Psychological Monographs, 77* (1–37, Whole No. 575).

White, C. W., Lockhead, G. R., & Evans, N. J. (1977). Multidimensional scaling of subjective color-blind observers. *Perception & Psychophysics, 21,* 522–526.

White, C. W., & Montgomery, D. A. (1976). Memory colours in afterimages: A bicentennial demonstration. *Perception & Psychophysics, 19,* 371–374.

Whitfield, I. C. (1967). *The auditory pathway.* London: Arnold.

Whitfield, I. C. (1968). The organization of the auditory pathways. *Journal of Sound and Vibration Research, 8,* 108–117.

Whitfield, I. C. (1978). The neural code. In E. C. Carterette & M. P. Friedman (Eds.), *Handbook of Perception: Vol. IV. Hearing* (pp. 163–183). New York: Academic Press.

Whitfield, I. C. (1980). Auditory cortex and the pitch of complex tones. *Journal of the Acoustical Society of America, 67,* 644–647.

Whitfield, I. C., & Evans, E. F. (1965). Responses of auditory cortical neurons to stimuli of changing frequency. *Journal of Neurophysiology, 28,* 655–672.

Whitsel, B. L., Dreyer, D. A., Hollins, M., & Young, M. G. (1979). The coding of direction of tactile stimulus movement: Correlative psychophysical and electrophysiological data. In D. R. Kenshalo (Ed.), *Sensory functions of the skin of humans* (pp. 79–108). New York: Plenum Press.

Whorf, B. L. (1956). Science and linguistics. In J. B. Carroll (Ed.), *Language, thought and reality: Selected writings of Benjamin Lee Whorf* (pp. 207–219). Cambridge, MA: MIT Press.

Whytt, R. (1751). *An essay on the vital and other involuntary motions of animals.* Edinburgh: Balfour & Neill.

Wickens, C. D. (1984). Processing resources in attention. In R. Parasuraman & D. R. Davies (Eds.), *Varieties of attention* (pp. 63–101). Orlando: Academic Press.

Wiener, N. (1961). *Cybernetics* (2nd ed.). Cambridge, MA: MIT Press.

Wier, C. C., Jesteadt, W., & Green, D. M. (1977). Frequency discrimination as a function of frequency and sensation level. *Journal of the Acoustical Society of America, 61,* 178–184.

Wier, C. C., Pasanen, E. G., & McFadden, D. (1988). Partial dissociation of spontaneous otoacoustic emissions and distortion products during aspirin use. *Journal of the Acoustical Society of America, 84,* 230–237.

Willer, J. C., Dehen, H., & Cambier, J. (1981). Stress-induced analgesia in humans: Endogenous opioids and naloxone-reversible depression of pain reflexes. *Science, 212,* 689–690.

Williams, D. R., MacLeod, D. I. A., Hayhoe, M. M. (1981). Foveal tritanopia. *Vision Research, 21,* 1341–1356.

Williams, J. M. (1979). Distortions of vision and pain: Two functional facets of D-Lysergic diethylamide. *Perceptual and Motor Skills, 49,* 499–528.

Williams, M. (1970). *Brain damage and the mind.* London: Penguin.

Willis, W. D. (1983). Descending control of nociceptive transmission by primate spinothalamic neurons. In C. von Euler, O. Franzen, U. Lindblom, & D. Ottoson (Eds.), *Somatosensory mechanisms* (pp. 296–308). New York: Plenum Press.

Willis, W. D. (1985). *The pain system: The neural basis of nococeptive transmission in the mammalian nervous system.* Basel: Karger.

Wilson, E. O. (1971). *The insect societies.* Cambridge, MA: Harvard University Press.

Wilson, H. C. (1987). Female axillary secretions influence women's menstrual cycles: A critique. *Hormones and Behavior, 21,* 536–546.

Wilson, H. C. (1988). Male axillary secretions influence women's menstrual cycles: A critique. *Hormones and Behavior, 22,* 266–271.

Wilson, H. R. (1986). Responses of spatial mechanisms can explain hyperacuity. *Vision Research, 26,* 453–469.

Wilson, H. R., & Bergen, J. R. (1979). A four mechanism model for threshold spatial vision. *Vision Research, 19,* 19–32.

Wilson, H. R., & Gelb, D. J. (1984). Modified line element theory for spatial frequency and width discrimination. *Journal of the Optical Society of America A, 1,* 124–131.

Wilson, H. R., Levi, D., Maffei, L., Rovamo, J., DeValois, R. (1990). The perception of form: Retina to striate cortex. In L. Spillman & J. S. Werner (Eds.), *Visual perception: The neurophysiological foundations* (pp. 231–272). New York: Academic Press.

Wilson, J. R., DeFries, J. C., McClearn, G. C., Vandenberg, S. G., Johnson, R. C., & Rashad, M. N. (1975). Cognitive abilities: Use of family data as a control to assess sex and age differences in two ethnic groups. *International Journal of Aging and Human Development, 6,* 261–275.

Wilson, M. (1957). Effects of circumscribed cortical lesions upon somesthetic and visual discrimination in the monkey. *Journal of Comparative and Physiological Psychology, 50,* 630–635.

Witkin, H. A., & Berry, J. W. (1975). Psychological differentiation in cross-cultural perspective. *Journal of Cross-Cultural Psychology, 6,* 4–87.

Wolfe, J. M., Cave, K. R., & Franzel, S. L. (1989). Guided search: An alternative to the feature integration model for visual search. *Journal of Experimental Psychology: Human Perception and Performance, 15,* 419–433.

Wolfe, J. M., & O'Connell, K. M. (1986). Fatigue and structural change: Two consequences of visual pattern adaptation. *Investigative Ophthalmology and Visual Science, 28,* 173–212.

Wolff, H. G., & Goodell, B. S. (1943). The relation of attitude and suggestion to the perception of and reaction to pain. *Research Publications, Association for Research in Nervous and Mental Disease, 23,* 434–448.

Wolff, P. H. (1987). *The development of behavioral states and the expression of emotions in early infancy.* Chicago: University of Chicago Press.

Wong, C., & Weisstein, N. (1982). A new perceptual context-superiority effect: Line segments are more visible against a figure than against a ground. *Science, 218,* 587–589.

Wong, E., & Weisstein, N. (1987). The effects of flicker on the perception of figure and ground. *Perception & Psychophysics, 41,* 440–448.

Wong-Riley, M. T. T. (1979). Changes in the visual system of monocularly sutured or enucleated cats demonstrable with cytochrome oxidase histochemistry. *Brain Research, 171,* 11–28.

Woo, G., & Bader, D. (1978). Age and its effect on vision. *Canadian Journal of Optometry, 40,* 29–34.

Woo, G. C., & Wilson, M. A. (1990). Current methods of treating and preventing myopia. *Optometry and Vision Science, 67,* 719–727.

Wood, R. W. (1985). The "haunted swing" illusion. *Psychological Review, 2,* 277–278.

Woodfield, R. L. (1984). Embedded figures test performance before and after childbirth. *British Journal of Psychology, 75,* 81–88.

Woodrow, H. (1951). Time perception. In S. S. Stevens (Ed.), *Handbook of experimental psychology* (pp. 1224–1236). New York: Wiley.

Woolard, H. H., Weddell, G., & Harpman, J. A. (1940). Observations of the neuro-historical basis of cutaneous pain. *Journal of Anatomy, 74,* 413–440.

Worchel, P., & Dallenbach, K. M. (1947). "Facial vision": Perception of obstacles by the deaf-blind. *American Journal of Psychology, 60,* 502–553.

Worthey, J. A., & Brill, M. H. (1986). Heuristic analysis of von Kries color constancy. *Journal of the Optical Society of America A, 3,* 1708–1712.

Wright, L. L., Elias, J. W. (1979). Age differences in the effects of perceptual noise. *Journal of Gerontology, 34,* 704–708.

Wright, M. J., & Johnston, A. (1985). Invariant tuning of motion aftereffect. *Vision Research, 25,* 1947–1955.

Wright, N. H. (1964). Temporal summation and backward masking. *Journal of the Acoustical Society of America, 36,* 927–932.

Wright, R. H. (1977). Odor and molecular vibration: Neural coding of olfactory information. *Journal of Theoretical Biology, 64,* 473–502.

Wright, R. H. (1978a). Specific anosmia: A clue to the olfactory code or to something much more important? *Chemical Senses and Flavor, 3,* 235–239.

Wright, R. H. (1978b). The perception of odor intensity: Physics or psychophysics? *Chemical Senses and Flavor, 3,* 73–79.

Wright, R. H. (1978c). The perception of odor intensity: Physics or psychophysics II. *Chemical Senses and Flavor, 3,* 241–245.

Wright, R. H. (1982). *The sense of smell.* Boca Raton, FL: CRC Press.

Wright, W. D. (1929). A re-determination of the trichromatic mixture data. *Medical Research Council (Great Britain), Special Report Series, SRS–139,* 1–38.

Wright, W. D. (1952). The characteristics of tritanopia. *Journal of the Optical Society of America, 42,* 509–521.

Wurtz, R. H., & Goldberg, M. E. (1971). Superior colliculus cell responses related to eye movements in awake monkeys. *Science, 171,* 82–84.

Wurtz, R. H., Goldberg, M. E., & Robinson, D. L. (1980). Behavioral modulation of visual responses in monkeys. *Progress in Psychobiology and Physiological Psychology, 9,* 42–83.

Wyburn, G. M., Pickford, R. W., & Hurst, R. J. (1964). *Human senses and perception.* Toronto: University of Toronto Press.

Wyszecki, G., & Stiles, W. S. (1967). *Color science: Concepts and methods, quantitative data and formulas.* New York: Wiley.

Yaksh, T. L. (1984). Multiple spinal opiate receptor systems in analgesia. In L. Kruger & J. C. Liebeskind (Eds.), *Neural mechanisms of pain* (pp. 197–216). New York: Raven Press.

Yamamamoto, T., Yayama, N. & Kawamura, Y. (1981). Central processing of taste perception: In Y. Katsuki, R. Norgren, & M. Sato (Eds.), *Brain mechanisms of sensation* (pp. 197–208). New York: Wiley.

Yantis, S. (1988). On analog movements of visual attention. *Perception & Psychophysics, 43,* 203–206.

Yantis, S., & Jonides, J. (1984). Abrupt onsets and selective attention: Evidence from visual search. *Journal of Experimental Psychology: Human Perception and Performance, 10,* 601–621.

Yarbus, A. L. (1967). *Eye movements and vision.* New York: Plenum Press.

Yarmey, A. (1979). *The psychology of eyewitness testimony.* New York: Free Press.

Ye, Q., Heck, G. L., & DeSimone, J. A. (1991). The anion paradox in sodium taste reception: Resolution by voltage clamp studies. *Science, 254,* 724–726.

Yen, W. (1975). Sex-linked major gene influence on selected types of spatial performance. *Behavior Genetics, 5,* 281–298.

Yerkes, R. M., & Dodson, J. D. (1908). The relation of strength of stimulus to rapidity of habit formation. *Journal of Comparative Neurology and Psychology, 18,* 459–482.

Yin, R. K. (1970). Face recognition by brain injured patients — a dissociable ability. *Neuropsychologia, 8,* 395.

Yodogawa, E. (1982). Symmetropy, an entropy-like measure of visual symmetry. *Perception & Psychophysics, 32,* 230–240.

Yonas, A. (1981). Infants' response to optical information for collision. In R. N. Aslin, J. R. Alberts, & M. R. Petersen (Eds.), *Development of perception.* (pp. 313–334.) New York: Academic Press.

Yonas, A., Cleaves, W., & Pettersen, L. (1978). Development of sensitivity to pictorial depth. *Science, 200,* 77–79.

Yonas, A., Goldsmith, L. T., & Hallstrom, J. (1978). Development of sensitivity to information provided by cast shadows in pictures. *Perception, 7,* 333–341.

Yonas, A., & Granrud, C. E. (1985a). Development of visual space perception in young infants. In J. Mehler & R. Fox (Eds.), *Neonate cognition: Beyond the blooming buzzing confusion* (pp. 45–68). Hillsdale, NJ: Erlbaum.

Yonas, A., & Granrud, C. E. (1985b). The development of sensitivity to kinetic, binocular and pictorial depth information in human infants. In D. Ingle, D. Lee, & M. Jeannerod (Eds.), *Brain mechanisms and spatial vision* (pp. 113–145). Dordrecht, The Netherlands: Nijoff.

Yonas, A., & Granrud, C. E. (1986). Infants' distance perception from linear perspective and texture gradients. *Infant Behavior and Development, 9,* 247–256.

Yoneshige, Y., & Elliott, L. L. (1981). Pure-tone sensitivity and ear canal pressure at threshold in children and adults. *Journal of the Acoustical Society of America, 70,* 1272–1276.

Young, F. A. (1981). Primate myopia. *American Journal of Optometry and Physiological Optics, 58,* 560–566.

Young, L. L., & Wilson, K. A. (1982). Effects of acetylsalicylic acid on speech discrimination. *Audiology, 21,* 342–349.

Young, L. R. (1971). Pursuit eye tracking movements. In P. Bach-y-Rita, C. C. Collins, & J. E. Hyde (Eds.), *The control of eye movements* (pp. 429–443). New York: Academic Press.

Young, R. A. (1977). Some observations on temporal coding of color vision: Psychophysical results. *Vision Research, 17,* 957–965.

Yuille, J. (1984). Research and teaching with police: A Canadian example. *International Review of Applied Psychology, 33,* 5–23.

Yund, E. W., Morgan, H., & Efron, R. (1983). The micropattern effect and visible persistence. *Perception & Psychophysics, 34,* 209–213.

Zakay, D., Nitzan, D., & Glicksohn, J. (1983). The influence of task difficulty and external tempo on subjective time estimation. *Perception & Psychophysics, 34,* 451–456.

Zaporozhets, A. V. (1965). The development of perception in the preschool child. *Monographs of the Society for Research in Child Development, 30,* 82–101.

Zaragoza, M. S., & McCloskey, M. (1989). Misleading postevent information and the memory impairment hypothesis: Comment on Belli and reply to Tversky and Tuchin. *Journal of Experimental Psychology: General, 118,* 92–99.

Zatorre, R. J. (1985). Discrimination and recognition of tonal melodies after unilateral cerebral excisions. *Neuropsychologia, 23,* 31–41.

Zatorre, R. J. (1988). Pitch perception of complex tones and human temporal-lobe function. *Journal of the Acoustical Society of America, 84,* 566–572.

Zatorre, R. J., Evans, A. C., Meyer, E., & Gjedde, A. (1992). Lateralization of phonetic and pitch discrimination in speech processing. *Science, 256,* 846–849.

Zatorre, R. J., & Jones-Gotman, M. (1990). Right-nostril advantage for discrimination of odors. *Perception & Psychophysics, 47,* 526–531.

Zeigler, H. P., & Leibowitz, H. (1957). Apparent visual size as a function of distance for children and adults. *American Journal of Psychology, 70,* 106–109.

Zellner, D. A., & Kautz, M. A. (1990). Color affects perceived odor intensity. *Journal of Experimental Psychology: Human Perception and Performance, 16,* 391–397.

Zigler, M. J. (1932). Pressure adaptation time: A function of intensity and extensity. *American Journal of Psychology, 44,* 709–720.

Zihl, J., von Cramon, D., & Mai, N. (1983). Selective disturbance of movement vision after bilateral brain damage. *Brain, 106,* 313–340.

Zimmerman, M. (1983). Centrifugal control of somatosensory inflow into the spinal cord. In C. von Euler, O. Franzen, U. Lindblom, & D. Ottoson (Eds.), *Somatosensory mechanisms* (pp. 285–296). New York: Plenum Press.

Zotterman, Y. (1959). Thermal sensations. In J. Fields, H. W. Magoun, & V. E. Hall (Eds.), *Handbook of Physiology: Section 1. Neurophysiology, 1,* 431–458.

Zrenner, E., Abramov, I., Akita, M., Cowey, A., Livingstone, M., & Valberg, A. (1990). Color perception: Retina to cortex. In L. Spillman & J. Werner (Eds.), *Visual perception: The neurophysiological foundations.* New York: Academic Press.

Zucker, I., Wade, G., & Ziegler, R. (1972). Sexual and hormonal influences on eating, taste preferences, and body weight of hamsters. *Physiology and Behavior, 8,* 101–111.

Zucker, S. (1987). Early vision. In S. C. Shapiro (Ed.), *The encyclopedia of artificial intelligence* (pp. 1131–1152). New York: Wiley.

Zuidema, P., Gresnight, A. M., Bouman, M. A., & Koenderink, J. J. (1978). A quanta coincidence model for absolute threshold vision incorporating deviations from Ricco's law. *Vision Research, 18,* 1685–1689.

Zurek, P. M. (1980). The precedence effect and its possible role in the avoidance of interaural ambiguities. *Journal of the Acoustical Society of America, 67,* 952–964.

Zwicker, E. (1958). Uber psychologische und methodosche Grundlagen der Lautheit. *Acustica, 8,* 237–258.

Zwicker, E. (1986). A hardware cochlear nonlinear preprocessing model with active feedback. *Journal of the Acoustical Society of America, 80,* 146–153.

Zwislocki, J. J. (1978). Masking: Experimental and theoretical aspects of simultaneous, forward, backward, and central masking. In E. C. Carterette & M. P. Friedman (Eds.), *Handbook of Perception: Vol. IV. Hearing* (pp. 283–336). New York: Academic Press.

Zwislocki, J. J., Damianopoulos, E. N., Buining, E., & Glantz, J. (1967). Central masking: Some steady-state and transient effects. *Perception & Psychophysics, 2,* 59–64.

AUTHOR INDEX

Page numbers in italics indicate figures; page numbers followed by "t" indicate tabular material.

Aantaa, E., 551, 647
Aaron, M., 649
Abbs, J. H., 430, 649
Abraham, H. D., 621, 649
Abramov, I., 169, 551, 649, 717
Abramson, A., 430, 685
Achorn, E., 634, 705
Adam, C. L., 429, 649
Adam, N., 429, 649
Adams, A. J., 619, 622, 640, 668
Adams, A. S., 622, 649
Adams, J., 557, 649, 661
Adams, J. A., 304, 649
Adams, R. D., 451, 649
Adams, R. J., 173, 688
Aitkin, L., 231, 649
Ajdukovic, D., 262, 266, 656
Akabas, M. H., 257, 649
Akerstrom, R. A., 336, 708
Akhtar, N., 568, 649
Akil, H., 321, 322, 649
Akita, M., 169, 717
Aks, D. J., 496, 497, 660
Albers, H. E., 447, 649, 669
Albrecht, D. G., 127, 661
Albrecht, R. E., 634, 661
Albright, T. D., 96, 663
Alcantara, J. I., 301, 661
Alexander, J. B., 634, 649
Alexander, K. R., 176, 649
Algom, D., 60, 235, 319, 649
Ali, M. R., 620, 649
Allan, L. G., 174t, 649
Allen, J. A., 493, 694
Allen, J. R., 622, 649
Allen, M., 574, 649
Allison, A. C., 273, 649
Allman, J., 456, 649
Allport, D. A., 528, 649
Allyn, M. R., 169, 595, 667
Alpern, M., 163, 650
Amerson, T. L., Jr., 230, 689
Ames, A., Jr., 389, 596, 650
Amir, T., 620, 649
Amoore, J. E., 272, 274, 277, 650

Amure, B. D., 619, 650
Anastaso poulos, D., 475, 688
Andersen, G. J., 476, 650
Anderson, C. H., 129, 710
Anderson, D. A., 568, 713
Anderson, D. J., 202, 699
Anderson, J. E., 564, 665
Anderson, N. H., 60, 650
Anderson, N. S., 39, 650
Andreasean, N. C., 650
Andrews, B. W., 117, 650
Anliker, M., 360, 694
Anstis, S. M., 135, 137, 462, 650
Anstis, T., 173, 374, 460, 593, 677, 697
Antes, J. R., 451, 529, 530, 566, 567, 650
Antonis, B., 528, 649
Aoki, C., 540, 701
Applebaum, S., 280, 627, 664, 665
Arend, L. E., 133, 650
Arlin, M., 452, 650
Arpajian, D. J., 298, 670
Arterberry, M., 360, 650
Arvidson, K., 258, 650
Asa, C. S., 279, 671
Asano, F., 227, 650
Aschoff, J., 446, 447, 450, 650
Ashby, F. G., 399, 650, 708
Ashmead, D. H., 230, 555, 650, 698
Aslin, R. N., 351, 359, 360, 555, 556, 565, 580, 583, 608, 651, 668, 703
Aspinall, P. A., 173
Atkin, L. M., 206, 714
Atkinson, J., 552, 553, 556, 557, 565, 655, 676
Attili, G., 279, 701
Attneave, F., 383, 386, 387, 651, 692
Aubert, H., 457, 651
Augenstine, L. G., 651
Avant, L. L., 370, 451, 651
Avolio, B., 574, 651
Al-Awqati, Q., 257, 649
Ayley, J. B., 605, 699

Bach-y-Rita, P., 299, 300, 301, 702, 714
Bacon, S. P., 220, 678
Baddeley, A. D., 449, 651

Bader, D., 572, 713
Bader, G. R., 656, 715
Bader, P., 580, 675
Baggen, S., 399, 680
Bailey, P., 343, 446, 669, 703
Bainard, D. H., 506, 651
Baird, J. C., 48, 55, 394, 651, 677
Bakalyar, H. A., 272, 671
Baker, C. L., 453, 460, 651, 675
Baldwin, B. A., 97, 680
Balint, R., 651
Ball, K., 453, 574, 651, 702
Ball, W., 360, 651
Ballard, D. H., 98, 651
Ballenger, W. L., 230, 688
Balogh, R. D., 280, 651, 696
Banks, M. S., 551, 552, 553, 556, 559, 651
Bannatyne, A., 570, 651
Baratz, S. S., 334, 651
Barbeito, D., 357, 651
Barclay, C. D., 465, 652
Barclay, P., 598, 653
Baribeau-Braun, J., 635, 657
Barlow, H. B., 98, 652, 694, 695
Barr, A., 565, 678
Barrera, M., 560, 657, 687
Barrie, D. L., 704
Bartleson, C. J., 174, 652
Bartlett, B., 605, 699
Barton, M., 624, 682
Bartoshuk, L. M., 254, 255, 259, 260, 261, 262, 263, 264t, 265, 652, 668, 673, 695
Baruch, C., 235, 654
Barz, K., 247, 652
Basala, M., 361, 431, 665
Bashford, J. A., 436, 652
Bass, E., 289, 343, 703
Bates, M. E., 619, 652
Batteau, D. W., 227, 652
Bauer, J. A., 476, 557, 590, 673, 675
Baum, J. M., 628, 712
Baumgartner, G., 104, 127, 139, 667, 694
Baylor, D. A., 77, 79, 701
Beauchamp, G. K., 564, 652
Bechtoldt, H. P., 360, 677
Beck, J., 374, 375, 504, 676, 707
Beck, N. C., 652

Becker, W., 475, 688
Beckett, P. A., 594, 652
Becklen, R., 457, 459, 711
Becklin, R., 522, 523, 526, 691
Bedford, W., 605, 699
Beeler, W. J., 319, 656
Beersma, D.G.M., 450, 662
Begleiter, S., 619, 652
Beidler, L. M., 256, 258, 652, 681
Bekesy, G. von, 24, 187, 188, 195, 230, 241, 242, 288, 295, 298, 652
Belkin, M., 610, 682
Bell, B., 572, 668
Belliveau, J. W., 652
Bem, S. L., 632, 652
Ben-Aharon, B., 235, 649
Bender, D. B., 96, 672
Bennedetti, F., 294t, 652
Bennett, T. L., 622, 652
Benson, A., 304, 700
Bentham, J. van, 444, 763
Bentin, S., 431, 652
Berbaum, K., 331, 332, 351, 373, 379, 463, 652
Berg, B. G., 223, 653
Berg, K. M., 562, 653
Bergeijk, W. A. van, 187, 653
Bergen, J. R., 127, 383, 679, 715
Berger, G. O., 653
Bergerone, C., 357, 700
Berglund, M. B., 55, 507, 653, 708
Berglund, U., 507, 708
Bergman, T., 566, 673
Berkley, M. A., 460, 469, 653, 710
Berlin, B., 176, 653
Berman, A. J., 66, 593, 707
Berman, K. F., 653
Berman, N., 582, 662
Bernhaus, I. J., 671
Bernstein, I. H., 496, 598, 653, 688
Bernstein, L. R., 223, 653
Berry, J. W., 634, 653, 715
Besser, G., 620, 653
Besso, M., 444, 665
Best, C. T., 434, 653
Best, H., 319, 661
Betke, K., 214, 653
Bever, T., 331, 332, 652, 653
Beverly, K., 351, 353, 476, 698
Bharucha, J. J., 411, 682
Bhatia, B., 455, 653
Bickel, W. K., 620, 676
Biddulph, R., 223, 224, 704
Biederman, I., 401, 451, 530, 653
Bierman, K., 653, 676
Bigiani, A. R., 257, 653

Billings, B. L., 221, 653
Bindra, D., 273, 657
Birch, E. E., 360, 653
Birmbaum, M. H., 609, 653
Birren, J. E., 576, 653
Bishop, P. O., 83, 86, 347, 653
Bissonnette, V., 223, 598, 653, 702
Blake, R., 217, 653, 673, 702
Blakemore, C., 137, 582, 654
Blakeslee, A. F., 260, 654
Blamey, P. J., 204, 301, 654, 661
Blasdel, G. G., 586, 654
Blazynski, C., 78, 654
Blecker, M. L., 628, 654
Bliss, J. C., 300, 654
Block, R. A., 451, 452, 558, 654
Block, S. S., 285, 701
Bloom, K., 563, 654
Blough, P. M., 629, 654
Blundo, C., 623, 654
Boardman, W. K., 217, 450, 671, 673
Bobbin, R. P., 195, 697
Boch, R., 513, 667
Boer, K., 394, 654
Bolanowski, S. J., Jr., 47, 51, 295, 299, 654, 670, 698, 710
Boll, F., 77, 654
Bolla-Wilson, K., 628, 654
Bolton, T. L., 416, 654
Bonnet, C., 457, 654
Bonsall, R. W., 279, 689
Booth, D. A., 323, 681
Borbely, A. A., 450, 653, 662
Borg, G., 55, 654
Boring, E. G., 265, 489, 676
Bornstein, M. H., 162, 163, 176, 654, 708
Borresen, C. R., 500, 684
Bose, H. E., 264, 265, 688
Bossom, J., 592, 593, 654, 675
Botstein, D., 159, 654
Botte, M. C., 235, 654
Botwinick, J., 576, 654, 655
Bouffard, J. A., 627, 686
Bouman, M. A., 114, 717
Bowen, R. W., 170, 655
Bowers, J. N., 230, 688
Bowker, D. O., 587, 655
Bowler, R., 173, 688
Bowmaker, J. K., 160, 161, 655
Bowman, K., 572, 661
Bownds, M. D., 503, 677
Boycott, B. B., 83, 139, 655, 694
Boyd, I. A., 303, 655
Boylan, A., 531, 557, 700
Boynton, R. M., 162, 163, 170, 176, 505, 655, 680, 709

Brabyn, L. B., 628, 655
Braddick, O. J., 360, 460, 552, 553, 556, 557, 565, 651, 655
Bradley, A., 126, 655
Bradley, D. R., 356, 467, 660
Bradley, R. M., 564, 655
Brady, T. J., 435, 652
Braff, D. L., 621, 655
Braida, L. D., 38, 306, 655, 692
Brainard, M. S., 231, 478, 681
Braine, L. G., 500, 655
Brand, J. G., 257, 272, 655, 707
Brandt, T., 118, 476, 664, 683
Brantley, M. A., 223, 681
Braun, A. M., 204, 654
Braun, C., 635, 655
Braun, C. M., 173, 655, 657
Braunstein, M. L., 476, 650
Braybyn, L. B., 655
Brazelton, T., 556, 655
Breen, T. J., 536, 659
Bregman, A. S., 245, 246, 378, 410, 413, 415, 417, 655, 708
Breitmeyer, B., 513, 517, 668
Brening, 82, 655
Brennan, P., 267, 655
Brenowitz, E. A., 417, 655
Brewster, M. M., 448, 682
Bridgeman, B., 356, 705
Bridges, C.D.B., 79, 655
Brill, M. H., 565, 587, 715
Brill, S., 506, 655, 683
Brillat-Savarin, J. A., 267, 655
Broadbent, D. E., 538, 542, 655, 656
Broadstone, S. M., 301, 713
Brodeur, D. A., 568, 666
Brodie, E., 304, 700
Brodmann, K., 88, 205, 656
Brody, B. A., 624, 682
Bronson, G. W., 566, 656
Brooks, B., 311, 385, 680
Brooks, P. L., 301, 680
Brooks, R. A., 399, 656
Brooks, V., 385, 602, 676
Brooksbank, B.W.L., 169, 661
Broota, K. D., 493, 666
Brou, P., 505, 657
Brown, A. C., 319, 657
Brown, A. M., 301, 654
Brown, B., 455, 572, 619, 622, 649, 656, 661, 668
Brown, J. M., 379, 656
Brown, J. W., 444, 656
Brown, M. E., 221, 683
Brown, P. E., 322, 656
Brown, P. K., 160, 161, 656
Brown, R. E., 279, 656, 686

Brown, S. W., 451, 656
Brown, T. S., 270, 656
Brown, V., 518, 683
Brown, W., 39, 656
Brownell, W. E., 656
Browse, R. A., 305, 375, 383, 673, 683
Bruce, C., 96, 97, 485, 491, 656, 663
Brugge, J. F., 202, 230, 695, 699
Bruner, J. S., 175, 566, 656, 686
Bruni, J. R., 574, 651
Bruno, M., 351, 656
Brunswick, E., 353, 485, 596, 656
Brussell, E. M., 165, 636
Bryden, M. P., 428, 629, 656
Buchanon, J. L., 230, 688
Buchbinder, R. R., 123, 652
Buchtel, H. A., 625, 656
Buckalew, L. W., 176, 659
Buckhout, R., 600, 656
Bucy, P. C., 94, 681
Buell, T., 231, 673
Buhrmann, K., 584, 707
Buining, E., 221, 717
Bujos, Z., 262, 266, 656
Bull, R., 612, 659
Bundesen, C., 462, 656
Bunt, A. A., 235, 684
Burg, A., 573, 628, 656
Burghauser, B., 628, 712
Burgland, B., 274, 656
Burke, R. J., 274, 706
Burl, M., 343, 703
Burnham, R. W., 174, 692
Burns, E. M., 409, 656
Burt, G. S., 496, 686
Burt, P., 348, 462, 657
Burton, G., 305, 657
Burton, G. J., 139, 657
Bushnell, M. C., 316, 317, 657, 689, 707
Butler, D. L., 389, 657
Butler, R. A., 227, 657, 668
Butter, C. M., 469, 682
Butters, N., 624, 657
Butterworth, G., 513, 562, 657
Buus, S., 222, 223, 668
Byrd, R., 411, 657, 685

Cacace, A. T., 236, 657
Caelli, T., 335, 375, 657
Cagen, R. H., 257, 269, 655, 657
Cahoon, D., 452, 657
Cain, D. P., 657
Cain, W. S., 262, 263, 267, 273, 274, 275, 276, 280, 575, 657, 673, 697
Cajal, S. R., 81, 657

Calderone, J. B., 457, 679
Calderone, L., 267, 677, 705
Caldwell, R., 561, 658
Calford, M. B., 224, 688
Calis, G., 657
Callaghan, T. C., 383, 657
Callender, M. G., 704
Calvanio, R., 625, 684
Cambier, J., 321, 714
Cameron, S., 568, 666
Campbell, D. T., 605, 606, 702
Campbell, F. W., 321, 657
Campbell, K. B., 634, 635, 705
Canevet, G., 233, 235, 655, 657
Canney, C., 560, 636, 702
Cannon, M. W., Jr., 657
Capaldi, E., 658
Cardillo, L., 353, 711
Carello, C., 328, 485, 491, 689
Carey, S., 570, 571, 658
Carlson, C. R., 116, 658
Carlson, V. R., 500, 658
Carlyon, R. P., 219, 221, 658
Carmichael, L., 600, 658
Caroll, D., 57, 658, 681
Caron, A., 561, 658
Caron, R., 561, 658
Carpenter, D. L., 341, 658
Carrell, T. D., 418, 698
Carroll, J. D., 314, 678
Carterette, E. C., 417, 665
Casey, K. L., 316, 318, 658, 688
Casperson, R. C., 653
Casseday, J. H., 229, 681
Cassone, V. M., 658
Cattell, J. M., 44, 658
Cavanagh, P., 170, 332, 374, 375, 455, 462, 658, 667, 709
Cavanaugh, P. H., 279, 688
Cave, K. R., 535, 715
Cegalis, J. A., 634, 658
Cei, A., 357, 700
Cerella, J., 573, 574, 576, 658
Ceridono, D., 357, 700
Cernoch, J. M., 280, 565, 658, 696
Chambers, D., 457, 686
Chamorro, A., 624, 658
Chang, J. J., 57, 658
Chapman, C. R., 322, 575, 658, 674
Charman, W. N., 117, 678
Checkosky, C. M., 299, 654
Cheeseman, J., 658
Cheng, P. W., 659
Cheng, T. O., 322, 659
Cherry, E. C., 43, 521, 522, 659
Chevrier, J., 489, 659
Choate, L. S., 531, 697

Chocolle, R., 44, 217, 659
Cholewiak, R. W., 301, 659
Chomsky, C., 692
Chomsky, N., 306, 425, 659
Chou, C. L., 619, 652
Choudhurt, B. P., 455, 659
Chung, S. S., 65, 331, 332, 652
Cicerone, C. M., 659
Ciner, E. B., 162, 565, 659
Clark, D. J., 146, 683
Clark, D. L., 450, 649
Clark, E. V., 419, 570, 659
Clark, G. M., 204, 301, 654, 655
Clark, H. H., 419, 659
Clark, J. C., 174, 659, 692
Clark, S. E., 593, 698
Clark, T. B., III, 265, 701
Clark, W. C., 314, 322, 659, 678
Clarkson, M. G., 562, 563, 659, 691
Clarkson-Smith, L., 379, 659
Cleaves, W., 360, 716
Clement, D. E., 317, 669
Clifford, B. R., 388, 612, 659
Clifton, R. K., 562, 563, 659, 691
Coats, A. C., 198, 687
Coffield, K. E., 176, 659
Cogan, R., 321, 659
Cohen, A., 521, 697
Cohen, A. J., 412, 661
Cohen, B., 478, 675
Cohen, K., 530, 562, 567, 659
Cohen, M. M., 430, 687
Cohen, M. S., 652
Cohen, S., 621, 665
Cohen, Y., 521, 531, 696
Cohen-Raz, L., 235, 319, 649
Cole, M., 624, 712
Cole, R. A., 424, 659
Coles, M. G., 634, 659
Collett, T. S., 351, 699
Collings, V. B., 260, 659
Collins, C. C., 299, 714
Collins, J. F., 448, 666
Collins, S. C., 431, 689
Comerford, J., 353, 693
Comfort, A., 277, 659
Comis, S. D., 193, 199, 693, 695
Condon, W. S., 433, 659
Cone, J., 173, 688
Conner, J. M., 632, 704
Constanzo, R. H., 669
Cook, J. E., 558, 710
Cooke, N. M., 536, 659
Cooke, V. T., 38, 685
Cooper, B. Y., 315, 659
Cooper, F. S., 439, 684
Cope, P., 169, 685

Corbit, J. D., 430, 438, 665
Coren, S., 14, 59, 71, 159, 160t, 171, 173, 208, 322, 329, 356, 360, 377, 379, 428, 466, 467, 494, *495*, 496, 497, 568, 569, 572, 593, 594, 595, 605, 606, 610, 613, 659, 660, 661, 665, 667, 670, 696, 712
Corkins, S., 573, 692
Cormack, R. H., 353, 660
Cornsweet, J. C., 370, 699
Cornsweet, T. N., 132, 133, 370, 503, 660, 699
Correia, M. J., 473, 660
Corso, J. F., 571, 572, 628, 660
Corwin, T. R., 587, 661
Costanzo, R. H., 269, 304, 661
Costiloe, J., 627, 702
Cotter, N., 204, 229, 708
Cotter, S. A., 558, 701
Cotzin, M. E., 459, 707
Couchman, D. H., 610, 699
Courage, M. L., 173, 557, 565, 661, 688
Covey, E., 221, 666
Cowan, R.S.C., 173, 301, 661
Cowan, W. B., 55, 712
Cowart, B. J., 564, 652
Cowen, G. N., Jr., 522, 671
Cowey, A., 98, 169, 661, 675
Cowley, J. J., 169, 661, 717
Craig, J. C., 301, 659, 661, 667
Craig, K. D., 322, 529, 661, 672
Craik, F., 576, 661
von Cramon, D., 453, 717
Craske, B., 593, 677
Crassini, B., 572, 661
Craton, L. G., 353, 561, 663
Cratty, B., 569, 661
Creed, R. S., *302*, 661
Crestoni, L., 304, 687
Creutzfeldt, O. D., 469, 692
Criss, G., 305, 713
Critchley, M., 622, 661
Crockett, L., 632, 694
Crommelink, M., 454, 694
Crook, C., 564, 661
Cross, I., 60, 417, 664, 667
Crossey, A. D., 455, 659
Crossman, E.R.F.W., 45, 661
Crowley, W. F., Jr., 630, 676
Cruchfield, R. S., 634, 661
Cuddy, L. L., 412, 661
Cunningham, V. J., 169, 685
Cunningham, W., 222, 661, 685
Curcio, C. A., 76, 661
Cutler, W. B., 662, 697

Cutting, J. E., 39, 351, 419, 465, 476, 652, 662
Cynader, M., 116, 353, 359, 582, 583, 662, 680

Daan, S., 662, 445, 450, 672, 699
Dacey, D. M., 81, 662
Dackis, C., 266, 701
Dadson, R. S., 699
Daher, M., 564, 669
Daigneault, S., 173, 655
Dallenbach, K. M., 229, 311, 662, 706, 707, 715
Dallos, P., 199, 662
D'Aloisio, A., 573, 574, 662
Dalton, K., 628, 662
Dalziel, C. C., 70, 338, 662
Damasio, A. R., 625, 662
Damianopoulos, E. N., 221, 717
Daniels, J. D., 552, 662
Dannemiller, J. L., 459, 506, 553, 651, 662
D'Aquila, J. M., 629, 701
Darian-Smith, I., 293, 662
Dark, V., 544, 598, 662
Dartnall, H.M.A., 79, 160, 161, 655, 662
Darwin, C. J., 206, 693
DaSilva, J. A., 493, 671
Daugman, J. G., 129, 662
Davidoff, J. B., 622, 662
Davies, A., 528, 709
Davies, P., 681
Dawson, J. L., 662
Dawson, M.R.W., 457, 462, 662, 663
Day, M. C., 566, 568, 663
Day, R. H., 174t, 305, 493, 663
Day, R. S., 663
DeCourten, C., 553, 677
Deekcke, L., 475, 688
Deering, L., 459, 674
DeGangi, G. A., 636, 663
Dehen, H., 321, 714
Delber, M. D., 169, 685
Delgutte, B., 219, 663
Delhorme, L. A., 175, 299, 476, 489, 665
Delk, J. L., 663
Delman, G., 136, 670
Delorme, A., 659, 663
Demarque, A., 575, 706
Demasio, A. R., 663
De Monasterio, F. M., 663, 681
Denier, C., 632, 705
Denny-Brown, D., *302,* 661
Deptula, D., 634, 658

Deregowski, J., 604, 663
De Renzi, D. E., 521, 663
De Ribaupierre, F., 207, 700
De Ribaupierre, Y., 207, 700
Derrington, A. M., 127, 663
Desaulniers, D. H., 230, 689
Desimone, R., 96, 97, 98, 255, 526, 656, 663
Deutsch, D., 409, 412, 413, 415, 416, 417, 428, 542, 543, 663, 690, 705, 716
Deutsch, G., 663, 705
Deutsch, J. A., 663
DeValois, K. K., 88, 127, 139, 165, 166, 351, 375, 663, 664
DeValois, R. L., 88, 91, 127, 129, 137, 165, 166, 168, 351, 375, 663, 664, 708, 715
Devaney, K. O., 225, 572, 664
De Vries, H., 274, 664
De Vries, J. V., 334, *492,* 664
DeWitt, L. A., 417, 664
Dewsbury, D., 359, 704
DeYoe, E. A., 88, 98, 454, 664
Diamant, H., 258, 265, 664
Diamond, R., 570, 571, 589, 658, 675
DiCarlo, L. T., 60, 664
Dichgans, J., 118, 476, 664, 683, 684
Dickhaus, H., 318, 664
Dickinson, R. G., 493, 663
Diehl, R. L., 429, 430, 664, 681
Diener, D., 613, 664
Dijkstra, C., 445, 699
Di Lollo, V., 457, 663
Dineen, I. T., 560, 664
Ditchburn, R. W., 473t, 664
DiZio, P. A., 477, 664
Djang, S., 599, 664
Dobelle, W. H., 160, 686
Dobson, V., 71, 649, 664
Dodd, J., 257, 649
Dodson, J. D., 538, 716
Dodwell, P. C., 174t, 560, 598, 664
Doetsch, G. S., 258, 664
Doherty, M. E., 598, 664
Domander, R., 288, 680
Domey, R. G., 572, 688
Donahy, T., 553, 665
Donaldson, I.M.L., 469, 664
Donchin, E., 514, 664
Donders, K., 600, 685
Doner, J., 341, 664
Dooley, G. J., 224, 664
Dorman, M. F., 221, 683
Doty, R. L., 279, 280, 627, 664, 665
Doughty, M. J., 704
Dowd, J. M., 563, 659

Dowell, R. C., 204, 654
Dowling, K., 556, 682
Dowling, W. J., 417, 665
Downing, C. J., 540, 665
Drance, S. M., 173
Dreyer, D. A., 293, 714
Driver, J., 531, 708
Droscher, V. B., 273, 665
Drum, B., 109, 110, 665
Dubin, M. W., 552, 690, 700
Duckman, R. H., 555, 682
Duffy, S. A., 536, 668
Dugan, M. P., 341, 658
Dumais, S. T., 351, 360, 535, 565, 651, 668, 689, 702, 703
Duncan, G. H., 316, 317, 707
Duncan, H. F., 604, 665
Duncan, J., 532, 665
Duncan, P., 357, 660
Duncker, K., 459, 665
Durlach, N. I., 38, 299, 304, 655, 692, 693, 697, 707
Dworkin, B., 320, 667

Easterbrook, J. A., 538, 665
Easton, M., 356, 431, 467, 667
Easton, R. D., 665
Ebert, L., 254, 704
Eccles, J. C., *302*, 661
Eddy, R. L., 159, 163, 691
Edmonds, E. M., 657
Edwards, A., 621, 665
Edwards, E. M., 452, 667
Efron, R., 448, 665, 716
Egan, D. J., 70, 338, 662
Egan, J. P., 26, 235, 665, 697
Egerman, B., 514, 703
Egeth, H. E., 535, 601, 665, 688
Ehrhardt, A. A., 630, 687
Eichengreen, J. M., 360, 665
Eijkman, E. G. J., 496, 665
Eilers, R., 417, 607, 665
Eimas, P. D., 430, 433, 438, 665
Einstein, A., 444, 665
Ekman, G., 57, 665
Eland, J. M., 564, 665
Elias, J. W., 715
Elkind, D., 665
Ellingson, R., 553, 665
Elliott, L. L., 565, 716
Ellis, H. C., 600, 665
Ellis, H. D., 625, 665
Ellis, S., 529, 567, 700
Elman, J. L., 439, 688
Emmerson, P. G., 170, 666
Emmerton, J., 666

Endman, M., 562, 709
Engen, T., 564, 657, 666, 686
Enns, J. T., 267, 274, 275, 331, 375, 379, 382, 383, 533, 568, 569, 570, 627, 666, 703
Enright, J. T., 339, 666
Enroth-Cugell, C., 106, 109, 649, 711
Epstein, W., 301, 334, 461, 466, 485, 492, 493, 501, 666, 702
Erickson, R. P., 258, 273, 664, 701, 702
Eriksen, C. W., 37, 448, 517, 518, 666, 667, 691
Ernst, M., 320, 667
Erulkar, S. C., 230, 667
Etheredge, 174t, 704
Evans, A. C., 428, 707, 716
Evans, E. F., 202, 207, 667, 714
Evans, J. J., 169, 714
Evans, P. M., 301, 661, 667
Evinger, C., 619, 704
Eysenck, H. J., 634, 667

Fabes, R. A., 667
Fagen, D., 620, 667
Fahle, M., 455, 709
Fallon, M., 195, 697
Falmagne, J. C., 667
Fant, G., 437, 440, 667
Fantz, R. L., 559, 667
Farah, M., 544, 662
Farber, J., 602, 700
Farkas, M., 576, 667
Farmer, R. M., 418, 712
Farrell, J. E., 460, 462, 656, 667
Farrimond, T., 619, 667
Favreau, O. E., 170, 455, 658, 667
Fechner, G. T., 14, 21, 41, 48, 667
Felleman, D. J., 129, 710
Fender, D. H., 467, 667
Fendrich, R., 457, 686
Fernald, A., 563, 667
Feroe, J., 415, 663
Festinger, L., 136, 168, 169, 356, 467, 555, 595, 656
Field, J., 513, 562, 691
Fields, R. W., 319, 656
Fillenbaum, S., 175, 663
Filsinger, E. E., 667
Findlay, J., 515, 529, 567, 667, 691
Fine, B. J., 619, 667
Finley, C., 477, 675
Fiorentini, A., 106, 127, 139, 667
Firestein, S., 272, 667
Fischer, B., 375, 513, 517, 667, 668, 695

Fisher, B., 306, 709
Fisher, D. L., 536, 668
Fisher, R. P., 601, 669
Fisher, R., 450, 668
Fishman, M., 173, 681
Fisk, A. D., 538, 668
Fisk, J. D., 356, 687
Fitts, P. M., 39, 650
Fitzhugh, A., 22, 711
Fitzpatrick, V., 334, 668
Flach, J. M., 476, 683
Flandrin, J. M., 454, 668
Flannery, R., 227, 668
Flin, R. H., 570, 668
Flock, A., 199, 662
Flock, H. R., 136, 504, 668
Flom, M. C., 609, 619, 622, 649, 672
Florentine, M., 222, 223, 668
Flynn, W. E., 707
Fodor, J., 668
Fogel, I., 668
Foley, J. E., 593, 668
Forman, E., 633, 682
Formby, C., 207, 683
Forrestor, L. J., 274, 650
Foulke, E., 418, 668
Fowler, C. A., 668
Fox, P. T., 360, 668
Fox, R., 379, 465, 565, 668, 703
Fozard, J., 572, 668
Frackowiak, R. S. J., 169, 685
Fraioli, A. J., *298*, 710
Fraisse, P., 444, 451, 668
Franchi, C., 280, 696
Frank, J. A., 690
Frank, M. E., 259, 668
Frankenhauser, M., 450, 668
Franzel, S. L., 535, 715
Fraser, J., 8t, 668
Frazier, N. I., 632, 705
Freedberg, E., 504, 668
Freedland, R. L., 459, 662
Freeman, D. M., 199, 668
Freeman, R., 583, 586, 668
Freeman, R. B., 469, 692
Freeman, S., 279, 671
Freeman, W. J., 104, 671
Freidman, E., 610, 668
French, J., 565, 651
Freud, S., 669
Frey, M. von, *293*, 669
Freyd, J., 387, 669
Friberg, U., 258, 650
Fridman, J., 645, 678
Friedman S. L., 399, 604, 669
Friedman, A., 530, 566, 669
Friedman, D. P., 290, 696

Friedman, R. B., 669
Friedrich, F. J., 521, 697
Frisby, J. P., 94, 347, 348, 351, 669, 687, 698
Frishkopf, L. S., 247, 704
Frison, K. J., 169, 685
Frost, B. J., 301, 650, 656
Frykholm, G., 465, 700
Fuchs, A. F., 127, 663
Fuld, K., 163, 669
Fuller, C. A., 447, 669
Fuller, J. E., 469, 689
Fulton, J. F., 446, 669
Funakoshi, M., 258, 260, 664, 669
Funkenstein, H. H., 208, 669

Gabor, D., 128
Gaddes, W. H., 570, 669
Gaes, G., 451, 676
Gagne, J. P., 218, 669
Galambos, R., 202, 207, 698, 700
Galanter, E., 25, 41, 47, 50, 53, 669, 696, 706
Gale, A., 634, 659
Ganchrow, J. R., 258, 564, 669
Ganz, L., 457, 702
Garaziano, J. A., 655
Garbart, H., 535, 665
Garbin, C. P., 305, 669
Garcia, C. R., 662, 697
Gardner, E. B., 288, 669
Gardner, E. P., 293, 304, 661, 669
Garey, L. J., 677
Garner, W. R., 37, 383, 387, 388, 396, 553, 628, 657, 673
Garraghty, P. E., 290, 696
Gates, G., 229, 676, 692
Gauss, C. F., 127
Geiselman, R. E., 601, 669
Geisler, C. D., 196, 220, 669, 670
Geiwitz, J., 574, 701
Gelade, G., 383, 709
Gelb, A., 127, 503, 670, 715
Geldard, F. A., 688, 670
Gent, J. F., 262, 670
George, E. J., 452, 629, 654, 656
Gerbino, W., 330, 670
Gerbrandt, L. K., 624, 670
Gerkemo, M. P., 446, 670
Gescheider, G. A., 26, 47, 51, 56, 298, 299, 654, 670
Gesteland, R. C., 270, 273, 670
Getchell, M. L., 270, 670
Getchell, T. V., 270, 670
Giachetti, I., 273, 670
Gibbons, B., 670

Gibson, E. J., 305, 328, 335, 341, 358, 359, 711
Gibson, J. J., 14, 305, 476, 485, 491, 601, 670
Gibson, M. M., 195, 681
Gibson, R. H., 53, 670
von Gierke, S. M., 222, 673
Gilbert, A. N., 267, 670
Gilbert, J., 607, 713
Gilchrist, A. L., 136, 314, 501, 503, 504, 670, 678
Gilger, J. W., 632, 670
Gilinsky, A. S., 500, 658
Gillam, B., 353, 494, 670, 711
Gilman, A., 622, 671
Gilmore, M. M., 264, 670
Ginsburg, A., 572, 684
Gintzler, A. R., 670
Girgus, J. S., 14, 59, 71, 173, 329, 356, 467, 494, 497, 568, 569, 570, 572, 594, 595, 605, 606, 610, 613, 618, 660, 666, 670
Giza, B. K., 260, 702
Gjedde, A., 428, 716
Glantz, J., 221, 717
Glanville, E., 619, 680
Glass, A. L., 530, 653, 670
Glassman, N., 413, 703
Glicksohn, J., 452, 716
Gliner, J. A., 619, 670
Glorig, A., 608, 670
Glucksberg, S., 522, 670
Gogel, W C., 339, 459, 493, 504, 671, 689
Goldberg, D., 379, 696
Goldberg, M. E., 518, 519, 520, 715
Golder, P., 379, 696
Goldman, A., 297, 669
Goldsmith, L. T., 360, 716
Goldstein, E. B., 671
Goldstein, J. L., 243, 244, 677, 705
Goldstein, R., 133, 650
Goldstone, S., 450, 671
Gombrich, E. H., 602, 671
Goodale, M. A., 623, 671
Goodell, B. S., 322, 673, 715
Goodell, H., 318, 319, 674
Goodfoot, D. A., 279, 674
Gooding, K. M., 279, 671
Goodman, G. S., 556, 673
Goodman, L., 622, 671
Goodman, N., 602, 671
Goodson, R., 610, 671
Goodwin, A., 293, 662
Goodwin, M., 279, 671
Goolkasian, P., 671
Gootlieb, G., 671

Gopher, D., 543, 691
Gordon, B., 586, 690
Gordon, J., 163, 649, 655
Gormican, S., 388, 709
Gorta, A., 415, 705
Goto, H., 607, 671
Gottlieb, M. D., 112, 580, 671
Gottschaldt, K., 287, 599, 671
Gouras, P., 165, 671
Gourlay, N., 604, 665
Gower, E. C., 588, 675
Goy, R. W., 279, 671
Graham, C. H., 159, 339, 671
Graham, E., 633, 684
Graham, N., 137, 375, 671, 707
Graham, N. V. S., 121, 671
Grahma, M., 341, 699
Grailet, J. M., 623, 671
Granger, G. W., 619, 671
Granrud, C. E., 360, 555, 671, 672, 716
Grant, B. F., 20, 478, 672
Grau, J. W., 232, 672
Gravetter, F., 38, 672
Graziade l, P. P. C., 269, 661
Green, B. G., 295, 313, 318, 672
Green, D. G., 109, 311, 672
Green, D. M., 26, 38, 43, 221, 222, 223, 224, 225, 242, 563, 651, 653, 672, 673, 678, 684, 689, 691, 699, 714
Green, D. W., 530, 672
Green, M., 462, 682
Green, M. A., 587, 661
Green, P. A., 665
Green, P., 485, 491, 656
Green, R. G., 674
Greenberg, M. J., 279, 672
Greene, H. A., 672, 724
Greene, S. I., 500, 655
Greenspan, S. I., 636, 663
Greenwood, D. D., 196, 672
Gregg, J. M., 339, 671
Gregory, M., 538, 655, 656
Gregory, R. L., 329, 457, 494, 496, 602, 672, 698
Gregory, W., 605, 699
Gresnight, A. M., 114, 717
Grice, G. R., 44, 672
Griffin, F., 584, 708
Griffith, B. C., 428, 684
Grings, W., 608, 670
Groep, J. C., 517, 710
Groos, G. A., 445, 446, 670, 672, 700
Gross, C. G., 96, 97, 656, 663, 672
Grossberg, J. M., 20, 672

Grossberg, S., 368, 672
Grosvenor, T., 609, 672
von Grunau, M., 462, 682
Grunau, R.V.E., 564, 672
Grzegorczyk, P. B., 575, 672
Gudeman, H. E., 575, 634, 649
Guedry, F. E., 473, 660
Guilbaud, G., 316, 683
Guirao, M., 245, 672
Guitton, D., 454, 672
Gulick, W. L., *228*, 239, 673
Gurnsey, R., 383, 673
Gustafson, R., 619, 673
Guttman, D., 525, 699
Guttman, N., 247, 704
Guzman, A., 401, 673
Gwiazda, J., 557, 565, 673

Haaf, R., 560, 673
Haake, R. J., 360, 672
Haas, E. M., 260, 694
Haber, R. N., 580, 598, 601, 673
Haegerstrom-Portnoy, G., 622, 649
Hafter, E. R., 231, 673, 701
Hagen, M., 602, 603, 673
Hagenaar, R., 517
Hahn, H., 262, 673
Hainline, L., 565, 649, 673
Haith, M. M., 556, 559, 566, 569,
   673, 680, 690
Hake, H. W., 37, 39, 666, 669
Hakstian, A. R., 159, 160t, 660
Hall, J. W., III, 243, 673
Hall, M. J., 261, 262, 673
Hall, W. G., 564, 673
Hallin, R. G., 315, 708
Hallstrom, J., 360, 716
Hallum, G., 605, 699
Halper, F., 466, 699
Halpern, B. P., 262, 673, 683, 704
Halpern, D. F., 379, 629, 632, 659
Halpern, D. L., 214, 673
Halsam, D., 634, 673
Hamalainen, H., 298, 673
Hamasaki, D. J., 552, 673
Hamernik, R. P., 202, 701
Hamid, P. N., 176, 673
Hamilton, S. L., 168, 708
Hammel, D. D., 632, 708
Hammond, E. J., 530, 672
Handel, S., 388, 673
Hanna, T. E., 222, 673
Hannon, D. J., 476, 712
Hanson, S., 466, 666
Hardie, R. C., 71, 673
Hardy, J. D., 318, 319, 673, 674
Hari, R., 674

Harkins, S. W., 575, 634, 674
Harmon, L. D., 244, 395t, 704
Harper, R. S., 175, 674
Harpman, J. A., *28*, 715
Harris, A. A., 632, 674
Harris, C., 373, 713
Harris, C. M., 79, 689
Harris, C. S., 137, 591, 593, 674
Harris, F. P., 197, *199*, 685
Harris, G., 319, 699
Harris, J. P., 621, 694
Harris, K. S., 428, 684
Harris, P., 555, 674
Harrison, R. V., 207, 674
Hartley, S., 573, 583, 668
Hartline, H. K., 80, 130, 674
Hartman, A., 621, 674
Hartmann, W. M., *228*, 674, 697
Harvey, L. O. Jr., 489, 674
Harwood, D. L., 417, 665
Hary, J. M., 430, 674
Hastings, J. W., 446, 678
Hatfield, G., 461, 666, 674
Hausfeld, S., 415, 705
Hawkins, M. D., 197, *199*, 685
Hay, J. C., 592, 694
Hayhoe, M. M., 162, 714
Hazan, C., 556, 673
He, L., 315, 674
Head, H., 624, 674
Heaton, J. M., 674
Hebb, D. O., 370, 697
Hecht, H., 463, 674
Hecht, S., 109, 114, 174, 674
Heck, G. F., 255, 716
Heckman, T., 459, 674
Heffner, H. E., 208, 674
Heffner, R. S., 208, 674
Heggelund, P., 91, 674
Hein, A., 582, 590, 662, 674, 675
Heintz, C., 265, 693
Held, R., 360, 476, 552, 555, 557,
   565, 568, 583, 587, 588, 589,
   590, 591, 592, 653, 673, 674,
   675,
Helekant, G., 233, 675
Heller, M. A., 233, 674
Hellman, R., 299, 657
Hellman, R. P., 675
Hellstrom, A., 41, 675
Helmholtz, H.E.F. von, 14, 44, 153,
   469, 675
Helson, H., 58, 675
Henderlite, 174t, 704
Henderson, A., 517, 649
Henderson, J. M., 517, 675
Hendricson, A. E., 76, 661

Henmon, V. A. C., 44, 675
Henn, V., 477, 675, 711
Henning, H., 265, *266*, 675
Henry, J., 173, 650
Hensel, H., 287, 290, 307, 311, 675
Hepler, N., 91, 664
Hering, E., 163
Herman, E., 356, 468, 686
Hernandez-Peon, R., 517, 675
Heron, W., 370, 697
Herscovitch, P., 207, 605, 606, 683
Hershberger, W., 675
Hershenson, M., 496, 497, 580, 598,
   673, 675
Hess, E., 453, 669
Hess, R. H., 358, 675
Heuer, F., 457, 686
Heywood, C. A., 169, 675
Heywood, J., 293, 662
Hick, W. E., 45, 675
Hickey, T. L., 551, 552, 582, 583,
   675
Hicks, R. E., 451, 452, 676
Hier, D. B., 630, 676
Higashiyama, A., 493, 676
Higgins, K. E., 681
Higgins, S. T., 620, 676
Hillenbrand, J., 214, 673
Hillyard, S. A., 541, 676, 686, 710
Hind, J. E., 195, 202, 681, 699
Hinton, G. E., 98, 651
Hirsch, H., 582, 584, 676, 684
Hirsh-Pasek, K., 564, 680
Hisa, Y., 159, 671
Ho, H., 632, 670
Hoagland, H., 449, 676
Hochberg, J., 339, 354, 385, 492,
   504, 565, 602, 676
Hockey, G. R., 538, 676
Hockey, R., 531, 687
Hoenig, P., 356, 476, 595, 660
Hoffer, A., 621, 676
Hoffman, D., 319, 673
Hoffman, H. A., 428, 684
Hoffman, J. E., 83, 174t, 396, 517,
   518, 536, 666, 676, 677, 681
Hoffmann, K. P., 556, 582, 585, 676
von Hofsten, C., 464, 678
Hogan, H. P., 600, 658
Hogman, L., 274, 656
Hogness, D. S., 159, 163, 691
Hoke, M., 241, 693
Hold, B., 279, 701
Holden, B. A., 67, 687
Holender, D., 542, 676
Holland, H., 676
Holland, H. L., 601, 620, 669

Hollerbach, J., 665
Hollins, M., 293, 714
Hollister, L., 621, 674
Holma, D., 451, 697
Holmes, D. L., 569, 690
Holmes, S. M., 169, 695
Holst, E. von, 588, 676
Holway, A. F., 489, 676
Holyoak, K. J., 670
Holzman, P. S., 635, 684
Honda, H., 356, 676
Hood, B., 557, 651, 676
Hood, D. C., 106, 711
Hooper, J. E., 262, 652
Horn, B. K. P., 368, 403, 676
Horner, D. T., 300, 676
Horton, J. C., 139, 677, 704
Horvath, S. M., 619, 670
Hosick, E. C., 450, 649
Houck, M. R., 174t, 536, 676, 677
House, A. S., 705
Houtsma, A. J. M., 243, 299, 677, 697
Howard, I. P., 354, 469, 476, 593, 677
Howell, P., 417, 627, 677, 702
Hoyer, W., 573, 575, 576, 667, 677, 695
Hu, S., 478, 677
Hubbell, W. L., 77, 677
Hubel, D. H., 13, 86, 90, 91, 94, 98, 454, 455, 552, 583, 677, 684, 685
Hudson, W., 604, 665, 677
Hudspeth, A. J., 182, 199, 215, 677
Huggins, G. R., 662, 697
Hughes, B., 301, 702
Hughes, H. C., 126, 394, 677
Hughes, J., 207, 700
Hughs, J., 202, 700
Hulse, S. H., 417, 677
Humphrey, D. E., 384, 560, 677
Humphrey, G. K., 174t, 560, 664, 677, 691
Humphrey, K., 607, 713
Humphreys, G. W., 500, 516, 532, 665, 677
Hunt, E., 535, 696
Hunzelmann, N., 456, 677
Hurlbert, A. C., 420, 677
Hurst, R. J., *257,* 716
Hurvich, L. M., 139, 166, 171, 173, 351, 677, 678, 681
Hutman, L. P., 573, 702
Huttenlocher, P. R., 553, 677
Hutz, C. S., 553, 677
Huxley, A., 677
Hwang, P. M., 269, 695
Hyman, A., 267, 677
Hynes, R., 681

Iacono, W. G., 635, 677
Iida, T., 339, 678
Ikeda, H., 619, 671
Imbert, M., 551, 552, 677
Ingram, R. M., 565, 677
Inhoff, A., 521, 697
Intraub, H., 448, 677
Ippolitov, F. W., 677
Irvin, L. K., 685
Irwin, R. J., 319, 610, 677
Isbey, S. C., 229, 681
Isensee, O., 316, 680
Ittelson, W. H., 333, 596, 677

Jacobs, G. H., 157, 163, 164, 677, 691
Jacobsen, A., 136, 501, 503, 504, 670, 677
Jahoda, G., 604, 677
James, W., 204, 677
Jameson, D., 139, 166, 172, 351, 677, 678
Jamison, W., 632, 708
Janal, M. N., 314, 678
Janowsky, D. S., 621, 655
Jansson, G., 464, 678
Jarvilehto, T., 298, 673
Jarvis, J. R., 169, 678
Jaschinski-Kruza, W., 610, 678
Jastrow, J., 23, 678
Javel, E., 243, 678
Jeannerod, M., 454, 668
Jeffress, L. A., 222, 672
Jenkins, B., 587, 678
Jenkins, J., 607, 705
Jennings, J. A. M., 117, 678
Jesteadt, W., 24, 220, 222, 223, 224, 678, 714
Johansson, I., 656, 678
John, E. R., 645, 678
Johnson, A. L., 346, 661
Johnson, C. H., 162, 446, 678
Johnson, D. H., 678
Johnson, E. F., Jr., 275, 657
Johnson, E. S., 629, 678
Johnson, H. A., 572, 664
Johnson, H. H., 556, 679
Johnson, R., 580, 598, 709
Johnson, R. C., 715
Johnson, S. C., 58, 678
Johnson, T. L., 703
Johnston, A., 715
Johnston, W., 544, 662
Johnstone, B., 202, 670
Jones, D. T., 272, 679
Jones, R., 602, 603, 673
Jones, R. T., 619, 622, 668

Jones, S. W., 575, 672
Jones-Gotman, M., 276, 717
Jongsma, H. J., 496, 665
Jonides, J., 514, 517, 540, 679, 716
Joubert, C. E., 453, 679
Judd, D. B., 150, 692
Julesz, B., 348, *350,* 360, 374, 375, 383, 385, 395t, 517, 532, 657, 674, 679, 694
Jung, R., 139, 679
Jusczyk, P. W., 433, 563, 564, 665, 679, 680, 682

Kaas, J. H., 290, 670, 696
Kaba, H., 267, 655
Kaernbach, 24, 25, 32, 679
Kaess, D. W., 500, 679
Kahneman, D., 116, 372, 389, 516, 536, 542, 543, 576, 679
Kail, R., 576, 701
Kaiser, P. K., 162, 163, 457, 679
Kalat, J. W., 640, 680
Kalina, R. E., 76, 662
Kaneko, A., 81, 680
Kanisza, G., 378, 680
Kaplan, A., 619, 680
Kaplan, E., 167, 703
Kaplan, G., 353, 680
Kaplan, H., 321, 680, 702
Kare, M. R., 257, 655
Karita, K., 293, 662, 680
Karmel, B. Z., 559, 680
Karvellas, 170t, 680
Kasahara, Y., 260, 669
Kasamatsu, T., 469, 680
Kasprzak, M., 279, 685
Katcher, M. H., 300, 654
Katsuki, Y., 207, 712
Kauer, J. S., 272, 273, 680
Kaufman, L., 207, 339, 341, 360, 680, 699
Kaufmann, R., 496, 680
Kautz, M. A., 176, 177, 276, 717
Kawabata, N., 353, 680
Kawamura, Y., 260, 669, 716
Kay, P., 176, 359, 653
Kaye, H., 564, 666
Kaye, M., 680
Kearny, J. K., 222, 672
Keeley, S. M., 598, 664
Keemink, C. J., 299, 683
Keiley, J. M., 573, 674
Keith, B., 171, 660
Kellman, P. J., 360, 379, 554, 561, 680
Kelly, S. A., 558, 701
Kelly, W. J., 221, 712

Kemler-Nelson, D. G., 564, 680
Kemp, D. T., 680
Kendrick, K. M., 97, 680
Kennard, C., 169, 685
Kennedy, D. N., 652
Kennedy, H., 455, 693
Kennedy, J. M., 602, 680
Kenshalo, D. R., 309, 311, 312t, 316, 680
Keren, G., 399, 680
Kessen, W., 163, 559, 654, 680, 700
Kessler, E. J., 410, 411, 682
Keuss, P., 394, 654
Keverne, E. B., 267, 279, 655
Khanna, S. N., 189, 202, 680, 706
Kiang, N.Y. S., 194, 202, 680, 700
Kidd, G., Jr., 223, 681
Kiefer, S. A., 230, 689
Kiesow, F., 293, 669
Kietzman, M. I., 112
Kilbride, P. E., 173, 681
Killbride, P. L., 681
Killeen, P. R., 429, 681
Kim, D. O., 194, 196, 197, 202, 619, 681, 698
Kim, Y., 619, 698
Kimchi, R., 392, 393, 396, 681
Kimura L., 258, 681
Kinchla, R. A., 396, 518, 681
King, K. A., 570, 666
King, L. E., 230, 688
King, M. C., 396, 685
Kingham, J. R., 169, 695
Kinnear, P. R., 173, 683
Kinsbourne, M., 451, 676
Kirk, B., 570, 704
Kirk-Smith, R. A., 681
Kirschfeld, K., 673
Kitzes, L. M., 195, 230, 231, 681, 703
Klatt, D. H., 681, 694
Klatzky, R. L., 299, 305, 681, 683
Klein, G. S., 634, 681
Klein, R., 531, 573, 574, 662, 681
Klein, S. A., 116, 681
Kletzman, M. I., 671
Kligman, A., 665
Kline, P., 634, 659
Kloka, A. G., 319, 656
Kluender, K. R., 429, 681
Klutky, N., 628, 681
Kluver, H., 96, 681
Klymenko, V., 385, 681
Knight, P. L., 207, 689
Knoblauch, K., 572, 681
Knudsen, E. I., 231, 681
Knudsen, P. E., 231, 681
Ko, W. Y., 665
Kobler, J. B., 229, 681

Kobrick, J. L., 619, 667
Koch, C. J., 379, 656
Koch, K., 478, 677, 706
Koenderink, J. J., 114, 717
Koffka, K., 133, 681
Kohler, W., 41, 682
Kohlston, P. J., 590, 682
Kolb, B., 96, 428, 681
Kolb, H., 73, 81, 96, 681, 691
Kolers, P. A., 448, 462, 682
Komoda, M. K., 555, 660, 682
Konishi, M., 231, 681
Konstadt, N., 633, 682
Koslow, M., 459, 671, 682
Koslowe, K. C., 610, 682
Kosterlitz, H. W., 321, 322, 682
Kowler, E., 555, 682
Kozlowski, L. T., 465, 662, 682
Kraepelin, E., 23, 683
Kratz, K. E., 86, 95, 683
Krauskopf, J., 114, 682
Kravetz, M. A., 279, 671
Kreiman, J., 626, 710
Kremenitzer, J. P., 682
Krieger, A., 662
Kries, J. von, 76, 682
Kring, A. M., 323, 389, 657
Kroek, K., 574, 651
Kropfl, W., 360, 694
Krueger, L. E., 299, 682
Kruger, J., 55, 83, 682
Krumhansl, C. L., 408, 409, 410, 413, 414, 416, 417, 563, 628, 693
Kruskal, J. B., 57, 682
Kryter, K. D., 609, 682
Kubovy, M., 116, 679
Kuffler, S. W., 80, 682
Kugler, B. T., 635, 709
Kuhl, P. K., 429, 562, 565, 607, 682
Kuhne, 77, 682
Kupchella, C., 176, 682
Kurtz, D., 469, 682
Kurtzberg, D., 553, 682, 710
Kusuda, M., 541, 588, 681, 691
Kutas, M., 676
Kuyk, T., 146, 409, 683
Kuyper, W. L., 663

LaBerge, D., 518, 683
La Brossiere, E., 649
Lacerda, F., 434, 682
Lackner, J. R., 477, 664
Ladavas, E., 624, 683
Ladefoged, P., 419, *422,* 683
Lahey, M. A., 146, 683
Lakowski, R., 173, 572
Lamaze, F., 683

Lammertsma, A. A., 169, 685
Lamore, P. J. J., 299, 683
Lamour, T., 683
Land, E. H., 316, 683
Landolt, E., 115, 503, 505, 506, 683
Lane, D. M., 568, 694
Lansman, M., 535, 696
Lappin, J. S., 341, 498, 500, 683
Larish, J. F., 476, 683
Larsen, A., 462, 656
Lasaga, M. L., 383, 657
Lathrop, G., 553, 665
Lauter, J. L., 207, 683
Lawless, H. T., 683
Lawley, H. J., 662, 697
Layton, W. M., 394, 677
Lea, S. E. G., 683
Le Bihan, D., 690
Leclerc, Y. G., 332, 658
Lederman, S. J., 299, 305, 681, 683
Lee, J. R., 375, 696
Lee, M. H. M., 320, 667
Leehey, S. C., 587, 683
Leek, M. R., 221, 683
Leeuwenberg, E., 385, 401, 657, 683
Lefton, L. A., 372, 683
Lehman, J. R., 220, 678
Lehmkuhle, S., 86, 95, 379, 683
Lehnertz, K., 241, 693
Leibowitz, H. W., 118, 467, 489, 490, 493, 498, 572, 603, 604, 674, 681, 683, 697
Leinonen, L., 683
Lemlich, R. N., 453, 684
Lenel, J. C., 463, 653
Lenneberg, E. H., 433, 684
Lennie, P., 86, 167, 684
Leonard, D.G.B., 680
LePage, E. L., 684
Lerdahl, F., 684
Lerman, S., 572, 684
LeRoy, D., 230, 650
Leshner, A. I., 279, 671
Lester, L. S., 394, 677
Lettvin, J. Y., 273, 505, 656, 670
LeVay, S., 583, 684
Levelt, W. J. M., 235, 684
Leventhal, A.,
Levi, D. M., 116, 129, 137, 681
Levin, A., 625, 635, 684
Levine, D. N., 526, 684
Levine, J. M., 279, 688
Levine, M. W., 121, 684
Levy, D. L., 684
Levy, E. T., 657
Levy, I., 688
Lewin, L. M., 610, 685
Lewis, J. W., 684

Lewis, M. E., 97, 689
Lewis, T. L., 552, 555, 556, 557, 559, 560, 561, 565, 684, 687
Lewis, V. G., 687
Leyden, J., 665
Lhamon, W. T., 450, 671
Li, X. F., 429, 694
Liberman, M. C., 194, 202, 418, 427, 428, 431, 435, 439, 440, 680, 684
Lichte, W. H., 500, 684
Lichtenstein, M., 455, 684
Liddell, E. G., *302*, 661
Lie, I., 113, 114, 116, 684
Liebelt, L., 530, 566, 669
Liebeskind, J. C., 321, 564, 684
Liebowitz, H. W., 706
Lim, A., 703
Lim, D. J., 193, 538, 684
Lindblad, I. M., 706
Lindbloom, B., 434, 682
Linden, L., 505, 656
Lindsay, P. H., *189, 201, 228,* 684
Lindsey, D. T., 455, 684
Linton, H., 633, 684
Lipsett, L. P., 564, 684
Lipsitt, L. P., 564, 666
Lipton, R. B., 635, 684
Lisker, L., 430, 685
Little, A. D., 230, 688
Livingston, M., 13, 86, 94, 98, 454, 685
Locke, J. L., 433, 685
Lockhead, G. R., 169, 396, 411, 672, 685, 690, 712, 714
Loewenstein, W. R., 685
Loftus, E. F., 685
Loftus, E., 600, 601, 685, 713
Loftus, G., 566, 685
Logan, J. S., 685, 713
Logothetis, 167, 169, 701
Lohman, D. F., 629, 685
Long, A. C., 469, 664
Long, G. M., 162, 685, 709
Long, G. R., 222, 685
Long, G., 198, 707
Longstreth, L. E., 46, 685
Lonsbury-Martin, B. L., 197, 198, *199,* 685, 687
Loomis, J. M., 301, 685
Loop, M. S., 112, 685, 702
Lorch, E. P., 568, 713
Lord, T., 279, 685
Lovegrove, 137, 685
Lovitts, B. E., 501, 666
Lowe, D., 399, 685
Lowenstein, D., 287, 475, 685
Lu, R., 322, 674
Luce, P. A., 437, 439, 695

Luce, R. D., 38, 46, 56, 651, 685, 691
Lucia, H. C., 593, 677
Ludemann, P. M., 560, 691
Ludman, E. J., 164, 691, 697
Lueck, C. J., 169, 685
Lummis, R. C., 244, 704
Lumry, A. E., 635, 677
Lumsden, E., 601, 685
Lundervold, D., 610, 685
Luria, A. R., 622, 624, 625, 685
Lustnauer, S., 698
Lutkenhoner, B., 241, 693
Lydic, R., 447, 669
Lyerly, O. G., 624, 651
Lyman, P. J., 451, 651
Lynch, M. P., 417, 686
Lynn, P. A., 686

MacArthur, R. O., 619, 686
MacDonald, D. W., 279, 656, 686
MacDonald, J., 431, 688
MacDonald, J. A., 188, 690
MacFarlane, A., 280, 555, 674, 686
Mach, E., 132, 686
Machmer, J., 453, 702
Mack, A., 356, 457, 468, 686
MacKain, K., 433, 686
MacKinnon, D. P., 473t, 601, 669
Macko, K. A., 95, 690
Mackworth, N. H., 537, 566, 686
Mackworth, V., 685
MacLeod, D.I.A., 162, 686, 714
MacLeod, P., 273, 686
Macleod, R., 686
MacNichol, E. F., 686
MacNichol, E. F., Jr., 164, *165,* 686, 707
Madden, D. J., 124, 672, 686
Madden, T. M., 496, 573, 686
Maes, H., 455, 693
Maffei, L., 129, 137, 455, 657, 715
Magnussen, S., 106, 127, 139, 667
Mai, N., 453, 717
Mair, R. G., 627, 686
Maire-Lepoivre, E., 586, 686
Maisel, E. B., 559, 680
Makous, J. C., 225, 686, 689
Maland, J., 360, 680
Malhotra, A. K., 622, 710
Mallach, R., 583, 668
Mandelbaum, M., 109, 886
Mandler, G., 391, 686
Mandler, M. B., 587, 655
Mangel, S. C., 86, 868
Mangen, G. L., 634, 686, 704
Mangun, G. R., 541, 696

Mann, V. A., 431, 652
Manning, K. A., 619, 704
Marcel, A. J., 542, 686
Maisel, E. B., 671
Maland, J., 356, 680
Mallach, R., 668
Mandelbaum, M., 674
Mandler, G., 221, 669
Mangel, S. C., 693
Marentette, P. F., 433, 694
Margolis, R. H., 236, 657
Mariani, A. P., 73, 81, 682, 691
Marks, L. E., 235, 262, 298, 652, 686, 688
Marks, W. B., 160, 232, 686
Marley, A. A. J., 38, 685, 686
Marr, D., 14, 127, 329, 347, 348, 368, 401, 403, 455, 486, 686, 687
Marre, M., 173, 695
Marrett, S., 707
Marshall, D. A., 274, 687
Marslen-Wilson, W. D., 438, 687
Martello, J., 559, 687
Martin, A. J., 555, 682
Martin, C., 476, 663
Martin, C., 687
Martin, D. K., 67, 687
Martin, G. K., 197, 198, *199,* 685, 687
Martin, K. D., 619, 687
Martin, M., 394, 687
Martin, R., 231, 649
Martin, R. L., 206, 687
Masica, D. N., 630, 687
Masin, S. C., 304, 687
Masland, R. H., 73, 81, 687
Mason, C. R., 222, 223, 668, 681
Massaro, D. W., 351, 430, 437, 440, 674, 687
Mather, G., 462, 658
Mather, J. A., 356, 687
Mathies, R. A., 77, 702
Matin, L., 356, 473t, 687
Matthews, B. H. C., 302, 687
Matthews, M., 379, 713
Mattingly, I. G., 418, 427, 431, 435, 439, 440, 684
Maunsell, J. H. R., 98, 139, 455, 687, 704
Maurer, D., 551, 552, 556, 559, 560, 561, 565, 684, 687
Maxwell, J. C., 66, 153, 687
May, B., 429, 687
Mayer, D., 262, 266, 656
Mayer, D. J., 322, 323, 687, 712
Mayfrank, L., 513, 687
Mayhew, J. E. W., 347, 348, 687
Maylor, E. A., 531, 687

McAnally, K. I., 224, 688
McBirdle, R. L., 688
McBride, R. L., 265, 688
McBurney, D. H., 260, 263, 266, 279, 688, 695
McCall, R. B., 554, 688
McCann, J. J., 503, 683
McClain, L., 451, 452, 688
McClellan, P. G., 496, 688
McClelland, J. L., 439, 688
McClintock, M. K., 601, 688, 716
McCloskey, M., 601, 688, 716
McColgin, F. H., 455, 688
McCray, E. E., 451, 712
McCready, D., 497, 688
McDaniel, C., 465, 668
McDonald, M., 558, 710
McElroy, A. E., 266, 701
McFadden, D., 198, 714
McFarland, R., 668
McFarland, R. A., 572, 688
McFarlane, A., 555, 674
McGee, M. G., 629, 688
McGlone, J., 629, 688
McGlothlin, W., 621, 690
McGuinness, D., 456, 655, 688
McGuinness, E., 649
McGurk, H., 431, 604, 678, 688
McHaftie, J. G., 90, 692
McKinstry, R. C., 652
McKnight, A., T., 321, 322, 682
McLean, J. P., 517, 704
McLeod, D. I., 106, 711
McLeod, P. J., 563, 713
McLeod, P., 670
McMahon, M., 593, 692
McMurty, P. L., 230, 688
McNichol, E. F., 160, 686
Meade, A. C., 629, 678
Meddis, R., 688
Meijer, J. H., 446, 672
Meiselman, H. L., 262, 264, 265, 673, 688
Melara, R. D., 232, 688
Meltzoff, A. N., 433, 682
Melzack, R., 314, 316, 318, 564, 684, 688
Mentyer, T,. 267, 677
Mercer, M. E., 173, 688
Mergler, D., 173, 688
Mergner, T., 475, 688
Merikle, P. M., 394, 542, 598, 658, 693
Merkel, J., 688
Mershon, D. H., 230, 504, 688, 689
Merzenich, M. M., 203, 207, 689
Metzger, V. A., 299, 681

Metzler, D. E., 79, 689
Mewhort, D. J. K., 412, 661
Meyer, E., 428, 707, 716
Meyer, G. E., 379, 694
Meyer, M., 560, 664
Michael, C. R., 168, 689
Michael, R. P., 279, 689
Michael, S., 689
Michaels, C. F., 328, 485, 491, 689
Michaud, A., 634, 705
Michell, J., 689
Michon, J., 689
Middlebrooks, J. C., 225, 228, 686, 689
Midgley, G., 359, 707
Miezin, F., 456, 649
Mihevic, P. M., 619, 670
Mikaelian, H., 592, 593, 689
Miles, F. A., 469, 689
Milewski, A., 556, 684
Milewski, A. E., 565, 689
Mill, J., 689
Millaer, D. L., 469, 689
Millan, M. J., 321, 689
Millar, J. M., 204, 428, 689
Miller, F. F., 139, 704
Miller, G. A., 37, 425, 659, 689
Miller, G. W., 451, 452, 676, 689
Miller, J., 528, 689
Miller, J. D., 665
Miller, N. D., 116, 689
Miller, R. J., 619, 689
Millis-Wright, M., 389, 697
Mills, A. W., 227, 689
Milne, J., 215, 689
Milne, M., 215, 689
Milner, A. D., 623, 671
Mintun, M. A., 668
Miranda, S. B., 559, 667
Mishkin, M., 90, 95, 97, 290, 454, 689, 690, 696, 710
Mistlin, A. M., 97, 694
Mistretta, C. M., 575, 672, 690, 708
Mitchel, D. E., 584, 708
Mitchell, D. E., 662, 680, 708
Mitchell, D., 584, 585, 586, 587, 690
Mitchell, M. S., 624, 712
Mittelstaedt, H., 588, 676
Mobashery, M., 513, 687
Mohindra, I., 565, 673
Molfese, D. L., 429, 649, 690
Monahan, J. S., 396, 690
Moncrieff, R. W., 275, 627, 630, 687
Monroe, M. D., 654
Montalvo, F. S., 330, 713
Montellese, S., 112, 690
Montgomery, J. C., 188, 690

Moody, D. B., 429, 687
Moonen, C. T. W., 690
Mooney, R. D., 552, 690
Moore, B., 563, 690
Moore, B. C. J., 224, 664
Moore, D., 490, 683
Moore, J. D., 280, 696
Moore, L. M., 575, 690
Moore, M. J., 566, 673
Moore, R. K., 469, 689
Moore, T., 607, 665
Moore-Ede, M. C., 447, 669
Moran, J., 96, 526, 586, 690, 705
Moray, N., 522, 695
Morgon, R. J., 622, 652
Mori, S., 540, 690
Morikawa, R. J., 496, 652, 660
Morish, R. B., 634, 704
Morrell, F., 553, 709
Morris, P. E., 601, 690
Morris, V., 569, 690
Morrison, F. J., 569, 690
Morrison, J. D., 339, 690
Morrongiello, B. A., 563, 659
Morrow, T. J., 316, 658
Morse, P. A., 429, 690
Morton, B. A., 173, 683
Morton, T., 627, 686
Morton-Cook, A., 690
Moskowitz, H., 621, 622, 703
Moskowitz-Cook, A., 558, 587, 683
Motter, B. C., 518, 690
Mouloua, M., 538, 694
Mount, R. J., 207, 674
Mountcastle, V. B., 303, 316, 518, 520, 690, 695
Mouton, D. G., 274, 687
Movshon, J. A., 71, 553, 557, 690, 708
Mozel, M. M., 268, 273, 690
Mroczek, K., 351, 653
Muir, D. W., 513, 560, 562, 586, 587, 654, 677, 691, 708
Muise, G., 666
Mullen, K. T., 157, 691
Muller, D. G., 517, 600, 665
Muller, H. J., 540, 691
Muller, J. J., 515, 516, 691
Mulligan, R. M., 451, 691
Munsell, A. H., 150, 691
Murphy, C., 264, 267, 670, 691
Murphy, T. D., 517, 666
Murray, J. B., 691
Mustillo, P., 691
Myers, A. K., 51, 691
Myles-Worsley, M., 544, 662

Nachmias, J., 137, 222, 654, 665, 673
Nafe, J. P., 311, 680
Nagasawa, A., 207, 674
Nagshineh, S., 139, 657
Nagy, A. L., 171, 691
Naka, K., 73, 691
Nakamura, C. Y., 633, 700
Nakayama, K., 330, 378, 379, 460, 517, 691
Narens, L., 46, 685, 691
Nathans, J., 159, 163, 691
Navon, D., 392, 543, 691
Neff, D. L., 221, 691
Neff, W. D., 657
Neisser, U., 39, 374, 522, 523, 531, 532, 536, 657
Neitz, J., 157, 163, 691
Nelson, B., 536, 676
Nelson, C. A., 560, 691
Nelson, D.G.K., 232, 672
Nelson, G., 553, 665
Nelson, J. N., 450, 712
Nelson, L. M., 664
Nelson, L. R., 321, 684
Nelson, P. G., 208, 258, 669
Nelson, R., 73, 81, 682, 691
Nerger, J. L., 162, 659
Nevatia, R., 368, 691
Neville, H. J., 691
Newhall, S. M., 150, 174, 692
Newland, J., 570, 692
Newman, E. B., 227, 228, 229, 237, 706, 711
Newman, J. D., 208, 669
Newport, A. G., 176, 576, 673
Newsome, W. T., 98, 454, 687, 692, 705
Niall, K. K., 498, 692
Nickerson, D., 150, 692
Nielson, C. R., 575, 690
Nijhawan, R., 496, 692
Nishimura, Y., 81, 680
Nissen, M. J., 573, 692
Nitzan, D., 452, 716
Nitzberg, D., 711
Noble, W., 229, 692
Noda, H., 469, 692
Noell, W., 609, 692
Noma, E., 49, 651
Nordby, K., 157, 703
Norgren, R., 259, 695
Norman, D. A., *189, 201, 228,* 397, 679, 692
Norman, J., 116, 679, 691
Norman, J. L., 542, 552, 679
Northrop, C. C., 194, 680
Norton, S. J., 306, 692

Norton, T. T., 551, 552, 582, 692
Norwich, K. H., 38, 43, 45, 264, 265, 371, 692
Nullmeyer, R., 44
Nunez, A. A., 446, 705
Nusbaum, H. C., 437, 439, 692, 695
Nusinowitz, S., 136, 668
Norman, J. L., 662
Nusinowitz, S., 668
Nullmeyer, R., 672
Nykvist, W. F., 264, 265, 688

Oakley, B., 263, 265, 654, 692
Oatley, M. W., 705
O'Brien, C. P., 321, 702
Obusek, C. J., 418, 712
Ochoa, J. L., 287, 708
O'Connell, L. M., 715
O'Connell, R. J., 174t, 273, 692
Odom, J. V., 230, 650
Oehler, R., 113, 114, 705
Ogasawara, K., 90, 692
Ohala, J. J., 692
Ohlott, P., 60, 686
Oldak, R., 628, 701
Oldfield, S. R., 227, 692
O'Leary, A., 593, 692
Olsho, L. W., 562, 692
Olson, R., 383, 692
Olzak, L., 126, 692
O'Mahony, M., 262, 265, 692, 693
Ommaya, A. K., 593, 654, 696
Ono, H., 341, 357, 494, 693
Ono, M. E., 341, 693
Oppenheim, R. W., 564, 673
Orban, G. A., 84, 89, 455, 587, 693, 710
Orndorff, M. M., 665
Ornstein, R. E., 447, 451, 693
Osaka, N., 110, 693
Osborne, M. P., 193, 199, 693, 695
O'Shaughnessy, M., 620, 698
Oshinsky, J. S., 416, 672
Osmond, H., 621, 676
Ost, 174t, 704
Oster, P. J., 575, 705
Osterberg, G., 75, 693
Ostfeld, A., 621, 693
Ostroy, S. E., 78, 602, 654
Ostry, D., 680
Otto, S. R., 204, 703
Ottoson, D., 273, 693
Over, R., 137, 379, 685, 705
Owens, D. A., 118, 683
Owens, M. E., 564, 693
Owsley, C., 124, 360, 693
Oyama, J., 55, 382, 693
Ozog, G., 372, 713

Packer, O., 76, 661
Padden, D. M., 429, 682
Page, S. C., 417, 677
Palmer, A. R., 206, 693
Palmer, C., 413, 416, 693
Palmer, J., 457
Palmer, S. E., 330, 397, 398, 702
Pan, X., 322, 674
Pandya, P. N., 699
Panek, P., 574, 651
Pang, X. D., 693
Pantev, C., 241, 693
Papert, S., 351, 693
Paquet, L., 394, 693
Parasuraman, R., 538, 693, 694
Parducci, A., 60, 694
Pare, E. B., 454, 692
Park, J. N., 666
Parker, D. E., 227, 467, 694
Parker, S., 53, 60, 696, 702
Parker, S.P.A., 692
Parks, T. E., 694
Parlee, M. B., 627, 694
Parrott, A. C., 622, 694
Pasanen, E. G., 198, 714
Pashler, H., 535, 694
Pasnak, R., 334, 493, 668
Pasternak, M., 575, 701
Pastore, R. E., 429, 431, 694
Patterson, R. D., 242, 243, 694
Patuzzi, R., 196, 202, 670, 703
Paulus, L., 260, 694
Pauser, G., 318, 664
Payne, R. A., 679
Peachly, N., 540, 701
Pearson, D. A., 568, 694
Peduzzi, J. D., 551, 552, 582, 675
Peeples, D. R., 558, 694
Peichl, L., 117, 139, 712
Pelosi, P., 269, 274, 694
Peloquin, L. J., 635, 677
Penfield, W., 290, *292,* 694
Penland, J., 529, 530, 567, 650
Pentland, A. P., 401, 403, 694
Perfetto, G., 341, 664
Perkell, J. S., 694
Perl, E. R., 287, 315, 694
Perrett, D. I, 97, 228, 694
Perrin, N. A., 399, 650
Perrott, D. R., 700
Perry, V. H., 139, 694
Peteanu, L. A., 77, 702
Peters, R. W., 243, 673
Petersen, M. R., 542, 632, 649
Petersik, J. T., 460, 694
Peterson, A. C., 630, 694
Peterson, S. E., 697
Peterzell, D. H., 571, 572, 713

Petitto, L. A., 433, 694
Petrig, B., 360, 694
Petronio, A., 624, 683
Petry, S., 379, 694
Pettersen, L., 360, 672, 716
Pettigrew, J. D., 347, 552, 583, 586, 653, 654, 662, 668, 694
Pevsner, J., 269, 695
Pfaff, D., 695
Pfaffman, C., 258, 259, 260, 264, 695
Pfeiffer, R. R., 206
Phillips, C. G., 98, 694, 695
Phillips, D. P., 250, 695
Phillips, L. J., 555, 682
Phillipson, O. T., 621, 636, 695
Piaget, J., 565, 695
Piantanida, T. P., 159, 163, 691
Pick, A. D., 695
Pick, H., 683
Pick, H. L., Jr., 592, 603, 604, 695
Picket, J. M., 436, 696
Pickford, R. W., 257, 716
Pickles, J. O., 189, 193, 195, 198, 199, 202, 207, 693, 695
Pierce, J. R., 417, 695
Piggins, D. J., 169, 695
Pigion, R. G., 619, 689
Pinel, J. P. J., 640, 695
Pinkers, A., 173, 695
Pionk, M., 628, 701
Pirenne, M. H., 114, 674
Pirozzolo, F. J., 625, 695
Pisanelli, A. M., 275, 694
Pisoni, D. B., 418, 437, 439, 440, 608, 695, 698, 711
Pitts, W. H., 273, 670
Plastow, E., 500, 655
Plateau, M. H., 695
Plude, D., 573, 575, 677, 695
Podgor, M., 681
Podgorny, P., 518, 695
Podolsky, S., 572, 668
Poggio, G. F., 303, 316, 351, 535, 695, 696, 698
Poggio, T., 347, 686, 696
Poggio, T. A., 677
Pohl, N., 97, 696
Pokorny, J., 170t, 171, 173, 696, 710
Pola, J., 466, 696
Pollack, I., 37, 38, 221, 409, 436, 696
Pollack, R. H., 606, 696
Pollatsek, A., 517, 536, 668, 675
Pollen, D. A., 117, 375, 650, 696
Poltrock, S. E., 535, 696
Pomerantz, J. R., 375, 379, 387, 396, 696
Pons, T. P., 290, 696
Poon, L., 576, 658

Poppel, E., 53, 444, 447, 696
Porac, C., 357, 379, 496, 569, 594, 613, 618, 660, 696, 712
Porjesz, B., 619, 652
Porter, R. H., 280, 565, 651, 658, 696
Poser, W. J., 709
Posner, M. I., 44, 504, 517, 521, 532, 539, 542, 557, 696, 697
Post, B., 467, 697
Post, R. B., 118, 459, 498, 572, 674, 683, 684
Postman, L., 175, 235, 656, 697
Poulton, E. C., 60, 697
Powell, T.P.S., 303, 690
Power, R. P., 415, 705
Powers, M. K., 109, 558, 672
Powley, T. L., 658
Poynter, W. D., 451, 697
Preble, L. D., 498, 500, 683
Predebon, J., 594, 697
Presti, D. E., 532, 697
Preti, G., 662, 697
Pribram, K. H., 624, 670
Price, J. L., 273, 697
Prichep, L. S., 645, 678
Priebe, F. A., 620, 711
Prinzmetal, W., 375, 389, 397, 532, 666, 697
Pritchard, R. M., 370, 697
Prkachin, K. M., 322, 661
Probst, R., 198, 687
Procter, M. M., 359, 704
Proffitt, D., 463, 465, 674
Przbyslawski, J., 586, 686
Puckett, J. de W, 467, 697
Puel, J. L., 195, 697
Puklin, J. E., 565, 699
Purcell, D. G., 628, 701
Purghe, F., 379, 697
Purkinje, J. E., 110
Pylyshyn, Z. W., 462, 663

Quigle, R., 608, 670
Quigley, S., 540, 701
Quinlan, P. T., 384, 677
Quinn, P. C., 164, 697

Rabbitt, P. M. A., 540, 573, 576, 697
Rabbitt, R. D., 189, 190, 530, 691, 697
Rabin, M. D., 267, 274, 280, 697
Rabinowicz, T., 697
Rabinowitz, W. M., 299, 306, 553, 665, 708
Rafal, R. D., 531, 697
Raftenberg, M. N., 199, 697

Rahe, A., 610, 671
Raichle, M. E., 207, 542, 683, 709
Rakerd, B., 228, 674, 697
Ram, C., 665
Ramachandran, V. S., 374, 379, 455, 462, 628, 697, 698, 709
Rammsayer, T., 698
Rand, T. C., 698
Randsom-Hogg, A., 113, 114, 698, 705
Raphaeli, N., 319, 649
Rashad, M. N., 715
Raslear, T. F., 449, 704
Rasmussen, T., 290, 292, 694
Ratliff, F., 130, 133, 370, 698, 699
Ratliff, R., 674
Rauth, J., 619, 704
Rayleigh, Lord, 698
Raymond, J. E., 467, 698
Rayner, K., 555, 698
Rea, M. M., 635, 698
Read, J. S., 173, 681
Reason, J., 478, 535, 698
Redding, G. M., 593, 698
Reddy, D. R., 424, 659, 698
Reddy, R., 436, 705
Reed, C., 305, 681
Reed, C. F., 299, 497, 681, 698
Reed, C. M., 306, 692
Reed, M. A., 452, 654
Reed, R. R., 272, 651
Reeves, A., 114, 540, 628, 701
Refinetti, R., 313, 698
Regal, D. M., 351, 555, 698
Regan, D., 476, 662
Regnier, F., 279, 671
Rehn, T., 506, 698
Reichardt, W., 455, 456, 698
Reid, F., 575, 765
Reid, R. C., 133, 703
Reilly, D. A., 701
Reiman, E. M., 620, 668
Reisberg, D., 698
Reisch, A. M., 260, 694
Reisz, 222
Remez, R. E., 418, 698
Remington, R., 517, 698, 704
Rensink, R. A., 331, 379, 568, 569, 570, 666
Repp, B. H., 698
Reschke, M. F., 304, 700
Reuter, G., 196, 698
Reynolds, M. L., 57, 704
Reynolds, P., 528, 649
Reynolds, R. I., 597, 698
Rhee, K., 619, 698
Rhein, L. D., 269, 657
Rhodes, G., 517, 698

Ricci, C., 623, 698
Rice, C. G., 605, 699
Richards, W., 503, 572, 609, 699
Riddoch, M. J., 677, 704
Riemersma, J. B., 384, 684
Riesen, A., 699
Rieser, J., 582, 699
Riesz, R. R., 699
Rifkin, B., 262, 652
Riggs, L. A., 370, 699
Rijnsdorp, A., 445, 699
Rivers, G., 136, 667
Rivest, J., 341, 693
Rizzo, M., 623, 699
Robbins, M., 604, 681
Roberts, J., 628, 699
Roberts, M., 432, 699
Roberts, T. D. M., *303*, 655
Robertson, P. W., 176, 699
Robey, J, 556, 655
Robins, D., 623, 699
Robinson, D. L., 518, 519, 520, 715
Robinson, D. W., 699
Robinson, L. R., 223, 699
Robinson, M. M., 81, 691
Robson, J. G., 117, 657, 699
Rocha-Miranda, E. C., 96, 672
Rock, I., 14, 329, 341, 461, 463, 466,
    485, 492, 496, 500, 680, 699
Rockland, K. S., 96, 699
Rodieck, R. W., 78, 82, 127, 699
Rodrigues, J., 175, 207, 656, 700
Roelofs, C. O., 356, 699
Roenker, D. L., 574, 651
Rogel, M. J., 699
Rogers, B., 173, 650
Rogers, B. J., 341, 351, 693, 699
Rogers, C. H., 300, 654
Rohrbaugh, J. W., 514, 699
Rojas, A., 273, 670
Rollman, G. B., 319, 699
Romani, G. L., 207, 699
Romano, J. A., 565, 699
Romano, P. E., 565, 699
Romer, D., 55
Root, W., 580, 699
Roper, S. D., 257, 653
Roscoe, S. N., 490, 610, 699
Rose, D. J., 467, 698
Rose, J. E., 195, 202, 207, 681, 699,
    700
Rosen, B. R., 652
Rosenblu, L. D., 668
Rosenblum, L., 431, 694
Rosenzweig, M. R., 228, 229, 711
Rosinki, R., 602, 700
Rosner, B. S., 649
Rosner, M., 450, 610, 682

Ross, H., 598, 700
Ross, H. E., 170, 304, 666, 700
Ross, N., 332, 700
Ross-Field, L., 632, 701
Roth, G. L., 207, 689
Rothbart, M. K., 531, 557, 700
Rothblat, L., 582, 584, 700
Roucoux, A., 454, 694
Rouiller, E. M., 207, 700
Rovamo, J., 129, 137, 715
Royster, J. D., 628, 700
Royster, L. H., 628, 700
Rozin, P., 254, 255, 267, 700
Rubin, A., 235, 649
Rubin, E., 377, 700
Rubin, P. E., 418, 698
Ruble, D. N., 633, 700
Ruddock, K. H., 139, 657
Rudnicky, A. I., 424, 659
Ruggieri, V., 357, 700
Rumelhart, D. E., 692
Runeson, S., 465, 700
Rusak, B., 446, 700
Rushton, W. A. H., 161, 162, 700
Russell, M. J., 279, 280, 565, 700
Russoff, A. C., 552, 690, 700
Ruthruff, A. M., 575, 705
Ryan, T. F., 298, 670
Ryugo, D. K., 194, 680

Saberi, K., 228, 684, 700
Sacco, R. L., 624, 658
Saccuzzo, D. P., 621, 655
Sachs, M. B., 202, 700
Sacks, O., 96, 700
Sager, L. C., 387, 696
Sagi, D., 375, 668
Saig, D., 668
St. James, J. D., 517, 518, 667
Salapatek, P., 555, 559, 561, 651,
    687, 688, 698, 700
Salmaso, D., 330, 670
Salmon, T. H., 654
Salthouse, T. A., 576, 700, 701
Samuel, A. G., 417, 430, 436, 664
Sand, A., 475, 685
Sandell, J. H., 139, 704
Sander, L. W., 433, 659
Sanders, A., 574, 701
Sanders, B., 629, 632, 701
Sanocki, T., 399, 701
Santos-Sacchi, J., 199, 662
Sapir, E., 701
Saunders, F., 681
Saunders, F. A., 299, 301, 713, 714
Sawusch, J. R., 430, 701
Sayers, B. M. A., 668

Scadden, L., 299, 714
Schab, R. F., 280, 701
Schady, W. J. L., 287, 708
Schaie, K. W., 574, 701
Schanel-Klitsch, E., 565, 659
Scharf, B., 217, *220*, 233, 234, 236,
    540, 655, 657, 701
Scharre, J. E., 558, 701
Schartz, D. W. F., 708
Schefrin, B. E., 173, 701
Scheiman, M., 565, 659
Schein, 96
Schenkel, K. D., 217, 701
Scher, D., 628, 700
Schiano, D., 595, 600, 660, 709
Schiff, W., 628, 701
Schiffman, H. R., 451, 691
Schiffman, S. S., 258, 265, 266, 273,
    278, 575, 666, 701, 705
Schiffren, R. M., 702
Schilder, P., 598, 700
Schiller, P. H., 83, 88, 167, 169, 701
Schindler, R. A., 203, 701
Schlaer, S., 114, 674
Schlauch, R. S., 701
Schleidt, M., 279, 280, 701
Schmeckler, M. A., 431, 694
Schmidt, A., 588, 691
Schmidt, H., 389, 532, 709
Schmiedt, R. A., 202, 701
Schnapf, J. L., 77, 79, 700
Schneck, M. E., 558, 697, 710
Schneider, B. A., 47, 60, 550, 562,
    702, 709
Schneider, D., 272, 702
Schneider, G. E., 702
Schneider, R., 627, 702
Schneider, S. L., 301, 702
Schneider, W., 536, 537, 538, 668,
    702, 704
Schnizlein, J. M., 44, 672
Schoenlein, R. W., 77, 702
Scholl, M., 556, 655
Schor, C. M., 351, 698
Schouten, M. E. H., 702
Schrott, A., 193, 705
Schubert, E. D., 702
Schull, J., 254, 321, 700, 702
Schulman, P. H., 459, 702
Schulte, R., 612, 708
Schultz, M. C., 306, 692
Schultze, M., 76
Schulze, H. H., 429, 702
Schvaneveldt, R. W., 536, 659
Schwab, E. C., 437, 692
Schwartz, C. B., 599, 702
Schwartz, M., 582, 584, 700
Schwartz, S. H., 112, 702

Schwartz, T., 114, 652
Schwarz, D. W. F., 241, 708
Scialfa, C. T., 573, 702
Sciasnia, T. R., 505, 656
Scott, H. A., Jr., 309, 311, 312t, 680
Scott, T. R., 254, 258, 259, 260, 702
Sedgwick, H., 702
Segall, M. H., 605, 702
Seggie, J., 636, 702
Sejnowski, T. J., 98, 651
Sekuler, R., 124, 330, 453, 574, 606, 617, 619, 693, 702
Selfridge, O. G., 399, 702
Seligman, P. M., 204, 654
Sellick, P. M., 196, 703
Semenza, C., 625, 703
Semple, M. N., 230, 231, 703, 705
Senden, M., von, 586, 703
Serafine, M. L., 625, 703
Serbin, L. A., 632, 705
Seron, X., 623, 671
Serpell, R., 570, 703
Sersen, E. A., 712
Service, J., 207, 687
Sestokas, A. K., 518, 690
Settle, R. G., 280, 664
Shaffer, H. L., 528, 703
Shaffer, L. H., 448, 703
Shah, 223
Shallice, T., 45, 703
Shamai, K., 81, 680
Shaman, P., 627, 665
Shank, C. V., 77, 305, 702, 711
Shankweiler, D. P., 439, 684
Shannon, C. E., 33, 703
Shannon, R. V., 204, 703
Shansky, M. S., 176, 649
Shapiro, K. L., 198, 467, 538, 679, 703
Shapley, R., 82, 83, 86, 94, 109, 133, 167, 168, 503, 703
Sharma, S., 621, 622, 690, 703
Sharpe, L. T., 112, 157, 690, 703
Shavit, Y., 321, 684
Shea, R. N., 360, 668
Shea, S. L., 359, 565, 703, 704
Shebilske, W. L., 343, 703
Sheedy, J. E., 518, 703
Sheehy, J. B., 704
Sheetz, A., J., 571, 572, 713
Shefner, J. M., 684
Sheingold, K., 703
Shepard, M., 409, 410, 695, 703
Shepard, R. N., 57, 463, 518, 540, 682, 703
Shepard, R. P., 300, 654
Shera, C. A., 191, 703
Sherk, H., 139, 677, 704

Sherman, S., 582, 585, 676
Sherman, S. M., 83, 84, 86, 95, 683, 704
Sherrick, M. F., 689
Sherrington, C. S., 302, 661, 704
Shiet, F. T., 575, 705, 706
Shiffman, S. S., 57, 704
Shiffrin, R. M., 535, 704
Shiller, P., 82, 86, 106, 127, 139, 552, 667, 704
Shimojo, S., 330, 360, 378, 379, 557, 653, 691, 704
Shinar, D., 574, 704
Shipley, T. F., 379, 680
Shlaer, S., 674
Shockey, L., 436, 704
Short, K. R., 561, 680
Shower, E. G., 223, 224, 704
Shows, T. B., 159, 691
Shulman, G. L., 517, 518, 704
Shulte, R., 708
Shupert, C. L., 684, 705, 706
Shurtleff, D., 449, 704
Sibony, P. A,. 619, 704
Siddle, D. A., 634, 704
Sidman, M., 570, 704
Sieg, D., 635, 711
Siegel, L. J., 652
Siegel, S., 174t, 649
Siemensen, D., 124, 693
Silvar, S. D., 606, 696
Silveira, L. C., 139, 694
Silver, W. L., 258, 704
Silverman, G., 691
Silverman, M. S., 168, 330, 378, 379, 517, 708
Silverton, L., 621, 655
Simm, G., 207, 700
Simmons, F. B., 229, 244, 704
Simmons, J. A., 704
Simmons, L., 449, 704
Simon, E., 576, 661
Simpson, W. A., 22, 704
Sinclair, D. C., 704
Sinnot, J., 619, 704
Siqueland, E. R., 433, 665
Sivak, J. G., 704
Sivian, L. S., 214, 217, 704
Skarda, C. A., 273, 704
Sklar, P. B., 269, 695
Skottun, B. C., 126, 655
Skowbo, D., 174t, 705
Schumer, R. A., 679
Slabach, E. H., 674
Slaback, E. H., 573, 674
Slaughter, M. M., 139, 704
Slavin, K., 629, 654
Sloan, K. R., 76, 661

Sloane, M. E., 704
Sloane, S. A., 359, 704
Sloboda, J. A., 417, 705
Slowiaczek, L. M., 439, 695
Small, L. H., 705
Smallman, R. L., 652
Smith, A., 379, 705
Smith, B., 268, 690
Smith, D. V., 259, 705
Smith, D. W., 207, 674
Smith, J., 415, 705
Smith, K. M., 562, 653
Smith, L. B., 651
Smith, M. C., 653
Smith, P., 268, 690
Smith, R. L., 298, 710, 714
Smith, V. C., 171, 173, 696, 710
Smith, W. S., 632, 705
Snellen, H., 114, 705
Snodgrass, J. G., 39, 704, 705
Snyder, S. H., 269, 321, 705
Soares, M. P., 629, 701
Sokolov, E. N., 514, 705
Solis-Macias, V., 396, 518, 681
Solomon, H. Y., 305, 657
Sone, T., 227, 650
Souther, J., 375, 709
Southwick, E., 277, 705
Spelke, E. S., 162, 561, 680
Spelman, F. A., 204, 554, 689
Sperling, G., 455, 462, 710
Sperling, H. G., 657, 705
Sperry, R. W., 358, 705
Spieker, R., 433, 686
Spierer, A., 610, 682
Spillman, L., 113, 114, 456, 698, 705
Spinelli, D. N., 624, 670, 676
Spinnato, J. A., 321, 659
Spitzer, H., 526, 705
Spitzer, M. W., 231, 705
Spoendlin, H. H., 193, 194, 705
Sprafkin, C., 632, 705
Spreen, O., 705
Springer, S. P., 428, 570, 705
Srulovicz, P., 243, 705
Stacey, E. W., Jr., 530, 653
Stagner, B. B., 197, 199, 685
Stanton, S., 207, 674
Stark, L., 356, 529, 567, 705
Stebbins, W. C., 187, 705
Stein, B. E., 90, 692
Steinberg, A., 705
Steiner, J. E., 564, 669
Steinfied, G. J., 597, 705
Steinman, R. M., 467, 697
Steinmetz, M. A., 518, 690
Stelmack, R. M., 634, 705
Stephan, F. K., 446, 705

Stephens, P. R., 471, 705
Stern, D., 433, 686
Stern, I. B., 564, 655
Stern, J. A., 576, 705
Stern, R. M., 478, 677, 706
Sternbach, R. A., 319, 706
Sternberg, S., 448, 706
Stevens, D. A., 683, 706
Stevens, J. C., 56, 261, 262, 274, 296, 311, 313, 575, 657, 673, 682, 706
Stevens, K. N., 232, 434, 682, 706
Stevens, S. S., 46, 50, 51, 53, 55, 227, *228*, 237, 239, 298, 313, 319, 706
Stevenson, M., 604, 669
Stewart, J. D., 625, 656
Stewart, W. R., 705
Sticht, T., 418, 668
Stiles, W. S., 104, 716
Stinson, M. R., 189, 706
Stoever, R. J., 387, 696
Stoffregen, T. A., 706
Stokes, B. A. R., 704
Stokinger, T. E., 221, 653
Stolwijk, J. A. J., 319, 673
Stone, C. A., 83, 568, 663
Stone, L. S., 358, 706
Strange, W., 607, 706
Stratton, G. M., 590, 706
Street, R. F., 706
Streitfeld, B., 59, 430, 707
Strom, L., 258, 654, 664
Stromeyer, C. F., III, 707
Stroop, J., 707
Stroud, J. M., 448, 707
Stryer, L., 77, 707
Stuart, G. W., 493, 663
Studdert-Kennedy, M., 433, 439, 686
Stuiver, M., 274, 664
Suedfeld, P., 707
Sugitani, M., 293, 662
Sullivan, R., *268*, 690
Sulzman, F. M., 447, 669
Summerfield, A., 432, 671, 699
Supra, M., 229, 707
Supramaniam, S., 530, 672
Sussman, H. M., 426, 430, 707
Sutija, V. G., 552, 673
Sutter, A., 375, 707
Suzuki, Y., 227, 650
Svaetichin, G., 164, *165,* 707
Swain, I. U., 562, 659
Swarbrick, L., 208, 707
Sweeny, J. A., *268,* 698
Swender, P., 690
Swensson, R. G., 31, 707
Swets, J. A., 26, 707

Swift, C. G., 620, 667, 707
Swindale, N. V., 116, 582, 707
Switkes, E., 168, 708
Symons, L. A., 584, 707
Szabo, S., 262, 266, 656
Szczesiul, R., 60, 431, 685
Szentagothai, J., 473, 707
Szoc, R., 372, 713

Tachibana, M., 81, 680
Talbot, J. D., 316, 353, 707
Talbot, W. H., 696
Talmadge, C. L., 198, 706
Tan, H. Z., 304, 306, 693, 707
Tanczos, 170t
Tangney, J., 373, 713
Tart, C., 622, 707
Taub, E., 593, 696, 707
Taylor, J. H., 375, 696
Taylor, S. P., 8, 707
Tedford, W. H., 707
Tees, R. C., 584, 607, 608, 707, 713
Teeter, J. H., 257, 655, 707
Teghtsoonian, M., 507, 550, 707, 708
Teghtsoonian, R., 56, 507, 694, 708
Teller, D. Y., 71, 113, 455, 557, 558, 664, 684, 708, 710
Templeton, W. B., 593, 677
Tepper, B., 447, 669
Terenius, L., 321, 708
Terheardt, E., 243, 708
Terman, G. W., 321, 684
Tetewsky, E., 379, 696
Tharp, D., 351, 653
Theodor, L. H., 613, 660
Thomas, E. A. C., 451, 708
Thomas, H., 53, 632, 708
Thomas, J. P., 106, 127, 139, 667
Thomas, W. G., 628, 700
Thorell, L. G., 127
Thornbury, J. M., 575, 708
Thornton, J. E., 279, 671
Thorpe, L. A., 563, 708
Timney, B. N., 359, 583, 584, 587, 662, 708
Tiplady, B., 707
Tipper, S. P., 620, 708
Tirindelli, R., 269, 694
Toch, H. H., 612, 708
Todd, J. T., 336, 465, 708
Tomko, D. L., 353, 670
Tomlinson, R. W. W., 241, 708
Tootell, R. B. H., 168, 708
Torebjork, H. E., 287, 315, 708
Torgerson, W. S., 708
Tougas, Y., 247, 708
Townsend, J., 244, 399, 708

Traior, L. J., 563, 709
Tranel, D., 625, 662, 663
Trehub, S. E., 550, 562, 563, 565, 607, 708, 709
Treisman, A., 375, 383, 384, 388, 389, 397, 403, 517, 528, 532, 542, 679, 709
Treisman, M., 447, 709
Tress, K. H., 635, 709
Trevarthen, C., 167, 684
Tronick, E., 709
Troscianko, T., 455, 709
Trout, J. D., 436, 709
Tsal, Y., 517, 709
Tsotsos, J. K., 368, 709
Tsvetkova, L. A., 625, 709
Tuason, V. B., 635, 677
Tubis, A., 198, 707
Tuck, J. P., 162, 709
Turnbull, C., 606, 709
Turner, P., 620, 709
Tursky, B., 319, 706
Turvey, M. T., 305, 657
Tversky, B., 58, 387, 600, 669, 709
Ty, T. C., 314, 688
Tyer, Z., 334, 493, 668, 694
Tyler, C. W., 351, 455, 658, 698, 709
Tynan, P., 453, 702

Uchanski, R. M., 223, 681
Uchicawa, H., 505, 709
Uchikawa, K., 505, 709
Uhlarik, J., 580, 598, 709
Ullman, S., 403, 455, 462, 709
Umezaki, H., 553, 709
Ungerleider, L. G., 90, 95, 96, 97, 454, 526, 709
Uttal, W., 329, 332, 333, 485, 492, 710
Ulrich, R., 448, 709

Vahle-Hinz, C., 287, 671
Valbo, A., 288, 295, 710
Valentine, R. H., 635, 677
Van Compernolle, D., 204, 708
Vandenberg, S. G., 715
van der Heijden, A. H. C., 517, 710
Van der Loos, H., 553, 677
van der Meer, H. C., 710
Van der Zwan, R., 305, 713
Van Dijk, P., 198, 710
Van Doren, C. L., 299, 710
Van Essen, D. C., 86, 88, 90, 98, 129, 167, 455, 456, 664, 684, 687, 710
Van Lacker, D. R., 626, 710
Van Santen, J. P. H., 455, 710

Van Sluyters, R. C., 553, 690
Van Voorhis, S., 541, 710
Varma, V. K., 622, 710
Varner, D., 558, 710
Vaughan, H. G., 531, 553, 682, 697, 710
Vautin, R. G., 460, 710
Velle, V., 627, 628, 710
Veres, J. G., III, 146, 683
Verriest, G., 173, 710
Verrillo, R. T., 293, 295, 298, 299, 654, 670, 710
Vevea, J. M., 652
Vickers, D., 45, 703
Viemeister, N. F., 203, 710
Vierck, C. J., Jr., 287, 303, 315, 659
Vigorito, J., 433, 665
Vilardi, K., 457, 686
Villa, A., 207, 700
Vimal, R. L. P., 171, 710
Vincent, J., 496, 665
Virzi, R. A., 535, 665
Vogels, R., 587, 710
Volkman, J., 227, 706
Volkmann, F. C., 237, 706
von der Heydt, R., 375, 709
Vurpillot, E., 360, 567, 651
Vyas, A., 223, 598, 653

Waber, D. P., 632, 710
Wade, G., 628, 717
Wade, N. J., 346, 710
Waespe, W., 473, 711
Waessle, 83, 86, 117, 167, 655, 684, 694
Wahl, O. F., 635, 711
Wahlstrom, A., 321, 708
Wainwright, A., 339, 671
Wald, G., 78, 160, 161, 656, 711
Walk, R. D., 358, 359, 711
Walker, J. L., 453, 711
Walker, J. T., 305, 457, 711
Wall, P. D., 314, 317, 416, 688, 711
Wallace, B., 593, 620, 698, 711
Wallace, P., 280, 711
Wallach, H., 228, 353, 457, 459, 468, 503, 711
Walley, A., 608, 711
Walls, G. L., 711
Walraven, J., 106, 505, 711, 713
Walter, A. A., 600, 658
Wandell, B. A., 651
Ward, D. C., 572, 688
Ward, L. M., 48, 53, 56, 60, 233, 319, 396, 540, 661, 690, 711, 712
Ward, S., 632, 705
Ward, T. B., 633, 712

Ward, W. D., 712
Ware, C., 173, 379, 712
Warm, J. S., 451, 712
Warren, A. B., 572, 688
Warren, D. E., 707
Warren, D. H., 247, 586, 712
Warren, R. M., 418, 436, 652, 712
Warren, R. P., 418, 712
Warren, W. H., 476, 712
Warshovsky, F., 706
Wassle, H., 139, 712
Watanabe, T., 207, 712
Watkins, L. R., 322, 323, 687, 712
Watson, A. B., 22, 129, 712
Watson, C. S., 221, 712
Watson, S. J., 321, 322, 649
Wattam-Bell, J., 552, 553, 557, 651, 655
Weale, R. A., 71, 132, 572, 712
Weaver, B., 708
Weaver, W., 703
Weaver, R. A., 451, 708
Webb, F., 632, 705
Weber, D. L., 38, 685
Weber, E. H., 712
Weber, E. U., 357, 693
Webster, M., 129, 712
Webster, W. R., 174t, 206, 663, 687, 712
Weddell, G., *287*, 715
Wegener, B., 712
Weiffenbach, J. M., 628, 712
Weil, A. T., 450, 712
Weinberger, D. R., 653
Weinstein, E. A.,712
Weinstein, N., 715
Weinstein, S., *295*, 296, 628, 712
Weisel, T. N., 552, 713
Weisenberg, M., 322, 713
Weisenberger, J. M., 301, 713
Weiskopf, S., 163, 654
Weiss, S., 199, 561, 658, 668
Weisskipff, R. M., 652
Weisstein, N. A., 121, 330, 372, 373, 377, 379, 385, 681, 713
Welch, R. B., 590, 591, 593, 713
Welford, A. T., 44, 713
Well, A. D., 568, 713
Wellen, D. G., 575, 706, 713
Wells, G. L., 600, 716
Wenderoth, P., 305, 713
Werblin, F., 272, 667
Werker, J. F., 434, 440, 563, 607, 608, 707, 713
Werner, G., 303, 690
Werner, H., 372, 505, 558, 713
Werner, J. S., 173, 571, 572, 701, 713

Wertheimer, M., 114, 380, 459, 562, 713, 714
West, J. A., 704
West, R., 417, 677
Westerman, L. A., 714
Westheimer, G., 135, 713
Wever, E. G., 242, 714
Wever, R. A., 446, 714
Whalen, D. H., 714
Whalen, J. J., 163, 669
Wheeler, D., *608*, 670
Whishaw, I. O., 97, 431, 682
Whitaker, H. A., 428, 689
White, B. L., 557, 590, 714
White, B. W., 299, 714
White, C. W., 169, 175, 595, 667, 714
White, K. D., 634, 704
White, R. L., 204, 708
White, S. D., 214, 217, 704
Whitehead, P. R., 319, 678
Whitehurst, G. S., 570, 659
Whiteside, T. C. D., 339, 690
Whitfield, I. C., 203, 207, 208, 707, 714
Whitsel, B. L., 293, 714
Whorf, B. L., 176, 714
Whytt, R., 714
Wickens, C. D., 714
Wiener, N., 33, 714
Wier, C. C., 198, 222, 224, 678, 714
Wiesel, T. N., 90, 91, 455, 583, 677, 684, 713
Wikner, K., 564, 699
Wilcox, S. B., 498, 684
Willer, J. C., 316, 321, 683, 714
Willette, M., 452, 689
Williams, A., 373, 713
Williams, D., 658
Williams, D. R., 162, 714
Williams, J. M., 621, 714
Williams, K. A., 434, 682
Williams, M., 96, 576, 623, 653, 714, 715
Williams, M. A., 715
Williamson, S. J., 207, 699
Willis, W. D., 315, 316, 317, 318, 323, 714
Wilson, B., 169, 675
Wilson, E. O., 279, 714
Wilson, H. C., 87, 88, 714
Wilson, H. R., 116, 126, 127, 129, 137, 714
Wilson, J., 518, 704
Wilson, K. A., 622, 716
Wilson, M., 59, 610, 707, 715
Wilson, W., 430, 607, 665
Winter, I. M., 206, 693
Winter, P. L., 208, 669

Wit, H. P, 198, 707, 710
Witkin, H. A., 634, 715
Wolberg, Z., 208, 669
Wolf, E., 572, 668
Wolf, S., 621, 627, 702
Wolfe, J., 174t, 681
Wolfe, J. M., 535, 715
Wolff, H. G., 318, 319, 322, 673, 715
Wolff, H. W., 674
Wolff, J. M., 715
Wolff, P. H., 563, 715
Wolters, G., 517, 710
Wong, A., 665, 715
Wong, C., 713, 715
Wong, E., 377, 713
Wong-Riley, M. T. T., 94, 715
Woo, G., 572, 610, 715
Wood, A., 576, 653
Wood, R. W., 476, 715
Woodfield, R. L., 632, 715
Woodhouse, J. M., 8, 707
Woodrow, H., 444, 451, 715
Woods, B., 658
Woodworth, D. G., 634, 661
Woolard, H. H., 287, 715
Wooten, B. R., 163, 164, 469, 558, 669, 697, 712, 713
Worchel, P., 229, 715
Worthey, J. A., 506, 715
Wright, L. L., 715
Wright, M. J., 715
Wright, N. H., 221, 715
Wright, R. H., 254, 269, 272, 275, 276, 715
Wright, W. D., 153, 158, 715
Wright-Cassidy, K., 564, 680
Wroten, H. W., 221, 712
Wurtz, R. H., 518, 519, 520, 715

Wyatt, H. J., 466, 696
Wyburn, G. M., 257, 716
Wysocki, C. J., 267, 670
Wyszecki, G., 104, 716

Yaksh, T. L., 321, 716
Yamamoto, T., 260, 669, 716
Yang, J. C., 322, 659
Yankell, S. L., 665
Yantis, S., 514, 517, 679, 716
Yarbus, A. L., 529, 716
Yarmey, A., 600, 716
Yates, G. K., 202, 670
Yayama, N., 260, 716
Ye, Q., 255, 716
Yeh, J., 517, 559, 661
Yeh, Y., 667
Yen, W., 716
Yeomans, D. C., 315, 659
Yerkes, R. M., 538, 716
Yin, R. K., 716
Yodogawa, E., 387, 716
Yonas, A., 353, 360, 517, 555, 561, 564, 650, 661, 672, 680, 716
Yoneshige, Y., 565, 716
Young, A. W., 625, 665
Young, C., 536, 668
Young, F. A., 610
Young, F. W., 57, 704
Young, J. Z., 471, 705
Young, L., 477, 675
Young, L. L., 622, 716
Young, L. R., 467, 716
Young, M. G., 293, 714
Young, R. A., 169, 555, 682, 716
Young, T., 157

Yuille, J., 601, 716
Yund, E. W., 91, 448, 664, 716

Zakay, D., 716
Zaporozhets, A. V., 567, 716
Zaragoza, M. S., 601, 716
Zare, S. L., 463, 703
Zaretsky, H. H., 330, 667
Zatorre, R. J., 208, 240, 276, 428, 716, 717
Zec, R. F., 653
Zeigler, H. P., 493, 717
Zeigler, R., 717
Zeki, S., 98, 169, 685, 694, 695
Zellner, D. A., 276, 717
Zenner, H. P., 196, 698
Zhang, X., 322, 674
Zhuang, S., 322, 674
Ziegler, R. O., 628
Zigler, M. J., 296, 717
Zihl, J., 453, 675, 717
Zilbert, D., 582, 699
Zimmerman, M., 318, 664, 717
Zinberg, E., 450, 712
Zotterman, Y., 258, 265, 307, 654, 664, 717
Zrenner, E., 164, 167, 169, 671, 717
Zucker, I., 402, 446, 628, 700, 717
Zue, V. W., 424, 659
Zuidema, P., 114, 717
Zurek, P. N., 208, 717
Zusho, H., 280, 664
Zweig, G., 191, 703
Zwicker, E., 196, 217, 218, 244, 704, 717
Zwislocki, J. J., 50, 55, 56, 202, 217, 221, 675, 717

SUBJECT INDEX

Page numbers in italics indicate figures; page numbers followed by "t" indicate tabular material; page numbers in boldface type indicate glossary definitions.

Aß fibers, 290, *291*, 315, 317
Aδ fibers, 290, *291*, 315, 317
AB,H system, 255, 257, **281**
Ablations, 644, **646**
Absolute distance, 328, **361**
Absolute threshold, measurement of, 21–32, 21t, **61**
  adaptive testing, 24–25, *25,* **61**
  method of constant stimuli, 21–23, *22,* **62**
  method of limits, 23–24, **62**
  signal detection theory, 26t, 27t, 26–32, **63**
Acceleration, 471, **479**
Accommodation, 70, **99**
  as depth cue, 338–39, **361**
Acoustic–phonetic invariance, 425, **441**
Across–fiber pattern, 258, *259,* **281**
Action potential, 641, **647**
Active process, 195, **209,** 437, **441**
Acupuncture, 321–22, *322*
Adaptation
  auditory, 235, **248**
  in brightness perception, 107–109, 136–37, *137,* 138t, **142**
  context and, 58–61
  dark, 107–108, *108,* 109t, **142**
  level, theory of, 59–61
  light, 107–108, **142,** 456
  pain, 319–20
  selective, 136–37, *137,* 138t, **142,** 456
  smell, 275, 276t
  taste, 262–64
  temperature, 309–13, *311*
  touch, 296–98, 297t
Adaptive testing, 24–25, *25,* **61**
Aerial perspective, as depth cue, 332, **361**
Affect, 13
Afference copy, 356, **361**

Affordances, 485, **508, 591, 615**
Afterimages, apparent movement and, 460, 461t, 472t, **479**
Aging, 571–76
  global changes of, 575–76
  hearing and, 574–75
  taste and smell and, 575
  visual function in, 571–74, *573*
Agnosia, 622–27, 626t, **637**
  autotopagnosia, 625, **637**
  prosopagnosia, 625, **637**
  simultagnosia, 623, **637**
  spatial, 624, **637**
  visual, 96, **101**
  visual integrative, 623, **637**
  visual object, 620, **637**
Alcohol, perceptual effects of, 619–20
Amacrine cells, 72, **99**
Ampulla, 471, **479**
Analgesia, 320–22
Anomalous trichromatism, 159, **177**
Anosmia, 275, **281**
APB (2–amino–4–phosphonobutyrate), 139, **141**
Aphasia, 625, **637**
Apparent movement, 459–61, 461t, 472t, **479**
Apprehension, of perceptual constancies, 486, **508**
Aqueous humor, 66, **99**
Area 17 (V1), 90, **99, 101**
Area 18 (V2), 90, **99, 101**
Area 19, 90, **99, 101**
Aristotle's illusion, 294t
Arousal, vigilance and, 536–39
Articulators, 420, **441**
Ascending series, 23
Astigmatism, 586, **615**
Attention, 512–44
  auditory, 516, 526–28
  divided, 512, 516, 526–28, **545**
  expecting and, 541–42
  extent of, 518, **546**
  filtering and, 512–28, **546**
    cocktail party phenomenon in, 521–22
    neurophysiology of, 525–26
    video overlap phenomenon in, 522–25

    focused, 512, **545**
  orienting and, 518–21
    covert, 514–16, **545**
    eye movements in, 513–14
    overt, 519–20
    visual capture and, 514, 515t, **547**
  searching and, 528–39
    automatic versus controlled, 535–36
    eye movements and, 528–31
    feature versus conjunction, 531–35
    vigilance and arousal in, 536–39
  selective, precedence effect in, 522, 523t
  shadowing and, 516, **546**
  size constancy and, 493, 494t
  structural theories of, 542–44, **546**
Attentional gaze, 517–18, **545**
Attentional resources, 543, **545**
Aubert–Fleischl effect, 467, 468t, **479**
Audible angle, minimum, 227, **250**
Audible field, minimum, 214, **250**
Audible pressure, 214, **250**
Auditory adaptation, 235, **248**
Auditory fatigue, 235, 236t, **248**
Auditory flutter fusion (AFF), 620, **637**
Auditory grouping, 563, **577**
Auditory masking, 217–21, 218t, 219t
  backward, 221, **248**
  central, 221, **249**
  forward, 219, **250**
  informational, 221, **250**
  simultaneous, 217, **250**
Auditory scene, 245–47, **245**
Auditory streams, 245, 248t, **248**
Auditory system, 201–208. *See also* Basilar membrane; Ear; Hearing; Sound(s)
  cortex, *205,* 207–208, *208*
  fatigue and, 235, 236t, **248**
  nerves of, 201–204
  pathways, *204,* 204–207

Auditory theories, of speech perception, 437–38
Autokinetic effect, 473t, **479**
Autotopagnosia, 625, **637**
Axon, 640, **647**
Azimuth, 225, **248**

Back projections, 88, **99**
Background stimuli, 59, **61**
Backward masking, 301, **324, 372, 404**
Basilar membrane, 191, 195, 197t, 199, **209**, 220
   mechanical tuning on, 195–98
   wave motion on, *195, 196, 196–98*
Bel, 184, **209**
Benefit, of information cues, 539, **545**
Benham's top, 170t
Beta (ß), 31, 35t, **61**
Bezold–Brucke effect, 171, **177**
Binocular perception, 360, **361.** *See also* Stereopsis
Binocular rivalry, 526, 527t, **545**
Biological clock, 445–50, **479**
   biological pacemaker and, 449–50
   circadian rhythms and, 445–47
   short–term timers and, 447–49
Biological reductionism, 13, **17**
Bipolar cells, of retina, 72, **99**
Bit, **61**
Blind spot, 79, 79t, **99**
Blindness
   color, 157, **178**
   day, 77, **100**
   night, 76
   psychic, 96, **101**
   snow, 370
Blobs, 94, **99**, 167, **178**
Bloch's law, 112, 116, **141**
Bodycentric direction, 354, **362**
Bony labyrinth, 471, **480**
Braille, 299–300
Brain activity, measurement of, 644–46
Brightness perception, *105,* 105–107, *107,* **141**, 501, **508**
   adaptation in, 107–109, 136–37, *137,* 138t, **142**
   dark, 107–108, *108,* 109t, **142**
   light, 107–108, **142**
   area and, 112–13
   assimilation, 133–36, **141**
   contrast and, 129–33, *135*
      simultaneous, *129,* 129–30
   retinal location and, 110, 117

rods and cones and, 108–109
sensitivity limit and, 114
spatial frequency analysis and, 118–29
time and, 111–12
visual acuity and, 114–18, 124, **143**
wavelength and, 110–11
Bril, 107, **141**
Bunsen–Roscoe law, 111, **141**

C fibers, 290, 315, 317
Carpentered world hypothesis, 605, **615**
Catch trials, 26, **61**
Category scaling, 50, **61**
Cell, body, 640, **647**
Central nervous system (CNS), 641, **647**
Change
   object–relative, 457, **480**
   subject–relative, 457, **481**
Channel capacity, 37–38, **61**
Childhood, 565–71. *See also* Infancy
   encoding and memory in, 569–71
   eye movement patterns in, 566–67
   orienting and filtering in, 568–69
Chlorolabe, 157, **178**
Choice reaction time, **61**
Chopper neuron, 206, 209
Chord, musical, 411, **441**
Chorda tympani, 257
Choroid coat, 72
Chromatic adaptation, 171, **178**
CIE. *See* Commission Internationale de l'Eclairage
Cilia, olfactory, 269, **283**
Circadian rhythm, 445–47, **480**
Circumvallate papillae, 256
CNS (central nervous system), 641, **647**
Cochlea, 188, *191, 192, 194*
Cochlear duct, 191, **209**
Cochlear implant, 203, **209**
Cochlear nucleus, 205, **209**
   dorsal, 205, **209**
   ventral, 205, **211**
Cognition, 12, **17**
Cognitive clock, 445, 450–53, **480**
   change monitoring and, 451, **480**
   processing effort and, 451–52
   temporal processing and, 452–53
Cognitive style, 634–37
Cold. *See* Temperature
Cold fibers, 307, **324**
Color(s). *See also* Color perception

additive, 150–53, **177**
atlas, 149, **178**
blindness, 157, **178**
complementary, 153, **178**
constancy, 504, 506t, **508**
hue and, **178**
memory, 173–75
metameric, 150, **178**
mixture, 150–53, 152t
   additive, 150–53, **177**
   subtractive, 151–53, **179**
spindle, 150, **178**
wheel, 148, *149, 153*
   purity in, 149, **178**
   saturation in, 149, **178**
Color perception. *See also* Color(s)
   abnormalities in, 157–60, *159,* 160t
   afterimages and, 172, **177**
   aging and physical condition and, 173
   brightness and, 149–50
   chromatic adapation in, 171, **178**
   CIE color space and, 153–56
   color channels and, 167–69, *168*
   cortical coding and, 167–69
   culture and, 147, 175–76
   defects in, 157–60, *159,* 160t
   emotion and, 176
   in infants, 163–64
   intensity and duration in, 170–73
   of males versus females, 159, 163
   monochromatic stimuli in, 149, **178**
   opponent–process theory of, 163–64
   physiology of, 156, 160–63
   primary, 153–56, *154, 155,* **178**
   simultaneous color contrast in, 172–73
   spectral, 149, **179**
   subjective, 169, 170t, **179**
   trichromatic theory and, 156–63, **179**
   tristimulus values and, 156, **179**
   wavelength and, 146–47, *147,* 149, 150–56, *154,* 160–61, *161, 163,* 164–67, *165, 166, 167,* 176
Commission Internationale de l'Eclairage (CIE), 104, **141**
   chromaticity space and, 155–56, *155*
   color space and, 153–56
Comparison stimuli, **61**
Complex cells, **99**
Computational theories, 14, **17,** 329, **362,** 485–86, **508**

Concentration test, **99**
Conceptually–driven processing, 392, 393t, **404**
Cones, **99**
Configural feature, 396, **404**
Confusion matrix, 37, **61**
Conjunction search, 532, **545**
Consonance, 232, **249**
Consonants, 419–20, 421t, **441**
Constancy scaling, 488, **508**. *See also* Size constancy
Constructive theories, 14, **17,** 329, **362, 485, 508**
Context, 58–61
  adaptation level and, 59
  meaning and, 595–601
    expectation and, 596–99
    eyewitness testimony and, 600–601
    language and, 599–601
  speech perception and, 435–37
  stimuli, classes of, 59, 486, **508**
  visual, and judged weight, 58t
Contour(s), 368–75, **404**
  emergence, 372–73
  extrinsic, 378, **404**
  illusory, 379, **405**
  intrinsic, 378, **404**
  in music, 412, **441**
  subjective, 379, **405**
Contrast
  brightness, 129–33, **135**
  matching, 123, **141**
  ratio, 123, **142**
Controlled processing, 535, **545**
Convergence, as depth cue, 339, **362**
Cooperative algorithms, 348, **362**
Cornea, 66, **99**
Correct negatives, signal detection theory, 27
Cortex
  auditory, *205, 207*–208, *208*
  extrastriate, 88, **100**
  inferotemporal, 96, **100**
  somatosensory, 290, 292, **325**
  striate, *86,* 88, **101**
  visual. *See* Visual system, cortex of
Cost, of information cues, 539, **545**
Covert attention, 514–16, **545**
Covert orienting, 568, **577**
Crista, 471, **480**
Critical flicker fusion frequency (CFF), **61,** 620, **637**
Critical period, in perceptual development, 583, **615**
Cross–adaptation
  of smell, 275, **283**
  to taste, 263, **282**

Crossed disparity, 344–45, **362**
Crossed olivocochlear bundle, 195, 209
Cross–modality matching, 55–56, **61**
Crystalline lens, 70–71, **338**
Cupola, 472, **480**
Cyanolabe, 157, **178**
Cycle(s)
  of sound waves, 182–84, **209**
  per second, 184, **209**
Cyclic adenosine monophosphate (cAMP), 270–72
Cyclopean eye, 355, **362**

d' (sensitivity), 32, 34t, 35t, **61**
Dark adaptation, *572*
Darkness perception, 139, 140t
Data–driven processing, 391–92, 397–98, **404**
Day blindness, 77, **100**
Decibel (dB), 184, **209**
Dendrites, 640, **647**
Density, of sound, 232, **249**
Depolarization, 641, **647**
Depth perception. *See also* Direction perception; Space perception
  absolute distance and, 328, **361**
  accommodation as, 338–39, **361**
  aerial perspective as, 332–33, **361**
  binocular. *See* Stereopsis
  combining and interaction of, 351–53
  convergence as, 339, **362**
  cues
    monocular, 329, **362**
    physiological, 338–39
    pictorial, 329–38, **362**
  divergence as, 339, **362**
  familiar size as, 333–34, 334t, **362**
  height in the plane as, 336–38, **362**
  interposition as, 330, **362**
  linear perspective as, 334–35, **362**
  motion parallax and, 339–41, **362**
  relative brightness and, 332, **363**
  relative distance and, 328, **363**
  retinal image size and, 333–34, **363**
  shading as, 330–32, *331*
  shadows as, 331–32
  size constancy and, 491–93
  subjective contours and, 379, **405**

texture gradients as, 335–36, **363**
theory(ies)
  computational, 329, **362**
  constructive, 329, **362**
  direct, 328–29, **362**
  intelligent perception, 329, **362**
Dermis, 286, **324**
Descending series, 23
Detail set, of attention, 518, **545**
Detection, 20–32, *21,* **61**
  adaptive testing and, 24–25, *25,* **61**
  method of contant stimuli and, 21–23, *21, 23,* 23–24
  method of limits and, 23t, 23–24
  signal detection theory and, *26,* 26–32, 27t, *28,* 29t, *30, 31, 32*
Deuteranomaly, 159, **178**
Deuteranopia, 158, **178**
Development. *See* Childhood; Infancy
Developmental approach theory, 550, **577**
Dichotic listening, 521–22, **545**
Dichromat, 158, **178**
Difference of Gaussian (DOG) filters, 127–29, **142**
Difference threshold, 39–40, **61**
Diplopia, 344, **362**
Direction perception, 354–57
  eye dominance and, 356–57
  eye movement and, 355–56
Direct perception, 14, **17,** 328, **362, 485, 508**
Direct scaling, 49–56, **61**
  category judgment and, 49–50
  cross–modality matching and, 55–56, **61**
  magnitude estimation and, 50–55, 52t, **52, 53**
Direction constancy, 468, **480,** 506, **508**
Directional acuity, 116, **143**
Discrimination, 20, 39–46, **61**
  pattern recognition and, 396–97
    during childhood, 570–71
  reaction time and, 44–46, 45t, *46*
  signal detection theory in, 43–44
  Weber's law and, 41–43, 42t, *43*
Disembedding, 629, **637**
Dissonance, 232, 249
Disparity, crossed versus uncrossed, 344–45, **362**
Distal stimulus, 485, **508**
Distance perception. *See also* Depth perception; Space perception
  absolute, 328, **361**

Distance perception *(continued)*
 apparent, 488–89, 489t
 cues
  physiological, 338–39
  pictorial, 329–38
  size constancy and, 488–90
 familiar size and, 333–34
 relative, 328, **363**
Distortions. *See* Illusion(s)
Divergence, as depth cue, 339, **362**
Divided attention, 512, 526–28, **545**
DOG filters, 127–29, **142**
Dol scale, 319, **324**
Dolorimeter, 318, **324**
Dominant wavelength, 150, **178**
Dorsal cochlear nucleus, 205, **209**
Dorsal column, 290, **324**
Double pain, 315, 316t, **324**
Drugs, perceptual effects of, 619–22
Duplex perception, 430, **441**
Duplex retina theory, 76, **100**
Duration. *See* Time perception
Dynamic range, of ear, 215, **249**
Dyschromatopsias, 173, **178**
Dyslexia, 570, **577**

Ear, 187–95. *See also* Auditory system; Hearing; Sound(s)
 canal (external auditory meatus),
  188, **209**
 eardrum (tympanum) of, 188–89,
  209
 evolution and anatomy of,
  187–88
 inner, 188–90, **210**, *474*
 mechanism of transduction in,
  199–201, *200*
 middle, 188–90, **210**
  bones of, 189
 outer, 188, **210**
 pinna of, 188, **210**
Early selection model, 542, **545**
Echolocation system, 229, **249**
Efference copy, 356, **362**
Efferent fibers, 473, **480**
Egocenter, 355, **362**
Egocentric localization, 328, **362**
Electroencephalogram (EEG), 645,
  647
Embedded figures test, 629, **637**
Emergent feature, 375, **404**
Emmert's law, 489, **508**
Emmetropic eye, 71, **100**
Encoding, memory and, 565, **577**
Endogenous noise, 24
Endogenous opiates, 321, **324**
Endorphins, 321, **324**
Enhancement, 580, **615**

Enkephalins, 321, **324**
Entrainment, 446, **480**
Environment and culture, 601–13
 illusion and constancy and,
  604–607
 occupational settings and, 608–10
 perceptual set and, 610–13
 picture perception and, 601–604
 speech and, 607–608
Epidermis, 286, **324**
Epithelium, olfactory, 269, *270, 283*
Equal loudness contour, 233, *234,
  235,* **249**
Equal pitch contour, **250**
Equal temperament scale, 237, **250**
Equal–interval scaling, 50, **61**
Erythrolabe, 157, **178**
Eustachian tube, 190, **209**
Event processing, 451, **480**
Event–related potentiation, 541, **546**
Evoked response, 634, **637**
Exafference, 588, **615**
Excitatory transmitter, 642, **647**
Exogenous noise, 24
Expecting, 512, 539–42, **542**
 information cues in, 539–40
 neurophysiology of, 540–42
Experience, 582–88
 restricted rearing and, 582, **615**
 selective rearing and, 588, **615**
Express saccades, 513, **546**
Extent, of attention, 518, **546**
External illuminance, 501, **508**
Extrastriate cortex, 88, **100**
Extrovert, 634, **637**
Eye, 66–70, **68**. *See also* Eye move-
  ment(s); Visual system
 compound, 130–32
 crystalline lens of, 70–71, **338**
 Cyclopean, 355, **362**
 dominance, 94, **100,** 356–57
 focusing ability of, 70–71
 form perception of, 366–68
 fovea of, 74–76
 mind's, 517
 movement of, 355–56, 370
 neural responses in, 79–84
 refractive, conditions of, *72*
 retina of. *See* Retina
 rods and cones of, 73–74, 76,
  76–79
 sighting–dominant, 357, **363**
Eye chart, 114–15
Eye movement(s)
 attention and, 565–67
 direction, 355–56
  constancy and, 468, **480**
 inflow theory of, 469, **480**

 motion perception and, 457–59,
  465–69
 optokinetic nystagmus, 556, **577**
 outflow theory of, 469, **480**
 position constancy in, 468, **480**
 reflex pursuit, 466, **480**
 saccadic, 528–31, 529t, 555, **577**
 smooth–pursuit, 466, **480**, 556,
  577
 vergence, 339, **363**
 vestibular sense and, 469–75,
  475t
 visual acuity and, 557, **577**
 visual attention and, 554–57
 voluntary pursuit and, 467, **481**
Eye–head system, 457, **480**
Eyewitness testimony, 600–601

Facilitation, 580, **615**
False alarm, signal detection theory,
  27–32, **61**
Familiar size, as distance cue,
  333–34, 334t, **362**, 603, **615**
Farsightedness, 71, **100**
Feature(s), 368–75, **404**
 configural, 396, **404**
 contour and, 370–73
 emergent, 375, **404**
 extraction tasks, 373–75
  texture segregation in,
   374–75, **405**
  visual search in, 373–75, **405**
 integration theory, 388–90, **404,**
  532, **546**
 relevant, 373, **405**
 search, 532, **546**
Fechner's law, 48–49, *49,* 53, 54t
Field dependency, 633, **637**
Field independency, 634, **637**
Figure(s), 376–79, *377,* **404**
 integration, 390t
 good, 382, 385–88
  information in, 385–88
  symmetry and, 387
 ground and, 376–79, *377, 378,*
  404
 grouping, 379–85
  by texture, 382–84
  spatial frequencies and,
   384–85
Filiform papillae, 256
Filled duration illusion, 451, **480**
Filtering, 512, 521–28, **546,** 568,
  577
 cocktail party phenomenon and,
  521–22
 divided attention and, 526–28

neurophysiology of, 525–26
orienting and, 568–69
video overlap phenomenon and,
    522–25
visual, 526–28
Flow, concept of, 444, **480**
Focal attention, 389, **404**
Focal stimulus, **61**, 486, **508**
Focus of expansion, 476, **480**
Foliate papillae, 256
Force, perception of, 304–306
Forced choice, **61**
Forced–choice preferential looking,
    554, **577**
Form perception, 366–75. *See also*
    Feature(s); Figure(s);
    Perceptual object
    contour in, 368–75
        change and, 370–72
        emergence, 372–73
    feature extraction in, 373–75
    viewing situation and, 366–68
    visual field and, 366, **405**
Formants, 421, **441**
Formant transitions, 423, *424,* **441**
Forward masking, 301, **325**
Fourier analysis, spatial, 118–22,
    127, 375
Fourier components, 186, *187,* **209,**
    375
Fourier synthesis, 122
Fourier's theorem, 118–21, **142**
Fovea centralis, 74–76, *75,* **100**
Free nerve endings, of skin, 287, **324**
Frequency (f), 184, **210**
Frequency sweep detector, 207, **210**
Fundamental frequency, 240, **250**
Fungiform papillae, 256

Gabor filter, *128,* 128–29, 142
Ganglion cells, of retina, 72, 81–84,
    82, 83, 83t, **100**
Ganzfeld, 370, 371t, **404**
Gate–control theory, 317–18,
    322–23, **324**
Gaussian distributions, 127
Gender differences, 627–32
    in taste and olfaction, 627–28
    in time and motion perception,
        628–29
    in touch sensitivity, 628
    in visual–spatial abilities, 628–32
Geniculostriate system, 84–88, *87,*
    100
Geons, 401, **404**
Gestalt, 380–82, *381,* **404**

law of good continuation, 381,
    404, 414
law of grouping, 413
law of proximity, 380, 405, 413
law of similarity, 380, **405,** 414
Glial cells, 640, **647**
Global precedence, 392–96, **404**
Golgi tendon organs, 303, **324**
Good continuation, law of, 381, **404,**
    414
Graded potential, 642, **647**
Grating acuity, 116, **142**
Ground, 376–79, *377,* **404**
Gustatory sense. *See* Taste

Habituation, 163, **178, ** 554, **577**
Hair bundle, 193, *194,* 210
Hair cells, 199–202, *200*
    model of transduction in, *199*
    of inner ear, 191, **210**
    of outer ear, 193, **210**
Haptic perception, 305–306, **325**
Harmonics, 240, **250**
Headcentric direction, 354, **362**
Hearing, 214–24. *See also* Auditory
        system; Sound(s)
    absolute threshold of, 21–22
    aging and, 574–75
    auditory masking and, 217–21
    high–frequency limits of, 215–16
    occupational noise and, 608–609
    range of, 214t, 214–16
    tactile perceptual systems and,
        300–301
Heat grill, 310t
Height in the plane, 336–38, **362**
Helicotrema, 190, **210**
Hemifield, 521, **546**
Hertz (Hz), 184, **210**
Hick's law, 46, **62**
Hidden figures test, 629, **637**
Hierarchial clustering, **62**
Hits, signal detection theory, 27–32,
    30, **62**
Homophenes, 435, **441**
Homophones, 435, **441**
Horopter, 345, *346,* **362**
Hue. *See* Color(s)
Hyperacuity, 116, **142**
Hypercolumn, 44, *95,* **100**
Hypercomplex cells, 92, **100**
Hypermetropia, 71, **100**
Hyperpolarization, 77, **100,** 641,
    647
Hz. *See* Hertz

Identification. *See* Perceptual object
Identification–by–components the-
    ory, 399–401, **404**
Illuminance, 105, **142**
Illusion(s), 9–11, **17**
    constancy and, 605–607
    decrement, 594, **615**
    filled duration, 451, **480**
    moon, 496, **508**
    Mueller–Lyer, 496, *497,* **508,** 568,
        577
    of movement, 459–63
    Poggendorff, 618, **637**
    Ponzo, 493, **508,** 568, **577**
    size constancy and, 493–97
    visual–geometric, 568, 577
Illusory conjunction, 389, **404**
Image–retina system, 457, *466,* **480**
Incus, 189, **210**
Indirect scaling, **62**
Induced movement, 459, 460t, **480**
Induction, 580, **615**
Infancy, 550–65
    brightness perception in, 558
    color perception in, 558
    eye movements in, 554–57, *566*
    hearing development in, 562–64
    pattern discrimination in, 558–60
    psychophysical testing methods
        and, 553–54
    smell development in, 564–65
    taste development in, 564–65
    touch and pain perception in,
        564–65
    visual system in, 550–53, 557–58
Infant directed talk, 563, **577**
Inferior colliculi, 205, **210**
Inferotemporal cortex, 96, **100**
Inflow theory, 469, **480**
Information
    bit, 36
    channels, 512, **546**
    cues, attention and, 516, **546**
    processing, 13, **17**
    theory, 33–39, **62**
    transmission, 36–39, **62**
        channel capacity and, 37–38
Inhibition of return response,
    530–31, **546**
Inhibitory transmitter, 642, **647**
Inner ear, 188–90, **210**
In phase, sound waves, 185, **210**
Instruction
    objective, 500, **508**
    projective, 500, **508**
Integral stimulus, 396–97, **404**
Integration, 565, **577**
Intensity difference, 225, **250**

Interblobs, 94, *100,* 168
Interposition as depth cue, 330, **362,** 603, **615**
Interstimulus interval, 219, **250,** 460, **480**
Interval of uncertainty, 40, **62**
Introvert, 634, **637**
Invariance, speech perception and, 425–26
Invariants, **17,** 485, **508**
Iodopsin, 78, **100**
Iris, 67, 100
Isoluminant stimuli, 455, **480**
Isosensitivity curve, 28

Just noticeable difference (jnd), 42, 48, **62**

Kinesthesis, 301–302, **325**
    haptic perception in, 305–306, **325**
    neural responses in, 303–304
    stimuli and receptors in, 302–303
    weight and force perception in, 304–306
Kinetic depth effect, 340, 342t, **362**

Labeled–line theory, 259, **282**
Labyrinth, 188, **210**
LAFS (Lexical Access From Spectra) model, 437, **441**
Late selection model, 542, **545**
Lateral geniculate nucleus, 84–88, 87, **100**
Lateral inhibition, *131,* 132, **142**
Lateral posterior nucleus, 90, **100**
Law of closure, 381, **404**
Law of good continuation, 381, **404,** 414
Law of Pragnanz, 382, 383t, **405**
Law of proximity, 380, **405,** 414
Law of similarity, 380, **405,** 414
Learning, sensory–motor, 588–95
Lemniscus, 641, **647**
Lens, **100**
    crystalline, 70–71, **338**
    zoom, 517
Lesions, 644, **647**
Levels–of–processing analysis, 13, **17**
Lexical Access From Spectra (LAFS) model, 437, **441**
Light, 66. See also Brightness perception; Lightness perception
    as wave phenomenon, 66

neural responses to, 79–80
    ganglion cells and, parvo and magno, 81–84
    receptive fields and, 79–81
    retina and, 79–81
photometric units of, 104–107, 106t
photosensitive pigment and, 72–74, 77
rods and cones and, 72, 76–79
source, 367, **405**
theory of, 66
wavelengths, reflectance and, 367
Lightness perception, 106–107, **142**
    constancy and, 501–504, 505t, **508**
    ratio principles, *502,* 502–504
Limbic system, 290, **325**
Linear perspective, as depth cue, 334–35, **362**
Linearity, speech perception and, 425, **441**
Localization(s)
    egocentric, 328, **362**
    object–relative, 328, **362**
    of sounds, 224–31
        complex sounds and, 228–30
        physiological mechanisms of, 230–31
        simple tones and, 225–28
    of touch sensation, 297
Lock–and–key theory, of smell, 272, **282**
Locus, of attention, 518, **546**
Long–range process, 460, **480**
Loudness, 231, 232–36, **250.** *See also* Sound(s)
    constancy, 506, **508**
    duration and, 234–35
    frequency and, 233–36
    magnitude estimation of, 51, 54t, 232–33, *233*
Lumen, 105, **142**
Luminance, 105, **142**
Luminosity curve, 110, **142**

Mach bands, *132,* 132–33, *134, 142*
Macula, 472, **480**
Macula lutea, 74, **100**
Macular spot, 75t
Magnetic resonance imaging (MRI), 646, **647**
Magnetoencephalography (MEG), 645, **647**
Magno cells, 81–84, *82, 83,* 83t, **100**
Magnocellular channel, 167, **178**

Maintenance, 580–81, **615**
Malleus, 189, **210**
Masking, 301
    auditory, 217–21, 218t, 219t
    backward, 301, **324,** 372, **404**
    contour emergence and, 372
    forward, 301, **325**
    simultaneous, 217, **250**
    touch and, 301, **324**
Matching
    contrast, 123, **141**
    cross–modality, 55–56, **61**
Maturation, 580, **615**
Maxwell's spot, 75t
McGurk effect, 431, **441**
Meaning, context and, 595–601
Medial geniculate, 205, **210**
Medial lemniscus, 258, **283,** 290, **325**
Mel scale, 237, **250**
Memory encoding, during childhood, 569–71
Mental rotation task, 629, 631t, **637**
Metacontrast, 372, *373,* **405**
Metameric colors, 150, **178**
Methathetic continuum, **62**
Method of constant stimuli, 21–23, *22,* **62**
Method of limits, 23–24, **62**
Microsaccades, 370, **405**
Microspectrophotometer, 160, **178**
Mind's eye, 517
Minimum audible angle, 227, **250**
Minimum audible field, 214, **250**
Minimum audible pressure, 214, **260**
Misses, signal detection theory, 27–32, **62**
Missing fundamental, 241, **250**
Mixed–modality scaling, 56, **62**
Model–based identification theory, 399, **405**
Modulation transfer function, 122–25, *124*
Moments, perceptual, 448, **480**
Monochromat, 158, **178**
Monocular cues, in depth perception, 329, **362**
Moon illusion, 496, **508**
Motion. *See also* Kinesthesis; Vestibular system
    aftereffect, 458t, 460
    apparent, 459–63, 472t, **479**
    biological, 463–65, **480**
    correspondence problem, 461, **480**
    induced, 459, **480**

parallax, 399–41, **362**
perception
    eye movements and, 457–59,
      465–69
    stimulus factors in, 457–50
rate of, 471, **479**
real, 460, **480**
self–, 475–78, 478t, **481**
Motives, payoff matrix and, 29
Motor neuron, 640, **647**
Motor theory, of speech perception,
    439
Movement. *See* Kinesthesis; Motion
Mueller–Lyer illusion, 496, *497,* **508,**
    568, **577**
Multidimensional interaction, 485,
    508
Multidimensional scaling, 56–58, **62**
    hierarchical clustering in, 58
    similarity matrix in, 56–57, **63**
Music, 408–17
    chords in, 411–12, **441**
    contour in, 412, **441**
    culture and, 417
    interval in, 411, **441**
    melody in, 412–17
    notes in, 408, 411–15
    pitch in, 237, 408–11, *409*
    rhythm in, 415, **441**
    space in, 410–11
    tempo in, 415, **441**
    tones in, 408–12, 410t
Myelin sheath, 640, **647**
Myopia, 71, **100,** 609, **615**
    night, 118

Nanometer (nm), 66, **100**
Near point distance, 71, **100**
Nearsightedness, 71, **100,** 609, 615
Necker cube, 620, **637**
Negative time error, 41, **62**
Neonates, 550, **577**
Neospinothalamic pathway, 290, **325**
Nervous system. *See* Neurophysiol-
    ogy
Neurophysiology. *See also specific*
    organ; specific system
    neural filters in, 127–29, *128,* **142**
    neural function, measurement of,
      643–46
    neural satiation in, 136–37, 138t,
      142
    neurons and, 640–41
      chopper, 206, **209**
      inter–, 640, **647**

motor, 640, **647**
off, 206, **210**
on, 206, **210**
pauser, 206, **210**
primarylike, 206, **210**
saturated, 203, **210**
sensory, 640, **647**
Neutral zone, skin temperature, 309,
    325
Night blindness, 76, **100**
Nodes of Ranvier, 641, **647**
Noise, 24
Nominal scale, **62**
Now, concept of, 444, **480**
Nuclear magnetic resonance (NMR),
    646, **647**
Nuclei, 641, **647**
Nystagmus, 475t, **480**

Object. *See* Perceptual object
Object properties, 486, **508**
Objective instruction, 500, **508**
Object–relative change, 457, **480**
Object–relative localizations, 328,
    362
Oblique effect, 587, **615**
Occipital lobe, 88, **100**
Occlusion, as depth cue, 330, **362**
Occupation, perceptual effects of,
    608–10
Odor
    absolute thresholds for, 274–75
    adaptation of smell sense and,
      275
    constancy, 506, **508**
    human, 279–81, 280t
    intensity and qualities of, 275–77
    pheromones and, 277–81
Off response, 80, **100**
Ogives, 22
Ohm's acoustical law, 187, 187t, **210**
Olfactory system, 269–74. *See also*
    Smell
    binding protein, 269, **283**
    bulb, 272, **283**
    cilia, 269, **283**
    epithelium, 269, *270,* **283**
    lateral tract, 273, **283**
    nerve, 272, **282**
    rod, 269, **283**
On response, 80, **100**
On–off response, 80, **100**
Opiates, endogenous, 320–22
Opponent process theory, color vi-
    sion, 163–67, **178**

Opsin, 77, **100**
Optacon, 300–301, **325**
Optic axis, **100**
Optic chiasm, 84, **100**
Optic disk, 79, **100**
Optic nerve, **100**
Optic radiations, 88, **100**
Optic tract, 84, **100**
Optokinetic nystagmus, 556, **577**
Ordinal scale, **62**
Organ of Corti, 191, *192, 193, 198,*
    210
Organization, 375–90
    figural goodness in, 385–88
    figural grouping in, 379–82
    figure and ground in, 376–79, *377*
Orientation specificity, **100**
Orienting, 518–21
    attentional gaze and, 517–18,
      545
    covert, 514–16, **545**
    neurophysiology of, 518–21
    reflex, 513–14, **546**
    response, 513, **546**
Oscilloscope, 643, *644,* **647**
Otoacoustic emissions, 197, **210**
Otocysts, 471, **480**
Otoliths, 471, **480**
Outcome matrix, 27, **62**
Outflow theory, 469, **480**
Out of phase, 185, **210**
Oval window, 189, **210**

Pacemaker, biological, 449–50, **480**
Pacinian corpuscle, 287–88, *288,*
    325
Pain, 313–23
    adaptation, 319–20
    alleviation of, 320–23
      acupuncture and, 321–22, *322*
      analgesics and, 320–22
    double, 315, 316t, **324**
    endogenous opiates and, 320–22
    gate–control theory of, 317–18,
      322–23
    intensity, 318–20
    neural responses to, 315–18,
    stimuli and receptors, 314–15
    thresholds, measurement of,
      318–20
Paleospinothalamic pathway, 290,
    325
Pandemonium theory, 399, *400,*
    405
Panum's area, 345, *346,* **362**

Papillae, 256, **283**
Paradoxical cold, 312, **325**
Paradoxical warmth, 312, **325**
Parallel search, 532, **546**
Parietal region, 81–84, *82, 83,* 83t, 97t, **100,** 290, **325**
Parvo cells, **101,** 117
Parvocellular channel, 167, *168,* **178**
Passive processing, 437, **441**
Pathology, physical, 622–28
Pattern perception. *See also* Feature(s); Figure(s)
  during childhood, 570–71
  discrimination and, 396–97
  tactile, 299–301
Pauser neurons, 206, **210**
Payoff matrix, 29, **62**
Perceived duration, of sound, 232, **250**
Perception, **17**
  direct, 14, **17,** 328, **362,** 485, **508**
    duplex, 430, **441**
    intelligent, 14, 17, 485, **508**
    picture, 601–604
  theories of, 484–86
    computational, 14, **17,** 329, **362,** 485–86, **508**
    constructive, 485, **508**
    feature integration, 388–90, **404**
    identification–by–components, 399–401, **404**
    information, 33–36
    model–based, 399, **405**
    pandemonium, 399, *400,* **405**
Perceptual distortions. *See* Illusion(s)
Perceptual learning approach, 550, **577**
Perceptual moments, 448, **480**
Perceptual object, 375–90, **405.** *See also* Form perception
  contours of, 378–79, 382, *384*
  figural grouping of, 379–85
    spatial frequencies and, 384–85
    texture and, 382–84
  figure and ground in, 376–79, *377,* **404**
  Gestalt principles of, 380–82
  in infants, 560–61
  identification and recognition, 20, 33–39, **62,** 390–92
    channel capacity and, 36–39
    context and, 397–98,

    conceptually–driven processing and, 391–92, 393t
    data–driven processing and, 391–92
    global processing and, 392–96
    local processing and, 392–96, 395t
  theory, 399–403
    computational, 401–403, *403*
    identification–by–components, 399–401, **404**
    information, 33–36
    model–based identification, 399, 405
    pandemonium, 399, *400,* **405**
Perceptual set, 610, **615**
Personality, cognitive style and, 632–36
Perspective
  aerial, 332–33, **363**
  linear, 334–35, **362**
  streaming, 476, *477,* **481**
Phase, of sound waves, 185, **210**
Phase angle, 184, **210**
Phase difference, 227, **250**
Phase–locking, 202, **210**
Pheromones, 267–69, 277–81, 283
Phone, 420, **441**
Phoneme, 420, **441,** 607, **615**
Phonemic boundary, 428, **441**
Phonemic restoration effect, 436, **441**
Phonemic shadowing, 522, **546**
Phonetic refinement theory, 439
Photometry, 104, 106t, **142**
  radiance and, 104–105, **142**
  standard units of, 104, **143**
Photon, 66, **101**
Photopic vision, **101,** 108, *111,* **142**
  luminosity curve and, 110, **142**
  rod and cone contribution in, 108–109
Photopsin, 79, **101**
Photoreceptors, in retina, 72, **101**
Phrase shadowing, 522, **546**
Physical condition, 622–28
Physiological zero, 309, 312t, **325**
Picture perception, 601–604
Pigment, visual, 77
Pigment epithelium, of retina, **101**
Pinna(ae) of ear, 188, **210**
Piper's law, 113, **142**
Pitch, 232, 237–40
  acoustical, 408–11
  contour, 239, **250**
  musical, 408–11
  theory of, 240–45
Poggenforff illusion, 618, **637**

Point of subjective equality, 40, **62**
Ponzo illusion, 493, **508,** 568, **577**
Pore, taste, 256, **283**
Position constancy, 468, **480,** 506, **508**
Positron emission tomography (PET) scan, 207, 316, 541, **546,** 645, **647**
Posterior parietal lobe, 520, **546**
Postsynaptic membrane, 642, **647**
Potentiation, taste, 263, **283**
Power law. *See* Stevens's law
Pragnanz, law of, 382, 383t, **405**
Preattentive process, 388–89, **405**
Precedence effect, 228, **250,** 523t
  Preferential looking procedure, 553, **577**
  forced–choice, 554, **577**
Presbyopia, 71, **101,** 572
Pressure amplitude, 184, **210**
Presynaptic membrane, 641, **647**
Primary auditory projection area, 205, **210**
Primary visual cortex, 88, **101**
Primarylike neuron, 206, **210**
Primers, 278, **283**
Probability distribution, 22, 29, **62**
Processing effort model, 451, **480**
Profile analysis, 223, **250**
Projective instruction, 500, **508**
Prosopagnosia, 625, **637**
Protanomaly, 159, **178**
Protanopia, 158, **178**
Prothetic continuum, **62**
Proximal stimulus, 485, **508**
Proximity, law of, 380, **405,** 414
Psychic blindness, 96, **101**
Psychometric function, 21, 21t, **62**
Psychophysics, 20–61
  detection task in, 21–27
  discrimination task in, 39–46
    reaction time and, 44–45
  fundamental, 20
  identification task in, 33–39
  scaling and, 46–49
    context and bias in, 58–66
    direct, 49–56
    Fechner's law and, 48–49
    multidimensional psychological, 56–58
  signal detection theory in, 43–44
  Weber's law and, 41–43
PTC (phenylthiocarbamide), 261, **283**
Pulvinar nucleus, 90, **101**
Pupil, 67, **101**
Pupillary light reflex, 67–68, 70t
Purkinje shift, 110–11, *112,* **142**

Quantum, 66, **101**

Radiance, 104–105, **142**
Random–dot stereopsis, 348, 349t, *350*
Ratio principle, of lightness constancy, 502, **508**
Reaction time, 44–46
  choice, 44–46, **61**
  simple, 44, **63**
  stimulus discriminability and, 45t, 45–46
Reafference, 588, **615**
Real movement, 460, **480**
Rearrangement, optical, 590, **615**
Receiver operating characteristic (ROC), curve, *28,* 28–32, **63**
Receptive fields, visual, 80–81, **101**
Recognition acuity, 114, **142**
Reduction conditions, 334, **363**
Reflectance, 105, **142,** 367, **405,** 501, **509**
Reflecting tapetum, 72, **101**
Reflex, orienting, 513–14, **546**
Reflex pursuit eye movement, 466, **480**
Refractive error, 71, **101**
Refractory period, 641, **647**
Regional cerebral blood flow (rCBF) method, 646, **647**
Registration, in information processing, 486, **508**
Reissner's membrane, 191, **210**
Relative brightness, aerial perspective and, 332–33, **363**
Relative distance, 328, **363**
Relative height. *See* Height in the plane
Releasers, 278, **283**
Residual stimuli, **63**
Resolution acuity, 116, **142**
Resting potential, 641, **647**
Restricted environmental stimulation technique, 451, **481**
Restricted rearing, 582–88, **615**
  human studies of, 586–88
  neurophysiological effects of, 582–84
  perceptual effects of, 584–86
Retina, 71–74, **101.** *See also* Retinal image
  acuity and, 117
  brightness perception and 110, 117
  cells, horizontal, 72, **100**
  cells, responses in, *80,* 80–81, *81*

darkness system in, 108–10, 109t, 139, 162t
duplex retina theory and, 76
illuminance and, 105, **142, 501, 509**
motion perception and, 457–59
structure of, 71–74, 73t, *74*
Retinal, 77–79, **101**
Retinal image, 366–68, **405**
  size constancy and, 487–88
  size cues and, 333–38
  stabilized, 370–72, **405,** 472t
  viewing situation and, 366–68, *369*
Retinal points, corresponding, 346, **362**
Reverberation, 230, **250**
Rhodopsin, 77, **101**
Rhythm, 415, **441**
  circadian, 445–47, **480**
ROC (receiver operating characteristic) curve, *28,* 28–32, **63**
Rods and cones, 73, 76–79, **101**
  in brightness perception, 108–109
  color response and, 156–67
  in human retina, 76
  hyperpolarization and, 77–78, *78*
  olfactory, 269, **283**
  pigment in, 77
Rooting response, in infants, 564, **577**
Round window, 191, **210**

Saccades, 513–14, **546**
  express, 513, **546**
Saccadic eye movements, 528–31, 529t, 555, **577**
Saccule, 471, **481**
Satiation, neural, 136–37, 138t, **142**
Saturated neuron, 203, **210**
Scala media. *See* Cochlear duct
Scale(s), 46–47, **63.** *See also* Scaling
  interval, 47, **62**
  nominal, 46, **62**
  ordinal, 47, **62**
  ratio, 47, **62**
Scaling, 20, 46–61, **63**
  adaptation level theory and, 59
  constancy, 488, **508**
  direct, 49–56, **61**
    category judgment and, 49–50
    cross–modality matching and, 55–56, **61**
    magnitude estimation and, 50–55, 52t, *52, 53*
  equal–interval, 50, **61**

indirect (Fechner's law), 48–49, 53, 54t
metathetic continuum of, 47, **62**
mixed–modality, 56, **62**
multidimensional psychological, 56–58, *57*
prothetic continuum in, 47, **62**
Schemata, 565, **577**
Schwann cells, 640, **647**
Sclera, 67, **101**
SCN (suprachiasmatic nucleus), 446, **481**
Scotoma, 90, **101**
Scotopic vision, **101,** 108–109, *111,* **142**
  luminosity curve and, 110, 142
  rod and cone contribution in, 108–109
Scotopsin, 79, 101
Search(ing), 512, 528–39, **546**
  automatic, 535–36
  conjunction, 532, **545**
  controlled, 535–36
  feature, 532, **546**
  guided, 535, **546**
  parallel, 532, **546**
  serial, 532, **546**
  vigilance arousal in, 536–39, **547**
  visual, eye movements and, 528–31, 529t, 566, **577**
Secondary visual cortex, 88, **101**
Selection model
  early, 542, **545**
  late, 542, **545**
Selective adaptation, 136–37, *137,* 138t, **142**
  of motion–specific cells, 456, **481**
  of spatial frequency channels, 138t
Selective attention, precedence effect and, 522, 523t
Selective rearing, 582, **615.** *See also* Restricted rearing
Self–motion, 475–78, 478t, **481**
Semicircular canals, 471, *474,* **481**
Sensation, defined, 12, **17**
Sensitive period, 359, **363**
Sensitivity (d'), 32, 34t, 35t, **61**
Sensory convergence, 478, **481**
Sensory neuron, 640, **647**
Sensory–motor learning, 588–95
  illusion decrement and, 594–95, **615**
  perceptual rearrangement and, 590–94
Separable stimulus, 396–97, **405**
Sequencial integration, 245, **250**
Serial search, 532, **546**

Set, perceptual, 610, **615**
Sexual attraction, pheromones and, 267
Shading, as depth cue, 330–32
Shadowing
    attention and, 516, 521, **546**
    phonemic, 522, **546**
    phrase, 522, **546**
Shadows, 330–32
    attached, 331–32, **361**
    cast, 332, **362**
Shape(s), 368, **405**
    constancy, 497–501, **509**
Short–range process, 460, **481**
SI System (Systeme International d'Unites), 104, **142**
Sighting–dominant eye, 357, **363**
Signal absent presentation, 26, *30, 32*
Signal detection theory, 26t, 27t, 26–32, **63**
    catch trials and, 26
    in discrimination, 43–44
Signal present presentation, 26–32, *30*
Similarity, law of, 380, **405**, 414
Similarity matrix, 56–57, **63**
Simple cell, **101**
Simple reaction time, **63**
Simultagnosia, 623, **637**
Simultaneous brightness contrast, *129,* 129–30
Simultaneous color contrast, 172–73
Simultaneous integration, 245, **250**
Simultaneous masking, 217, **250**
Sine wave grating, *119,* 119–20
Situation properties, 486, **509**
Size, familiar, 333–34, 488, 492
Size constancy, 487–96, **509**
    attention, 493, 494t
    direct and constructive aspects of, 491–93
    distance cues, 488–90
    illusion, 493–97
Skill, perceptual tasks and, 536, **546**
Skin, 286–93. *See also* Kinesthesis; Pain; Temperature; Touch
    dermis of, 286, **324**
    epidermis of, 286, **324**
    free nerve endings in, 287, **324**
    glabrous, 286, *287,* **324**
    hairy, 286, *287,* **324**
    inhibitory interactions on, 288, 289t
    neural pathways of, 288–93, *293*
    stimuli and receptors, 286–88
Smell, 267–82. *See also* Odor; Olfactory system

adaptation, 275, 276t
aging and, 575
flavor and, 267–69, *268*
gender differences and, 627–28
intensity and qualities, 275–77
neural responses in, 272–74
pheromones and, 267–69, 277–81, **283**
    primer, 278, **283**
    releaser, 278, **283**
    receptors, 269–74, *273*
    sensitivity, 274–75
    stimuli, 269–74, *273*
    taste and, 267
    thresholds, 274–75
Smoking, perceptual effects of, 619
Smooth–pursuit eye movement, 466, **480**, 556, **577**
Snellen eye chart, 114–15
Sodium–potassium pump, 641, **647**
Solitary tract, 257–58, **283**
Somatosensory cortex, *282,* 290, **325**
Sone, **250**
Sound(s), 182–87. *See also* Ear; Hearing; Speech perception
    auditory masking and, 214–16, *214,* 215t
    auditory scene analysis and, 245–47
    auditory stream and, 245, **248**
    auditory threshold of, 214–16, *214,* 215t
    complex, 228–30
    detection, 214–16, *214, 215*
        auditory masking and, 217–21, 218t, 219t
    discrimination, 222–24
    duration, perceived, 232, **250**
    intensity, 222–23, *222*
        differences, 225–26, **250**
    frequency, 215–16, 223–28, *224*
    location, perceived, 232, **250**
    localization, 224–28
    loudness and, 231, 232–36, **250**
    physiological mechanisms of, 230–31
    pitch and, *237,* 237–45, **250**
    shadow, 225, **250**
    threshold, 214–16, 215t
    tones, 225–28
    waves, **211**
        complex, 185–86, *187*
        fundamental frequency of, 24, **250**
        in phase, 185, **210**
        out of phase, 185, **210**
        simple, 182–87, *183*

traveling, along basilar membrane, *195, 196,* 196–98
Sound pressure level (SPL), 184, **210**
Space perception, 357–60. *See also* Depth perception; Distance perception
    experience and, 359–60
    motion and, 339–41
    species differences in, 357–59
Spatial agnosia, 624, **637**
Spatial context effects
    of brightness assimilation, 133–36, *141*
    of brightness contrast, 129–33, *135*
    simultaneous, *129,* 129–30
Spatial agnosia, 624, **637**
Spatial frequency
    analysis, 118–29
    channels, selective adaptation of, 138t
    contrast ratio in, 123, **142**
    figural organization and, Fourier's theorem and, 118–21, **142**
    low and high, 122–25, *127*
    modulation transfer function and, 122–25, *124,* **142**
    neural channels and, 125–29, *126*
    neural filters and, 127–29, *128,* **142**
    sine wave grating and, *119,* 119–20
    square wave grating and, 120, **142**
Spatial modulation transfer function, 122–25, *124,* **142**
Speech perception, 417–37
    acoustic properties of, 421–25
    ambiguity and invariance in, 425–26
    articulators, 420, **441**
    categorical, 428–30, **441**
    context and, 435–37
    cross–model integration and, 431–32
    development of, 433–35
    duplex, 430–31, **441**
    environment and culture in, 607–608
    signal segmentation in, 426, 427t
    spectrogram, 421, *422,* **441**
        formants, 421, 423, **441**
    stimulus and, 418–25
        acoustic properties and, 421–25
        consonants and vowels as, 419–20

phonemes as, 420–21, **441**
theory, 437–40
  auditory, 437–38
  active processing, 437, **441**
  motor, 439
  passive processing, 437, **441**
  phonetic refinement, 439
Spike potential, 641, **647**
Spindle organs. *See* Stretch receptors
Spinothalamic pathway, 290, **325**
Spiral ganglion, 193, **210**
SPL (sound pressure level), 184, **210**
Square wave grating, 120, **143**
Stabilized retinal image, 370–72, **405**
Staircase method, 24–25, **63**
Standard, stimulus intensity, 39–41, **63**
Stapes, 189, **210**
Statocysts, 470, **481**
Statolith, 471, **481**
Stereomotion, 353, **363**
Stereopsis, 124, 339, 341–51, 342t, 343t
  binocular disparity, 343, 344t, **361**
  diplopia, 344, **362**
  fusion and, 344–46, **362**
  global, 348, 349t, **362**
  random–dot, 348, 349t, *350*
Stereoscope, 346, **363**
Stereotaxic instrument, 644, **647**
Stevens's law, 50–55, 52t, *52, 53*
Stimulants, **63.** *See also* Drugs
Stimulus(i). *See also specific perception; specific sense*
  adaptation levels and, 59–61
  apprehended, 486, 487t, **598**
  background, 59, **61**
  constant, method of, 21–23, 39–40, *40*
  context, 58–61, 486, **508**
  cue, attention and, 516, **546**
  discrimination, 39–46
  distal, 485, **508**
  focal, 59, **61**
  integral, 396–97
  intensity
    comparison, 39
    measurement. *See* Threshold
    standard, 39
  proximal, 485, **508**
  reaction time and, 45t, 45–46
  registered, 486, 487t, **598**
  residual, 59, 63
  scaling. *See* Scaling
  signal detection theory and, 26t, 27t, 26–32, 43–44, **63**

threshold. *See* Threshold
  Weber's law and, 41–43
Storage size model, time perception, 451–52, **481**
Streaming perspective, 476, *477,* **481**
Stretch receptors, 303, **325**
Striate cortex, 88, **101**
Stroop effect, 535, **546**
Structural theories, of attention, 542, **546**
Subjective colors, 169, 170t, **179**
Subjective contours, 379, **405**
Subject–relative change, 457, **481**
Substantia gelantinosa, 317, **325**
Subtractive color mixture, 151–53, **179**
Superior colliculus(i), 89, 519, **546**
Superior olives, 195, **210**
Superior temporal cortex, **101**
Suprachiasmatic nucleus (SCN), 446, **481**
Surface
  accretion, 353, **363**
  deletion, 353, **363**
  orientation, 367, **405**
Symmetry, figural goodness and, 385–88, *387*
Synapse, 641, **647**
Synaptic cleft, 641, **647**
Synaptic knob, 641, **647**
Synaptic vesicle, 641, **647**
Systeme International d'Unites (SI System), 104, **142**

T cells, 317, **325**
Tacile perception. *See* Touch
Tadoma, 306, 308t, **325**
Taste, 254–66
  adaptation, 262–64
  aging and, 264–65
  blindness, 261–62
  buds, 256, *257, 283*
  cross–adaption, 263, **282**
  intensity, 264–66
  introversion–extroversion and, labeled–line theory of, 259, **282**
  neural responses in, 257–60, 265
  pore, 256, **283**
  potentiation, 263, **283**
  qualities, 255–56, 265–66
  smell and, 267
  stimuli for, 255–60
  thresholds for, *260, 261,* 260–62
Tectopulvinar system, 84, 88–90, *89, 98,* **101**
Tectorial membrane, 191, **211**

Tectum, **101**
Temperature
  adaptation to thermal stimuli, 309–13, *311*
  cold, paradoxical, 312, **325**
  neural coding of, 307–309
  physiological zero, 309, 312t, **325**
  stimulus intensity and, 312–13
  thermal thresholds and, 309–11
  warmth, paradoxical, 312, **325**
Tempo, 415, **441**
Temporal context effects, 136–38
Temporal lobes, 526, **546**
Temporal processing model, 452, **481**
Temporal summation, 216, **250**
Temporal visual field, 556, **577**
Textons, 383, **405**
Textural contour, 382, **405**
Texture, visual, 382, **405**
Texture gradient, as distance cue, 335–36, **363**
Texture segregation, 374, 382, **405**
Thalamus, 84, **101,** 258, 283, 290, **325**
Three–dimensional response, 604, **615**
Threshold(s). *See also specific perception; specific sensation*
  absolute. *See* Absolute threshold
  difference, 39–43
  response curve, 201, **211**
  stimulus, defined, 21
Timbre, 185, 186t, 211, 232, 240, **251**
Time perception, 445–53. *See also* Duration
  biological clock and, 445–50
  biological pacemaker and, 440–50
  body temperature and, 449–50, 450t
  brightness perception and, 111–12
  circadian rhythm and, 445–47, **480**
  clock theories of, 445
  cognitive clocks and, 450–53
  contour emergence and, 372–73
  difference, and sound source, 226, **254**
  event processing and, 451, **480**
  flow concept in, 444–45
  now concept in, 444–45
  perceptual moments and, 448–49, **480**
  processing effort in, 451
  storage size model of, 451, **481**

Time perception (*continued*)
temporal versus nontemporal attention in, 452–53
Tinnitus, 203
Tone, musical, 411–12
Tone chroma, 409, **441**
Tone height, 408, **441**
Tonotopic response, 206, **211**
Topographic map, **101**
Touch, 293–301. *See also* Skin
adaptation, 296–98, 297t
hearing and, 300–301
intensity, 298–99
localization, 297t
masking patterns and, 301
tactile pattern perception in, 299–301
thresholds for, 293–96
vision and, 299–300
Trace model, of speech perception, 439, **441**
Transactional viewpoint, 596, **615**
Transduction, olfactory, 199–201, *220*
Transmission (T) cells, 317, **325**
Transmitter(s)
excitatory, 642, **647**
inhibitory, 642, **647**
substance, 641, **647**
Trichromatic color theory, 156–63, **179**
Tritanopia, **179**
Tuned neuron, 201, **211**
Tuning curve, *201*, **211**
Tunnel of Corti, 191, **211**
Two–dimensional response, 604, **615**
Two–point threshold, of touch, 295, *296*, **325**
Two–tone suppression, 202, 211
Tympanic canal, 190, **211**
Tympanum, 188–89, **209**
Type I and II fibers, 193, **211**

Unconscious inference, 485, **509**
Uncrossed disparity, 344–45, **362**
Useful field of view (UFOV), 574, **577**
Utricle, 471, **481**

V1 (Area 17), 90, **101**
V2 (Area 18), 90, **101**
V3 (Area 19), 90, **101**
Vanishing point, 334, **362**
Vection, 476, **481**
Ventral cochlear nucleus, 205, **211**

VEP (visually–evoked potential), 557, **577**
Vergence movements, 339, **363**
Vernier acuity, 116, **143**
Vestibular system, 469–75, **481.** *See also* Motion
canal, 190, **211**
neural responses in, 473–75
nuclei of, 473, **481**
stimuli and receptors in, 471–73, 475t
Video overlap phenomenon, 522–25
Viewing position, 368, **405**
Vigilance, 536–39, **547**
Vision. *See also* Visual system
blindness and, 77
color, 157, **178**
day, 77, **100**
night, 76
psychic, 96, **101**
snow, 370
color. *See* Color perception
double, 344, **362**
farsightedness in, 71, **100**
form perception and, 366–68
night myopia in, 118
photopic, 76, 108, *111, 142*
scotopic, 76, 108, *111, 142*
substitution system, 299–300, *300*, **325**
visual–spatial abilities by gender, 629–32
Visual system. *See also* Brightness perception; Eye; Vision
acuity in, **99,** 114–21, **143,** 156–57
directional, 116, **143**
grating, 116, **142**
illumination and, 117–18, *118*
in infants, 557–58
measurement of, 115–21
recognition, 114–15, **142**
retinal position and, 117, 117t
Vernier, 116, **143**
visual angle and, 115, **143**
aging and, *124,* 124–25, 571–74
agnosia, 96, **101,** 622, **637**
blind spot and, 79, 79t, **99**
capture, visual, 514, 515t, **547**
cliff, visual, 358, **362**
cortex of, *86,* 90
color perception and, 167–69
maps of, alternate, 97–99
parietal lobes of, 97
primary, organization of, *93,* 93–95

receptive fields of, 90–92, *91*
temporal lobes in, 95–97
development of, in infants, 550–53
divided attention and, 512, 526–28, **545**
duplex retina theory of, 76
field, 366, 368–70, **405,** 585, **615**
contour in, 340–42, 368–73, **404**
nasal, 556, **577**
shapes in, 368, **405**
temporal, 556, **577**
filtering and, 526–28
hemineglect, visual, and 624, **637**
illusions, visual–geometric, 568, 577
pathways in, 84, *85*
geniculostriate system in, 84–88, *87*
tectopulvinar system in, 84, 88–90, *89*
perceptual organization of, 375–90
figural grouping in, 379–82
figure and ground in, 376–79, *377, 404*
search, visual, 373, **405**
texture, visual, 382, **405**
topographic mapping of, 84–99
Visually evoked potential (VEP), 557, **577**
Vitreous humor, 71, **101**
Voice onset time, 428, **441**
Volume, 232, **251**
Voluntary pursuit eye movements, 467, **481**
Vowels, 419, 421t, **441**

W cells, 83–84, **101**
Warm fibers, 307, **325**
Warmth. *See* Temperature
Wavelength, **211**
brightness perception and, 110–11
color perception and, 146–47, *147,* 149, 150–56, *154,* 160–61, *163,* 164–67
dominant, 150, **178**
of electromagnetic energy, 66, *67*
luminosity curve and, 110, **142**
primary, 153–56, **178**
Purkinje shift and, 110–11, *112,* **142**
of sound waves, 183, 185, 185–87, *187,* **211**

Weber fraction, *43,* **63**
Weber's law, 41–43, 42t, 48
Weight
    judged, effect of visual context
        on, 58t
    perception of, 304–306

Westheimer function, 114, **143**
Whiteness perception. *See* Lightness
    perception
Whytt's reflex, 67–68, 70t

X cells, **101**

Y cells, **101**
Yerkes–Dodson law, 538, **547**

Zeitgeber, 446, **481**
Zoom lens, 517